Brian Fleming Research & Learning Library
Ministry of Education
Ministry of Training, Colleges & Universities
900 Bay St. 13th Floor, Mowat Block
Toronto, ON M7A 1L2

Education for All
THE QUALITY IMPERATIVE

EFA Global Monitoring Report 2005

Education for All
THE QUALITY IMPERATIVE

UNESCO Publishing

The designations employed and the presentation of the material
in this publication do not imply the expression of any opinion
whatsoever on the part of UNESCO concerning the legal status
of any country, territory, city or area, or of its authorities, or
concerning the delimitation of its frontiers or boundaries.

Published in 2004 by the United Nations Educational,
Scientific and Cultural Organization
7, Place de Fontenoy, 75352 Paris 07 SP

Graphic design by Sylvaine Baeyens
Iconographer: Delphine Gaillard
Printed by Graphoprint, Paris
Second printing
ISBN 92-3-103976-8

©UNESCO 2004
Printed in France

Foreword

The quest to achieve Education for All (EFA) is fundamentally about assuring that children, youth and adults gain the knowledge and skills they need to better their lives and to play a role in building more peaceful and equitable societies. This is why focusing on quality is an imperative for achieving EFA. As many societies strive to universalise basic education, they face the momentous challenge of providing conditions where genuine learning can take place for each and every learner.

The six goals adopted at the World Education Forum in Dakar, Senegal, in April 2000, implicitly or explicitly integrate a quality dimension. Goal 6, in particular, commits countries, with the support of their EFA partners, to improve all aspects of the quality of education. The benefits of early childhood, literacy and life-skills programmes largely depend on the quality of their contents and of their teachers. Reducing gender disparities in education relies strongly on strategies that address inequalities in the classroom and in society. Primary and secondary education – the central planks of most education systems – are expected to ensure that all pupils acquire the knowledge, skills and values necessary for the exercise of responsible citizenship.

Although much debate surrounds attempts to define education quality, solid common ground exists, as this third issue of the *EFA Global Monitoring Report* makes clear. Quality must be seen in light of how societies define the purpose of education. In most, two principal objectives are at stake: the first is to ensure the cognitive development of learners. The second emphasises the role of education in nurturing the creative and emotional growth of learners and in helping them to acquire values and attitudes for responsible citizenship. Finally, quality must pass the test of equity: an education system characterized by discrimination against any particular group is not fulfilling its mission. The *EFA Global Monitoring Report 2005* gives powerful evidence of why quality matters for reaching a wide set of individual and development goals, and identifies policy areas that directly impact on learning.

This Report tells both a quantitative and a qualitative story. First, that the number of out-of-school children is declining too slowly to achieve universal primary education by 2015. Second, that despite progress, no country outside the developed word has achieved the four measurable EFA goals. Improving the quality of learning through inclusive, holistic policies is an overriding priority in a majority of countries. The Report highlights a number of urgent needs – for more and better trained teachers, for improved textbooks available to all learners, for pedagogical renewal and for more welcoming learning environments. While no reform comes without cost, better learning outcomes have been achieved in very diverse political contexts, and in societies with greatly varying degrees of wealth.

UNESCO gives very high priority to improving the quality of education. The prestigious International Commission on Education for the Twenty-first Century (1996), under the chairmanship of Jacques Delors, gave an important and influential lead. My structural reform of the Education Sector at UNESCO included the creation of a transversal Division for the Promotion of Quality Education. In 2003, during the 32nd Session of UNESCO's General Conference, Ministers of Education from over 100 countries participated in a round table to reflect on strategies for steering their systems towards better quality. And, most recently, the 47th session of the International Conference on Education, held in Geneva on 8-11 September 2004 and organized by the UNESCO International Bureau of Education, was devoted to the theme of 'Quality education for all young people: challenges, trends and priorities'.

Every investment in basic education must be measured against how well it serves both to expand access to education and to improve learning for all children, youth and adults. This endeavour begins at home, with a national consensus on quality and a robust long-term commitment to achieve excellence. However, the international community must also give strong and consistent support to countries that are boldly seeking to expand and improve learning for all of their citizens.

I am confident that this Report provides a comprehensive reference to assist national and international decision-makers in defining education priorities that will ultimately shape the well-being of our societies.

Koïchiro Matsuura
Director-General of UNESCO

Acknowledgements

We are indebted to John Daniel and Aicha Bah Diallo, former and acting Assistant Directors-General for Education, and to Abhimanyu Singh, Director of UNESCO's Division of International Coordination and Monitoring for Education for All, and their colleagues for their support in the preparation of this Report.

The Report benefited strongly from the advice of the international Editorial Board and its former and present chairpersons Anil Bordia and Ingemar Gustafsson, as well as from in-depth guidance from a small advisory group composed of Beatrice Avalos, Martin Carnoy, Krishna Kumar, Marlaine Lockheed, Jaap Scheerens, and Mary Joy Pigozzi from UNESCO.

The EFA Report depends greatly on the work of the UNESCO Institute for Statistics (UIS). Denise Lievesley, Simon Ellis, Albert Motivans, Alison Kennedy, Said Belkachla, Said Ould Voffal, Ioulia Sementchouk, Weixin Lu and their colleagues contributed significantly to this Report, particularly in the preparation of chapter 3 and the statistical tables.

Special thanks are due to all those who prepared background papers, notes and boxes for the Report. These were:

Kwame Albert Akyeampong, Terry Allsop, Massimo Amadio, Allison Andersen-Pillsbury, David Atchoarena, Peter Badcock-Walters, Aaron Benavot, Paul Bennell, Carol Benson, Roy Carr-Hill, Linda Chisholm, Mariana Cifuentes, Christián Cox, Charlotte Creed, Anton De Grauwe, Jean-Marie De Ketele, Martial Dembélé, Gusso Divonzir, Alicia Fentiman, Clermont Gauthier, Marelize Görgens, Gilbert Grandguillaume, Sky Gross, Jacques Hallak, Eric Hanushek, Wim Hoppers, Michael Kelly, Krishna Kumar, Sylvie Lambert, Scherezad Latif, Keith Lewin, Shay Linehan, Robert Litteral, Angela Little, Todd Lubart, Phyllis Magrab, Robert Myers, Boubacar Niane, Kicki Nordström, Miki Nozawa, John Oxenham, Christine Panchaud, Kamala Peiris, Joel Pii, Muriel Poisson, Mathilde Poncet, Neville Postlethwaite, Bill Ratteree, Patrick Ressler, Diane Richler, Padma Sarangapani, Jaap Scheerens, Ernesto Schiefelbein, Maria Teresa Siniscalco, Tuomas Takala, Peter Taylor, Nhung Truong, Duncan Wilson, Siri Wormnæs.

The Report also benefited considerably from the advice and support of individuals, Divisions and Units within UNESCO's Education Sector, the International Institute of Educational Planning, IIEP, the International Bureau of Education, IBE, and the UNESCO Institute of Education, UIE. UNESCO's Regional Offices provided helpful advice on country-level activites and helped facilitate commissioned studies.

A number of individuals also contributed valuable advice and comments. These were:

Eric Allemano, Samer Al-Samarrai, David Atchoarena, Rosemary Bellew, Julia Benn, Nancy Birdsall, Cecilia Braslavsky, Mark Bray, Françoise Caillods, Luis Crouch, Bridget Crumpton, Michel Debeauvais, Kenneth Eklind, Dalia Elbatal, Robin Ellison, Paolo Fontani, Richard Halperin, Steve Heineman, Yoshie Kaga, Stefan Lock, Ute Meir, Peter Moock, Hena Mukerjee, Saul Murimba, Paud Murphy, Miki Nozawa, Petra Packalén, Chantal Pacteau, Ioana Parlea, Mary Joy Pigozzi, Robert Prouty, Abby Riddell, Beverly Roberts, Mark Richmond, Clinton Robinson, Kenn Ross, Paolo Santiago, Simon Scott, Francisco Seddoh, Sheldon Shaeffer, Madhu Singh, Soo Hyang Choi, Benoît Sossou, Adriaan Verspoor, Sue Williams, Cream Wright.

The production of the Report benefited greatly from the editorial expertise of Rebecca Brite. Wenda McNevin and Paul Snelgrove also provided valuable support. We would also like to thank Sonia Fernandez-Lauro and her colleagues in the Education Documentation Centre for their considerable support and assistance.

The analysis and policy recommendations of this Report do not necessarily reflect the views of UNESCO. The Report is an independent publication commissioned by UNESCO on behalf of the international community. It is the product of a collaborative effort involving members of the Report Team and many other people, agencies, institutions and governments. Overall responsibility for the views and opinions expressed in the Report is taken by its Director.

The EFA Global Monitoring Report Team

Director
Christopher Colclough

Steve Packer (Deputy Director),
Albert Motivans (UIS),
Jan Van Ravens, Ulrika Peppler Barry, Lene Buchert,
Nicole Bella, Cynthia Guttman,
Vittoria Cavicchioni, Yusuf Sayed, Valerie Djioze, Carlos Aggio,
Jude Fransman, Ikuko Suzuki, Delphine Nsengimana,
Liliane Phuong, François Leclercq, Fadila Caillaud, Roser Cusso

For more information about the Report,
please contact:
The Director
EFA Global Monitoring Report Team
c/o UNESCO, 7 place de Fontenoy
75352 Paris 07, France
e-mail: efareport@unesco.org
Tel.: +33 1 45 68 21 28
Fax: +33 1 45 68 56 27
www.efareport.unesco.org

Previous EFA Global Monitoring Reports
2003/4. Gender and Education for All – THE LEAP TO EQUALITY
2002. Education for All – IS THE WORLD ON TRACK?

Contents

	Headline messages	16
	Executive summary	18

Chapter 1 — Understanding education quality — 27
- Why focus on quality? — 28
- Quality for whom and what? Rights, equity and relevance — 30
- Education traditions and associated notions of quality — 32
- A framework for understanding, monitoring and improving education quality — 35
- Using the framework — 37
- The structure of the Report — 37

Chapter 2 — The importance of good quality: what research tells us — 38
- The impact of education quality on development goals — 40
- International assessments of cognitive achievement — 44
- What determines quality? Lessons from eleven countries — 49
- The quality of ECCE and literacy programmes — 56
- The quality of schooling — 60
- The role of the organization and social context of schools — 75
- Conclusion: what we know about what matters for education quality — 77

Chapter 3 — Assessing progress towards the EFA goals — 81
- Early childhood care and education — 82
- School participation — 90
- Teachers, finance and quality — 107
- Quality and equality of learning — 119
- Literacy and skills development — 126
- The Education for All Development Index — 136

Chapter 4 — Policies for better quality — 140
- Setting a policy framework — 142
- Start with learners — 143
- Improving teaching and learning — 146
- Better teachers — 161
- Better schools — 168
- Support schools, inform policy — 177
- Building support for systemic reform — 181
- Conclusions — 185

Chapter 5 — Meeting our international commitments 186
- Aid flows to education 188
- Using aid effectively for EFA 196
- Plans, partnerships and quality 205
- International coordination 213

Chapter 6 — Towards EFA: the quality imperative 223
- Progress towards the EFA goals 224
- What is an education of good quality worth? 226
- Quantity alone is not enough 226
- The main determinants of better quality in education 228
- Policies for improved learning 229
- International dimensions 231

Annex
- Appendix 236
- Statistical annex 248
- Glossary 394
- References 398
- Abbreviations 428

List of figures, tables and text boxes

Figures

1.1:	A framework for understanding education quality	36
2.1:	HIV prevalence in rural Uganda (%) by education category, 1990-2001 (individuals aged 18-29)	45
2.2:	Percentage of women who used a condom during sex in previous month	45
2.3:	Percentage of men who used a condom with a recent non-regular partner	45
2.4:	Changes in literacy scores between SACMEQ I and II in six African countries	46
2.5:	Performance indicators for primary education in eleven countries	50
3.1:	Distribution of countries by the number of years of pre-primary education provided, 2001	82
3.2:	Gross and net pre-primary enrolment ratios, 2001	83
3.3:	Age-specific enrolment ratios for pre-primary and primary education, 2001	84
3.4:	Pre-primary school life expectancy in selected countries by region, 2001 (regional averages and countries with the highest and lowest values)	85
3.5:	Pre-primary gross enrolment ratios in 2001 and change since 1998 (countries with GER below 30%)	86
3.6:	Net ECCE attendance rates for 3- and 4-year-olds by urban or rural residence, 2000	88
3.7:	Net ECCE attendance rates for 3- and 4-year-olds by household wealth, 2000	88
3.8:	Comparison of per-child expenditure at pre-primary and primary levels, 2001 (primary education = 100)	90
3.9:	Net and gross enrolment ratios in primary education for countries with NER below 95%, 2001	92
3.10:	Net enrolment ratios in primary education, 1990-2001 and 1998-2001	94
3.11:	Gender disparities in gross enrolment ratio in primary education, 1990, 1998 and 2001 (countries with GPI below 0.97 in 1998 or 2001)	96
3.12:	Characteristics of pupils entering school late in Uganda and Zambia	97
3.13:	Distribution of countries by GIR, medians, quartiles and highest and lowest deciles, by region, 2001	98
3.14:	Cumulative net intake rates by age, in selected countries, 2001	99
3.15:	Survival rates to grade 5 and average number of grades reached when dropping out of primary school, 2001	100
3.16:	Percentage of repeaters in primary schools, 1991 and 2001	101
3.17:	Secondary gross enrolment ratios, 1998 and 2001	103
3.18:	Tertiary gross enrolment ratios, 1998 and 2001	104
3.19:	Gender parity and secondary gross enrolment ratios, 2001	105
3.20:	Gender parity and tertiary gross enrolment ratios, 2001	106
3.21:	School life expectancy by region, 2001 (regional averages and countries with the highest and lowest values)	107
3.22:	Percentage of primary-school teachers meeting national qualification standards in sub-Saharan Africa, 2001	109
3.23:	Trained teachers in primary education, 2001	110
3.24:	Primary teachers meeting national standards and adult illiteracy in Brazil, by state, 2000	110
3.25:	Median pupil/teacher ratios in primary education by region, 1990, 1998 and 2001 (countries with data for all three years; number per region in brackets)	114
3.26:	Primary education: pupil/teacher ratios and survival to the last grade, 2001	116
3.27:	Public expenditure on education as a percentage of GDP, by education level, 2001 (regional medians and countries with the highest and lowest values)	117
3.28:	Change in total education expenditure in real terms, selected countries, 1998 to 2001	118
3.29:	Combined literacy performance and cumulative education expenditure to age 15, PISA, 2000/2001	119

3.30: Grade 6 assessment results in four Latin American countries, various years 121

3.31: SACMEQ. Percentage of grade 6 pupils reaching proficiency levels in reading in seven African countries, 1995-1998 121

3.32: PASEC. Percentage of grade 5 pupils with low achievement in six African countries, 1996-2001 122

3.33: PIRLS. Percentage of grade 4 pupils in the lowest quartile of the international reading literacy scale, 2001 122

3.34: PISA. Percentage of 15-year-old students in five proficiency levels for reading, 2000-2002 (selected countries) 123

3.35: Socio-economic gradients for literacy performance 124

3.36: Which countries meet the goals of quantity and quality of education? 125

3.37: Adults with primary as their highest education level who report being unable to read, 2000 128

3.38: Measures of literacy in Ghana among people aged 15 and over, 1989 and 2003 129

3.39: Mothers' literacy and schooling status in the Niger, the Lao PDR and Bolivia, 2000 130

3.40: World adult illiterate population, percentage by country, 2000-2004 131

3.41: Literacy rates for ages 15 to 24 by gender and rural or urban residence in sub-Saharan Africa, 2000 133

3.42: Lao PDR. Out-of-school youth by age and gender, 2001 134

3.43: EFA Development Index in 2001 and change since 1998 (countries with EDI less than 0.80 in 2001) 139

4.1: Policy framework for improving the quality of teaching and learning 143

4.2: Real salary index for primary and secondary (language and mathematics) teachers, selected countries, 1998 or latest available year (1990=100) 166

4.3: Mid-career salaries for primary teachers and GDP per capita, 2001 167

5.1: Total official development assistance (net disbursements in US$ billions), 1992-2002 188

5.2: Bilateral aid commitments to education, 1990-2002 189

5.3: Bilateral education aid commitments: percentage of donor's education aid to its most favoured region, two-year averages for 2001-2002 191

5.4: Comparison of priorities assigned to overall education aid and basic education aid, 2001-2002 192

5.5: World Bank education lending per year, 1963-2003 194

5.6: World Bank education lending as proportion of total lending, 1960s to 1990s 195

5.7: Composition of total World Bank education lending, three-year averages for 1992-2003 195

5.8: Harmonization and alignment 197

5.9: Education Index of Donor Proliferation for 2001-2002 against total Index of Donor Proliferation for 1999-2001 200

5.10: Recipient countries by region and number of bilateral donors making education aid commitments, 2001-2002 200

5.11: The EFA-FTI process 215

Tables

2.1: Estimated returns to a standard deviation increase in cognitive skills 42

2.2: Percentage and mean differences in selected variables between SACMEQ I and II 47

2.3: Education system and background characteristics in eleven countries 50

2.4: Test scores and changes in real expenditure per pupil, 1970-94 (percentages) 60

2.5: Results of studies investigating the relationship between educational expenditures and outcomes 62

2.6: Percentage distribution of estimated effect of key resources on student performance, based on 376 production function estimates (United States) 65

2.7: Percentage distribution of estimated expenditure parameter coefficients from ninety-six education production function estimates (developing countries)	65
2.8: Effectiveness-enhancing conditions of schooling: results of five review studies	66
2.9: Comparison of traditional and constructivist instructional models	69
2.10: The most important conditions for enhancing teaching effectiveness	71
3.1: Net ECCE attendance rates for 3- and 4-year-olds by gender and number of hours attended, 2000	87
3.2: Grouping of countries by levels of primary net and gross enrolment ratios, 2001	91
3.3: Number of out-of-school children by region, 1998 and 2001	95
3.4: Expected years of schooling by region, 2001, and change since 1990	106
3.5: Primary teacher qualification and training levels in fourteen low-income countries, 1995	109
3.6: Distribution of countries according to primary pupil/teacher ratios, 2001	113
3.7: Adult literacy (age 15 and over) by gender and region, 2000-2004	129
3.8: Adult literacy rates in five high-population countries by gender, 1990-1994 and 2000-2004	131
3.9: Youth literacy (15-24) by gender and region, 2000-2004	132
3.10: Distribution of countries by their mean distance from the EFA goals in 2001	137
3.11: Distribution of countries by change in their mean distance vis-à-vis the EFA goals from 1998 to 2001	137
4.1: Policy choices in determining national curriculum goals as reflected in the Convention on the Rights of the Child	147
4.2: Trends in curriculum statements, 1980s to 2000s	148
4.3: Mean percentage of total instructional time allocated to mathematics in primary and lower secondary education, by grade level and time period (constant cases within grade levels)	149
4.4: Mean percentage of countries requiring instruction in selected newer subjects in primary and lower secondary education, by grade level and time period	151
4.5: Global average of annual instructional time, by grade level and time period	151
4.6: Regional average yearly instructional time by grade level in 2000	152
4.7: Languages used in education in China and South-East Asia	155
4.8: Summative and formative assessment	158
4.9: Main models of initial teacher training	162
4.10: Average primary-school teacher salary (ratio to per capita GDP) by world region, 1975-2000 (countries with per capita GDP below US$2,000 in 1993)	165
4.11: School improvement: policy implications	170
4.12: Child-Friendly School Framework	172
4.13: The main forms of corruption in the education sector	185
5.1: Bilateral aid commitments (total and education), two-year averages for 2001-2002	189
5.2: Bilateral aid commitments to education and to basic education, two-year averages for 2001-2002	191
5.3: Bilateral aid priorities for education and basic education, 2001-2002	192
5.4: Composition of bilateral education assistance, two-year averages for 2001-2002 (percentage)	193
5.5: Average annual multilateral aid commitments (excluding World Bank), two-year averages for 1999-2000 and 2001-2002	194
5.6: Bilateral and multilateral commitments to education, two-year averages for 1999-2000 and 2001-2002 (Constant 2001 US$ billions)	195
5.7: Recipients of bilateral aid, 2001-2002	198
5.8: Index of donor proliferation in education aid	199
5.9: PRSPs and education plans by EFA region	205

5.10: PRSPs and education plans by country classification ... 206
5.11: Aid dependence in education in three African countries: budgets and agencies ... 208
5.12: Types of funding under BESSIP, 2001 ... 209
5.13: BESSIP budget by component and funding type, 2002 ... 209
5.14: Zambia Ministry of Education expenditure, 1998-2002 (Constant 2001 Kwacha billions) ... 209
5.15: Initial ESIP indicators relating to quality, 2000/2001-2003/2004 ... 211
5.16: Status of countries in relation to FTI, February 2004 ... 216
5.17: Policy benchmarks for universal primary completion by 2015 ... 216
6.1: Quantitative versus qualitative indicators of participation in primary schooling ... 227

Text boxes

1.1: The Dakar Framework for Action and Millennium Development Goals ... 28
1.2: Education quality as defined in Jomtien and Dakar ... 29
1.3: The evolution of UNESCO's conceptualization of quality ... 30
1.4: The aims of education, from the Convention on the Rights of the Child, Article 29 (1) ... 31
1.5: The UNICEF approach to quality ... 31
1.6: Quality in the humanist tradition ... 32
1.7: Quality in the behaviourist tradition ... 33
1.8: Quality in the critical tradition ... 34
1.9: Quality in the indigenous tradition ... 34
1.10: Quality in adult education approaches ... 34
2.1: Education and HIV/AIDS risk avoidance: does knowledge equal change? ... 45
2.2: Major conclusions from more than forty years of international achievement surveys ... 48
2.3: Constructivism ... 69
2.4: The impact of a remedial education programme in India's urban slums ... 74
3.1: Late entry into schooling and concerns about equity ... 97
3.2: Towards a better international measure of primary education completion ... 102
3.3: How can we measure teacher quality? ... 108
3.4: Determining and promoting good-quality teaching in especially difficult circumstances ... 111
3.5: HIV/AIDS and teacher attrition trends in Kenya ... 112
3.6: Expanding access to primary education: quantity and quality factors ... 115
3.7: Defining low achievement ... 120
3.8: International goals and indicators ... 127
3.9: Measuring 'good-quality literacy' in developing countries ... 128
3.10: Links between mothers' literacy skills and child schooling status ... 130
3.11: Literacy-related activities in the home: cross-national evidence from PIRLS ... 132
3.12: Reducing illiteracy and improving gender parity are the best predictors of progress towards EFA ... 138
4.1: School health and nutrition in Burkina Faso ... 144
4.2: Inclusive education or special education? ... 145
4.3: Distance learning for disadvantaged learners ... 145
4.4: The currency of a selection of newer subjects and subject areas at global level ... 150

4.5:	Open-ended and discovery-based instruction	153
4.6:	Structured teaching	154
4.7:	Multigrade teaching	155
4.8:	Initial literacy and the medium of instruction in Zambia	156
4.9:	Elementary schools in Papua New Guinea	157
4.10:	'Unfriendly' schools	160
4.11:	Best practice in ongoing professional support	163
4.12:	New career paths for teachers in South Africa	163
4.13:	Primary school teachers in Sierra Leone	164
4.14:	Negotiating salaries, careers and professional concerns in Chile	167
4.15:	Teacher supply and demand in four African countries	168
4.16:	Whole school development in Ghana	171
4.17:	Child-seeking, child-centred schools	171
4.18:	School-based management and better learning	173
4.19:	Organizing the school day in multi-shift systems	177
4.20:	Teacher resource centres	178
4.21:	Cuba: school improvement as a collective effort	179
4.22:	English-language curriculum development in the Gambia	180
4.23:	Nine ways to make changes happen	182
4.24:	Involving the Tanzanian Teachers Union in basic education planning	183
4.25:	Bargaining and social dialogue in South African education	183
5.1:	Notional sector classification of budget support: the DFID experience	190
5.2:	Philanthropic funding of education	196
5.3:	Coordination and harmonization of government and donor practices in Zambia	198
5.4:	European Development Funds: relevance and effectiveness of programme and project aid to education	202
5.5:	Conclusions of Joint Evaluation of External Support to Basic Education in Developing Countries	202
5.6:	DFID aid to primary schooling: issues and lessons	203
5.7:	How should financial aid for education be provided?	204
5.8:	EFA plan developments: some regional experiences	207
5.9:	Evolution of the sector approach in education in Mozambique	208
5.10:	Policy dialogue on quality in Mozambique	210
5.11:	Fast-Track Initiative: goals and principles	214

Headline messages

The six goals: where the world stands

Goal 1 **Early childhood care and education.** Progress towards wider access remains slow, with children from disadvantaged backgrounds more likely to be excluded from ECCE. A child in sub-Saharan Africa can expect only 0.3 years of pre-primary schooling, compared to 1.6 years in Latin America and the Caribbean and 2.3 years in North America and Western Europe. In many developing countries, ECCE programmes are staffed by teachers with low qualifications.

Goal 2 **Universal primary education.** The number of out-of-school children is declining, having fallen from 106.9 million in 1998 to 103.5 million in 2001. While progress has been made globally, over the past decade, in getting more children into school, the pace remains too slow to achieve UPE by 2015. If past trends continue, the world net enrolment ratio will be about 85% in 2005 and 87% in 2015. Completion of primary schooling remains a major concern: delayed enrolment is widespread, survival rates to grade 5 are low (below 75% in thirty of ninety-one countries for which data are available) and grade repetition is frequent.

Goal 3 **Youth and adult learning.** Efforts to raise the level of skills among youths and adults are marginal in the few developing countries that have conducted evaluations of skills development programmes. Progress remains difficult to assess on a global basis.

Goal 4 **Literacy.** About 800 million adults were illiterate in 2002;[1] 70% of them live in nine countries belonging mostly to sub-Saharan Africa and East and South Asia, notably India, China, Bangladesh and Pakistan.

Goal 5 **Gender.** Although many countries around the world have made significant progress towards gender parity at primary and secondary levels over the past decade, large gaps remain, particularly in the Arab States, sub-Saharan Africa and South and West Asia. Girls accounted for 57% of the out-of-school children of primary school age worldwide in 2001 and for more than 60% in the Arab States and in South and West Asia. Girls' participation remains substantially lower than boys' (a gender parity index below 0.97) in seventy-one out of 175 countries at primary level. Gender disparities become more extreme at secondary level and in higher education. Of eighty-three developing countries with data, half have achieved gender parity at primary level, fewer than one-fifth at secondary and only four at tertiary. Almost two-thirds of the world's adult illiterates (64%) are women.

Goal 6 **Quality.** Countries that are farthest from achieving goals 1 to 5 are also farthest from achieving goal 6. Several indicators provide information on dimensions of quality. Public expenditure on education represents a higher proportion of GDP in rich countries, where the EFA goals are already achieved, than in poorer ones, where the coverage of under-resourced systems needs to be both expanded and improved. Spending has increased over the past decade in many developing countries, notably in East Asia and the Pacific and in Latin America and the Caribbean. Pupil/teacher ratios remain higher than is desirable in many countries of sub-Saharan Africa (regional median: 44:1) and South and West Asia (40:1). In many low-income countries, teachers do not meet even the minimum standards for entry into teaching and many have not fully mastered the curriculum. The HIV/AIDS pandemic is severely undermining the provision of good education and contributing significantly to teacher absenteeism. Data from national and international test scores show that low achievement is widespread in most developing regions.

---

1. UIS has re-estimated the number of illiterates, using the latest data revisions. The present estimate is considerably lower than the 862 million for 2000 given in *EFA Global Monitoring Report 2003/4*. This is a consequence of several factors, notably the release of literacy data from recent censuses and surveys in many countries. For instance, China's 2000 census resulted in the UIS estimate of the number of adult illiterates in the country decreasing by over 50 million.

2. EDI value can range from 0 to 1. The closer the value is to 1, the closer a country is to meeting its goals and the greater is its EFA achievement.

The Education for All Development Index measures the extent to which countries are meeting four of the six EFA goals: UPE, gender parity, literacy and quality. Several countries – including some of the poorest – sharply improved their EFA achievement levels between 1998 and 2001. This indicates that poverty is not an unavoidable barrier to rapid progress towards EFA. On the other hand, massive educational deprivation continues to be concentrated in sub-Saharan Africa, the Arab States and South and West Asia.

- Forty-one countries (one-third of those for which the index can be calculated), most of them in North America and Western Europe and Central and Eastern Europe, have achieved the goals or are close to doing so.

- Fifty-one countries have EDI values between 0.80 and 0.94.[2] In about half of these, mostly in Latin America, the quality of education is lagging behind the other goals.

- Thirty-five countries are far from meeting the goals, with EDI values below 0.80. Twenty-two of these countries are in sub-Saharan Africa. Three very high-population countries of South Asia – Bangladesh, India and Pakistan – are also in this group.

Better quality education for all

■ **The challenge**: Education for all cannot be achieved without improving quality. In many parts of the world, an enormous gap persists between the numbers of students graduating from school and those among them who master a minimum set of cognitive skills. Any policy aimed at pushing net enrolments towards 100% must also assure decent learning conditions and opportunities. Lessons can be drawn from countries that have successfully addressed this dual challenge.

■ **Benefits**: Better education contributes to higher lifetime earnings and more robust national economic growth, and helps individuals make more informed choices about fertility and other matters important to their welfare. For example, it reduces exposure to HIV/AIDS: research shows that cognitive gains from basic education are the most important factor in protecting teenagers from infection. Such benefits are closely linked to the education levels achieved.

■ **Test scores**: International achievement tests reveal that socio-economic status has a strong influence on levels of school outcomes. Both educational and economic policies need to address initial and ongoing socio-economic inequalities among learners.

■ **Inclusion**: Uniform models of reform that ignore the multiple disadvantages faced by many learners will fail. Educational approaches for those who live with HIV/AIDS, emergency, disability and child labour should be given more support.

■ **Defining quality**: Two principles characterize most attempts to define quality in education: the first identifies learners' cognitive development as the major explicit objective of all education systems. Accordingly, the success with which systems achieve this is one indicator of their quality. The second emphasizes education's role in promoting values and attitudes of responsible citizenship and in nurturing creative and emotional development. The achievement of these objectives is more difficult to assess and compare across countries.

■ **Years in school**: Higher quality in education improves school life expectancy, though opportunities differ widely by region. On average for all countries, pupils can expect 9.2 years of primary plus secondary education; a child in sub-Saharan Africa, however, can expect to receive five to six fewer years of schooling than one in Western Europe and the Americas. People in countries with the highest levels of school life expectancy can expect to stay in school up to five times as long as those in countries at the bottom of the range.

■ **Resources**: In low-income countries, increasing spending to provide more textbooks, reduce class size and improve teacher education and school facilities has a positive impact on learners' cognitive achievement, though the relationship is weaker in richer countries where overall standards of provision are much higher. Improvements in quality can often be achieved at modest cost and are within reach even in the poorest countries. Where repetition rates in schools are very high, modest increases in quality can be partly self-financing because they reduce the length of time pupils take to complete the cycle.

■ **Coordination**: Stronger links among government departments responsible for early childhood care and education, literacy and health can help improve quality. In addition, gender-sensitive policies in education and broadly-based gender reforms in society can directly improve the quality of education.

■ **Better learning**: A solid body of evidence provides guidance on what makes schools effective. It emphasizes the dynamics of the teaching and learning process: how teachers and learners interact in the classroom and how well they use instructional materials. Policies for better learning must focus on:

● *Teachers*. Achieving UPE alone calls for more and better-trained teachers. Countries that have achieved high learning standards have invested steadily in the teaching profession. But in many countries, teachers' salaries relative to those of other professions have declined over the past two decades and are often too low to provide a reasonable standard of living. Training models for teachers should be reconsidered, in many countries, to strengthen school-based pre- and in-service training rather than rely on lengthy traditional, institutional pre-service training.

● *Learning time*. Instruction time is a crucial correlate of achievement: the broadly agreed benchmark of 850–1,000 hours of instruction per year for all pupils is not reached in many countries. Test scores clearly show that the amount of class time spent on mathematics, science and language strongly affects performance in these subjects.

● *Core subjects*. Literacy is a critical tool for the mastery of other subjects and one of the best predictors of longer-term learning achievement. Reading must be considered a priority area in efforts to improve the quality of basic education, particularly for learners from disadvantaged backgrounds.

● *Pedagogy*. Many commonly used teaching styles do not serve children well: they are often too rigid and rely heavily on rote learning, placing students in a passive role. Many educational researchers advocate structured teaching – a combination of direct instruction, guided practice and independent learning – in a child-friendly environment.

● *Language*. The choice of the language of instruction used in school is of utmost importance. Initial instruction in the learner's first language improves learning outcomes and reduces subsequent grade repetition and dropout rates.

● *Learning materials*. The quality and availability of learning materials strongly affect what teachers can do. Lack of textbooks can result from an inefficient distribution system, malpractice and corruption.

● *Facilities*. To achieve UPE, unprecedented refurbishing and building of classrooms is needed in many countries. Clean water, sanitation and access for disabled students are vital.

● *Leadership*. Central governments must be ready to give greater freedom to schools, provided that adequate resources are available and that roles and responsibilities are clearly defined. Head teachers/principals can have a strong influence on the quality of schools.

Executive Summary

In the many countries that are striving to guarantee all children the right to education, the focus on access often overshadows the issue of quality. Yet quality stands at the heart of Education for All. It determines how much and how well students learn, and the extent to which their education achieves a range of personal, social and development goals. This Report sets the quality debate in its historical context and offers a map for understanding, monitoring and improving quality (Chapter 1). It synthesizes current knowledge about the factors that influence quality (Chapter 2) and describes policy options for improving it, focusing on resource-constrained countries (Chapter 4). The extent to which the international community is supporting education in these countries is then analyzed (Chapter 5). As in the two previous editions, the Report monitors progress towards the six EFA goals adopted at Dakar in 2000, with more in-depth attention to quality indicators (Chapter 3). The Education for All Development Index, introduced in the previous Report, provides a summary overview of progress towards four of the Dakar goals in 127 countries.

Chapter 1

Understanding education quality

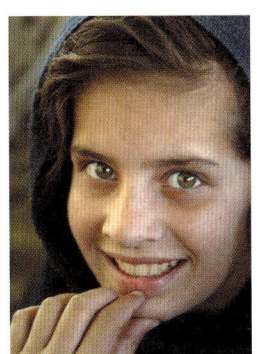

The goal of achieving universal primary education (UPE) has been on the international agenda since the Universal Declaration of Human Rights affirmed, in 1948, that elementary education was to be made free and compulsory for all children. This objective has been restated many times in international treaties and United Nations conference declarations. Many of these instruments, however, remain focused upon the quantitative aspects of education policy. Most recently, the United Nations Millennium Declaration set out the commitment to achieve UPE by 2015, without specific reference to its quality.

Other important instruments do emphasize the importance of quality, however. Goal 2 of the Dakar Framework for Action (2000) commits nations to the provision of primary education 'of good quality', and goal 6 includes commitments to improve all aspects of education quality 'so that recognized and measurable learning outcomes are achieved by all, especially in literacy, numeracy and essential life skills.'

A new consensus and impetus is building up around the imperative to improve the quality of education. How well students are taught and how much they learn are likely to have a crucial impact upon the length and value of their schooling experience. Quality can influence parents' choice to invest in their children's education. The range of intrinsic and social benefits associated with education, from better protection against disease to higher personal income, is strongly dependent on the quality of the teaching-learning process.

Although there is no single definition of quality, two principles characterize most attempts to define the objectives of education. The first, which identifies learners' cognitive development as the major explicit objective of all education systems, sees the success with which systems achieve this as one indicator of their quality. The second emphasizes the role of education in promoting commonly shared values along with creative and emotional development – objectives whose achievement is much more difficult to assess. Common ground is also found in the broadly shared objectives that tend to underpin debates about quality: respect for individual rights, improved equity of access and of learning outcomes, and increased relevance. These principles have been integrated into the aims of education set out in the Convention on the Rights of the Child (1990), which underpins the current positions on quality held by UNESCO and UNICEF.

The various approaches regarding quality have their roots in different traditions of educational thought. Humanist approaches, behaviourist theory, sociological critiques of education and challenges to the legacies of colonialism have each enriched the quality debate and spawned distinct visions of how the objectives of education should be achieved.

To reconcile a range of approaches, the Report adopts a framework that takes into account five major factors affecting quality: learners, whose diversity must be recognized; the national economic and social context; material and human resources; the teaching and learning process and the outcomes and benefits of education. By focusing on these dimensions and how they interact, it is possible to draw up a comprehensive map for understanding, monitoring and improving quality.

Chapter 2

The importance of good quality: what research tells us

Extensive research in a range of traditions has been conducted over the past forty years on how better education affects development outcomes and what factors are influential in improving quality.

The evidence is clear-cut on the links between good education and a wide range of economic and social development benefits. Better school outcomes – as represented by pupils' achievement test scores –

are closely related to higher income in later life. Empirical work has also demonstrated that high-quality schooling improves national economic potential. Strong social benefits are equally significant. It is well known that the acquisition of literacy and numeracy, especially by women, has an impact upon fertility. More recently, it has become clear that the cognitive skills required to make informed choices about HIV/AIDS risk and behaviour are strongly related to levels of education and literacy.

Test scores provide one important measure of how well the curriculum is being learned, and help to indicate achievement at the main exit points of the school system. A number of international assessments facilitate comparisons of learning achievements among countries and over time. They reveal, for example, that education quality in Africa has been particularly challenged in recent years, with declines in literacy achievement scores between 1995/96 and 2000/01 in one sample of countries. Several lessons can be drawn from studying the results of international tests over time. First, socio-economic status is very influential in determining achievement in all contexts. Second, the class time spent on mathematics, science and language strongly affects performance. Third, the teacher's gender has an impact in many lower-income countries. Several studies also show that the impact of pupils' socio-economic background can be partly offset by a better school climate, stronger support to teachers, greater school autonomy and additional resources, especially textbooks.

Identifying the best ways to improve learning outcomes has been tackled in many different ways. No general theory as to what determines the quality of education has been validated by empirical research. Many approaches in the economic tradition have assumed there is a workable analogy between schools and industrial production, in the sense that a set of inputs to schooling is transformed by teachers and pupils into a set of products, or outputs, in a fairly uniform way.

Common sense would suggest that the more resources spent per student, the better their performance. In eleven OECD countries, however, mathematics and science test scores generally fell over the quarter century ending in 1995, even though in many cases per pupil spending more than doubled. In developing countries, more positive links are apparent: a majority of studies suggest that cognitive achievement (as measured by standardized tests) increases as school expenditure, teacher education and school facilities are enhanced. Even here, however, there are few uncontested results. Other evidence from a growing body of experimental studies conducted in low-income countries shows that achievement is significantly improved by textbook provision, reduction of class size and child-friendly remedial education.

And yet schools are not factories producing outputs according to recipe in a technically deterministic way. A strong research tradition has sought to unpack the 'black box' of education by focusing on the learning process itself – the creative interaction between pupils and teachers in the classroom – with a view to drawing lessons from success. This research shows that good primary schools are typically characterized by strong leadership, an orderly and secure classroom environment, emphasis on acquiring basic skills, high expectations regarding pupils' attainment and frequent assessment of their progress. How well teachers master the curriculum, the level of their verbal skills and their expectations of students all contribute to school quality.

Finally, the social context of the school deserves attention. Studies in the sociology of education suggest that students whose family background and peer group have ideals close to those promoted by their school will tend to achieve higher levels of cognitive skills than others, who may try to escape the contradiction by rebelling. The need for education to be built around an explicit social goal presents challenges for the quality of schooling that cannot be addressed by technical means alone.

Case studies from eleven countries provide insights into how both rich and lower-income nations tackle quality. In countries with high rates of achievement, the quality of the teaching profession receives consistent attention. The experience of such countries also suggests that successful qualitative reforms require a strong leading role by government and a robust long-term vision for education.

Chapter 3

Assessing progress towards the EFA goals

This chapter provides an account of progress towards the six EFA goals based on the most recent global education data, for the 2001/02 school year, with particular attention to quality indicators (see box, p. 25).

The expansion of schooling is leading to a slow reduction in the number of out-of-school children of primary-school age, which dropped from 106.9 million in 1998 to 103.5 million in 2001 – a rate that appears insufficient to achieve UPE by 2015. Girls account for 57% of this group (more than 60% in the Arab States and in South and West Asia), and their participation in primary education is still substantially lower than that of boys in seventy-one out of 175 countries. With only three exceptions, all the countries with a gender parity index below 0.90 are in sub-Saharan Africa, the Arab States and South and West Asia. Completion of primary schooling remains a major cause for concern: delayed enrolment is widespread, survival rates to grade 5 are low (below 75% in thirty of the ninety-one countries with data) and grade repetition is frequent.

Quality is reflected by a range of indicators, including government spending on education, pupil/teacher ratios, teacher qualifications, test scores and the length of time pupils spend in school. Public expenditure on education represent a higher proportion of GDP in rich countries that have already achieved EFA goals (regional median: 5.52% in North America and Western Europe) than in poorer countries that need to sharply expand under-resourced school systems (regional medians: 3.3% in sub-Saharan Africa, 3.9% in East Asia and the Pacific).

The quality of teachers remains poor in many resource-constrained systems. The qualifications required to become a government primary-school teacher are variable, but they are often not met. Insufficient mastery of the curriculum is widespread. The HIV/AIDS crisis is aggravating teacher absenteeism. The large class sizes observed in primary schools of many low-income countries (e.g. one teacher for sixty pupils) are not conducive to adequate learning. In countries with the highest pupil-teacher ratios, barely one in three students who starts primary reaches grade 5. The absolute number of teachers also remains problematic in the countries that still need to significantly expand coverage.

Evidence from data on national and international assessments suggests that in too many countries, children are not mastering basic skills. Low achievement is widespread and most seriously affects countries where school systems are weak in terms of enrolment and available school resources.

Combining enrolments by age at primary, secondary and tertiary levels of education shows that the world's children gained a year of school life expectancy in the 1990s. The world average is 9.2 years of primary plus secondary education. A child in sub-Saharan Africa can expect to receive, on average, five to six fewer years of primary and secondary schooling than a child in Western Europe or the Americas.

Achieving higher levels of school participation is also tied to improving early childhood care and education programmes, yet progress towards wider access to them remains slow. Adult literacy, a desirable goal in its own right, also has a strong impact on children's education. Yet the world counts about 800 million illiterate adults;[1] 70% of them living in just nine countries belonging mostly to sub-Saharan Africa and East, South and West Asia.

Introduced in the 2003 EFA Global Monitoring Report, the Education for All Development Index (EDI) provides a summary quantitative measure of the extent to which countries are meeting four of the six EFA goals (UPE, gender, literacy and quality).

---

1. UIS has re-estimated the number of illiterates, using the latest data revisions. The present estimate is considerably lower than the 862 million for 2000 given in *EFA Global Monitoring Report 2003/4*. This is a consequence of several factors, notably the release of literacy data from recent censuses and surveys in many countries. For instance, China's 2000 census resulted in the UIS estimate of the number of adult illiterates in the country decreasing by over 50 million.

It shows that massive educational deprivation continues to be concentrated in sub-Saharan Africa, some of the Arab States and South and West Asia. Progress between 1998 and 2001 was widespread but not universal. About three-quarters of the seventy-four countries having the data registered a modest increase in their index value but at a rate insufficient to reach the EFA goals.

Chapter 4

Policies for better quality

Governments of low-income countries and others with severe resource constraints face difficult choices. This chapter sets out some priorities for policy that are not necessarily beyond such countries' reach. It starts by positioning learners at the heart of the learning experience. This may seem obvious but it is not always the reality. HIV/AIDS, disability, conflict and child labour place millions of children in a state of extreme vulnerability. Accordingly, policies must be inclusive, responding to the diverse needs and circumstances of all learners.

Priority must be given first and foremost to the spaces where teaching and learning actually take place. This includes attention to defining appropriate goals and relevant content. As a crucial correlate of achievement, instruction time deserves attention. Although 850-1,000 hours per year is a broadly agreed benchmark for minimum instruction time, this goal is not reached in many countries.

Across the world, commonly used styles and methods of teaching are not serving children well. In the spectrum running from traditional 'chalk-and-talk' teaching to 'open-ended instruction', many educators advocate structured teaching – a combination of direct instruction, guided practice and independent learning. Pedagogically sound language policy – allowing children to learn in their mother tongue for at least their first few school years – has a positive impact on learning. Regular assessments are also key to improving both teaching and learning.

Investment in teachers is critical. Balancing time and money spent on initial training and ongoing professional support is a key policy question. There is room to strengthen the emphasis on school-based training. Incentives to join the profession are closely tied to pay and conditions of service. In many resource-constrained countries, teachers' earnings are too low to provide a reasonable standard of living. What is more, teachers' pay has tended to decline over time relative to that of comparable groups. In some cases the problem can be lessened by improving central support to the management and supervision of schools and by assuring more timely payment of salaries. In other cases, multigrade and double-shift teaching can reduce unit costs if carefully implemented. Ensuring that all schools have teachers may also require incentives to work in rural environments.

Learning materials strongly affect what teachers can do. In this regard, national policies can encourage local publishing and increase the availability of textbooks. Equally important is the provision of basic sanitation, a sound infrastructure and other facilities to make schools safe and welcoming.

Schools need help to find their own solutions to improving quality, within well-defined accountability frameworks. Head teachers are critically important to this endeavour. Greater autonomy can make a difference provided that schools are well supported and have established capacity and strong leadership. Investment in services, networks and structures to develop and share educational knowledge can enable schools to make much better use of their resources, to learn from each other and to better inform policy.

Although all these policy reforms entail costs, a first step is to create a national consensus concerning quality. From this basis, priorities in a given society can be addressed. Any reform to improve quality should pay attention to establishing dialogue with teachers, strengthening accountability and combating corruption. Strategies must fit into a sound, coherent long-term vision of education and be backed by strong political commitment.

EXECUTIVE SUMMARY / 23

Chapter 5

Meeting our international commitments

The dual challenge of improving quality and expanding access in an equitable way requires a level of sustained investment that is currently beyond the reach of a large number of countries. This chapter takes stock of aid flows, analyses efforts to improve coordination among donors and with governments, and reviews evidence on the effectiveness of aid for education.

Recent estimates of the additional resources likely to be forthcoming in the follow-up to the 2002 International Conference on Finance for Development in Monterrey, together with those that could arise if the proposed International Finance Facility comes into existence, suggest that total aid to basic education could double, reaching about US$3–3.5 billion by 2006. This represents a substantial, if theoretical, level of increase. However, it remains well short of the US$7 billion per year in external aid to basic education that is likely to be required if universal participation in primary education of a reasonable quality is to be achieved by 2015, let alone the other EFA goals. The likely shortage of resources means a particular premium on ensuring that aid is used as effectively as possible and that it is directed towards the countries that most need it.

The objective of improving education quality is often not well served by current aid practice. First, many donors spread their aid across a large number of countries. This results in relatively high transaction costs within agencies. It can also place a heavy administrative burden on recipient governments dealing with multiple donors, each with its own procedures. Better coordinated aid provided by fewer agencies in individual countries is needed. Second, external models of good practice in education, advocated without any particular consistency by different groups of agencies, are often insufficiently attuned to local circumstances.

Sector-wide approaches are strengthening national ownership of policy and providing opportunities for donors to address the issue of quality holistically. On the other hand, this process involves intensive policy dialogue and the potential for undue donor influence, which can challenge local ownership of the process. Better harmonization and coordination among donors, support to governments where financial management is weak, and closer monitoring of the quality dimension are ways to make aid contribute more effectively to better learning outcomes.

Chapter 6

Towards EFA: the quality imperative

Whether a particular education system is of high or low quality can be judged only in terms of the extent to which its objectives are being met. Quality must also be judged in the mirror of equity. An education system in which there is gender inequality or discrimination against particular groups on ethical or cultural grounds is not a high-quality system. A shift towards equity represents, in itself, an improvement in the quality of education.

From a policy perspective, one fundamental reason why simply focusing upon the quantitative dimension of UPE and the other goals will not deliver EFA is that, in many parts of the world, an enormous gap prevails between the numbers graduating from schools and those among them who can master a minimum set of cognitive skills.

Governments committed to improving learning outcomes face difficult choices, but policies exist that are not necessarily beyond the reach of the most resource-constrained countries. They start with a focus on the learner and place emphasis on the dynamics of teaching and learning, supported by a growing body of research on what makes schools and teachers effective.

Links among different parts of the education sector can help improve quality but they are often hidden or ignored by the compartmentalised machinery of government. ECCE helps with subsequent achievement in school and further lifelong learning. Literacy improves adults' commitment to their children's education and is desirable in its own right. Gender-sensitive and inclusive policies directly improve the quality and outcomes of education.

Successful qualitative reforms require government to play a strong leading role. Although external assistance can boost resource levels and help in managing school systems, it cannot make up for the absence of a societal project for educational improvement. Accordingly, the domestic political process is ultimately the guarantor of successful reform. If it favours educational change, the chances that external assistance will facilitate a move towards higher-quality universal education are profoundly better than is the case where such political circumstances are absent.

Accurate, timely and consistent data

The availability of accurate, timely and consistent data, both quantitative and qualitative, is essential for the effective monitoring of progress towards the EFA goals. Such data are also vital for evidenced-based education policy and for the rigorous evaluation of practice. Disaggregated data are needed to identify areas of greatest inequality and to facilitate better national and local planning and evaluation.

This Report draws heavily on administrative data provided annually by national governments to the UNESCO Institute for Statistics (UIS). Those for the 2001/02 school year are the latest available from this source. They comprise a quality-assured data set, compiled in such a way that statistics are comparable for the majority of countries, using the International Standard Classification of Education. Inevitably, there is some time lag between the collection (and often the publication) of data by national governments and their release by UIS for use in this and other reports.

The annex tables demonstrate that some major limitations exist in the coverage of data, for example on the financing of education. These make it difficult to monitor several dimensions of EFA both nationally and globally, to undertake up-to-date trend analyses and, consequently, to monitor progress towards some EFA goals. Data gaps may also hinder aspects of national policy development in some countries, though information may be available at national level but not reported to UNESCO or not easily transferable into an internationally comparable framework.

Major efforts are under way by UIS to accelerate data collection and halve the current two-year time lag. Success in this endeavour will depend in many cases upon governments strengthening their own data collection and analysis capacities, with assistance from UIS and other agencies. UIS is also seeking to put in place a major programme of statistical capacity building, since the quality of data published reflects the quality of data that countries provide.

It should be noted that the Report also uses many other data sources, including national household surveys and specially commissioned studies. These enrich its analysis and enable it to map recent policy changes in countries and their potential impact on progress towards the achievement of EFA goals.

EFA Global Monitoring Report 2005

The smile of renewed hope in Afghanistan

© Radu Sigheti / REUTERS

Chapter 1

Understanding education quality

The goal of achieving universal primary education (UPE) has been on the international agenda since the Universal Declaration of Human Rights affirmed, in 1948, that elementary education was to be made freely and compulsorily available for all children in all nations. This objective was restated subsequently on many occasions, by international treaties and in United Nations conference declarations.[1] Most of these declarations and commitments are silent about the quality of education to be provided.

Why focus on quality?

Although some of the international treaties, by specifying the need to provide education on human rights, reproductive health, sports and gender awareness, touched on educational quality,[2] they were generally silent about how well education systems could and should be expected to perform in meeting these objectives. This remained true as recently as 2000, when the United Nations Millennium Declaration's commitment to achieve UPE by 2015 was directly and simply set out without explicit reference to quality (see Box 1.1). Thus, in placing the emphasis upon assuring access for all, these instruments mainly focused on the quantitative aspects of education policy.

It seems highly likely, however, that the achievement of universal participation in education will be fundamentally dependent upon the quality of education available. For example, how well pupils are taught and how much they learn, can have a crucial impact on how long they stay in school and how regularly they attend. Furthermore, whether parents send their children to school at all is likely to depend on judgements they make about the quality of teaching and learning provided – upon whether attending school is worth the time and cost for their children and for themselves. The instrumental roles of schooling – helping individuals achieve their own economic, social and cultural objectives and helping society to be better protected, better served by its leaders and more equitable in important ways – will be strengthened if education is of higher quality.[3] Schooling helps children develop creatively and emotionally and acquire the skills, knowledge, values and attitudes necessary for responsible, active and productive citizenship. How well education achieves these outcomes is important to those who use it. Accordingly, analysts and policy makers alike should also find the issue of quality difficult to ignore.

More fundamentally, education is a set of processes and outcomes that are *defined* qualitatively. The *quantity* of children who participate is by definition a secondary consideration: merely filling spaces called 'schools' with children would not address even

> The achievement of universal participation in education will be fundamentally dependent upon the quality of education available

---

1. Such statements are found in the declarations that emerged from a series of United Nations regional conferences on education in the early 1960s, in the treaties that formed the International Bill of Human Rights in the 1970s, in the World Declaration on Education for All adopted at the World Conference on Education for All in Jomtien, Thailand, 1990 and in the Millennium Declaration and the Dakar Framework for Action in 2000 (for details see UNESCO, 2003a: 24-8). The last two reaffirmed the commitment to achieve universal provision and access to primary schooling and added a target year: 2015.

2. This was most notably so with the Convention on the Rights of the Child, which came into force in 1990.

3. This categorization of the ways in which education is valuable to individuals and society is informed by the classification suggested by Drèze and Sen (2002: 38-40).

Box 1.1 The Dakar Framework for Action and Millennium Development Goals

■ **EFA Dakar goals**

1. Expanding and improving comprehensive **early childhood care and education**, especially for the most vulnerable and disadvantaged children.

2. Ensuring that by 2015 all children, particularly girls, children in difficult circumstances and those belonging to ethnic minorities have access to complete **free and compulsory primary education of good quality**.

3. Ensuring that the learning needs of all young people and adults are met through equitable access to appropriate learning and **life skills** programmes.

4. Achieving a 50 per cent improvement in levels of adult **literacy** by 2015, especially for women, and equitable access to basic and continuing education for all adults.

5. Eliminating gender disparities in primary and secondary education by 2005 and achieving **gender equality** in education by 2015, with a focus on ensuring girls' full and equal access to (and achievement in) basic education of good quality.

6. Improving all aspects of the **quality of education** and ensuring excellence of all so that recognized and measurable learning outcomes are achieved by all, especially in literacy, numeracy and essential life skills.

■ **Millennium Development Goals**

Goal 2. Achieve universal primary education
Target 3. Ensure that by 2015 children everywhere, boys and girls alike, will be able to complete a full course of primary schooling.

Goal 3. Promote gender equality and empower women
Target 4. Eliminate gender disparity in primary and secondary education, preferably by 2005, and at all levels of education no later than 2015.

> Box 1.2 **Education quality as defined in Jomtien and Dakar**
>
> In 1990, the World Declaration on Education for All noted that the generally poor quality of education needed to be improved and recommended that education be made both universally available and more relevant. The Declaration also identified quality as a prerequisite for achieving the fundamental goal of equity. While the notion of quality was not fully developed, it was recognized that expanding access alone would be insufficient for education to contribute fully to the development of the individual and society. Emphasis was accordingly placed on assuring an increase in children's cognitive development by improving the quality of their education.
>
> A decade later, the Dakar Framework for Action declared that access to quality education was the right of every child. It affirmed that quality was '*at the heart of education*' – a fundamental determinant of enrolment, retention and achievement. Its expanded definition of quality set out the desirable characteristics of learners (healthy, motivated students), processes (competent teachers using active pedagogies), content (relevant curricula) and systems (good governance and equitable resource allocation). Although this established an agenda for achieving good education quality, it did not ascribe any relative weighting to the various dimensions identified.

quantitative objectives if no real education occurred. Thus, the number of years of school is a practically useful but conceptually dubious proxy for the processes that take place there and the outcomes that result. In that sense, it could be judged unfortunate that the quantitative aspects of education have become the main focus of attention in recent years for policy makers (and many quantitatively inclined social scientists).

It should come as no surprise, therefore, that the two most recent United Nations international conference declarations focusing on education gave some importance to its qualitative dimension (Box 1.2). The Jomtien Declaration in 1990 and, more particularly, the Dakar Framework for Action in 2000 recognized the quality of education as a prime determinant of whether Education for All is achieved. More specifically than earlier pledges, the second of the six goals set out in the Dakar Framework commits nations to the provision of primary education 'of good quality' (Box 1.1). Moreover, the sixth goal includes commitments to improve all aspects of education quality so that everyone can achieve better learning outcomes, 'especially in literacy, numeracy and essential life skills'.

Notwithstanding the growing consensus about the need to provide access to education of 'good quality', there is much less agreement about what the term actually means in practice.[4] Box 1.3 summarizes the evolution of UNESCO's understanding of education quality. This effort in definition goes beyond the intrinsic and instrumental goals of education mentioned earlier. It seeks to identify unambiguously the important attributes or qualities of education that can best ensure that those goals are actually met. Similar formulations can be found in documents produced by other international organizations and in the vast array of literature dealing with the content and practice of education. Although the details differ, two key elements characterize such approaches:

- First, cognitive development is identified as a major explicit objective of all education systems. The degree to which systems actually achieve this is one indicator of their quality. While this indicator can be measured relatively easily – at least within individual societies, if not through international comparison – it is much more difficult to determine how to improve the results. Thus, if quality is defined in terms of cognitive achievement, ways of securing increased quality are neither straightforward nor universal.

- The second element is education's role in encouraging learners' creative and emotional development, in supporting objectives of peace, citizenship and security, in promoting equality and in passing global and local cultural values down to future generations. Many of these objectives are defined and approached in diverse ways around the world. Compared with cognitive development, the extent to which they are achieved is harder to determine.

It could be judged unfortunate that the quantitative aspects of education have become the main focus of attention in recent years for policy makers

[4]. Adams (1993) identifies about fifty different definitions of the term.

Box 1.3 The evolution of UNESCO's conceptualization of quality

One of UNESCO's first position statements on quality in education appeared in *Learning to Be: The World of Education Today and Tomorrow*, the report of the International Commission on the Development of Education chaired by the former French minister Edgar Faure. The commission identified the fundamental goal of social change as the eradication of inequality and the establishment of an equitable democracy. Consequently, it reported, 'the aim and content of education must be recreated, to allow both for the new features of society and the new features of democracy' (Faure et al., 1972: xxvi). The notions of 'lifelong learning' and 'relevance', it noted, were particularly important. The Report strongly emphasized science and technology as well. Improving the quality of education, it stated, would require systems in which the principles of scientific development and modernization could be learned in ways that respected learners' socio-cultural contexts.

More than two decades later came *Learning: The Treasure Within, Report to UNESCO of the International Commission on Education for the Twenty-first Century*, chaired by another French statesman, Jacques Delors. This commission saw education throughout life as based upon four pillars:

- *Learning to know* acknowledges that learners build their own knowledge daily, combining indigenous and 'external' elements.

- *Learning to do* focuses on the practical application of what is learned.

- *Learning to live together* addresses the critical skills for a life free from discrimination, where all have equal opportunity to develop themselves, their families and their communities.

- *Learning to be* emphasizes the skills needed for individuals to develop their full potential.

This conceptualization of education provided an integrated and comprehensive view of learning and, therefore, of what constitutes education quality (Delors et al., 1996).

The importance of good quality education was resolutely reaffirmed as a priority for UNESCO at a Ministerial Round Table on Quality of Education, held in Paris in 2003.

UNESCO promotes access to good-quality education as a human right and supports a rights-based approach to all educational activities (Pigozzi, 2004). Within this approach, learning is perceived to be affected at two levels. At the level of the *learner*, education needs to seek out and acknowledge learners' prior knowledge, to recognize formal and informal modes, to practise non-discrimination and to provide a safe and supportive learning environment. At the level of the *learning system*, a support structure is needed to implement policies, enact legislation, distribute resources and measure learning outcomes, so as to have the best possible impact on learning for all.

Quality for whom and what? Rights, equity and relevance

Although opinions about quality in education are by no means unified, at the level of international debate and action three principles tend to be broadly shared. They can be summarized as the need for more relevance, for greater equity of access and outcome and for proper observance of individual rights. In much current international thinking, these principles guide and inform educational content and processes and represent more general social goals to which education itself should contribute.

Of these, the question of *rights* is at the apex. Although, as indicated earlier, most human rights legislation focuses upon access to education and is comparatively silent about its quality, the Convention on the Rights of the Child is an important exception. It expresses strong, detailed commitments about the aims of education. These commitments, in turn, have implications for the content and quality of education. Box 1.4 summarizes the relevant sections.

The Convention takes the educational development of the individual as a central aim. It indicates that education should allow children to reach their fullest potential in terms of cognitive, emotional and creative capacities. The learner is at the centre of the educational experience, in a context also characterized by respect for others and for the environment.

The Convention has important implications for both the content and the process of education. It implies that the learning experience should be not simply a means but also an end in itself, having intrinsic worth. It suggests an approach to teaching (and the development of textbooks and learning materials) that upholds the idea of a child-centred education, using teaching

> **Education should allow children to reach their fullest potential in terms of cognitive, emotional and creative capacities**

> **Box 1.4 The aims of education, from the Convention on the Rights of the Child, Article 29 (1)**
>
> 1. States Parties agree that the education of the child shall be directed to:
>
> (a) The development of the child's personality, talents and mental and physical abilities to their fullest potential;
>
> (b) The development of respect for human rights and fundamental freedoms, and for the principles enshrined in the Charter of the United Nations;
>
> (c) The development of respect for the child's parents, his or her own cultural identity, language and values, for the national values of the country in which the child is living, the country from which he or she may originate, and for civilizations different from his or her own;
>
> (d) The preparation of the child for responsible life in a free society, in the spirit of understanding, peace, tolerance, equality of sexes, and friendship among all peoples, ethnic, national and religious groups and persons of indigenous origin;
>
> (e) The development of respect for the natural environment.

processes that promote – or at least do not undermine – children's rights. Corporal punishment is deemed here to be a clear violation of these rights. Some dimensions of this 'rights-based approach' to education is evident in the position adopted by UNICEF (Box 1.5).

Other international legislation, such as the International Covenant on Civil and Political Rights and the International Covenant on Economic, Social and Cultural Rights, addresses the principle of equity by stressing government's responsibility to ensure that all children have access to education of an acceptable quality. Brazil, Costa Rica and the Philippines provide three examples of countries that have constitutional provisions guaranteeing a percentage of the budget for education, in accordance with the International Covenant on Economic, Social and Cultural Rights. Such legal safeguards permit stakeholders to hold governments accountable for progressive realization of the right to education and for aspects of its quality. (Wilson, 2004)

Where human rights legislation deals with education, its central concern is *equity*: the objective of increasing equality in learning outcomes, access and retention. This ambition reflects a belief that all children can develop basic cognitive skills, given the right learning environment. That many who go to school fail to develop these skills is due in part to a deficiency in education quality. Recent analyses confirm that poverty, rural residence and gender inequality persist as the strongest inverse correlates of school attendance and performance (UNESCO, 2003a) and that poor instruction is a significant source of this inequality. Quality and equity are inextricably linked.

The notion of *relevance* has always attended debates about the quality of education. In the past, and particularly in developing countries, imported or inherited curricula have often been judged insufficiently sensitive to the local context and to learners' socio-cultural circumstances. The Convention on the Rights of the Child stresses a child-centred approach to teaching and learning.[5] This in turn emphasises the importance of curricula that as far as possible respond to the needs and priorities of the learners, their families, and communities.

Relevance is also an issue for national policy. With the acceleration of global economic integration, governments have become more

The Convention on the Rights of the Child stresses a child-centred approach to teaching and learning

> **Box 1.5 The UNICEF approach to quality**
>
> UNICEF strongly emphasizes what might be called desirable dimensions of quality, as identified in the Dakar Framework. Its paper *Defining Quality in Education* recognizes five dimensions of quality: learners, environments, content, processes and outcomes, founded on 'the rights of the whole child, and all children, to survival, protection, development and participation' (UNICEF, 2000). Like the dimensions of education quality identified by UNESCO (Pigozzi, 2004), those recognized by UNICEF draw on the philosophy of the Convention on the Rights of the Child.

---

5. According to the Appendix to General Comment No. 1 on Article 29 (1) of the Convention on the Rights of the Child (United Nations, 2001a), "this article emphasizes the message of child-centred education: that the key goal of education is the development of the individual child's personality, talents and abilities, in recognition of the fact that every child has unique characteristics, interests, abilities, and learning needs. Thus, the curriculum must be of direct relevance to the child's social, cultural, environmental and economic context..."

preoccupied with whether their education systems produce the skills necessary for economic growth in an increasingly competitive environment. Increasing mobility has also brought concerns about the extent to which learning, measured in terms of qualifications, is transferable. This has led to increased monitoring and regulation of education systems and to a flourishing industry of cross-national learning assessment using comparative benchmarks. Critics have voiced caution that such studies, such as those discussed in Chapters 2 and 3 of this Report, may contribute to the standardization of cognitive skills informed by a set of culturally exclusive principles and knowledge. Recent research has shown that even skills as basic as literacy and numeracy can be conceived and taught in quite varied ways[6] and thus run the risk of misrepresentation by culturally insensitive assessment.

As with all aspects of development, a balance should be struck between ensuring the relevance of education to the socio-cultural realities of learners, to their aspirations, and to the well-being of the nation.

Education traditions and associated notions of quality[7]

When thinking about the quality of education it is useful to distinguish between educational outcomes and the processes leading to them. People who seek particular, defined outcomes may rate quality in those terms, ranking educational institutions according to the extent to which their graduates meet 'absolute' criteria concerning, for example, academic achievement, sporting prowess, musical success, or pupil behaviour and values. The standard of comparison would be in some sense fixed, and separate from the values, wishes and opinions of the learners themselves.[8] By contrast, relativist approaches emphasize that the perceptions, experiences and needs of those involved in the learning experience mainly determine its quality.[9] Drawing on a business analogy, 'client orientation' in education puts strong emphasis upon whether a programme fits its purposes in ways that reflect the needs of those who use it. These different emphases have deep roots, and are reflected in major alternative traditions of educational thought.

Humanist approaches

The ideas that human nature is essentially good, that individual behaviour is autonomous (within the constraints of heredity and environment), that everyone is unique, that all people are born equal and subsequent inequality is a product of circumstance and that reality for each person is defined by himself or herself characterize a range of liberal humanist philosophers from Locke to Rousseau.[10] Such principles, where accepted, have immediate relevance for educational practice. Learners, for humanists, are at the centre of 'meaning-making', which implies a relativist interpretation of quality. Education, strongly influenced by learner actions, is judged central to developing the potential of the child.[11]

The notion that acquisition of knowledge and skills requires the active participation of individual learners is a central link between humanism and constructivist learning theory. The latter was influenced strongly by the work of John Dewey, who emphasized the ways in which people learn how to construct their own meanings and to integrate theory and practice as a basis for social action.[12] Piaget (1971) was also influential in developing a more 'active'

Box 1.6 Quality in the humanist tradition

● Standardized, prescribed, externally defined or controlled curricula are rejected. They are seen as undermining the possibilities for learners to construct their own meanings and for educational programmes to remain responsive to individual learners' circumstances and needs.

● The role of assessment is to give learners information and feedback about the quality of their individual learning. It is integral to the learning process. Self-assessment and peer assessment are welcomed as ways of developing deeper awareness of learning.

● The teacher's role is more that of facilitator than instructor.

● Social constructivism, while accepting these tenets, emphasizes learning as a process of social practice rather than the result of individual intervention.

---

6. See footnote 24.

7. The 'traditions' discussed here entail different ideas of what constitutes quality in teaching and learning. While each differs in its ideology, epistemology and disciplinary composition, all ask what individual or social purposes education should serve and how teaching and learning should occur. It is important to distinguish between these broad traditions and the more specific pedagogies discussed later in the Report. While few pedagogies are value-neutral, none is restricted to one tradition. Nor do education systems usually reflect a single model of education. Accordingly, this Report will consider pedagogies in functional terms rather than from the philosophical perspectives that inform them.

8. Focusing on absolute output characteristics of education programmes does not preclude a 'value-added' approach that takes differences in ability into account.

9. Some writers distinguish between two relative approaches. One, emphasizing the extent to which an education programme suits its intended purpose, might focus on organizational processes; the other, emphasizing learners' needs and capacities, would be strongly responsive to particular 'client groups' (Sallis, 1996: 15-7).

10. See Russell (1961: 577-83) and Elias and Merriam (1980).

11. In this context, Rousseau believed there was one developmental process common to all humans. This, he asserted, was an intrinsic, natural process whose primary behavioural motivation was curiosity. An advocate of universal schooling, Rousseau designed a method that involved removing children from society (for example, to a country home) and exposing them to changed environments and problems to solve or overcome. Once children reached the age of reason (about 12 years), they were considered capable of engaging as 'free' individuals in a continuing process of education (Rousseau, 1911).

12. Dewey (1916) saw pupils as creating knowledge in the classroom and transforming their identities through 'a process of learning by performing new roles' (Fenwick, 2001: 3).

> **Box 1.7 Quality in the behaviourist tradition**
>
> - Standardized, externally defined and controlled curricula, based on prescribed objectives and defined independently of the learner, are endorsed.
> - Assessment is seen as an objective measurement of learned behaviour against preset assessment criteria.
> - Tests and examinations are considered central features of learning and the main means of planning and delivering rewards and punishments.
> - The teacher directs learning, as the expert who controls stimuli and responses.
> - Incremental learning tasks that reinforce desired associations in the mind of the learner are favoured.

and 'participatory' role for children in their learning.[13] More recently, social constructivism, which regards learning as intrinsically a social – and, therefore, interactive – process, has tended to supersede more conventional constructivist approaches.[14] Box 1.6 summarizes the approach to education quality in the humanist tradition.

Behaviourist approaches

Behaviourist theory leads in the opposite direction to humanism. It is based on manipulation of behaviour via specific stimuli.[15] Behaviourism exerted a significant influence on educational reform during the first half of the twentieth century (Blackman, 1995). Its main tenets were that:

- Learners are not intrinsically motivated or able to construct meaning for themselves.
- Human behaviour can be predicted and controlled through reward and punishment.
- Cognition is based on the shaping of behaviour.
- Deductive and didactic pedagogies, such as graded tasks, rote learning and memorization, are helpful.[16]

Although few educationists accept the full behaviourist agenda in its pure form, elements of behaviourist practice can be observed in many countries in teacher-training programmes, curricula and the ways teachers actually operate in classrooms.[17] Forms of direct or structured instruction, which have an important place in this Report, share a key element with the behaviourist tradition: the belief that learning achievement must be monitored and that frequent feedback is crucial in motivating and guiding the learner. Box 1.7 summarizes the behaviourist approach to education quality.

Critical approaches

Over the final quarter of the twentieth century, several important critiques of the precepts of humanism and behaviourism emerged. Sociologists had already perceived society as a system of interrelated parts, with order and stability maintained by commonly held values.[18] Since the role of education is to transmit these values, quality in this approach would be measured by the effectiveness of the processes of value transmission. In the latter part of the twentieth century, critics began to acknowledge these processes as highly political. Some neo-Marxist approaches characterized education in capitalist societies as the main mechanism for legitimizing and reproducing social inequality.[19] Others, in the 'new sociology of education' movement of the 1970s and 1980s, focused their critiques on the role of the curriculum as a social and political means of transmitting power and knowledge.[20] A separate group of critical writers, known as the 'de-schoolers', called for the abandonment of schooling in favour of more community-organized forms of formal education.[21] Other critiques of orthodox approaches included various postmodern and feminist views.[22]

While the critical approaches encompass a vast array of philosophies, they share a concern that education tends to reproduce the structures and inequalities of the wider society. Though many retain the founding humanist principle that human development is the ultimate end of thought and action, they question the belief that universal schooling will result automatically in equal development of learners' potential. As a reaction against this, advocates of an 'emancipatory pedagogy' suggested that 'critical intellectuals' should work to empower

13. Piaget (1972), in his theory of 'genetic epistemology', identifies patterns of physical and mental activity corresponding to stages of child development. Rather than seeing new learning as simply linking to prior learning, Piaget argues that learners need to be faced with a conflict between the two; otherwise, knowledge is static and learning cannot take place.

14. These approaches derive largely from Dewey's pragmatism and the 'social development theory' of Vygotsky (1978). The latter advances the notion that learning happens first in relation to others, only later being internalized individually. Thus, social interaction leads to cognitive development. This is the opposite of Piaget's standpoint.

15. As an example of 'classic' behaviourist theory, consider two types of conditioning – 'respondant' and 'operant' (Skinner, 1968). The first refers to a process by which a subject is conditioned to respond to an external stimulus (for example, Pavlov's dog salivating at the sound of the bell announcing feeding time). Operant conditioning refers to reinforcement of such a response through reward/punishment systems (for example, feeding the dog or withholding food) that stimulate new learning and/or the abandonment of old behaviour.

16. These notions generated the 'objective' school of education, first manifested in attempts by Bobbitt (1918) to apply the ideas of the management expert F. W. Taylor to school curricula. Other noteworthy approaches are Tyler's *Basic Principles of Curriculum and Instruction* (1949) and Bloom's taxonomy (1956), which set out educational objectives against which finely tuned testing instruments could be developed.

17. Jarvis (1983: 61) suggests that even seemingly 'innocent' practices such as 'praising a reticent student for contributing to a group discussion' have underpinnings in Skinner's operant conditioning.

18. These included functionalist theorists (e.g. Parsons, 1959) and some structuralists (e.g. Durkheim, 1956).

19. Notably Bourdieu and Passeron (1964), Bowles and Gintis (1976), Apple (1978), Spring (1972) and Michéa (1999).

20. Notably Young (1971), Keddie (1971) and Bourdieu (1977).

21. Notably Illich (1971).

22. 'Postmodernism' and 'post-structuralism' are often used interchangeably. Their common theme is that power and knowledge reside in discourse, not in structures. Foucault (1977) argues that power and power relationships create the conditions for the production of knowledge. This is reflected at a deep level within curricula.

Box 1.8 Quality in the critical tradition

Critical theorists focus on inequality in access to and outcomes of education and on education's role in legitimizing and reproducing social structures through its transmission of a certain type of knowledge that serves certain social groups. Accordingly, these sociologists and critical pedagogues tend to equate good quality with:

- education that prompts social change;
- a curriculum and teaching methods that encourage critical analysis of social power relations and of ways in which formal knowledge is produced and transmitted;
- active participation by learners in the design of their own learning experience.

---

marginalized students by helping them analyse their experience – and thus redress social inequality and injustice. Critical pedagogy, in this view, is emancipatory in the sense that it lets students find their own voices (Freire, 1985), frees them from externally defined needs (Giroux, 1993) and helps them to explore alternative ways of thinking that may have been buried under dominant norms (McLaren, 1994). Box 1.8 outlines the key features of the critical approaches as regards education quality.

Indigenous approaches

Some important efforts to develop alternative educational ideas are rooted in the realities of lower-income countries and have often arisen as challenges to the legacies of colonialism. Prominent examples include the approaches of Mahatma Gandhi and Julius Nyerere, both of whom proposed new and alternative education systems with culturally relevant emphases on self-reliance, equity and rural employment.[23]

Such indigenous approaches challenged the 'imported' knowledge, images, ideas, values and beliefs reflected in mainstream curricula. A positive example of the alternatives offered, in curriculum terms, is in the field of mathematics. 'Ethno-mathematicians' claim that 'standard' mathematics is neither neutral nor objective, but culturally biaised and that alternative forms exist that have implications for teaching and learning.[24] Box 1.9 presents some important features common to indigenous approaches.

Adult education approaches

Adult education is frequently ignored in debates about education quality, but it has its share of behaviourist, humanist and critical approaches (see Box 1.10). Some writers, with roots in humanism and constructivism, emphasize the experience of adults as a central learning

Box 1.10 Quality in adult education approaches

In the adult education tradition, experience and critical reflection in learning is an important aspect of quality. Radical theorists see learners as socially situated, with the potential to use their experience and learning as a basis for social action and social change.

---

23. Gandhi and Nyerere both incorporated the teaching of simple vocational skills in formal curricula. Nyerere (1968) set out a vision of 'Education for Self Reliance' for the United Republic of Tanzania. His vision rested on several key educational aims: preserving and transmitting traditional values, promoting national and local self-reliance, fostering co-operation and promoting equality. In southern Africa, the notion of *ubuntu*, with its connotations of community, informs an alternative vision of education as embracing the social nature of being, rather than individual advancement (Tutu, 2000).

24. Examples of this approach, as identified by Gerdes (2001), include:
- Sociomathematics of Africa: Zaslavsky (1973: 7) examines 'the applications of mathematics in the lives of African people and, conversely, the influence that African institutions had upon the evolution of their mathematics'.
- Mathematics in the (African) socio-cultural environment: Touré (1984: 1-2) draws attention to the mathematics of African games in Côte d'Ivoire and suggest that crafts belonging to learners' socio-cultural environment should be integrated in the mathematics curriculum.

Box 1.9 Quality in the indigenous tradition

Challenging dominant Northern ideas about the quality of education, indigenous approaches reassert the importance of education's relevance to the socio-cultural circumstances of the nation and learner.

The following principles are implied:

- Mainstream approaches imported from Europe are not necessarily relevant in very different social and economic circumstances.

- Assuring relevance implies local design of curriculum content, pedagogies and assessment.

- All learners have rich sources of prior knowledge, accumulated through a variety of experiences, which educators should draw out and nourish.

- Learners should play a role in defining their own curriculum.

- Learning should move beyond the boundaries of the classroom/school through non-formal and lifelong learning activities.

resource.[25] Others see adult education as an essential part of socio-cultural, political and historical transformation.[26] The latter view is most famously associated with literacy programmes and with the work of the radical theorist Paulo Freire, for whom education was an intensely important mechanism for awakening political awareness.[27] His work urges adult educators not only to engage learners in dialogue, to name oppressive experiences, but also, through 'problem posing' and 'conscientization', to realize the extent to which they themselves have been influenced by repressive societal forces.

A framework for understanding, monitoring and improving education quality

Given the diversity of understanding and interpretation of quality evident in the different traditions discussed above, defining quality and developing approaches to monitoring and improving it requires dialogue designed to achieve:

- broad agreement about the aims and objectives of education;
- a framework for the analysis of quality that enables its various dimensions to be specified;
- an approach to measurement that enables the important variables to be identified and assessed;
- a framework for improvement that comprehensively covers the interrelated components of the education system and allows opportunities for change and reform to be identified.

As earlier sections of this chapter have indicated, cognitive development and the accumulation of particular values, attitudes and skills are important objectives of education systems in most societies. Their content may differ but their broad structure is similar throughout the world. This may suggest that in one sense the key to improving the quality of education – to helping education systems better achieve these objectives – could be equally universal. Considerable research has been directed towards this question in recent years. As Chapter 2 shows, however, the number of factors that can affect educational outcomes is so vast that straightforward relationships between the conditions of education and its products are not easy to determine.

Nevertheless, it helps to begin by thinking about the main elements of education systems and how they interact. To this end, we might characterize the central dimensions influencing the core processes of teaching and learning as follows:

- learner characteristics dimension;
- contextual dimension;
- enabling inputs dimension;
- teaching and learning dimension.
- outcomes dimension.

Figure 1.1 illustrates these dimensions and their relationships, and the following subsections discuss their characteristics and interactions.

Learner characteristics

How people learn – and how quickly – is strongly influenced by their capacities and experience. Assessments of the quality of education outputs that ignore initial differences among learners are likely to be misleading. Important determining characteristics can include socio-economic background, health, place of residence, cultural and religious background and the amount and nature of prior learning. It is therefore important that potential inequalities among students, deriving from gender, disability, race and ethnicity, HIV/AIDS status and situations of emergency are recognized. These differences in learner characteristics often require special responses if quality is to be improved.

Context

Links between education and society are strong, and each influences the other. Education can help change society by improving and strengthening skills, values, communications, mobility (link with personal opportunity and prosperity), personal prosperity and freedom. In the short term, however, education usually reflects society rather strongly: the values and attitudes that inform it are those of society at large. Equally important is whether education takes place in the context of an affluent society or one where poverty is widespread. In the latter case, opportunities to increase resources for education are likely to be constrained.

Links between education and society are strong, and each influences the other

---

25. Knowles (1980) lists experience as one of five principles of adult learning theory in which reflection by individuals is a central part of the educational process. The learning cycle developed by Kolb (1984) also has 'concrete experience' as the starting point for learning, based on reflection.

26. For an overview of paradigms in adult learning, see UIE (2004).

27. In his most influential work, *Pedagogy of the Oppressed*, Freire characterized the education normally provided to the poor as 'banking education', seeing it as being of inferior quality and irrelevant to learners' needs. He argued that educational practice that excludes alternative interpretations of a particular reality reinforces the power of the teacher and encourages non-critical analysis by students. Freire saw the agency of the learner and her or his prior knowledge as central to the learning process, maintaining that the learner must take on 'full responsibility as an actor with knowledge and not as recipient of the teacher's discourse' (Freire, 1985: 47-8). This activist perspective drew attention to the deeper political changes and reforms necessary for improvement in education quality. Newer approaches include those of Usher and Edwards (1994), who bring post-structural and postmodern perspectives to bear on adult education and learning, and Fenwick (2001), who draws on experiential learning in innovative ways.

Figure 1.1: A framework for understanding education quality

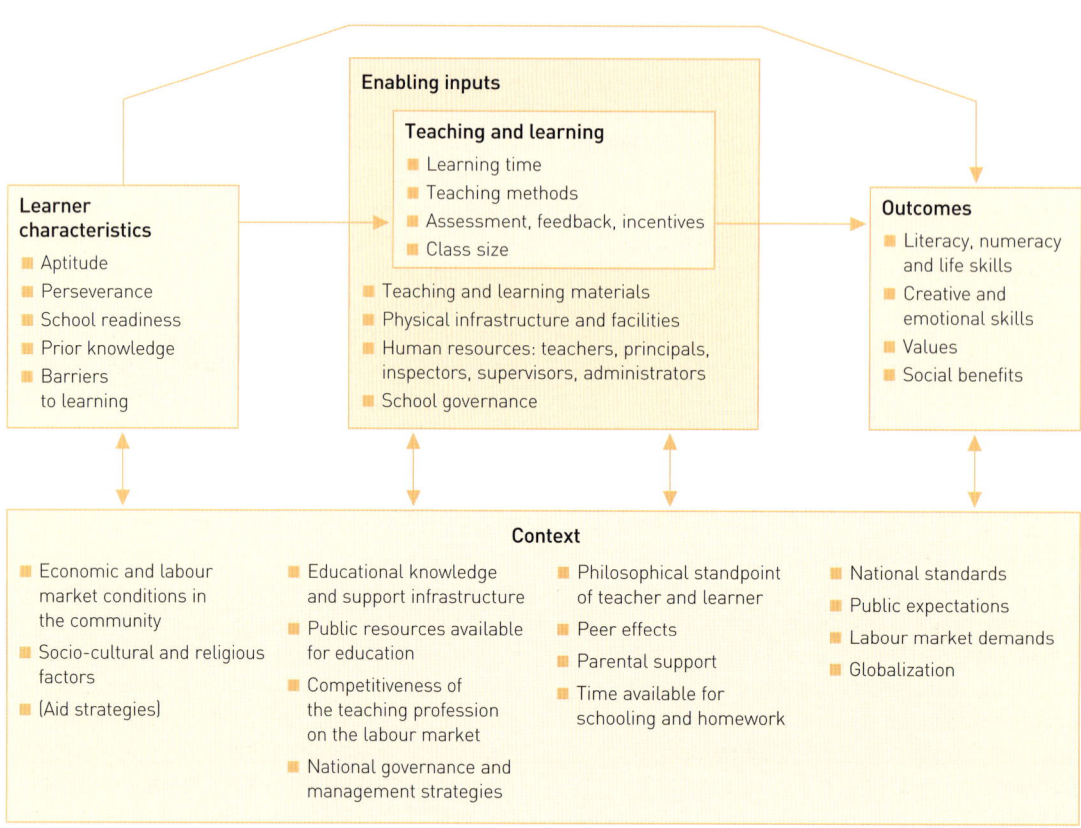

It is obvious that schools without teachers, textbooks or learning materials will not be able to do an effective job

More directly, national policies for education also provide an influential context. For example, goals and standards, curricula and teacher policies set the enabling conditions within which educational practice occurs. These contextual circumstances have an important potential influence upon education quality. International aid strategies are also influential in most developing countries.

Enabling inputs

Other things being equal, the success of teaching and learning is likely to be strongly influenced by the resources made available to support the process and the direct ways in which these resources are managed. It is obvious that schools without teachers, textbooks or learning materials will not be able to do an effective job. In that sense, resources are important for education quality – although how and to what extent this is so has not yet been fully determined. Inputs are *enabling* in that they underpin and are intrinsically interrelated to teaching and learning processes, which in turn affects the range and the type of inputs used and how effectively they are employed. The main input variables are material and human resources, with the governance of these resources as an important additional dimension:

■ Material resources, provided both by governments and households, include textbooks and other learning materials and the availability of classrooms, libraries, school facilities and other infrastructure.

■ Human resource inputs include managers, administrators, other support staff, supervisors, inspectors and, most importantly, teachers. Teachers are vital to the education process. They are both affected by the macro context in which it takes place and central to its successful outcomes. Useful proxies here are pupil/teacher ratio, average teacher salaries and the proportion of education spending allocated to various items. Material and human resources together are often measured by expenditure indicators, including public current expenditure per pupil and the proportion of GDP spent on education.

- Enabling school-level governance concerns the ways in which the school is organized and managed. Examples of potentially important factors having an indirect impact on teaching and learning are strong leadership, a safe and welcoming school environment, good community involvement and incentives for achieving good results.

Teaching and learning

As Figure 1.1 indicates, the teaching and learning process is closely nested within the support system of inputs and other contextual factors. Teaching and learning is the key arena for human development and change. It is here that the impact of curricula is felt, that teacher methods work well or not and that learners are motivated to participate and learn how to learn. While the indirect enabling inputs discussed above are closely related to this dimension, the actual teaching and learning processes (as these occur in the classroom) include student time spent learning, assessment methods for monitoring student progress, styles of teaching, the language of instruction and classroom organization strategies.

Outcomes

The outcomes of education should be assessed in the context of its agreed objectives. They are most easily expressed in terms of academic achievement (sometimes as test grades, but more usually and popularly in terms of examination performance), though ways of assessing creative and emotional development as well as changes in values, attitudes and behaviour have also been devised. Other proxies for learner achievement and for broader social or economic gains can be used; an example is labour market success. It is useful to distinguish between achievement, attainment and other outcome measures – which can include broader benefits to society.

Using the framework

This framework provides a means of organizing and understanding the different variables of education quality. The framework is comprehensive, in that the quality of education is seen as encompassing access, teaching and learning processes and outcomes in ways that are influenced both by context and by the range and quality of inputs available. It should be remembered that agreement about the objectives and aims of education will frame any discussion of quality and that such agreement embodies moral, political and epistemological issues that are frequently invisible or ignored.

While the framework is by no means the only one available or possible, it does provide a broad structure which can be used for the dual purposes of monitoring education quality and analysing policy choices for its improvement. In Chapters 2 and 3 of this Report, the determinants of education quality are analysed according to the extent to which variables from different dimensions result in improved learning outcomes (measured primarily in terms of cognitive achievement). Chapter 4 then adapts and modifies the framework to facilitate a more holistic discussion of policy strategies for the improvement of education quality. It focuses on the central teaching and learning dimension of Figure 1.1, placing the learner at the core.

The structure of the Report

The primary purpose of the EFA Global Monitoring Report is to monitor changes in education around the world in the light of the Dakar goals. As in the earlier volumes, a substantial amount of attention is given (particularly in Chapter 3) to analysing progress towards the goals – mainly in a quantitative sense. In taking the quality of education as its theme and thus focusing attention particularly upon progress and prospects for achieving the sixth Dakar goal, the Report has already illustrated the importance of education quality to EFA and addressed questions of how it can be defined and monitored (Chapter 1). It now goes on to identify what factors particularly affect education quality (Chapter 2), what strategies for improvement can be adopted, particularly by developing countries[28] (Chapter 4), and how the international community is meeting its international commitments to EFA (Chapter 5).

> Agreement about the objectives and aims of education embodies moral, political and epistemological issues that are frequently invisible or ignored

28. Throughout the Report, the word 'countries' should generally be understood as meaning 'countries and territories'.

Chapter 2
The importance of good

Learning together, living together: a school playground in Senegal

quality: what research tells us

Recent debates about the quality of education, reviewed in Chapter 1, indicate that its meaning is not a settled matter. However, one clear conclusion is that good quality in education (in schools or other forms of organized learning) should facilitate the acquisition of knowledge, skills and attitudes that have intrinsic value and also help in addressing important human goals. This chapter begins by examining the evidence about these links and shows that better cognitive and non-cognitive skills acquired in schooling contribute to economic and social development. The question as to how best to improve the quality of education, therefore, takes on some urgency. Accordingly, the main objective of this chapter is to identify and synthesize the available evidence about the determinants of education quality. It is only by knowing how the quality of schooling and other forms of organized learning are determined that policies to secure and improve the quality of education can be designed.[1]

The impact of education quality on development goals

It is commonly presumed that formal schooling is one of several important contributors to the skills of an individual and to human capital. It is not the only factor. Parents, individual abilities and friends undoubtedly contribute. Schools nonetheless have a special place, not only because education and 'skill creation' are among their prime explicit objectives, but also because they are the factor most directly affected by public policies. It is well established that the distribution of personal incomes in society is strongly related to the amount of education people have had. Generally speaking more schooling means higher lifetime incomes. These outcomes emerge over the long term. It is not people's income while in school that is affected, nor their income in their first job, but their income over the course of their working life. Thus, any noticeable effects of the current quality of schooling on the distribution of skills and income will become apparent some years in the future, when those now in school become a significant part of the labour force.

Impact of quality on individual incomes

One challenge in documenting the impact of differences in the quality of human capital has been its measurement. Much of the discussion of quality – in part related to new efforts to improve accountability – has identified the importance of enhancing cognitive skills via schooling, and most parents and policy makers accept that such skills represent a key dimension of schooling outcomes. If cognitive skills do provide proxy evidence, however incomplete, for school quality, the question arises as to whether these skills are correlated with students' subsequent performance in the labour market and with the economy's ability to grow.

There is mounting evidence that the quality of human resources, as measured by test scores, is directly related to individual earnings, productivity and economic growth. A range of research results from the United States shows that the earnings advantages due to higher achievement on standardized tests are quite substantial.[2] These studies typically find that measured achievement has a clear impact on earnings, after allowing for differences in the quantity of schooling, age or work experience, and for other factors that might influence earnings. In other words, for those leaving school at a given grade, higher-quality school outcomes (represented by test scores) are closely related to subsequent earnings differences and, we therefore suppose, to differences in individual productivity.

Three recent studies from the United States provide direct and quite consistent estimates of the impact of test performance on earnings (Mulligan, 1999; Murnane et al., 2000; Lazear, 2003). They use different data sets – each of them nationally representative – following students after they leave school and enter the labour force. They suggest that one standard deviation increase in mathematics performance at the end of high school translates into 12% higher annual earnings.[3] By way of comparison, estimates of the average value of an additional year of school attainment in the United States are typically 7–10%.

There are reasons to believe that these estimates provide a lower boundary for the impact of higher cognitive achievement on earnings. First, they are obtained fairly early in the working lives of the sampled people, who were generally 25 to 35 years old at the dates to which the data refer, and evidence suggests that the impact of test performance increases with work experience.[4] Second, the observed labour market experiences cover 1985–95, and other evidence suggests that the value of skills and schooling has grown since

> It is well established that the distribution of personal incomes in society is strongly related to the amount of education people have had

---

1. The existing literature, whether in economics or in education science, has focused on educational outcomes rather than inputs and processes, and indeed on one type of outcome only: cognitive skills. Accordingly, most of this chapter focuses on cognitive achievement, though it also mentions the importance of non-cognitive skills and other outcomes of schooling whose value is increasingly recognised.

2. These results are derived from different approaches, but the underlying analysis involves estimating a standard Mincer earnings function and adding a measure of individual cognitive skills. This approach relates the logarithm of earnings to years of schooling, experience and other factors that might yield individual earnings differences. The clearest analyses are found in Bishop (1989, 1991), O'Neill (1990), Grogger and Eide (1993), Blackburn and Neumark (1993, 1995), Murnane, Willett and Levy (1995), Neal and Johnson (1996), Mulligan (1999), Murnane et al. (2000), Altonji and Pierret (2001), Murnane et al. (2001) and Lazear (2003).

3. One standard deviation increase from the mean would be an achievement level equivalent to the eighty-fifth percentile of the distribution; i.e. 15% of students would normally achieve higher test scores than this. Murnane et al. (2000) provide evidence from the High School and Beyond study and the National Longitudinal Survey of the High School Class of 1972. Their estimates suggest some variation, with males obtaining a 15% increase and females a 10% increase per standard deviation of test performance. Lazear (2003), relying on a somewhat younger sample from the National Education Longitudinal Study of 1988, provides a single estimate of 12%. Similarly, Mulligan (1999) finds 11% for the normalized Armed Forces Qualification Test score in the National Longitudinal Survey of Youth data.

4. Altonji and Pierret (2001) find that the impact of achievement on earnings grows with experience partly because the employer has more chance to observe performance.

then. Third, future general improvements in productivity throughout the economy are likely to lead to larger returns to higher skill levels.[5]

As regards other direct benefits, research has established strong returns to both numeracy and literacy in the United Kingdom[6] and to literacy in Canada.[7] Accordingly, educational programmes that deliver these skills will bring higher individual economic benefits than those that do not.

Part of the returns to school quality comes through continuation in school.[8] Obviously, students who do better in school, as evidenced by either examination grades or scores on standardized achievement tests, tend to go further in school or university.[9] By the same token, the net costs of improvements in school quality, if reflected in increased attainment by learners, are less than they appear – perhaps substantially so – because of the resulting reductions in rates of repetition and dropout. Thus, higher student achievement keeps students in school longer, which leads, among other things, to higher completion rates at all levels of schooling. Accordingly, in countries where schools are dysfunctional and grade repetition is high, some improvements in quality may be largely self-financing, by reducing the average time completers spend in school.

As regards these relationships in developing countries, it appears likely, on the basis of somewhat limited evidence, that the returns to school quality are, if anything, higher than in more industrialized contexts. Table 2.1 provides a simple summary of research results for six countries, mainly in Africa. Using simple measures of basic cognitive skills, these studies show that such skills are separately important in determining earnings, apart from the effect of years of schooling attained. Although there are reasons for caution in interpreting the results,[10] the table suggests the presence of strong economic returns to education quality. Only the studies for Ghana and the United Republic of Tanzania had ranges of returns that were less than or similar to the United States estimates. Elsewhere, one standard deviation increase in test scores was associated with wage increases ranging from 12% to 48%, suggesting a substantial return to higher levels of cognitive skills and probably, therefore, to higher levels of school quality.

Impact of quality on economic growth

The relationship between measured labour force quality and economic growth is perhaps even more important than the impact of human capital and school quality on individual productivity and incomes. Economic growth determines how much improvement can occur in the overall standard of living of a society. Moreover, the education of each individual has the possibility of making others better off (in addition to the individual benefits just discussed). Specifically, a more educated society may translate into higher rates of innovation, higher overall productivity through firms' ability to introduce new and better production methods, and faster introduction of new technology. These externalities provide extra reason for being concerned about the quality of schooling.

Economists have developed a variety of models and ideas to explain differences in growth rates among countries, invariably featuring the

A more educated society may translate into higher rates of innovation, higher overall productivity and faster introduction of new technology

---

5. Studies on the impact of achievement on earnings typically compare workers of different ages at one point in time, in order to obtain an estimate of how earnings will change for any individual. Any productivity improvements in the economy, however, will tend to raise the earnings of individuals over time. Thus, the benefits of improvements in student skills are likely to grow over a person's working life, rather than remain constant.

6. See McIntosh and Vignoles (2001). Because they look at discrete levels of skills, it is difficult to compare the quantitative magnitudes directly with the United States work.

7. Finnie and Meng (2002) and Green and Riddell (2003) both suggest that literacy has a significant return, but Finnie and Meng find an insignificant return to numeracy, a finding at odds with most other analyses focusing on numeracy or mathematics skills.

8. Much of the work by economists on differences in worker skills has been directed at determining the average labour market returns to additional schooling. The argument has been that, as higher-ability students are more likely to continue in schooling, part of the higher earnings observed for those with additional schooling really reflects pay for added ability rather than additional schooling. Economists have pursued a variety of analytical approaches for dealing with this, including adjusting for measured cognitive test scores, but this work generally ignores issues of variation in school quality. The approaches have included looking for circumstances where the amount of schooling is affected by things other than the student's valuation of continuing, and considering the income differences among twins (see Card, 1999). The various adjustments for ability differences typically result in small changes to the estimates of the value of schooling, and Heckman and Vytlacil (2001) argue that it is not possible to separate the effects of ability and schooling. The only explicit consideration of school quality typically investigates expenditure and resource differences among schools, but these are known to be poor measures of school quality differences (Hanushek, 2002a).

9. Though the point may indeed be obvious, a significant amount of research evidence also documents it. See, for example, Dugan (1976) and Manski and Wise (1983). Rivkin (1995) finds that variations in test scores in the USA capture a considerable proportion of the systematic variation in high school completion and college continuation. Bishop (1991) and Hanushek, Rivkin and Taylor (1996), in considering the factors that influence school attainment, find that individual achievement scores are highly correlated with continued school attendance. Behrman et al. (1998) find strong achievement effects on both continuation into college and college quality; moreover, the effects are greater when proper account is taken of the various determinants of achievement. Hanushek and Pace (1995) find that college completion is significantly related to higher test scores at the end of high school.

10. The estimates appear to be quite sensitive to the estimation methodology. Both within individual studies and across studies using the same basic data, the results are quite sensitive to the techniques employed in revealing the fundamental parameter for cognitive skills. See Glewwe (2002).

Table 2.1: Estimated returns to a standard deviation increase in cognitive skills

Study	Country	Estimated effect[1]	Notes
Glewwe (1996)	Ghana	0.21** to 0.3** (government) 0.14 to 0.17 (private)	Alternative estimation approaches yield some differences; mathematics effects shown to be generally more important than reading effects, and all hold even with Raven's test for ability.
Jolliffe (1998)	Ghana	0.05 to 0.07*	Household income related to average mathematics score with relatively small variation by estimation approach; effect from off-farm income with on-farm income unrelated to skills.
Vijverberg (1999)	Ghana	uncertain	Income estimates for mathematics and reading with non-farm self-employment; highly variable estimates (including both positive and negative effects) but effects not generally statistically significant.
Boissiere, Knight and Sabot (1985); Knight and Sabot (1990)	Kenya	0.19** to 0.22**	Total sample estimates: small variation by primary and secondary school leavers.
Angrist and Lavy (1997)	Morocco	uncertain	Cannot convert to standardized scores because use indexes of performance; French writing skills appear most important for earnings, but results depend on estimation approach.
Alderman et al. (1996)	Pakistan	0.12 to 0.28*	Variation by alternative approaches and by controls for ability and health; larger and more significant without ability and health controls.
Behrman, Ross and Sabot (forthcoming)	Pakistan	uncertain	Estimates of structural model with combined scores for cognitive skill; index significant at .01 level but cannot translate directly into estimated effect size.
Moll (1998)	South Africa	0.34** to 0.48**	Depending on estimation method, varying impact of computation; comprehension (not shown) generally insignificant.
Boissiere, Knight and Sabot (1985); Knight and Sabot (1990)	UR Tanzania	0.07 to 0.13*	Total sample estimates: smaller for primary than secondary school leavers.

Notes: *significant at .05 level; **significant at .01 level.
1. Estimates indicate proportional increase in wages from an increase of one standard deviation in measured test scores.
Source: Hanushek (2004)

---

11. For a review of analyses and of the range of factors they include, see Barro and Sala-i-Martin (2003).

12. See also Barro and Lee (2001), whose analysis of qualitative differences includes literacy.

13. For details of this work see Hanushek and Kimko (2000) and Hanushek (2003b). Significantly, adding other factors potentially related to growth, including aspects of international trade, private and public investment and political instability, leaves the effects of labour force quality unchanged. The results also prove robust after allowing for other factors that can cause both higher growth and better educational performance.

14. Other desirable outcomes, apart from those relating to the competence of the labour force, that stem from improvements in education quality are discussed below.

importance of human capital.[11] In testing these models, empirical work has emphasized school attainment differences as a proxy for differences in human capital. Many studies find that the quantity of schooling, measured this way, is closely related to economic growth rates. The quantity of schooling, however, is a very crude measure of knowledge and cognitive skills – particularly in an international context, where wide differences exist as regards the resources available to school systems and the levels of household poverty.

Difficulties in international comparison of education quality have hampered attempts to incorporate measures of the quality of schooling in empirical analyses. In recent years, however, the existence of international achievement tests, administered in a consistent way to a growing group of countries, has begun to make such comparison possible. Hanushek and Kimko (2000), for example, incorporate information about international differences in mathematics and science knowledge by developing a common scale across all countries and tests and including a composite measure of quality as an additional determining variable in cross-country growth equations.[12] Their results suggest a strong impact of differences in school quality on economic growth: a difference of one standard deviation on test performance is related to a 1% difference in annual growth rates of GDP per capita.[13] That may sound small, but it is actually very significant. Because the added growth has a compound effect, it brings powerful incremental results for national income and societal well-being. Thus, the quality of the labour force, as measured by mathematics and science scores, appears to be an important determinant of growth, and thus of the potential to alleviate poverty.[14]

Quality and non-cognitive skills

There is a whole set of non-cognitive skills that are important for success in economic life. As Aesop's fable of the Tortoise and the Hare sets out to demonstrate, those with motivation and perseverance are likely to do better, other things being equal, than people of similar intelligence but less staying power. It has become increasingly clear that society rewards these and other non-cognitive skills such as honesty, reliability, determination and personal efficacy.

Early research found that personality and behavioural traits such as perseverance and leadership qualities had a significant influence upon labour market success, including earnings (Jencks et al., 1979). Personal stability, dependability, willingness to adopt the norms of institutions and hierarchies – these were shown to be important conditions for getting on in life and winning employer approval (Bowles and Gintis, 1976). Until recently, data and measurement problems largely discouraged further attempts to estimate the effects of such characteristics. However, a recent study of United States and United Kingdom data finds that individual differences in personality account for substantial differences in earnings, and that the way such characteristics affect earnings differs between the sexes (Bowles, Gintis and Osborne, 2001). In high-status jobs, women are penalized for having aggressive personalities, whereas men are rewarded, the study finds (after controlling for education, measured ability, exam success and other factors affecting earnings). The pattern is reversed for passive, withdrawing personalities, with men losing and women gaining income. The study also finds, again after controlling for other income-related factors, that women in the United States with a lower sense of their own ability to influence their destinies have lower earnings. Other recent research from the United States shows that bright but undisciplined male school dropouts who lack persistence and adaptability earn less than others with the same levels of ability and cognitive achievement and will continue to do so, beyond school (Heckman and Rubenstein, 2001). These types of enquiry are increasingly demonstrating the importance of non-cognitive skills in economic life.

Such skills are imparted and nourished by schools, at least in part. Not all are necessarily desirable; some (honesty, determination, reliability) are encouraged and rewarded by schools while other non-cognitive traits that the labour market appears to value (passivity in women, aggressiveness in men) are targeted by many schools as undesirable outcomes that strengthen inequalities in society. On average, the possession of useful non-cognitive skills may be approximated by test scores, in that higher cognitive achievers may have more of these 'valuable' non-cognitive skills too. But it is likely that their distribution explains some of the variation in earnings among those with similar cognitive achievement levels, indicating that these skills and traits are separately valued in the labour market.

The impact of quality on behavioural change

It seems, then, that there is good evidence to suggest that the quality of education – as measured by test scores – has an influence upon the speed with which societies can become richer and the extent to which individuals can improve their own productivity and incomes. We also know that years of education and acquisition of cognitive skills – particularly the core skills of literacy and numeracy – have economic and social pay-offs as regards income enhancement, improved productivity in both rural non-farm and urban environments and strengthened efficacy of household behaviour and family life (Jolliffe, 1998; Rosenzweig, 1995). In South Africa and Ghana, the number of years spent at school is negatively correlated with fertility rates, a relationship partly deriving from links between cognitive achievement and fertility (Thomas, 1999; Oliver, 1999).[15] Education systems that are more effective in establishing cognitive skills to an advanced level and distributing them broadly through the population will bring stronger social and economic benefits than less effective systems. This implies that the subject structure of the curriculum is important, in that school systems that do not impart literacy and numeracy would not be associated with these benefits – and those that do so more effectively (i.e. those that are of higher quality) are associated with larger benefits.

Clearly, then, differences in education quality can affect human behaviour in ways that facilitate the achievement of a wide range of human goals.

In high-status jobs, women are penalized for having aggressive personalities, whereas men are rewarded

---

15. The exceedingly complex links between education and fertility have been researched for many years. It is not only cognitive skills but also the process of socialization through schooling that can help give women the autonomy to change fertility outcomes (see Basu, 2002).

44 / CHAPTER 2

Granted, knowledge, even when widely shared, is not sufficient in and of itself to change behaviour. Opportunities of many kinds, however, can be found to improve the quality of schooling so as to facilitate such consequences. One important current example concerns health behaviour – specifically the challenge of responding to the HIV/AIDS pandemic.[16]

The mounting evidence of HIV/AIDS' impact in many countries indicates the potential importance of links between HIV/AIDS education and behavioural change. We readily and reasonably assume that the provision of clear information about the sources of HIV/AIDS infection and, indeed, improved general levels of literacy, will allow those at risk to understand and judge their options better. Are we right to do so? Box 2.1 indicates that knowledge and risk-reducing skills are acquired through a complex network of formal and informal sources, of which the education system is only one. Nevertheless, the cognitive skills required for informed choices in respect of HIV/AIDS risk – and for behavioural change – appear to be substantively based on levels of education and literacy. Thus, the primary inherent value of formal education in this context is to enhance the learning skills required to understand the HIV/AIDS education on offer and make sense of the many related messages from other sources (Badcock-Walters, Kelly and Görgens, 2004). This suggests that access to and retention in the school system is indeed the uniquely important 'social vaccine' to which many refer (Kelly, 2000; Low-Beer and Stoneburner, 2001). Helping schools deliver effective messages about HIV/AIDS prevention can only enhance their beneficial impact.

International assessments of cognitive achievement

In much of the evidence on the relationships between education quality and levels of economic growth and personal incomes, reviewed earlier, test scores serve as a proxy for education quality. Assessment of learners' progress, using cognitive tests, serves a number of purposes. It can provide an indication of how well items in the curriculum are being learned and understood, for example – a 'formative' influence for teaching and learning policies at local or national level. Equally, it can provide a signal as to how well learners have done at the main exit points from the school system, thereby typically helping educational institutions or employers to select those best qualified for further education or for various kinds of work. This type of 'summative' assessment is used as a means of facilitating (and legitimizing) access to social and economic hierarchies. Precisely because of their role in rationing access to scarce opportunities, such assessments can have an important impact on what goes on in schools. They may have beneficial effects by helping to ensure that the intended curriculum is taught and learned, but they can bring unintended, detrimental effects where the pressure to succeed encourages excessive attention to passing examinations rather than to broader aspects of learning.

These and other aspects of national educational assessment systems, and the impact they can have upon the quality of education, are discussed further in Chapter 4. Here we are interested in the large – and growing – body of information available from international surveys of cognitive achievement, upon which most international comparisons of education quality draw. What can their results tell us about the determinants of education quality?

The studies

In the late 1950s, the International Association for the Evaluation of Educational Achievement (IEA) was formed. It initiated what would become a major set of studies aiming to measure cognitive achievement at various levels of education in several countries and to identify the main causes of differences in outcomes. Twelve countries joined its first mathematics study. By 2000, some fifty countries were participating in surveys covering mathematics and science (now called the Trends in International Mathematics and Science Study or TIMSS), science, reading (the Progress in International Reading Literacy Study or PIRLS) and other subjects. Strongly influenced by the IEA experience, several other such studies, usually of regional focus, have since been established. They include the Programme for International Student Assessment (PISA), set up by the OECD in 1998 and now covering fifty-nine mainly industrialized and middle-income countries; the Southern and Eastern African Consortium for Monitoring

> The cognitive skills required for informed choices in respect of HIV/AIDS risk appear to be based on levels of education and literacy

---

16. A second example is the impact of educational change on gender relations in school and in society. It is clear that changes in school location planning, reforms to curricula and textbook development, widening subject options for girls, changing the nature of school chores, improving teacher training and sensitization, ensuring that school facilities are girl-friendly, making timetables more flexible to respond to the demands of households, and a wide range of other, more detailed reforms can help reduce gender inequality in school and beyond. These matters comprised the major theme of the *EFA Global Monitoring Report 2003/4* (UNESCO, 2003a). See that volume for extensive discussion and evidence on these issues.

Box 2.1 Education and HIV/AIDS risk avoidance: does knowledge equal change?

A recent study of six African countries – Kenya, Malawi, Uganda, the U. R. Tanzania, Zambia and Zimbabwe – found high levels of HIV/AIDS awareness in the population (more than 90% of those surveyed) in each country but considerable differences as to the sources of this knowledge (Low-Beer and Stoneburner, 2000). Social networks of friends and family were the main sources in Uganda, whereas in the other countries the mass media and institutional sources (schools, churches, clinics) predominated.

The percentage of respondents who had known someone with HIV/AIDS was substantially higher in Uganda (91.5% of men and 86.4% of women) than in the five other countries. This direct experience appears to have acted as a spur to behavioural change. For example, about 20% of Ugandan men aged 15 to 24 who knew someone with AIDS had started using condoms, whereas only some 5% of those who did not know an AIDS sufferer used them.

In a South African study, almost one-fifth of 15- to 24-year-olds indicated that they talk to teachers and classmates about HIV/AIDS, and about one-third of them reported learning most about HIV/AIDS from school sources (Pettifor et al., 2004). On the other hand, among secondary school students in Botswana, Malawi and Uganda, radio was the most widely cited source (Bennell, Hyde and Swainson, 2002). Teachers ranked second in Botswana and Malawi for both genders, yet in Uganda they were ranked fifth by male students and second by female students, reinforcing the view that education in schools is not necessarily the principal source of information about HIV/AIDS in that country.

Even in Uganda, though, clear evidence exists of strong and increasing links between HIV/AIDS education, increased general knowledge and risk-avoidance behaviour. Figure 2.1 shows that rates of HIV prevalence in rural Uganda were initially closely comparable for all education levels, but separation began in 1995, and by the turn of the century those with some secondary education had much lower prevalence rates than those with less schooling. This evidence is mirrored in other African countries, where condom use is rising sharply among both men and women with higher levels of schooling (Figures 2.2 and 2.3). Thus, retention in a functional education system seems likely to provide the quality of education and skills development necessary to reduce or eliminate sexual and lifestyle risk. The general cognitive and social gains from a basic education seem to be the main factor in protecting adolescents and young adults from infection.

Figure 2.2: Percentage of women who used a condom during sex in previous month

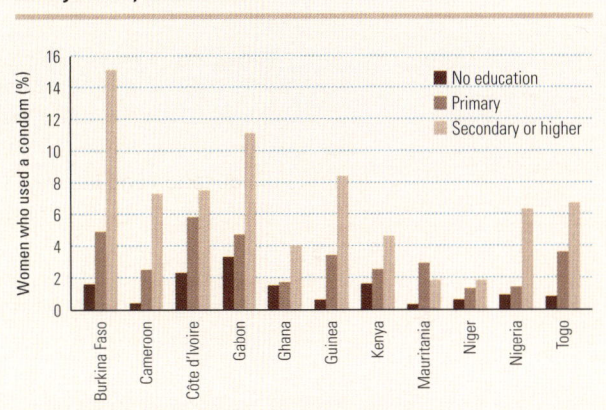

Source: GCE graphic using DHS data from www.statcompiler.com

Figure 2.1: HIV prevalence in rural Uganda (%) by education category, 1990-2001 (individuals aged 18-29)

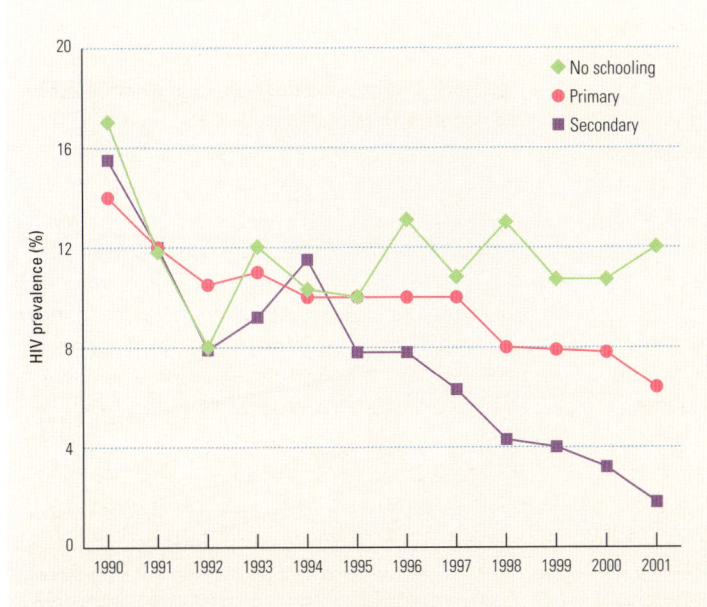

Note: Primary means having attended any or all of grades 1–7; Secondary means having attended any or all of grades 8–13 or above.
Source: De Walque (2004)

Figure 2.3: Percentage of men who used a condom with a recent non-regular partner

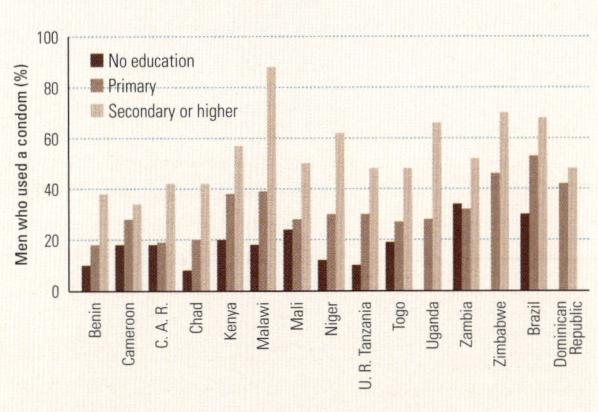

Source: UNAIDS/WHO graphic using DHS and UNICEF data from www.macrointernational.com

Tests of cognitive achievement are incomplete proxies for the quality of education

Educational Quality (SACMEQ), which since its first survey in Zimbabwe in 1991 has expanded to fifteen African countries; the Latin American Laboratory for the Assessment of Quality in Education (LLECE), which began in 1997 and covers sixteen countries; the UNESCO Monitoring Learning Achievement (MLA) project and the survey in French-speaking Africa known as the *Programme d'analyse des systèmes éducatifs de la CONFEMEN* (PASEC).

Comparisons across countries and over time

Tests of cognitive achievement are incomplete proxies for the quality of education. They tell nothing about values, capacities or other non-cognitive skills that are important aims of education. Moreover, if the extent of value added by schooling, even in the cognitive domain, is to be known, such tests need to be supplemented by measures of the background characteristics that learners bring to formal education. The aforementioned studies differ in the extent to which their methodologies allow for these dimensions. They also differ as to whether comparisons over time, and across countries, can be made.

It is possible to compare learning achievement scores among the countries within each study, but not among the studies themselves.[17] This is partly because they examine different age or education groups: PISA, for example, focuses on 15-year-olds while the others concentrate on primary school pupils. There are grounds for believing that many of the African countries included in SACMEQ have much poorer reading achievement than the IEA countries, but, in the absence of a common scale, this cannot be properly demonstrated.

The second IEA science study was the first to allow achievement over time to be compared (Keeves and Schleicher, 1992). It found that, from 1970 to 1984, general science achievement scores at mid-secondary level increased for England, Finland, Hungary, Italy, Japan, the Netherlands, Sweden and Thailand, were roughly unchanged for Australia and decreased for the United States. The causes of the changes were unclear in the absence of information about system change and curricular modifications in these countries.

Results from PIRLS allowed comparison of changes in reading comprehension between 1991 and 2001 for the grade covering 9-year-olds. It indicated that achievement levels increased significantly in Greece, Slovenia, Iceland and Hungary, changed insignificantly in Italy, New Zealand, Singapore and the United States and fell in Sweden.

As regards developing countries, some strong and interesting comparisons emerge from SACMEQ I (1995/96) and II (2000/01).[18] As Figure 2.4 shows, five of the six countries included in both rounds of SACMEQ had declines in literacy achievement scores, although these differences were statistically significant only in Malawi, Namibia and Zambia. In Kenya, SACMEQ II was conducted in 1998, so the interval between the two surveys was three years rather than four to six years for the others. Here again there was no significant change. The bold line showing the average for all six countries indicates a 4% decline in achievement scores. In view of the comparatively short period covered, the consistency of these results across the region is compelling.

Table 2.2 shows changes in important contextual circumstances for the sampled schools in Malawi, Namibia and Zambia. The age of pupils in grade 6 decreased over the period, which in some circumstances could have a bearing on

Figure 2.4: Changes in literacy scores between SACMEQ I and II in six African countries

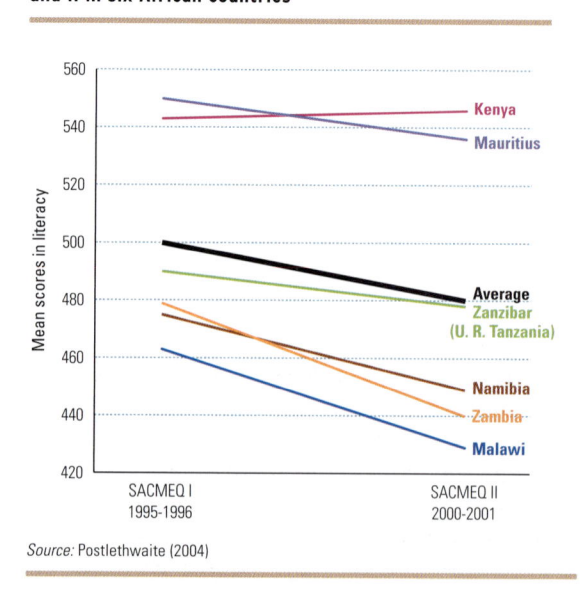

Source: Postlethwaite (2004)

---

17. Some analysts are testing such comparisons (e.g. Hanushek, 2004; Pritchett, 2004; Crouch and Fasih, 2004), but interpreting them requires making strong assumptions.

18. Measurement across time is also a major focus of the PISA research, but the results comparing the 2003 testing with that of 2000 were published too late for inclusion in this Report.

Table 2.2: Percentage and mean differences in selected variables between SACMEQ I and II

Variable	Malawi	Namibia	Zambia
Pupil age in months	–7.1*	–11.9*	–4.9*
Pupil sex, % female	1.3	0.7	2.6
Pupil possessions	–0.04	–0.04*	–0.07*
Parental education	0.2	0.1	0.2
% sitting places	21.4*	–2.0	5.4*
% writing places	26.0*	1.4	32.2*
Own reading book	–5.6	–5.9	0.7
Teacher age in years	1.7	1.5	4.0*
Teacher sex, % female	1.8	–8.6	13.5*
Teacher years experience	0.9	0.7	3.8*
School resources (22)	–0.42	0.10	0.15
Class resources (8)	0.7	–0.3	0.0
Lack of pupil materials	0.09	–1.05	0.30

Note: Asterisks indicate that differences were statistically significant at the 95% level of confidence.
Source: Postlethwaite (2004)

performance. Here, however, the number of over-age pupils was declining – a fact that could be counted as progress from the perspective of ministries of education and that was unlikely to lead to negative reading performance. On the other hand, household income (measured by whether pupils had particular possessions or amenities at home[19]) also appears to have fallen over the period, particularly in Namibia and Zambia – indicating economic decline or enrolment of pupils from poorer homes, or both.

Some aspects of the school environments appear to have improved over the period. A significantly higher proportion of pupils in Malawi and Zambia had their own seats and a desk or table on which to write. The age and experience of teachers were higher in Zambia, and a greater proportion of them were female (not the case in the other countries). The percentages of pupils having their own textbooks (i.e. not having to share) were virtually unchanged, however, as were the schools' physical resources.[20]

Overall, what accounts for the decrease in achievement in these three countries is not entirely clear. It is likely that the reduced average income of pupils' households was a factor in all three cases. In Zambia, per capita income declined sharply during the 1990s and demands on pupils to supplement incomes – at the cost of their school performance – probably increased. In Namibia, a higher proportion of poorer households were sending their children to school. In Malawi, rapid expansion, which led to the number of primary pupils almost doubling over the decade, was a significant factor in the qualitative decline. The abolition of school fees there led to a much greater proportion of children from lower socio-economic backgrounds attending school. In addition, Malawi's performance on school resources was the lowest for all six countries. It was significantly worse than in Namibia and Zambia and had fallen in absolute terms over the years between SACMEQ I and II.

More general explanations for pupil achievement

Each study made great efforts to identify the major factors influencing achievement. What were the main results? In nearly all education systems, pupils' home background was found to be important. Those from higher socio-economic backgrounds – where parents had more education and households had more material possessions, including more books – tended to perform better than those from poorer homes. In the African and Latin American studies there were also strong urban-rural differences, reflecting both higher incomes and better education facilities in urban areas.

In many developing countries, the material resources in schools are inadequate. In the SACMEQ studies the average child was in a school with 8.7 of the twenty-two desirable school resource items; the range was from 4.3 items in Malawi to 16.7 in the Seychelles, with wide urban-rural variation within countries. Even in countries that had achieved some degree of equity in the provision of material resources, the teachers in urban schools tended to be better qualified and more experienced than those in rural areas. Some schools did not even have enough seats for all pupils. On average, for all fifteen SACMEQ countries, 10% of pupils lacked a place to sit. By country the proportion ranged from 45% in Zanzibar to zero in Botswana, Lesotho, Mauritius and Seychelles.

The sex of primary teachers has an influence on performance, particularly of girls. The SACMEQ studies showed wide variations by country. For all countries, 53% of pupils surveyed were taught by female teachers, on average, but the share

In all fifteen SACMEQ countries, 10% of pupils lacked a place to sit

---

19. Pupils were asked which of the following they had at home: daily newspaper, weekly or monthly magazine, radio, TV set, video recorder, cassette player, telephone, refrigerator, car, motorcycle, bicycle, piped water, electricity (main, generator or solar) and a table at which they could write.

---

20. School heads were asked which of the following were available to them: school library, school hall, staff room, head's office, storeroom, cafeteria, sports area/playground, school garden, piped water/well or bore-hole, electricity, telephone, first-aid kit, fax machine, typewriter, duplicator, radio, tape recorder, overhead projector, television set, video recorder, photocopier and computer.

ranged from 17% in Uganda to 99% in Seychelles. Pupils taught by females scored, on average, three-tenths of a standard deviation higher than pupils with male teachers.

Pupils taught by females scored higher than pupils with male teachers

Other items prominent in the African studies were behavioural problems of pupils (and teachers): late arrival, absenteeism and pupil dropout were all correlates of poor performance. In the PISA studies, where socio-economic advantage improved performance, changes in the school climate, teacher morale and commitment, school autonomy, teacher-pupil relations and disciplinary regime had some compensatory influence towards greater equity. In the Latin American countries covered in the LLECE studies, pupil socio-economic background and classroom climate appeared to be the most important predictors of achievement.

Box 2.2 summarizes some of the major findings from more than forty years of research conducted through the IEA programme. Three have particular importance for policies aimed at improving education quality. First, the distribution of abilities in the population has a significant impact on average achievement levels. The greater the overall proportion of children enrolled, the lower average achievement levels tend to be. The achievement levels of particular cohorts of ability, however, are not affected – the cognitive achievement levels of the most able decile are unchanged by expansion. Second, time spent actually working on particular subjects, either in school or as homework, affects performance, especially in mathematics, science and languages. Third, although socio-economic status is influential in determining achievement in all contexts, textbook availability and school resources appear to be capable of countering socio-economic disadvantage, particularly in low-income settings.

Box 2.2 Major conclusions from more than forty years of international achievement surveys

Results of the IEA studies, now covering fifty countries and carried out over more than forty years, suggest the following conclusions:

- Marked differences exist between average levels of pupil achievement in the industrialized countries and those in less developed countries (LDCs) even though not all pupils in the various school-age groups were enrolled in the LDCs.
- The average level of achievement within a country at the terminal secondary school stage is inversely related to the proportion of the age group enrolled (or the age group studying the subject surveyed).*
- At the terminal level, when equal proportions of the age group are compared, only small differences in levels of achievement are found, irrespective of the proportion of the age group enrolled at that level. Thus, the best students do not suffer as retention rates increase.
- Student achievement in mathematics, science and French as a foreign language is positively related to the time spent studying the subject at school, both across and within countries.
- Student achievement in mathematics, science and French as a foreign language is also positively associated with the time spent on homework, after other factors influencing achievement are taken into account.
- The average level of student achievement across countries is positively related to the time spent in class studying the content of the items tested.
- The impact of increased textbook use on student learning in LDCs is strong. The same effects are not detected in richer countries, probably because of the wider availability of textbooks in those countries.
- Measures of the socioeconomic status of pupils' families are positively related to student achievement in all countries, at all age levels and for all subjects.
- Although the effects of home background variables on student achievement are similar for all subject areas, the effects of learning conditions in the schools differ by subject and are sometimes equivalent to or greater than the influence of home background on student achievement.

* Among the participating countries, the correlation between the proportion of an age group enrolled in a particular grade and the average measured achievement in mathematics and science, and that between the proportion of an age group specializing in one of the sciences and achievement in it, range from -0.69 and -0.88.

Sources: Keeves (1995: 2-23); Mullis et al. (2003: 36-38); Postlethwaite (2004).

What determines quality? Lessons from eleven countries

Lessons to aid understanding and improvement of the quality of education can be gained in a wide range of ways. Quantitative international analysis, discussed above, is one approach. Country case studies provide a different way of profiting from national experiences, using both qualitative and quantitative information. In this section, eleven countries have been selected for such analysis. Four of them – Canada, Cuba, Finland and the Republic of Korea – have achieved high standards of education quality. They have shown leading performance in achievement surveys,[21] a criterion that admittedly is just one aspect of education quality. Cuba and the Republic of Korea have achieved high standards in the past two or three decades, the former inspired by a strong belief that education helps it achieve the objectives of its 1959 revolution, the latter viewing education as fundamental to its post-war economic expansion. In Finland, an industrialized country with a longstanding tradition in education (Finland Ministry for Foreign Affairs, 2002), the economic crisis of the 1990s provided a more recent impetus for a knowledge-based economic strategy.[22] Canada is a country where immigration has underpinned socio-economic development and education is judged to be the key to nation building.[23]

The seven other countries discussed – Bangladesh, Brazil, Chile, Egypt, Senegal, South Africa and Sri Lanka – have demonstrated strong commitment to EFA. All are developing countries that have been successful in expanding access to primary education. They have also made strong progress towards gender parity, or have achieved it. All seven have made big efforts to increase the quality of education in terms of learning outcomes, even if substantial, measurable progress has not yet materialized in all cases.

Senegal and Bangladesh are the poorest of these countries. There, the major challenge is to close the enrolment gap in primary education while at the same time addressing quality. In both countries the non-formal sector plays an important role. For Sri Lanka and Egypt, universal primary enrolment (UPE) is within reach; the keys to raising quality include greater consultation with civil society on national reforms (Sri Lanka) and a business approach (Egypt). In South Africa, equity has driven education development over the last decade. Brazil and Chile, countries on the threshold of industrialization, are aiming to improve education further through large projects (Brazil) or major financial investments (Chile).

Table 2.3 and Figure 2.5 compare the educational profiles of the eleven countries. It can be seen that the four 'high-performance' countries are ahead of the others in terms of primary and secondary enrolment. Their pupil survival rates to grade 5 also tend to be higher, and the gender ratios of enrolment more equal, than in the seven countries here labelled 'ambitious'. However, when comparative performance on international achievement tests is examined, more substantial gaps appear, in general between high-performing and less developed countries.[24]

The four 'high performance' countries: how did they do it?

For some decades, several South-east and East Asian countries pursued a strategy of building a larger 'stock' of trained human resources than strictly needed in the short term, in order to attract knowledge-intensive investment and thus boost economic expansion.[25] The Republic of Korea was one of this group. As early as 1959 it had managed to enrol 96% of its children in primary school. The following three decades saw rapid development of education, large increases in the availability of educated youth and adults, and sustained economic growth.

By 1980, the Republic of Korea had shifted its emphasis in education from expansion towards a focus on quality, giving more importance to students' 'sense of the future and ... social and moral responsibilities' (KEDI, 1979). The exploding demand for schooling had resulted in overcrowded classrooms[26] and excessive competition for scarce places in secondary and tertiary education. The degree of competition was felt to be harmful for learners and parents. Distance education and adult education were expanded during the 1980s, to ease the pressure on the regular school system. Entrance examinations were reformed or abolished. Teachers received longer training and better incentives, while physical facilities in schools were improved. An infrastructure of research institutes at national level – including the Korean

---

21. Canada, Finland and the Republic of Korea, as this chapter notes, performed well in the first round of PISA, for which data were collected in 2000 (OECD/UNESCO Institute for Statistics, 2003), and in various earlier international assessments. Cuba participated in a survey conducted by OREALC, the UNESCO regional office for Latin America and the Caribbean (Casassus et al., 2002). The average performance level of its pupils was remarkably high compared to that of other countries in the region.

22. The developments in the Soviet Union in the early 1990s caused a deep crisis in Finland: GDP dropped by 14% and unemployment rose to 20%. Yet, by 2003, its economic competitiveness had been restored. Knowledge – particularly education and research and development – is said to have played a major role in the recovery. See, for example, www.warsawvoice.pl/view/4268.

23. The children of immigrants in Canada perform better on standardized tests than those in other countries participating in PISA (Döebert, Klieme and Sroka, 2004).

24. Pritchett (2004) found, for instance, that only the 3.2% best-performing Brazilian children were better in mathematics than the average Danish pupil. Comparisons of Indonesia with France and of Peru with the United States revealed very similar differences between these middle- and high-income countries.

25. Wade (1990) and the World Bank (1993) indicate that several countries and territories, including the Republic of Korea, Singapore, Taiwan (China) and Hong Kong (China), have seen rapid economic expansion associated partly with certain monetary and macroeconomic policies, and partly with public investment in social infrastructure, particularly education (see also Republic of Korea, 2003: 12 and Corrales, 1999: 24–5.)

26. In 1978, the rural average was 44.8 pupils per class and the urban average was 61.0 (excluding Seoul and Busan, where the figure was 71.8). The national average was 52.8; for comparison, the figure in Japan was 32.9 and in China 47.9 (KEDI, 1979: 77). Reducing class size has been a priority ever since. In 2004, classes are expected to have thirty-six pupils or fewer, according to the Presidential Commission on Education and Human Resource Policy (2002: 61). The commission recommends adding assistant teachers for classrooms with more than thirty pupils.

Table 2.3: Education system and background characteristics in eleven countries

	Background		Adult literacy[1]		Primary		Secondary		Teaching staff		Finance
	Population in thousands	GNP per capita (PPP)	Total %	GPI (F/M)	GER (%)	GPI (F/M)	GER (%)	GPI (F/M)	Primary school teachers, female %	Pupil/teacher ratio in primary	Total public expenditure on education as a % of GNP
Ambitious											
Bangladesh	140 880	1 710	41.1	0.62	97.5	1.02	46.9	1.10	36.0	55.1	2.2
Brazil	174 029	7 350	86.4	1.00	148.5	0.94	107.5	1.10	92.1	23.0	4.2
Chile	15 419	9 240	95.7	1.00	102.7	0.98	85.5	1.02	77.6	32.2	4.0
Egypt	69 124	3 720	55.6	0.65	96.9	0.94	88.1	0.93	53.3	22.5	...
Senegal	9 621	1 540	39.3	0.61	75.3	0.91	18.7	0.67	22.8	48.9	3.2
South Africa	44 416	9 530	86.0	0.98	105.1	0.96	86.4	1.09	77.8	37.1	5.8
Sri Lanka	18 752	3 380	92.1	0.95	110.4	0.99	80.8	...	...	...	1.3
High performance											
Canada	31 025	28 570	...	...	99.6	1.00	106.2	0.99	68.1	17.4	5.3
Cuba	11 238	...	96.9	1.00	100.3	0.96	89.1	0.99	78.9	13.5	8.7
Finland	5 188	25 500	99.7[2]	0.99	102.0	0.99	126.5	1.11	74.2	15.6	6.4
Republic of Korea	47 142	15 060	98.0	0.98	102.1	1.00	91.1	1.00	71.6	32.0	3.6

Notes: see source tables for detailed country notes.
1. Adult literacy rate is for the period of 2000-2004.
2. Adult literacy rate for Finland is based on the rates of 0-3 years of schooling.
Source: Statistical annex, Tables 1, 2, 5, 7, 8 and 14. Adult literacy rate for Finland: European Social Survey (www.europeansurvey.org).

Figure 2.5: Performance indicators for primary education in eleven countries

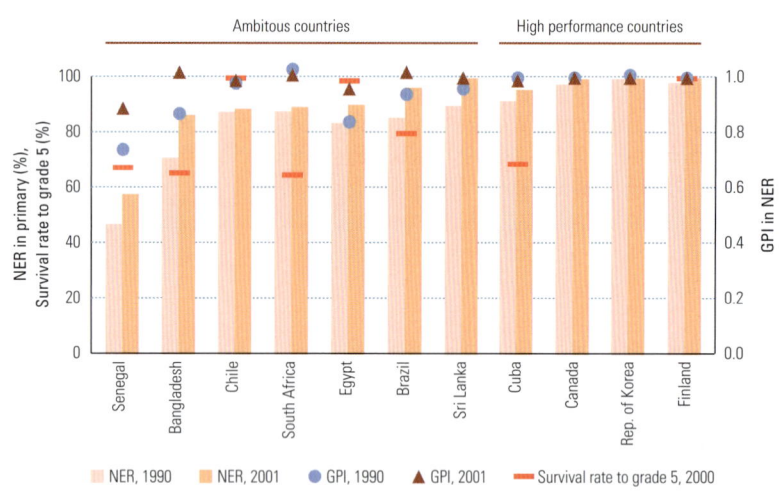

Note: For Cuba, the survival rate is to the *last grade* (not grade 5, which is unavailable).
See source tables for detailed country notes.
Source: Statistical annex, Tables 5 and 7.

Educational Development Institute – served to guide this reform process, while an education tax was introduced to finance it. Through the 1990s, these initiatives were consolidated – a process reinforced by the founding of advisory bodies that transcended political regimes and sought consistency in education policy (Republic of Korea, 2003: 23–5).[27]

Notwithstanding these efforts, class size remains large, even though it has been almost halved. In an important sense, being taught in a smaller group is a quality gain in its own right. Whatever disadvantage larger classes entail, though, it is overcome in the Republic of Korea through the willingness of pupils (and parents) to make extra efforts and through pedagogies and classroom climates that facilitate learning in large groups. Still, the Republic of Korea's first place for science, third place for mathematics and seventh place for reading in the PISA study covering forty-one high- and middle-income countries (OECD/UNESCO Institute for Statistics, 2003) are remarkable, especially given PISA's adoption of more contextual (less 'schoolish') testing methods. These rankings suggest that the Republic of Korea has reached a broader interpretation of learning outcomes than other countries, including many at higher income levels.

At an earlier stage than the Republic of Korea, Cuba was emphasizing education's role in developing the whole individual (including physical education, sports, recreation and artistic education) while explicitly linking education with life, work and production (Amadio et al., 2004). Following the Cuban Revolution, education and health care were strongly prioritized (Ritzen,

27. See also Corrales (1999: 27) and Amadio et al. (2004).

1999) to support human development. They were seen both as desirable ends in themselves and as a means of assuring the country's economic and political independence. The balance between these two types of value, which the Republic of Korea sought in the 1980s, was present in Cuba from the start of its development process.

In both countries, competition plays an important role, but it does so in very different ways. While competition for places arose as an unintended effect of scarce provision in the Republic of Korea, educational opportunities in Cuba have been abundant and freely accessible at each level, partly because investment in education is high, amounting to 10–11% of GDP (Gasperini, 2000: 7). The Cuban form of competition, 'emulation', is conceived of as self-improvement through solidarity and collaboration among peers. Emulation occurs among pupils, among teachers and among schools. For each group, incentives reward excellence, and mechanisms are in place to make sure others benefit from the experience. An example is the *colectivo pedagógico*, a group of subject teachers meeting frequently for mutual learning and joint development of curricula, methods and materials (Gasperini, 2000: 9–14). The result is an education system that stakeholders are encouraged to improve. Extra-curricular contributions, such as to school maintenance, are common, and the system is characterized by a high level of discipline and classroom order (Carnoy, Gove and Marshall, forthcoming). Cuba's educational feats are impressive: it reduced illiteracy from 40% to near zero in ten years (Ritzen, 1999), and in the recent OREALC/UNESCO study the average performance of the bottom quartile of its tested students was higher than the average of the top quartile for any other country in the survey.[28]

Can other countries emulate Cuba's policies? The revolutionary spirit that inspired teachers, pupils and parents to make great efforts for the benefit of the schools may prove to be unique. Nevertheless, learning communities of teachers can be created, and schools' performance scrutinized, in other contexts.[29] The high esteem in which the teaching profession is held in Cuba seems crucial to its success. This could be a potentially vulnerable point: as the country opens up to tourism and foreign investment, teacher salaries – very low when expressed in foreign currency – might not be able to compete with salaries in other sectors (Gasperini, 2000: 21). Moreover, the availability of relatively well-paid tourism jobs for which few qualifications are needed could encourage youth not to continue their education.

Canada[30] is another country where the teaching profession is held in high esteem. Despite teacher shortages, admission to teacher training is highly competitive, and only 10% of applicants succeed. Even pre-primary teachers need a university degree. In-service training amounts to forty days per year in some parts of the country; participation is often obligatory or a condition for promotion, and is financially rewarded. A system of accreditation in Ontario, which is under consideration elsewhere, tests teachers every five years, and those who fail lose their teaching certificate.

Canada not only maintains high standards for teachers, it also provides a well-developed support system. Its school development teams (at district level) and school advisory councils (bringing local stakeholders together in support of the school) are reminiscent of some Cuban institutions. Monitoring is a third hallmark of Canadian education. A culture of indicator use has developed at all levels. The performance of students, schools, districts and even provinces is tracked closely. This is seen as a way of revealing both excellence and underperformance and as a basis for designing policy interventions.

Despite a decline in investment in education from 9% of GNP in 1970 (Wisenthal, 1983) to 6.6% of GDP in 1999, Canada performed very well in PISA, ranking second for reading, seventh for mathematics and sixth for science (out of forty-one high- and middle-income countries). Most notable is the excellent performance of immigrant children in Canada compared to those in other industrialized countries. This underlines one of the characteristic objectives of Canadian education: to build a nation while cherishing the cultural diversity of the population.

Finland[31] had the highest overall outcomes in the PISA tests, ranking first out of the forty-one countries for reading, fifth for mathematics and fourth for science. Disparities in student achievement are very small, as is the impact of social background on achievement (Välijärvi et al., 2002: 28). That is what Finland intended

The high esteem in which the teaching profession is held in Cuba seems crucial to its success

---

28. We should continue to bear in mind the point made in footnote 1, however: that achievement scores are far from the whole picture.

29. See, for example, the discussion of Canada below, and UNESCO (2003a: 216).

30. Unless indicated otherwise, the information on Canada is derived from a comparative study of seven countries, based on PISA, written by several national teams and edited by Döebert, Klieme and Sroka (2004).

31. Except where indicated otherwise, the information on Finland is also derived from Döebert, Klieme and Sroka (2004).

> The combination of high performance and moderate expenditure has made Finnish education an interesting benchmark for many countries

in investing consistently and for many decades in human development, pursuing both equality of opportunity and inclusion. Economic competitiveness and education sector performance, however, are also key areas in the country's education strategy for 2015 (Finland Ministry of Education, 2003). This emphasis on the more utilitarian objectives of education was absent in the 1980s (Amadio et al., 2004) and may be a consequence of Finland's economic crisis in the 1990s after the collapse of the Soviet Union. Finland consciously chose a knowledge-based recovery strategy, but could not afford high investment in education. The 5.8% of GDP that it invests in education is only slightly above the OECD average and clearly below Scandinavian standards. The combination of high performance and moderate expenditure has made Finnish education an interesting benchmark for many countries.

As in Canada, selection for teacher training is very rigorous. Every teacher has masters' degrees in two subjects. Other factors that are said to explain Finland's high performance in PISA are its comprehensive pedagogies, students' own interests and leisure activities, the structure of the education system, school practices and Finnish culture[32] (Välijävi et al., 2003: 4).

The experiences of these four countries suggest three common characteristics. The first concerns teachers. High esteem for the teaching profession, thorough pre-service training and sometimes restrictive admission, and a well-developed constellation of in-service training, plus mechanisms for mutual learning and teacher support are evident in all these countries. There are no concessions on teacher quality, even where teacher shortages exist.

The second is continuity of policy. The Republic of Korea consciously sought to neutralize the impact of political change by establishing advisory bodies. In Cuba, continuity is implied in the political system. Canada and Finland have strong education knowledge bases (within institutions for teacher training and support) that seem to prevent governments changing course too frequently and radically.

The third characteristic is the high level of public commitment to education, which seems to emanate from a strong political vision. The Republic of Korea's determination to become and remain globally competitive, Cuba's will to defend the revolution, Canada's belief that its strength as a nation lies in cultural diversity, and Finland's deep commitment to human development and equality – each, in its own way, has profoundly affected education policies and outcomes.

One other characteristic, in the Republic of Korea and Cuba, is an extremely high level of energy among learners, teachers and parents. In both countries it is associated with an atmosphere of competition, albeit from very different standpoints and in very different forms. Whether and how this can be mirrored in other developing country contexts is an open question.

The seven ambitious countries: what can they learn?

Senegal[33] has been strongly committed to basic education and has rapidly expanded access. Between 1990 and 2000, its net enrolment ratio rose from 48.2 to 63.1, with the gender parity index increasing from 0.75 to 0.90. The country is now looking for a better balance between quantity and quality. Indicators of quality still seem to lag behind, however, with relatively high repetition rates in the higher grades, a low ranking in the PASEC survey[34] and little progress according to the national assessment system – the *Système national d'évaluation des rendements scolaires* (SNERS). Transition to secondary education is low compared to other countries in sub-Saharan Africa. Unlike the Republic of Korea, Senegal has not been able to benefit from economic growth when raising quality; in fact, growth was negative between 1990 and 2000.

With limited money to fight illiteracy and with current efforts to do so widely scattered, the government adopted an innovative approach called *faire-faire*, or 'getting it done' (Niane, 2004: 12). It is based on bringing relevant partners together, sharing out duties and responsibilities to local actors, giving a voice to stakeholders and decentralizing the education system. The *faire-faire* approach has been applied to literacy programmes in which over a million adult women were enrolled in 2003, along with almost half a million boys and girls who missed out on regular school. While achievement in regular education was stagnant, progress in

---

32. The importance of Finnish culture and students' interests and leisure activities points to the cumulative intergenerational effects of sustained support to education. It is known that student performance is driven by the cultural capital and the interests students bring from home to the classroom, which in turn are strongly linked to parent's education attainment Thus, if a country invests long enough in good education, its quality may to some extent become self-sustaining.

33. Unless otherwise indicated, the information on Senegal is from Niane (2004) and the Statistical annex of this Report.

34. PASEC, discussed in the section on international assessments, was conducted in Burkina Faso, Cameroon, Ivory Coast, Madagascar and Senegal in 1996 and (for Madagascar) 1998. The results for Senegal were the lowest among the five countries.

these literacy programmes was remarkable between 1998 and 2001. Another innovation is the formation of *collectifs des directeurs*, or regional groups of school principals, which echo the Cuban concept of stimulating mutual learning among peers and provide a way to make decentralization work. Senegal realized that school autonomy should not leave schools in isolation and that networks are important.[35]

On balance, the Senegalese experience seems to reflect a sense of dissatisfaction with the bureaucratic nature of the formal school system. Schools remain passive, expecting initiatives to come from above rather than be self-generated. Hence, there is a tendency to operate outside the formal system (*faire-faire*) or independently from it (*collectifs des directeurs*) to accomplish change. While some high-performing countries pursue similar strategies, few of them made this choice at such an early stage of education development. The chances for a robust, vision-led, consistent national education strategy thus seem limited, although the Education and Training Programme (2000–10) does chart a course for the longer term. One strong point is the high proportion of teachers in Senegal with good academic backgrounds. The number of teachers who actually have a teaching certificate, however, has fallen.

Bangladesh[36] also made impressive progress in access to primary education between 1990 and 2000, possibly as a result of the advent of democratic government at the beginning of that decade. In this large and poor country – it has 130 million inhabitants, half of whom live below the poverty line – the net enrolment ratio went up from 71.1 to 88.9 over the decade and gender parity was achieved by the turn of the century. The ten-year rise in the gender parity index from 0.87 to 1.02 implies an increase in quality in its own right. But, as in Senegal, learning achievement is still a problem. Although it is not possible to assess developments over time,[37] the proportion of pupils demonstrating specified minimum levels of mastery for basic subjects may be as high as 50%, as reported by the government (Latif, 2004: 9), or as low as the 9% that independent sources report (Education Watch, 2000). That three-quarters of pupils nevertheless complete primary education points to weaknesses in curricula, teaching and quality assurance.

Another similarity with Senegal is the large non-formal education sector. NGO-supported schools in Bangladesh cater for 2 million children, against 19 million in the formal system. BRAC (formerly the Bangladesh Rural Advancement Committee) is an NGO focusing on children who did not enrol at the normal entry age. Teachers receive very short preparatory training (twelve days) but ongoing support is well-organized and supervision is given weekly. BRAC children perform significantly better on life skills and writing than their peers in normal schools and do equally well in reading and numeracy. In 1999, transition to secondary school was also higher for BRAC children: 95.3%, against 81.9% for children in the formal system.

The non-formal sector is large and diverse. With eleven types of primary education and many partners, it is hard to develop and implement a robust national policy, the more so because the education data system does not yet allow close monitoring and precise target setting. The low student attendance rate (62%), high teacher absenteeism and relatively low number of contact hours (World Bank/Asian Development Bank, 2003), together with relatively low interest in teacher training (Latif, 2004: 8), stand in contrast to the high levels of engagement in Cuban schools and those of the Republic of Korea. Nonetheless, the government of Bangladesh is continuing its strong commitment to education reform into the second phase of the Primary Education Development Programme.[38]

Sri Lanka[39] is making progress in both access and quality. UPE is within reach, and gender parity has been achieved. Grade repetition and dropout have declined rapidly and the promotion rate stood at 98.4% in 2001. The pupil/teacher ratio (PTR) fell from 24:1 to 22:1 between 1992 and 1999. Exclusion of Tamil children in the country's tea plantation area is being addressed. Expenditure as a percentage of GDP has been constant in recent years at around 3%, but education's share in the government's budget has fallen, in line with a decrease in the school population. Indications of achievement diverge strongly, as in Bangladesh. While evaluation of a pilot project in the Gamphala district found that 80% of the students reached mastery level (Little, 2000), a national study found 37.2% at mastery level for literacy and 22.6% for numeracy (National Institute of Education of Sri Lanka, 2002).

Sri Lanka is making progress in both access and quality. UPE is within reach, and gender parity has been achieved

35. See also UNESCO (2003a: 216).

36. Unless otherwise indicated, the information on Bangladesh is derived from Latif (2004) and the Statistical annex.

37. Several assessments of learning achievement have taken place in Bangladesh in recent years, but as a result of methodological differences it is not possible to compare these and identify trends. In fact, the outcomes of the various studies are remarkably different; see Latif (2004: 9–10).

38. The first phase, from 1997 to 2003, comprised twenty-seven projects. Its evaluation informed the design of the second phase (2003–08). A pool fund established jointly by donors and the government will support implementation of phase II.

39. Unless otherwise indicated, the information on Sri Lanka is derived from Peiris (2004) and the Statistical annex.

However, recent years have seen a modest upward trend in achievement and in examination results, especially among poor children, although less so among the Tamil population in conflict-ridden northern Sri Lanka.

There are good prospects for further advances. Achievement levels for 2002 may not yet fully reflect the primary education reforms instituted in 1998 in response to alarm over Sri Lanka's international standing resulting from 1997 primary education test scores. The reform process involved consultation and mobilization of society (including children). The comprehensive approach addressed all issues believed to make a difference for quality and focused on changing teacher behaviour and developing built-in monitoring and evaluation capacity.[40]

Egypt's stage of educational development is comparable to that of Sri Lanka. Expansion of access between 1990 and 2000, in the largest education system of the Arab world, brought UPE and gender parity within reach (Arab Republic of Egypt Ministry of Education, 2002). Quality was placed high on the agenda. While grade repetition and dropout have been declining since the early 1990s, achievement tests did not indicate progress between 1997 and 2001 (World Bank, 2002a). But performance may soon show the effects of measures taken in the late 1990s, such as increased expenditure on teacher salaries, modest reductions in class size, 'aggressive' in-service teacher training and strengthened support systems. The latest five-year plan (2002–07) involves further efforts to achieve 'excellence for all' in 'beautiful, clean, developed and productive schools' as the government puts it (UNESCO, 2003c).

Egypt is remarkable for the business-style approach to quality assurance that it has chosen.[41] Possibly inspired by foreign donors, the country sees the challenge of improving education as one in which clear targets need to be set (Arab Republic of Egypt Ministry of Education, 2002: 128-134). Decentralized management based on information and communications technology (ICT) is expected to be key in meeting these targets. 'School improvement plans' unite all elements of the strategy. Periodic evaluation of school performance and participation by civil society are seen as instrumental in holding schools accountable. With its businesslike approach, Egypt seems to have a strong vision of educational development. This vision may stabilize education policy over the longer term, as was the case for the four high-performance countries discussed above. One area in which Egypt stands out is that of its emphasis on early childhood care and education (ECCE). It has set an intermediate target of enrolling 60% of 4- to 6-year-olds by 2010, and intends kindergarten to eventually be an integral part of the system of free compulsory education.

For South Africa[42] the challenge has been to address access, equity and quality at the same time. The 1990s saw the net enrolment ratio stagnant at just below 90%, while the gender parity index dropped slightly, from 1.02 in 1990 to 0.98 in 2000. Apartheid left the country with large inequalities along racial lines, reflecting stark differences between rich and poor schools and districts. Results from the SACMEQ, MLA and TIMSS surveys revealed striking underperformance of South African youth compared to other countries in the region – even those investing less in education. South Africa's own expenditure decreased from a relatively high 7.3% of GDP in 1991/92 to 5.5% in 2001–04.

Measures taken soon after the abolition of apartheid in 1994 included ending resource allocation based on racial criteria and democratizing control over schools by introducing school governing bodies. In addition, a remarkable teacher redistribution and deployment project aimed at moving the better teachers to the poorer schools was undertaken. Policy makers had to arrive at a new balance between public and private resources. Nine years of basic education was made compulsory, and expenditure on schooling was equalized for all racial groups. To avert flight to private schools, the government introduced an approach to financing whereby schools could introduce fees to supplement state resources, if their governing bodies deemed it appropriate. No child, however, can be denied access to schooling on grounds of inability to pay the fees, and all or part of the amount is waived for children from families whose income is less than thirty times the fees charged. As intended, this policy has kept fees from deterring enrolment among the poor, while also maintaining participation by richer families in the state education system (Fiske and Ladd, 2004).

> For South Africa the challenge has been to address access, equity and quality at the same time

---

40. For a detailed account and evaluation of the education reform process in Sri Lanka, see Little (2003o).

41. See also the Hungarian experience (UNESCO, 2003a: 216).

42. Unless otherwise indicated, the information on South Africa is from Chisholm (2004) and the Statistical annex.

A new curriculum was launched in 1997. To accelerate its use and enhance its impact on quality, a plan for 2000–04 gave special attention to building teacher self-esteem, developing a professional body for teachers and providing better support. The central role accorded to securing the commitment and quality of teachers is consistent with the lessons from the high-performance countries discussed earlier.

Brazil[43] and Chile[44] are among the countries that symbolize the enormous progress towards EFA in Latin America and the Caribbean. While Cuba is clearly the region's star, Brazil and Chile, along with Argentina, performed relatively well in the OREALC/UNESCO survey.[45] But, measured over time, achievement has been stagnant in Brazil and Chile, despite ambitious efforts to improve.

In the case of Brazil this must be seen against the backdrop of expansion: NER rose from 86.4 in 1990 to 96.7 in 2000. Most new entrants are likely to come from marginalized groups. Their 'school-readiness'[46] will generally be lower than that of children from groups that have been included in education longer. Keeping average achievement constant over the period of expansion can thus be seen as improvement. Moreover, the achievement gap between the highest and lowest performers is relatively small in Brazil. The country has made strong policy efforts to address regional and social inequalities in inputs (especially funding) and achievement. Two flagship projects under the Ten-Year Plan for Education For All (1993–2003) were FUNDEF and Bolsa Escola/PETI. The former is an equalization fund that reduced regional inequalities in the funding of primary education, despite the complex three-level governance structure (local, state, federal). Funding for the poorest schools increased significantly, explaining the growth of enrolment and boosting teachers' salaries and training. Bolsa Escola and PETI are widely praised initiatives to boost schooling among poor families (UNESCO, 2003a: 169). Other projects under the aegis of the ten-year plan are FUNDESCOLA, to enhance school attendance and combat dropping out; PROFORMACAO, to train unlicensed teachers through distance learning; the National Schoolbook Programme, which increased the number of textbooks in terms both of copies and titles; School Cycles implying automatic promotion from first to second grade; and Accelerated Learning Programmes, to give late entrants a chance to catch up. These illustrate a difference between the ways Brazil and South Africa address inequalities. Brazil has selected several large projects, each addressing an aspect of the education system or its context. South Africa has followed a broader strategy, focusing on equalizing resource inputs among schools, and making teacher quality a key element of reform.

Chile, like Finland, consciously chose education as a core strategy for socio-economic development. In the early 1990s, the former military regime had left the country with the challenge of revitalizing and modernizing the economy, enhancing social cohesion and building a democratic citizenry. Public expenditure on education rose from 2.4% of GDP in 1990 to 4.4% in 2001. In absolute terms it more than tripled between 1990 and 2003, and private expenditure also increased strongly. An expansion of the annual number of school hours, from 880 to 1,200, is on course, the idea being eventually to end the practice of multi-shift teaching. Social assistance has been improved, enhancing enrolment of poorer children. ICT is seen as key to modernizing education. Authoritarian teaching styles, mainly aimed at keeping order in the classroom (Carnoy, Gove and Marshall, forthcoming; OECD, 2004d: 36–7), are slowly giving way to more advanced approaches aimed at activating students. However, all this remains weakly associated with learning targets (OECD, 2004d: 36–7). Indeed, Chile's national student monitoring system (*Sistema de medición de la calidad de la educación*, or SIMCE) reveals only modest gains. Much more progress in achievement is reported from compensatory programmes such as P.900, which targets the schools in the lowest-performing decile, and the rural programme of MECE,[47] for small multigrade schools. Thus, as in Senegal, progress is found in special settings and has not yet spread throughout the system. Low self-confidence among Chilean teachers, reported in 1999,[48] may play a role in the lack of progress, given the importance of teacher esteem in the four high-performance countries.

Taking stock of the experience of the seven ambitious countries, we can observe a number of common characteristics. All seven have made significant progress in expanding access, and are

Brazil and Chile are among the countries that symbolize the enormous progress towards EFA in Latin America and the Caribbean

43. Unless otherwise indicated, the information on Brazil is from Gusso (2004) and the Statistical annex.

44. Unless otherwise indicated, the information on Chile is from Cox (2004) and the Statistical annex.

45. Again, though, it is worth recalling that achievement scores do not give the whole picture.

46. See 'Start with learners' in Chapter 4. The extent to which children are sufficiently prepared for school varies significantly, with social background playing an important role.

47. 'Mejoramiento de la calidad y equidad de la educación' (improvement of quality and equity in education) is a series of programmes aimed at improving education at various levels.

48. This was among the findings of the 1999 TIMSS survey. Of the thirty-eight countries covered, Chile and the Philippines shared the lowest position concerning the number of teachers who are confident about their mastery of mathematics, and Chile and Italy shared the lowest position regarding science mastery. Self-confidence regarding teaching skills was also lower in Chile than in most of the other countries.

Successful qualitative reforms require a very strong leading role by government and a robust long-term vision for education

now shifting the balance between quantity and quality. Indeed, raising quality generally seems to *follow* the expansion of access, up to a certain level. While the achievement of higher quality is implied by progress on gender parity and better-equipped schools, the picture as regards learning achievement is less favourable. Progress in cognitive outcomes has been modest, absent or restricted to certain projects, though some countries can expect broader, more substantial improvement as a result of recent policy initiatives.

Judging from the experience of the four high-performance countries, successful qualitative reforms, in the context of systems characterized by universal access, seem to require a very strong leading role by government and a robust long-term vision for education. These characteristics are less prominent in the seven ambitious cases, where another key requirement – having sufficiently motivated, well-supported teachers – also seems insufficiently fulfilled.

Although these characteristics and similarities are important, it seems clear from this discussion of eleven very different countries that a search for any general theory of successful educational reform is unlikely to succeed. Contextual differences limit the transferability of policy lessons from one country to another (OECD, 2004a), even among relatively comparable countries.[49] Usually, reforms that aim to raise the quality of education are politically even more difficult to pursue than those that aim at expansion.[50] This means the political context is likely to have a strong impact on prospects for reform, irrespective of the technical and resource context of the school system. The time factor also complicates the analysis: the impact of an education policy may not become apparent until years after it is implemented, and is never in isolation from other policies and trends. This makes one-to-one relationships between measures and effects difficult, though not impossible, to establish.[51]

The quality of ECCE and literacy programmes

As the above review of country experience illustrates, most discussions and evidence of the quality of education focus on the school system. Very many youths and adults in developing countries have had little or no access to schooling, yet the attention and resources given to literacy and skills development programmes are much lower than what is given to schooling. When such programmes do receive emphasis, it tends to be on the expansion of provision rather than on quality.

This section takes a closer look at the quality of the learning that takes place before and after primary school age.[52] It asks several questions: What can be said about the quality of programmes? What are characteristics of good programmes? How can quality be enhanced affordably? Do better-quality programmes have a correspondingly stronger impact on the individual, community and society?

Does the quality of ECCE programmes make a difference?[53]

Assessing the quality of provision in early childhood care and education is more challenging than for schooling. Achievement tests, examinations and diplomas are largely absent at this level. National data showing provision and inputs are limited and often not easily comparable, although at programme level various quality assessment instruments have been developed.[54]

ECCE provides a good example of programmes where relative interpretations of quality are necessary. For example, in the early years of learning, parents involve themselves more intensively and in different ways than they do later in their children's education. Young children have a right to spend their first years in a peaceful, safe and playful environment. As the quality of ECCE depends strongly on programme context, it can be argued that the definition of quality in this area should vary and be subject to negotiation among parents, practitioners and policy makers.

Common sense suggests that the early years – when the brain matures, when we first learn to walk and talk, when self-control begins, when the first social relationships are formed – must be regarded as important. It also suggests that children whose basic health, nutritional and psycho-social needs are being met will develop and perform better than those less fortunate. Common sense also suggests that a child who

---

49. Germany is making an encouraging attempt to overcome this difficulty. Concerned about its PISA results, it conducted an in-depth study of a few relatively comparable but better-performing countries (Döebert, Klieme and Sroka, 2004). The design of this study could serve as a model for those wishing to learn from other countries.

50. See Corrales (1999) for a useful analysis of why this is so.

51. See the section below on the experimental evaluation of education policy interventions.

52. Previous Global Monitoring Reports have focused on the impact of ECCE and learning programmes, on the importance of ECCE for gender equality, and on conceptual issues (UNESCO, 2002a: 38–43 and 56–67; UNESCO, 2003a: 34–43, 84–95 and 181–8).

53. Unless otherwise indicated, the information on ECCE is from Myers (2004).

54. Examples are the Early Childhood Environmental Rating Scale (ECERS), the High/Scope Program Quality Assessment (PQA) and an observational instrument developed for the IEA Preschool Project.

develops well physically, mentally, socially and emotionally during the early years is more likely to be a happy and productive member of society than one who does not.

Research on early childhood development confirms common sense. The literature is vast and varied, encompassing research carried out by psychologists, medical doctors, anthropologists, neurobiologists, educators, sociologists, nutritionists and others. In general, this research supports the following propositions:[55]

- The early years of life are a key period for the development of intelligence, personality and behaviour.

- Early childhood learning and development can be enhanced by ECCE programmes.

- The effects of such programmes are likely to be greater for children from disadvantaged backgrounds than for their more privileged peers.

- Good programmes are sensitive to differences in cultural, social and economic contexts.

Given that ECCE matters and that ECCE programmes differ enormously in design and quality,[56] the question becomes whether their design and quality make a difference. The answer seems to be that they do, for most desired outcomes, even when the tendency for privileged families to choose higher-quality programmes is taken into account.

While most of the research compares children who followed a certain programme with those who did not, another kind of study has emerged over the last two decades that focuses explicitly on quality, comparing outcomes for children in ECCE centres that differ in the level of quality attributed to them.

A Turkish study, for example, compared children who received no form of care, those who were looked after by child minders and those who attended some type of preschool centre (Kagitçbasi, 1996). Although quality was not defined explicitly, the results were better for the third group. Another feature of this study was the inclusion of a parental education and support component. This was found to produce important results regarding children's cognitive development and school performance as well as child-rearing practices in the family – the latter related in part to changes in the self-image and knowledge of the participating mothers.

In Mauritius, eighty-three children were assigned to a good preschool from ages 3 to 5, and matched on temperament, nutritional, cognitive, autonomic and demographic variables with a control group of 355 children given no special schooling. By age 10, the children who had attended the quality preschool showed better social skills and more organized thinking and had more friends than those in the control group. At age 17 and age 23, the positive effects were still pronounced: the researchers found these young adults to be more socially adjusted, calmer, better able to get along with peers and up to 52% less likely to commit a crime (Raine et al., 2003).

A fifteen-year IEA study in ten high- and middle-income countries[57] found similar results (Weikart, Olmsted and Montie, 2003). It sought to determine how process and structural characteristics of community pre-primary settings affected language and cognitive development. Based on a study of more than 5,000 children aged 4 and 7, in 1,800 different settings, it was found that language performance at age 7 was better the more autonomy children had been given in preschool and the higher the preschool teacher's educational level. Another study found that cognitive performance improves the less time children spend in whole-group activities and the more and better equipment and materials to which they have access. (High/Scope Educational Research Foundation, 2004).

Although most of these studies did not treat quality explicitly, it was nevertheless evident that even where pre-primary programmes operated with modest resources (using paraprofessionals and sometimes with unfavourable class sizes) they often showed a positive impact on children,[58] and work with parents seemed to be a factor in this effect. This is not to say that better quality would not have produced even better results, but it serves to emphasize that it is not always necessary to apply high and probably unaffordable quality standards uniformly in all settings.

Even where pre-primary programmes operated with modest resources they often showed a positive impact on children

---

55. See, for instance, Hunt (1961), Vygotsky (1962), Bloom (1964) and Piaget and Inhelder (1969), and more recent work on brain development (summarized in Mustard, 2002), the roots of antisocial behaviour (Rutter, Giller and Hagell, 1998), the prevention of intellectual disabilities (Ramey and Ramey, 1998), resilience and 'positive deviance' (Werner and Smith, 1982; Zeitlin, Ghassemi and Mansour, 1990) and nutrition and cognitive development (McKay et al., 1978), recent reviews by the National Research Council (2001), the Carnegie Corporation of New York (1994) and the Centre of Excellence for Early Childhood Development (2004), and volumes edited by Keating and Hertzman (1999) and Young (2002), among many others.

56. They may involve direct attention to children, or indirect attention via work with their parents, or be child-centred community programmes, or a combination of these. They may involve health, nutrition or education components, or a combination. They may be publicly or privately run. A range of curricula can be found.

57. Finland, Greece, Hong Kong, Indonesia, Ireland, Italy, Poland, Spain, Thailand and the United States.

58. Martínez and Myers (2003) found in Mexico that the larger urban classes reached better outcomes than smaller rural classes, since other factors appeared to be stronger, such as teacher preparation, resource availability, multigrade classes and the quality of management.

The research evidence indicates that better child care for children of preschool age is associated with better cognitive and social development

59. See Peisner-Feinberg (2004) for a recent review.

60. Unless otherwise indicated, the information on Literacy Skills Development is from Oxenham (2004).

61. Literacy and various other kinds of skill often go hand in hand, both in acquisition and application, though it remains important to distinguish them clearly (see UNESCO, 2003a: 84–6).

62. There is also increasing agreement on the rights of adults to empowering and relevant basic education and on the importance of participating in dynamic, rich, inclusive learning environments (UIE, 2004: 1).

63. See Arnove and Graff (1987) for evaluations of several campaigns.

64. For example, in the United Republic of Tanzania out of the 466,000 people enrolled in a literacy project carried out between 1967 and 1973 within the framework of the Experimental World Literacy Programme, 293,000 took the final examination and 96,000 passed, at an average cost of US$32 per new literate, US$10 of which came from the United Nations (UNESCO/UNDP, 1976).

Most of the present 'success stories' of ECCE come from high- and middle-income countries where resources are less scarce. India and Nepal are exceptions. Both have low-cost programmes that nevertheless have a relatively strong positive impact on children and their families (UNESCO, 2003a: 182–3). In the Nepalese 'Entry Point Programme', a well-designed four-day training programme and a toolkit enabled mothers to educate each others' children one day a week, freeing them to generate income on the other days. In countries where achieving UPE is the main challenge, such low-cost measures offer an interesting option.

In conclusion, the research evidence indicates that better child care for children of preschool age is associated with better cognitive and social development. Organized preschool care and education, with some material resources and qualified teachers giving children stimulation and some choice of activities, seems to lead to better cognitive and social development later in life than does an absence of such programmes.[59] The impact of quality in ECCE appears to be important for children from all backgrounds, but particularly for the least advantaged.

Literacy and skills development programmes for youth and adults[60]

The debate on the quality of literacy and skills development[61] has its own history, distinct from that on schooling. The importance of strong, widely distributed reading, writing and calculation skills in societies aiming for democracy, industrialization and farm modernization has long been recognized.[62] However, in the praxis of adult learning, many paradigms have come and gone over the years.

Until the 1950s, literacy skills were widely assumed to be general. Reading a manual was judged no different from reading a newspaper. An effective text or curriculum would thus serve all learners equally well, it was thought. This 'one size fits all' approach underlay government and other agency efforts, whether in campaigns,[63] national programmes or missionary classes. Although good evaluations of these early programmes are scarce, it is clear that their effectiveness varied widely.

Doubts about their efficacy prompted UNESCO to propose a new strategy in the 1960s. It was based upon the premise that literacy skills, being means to ends, required clear purposes and almost immediate applicability. The new approach was to be 'functional, selective, intensive and work-oriented'. Instead of one curriculum to fit all, many were developed to fit particular groups or occupations where literacy skills could raise productivity. The occupations ranged across household, agricultural and industrial situations in rural and urban areas, and addressed the interests of both women and men. However, a 1976 UNESCO/UNDP evaluation of these 'functional literacy' approaches found only modest benefits,[64] and confidence in such programmes' worth declined as a result.

Nevertheless, the idea of 'functional' literacy has remained central to subsequent approaches, and its main assumptions have been validated. Functional content has usually included rudimentary information on health, hygiene, nutrition, child care, agriculture, environmental concerns, savings, credit and other topics judged important and useful for unschooled and poor people, especially women. Many governments and international agencies have supported programmes with these central themes.

On a parallel though much smaller scale, some work has aimed at using literacy to address more political objectives. Where earlier literacy programmes sometimes espoused political content to encourage nation building, the Brazilian educator Paolo Freire sought to use literacy to generate political and social change from below. He developed a pedagogical strategy that would lead people to reflect on their predicaments and their causes. Learners were expected to use literacy to articulate their concerns and initiate political action to ameliorate their conditions. Although the strategy appealed to adult educators and to government departments of adult education, the scope for using it for political ends was limited, and its legacy was absorbed within the functional approach.

Since the early 1990s, however, ActionAid, an international NGO, has taken Freire's strategy a step further. Whereas Freire derived conventional texts and exercises from words and phrases of special significance in local vocabularies, ActionAid has gradually dispensed with prepared materials. It uses the techniques of 'participatory rural appraisal' to introduce participants to ways of representing their neighbourhoods and practices symbolically – e.g. maps and calendars – and to progress from there, by way of reflections on their situation, to words and numbers. Literacy is subordinated to empowering the poor to take action to improve their situation; learning sessions are expected to end with identification of action points.[65]

What counts in designing effective programmes? Programmes aimed at helping people acquire the skills they need to sustain a livelihood stand a stronger chance of success than those led by literacy as such;[66] demand is stronger in such cases. Development organizations seem better able than non-specialized educational organizations to design and deliver effective combinations of livelihood and literacy.[67]

Instructors' own skills have a pay-off in terms of skill mastery by learners. The skills most needed in instructors include reliability; mastery of their subject matter, methods and skills; rapport with learners and the ability to sustain learners' interest and engagement.

In many cultures, teaching adults appears to work best when instructor and learners are of the same sex, yet in most countries more men than women are available as instructors while most learners tend to be female. Among the various training models available, recurrent, brief training supports instructors better than initial training followed by irregular supervision. While most people who are literate can be trained to teach literacy effectively to others, livelihood skills require more specialized instructors, preferably selected locally by the learners themselves.

Ideally a group of learners should be served by at least two instructors, each covering selected skills within a coordinated curriculum. Outcomes of adult learning seem to be independent of pedagogical methods: a variety of approaches seems equally effective. That said, it is important for technical materials to both support what the learners wish to learn and to be in advance of what the learners know already. That requires thorough needs assessment, covering both content and qualitative objectives.[68]

Most programmes arrange for learners to undergo some form of assessment and receive certification of their attainments as a means of sustaining motivation. Some recognize the basic literacy course as equivalent to some level of primary schooling, perhaps qualifying learners to enter more formal education.[69] People acquire literacy most easily in their mother language, the next best option being a language with which they are familiar. Ghana has delivered programmes in as many as fifteen languages, and larger countries like India and Nigeria offer even more. Multilingualism, then, is not an insuperable problem even where it adds to programme complexity and cost. Where an international language is the medium for government, education, law and commerce, tuition in that language is sometimes offered as a follow-on to the basic literacy course. Namibia again provides a recent example.

The evidence shows that up to 80% of the people who enrol in well-run literacy classes complete their courses, and half or more of the enrolees pass the local assessment tests. The 'unsuccessful' completers or dropouts may also learn and use some skills. Even better results can be expected from programmes that bring learners together around a common purpose.[70]

The desirable duration of programmes depends on context, but it seems that 400 hours of structured learning can be sufficient to bring totally unschooled and illiterate adults to some basic level of mastery (Oxenham et al., 2002: 38). Similar levels of proficiency have been shown (e.g. in Bangladesh, Indonesia and Uganda) to require some 1,700 to 3,400 hours of primary school instruction (two to four years).[71] This does not imply that adults or schoolchildren are *fully* literate after 400 hours, or two to four years (see UNESCO, 2003*a*: 60, Figure 2.14) Furthermore, without continued practice, much of what is learned may fall into disuse over the years.[72]

Whether people who attain literacy actually make much use of it is subject to debate.[73] On balance, however, literacy seems more used where economic development is better established.[74] This supports the argument that some degree of economic and political improvement is necessary to sustain literacy (Torres, 2003: 141): people will use their literacy skills where conditions make it useful or desirable for them to do so.

In many cultures, teaching adults appears to work best when instructor and learners are of the same sex

65. This strategy is called REFLECT (for 'Regenerated Freirean Literacy through Empowering Community Techniques'). Some 350 organizations in at least sixty countries have adopted it (see www.reflect-action.org).

66. See, for instance, Oxenham et al. (2002) and Oxenham (forthcoming).

67. An example is provided by the Farmers' Field Schools in Nepal; see World Education (2000).

68. In a pioneering 1970s example, Indonesia's Paket A project offered 100 booklets on several topics, graded by reading difficulty, from beginners to more fluent readers (Indonesia Ministry of Education and Culture, 1998).

69. In Namibia, literacy programmes are tied in with a national system of vocational qualifications (see Chapter 4).

70. See, for instance, Nirantar (1997) and Oxenham et al. (2002).

71. Bear in mind that literacy is only part of the primary school curriculum.

72. Several studies suggest, however, that the rate of forgetting skills may be faster than had been feared; see, for instance, Kapoor and Roy (1970), Indonesia Ministry of Education and Culture (1998), Cawthera (2003) and Okech et al. (2001).

73. Somewhat negative conclusions are found in Karlekar (2000) on India, and Fiedrich and Jellema (2003) on REFLECT projects in Bangladesh and Uganda. Okech et al. (2001) have more positive observations on other projects in Uganda.

74. See, for instance, Carron, Mwiria and Righa (1989) and Carr-Hill et al. (1991) on their evaluations of literacy programmes in Kenya and Tanzania.

> Better programmes are not necessarily more expensive, from the perspective of society, given the links between learning and income generation

Conclusion

Where formal education systems are flanked by programmes of early learning and literacy and skills development, additional benefits accrue to the individual, the community, society, and formal education itself. Children who enjoyed early learning opportunities learn better in formal education, while educated adults, as parents, make bigger efforts to enrol their children and to support them when in school.[75] In this section we have seen that better programmes have a stronger impact on schooling and other developmental objectives than do weak programmes. Furthermore, better programmes are not necessarily more expensive, from the perspective of society, given the links between learning and income generation.

The quality of schooling

As the two previous sections indicate, qualitative study of country experience and investigation of lessons from particular types of educational programme can bring important insights. This synthetic work, however, is not always as rigorous as is needed to form the basis for educational innovation and policy reform. To establish a better basis for generalization about what policies count, it is necessary to assess the results of a large body of scientific work on what makes a difference for the quality of education. Most of this literature relates to schools, as the major institutions for learning in all societies.

The paradox

Schooling is a social process, and improvements in resources, technology and the quality of student and teaching inputs should in principle be able to enhance its overall quality. Even a casual look at the history of test scores around the world, however, reveals a central and, at first sight, baffling paradox. In a good number of countries, large increases in average real expenditure per student and other measures of school resources in primary and secondary schools over the last four or five decades have not remotely been matched by a comparable increase in average test scores.

Table 2.4 makes this clear. The first column shows that mathematics and science test scores in eleven OECD countries mainly fell, over the quarter-century ending in 1995,[76] the exception being increases in Sweden, the Netherlands and Italy. Over the same period, however, as the second column shows, six of the eleven countries increased real expenditure per pupil by more than 100%, and the remaining countries also increased spending significantly.

As examples of particular resource changes, PTRs in the United States fell by almost 40% between 1960 and 2000, the proportion of teachers with at least a master's degree doubled and average teacher experience increased similarly. And yet, the mathematics and reading performance of 17-year-old students was only slightly higher in 1999 than it had been 30 years

Table 2.4: Test scores and changes in real expenditure per pupil, 1970–94 (percentages)

Country	Change in mathematics and science score, 1970–94	Increase in real spending per pupil, 1970–94	Increase in real GDP per capita, 1970–94	Staff compensation as % of current expenditure on primary education, 1995
Australia	−2.3	269.8	46.4	79
New Zealand	−9.7	222.5	24.3	n.a.
France	−6.6	211.6	60.7	79
Italy	1.3	125.7	74.6	89
Germany	−4.8	108.1	66.8	76
Japan	−1.9	103.3	100.7	87
United Kingdom	−8.2	76.7	58.3	70
Belgium	−4.7	64.7	68	86
Netherlands	1.7	36.3	52.9	78
United States	0	33.1	70.5	80
Sweden	4.3	28.5	35.1	56

Sources: GDP data: constant price chain series (1996 US$) provided by Heston, Summers and Aten (2002). Other data: Pritchett (2003); OECD (1998: Table B5.1a).

---

75. Oxenham (2004: 8–11), using the Millennium Development Goals as a framework, shows the positive impact of adult learning on each goal, including UPE and gender equality. Myers (2004: 5–6) points to the well-researched benefits of early learning.

76. For the assumptions involved, see Pritchett (2003). Although the calculations are subject to error, this does not affect the broad picture.

before, when spending was dramatically lower, and the performance of students in science was significantly lower in 1999 than in 1970.[77] As the table shows, the decline was even sharper in some other OECD countries.[78] Despite this evidence, however, popular policy prescriptions for improving school quality focus particularly on further increasing expenditure and resource levels.

Explanations

Why have countries had such a difficult time increasing average test scores? Some authors have argued that the impact of television on children and their use of time, changes in pedagogy towards less test-oriented teaching methods, the power of teachers' unions and improvements in labour market opportunities for women – allowing highly capable women to move into professions other than teaching – have each had a negative impact on the prospects for learning in schools.[79]

Part of the increase in unit expenditure arises from the growth in societies' wealth since 1970. Column 3 in Table 2.4 shows that all the countries grew richer and, in the last five of those shown, the rise in real GDP per capita was actually greater than the increase in per-pupil spending. This income growth would also have been reflected in individual earnings, and since staff salaries account for 60–90% of unit expenditure (see column 4), the general increase in teacher earnings must account for a significant part of the rise in real expenditure per pupil.

Earnings provide an important incentive mechanism, which can influence both the quality and motivation of teachers. If teachers' real average earnings had kept pace with other professional groups over the period, the productivity impact of their earnings growth would likely have been small. In fact, however, in many countries, teachers' earnings have increased considerably less sharply than those of other groups.[80] So while teachers may actually be better off in real terms than they were in 1970, they may feel worse off, because of their decline in status relative to other professional groups. This circumstance could well explain part – perhaps an important part – of the apparent lack of impact on learning outcomes of increases in real per-student spending over time.

Other things may also make it impossible to observe a strong but simple relationship between resource inputs to schooling and test scores. Changes in other inputs (teaching time, curricula requirements, school sizes, etc.) could have affected test scores as well. The second half of the twentieth century was a period of strong expansion of school systems throughout the world. In many countries the original social roles of schooling have changed, yet expectations have been slower to adjust as a greater mix of ability groups has proceeded through to the higher levels of schooling.

Many studies have been conducted in the past twenty years to discover the extent to which such disturbances explain why the expected relationship between inputs and outputs is concealed. In the economics literature there have been two main types of investigation. The first involves cross-country studies of the relationship between educational expenditure and test scores. The second, now comprising numerous articles and papers, takes a more micro approach and is based on the idea of an education production function to inform the analysis. The results of both types of work are briefly discussed below.

Results from macro studies

Table 2.5 summarizes the main results of the small number of empirical papers that have sought to establish whether there is a positive, strong and significant causal relationship between educational expenditure and outcomes at the aggregate level. The table shows the dependent variables that were taken as proxies for school quantity or quality in each study: test scores, repetition and dropout rates, completion rates, enrolment ratios at primary, and sometimes secondary, level. The studies aim to establish the extent to which increases in school resources – usually measured as PTRs, expenditure per pupil, proportion of GDP or average teacher salaries – enhance educational outcomes.

The strongest set of results seeming to establish the importance of school resources for test scores emerges from the work of Lee and Barro (2001). They find, first, that increases in PTR result in a decrease in average test scores, thereby indicating that smaller classes are associated with better pupil achievement; their

The second half of the twentieth century was a period of strong expansion of school systems throughout the world

---
77. Expenditure and input figures are from US Department of Education data, while scores are the results of tests administered to a random sample of students aged 17 by the National Assessment of Educational Progress. See Hanushek, 2003: 67–9.

78. See also Gundlach, Woessmann and Gmelin (2001) and Carnoy (2004).

79. Pritchett (2003). See also Carnoy (2004).

80. See the section on teacher earnings in Chapter 4.

Table 2.5: Results of studies investigating the relationship between educational expenditures and outcomes

Study	Type of data, year, number of observations	Educational outcome	Educational expenditure	Results
Al-Samarrai (2002)	Cross-country; 1996; 33 to 90	■ Primary gross and net enrolment ratios ■ Survival rate to primary grade 5 ■ Primary school completion rate	■ Public primary education spending (% GNP) ■ Primary expenditure per pupil ■ Primary PTR	■ Primary expenditure per pupil has a positive and significant impact on survival rate to grade five only (10%), and a negative and significant impact on the enrolment ratios (1% and 5%, respectively). ■ All other coefficients are insignificant.
Hanushek and Kimko (2000)	Cross-country panel; 1965, 1970, 1988, 1991; 67 to 70	■ IEA and IAEP[1] mathematics and science tests	■ PTR ■ Current education spending per pupil ■ Total expenditure on education (% GDP)	■ Insignificant ■ Negative impact, 1% ■ Negative impact, 5%
Woessmann (2000)	Cross-country; 1995; 39	■ TIMSS mathematics and science scores	■ Class size	■ Positive impact, 1%
Lee and Barro (2001)	Cross-country panel: 1964, 1970, 1975, 1980, 1982, 1984, 1985, 1990 (depending on the outcome considered) 214 to 346	■ Test scores ■ Primary school repetition rates ■ Primary school dropout rates	■ PTR ■ Average teacher salary ■ Current education spending per pupil	■ PTR has a negative and significant impact on all three variables (5%, 1% and 5%). ■ Average teacher salary has a positive and significant impact on test scores (10%). ■ All other coefficients insignificant.
McMahon (1999)	Cross-country; early 1990s; 44 to 50	■ Primary male and female gross enrolment ratios ■ Male and female grade 5 completion rate	■ Public current expenditure on primary education (% GNP) ■ Public current expenditure per primary student (% GNP per capita) ■ Public current expenditure per primary student (level)	■ Total expenditure has a positive and significant impact (1%). ■ Per capita expenditure has a negative and significant impact (1%). ■ Positive impact, 1%
Gupta, Verhoeven and Tiongson (1999)	Cross-country: 1993/94 23 to 42	■ Primary and secondary gross enrolment ratios ■ Persistence through grade 4	■ Primary and secondary education spending (% total education spending) ■ Education spending (% GDP)	■ Expenditure on primary and secondary education has a positive and significant impact on all three variables (1–5%, 5–10%, 5–10%) ■ Total education spending has a significant and positive impact on secondary enrolment only (5%); insignificant for the other two variables.
Schultz (1996)	Country panel; 1965–80; 60 to 191	■ Primary gross enrolment ratio	■ Public teacher compensation as (% GNP per working age adult)	■ Negative impact, 1%
Colclough with Lewin (1993)	Cross-country; 1986; 82	■ Primary gross enrolment ratio	■ Public current expenditure on primary (% GNP) ■ Public current expenditure per primary student (% GNP per capita)	■ Insignificant ■ Negative impact, 1–5%

Notes and sources: Table: Al-Samarrai (2002), with additional results from Gupta, Verhoeven and Tiongson (1999). Detailed sources: Hanushek and Kimko (2000: Table 3); Woessmann (2000: Table 1); Lee and Barro (2001: Table 3); McMahon (1999: 164 and 166); Schultz (1996: Tables 2 and 3); Colclough with Lewin (1993: Table 2.6a); Gupta, Verhoeven and Tiongson (1999: Table 1); Al Samarrai (2002: Tables 4.1 and 4.2). Lee and Barro (2001) present other specifications but the results do not differ markedly.
Colclough with Lewin (1993) also present results for developing countries and African countries separately, but the results on the resource variables are similar.
1. International Assessment of Educational Progress.

results suggest that a decrease in the average PTR (by 12.3 in 1990) raises test scores by 1.8 percentage points. Second, higher teacher salaries in their sample of fifty-eight countries were associated with a significant increase in test scores. Third, the results for repetition and dropout rates are consistent with their being affected by school resources: reductions in PTR are associated with reduced rates of dropout and repetition. Lee and Barro conclude that school inputs (especially smaller class sizes, but probably also higher teacher salaries and more years of schooling) enhance educational outcomes.

Two studies produce evidence that spending on the primary system – but not total education spending – affects the retention rate to grades 4 and 5 (Gupta, Verhoeven and Tiongson, 1999; McMahon, 1999). Not surprisingly, it is the share of resources devoted to primary schools that affects their functioning, total resources going to education being too approximate a measure to be relevant.

Other results, however, are rather different. As the table shows, Hanushek and Kimko (2000) found that variations in school resources do not have strong effects on test performance. By their estimates, the effects of various types of resources are either statistically insignificant or, more frequently, statistically significant but with an unexpected sign – in other words, suggesting that increased resources actually results in lower test scores. This finding holds regardless of the measure of resources used: PTR, current expenditure per student, total expenditure per student and a variety of others not shown in the table.

A later study (Hanushek and Luque, 2003) uses data from the TIMSS, taken from representative samples of schools in 1995 in more than forty countries for pupils aged 9, 13 and 17. The paper examines the determinants of pupil achievement, focusing on the class-level averages of mathematics test results for 9- and 13-year-olds. It finds that almost all the coefficients associated with school characteristics are insignificant and divided almost equally between negative and positive ones. Only five countries exhibit the 'expected' negative and significant relationship between achievement and class size; none exhibits a positive and significant relationship between achievement and teacher education or experience. The authors conclude that, overall, for the countries sampled, resources' power to produce better student performance is rather limited. While certain countries do stand out for having significant effects, these results do not suggest that outcomes related to school resource differences are more positive in poorer countries or in those that begin with lower levels of resources.

The other studies reported in the table deal with educational outcomes expressed in terms of enrolment ratios, rather than qualitative indicators. Here, too, the results conflict. Some studies consistently find that expenditure increases are associated with increased enrolments, and others find the opposite.

In general, no consistent relationship is discernable across these studies. Those using internationally comparable test scores tend to show that resources have a significant impact on educational outcomes, but the direction of the impact differs among the studies and is often counter-intuitive. Taken as a whole, this group of studies does not suggest that a positive, strong and significant relationship between educational expenditure and outcomes can yet be identified using aggregate, country-level data.

Results from micro studies

Addressing questions about the relative importance of schools and families in determining cognitive achievement and subsequent success in life is not a new activity. For example, a century ago French sociologist Paul Lapie studied the life histories of 722 men who had been enrolled between 1872 and 1893 at the primary school in Ay, a small town in eastern France. He concluded, on the basis of this work: 'Schooling sometimes succeeds in breaking the strings of the net by which economic circumstances control our destinies. Its impact is not great, but it is not nothing.'[81] The notion that education in general, and school in particular, makes a difference to people's lives informed politics and public policy throughout the 20th century. Research on the matter was given a strong stimulus in the mid-1960s by the publication of an influential report concluding that, in the USA, family background and the composition of peer groups in school had a much larger impact on educational outcomes and on subsequent economic success than did variations in the characteristics of the schools themselves (Coleman et al., 1966). The profoundly radical implication was that schools simply helped reproduce inequalities in society that already existed. One result was an outpouring of research aimed at establishing a firmer basis for these findings or refuting them.

This modern economic approach to investigating the determinants of educational outcomes has borrowed well-established techniques from other economic applications. The idea that there is a determinate relationship between inputs to a production process and the outputs that subsequently emerge has long been important in microeconomic analysis. If a firm's production possibilities are governed by certain technical

> **The profoundly radical implication of the Coleman report was that schools simply helped reproduce inequalities in society that already existed**

[81]. 'Ainsi, l'école réussit parfois à rompre les mailles du réseau dans lequel des causes d'ordre économique enferment nos destinées. Son action n'est pas considérable, mais elle n'est pas nulle'. Paul Lapie. 1904. 'Les Effets sociaux de l'école' ['The Social Effects of Schooling'], *La Revue scientifique* (Revue rose), 41 (2); cited in Baudelot et al. (2004).

The application of production function analysis to education is somewhat hazardous

relationships between factors of production – e.g. it takes a bag of nails, some tools, some planks of wood and some days of labour to produce a fence – the 'production function' describes the maximum feasible output (fence) obtainable from alternative combinations of these inputs. Production functions are powerful analytic tools, which have been applied to the analysis of most forms of economic production. Since the mid-1960s, they have also been widely used in the economic analysis of education.

The application of this idea to education is, however, somewhat hazardous. While it may be reasonable to assume that managers of firms in some sense 'know' the shape and characteristics of the production function they face in their industry, this is not the case with education managers. Furthermore, the inputs to the schooling process are much less homogeneous (teachers, goals, pupils) than in industry, where labour usually faces more defined tasks than do teachers. Nor can the characteristics of the outputs (more schooled pupils) be unambiguously compared with earlier pupil inputs for 'value added' purposes. But the main difficulty with representing education as a production process is that some of its inputs and all of its outcomes are embodied in pupils, who have their own autonomous behaviour. Planks of wood cannot decide that they do not want to be assembled, avoid coming to the construction site or refuse to interact with construction workers. Unfortunately, the production function literature has comprehensively failed to model pupil behaviour.

Notwithstanding these and other difficulties,[82] this literature has burgeoned, with the explicit aim of guiding education policies around the world by identifying which policy-controlled inputs have the largest marginal impact on achievement. Would a greater impact on learning, for example, arise from providing more textbooks, increasing teacher salaries or improving teacher training? In the absence of proper theories of cognitive processes, pupil-teacher interactions and schools as institutions, the usual assumption has been that higher expenditure and input provision will automatically lead to better educational outcomes. From what has already been said at the macro level, it is perhaps not surprising that such a clear picture does not emerge from the research results at the micro level.

Results from education production function studies

Since the education production function literature now includes numerous studies, a summary analysis of this evidence might be expected to provide robust empirical regularities as to which inputs stimulate achievement, and to what extent.[83] Table 2.6 shows a meta-analysis of all published estimates up to 1995 for the USA. It covers eighty-nine individual publications containing 376 production function estimates. The educational outcomes considered in three-quarters of these studies are test scores; the rest used other outcomes, such as rates of continuation in school or drop-out rates. Resources considered are real classroom resources (PTR, teacher education, teacher experience), financial aggregates (teacher salary, expenditure per pupil) and other resources (facilities, administration, teacher test scores).

The results show that for between 9% and 37% of these cases, resource inputs had a positive effect upon measured student achievement. Their frequency was often not much greater than the number of negative cases, however: most notably, improving PTR had a negative impact upon achievement as often as it had a positive one.[84] Furthermore, although the proportion of positive and significant estimates was, on the whole, much greater than that of the negative ones, in a considerable majority of all cases there was no significant measured relationship between resource inputs and student performance.

The developing-country sample, shown in Table 2.7, summarizes ninety-six estimates of the impact on student performance of up to six resource inputs (PTR; teacher education, experience and salary; expenditure per pupil; and school facilities). Here, there are twelve to sixty-three estimates per variable, and the results are much more varied than those derived from the US studies. First, there are proportionately fewer statistically insignificant estimates: in only two cases do these represent a majority. Second, among the significant estimates, a strong majority are positive, and the proportion of negative estimates is below 10% except in the cases of the PTR and teacher salary. Third, an absolute majority of the estimates are significant and positive for teacher education, expenditure per pupil and school facilities.

---

82. See Glewwe (2002) for discussion of the technical problems underlying the methodology.

83. It does so if one accepts the implicit assumption that a homogenous 'technology' exists, whose parameters would be common to all education systems across the world, conditional on a sufficient number of adequately selected control variables.

84. The regression coefficient may be of the opposite sign, e.g. a negative coefficient associated with the PTR is considered a positive estimate, for it implies that teacher resources are positively associated with achievement.

The literature contains much debate as to the implications of all these research results. Some argue that the glass is half full, others that it is half empty. Alternative ways of grouping and summarizing the results, however, suggest that improvements to the resources available to developing country schools are more likely than not to improve the levels of cognitive achievement of pupils.[85] This suggests grounds for confidence that, in developing countries, increased resources for schools do influence student performance positively – more strongly than in the case of the USA, with its already high average resource levels.

That being said, dozens of production function studies for education have been published over the last three decades for the USA, a few other developed countries and a relatively large number of developing countries. They have yielded few uncontroversial empirical regularities on which education policies can be based. Quite apart from the considerable technical problems involved in interpreting individual estimates, there is no real consensus on whether it makes sense to summarize them through meta-analytical techniques (as in Tables 2.6 and 2.7) rather than surveying a few key studies, nor on how the meta-analysis should be conducted and its results interpreted. Given this level of uncertainty, at least some of the conclusions that the various authors in this field have drawn depend on their *a priori* opinions, as much as anything, and cannot be unquestioningly used to guide policies.

Effective schools research

In parallel with this economic tradition, a rather different empirical approach to the study of schools and classrooms began to emerge. Education researchers became increasingly concerned that standard production function approaches ignored important aspects of the processes of learning and teaching in schools. These approaches tended to treat what happened in schools – the quality and nature of teacher-pupil interactions, the ways resource inputs were actually used – as being of little consequence. Yet it appeared obvious that ways of organizing schooling – e.g. time spent in class, amount of homework, ways of assessing pupil progress, and teacher expectations, experience and in-service training – were likely to affect student outcomes quite apart from the resource inputs to schooling, and that this might account for the often ambiguous results of production function studies.

The studies in this emerging 'school effectiveness' approach[86] remained quantitative in orientation, and mainly focused on the school as the unit of analysis. Generally, too, the concern was to explain pupils' academic outcomes. Their main innovation was to add new school-level factors to the earlier analyses that had looked at processes within schools only to the extent that they were believed to be important for academic outcomes. Taking a broader perspective, it became increasingly clear that different patterns of school organization and teacher behaviour had different effects on

Table 2.6: Percentage distribution of estimated effect of key resources on student performance, based on 376 production function estimates (United States)

Resources	Number of estimates	Statistically significant (%) Positive	Statistically significant (%) Negative	Statistically insignificant (%)
Real classroom resources				
PTR	276	14	14	72
Teacher education	170	9	5	86
Teacher experience	206	29	5	66
Financial aggregates				
Teacher salary	118	20	7	73
Expenditure per pupil	163	27	7	66
Other				
Facilities	91	9	5	86
Administration	75	12	5	83
Teacher test scores	41	37	10	53

Source: Hanushek (2003a), based on Hanushek (1997).

Table 2.7: Percentage distribution of estimated expenditure parameter coefficients from ninety-six education production function estimates (developing countries)

Inputs	Number of estimates	Statistically significant (%) Positive	Statistically significant (%) Negative	Statistically insignificant (%)
PTR	30	27	27	46
Teacher education	63	56	3	41
Teacher experience	46	35	4	61
Teacher salary	13	31	15	54
Expenditure per pupil	12	50	0	50
Facilities	34	65	9	26

Source: Hanushek (2003a), based on Hanushek (1995).

85. The approach used in Tables 2.6 and 2.7 can be challenged on the grounds that giving equal weight to all estimates made in each study, as opposed to counting only the major results, of each, biases the results, because studies with many estimates are likely to include a greater proportion of negative or insignificant relationships. Krueger (2003) finds that the incidence of studies with positive results is twice as high as the incidence of those with negative results, and that the probability of this occurring by chance is very small. Accordingly, marginal increases in resource inputs, on this interpretation of the production function evidence, are very important for improving cognitive achievement.

86. Brookover et al. (1979) and Mortimore et al. (1988) were early examples.

learning outcomes.[87] Results for industrialized countries converged around the importance of five factors:

- strong educational leadership;
- emphasis on acquiring basic skills;
- an orderly and secure environment;
- high expectations of pupil attainment;
- frequent assessment of pupil progress.

Most of the many reviews of this large body of literature focus on 'what works'.[88] Table 2.8 summarizes results from five such reviews.

Although the emphasis in these studies varies, consensus is strong with respect to the aforementioned five factors (represented in the first five rows of the table). Other factors increasingly being found to be important are school-based in-service development of teachers, the use of well-structured, purposeful and sustained teaching time and the beneficial influence of parental support and involvement with the school.

On the other hand, the amount of variation in pupil achievement that these empirical studies in industrialized countries typically explain is comparatively low, seldom more than 15%. Although this phenomenon is partly due to measurement error, to the lack of an underlying theoretical model that can effectively capture all the influences upon student learning and to the lack of direct value-added measures in most studies, the power of school and classroom variables to explain achievement remains limited.

Table 2.8: Effectiveness-enhancing conditions of schooling: results of five review studies

Purkey & Smith, 1983	Levine & Lezotte, 1990	Scheerens, 1992	Cotton, 1995	Sammons, Hillman & Mortimore, 1995
Strong leadership	Outstanding leadership	Educational leadership	School management and organization, leadership and school improvement, leadership and planning	Professional leadership
Clear goals on basic skills	Focus on central learning skills		Planning and learning goals and school-wide emphasis on learning	Concentration on teaching and learning
Orderly climate; achievement-oriented policy; cooperative atmosphere	Productive climate and culture	Pressure to achieve, consensus, cooperative planning, orderly atmosphere	Planning and learning goals, curriculum planning and development	Shared vision and goals, a learning environment, positive reinforcement
High expectations	High expectations		Strong teacher-student interaction	High expectations
Frequent evaluation	Appropriate monitoring	Evaluative potential of the school, monitoring of pupils' progress	Assessment (district, school, classroom level)	Monitoring progress
Time on task, reinforcement, streaming	Effective instructional arrangements	Structured teaching, effective learning time, opportunity to learn	Classroom management and organization, instruction	Purposeful teaching
In-service training/ staff development	Practice-oriented staff development		Professional development and collegial learning	A learning organization
	Salient parental involvement	Parent support	Parent-community involvement	Home-school partnership
		External stimuli to make schools effective; Physical and material school characteristics; Teacher experience; School context characteristics	Distinct school interactions; Equity; Special programmes	Pupil rights and responsibilities

---

87. A related body of literature on 'school improvement' is mainly concerned with praxis, adopting a particular set of tenets about how to improve conditions in schools. In that sense it represents more a set of policy choices than an established body of knowledge about how schools improve. Chapter 4 discusses some implications of this literature.

88. Numerous reviews on school effectiveness have been published since the late 1970s. Early reviews are those by Anderson (1982), Cohen (1982), Dougherty (1981), Edmonds (1979), Murnane (1981), Neufeld, Farrar and Miles (1983), Purkey and Smith (1983), Rutter (1983), Good and Brophy (1986), Ralph and Fennessey (1983), Kyle (1985) and Sweeney (1982). More recent reviews are those by Levine and Lezotte (1990), Scheerens (1992), Creemers (1994), Reynolds, Hopkins and Stoll (1993), Sammons, Hillman and Mortimore (1995) and Cotton (1995). A comprehensive overview of methodology and results is provided in Teddlie and Reynolds (2000).

Of course, classroom resources typically vary less in rich countries than in developing countries. The impact of class size on pupil learning when the range is fifteen to thirty-five students is different than when the upper limit is as high as 100, as may occur in many developing countries. Studies do seem to suggest that school-related factors explain more of the variation in achievement in developing countries than in industrialized countries, that the impact of socio-economic background is less in the former and that the factors with the greatest importance for student achievement appear to be somewhat different. A review of research on the factors promoting science achievement in developing countries found that in over four-fifths of the studies the length of instructional programmes, use of a school library and school meals were important factors, and that over two-thirds identified teacher training and the presence of textbooks and instructional materials as important (Walberg, 1991). By contrast, only one-quarter to one-third of the studies found the presence of science laboratories, increases in teacher salaries and reductions in class size to be important.

This evidence suggests that, as we would expect, resources are more important determinants of pupil achievement in resource-poor environments than in richer ones. The importance of teacher quality also tends to emerge more clearly, no doubt because the variation in levels and quality of teacher training, competence and initial educational background is generally much greater in developing countries.

Evidence on instructional effectiveness

School resources provide a framework within which teachers can guide students in their learning. In a more fundamental sense, however, the effectiveness of learning depends on what pupils, as well as teachers, bring to the task. Early attempts to understand the learning process emphasized both aspects. It became clear that the following five elements were likely to have an important influence on learning outcomes (Carroll, 1963 and 1989):

■ *aptitude*, which determines the amount of time a pupil or student needs to learn a given task under optimal conditions of instruction and student motivation;

■ *opportunity to learn*, measured as the amount of time available for learning;

■ *perseverance*, or the amount of time a pupil or student is willing to spend on learning;

■ *quality of instruction*, which, when sub-optimal, increases the time needed for learning;

■ *ability to understand instruction*, which includes language comprehension and the ability to understand the nature of the task and how to go about it.

Although the above formulation is not specific as to what determines high-quality instruction, teachers have long been believed to be the key to education quality. Accordingly, education researchers have focused extensively on the best ways to improve teacher effectiveness. Early work found little consistency in the relationships between teachers' personal characteristics (e.g. warm and open or strict and inflexible) and pupil achievement (Medley and Mitzel, 1963; Rosenshine and Furst, 1973; Gage, 1965). As later research focused on classroom observation of teacher behaviour, more systematic links between some teacher characteristics (e.g. clarity, flexibility, enthusiasm, ordered preparation) and pupil performance were suggested. The research methodologies remained controversial (Weeda, 1986), however, and no decisive commonalities had yet emerged.

Over the 1980s, studies of the determinants of effective instruction began to show more consistent results. It seemed that, at primary level, effective learning time, class organization and management, teaching strategies and instruction, and assessments and teachers' expectations were all significant factors in improving pupil performance (Stallings, 1985). As regards *effective learning time*, it became clear that simply making the school day longer did not necessarily lead to better performance. More important, ultimately, is how effectively time is spent. Studies of effective teachers (Stallings and Mohlman, 1981) showed that they spent some 15% of the school day on organization, management and lesson planning; 50% on interactive teaching and 35% on monitoring pupils' work.

Resources are more important determinants of pupil achievement in resource-poor environments than in richer ones

As regards *class organisation and management*, streaming on the basis of ability appears to work for more gifted pupils, but evidence from a large number of surveys indicated hardly any effect for less able groups (Kulik and Kulik, 1982; van Laarhoven and de Vries, 1987; Reezigt, 1993; Slavin, 1987). Not surprisingly, in classes where there is disruptive behaviour, effective learning time is reduced and pupil performance is lower.

Appropriate *teaching strategies* depend upon the type of learning tasks targeted. For example, those largely depending on memory are most effectively taught with a highly ordered and consistent approach. For acquisition of new understanding, a clear presentation of the information is crucial, as are questions to check whether pupils have absorbed specific insights. With regard to problem solving, evidence suggests that it is desirable for pupils to take much of the initiative.[89]

Studies on *teacher assessments and teachers' expectations* of pupils underline the danger of self-fulfilling prophecies. Where teachers form negative expectations of certain pupils, they are likely to give them less attention and expose them less to more challenging tasks. This kind of stereotyping can have highly negative consequences for some pupils. (Hoeven-Van Doornum and Jungbluth, 1987). High teacher expectations, on the other hand, contribute significantly to pupil performance.

A typical list of steps/characteristics required for effective teaching, based on these and other research results, is the following (in this case, from Doyle, 1985):

■ clearly formulated teaching goals;

■ course material carefully split into sequenced learning tasks;

■ clear explanations from the teacher as to what pupils must learn;

■ regular questioning by teachers to gauge pupils' progress and whether they have understood material covered;

■ ample time for pupils to practice what has been taught, with much use of 'prompts' and feedback;

■ skills being taught until mastery of them is automatic;

■ regular testing, and expectations that pupils will be accountable for their work.

This highly structured approach to teaching[90] appears to work equally well for primary and secondary education. Of course, at secondary level, the range of subject options is greater, children are older and a stronger emphasis is needed on more advanced cognitive processes (Brophy and Good, 1986: 367). Furthermore, progress through the subject matter can be quicker, and testing need not be so frequent. The importance of varying learning tasks and of providing intellectual challenges is clear. An evaluative climate in the classroom, with pupils encouraged to take risks even in complicated tasks, is helpful. The evidence on the impact of individual teaching and of working together in small groups is mixed. In general, it is difficult to point to clear evidence of higher achievement deriving from either mode.[91] It seems, however, that group work can be beneficial where group rewards are introduced, based on the individual learning of all group members, and where students are taught how to work together in ways that closely reflect their instructional objectives (Slavin, 1996: 57).

Not all education analysts, however, accept the value of the notion of structured teaching. Constructivists, for example, believe learners should be the main instigators and designers of learning processes. Box 2.3, Table 2.9 contrasts some major distinguishing features of learning and instruction according to the constructivist position with characteristics of more traditional models. Such comparisons, of course, risk oversimplification. Furthermore, less extreme constructivist views can be reconciled with other approaches (Merrill, 1991), for example, when teacher-controlled and learner-controlled instructional situations are used alternately (Boekaerts and Simons, 1993). However, it is difficult to avoid the conclusion that such approaches to teaching presuppose levels of student competence and classroom facilities that may not be compatible with low-resource environments, where many pupils come from poor or non-literate backgrounds. This debate may therefore be particularly relevant to the circumstances of richer nations and communities.

High teacher expectations contribute significantly to pupil performance

---

89. Collins and Stevens (1982) list five teaching strategies to support problem solving:
a) systematic variation of examples;
b) counterexamples;
c) entrapment strategies;
d) hypothesis identification strategies; and
e) hypothesis evaluation strategies.

90. See also Bloom (1968) on the notion of 'mastery learning' and Rosenshine (1983) on 'direct instruction'; both suggest characteristics of effective teaching that are quite similar to this list.

91. Bangert, Kulik and Kulik (1983) found individualized teaching in secondary education had little or no impact on achievement or on pupil self-esteem and attitudes. Vedder (1985) suggested that the lack of a clear positive influence of group work was due to the way pupils work together, there being insufficient cognitive stimulation in such circumstances.

Box 2.3 Constructivism

An important group of analysts stress the key role of the learner rather more than that of the teacher. These 'constructivists' argue that learning needs to be largely self-directed, with an emphasis on discovery, and with particular value being ascribed to the students' interpretation of events and facts. Learning strategies, and reflection upon them, are as important as mastering content. Recognizing different ways of finding a solution is as important as the solution itself. Terms like 'active learning' (Cohen, 1988), 'situated cognition' (Resnick, 1987) and 'cognitive apprenticeship' (Collins, Brown and Newman, 1989) are used.

Consistent with this approach, teaching strategies need to enable students 'to construct their own meaningful and conceptually functional representations of the external world' (Duffy and Jonassen, 1992: 11). The teacher becomes more of a coach, who assists students in 'criss-crossing the landscape of contexts' (Spiro et al., 1992: 8). Some have used the term 'adventurous teaching' to describe this approach (Cohen, 1988).

There is less emphasis here on prior structuring of goals, learning tasks and plans; goals are supposed to emerge when 'situated learning' takes place and plans are not so much supposed to be submitted to the learner as constructed in response to changing demands and opportunities. Learning situations should encourage students to engage in sustained exploration. Some authors writing from this perspective state that 'transfer' is the most distinguishing feature (Tobias, 1991), whereas others mention argument, discussion and debate to arrive at 'socially constructed meaning' (see Cunningham, 1991).

In this context, the role of assessment and the evaluation of students' progress is hotly debated. Radical constructivists take the position that performance on an actual learning task is the only legitimate form of assessment, since distinct 'external' evaluation procedures could not do justice to the specific meaning of a particular learning experience for the student. Others (e.g. Jonassen, 1992) judge that assessment procedures should merely be different: goal-free, rather than fixed on particular objectives, formative rather than summative and oriented towards assessing learning processes rather than mastery of subject matter. Appraisals of samples of products and portfolios qualify as acceptable assessment procedures.

Classroom practices have the strongest association with achievement

Research evidence has continued to accumulate. A review of the influence of educational, psychological and social factors on learning (Wang, Haertel and Walberg, 1993) ranks factors that have been found to influence student achievement as follows (from high to low):

- student characteristics;
- classroom practices;
- home and community educational contexts;
- design and delivery of curriculum and instruction;
- school demographics, culture, climate, policies and practices;
- state and district governance and organization.

Apart from the characteristics of the students themselves, classroom practices have the strongest association with achievement. Within this category are classroom management and student and teacher social interaction (e.g. 'students respond positively to questions from other students and from the teacher'). An illustrative variable within classroom management is 'group alerting' (teachers using

Table 2.9: Comparison of traditional and constructivist instructional models

Traditional instruction	Instruction inspired by constructivism
Emphasis on basic skills	Bias towards higher-order skills
Subject matter orientation	Emphasis on learning process
Structured approach ■ pre-specified objectives ■ small steps ■ frequent questioning/feedback ■ reinforcement through high level of mastery	Discovery-learning ■ 'rich' learning environment ■ intrinsic motivation ■ challenging problems
Abstract-generalizable knowledge	Situation-specific knowledge, learning from cases
Standardized achievement tests	Assessment; less circumscribed alternative procedures

Source: Scheerens (2004)

questioning/recitation strategies that maintain active participation by all students). Other relatively influential aspects of classroom practice are classroom climate, classroom assessment and quantity of instruction (e.g. time on task). In summary, it appears that, as far as classroom instruction is concerned, general instructional approaches that are relatively structured bring important pay-offs for learning.

One study (Slavin, 1996), using a combination of systematic literature review and meta-analysis, has analyzed research in which pupil outcomes among those grouped according to ability were compared with those from heterogeneously grouped classes. It concludes that *whole-class ability grouping*, with the aim of creating groups that are homogeneous in ability level ('ability-grouped class assignment'), is generally ineffective: in the studies surveyed, effects were either negative or close to zero, with only a few cases reporting small positive effects. On the other hand, grouping for reading across grades appears to have a consistently positive effect, and it appears that *within-class ability grouping in mathematics* at primary level is also effective.[92] These results suggest that successful ability grouping requires:

- reduced heterogeneity of aptitudes for the skill being taught;

- mechanisms to deal with errors in assignment to ability groups and changes in student performance;

- teachers varying their pace and level of instruction to correspond to students' levels of readiness and ability to learn.

Ability-grouped class assignment, regardless of the skills, probably fails the first and often fails the second of these criteria (Slavin, 1996: 158).

Within-class ability grouping entails some loss of teaching time during transition of the teacher from one group to the next. It also implies that groups will have to work a considerable amount of time without direct teacher instruction. Nevertheless, the above results indicate that within-class ability grouping is more effective despite a certain loss of direct instructional time. It would seem advisable, then, not to allow too many ability groups within classes, to minimize the negative impact of such loss. Other implications are (Slavin, 1996: 164):

- students should be assigned to heterogeneous classes most of the time and be regrouped by ability only in subjects in which low heterogeneity is particularly important (e.g. reading, mathematics);

- grouping plans should reduce heterogeneity in the skill being taught;

- grouping plans should be flexible and allow for easy reassignment;

- teachers should vary their level and pace of instruction so as to be consistent with students' levels of performance;

- the number of groups should be minimized.

More recent contributions to the study of instructional effectiveness have returned to examination of the personal characteristics of effective teachers. They reaffirm the importance of subject matter mastery and verbal skills (Darling-Hammond, 2000) and the strong impact on pupil performance of teachers' expectations, their drive for improvement amongst their pupils and their passion for learning (McBer, 2000). Another emerging theme is the importance of structured teaching mixed with respect for the self-regulated learning of pupils (Brophy, 2001; Baumert, Blum and Neubrand, 2000; Anderson, 2004).

Implications for the major determinants of effective teaching

If learning outcomes depend on student learning strategies and students' motivation to learn (engagement), the teaching conditions summarized in Table 2.10 are also important, particularly the top three: relevance, time and structure.

First, relevance includes keeping subject matter selection well aligned to the intended curriculum – including between grades and classes – and ensuring that the contents of teaching and learning assignments match those of tests and other assessment instruments.

The second condition requires attention to the time to be spent on major curriculum areas and

---

92. The median sizes for these effects were + 0.44 standard deviation for reading and +0.34 standard deviation for mathematics.

Table 2.10: The most important conditions for enhancing teaching effectiveness

Relevance	Curriculum alignment
Time	Learning time
Structure	Structured teaching Stimulating engagement Monitoring and questioning Feedback and reinforcement Modelling learning/self-regulation
Classroom environment	Task-oriented climate Mutual respect Orderliness, safety
Teacher characteristics	Subject matter mastery Verbal intelligence Teaching repertoire Achievement orientation

Source: Scheerens (2004)

subjects according to official timetables. At school level, 'net teaching time' in the classroom – i.e. official teaching time minus time 'lost' to other activities – is a key quality variable. Ultimately, optimizing the time students spend actively involved in learning activities has a significant impact on pupil achievement.

Third, structured teaching emerges as being important to pupil performance in many instructional effectiveness studies, perhaps most strongly for less-able learners in primary schools, but also more generally at higher levels of schooling where more advanced cognitive skills are targeted. Debates inspired by constructivism suggest a continuum running from a highly structured teaching process to one characterized by a high level of learner independence. The key to effective teaching lies in selecting the appropriate extent of structure, in the light of learner' characteristics, learning tasks and educational objectives. Structural dimensions also include frequent monitoring of students' progress, provision of feedback and reinforcement related to assessment outcomes, provision of cognitive support and fostering of student engagement.

Fourth, classroom climate and organization, the extent of mutual trust, and safety and discipline factors can have a direct impact on student learning. Fifth, strong teacher characteristics are prerequisites for delivering relevant teaching, using time efficiently and providing an appropriate level of structure. As discussed earlier, broader conditions for effective schooling, such as school organization and educational leadership, are necessary supportive conditions for effective teaching.

The experimental evaluation of education policy interventions

The difficulty of estimating education production functions has led to the development of a new approach to measurement of the impact of school resources on education outcomes: the experimental evaluation of policy interventions. Rather than seeking to identify the parameters of a theoretical model of education production that might have universal relevance, this approach attempts to measure the impact of a given change in school resources on education outcomes in a specific institutional context. If the former model was empirical testing of economic theory, the new one is the practice of randomized trials, as in biology and medicine. Random selection of students who are to participate in a policy intervention allows relatively simple measures of the difference between students belonging to the 'treatment group' (who benefited from the intervention) and the 'control group' (who did not) to yield unbiased estimates of the intervention's impact.[93]

Randomized experiments belong to the field of policy evaluation as much as to economics.[94] The evaluation of many types of policy intervention through randomized experiments, long practiced in the USA, is becoming a standard tool in development programmes, notably World Bank-funded projects. Such experiments remain less frequent in the field of education, but have already provided some credible evidence about the effectiveness and cost-efficiency of alternative policy interventions. Experiments are not without their weaknesses, however. They are usually small scale, so the generality of their results and the possibility of scaling up are not guaranteed.[95] Where benefits are widely expected, they may induce selective migration, and other practical difficulties can also result in the selection of students 'for treatment' not being fully random. Furthermore, conducting experiments in education may be difficult on ethical, political or financial grounds, e.g. it can be difficult to justify the exclusion of some people from a potentially beneficial intervention.

> The evaluation of many types of policy intervention through randomized experiments is becoming a standard tool in development programmes

93. Todd and Wolpin (2003) demonstrate that structural estimates of education production function parameters and experimental estimates of policy intervention effects are not directly comparable. The former reflect a technical relationship between inputs and outputs and answer such questions as 'How would a change in class size, holding all other inputs constant, affect achievement?' The latter measure the total direct and indirect effects of an intervention, answering such questions as 'What would be the total effect of a change in class size on achievement, that is, not holding other inputs constant?' This difference, and the fact that structuralists and 'experimentalists' tend to form separate scientific communities, justifies their separate consideration.

94. See Burtless (1995), Duflo and Kremer (2003) and Newman, Rawlings and Gertler (1994) for further discussion of this point.

95. On this, see Duflo (2003).

Children belonging to disadvantaged social backgrounds benefit most from reduced class size

One way to generate experimental data without raising such issues is to randomize the phasing in of programmes that are in any case to be gradually introduced.

Experimental estimation techniques may find another application in non-experimental settings where history or institutions have caused variation in education policies. Such circumstances are termed 'natural experiments' or 'quasi-experiments'.

Better evidence as to the efficacy of resource improvements to schooling is emerging from recent country studies using the new approach. Where key differences in schooling conditions, as between different groups of pupils, have been sharply controlled, stronger contrasts in inputs and outcomes can be seen. Results from some 'random' and 'natural' experiments, briefly discussed below, suggest, somewhat more clearly than production function evidence, that well-designed resource policies can have a strong qualitative impact on the outcomes of schooling.

Randomized experiments

Experience from industrialized countries is available from as early as the late 1980s. The Tennessee Student-Teacher Achievement Ratio (STAR) project was a large-scale randomized experiment on the impact of class size on pupil achievement. It followed almost 12,000 pupils from kindergarten to grade 3. The chosen schools were large, with at least three classes per grade. Pupils were randomly divided between a treatment group with small classes of thirteen to seventeen students and a control group with regular classes of twenty-two to twenty-five students, with or without a full-time teacher's aide. Standardized tests were administered to all students at the end of each year. Estimates of the project's impact were made on the basis of differences in test scores, within each of the seventy-nine participating schools, between pupils belonging to the treatment and control groups.

The results show that pupils in small classes perform better than those in regular classes and than those in regular classes with aides. The difference is established in the kindergarten class at about five percentage points. It widens to 8.6 points in the first grade, and stays at five or six points in the second and third grades (Krueger, 1999: 511). Thus, most of the impact is observed after the first year, with the additional impact of subsequent years still being positive, but smaller. Finally, the impact tends to be larger for students who were eligible for free lunches and for black students and inner-city students, which suggests that children belonging to disadvantaged social backgrounds benefit most from reduced class size.

These differences appear to have continued throughout the students' subsequent school careers. The test scores of black students included in the initial study increased by seven to ten percentage points from kindergarten to grade 3, as against three to four percentage points for white students. Test scores in further grades, after the end of the experiment, increased by five points per year for black students and 1.5 points for white students. The probability of the black students taking entrance examinations for college was also increased much more substantially than that of the white students (Krueger and Whitmore, 2002).

The results of STAR provide robust evidence that class size affects achievement in the context of a high income country. It shows that reducing class size in the early school years appears to have long-run effects, especially in terms of reducing social inequalities in test scores and access to higher education. If this were generally true, developing preschools and improving primary schools could be expected to have larger returns than targeted cognitive-skill-based policies for adolescents (Carneiro and Heckman, 2003).[96]

In the last few years, studies related to developing countries have also begun to appear. In Kenya, the impact of school meals in a sample of twenty-five treatment and twenty-five control preschools was examined (Vermeersch, 2002). It was found that attendance increased by 30%. The programme was also expected to have an impact on test scores, but because organization of the meals cut into instruction time, an increase in test scores (by 0.4 standard deviation) was observed only in schools in which teachers had received substantial training. A separate study assessed the impact of provision by an NGO of free uniforms, textbooks and classroom construction, using fourteen poorly performing

---

96. The benefits of early childhood intervention in the United States are the focus of a sizeable literature that includes randomized experiments. See Currie (2001) for a survey.

Kenyan schools, half being the control group (Kremer et al., 1997). The intervention reduced dropout rates in treated schools, resulting over five years in a 15% increase in the average amount of schooling completed. Furthermore, many parents transferred their children from nearby schools to treatment schools, leading to an increase in class size by 50%, without deterioration in test scores. Thus, parents were willing to accept larger class sizes in return for lower direct costs as long as the increase in size did not have a major impact on achievement. This suggests that, in some contexts, a strategy of increasing class size so as to spend more on improving school inputs and reducing fees would be beneficial.

Again in Kenya, it was found that the provision of textbooks to schools increased test scores by about 0.2 standard deviation. The impact was concentrated among students who had scored in the top two quintiles in tests administered before the programme was started, however, and there was no impact on the other 60% of pupils. The intervention tended to be biased towards children belonging to relatively privileged families (Glewwe, Kremer and Moulin, 2002).[97]

In a randomised experiment conducted in the Philippines, thirty schools were allocated either to a control group or to one of four treatment groups, which received school meals, pedagogical materials for teachers, or structured meetings between parents and school officials combined with one of the other interventions. The provision of pedagogical materials had a considerable impact on dropout rates after one year, and all interventions significantly affected test scores (Tan, Lane and Lassibille, 1999).

A range of randomized experiments has been conducted in India. Among the studies was one showing that appointing a second teacher to single-teacher schools increased females' school participation but had no impact on test scores. A programme that provided teacher training and other inputs to preschool teachers who had begun teaching after receiving only minimal training was also found to have little impact on test scores (Banerjee and Kremer, 2002). However, a large and innovative experiment begun during the 1990s in urban Indian schools demonstrates the positive impact on learning of reducing class size, targeting

attention to ability groupings and, especially, providing child-friendly teaching. In this programme, lagging pupils are taken out of school for two hours per day to be taught by educated young local women who have undergone a short training programme. Existing classes are thus reduced in size for a time, for both low- and high-achieving pupils. The former group also benefits from more focused attention on their difficulties and the latter benefit from higher average abilities among their peers. As Box 2.4 reports, the test scores of both groups increased significantly – but particularly so for those in the lower-achieving category. It is likely that a crucial ingredient for success was the selection of local women who were strongly motivated to work with the children in the schools concerned. The experiment nonetheless demonstrates both the potential impact of class size on achievement and the potential effectiveness of using lower-cost teaching solutions for targeted purposes.

Natural experiments

Studies involving natural experiments are based on similar techniques to those used in studies based on randomized experiments: in both cases, a specific source of variation in a potential determinant of achievement can be identified and studied. Natural experiments in education are usually the result of the application of some policy rule that is independent of the usual functioning of schools. Their obvious disadvantage relative to randomized experiments is that researchers do not have control over them, and data may be lacking. Thus, the number of exploitable natural experiments may not be very high.

The case of Israel affords an opportunity to investigate the impact of class size on pupil performance. Israeli schools are allocated teachers according to a rule formulated by the medieval scholar Maimonides, which says that class size should not exceed forty pupils. As a result, a school with, say, thirty-nine pupils will have one teacher, but a school with forty-one pupils will have two. This generates a systematic, predictable relationship between the number of pupils enrolled in a school and the PTR that is uncorrelated with unobserved characteristics of pupils that affect learning.[98] When comparing class-size data with test scores for 2,000 classes of third- to fifth-grade pupils, a significant

The provision of pedagogical materials had a considerable impact on dropout rates after one year

---

97. The authors note that Kenyan textbooks are written in English and reflect a curriculum designed for elite families in Nairobi, so they may be difficult for rural children to grapple with.

98. Such a correlation could still exist if application of the rule differed by neighbourhoods' socio-economic makeup – for example if privileged areas more easily obtained additional teachers as the PTR neared 40:1. Angrist and Lavy (1999), however, provide evidence that the rule is quite strictly observed.

> **Box 2.4 The impact of a remedial education programme in India's urban slums**
>
> In the slums of a number of Indian cities, Pratham, an NGO, runs a remedial education programme in primary schools. Pratham hires young women (*balskahi*), holding the equivalent of a high school degree, who belong to the same community as the children. They teach one group of fifteen to twenty lagging children, who are withdrawn from their normal classes for two hours every morning, and another group in the afternoon. Teachers receive two weeks of initial training and further training during the year. The balskahis focus on basic numeracy and literacy, which children should have learned in the second and third grades. The expected benefits of the intervention include the impact of remedial education on the children who attend the special classes and the impact of reduced class size for all.
>
> The programme was used to conduct a randomized experiment in the cities of Mumbai, where the balsakhi programme started in 1994, and Vadodara, where it started in 1999. In Vadodara, the programme was extended over 2000-02 to the ninety-eight eligible schools not yet covered. Half were randomly selected to receive balskahis, and their results were compared with those of the half that did not receive the intervention. A similar procedure was followed in Mumbai. Literacy and numeracy tests were administered in all schools before the intervention began and at the end of each school year. More than 15,000 students were included, which allowed a reliable estimation of its impact.
>
> The results revealed a significant impact on achievement, which was remarkably similar in both cities. Test scores of children who benefited from the programme improved by 0.12 to 0.16 standard deviation in the first year and 0.15 to 0.30 in the second year. The results were even stronger for the lowest achievers. Children in the bottom third of the distribution improved their test scores by 0.22 standard deviation in the first year and 0.58 in the second. Moreover, the results suggest that the direct impact of balsakhi sessions on children who attended them accounts for most of this improvement, rather than the impact of reduced class size for the other children. This implies that balsakhis were more effective in their separate classes than regular teachers were in the combined classes. The study concludes that both the efficacy of the remedial education programme and, more generally, the feasibility of strongly improving test scores at very low cost have been demonstrated. The estimates suggest that reducing class size by hiring a balsakhi is at least twice as effective as reducing class size by keeping children with regular teachers, even though balsakhis are paid only a fraction of teachers' salaries.
>
> *Source:* Banerjee et al. (2003)

negative impact of class size on the reading and mathematics scores of fifth-graders is found: a decrease in class size by a standard deviation (6.5 pupils) results in an increase in reading test scores by 0.2 to 0.5 standard deviation and an increase in mathematics test scores by 0.1 to 0.3 standard deviation. The effects on the achievement of third- and fourth-graders, however, were often insignificant.[99]

As regards developing countries, the notion that class size is important for cognitive achievement is further strengthened by a study of South Africa at the end of the apartheid regime (Case and Deaton, 1999). During the apartheid period, blacks had no political representation and therefore no control over government funding of education, which was heavily centralized. Furthermore, controls were imposed on their place of residence, preventing internal migration, except under tightly defined circumstances. Consequently, parents of black children had no influence on the quality of the schools their children attended.[100] Data collected in 1993 revealed a significant impact of PTR variation on years of schooling completed, on current enrolment status and on test scores of black children. For example, decreasing the PTR from forty (the mean value for black schools) to twenty (the mean for white schools) increased schooling by 1.5 to 2.5 years and reading test scores by the equivalent of what was usually delivered by two additional years of schooling.[101]

This approach has also been used, with data from the 1996 South African census, to estimate the impact of school quality. Significant negative effects of the PTR on educational attainment, on

---

99. Angrist and Lavy (1999) discuss the results, which are subject to debate. Similar studies sometimes produce conflicting results. In the state of Connecticut, United States, where similar maximum class-size rules allow comparison, no impact on test scores was found for variations ranging from ten to thirty pupils (Hoxby, 2000). Comparing primary schools in Connecticut and Israel is not straightforward, however, if only because class size is much larger in average Israeli schools.

100. The authors state that interviews with officials then in charge revealed that there were no consistent rules for allocating resources to schools for black children. Hence, they argue, the wide variations in PTR observed between those schools can be considered random, and exogenous with respect to family characteristics affecting learning. The natural experiment here is, somewhat paradoxically, the absence of a well-defined school policy due to neglect of the well-being of the black population under apartheid.

101. The impact on mathematics scores was not significant.

the probability of employment and on the returns to education are revealed. For example, reducing the PTR by five students would increase the return to education by 1% (Case and Yogo, 1999).

Other research using these methods addressed the effectiveness of in-service teacher training (Angrist and Lavy, 2001). As with class size, production function evidence on teacher training is mixed, but it tends to focus on initial training, while in-service training could plausibly have a stronger impact. A few Jerusalem schools received funds earmarked for in-service teacher training in 1995, and the study matched these schools with comparable schools in the same area that did not receive such funds.[102] It found that teacher training improved test scores by 0.2 to 0.4 standard deviation in secular schools. The training programme focused on pedagogy rather than subject content, and was inexpensive compared to class-size reduction.

In summary, it appears that this newer evidence deriving from random or natural experiments can indeed reveal the impact of particular policy changes on learning achievement, at least in particular contexts. These studies do not rely on theoretical modelling, so a wider range of interventions has already been considered than in the education production function literature. Empirical modelling is made simpler by the identification of a particular, externally determined source of variation in school resources, which is a matter of policy analysis, not of statistics or econometrics. The dissemination of the results beyond academic circles is thus bound to be easier.

The application of these methods is as yet in its infancy. Yet it is already clear that strong evidence of the importance of school resources in affecting learning outcomes has been demonstrated in industrialized countries and, even more so, in developing countries. The case here is considerably stronger than that provided by the production function literature for the notion that smaller class size, more textbooks, teacher in-service training and teaching strategies that focus upon the needs of the learner are resource strategies that make a difference, particularly in poorer countries and particularly for less able groups.

The role of the organization and social context of schools

Teaching and learning in the classroom do not take place in isolation from the functioning of schools as organizations, nor from their social context. Organizational weaknesses of schools are increasingly being pointed to as a major cause of low learning achievement, especially in the case of government schools in developing countries. For example, a landmark field study of rural primary schools in northern India (PROBE Team, 1999) provided striking evidence of a lack of teacher motivation (e.g. absenteeism and a tendency to supervise rather than actually teach) but also noted the difficult working conditions teachers face and the lack of control and support from education authorities. Meanwhile, education expansion, whether at primary level in developing countries or at secondary and higher levels in industrialized countries, results in changes in the social composition of the student population. The functioning of schools can be affected by this in ways that are quite separate from the impact of resources or teaching practices.

This section examines recent evidence concerning the functioning of schools as organizations and their interaction with their social context. One approach proposes radical changes in the structure of teacher incentives, arguing that this could have a more effective impact on learning outcomes than would further rises in expenditure or changes in teaching practices. Increasingly popular among economists and policy makers, such 'incentive-based' policies have been implemented in industrialized and developing countries, so there is growing evidence concerning their benefits and shortcomings. A second approach, maintaining that neither resource levels nor incentive structures can properly account for differences in schooling outcomes, gives weight to political and sociological factors.

Promises and pitfalls of incentive-based policies

While research on school and teacher effectiveness has addressed the behaviour of teachers as pedagogues, economists have investigated their behaviour as employees of schools or of education authorities. This work has typically examined the extent to which a

Organizational weaknesses of schools are increasingly being pointed to as a major cause of low learning achievement

---

102. 'Matching' is an econometric technique that does not explicitly rely on the experimental paradigm but similarly allows a reduction in endogenous biases. While it has become extremely common in labour economics, its use in the economics of education is still infrequent, as Glewwe (2002) notes.

teacher's 'productivity' in the classroom is linked with remuneration and whether reinforcing any such link can improve learning outcomes.[103] There is some evidence that this link is, at present, weak. For example, in urban state-run secondary schools of northern India, teacher characteristics that determine pay, such as the quantity of education, training and experience, have little impact on pupil achievement, while the quality of teacher education, represented by cognitive skills, affects achievement but not pay (Kingdon, 1996). By contrast, in private schools a direct relationship between pupil achievement and teacher pay appears to at least partly explain why they are more efficient than state schools (Kingdon and Teal, 2003).

'Merit pay' systems tested in the United States do not seem to have been successful

'Merit pay' systems tested in the United States do not seem to have been successful. Teachers generally responded by increasing the quantity rather than the quality of teaching, and uniform pay structures evolved, defeating the purpose of the reforms.[104] On the other hand, a programme introduced in Israeli high schools, whereby teachers received cash bonuses for improvements in their students' performance on matriculation examinations, had a significant impact on English and mathematics results (Lavy, 2003).

Merit pay nevertheless seems quite a narrow approach to teacher incentives. First, it can have perverse side-effects. For example, in a randomized experiment conducted in Kenya, prizes were attributed by parent-run school committees to teachers whose pupils had low dropout rates and performed well on exams. Teachers responded by manipulating exam results rather than teaching better, and there was little impact on real achievement (Glewwe, Nauman and Kremer, 2003). Second, where salaries are relatively high, additional pay may not be a major motivating factor for teachers, given the specificity of their profession.[105] Recent research in public schools in the United States suggests that, while institutional arrangements do result in a weak relationship between teacher salaries and performance, student characteristics rather than salary differentials explain teachers' decisions to change schools.[106] Meanwhile, recent evidence from Mexico's Carrera Magisterial programme indicates that providing additional training while raising salaries and improving school resources can increase pupil achievement. The impact of that programme appeared greatest when training was aimed at increasing teachers' practical experience and developing content-specific knowledge, and when supervision by school administrators was high (Lopez-Acevedo, 2004). This finding suggests that policies focusing on teaching practices, resources and incentives may be complements rather than substitutes.

Similar remarks apply to decentralization and privatization, which have been advocated as giving parents more control over the functioning of schools and over teacher behaviour. There is indeed evidence that increasing local financing can improve learning, and several studies have found private schools to be more efficient than public ones.[107] But any general appraisal of such radical changes in school system organization involves considering other outcomes of schooling than cognitive achievement, given the much broader socio-political impact of such reforms. In Kenya, decentralization is reported to have created incentives for local communities to build too many small schools, to spend too much on teachers relative to other inputs and to set school fees at levels that prevent many children from attending (Kremer, Moulin and Namunyu, 2003). While the case for increasing teacher and school accountability to parents is simple enough, designing reforms to this end appears to be a difficult task.

Schools as social institutions

Explaining how and why changes in resource allocation or teaching practices have – or fail to have – an impact on cognitive achievement requires understanding how teachers and students interact, not only as teachers and learners but also as persons in the social context of the school. Education is not only a set of outcomes, it is also a process. Given the amount of time spent in it, the behaviour of teachers and students is bound to be determined as much by the quality of this process as by its anticipated returns. Improving learning outcomes thus does not only involve providing sufficient resources for efficient use by teachers who use best-practice methods, with an adequate incentive structure. It can also involve affecting the way students and teachers experience life and work at school throughout its duration.

---

103. Much of this literature assumes that schools *should* be likened to achievement-maximizing private firms in a competitive market, and is thus not neutral ideologically. Whatever one's opinion about this assumption, the gathering of evidence on implementation of the increasingly frequent reforms using this approach remains important.

104. The evidence is surveyed by Hanushek (2002b).

105. This, of course, is far from being the case in many developing countries. In recent years, salary levels have often sunk so low that the very subsistence of teachers and their families is threatened. Under these circumstances the link between pay and performance is difficult to deny. See the discussion on teacher earnings in Chapter 4.

106. See Hanushek and Rivkin (2003), Hanushek, Kain and Rivkin (1999), Hanushek, Kain and Rivkin (2004) and Jepsen and Rivkin (2002).

107. On both points, see Glewwe (2002).

Studies in the sociology of education suggest, first, that the quality of learning depends on student behaviour more than on anything else, and that student behaviour responds directly to socialization processes that take place at school.[108] Ethnographic and sociological studies of high schools in the United States have shown that students divide into distinct social groups, each associated with an ideal behaviour to which its members strive to conform. Ideals include the attitude towards the school in general and towards learning in particular. Student effort is influenced by the social group to which a student belongs and by the ideal of that social group. Second, schools are not neutral vis-à-vis student behaviour. They try to impart not just cognitive skills but also a series of psychological and behavioural traits that define their own social ideal. Students whose family and peer group have ideals close to that promoted by their school will tend to demonstrate greater learning effort and achieve higher levels of cognitive skills. Others will try to escape the contradiction between their own and their school's ideals by rebelling – reducing learning effort, among other things.[109] Thus, an important way for schools to improve learning achievement is to reduce the social distance between their own social ideal and that of their students, so that fewer students choose to belong to social groups whose attitude clashes with learning.[110]

This conceptual framework may shed new light on the situation in many developing countries. The education policies pursued after independence in many states often explicitly promoted a social ideal, whether expressed in terms of national unity or a more explicitly socialist or other ideology. Initially this concerned only the parts of the population that happened to be able to attend school, whether groups with elite status or ethnic or other favoured social groups. Expansion of the school system beyond those groups raised crucial issues concerning the content of teaching. Meanwhile, the ideological wave that had accompanied decolonization receded, and resources also became scarcer during the 1980s. Today, an array of factors – continued resource scarcity, discrepancies between teachers' and students' social backgrounds, clashes between the social content of the curriculum and students' family backgrounds, the lack of an explicit social goal for education policy – may help explain the widespread inefficiency of state school systems in developing countries in a subtler and more relevant way than single-factor explanations such as inadequacy of teacher pay.

Conclusion: what we know about what matters for education quality

There is ample evidence that the quantity of education a person receives (measured as the number of years spent in the school system) goes hand in hand with the quality of that education (usually somewhat narrowly defined as cognitive skills but in fact including non-cognitive skills, values and other psychological and behavioural traits acquired through schooling). The latter aspect has intrinsic value and is also associated with many and various private and social returns. These are not limited to income but also include advantages derived from a range of market and non-market activities.

International assessments of cognitive skills suggest that school quality differs widely among and within countries. In particular, children who live in developing countries not only receive fewer years of education but also reach lower achievement levels. Meanwhile, though the evolution of test scores over the years is difficult to assess and interpret, clearly their stagnation in developed countries in recent decades represents an important puzzle.

Identifying the determinants of better learning outcomes so as to produce policy-relevant conclusions is an arduous task that requires using approaches from different social sciences. The learning process is extremely complex. It first and foremost involves relationships between teachers and students following a given curriculum and teaching practices, but it also takes place in a broader social context. These relationships are further conditioned by the resources available to schools, the incentive structure teachers face as employees of schools or education authorities, and the correspondence between the values promoted by schools as social institutions and those that prevail in students' families and society at large.

The stagnation of test scores in developed countries in recent decades represents an important puzzle

108. This approach has been explored recently by Akerlof and Kranton (2002).

109. A similar representation could be given of teacher behaviour.

110. This concept can be applied to the history of secondary education in a number of industrialized countries. Akerlof and Kranton (2002) show that the democratization of school systems in the last third of the twentieth century led to growing clashes between earlier ideologies – that of the French republican bourgeois elite, for instance – and those of the more socially diverse population that was increasingly entering schools.

> Designing more adequate incentive structures for teachers appears a natural complement to resource policies

This complexity is reflected in the findings of this chapter.

- First, an examination of country-specific experience reveals that very different school systems have produced either low or high average levels of achievement. Much is to be learned from further comparisons among and within countries.

- Second, debates within the education community regarding adequate teaching practices are not settled. Hence, experimenting with alternative practices is necessary, especially as progress towards Education for All results in enrolment of children from communities that were formerly socially distant from the school system.

- Third, while the education production function literature has yielded no easy consensus on the impact of specific resource policies on achievement, there is evidence, especially from recent experimental studies, that sufficient resources are necessary if education of acceptable quality is to be attained, and that well-implemented increases in resources are an important means of improving educational quality in developing countries.

- Fourth, education policies need to address the efficiency of resource use in schools. Designing more adequate incentive structures for teachers appears a natural complement to resource policies. However, the limited evidence on ideas such as merit pay, decentralization and privatization show that they can have perverse side effects that either reduce their impact on cognitive skills or affect other educational outcomes.

In the end, improving learning outcomes in schools around the world is not only a matter of implementing a set of adequately designed technical measures. That the experimental evaluation of policy interventions is becoming a standard tool in policy design is certainly a welcome development, but it does not solve the question of which interventions are tested or what their goals are. Schools are social institutions in which day-to-day educational processes interact with the shaping of educational outcomes. The cognitive and non-cognitive outcomes of this process may sometimes conflict. As a larger proportion of children are socialized for an increasingly extended part of their childhood, adolescence and early adulthood, questions of curriculum content and of contrast between student background and aspiration present new challenges for the quality of schooling that cannot be addressed only by technical means. The politics of the process, as well as the details of its resourcing and pedagogy, have become increasingly important to its solution.

Strong dynamics: after overcoming multiple social barriers, Lalita, a woman from one of the lowest castes in India shows pleasure in teaching mathematics to young girls in her village of Koprah.

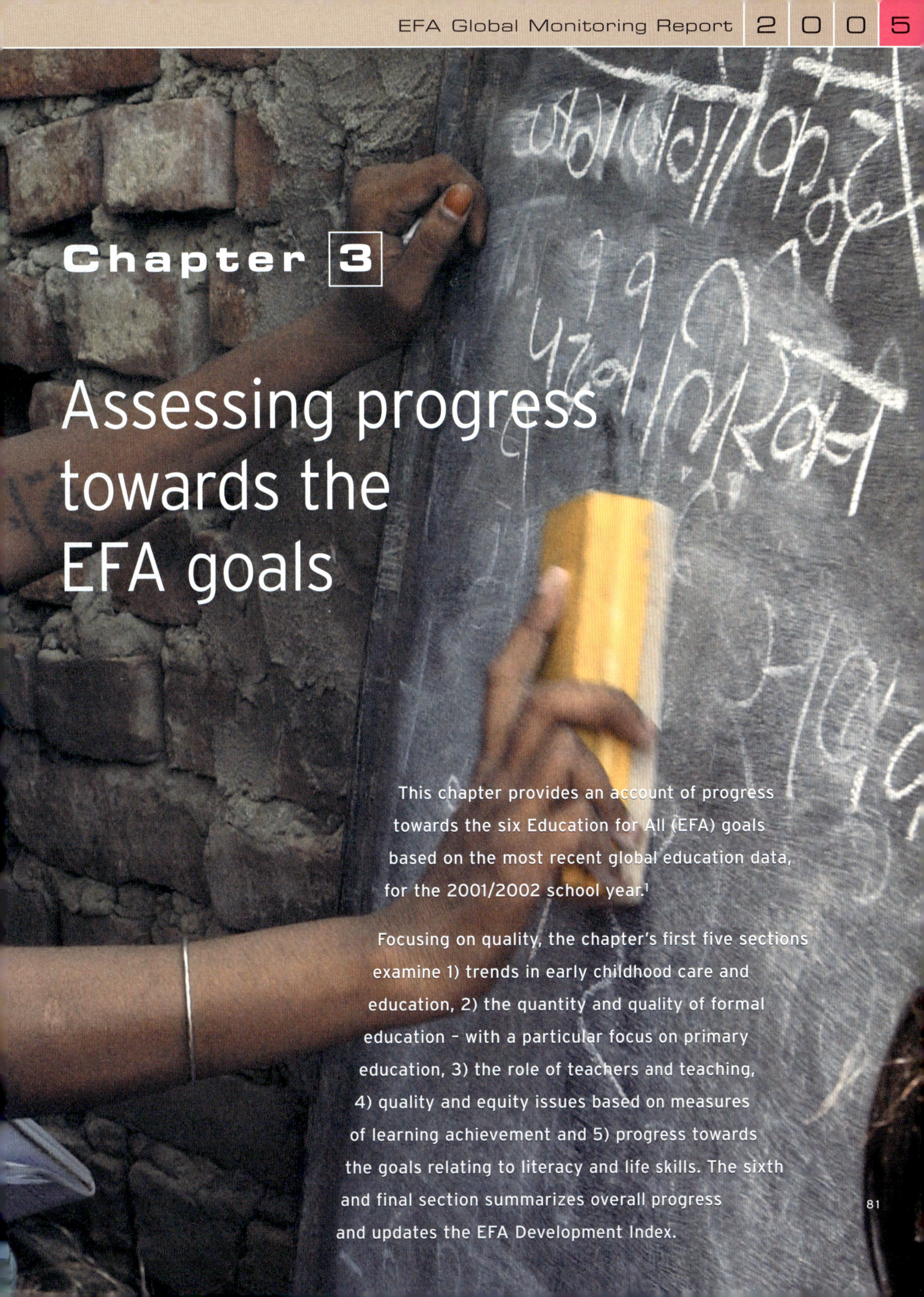

Chapter 3

Assessing progress towards the EFA goals

This chapter provides an account of progress towards the six Education for All (EFA) goals based on the most recent global education data, for the 2001/2002 school year.[1]

Focusing on quality, the chapter's first five sections examine 1) trends in early childhood care and education, 2) the quantity and quality of formal education – with a particular focus on primary education, 3) the role of teachers and teaching, 4) quality and equity issues based on measures of learning achievement and 5) progress towards the goals relating to literacy and life skills. The sixth and final section summarizes overall progress and updates the EFA Development Index.

Early childhood care and education

Early childhood care and education (ECCE) refers to a wide range of programmes, all aimed at the physical, cognitive and social development of children before they enter primary school – theoretically from birth to about age 7 or 8. The benefits of ECCE programmes, which extend into adulthood, are well documented, as Chapter 2 shows. They contribute to good child development outcomes that set the foundation for lifelong learning and help in the monitoring of health and nutrition status during this critical period of development.

The provision of ECCE programmes can free members of the household from childcare responsibilities, allowing a parent to work or an older sibling to attend school. Of course, early childhood care also takes place in the context of families. Parenting practices have strong effects on learning and development (Myers, 2004).

Monitoring early childhood care and education

To monitor progress towards the goal stated in the Dakar Framework as 'expanding and improving comprehensive early childhood care and education, especially for the most vulnerable and disadvantaged children', it is important to distinguish between care and education and to identify the typical age groups that programmes serve and the extent to which statistical reporting covers formal and non-formal programmes.

The International Standard Classification of Education (ISCED) defines pre-primary education, or ISCED level 0, as comprising programmes that offer structured, purposeful learning activities in a school or a centre (as opposed to the home) to children aged at least 3 years (UNESCO, 1997). Such programmes are normally held to include organized learning activities that occupy on average the equivalent of at least two hours per day and 100 days per year.

These criteria may not reflect the full extent of participation in ECCE programmes, as they exclude care and education provided below age 3. Moreover, data collection systems that focus largely on state or state-regulated providers may not cover non-formal care and educational activities administered by other state authorities or private entities for children aged 3 and up.

Assessing quality in ECCE provision is difficult, both conceptually and empirically, and has been insufficiently addressed at the global level. There is a real lack of information about inputs and about how they are used to achieve good outcomes in programmes for young children. The use of standards is increasingly the norm in more developed countries, as is the use of assessment instruments to measure outcomes. But learning achievement alone is an inadequate basis on which to judge programme quality, especially in developing countries, where the focus is on ensuring a wider range of child development outcomes.

An important part of assessing ECCE provision is determining how well programmes reach the most vulnerable and disadvantaged children. This has become more feasible with the greater availability of household survey results that allow the disaggregation of participation data by gender, household wealth and rural or urban residence. At the same time, however, these results may underestimate the extent of the differences, as national surveys are not typically used to collect information about the most marginalized populations.

Participation in ECCE programmes

National ECCE systems vary considerably in terms of age group served, number of years provided and content. The intended age group

Figure 3.1: Distribution of countries by the number of years of pre-primary education provided, 2001

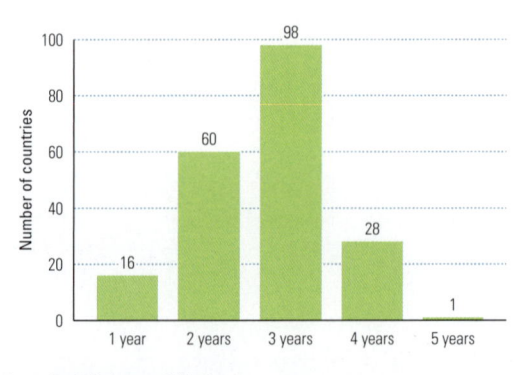

Years	Number of countries
1 year	16
2 years	60
3 years	98
4 years	28
5 years	1

Source: Statistical annex, Table 3.

---

1. The analysis primarily covers 1998–2001; 1998 was selected as a base because it was the latest year covered by the EFA 2000 assessment presented at the 2000 World Education Forum. It was also the first year for which data were collected after the 1997 ISCED revision, so all data from 1998 onward are comparable over time.

ASSESSING PROGRESS TOWARDS THE EFA GOALS / 83

Early childhood care and education

for pre-primary programmes varies widely, as Figure 3.1 shows. However, in most countries, participation is not obligatory and children may start programmes at any age. In some cases, programmes can be taken for only one year, as in Sri Lanka and the Philippines. In other cases, they can be taken for up to four years, as in many Central and Eastern European countries, or even five years, as in Mongolia. The most common duration is three years, typically serving ages 3 to 5 or, less frequently, 4 to 6. In a few countries, the year before the official entrance age for primary education is compulsory.

The annual statutory number of hours of pre-primary schooling in developing countries in 1999 ranged from 195 hours in Iraq to more than 1,250 hours in Colombia, Cuba and Saint Kitts and Nevis – a ratio of 1:8 between minimum and maximum (UNESCO, 2003a). Programmes in about half the countries for which data are available fell in the range of 700 to 999 hours per year. Programmes of longer duration are not necessarily of better quality – their impact on child outcomes also depends on support provided in the home and on the quality of the activities provided.

Gross and net enrolment ratios (GER and NER) – explained in the section below on school participation – are typically used to measure levels of participation in ECCE programmes. The GER should be interpreted within the context of the official age groups for pre-primary education (they are found in the Statistical annex, Table 3). Figure 3.2 shows enrolment ratios in selected

The impact of ECCE programmes depends on support provided in the home and on the quality of the activities provided

Figure 3.2: Gross and net pre-primary enrolment ratios, 2001

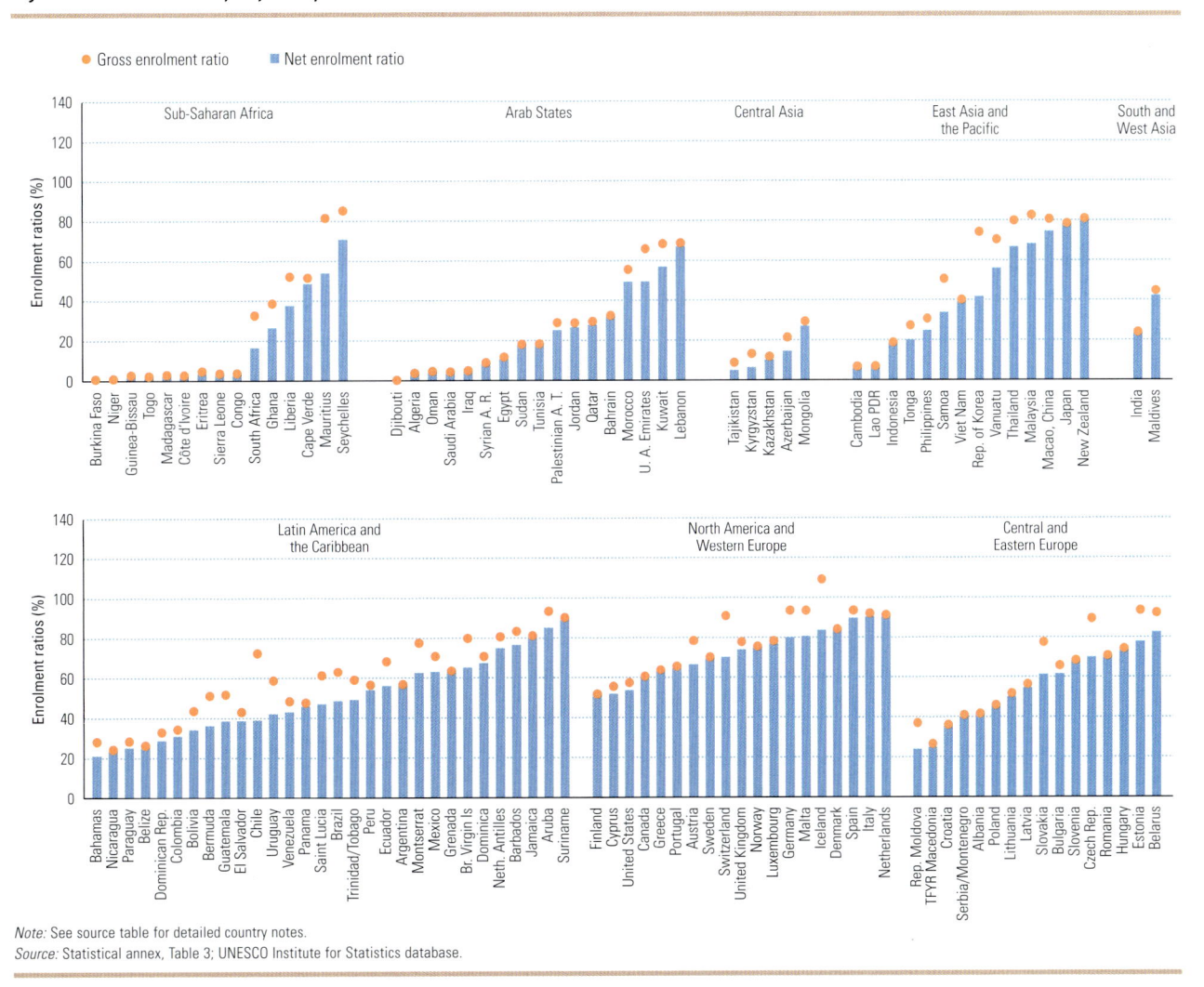

Note: See source table for detailed country notes.
Source: Statistical annex, Table 3; UNESCO Institute for Statistics database.

84 / CHAPTER 3

countries for the 2001/2002 school year. Most countries in the EFA[2] regions of sub-Saharan Africa, the Arab States, Central Asia and South and West Asia have low enrolment levels, while those in the Latin America and the Caribbean region and the North America and Western Europe region have generally higher levels. The considerable difference between the GER and the NER in several countries indicates that a large proportion of those enrolled are outside the intended age group.

The countries shown in Figure 3.3 illustrate three typical patterns in terms of participation by age. In the most common pattern, participation rates increase with age, and peak in the year before entry into primary school. In Poland, the peak covers practically all 6-year-olds, because the last year of pre-primary is compulsory. One year of compulsory pre-primary education has become the norm for most European countries (OECD, 2001). While almost all children in Poland enter primary school at age 7, in Colombia and Ghana there is a greater mix of pre-primary and primary school participation among children of the same age, even at the official entry age for primary school. By contrast, in Côte d'Ivoire, as in many other sub-Saharan African countries, pre-primary participation levels are extremely low at all ages. Levels of participation in primary school are also relatively low.

Pre-primary school life expectancy summarizes these diverse participation patterns into the average number of years of pre-primary education that a child could expect to receive if current participation rates remain constant. Figure 3.4 shows countries with the highest and lowest levels of ECCE participation in each EFA region, together with the average of a larger group of countries in that region. It indicates that the highest levels of pre-primary school life

One year of compulsory pre-primary education has become the norm for most European countries

Figure 3.3: Age-specific enrolment ratios for pre-primary and primary education, 2001

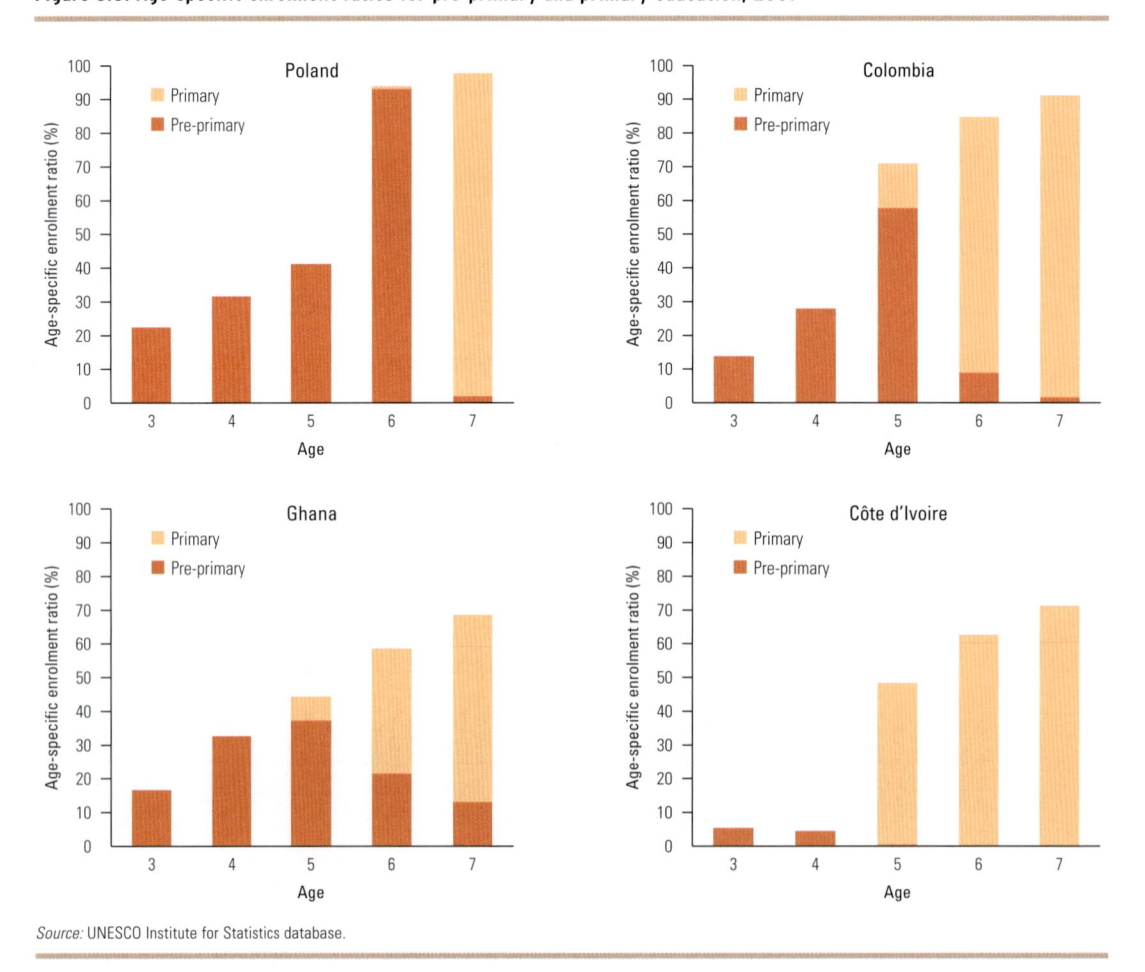

Source: UNESCO Institute for Statistics database.

2. See the introduction to the Statistical annex for the composition of the EFA regions.

Early childhood care and education

Figure 3.4: Pre-primary school life expectancy in selected countries by region, 2001
(regional averages and countries with the highest and lowest values)

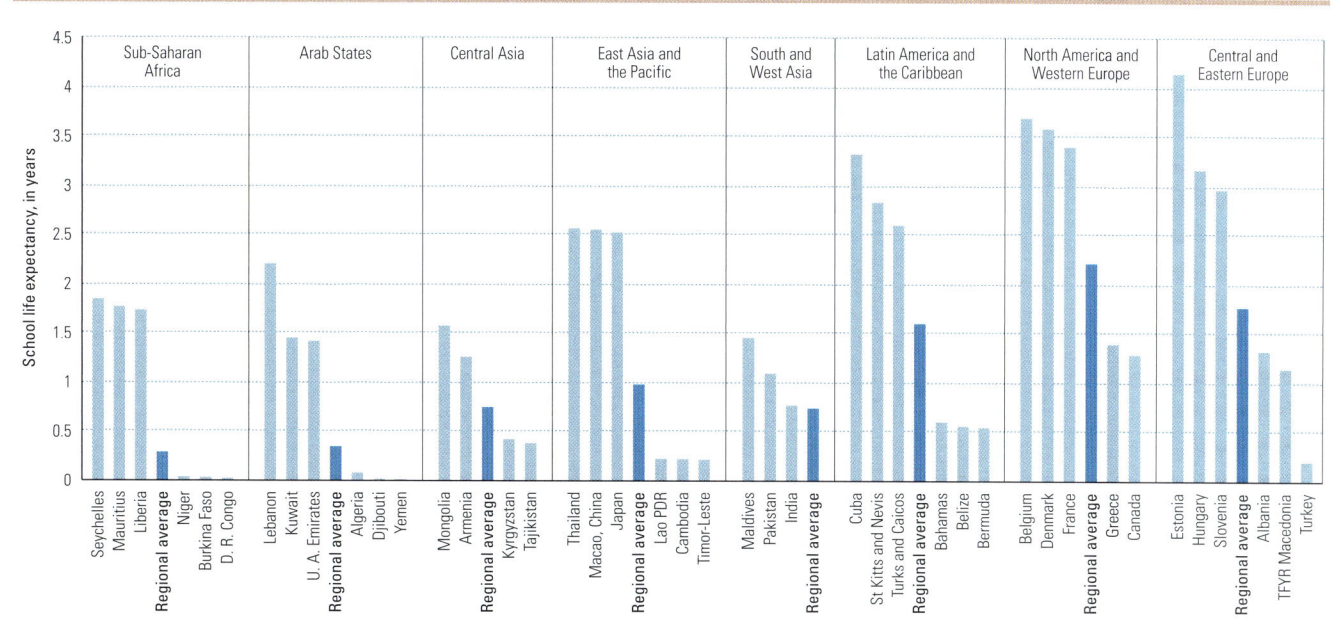

Notes: Regional averages are unweighted. They are based on the following number of countries: Sub-Saharan Africa: 34; Arab States: 19; Central Asia: 8; East Asia and Pacific: 22; South and West Asia: 8; Latin America and the Caribbean: 3; North America and Western Europe: 23; Central and Eastern Europe: 19.
Source: UNESCO Institute for Statistics database.

expectancy are found in North America and Western Europe (2.2 years), followed by Central and Eastern Europe (1.8 years) and Latin America and the Caribbean (1.6 years). The high rates in Central and Eastern Europe partly reflect the legacy of heavily subsidized pre-primary programmes accompanying high female labour force participation (UNICEF, 1999b). In the best-performing countries of sub-Saharan Africa a child could be expected to attend almost two years of pre-primary programmes, but the numbers drop off sharply and the regional average is only about 0.3 years. Despite high values in Lebanon and Kuwait, the Arab States' regional average closely follows sub-Saharan Africa's. Pre-school life expectancy is a measure of the quantity of programme provision and does not necessarily reflect programme quality, but extremely low participation levels indicate that ECCE in the countries concerned may bring few benefits to society.

Progress towards wider access to pre-primary programmes since 1998 has been slow. Gross enrolment ratios have increased by more than 10% in fourteen countries of sub-Saharan Africa, although they started from very low levels.

The GER rose by 133% in Congo (from 1.8% to 4.2%), due to recovery after the disruption caused by conflict. Increases above 50% were reported in Algeria, Burundi, the Libyan Arab Jamahiriya and the Islamic Republic of Iran. The decline experienced in countries of Eastern Europe and Central Asia during the 1990s has stabilized and the situation has started to improve in most countries (UNESCO, 2003a).

Figure 3.5 shows the rates of change in participation for countries with GERs of less than 30%. The biggest gains were in countries with an established base to build on (GER between 20% and 30%): Azerbaijan, India, the Islamic Republic of Iran, Tonga and Tunisia. However, in other countries in the same group, such as China and Lesotho, levels were stable or declined. Most sub-Saharan African and other 'least-developed' countries showed low participation levels (often below 10%) and, in some cases, declines. Most of these countries belong to the 'heavily indebted poor countries' group and are generally affected by the HIV/AIDS pandemic and high levels of poverty. They face the greatest challenge when it comes to achieving the good care, health, education and development of young children.

Most sub-Saharan African and other 'least-developed' countries showed low participation levels (often below 10%) in pre-primary enrolments

86 / CHAPTER 3

Figure 3.5: Pre-primary gross enrolment ratios in 2001 and change since 1998 (countries with GER below 30%)

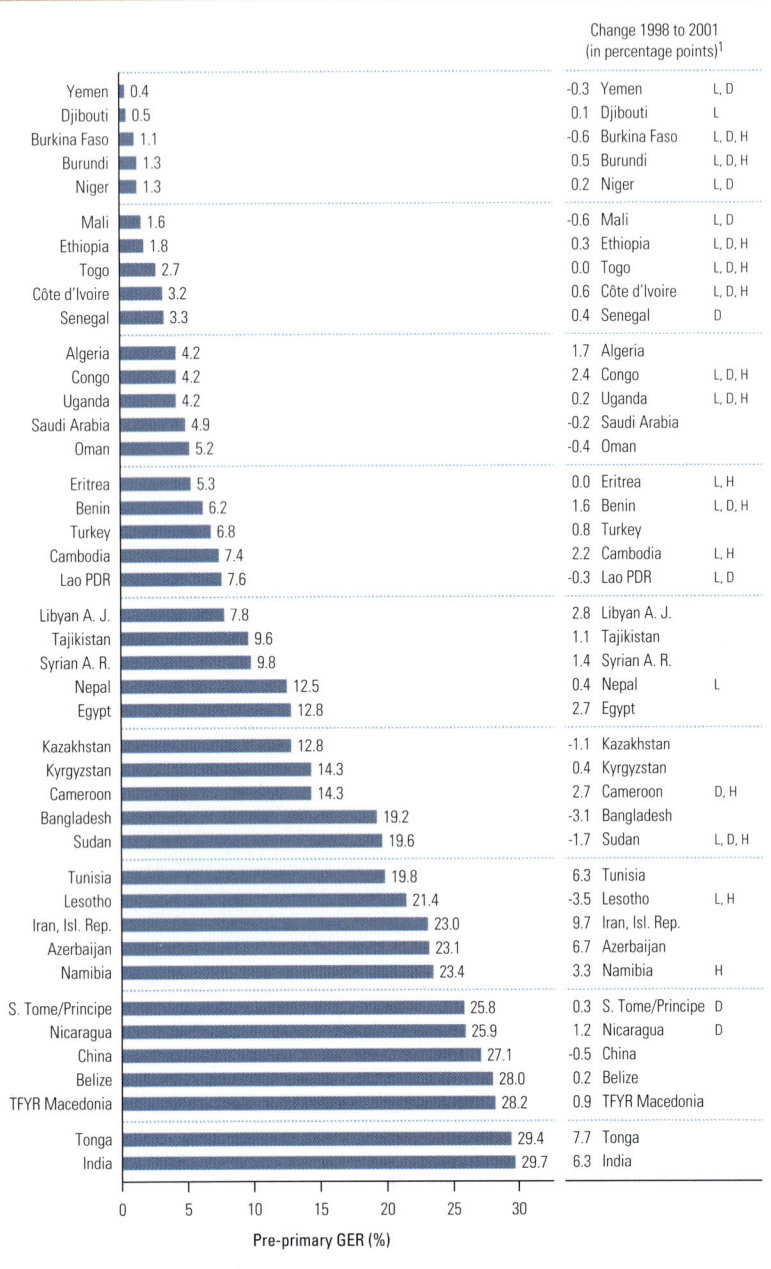

Country	Pre-primary GER (%)	Change 1998 to 2001 (in percentage points)[1]	
Yemen	0.4	-0.3	L, D
Djibouti	0.5	0.1	L
Burkina Faso	1.1	-0.6	L, D, H
Burundi	1.3	0.5	L, D, H
Niger	1.3	0.2	L, D
Mali	1.6	-0.6	L, D
Ethiopia	1.8	0.3	L, D, H
Togo	2.7	0.0	L, D, H
Côte d'Ivoire	3.2	0.6	L, D, H
Senegal	3.3	0.4	D
Algeria	4.2	1.7	
Congo	4.2	2.4	L, D, H
Uganda	4.2	0.2	L, D, H
Saudi Arabia	4.9	-0.2	
Oman	5.2	-0.4	
Eritrea	5.3	0.0	L, H
Benin	6.2	1.6	L, D, H
Turkey	6.8	0.8	
Cambodia	7.4	2.2	L, H
Lao PDR	7.6	-0.3	L, D
Libyan A. J.	7.8	2.8	
Tajikistan	9.6	1.1	
Syrian A. R.	9.8	1.4	
Nepal	12.5	0.4	L
Egypt	12.8	2.7	
Kazakhstan	12.8	-1.1	
Kyrgyzstan	14.3	0.4	
Cameroon	14.3	2.7	D, H
Bangladesh	19.2	-3.1	
Sudan	19.6	-1.7	L, D, H
Tunisia	19.8	6.3	
Lesotho	21.4	-3.5	L, H
Iran, Isl. Rep.	23.0	9.7	
Azerbaijan	23.1	6.7	
Namibia	23.4	3.3	H
S. Tome/Principe	25.8	0.3	D
Nicaragua	25.9	1.2	D
China	27.1	-0.5	
Belize	28.0	0.2	
TFYR Macedonia	28.2	0.9	
Tonga	29.4	7.7	
India	29.7	6.3	

Note: See source tables for detailed country notes.
1. L = least developed countries, D = highly indebted poor countries (HIPC), H = HIV prevalence in adults (ages 15–49) >2%.
Source: Statistical annex, Tables 1 and 3; HIPC classification available at www.worldbank.org/hipc.

3. The GPI is the ratio of female to male values of a given indicator. A GPI of 1 indicates parity between sexes; a GPI between 0 and 1 means a disparity in favour of boys/men; a GPI greater than 1 indicates a disparity in favour of girls/women.

The difficulty of expanding access to ECCE programmes in the least developed countries is the focus of a recent World Bank study (Jaramillo and Mingat, 2003). Almost half of the 133 developing countries considered in the study would not achieve a pre-primary GER of even 25% by 2015, based on current trends. The study suggests that one of the main ways for poor countries to increase ECCE is by expanding the role of the private sector via community-based provision. One danger of such a strategy, however, is greater inequality, since generally only the better-off communities and households are able to invest in ECCE programmes.

Achieving gender equality in access and provision is especially important during this critical period of child development. The countries for which data are available are divided almost evenly between those where gender disparities in pre-primary education, as measured by the gender parity index (GPI),[3] favour boys and those where they favour girls. The disparities in favour of boys are generally less striking than those for primary education in South and West Asia, sub-Saharan Africa and certain Arab States. One possible explanation is the degree of civil society participation in ECCE provision (UNESCO, 2003a). Many non-governmental organizations (NGOs) and other associations are concerned with the interests of women and young children and seek to ensure that girls participate at least as much as boys. Nevertheless, in some countries, such as Morocco and Pakistan, the GER for girls is still no more than three-quarters of the ratio for boys. In the British Virgin Islands, Nepal, Oman, Tajikistan and the Turks and Caicos Islands, girls' participation remains 12%–15% below that of boys.

Table 3.1 presents data on attendance in early childhood programmes by 3- and 4-year-olds, collected in household surveys. The UNICEF Multiple Indicator Cluster Surveys (MICS), conducted in or around 2000, collected data on the percentage of children aged 3 and 4 who attended organized learning or early childhood education programmes, along with the average number of hours attended in the week before the survey.

The number of hours attended ranged from ten or fewer in sub-Saharan African countries such as Burundi, Chad, Guinea-Bissau and Sierra Leone to more than thirty in Azerbaijan, Mongolia and Tajikistan. Countries whose attendance rates and hours attended were both relatively high included the Dominican Republic, the Republic of Moldova, Suriname, Trinidad and Tobago and Viet Nam. By contrast, in Burundi, Chad, the Central African Republic, the Democratic Republic of the Congo, Guinea-Bissau and the Niger, only a

Early childhood care and education

small proportion of 3- and 4-year-olds attended and for only a few hours per week.

Who benefits from ECCE programmes?

While countries providing GERs are evenly divided between those favouring boys and those favouring girls, disparity in net attendance rates among 3- and 4-year-olds in the surveyed countries is more often in favour of girls. In almost two thirds of the surveyed countries, they attend ECCE programmes more than boys. Furthermore, disparities in favour of either sex are more pronounced for attendance rates than for GERs. The disparity in favour of girls is highest in the Lao People's Democratic Republic, the Philippines and Botswana; the disparity in favour of boys is highest in Chad, the Niger and Tajikistan.

Attendance rates in pre-primary programmes are considerably higher for urban children than for those living in rural areas (Figure 3.6) and higher for children from better-off households than poor ones (Figure 3.7). Countries with higher-than-average attendance rates that have minimized differences in urban versus rural attendance include Equatorial Guinea and Suriname. The greatest differences in attendance between rich and poor were found in the Dominican Republic, Viet Nam and the Republic of Moldova. Research has shown that children from the poorest backgrounds benefit the most from ECCE provision in terms of care, health and education (Jarousse, Mingat and Richard, 1992), yet UNICEF MICS and other studies show that they are also more likely to be excluded from it.

Assessing the quality and cost of ECCE

It is difficult to assess the quality of ECCE provision, as outcomes are hard to measure, although projects using increasingly refined instruments are being carried out.[4] Most such studies measure the impact of ECCE participation on the progression of pupils through the primary school grades and on their overall achievement. Chapter 2 of this report discusses evidence from developed and developing countries (see also Myers, 2004). Indicators that can assist in assessing the quality of early childhood programmes cover such aspects as physical environments, staff training and qualification levels and numbers of children per class and per caregiver. The characteristics of how provision is organized and managed, the clarity of curricular goals and the quality of the education process are also keys to good child development outcomes. But data for these indicators are often difficult to collect and interpret in a comparative framework.

Table 3.1: Net ECCE attendance rates for 3- and 4-year-olds by gender and number of hours attended, 2000

Country	Total	Male	Female	GPI (F/M)	Mean number of hours attended[1]
Albania	16.1	15.9	16.2	1.02	14.9
Angola	6.7	6.8	6.7	0.99	...
Azerbaijan	11.6	12.3	10.9	0.89	32.5
Bolivia	17.6	16.9	18.2	1.08	19.1
Bosnia/Herzeg.	8.9	8.3	9.7	1.17	21.8
Botswana	14.5	11.8	17.0	1.44	...
Burundi	4.5	3.9	5.0	1.28	8.4
Cameroon	15.9	16.7	18.4	1.10	...
C. A. R.	2.8	2.7	2.9	1.07	13.0
Chad	0.8	1.0	0.6	0.60	7.3
Comoros	16.5	15.7	17.3	1.10	13.4
Côte d'Ivoire	6.6	7.2	5.9	0.82	16.6
D. R. Congo	3.0	3.1	2.9	0.94	15.1
Dominican Rep.	49.8	48.3	51.5	1.07	16.1
Equat. Guinea	45.8	46.5	44.9	0.97	15.5
Gambia	17.2	16.6	17.6	1.06	20.1
Guinea-Bissau	6.7	7.2	6.1	0.85	9.4
Guyana	36.1	36.9	35.1	0.95	...
Kenya	17.9	15.9	19.9	1.25	28.5
Lao PDR	7.0	5.2	8.9	1.71	25.0
Lesotho	22.6	21.6	23.7	1.10	19.6
Madagascar	5.6	5.6	5.5	0.98	15.5
Mongolia	21.8	21.7	21.8	1.00	32.7
Myanmar	9.7	9.1	10.4	1.14	22.5
Niger	2.6	3.4	1.7	0.50	19.9
Philippines[2]	10.9	8.6	13.3	1.55	...
Rep. Moldova	30.3	28.7	32.1	1.12	27.0
Rwanda	2.7	2.5	2.9	1.16	...
S. Tome/Principe	19.4	20.3	19.3	0.95	15.2
Senegal	9.1	9.7	8.6	0.89	17.7
Sierra Leone	11.5	11.4	11.5	1.01	10.0
Suriname[2]	40.1	42.2	38.1	0.90	19.8
Swaziland	12.6	11.7	13.7	1.17	16.0
Tajikistan	4.1	4.6	3.5	0.76	32.2
Togo	8.6	8.3	8.9	1.07	...
Trinidad/Tobago	71.5	67.9	75.4	1.11	24.7
Uzbekistan	20.7	18.2	23.3	1.28	17.3
Venezuela	33.1	32.5	33.9	1.04	...
Viet Nam	32.5	30.6	34.6	1.13	24.4
Zambia[2]	8.0	7.6	8.5	1.12	...
Average	**17.1**	**16.6**	**17.7**	**1.06**	**19.1**

1. Number of hours attended in the week preceding the interview.
2. Data are for 1999.
Source: Calculations based on UNICEF MICS database.

4. An example is the Pre-Primary Project of the International Association for the Evaluation of Educational Achievement (IEA). This longitudinal study is designed to explore the quality of life of pre-school children in various care and education environments. The recently completed final phase examined the relationship between experiences at age 4 and cognitive and language development at age 7 (Weikart, Montie and Xiang, 2004).

88 / CHAPTER 3

Figure 3.6: Net ECCE attendance rates for 3- and 4-year-olds by urban or rural residence, 2000

Source: Calculations based on UNICEF MICS database.

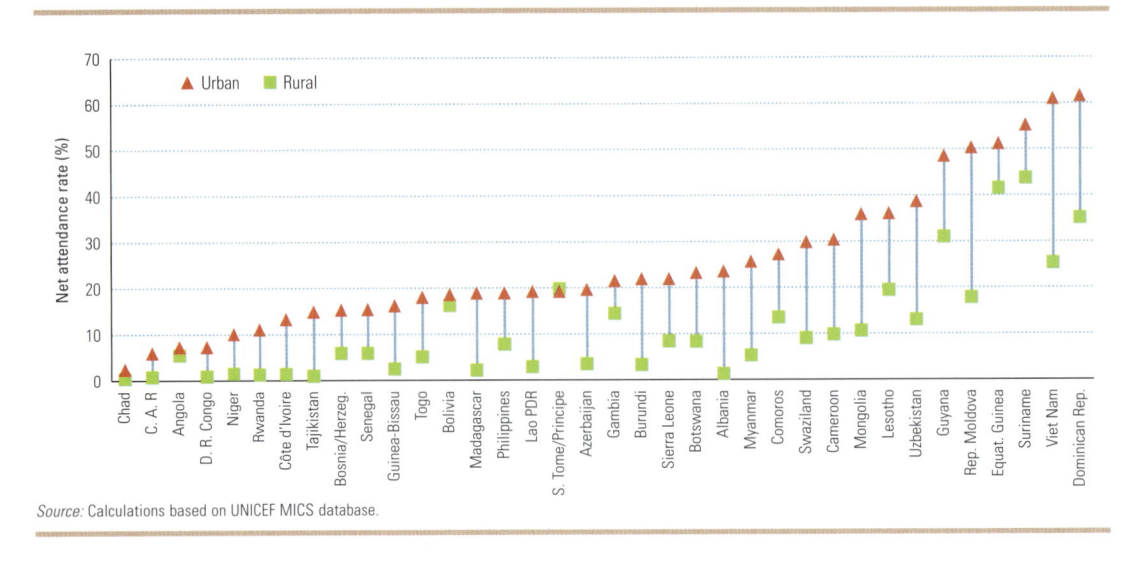

Figure 3.7: Net ECCE attendance rates for 3- and 4-year-olds by household wealth, 2000

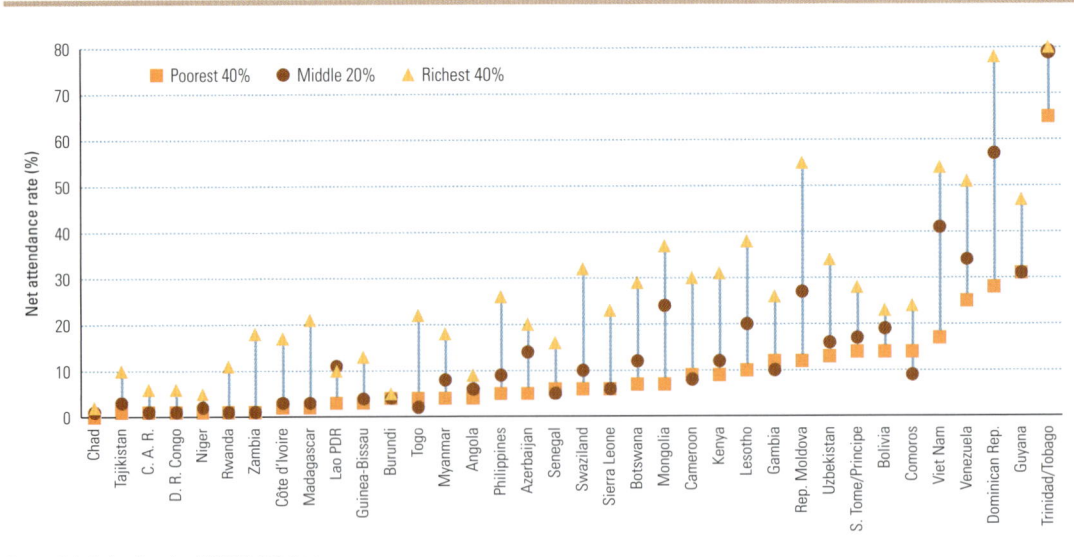

Source: Calculations based on UNICEF MICS database.

Many teachers are employed on a contract basis, receive low salaries and have limited or no professional training

Pupil/teacher ratios (PTRs) vary greatly in pre-primary education. The PTR is the ratio of the total number of pupils to the total number of teachers at a given level. PTRs are highest in sub-Saharan Africa, where 40% of the countries for which data are available have between twenty-five and thirty-four children per teacher, and lowest in Central and Eastern Europe and Central Asia, where the ratio is below 15:1 in seven out of ten countries. In general, PTRs tend to be higher in primary than in pre-primary education, as younger children need more individual care and attention. For instance, in sub-Saharan Africa, over three-quarters of the countries have PTRs over 35:1 in primary education, while only one in ten does at the pre-primary level. In Central and Eastern Europe and Central Asia, over 70% of the countries have fewer than fifteen pupils per teacher in pre-primary but fifteen to twenty-four in primary. This pattern is less clear-cut in the Arab States and in North America and Western Europe.

These averages represent only rough indications of the quality of processes and outcomes. A recent study, covering mostly industrialized countries, reports that ten out of twenty-one countries had child/staff ratios that differed according to children's age, socio-economic background, home location, staff qualifications and location of institution (Bertram and Pascal, 2002). These ratios varied from an average of 25–30:1 for 5- and 6-year-olds to 15:1 for 3- and 4-year-olds. Crèches, catering to 0- to 2-year-olds, generally had fewer than eight children per adult. For 4- to 6-year-olds, the average ratio was as low as 15:1 in programmes targeting the socially and economically disadvantaged. According to another source, national standards for child/staff ratios in OECD countries for 0- to 3-year-olds range from 3:1 in Denmark to 10:1 in Portugal, and for 3- to 6-year-olds from 6:1 in Denmark and Sweden to 20–28:1 in Italy (OECD, 2001).

The quality of ECCE programmes is limited in some countries by low staff qualifications. Many teachers are employed on a contract basis, receive low salaries and have limited or no professional training. Among sixty-nine countries providing data, 20% report that all ECCE teachers have received training, while in another 20% fewer than half are trained. Trained personnel make up less than one quarter of teaching staff in Trinidad and Tobago, Cape Verde and Ghana (see Statistical annex, Table 13A). In three quarters of these sixty-nine countries, the proportion of untrained teachers at pre-primary level is higher, and sometimes much higher, than at primary level.

In OECD countries, pre-primary staff are generally well qualified. In most Western European countries and Japan, staff need university qualification, while in the United States lower qualification is sufficient (CERI, 1999). A review of staff qualifications in nineteen developed countries conveys a picture of pre-primary programmes delivered by highly qualified staff (Bertram and Pascal, 2002). Recent changes to qualification requirements pointed to increasing professionalization. Staff dealing with 4-year-olds in all but two of the countries had qualifications similar to those of primary school teachers – usually at least three years of university training.

Among middle-income countries for which data are available, teacher qualification standards and salary levels (entry level with minimum qualification) do not differ greatly between pre-primary and primary levels. In lower-income developing countries, qualifications and salaries are lower at pre-primary than at primary level. Minimum salaries at both levels are reported to be similar in, for instance, India, Indonesia, Malaysia, Paraguay and the Philippines, but the number of hours of instruction is lower in pre-primary than in primary school, which results in higher pre-primary unit costs. Pre-primary expenditure per child is also higher where pre-primary PTRs are lower than in primary school, e.g. in Brazil, Chile, Indonesia, the Philippines and Tunisia (UNESCO Institute for Statistics/OECD, 2003).

As Figure 3.8 shows, pre-primary unit costs are also substantially higher than primary costs in the Czech Republic, Slovakia and the United Kingdom. While in Slovakia pupil/teacher ratios (10:1 in pre-primary, 19:1 in primary) may explain the cost level, this explanation may not hold true in the United Kingdom, which has PTRs of 24:1 in pre-primary and 17:1 in primary school. Nevertheless, it can be seen that unit costs are lower at pre-primary level than at primary level in almost two thirds of the countries providing data (sixteen countries out of twenty-seven).

Conclusion

Progress towards the ECCE goal has been slow, especially as it relates to reaching marginalized populations. The number of countries reporting GERs lower than 15% has changed little since 1998. Increases are found in particular among countries with an established base of participation, but some countries in this group report decreases. Participation as measured by GER is more gender-balanced than in primary school, though girls are still at a disadvantage in several countries. The evidence of household surveys, however, suggests that girls' attendance is higher than boys' (Table 3.1). ECCE programmes are unequally accessible within countries, with provision biased towards urban dwellers and richer households. In several countries, GER and NER differ considerably, indicating that a large proportion of those enrolled are outside the official age group.

Progress towards the ECCE goal has been slow, especially as it relates to reaching marginalized populations

Figure 3.8: Comparison of per-child expenditure at pre-primary and primary levels, 2001
(primary education = 100)

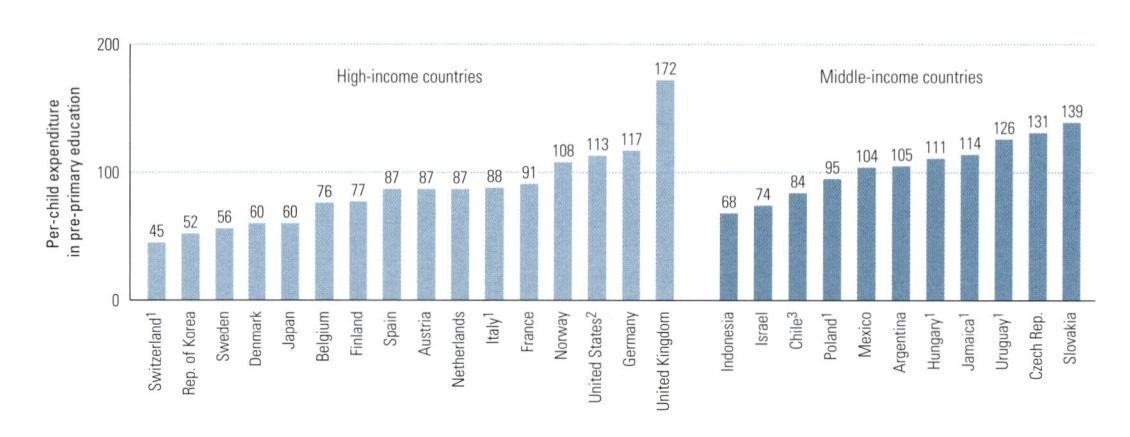

Country	Per-child expenditure in pre-primary education
Switzerland[1]	45
Rep. of Korea	52
Sweden	56
Denmark	60
Japan	60
Belgium	76
Finland	77
Spain	87
Austria	87
Netherlands	87
Italy[1]	88
France	91
Norway	108
United States[2]	113
Germany	117
United Kingdom	172
Indonesia	68
Israel	74
Chile[3]	84
Poland[1]	95
Mexico	104
Argentina	105
Hungary[1]	111
Jamaica[1]	114
Uruguay[1]	126
Czech Rep.	131
Slovakia	139

High-income countries / Middle-income countries

Note: Calculation based on expenditure per child in US dollars at PPP, using full-time equivalents.
1. Public institutions only.
2. Public and independent private institutions only.
3. Based on 2002 data.
Source: UNESCO Institute for Statistics database.

In terms of defining and monitoring ECCE programme quality, much unexplored territory remains. More evidence is required to assess progress towards the goal in terms of quality in low-income countries.

School participation

Universal primary education (UPE) means that all children of primary-school age participate in the school system and complete primary school

This section focuses on pupil participation at primary level and briefly discusses participation at secondary and tertiary levels. Universal primary education (UPE) means that all children of primary-school age participate in the school system and complete primary school. This requires initial enrolment at the officially prescribed age, regular attendance and the progression of most pupils from one grade to another at the appropriate time, so that everyone completes the curriculum. Such results are possible only if the school system has the capacity to accommodate entire cohorts of children and deliver decent-quality teaching. Timely completion of primary schooling with a reasonable degree of mastery of the curriculum – notably basic cognitive skills such as literacy and numeracy – appears to be necessary for primary education to yield the expected benefits over the long run, and is obviously a condition for successful participation in post-primary education.

As far as UPE is concerned, quantitative and qualitative objectives are inseparable. For example, improving school quality is one way to increase demand for education and improve school participation. The returns accruing to children from a given amount of schooling will also be crucially affected by its quality.

How close is the world to universal primary education?

Enrolment
Enrolment is the most basic element of school participation. It is also the most easily measurable indicator of progress towards UPE. As noted earlier, two enrolment ratios are usually distinguished. The gross enrolment ratio (GER) is the ratio of the number of children enrolled at a given level (e.g. in primary school), whatever their age, to the number in the age range officially corresponding to that level (e.g. ages 6 to 12). The GER is expressed as a percentage. It can exceed 100%, because of early or, more frequently, delayed enrolment, as well as grade repetition – which result in children other than those of the official age(s) being enrolled at a given level. GERs measure the overall capacity of school systems in purely quantitative terms, though wide differences in levels of resources per pupil often make broad comparisons difficult.

Table 3.2: Grouping of countries by levels of primary net and gross enrolment ratios, 2001

		Level of NER				
		<50%	50.1%-70%	70.1%-90%	90.1%-100%	NER not available
GER<100%	Sub-Saharan Africa	Burkina Faso, Eritrea, Ethiopia, Guinea-Bissau, Niger	Burundi, Chad, Côte d'Ivoire, Ghana, Guinea, Kenya, Mozambique, Senegal, United Republic of Tanzania, Zambia	Gambia, Zimbabwe		Central African Republic, Comoros, Congo, Mali, Nigeria, Sierra Leone
	Arab States	Djibouti	Mauritania, Saudi Arabia, Yemen	Kuwait, Oman, United Arab Emirates	Bahrain, Egypt, Iraq, Jordan	Sudan
	Central Asia			Armenia, Azerbaijan, Kazakhstan, Mongolia	Georgia	
	East Asia and the Pacific			Myanmar, Papua N. Guinea, Thailand, Cook Islands	Malaysia, New Zealand	
	South and West Asia		Pakistan	Bangladesh, India, Islamic Republic of Iran		Afghanistan
	Latin America and the Caribbean			Bahamas	Anguilla	
	North America and Western Europe				Canada, Cyprus, Greece, Iceland, United States	
	Central and Eastern Europe			Croatia, Latvia, Rep. Moldova, Romania, Serbia/Montenegro, Turkey, Ukraine	Bulgaria, Poland, TFYR Macedonia	
GER>100%	Sub-Saharan Africa		Liberia, Madagascar	Benin, Botswana, Equatorial Guinea, Gabon, Lesotho, Malawi, Namibia, Rwanda, South Africa, Swaziland	Cape Verde, Mauritius, S. Tome/Principe, Seychelles, Togo	Cameroon, Uganda
	Arab States			Lebanon, Morocco	Algeria, Palestinian A. T., Qatar, Syrian A. R., Tunisia	Libyan A. J.
	Central Asia				Kyrgyzstan, Tajikistan	Uzbekistan
	East Asia and the Pacific			Cambodia, Lao PDR, Macao (China)	Australia, China, Fiji, Indonesia, Japan, Niue, Palau, Philippines, Rep. of Korea, Samoa, Tonga, Vanuatu, Viet Nam	Brunei Darussalam, Timor-Leste
	South and West Asia			Nepal	Maldives, Sri Lanka	
	Latin America and the Caribbean			Chile, Colombia, El Salvador, Guatemala, Honduras, Netherlands Antilles, Nicaragua, Turks and Caicos Islands, Uruguay	Argentina, Aruba, Barbados, Belize, Bermuda, Bolivia, Brazil, Br. Virgin Is, Costa Rica, Cuba, Dominican Republic, Ecuador, Guyana, Jamaica, Mexico, Montserrat, Panama, Paraguay, Peru, Saint Lucia, Saint Vincent/Grenadines, Suriname, Trinidad and Tobago, Venezuela	
	North America and Western Europe			Austria	Belgium, Denmark, Finland, France, Ireland, Israel, Italy, Luxembourg, Malta, Netherlands, Norway, Portugal, Spain, Sweden, Switzerland, United Kingdom	Germany
	Central and Eastern Europe			Czech Republic, Slovakia	Albania, Belarus, Estonia, Hungary, Lithuania, Slovenia	Russian Federation

Note: See source table for detailed country notes.
Source: Statistical annex, Table 5.

The net enrolment ratio (NER) only takes into account enrolled children who belong to the official age range (e.g. 6- to 12-year-olds enrolled in primary school), regardless of whether younger or older children are also enrolled; thus it cannot exceed 100%. As a measure of the coverage of children in the age range officially associated with a given level of education, the NER comes closer to being an indicator of school quality. UPE implies a NER at or near 100%. A high GER is not necessarily a sign of progress towards UPE if the NER is much lower.[5]

Table 3.2 groups countries according to their GERs and NERs in primary education in 2001. Figure 3.9 displays GERs and NERs for the 100-plus countries that had not reached an NER of 95% by 2001. More than one-third of the countries for which data are available still have GERs below 100%, although those with NERs above 90% may have sufficient capacity for UPE.

In the more than forty countries with GERs below 100% and NERs below 90%, capacity will need to increase strongly for UPE to be reached. Figure 3.9 further suggests that the gap between GER and NER is often large for countries with low NERs. This shows that lack of coverage and inefficiency in primary education tend to occur together.

Striking regional patterns emerge. The greatest concentration of educational deprivation (and poverty in general) is found in Africa and South Asia. In sub-Saharan Africa, only a handful of small countries both reach GERs of 100% or more and have NERs above 90%. Some larger countries combine GERs below 100% with NERs below 70% or even below 50%. The only other countries reporting NERs below 70% are a few Arab States and Pakistan. Just six countries, all in Africa, have primary education NERs below 50%. Dealing with these data at the country level, however, masks the extent of educational deprivation in South and West Asia. There, despite somewhat higher national GERs and NERs, highly populated regions within countries have lower enrolment levels than do many African states.

Most of the world's countries, however, have attained NERs of at least 70%, and in North America and Western Europe, Latin America and the Caribbean and East Asia and the Pacific, most countries combine GERs above 100% with NERs above 90%. In Central and Eastern Europe, however, the situation is problematic: more than half the countries in the region have GERs below 100%, and some have NERs between 70% and 90%.

Unsatisfactory as the current situation may be, there was much progress in enrolment during

Figure 3.9: Net and gross enrolment ratios in primary education for countries with NER below 95%, 2001

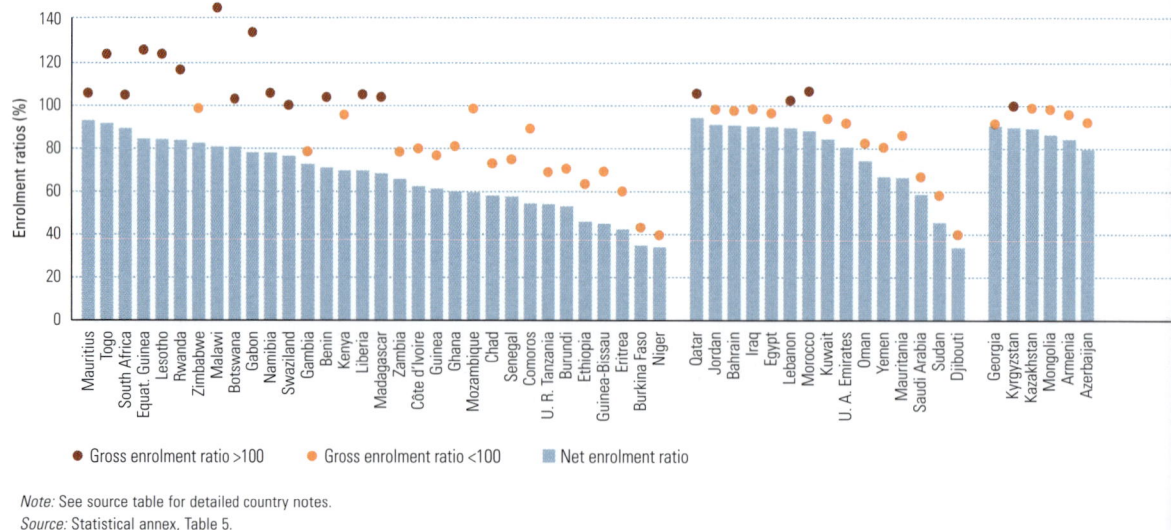

5. For example, GERs in primary education exceed 120% in Cambodia, Equatorial Guinea, Gabon, Lesotho, Malawi, Nepal and Togo, but all those countries have NERs between 70% and 89% except Togo, whose NER is above 90% (see Table 3.2). Countries in such a situation probably need to improve the coverage of primary education while reducing delayed enrolment and grade repetition. Thus, contrary to what the high GERs might suggest, major changes in school system organization and improvements in teaching quality may be needed in such countries.

Note: See source table for detailed country notes.
Source: Statistical annex, Table 5.

Universal primary education and gender parity

the 1990s, both over the whole decade (1990–2001) and its last third (1998–2001), as Figure 3.10 shows. By 2001, NERs had increased in nearly all countries that started the decade below 70%, leading to some convergence at the global level – NERs in primary education ranged from 16% to 100% in 1990, but from 34% to 100% in 2001. In twenty countries NERs increased beyond 90% and several countries that still had not reached 90% in 2001 nevertheless showed dramatic progress since 1998, with increases of over 10 percentage points (Burundi, Ethiopia, Guinea, Lesotho, Morocco, Mozambique and Sao Tome and Principe).

On the other hand, in about one fifth of all countries providing data, NERs declined more than two percentage points between 1990 and 2001. In many cases these were Central and Eastern European or Central Asian countries that had had relatively high NERs at the beginning of the period. Others were developing countries, especially in sub-Saharan Africa, that experienced prolonged economic crisis during the decade. In Nepal, the Republic of Moldova and Zambia, whose NERs were already below 90% in 1990, enrolment had dropped by more than 10 percentage points by 2001.

Similar changes occurred between 1998 and 2001, although on a smaller scale. As things stand, the world appears divided between a large group of countries with high and stable NERs and a smaller (but still relatively large) group of countries with low NERs, only some of which are making quick progress towards joining the first group. This is definitely a cause for concern, as is the fact that significant fractions of the population remain excluded from primary school in countries with higher NERs, especially in disadvantaged areas or communities.

By definition, achieving UPE entails achieving gender parity in enrolment. When initial enrolment is low, its growth is often gender-imbalanced, with enrolment ratios for males increasing much earlier than those for females. Figure 3.11 displays the evolution from 1990 to 1998 and to 2001 of the gender parity index, which is the ratio of the GER for girls to that for boys. A GPI between 0.97 and 1.03 is considered as reflecting gender parity. Figure 3.11 focuses on countries that had GPIs below 0.97 in 1998 or 2001, or both, reflecting a gender imbalance in favour of boys. In 2001, there were seventy-one such countries, or about 40% of the countries for which data are available.

Gender disparity in enrolment is characteristic of many of the countries with low overall enrolment. All but three of the countries with a GPI below 0.90 are in sub-Saharan Africa

Gender disparity in enrolment is characteristic of many of the countries with low overall enrolment

Figure 3.9 (continued)

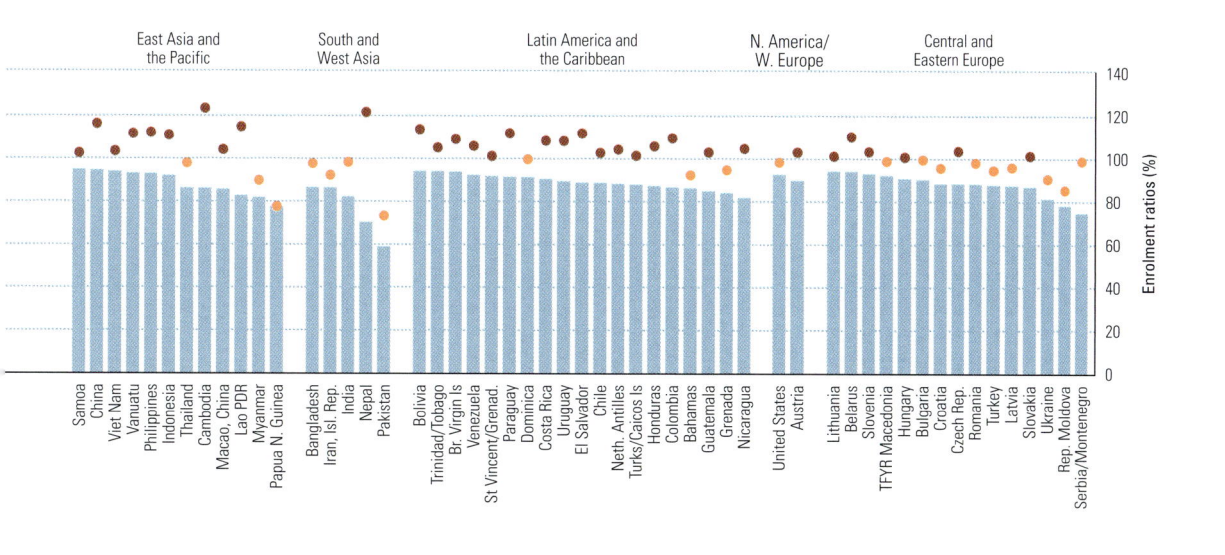

Figure 3.10: Net enrolment ratios in primary education, 1990-2001 and 1998-2001

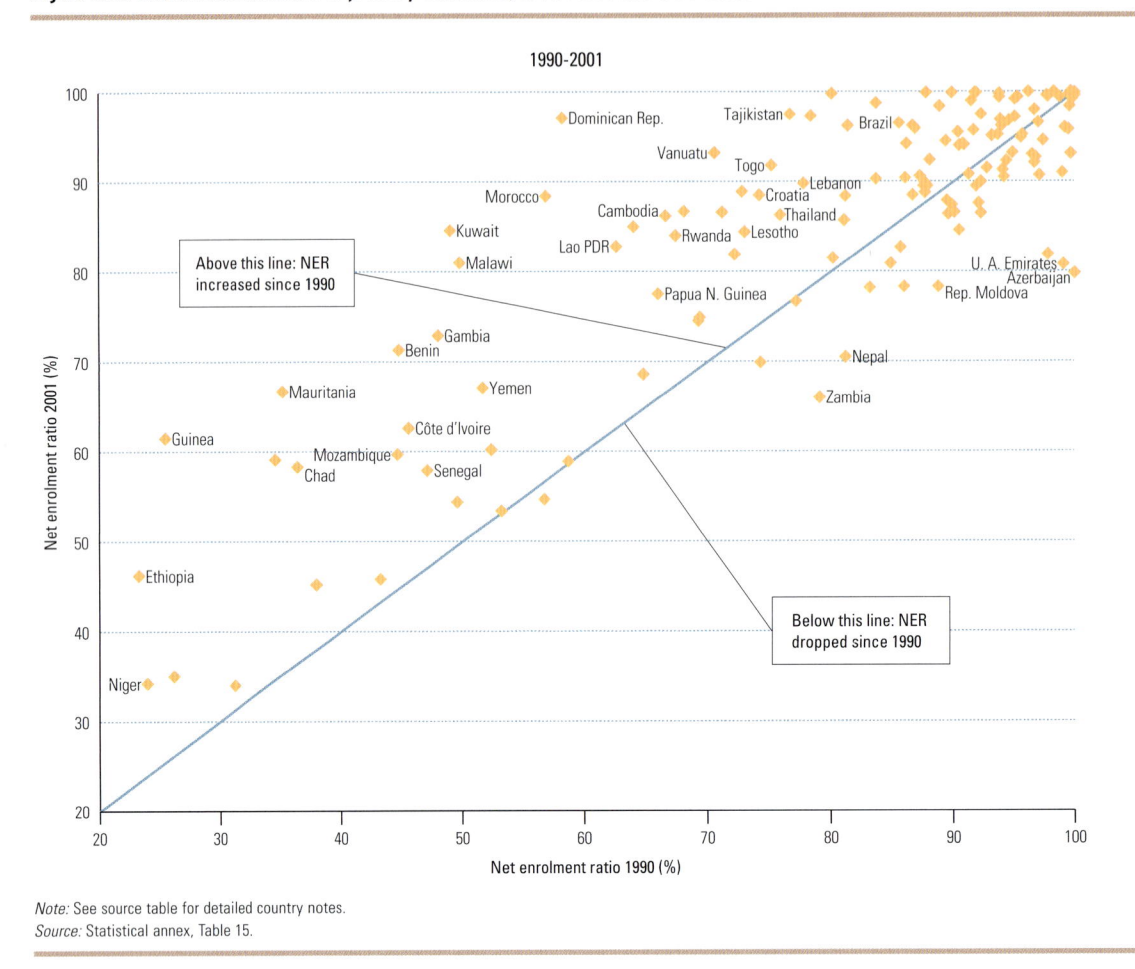

Note: See source table for detailed country notes.
Source: Statistical annex, Table 15.

Enrolment ratios are not increasing quickly enough for universal enrolment to be achieved in the short or even medium term

(notably West Africa), the Arab States, and South and West Asia. Progress towards gender parity was notable since 1990 and the trend has continued in 1998–2001. Thus, quick progress in gender parity can be achieved even in poor countries with low enrolment ratios.[6] Nevertheless, the GPI fell recently in several countries.

Out-of-school children

Despite the progress in enrolment made throughout the 1990s in a majority of developing countries, large numbers of children of primary-school age are still not participating. The most easily available estimate of the number of these 'out-of-school children' is calculated from the NER, although, since some children of primary age are enrolled in pre-primary schooling and, occasionally, at secondary level, this method slightly overestimates the actual number of children who are out of the school system.

Table 3.3 presents estimates of the number of out-of-school children in 1998 and 2001.[7] Worldwide, there were about 103 million of them in 2001, after a slow decline since 1998 (106.9 million) and 2000 (104.1 million). Clearly, enrolment ratios are not increasing quickly enough for universal enrolment to be achieved in the short or even medium term. At the world level, the NER rose from 81.7% in 1990 to 84% in 2001. Should this trend continue, the NER would reach 85% in 2005 and 87% in 2015. The regional distribution of out-of-school children naturally reflects NER and population figures. Some 96% of out-of-school children live in developing countries. Sub-Saharan Africa and South and West Asia together account for almost three quarters of unenrolled children. About 57% of such children are girls. The proportion is 60% or higher in the Arab States and South and West Asia.

---

6. See the extensive discussion of these issues in UNESCO, 2003a.

7. The numbers of out-of-school children are 2004 UIS estimates based on the latest data revision. For an explanation of previous estimate revisions, see UNESCO, 2003a: 49.

ASSESSING PROGRESS TOWARDS THE EFA GOALS / 95
Universal primary education and gender parity

Figure 3.10 (continued)

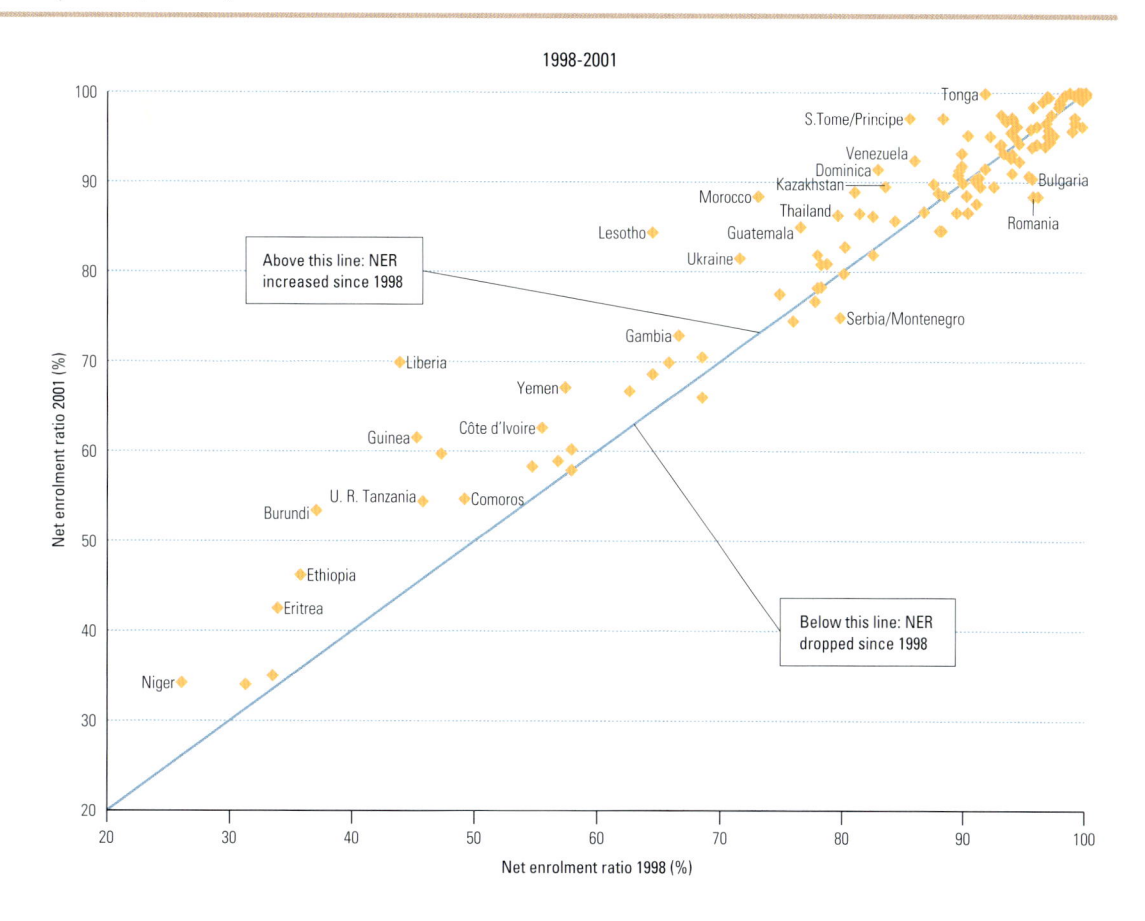

1998-2001

[Scatter plot of Net enrolment ratio 2001 (%) vs Net enrolment ratio 1998 (%), with diagonal line. Labels: "Above this line: NER increased since 1998" and "Below this line: NER dropped since 1998". Countries labeled include: Tonga, S.Tome/Principe, Venezuela, Dominica, Kazakhstan, Bulgaria, Morocco, Thailand, Romania, Lesotho, Guatemala, Ukraine, Serbia/Montenegro, Gambia, Liberia, Yemen, Guinea, Côte d'Ivoire, U. R. Tanzania, Comoros, Burundi, Ethiopia, Eritrea, Niger.]

Sub-Saharan Africa and South and West Asia together account for almost three quarters of unenrolled children

Table 3.3: Number of out-of-school children by region, 1998 and 2001

	1998				2001			
	Total	Male	Female	% female	Total	Male	Female	% female
	Thousands				Thousands			
World	106 916	44 062	62 853	59	103 466	44 985	58 481	57
Developing countries	101 905	41 537	60 368	59	99 056	42 667	56 389	57
Developed countries	2 447	1 251	1 196	49	2 992	1 612	1 380	46
Countries in transition	2 563	1 274	1 289	50	1 419	706	713	50
Sub-Saharan Africa	43 082	19 736	23 346	54	40 291	18 301	21 990	55
Arab States	8 491	3 501	4 991	59	7 441	2 992	4 450	60
Central Asia	879	429	450	51	390	169	222	57
East Asia and the Pacific	7 830	3 912	3 917	50	11 993	6 159	5 835	49
South and West Asia	37 410	12 179	25 231	67	35 808	13 518	22 289	62
Latin America and the Caribbean	3 759	1 699	2 059	55	2 468	1 300	1 168	47
North America and Western Europe	1 884	967	917	49	2 386	1 301	1 085	45
Central and Eastern Europe	3 581	1 640	1 941	54	2 688	1 245	1 443	54

Note: Figures may not add to totals, because of rounding.
Source: Statistical annex, Table 5.

96 / CHAPTER 3

Figure 3.11: Gender disparities in gross enrolment ratio in primary education, 1990, 1998 and 2001
(countries with GPI below 0.97 in 1998 or 2001)

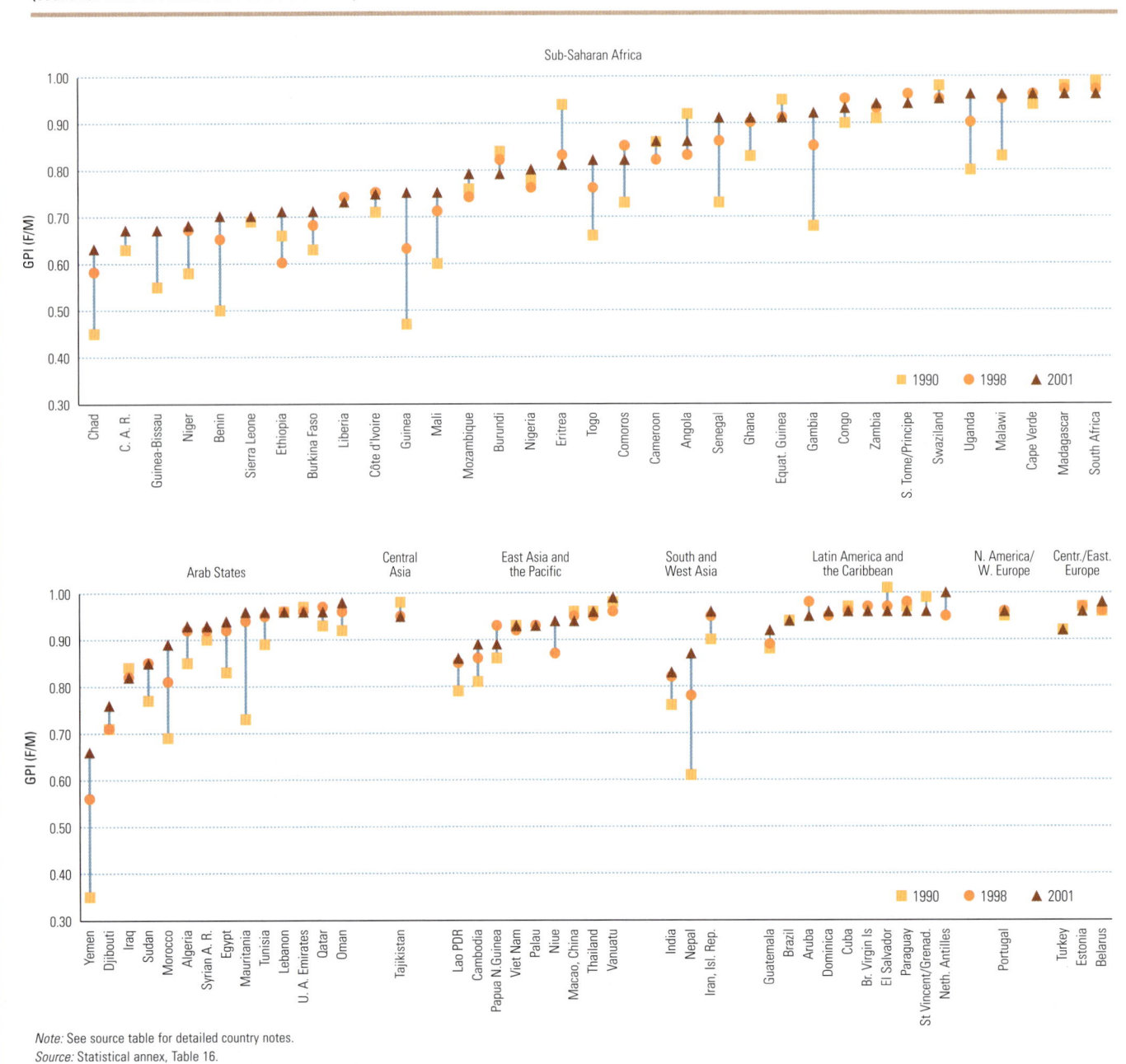

Note: See source table for detailed country notes.
Source: Statistical annex, Table 16.

Pupil progression: where quantity and quality meet

Reaching universal enrolment in primary schools is necessary for UPE, though not in itself sufficient. UPE also requires universal (or, more realistically, near-universal) completion of the primary curriculum, which can be achieved only if schools are of sufficient quality. Assessing the progression of pupils through primary schooling provides information on further quantitative aspects of the school system, as well as a first approach to assessing quality.

Late enrolment

One initial issue is the age at which children are enrolled for the first time. While primary education is officially meant to start at age 5

ASSESSING PROGRESS TOWARDS THE EFA GOALS / 97
Universal primary education and gender parity

Box 3.1 Late entry into schooling and concerns about equity

Household surveys, such as the DHS EdData surveys conducted in Uganda in 2001 and in Zambia in 2002, provide information on individual children's school careers and reflect the socio-demographic characteristics of children who enter school late. Although data are not available for many countries, the findings from these surveys indicate that late entry is an important equity issue.

Figure 3.12 compares late entry rates among various population groups. It considers children (6- to 18-year-olds in Zambia and 6- to 14-year-olds in Uganda) who started late and are still in school and those who have already left school. In Uganda, children living in rural areas are more than twice as likely to start late than are urban children. In Zambia, rural children are three times as likely to start late. National averages mask significant sub-national differences in school capacity and demand for education.

Late entry is also linked to household wealth. In Uganda, the proportion of children from poor households who start school late is five times higher than the proportion among the richest households. In Zambia, the share is ten times higher.

Why do children start late? When parents and guardians of late entrants in Uganda were asked, they cited cost of schooling as an important factor for about half the children who started late. The second most cited reason – that the school was too far away – affected 22% of rural children who started late, compared to 11% in urban areas. A further 20% of children who started school late did so at least partly because the household needed them to work.

Figure 3.12: Characteristics of pupils entering school late in Uganda and Zambia

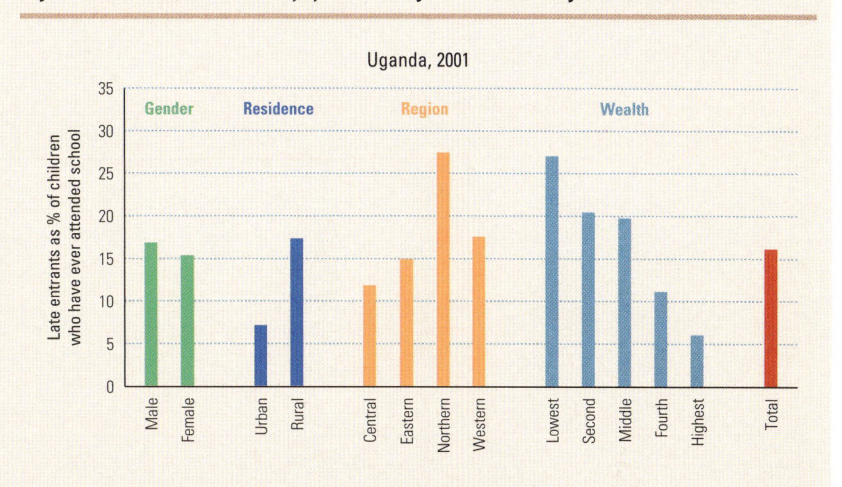

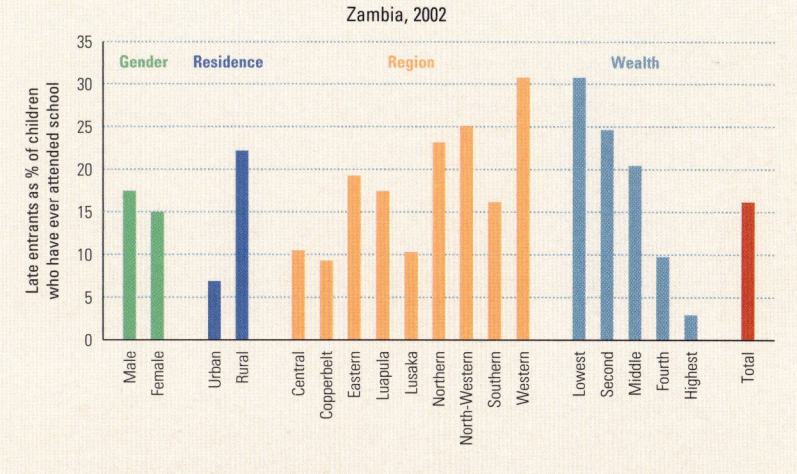

Sources: Uganda Bureau of Statistics and ORC Macro (2002); Zambia Central Statistical Office and ORC Macro (2003).

or 6 in most countries, late enrolment is common throughout the developing world, for a variety of reasons, e.g. children's participation in family economic activities and the difficulty of walking to distant schools. Box 3.1 examines the patterns and causes of late enrolment in two countries of sub-Saharan Africa.

Late enrolment means children would be completing their primary education at an age when constraints on school participation become stronger than during early childhood: more opportunities or pressure to work or get married and more limitations on girls' mobility, may reduce the probability of completing primary school. Moreover, late mastery of basic cognitive skills provides weaker foundations for further learning.

Intake rates can be used to assess the extent of late versus timely enrolment. The gross intake rate (GIR) is the number of new entrants to the first grade of primary school, regardless of age, as a percentage of the number of children at the official primary-school entrance age. The net intake rate (NIR) takes into account only those new entrants who are of the official entrance age. Like the NER, the NIR cannot exceed 100%, while the GIR can, where early or late enrolment is common. Figure 3.13 shows the distribution of

98 / CHAPTER 3

Figure 3.13: Distribution of countries by GIR, medians, quartiles and highest and lowest deciles, by region, 2001

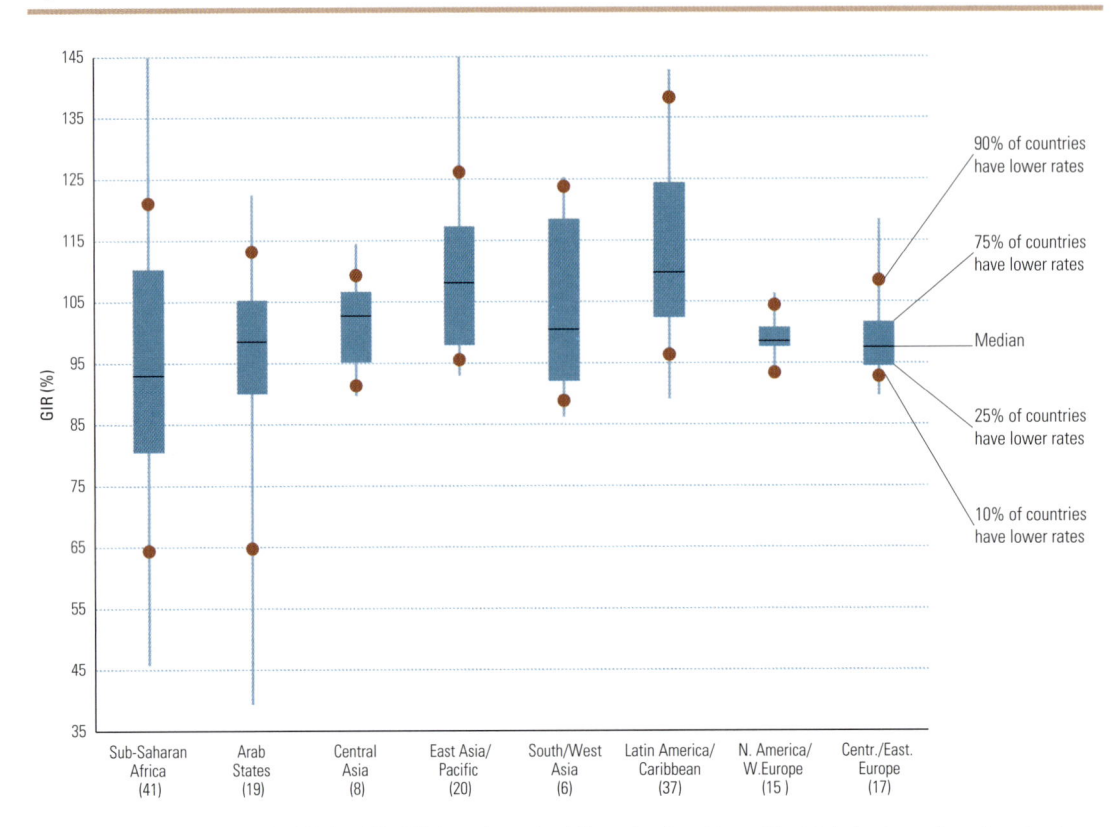

Notes: The boxes represent the range in which the middle 50% of countries are found. The number of countries providing data is given in parentheses for each region.
Source: Statistical annex, Table 4.

Once children are enrolled, it is crucial to ensure that they remain at school long enough to complete the curriculum and acquire basic skills

GIRs among the regions. It is remarkably complex. All Western European and North American countries have GIRs close to 100%, indicating school systems with the capacity to enrol all children and where the official age for initial enrolment is enforced. To some extent, the same situation prevails in Central and Eastern Europe and Central Asia, although with somewhat higher GIRs. Countries of East Asia and the Pacific and of Latin America and the Caribbean have generally higher GIRs – with a median above 105% and hardly any country having a GIR below 95% – indicating either that insufficient access to pre-primary schooling leads to early enrolment, or that many children enrol late, or both. The situation is similar in South and West Asia, although with lower rates. The Arab States and, especially, sub-Saharan Africa include some countries with very high GIRs and some with very low ones. Many school systems in these two regions have probably not yet reached the capacity to enrol all children in the first grade, while others are overloaded with late enrollers. Low GIRs are, by and large, specific to these two regions; out of the 107 countries for which data are available, the only ones outside these regions with GIRs below 90% are Azerbaijan, the Islamic Republic of Iran, Latvia and the Netherlands Antilles. The rate falls below 65% in eight countries: Burkina Faso, the Central African Republic, Congo, Eritrea, Mali and the Niger in sub-Saharan Africa and Djibouti and Sudan in the Arab States.

More direct evidence on late enrolment can be gained by examining NIRs. Figure 3.14 illustrates the situation of five countries of sub-Saharan Africa and one of Central and Eastern Europe, displaying the evolution of the NIRs as children older than the official first-grade age are progressively taken into account. Slovakia's profile is typical of most high- and middle-income countries: 90% of the children enrolled in the first grade are the official age or one year older. Against this benchmark, the extent of late enrolment in sub-Saharan African countries

Figure 3.14: Cumulative net intake rates by age, in selected countries, 2001

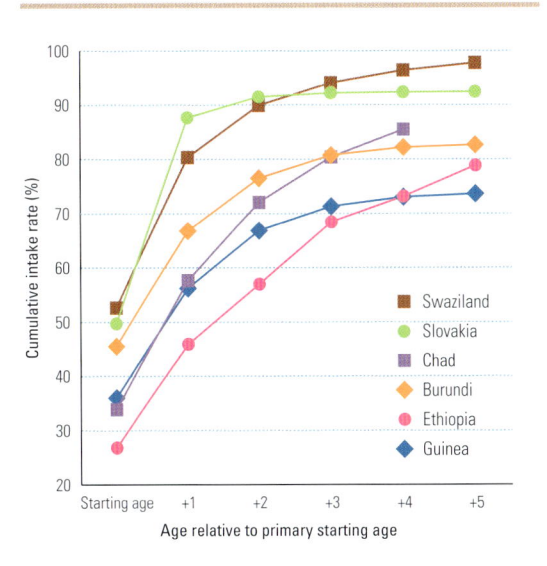

Note: Children entering early are included in the cumulative rate for the starting age.
Source: UNESCO Institute for Statistics database.

appears clearly: children two or more years older than the official age represent about 20% to 40% of first-grade pupils.

Retention

Once children are enrolled, it is crucial to ensure that they remain at school long enough to complete the curriculum and acquire basic skills. For a variety of school- or family-related reasons, large numbers of children drop out of school, or more accurately, are 'pushed out' (e.g. by the costs of schooling or by a child-unfriendly environment in the classroom) or 'drawn out' (to participate in household economic activities) before completing the fifth grade. These children are likely to be those who found it most difficult to cope with school and whose achievement levels are especially low. The returns they will have from a couple of unsuccessful years of school attendance may be insignificant, compared with those that completion of primary schooling would bring. Reducing dropout rates is thus crucial.

Figure 3.15, covering ninety-one countries, shows that the survival rate to grade 5 (the proportion of children enrolled in grade 1 who eventually reach grade 5) varies considerably and is especially low in sub-Saharan Africa. The survival rate is below 75% in thirty countries and below 66% in half of the sub-Saharan African countries for which data are available. The figure further shows the relationship between survival rate and the number of grades reached before dropping out: the latter typically varies between 1.5 and 2.5 when the former is below 80%. There is much more variation in countries with high survival rates, however.

Survival rates tend to be higher for girls than for boys, in all regions. This fact is not inconsistent with the typical gender gap in enrolment; in countries where parental preference for sons is strong and/or the school system and society discriminate against girls, families that manage to send their daughters to school tend to be more advantaged than those who send only their sons. Thus, on average, female pupils have more favourable family backgrounds than male pupils.[8] Survival rates increased in many countries during the 1990s (see Statistical annex, Table 17). For example, between 1998 and 2001, the increase was about 10 percentage points in Cambodia, Djibouti, the Lao People's Democratic Republic, Malawi, Mozambique, Namibia and Samoa. At the same time, however, substantial declines were registered in Chad, Colombia, Eritrea, Ghana,[9] Madagascar, Mauritania, Rwanda and South Africa.

Grade repetition

Grade repetition is another indicator of pupils' progress, although it can be difficult to interpret, because it depends on policy: some countries systematically promote pupils to the next grade while others apply stringent achievement criteria. Where grade repetition is possible, however, its incidence is a measure of the proportion of children who do not master the curriculum (e.g. because school quality was insufficient). A high level of grade repetition is a sign of a dysfunctional school system often exacerbating dropout and resulting in overcrowded schools. In Senegal, where 14% of primary school pupils repeat grades, a cohort study of some 2,000 pupils in nearly 100 schools (1995 to 2000) found that repeating a grade at an early stage increased the risk of dropping out the following year by 11% (CONFEMEN, 2004).

Figure 3.16 displays the percentage of repeaters in primary education in 1991 and 2001 for eighty-one countries. Relatively few countries are affected by very high levels of grade repetition: two-thirds of the countries displayed have rates

A high level of grade repetition is a sign of a dysfunctional school system

---
8. For more discussion of this and related matters, see UNESCO (2003a).

9. The survival rate in this country went from 98% in 1998 to 66% in 2000. It seems, however, that the 1998 value is inflated, because substantially more children were reported in several grades in 1999 than 1998. This suggests that relatively large numbers of children who had previously dropped out re-entered school that year.

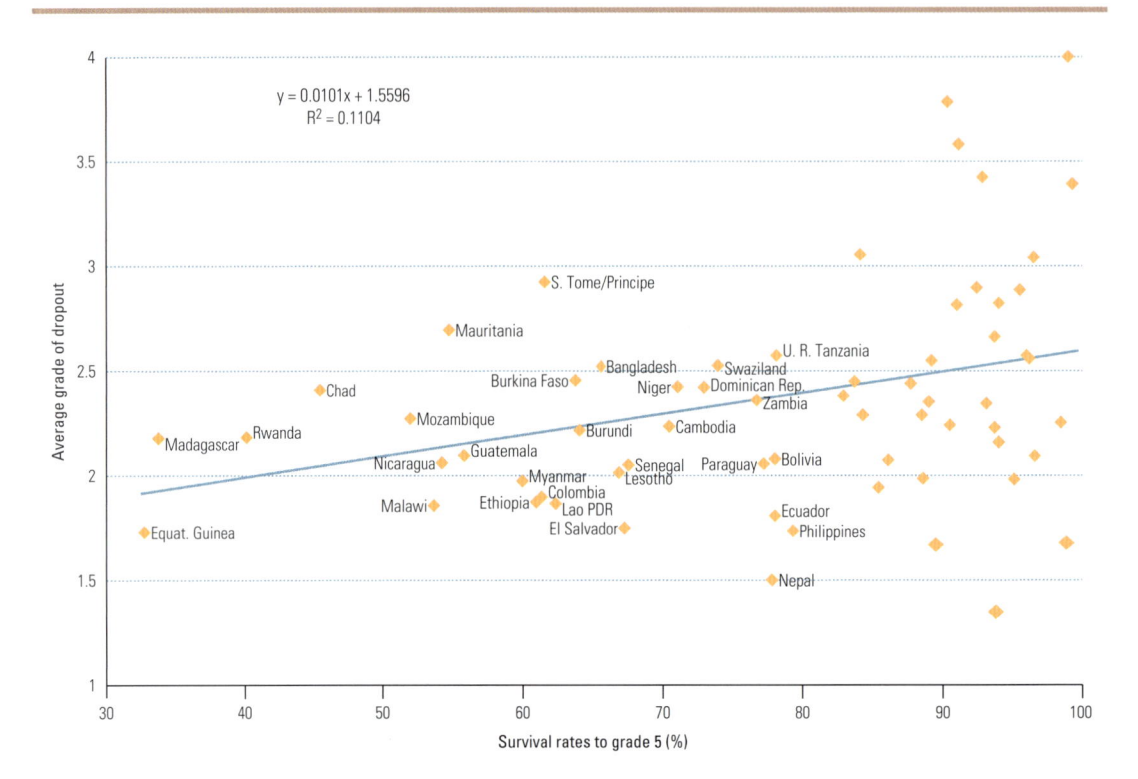

Figure 3.15: Survival rates to grade 5 and average number of grades reached when dropping out of primary school, 2001

$y = 0.0101x + 1.5596$
$R^2 = 0.1104$

Notes: The average number of grades reached before dropping out of primary school is weighted by the proportion of a school cohort that drops out at that grade. The proportion is estimated from survival rates by single grade based on the reconstructed cohort method. Countries with survival rates distorted by migration are excluded. Countries with survival rates below 80% are labelled.
See source table for detailed country notes.
Source: Statistical annex, Table 7; UNESCO Institute for Statistics database.

Education for All extends well beyond primary education

below 10%. There is much diversity among the remaining countries, however, and in those where more than a quarter of pupils are repeating grades (such as Chad, Comoros, Gabon, Madagascar and Rwanda), repetition is equivalent to an additional year of participation per child (UNESCO Institute for Statistics, 2004a). The figure further suggests that grade repetition became less frequent during the 1990s, but this may be a result of changes in promotion rules as well as of improved learning achievements.

Finally, the condition of a primary education system is best judged by the proportion of children of each age cohort who complete the cycle and the level and distribution of their learning achievement. The latter is discussed in the fourth section of this chapter. The former is more difficult to measure than the other indicators mentioned in this subsection. Box 3.2 discusses efforts to arrive at internationally comparable measures of primary education completion.

Meeting learning needs beyond primary education

Education for All extends well beyond primary education. Secondary education has been the standard minimum level of education for many years in most high-income countries and is increasingly required in developing countries for access to most jobs. Developing good-quality secondary school systems is thus an important policy objective, especially for countries that, by and large, have achieved UPE.

At least some secondary education is compulsory in 144 of the 183 countries for which data are available (most of the exceptions are countries of sub-Saharan Africa and South and West Asia). However, the rules are not enforced in many countries and international standards are less explicit for secondary than for primary education. For example, the 1950 Constitution of India (a country that is still far from having reached UPE)

Universal primary education and gender parity

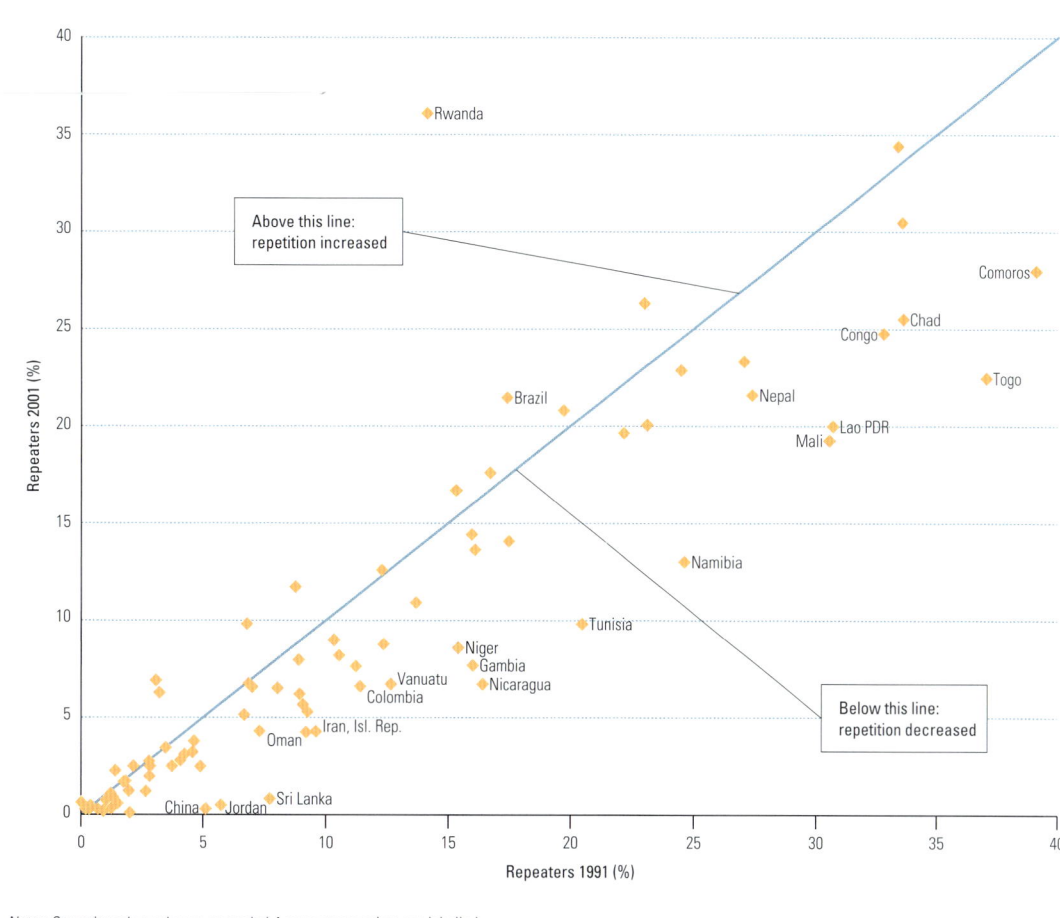

Figure 3.16: Percentage of repeaters in primary schools, 1991 and 2001

Notes: Countries where change exceeded 4 percentage points are labelled.
See source table for detailed country notes.
Source: Statistical annex, Table 6; UNESCO Institute for Statistics database.

---

mandates free and compulsory education up to age 14. A recent constitutional amendment made education for ages 6 to 14 a 'fundamental right'.

In most developing countries, a large proportion of primary-school graduates do not make the transition to post-primary education. Among countries in which lower-secondary education is supposed to be compulsory, only one-third have secondary-level GERs higher than 80%. Unfortunately, data on secondary and higher education are less available than those pertaining to primary education. The following discussion focuses on enrolment.

As Table 3.2 and Figure 3.9 suggest, most countries in the world had reached primary GERs of 80% or more by 2001, with exceptions in sub-Saharan Africa, South and West Asia and the Arab States. By contrast, the median secondary GER for developing countries in 2001 (57%) was about half that for developed countries (106%), and the only developing countries with GERs above the developed-country median were Brazil and Seychelles (see Statistical annex, Table 8).

Figure 3.17 shows that regional patterns are similar to those observed for primary education, but the contrasts are sharper. The industrialized countries of Western Europe and North America have almost reached universal secondary education, with GERs often above 100% and NERs above 90% (see also Statistical annex, Table 8). Secondary education is also well advanced in Central and Eastern Europe, where most GERs range from 80% to 100%. These levels are also reached by a few countries of East Asia and the Pacific, Latin America and the

In most developing countries, a large proportion of primary-school graduates do not make the transition to post-primary education

The vast majority of the youth in sub-Saharan Africa has little access to secondary education

Box 3.2 Towards a better international measure of primary education completion

The World Bank and the UNESCO Institute for Statistics (UIS) are endeavouring to improve comparative measures for monitoring primary school completion. A principal goal of Education for All is for all children to access and complete school and acquire basic skills – reading, writing and numeracy – to improve both individual and societal outcomes. In the Millennium Development Goals, Target 3 reads: 'Ensure that by 2015, children everywhere, boys and girls alike, will be able to complete a full course of primary schooling.' While completing primary school appears to be a condition for achieving and retaining basic cognitive skills, it is often not sufficient; where school quality is inadequate, many children complete the primary cycle without mastering basic skills or the rest of the curriculum.

The indicator currently used to measure primary school completion is a proxy that expresses the number of pupils in the last primary grade minus repeaters in this grade as a proportion of the number of children at the expected graduation age. A better proxy would express the number of pupils graduating from the last grade of primary school as a proportion of the total number of children at the typical graduation age. But countries often do not report the number of primary graduates.

As earlier monitoring reports noted, there are several important limitations related to the proxy measure of completion. For instance, it ignores pupils who drop out during the final year of primary school, and thus may overestimate completion levels (UNESCO, 2003a). To address this issue, the UIS is collecting data on final-year dropout.

While a national measure based on graduates could provide a reasonable estimate of completion, it would entail two limitations in terms of comparisons among countries. First, the criteria used to define graduation can differ markedly. Pupils may need to meet a variety of requirements to be recognized as 'graduates'. Among eighty-seven countries responding to a UIS survey, 67% indicated that passing a final exam was a requirement for graduation. Other criteria included teacher evaluation (29%) and accumulation of a designated number of course hours (18%). Thirteen countries indicated that there were still other criteria. In fifteen of the countries (17%), pupils enrolled in the last grade of primary were automatically promoted to secondary school (UNESCO Institute for Statistics, 2004a).

Second, it is difficult to reconcile the national definitions of primary education duration in an international comparative framework, such as the ISCED. Among countries responding to a UIS survey, 54% indicated that grade 6 was the final year of primary school in their national system. The range in other countries, however, was from grade 3 to grade 10.

While indicators based on administrative data are being improved, other efforts to examine trends in completion rates have focused on household survey data. Here, one main limitation has been related to the age group under study. Initially, primary completion rates were examined among all adults (Bruns, Mingat and Rakotomalala, 2003), or adults in the labour force. Such assessments, however, reflect the education system a decade or more in the past and are of limited use in guiding current policy. To address this issue, other studies have projected completion rates from adult cohorts to younger age cohorts (Guadalupe and Louzano, 2003) or analysed younger age cohorts, such as 16- and 17-year-olds. These measures better reflect more recent trends in the education system, though the fact that many youths aged 16 and older are still in primary school in developing countries will affect their accuracy.

Work continues, using a range of data sources and approaches, to improve the calculation and interpretation of the primary completion rate, together with indicators of participation and progression, for the purpose of monitoring progress towards UPE.

Caribbean and the Arab States, but those regions also include many countries with GERs around or even below 60%. Meanwhile, there is extreme diversity within sub-Saharan Africa, which, like South and West Asia, some Arab States and a few countries of East Asia and the Pacific, has a concentration of countries with GERs below 40%.

With the notable exception of South Africa, sub-Saharan African countries with high secondary GERs have small populations. The vast majority of the sub-continent's youth thus have little access to secondary education. Much the same is true for South and West Asia, where the countries with larger populations, such as

Figure 3.17: Secondary gross enrolment ratios, 1998 and 2001

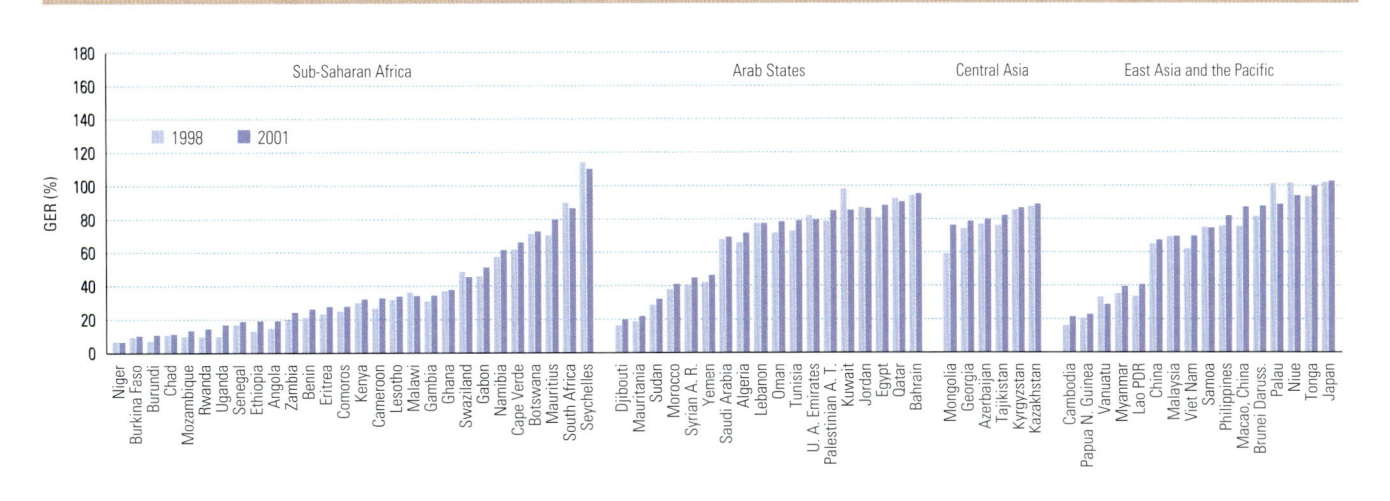

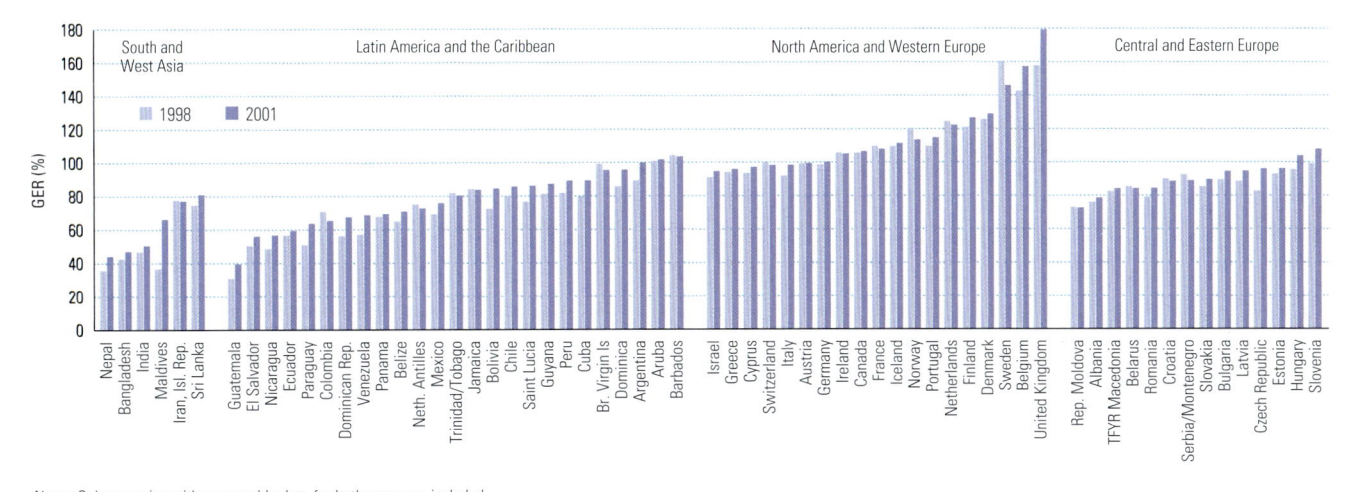

Notes: Only countries with comparable data for both years are included.
See source table for detailed country notes.
Source: Statistical annex, Table 8.

Bangladesh, India and Pakistan, have secondary GERs between 24% and 50%.

Figure 3.18 shows tertiary enrolment ratios. Here the gap between developed and developing countries is even more pronounced: the median GER is 55% among the former, 11% among the latter (see Statistical annex, Table 9). With a few exceptions, countries in Western Europe and North America achieve ratios of 40% or more, as do some countries in Central and Eastern Europe and a handful of developed countries in East Asia and the Pacific. Elsewhere, higher education systems are far less developed. China's and India's tertiary GERs are substantially below 15%. In more than a third of all developing countries for which data are available, GERs are below 5%.

This is the case in most sub-Saharan African countries. By and large, widespread access to higher education remains a privilege of high-income-country residents.

On the other hand, participation in secondary and tertiary education is growing, in many countries. Between 1998 and 2001, GERs rose by more than 2 percentage points in 80 out of 131 countries at the secondary level and 56 out of 95 countries at the tertiary level.

Gender disparities in secondary and higher education

Disparities between the sexes are even more prevalent in secondary and higher education than in primary education. Among the eighty-three

By and large, widespread access to higher education remains a privilege of high-income-country residents

Figure 3.18: Tertiary gross enrolment ratios, 1998 and 2001

Notes: Only countries with comparable data for both years are included.
See source table for detailed country notes.
Source: Statistical annex, Table 9.

Only four of eighty-three developing countries have achieved gender parity in higher education

developing countries for which data are available for all three levels, about 50% have achieved gender parity (i.e. GPIs falling between 0.97 and 1.03) in gross enrolment in primary education. The share drops, however, to less than 20% in secondary education and barely 5% in higher education. Of the thirty-seven developed countries with data, some 95% (all except Estonia and Portugal) have achieved gender parity in primary education, around 66% have achieved it in secondary education and about 60% in higher education. Finally, of the ten countries in transition for which data are available, all except Tajikistan have achieved parity at both primary and secondary levels, and half have done so in tertiary education.

Figure 3.19 displays ratios of female to male and male to female GERs in secondary education and Figure 3.20 does the same for GERs in higher education. A large group has low enrolment combined with gender imbalance (in favour of men) of widely differing magnitude – there is little association between enrolment and the *depth* of gender disparity at low levels of enrolment. Of the forty-six countries with secondary-level GERs below 50%, forty-two show gender disparity favouring men. On the other hand, a large group of countries has a gender imbalance in favour of women, associated in most cases with high overall enrolment: most of the fifty-three countries with GERs above 90% show gender disparity in favour of women. The picture is very similar at the tertiary level.

Universal primary education and gender parity

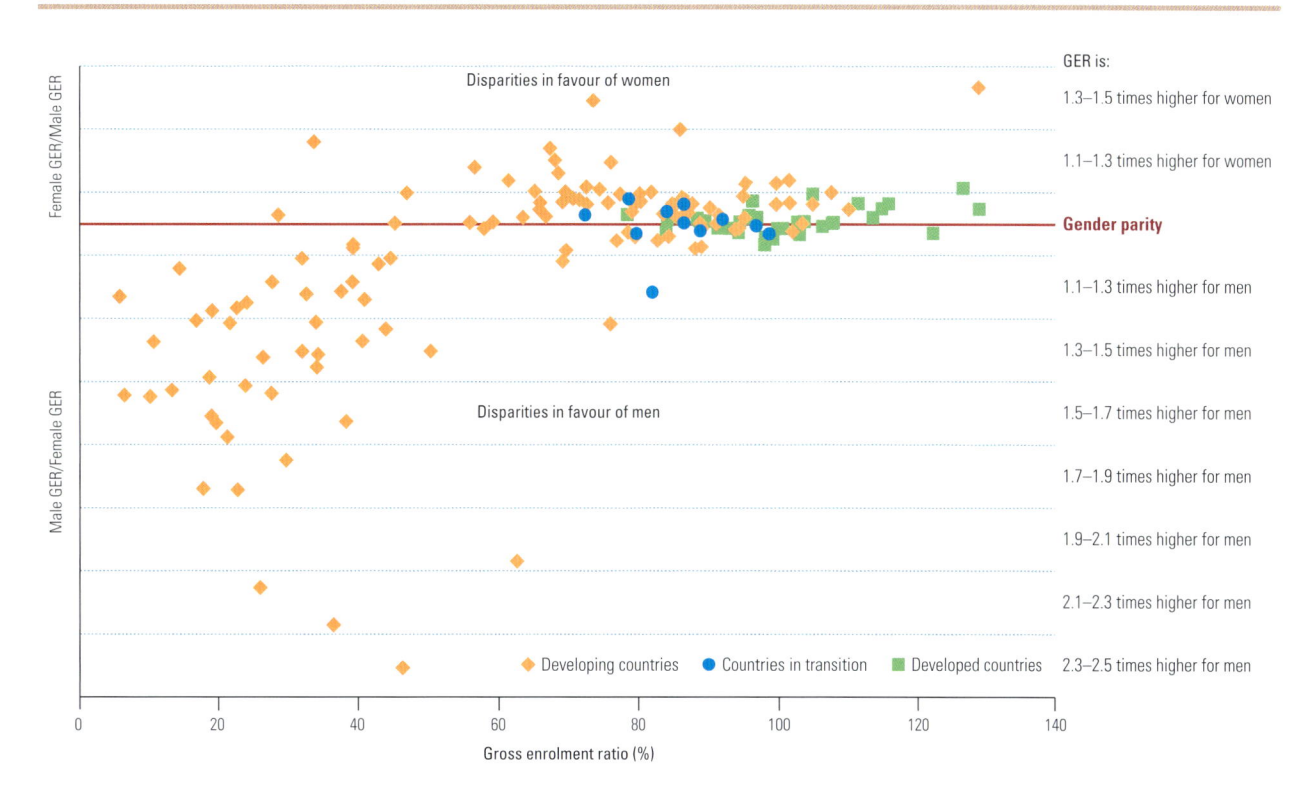

Figure 3.19: Gender parity and secondary gross enrolment ratios, 2001

Note: Disparities are presented on a comparable scale for both sexes: those favouring women are expressed as the ratio of the female GER to the male GER while those favouring men are expressed as the ratio of the male GER to the female GER.
Source: Statistical annex, Table 8.

School life expectancy

A good synthetic measure of enrolment patterns can be obtained by combining enrolment ratios by age at the different levels of the education system. The resulting indicator, school life expectancy (SLE), represents the average number of years of schooling that individuals can expect to receive.

Caution is required when using SLE, however; like GER, it is sensitive to the extent of grade repetition. In at least twenty countries, repetition contributes more than one year to school life expectancy – and up to two years in Algeria, Brazil, Gabon, Rwanda and Togo (UNESCO Institute for Statistics, 2004*b*).

Figure 3.21 displays regional SLE averages and the countries with the highest and lowest values, both for primary and secondary education and for post-secondary education.

Regional patterns are consistent with those discussed earlier: a child in sub-Saharan Africa can expect to attend an average of five to six fewer years of primary and secondary schooling than a child in Western Europe or the Americas. Dramatic subregional disparities are found in sub-Saharan Africa and the Arab States, the difference between the countries with the highest and lowest SLEs being up to fivefold.

The world average is 10.3 years – 9.2 years of primary plus secondary and 1.1 of post-secondary education – as shown in Table 3.4, which also presents the change in SLE between 1990 and 2001 and between 1998 and 2001. Globally, the world's children gained a year of school life expectancy during the 1990s. Progress was quickest in regions with already high SLEs, such as Latin America and the Caribbean (where grade repetition is very common) and North America and Western Europe. Less progress was registered in sub-Saharan Africa, and South and West Asia. Unsurprisingly, most of the progress

A child in sub-Saharan Africa can expect to attend five to six fewer years of primary and secondary schooling than a child in Western Europe or the Americas

Figure 3.20: Gender parity and tertiary gross enrolment ratios, 2001

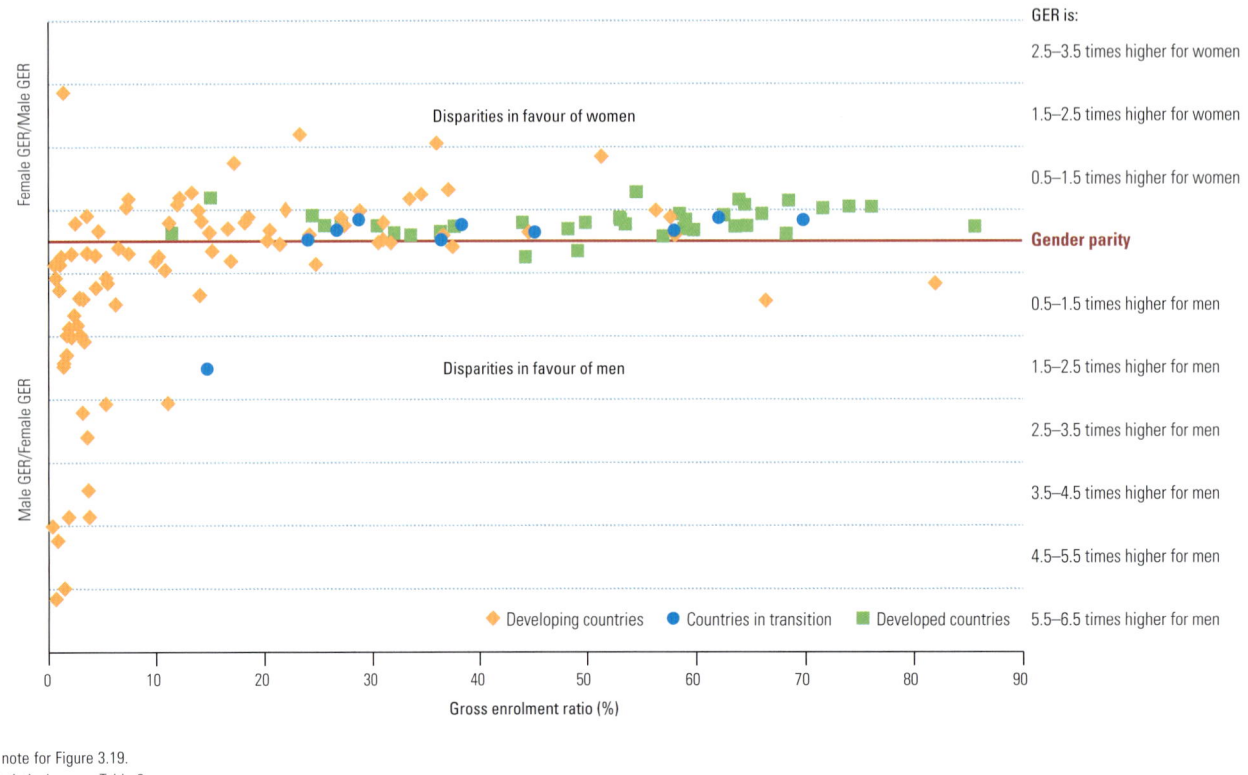

Note: See note for Figure 3.19.
Source: Statistical annex, Table 9.

Table 3.4: Expected years of schooling by region, 2001, and change since 1990

	School life expectancy, in years						
	2001			Change since 1990			Change since 1998
	Primary/ secondary	Post- secondary	All levels	Primary/ secondary	Post- secondary	All levels	All levels
Sub-Saharan Africa	6.8	0.2	7.1	+0.9	+0.1	+1.0	+0.3
Arab States	9.0	1.0	10.0	+1.0	+0.4	+1.4	+0.2
Central Asia	10.1	1.3	11.4	+0.0	−0.1	−0.2	+0.3
East Asia/Pacific	10.0	1.0	10.9	+0.7	+0.6	+1.3	+0.4
South/West Asia	8.0	0.6	8.6	+0.5	+0.5	+1.0	+0.2
Latin America/Caribbean	11.6	1.4	13.0	+2.1	+0.5	+2.6	+0.9
N. America/W. Europe	12.8	3.5	16.3	+0.7	+0.8	+1.5	+0.1
Central/Eastern Europe	10.2	2.5	12.7	+0.5	+0.8	+1.3	+0.9
World	9.2	1.1	10.3	+0.6	+0.4	+1.0	+0.3

Source: Statistical annex, Table 17; UNESCO Institute for Statistics database.

took place in primary and secondary education in developing countries and in higher education in developed countries.

Conclusion

While the world average of 10.3 years of education per child in 2001 is relatively high, participation is very unevenly distributed. Severe educational deprivation persists in sub-Saharan Africa, South and West Asia and some Arab States, where UPE is far from being reached. The dual task of targeting specific sections of society that still lack access to primary education, while expanding the general supply of secondary education, is growing urgent in Latin America and the Caribbean as well as in many developing countries of East Asia and the Pacific. Finally, while higher education might appear a lesser priority in developing countries – especially as it has often received a disproportionate share of education expenditure – the extremely low tertiary-level enrolment ratios in some developing countries are a cause for concern.

The quality of education

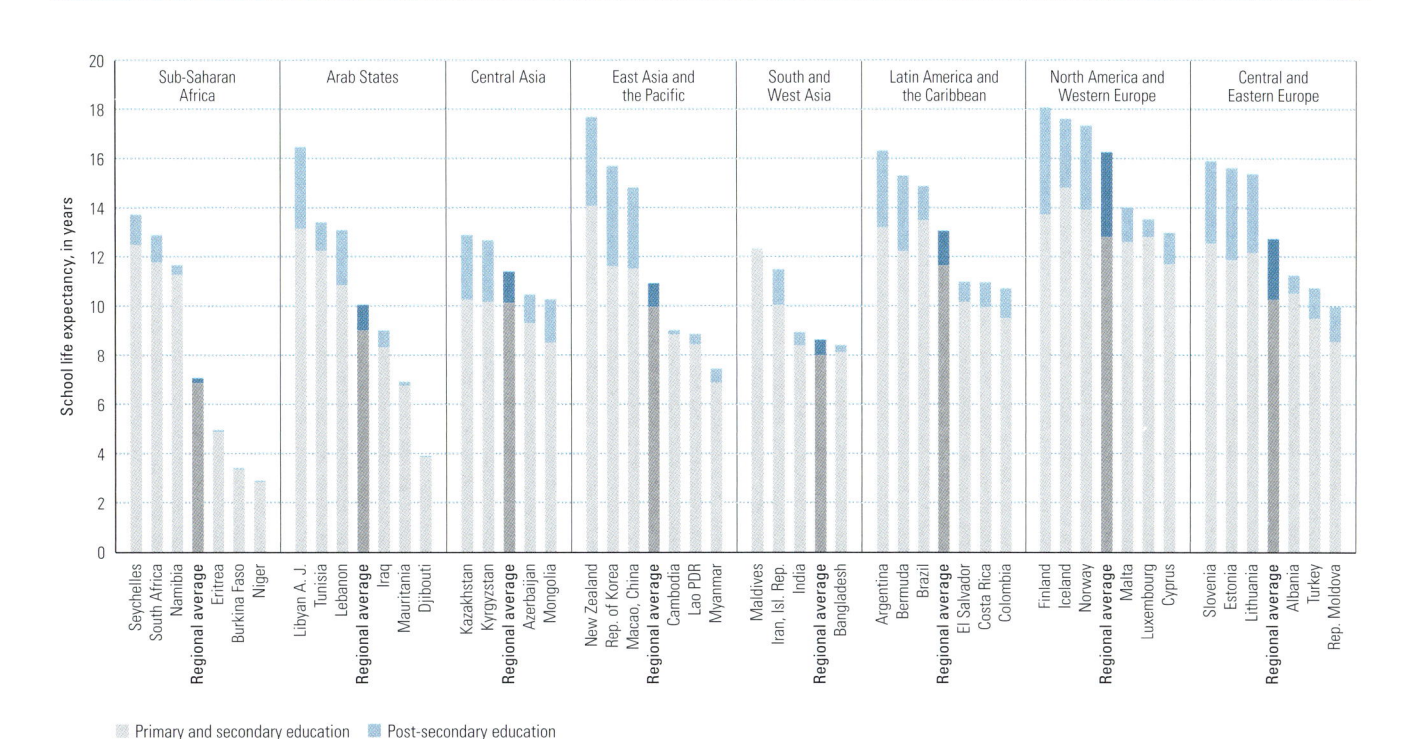

Figure 3.21: School life expectancy by region, 2001 (regional averages and countries with the highest and lowest values)

Notes: Regional averages are weighted by population of children aged 5. 194 countries and 99.7% of world population are covered. All regions are covered by more than 98% of their population. See source table for detailed country notes.
Source: Statistical annex, Table 17; UNESCO Institute for Statistics database.

Teachers, finance and quality

The relatively high primary-school enrolment ratios around the world today are the result of rapid expansion of school supply over the twentieth century, especially in the second half. There is much debate about the relationship between, on the one hand, the rapid increases in enrolment and in the quantity of education provided (in terms of years of school completed), and, on the other, the quality of that education, whether in terms of a school system's characteristics or of the achievement of its pupils. The view that emphasis on access to education has led to inadequate attention being paid to quality, and that improving the quality of existing schools should now be a policy priority, is gaining ground. But even if some trade-off exists between the coverage and the level of per-pupil funding of a school system, this does not necessarily imply that developing countries have to choose between further expanding access to primary schooling and improving its quality.

When expressed as a percentage of GDP, the increase in education expenditure required to improve both coverage and per-pupil funding is not insurmountable when seen in light of total government expenditure. The real issue is the political economy of allocating public expenditure among sectors, rather than constraints on education budgets per se. Moreover, there is much scope for reducing inefficiency in existing school systems. In particular, developing ECCE programmes while improving the functioning of primary schools is likely to result in more timely entry into the school system and less grade repetition, thus allowing additional enrolment. And while per-pupil funding may not increase as quickly as enrolment when, for instance, major school construction programmes are under way, some countries may have both higher enrolment ratios and better schools than others, as a result of policies giving priority to education.

Increased concern for education quality has been reflected in growing pressure to collect data on,

There is much scope for reducing inefficiency in existing school systems

and develop adequate indicators of, school quality. Some of this pressure results from global initiatives such as Education for All. Change is also taking place at the national level, where policy-makers need better understanding of the factors that are most effective in improving learning outcomes. Given the discussion of the concept of the quality of education in Chapter 1, it should be clear that no single or simple set of indicators will enable policy-makers to assess progress towards improved quality. Instead, a range of indicators is needed to capture the complex, multi-level nature of the concept. Moreover, some aspects of a broadened vision of education quality are difficult to quantify in internationally comparable ways.

This section looks at indicators related to quality that are readily available and internationally comparable. It thus tends to focus on inputs, such as numbers and characteristics of teachers, and the level and allocation of education funding. Many other aspects, such as teaching practices and teacher incentives, are known to matter just as much (see Chapter 2), but data on them are insufficient. Resources, however, are a necessary albeit insufficient condition for learning, and the inadequate resource levels found in many developing countries imply that school reform should include additional funding, alongside attention to more complex considerations. Considerable evidence indicates not only that children from poor families have less access to education than those who are better off, but also that those who do participate receive a lower-quality education. Even countries that have achieved some degree of equity in terms of overall access still tend to favour certain population groups or areas in the allocation of education resources.

> How teachers are prepared for teaching is a critical indicator of education quality

Monitoring the quality of teachers and teaching

As Chapter 2 demonstrates, teacher and teaching quality, broadly defined, have often been identified as the most important organizational factors associated with student achievement. Unfortunately, they are difficult to measure and monitor, as Box 3.3 shows.

How teachers are prepared for teaching is a critical indicator of education quality. Preparing teachers for the challenges of a changing world means equipping them with subject-specific expertise, effective teaching practices, an understanding of technology and the ability to work collaboratively with other teachers, members of the community and parents.

Teacher qualifications, training and content knowledge in primary education

Available data suggest that large proportions of primary-school teachers lack adequate academic qualifications, training and content knowledge, especially in developing countries. This suggests that much pre-service training may be ineffective. Pre-service training usually combines theoretical and content knowledge with teaching practice in schools but there are wide variations in the relative weight given to these two elements and in their modes of delivery. In some countries, where there is a pressure to recruit new teachers quickly, the length of college-based training is shortening and the sequencing of practical and academic training changing (Lewin, 1999).

As a starting point, Figure 3.22 shows the level of education (classified according to ISCED levels)

Box 3.3 How can we measure teacher quality?

Teacher quality is extremely difficult to define, as it depends not only on observable and stable indicators but also on behaviour and the nature of the relationship teachers maintain with their pupils or students. Teaching qualifications, however, are administratively defined; they are grounded on relatively objective assessments of skills, abilities and knowledge that are recognized as important (though this is subject to continuous debate). Moreover, despite the measurement limitations and data challenges, 'teacher qualifications' is conceptually and practically more approachable than 'teacher quality' or 'teaching quality'.

Potential indicators deal with:
- academic qualification;
- pedagogical training;
- years of service/experience;
- ability or aptitude;
- content knowledge.

The last two can be measured through individual assessment.

These indicators have the advantage that they can be governed by policy. Governments can set and regulate standards on academic qualifications, adjust salary scales so that experience is rewarded and improve teacher development and motivation through testing and rewarding of competence.

Source: Kasprzyk (1999)

The quality of education

Figure 3.22: Percentage of primary-school teachers meeting national qualification standards in sub-Saharan Africa, 2001

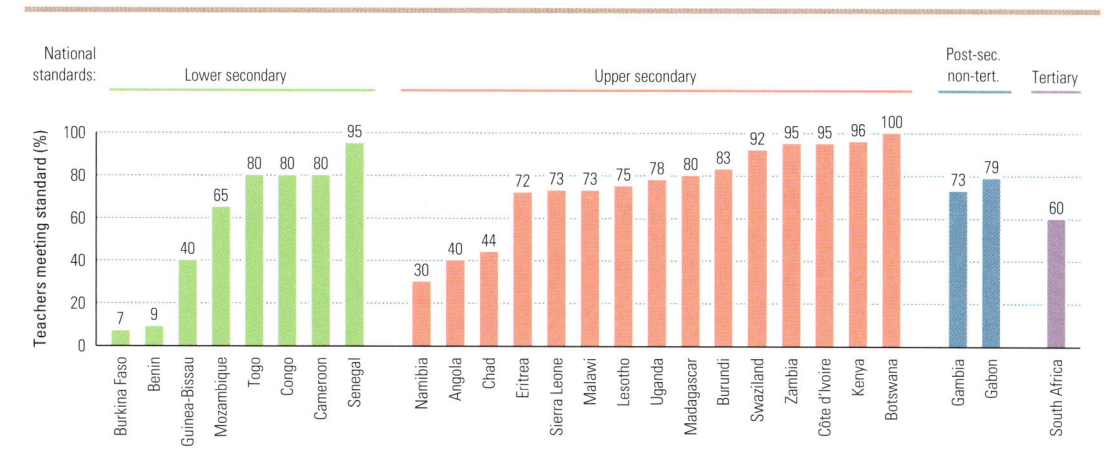

National standards: Lower secondary | Upper secondary | Post-sec. non-tert. | Tertiary

Teachers meeting standard (%):
- Burkina Faso: 7 (Lower secondary)
- Benin: 9
- Guinea-Bissau: 40
- Mozambique: 65
- Togo: 80
- Congo: 80
- Cameroon: 80
- Senegal: 95
- Namibia: 30 (Upper secondary)
- Angola: 40
- Chad: 44
- Eritrea: 72
- Sierra Leone: 73
- Malawi: 73
- Lesotho: 75
- Uganda: 78
- Madagascar: 80
- Burundi: 83
- Swaziland: 92
- Zambia: 95
- Côte d'Ivoire: 95
- Kenya: 96
- Botswana: 100
- Gambia: 73 (Post-sec. non-tert.)
- Gabon: 79
- South Africa: 60 (Tertiary)

Notes: Lower secondary = ISCED 2; Upper secondary = ISCED 3; Post-secondary non-tertiary = ISCED 4; Tertiary = ISCED 5.
Source: UNESCO Institute for Statistics (2001)

---

required by national qualification standards for entering primary school teaching and the proportion of the teaching force that meets this requirement, in twenty-six sub-Saharan African countries. National standards vary considerably, from lower secondary (equivalent to nine or ten grades of basic schooling plus one or two years of training) to a tertiary degree (in South Africa). The average number of years of academic study and teacher training required to become a primary school teacher ranges from just over twelve years among countries where the standard is lower secondary to seventeen years where it is higher education.

How well countries meet their own standards can also vary considerably. Less than 10% of the teaching force meets even the low minimum standard of lower secondary in Benin or Burkina Faso, and many other countries fall short of standards set at the upper secondary level, notably Angola, Chad and Namibia. In Botswana, Côte d'Ivoire, Kenya and Zambia, however, almost the entire teaching force reaches the upper secondary standard.

Furthermore, while the growing supply of educated youth in most countries may be thought to imply that newly recruited teachers will have higher qualification levels, the proportion of new primary-school teachers meeting national standards has actually been falling in several countries. For example, only 30% of teachers in their first year of experience met the standards (post-secondary non-tertiary) in the Gambia. The proportions were even lower in Botswana (10%), Lesotho (11%) and Chad (19%), where the standard was an upper-secondary qualification, and in Togo (2%), Guinea-Bissau (15%) and Cameroon (15%), where it was lower-secondary. This phenomenon may reflect the increasingly common practice of recruiting teachers without the necessary qualifications in response to pressures caused by expanding levels of enrolment.

Further evidence comes from primary-school surveys conducted in 1995 in fourteen of the

Table 3.5: Primary teacher qualification and training levels in fourteen low-income countries, 1995

	Teachers with nine years of education or less (%)	Teachers with no training (%)
Bangladesh	44	18
Benin	92	1
Bhutan	30	8
Burkina Faso	70	27
Cape Verde	87	35
Equat. Guinea	77	8
Ethiopia	0	13
Madagascar	46	10
Maldives	89	22
Nepal	32	3
Togo	77	41
Uganda	91	50
U. R. Tanzania	91	0
Zambia	24	14

Source: Schleicher, Siniscalco and Postlethwaite (1995)

The proportion of new primary-school teachers meeting national standards has actually been falling in several countries

110 / CHAPTER 3

Figure 3.23: Trained teachers in primary education, 2001

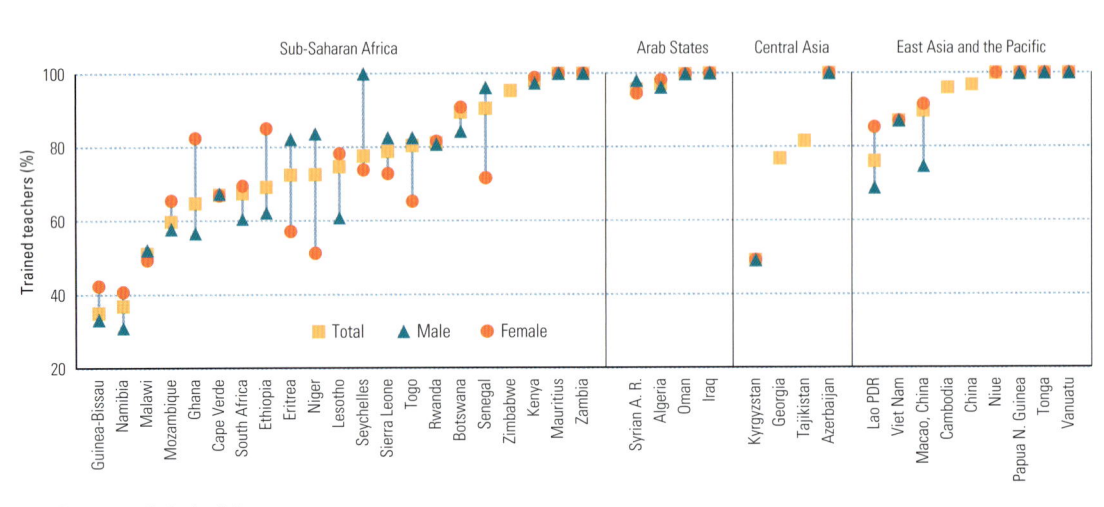

Note: See source table for detailed country notes.
Source: Statistical annex, Table 13A.

In Brazil, most trained teachers tend to be in the parts of the country that need them least

world's poorest countries – in sub-Saharan Africa and South and West Asia. Table 3.5 shows variable but generally low levels of education and training among primary-school teachers in these countries. Interestingly, in most of them a majority of teachers had received at least some training even though they had very low academic qualifications (an extreme case is Benin, where 92% of primary-school teachers had less than ten years of education but 99% had received training). Ethiopia and Uganda stand out, the former owing to above average and the latter to below average proportions of educated and trained teachers.

Figure 3.23 broadens the picture, as it covers seventy-two countries with data on teacher training for 2001. Although the coverage is insufficient for general patterns to emerge (e.g. no data are available for OECD countries or most large countries of Latin America and the Caribbean), large disparities between countries can be seen; a minority of countries provide training to almost all their teachers. Several countries, notably in sub-Saharan Africa, feature large gender gaps, though sometimes it is women who are favoured (this is the case to some extent in one-third of the sample).

Having low average levels of teacher qualification and training leaves much scope for unequal distribution within countries. As a striking example, Figure 3.24 displays the relationship between the proportion of primary-school teachers who meet national qualification standards and the adult illiteracy rate for the twenty-seven states of Brazil. High levels of adult illiteracy are a good indicator of socio-economic and educational deprivation, for they reflect the history of local school systems as well as what families invest in children's education. Most trained teachers tend to be in the parts of the country that need them least. In the states with, at worst, 12% illiteracy, 60% or more of the teachers meet the national training standards,

Figure 3.24: Primary teachers meeting national standards and adult illiteracy in Brazil, by state, 2000

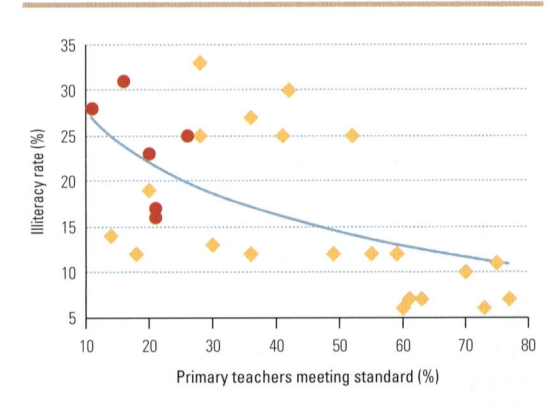

Note: Red dots represent the states of the Nordeste region.
Source: INEP (2002).

The quality of education

Figure 3.23 (continued)

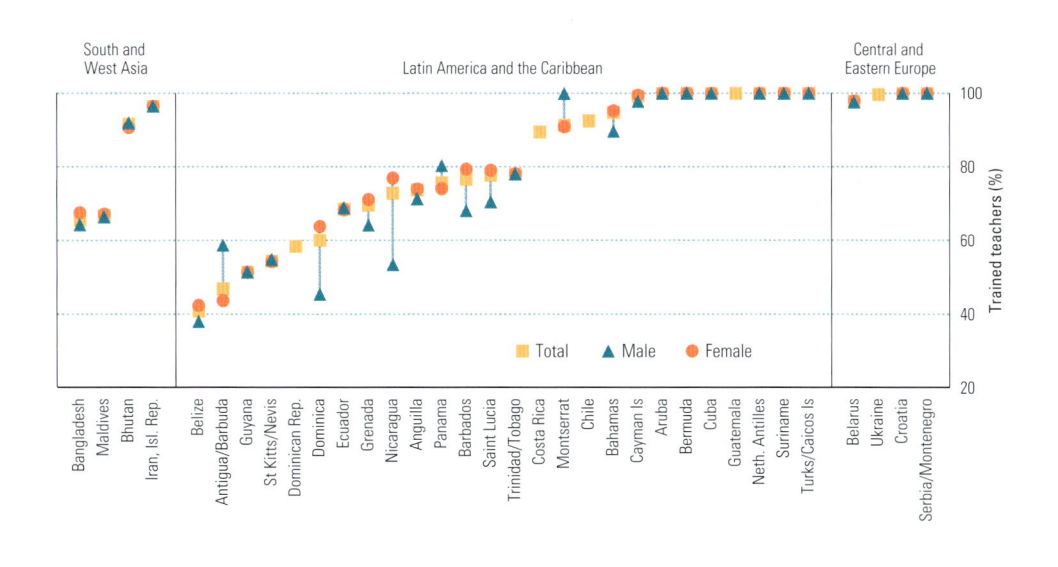

but elsewhere the situation is extremely variable. The six states of the Nordeste region, generally the most disadvantaged area of Brazil, have among the lowest proportions of trained teachers.

Teachers' formal qualifications however may not reflect teacher quality as adequately as the ability to make the best use of learning materials, students' work and their own subject knowledge. These skills are even more salient in especially difficult situations, such as countries in conflict (see Box 3.4).

Box 3.4 Determining and promoting good-quality teaching in especially difficult circumstances

In many conflict and post-conflict countries, the education system cannot provide for all children. The system may have collapsed or, in a situation like that of Afghanistan, the Ministry of Education's post-conflict reconstruction process cannot keep pace with increased demand. In addition, refugee children, especially those living in camps, are unlikely to be served directly by the state education system. In such situations, communities, often with the support of international bodies, may take the situation into their own hands and recruit community members as teachers. Although they may receive some training, many will have completed only primary schooling.

Can good-quality teaching and learning take place in such situations, where traditional indicators of teacher quality such as academic qualifications seem less relevant? The International Rescue Committee (IRC) – an NGO based in the United States that works with refugees – helps underqualified teachers set locally appropriate objectives for quality teaching and identify indicators (teacher methodologies, behaviours and activities) that can help them assess whether these objectives are met.

In a refugee camp school in northern Ethiopia, where the IRC runs education and other programmes, few teachers have completed secondary school or feel confident in a role for which they are underqualified, though self-confidence is an important aspect of being a good teacher. Other elements of good teaching that are critical in classrooms where children have been affected by war are creativity and the promotion of social cohesion. Where children of different ethnic groups with different languages, backgrounds and experiences are living and attending school together, it is important to promote understanding – for instance by having some children translate to ensure that all have understood. Such creativity is not only important in encouraging children's freedom of expression, it can also be more generally important in resource-poor environments. Teaching a science lesson with minimal resources and with only locally available materials often requires great originality.

Source: Kirk and Winthrop (2004)

Teacher subject knowledge is crucial and has been shown to be a good predictor of student achievement (Darling-Hammond, 2000). In many developing countries, levels of subject knowledge are a problem. A recent study in seven southern African countries finds that some primary-school mathematics teachers possess only basic numeracy, actually scoring less in tests than students (Postlethwaite, 2004). Provision of training and other forms of support based on relevant quality indicators can help build the confidence of undertrained teachers and enable them to become more competent.

Teacher absenteeism

Teacher absenteeism, a persistent problem in many countries, reduces the quality of education and results in a waste of resources. In 2003, investigators for a World Bank study who made random visits to 200 primary schools in India found no teaching activity in half of them. Up to 45% of teachers in Ethiopia had been absent at least one day in the week before a visit – 10% of them for three days or more, and in Uganda and Zambia the shares of teachers who had been absent in the previous week were 26% and 17%, respectively (World Bank, 2004j). This continues to confirm the findings of school surveys conducted in fourteen low-income countries in 1995, which showed high rates of absenteeism, especially in sub-Saharan African countries, e.g. the United Republic of Tanzania (38%), Uganda (30%) and Zambia (25%), and in South and West Asia, e.g. Bhutan (14%), Nepal (11%) and Bangladesh (8%), (Schleicher, Siniscalco and Postlethwaite, 1995).

High levels of teacher absenteeism generally indicate severe dysfunctions in the school system, but they may have many different direct causes. Lax professional standards and lack of support and control by education authorities are major issues in many countries. Education policy deficiencies can also play a role, for instance where teachers are reassigned to other classrooms or schools (Jessee et al., 2003), must travel to obtain their monthly pay (Moses, 2000), or need to take a second job to supplement insufficient salaries (Michaelowa, 2002). Appropriate support and better incentive structures may help reduce levels of teacher absenteeism.

The high level of prevalence of HIV/AIDS in a growing number of developing countries, especially in sub-Saharan Africa, is a major factor influencing teacher absenteeism and lack of effectiveness, sometimes leading to high teaching-staff attrition rates (see Box 3.5).

Box 3.5 HIV/AIDS and teacher attrition trends in Kenya

The impact of the HIV/AIDS epidemic on the teaching force has at least three dimensions. First, teacher mortality rate is likely to grow over time, assuming the infection rate is similar to that in the general population. Second, since the private sector has traditionally recruited skilled human resources from the teaching profession, AIDS deaths in the general workforce could result in a further drain on the availability of skilled teachers. Third, the long, debilitating illness that generally precedes death from AIDS implies loss of teacher contact time, quality, continuity and experience (Badcock-Walters et al., 2003).

The first aspect is perhaps the easiest to quantify. In Kenya, for example, the Ministry of Health has stated that HIV/AIDS has impaired the effectiveness of the education sector by increasing the rate of teachers' deaths and attrition over the past decade. According to the Teachers Service Commission, the reported number of teacher deaths rose from 450 in 1995 to 1,400 in 1999. Although data on causes of teacher mortality are not kept, the high increase is probably due to HIV/AIDS.

A survey in four districts in Kenya found that in Kisumu, the district most affected by HIV/AIDS, the primary teacher attrition rate had risen from 1% in 1998 to around 5% in 1999 and had remained at that level since. At that rate, a quarter of the teaching force would disappear within five years. While it is difficult to say for certain how many deaths are AIDS-related, most are occurring in districts with high HIV prevalence rates, supporting the hypothesis that AIDS is a major cause of mortality. The retirement rate also increased, from less than 0.5% in 1998 to 2% in 2001. The hypothesis that some of the extra retirements were on medical grounds is quite plausible.

Source: Carr-Hill (2004a)

The quality of education

Table 3.6: Distribution of countries according to primary pupil/teacher ratios, 2001

Regions	Below 15	15-24	25-34	35-44	45-54	55 and above
Sub-Saharan Africa	Seychelles (1)	Mauritius (1)	Botswana, Cape Verde, Ghana, Kenya, Namibia, Sao Tome and Principe, Swaziland (7)	Togo, Angola, South Africa, Sierra Leone, Gambia, Zimbabwe, Liberia, Comoros, Nigeria, Niger, Equat. Guinea, Côte d'Ivoire, Eritrea (13)	Guinea-Bissau, Zambia, U. Rep. Tanzania, Guinea, Burkina Faso, Lesotho, Madagascar, Senegal, Burundi, Gabon, Benin, Uganda (12)	Congo, Mali, Ethiopia, Rwanda, Cameroon, Malawi, Mozambique, Chad, Central African Republic (9)
Arab States	Libyan A. J., Saudi Arabia, Qatar, Kuwait (4)	U. A. Emirates, Bahrain, Lebanon, Jordan, Iraq, Tunisia, Egypt, Oman, Syrian A. R. (9)	Algeria, Morocco, Palestinian A. T., Djibouti (4)	Mauritania (1)		
Central Asia	Georgia (1)	Azerbaijan, Armenia, Kazakhstan, Tajikistan, Kyrgyzstan (5)	Mongolia (1)			
East Asia and the Pacific	Brunei Darussalam (1)	Marshall Is, New Zealand, Palau, Cook Islands, Niue, Thailand, China, Malaysia, Japan, Tonga, Indonesia (11)	Samoa, Tuvalu, Viet Nam, Macao (China), Fiji, Vanuatu, Lao PDR, Rep. of Korea, Myanmar (9)	Papua New Guinea, Philippines (2)	Timor-Leste (1)	Cambodia (1)
South and West Asia		Maldives, Islamic Republic of Iran (2)		Bhutan, Nepal, India, Afghanistan, Pakistan (5)		Bangladesh (1)
Latin America and the Caribbean	Bermuda, Cuba, Cayman Islands (3)	Barbados, St Kitts/Nevis, Bahamas, Br. Virgin Is, Anguilla, St Vincent/Grenadines, Turks/Caicos Is, Dominica, Antigua/Barbuda, Aruba, Trinidad/Tobago, Suriname, Montserrat, Argentina, Neth. Antilles, Uruguay, Grenada, Belize, Brazil, Saint Lucia, Costa Rica, Panama, Ecuador (23)	Boliva, El Salvador, Colombia, Guyana, Mexico, Peru, Guatemala, Chile, Jamaica, Honduras (10)	Nicaragua, Dominican Rep. (2)		
North America and Western Europe	San Marino, Netherlands, Denmark, Italy, Portugal, Iceland, Sweden, Luxembourg, Andorra, Belgium, Israel, Greece, Austria, Switzerland, Spain, Germany (16)	United States, Finland, United Kingdom, Canada, France, Cyprus, Malta, Ireland, Monaco (9)				
Central and Eastern Europe	Hungary, Slovenia, Estonia, Latvia, Poland (5)	Lithuania, Belarus, Bulgaria, Russian Fed., Czech Rep., Romania, Croatia, Slovakia, Rep. Moldova, Ukraine, Serbia/Montenegro, TFYR Macedonia, Albania (13)				
Total number of countries 182	31	74	30	23	13	11

Note: In each box, countries are listed in increasing order of pupil/teacher ratio.
Source: Statistical annex, Table 13A.

About 815 primary-school teachers in Zambia died from AIDS in 2000 – the equivalent of 45% of the teachers trained that year

The impact on efforts to extend or improve the national school system can be dramatic. For example, it is estimated that 815 primary-school teachers in Zambia died from AIDS in 2000 – the equivalent of 45% of the teachers trained that year. The disease's impact on school systems is a major reason that HIV/AIDS has wide-ranging effects over the long run. With epidemics developing in many countries of South and West Asia, East Asia and the Pacific, Central Asia, and Central and Eastern Europe, HIV/AIDS is a major global constraint on the provision of good-quality education.

Teacher deployment and education outcomes

Besides qualifications and training, the number and distribution of teachers are important policy parameters helping to determine the quality of education pupils and students receive. At the school level, the most visible element of teacher deployment is class size, or the number of pupils a teacher has to teach. While the impact of class size on educational outcomes remains a matter of debate (see Chapter 2) and depends on the pedagogy used, the very large class sizes observed in primary schools in many developing countries are clearly not conducive to adequate learning. Children in areas not yet covered by primary-school systems probably need smaller class sizes than the average because they are often first-generation learners from underprivileged social groups and are more likely to belong to a minority whose language is not used as a medium of instruction. Furthermore, curricula are usually divided into grades, requiring one teacher per grade for effective teaching or requiring special training in the case of multigrade teaching. While data on class sizes and the number of teachers per grade in each school are not widely available, teacher deployment policies can be approached through the pupil/teacher ratio.

High PTRs may signify an overstretched teaching staff, while low ratios may mean there is additional capacity. However, the PTR measured at the national level can mask disparities among regions and schools. For instance, the national primary PTR in Mauritania is 35:1, but some schools may have one teacher for every ten pupils while others have one for every sixty pupils. Moreover, the ratio depends on an accurate count of teachers who have classroom responsibilities, and should be adjusted, as far as possible, to account for part-time teaching, teaching in shifts and multigrade classes.

Keeping in mind these caveats, Table 3.6 provides a classification of countries according to national PTR. The ratios are low (less than 20:1) in regions where enrolment ratios are high – in particular North America and Western Europe, Central and Eastern Europe, and Central Asia – and high in regions where enrolments are low, notably South and West Asia and sub-Saharan Africa, with median values of 40:1 and 44:1, respectively. This implies that teacher numbers are a problem in the very countries that most need more teachers in order to increase significantly the coverage of their primary school systems. In the Arab States, East Asia and the Pacific and in Latin America and the Caribbean, most countries have fifteen to thirty-four pupils per teacher. Unacceptably high PTRs exist in many schools and districts of individual countries, of course, but this is more a matter of the distribution of teachers than of their total number.

Figure 3.25, which shows the evolution of the median PTR by region from 1990 to 1998 and 2001, for countries with data available for all three years, makes these regional patterns even

Figure 3.25: Median pupil/teacher ratios in primary education by region, 1990, 1998 and 2001 (countries with data for all three years; number per region in brackets)

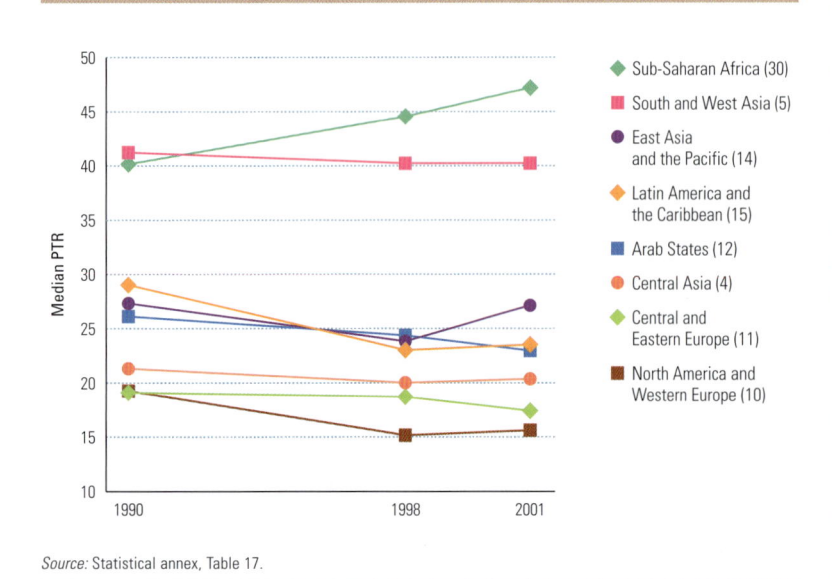

Source: Statistical annex, Table 17.

Box 3.6 Expanding access to primary education: quantity and quality factors

How do trends in enrolment, teacher recruitment and pupil/teacher ratios relate? The experience of three countries sheds some light on the kind of trade-offs policy-makers face, e.g. between expanding the school system and maintaining stable PTRs, or between improving education quality by reducing the PTR or increasing expenditure on other items. Between 1998 and 2001, the number of primary-school pupils in Cambodia rose substantially, by 28%, and the primary-school NER increased from 82% to 86%. The number of teachers increased by only 9%, so the PTR rose from 48:1 to 56:1. Although public spending on education increased steadily, education policies sought to improve education quality by channelling existing funding into retraining teachers, buying more up-to-date textbooks, reforming evaluation methods and improving infrastructure. Hence teacher recruitment was limited and teachers could not keep pace with the growth in enrolment (Cambodia, 1999).

In Ethiopia during the same period, the number of pupils rose by 40%, boosting the primary-school NER from 36% to 46%. Policy decisions led to the primary PTR rising by 24%, from 46:1 to 57:1, as the number of teachers increased by only 13%. The Ministry of Education decided to allow class size to increase in order to reallocate funding to books, desks and other needs, with the aim of increasing the effectiveness of existing teachers and the efficiency of the overall system (Ethiopia Ministry of Education, 1999).

Unlike most sub-Saharan African countries, Togo experienced a substantial decrease in the primary PTR between 1998 and 2001, from 41:1 to 35:1, while its NER rose from 90% to 92%. While total education expenditure is reported to have increased by 18% between 1998 and 2000, one-fourth of all new teachers were placed on short-term contracts that paid significantly less than those of their permanent counterparts (Kigotho, 2004). While the decision to hire more teachers resulted in declining PTRs, which should improve overall instructional and educational quality, a study conducted in Togo suggests that the contract teachers were less effective than other teachers (Vegas and De Laat, 2003).

---

clearer. It shows PTRs that are relatively low and have been declining or fairly stable in all regions except sub-Saharan Africa, where the median rose from 40:1 in 1990 to 47:1 in 2001. The situation in this region may be explained by demography: high population growth translates into larger cohorts of potential primary-school pupils and increasing enrolment – with which the school system cannot keep pace. In three sub-Saharan countries that saw an especially steep rise in PTRs between 1998 and 2001 – Ethiopia (23%), Nigeria (28%) and the United Republic of Tanzania (22%) – efforts to widen access to primary education partly explain the rise. Indeed, the PTR increased in almost every country where the net enrolment ratio increased, e.g. in Ethiopia from 46:1 to 57:1 and the United Republic of Tanzania from 38:1 to 46:1. More generally, in sub-Saharan African countries whose PTR grew over the decade, that growth slightly accelerated after 1998. The PTR also increased between 1998 and 2001 in East Asia and the Pacific (from 24:1 to 27:1), reversing the trend of the early and mid-1990s.

Once again, while countries with a strong political commitment towards education have both high enrolment and low PTRs, those starting with low enrolment ratios may face severe quantity/quality trade-offs, in the short run. These can be avoided only if countries can mobilize substantially more resources for education or recruit additional teachers at lower salaries without compromising teaching quality. The latter course has been tried in many countries, but more evidence as to its effectiveness is needed than is yet available (see also Chapter 4). Indeed, expansion of educational opportunity and the concomitant demand for teachers tend to put quality at risk if entry requirements for teachers are relaxed and/or the workload of the current teaching force increases (see Box 3.6). In countries where PTRs are already very high, further demands on teachers could be detrimental to teacher capacity and morale and result in diminished learning outcomes among students (see the Appendix, which shows the relationship between PTRs and learning outcomes).

Figure 3.26 shows that, in general, low PTRs are associated with high survival rates to the last grade of primary school. However, the dispersion in the survival rate is higher within the group of

High population growth causes increasing enrolment, with which the school system cannot keep pace

116 / CHAPTER 3

Figure 3.26: Primary education: pupil/teacher ratios and survival to the last grade, 2001

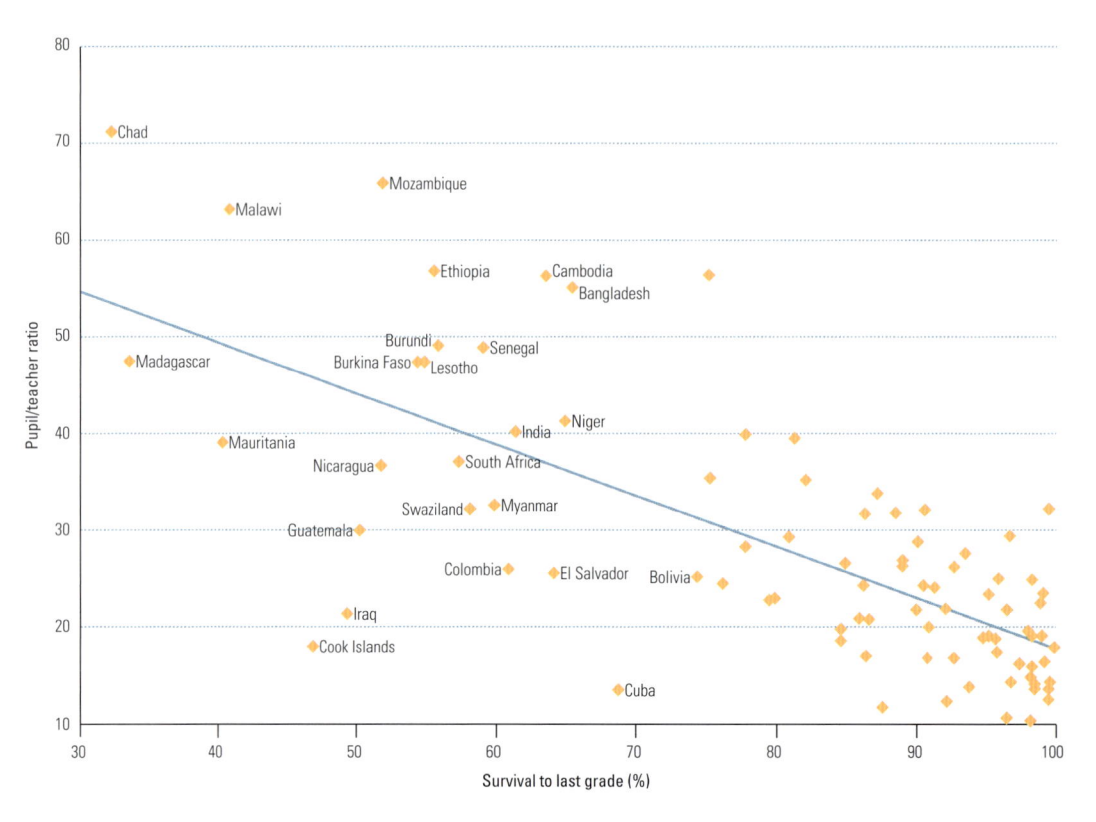

Notes: Countries with a survival rate of less than 75% are labelled.
See source tables for detailed country notes.
Source: Statistical annex, Tables 7 and 13A.

In Chad, only one in three pupils starting school reaches the final grade

countries with high PTRs than within that with low PTRs. Thus, the negative relationship appears to be between these two groups rather than within them. The PTR here should be interpreted more as a general indicator of the state of the school system than as a cause of low survival rates, as countries with comparable PTRs achieve dramatically different survival rates. Many other factors enter the picture. On the other hand, it is difficult to believe that high PTRs are not an issue in countries such as Chad, where the PTR exceeds 70:1 and where only one in three pupils starting school reaches the final grade.

When money matters: investing in education

While teachers are the most important resource in education, it is worth looking at other resources available to schools that have an important impact on prospects for high-quality teaching. Detailed data on factors such as school buildings and equipment or teaching/learning materials may not be available for a large sample of countries, nor would they be very informative on their own. Aggregate expenditure on education, however, is a good indicator of policy-makers' commitment to education quality.

Figure 3.27 presents total public expenditure on education as a percentage of GDP, showing regional medians and the highest and lowest country figures. This indicator of policy preferences may not have the same significance everywhere. Differences in relative prices of education inputs, allocation of funding between teacher salaries and other inputs, and demographic structure mean different countries may have to spend at different levels to achieve comparable quality. For example, Germany and India spend comparable proportions of their GDP on education (slightly more than 4%) but Germany's wealthy, ageing population has

The quality of education

Figure 3.27: Public expenditure on education as a percentage of GDP, by education level, 2001
(regional medians and countries with the highest and lowest values)

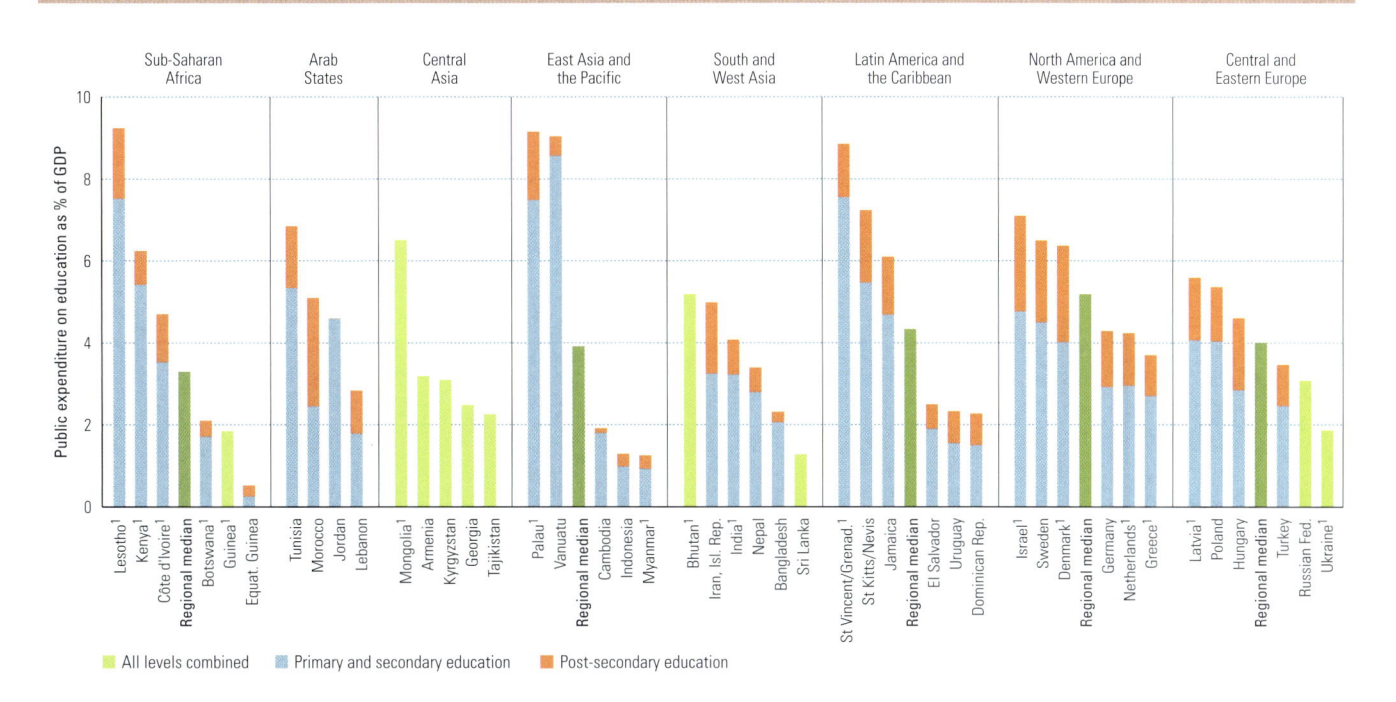

■ All levels combined   ■ Primary and secondary education   ■ Post-secondary education

Note: Regional medians based on the following country numbers: sub-Saharan Africa: 19; East Asia and the Pacific: 17; Latin America and the Caribbean: 20; North America and Western Europe: 17; Central and Eastern Europe: 8. Regional medians not calculated for Arab States, Central Asia, and South and West Asia because data were available for too few countries.
1. Data are for 2000.
Source: UNESCO Institute for Statistics (2004b).

access to a completely different education system than India's poor, young and still quickly growing population. Regional patterns are consistent with those observed for enrolment ratios and teacher deployment: the highest median is that of North America and Western Europe and the lowest that of sub-Saharan Africa. Given differences in GDP levels and the proportions of school-age children in the population, this implies dramatic differences in per-pupil resources between the two regions. Several large countries of South and West Asia and of East Asia and the Pacific are also notable for low levels of expenditure. The high levels found in a few island states can be explained by specific factors. For example, the GDP of the countries may be small, or they do not benefit from economies of scale because their school-age population is small, or students have to leave the country for higher education, implying substantial costs if this is subsidized by the state.

While most countries have predominantly public education systems, government expenditure is not total expenditure. A different picture would emerge if data on private expenditure on education were available. Countries have different mixes of public and private schooling, and a shift of emphasis from what *governments* invest in education to what *societies* invest is needed to take this into account. Household expenditure on education, for instance, is generally substantial even in many countries where at least primary schooling is officially provided free by the state. The share of private expenditure in primary and secondary education has been estimated at 42% in Jamaica, 33% in the Philippines, 30% in Chile, 24% in Indonesia and 21% in Colombia, to take but a few examples (UNESCO Institute for Statistics/OECD, 2003).

Figure 3.28 tracks trends in public expenditure on education during the late 1990s, showing changes in real expenditure in the relatively few countries that provided data for both 1998 and 2001. Spending levels were generally stable in North America and Western Europe but quite a few developing countries increased spending

Household expenditure on education is generally substantial even in countries where primary education is free

118 / CHAPTER 3

Figure 3.28: Change in total education expenditure in real terms, selected countries, 1998 to 2001

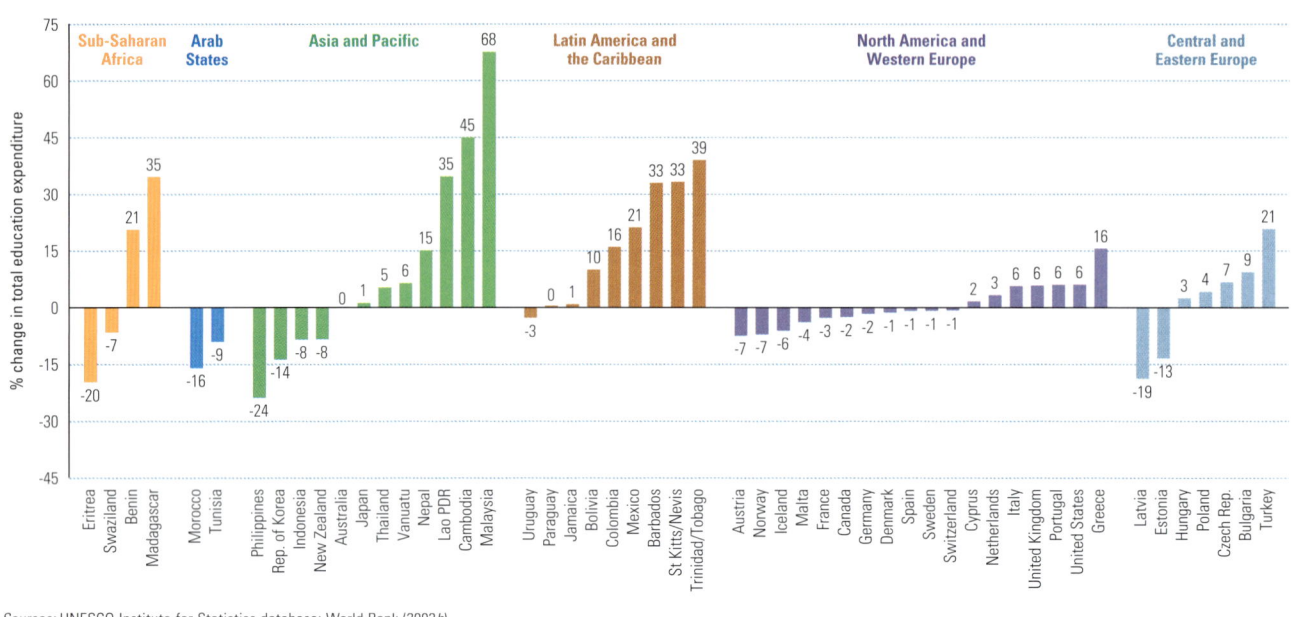

Sources: UNESCO Institute for Statistics database; World Bank (2003b).

Public/private partnerships raise quality and equity issues

considerably, notably in East Asia and the Pacific, and Latin America and the Caribbean. A few large countries reduced expenditure significantly, however, e.g. the Philippines (–24%) and Indonesia (–8%).

Public and private expenditures on education are often intertwined and complementary, notably where governments provide partial funding to private institutions. For instance, in Zimbabwe, 80% of primary-school pupils attend government-dependent private schools whose teachers are paid by the government, while other costs are borne by local communities. Such public/private partnerships are being promoted increasingly as a way to mitigate the impact of uncertainties and insufficiencies in public expenditure. They raise quality and equity issues, however, since communities differ in their ability to attract government expenditure as well as raise private funds.

The allocation of education expenditure matters a great deal in translating funds into education outcomes. Teachers' salaries tend to account for by far the greatest item of expenditure, especially in developing countries. Debates have been raging about differences in salary costs among countries and whether high salaries impede

efforts to expand and improve school systems so as to achieve EFA goals. Data on the share of primary teachers' salaries in total public current expenditure for primary education are available for fifty-one countries; among these, the shares exceed 90% in eleven countries. By comparison, figures for the share of textbooks and other teaching materials in public current expenditure for primary education, among the twenty countries providing such data, range from 0.8% in Belize to 12% in the Republic of Moldova. Clearly, teachers' salaries are a central issue in the political economy of education. More generally, it has been suggested that teacher-related inputs receive a disproportionate share of expenditure. Designing adequate salary and non-salary incentives to motivate teachers appears to be a priority, as the need to save resources for other inputs has to be balanced against the need to pay teachers well enough to attract and retain qualified individuals.

While the degree of causal relationship between education expenditure and outcomes has proved difficult to estimate (see Chapter 2), the two are clearly related. Based on results of tests administered to 15-year-old students as part of the Programme for International Student Assessment (PISA), Figure 3.29 shows that

The quality of education

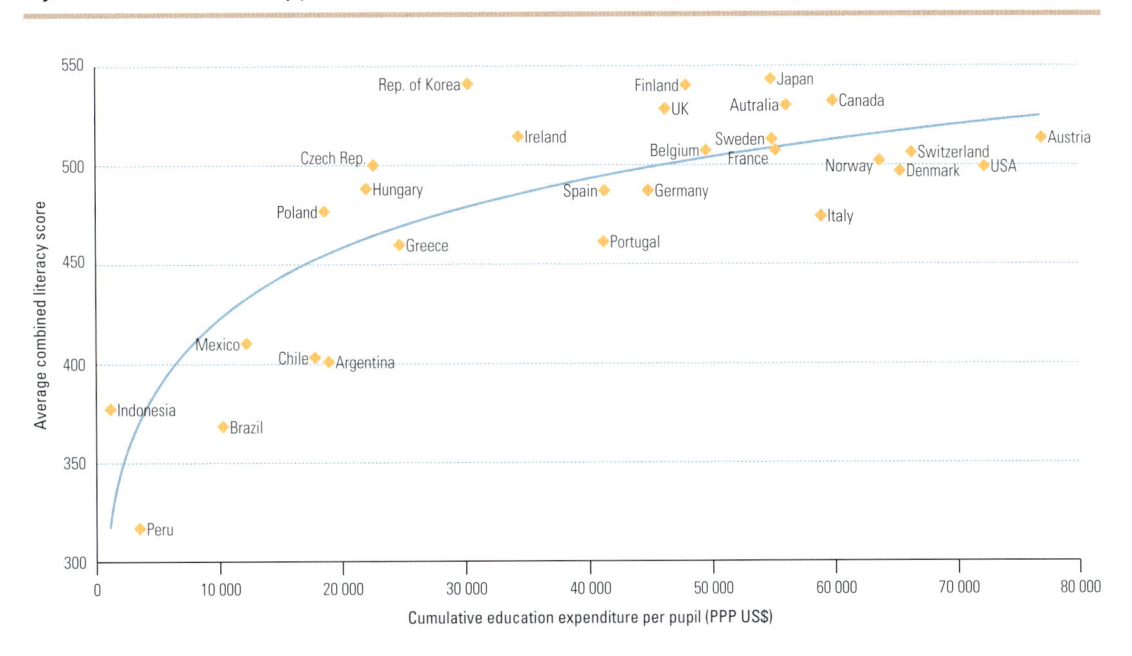

Figure 3.29: Combined literacy performance and cumulative education expenditure to age 15, PISA, 2000/2001

Source: UNESCO Institute for Statistics, based on OECD/UNESCO Institute for Statistics (2003).

students in countries that invest more in education (measured as cumulative per-pupil expenditure up to age 15) tend to have better literacy skills. The relationship is most evident for the few developing countries participating in the study, countries of Central and Eastern Europe and countries of Western Europe with relatively low expenditure levels, such as Greece and Ireland. Among other countries of Western Europe, variation in literacy scores is limited even as expenditure doubles from about PPP US$40,000 to about PPP US$80,000.[10] This suggests that resources can have a strong impact on outcomes when initial spending is low, but that the impact levels off as spending increases: additional resources might be wasted or devoted to other purposes than improving the kind of performance measured by literacy tests.

As the graph does not take into account factors such as the efficiency of resource allocation and use or family background, large differences in literacy scores may be observed between countries with similar spending levels, e.g. Poland and Chile or Argentina. Note also, that Mexico, Chile and Argentina reach similar average scores, even though Mexico spends only PPP US$12,189 per student, compared with PPP US$17,820 in Chile and PPP $18,893 in Argentina. The graph is also silent about whether there is a causal relationship or just a correlation between expenditure and performance. What matters is rather the consistency of regional patterns regarding the variables analysed in this chapter. Some countries have high achievement levels coupled with high enrolment ratios and high expenditure; others combine low enrolment with low expenditure and low achievement. Thus, while it is true that increasing resources remains fundamental in many countries, it is unlikely to improve performance significantly if other factors behind the differences are not addressed.

Quality and equality of learning

School systems are meant to produce a multitude of outputs, from equipping students with knowledge and cognitive skills to cultivating creative minds and fostering civic and moral values. Assessing their success in doing so is difficult, for two reasons. First, different stakeholders assign their own values to different objectives (World Bank, 2004j), and maximizing one kind of output may not be consistent with maximizing others: e.g. creative thinking may conflict with values emphasized by authoritarian

> **Increasing resources remains fundamental, but is unlikely to significantly improve performance if other factors are not addressed**

---

10. PPP means purchasing power parity. See glossary in Annexes.

curricula. Comparing school systems on the basis of one type of output may not do justice to those who emphasize other types. Second, some outputs are easier to measure and compare than others. It is relatively straightforward to measure mastery of simple skills through standardized testing, but more difficult to do the same for critical thinking and creativity.

Although knowledge and cognitive skills have not necessarily been the only priority of many government school systems, they have received the lion's share of attention in assessment exercises that have provided internationally comparable data. While each country has its own system of classroom-based assessment and public examinations, national and international assessments of student learning through standardized tests are increasingly used to monitor and evaluate the overall quality of education systems, to diagnose their relative strengths and weaknesses and to shed light on policy options that could enable good-quality learning for all (Kellaghan and Greaney, 2001). This section focuses on the evidence emerging from such assessments. It should be noted that although cognitive skills can be measured, defining which achievement levels can be deemed satisfactory is a complex issue (see Box 3.7).

Box 3.7 Defining low achievement

A number of studies have explicitly defined achievement or proficiency levels reflecting targets and expectations represented by national curricula or international standards. Where such definitions are available, the lowest band of test scores represents low achievement. Examples of such assessments include national assessments in four Latin American countries (Figure 3.30), the Southern and Eastern African Consortium for Monitoring Educational Quality (SACMEQ) (Figure 3.31) and the Programme for International Student Assessment (PISA), mentioned earlier (Figure 3.34).

Two other assessments, the *Programme d'Analyse des Systèmes Éducatifs de la CONFEMEN** (PASEC) (Figure 3.32) and the Progress in International Reading Literacy Study (PIRLS) (Figure 3.33), do not provide explicit achievement levels. For these assessments, students performing at or below the 25th percentile on the achievement scale are considered low achievers. For example, in PASEC, fewer than half of such students could correctly perform the following task:

Sort the numbers from highest to lowest value
    35.7   25.9   35.8   35.6

The SACMEQ study was first carried out in 1995 in seven countries. Fifty-nine items were used to test the reading literacy of grade 6 pupils in three types of text: narrative and expository texts and documents. National experts selected a subset of 'essential items' and established 'minimum' and 'desirable' performance levels based on how many essential items students answered correctly. The number of essential items and the cut-off-points for proficiency levels varied by country.

For example:

	Essential items	Number of correct answers required	
		Minimum level	Desirable level
Zimbabwe	34	14	17
Zambia	46	23	37

PIRLS was carried out in thirty-five countries in 2001, under the auspices of the International Association for the Evaluation of Educational Achievement. It assessed a range of reading comprehension strategies among grade 4 pupils in literary and informational texts. More than half the questions required students to generate and write answers; the rest were multiple-choice items. The 25th percentile on the reading literacy score is used as the cut-off point. The study report noted that items at or below this level required 'retrieval of explicitly stated details from the various literary and informational texts' and that 'generally this process needs little or no inferring or interpreting' (Mullis et al., 2003).

PISA studies the 'preparedness for adult life' of 15-year-olds, who are near the end of compulsory schooling in most OECD countries and a number of non-OECD countries. It assesses literacy, knowledge and skills in reading, mathematics and science. PISA aims to measure how well students can use what they have learned in school in real-life situations. The first PISA assessment, carried out in 2000 and 2002 in forty-three countries, focused on reading literacy. PISA divides reading proficiency performance into five levels, based on the complexity and difficulty of the tasks, with level 1 being the lowest level of reading ability and level 5 the highest. Students performing at level 1 may be able to complete only the most basic reading tasks.

* CONFEMEN stands for *Conférence des ministres de l'Education des pays ayant le français en partage* (Conference of Education Ministers of French-speaking Countries).

Figure 3.30: Grade 6 assessment results in four Latin American countries, various years

a. Nicaragua, 2002
- Proficient
- Intermediate
- Basic

b. Uruguay, 1999
- Highly satisfactory
- Satisfactory
- Unsatisfactory
- Highly unsatisfactory

c. El Salvador, 1999
- Superior
- Intermediate
- Basic

d. Honduras, 2002
- High
- Medium
- Low
- Insufficient

Sources: a. Nicaragua Ministry of Education (2003); b. Ravela (2002); c. El Salvador (2003); d. Honduras Ministry of Education (2003).

National and international assessments of cognitive skills

National assessment exercises such as those described in Box 3.7 are not easily comparable among countries, but they indicate how educational authorities evaluate the results of the system they manage. Figure 3.30 displays the percentage of pupils around the end of primary schooling who reached nationally defined performance levels in four countries of Latin America. In Nicaragua in 2002, 70% of students reached only the 'basic' level in language and more than 80% did so in mathematics. In Uruguay in 1999, the performance of 40% of sixth-graders was considered 'unsatisfactory' or 'highly unsatisfactory' in language and the share was 60% in mathematics. In El Salvador in 1999, 40% of sixth-graders reached only the 'basic' level in language, mathematics, science and social studies. In Honduras in 2002, 90% of sixth-graders performed at 'low' or 'insufficient' level in language and mathematics. Thus, whatever the relevance of the criteria used, all four countries consider the overall performance of their school system unsatisfactory.

The SACMEQ study showed poor performance among primary school students in reading literacy, according to standards established by national reading experts and sixth-grade teachers. In four out of seven countries, fewer than half of sixth-graders achieved the minimum level in reading (see Figure 3.31). Only 1% of sixth-graders tested in Malawi and 37% in

Figure 3.31: SACMEQ. Percentage of grade 6 pupils reaching proficiency levels in reading in seven African countries, 1995-1998

Country	Desirable	Minimum
Kenya	23	65
Zimbabwe	37	56
Mauritius	27	53
Zanzibar (U. R. Tanzania)	5	46
Namibia	8	26
Zambia	2	26
Malawi	1	22

Students reaching proficiency levels in reading (%)

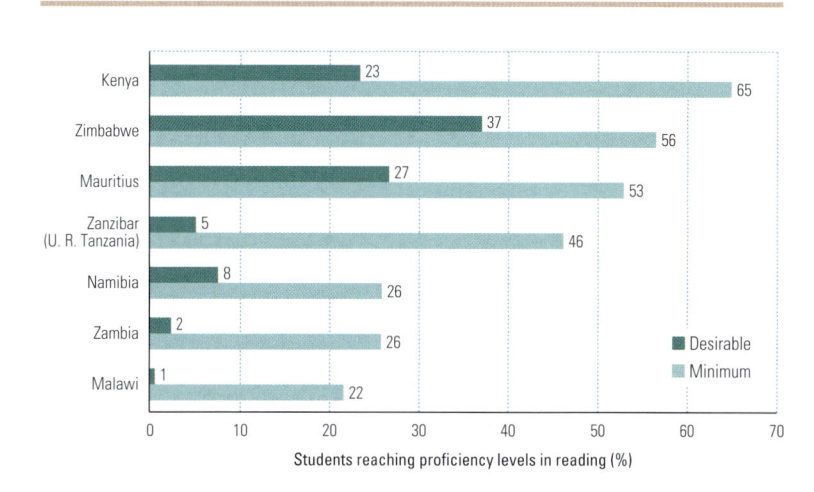

Note: Countries are ranked by proportion of pupils meeting minimum proficiency levels.
Sources: Kulpoo (1998); Machingaidze, Pfukani and Shumba (1998); Milner et al. (2001); Nassor and Mohammed (1998); Nkamba and Kanyika (1998); Nzomo, Kariuki and Guantai (2001); Voigts (1998).

122 / CHAPTER 3

Figure 3.32: PASEC. Percentage of grade 5 pupils with low achievement in six African countries, 1996-2001

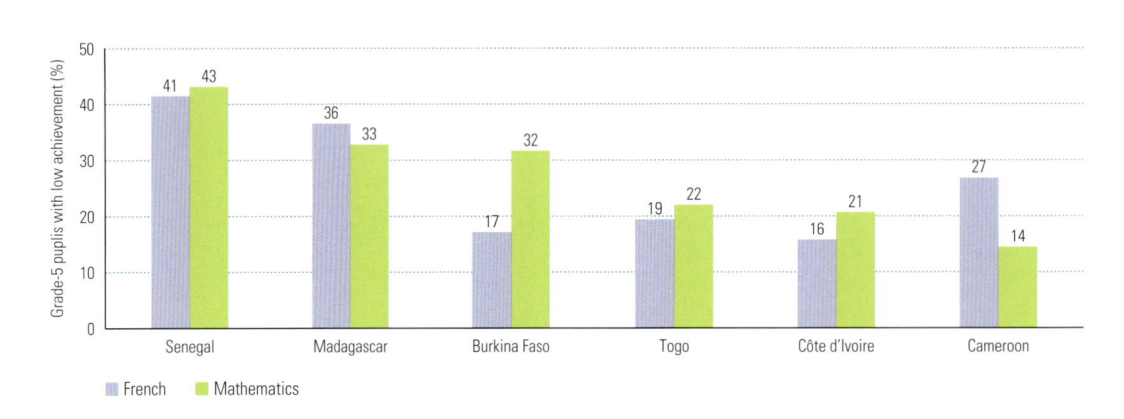

Country	French	Mathematics
Senegal	41	43
Madagascar	36	33
Burkina Faso	17	32
Togo	19	22
Côte d'Ivoire	16	21
Cameroon	27	14

Notes: The assessment was carried out in Burkina Faso, Cameroon, Côte d'Ivoire and Senegal in 1995/1996, in Madagascar in 1997/1998 and in Togo in 2000/2001. Countries are ranked by proportion of low-achieving pupils in mathematics. Low achievement is defined as a score below the 25th percentile on reading and mathematics.
Sources: Bernard (2003); Michaelowa (2004).

Figure 3.33: PIRLS. Percentage of grade 4 pupils in the lowest quartile of the international reading literacy scale, 2001

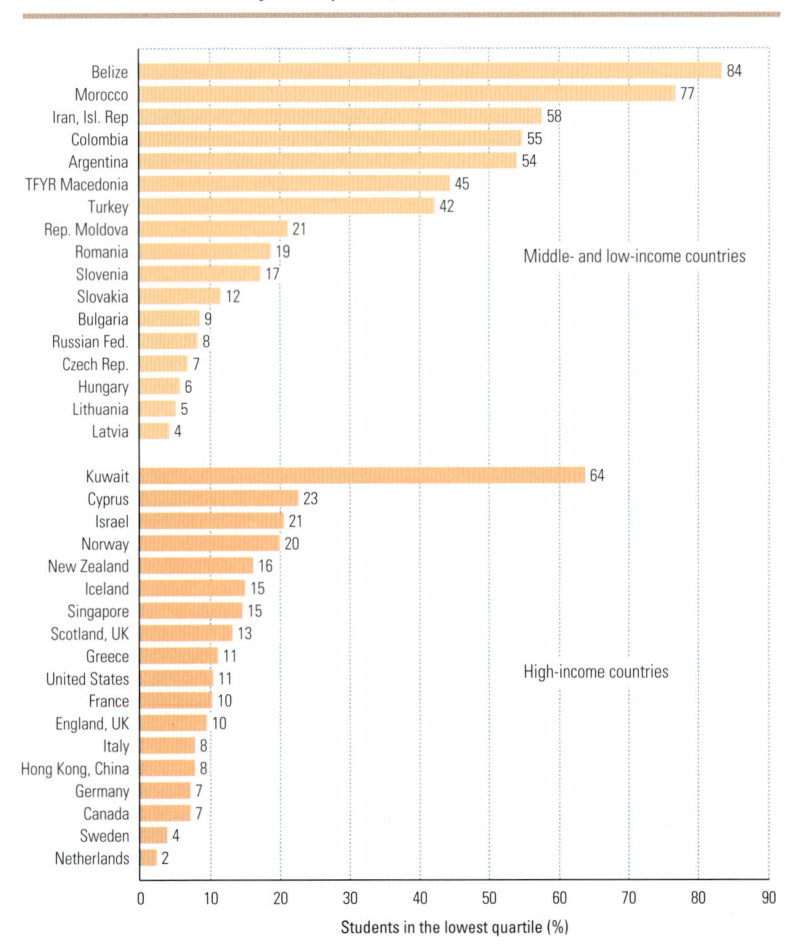

Middle- and low-income countries

Country	%
Belize	84
Morocco	77
Iran, Isl. Rep	58
Colombia	55
Argentina	54
TFYR Macedonia	45
Turkey	42
Rep. Moldova	21
Romania	19
Slovenia	17
Slovakia	12
Bulgaria	9
Russian Fed.	8
Czech Rep.	7
Hungary	6
Lithuania	5
Latvia	4

High-income countries

Country	%
Kuwait	64
Cyprus	23
Israel	21
Norway	20
New Zealand	16
Iceland	15
Singapore	15
Scotland, UK	13
Greece	11
United States	11
France	10
England, UK	10
Italy	8
Hong Kong, China	8
Germany	7
Canada	7
Sweden	4
Netherlands	2

Note: The classification by income level is based on World Bank, 2003.
Source: Mullis et al. (2003)

Zimbabwe achieved the desirable level in reading. Thus, no country in this study met the target suggested in 1990 at Jomtien for 2000 (at least 80% of students reaching a defined minimum achievement level) with respect to reading skills.

Low achievement is also evident from the PASEC study (Figure 3.32), which shows, for example, that over 40% of grade 5 pupils in Senegal had difficulty with the problem shown in Box 3.8: ordering numbers with one decimal point.

Although average achievement is much higher in developed than in developing countries, low achievement is an issue in many middle-income countries and affects significant minorities of the population in high-income countries. The PIRLS results indicate that large numbers of fourth-graders in several of the thirty-five countries participating in the study have limited reading skills (see Figure 3.33). More than half the students failed to reach the bottom quartile (the international benchmark) in Argentina, Belize, Colombia, the Islamic Republic of Iran and Morocco, among the middle-income countries, and in Kuwait, among the high-income countries – which typically have a less-than-20% share of low achievers.

According to PISA, 18% of 15-year-old students in the OECD as a whole (mostly high-income countries and a few middle-income ones) performed at or below level 1, indicating very low

ASSESSING PROGRESS TOWARDS THE EFA GOALS / 123

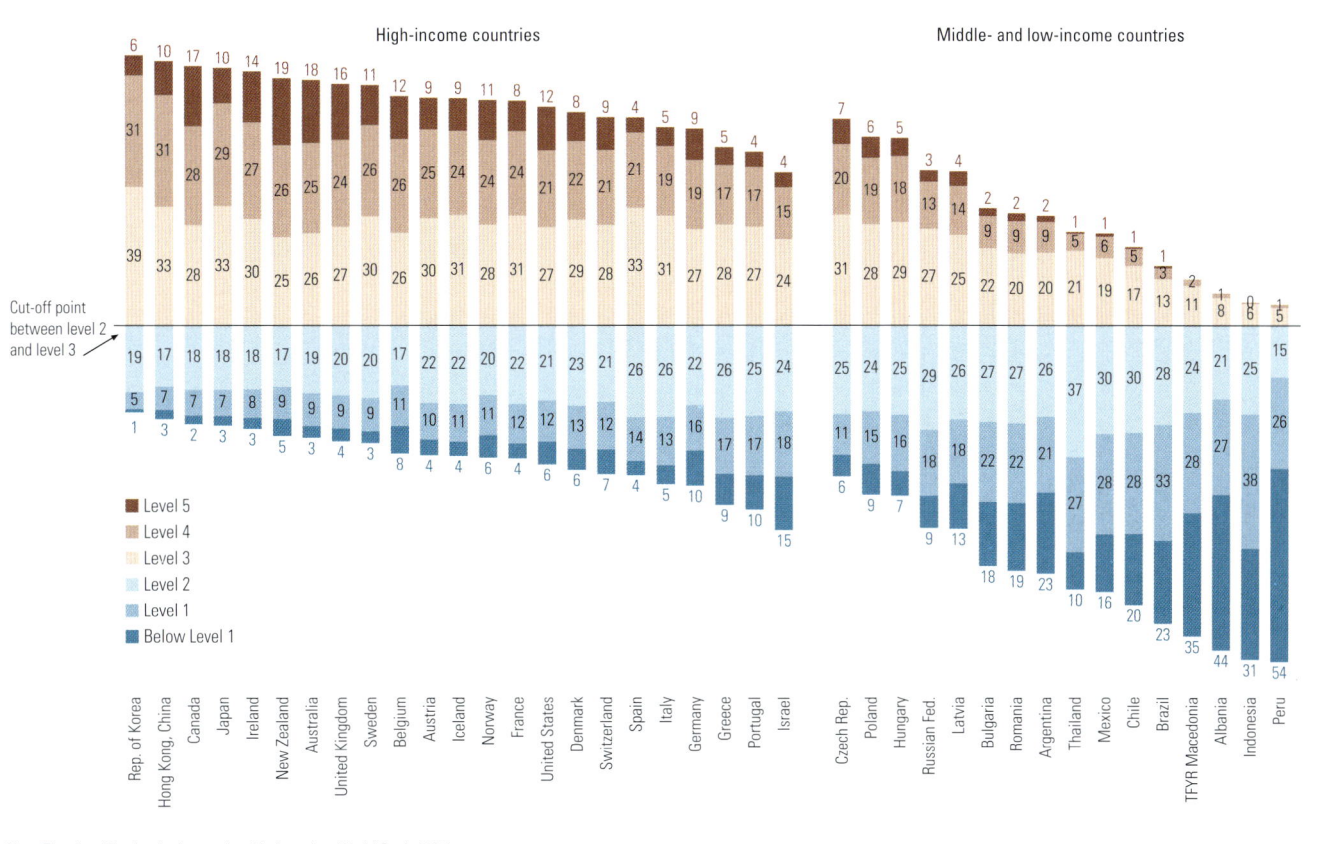

The quality of education

Figure 3.34: PISA. Percentage of 15-year-old students in five proficiency levels for reading, 2000-2002 (selected countries)

[Stacked bar chart showing percentage distribution across proficiency levels (Below Level 1, Level 1, Level 2, Level 3, Level 4, Level 5) for high-income countries and middle- and low-income countries. A cut-off point between level 2 and level 3 is marked. High-income countries listed: Rep. of Korea, Hong Kong China, Canada, Japan, Ireland, New Zealand, Australia, United Kingdom, Sweden, Belgium, Austria, Iceland, Norway, France, United States, Denmark, Switzerland, Spain, Italy, Germany, Greece, Portugal, Israel. Middle- and low-income countries listed: Czech Rep., Poland, Hungary, Russian Fed., Latvia, Bulgaria, Romania, Argentina, Thailand, Mexico, Chile, Brazil, TFYR Macedonia, Albania, Indonesia, Peru.]

Note: The classification by income level is based on World Bank, 2003.
Source: OECD/UNESCO Institute for Statistics (2003)

reading ability. Among students in middle- and low-income countries, 40% or more performed at or below level 1 – for example, more than 60% in Albania, Indonesia and the former Yugoslav Republic of Macedonia, and as high as 80% in Peru (see Figure 3.34).

Disparities in achievement within countries

The data presented above consistently suggest that low achievement is widespread and that it most seriously affects countries whose school systems are weak in terms of enrolment and resources. The distribution of achievement levels within countries is another cause for concern, as low-achieving pupils never represent a random sample of the population. Although the specific determinants of low achievement are best examined in a national context, results from national and international assessments suggest that pupils from rural areas and from socio-economically disadvantaged backgrounds are particularly vulnerable.

Learning disparities associated with socio-economic status begin in the early grades and continue through all levels of education. Children with low academic achievement may be more vulnerable to grade repetition and dropout. Since most school subjects build on fundamentals introduced in early grades, low-achieving primary school pupils may also face difficulties in later grades. Indeed, poor learning outcomes in early school years are often a good predictor of educational, social and economic disadvantages in adulthood.

The relationship between academic performance and socio-economic status varies by country as much as average achievement itself. Figure 3.35 displays this relationship for twelve Latin American

124 / CHAPTER 3

Figure 3.35: Socio-economic gradients for literacy performance[1]

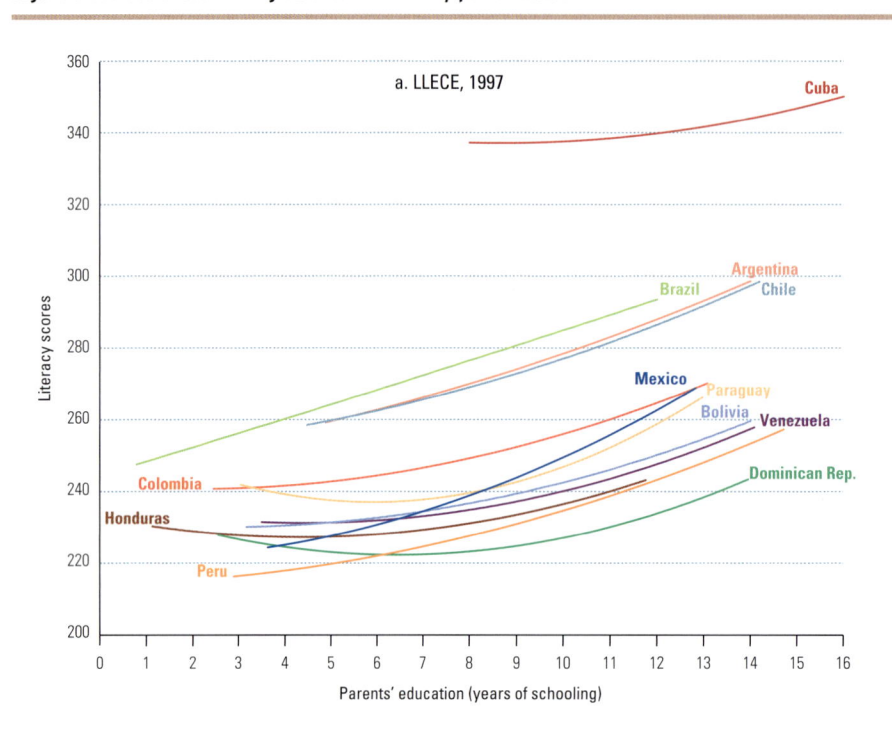

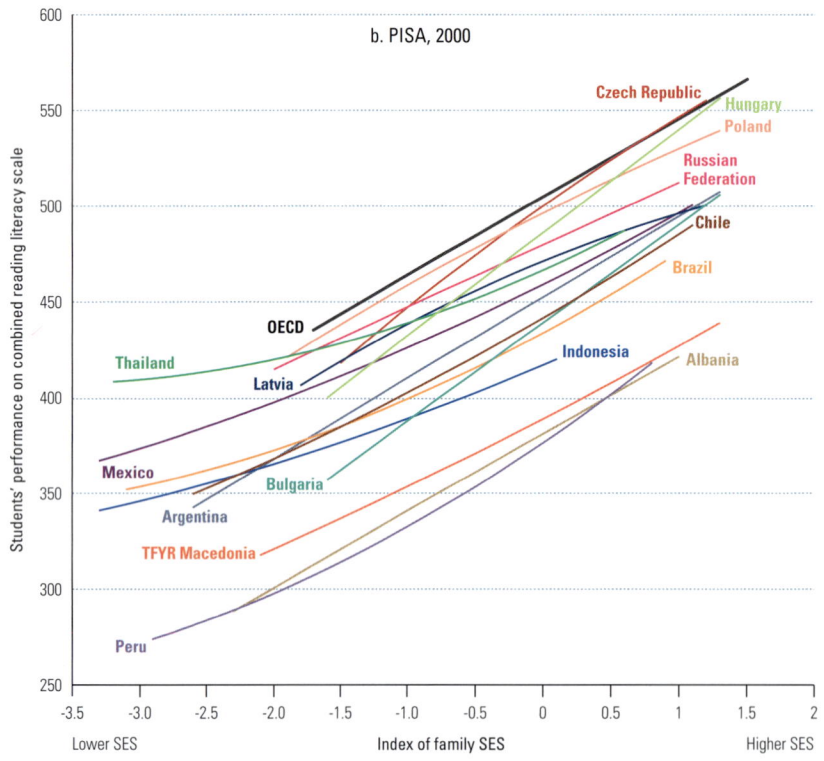

a. LLECE, 1997

b. PISA, 2000

Note: SES: socio-economic status.
1. The gradients, or "learning bars", are the best-fitting lines. This means that points on the line do not necessarily represent an empirical observation. Rather, the lines indicate the association between students' academic achievement and family background for each country. The *slope* of each gradient line is an indication of the extent of inequality in academic achievement attributable to family background. The *length* of each gradient line is determined by the range of the family background measure used in each study and by the slope. It indicates how the student population varies in terms of family background.
Sources: **a**. Willms and Somers (2001); **b**. OECD/UNESCO Institute for Statistics (2003).

and Caribbean countries that participated in a study conducted in 1997 by the *Laboratorio Latinoamericano de Evaluación de la Calidad de la Educación* (LLECE), and for a group of middle-income countries that participated in PISA in 2000. The relationship is sometimes termed a 'socio-economic gradient' or 'learning bar' (Willms, 2003; OECD/UNESCO Institute for Statistics, 2003). In the graph illustrating the LLECE results, the learning bars show the relationship between reading achievement of third and fourth graders and the years of schooling completed by their parents. The PISA graph shows the relationship between reading performance and a statistical composite indicating socio-economic status (SES), made up of the parents' level of education and occupation and indices of the family's material, educational and cultural possessions.

As noted above, socio-economic gradients vary considerably among countries. In the LLECE study, Cuba had the highest level of student achievement and the smallest variation in parents' educational attainment. Detailed analyses of the LLECE data revealed several factors in Cuba's success, including universal day care, more prevalence of home educational activities, smaller class sizes, higher levels of school and classroom material resources, better-trained teachers, greater parental involvement in school, a strong classroom disciplinary climate and relatively few multigrade

Figure 3.36: Which countries meet the goals of quantity and quality of education?

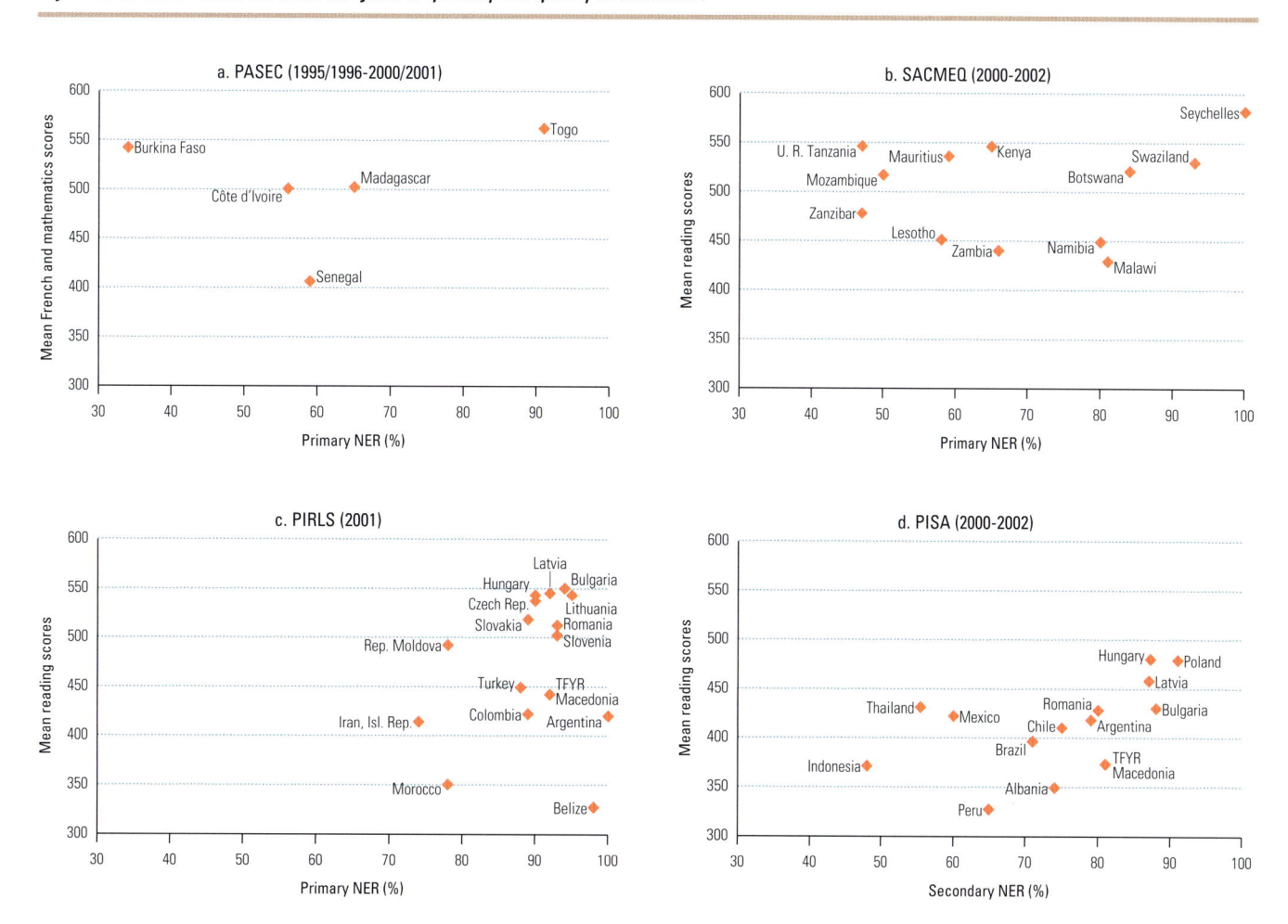

Notes: **a.** Primary NERs are for 1998/1999 except: Togo (2000/2001). **b.** Primary NERs are for 1999/2000 except: Malawi (2001/2002) and Seychelles (2000/2001).
c. Primary NERs are for to 2000/2001 except: Turkey (2001/2002). **d.** Secondary NERs are for 2000/2001 except: Indonesia and TFYR Macedonia (1999/2000).
Sources: NER data: UNESCO Institute for Statistics database; learning achievement data: **a.** Bernard (2003) and Michaelowa (2004); **b.** Dolata, Ikeda and Murimba (2004); **c.** Mullis et al. (2003); **d.** OECD/UNESCO Institute for Statistics (2003).

or ability-grouped classes (Willms and Somers, 2001). Figure 3.35 shows that students in middle-income countries perform below the OECD average corresponding to their socio-economic status. In several large countries, such as Indonesia, on average, students from the most favourable backgrounds perform worse than OECD students from the least favourable backgrounds, clearly suggesting unsatisfactory performance of the school system itself.

Assuring quality while expanding access: a dual challenge

Achieving good-quality learning for all requires that all school-age children have access to learning opportunities and that all students receive good-quality schooling. In reality, countries achieve various mixes of attainment and achievement. Figure 3.36 presents proxies for these, with scatter diagrams of net enrolment ratios and mean test scores, again based on SACMEQ, PASEC, PIRLS and PISA data. Four scenarios may be distinguished: some school systems combine quantity and quality, others fail either on quantity or on quality and others combine low quantity with unsatisfactory quality. Policy priorities may vary accordingly, from mere adjustments to further improvement of already high-quality schooling to complete reshaping of the system. The standard notion of a quantity-quality trade-off is often thought of as implying that countries cannot combine high quantity and high quality, but the concept is probably more relevant in a short-term, dynamic perspective. Thus within a country, quickly expanding the school system without reducing its quality, or immediately achieving high quality in new schools, may be difficult.

Indeed, no trade-off appears on any of the panels. There is no clear pattern for SACMEQ and PASEC, and PIRLS countries achieve widely variable quality for comparably high enrolment ratios. There is more variation in the PISA sample, in which it appears clearly, once again, that countries with stronger school systems combine better quality and quantity than others. The key question for achieving EFA, then, is not whether existing school systems should be expanded, given that this may put quality at risk, but rather how countries that combine high quantity and quality have arrived at this satisfactory situation.

Quickly expanding a school system without reducing its quality may be difficult

Conclusion

This section concludes the discussion of schooling that started with the sections on participation patterns and on teachers and other school resources. In summary, the various indicators that depict progress towards EFA, whether quantitative or qualitative, are positively correlated: regions where access to primary education is still restricted to a fraction of the population – in particular sub-Saharan Africa, South and West Asia and some of the Arab States – need holistic policies to rebuild their school systems, while other countries may focus on specific aspects of education policies, notably achievement or access for disadvantaged segments of the population. The next section shifts the emphasis away from formal education, discussing literacy programmes and skill development for youth and adults.

Literacy and skills development

The spread of basic cognitive skills such as literacy and numeracy is key to individual and societal development. Universalizing quality education implies that the children who benefit from it will become literate adults, though, of course, elementary education should include more than the mere mastery of basic cognitive skills. But much can also be done outside the formal school system to help youth and adults who have never been enrolled or have not completed enough schooling to become literate. Whether the immediate benefits of adult literacy programmes are of the same magnitude as the future benefits of formal schooling is a difficult question, but opportunities to reduce the proportion of the adult population that is illiterate should not be neglected, as this is an important complement to EFA in the child population. The spread of literacy is a major societal change, but its nature is bound to be country-specific, given the history of each written language and the individual and collective uses of literacy that will arise. Literacy thus depends not only on efforts by governments, international organizations and NGOs to provide primary schooling and literacy education, but also on individuals' family and socio-cultural context and their attitudes towards written matter. A related process is the teaching of life skills, which are meant to help individuals function effectively in society.

Defining and measuring literacy

Measuring EFA and other international goals concerning literacy requires agreement on operational definitions of the literacy status of an individual. As Box 3.8 explains, this is a difficult exercise and several indicators are in use. Data typically originate in censuses or, more rarely, household surveys. As a general principle, these indicators are predicated on the traditional UNESCO definition of literacy, i.e. 'the ability to read and write, with understanding, a short simple sentence about one's everyday life'. Other definitions are also used. (For details on UNESCO Institute for Statistics reporting of literacy data, see the Introduction to the Statistical annex).

A recent shift in the discourse of international organizations, from a dichotomous approach (literate and illiterate) to recognition of the existence of a continuum of literacy levels, is reflected in the notion of 'good-quality literacy', discussed in Box 3.9. This notion tries to take into account the range of functional skills applicable in a variety of situations (e.g. reading a legal contract or a newspaper or using a computer) and the fact that what ultimately matters is the ability to grasp the meaning(s) of a text and develop critical judgement.

Most discussions of literacy emphasize reading, but the ability to write correctly is as important, and complementary numeracy skills should not be overlooked. The literacy data currently available are too narrowly focused to reflect a set of skills that includes much more than the ability to decipher a text.

One of the practical difficulties met with when assessing literacy is that different methods may yield different literacy rates. Sometimes a test is administered in which respondents have to read a sentence from a printed card and the interviewer judges whether they can read it aloud correctly. Most available data sets, however, rely on the respondent's answer to a question regarding his or her own literacy (sometimes quoting the UNESCO definition). Often the head of the household responds for all members of the household. Significant distortions may arise because, for instance, respondents consider themselves literate since they can write their name or are reluctant to admit they cannot read. In a study in rural Bangladesh, more than half of those who asserted that they could write were not recognized as being able to do so according to a minimum standard (Greaney, Khandker and Alam, 1999).

Many countries do not collect national literacy data, but use educational attainment levels as a proxy. For example, in some countries, all those who have completed a certain number of years of school or reached a particular grade are considered literate. Using attainment as a proxy

Most available data sets rely on the respondent's answer to a question regarding his or her own literacy

---

Box 3.8 International goals and indicators

The United Nations Literacy Decade was launched in 2003 to renew the commitment and efforts to improve literacy around the world. The Decade takes place in the context of the Education for All compact, which sets targets for literacy (EFA goal 4): 'achieving a 50% improvement in levels of adult literacy by 2015, especially for women, and equitable access to basic and continuing education for all adults'. In a country with an adult literacy rate of 40%, the goal for 2015 would be to achieve a rate of 60%. For countries with rates above 66%, the goal for 2015 is universal literacy.

Progress towards this goal is monitored through three indicators:
- youth literacy rate (ages 15 to 24);
- adult literacy rate (age 15 and over);
- ratio of female to male literacy rates.

Similarly, the Millennium Development Goals, which cover not just education but also health, economic well-being, gender equality and other basic human needs or rights, use two literacy indicators:
- youth literacy rate (same as for the EFA goal);
- ratio of literate females to males among 15- to 24-year-olds.

The usefulness of these indicators is limited because they suggest a dichotomy between literate and illiterate individuals when the reality is a continuum of proficiency or competence. They do not account for levels of literacy skills (e.g. reading speed) that are fundamental in everyday life, nor do they reflect the different types of literacy skills needed in various situations, e.g. at work or at home. Global literacy measures are in critical need of improvement.

The measured increase in literacy over the 1990s is highly dependent on the method used

Box 3.9 Measuring 'good-quality literacy' in developing countries

To quantify the idea of 'good-quality literacy', many countries turn to assessment surveys rather than traditional data collection methods. Through the Literacy Assessment Monitoring Programme (LAMP), the UNESCO Institute for Statistics aims to promote literacy assessment surveys that can yield comparable results even given differing socio-cultural and linguistic backgrounds, and that rely on a robust and technically sound methodology. LAMP builds upon the methods used in the International Adult Literacy Survey (IALS) – a literacy assessment conducted in developed countries.

LAMP has developed data collection instruments that are particularly sensitive to the lower end of the proficiency scale, partly in response to issues related to the broadness of the lowest proficiency level in IALS (about 40% of adults in Chile and Poland, for instance, read at that level). To compile a meaningful picture of literacy in developing countries it is important to distinguish various levels or components of literacy skills at this end of the scale.

LAMP assesses functional skills. The assessment instruments are designed to present the respondent with real-life situations, as much as possible, within practical limits. Certain parts of the test measure speed, in order to gather data indicative of word recognition and fluency. LAMP also collects information on the languages the respondent speaks and writes, in order to document issues related to dominant and more local languages. While practical constraints prevent a full assessment of writing skills, the test does require some writing, in an attempt, however limited, to take writing skills into account in acknowledgment of their importance.

Source: UNESCO Institute for Statistics.

---

for literacy, however, can result in a sharp underestimation of illiteracy levels, since it is not uncommon for residents of countries with weak education systems to attend or even complete primary school without acquiring lasting literacy skills. For example, Figure 3.37 presents household survey data showing that more than one in three adults with a fifth-grade education in Chad and the Niger reported that they could not read.

Figure 3.37: Adults with primary as their highest education level who report being unable to read, 2000

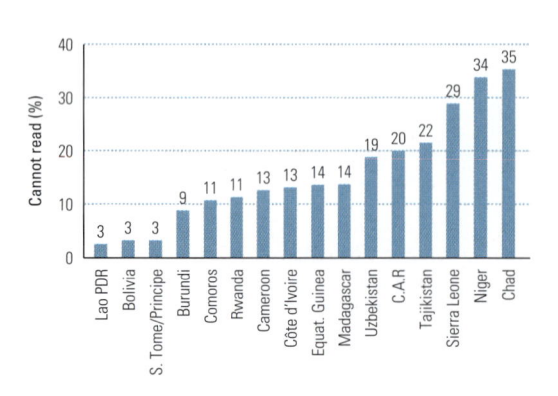

Country	Cannot read (%)
Lao PDR	3
Bolivia	3
S. Tome/Principe	3
Burundi	9
Comoros	11
Rwanda	11
Cameroon	13
Côte d'Ivoire	13
Equat. Guinea	14
Madagascar	14
Uzbekistan	19
C.A.R	20
Tajikistan	22
Sierra Leone	29
Niger	34
Chad	35

Source: Calculations based on UNICEF MICS database.

The case of Ghana, shown in Figure 3.38, illustrates the difficulty of reaching an unambiguous measure of literacy. Not only do census- and survey-based figures pertaining to the early 1990s and 2000s differ from each other, but self-reported literacy also differs from grade 5 completion and a language test. Both sources suggest that self-reported literacy is higher than the actual figure, and the language test, which may be considered the most accurate of the three measures, yields the lowest literacy levels. The measured increase in literacy over the 1990s is also highly dependent on the method used; by self-reporting on the census the increase is 3 percentage points, compared with 8 percentage points according to a language test in the household survey.

The above examples illustrate the diversity of current definitions and measurements, which contributes to the difficulties in making comparisons and drawing conclusions about the global state of literacy. These caveats should be kept in mind when examining available literacy figures, as in the following subsection.

Literacy and skills development

Figure 3.38: Measures of literacy in Ghana among people aged 15 and over, 1989 and 2003

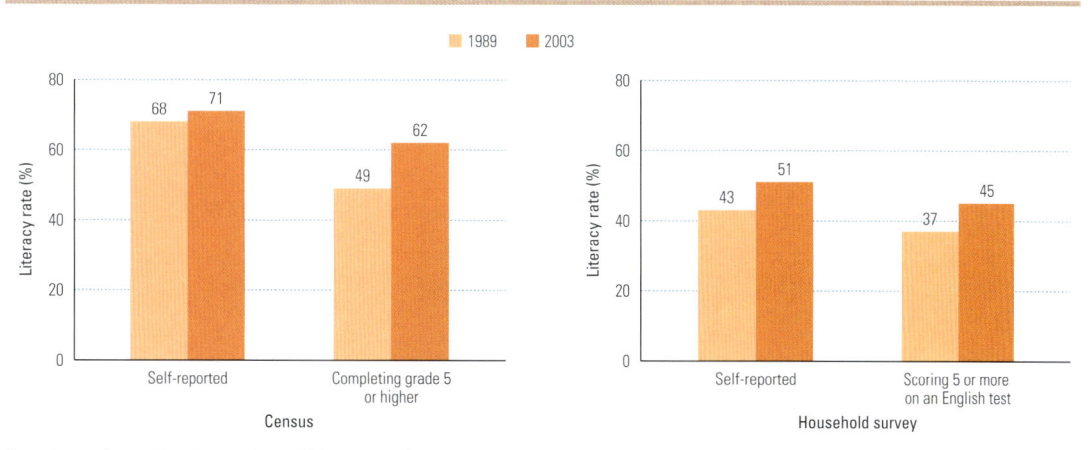

Census — Self-reported: 1989 = 68, 2003 = 71; Completing grade 5 or higher: 1989 = 49, 2003 = 62.

Household survey — Self-reported: 1989 = 43, 2003 = 51; Scoring 5 or more on an English test: 1989 = 37, 2003 = 45.

Notes: Census data are from January 1990 and February 2000. Survey data were calculated from Ghana Living Standards Survey 2 and Ghana Statistical Service/OED survey. In comparing census and survey results, it is important to note that the questions used to collect data, along with coverage and the target group, may differ.
Source: White (2004)

Table 3.7: Adult literacy (age 15 and over) by gender and region, 2000–2004[1]

	Total	Male	Female	GPI (F/M)	Total (thousands)	% female
World	82	87	77	0.88	799 147	64
Developing countries	76	83	69	0.83	788 999	64
Developed countries	99	99	99	1.00	9 151	62
Countries in transition	100	100	99	1.00	998	70
Sub-Saharan Africa	62	70	54	0.77	137 000	61
Arab States	62	73	51	0.69	69 298	64
Central Asia	99	100	99	1.00	333	70
East Asia and the Pacific	91	95	88	0.92	134 978	71
South and West Asia	58	71	45	0.63	402 744	64
Latin America and the Caribbean	89	90	88	0.98	39 383	55
North America and Western Europe	99	99	99	1.00	6 946	61
Central and Eastern Europe	97	99	96	0.97	8 464	77

Note: Figures may not add to totals because of rounding.
1. 2000-2004 data are derived from the March 2004 literacy assessment by the UNESCO Institute for Statistics, which uses directly reported national figures together with UIS estimates. For countries that did not report literacy data for the 2000-2004 reference period, UIS estimates for 2002 were used. See introduction to the Statistical annex for further details on the estimation of literacy data.
Source: Statistical annex, Table 2.

Global estimates of adult and youth literacy

Patterns of adult literacy

Table 3.7 displays the latest available estimates (based on data from the early 2000s) of literacy rates and numbers of adult illiterates by gender, for the world and the EFA regions, with adult defined as age 15 and above and literacy defined as the ability to read and write, with understanding, a simple statement about one's everyday life.

According to these estimates, there are nearly 800 million adult illiterates in the world, representing 18% of the adult population.[11] Two facts stand out. First, 64% of adult illiterates are women. The proportion varies widely by region, from 55% in Latin America and the Caribbean to 77% in Central and Eastern Europe and close to the world average in sub-Saharan Africa, the Arab States and South and West Asia. Absolute numbers may be influenced by demographic characteristics, however; the ratio of the literacy rate for females to that for males (i.e. the gender

11. The number of illiterates has been re-estimated by UIS in 2004 based on the latest data revisions. The present estimate of nearly 800 million adult illiterates in the reference period 2000-2004 is considerably lower than the estimate of 862 million for 2000 given by the *EFA Global Monitoring Report 2003/4.* (UNESCO 2003a: 86). This is a consequence of several factors notably the release of recent literacy data from the latest census and survey in a number of countries. For instance, the China 2000 census results in a decrease in the number of adult illiterates of over 50 million compared to the previous UIS estimate for that country.

130 / CHAPTER 3

> **Box 3.10 Links between mothers' literacy skills and child schooling status**
>
> Adult literacy skills are linked to progress towards UPE. The education level or literacy skills of a mother or caregiver can increase the probability of a child participating in or completing primary education. Among the factors probably involved are those of increased income levels (which lower opportunity costs or enable payment of school fees), greater appreciation of the value of education, and ability to help children learn. Household surveys provide evidence that mothers' literacy skills are often associated with their school-age children's participation in education.
>
> Figure 3.39 shows, for the Niger, the Lao People's Democratic Republic and Bolivia, the relationship between the mother's (or caregiver's) self-reported literacy status and the risk of the children not attending school. In each case, the risk is highest among mothers with low literacy skills. In the Niger, 70% of the primary school-age children of illiterate mothers are not in school, compared to 30% among those whose mothers are able to read easily.
>
> **Figure 3.39: Mothers' literacy and schooling status in the Niger, the Lao PDR and Bolivia, 2000**
>
> *Source:* Calculations based on the UNICEF MICS database.

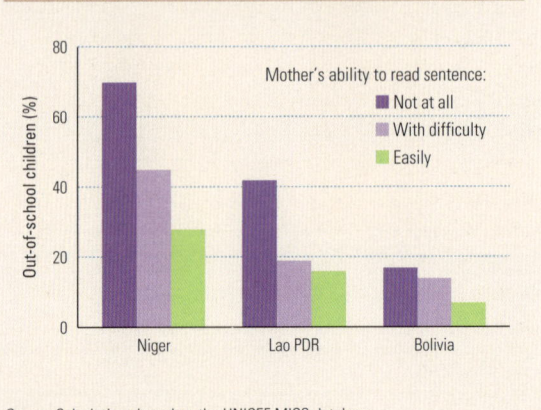

About a quarter of the adult population of the developing world is illiterate

parity index) is a better measure of gender disparities. It ranges from 0.63 to 0.77 in South and West Asia, the Arab States and sub-Saharan Africa, and is above 0.90 in the rest of the world. Indeed, the GPI is lowest where average literacy is also lowest, e.g. 0.53 in Pakistan and below 0.50 in countries such as Benin, Burkina Faso, Mali, Nepal, the Niger and Yemen, where total adult literacy is below 50% (see Table 2 of the Statistical annex). Given the impact of literacy on female well-being, autonomy and empowerment, actions aimed at achieving gender parity are urgently needed. They would yield comprehensive benefits in the long run as well, given the relationship between women's education, their fertility and the development of their children (see Box 3.10).

The second striking fact that emerges from Table 3.7 is that adult illiteracy is very unevenly distributed geographically, though it is almost exclusively a developing-country phenomenon: developed countries and countries in transition have literacy rates close to 99%, and together account for just 1.3% of the world's illiterates. About a quarter of the adult population of the developing world is illiterate. Latin America and the Caribbean and East Asia and the Pacific both have literacy rates in the neighbourhood of 90% but, as relatively populous regions, they account

for 22% of the world's illiterates. Truly severe illiteracy is concentrated in the three regions whose school systems have been shown in previous sections to be the weakest: sub-Saharan Africa, the Arab States and South and West Asia, which have literacy rates of around 60%. These regions account for three-quarters of the world's illiterates. South and West Asia alone, with its very large population, accounts for more than half. Literacy rates below 60% are found in 22 of the 119 countries for which data are available. With the exception of Haiti, all are located in those three regions. The lowest rates are found in Burkina Faso (13%), the Niger (17%) and Mali (19%), in sub-Saharan Africa. Note that some sub-national entities in South and West Asia have populations and literacy rates comparable to those of these entire countries.

Of the world's adult illiterates, over 70%, or 562 million persons, live in only nine countries, as Figure 3.40 shows, with some 34% in India alone. The other countries are either countries of sub-Saharan Africa, the Arab States or South and West Asia with low literacy rates (below 70%) and sizeable populations (Bangladesh, Egypt, Pakistan, Nigeria, Ethiopia), or populous countries of Latin America and the Caribbean and East Asia and the Pacific with high literacy rates but large absolute numbers of illiterates

Literacy and skills development

(mostly China, with a literacy rate of 91%, but also Indonesia and Brazil, both with a literacy rate of 88%).

There has been significant progress in levels of literacy over the 1990s, as exemplified by census results available for five countries that account for 46% of the world's population and 56% of the world's adult illiterates (Table 3.8). China has dramatically reduced female illiteracy through early and sustained efforts promoting school for girls and women, and the gender gap has shrunk from 18.9 to 8.6 percentage points. It has started narrowing in India, where male and female literacy rates increased quickly between the last two censuses.[12] Yet a striking contrast remains between, on the one hand, Pakistan (where literacy essentially stagnated, especially among men) and, on the other, Brazil, China and Indonesia, with literacy now above 80% for both sexes.

Youth literacy

The literacy rate among the population aged 15 to 24 is another indicator of progress towards Education for All and the Millennium Development Goals. Youth literacy reflects the education system's ability to deliver basic literacy skills, as well as the extent of literacy-related activities and other forms of support that children and youth receive at home (see Box 3.11).

In general, literacy rates tend to be higher among youth than adults, because of recent expansion of access to basic education. The latest available estimates indicate that there are nearly 137 million illiterate youths in the world (17% of all adult illiterates), 85 million of them (63%) female. As Table 3.9 shows, youth literacy rates are above 70% in all regions, though individual countries fall below the average. In developing regions, youth illiteracy rates range from 2% in East Asia and the Pacific to 28% in South and West Asia. Gender disparities are generally less pronounced in youth literacy than in adult literacy, but regional variations follow the same line as for adults, with gaps between men and women still notable among youth in South and West Asia, the Arab States and sub-Saharan Africa.

While national literacy rates vary widely by region and country, even greater variation exists in their distribution within countries. Figure 3.41 looks at differences in self-reported literacy of young women and men in urban and rural areas of twelve sub-Saharan African countries. In small island states such as Sao Tome and Principe and Comoros, there are very minor differences in the literacy status of young women and men, particularly in urban areas. In larger, more heterogeneous countries, the gaps between women and men and between rural and urban are considerable.

In the six countries with relatively high primary enrolment ratios (Cameroon, Comoros, Equatorial Guinea, Madagascar, Rwanda,

Figure 3.40: World adult illiterate population, percentage by country, 2000-2004[1]

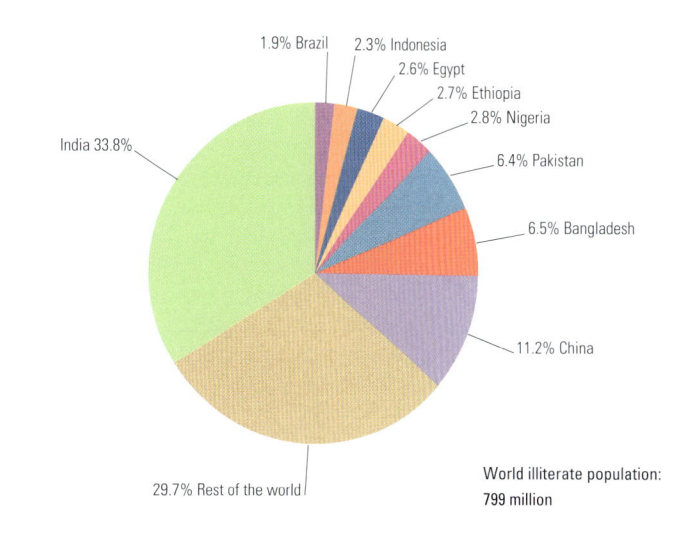

- 1.9% Brazil
- 2.3% Indonesia
- 2.6% Egypt
- 2.7% Ethiopia
- 2.8% Nigeria
- 6.4% Pakistan
- 6.5% Bangladesh
- 11.2% China
- 29.7% Rest of the world
- India 33.8%

World illiterate population: 799 million

1. See Note 1 in Table 3.7.
Source: Statistical annex, Table 2.

Table 3.8: Adult literacy rates in five high-population countries by gender, 1990-1994 and 2000-2004[1]

	Men			Women		
	Literacy rates (%)		Change (percentage points)	Literacy rates (%)		Change (percentage points)
	1990-1994	2000-2004		1990-1994	2000-2004	
Brazil	80.1	88.0	7.9	79.7	88.3	8.6
China	87.0	95.1	8.1	68.1	86.5	18.4
India	61.6	…	…	33.7	…	…
Indonesia	88.0	92.5	4.5	75.3	83.4	8.1
Pakistan	52.8	53.4	0.6	23.8	28.5	4.7

1. See Note 1 in Table 3.7.
Sources: 2000–2004: Statistical annex, Table 2; 1990–1994: national estimates provided to the UNESCO Institute for Statistics.

12. Literacy rates among the population aged 7 and above increased by 11.2 percentage points for men/boys and 14.4 points for women/girls between the 1991 and 2001 censuses.

Box 3.11 Literacy-related activities in the home: cross-national evidence from PIRLS

The Progress in International Reading Literacy Study (a cross-national assessment of reading literacy among fourth-grade students in thirty-five countries) also sought to measure literacy-related activities in the home by devising an index based on parents' reporting of how often they took part in the following activities with their pre-school child: reading books, telling stories, singing songs, playing with alphabet toys, playing word games and reading aloud signs and labels. The highest levels were reported in England and Scotland, where more than 80% of students were in the high early activity category. Among the countries where parents reported lower levels of engagement were Turkey, the Islamic Republic of Iran and Hong Kong (China), with parents of 30% or more of students in the low category, meaning they reported that they never or almost never engaged in these activities before children began school.

Countries with the highest average reading scores (Sweden and the Netherlands) were not necessarily those with the highest percentages of students in the high early activity category. Nevertheless, there was a positive relationship between engaging in early literacy activities and reading performance in every country. On average, internationally, students in the high index category enjoyed a twenty-point advantage in reading performance over those in the medium category, who in turn scored about twenty points above students in the low category. Countries where students in the high category had the greatest advantage over those in the medium category (thirty points or more) included England, New Zealand, Belize, Singapore and the Islamic Republic of Iran.

Source: Mullis et al. (2003)

Table 3.9: Youth literacy (15-24) by gender and region, 2000-2004[1]

	Youth literacy rates				Youth illiterates	
	% Total	Male	Female	GPI (F/M)	Total (thousands)	% female
World	88	91	84	0.92	136 710	63
Developing countries	85	89	81	0.91	136 052	63
Developed countries	100	100	100	1.00	354	49
Countries in transition	99	99	99	1.00	304	50
Sub-Saharan Africa	77	81	72	0.89	31 135	59
Arab states	78	84	72	0.85	12 946	64
Central Asia	98	98	98	1.00	257	50
East Asia and the Pacific	98	98	97	0.99	7 446	58
South and West Asia	72	82	63	0.77	79 344	65
Latin America and the Caribbean	96	95	96	1.01	4 589	46
North America and Western Europe	100	100	100	1.00	203	49
Central and Eastern Europe	99	99	98	0.99	790	69

Note: Figures may not add to totals, because of rounding.
1. See Note 1 in Table 3.7.
Source: Statistical annex, Table 2.

Sao Tome and Principe, with GER close to, or above, 90%), the differences in literacy rates by gender are relatively minor. Nevertheless, there are enormous rural-urban differences, e.g. in Madagascar, Cameroon and Rwanda. In the remaining six countries, overall youth literacy rates are lower and the rates by gender and rural residence are startlingly different, except in Burundi. There are more likely to be differences between urban youth by gender. For instance: literacy rates are 10 to 20 percentage points less for urban girls than for urban boys. In the Central African Republic, Sierra Leone, Chad and the Niger, fewer than one in four rural youths are literate, compared to one in ten young women, or fewer. These data reflect narrow, stratified access to learning opportunities and underline the importance of going beyond national

Literacy and skills development

Figure 3.41: Literacy rates for ages 15 to 24 by gender and rural or urban residence in sub-Saharan Africa, 2000

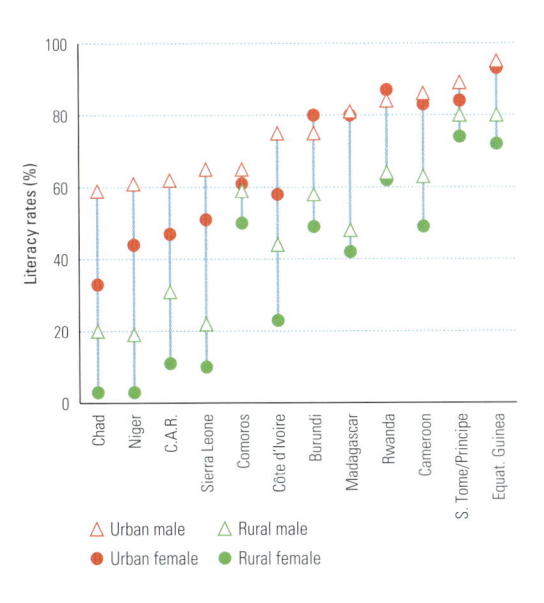

[Chart showing literacy rates (%) for Chad, Niger, C.A.R., Sierra Leone, Comoros, Côte d'Ivoire, Burundi, Madagascar, Rwanda, Cameroon, S. Tome/Principe, Equat. Guinea, with categories: Urban male, Rural male, Urban female, Rural female]

Source: Calculations based on UNICEF MICS database.

averages to identify populations that are marginalized by low literacy skills.

Skills development in four countries

Goal 3 of the Dakar Framework for Action addresses the learning needs of all young people and adults, especially those who missed out on a good basic education. It concerns various sorts of skills: the generic skills, more context-specific skills (including livelihood skills) and vocational skills, which are usually acquired in more formal settings.[13] Efforts to systematically enhance these skills are increasingly referred to collectively as skills development.[14] Literacy is not always seen as part of skills development, though as Chapter 2 shows there are important links between the two.[15]

Four countries recently reviewed their skills development activities. Assisted by UNESCO and its International Institute for Educational Planning (IIEP), the Lao People's Democratic Republic, Mali, Nepal and Senegal have developed a common framework to assess youth and adult learning needs and the provision of relevant learning opportunities. The aim is to identify gaps between the two and, after consultative meetings, prepare an Education for All Skills Development Plan.[16] This approach is intended to be applied in the near future in other countries, in the first instance the Pacific subregion, so that a more or less standardized instrument emerges for the monitoring of goal 3.[17]

In all four countries, national review teams found that governments tend to give little attention to disadvantaged and vulnerable young people who are not in school. Their needs are commonly left to NGOs. Many initiatives exist to reach and empower the marginalized through non-formal vocational skills training, but they are often locally based, may be short-lived and are not part of a comprehensive national strategy. Government-sponsored skills training is often scattered in nature and not well coordinated, involving not only the ministry dealing with education but also those handling other sectors and issues (e.g. labour, agriculture, women, youth).

Defining skills development programmes

The four countries looked at the following issues:
- Who are the target groups?
- What skills are relevant in specific contexts?
- What programmes are being provided in formal and non-formal settings, public and private?
- Which training methods work best in centre-based programmes, which in community-based programmes and which in distance education?
- What are the roles of government and NGOs?
- Who are the trainers? How can they be better recruited, trained and supported?
- What languages should be used?
- What are the financing sources and mechanisms for skills development?
- How can skills development strategies and programmes best be monitored and evaluated?

The rest of this section summarizes some of the findings.

Young people who drop out of primary school or never attended one are a major target group for skills development (although in countries or regions where most children complete primary school, secondary-school dropouts can have a relative disadvantage). Irrespective of educational

> **Young people who drop out of primary school or never attended one are a major target group for skills development**

---

13. Generic skills include problem-solving, working in teams, networking, communicating, negotiating, etc. For a more extensive discussion of all these skills, often referred to as 'life skills', see UNESCO (2003a): 84–86.

14. See, for instance, Working Group for International Cooperation in Skills Development (2002).

15. See the section titled 'The quality of ECCE and literacy programmes' in Chapter 2.

16. UNESCO/IIEP (2004) describes the project briefly. The information in this section is largely derived from Atchoarena and Nozawa (2004) – a commissioned paper based on the four country reports.

17. Other countries may issue reports with a view to making skills development more transparent, even if they do not follow the UNESCO/IIEP format.

134 / CHAPTER 3

background, certain groups have been identified as vulnerable. These mainly include those living in a difficult environment (Lao People's Democratic Republic); sensitive occupational groups, e.g. apprentices in the informal sector (Mali and Senegal); marginalized minority groups (low-caste persons in Nepal); various ethnic minorities (Lao People's Democratic Republic and Nepal); street children (Mali and Senegal) and disabled youth (all four countries).

Only scattered indications of the size of these out-of-school groups are available, as reliable data are scarce. In Nepal, some 80% of adolescents are neither in school nor in a training institution. In the Lao People's Democratic Republic, about 53% of 15-year-olds, 67% of 16-year-olds and 75% of 17-year-olds are out of school (Figure 3.42).

In each country, the review teams identified a set of skills important for social inclusion and poverty reduction in the local context. Agricultural and artisan skills were particularly emphasized. In many cases, especially in poor rural areas, wage employment is rare so skills development must focus on livelihoods – the activities and means by which individuals make a living independently. Household and community needs have to be taken into account. In an effort to improve the impact of skills development programmes, countries (e.g. the Lao People's Democratic Republic) sometimes include post-training microcredit initiatives, which pose additional challenges for programme management and the development of monitoring and evaluation tools.

Countries can begin to design national skills development strategies only if there is adequate information on programme providers, course content and duration, enrolment, costs and fees. Among the many ministries that may be involved, those in charge of education tend to have the best data on skills development. As regards NGO participation, some programmes are supported by large international organizations and others by local, community-based groups. In all four countries, the latter type makes up the larger part of the NGO sector, but data are usually scarce. The former type, while smaller, is generally more transparent.

In Mali and Senegal, contracting to NGOs is an important means of implementing skills development programmes, particularly those aimed at reaching apprentices in the informal sector. Nepal is considering this approach, possibly via a skills development fund. The involvement of subcontractors increases the

In Nepal, some 80% of adolescents are neither in school nor in a training institution

Figure 3.42: Lao PDR. Out-of-school youth by age and gender, 2001

■ Out-of-school boys
■ Out-of-school girls
■ Total out-of-school

Source: Lao PDR Ministry of Education, 2001 school census.

need for tight monitoring. The allocation of public resources to private providers normally necessitates the establishment of mechanisms to assure quality, efficiency and transparency. Such control is easier when some support functions are publicly provided, such as funding or training of trainers.

Locating the most vulnerable groups is another challenge, especially in large and culturally diverse countries with strong disparities between richer and poorer areas. The Lao People's Democratic Republic is using a geographical information system to chart the areas where poverty, school dropout rates and gender disparities need most urgently to be addressed and where there is a risk of learning opportunities being insufficient.

Assessing skills development programmes

As with other educational programmes, efficiency of skills development programmes can be measured by dropout and completion rates, while effectiveness should be measured through direct assessment of the skills and knowledge acquired. However, as with literacy programmes, such data are seldom available. Short skills programmes are rarely followed by an exam, and where they are, the results are not often recorded.

Nevertheless, in Mali and Nepal there is increasing interest in awarding certificates for successful completion of longer programmes, and the Lao People's Democratic Republic is also interested in defining the equivalence of such certificates to formal qualifications. Equivalence policies should allow learners to build their own pathways, for instance by first attending non-formal learning and then making a transition (back) to school (an option that is mainly realistic for younger members of target groups). Discussions in the Lao People's Democratic Republic and Nepal on establishing a national qualification framework suggest that eventually more systematic data collection on achievement will be possible.

Non-formal skills development programmes tend to cost less than formal vocational education, though precise information about costs is difficult to obtain, because such programmes are often subsidized by external donors and not covered by national statistics.

Furthermore, the diversity of programmes offered by a given provider (long-term/short-term, centre-based/community-based, agricultural skills/industrial skills) often makes it difficult to assess unit cost. The government of Nepal estimates that 47,000 students are enrolled in training programmes offered by ministries other than the Ministry of Education. Although cost data are available, they are not related to course length and thus are difficult to compare with costs in formal education.

The Lao Ministry of Education has estimated the unit costs of non-formal basic vocational skills programmes, vocational programmes delivered by community learning centres and outreach programmes conducted by technical and vocational schools. These estimates are being used in an EFA simulation model that allows various policy options' cost implications and likely results to be assessed.

Skills development represents a marginal share of national education budgets in the four countries. In Mali and Nepal, non-formal education accounts for less than 1% of public current expenditure on education. Technical and vocational education constitutes 2.6% of the education budget in the Lao People's Democratic Republic and 1.4% in Nepal. As in most countries, this segment of educational provision continues to be very much a junior partner of the formal system.

Decentralization is under way in the four countries, and the provincial and district levels enjoy increasing responsibilities. Given the contextual nature of many learning needs, there is every reason to differentiate skills development programmes at local level. Information systems at the grass roots, however, do not easily provide the summary information that national policy-makers need for effective monitoring, evaluation and policy development. Locally relevant data need to be aggregated to be of use in analytical and diagnostic tools at the national level. The Lao People's Democratic Republic and Senegal are working on this step.

> **Locating the most vulnerable groups is a challenge, especially in large and culturally diverse countries with strong disparities between richer and poorer areas**

The Education for All Development Index

At the Dakar Forum in 2000, participating countries and agencies committed themselves to achieving the six EFA goals by 2015. While all these goals are important individually, it is useful to have a summary means of indicating progress towards EFA as a whole. The EFA Development Index (EDI), a composite of relevant indicators, provides one way of doing this.

There are well-known problems associated with the construction and interpretation of indices. These relate to which elements and indicators to select, how they should be aggregated and weighted across different fields and how the results should be used. For example, the constituents of a human development index can be debated in terms of the meaning of the concept, what should constitute its most important elements, the possible proxies for these elements and, more fundamentally, whether there are more important objectives of development policy that vitiate the need for such an index. In the case of EFA, some of these problems are less pressing. The international community has defined EFA in terms of a set of six time-bound goals. At least some of these goals can be quantified and a set of indicators has been agreed as regards what variables best proxy their attainment. Thus, in the case of the EFA development index, some of the problems of indicator selection, weighting and interpretation are less difficult to resolve.

The constituents of the EDI should ideally reflect all six Dakar goals, but this is difficult in practice. Goal 3 on learning and life-skills programmes is not easy to quantify, while goal 1 on ECCE cannot be incorporated yet because national enrolment data are available for only a few countries and are insufficiently standardized. Thus the EDI currently incorporates indicators for UPE, adult literacy, gender parity and education quality.

All the EFA goals are considered equally important, so, in order to give the same weight to each of the four EDI components, each is represented by one proxy indicator. The EDI value for a particular country is the arithmetical mean of the observed values for each of these indicators. The EDI's value falls between 0 and 1. The closer it is to the latter, the higher the country's EFA achievement.

The EDI constituents and related indicators[18] are:

- universal primary education: net enrolment ratio;
- adult literacy: literacy rate of the group aged 15 and over;
- gender: gender-specific EFA index (GEI, the arithmetical mean of the GPIs for the primary and secondary gross enrolment ratios and the adult literacy rate);
- education quality: survival rate to grade 5.

The data used are for 1998 and 2001 (or 2000 where more recent data are not available). Only those countries with a complete set of the indicators required to calculate the EDI are included in this analysis. Although the number of such countries rose from 94 to 127 between 2000 and 2001, coverage is still incomplete, so no comprehensive global overview of progress towards the goals can be given as yet.

How close are we to EFA?

The EDI can be calculated for 2001 for 127 countries, i.e. nearly two-thirds of the world's countries. Table 1 of the Appendix presents the index values for these countries. Table 3.10 summarizes the values for the EFA regions. Estimates are available for one-half to four-fifths of the countries in all eight regions. A special effort was made to include more OECD countries and more Central and Eastern Europe countries by filling the gaps in their data for adult literacy and survival to grade 5. The Appendix discusses the methodology further.

Forty-one countries, or one-third of those with data, have either achieved the four most quantifiable EFA goals or are close to doing so. Not surprisingly, most of these countries are in North America and Western Europe and Central and Eastern Europe – regions where compulsory education has been in force for more than a century in some cases. No country from the Arab States is close to achieving the goals. Countries that have achieved the goals or are close to doing so include several in Latin America and the Caribbean and in Central Asia that have a long-established tradition of emphasizing widespread

The EDI can be calculated for 2001 for 127 countries, i.e. nearly two-thirds of the world's countries

18. The Appendix explains why these particular indicators were chosen.

The Education for All Development Index

Table 3.10: Distribution of countries by their mean distance from the EFA goals in 2001

	Achieved EDI: 0.98–1.00	Close to the goals EDI: 0.95–0.97	Intermediate position EDI: 0.80–0.94	Far from the goals EDI: less than 0.80	Subtotal sample	Total number of countries
Arab States			12	4	16	20
Central and Eastern Europe	3	8	3		14	20
Central Asia		3	4		7	9
East Asia and the Pacific	1	1	9	3	14	33
Latin America and the Caribbean	1	4	15	2	22	41
North America and Western Europe	11	7			18	26
South and West Asia		1	1	4	6	9
Sub-Saharan Africa		1	7	22	30	45
Total	**16**	**25**	**51**	**35**	**127**	**203**

Source: Appendix, Table 1.

participation in basic education. They also include Fiji in East Asia and the Pacific, Maldives in South and West Asia and Seychelles in sub-Saharan Africa.

Fifty-one countries have intermediate EDI values (0.80–0.94). They are found in all regions except North America and Western Europe. Clearly several of them do not perform equally in all the EFA goals represented in the EDI. Often the expansion of education does not balance the attention being given to its quality: in almost half the countries with EDIs at intermediate level (mostly in Latin America), education quality as measured by survival rate to grade 5 lags behind. In these cases, many children who have access to school leave prematurely, partly because of poor education quality.

Thirty-five countries, or more than 25% of those with EDI data, are very far from achieving the EFA goals, with EDI values lower than 0.80. As many as twenty-two of these low-EDI countries (more than 60% of the category) are in sub-Saharan Africa. The category also includes three participants in UNESCO's E-9 initiative of high-population countries: Bangladesh, India and Pakistan. Table 1 of the Appendix reveals that most of these thirty-five countries are characterized by low achievement on each of the four EFA goals. Primary-school enrolments are low, gender ratios are highly unequal, illiteracy is widespread and education quality is poor, leading to high dropout rates, which means many pupils never reach grade 5. Countries in the low-EDI group face multiple challenges that must be tackled simultaneously if EFA is to be reached (Box 3.12).

Progress towards EFA from 1998 to 2001

The EDI's value depends on the levels of its constituents, and changes in it can be explained by countries' progress, or lack of progress, towards the four goals. How are countries moving towards EFA since Dakar? Are they paying equal attention to all the EFA goals, as the Dakar Framework for Action recommends?

A trend analysis of the EFA Development Index is possible only for the seventy-four countries having data on all four constituents for both 1998 and 2001. Table 3.11 demonstrates that there is a clear general movement towards achievement of EFA. For fifty-four of these countries, or nearly three-quarters of those in the sample, the EDI has risen. Progress has been relatively important, in particular for countries with low EDI or those that are far from EFA, such as the Comoros, Liberia, Mozambique, Togo and Yemen,

> Thirty-five countries, or more than 25% of those with EDI data, are very far from achieving the EFA goals

Table 3.11: Distribution of countries by change in their mean distance vis-à-vis the EFA goals from 1998 to 2001

	Towards the EFA goals EDI has increased	Away from the EFA goals EDI has declined	Total
Achieved [EDI: 0.98–1.00]	1	1	2
Close to the goals [EDI: 0.95–0.97]	6	5	11
Intermediate position [EDI: 0.80–0.94]	26	8	34
Far from the goals [EDI: less than 0.80]	21	6	27
Total	**54**	**20**	**74**

Source: Appendix, Table 3.

Box 3.12 Reducing illiteracy and improving gender parity are the best predictors of progress towards EFA

The extent to which achieving any one EFA goal is intertwined with achieving the rest can easily be demonstrated. The graphs below show how variation in each EDI constituent is associated with variation in the other three. In general, countries doing well on one EFA goal also tend to do well on the others. This also implies, however, that countries at low levels of EFA achievement face multiple aspects of educational deprivation, severely complicating the tasks they must carry out to meet time-bound goals.

The results also show that the indicators that have the strongest associations with other EDI constituents are the GEI and adult literacy.* Each of these variables explains more than 75% of the variance of the combined mean scores of the others. NER and survival rate to grade 5 are somewhat less strongly associated with the other elements, explaining 58% and 42% of their respective variance.

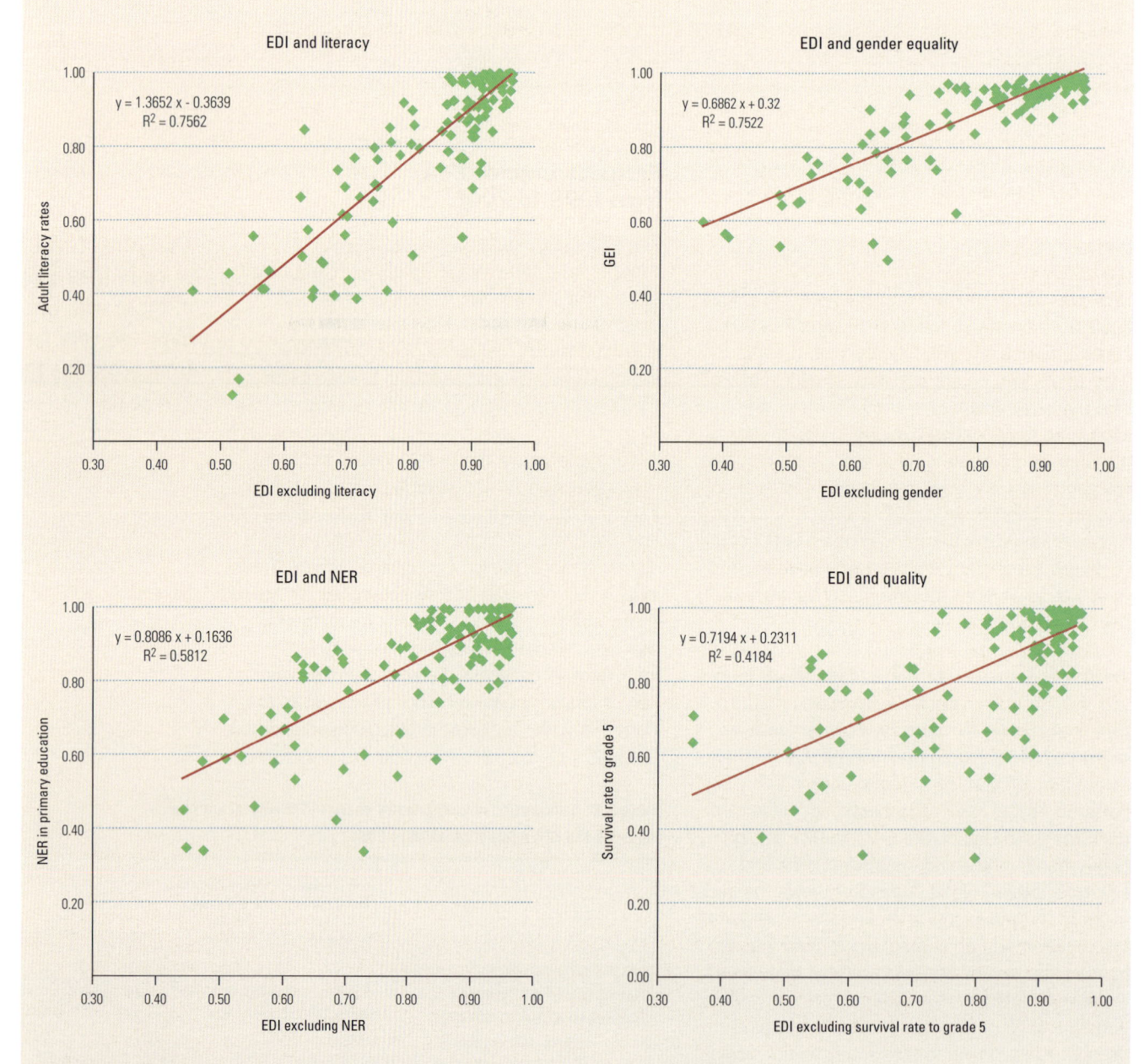

EDI and literacy
$y = 1.3652 x - 0.3639$
$R^2 = 0.7562$

EDI and gender equality
$y = 0.6862 x + 0.32$
$R^2 = 0.7522$

EDI and NER
$y = 0.8086 x + 0.1636$
$R^2 = 0.5812$

EDI and quality
$y = 0.7194 x + 0.2311$
$R^2 = 0.4184$

* The higher correlation between literacy and the three other EDI components compared with that presented in the *EFA Global Monitoring Report 2003/4* is mainly due to changes in adult literacy rate values for a number of countries and to improved literacy data coverage, in particular for OECD countries.

each of which saw an increase of 15% or more between 1998 and 2001 (Figure 3.43).

In the remaining twenty countries, however, the EDI declined over the period. The change was small in most cases, but in South Africa, Ghana and Burundi the value of the index fell by between 3% and 7%, with the rate of survival to grade 5 being a particularly weak point.[19]

Countries' overall EDI ranking did not change markedly and most of those in the high, medium and low EDI categories stayed in those groupings. Venezuela, Namibia and Togo improved their rankings by more than five places, showing that even poor countries that are far from achieving the goals can make rapid progress towards EFA. Only Ghana, South Africa, Mongolia, Azerbaijan and Georgia fell in rank by more than five places. In general, the extent of movement in the EDI over the period was relatively small: the (unweighted) index as a whole rose by 2.2% and the mean individual change per country (positive or negative) was 2.8%. In some cases, countries making rapid progress on some indicators did so at the expense of other indicators. As Table 3 in the Appendix shows, in almost two-thirds of the countries (forty-eight out of seventy-four), at least one indicator moved in the opposite direction to the others.

This implies that, when monitoring overall progress towards EFA, one needs to return to the individual EDI constituents to understand how progress is being made. Most countries where EFA has been achieved pay equal attention to questions of access and participation in education, to the gender parity issue, to literacy and to retention of children in school.[20] The right to education in these countries goes beyond rhetoric; compulsory education is a long-established and rigorously enforced institution and schooling is free. In many countries that are still far from the goal, both the EDI and trends in the EDI mask significant variations between its constituents that result partly from a lack of balance in education policies. Where education is expanded without due attention to quality or to enrolling the poorest, it is harder to achieve and maintain EFA. It is possible, however, to avoid such a lack of balance. Yemen, for instance, was able to increase the value of its EDI by more than 15%, from 0.546 in 1998 to 0.629 in 2001, by

Figure 3.43: EFA Development Index in 2001 and change since 1998
(countries with EDI less than 0.80 in 2001)

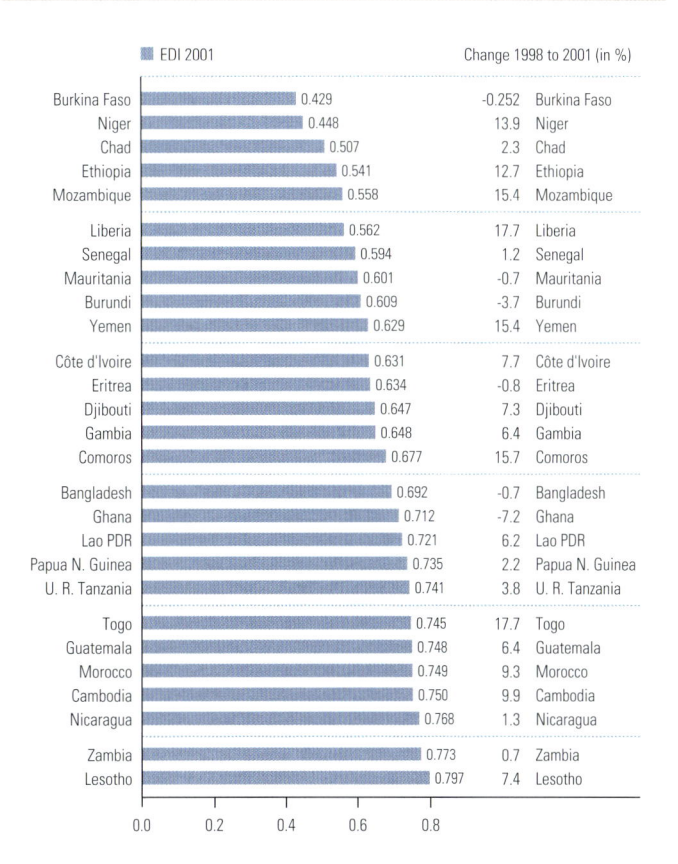

Country	EDI 2001	Change 1998 to 2001 (in %)
Burkina Faso	0.429	-0.252
Niger	0.448	13.9
Chad	0.507	2.3
Ethiopia	0.541	12.7
Mozambique	0.558	15.4
Liberia	0.562	17.7
Senegal	0.594	1.2
Mauritania	0.601	-0.7
Burundi	0.609	-3.7
Yemen	0.629	15.4
Côte d'Ivoire	0.631	7.7
Eritrea	0.634	-0.8
Djibouti	0.647	7.3
Gambia	0.648	6.4
Comoros	0.677	15.7
Bangladesh	0.692	-0.7
Ghana	0.712	-7.2
Lao PDR	0.721	6.2
Papua N. Guinea	0.735	2.2
U. R. Tanzania	0.741	3.8
Togo	0.745	17.7
Guatemala	0.748	6.4
Morocco	0.749	9.3
Cambodia	0.750	9.9
Nicaragua	0.768	1.3
Zambia	0.773	0.7
Lesotho	0.797	7.4

Source: Appendix, Table 3.

improving all four EDI components, achieving strong increases in its primary-level NER, adult literacy rate, GPI and survival rate to grade 5 over the three years. This and other examples show that attention to all goals is not incompatible with achieving and sustaining sharp gains in EDI.

---

19. For an explanation of the change in survival rate in Ghana, see footnote 9, p. 99.

20. The main exception in the industrialized countries concerns gender. In several countries, girls have consistently been outperforming boys in the upper levels of schooling, so these countries remain some distance from achieving gender parity. For further discussion of this issue, see UNESCO (2003a).

Chapter 4

Policies for better quality

Raising the quality of education pays off. Chapter 2 summarizes the evidence that demonstrates that improving education quality has significant effects on individual earnings, economic growth, fertility and health. Better education enables people to live more productive lives, extend their freedoms strengthen their values and expand their life choices.

There is considerable scope for improving the quality of education. Many children and adults in the developing world do not master basic literacy and numeracy skills, even if they complete primary education. And although the average level of achievement is higher in the developed world, low achievement also affects significant minorities in high-income countries.[1] Furthermore, in all eight EFA regions, disparities within countries are often marked. This evidence makes it clear that education's mission to counteract the multiple disadvantages of poverty, illiteracy and gender inequity has nowhere been completed.

EFA Global Monitoring Report 2 0 0 5

An enthusiastic pupil in Eritrea

Setting a policy framework

There is every reason to invest further in improving the quality of education. However, it is not an investment than can be borne easily by those who stand to benefit most. Poor people already bear heavy costs for their children's education, the benefits of which may accrue long after the investments have been made. Furthermore, because many of the benefits of a good basic education are broad and general, it is difficult to mobilize significant private resources for improving the quality of basic education. Hence, the role of government, as the actor most able to transcend short-term realities and interests and invest in quality, becomes crucial.

It has been argued that governments should invest at least 6% of GNP in education (Delors et al., 1996). While this level of investment is not itself a guarantor of quality, the idea of a benchmark has considerable political value[2] and in many countries meeting such a target would be a boost to the level of available resources.[3] For each country there is clearly a minimum level below which government expenditure cannot sink without serious consequences for quality. This Report, however, cannot confirm a more general rule of thumb for investments at the macro level. (See Chapter 3, Figure 3.27, for a macro overview of public expenditure on education and Figure 3.29 on expenditure and achievement.) As Chapter 2 points out, the relationship between investment and quality – measured in terms of achievement – is not straightforward. Moreover, many factors affect levels of investment, including size of GNP, demography and public investments in other social sectors. Where measurable economic production is low and where children are a significant proportion of the population, the share of GNP devoted to education may need to be higher. In the case of major health deficits, hard choices have to be made regarding the allocation of resources among social sectors. Such choices should be informed by the knowledge that good education can help address broader social and economic challenges, including poor health and nutrition, conflict and HIV/AIDS.

Even at existing levels of investment, including aid in highly aid-dependent countries, governments and stakeholders can make significant choices to improve quality. Those choices are the focus of this chapter. It explores what governments can do to create greatly improved conditions for learning while remaining mindful of budget limitations. Led by the evidence in Chapter 2 on what determines quality, and drawing on the experience of countries that have made significant progress, it examines key policy options at various levels in the education system, with quality as the objective.

Recognizing the importance of contextual circumstances, and employing evidence from earlier chapters, this chapter is guided by a framework for improving the quality of teaching and learning, presented in Figure 4.1.

This model reorganizes the five dimensions of the heuristic framework in Chapter 1 (context, learner characteristics, teaching and learning, enabling inputs, outcomes) to provide a more systemic and holistic structure for analysis. While Chapter 2 examines various indicators in terms of what determines quality, this chapter focuses on what actors at various levels in education systems can do to actually improve education.

The policy framework places **learners** at the heart of the teaching and learning process, emphasizing that, from the outset, policy must acknowledge their diverse characteristics, circumstances and learning needs. This emphasis is important in establishing objectives for better quality and defining strategies to improve education. The central role of learners, therefore, is the starting point for this chapter. It leads to a consideration of the ways in which *teaching and learning* in the classroom can be genuinely responsive to learners through curriculum development and application. This ring of Figure 4.1 also covers *outcomes* (both skills and values), as envisaged in curriculum goals and realized through the teaching and learning process. Beyond the classroom, there are many ways to create an *enabling environment* that is conducive to teaching and learning. Better teachers, better schools and a strong knowledge infrastructure can all make a considerable difference to the quality of education. Finally in this teaching and learning framework comes the umbrella of a coherent *education sector policy* and the *reforms* that governments can initiate at the national level.

The role of government, as the actor most able to transcend short-term realities and interests and invest in quality, is crucial

---

1. See the section on national and international assessments of cognitive skills in Chapter 3.

2. See, for instance, the NGO Declaration on Education for All, International Consultation of Non-Governmental Organizations, Dakar, 25 April 2000 (www.unesco.org/education/efa/wef_2000/cov_ngo_declaration.shtml).

3. See Chapter 2, Table 2.3: all the 'ambitious' countries are well below this benchmark (the share ranges from 1.3% of GNP in Sri Lanka to 4.2% in Brazil), except South Africa (5.8%). Of the 'high-performing' countries, Cuba (8.7%) and Finland (6.4%) exceed the benchmark, while Canada (5.3%) and the Republic of Korea (3.6%) invest below the threshold.

Thus, this chapter focuses primarily on actors: the learner, the teacher, the school leader or manager, the specialist and the policy-maker. Its mode of analysis differs from that of earlier chapters in that it builds partly on lessons of experience, learning from initiatives that have worked or failed and accepting that causal relations are often far less clear-cut than in analysis based more on quantitative data. The chapter does not attempt to be comprehensive. It looks for the attainable, not the ideal. It looks at making difficult choices about priorities. Its focus is primarily, but not exclusively, on formal schooling.

Start with learners

The quality of learning is and must be at the heart of EFA (UNESCO, 2000a). This being so, learners are central to attempts to improve the quality of education. While this may appear obvious, it is not always reflected in practice. All learning activities designed to offer meaningful learning outcomes should start with the clear understanding that learners are individuals, with different aptitudes and learning styles and with personal attributes influenced by their home and social backgrounds (Lubart, 2004).

It follows that strategies to improve quality should draw on the strengths of learners and on their knowledge, interests and capacities. As the previous edition of this Report on gender equality stressed, learners should not be treated as standard units in a uniform process. Education should be inclusive, responding to the diverse needs and circumstances of learners and giving appropriate weight to the abilities, skills and knowledge they bring to the teaching and learning process. The Dakar Framework makes clear that an inclusive learning environment is an essential attribute of high-quality education.[4]

In this context it is important to restate briefly the circumstances in which millions of children live:

■ In sub-Saharan Africa, more than 11 million children under 15 have lost at least one parent to HIV/AIDS, and the number is projected to reach 20 million by 2010 (UNAIDS/UNICEF, 2003).[5] Their access to learning opportunities is significantly constrained by the need to care for sick family members and younger siblings, by reductions in household income, by the burdens of loss and grief and by the stigma and discrimination that AIDS can bring.

■ Estimates suggest that there are 150 million children with *disabilities* worldwide and that fewer than 2% of them are enrolled in school. This is a diverse category, covering intellectual, physical, sensory and psychiatric disabilities (Disability Awareness in Action, 2004).

■ A recent survey of ten countries affected by or emerging from *conflict* found that more than 27 million children and young people, including refugees and internally displaced persons, lacked access to formal education (Women's Commission for Refugee Women and Children, 2004). The insecurity to which emergency gives rise particularly affects girls' education (UNESCO, 2003a). Moreover, experience of violence and the loss of family and friends have a major impact on children's emotional development.

■ The International Labour Office estimates that 16% of 5- to 14-year-olds worldwide were engaged in work in 2000, and that 7% of 5- to 9-year-olds and 10% of 10- to 14-year-olds combined work with schooling (ILO, 2002).[6] Work has an adverse impact on attendance, attainment

Figure 4.1: Policy framework for improving the quality of teaching and learning

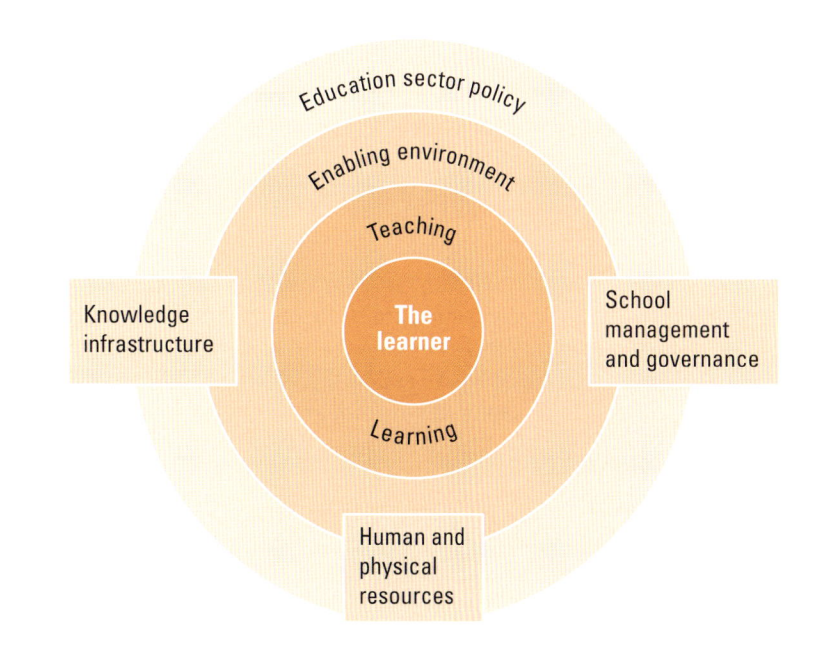

(concentric circles diagram: *The learner* at center, surrounded by *Teaching / Learning*, then *Enabling environment*, then *Education sector policy*; with external labels *Knowledge infrastructure*, *School management and governance*, *Human and physical resources*)

The Dakar Framework makes clear that an inclusive learning environment is an essential attribute of high-quality education

---

4. See strategy viii: 'Create safe, healthy, inclusive and equitably resourced educational environments conducive to excellence in learning, with clearly defined levels of achievement for all' (UNESCO, 2000a: 20).

5. The estimates of orphan populations vary depending on the methodology.

6. These figures exclude children working at home on household chores, so the actual number working and attending school is probably much larger, particularly for girls (UNESCO, 2003a).

> There is strong evidence that poor nutrition and health in early childhood severely affect cognitive development in later years

and achievement, especially when children work away from home for long hours (Orazem and Gunnarsson, 2003).

■ In all these circumstances, disadvantages linked to gender, race and ethnicity, culture and language, religion, social status and migration are likely to be exacerbated.

It follows that schools need to respond to these conditions of severe disadvantage and be proactive in helping to mitigate their impact on children. An essential starting point is assuring good health and safety, while recognizing that some problems require particular types of educational response.

Healthy and safe learners

The link between health and learning is well established (WHO, 1997). Ill health affects attendance, retention, cognitive development and academic performance. There is strong evidence that poor nutrition and health in early childhood severely affect cognitive development in later years.[7] Recent studies also reveal negative relationships between health and nutritional status and learners' school achievement.

This points to the importance of good early childhood care and the school's role in promoting good health and nutrition. School-based health programmes can be a cost-effective way to improve the health of learners at school and the community,[8] particularly when good use is made of local resources and networks, as a Burkina Faso programme illustrates (Box 4.1).

Internationally, the FRESH programme (Focusing Resources on Effective School Health), launched at Dakar, has developed a strategic framework to encourage health-promoting schools.[9] It has four main components:

■ **Health-related school policies**: Education policy should address issues of health, harassment, violence, inclusion and equity.

■ **Healthy learning environments**: Provision of safe water and adequate sanitation is the first step for a healthy learning environment.

■ **Skills-based health education**: Schools should promote balanced development of knowledge, attitudes, values and life skills covering social behaviours associated with factors such as HIV/AIDS, family life and reproductive health.

■ **School health and nutrition services**: School meals, deworming and other services are delivered effectively through school networks.

The strength of this initiative lies in its integrated approach to health promotion and its broad definition of a healthy school environment, addressing issues of violence, equity and inclusion.

Tragically, violence is endemic in many schools worldwide. Such behaviour as bullying, sexual harassment, abuse and vandalism increase anxiety and adversely affect attendance and performance. Violence can lead to serious psychological problems (WHO, 1998; Currie et al., 2004). Dealing effectively with violence requires a strong commitment to change by the whole school community. For example, a strategy developed in Norway for coping with bullying involves intervention by teachers, pupils and parents, clear school and classroom rules against bullying and

---

7. For details see Pollitt (1990), Levinger (1994), Rosso and Marek (1996), Drake et al. (2002), Vince-Whitman et al. (2001) and World Bank (2004h).

8. Miguel and Kremer (2004) found that a school deworming programme in Kenya reduced absenteeism among treated pupils by at least 25% and improved attendance of children in neighbouring schools as well. Given the low cost of mass treatment (US$0.49 per child in the United Republic of Tanzania, for instance), they argue that deworming is highly cost-effective and deserves government subsidy. For other studies on the effectiveness of school-based health and nutrition programmes, see Bennett (2003).

9. FRESH is a joint initiative of the World Health Organization, UNICEF, UNESCO and the World Bank. For details on its four core components and other information, see www.freshschools.org.

Box 4.1 School health and nutrition in Burkina Faso

Many school-aged children in Bazega province suffer from health problems. After a situation analysis, Save the Children (USA), in collaboration with the health and education ministries, launched a school-based health and nutrition programme in 1999. The programme comprises deworming, vitamin A and iodine supplementation, provision of latrines and safe drinking water and skills-based health education.

A study conducted after the first year in five schools found a significant reduction in the prevalence of malnutrition, anaemia and parasite infection, as well as a 20% increase in school attendance and improved performance in end-of-year exams. The programme has since expanded to cover the whole province, reaching nearly 15,000 children in 174 schools.

Sources: World Bank (2004i); Save the Children (2004).

> **Box 4.2 Inclusive education or special education?**
>
> Studies in both OECD and non-OECD countries indicate that students with disabilities achieve better school results in inclusive settings. Inclusive education also provides opportunities to build 'social networks, norms of reciprocity, mutual assistance and trustworthiness' (Putnam and Feldstein, 2003). Special schools tend to perpetuate the segregation of disabled people, yet, for students with some types of disabilities, provision of high-quality education in special schools may be more appropriate than 'inclusion' in a regular school that does not provide meaningful interaction with classmates and professionals. Ensuring that inclusive education is of good quality entails costs – for adapting curricula, training teachers,* developing teaching and learning materials, and providing transport and accessible facilities – that many countries may have trouble meeting. A third option is to reconcile the inclusive and specialized approaches in a 'twin track' approach in which parents and learners decide whether to opt for an inclusive regular school or a special school initially, with inclusive education remaining the ultimate goal.
>
> *In some countries, specially trained teachers are paid less than other teachers because they have fewer pupils. This discourages teachers from training for special needs (Nordström, 2004).
>
> Sources: Nordström (2004); Richler (2004); Magrab (2004); Wormnaes (2004).

the establishment of school committees to handle the problem (Olweus, 2001).[10]

Responsive and inclusive schools

Proactive measures can also be taken to address disadvantages afflicting many millions of children. Four brief examples make this point.

Meeting the needs of *learners with disabilities* is particularly challenging, given the unresolved debate between proponents of a strong inclusive approach and those who argue for special needs provision (Box 4.2). In large measure this controversy reflects the many definitions and types of disability. Each type requires learner-specific responses, whether in mainstream or special schools.

As Chapter 2 shows, the cognitive skills required to make informed choices in respect of *HIV/AIDS* risk and behavioural change appear to be closely linked to levels of education and literacy. But schools must also find responsive and flexible ways to meet the needs of learners already affected by HIV/AIDS either directly or indirectly, e.g. through being orphaned and taking on wider family responsibilities.[11] For example, peer support can help address the psychological burden of orphanhood and the social stigma and sense of exclusion it may bring. Measures to reduce the financial burden of schooling, such as provision of stipends, will increase retention and completion among learners affected by HIV/AIDS.[12]

Flexible timetables and enrolment schedules, and special out-of-school learning groups can also help, as they do for children who work or have never attended school (UNICEF, 1999a; ILO, 2004). Above all, schools should not expel children on the grounds of HIV/AIDS status – nor because of race, ethnicity, religion, early pregnancy or sexual orientation. The school environment should be inclusive, safe and welcoming, and should respect human rights (World Bank, 2002b; Pigozzi, 2004).[13]

In some circumstances, the inclusion of disadvantaged learners may require alternatives to formal schools and full-time schooling. *Distance learning* is one such option, especially where it can be made highly flexible and context-specific. Examples from India and Somalia illustrate the point (Box 4.3).

> **Box 4.3 Distance learning for disadvantaged learners**
>
> The Open School Society in the Indian state of Andhra Pradesh was founded in 1991 and now comprises 4,700 centres, reaching over 100,000 learners, many of them dropouts, children from scheduled castes and learners with disabilities. It offers a condensed curriculum of language, mathematics and environmental studies in flexible, face-to-face instruction and in regional languages, several times a week. The programme provides regular training for teachers and community members. It has the advantage of being able to provide equivalence with the formal primary education system while remaining culturally and linguistically relevant to local needs.
>
> The Somali Distance Education for Literacy programme teaches literacy, numeracy and life skills through weekly radio programmes, print materials and face-to-face instruction. It has over 10,000 registered learners, 70% of them women and girls, in some 350 classes.
>
> Source: IRFOL (2004)

10. For details, see www.colorado.edu/cspv/safeschools/bullying/overview.html and http://modelprograms.samhsa.gov.

11. The impact of orphanhood on enrolment and attendance has yet to be established. Studies show lower enrolment and attendance among orphans in many countries, but the pattern varies by country, suggesting differing local responses (World Bank, 2002b).

12. For a detailed examination of these issues, see Pigozzi (2004).

13. Also see the section below on better schools.

> In situations of conflict and emergency, education is particularly important for children because it can provide stability and hope

In situations of *conflict and emergency*, education tends to be a low priority. Yet it is particularly important for children in such situations because it can provide stability and hope. Learning activities and knowledge that can help children cope mentally and physically with stress, while building values and attitudes that promote peace, should be emphasized. Key elements in fostering a sense of safety and personal well-being include safe play, sport and cultural activities; strong messages on health, nutrition and sanitation; mine awareness and other types of safety information; and development of communication and negotiation skills as a foundation for a peaceful and secure society.[14] The Inter-Agency Network for Education in Emergencies (INEE) is developing a set of minimum standards designed to help the international community and other actors provide education of sufficient quality in situations of emergency and early reconstruction (Anderson Pillsbury, 2004).

Learner readiness

It is now widely recognized that early childhood care and education (ECCE) substantially enhances children's school readiness,[15] yet this is not an area of significant investment by governments in most countries, despite evidence suggesting that such investment is a cost-effective way to improve education quality. A cross-country study in sub-Saharan Africa shows clear relationships between preschool coverage and repetition and survival rates as well as children's physical development (Jaramillo and Mingat, 2003).[16] The study concludes that 87% of investment in preschool will be repaid in the form of increased efficiency in primary education.[17] Other individual and social returns – such as better health, higher income and greater social cohesion – will most likely offset the remaining 13%, and possibly much more. While formal preschool is the most costly form of ECCE, cheaper options exist, such as mobilizing parents (see Chapter 2), and such informal ECCE activities may bring no less impressive benefits. Ways to provide affordable ECCE should receive greater attention.

Conclusion

Understanding learners' needs, circumstances, strengths and capacities should underpin the development and implementation of all education programmes. Education that is not inclusive, in the broadest sense of that term, is unlikely to bring or sustain improvements in learning quality. The challenge for governments is to develop teaching and learning strategies that recognize this.

Improving teaching and learning

Teaching and learning are what learners experience. Together they form a process that takes place in classrooms and other learning settings. It is by this complex process that learners acquire the knowledge, skills, values and beliefs that constitute a good education. Consequently, policy decisions on teaching and learning are of the utmost importance. This section highlights seven major policy areas for attention. The first six are directly related to teaching and learning: establishing *appropriate goals* for the curriculum, developing *relevant content*, *using time well*, ensuring that *teaching styles are effective*, carefully considering the *language of instruction* and developing a sound *assessment* policy. The final policy area deals with enabling inputs that indirectly support quality teaching and learning: the supply, distribution and use of *learning materials* and a secure, accessible *physical environment* with appropriate facilities.

Appropriate, relevant aims

What happens in classrooms should reflect agreement as to what learners should learn and why. This is a matter of major interest in all societies. Invariably, weight is given to the knowledge and skills necessary for productive lives and livelihoods. But there is also strong concern for social and cultural values, human rights, greater equity and equality, and, increasingly, good citizenship, democracy and world peace.[18] Clarity about the aims of education strengthens the coherence of the education system and helps in itself to improve quality.

Arriving at an appropriate set of educational aims largely involves striking a good balance between global or generic and local or more contextual skills and values. In many countries there is likely to be a need to refine this process by balancing general educational aims that stress national

---

14. See, for example, Sinclair (2001, 2002).

15. See Myers (2004) and UNESCO (2002*a*, 2003*a*).

16. The study cited here focuses on formal preschool because too few data on other forms of ECCE were available.

17. The authors estimate that if African countries expand preschool coverage to 40% by 2015, primary school repetition rates will fall to 15%, from 20% in 2000, and survival to grade 5 will rise from 65% to 78%.

18. See, for example, Weva (2003*a*).

Table 4.1: Policy choices in determining national curriculum goals as reflected in the Convention on the Rights of the Child

	Generic/global	Country/local
Cognitive skills development	'The development of the child's personality, talents and mental and physical abilities to their fullest potential' (Article 29.1.a.) The rights to literacy, numeracy and life skills, 'such as the ability to make well-balanced decisions; to resolve conflicts in a non-violent manner; and to develop a healthy lifestyle, good social relationships and responsibility, critical thinking, creative talents, and other abilities which give children the tools needed to pursue their options in life'[1]	'...[T]he development of the individual child's personality, talents and abilities, in recognition of the fact that every child has unique characteristics, interests, abilities, and learning needs. Thus, the curriculum must be of direct relevance to the child's social, cultural, environmental and economic context and to his or her present and future needs and take full account of the child's evolving capacities; teaching methods should be tailored to the different needs of different children'[1]
Values development	'The development of respect for human rights...' (Article 29.1.b.) 'The preparation of the child for responsible life in a free society, in the spirit of understanding, peace, tolerance, equality of sexes, and friendship among all peoples, ethnic, national and religious groups and persons of indigenous origin' (Article 29.1.d.) 'The development of respect for the natural environment' (Article 29.1.e.)	'The development of respect for the child's parents, his or her own cultural identity, language and values, for the national values of the country in which the child is living, the country from which he or she may originate, and for civilizations different from his or her own' (Article 29.1.c.) '...the right [of the child belonging to minority groups], in community with other members of his or her group, to enjoy his or her own culture, to profess and practice his or her own religion, or to use his or her own language.' (Article 30)

1. Appendix, para. 9. (CRC/GC/2001/1) Committee on the Rights of the Child, General Comment 1: The Aims of Education

---

unity and identity with aims that reflect the needs of particular groups. These choices are extremely important in defining the school curriculum.

Table 4.1 draws on the Convention on the Rights of the Child (see Chapter 1) to present important areas for policy debate on curriculum design, classifying them by whether they relate to generic/global aims or country/local goals and indicating the balance between cognitive skills and values development.[19]

Using data from the national curricula of 108 countries, held by the UNESCO International Bureau of Education (IBE), we can gauge shifts in the weight that countries accord to different objectives, from the mid-1980s to the early years of the new millennium. The right-hand column of Table 4.2 sets out some of the more significant changes. In essence, while basic skills retain a strong place in national curriculum objectives, increased prominence is being given to values associated with citizenship and democracy, as well as to education as a human right and education for sustainable development.

This evidence suggests that countries do review the mix between global and local, and the balance between values and cognitive skills and knowledge. The table also offers some insight on the extent to which educational aims and the goals of curricula are designed to address the social and economic imperatives of life locally, nationally and globally. While radical, transformative changes occasionally occur,[20] adaptation and reshaping of existing curricula are more usual.[21]

One way to move towards a relevant, balanced set of aims is to analyse the curriculum in terms of inclusion. An inclusive approach to curriculum policy recognizes that while every learner has multiple needs – even more so in situations of vulnerability and disadvantage – everyone should benefit from a commonly accepted basic level of education quality. In the United Kingdom, a government-supported 'Index for Inclusion'[22] identifies three dimensions of inclusion: creating inclusive cultures, producing inclusive policies and evolving inclusive practices (Booth and Ainscow, 2000).

The debate about the aims of education may seem remote from the practice of classroom teaching and learning. But without an educational vision and a sense of direction and purpose, it is impossible to arrive at nationally accepted approaches to content, pedagogy and assessment.

---

19. Some observers identify a strong tendency to adopt global/generic standards and skills, maintaining that international accountability legislation fuels this trend. It is sometimes seen as resulting in greater uniformity of education (Ohanian, 1999) and insufficient attention to local aims related to social change and human development.

20. One example is Paolo Freire's reading method, in which the teaching and learning of literacy centres on words with strong social and economic implications. Freire claims reading can be taught more effectively if the words being learned have important meaning to the learners and are in themselves empowering.

21. Current initiatives tend to be less radical than those of the 1960s and 1970s, such as Julius Nyerere's vision of Education for Self-Reliance (see Chapter 1: 34 and Kassam, 1995).

22. The index is an evaluation tool, designed to facilitate a participatory approach to developing inclusive education. This approach stresses the importance of examining the social and cultural purposes of the evaluation before considering such areas as schools, programmes and assessment (Lynch, 2000).

Table 4.2: Trends in curriculum statements, 1980s[1] to 2000s[2]

Aims of education as set out in Article 29 of the Convention on the Rights of the Child	Trends in objectives of education drawn from curriculum documents of 108 countries, over two periods, mid-1980s and early 2000s
'The development of respect for human rights...'	The number of countries emphasizing education as the fulfilment of a human right has increased. It is prominent in developing countries but the emphasis has declined in developed countries.
'The development of the child's personality, talents and mental and physical abilities to their fullest potential'	More countries now include development of individuals' capabilities, including skills and attitudes for critical thinking and problem-solving. In general, the development of personal capabilities, including emotional, creative and cognitive development, is given more attention at the primary level than in formal education as a whole. All world regions continue to put high priority on these non-cognitive skills. Attention to 'cognitive development and intellectual capacity' also increased, with basic skills such as literacy and numeracy emphasized across all regions and over time.
'The development of respect for the child's parents, his or her own cultural identity, language and values, for the national values of the country in which the child is living...'	The number of countries including religions and national identity as educational aims declined slightly overall, but trends in the regions reflect different social and political situations. Religion is strongly emphasized in the Arab States and in South and West Asia, while more countries in Central and Eastern Europe place importance on national identity.
'The preparation of the child for responsible life in a free society, in the spirit of understanding, peace, tolerance, equality of sexes...'	Greater attention is now being given to values, including democracy, citizenship and equality.
'The development of respect for the natural environment'	The number of countries including sustainable development as an aim of education tripled between the 1980s and the 2000s, albeit from a low base. The trend is particularly prominent in developing countries.

Note: For methodological detail see the source document.
1. Refers to 1980-85.
2. Refers to 1996-2001.
Source: Amadio et al. (2004)

> Central to the curriculum is the teaching and learning of reading and writing. Literacy is a critical tool for the mastery of other subjects

Relevant content

The goals of the curriculum take shape in the subjects taught in schools. This fact gives rise to a policy debate regarding the definition of subjects, their number and the allocation of time to each. Opinion remains divided over the trade-offs between a curriculum with broad subject coverage and one defined more narrowly, focusing on a small set of priority goals and core subjects.

In practice, the mean numbers of subjects or subject areas listed in official curricula around the world have changed relatively little over the past two decades, for all grade levels (Benavot, 2004a). The *composition* of these subjects does appear to be changing, however, especially in relation to 'newer' subjects.[23] Consequently, a broad distinction can be made between these additions to the curriculum and subjects that contribute more directly to literacy and numeracy.

Central to the curriculum is the teaching and learning of reading and writing. Literacy is a critical tool for the mastery of other subjects.

It is also one of the best predictors of longer-term learning achievement.[24] Literacy must therefore be considered a priority area in efforts to improve the quality of basic education, particularly for learners from disadvantaged backgrounds (Gauthier and Dembélé, 2004).

While classroom time allocated to literacy skills has generally remained stable worldwide over the past two decades, the mean percentage of total instruction time allocated to mathematics instruction has declined slightly in the upper grades of primary education and increased marginally in lower primary education (Table 4.3). By and large, the patterns noted at the global level for mathematics are also apparent in each EFA region.[25] Conversely, the trend of incorporating and assigning greater priority to other subjects than literacy and mathematics in the curriculum is on the increase (Box 4.4 and Table 4.4).

Overall, the most notable increases are in the time allocated to environmental education and technology-related education. Vocational

---

23. 'Newer' refers here to subjects other than reading, writing and mathematics.

24. An analysis from North America reports that if a student has reading difficulties at the end of the first year of formal schooling, the probability of this student having difficulty at the end of grade 4 and at secondary level is as high as 90% (Juel, 1991).

25. Some regions saw a very slight increase between grades 1 and 2, but the overall trend of decline between primary (grades 1–6) and lower secondary education (grades 7–9) occurred clearly worldwide.

Table 4.3: Mean percentage of total instructional time allocated to mathematics in primary and lower secondary education, by grade level and time period
(constant cases within grade levels[1])

EFA Region	Time[2] period	Grade 1[3]	Grade 2	Grade 3	Grade 4	Grade 5	Grade 6	Grade 7	Grade 8	Grade 9
Sub-Saharan Africa	1980s	20.8	20.2	19.6	18.6	20.3	20.5	16.6	16.1	16.1
	2000s	19.2	19.2	19	18.2	18.1	17.7	16.5	16	17.2
	(n)	12	12	12	12	12	11	10	8	5
Arab States	1980s	18.1	17.9	17.4	16.9	15.3	16.3	14.4	14	13.9
	2000s	17.6	18.5	17.1	17	16.8	16.6	14.2	14	14.3
	(n)	12	13	13	13	12	13	12	12	12
East Asia and the Pacific	1980s	17.5	20.5	19.8	19.6	18.3	15.9	13.8	14.2	14.3
	2000s	21	22.5	17.9	17.1	15.5	15.9	13.3	13.2	12
	(n)	7	7	7	6	6	5	7	7	7
South and West Asia	1980s	17.8	17.8	16.5	16.4	15.9	15.9	12.4	12.4	–
	2000s	19.1	19.8	15.7	16.4	16.4	12	11	11	10
	(n)	4	4	4	4	3	1	2	2	0
Latin America and the Caribbean	1980s	17.7	17.7	18	17.5	16.5	17.1	15.4	14.3	14.3
	2000s	23.4	23.4	23.3	21.8	21.6	21.1	14.6	14.5	13.4
	(n)	9	9	9	9	10	10	13	13	12
North America and Western Europe	1980s	18.4	18.2	18	16.6	16	15.1	14	12.8	13.2
	2000s	17.7	17.6	16.8	16.7	15.9	15.4	13.8	13	13
	(n)	11	11	11	11	11	11	9	7	6
Central and Eastern Europe	1980s	22.3	21.9	20	20	18.3	16.4	14.5	13.8	–
	2000s	19.3	19	17.8	17.4	15.2	14.2	13.4	13	–
	(n)	9	9	8	8	8	8	8	8	0
Global Mean	1980s	19.1	19.2	18.5	17.9	17.3	17	14.8	14.1	14.3
	2000s	19.4	19.7	18.4	17.9	17.3	16.9	14.3	13.9	13.9
	(n)	64	65	64	63	62	59	61	57	42

Note: For methodological detail see the source document. Data is not available for Central Asia.
1. The calculations are based on the data sets of the number of countries (n) for which the relevant data are available for both periods for a given grade. For example, nine countries in Latin America and the Caribbean have data on instruction time for grade 1 for both the 1980s and the 2000s. Countries with data for only one period are excluded from the analysis.
2. '1980s' refers to 1980–85; '2000s' refers to 1996–2001.
3. 'Grade I' is the first year of primary education.
Source: Benavot (2004a)

education is losing currency, while the social sciences are little changed. Civics and citizenship education has gained ground in Latin America and the Caribbean and in East Asia and the Pacific but is less evident in Central and Eastern Europe, the higher grades in sub-Saharan Africa and the lower grades in North America and Western Europe. The time allotted to subjects relating to moral values, as opposed to skills-based subjects, increased in sub-Saharan Africa and in North America and Western Europe but decreased elsewhere, though countries in East Asia and the Pacific, while experiencing this decline, still give weight to these subjects. Surprisingly, health education appears to have decreased in Latin America and the Caribbean and in the Arab States, as well as in the lower grades in sub-Saharan Africa and East Asia and the Pacific. Trends in the higher grades are not consistent within regions. North America and Western Europe have increased instruction in health education at all levels (Benavot, 2004a).

Although these trends can be mapped, little can be said about the learning implications of increasing the quantity of subjects within the curriculum, or about the trade-off between literacy and mathematics versus other subjects as manifested in learning outcomes.[26] What can be stressed is the importance of weighing the options carefully, especially as regards available instructional time.

26. The ways 'newer' subjects are actually taught varies. For example, HIV AIDS prevention education may be integrated into any of several subjects or 'infused' throughout the curriculum. Many countries teach HIV/AIDS prevention as part of life skills development (Panchaud, Pii and Poncet, 2004; Smith, Kippax and Aggleton, 2000).

> **Box 4.4 The currency of a selection of newer subjects and subject areas# at global level**
>
> ■ **Health education or hygiene**
>
> In one-fourth to one-third of countries globally, some form of health education is required during primary and (lower) secondary education. Its prevalence in primary school curricula has declined slightly since the 1980s, but this trend is less apparent in secondary school curricula. The content of health education varies greatly. It can include family planning, HIV/AIDS prevention education, sex education, drug prevention and personal hygiene. The prevalence of health education in national curricula may reflect, in part, the broad-based content possible under this catch-all subject label.
>
> ■ **Human rights education***
>
> Considered an integral part of the right to education, this area has gained some recognition as a human right in itself. It is designed to increase knowledge of and respect for the rights and freedoms of each and every person, including the individual learner.
>
> ■ **Multicultural education***
>
> Multicultural education promotes knowledge and understanding of the cultures of fellow learners and citizens. It has gained considerable prominence in the past two decades.
>
> ■ **Environmental subjects and education for sustainable development**
>
> Pollution, concerns over population and food supplies, depletion of natural resources and the ozone layer, the greenhouse effect and possible solutions for such environmental concerns are being covered in the primary school curricula of many industrialized and, to a lesser extent, developing countries. Overall the prevalence of this subject in national curricula has increased notably in the past fifteen years. While it is given greater prominence during the first five grades of primary school, the proportion of countries requiring instruction in environment-related topics has increased in all grades.
>
> ■ **Citizenship and global citizenship education: educating for democracy and peace**
>
> Civics and citizenship education has increased in almost all grade levels since the 1980s. Attention given to citizenship education is particularly apparent in the lower grades of primary education. On average, one-fifth to one-third of all countries require the teaching of this subject in primary school and close to half of all countries require it to be taught in the (lower) secondary grades.
>
> ■ **Technology**
>
> On average, technology-related topics – excluding computer instruction – accounted for 5%–6% of primary-grade timetables in the 1980s but is now required in 16%–27% of all primary-level timetables. Its prevalence as a required subject area has more than doubled in the lower secondary grades. Overall, in both the early 1980s and today, the importance of this subject increases with grade level. Factoring-in computer instruction would heighten this trend.
>
> ■ **Development or global education**
>
> Development of global education is largely specific to industrialized countries. Comprising elements from education for sustainable development, human rights education, citizenship education, world studies, civics education, anti-racist education and peace education, it encourages learners to critically explore the relationship between North and South, understand global interdependences and work towards change in attitudes, values and behaviour (DEA, 1996). There is some evidence that development education is contributing to changing attitudes, thereby enhancing public support for development (McDonnell, Lecomte and Wegimont, 2003).
>
> #These subjects may also be categorized as life skills and receive attention in the area of non-formal and adult education (UNESCO, 2003a).
>
> *No trend data are available for these subjects.
>
> *Source:* Benavot (2004a)

Using time well

Instructional time is an aspect of the curriculum that deserves special attention. The length of time required to achieve educational goals is a matter of considerable significance and a strong indicator of students' access to learning opportunities. School effectiveness research (Chapter 2) shows consistent positive correlations between instructional time and students' achievement at both primary and secondary levels. Significantly, this relationship appears stronger in developing countries; Fuller and Clarke (1994) report this finding to hold good in twelve out of fourteen studies. The World Bank estimates that 850 to 1,000 effective hours (not necessarily official hours) of schooling per year is optimal in publicly financed primary schools (World Bank, 2004a). Increased instructional time enhances learners' exposure to knowledge and

Table 4.4: Mean percentage of countries requiring instruction in selected newer subjects in primary and lower secondary education, by grade level and time period

Subject areas	Time Period[1]	Grade 1	Grade 2	Grade 3	Grade 4	Grade 5	Grade 6	Grade 7	Grade 8	Grade 9	Number of countries
Hygiene/Health Education	1980s	26.2	29.4	31.8	35.3	31.7	32.9	25.9	24.1	16.7	72–85
	2000s	25.0	25.0	26.4	25.0	27.6	27.2	21.3	23.7	22.3	93–127
Environmental Science/Ecology	1980s	17.9	17.6	15.3	12.9	9.8	7.6	1.2	1.2	0.0	72–85
	2000s	24.4	26.0	25.6	23.4	16.5	11.2	7.4	5.1	6.5	93–127
Civics/Citizenship Education	1980s	13.1	14.1	17.6	21.2	26.5	34.1	40.2	45.9	39.7	73–85
	2000s	21.0	21.8	25.6	28.2	31.5	35.2	39.3	38.7	51.1	93–127
Social Studies	1980s	31.3	33.3	40.0	43.5	46.9	43.0	43.5	42.2	40.3	72–85
	2000s	32.0	31.2	39.7	46.0	42.5	43.7	49.6	46.7	45.3	94–127
Moral or Values Education	1980s	25.0	25.9	23.5	24.7	25.6	20.3	16.7	18.3	13.9	72–86
	2000s	24.2	25.0	26.4	26.6	27.6	27.2	23.8	21.0	21.3	94–127
Technology and Related Subjects[2]	1980s	4.8	5.9	5.9	5.9	6.1	5.1	14.1	15.7	16.7	72–86
	2000s	16.1	16.1	18.4	21.0	25.2	27.2	35.0	35.8	37.9	95–127
Vocational Education/Skills	1980s	21.4	21.2	22.4	21.2	22.0	26.6	32.6	38.6	36.1	72–86
	2000s	17.1	17.1	17.7	19.5	21.4	23.4	30.6	28.8	25.8	93–126

Note: For methodological detail see the source document.
1. '1980s' refers to 1980–85; '2000s' refers to 1996–2001.
2. Excludes computer instruction.
Source: Benavot (2004a)

---

results in correspondingly significant learning gains (Benavot, 2004b). Recent analysis suggests, however, that global annual intended instructional time has not increased since the mid-1980s and is often well below 1,000 hours (Table 4.5). In many countries instructional time has declined. In some cases (e.g. Japan) this may be an outcome of curriculum reform in which the number of subjects has been reduced. In others, particularly developing countries, meeting demand for increased access under resource constraints may have resulted in reductions in instructional time (Benavot, 2004a).

Table 4.6 shows annual instructional time by region. In all regions, it increases with grade. Sub-Saharan Africa has the highest values in all grades. Latin America and the Caribbean, East Asia and the Pacific and North America and Western Europe score high as well.

Intended instructional time – the maximum amount set out in national curriculum statements – is not the same as actual learning time. Studies in developed countries (OECD, 1996; Doll, 1996) reveal disparities between intended instruction time, actual time allocated in schools, the time learners spend actually learning ('time on task') and the time they spend on academic tasks ('academic learning time').[27] The amount of time decreases from the first to the fourth of these categories, especially in schools in poor communities. Micro studies have shown that in developing countries considerable amounts of time allocated for instruction are lost because of teacher and learner absenteeism, classroom shortages and lack of learning materials, as well as more universal phenomena such as lack of discipline and difficulty in maintaining learners' attention (Benavot, 2004b). Loss of instructional time deserves a high degree of attention, as it is a major constraint on improving quality. It can be remedied, however, primarily through better school management and organization and more effective teaching strategies.[28]

Table 4.5: Global average of annual instructional time,[1] by grade level and time period

	Grade 1	Grade 2	Grade 3	Grade 4	Grade 5	Grade 6	Grade 7	Grade 8	Grade 9
1985	710	720	760	791	817	844	896	908	900
2000	705	717	754	780	811	825	900	904	940
Number of countries	79	79	79	79	78	77	71	69	54

Note: For methodological detail see the source document.
1. Annual instructional time for each country is estimated, based on national documents submitted to UNESCO and supplementary sources. As the precision of these documents varies, the data should be interpreted with caution.
Source: Benavot (2004a)

27. See also Benavot (2004b).

28. Carnoy, Gove and Marshall (forthcoming) note remarkable differences in time use among schools in Brazil, Chile and Cuba and among different types of school within Chile, and report that the differences seem to be associated with learning achievement.

Table 4.6: Regional average yearly instructional time by grade level in 2000

EFA Regions	Grade 1	Grade 2	Grade 3	Grade 4	Grade 5	Grade 6	Grade 7	Grade 8	Grade 9	Number of countries
Sub-Saharan Africa	755	775	812	847	872	871	951	946	965	16-18
Arab States	725	732	752	792	813	820	862	868	880	17
Central Asia	533	575	620	647	740	754	798	812	830	9
East Asia and the Pacific	704	710	764	784	814	826	911	918	918	14
South and West Asia	646	646	730	769	771	856	885	890	907	7-5
Latin America and the Caribbean	761	764	781	783	792	796	921	928	943	17-18
North America and Western Europe	743	748	790	799	845	847	894	906	933	23
Central and Eastern Europe	549	597	624	658	734	773	811	830	855	20
Total	689	705	742	766	804	819	883	891	908	122-125

Source: Benavot (2004a).

Effective teaching styles

What goes on in the classroom, and the impact of the teacher and teaching, has been identified in numerous studies as *the* crucial variable for improving learning outcomes. The way teachers teach is of critical concern in any reform designed to improve quality.

In an influential study, Coleman et al. (1966; cited in Gauthier and Dembélé, 2004: 2–4) identified the teacher variable as having the most pronounced effect on school achievement among pupils from modest backgrounds and ethnic minorities. More recent meta-analysis designed to assess the factors that are most likely to help children learn has confirmed the significance of the teacher effect. In a rigorous study of twenty-eight such factors, the two most prominent were found to be directly related to the teacher (Wang, Haertel and Walberg, 1994). A synthesis of 134 meta-analyses (Hattie, 1992; cited in Dembélé and Miaro-II, 2003) reached similar conclusions, indicating that even when there are significant differences in learners' backgrounds, teachers can exert a powerful influence, raising levels of achievement (Crahay, 2000).

Further research, however, indicates a wide variation in effectiveness among teachers. Good teachers appear to be effective with learners of all achievement levels no matter how heterogeneous their classrooms. If the teacher is ineffective, his or her students are more likely to perform at lower levels (Wright, Horn and Sanders, 1997; cited in Gauthier and Dembélé, 2004). More recent work (Babu and Mendro, 2003; Rivkin, Hanushek and Kain, 2002:

3; both cited in Gauthier and Dembélé, 2004) confirms these findings. The immediate and clear implication is that much can be done to significantly improve education by improving teacher effectiveness. This in turn requires attention to pedagogy and the way teachers teach.

Recent findings on the theme of pedagogical renewal and teacher development in sub-Saharan Africa[29] conclude that:

- Undesirable teaching practices persist.

- They can be described as following a rigid, chalk-and-talk, teacher centred/dominated, lecture-driven pedagogy or rote learning.

- Such pedagogy places students in a passive role, limiting their activity to memorizing facts and reciting them to the teacher. It is also reflected in classroom assessment practices.

- Such teaching practices are the norm in the vast majority of classrooms in sub-Saharan Africa and elsewhere, even in the most affluent countries (Dembélé and Miaro-II, 2003).

Pedagogical renewal across sub-Saharan Africa has included many attempts to switch to learner-centred, activity-oriented pedagogy and away from teacher-dominated instructional practices (Anderson, 2002; Kotta, 1986; Tabulawa, 1997; Storeng, 2001; van Graan et al., 2003; all cited in Dembélé and Miaro-II, 2003). Such efforts may be explained in part by the current tendency of some international agencies to favour such pedagogies. In most of the countries concerned, however,

> Good teachers appear to be effective with learners of all achievement levels no matter how heterogeneous their classrooms

---

29. Case studies, background papers and literature reviews by the African education research networks ERNESA and ERNWACA, produced for the 2003 Biennial Meeting on Quality held by the Association for the Development of Education in Africa, are available at www.adeanet.org/publications_biennale/en_2003 bienpubs.html.

> **Box 4.5 Open-ended and discovery-based instruction**
>
> Open-ended and discovery-based pedagogies involve high-level cognitive skills such as comprehension, the application of knowledge, divergent thinking and problem solving. Examples of programmes that have adopted these pedagogies include:
>
> - the **Escuela Nueva programme** in Colombia;
> - the **Non-Formal Primary Education programme** of the Bangladesh Rural Advancement Committee;
> - the **Escuela Nueva Unitaria programme** in Guatemala;
> - the **Fe y Alegria schools** in Latin America;
> - **multigrade programmes** in Guinea and Zambia;
> - **Convergent Pedagogy** in Mali;
> - the UNICEF-sponsored **Community Schools programme** in Egypt;
> - the **MECE programme** in Chile;
> - a **network of 'education for production' programmes** in Latin America;
> - Namibia's **Basic Education Teacher Diploma**;
> - the Aga Khan Foundation-supported **Dar-es-Salaam Primary Schools Projects**;
> - Botswana's **University-Based Teacher Education Model**.
>
> Typically, these programmes have some or all of the following characteristics:
>
> - child-centred rather than teacher-driven pedagogy;
> - active rather than passive learning;
> - multigrade classrooms with continuously assessed learning;
> - combinations of fully trained teachers, partly trained teachers and community resource people, all of them heavily involved in learning and in school management;
> - peer tutoring among learners;
> - carefully developed self-guided learning materials;
> - teacher- and student-constructed learning materials;
> - active student involvement in school governance and management;
> - use of radio, correspondence materials, television in some cases and computers in a few cases;
> - ongoing and regular in-service training and peer mentoring for teachers;
> - ongoing monitoring, evaluation and feedback systems;
> - strong links between the school and the community;
> - attention by the community to children's nutrition and health long before they reach school age;
> - local adaptations of the school day or school year cycle;
> - a school focus on learning rather than teaching.
>
> *Sources:* Avalos (1980); Farrell (2002); Anderson (2002); Craig, Kraft and du Plessis (1998); Hopkin (1997).

attempts to institutionalize child-centred pedagogy in schools and teacher-training institutions have produced inconclusive results. One investigation into why this is so, in Botswana (Tabulawa, 1997), cites deeply engrained epistemological assumptions by teachers and students, as well as social factors inherent in Tswana society. The assumptions were found to conflict with the basic tenets of child-centred pedagogy. If confirmed, this finding would indicate that, for open-ended pedagogies to be successful, significant change in the culture of knowledge acquisition may be required.

A further body of knowledge says that teaching practices are informed by ideas and beliefs that teachers begin to develop long before embracing teaching as a career and that traditional teacher preparation does not successfully challenge these beliefs (Dembélé and Miaro-II, 2003). Experts broadly agree on what constitutes *undesirable* practice: a teacher-centred pedagogy, which places students in a passive role. There is also some consensus on the desirability of a participatory, interactive, child-centred, active pedagogy that is characterized by cooperative learning and inquiry and fosters conceptual understanding, critical thinking and problem-solving skills (ibid.). These desirable practices fall under the general category of 'open-ended' instruction (Box 4.5).

In the spectrum between 'traditional' chalk-and-talk teaching and open-ended instruction, some educators advocate structured teaching, a combination of direct instruction, guided practice and independent learning (Box 4.6).[30]

Discovery-based pedagogies have proved extremely difficult to implement on a national scale. Moreover, their success relies heavily on appropriate levels of physical resources, strong

Structured teaching is a combination of direct instruction, guided practice and independent learning

[30]. Evidence from North America and the United Kingdom suggests that structured pedagogies work far better than open-ended approaches for children from socio-economically disadvantaged backgrounds and those excluded on the grounds of race or ethnicity, as well as slower learners, those with learning difficulties and underachievers. The research also indicates that this approach is not prejudicial to high achievers (Gauthier and Dembélé, 2004).

> **Box 4.6 Structured teaching**
>
> The concept of structured teaching stems from research identifying the teaching strategies and techniques used by experienced teachers and comparing them with those used by inexperienced teachers. The research highlights the practices that most help learning. Experiments have demonstrated that when inexperienced teachers are trained to use effective techniques, student achievement improves significantly.
>
> Structured and systematic teaching consists of presenting material in small steps, pausing to check for student understanding and eliciting active and successful participation from all students. It is a particularly appropriate method for learning reading, mathematics, grammar, mother tongue, sciences, history and, to some extent, foreign languages. It can be adapted to young pupils as well as to slow learners of any age.
>
> Structured instruction has proved most effective for teaching literacy. After a review of 1,056 experimental studies conducted over thirty years in the United States on the processes of learning to read, the National Reading Panel recommended explicit, systematic and intensive teaching of the various components of reading: phonological awareness and phonemes, grapho-phonetic entry points, guided oral and silent reading, and vocabulary. The panel recommended teaching reading by modelling, a technique in which the teacher illustrates links between new and prior knowledge and demonstrates forms of reasoning that foster better understanding. This requires providing many occasions for guided practice, during which students should receive feedback, so that later they can read successfully on their own.
>
> *Sources:* Brophy and Good (1986); Gage (1986); Good, Biddle and Brophy (1983); Rosenshine and Stevens (1986); all cited in Gauthier and Dembélé (2004).

support and well-motivated, enthusiastic teachers. This does not mean that the idea of open-ended pedagogy should be abandoned in resourced-constrained situations, but it does face formidable challenges, even in optimal conditions. Thus, structured instruction may be the more pragmatic option for providing satisfactory quality in education in situations of severe resource constraints, high pupil/teacher ratios (which complicate classroom management and individual learning strategies) and underqualified or unmotivated teachers.[31] With an approach to structured teaching that leaves space for individual discovery, good teachers can create a child-centred environment even in adverse circumstances. Child-centred in this context suggests respect for children and encouraging their involvement in their own learning (Croft, 2002).

Pedagogies for non-conventional settings

For people living where there is no school because of geographical isolation or low population density, or for those with nomadic lifestyles, alternative pedagogies are likely to be needed. Distance learning for conflict areas (discussed earlier in this chapter), mobile classrooms for nomadic communities and non-formal schools with teachers recruited from the community are among the possible responses.[32]

Where schools do exist but are extremely underpopulated, multigrade teaching is an option. Although sheer logistical and economic factors can make multigrade teaching a necessity, it can also be a choice as an effective pedagogy for addressing the needs of a diversity of learners. Box 4.7 summarises the main conditions for effective multigrade teaching.

Language of instruction matters

Most countries in the world are bilingual or multilingual.[33] Hence, national language policy and the selection of languages to be taught in school and used as the media of instruction is of considerable importance for the quality of teaching and learning. It is a policy choice with implications for curriculum goals, content and pedagogy. It is also an intensely political matter. As UNECSO notes (UNESCO, 2003b):

> Educational policy makers have difficult decisions to make with regard to languages, schooling and the curriculum in which the technical and the political overlap. While there are strong educational arguments in favour of mother tongue (or first language) instruction, a careful balance also needs to be made between enabling people to use local languages in learning and providing access to global languages of communication through education.

The situation in South-East Asia and China illustrates the diversity of languages and of patterns of language use in school (Table 4.7). In this part of the world there is a general trend towards more widespread use of local languages in the first few years of primary education.

There is now a strong body of evidence that bilingual schooling offers significant benefits in

---

31. For a detailed discussion of structured teaching, see Gauthier and Dembélé (2004: 27–32).

32. For more detail on these alternative strategies, see ADEA (2003) and UNESCO (2003a).

33. Some 6,000 to 7,000 languages are spoken in the world (UNESCO, 2003b). About 1.3 billion people, or 20% of the world's population, speak a local vernacular as their first language (Walter, forthcoming; cited in Kosonen, 2004). Worldwide, twenty countries have more than one official language. In major urban areas, schools may have children speaking thirty or forty languages.

Box 4.7 Multigrade teaching

Multigrade teaching is found in many parts of the world. It is believed to have positive impacts on cognitive achievement and on social and behavioural development, though these have not been confirmed. While multigrade teaching in wealthier countries is generally a pedagogic choice, in resource-constrained situations it is usually a necessity, and teachers may have negative attitudes towards teaching in multigrade classes with few resources available. For multigrade teaching to be beneficial for learners, the following conditions need to be met:

- Teachers and policy makers should be aware of the special needs involved.
- Curriculum should be specially adapted. Experimental work has been undertaken in Nepal and Sri Lanka to reorganize the national curricula in relation to core concepts and skills.
- Teachers should develop a range of teaching approaches to meet the needs of a multigrade setting, including peer learning, group learning and self-study.
- Adequate supplies of learning materials designed for individual and group learning are essential. Self-study materials cannot be a substitute for teachers, however; teachers should use the materials as part of an integrated teaching strategy.
- Learners should be involved in the general classroom management.
- Pre-service and in-service training should be designed to prepare teachers.
- Regular, frequent formative assessment by teachers is essential.

Curriculum, learning materials, teacher education and assessment are the most important components of an integrated strategy for quality improvement through multigrade teaching.

Source: Little (2004)

Table 4.7: Languages used in education in China and South-East Asia

Country	Local languages used in education[1]	Multiple languages in government system of education[2]	Local languages used as medium of instruction[3]	Languages used in government system of education[4]	Access to education in L1 languages (%)[5]	Total number of languages spoken[6]
China	Yes	Yes	Yes	Mandarin, LWCs, local languages	69	201
Brunei	No	**Yes**	No	Malay, English	2	17
Cambodia	Yes	Yes	Yes	Khmer, local languages	90	19
Indonesia	Yes	Yes	No	Indonesian, LWCs	10	726
Lao PDR	No	No	No	Lao	<50	82
Malaysia	Yes	Yes	No	Malay, English, Mandarin, Tamil, Telugu, Punjabi, local languages	45	139
Myanmar	Yes	No	**Yes**	Myanma	61	107
Philippines	Yes	Yes	Yes	Filipino, English, LWCs	26	169
Singapore	No	**Yes**	No	English, Mandarin, Malay, Tamil	33	21
Thailand	Yes	Yes	**Yes**	Thai, local languages	<50	75
Viet Nam	Yes	Yes	No	Vietnamese, local languages	91	93

Notes:
1. *Local languages used in education* indicates whether local languages or languages of wider communication (LWCs), other than a national or official language, are used in education practice at any level or in any system of basic education – pre-primary, primary, lower secondary, formal or non-formal – run by government, local communities, NGOs, etc. 'Yes' means both instruction and some learning materials are in local languages and/or LWCs. Situations in which teachers use a local language or a LWC orally in addition to the official language of instruction are not included.
2. *Multiple languages in government system of education* indicates whether more than one language is used in the government education system (formal or non-formal) at any level of basic education. Private schools and NGO education projects are not included. 'Yes' in bold means more than one language is used, but no local languages are included.
3. *Local languages used as media of instruction* shows where local languages are the daily media of instruction at any level or system of basic education. 'Yes' in bold means local languages are used only in non-formal education by NGOs.
4. *Languages used in government system of education* lists the languages used in the government system. Details of other languages are given in each country case.
5. *Access to education in L1 (%)* is the estimated proportion of a country's population having access to education in the learners' first language (L1) – i.e. the proportion of the population having as mother tongue one of the languages used in education (Walter, forthcoming; except Cambodia, Lao PDR and Thailand estimates by Kosonen using data from Chazée, 1999; Grimes, 2000; Kingsada, 2003; National Statistical Centre, 1997; Schliesinger, 2000, 2003; Smalley, 1994).
6. *Total number of languages* spoken in a given country (Grimes, 2000).

Source: Kosonen (2004)

Initial literacy is acquired more easily in the mother tongue

learning outcomes.[34] In the most successful models, the mother tongue is used in the early years of schooling so that children can acquire and develop the literacy skills that enable fuller participation in learning activities (Benson, 2004). In a growing number of countries, after four or five years (earlier in some cases) there is a transition to learning and using the second or foreign language as the medium of instruction. In this way initial literacy is acquired more easily, facilitating the acquisition of the language that will become the medium of instruction for the rest of the school years.[35]

Zambia recently adopted a new policy on initial literacy. English had been its medium of instruction for primary education, at the expense of all vernacular languages, since 1965, the primary reason being promotion of national unity, allied to the economic and political value accorded to an international language.[36] Many educators lobbied for years to reverse this policy, arguing that it impeded the acquisition of literacy and mastery of the whole curriculum. Poor learning outcomes were used to support the argument.[37] Box 4.8 shows how Zambia is developing its own bilingual model (Linehan, 2004; Sampa, 2003).

Papua New Guinea (PNG) has over 830 languages, and at least 434 local languages are used for initial instruction in schools (Litteral, 2004). Popular demand for the use of local languages spearheaded a remarkable reform story that has had broader implications for the primary school system. In the late 1970s and early 1980s, village vernacular schools were introduced in Bougainville province, where

---

Box 4.8 Initial literacy and the medium of instruction in Zambia

The implications of the decision to use English in 1965 were eased slightly in a 1977 policy paper, 'Educational Reform: Proposals and Recommendations', which allowed teachers to use one of the seven official local languages to explain concepts that might not be understood in English, provided a majority of pupils in a class understood the vernacular chosen.

After studies in the early-1990s highlighted low levels of reading, in 1995, the National Reading Committee (NRC) concluded that a compromise was needed that would separate the medium of instruction from the language of initial literacy. The idea was to allow children to learn to read and write in a familiar language within a system where the official medium of instruction was English. This would meet both educational and political requirements, offering pedagogical innovation within a stable linguistic context.

A 1996 policy statement, 'Educating Our Future', agreed with the NRC's conclusions. With external assistance from the United Kingdom's Department for International Development (DFID), the Ministry of Education initiated the Zambia Primary Reading Programme (PRP). This programme was a systematic attempt to improve reading and writing in all primary schools, with goals for each grade level: basic literacy in a familiar language by the end of the first year of primary education, basic literacy in English by the end of the second year and improvement in the teaching of reading at all grade levels through appropriate training and materials.

Early assessments and evaluations have been encouraging.* More broadly, the focus on literacy has helped secure observable success, in that parents and communities have responded warmly to the change. It has also raised teachers' expectations for themselves and their pupils. The PRP integrates methodology, assessment and classroom management into its courses and training programmes in a way that allows for practical demonstration of good practice and facilitates a process where teachers can theorize from practice (DFID/Ministry of Education, 2002). There is some evidence that enrolment levels are rising and absenteeism is on the wane in schools that are spearheading PRP strategies (Kotze and Higgins, 1999). The Permanent Secretary of the Ministry of Education stated in December 2003 that the PRP was the single most effective change agent for achieving quality education in Zambia.

* Grade 1 test scores in Zambian Languages improved dramatically, from a very low baseline, in districts where initial literacy was taught in the vernacular. In grade 2, scores in English resulted, on average, in learners reading above the expected level for the grade. In September 2003, grade 4 children from forty-five schools in the PRP pilot programme were found to be outperforming non-PRP pupils at grade 5 in literacy and numeracy. In all grades, the gender differences in performance found in the non-PRP sample had all but vanished (Kanyika, 2004).

Source: Linehan (2004)

---

34. Benson (2004) summarizes this literature, highlighting the many benefits of becoming literate in a familiar language. These include having easier access to communications and literacy skills in a second language, having a language and culture that are valued by schools, feeling good about school and teachers, being able to demonstrate knowledge, participating in learning, having the courage to ask questions and lessening the likelihood of unfair advantage being taken (a point especially pertinent for girls).

35. Bolivia may have the most advanced development and maintenance model for long-term continued study of the mother tongue and Spanish, which, being initially taught as a second language, moves up to 50/50 status in grade 4. Nigeria follows a slightly different model: in Yoruba-speaking districts, Yoruba is used throughout the six years of primary education, with English taught as a subject and gradually phased in.

36. Linehan (2004), in a paper commissioned as background for this report, outlines the history of language policy in Zambia since 1927.

37. For example, Williams (1998; cited in Linehan, 2004) notes that particular concern arose after test results in 1995 showed that only 3% of grade 6 pupils could read at desirable levels in English.

> **Box 4.9 Elementary schools in Papua New Guinea**
>
> **Governance**
>
> Through a successful preschool system, Itok Pies Pri Skul (also known as TPPS), vernacular education was already familiar to the population of Papua New Guinea, so introducing vernacular education at primary level met with no major resistance. The main challenge has been to marry the decentralized, non-formal TPPS network with the highly centralized national education system. The pace of implementation varies by province and according to capacity. At village level, elementary schools are managed by a board designed to empower parents and communities in a way that is not possible with English-medium education. The boards vary in their ability to provide direction and implement policy. Communities select those to be trained as teachers and choose the language to be used for instruction.
>
> **Educational challenges**
>
> - *Personnel at all levels* must be competent to operate a vernacular education system. In the non-formal system, NGOs with vernacular education experience provided assistance from national to village level, focusing on language and culture.
> - *Elementary teachers* must be prepared. Recruiting teachers with knowledge of local language and culture is most important. Selected teacher trainers with experience in the English system received short training courses on vernacular education. The courses, while practical and intended to emphasize materials production and teaching in the vernacular, had disappointing results.
> - *Alphabets* were developed for 135 languages. Where there is no alphabet a lingua franca is used instead of the vernacular. Most provinces lack trained personnel who can assist in alphabet development.
> - *Vernacular materials* need to be developed. Early local programmes developed separate materials for each language, but, in the 1980s, sets of printed pictures were produced that could be made into simple books by adding text in any language. This model is now used widely. The method of teaching literacy is interactive, with the integration of phonics and whole language approaches, which saves on materials costs.
> - *Assessment and monitoring* are obviously more complicated in multilingual contexts. In elementary schools, teachers are responsible for their own assessment, taking for granted that comparability is problematic. For the primary system, a pilot project was started to monitor the progress of students in grades 3, 5 and 8 in four vernacular languages.
>
> **Financial challenges**
>
> During the TPPS period, each province or language community was mainly responsible for financing vernacular programmes and had its own policy. The introduction of formal elementary education put the financial burden on the national government. AusAID provided grants to cover the costs of training and materials from 1997 to 2002; since then, fewer teachers have been trained and the expansion and introduction of new schools has slowed.
>
> *Source:* Litteral (2004)

parents felt strongly that their language and culture should figure more prominently in education to counter evidence of alienation and social problems among young people. This was the beginning of a movement that, with the aid of SIL International, an NGO, led ultimately to the national Education Reform Agenda in 1995. The agenda provided for a new level of education in which the language of the community is the language of instruction (vernacular in rural areas, lingua franca in urban areas), with the introduction of oral English at the end of the third year. Box 4.9 shows how the political, educational and financial challenges were overcome in PNG. As in Zambia, this is a relatively 'young' experience, but already some important lessons have been learned (Litteral, 2004):

■ To be sustained, vernacular education must be successful in the eyes of communities and the educational establishment.

■ A large number of languages is not in itself an obstacle to vernacular education if language communities and the government give practical, political and technical support.

■ Aid agencies and NGOs can make significant contributions of technical skills, local knowledge and financial resources, though care should be taken to avoid dependence.

■ Long-term commitment is essential. It will be sustained by improved student achievement and a strong sense of community responsibility. Teachers must be trained for bilingual education.

■ Growth should be gradual and planned.[38]

It seems clear both from the technical literature and experience on the ground that initial first language instruction improves the quality of education cost-effectively,[39] at best by building on

---

38. This section draws on Litteral (2004), a paper prepared for this report. PNG's primary system has three levels, each of three years: elementary (preschool to grade 2), using vernacular languages and a bridge to English in the third year; lower primary, where a bilingual policy prevails; and upper primary, in which English is the medium of instruction but vernacular languages are maintained.

39. Studies indicate that decreases in grade repetition and dropout outweigh the extra costs of vernacular education; see Benson (2004), who cites work by Chiswick, Patrinos and Tamyo (1996), Patrinos and Velez (1996) and Vawda and Patrinos (1998). Patrinos and Velez found that in Guatemala the benefits of implementing mother tongue programmes outweighed the costs after only two years.

Table 4.8: Summative and formative assessment

	Summative assessment	Formative assessment
Purpose	To evaluate and record a learner's achievement.	To diagnose how a learner learns and to improve learning and teaching.
Judgement	Criterion-referenced or norm-referenced; progression in learning against public criteria.	Criterion-referenced and pupil-referenced.
Method	Externally devised tasks or tests. Reviewing written work and other products (portfolio) against criteria applied uniformly for all learners.	Observing learning activities, discussing with learners, reviewing written work and other products (portfolio), learner self-assessment and peer assessment.

Sources: Harlen and James (1997); Black and Wiliam (2002).

the knowledge and experience of students and teachers, encouraging understanding through intercultural education and promoting gender and social equality (UNESCO, 2003b).

Assessment for better practice

Regular, reliable and timely assessment is key to improving learning achievement

As Chapter 2 indicates, regular, reliable and timely assessment is key to improving learning achievement.[40] It is the bedrock of an effective teaching and learning environment, whether it takes place at international or regional level (e.g. PISA, SACMEQ), national level (e.g. Key Stage tests in England and Wales) or school/classroom level (e.g. end-of-term tests). Assessment should allow those working in the education system to diagnose, monitor and assure the quality of the education they provide. International/regional and national assessment is discussed in Chapter 2. This section reviews the types of assessment designed to improve education at the classroom level, which we may characterize as either formative or summative (Table 4.8).

National and international assessments are summative in nature. Classroom-level assessments by teachers can be summative or formative. Formative assessment looks at how each learner learns and the problems she or he encounters, so teachers can adjust their teaching to observed learning progress. Evidence shows, too, that by giving feedback to learners, formative assessment can help improve their learning and performance (Black and Wiliam, 1998). Where practical, it should also draw on learner self-assessment, which can empower learners to assess their own progress and reflect on how they could improve their learning.

Summative assessment is often used to determine whether students are promoted to a higher grade or education level, or awarded certificates or diplomas. This usually relies on one-off examinations. Increasingly, however, ministries of education are opting for a continuous assessment, which is a combination of summative and formative assessments. Countries including Sri Lanka, South Africa and Ghana have introduced such systems to supplement the national examination. The idea is to facilitate more holistic judgement of learners' progress and achievement and lessen incentives to 'teach to exams'.

In practice, however, 'continuous assessment' often amounts to 'repeated summative assessment', with teachers filling in record forms, while no specific feedback is given to learners. This situation is partly attributable to lack of understanding on the part of teachers about formative assessment, but also reflects the pressure of external summative assessment on teaching and learning. Moreover, effective formative assessment requires adequate resources, teachers trained in assessment techniques and relatively small class sizes – requirements which do not fit the realities in many countries.

For governments seeking to improve education quality, a sound assessment policy is crucial. For school-level assessment to be influential, it should be consistent, regular and reliable, part of an overall school development policy and reconcile both formative and summative assessments with a strong focus on providing feedback to the learner and teacher. The actual mix of formative and summative assessment will take into account the constraints in particular contexts.

Enabling inputs for quality teaching and learning

Teaching and learning in the classroom are supported by a broader enabling environment, as Figure 4.1 illustrates. It essentially consists of good teachers, strong schools and a coherent national support infrastructure (discussed below). Also important is the provision, distribution and delivery of resources (including textbooks and other materials) and the physical structure of classrooms and schools.

---

40. It is crucial here to distinguish between the terms 'assessment' and 'examination', the latter being a specific form of summative assessment mainly used to differentiate among learners for selection or certification (Somerset, 1996).

Learning materials must be there

Effective teaching and learning require wide and equitable availability of learning materials. In many countries this is not the case. This situation calls for urgent attention, including the rethinking of policies governing production and distribution of textbooks and other learning materials and the training of teachers in how to use learning materials more effectively, in line with good teaching practice.

For many countries, providing every pupil with a complete set of textbooks is only an 'ideal target' (Montagnes, 2001). Moreover, accurate data on textbook availability is often scarce or non-existent. Often the lack of textbooks in classrooms is a result of an inefficient distribution system, not a shortage of resources. A study in Zambia indicated that less than 10% of books procured had actually reached classrooms (Silanda, 2000). A survey in Guinea found wastage of up to 67% of textbook stock (Sow, Brunswic and Valérien, 2001). The multiplicity of interests involved in textbook provision can lead to malpractice and corruption, which also contribute to inefficiency (Leguéré, 2003). To address this problem, the worldwide trend is to liberalize textbook production and distribution and decentralize procurement.

This opening of the textbook market has helped increase availability and decrease prices in many countries. In Uganda, textbook prices have been reduced by 50% as a result of liberalization (Eilor et al., 2003). Liberalization is not a panacea, though. In Russia it has led to regional inequity in availability and price (Borovikova, 2004). Liberalization can also result in replacement of a state monopoly by a few large, often international publishing houses, to the detriment of local publishers. High import taxation on paper, printing equipment and the like also hurts local textbook production (Montagnes, 2001).

Sustainable and equitable textbook development requires strong coordination by the state, preferably through a national body for book development, involving relevant ministries (e.g. those handling trade and finance), the private sector and NGOs, as well as the formulation of a national policy on textbooks (Salzano, 2002). Liberalization should be accompanied by the development of local private publishers in general.

School effectiveness research, including several studies in the 1970s and early 1980s, shows the availability of relevant, good-quality, affordable textbooks having a positive impact on achievement.[41] Later studies indicate that, once schools have an acceptable level of textbooks, it is teacher practice that makes the difference.[42] Studies in Kenya, Ghana and Australia (Glewwe, Kremer and Moulin, 2000; Okyere et al., 1997; Horsley, 2004; Laws and Horsley, 2004) are instructive in this respect. They demonstrate that, while textbook availability does affect the quality of teaching and learning, the ways teachers use textbooks vary considerably. This confirms the importance of support for teachers on effective use of textbooks.

Materials other than textbooks are also important. While the use of computers is spreading rapidly in schools in the industrialized world, most classrooms in developing countries may barely have a blackboard and a few textbooks. Teachers' guides are rare. Home-made teaching aids sometimes supplement meagre classroom resources, often with support from teacher resource centres (discussed below). In some countries, libraries are set up to provide supplementary reading material.[43] Such teaching materials and supplementary books are often underused, however (Knamiller, 1999; Rosenberg, 1998). The effectiveness of teaching and learning materials depends on teachers' ability and willingness to use them (Askerud, 1997; Rosenberg, 1998). Training in the use of newly introduced materials and continuous support to teachers should be an integral part of teaching and learning materials development.

Good places to learn

Attention has already been drawn to the importance of learner-friendly schools. Good school infrastructure is important to effective teaching and learning, as a recent World Bank evaluation on Ghana indicates (World Bank, 2004a). Achieving UPE will require unprecedented development and refurbishment of classrooms in many countries. A priority in remote and rural areas, it is also important in many cities, to avoid overcrowding. School buildings should also be accessible to disabled people. Clean water and sanitation facilities for girls and boys are basic elements of a healthy, safe and secure learning environment, but, as Box 4.10 shows, schools often do not meet these needs.

> **Once schools have an acceptable level of textbooks, it is teacher practice that makes the difference**

41. Findings from later studies suggest, however, that the reported gains were largely due to learners' family backgrounds and other factors. Fuller and Clarke (1994) review studies on textbook availability and pupil achievement. For a recent study on the impact of textbook availability, see World Bank (2004a).

42. Fuller and Clarke (1994) reviewed school effectiveness research, focusing on sociological aspects. They argue that both the 'minimum' level of inputs and teachers' response to the availability of inputs are specific to context.

43. Strong political support made it possible for Brazil's government to supply nearly all its primary schools with library books – over 8 million to date – at a cost of US$20 million (Gusso, 2004). In South Africa, classroom libraries have been set up through READ Trust, which also provides teacher training. For an estimated cost of US$18 per learner, the programme seems to have successfully encouraged reading culture and improved reading and writing abilities (Radebe, 1998).

The formulation of clear norms and standards regarding the technical specifications and location of schools should take into account the need for a good physical learning environment for all pupils and students. However, flexibility in norms for school location and due attention to such future contingencies as the introduction of multigrade schooling or the addition of a lower secondary class are critical. Local school mapping is an important tool in this regard. Finally, more attention must be paid to maintenance of school facilities, an issue too often neglected in aid projects and government budgets. Communities with limited resources can perform only basic maintenance tasks. Good maintenance is a cost-effective measure that expands the lifetime and quality of school buildings.

> More attention must be paid to maintenance of school facilities, an issue too often neglected in aid projects and government budgets

Policy choices

There is enormous potential to increase the quality of teaching and learning in every school and classroom. A rich body of knowledge and experience shows what should be done. Whether the poorest countries can or even should address the full menu of policy issues discussed here is another matter. Through striving for coherence and consistency among the major components of the teaching and learning process, however, significant improvement in education quality is nonetheless possible. Another key is well-defined, well-balanced aims for education that give due attention to both cognitive skills and values development, through traditional core subjects and, where relevant, new areas of study. Sufficient learning time is critical: 850-1,000 hours of effective instructional time is a good target. Much more attention to teaching styles is needed. Structured teaching may be the most effective option for resource-constrained systems, but this does not mean the classroom cannot be child centred. In multilingual societies, the choice of language of instruction and language policy in schools is critical for effective learning. And assessment is important if lessons are to be learned for good classroom practice. Carefully considered options for providing and distributing learning materials, classroom facilities and physical infrastructure also play their part in better learning.

Box 4.10 'Unfriendly' schools

■ Sub-Saharan Africa

Historically, school construction projects rarely included latrines or water supply. In *Mauritania* and *Chad*, for example, inclusion of latrines and water in primary school construction projects dates only from 2001 and 2002, respectively, with the sixth World Bank education project. In Chad, one-third of schools have latrines and two-thirds drinking water. In *Guinea*, latrines and water supply were required in all new schools by 1989 but the retrofitting of older schools – 2,000 lacking latrines and 2,900 without water – was launched only with the ten-year Education for All Programme of 2001. In *Senegal*, 39% of classrooms have sanitation and 33% access to drinking water – facilities that still are not systematically included in school construction projects.

■ South Asia

In 1993, in the Indian state of Uttar Pradesh, 64% of the 73,000 primary schools lacked latrines and 43% water supply. By 2001, with the support of three World Bank-financed projects, more than 41,000 toilets had been built – not far from the initial need – and drinking water provided to more than 17,000 primary schools. For *India* as a whole, eight projects financed by the World Bank built 91,000 toilets – more than the number of new classrooms in the same projects – and equipped 57,000 schools with drinking water. In *Pakistan*, as of 1990, more than 51% of primary schools in Sindh province had no sanitation and 42% were without water supply. The situation in North-West province, as of 1995, was even worse: more than 80% of primary schools had no sanitation and half lacked drinking water.

■ Latin America

School latrines and drinking water have received more attention in Latin America. *Mexico*, for instance, added almost 3,200 latrines to primary schools, in four states targeted by the Primary Education Project of 1991-98. The Second Primary Education Project (1994-99) provided ten other states with latrines.

Source: Theunynck (2003)

Better teachers

Teachers are a key enabling factor in improving the quality of education. The evidence of this and many other reports is that teachers are critical to any reforms designed to improve quality. Moreover, teachers represent by far the most significant investment in public sector budgets. This section addresses ways in which countries with limited means could improve the recruitment of teachers, their initial training and ongoing support, their earnings and their deployment and conditions of service. It concludes by addressing a central dilemma: how to pay for an expanded teaching force.

Finding the right recruits

Preparing teachers begins with the selection of those who are to enter teacher training. Most governments have set standards that vary with the kind of schooling for which the training is designed. Both in developing and developed countries there is a temptation to lower these standards. In the developing world, it stems from a need in many countries to attract large numbers of teachers, in order to expand access to education quickly and reduce class size. In the industrialized world, some countries face ageing teaching forces and shortages of people interested in a teaching career, especially in mathematics, foreign languages, sciences, business studies and the technology fields, including information and communications technology (OECD, 2004e). The 'high performing countries' discussed in Chapter 2 have resisted the temptation to lower standards, keeping access to teacher training selective in order to maintain quality and the esteem in which the profession is held. But in some other countries people with low academic qualifications do enter teacher training (Lewin, 2004).[44]

Countries with sufficient means might consider publicity campaigns and financial incentives to attract trainees. An alternative approach to recruiting the right candidates involves rethinking the criteria and procedures for admission to teacher training.[45] One possibility is to develop technically sound aptitude and motivation tests. Another is to make more use of interviews, though this is often time consuming.

In the On the Job Training programme in Trinidad and Tobago, people who are considering a career in teaching are given a chance to practise as a class assistant, so that a more informed decision can be made (George and Quamina-Aiyejina, 2003). South Africa also offers an example of making the training pathways towards the teaching profession more flexible: its 2000 Act on Adult Basic Education and Training gives adult educators the possibility of having relevant learning experiences and qualifications validated as 'building stones' for formal qualification (UIE, 2004).

Improving initial training

Initial teacher training can take a variety of forms. Its duration, curriculum focus, teaching practice and other aspects differ strongly from country to country. Table 4.9 illustrates the diversity in a framework of four main models.

In models 1 and 2, the training is predominantly or entirely pre-career, and usually full-time and residential. This leaves few resources for ongoing professional development – in particular the crucial support of newly qualified teachers in their first years of teaching. Moreover, it often ignores long-term professional development, and teacher training institutions tend to be isolated from schools. This can be mitigated by extending the teaching-practice part of the curriculum. In the United Kingdom, for instance, trainees spend two-thirds of their time in schools,[46] and in Cuba the entire pre-service training is school-based (Gasperini, 2000). Such models require a sufficient number of schools with the capacity to coach and counsel trainees; related costs will diminish somewhat with the gains made by reducing the off-the-job part of the curriculum.

School-based training can be combined with distance education, which saves travel and replacement costs[47] and can reduce direct costs if part of the training is self-instructional and based on print or other low-cost media. However, distance learning also entails problems (Sayed, Heystek and Smit, 2002), as observed with primary teachers in rural Africa. The materials need to be in the right language and address a wide range of topics, the trainees must be supported by both the school and the training institution and administrative support must be assured.[48]

Both in developing and developed countries there is a temptation to lower teacher training standards

44. The literature identifies several cases in which the expansion of the teaching force required to staff the policy of smaller classes appears to have led to deterioration in average teacher quality in schools – and thereby put at risk the hoped-for benefits of smaller classes (OECD, 2004e).

45. Examples may be found in information on the OECD project *Attracting, Developing and Retaining Effective Teachers*, which involved twenty-two OECD member states and Chile. The participants' Country Background reports, describing their policies and innovations in the area of teacher supply and professional development, are available via www.oecd.org.

46. Döbert, Klieme and Sroka (2004) note that the advantages of school-based preparation should be weighed against the risk of reducing the critical edge that teacher training in colleges and universities can provide. Immersion in daily practice may to some extent prevent trainees from seeing failures and seeking alternatives.

47. This was the case, for instance, in the Malawi Integrated In-service Teacher Education Programme (MITTEP) described by Kunje (2002).

48. See Kunje and Chirembo (2000), Kunje (2002) and Kunje, Lewin and Stuart (2003) for more detailed discussions.

Table 4.9: Main models of initial teacher training

Description	Duration	Entry	Curriculum	Teaching practice	Cost per student
Model 1 College certificate or diploma (e.g. Bachelor of Education)	1–4 years full-time residential	Junior or senior secondary school leavers with or without experience	Subject upgrading, subject methods, professional studies	Block practice 4–12 weeks in one or more years, sometimes followed by internships	Relatively high
Model 2 University post-graduate certificate of education	1–2 years full-time residential after first degree	University degree, mostly undergraduates without experience	Subject methods, professional studies	Block practice 2–10 weeks, sometimes followed by internships	Relatively high but for less time
Model 3 In-service training of untrained teachers based in schools, leading to initial qualification	1–5 years part-time residential and/or non-residential workshops, etc.	Junior or senior secondary school leavers with experience as untrained teachers	Subject upgrading, subject methods, professional studies	Teaching in schools in normal employment	High or low depending on duration and intensity of contact with tutors
Model 4 Direct entry	0–4 years probation	Senior secondary, college or university graduates	None, or supervised induction	Teaching in schools in normal employment	Low

Source: Lewin (2004)

The importance of subject knowledge tends to be underestimated, given that many trainees lack basic knowledge

The curriculum of teacher training usually has four components: knowledge of the subjects that are to be taught, teaching methods, knowledge about how children learn and teaching practice. The time allocated to each varies considerably (Lewin, 2004) and the importance of the first, subject knowledge, tends to be underestimated, given that many trainees lack basic knowledge.

Findings from the five-country MUSTER project[49] suggest that an improved teacher education curriculum should have the following aspects (Lewin, 2004):

- It should equip trainees with the necessary language fluency and capability to serve the needs of the school to which they will be posted.

- Training material should be locally written and produced if externally produced materials are scarce or insufficiently relevant.

- The curriculum should challenge the trainee to reflect on his or her own practice. Learning to teach means acquiring not only knowledge and skills but also an understanding of learners and how they learn, along with repertoires of strategies for dealing with unique and ever-changing circumstances.

- The curriculum must have the flexibility to take the trainee's prior experiences into account.

Consideration should also be given to the people who train teachers. They tend to be recruited from the ranks of practising, mid-career teachers, and many stay in teacher training until retirement, gradually losing contact with schools.[50] This problem is exacerbated by a preference for secondary-school teachers, who are seldom familiar with the realities of primary education. One solution could be short-term appointments of experienced primary teachers as teacher trainers.

Ongoing professional support

Education policy has long put more priority on initial teacher training than on continuing, in-service education, but this balance is now changing (OECD, 2004e: 6), both in industrialized and developing countries (ADEA, 2003: 19). Research shows that newly qualified teachers require a great deal of support from experienced colleagues and the teacher training institution, especially during their first year of practice (Lewin and Stuart, 2003; Lewin, Samuel and Sayed, 2003). Their early experiences also determine to a large extent whether they remain in teaching.

---

49. For details and discussion papers on MUSTER (Multi-site Teacher Education Research Project), carried out between 1998 and 2000 in Ghana, Lesotho, Malawi, Trinidad and Tobago and South Africa, see www.sussex.ac.uk/usie/muster.

50. MUSTER found that teacher trainers were not often focused on trainees' needs, lacked links with schools, could be better managed to play a useful role in curriculum development and implementation, and could be more effective in providing continuing professional development and support.

> **Box 4.11 Best practice in ongoing professional support**
>
> Ongoing professional support may include study opportunities for teachers, training workshops, support from in-service advisers and inspectors, inter-school visits and peer consultation in teacher clusters. Such activities have the following characteristics:
>
> - They require schools to become learning organizations in which teacher development activities are geared towards improving student learning. This means school leadership prioritizes learning and harnesses the different capacities of teachers to address common learning difficulties.
> - They need to be part of a systemic process of education reform.
> - They require an incentive structure that rewards individuals and promotes collective improvements in performance. Teachers must see the need to change their practice, be rewarded if they do so, and appreciate the benefits this brings to the school.
> - They should be based on a holistic change strategy bringing other aspects of education into harmony with changes in teacher training and support. For example, deploying newly qualified teachers to schools where many staff lack skills will demotivate new staff and discourage them from engaging in continuous learning.
> - They require government to assure the needed financial and other resources.
> - They should focus on a few programmes and targets that can show improvement in small ways and be diffused to more schools.
>
> *Source:* Sayed (2001)

Balancing time and money spent on initial training and ongoing professional support is a critical policy question. One consideration is that primary school teachers tend to have relatively short careers.[51] Ongoing professional development directs more training resources towards those who are on the job and likely to remain so. It also allows for more incremental training via several routes (full-time, part-time, day release, residential, distance, etc.) and in a variety of locations (in school, at teacher centres and at colleges and universities). Box 4.11 outlines best practice with regard to ongoing professional support. The 'knowledge infrastructure' vital to such support is discussed below under 'Support schools, inform policy'.

Teachers' career perspectives matter. Professional development does not work if teachers have few promotion opportunities other than in school administration or the education bureaucracy. In Sri Lanka, teachers can qualify as 'in-service advisers' who use their professional skills to benefit other teachers (Malderez, 2002). Box 4.12 describes a South African initiative that gives teachers a choice between promotions in teaching and in management.

Teacher earnings

As in all jobs requiring a qualification that provides access to multiple career paths, the salaries and conditions of service offered to teachers can have a significant impact on the composition of the profession and the quality of teaching. Teachers' salaries and earnings prospects, relative to those in other comparable jobs, can affect the decision by qualified individuals to enter or to remain in the teaching profession. They can also affect how hard people work at teaching and how motivated they are.

> **Box 4.12 New career paths for teachers in South Africa**
>
> In April 2003, South Africa established a new post and salary structure for teachers. This involves performance-related salary increases and two promotion routes for teachers: one in teaching and one in management. In the teaching route, one can become a senior education specialist in schools while staying active as a teacher. Another option is to become an adviser to the Department of Education. The management route incorporates the more traditional forms of promotion, such as promotion to head teacher or official. The opportunities opened up by the teaching route are seen as an enrichment of the support structure, enhancing evidence-based practice in schools and strengthening links between daily practice and national policy.
>
> *Source:* ELRC (2003)

The salaries and conditions of service offered to teachers can have a significant impact on the composition of the profession and the quality of teaching

---

51. Among the possible explanations of this trend are increased attrition rates in countries with high HIV/AIDS prevalence, a tendency in some countries to regard primary school teaching as a stepping stone to better opportunities in the education system, and, where pay and conditions of service for primary school teachers are poor, migration to adjacent countries with better incentives or switching to more attractive occupations.

Box 4.13 Primary school teachers in Sierra Leone

The ending of Sierra Leone's eleven-year civil war in 2001, along with major changes in education policy (including abolition of tuition fees and introduction of universal school meals), led to a dramatic expansion of primary school enrolment. The number of pupils tripled in fewer than four years, while budget constraints led to the pupil/(payroll) teacher ratio increasing to 72:1 by 2003 (it had been 32:1 in 1992). One consequence is that around 20% of primary school teachers at government-funded primary schools are not on the public payroll. Many are 'volunteer' or 'community' teachers with little or no professional training, who are paid very little by their schools. They often account for over half of the teachers in government primary schools in remote rural areas. Severe crowding in classrooms, combined with lack of basic equipment and teaching materials, has resulted in the quality of primary schooling being very low.

Although teachers' salaries compare relatively well with those of equivalent occupations in the public service, most primary school teachers live in poverty. The average salary (plus allowances) for government primary school teachers in late 2003 was US$50 per month. 'Community' teachers at government schools earned much less. Community schools have also been established, but rural parents are too poor to contribute much towards supporting them. At many of these schools, the community pays teachers in kind by working on their farms. Their low and usually irregular remuneration raises major questions about the sustainability of community schools.

Primary school teachers are increasingly demoralized. Most would leave the profession if they could. Teachers typically have to maintain a household of four or five people on a salary of less than US$2 a day. Pay levels, even for qualified teachers, are only about one quarter of the cost of a minimum-needs wage basket for a four-person household. In real terms, teachers' pay has fallen by over half since the mid-1990s, while workloads have increased appreciably, especially for teachers in the infant classes.

Low pay is compounded by very late payment of salaries. Both urban and rural housing conditions are quite poor. Many urban teachers have to commute long distances. Nevertheless, teachers want to work in urban areas, where they can earn additional income through private tuition and other work. This practice tends to undermine commitment. It has been suggested that some teachers deliberately do not teach the full syllabus, thus forcing students to attend private classes. Even in rural primary schools, 'extension classes' after the end of the school day are the norm for grades 5 and 6. The charges for these classes, which supplement teachers' salaries, are a major burden for poorer households and contribute to high dropout rates from these classes.

In rural areas the high incidence of poverty makes it hard for teachers to increase their income much with private tuition. But teachers commonly sell cakes and sweets to their pupils during break times, and pupils frequently work on teacher's farms. In some schools the latter activity is actually part of the school timetable.

Despite the growing demoralization, the overall rate of teacher absenteeism appears to have fallen in recent years: it was around 20% in late 2001, when peace was returning to much of the country, and is now perhaps half that. No reliable information is available on levels of and trends in teacher attrition, but the EFA National Action Plan notes the 'high mobility' of teachers. Given limited opportunities for tertiary education, many students opt for teacher training courses with little or no intention of taking up teaching as a lifelong profession.

Source: Bennell (2004)

Teachers' earnings are often insufficient to provide a reasonable standard of living

All governments face a balancing act. On the one hand, expenditure on education is often subject to tight fiscal constraints, and teachers' salaries and allowances already typically account for two-thirds (often much more) of current public expenditure on education (see Statistical annex, Table 14). Increases in teachers' salaries may not be possible without sacrificing other important school resources. On the other hand, particularly in developing countries, teachers' earnings are often insufficient to provide a reasonable standard of living. As Box 4.13 illustrates, with the case of Sierra Leone, salaries may be too low to enable teachers to concentrate fully on their professional duties, which may encourage absenteeism, if teachers supplement their earnings from other sources (Mehrotra and Buckland, 1998).

Over time, teacher earnings have tended to decline, relative to those of comparable groups.

This is to some extent a natural result of the global increase in numbers of educated and trained people: the relative scarcity of people potentially able to join the profession has lessened. Similarly, progress towards universal provision has limited the ability of governments to increase real average salary levels regularly. Table 4.10 shows the trend in average primary school teachers' salaries in developing countries from 1975 to 2000 in relation to per capita GDP. They began the period more than six times as high as per capita GDP, but by the turn of the century the ratio had been nearly halved. The decline was particularly marked in Africa, especially in the French-speaking countries and in those of the Sahel, where the ratio fell to around one-third of its former level. It is not insignificant that the countries where salary ratios are among the highest are also those where the coverage of primary education systems remains low.[52]

Comparisons with per capita GDP provide only a rough proxy for the extent to which teachers feel themselves better off or worse off than they were. It is also important to establish whether teachers' real earnings have risen over time. Figure 4.2 indicates that, in a selection of high- and middle-income countries where data are available, teachers mainly became better off in real terms over the 1990s.[53] Lower-income countries saw reductions in real earnings, with falls in excess of 20% in some cases. Data for 1998–2001 show these patterns continuing, with significant reductions in real salaries in Indonesia, the Philippines, Tunisia, Uruguay, Chile, Argentina, Senegal and the United Republic of Tanzania.[54] In much of Africa, teacher earnings were actually lower in real terms by 2000 than in 1970; the recent figures are often just the latest manifestation of decline.[55]

There are also, of course, huge absolute differences in teachers' earnings among countries, due most notably to differences in standards of living: even after adjustment by purchasing power, real average teacher salaries in China are only one-tenth of the average for OECD countries. But even countries at similar levels of income pay their teachers differently, as can be seen from Figure 4.3. Thus, salaries paid in the Philippines are two to three times those paid in Egypt and Peru, even though per capita incomes are similar between these states. It seems, then, that there may be room for manoeuvre, in many societies, concerning the affordability and desirability of improvements to levels of teachers' salaries and conditions of service.

Table 4.10: Average primary-school teacher salary (ratio to per capita GDP) by world region, 1975–2000
(countries with per capita GDP below US$2,000 in 1993)

	1975	1985	1992	2000
All countries with per capita GDP below US$2 000	6.6	4.6	4.3	3.7
Africa	8.6	6.3	6.0	4.4
English speaking	4.4	3.5	3.6	4.2
French speaking	11.5	8.0	6.3	4.8
Sahel	17.6	11.8	8.2	6.4
Asia	3.7	2.7	2.5	2.9
Latin America	2.7	2.9	2.3	2.3
Middle-East and North Africa	5.6	2.8	3.3	3.3

Source: Mingat (2002)

Teacher deployment and conditions of service

Practices concerning teacher deployment also differ. Some systems are centralized, others devolved to regions, districts or even schools. Certain practices can have a detrimental impact on the quality of education. In Ghana, for example, teachers may be posted to rural schools where they are not fluent in the medium of instruction (Hedges, 2002). The pull of town and city can distort efforts to deploy good teachers to schools in rural areas, compounding problems associated with poor living environments and housing shortages in rural areas.

To assure equitable allocation of teachers according to need, a prerequisite is a consistent, well-defined, honestly executed national framework for posting new and experienced teachers, to meet the needs of each and every school. Deployment cannot be left to individual decisions at local levels.[56] In many cases, incentives will be needed to attract teachers to difficult areas. Appropriate incentives can include opportunities for further study, leading to university degrees or postgraduate studies, and, for remote rural environments, housing or housing subsidies.

---

52. The origins of this differential date back to the colonial period. Under France's colonial policy, the only medium of instruction was French, schools were secular institutions and teachers were paid the same as their metropolitan counterparts. In countries under British rule, missionary schools were an integral part of the education system and benefited from state subsidies, and there was no equivalence between local wages and those in Britain. Thus British colonies had more primary school coverage at lower cost than did French colonies (see Cogneau, 2003).

53. In relative terms, however, teachers' salaries declined between 1994 and 2001 in fourteen of the nineteen OECD countries where data is available (see OECD, 2004e: 4).

54. The data for the first six countries are in Siniscalco (2004: Figure 7) and those for Senegal and the United Republic of Tanzania, covering the decade to 2000, are in Lambert (2004: Table 3).

55. See Lambert (2004: Table 3) and Colclough (1997, 1991).

56. De Ketele (2004) notes that a key problem with assuring effective deployment in the developing world is that systems are often decentralized, with individual districts or schools making decisions that affect national needs. He advocates centralized systems, though it may be more appropriate to develop a national deployment framework to handle applications and appointments.

166 / CHAPTER 4

Figure 4.2: Real salary index for primary and secondary (language and mathematics) teachers, selected countries, 1998 or latest available year (1990=100)

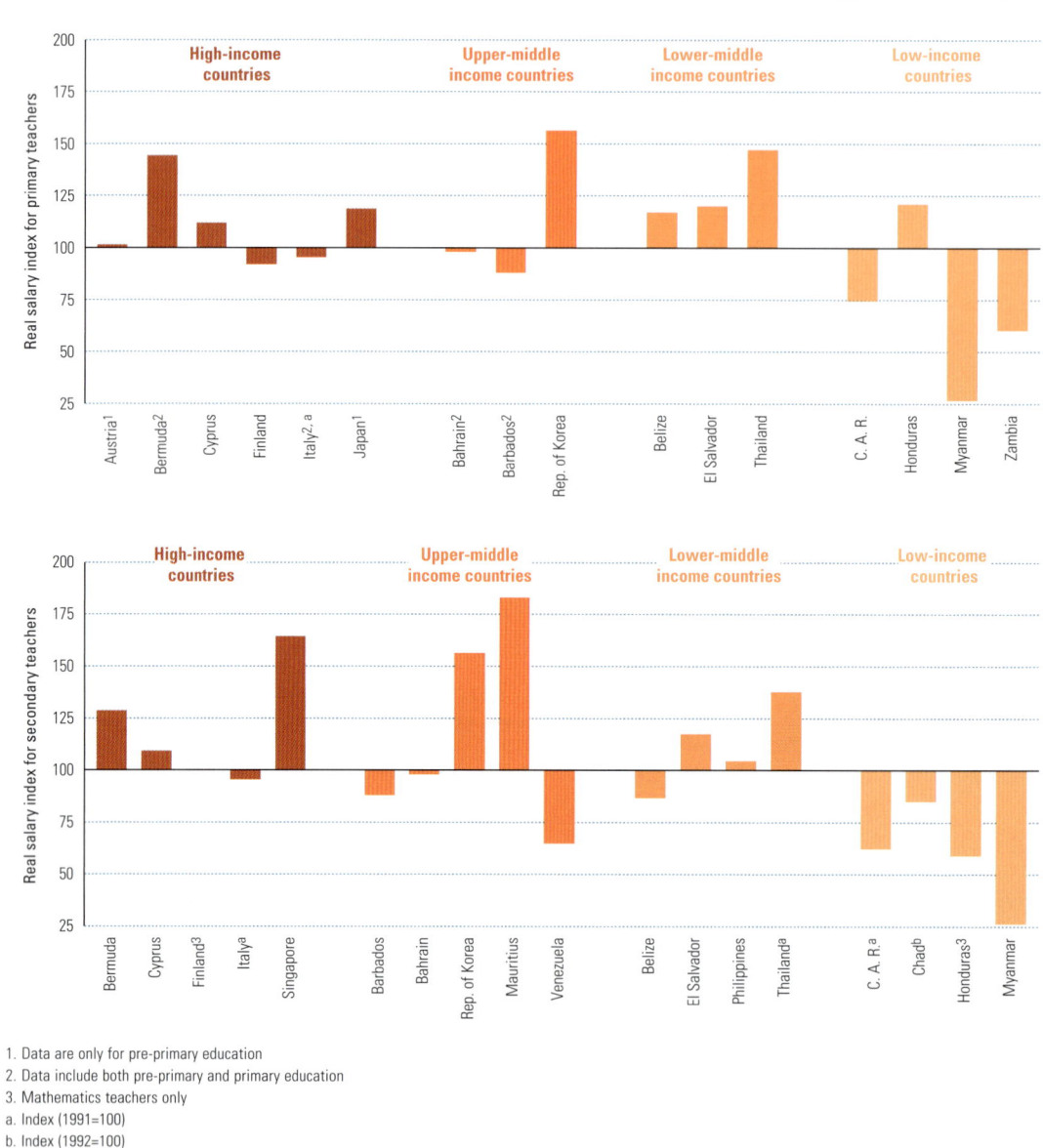

[Bar chart showing Real salary index for primary teachers across High-income countries (Austria[1], Bermuda[2], Cyprus, Finland, Italy[2,a], Japan[1]), Upper-middle income countries (Bahrain[2], Barbados[2], Rep. of Korea), Lower-middle income countries (Belize, El Salvador, Thailand), and Low-income countries (C.A.R., Honduras, Myanmar, Zambia).]

[Bar chart showing Real salary index for secondary teachers across High-income countries (Bermuda, Cyprus, Finland[3], Italy[a], Singapore), Upper-middle income countries (Barbados, Bahrain, Rep. of Korea, Mauritius, Venezuela), Lower-middle income countries (Belize, El Salvador, Philippines, Thailand[a]), and Low-income countries (C.A.R.[a], Chad[b], Honduras[3], Myanmar).]

1. Data are only for pre-primary education
2. Data include both pre-primary and primary education
3. Mathematics teachers only
a. Index (1991=100)
b. Index (1992=100)
Source: ILO (2000)

Concern about teachers' salaries and deployment features crucially in discussions about conditions of service of teachers. In a survey by Voluntary Services Overseas of teachers in Malawi, Zambia and Papua New Guinea (VSO, 2002), three primary concerns emerged other than low pay. Allowances and incentives were considered insecure, inequitable and often not included in pension plans; payment of salaries and allowances was late; and accommodation, where available, was in poor condition.[57] The survey also noted the scarcity of promotion opportunities, the personal costs of furthering professional development through study, and a lack of transparency and equity in promotion processes.

Collectively, such conditions help explain why some teachers leave the profession and many feel their professional status is undermined. Positive signs are appearing in some countries, where improved morale and motivation have

57. In some cases, notably in Zambia, female teachers were adversely affected when it came to accommodation, since the official view was that they had no need of housing and that their husbands would provide for them (VSO, 2002).

POLICIES FOR BETTER QUALITY / 167

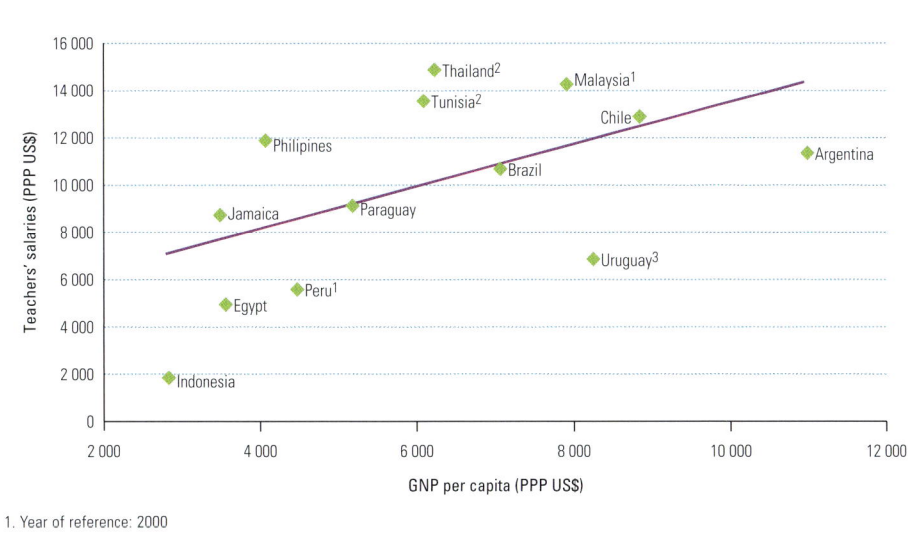

Figure 4.3: Mid-career salaries for primary teachers and GDP per capita, 2001

[Scatter plot: Teachers' salaries (PPP US$) on y-axis (0 to 16 000) vs GNP per capita (PPP US$) on x-axis (2 000 to 12 000). Data points: Indonesia, Egypt, Jamaica, Peru¹, Philippines, Paraguay, Tunisia², Thailand², Brazil, Uruguay³, Malaysia¹, Chile, Argentina.]

1. Year of reference: 2000
2. Including additional bonuses
3. Salaries for a position of 20 hours per week. Most teachers hold two positions.
Sources: OECD (2003c); OECD/UNESCO database.

resulted from teacher unions having negotiated with governments for improvements in conditions of service. As the example in Box 4.14 demonstrates, however, it can be a long, time-consuming process.

Developing national teacher policies

A key challenge for many governments in meeting the Dakar goals is to assure an adequate supply of teachers. The magnitude of the challenge can be considerable. In sub-Saharan Africa, for example, ten countries have net enrolment rates below 60%, fourteen below 80% and seven below 95% (see Statistical annex, Table 5). Many additional teachers will be needed to achieve UPE, unless dramatic efficiency gains from reduced grade repetition can be achieved. Moreover, pupil/teacher ratios exceed 60:1 in several low-enrolment countries and in countries that have seen rapid increases in enrolments related to EFA programmes. To reduce these ratios requires *pro rata* increases in the numbers of teachers. Untrained teachers make up as much as 40% of the cadre of primary teachers in some countries in sub-Saharan Africa. Upgrading these teachers' knowledge and skills creates additional demand for teacher training capacity, on top of the need for regular initial training. Box 4.15 shows the extent of this double challenge in four countries.

Box 4.14 Negotiating salaries, careers and professional concerns in Chile

The emergence of new career structures and a move linking teacher pay to performance in Chile offers a glimpse of what is possible when dialogue on education is mature and takes a 'high road' option towards quality objectives.

Chile adopted a comprehensive career plan, the Estatuto Docente (Teachers' Statute), following negotiations and broad social dialogue on modifying teachers' salaries and employment conditions. The negotiations took almost a decade and resulted in three national laws. The first, signed in 1991, regulated employment conditions and established a common structure for salaries and employment stability for teachers employed by local authorities and private schools. In 1995, modifications were made to local educational planning and to labour relations between teachers and employers. In 2001, salary improvements were agreed and new criteria established that linked progress in the teaching profession to assessments and voluntary accreditation. Coupled with these laws is a programme on teacher assessment, featuring peer assessment, agreed by the Ministry of Education, National Association of Municipalities and Colegio de Profesores (teachers' union). It is part of the Teachers' Statute. A national teachers' network for excellent teaching, called EDUCAR, was also established.

Sources: Gajardo and Gómez (2003); Liang (1999); both cited in Ratteree (2004).

Faced with this challenge, a number of African and South Asian countries have appointed parateachers, who are not given full civil-servant status. Sometimes called 'volunteers', they are typically hired for a short-term contract and offered lower wages and other benefits than

> **Box 4.15 Teacher supply and demand in four African countries**
>
> In **Ghana**, if the Free Compulsory Universal Basic Education programme is to achieve its objectives, the number of additional teachers needed will rise dramatically, to between three and four times the current output of teacher training. In **Lesotho**, the numbers needed represent as much as five times the historic output of the conventional initial teacher training system. In **Malawi**, which has adopted a mixed-mode in-service training system split between colleges and schools in order to increase output, numbers need to double. Projections of teacher demand in **South Africa** are complex, and so is the restructuring of providers. Nevertheless recent estimates suggest both a considerable shortfall in output related to need, and a crisis in supply of willing and qualified applicants.
>
> *Sources:* Lewin (2002); Akyeampong, Furlong and Lewin (2000); Lewin et al. (2000); Kunje and Lewin (2000); Sayed (2002); Parker (2003); Steele (2003); Crouch and Lewin (2003).

The long-term sustainability of a policy maintaining two groups of teachers with blatantly unequal status is questionable

those for which their career-teacher counterparts are eligible. In India, as the discussion of the 'balskahi' teachers in Chapter 2 indicates, a critical feature of success has been the identification and local hiring of well-motivated individuals who are particularly suited to their jobs. In the Niger, on the other hand, where the vast majority of new teachers are now hired on a 'voluntary' basis, teachers' unions express outrage over the segmentation between civil servants and volunteers. The long-term sustainability of a policy maintaining two groups of teachers with blatantly unequal status is questionable. Senegalese experience suggests that the eventual absorption of 'volunteer' teachers within the civil service may be difficult to avoid.[58] The use of paraprofessionals is not restricted to developing countries. In the UK, for example, classroom assistants work alongside experienced and qualified teachers. The UK has begun to formalize the work of parateachers by offering training and qualifications for this work. The policy challenge that governments face is how to support 'volunteer' teachers while ensuring that the conditions of service of regular teachers are not undermined and that parateachers are not exploited.

Moves to reduce average levels of teacher earnings in ways envisaged by a mechanistic application of the Fast-Track Initiative's Indicative Framework[59] can be fraught with difficulty. They may increase the affordability of extending education to all, yet seriously undermine the quality of schooling by hurting teacher morale.[60] At best, where structural rigidities have continued to hold teacher salaries at higher levels than market principles would otherwise support, governments need a long-term strategy to tackle them. Sudden shifts in policy are likely to threaten quality in the short term. Meanwhile, however, many countries can use other means of reducing the burden of salary costs: increases in class size, multigrade classes and double shifts can help reduce unit costs if carefully implemented in the right context.

Better schools

Chapter 2 reviews evidence on what makes a difference in improving the quality of education in schools. One important conclusion is that there are significant opportunities to improve the ways human and material resources are managed and used in schools, recognizing that the school is a complex social institution that operates within a wider socio-cultural and political context.

This section looks at the policy implications of approaches to making schools work better. It addresses two main issues. First, it examines how governments can develop policies that place schools at the forefront of improving education quality. Among the countries discussed in Chapter 2, for example, Egypt defines schools in terms of being 'beautiful, clean, developed and productive', while in Cuba collective ownership of schools is important and in Canada the notion of 'schools as habitat' has gained currency. Education policy in these countries embodies a sense of what a school should be and how it can improve.

The second issue is the extent to which improving quality requires greater school autonomy and better leadership. It involves important questions regarding the levels of authority, responsibility and accountability that should lie with those who work directly in and with schools. This issue is invariably part of a wider national debate on decentralization of public services, and so is unlikely to be resolved within the education sector alone.[61]

---

58. See Lambert (2004) for further discussion.

59. The framework advocates an 'optimal' ratio between average teacher salaries and per capita GDP of no more than 3.5. For further discussion see Chapter 5 and UNESCO (2003a: 250).

60. As noted earlier, low wages drive teachers into higher-status occupations, and in recent years high levels of teacher turnover and absenteeism have become entrenched, particularly in Africa (UNICEF, 1999c; AfDB, 1998). Glewwe, Nauman and Kremer (2003) find that teachers in Kenya are absent 20% of the time, and even higher rates are recorded in Uganda and Madagascar. Bernard (1999) notes that 74.2% of the teachers in the PASEC sample in Cameroon hold a second job.

61. For a broader discussion of decentralization in education see UNESCO (2003a).

Promoting better schools

As the learner is at the heart of the learning process, so the school is at the centre of the education system. It is where investments designed to improve the quality of education come together in the teaching and learning process. Reforms to improve quality should give appropriate weight to enabling schools to improve their own performance. Schools however, cannot effect meaningful change without sufficient capacity and considerable ongoing support. The question, then, is how to ensure that complex but necessary changes come about within a well-defined policy framework designed to develop better schools.

The notion of improving a school in its totality, as distinct from strengthening individual inputs or processes, has gained ground in both the industrialized and developing worlds. It finds expression in many different but related conceptual frameworks. Three examples are 'school improvement', which is largely a product of Western discourse and argues that schools should be significant agents in the management of their own change; 'whole school development', which takes a holistic approach to implementing systemic changes; and 'child-friendly schools' – a rights-based model that owes much to the work of United Nations bodies, especially UNICEF. All three ideas build on the premise that the school should be more central to reform and improvement.

School improvement

School improvement has been described as a branch of the study of educational change.[62] While school effectiveness research (described in Chapter 2) looks at what counts, school improvement considers how to bring about change. That is its defining characteristic, and although there are variations in emphasis and focus, a broad set of principles underpins its philosophy:

■ The school should be the focus of *education change strategies*.

■ The *processes of education change* are important.

■ Schools should be part of, and *own* attempts at, education reform.

■ Real improvements require strong *group dynamics*, *teacher empowerment* and *capacity building*.

■ *'Bottom up'* processes of education planning and curriculum development are most effective.

It is clear from the nature of these principles that an enabling policy environment is a prerequisite for school-driven school improvement. In many countries this requires a more proactive way of looking at schools and at those who work in and for them. In some industrialized countries, the concept of school improvement has been invoked as part of reforms designed around nationally agreed student and school performance benchmarks. In such circumstances, school improvement risks being 'little more than a quick fix and expedient response to the demands for change and the setting of targets by external agencies' (Hopkins, 2001). Insufficient attention is paid in such cases to the context of the school, to incentives that make a long-term difference and to capacity building.[63]

A more 'authentic' form of school improvement emphasizes the skills, aspirations and energy of those closest to the school, rather than a centrally driven set of prescriptive changes. It recognizes that teachers and learners can learn from one another and in so doing improve interpersonal relationships and the culture of the school. This is a prerequisite for enhancing the nature and quality of learning experiences.[64]

Conceived of in this light, school improvement is a way of designing and providing conditions that enable teachers, other adults and learners to promote and sustain learning among themselves within schools. Drawing on the work of Hopkins, Table 4.11 shows one school improvement framework and the major policy implications derived from it. The implications, in the right-hand column, will not be unfamiliar to education policy makers: all are objectives to which most systems aspire. The particular import of the school improvement model is the centrality of learning, learners and learning achievement and the focus this gives to school-driven change strategies.

Some critics ask whether such an all-encompassing model can be applied systemically where resource constraints exist. Even in more

> As the learner is at the heart of the learning process, so the school is at the centre of the education system

---

62. See Miles, Saxl and Lieberman (1998), Hargreaves et al. (1998) and Hopkins (2001) for recent overviews of the literature on school improvement.

63. See, for example, work on performance-based reforms in the US, New Zealand and Australia, which concluded that no real gains in student performance resulted from major reforms that neglected to focus on instruction and capacity building (Leithwood, Jantzi and Steinbach, 1999).

64. See, for example, Barth (1990) and Hopkins (2001).

Table 4.11: School improvement: policy implications

Strategies	Policy implications
Focus on student achievement, learning and empowerment	• Keep an unrelenting focus on student achievement and learning • Develop curriculum and teaching programmes that are based on what is known about learning
Develop curriculum and teaching programmes that are based on what is known about learning	• Pay attention to context – develop knowledge about what works and where • Build capacity and strengthen known capacity-creating components
Create the conditions and capacity for school improvement	• Nurture professional learning communities and provide incentives for teacher and school enquiry • Improve research and dissemination of its results and make it relevant to practitioners
Implement focused change strategies	• Make a commitment to, and allow time for, effective implementation • Link pressure and support at all levels of the system
Build policy context and external support networks	• Establish local infrastructure and networks, supported by good external facilitation • Assure policy coherence

Source: Hopkins (2001)

---

65. This is based on Hopkins (2001), drawing on Dalin (1994).

66. See Akyeampong (2004), World Bank (2004f), Akyeampong et al. (2000) and Sayed, Akyeampong and Ampiah (2000). World Bank (2004f) suggests that school participation in whole school development has enhanced English and mathematics scores.

67. Sayed, Akyeampong and Ampiah (2000) found that head teachers who tried to organize on-site teacher development often lacked resources and/or had trouble motivating teachers in the absence of rewards and incentives. Moreover, although structures for supporting and training teachers, such as district teacher support teams and clusters, had been established, they had not necessarily developed a set of activities. Akyeampong (2004) also discusses challenges facing the programme.

68. World Bank (2004f) found that about one-third of teachers 'use a student-centred learning approach and use simulations on a regular basis, though about a fifth of the latter could not explain them properly. And about one fifth use cues to help explain difficult words. In summary, modern methods are far from unknown, but their use cannot be described as widespread, being utilized by a minority of teachers.'

---

developed countries it has been suggested that emphasis on school-level change strategies is too time consuming and expensive and is most likely to be effective for schools that already have a strong capacity or propensity for change (Slavin, 1998). The model has also been criticised for a lack of attention to broader policy frameworks and the contexts in which they are developed. As a recent overview of school improvement notes, however, although national contexts differ it is unlikely that those concerned with education reform in developing countries would disagree with all or most of the following propositions:

■ Education reform has to work at the level of the school.
■ A multi-agency approach should support schools.
■ System linkages should be 'wide' and 'deep'.
■ Reform itself is a learning process.
■ A strong vision of reform is needed.
■ A strong focus on classroom practice is needed.
■ Teachers are learners.
■ Commitment comes from empowerment.
■ Both local and central initiatives can work.
■ Parents and communities make a difference.[65]

If these propositions are accepted, school improvement does have insights from which all systems can benefit. Perhaps the key message of the concept for some of the world's poorest countries is that this framework helps people think through the actions that are required to make schools part of the process of change. How comprehensively it can be applied may be unclear, but it provides a basis for analyzing whether schools can make a significant difference when they are placed at the centre of a reform model.

Whole school development

In some developing countries, the approach being adopted for comprehensive projects or national reforms is 'whole school development' or 'reform', which draws on insights generated by work on the school improvement concept. Examples include Aga Khan-supported projects in East African countries and in South Africa, Sri Lanka and Ghana (Akyeampong, 2004; and Sayed, Akyeampong and Ampiah, 2000).

Ghana's Whole School Development Programme is geared to meet the objectives of the government's Free Compulsory Universal Basic Education reforms. Increased authority and responsibility are being given to schools, communities and district authorities to improve the quality of teaching and learning, with a focus on:

■ child-centred practice in the acquisition of literacy, numeracy and problem-solving;
■ community participation in the delivery of education;
■ school-based in-service teacher training;
■ participatory planning and resource management;
■ greater efficiency in resource management.

These objectives (Ghana Education Service, 2004) underpin the strategies shown in Box 4.16.

The programme has given rise to a range of positive intermediate developments and shows some signs of affecting the quality of student learning in Ghana.[66] But it is not without its challenges. For example, the cascade approach to training is not proving as effective as expected,[67] and some doubts have been raised about the extent to which there has been a real change in pedagogy in the classroom.[68]

Box 4.16 Whole school development in Ghana

Among the strategies in the Whole School Development Programme in Ghana, three key strategies involve teacher professional development, school-based action plans and the formation of school clusters.*

- The programme provides support to **head teachers and teachers**. In-service training follows a 'cascade' model: head teachers and district school circuit supervisors receive training, then are required to provide training at district and school levels. The training emphasizes child-centred pedagogy, effective use of appropriate teaching and learning materials and use of the local environment as a learning resource.

- To improve the partnership between head teachers, teachers and the community, workshops teach participants how to develop a '**Whole School Action Plan**' emphasizing the importance of this tripartite partnership in addressing teaching and learning needs. Action plans set targets, guide preparation of school budgets and include plans for ways to involve the community.

- To foster in-service training, the programme organizes schools in **clusters** of five to eight institutions. The cluster has become the primary unit of change for school improvement. Cluster in-service workshops are intended to provide the focus for school improvement activities.

*For details of training and other activities see Ghana Education Service (1999).

Source: Ghana Education Service (1999)

Nevertheless, the Ghana experience underlines the value of a long-term school-focused approach to reform that recognizes the importance of continual capacity building. Roles have to be defined clearly and responsibilities agreed and accepted. Strong partnerships are essential: within schools, between the head teacher and classroom teachers and between the school and the local community, with proactive support from district education authorities.

Child-friendly schools

The child-friendly school is a rights-based model that draws its authority from the Convention on the Rights of the Child. It promotes the view that good schools should be child-seeking and child-centred (Box 4.17).

In terms of national policies and programmes, child-friendly schooling can be a normative goal and thus a framework for programming and resource allocation, including for training. For individual schools and communities it can be both a goal and a tool for improving quality through self-assessment, school planning and management, as well as a way of mobilizing the community around education and child rights.

The model emphasizes the school as a place providing learning opportunities relevant to life and livelihood, in a healthy, safe environment that is inclusive and protective, is sensitive to gender equity and equality and involves the participation of students, families and communities (Chabbott, 2004). These ideas are given expression in the Child-Friendly School Framework (Table 4.12), which is a matrix juxtaposing quality-related issues with child-related concerns.

Box 4.17 Child-seeking, child-centred schools

Rights-based or child-friendly schools not only help children enjoy their right to a good basic education, they also help children learn what they need to know to face the challenges of the new century; enhance children's health and well-being; guarantee them safe, protective spaces for learning, free from violence and abuse; raise teacher morale and motivation and mobilize community support for education.

A rights-based, child-friendly school has two basic characteristics:

- It is **child-seeking**, actively identifying excluded children and working to get them enrolled in school and included in learning. It treats children as subjects with rights and treats the state as under obligation to fulfil these rights. It demonstrates, promotes and helps monitor the rights and well-being of all children in the community.

- It is **child-centred**, acting in children's best interests so that they may realize their full potential, and it is concerned both about the 'whole' child (including health, nutritional status and well-being) and about what happens to children in their families and communities before they enter school and after they leave.

Source: www.unicef.org/lifeskills/index

Table 4.12: Child-Friendly School Framework

Quality issues \ Child-friendly issues	Inclusive/ gender-sensitive	Healthy/safe/ protective	Effective	Involved with the community
Learners				
Content				
Teaching/learning processes				
Environments				
Outcomes				

Source: Chabbott (2004)

> School-based management undoubtedly has an impact on quality, regardless of whether that is its ultimate goal

Several projects around the world are using the framework. A recent overview suggests it is too early to assess the results; most of the projects are relatively small and baseline data on learning levels and outcomes are insufficient. Nevertheless, some initial evidence suggests that the framework is proving to be valuable in enabling some policy makers to work through the implications of decentralization and school-based management (Chabbott, 2004).

A study of child-friendly school initiatives in East Asia and the Pacific[69] draws four main conclusions (Bernard, 2004):

- The focus on learners, content, teaching and learning processes, environments and outcomes remains fundamental to the definition and realization of child-friendly schools, but flexibility is the key to implementation.

- The concept of the child-friendly school may be desirable in principle but it is difficult to maintain in practice.

- Single initiatives cannot be sustained in isolation. They must build on existing systems and work with 'like-minded' activities and partners.

- The concept has the potential to offer an entry point for addressing school level and systemic issues, but it requires a proactive, creative approach.

This study seems to suggest that the extent to which the concept of child-friendly schools provides an overarching framework for implementation of national policies and strategies – as distinct from an analytical tool that sharpens understanding of whether children are genuinely at the heart of learning processes – remains to be tested fully. At present, as with EFA more generally, it is not surprising if governments embrace the concept as a general principle but do not as yet apply it in organizing school development and management. Still, its close attention to inclusion, diversity, security, health and gender equality make it an important framework for overcoming disadvantage and encouraging more effective learning environments.

School autonomy: challenges for management and leadership

One implication of reforms driven by school improvement, however interpreted and applied, is greater school autonomy. Such reforms are usually associated with decentralization. School-based management and leadership are crucial aspects of any reform strategy in which control and responsibility are devolved.

School-based management[70]

In school-based management, responsibilities are transferred from central level to professionals within the school (generally the head teacher and senior teachers) and greater authority is given to elected school boards representing parents and the wider community. The concept is of increasing significance worldwide and undoubtedly has an impact on quality, regardless of whether that is its ultimate goal (Caldwell, 1998).

---

69. The countries involved are Cambodia, China, Indonesia, Mongolia, Myanmar, the Philippines, Thailand, Vanuatu and Viet Nam.

70. This sub-section mainly draws on de Grauwe (2004) – a background paper prepared for this report. School-based management is often used interchangeably with the terms school based governance, school self-management and school site management.

> **Box 4.18 School-based management and better learning**
>
> In **Israel**, greater school autonomy has had a positive impact on teachers' motivation and sense of commitment and on schools' achievement orientation, but only 4% of the variance in the effectiveness between autonomous and less autonomous schools could be explained by school-based management.
>
> Autonomous schools in **Nicaragua**, most of which serve deprived areas, have results as good as other schools. This positive finding is related to their relative autonomy in staff selection and staff monitoring.
>
> **El Salvador**'s Community Managed Schools Programme, or EDUCO, gives communities significant authority over schools, including in finance and staffing. An early evaluation found that enhanced community and parental involvement improved students' language skills and diminished absenteeism, which could have long-term effects on achievement.
>
> The results of the **OECD**'s Programme for International Student Assessment (PISA) in 2000 suggests that 'in those countries in which principals report, on average, a higher degree of school autonomy with regard to choice of courses, the average performance in reading literacy tends to be significantly higher. The picture is similar, though less pronounced, for other aspects of school autonomy, including the relationship between mean performance and the degree of school autonomy in budget allocation.' The OECD warns, however, against a cause-effect interpretation, since, 'for example, school autonomy and performance could well be mutually reinforcing or influenced by other factors'.
>
> Studies in **New Zealand** and in several countries of **West Africa** found that, in general, school-based management led to few changes in pedagogical practices.
>
> *Sources*: Israel: Gaziel (1998); Nicaragua: King and Ozler (1998); El Salvador: Jiminez and Sawada (1998); PISA: OECD (2004c); New Zealand and West Africa: de Grauwe (2004).

Some commentators see it as a means of improving quality even when that is not the primary focus.[71] Others[72] express concern that introducing school-based management nationally can hurt the performance of weak schools where resource management capacity is most limited. Most, however, say there is simply not enough evidence-based knowledge about the direct or indirect impact of school-based management on learning outcomes.[73]

The main arguments made for greater school autonomy are compelling and include the ideas that it is:

- more democratic, allowing teachers and parents to take school-based decisions;

- more relevant, since decision-making powers are closer to where problems are experienced, leading to more appropriate and relevant policies;

- less bureaucratic, since decisions are taken more quickly;

- more accountable, as allowing schools and teachers a greater say in decisions implies greater responsibility for their performance;

- more likely to yield additional resources, especially where giving parents a say in school management encourages them to contribute to it.

In themselves, these benefits do not lead to better quality. A recent macro study of school-based management, drawing on eighty-three empirical studies, concludes: 'There is virtually no firm, research-based knowledge about the direct or indirect effects of school based management on students...[T]he little research-based evidence that does exist suggest[s] that the effects on students are just as likely to be negative as positive' (Leithwood and Menzies, 1998).[74] Studies from several countries give some, if not total, support to this conclusion (Box 4.18).

These potentially dispiriting findings lead naturally to the question of what strategies and actions need to accompany the introduction of school-based management for quality to be improved, or at least not threatened. The literature to date has identified at least six main requirements:

- School-based management must be accompanied by strategies to strengthen capacities and *leadership* (see below).

- Schools need *information* on their performance so as to identify their strengths, weaknesses and priorities, in motivating rather than demotivating ways. This requires capacity building on basic data analysis and support on school improvement strategies. The role of local and district offices is key.

Schools need information on their performance so as to identify their strengths, weaknesses and priorities, in motivating rather than demotivating ways

---

71. See, for instance, Gaziel (1998), Williams et al. (1997), King and Ozler (1998), Jimenez and Sawada (1998) and OECD (2004c).

72. For example, Odden and Busch (1998), Asian Network of Research and Training Institutions in Educational Planning (forthcoming) and de Grauwe (2004).

73. See, for instance, Leithwood and Menzies (1998), Fullan and Watson (2000) and Caldwell (1998).

74. Caldwell (1998) and Fullan (1993) arrive at similar conclusions.

- Schools need professional, well-managed structures offering constant *support*.

- Central authorities must continue to play a critical role, especially in *monitoring* school performance for any patterns of low quality and inequality.

- Schools need control over resources.

- School-based management must be transparent.

Also required are strong accountability mechanisms. At the national level, these are likely to include curriculum guidelines, regular national examinations and audits to assure propriety in expenditure. At the local level, too, the effectiveness of school-based management depends strongly on the accountability the school feels towards the community, as well as the influence the community can exercise on the school through knowledge and skills, power, information and rewards (Lawler, 1986). More concretely, the community generally exercises its influence through involvement in the school board or council. The precise powers of such bodies vary. In Australia and the USA, for instance, boards can play a positive role in recruitment of principals/head teachers, in some budgetary decisions and in extra-curricular matters. But constructive engagement is not always present; at worst, boards provide opportunities for misuse of community resources, and transparency may be lacking especially in the use of funds.[75] In addition, communities are far from homogeneous. Elites can manipulate boards to reinforce their power. Evidence from New Zealand and Australia shows under-representation of minority groups in the composition of school boards (de Grauwe, 2004).

Tensions may exist within schools, too. Putting school budgets in the hands of communities can be unpopular with teachers, as was the case, for instance, in some districts of India and with EDUCO schools in El Salvador (Jimenez and Sawada, 1998). And while head teachers may support in-school supervision, teachers may be more antagonistic.

These significant challenges suggest that without major government undertakings for systemic reform to strengthen individual and institutional capacities, the impact of school autonomy on the quality of education may be limited. Where the capacity of schools and governments alike is extremely weak, the main priority may be for central government to ensure that all schools have a minimum level of key resources – teachers, learning materials and infrastructure. Giving schools freedom to develop some of their own solutions may nevertheless be appropriate where communities are strong and NGOs active, but whether it is a long-term, sustainable grass-roots option is more doubtful. As the examples of countries cited in Chapter 2 suggest, greater autonomy may work best when education systems have basic infrastructure and capacities in place. Otherwise the absence of an efficient, supportive state structure is risky, not only for individual schools but also for the system as a whole, with a threat of increasing disparities in performance. For real benefits to accrue, greater school autonomy must be accompanied by strategies to build the capacities of schools, head teachers and communities, inspired by a focus on quality improvement and concern for equity.

School leadership[76]

The preceding sections on school improvement, and the school effectiveness literature cited in Chapter 2, point clearly to the importance of strong educational leadership in improving learning outcomes and creating a culture of school development. In both cases, leadership is seen in terms of transformation rather than control or maintenance. Thus, the ability of schools to improve teaching and learning can depend significantly on the quality of the professional leadership provided by senior school staff and, to a certain extent, by people from outside of day-to-day school operations.

In many industrialized countries, recognition of the importance of developing leadership skills is reflected in specialized institutions and research programmes such as the National College for School Leadership in the United Kingdom, the proposed National Institute for Quality Teaching and School Leadership in Australia and the international research project on Successful School Leadership at the Ontario Institute for Studies in Education at the University of Toronto, Canada.

Building capacity for school leadership systemically and sustainably is much more

> Evidence from New Zealand and Australia shows under-representation of minority groups in the composition of school boards

---

75. Research by UNESCO's International Institute for Educational Planning (IIEP) on school functioning in a context of decentralization in West Africa shows that parents and teachers have scarcely any knowledge or control of the use of the money paid for children's schooling. Thus, where accountability at local and central level is weak, school-based management is unlikely to lead to better use of funds (de Grauwe, 2004).

76. This sub-section draws largely on the background paper by de Grauwe (2004).

difficult in education systems with limited resources available for professional development.[77] Few senior staff members in such systems can be classified as well-trained professionals. They are often classroom teachers who have been promoted near the end of their teaching careers. Selection and recruitment practices may favour long service, convey a gender bias and take account of factors extraneous to the demands of school leadership. Professional development opportunities are often limited in coverage, and in highly aid-dependent countries they may be associated with donor-supported projects whose methods may not mesh well with the practice of national systems.

The trend towards greater school autonomy and school-based management has significant implications for head teachers in terms of their workload, the nature of their responsibilities and the skills and knowledge required to fulfil new and more complex roles. Good school leadership is about transforming feelings, attitudes and beliefs, as well as practice, to improve the culture of the school (Hopkins, 2001); promoting teacher behaviour that focuses on a broad spectrum of learning outcomes (Leithwood, Jantzi and Steinbach, 1999) and building close working relationships with all stakeholders – parents, teachers, learners. But for head teachers working in relatively isolated, poorly supported schools with resource constraints, the motivation and incentive to become an innovative pedagogical leader and a proactive, participatory manager may be severely limited. Indeed, pressure to fulfil new roles without support may be a disincentive to becoming or remaining a head teacher.

In both developing and developed countries, the demands that reforms place on senior school staff may limit the time and the energy they can give for quality improvement (Leithwood and Menzies, 1998). Many new management tasks, especially those concerning financing and staffing, are complex. Studies covering four OECD countries found that administrators were 'troubled by ethical dilemmas…and some reported an increase in the frequency with which they were confronted with difficult decisions in recent years' (Dempster, 2000).

What can be done? Few countries have explicit policies on the professional development of head teachers that are linked to a wider reform agenda, even where major programmes of decentralization and delegation of authority to schools are under way. And few ministries of education have one of the chief prerequisites for drawing up a professional development strategy: a national or district profile of head teachers, deputies, and teachers with school leadership potential.

At a minimum, clarity on the following issues is needed:

■ what is expected and required of existing head teachers; what their areas of autonomy and levels of accountability are and what the roles and responsibilities are of decision-makers in the school and community;

■ what head teachers, especially those newly appointed and/or isolated, can rightfully expect from local and national support structures;

■ recruitment and selection procedures, including mechanisms for early identification of potential head teachers and, preferably, a system of mentoring by practising head teachers;

■ career paths through regular professional development opportunities and in-service training;

■ the importance of learning from one another in school- and cluster-based activities, through mutual support systems, including shared use of self-learning modules and materials.

Some countries have elements of this menu in place. In the Republic of Korea, recruitment patterns have been changed to attract younger candidates and some school communities have been given a say in the selection of head teachers. In Sri Lanka, a 'school-based management policy' has redesigned areas of responsibility at different management levels, including that of head teacher. In Malaysia, a system of early identification of promising future head teachers includes training and mentoring by practising head teachers. In Senegal, which has no nationally organised support systems, school directors on their own initiative have set up groups to share experience and advice through visits and seminars to which they all contribute.

> Good school leadership is about transforming feelings, attitudes and beliefs, as well as practice, to improve the culture of the school

77. Some significant developments in this regard, such as the PRISM project in Kenya (discussed later), are emerging, however.

A recent overview of seventeen school improvement programmes in sub-Saharan Africa found twelve with school leadership components (ADEA, 2003). The Primary School Management Programme in Kenya, known as PRISM, has undertaken school management competency development activities for 16,700 primary school head teachers. Drawing on local resources and communities, it came up with a sustainable approach to school improvement. Head teacher support groups, led by zone inspectors, were the key development mechanism. Evaluations of PRISM reveal that these groups 'have a positive impact on several indicators...including school governance; student participation and achievement; admission and retention rates; parent and community participation in school life and activities; gender equity in access; parental financial contributions; instructional leadership by school heads...and the design and implementation of teacher development activities by school heads' (Weva, 2003b).

School-based leadership is unlikely to be achieved by formal training alone, although acquisition of new skills and knowledge is clearly important. South Africa has begun introducing a policy framework for Education Management and Leadership Development to develop national and provincial institutional focal points for management development, build strong networks of professional and community associations, establish quality assurance practices, use existing resources as much as possible and develop more cost-effective training methodologies (South Africa Department of Education, 2004). This broad-based approach suggests that effective school leadership flourishes where there are positive working conditions, incentives for change, a collegial environment and strong partnerships between schools and communities.

Multi-shift schooling

The previous sections draw on analyses of schools that conform to a broadly standard model. In many resource-constrained countries, however, organizing schooling means making difficult decisions about how to maximize scarce resources, especially where primary school enrolment has risen rapidly but new funding has not.

Multi-shift schooling is an option in such situations. It is a way of increasing the supply of school places by using existing resources efficiently. Double or even triple shifts make it possible for a single set of buildings, facilities, books and teachers to serve many more pupils and thus meet increased demand for schooling and for greater equity in the provision of primary education. Multi-shift schooling may also provide opportunities for disadvantaged children to go to school. For example, children in work may be able to attend only in the morning or afternoon and still follow a complete curriculum.

Multi-shift schooling places enormous pressure on those charged with managing and leading schools, and this has significant implications for the quality of education. However, it can bring benefits. For example, in areas where access is not a major issue, multi-shifting may help improve quality by significantly reducing class size and thereby alleviating pressure on school facilities. On the other hand, quality is clearly threatened if instruction time is severely curtailed and/or condensed. And, depending on how they are deployed, teachers may be overworked and tired. These drawbacks are not always serious, however; indeed, some research has indicated that academic achievement in double-shift schools may be just as high as in single-shift schools, and administrators with imagination may find ways to get round the problems of shorter school days and congested school compounds.[78]

Like many strategies for reconciling tensions between access and quality in education, multi-shifting is most effective when tailored to a specific context. Variations on the concept range from choices between overlapping and 'end-on' shifts to changes in the length of the school week and rotation systems in which classes might alternate by day, week or month. The brief examples in Box 4.19 illustrate this variety.

Nevertheless, school managers and supervisors and local authorities cannot simply assume that multi-shift systems will operate cost-effectively. Efficient operation requires attention to the model that is to be used and the management structures that are needed (as well as their implications for recruitment and training), along with meticulous scheduling to assure efficient use of the school day. Learning at home and

---

78. For an extended examination of shift schooling and its implications for quality, see Bray (2000).

> **Box 4.19 Organizing the school day in multi-shift systems**
>
> - Sabelas Maret is a secondary school in **Indonesia**. With overlapping shifts and efficient scheduling, the school expanded its enrolment by 25% without major changes to the learning process.
>
> - In **Hong Kong, China**, different teachers teach morning and afternoon sessions.
>
> - In **Senegal**, which is short of qualified teachers, the same teachers are used for multiple shifts. Some teachers welcome this, as it enables them to increase their earnings.
>
> - In **Bangladesh**, grades 1 and 2 are taught in the morning and grades 3, 4 and 5 in the afternoon.
>
> - In **Puerto Rico**, elementary-level pupils are accommodated in the morning and intermediate-level pupils in the afternoon. Some schools are used by children during the day and by adults at night.
>
> *Source:* Bray (2000)

better use of community facilities can also support multi-shift schooling.

Conclusion

Making schools work better is not easy, but is at the heart of the educational enterprise. It is important to have a vision of what a good school is. Greater autonomy can make a difference if schools are well supported. Leadership is critical, whether in the context of greater school autonomy or not.

Support schools, inform policy

Better teachers and better schools are essential ingredients of the enabling environment that contributes to improving the quality of teaching and learning (Figure 4.1). A third enabling component is professional support for teachers and schools, and, more broadly, the circulation of knowledge and experience among all major education stakeholders.

Like any other learning organization, schools need to reflect constantly on their activities and improve their performance. To do so, they must have regular access to evidence-based, practical knowledge about what works best in classrooms. Professional support to schools and teachers is therefore vital. Services that offer advice, promote developmental activity and manage in-service training have to be responsive to issues that are specific to schools, especially in resource-constrained systems where the need for support is often most critical. National, regional and global policy networks can also benefit from knowledge drawn from local experiences and innovations, using it to inform their understanding of the strategies needed to improve teaching and learning.

There is merit in seeing the institutions and bodies involved in these two functions – supporting schools and informing policy – as part of a 'knowledge infrastructure'[79] (Hoppers, 2004) that contributes to the production and use of professional knowledge (Hargreaves, 2000). This view stresses the generation, mediation and dissemination of educational knowledge in such a way that it is useful for teachers, school managers and policy makers.

The elements of this infrastructure can be conceptualized in two ways. First, they can be seen as a set of institutions and bodies established specifically to provide direct professional support to schools. They include school advisory services, teacher resource centres, school clusters, counsellors and school inspectors (in their advisory and reporting functions). The second understanding is broader and concerns upward and downward flows of knowledge, mediated by those who generate and disseminate outcomes of research on how to improve teaching and learning, whether for application in schools or to inform policy development. These actors include universities, research institutes, teacher training colleges and curriculum development centres. They may also include teachers' unions, head teachers' associations and community-based organizations providing professional support or generating knowledge. International organizations and networks may also make important contributions.

National, regional and global policy networks can benefit from local experiences and innovations, to inform their strategies

---

79. In this context, this term is preferred to the somewhat narrower concept 'educational research and development' used by the OECD (2004b). In addition to research and development, the notion of knowledge infrastructure includes training, advisory work and quality assurance.

In reality, these two dimensions are interlinked. A well-functioning knowledge infrastructure will support the development of a culture that encourages cooperation, sharing of knowledge and experience and, eventually, evidence-based classroom practice, school management and policy development. Common understandings at various levels of the education system enhance mutual learning and strengthen the coherence between national policy and local practice.

Keeping in mind the interplay between institutions of professional support and less tangible knowledge processes, this section addresses five major components of the knowledge infrastructure: advisory work, training, developmental activities, research and quality assurance. Understanding the interrelations between these functions and assuring some consistency and coherence throughout is a key step in strengthening the capacity of the education knowledge infrastructure and increasing the benefits that flow from it.

Advising teachers

Advising teachers and schools is an essential activity of professional support and guidance. Advisers should be able to translate the knowledge available from research, local experience, ministry directives and the like into a form that will benefit schools and their teachers. Increasing school autonomy makes this function even more important, since more autonomous schools will need more 'customized' knowledge. Such outreach to schools, where it exists, is usually in the hands of advisors and managers operating at regional or district level – or even closer to schools, with NGOs and for-profit organizations increasingly becoming active in the field (Hoppers, 2004). In addition, teachers' centres or teacher resource centres (Box 4.20), operating at intermediate and/or local levels, have become important elements of the teacher's support infrastructure in many countries.

A more informal type of advisory work is carried out by selected teachers, usually referred to as resource or staff development coordinators, change agents or leader teachers. Often informally appointed by school administrators or local authorities, they advise schools or networks of schools, thus enhancing cooperation between teachers and administrators at local level (Hoppers, 2004). Training and formal recognition may be as important as material rewards in promoting this form of pedagogical leadership (Chelu and Mbulwe, 1994).

In-service training

Earlier sections of this chapter discuss the professional development of teachers and school leaders, both pre-service and in-service. Here we take another look at in-service training, focusing on its importance as a vehicle for the transmission of knowledge regarding good practice and on its synergies with other functions of the support structure.

Here, too, one can see a transition from a more traditional institutional model to a variety of arrangements involving several stakeholders, including schools themselves. An emerging view is of the school as a professional learning community where staff development involves not only formal off-the-job training but also peer coaching and action research (Hopkins, 2001).[80]

> **Box 4.20 Teacher resource centres**
>
> Teacher resource centres (TRCs) offer in-service training, develop and provide resources for teaching and enhance the exchange of ideas among teachers. They are often integrated in school cluster systems and linked to institutions responsible for supervision or teacher education. In-service training is often provided through the 'cascade' model in which, for instance, head teachers are trained and then train teachers. The primary aim is improving pedagogy. Studies in some countries, however, show only a limited impact on classroom practice from this type of in-service training, raising questions about how appropriate one-way knowledge transfer is as a mode of professional development. The experience of early forms of TRCs in African countries indicates that such centres may be more successful when they are given greater pedagogical autonomy. TRCs can be effective when they facilitate knowledge development at the classroom level and encourage knowledge sharing among teachers, managers, advisors and inspectors.
>
> *Sources:* De Grauwe (2001); Knamiller (1999); Hoppers (1998); de Grauwe and Carron (undated).

---

80. See also Aspland and Brown (1993) and ERNWACA (2003).

As noted earlier, pre-service training increasingly tends to involve new pathways into teaching. Partly inspired by pedagogical insights but also influenced by teacher shortage and limited resources, low-income and industrialized countries alike are showing a growing interest in work-based learning for teachers and in appointing trainee teachers or apprentices as classroom assistants.[81] Their further development into professionals then takes place partly on the job, with training institutions playing an important supportive role and the trainees learning from closer contact with teachers' workplaces.

Experience in Cuba demonstrates that such arrangements are by no means limited to rich countries (Box 4.21). The costs of freeing up the time of teachers, principals and consultants can be offset by the benefits of greater synergies between schools and supporting institutions. Moreover, collaborating with schools rather than individual teachers makes it possible to look at school development in its totality (Hopkins, Ainscow and West, 1994). This is also the background to the 'whole school' movement (see 'Better schools', above) in South Africa, where schools link up with universities, NGOs and provincial Departments of Education.

Box 4.21 Cuba: school improvement as a collective effort

Cuba's national curriculum continually undergoes reform and adaptation to respond to local realities. Teachers and students take an active role and support the school in producing learning materials. Teachers exchange experience on teaching methods and materials in *colectivos pedagógicos*, which are organized by subject; each collective is supported by an expert in methodology. Every teacher is expected to carry out applied research, and the best results are shared at municipal education conferences. Specialized institutes guide the research. Strong links with the community are assured through home visits by teachers, homework sessions by students (three times per week) and mass gatherings and other participatory activities. Both pre- and in-service training (lasting five and six years, respectively) are school-based, assuring links between schools and training institutions.

Source: Gasperini (2000)

Developing curricula

In most developing countries, ministries take direct responsibility for the development of curricula, content and assessment instruments, sometimes supported by ministerial committees, as in South Africa (Hoppers, 2004). This model reflects a relatively high degree of centralization. In some circumstances it is susceptible to political influence on content. Ministries in countries with more decentralized systems have outsourced these functions and in some cases partly privatized them[82] (Kloprogge et al., 1995), with schools free to choose the types of support they want.

In Finland, greater school autonomy has led to the development of horizontal networks of schools, combined with assistance from specialized experts (Hopkins, 2001, citing Fullan, 2000; UNESCO, 2003a).[83] The Senegalese *Collectifs des Directeurs* work on a similar principle (Niane, 2004), while Cuba is noteworthy for the concerted way in which actors at all levels are engaged in continuous school improvement as Box 4.21 already illustrated.

Participatory curriculum development (PCD) is a further example of developmental work involving local stakeholders. It suggests that, since successful use of the national curriculum in schools depends on the capacity, motivation and commitment of those who teach and directly support schools, the participation of these actors in curriculum development can reap learning dividends (McLaughlin, 1987; cited in Weva, 2003a). An example from the Gambia illustrates PCD at work (Box 4.22).

PCD has its critics. As the example from the Gambia suggests, it is not without costs, especially if there is a significant initial investment in establishing networks, systems and structures. Proponents argue, however, that the long-term benefits outweigh the costs and that the latter gradually decrease as the pool of skilled people grows and learning materials are put to use (Taylor, 2004; Helvetas, 2002). Perhaps the critical point for most resource-constrained systems is that this approach has benefits where there is already a clear, well-defined national core curriculum on which to build.

In South Africa, schools link up with universities, NGOs and provincial Departments of Education

---

81. For instance, the Bangladesh Rural Advancement Committee (BRAC) carries out initial training of teachers in as little as 12 days but provides well-organized ongoing support and weekly supervision. The level of pupil achievement in BRAC schools is generally better than in schools in the formal system (Latif, 2004). Systems in industrialized countries may use teacher shortages as an argument for shorter, more flexible pre-service training but pedagogical considerations also play a role (see, for instance, OECD, 2003b). Citing studies in developing countries, ADEA (2003) advises against lengthy pre-service training; it recommends continuous professional development in close interaction with teacher resource centres (for example) and making good use of information and communications technology.

82. Privatization does not necessarily exclude sustained subsidization, either direct or via schools. In the latter case, schools receive funds to 'buy' developmental services on a more or less free market.

83. The Finnish approach is based on the idea that 'it is possible for the school with its support networks to create visions of the future, (and to) reinforce (the) morals and (the) know how, which man (sic) needs as a member of society'. (Finland National Board of Education, 1996). Accordingly, Finland has opted for 'curriculum planning and implementation at the school level', which has important implications for the support structure (ibid.).

> **Box 4.22 English-language curriculum development in the Gambia**
>
> A participatory curriculum development approach was applied in the Gambia in the development of English-language teaching in primary schools. The following steps were critical:
>
> - a small awareness raising workshop on the PCD approach, involving key stakeholders and resulting in an action plan for the curriculum development process;
> - stakeholder analysis, followed by individual meetings with key individuals, focusing on their roles and their views on the current curriculum;
> - a wider survey of stakeholders (teachers, parents, employers) from schools around the country;
> - development of a thematic, child-centred approach to the new curriculum, integrating appropriate teaching and learning methods and materials into the content, and elaboration of a general outline through a departmental workshop, after which panels of serving teachers worked to develop the detailed curriculum;
> - teacher participation in writers' workshops, where they produced pupils' books and teachers' guides.
>
> The engagement of stakeholders throughout the process resulted in a high degree of interest, especially from teachers, in the development of the curriculum. Those involved agreed and followed a work plan. The main challenges included:
>
> - dealing with regular turnover of staff;
> - getting people together for key events;
> - a need to build educational and pedagogical abilities and capacities, and reluctance by some participants to admit to this need;
> - belated recognition of the need to engage more with learners and parents;
> - difficulty in processing the large needs survey; a smaller sample survey would have been equally effective.
>
> *Source:* Taylor (2004)

Research

A radical approach to addressing the issue of relevance and applicability of research involves changing the very nature of research

Generating knowledge about education has traditionally been the mission of universities and national institutes for education research. Such institutions traditionally investigate the practice of teaching and learning on the ground, combine the findings with existing bodies of knowledge and disseminate the results to the academic world, policy makers and, more rarely, directly to schools, teachers and/or intermediate organizations. A fundamental problem in this paradigm is that knowledge generated in one context may have limited application elsewhere. The problem exists both within developing countries (Hoppers, 2001) and within industrialized countries (OECD, 2004b), but it is exacerbated when the existence of an 'international state of practice' is suggested (Samoff, 1993) and is transferred by researchers and consultants from a Northern context to countries in the South. To enhance the relevance of education research, some countries have established bodies bringing together a variety of stakeholders – e.g. policy makers, practitioners, academics, NGOs and funding agencies. Examples include the Commission on Values in Education in South Africa and the Primary Education Development Programme in the United Republic of Tanzania (Hoppers, 2004).

At subregional level, member states of the Southern African Development Community (SADC) have started the Education Policy Support Initiative to review one another's educational knowledge bases, in order to inform future research (Hoppers, 2004).[84] Another international mechanism is the OECD Education Committee, where member states negotiate a common agenda of activities in the areas of research, policy review and indicator development.

A more radical approach to addressing the issue of relevance and applicability of research involves changing the very nature of research. Increasingly, practitioners recognize the value of reflecting on their own work and exchanging experiences in circles of peers that operate in comparable circumstances.[85] Action research is a more specific form of knowledge creation at grass-roots level, serving both to improve education directly and to feed outcomes upward in the national policy process (Van Graan et al., 2003). Central to these approaches is the aim of bridging theory and practice in efforts to enhance the value of education research.

Quality assurance

Strictly speaking, quality assurance is not an aspect of providing professional support to

---

84. For further information, see www.sadceducation.com

85. Gibbons et al. (1994) conceptualize such forms of interaction as 'Mode 2 knowledge production' – knowledge that is generated in the context of its application, possibly unintentionally and often by practitioners themselves. As traditional research institutions become aware of the more experiential forms of knowledge production, they may develop ways of interacting with practitioners on the ground to bridge the gap between traditional and alternative methods. See, for instance, Taylor and Fransman (2004) on participatory methods for effective learning.

schools or generating knowledge to inform policy. It is about measuring quality *ex post* and holding schools accountable – not about increasing quality *ex ante*. In practice, however, it is difficult, if not undesirable, to separate the functions of advising schools and informing policy from the function of controlling them, the more so because 'tight inspection and control are essential for success' in school improvement (Hopkins, 2001, citing Dalin, 1994). The advice to 'link pressure and support at all levels in the system' (Hopkins, 2001) is supported by various authors,[86] while Fullan (2000) notes that such linkage works best when systems of pressure and support are integrated.

For instance, benchmarked school performance indicators not only help inspectors hold schools accountable but should also serve as vital, more direct feedback to teachers, helping them identify their strengths and weaknesses (Hopkins, 2001). This scenario gives the inspector something of a hybrid role, sometimes referred to as that of the 'critical friend'. On the one hand, the inspector uses information about school performance to make comparisons with other schools, to point at good practice and thus to truly support the school; on the other hand, the inspector needs to report any failure. Some countries accept or mitigate the resulting tension,[87] while others – e.g. Botswana and Namibia – avoid it by allocating the reporting function to a separate cadre (de Grauwe, 2001).

A good investment

The development of infrastructure that provides professional support and generates and mediates knowledge for better learning is resulting in a general trend towards much greater interaction at all levels among practitioners, experts, inspectors, policy makers and researchers, accompanied by increased mutual learning in networks and a higher level of engagement. Investment in such infrastructure remains low, however. Some commentators attribute this to a certain resistance in the education field to evidence-based practice (Hargreaves, 1999).[88] Everything that has been said in this chapter nevertheless indicates that improving schools and the teaching and learning that goes on within them requires a culture of working on the basis of knowledge and evidence (Hopkins, 2001).

Building support for systemic reform

Starting with the learner, this chapter has looked at how the quality of education can be enhanced in an operational sense: in the classroom, in and around the school, through professional advice and support and through wider application of evidenced-based knowledge. But as was made clear at the outset (Figure 4.1), any intervention should be set very firmly within the context of wider education sector policies and frameworks. Innovation at local level will not in itself give rise to more improvement in education. Raising the quality of education requires a broad, systemic approach sustained by political support and backed by sufficient investment to sustain key policy interventions, even if allocations to specific improvements are modest.

However, even assuming that policies and budgets are in place, national governments face other significant challenges in implementing reforms aimed at improving the quality of education. Politically, such reforms seem more difficult to pursue than policies to enhance access (Corrales, 1999: 5). Parents, for instance, will immediately note and enjoy a capacity expansion at a nearby school and the abolition of fees. Improving education takes more time, and although the benefits are considerable (as Chapter 2 shows), they are also more general, involving effects such as the long-term impact on economic growth, fertility and health and changes in values. Consequently it is often more difficult to build a strong national alliance of interest groups around quality. But the examples of countries where progress is being made suggest that such alliance building is important.

Reform strategies

Successful education reforms have been achieved in rich and poor countries, in democratic and non-democratic states and under political parties with very different ideologies. Some reforms have been part of broader national reform strategies, while others are very specific (Corrales, 1999: 15–16). National experiences point to a set of promising strategies, summarized in Box 4.23.

Drawing on these broad ideas about reform, this section looks at three issues with a direct impact

---

86. Barber (2000), for instance, promotes the principle of 'maximum challenge, maximum support' in relation to the English education system.

87. In the United Kingdom, Australia and New Zealand, the initiative in supervision lies with schools (self-evaluation). They must establish School Development Plans, which inform subsequent school-based reviews by external actors (Hargreaves and Hopkins, 1994). The reviews serve both to provide feedback to schools and to make them accountable to the government and the general public. There is debate about the disclosure of information on school performance. Full transparency could raise the pressure on weaker schools to improve but could also lead parents to avoid these schools, resulting in a downward spiral. Cuba's 'emulation' principle anticipated Barber's 'maximum challenge, maximum support': it integrates both extreme pressure (in the form of competition) and peer support. Cuban teachers seem to receive all the help they need, yet their careers and even their salaries may be influenced by pupils' achievement (Gasperini, 2000).

88. The level of investment in educational R&D – a narrower concept than the whole educational knowledge infrastructure – is known for seven industrialized countries (Australia, Canada, Finland, Ireland, Netherlands, Sweden and the United Kingdom). The average for these countries is 0.3% of total educational expenditure, which is far less than the comparable figure for other knowledge intensive sectors (CERI, 2002).

> **Box 4.23 Nine ways to make changes happen**
>
> Change requires political initiative, followed by continuous political support through:
>
> - formation of independent advisory councils that can sustain the impetus for reform despite any eventual political change;
> - work towards consensus agreement with opposition political parties;
> - linkage of education reform with other issues, such as economic competitiveness, social cohesion and nation building.
>
> Demand for change needs to be strengthened:
>
> - Information campaigns can help make parents and employers aware that reform is in their interest.
> - Stakeholders can be actively involved, e.g. teachers, through participation in policy development, and parents, through participation in school boards.
> - As a further step, actors at local level can be given financial autonomy.
>
> Opposition to change needs to be addressed:
>
> - Incremental implementation may ease the tensions raised by change, though reform then runs a risk of losing momentum.
> - Opponents need to be turned into allies through early consultation and adaptation of plans to address their concerns.
> - In some cases, salary increases or other incentives may need to be given to teachers, and the role of their unions better acknowledged.
>
> *Sources:* Corrales (1999); Chapter 2 (see 'What determines quality? Lessons from eleven countries').

The situation of teachers has improved considerably in Latin America with the advent of more democratic government

on whether reforms designed to improve quality will make a difference: partnerships with teachers, strengthening of accountability and the need to combat corruption. As Box 4.23 makes clear, this not an exhaustive list, but it illustrates the equilibrium needed in the politics and practice of education if quality is to have a chance.

Partnerships with teachers

Given the central role of teachers in improving quality, their involvement as a profession, particularly through their unions and professional associations, is important. We have already seen how teachers can participate in non-teaching activities through work for school councils and governing bodies.[89] This type of local activity is more common than consultation at national level on the curriculum, pedagogical practice or other professional responsibilities.

The extent to which teachers' unions or associations can and do negotiate their employment terms and working conditions varies enormously by region and country, as noted earlier in the section on teacher deployment and conditions of service. Yet, like any other category of workers, teachers should benefit from the minimum international labour standards (freedom of association, right to organize and right to bargain collectively on conditions of employment).[90] Overall, the situation is most positive in North America and Western Europe. It has improved considerably in Latin America with the advent of more democratic government, and shows signs of improving in sub-Saharan Africa, Central and Eastern Europe, Central Asia and the Pacific. It seems to have furthest to go in the Arab States and some Asian countries, despite significant improvements in particular cases (Ratteree, 2004: 16). But even in the more positive circumstances a shift is needed, from a bargaining positioning towards more of a proactive partnership that gives more attention to professional ethics and mutual accountability.

Nevertheless, there are other ways of motivating and enabling teachers to participate in dialogue on reform. Decentralization of authority regarding curricula and pedagogies can broaden the scope for stronger, more direct involvement of teachers at district or local level, although, as the experience of Indonesia in the 1990s revealed, this in itself is not sufficient (Ratteree, 2004: 11). Box 4.24 shows how stakeholders in the United Republic of Tanzania discovered that additional measures needed to be taken.

A key lesson from the Tanzanian experience is that formal communication channels, while important, are not enough to incorporate teachers' voices in educational decision making. Extra steps are needed to overcome misunderstandings and bring in the views of local and district union leaders. The capacity of teachers' organizations for research and for development and defence of policy positions must be strengthened. A legal and institutional framework to make dialogue predictable and to settle any disputes is also needed.

---

89. Such contributions are less prominent when teachers work in small and isolated rural schools (Ratteree, 2004).

90. International Labour Office Conventions: Freedom of Association and Protection of the Right to Organize, 1948 (No. 87); the Right to Organize and Collective Bargaining, 1949 (No. 98); Labour Relations (Public Service), 1978 (No. 151); the Collective Bargaining Convention, 1981 (No. 154).

> **Box 4.24 Involving the Tanzanian Teachers Union in basic education planning**
>
> When the United Republic of Tanzania developed its comprehensive Education Sector Development Plan and Primary Education Development Programme (PEDP), the government and donors initially thought the Tanzanian Teachers Union (TTU) was sufficiently involved in the process. But the TTU insisted that it was not fully involved in all the technical committees and district-level decision making. This difference in perception had to do with the union's limited capacity for response to all the invitations to participate in the process and to bring to the table its own vision of how the PEDP could be implemented. A series of policy dialogue seminars, supported by the ILO and UNESCO, brought together key government officials and the TTU's top national and district leadership. The union then changed its approach to policy analysis, created a focal point for the poverty reduction strategy, expanded its research capacity, reflected on its position regarding education and poverty issues, and strengthened its coordination in these areas.
>
> *Source*: Ratteree (2004)

Countries that are strengthening democracy, as in Eastern Europe and during the 1990s in South Africa, face the additional challenge of building a culture of dialogue. Box 4.25 shows how South Africa set about this task.

International organizations also have a role to play, whether from an international base or locally, in supporting national bodies. This is far from a universal trend, but change is in the air in the form of a fragile but promising dialogue involving international financial institutions, bilateral donors, international teachers' organizations and NGOs. Since 2002, the World Bank has stepped up its dialogue with trade unions. A reflection of these efforts is the review of trade union participation in the Poverty Reduction Strategy Paper (PRSP) processes in twenty-three countries (Egulu, 2004). Gaps in union participation were identified and suggestions put forward on how to improve not only the World Bank/International Monetary Fund partnership with unions but also participation in PRSP development more generally.

Codes of conduct[91]

The concept of mutual accountability and the responsibilities that lie with everyone charged with enabling good-quality education is implicit in much of the preceding analysis. In some countries this concern has resulted in the development of professional codes of conduct in education. Some deal with the whole education system while others focus on teachers, but in general their aims are to:

■ enhance commitments, dedication and efficiency of service among members of the teaching profession, and in education more

> **Box 4.25 Bargaining and social dialogue in South African education**
>
> When its first democratically elected government came to power in 1994, South Africa began to regularize public sector labour relations and established the Public Service Co-ordinating Bargaining Council. The council's aim is to enhance workers' well-being and build sound relationships between the state, as an employer, and its employees. It also provides a forum for negotiations and collective bargaining. To accommodate the specific service needs and employment conditions of various categories in the public service, sector-specific bargaining frameworks were established, among them the Education Labour Relations Council (ELRC). Teachers' unions are represented on a proportional basis corresponding to the percentage of education sector workers they represent. Wages and conditions of service are the main bargaining topics but the parties also discuss the longer-term development of the education system. They can involve external stakeholders in these discussions in order to achieve their common goals.
>
> *Source*: Ratteree (2004)

broadly, by formulating a set of recognized ethical standards to which everyone should adhere;

■ provide self-disciplinary guidelines by establishing norms of professional conduct;

■ gain community confidence in and support for the teaching profession by emphasizing social responsibilities towards the community.

The codes usually cover issues such as school admission policies, management of teachers, service conditions of teachers and staff, examinations, evaluation and certification procedures, and the mobilization and allocation of financial and other resources.

91. This section mainly draws on Hallak and Poisson (2004a), a background paper prepared for this report. For more information, see www.unesco.org/iiep/eng/focus/etico

Several studies conducted in the 1990s emphasize the negative influence of corruption on economic, political and social development

Usually, ministries of education are responsible for enforcing the code. Special bodies may have an advisory role – an example is the Ontario Teachers' Federation – or play a more far-reaching part, as in the case of the Council of Professional Conduct in Education, in Hong Kong, China, which is responsible for ensuring that teachers comply with professional codes of practice. Another example is Scotland's General Teaching Council – a self-regulatory body with the power to cancel a teacher's registration.

Such codes can contribute significantly to the quality of the school environment and hence the quality of learning. Moreover, for teaching of norms and values to be credible, the school itself must be a place where honesty is the rule.

In Bangladesh, India and Nepal, codes of conduct are seen to have a significant positive impact on the commitment, professional behaviour and performance of teachers and staff, and to contribute to a reduction in teacher absenteeism.

Codes of conduct function less well when staff do not know about or understand them, and where complaint procedures are not well known or enforcement capacity is lacking. Some of these problems can be addressed by simplifying codes and making them more relevant, by involving teachers in their design and implementation so as to assure ownership, by making sure they are widely disseminated, by strengthening mechanisms for dealing with complaints and by integrating issues related to professional conduct into pre-service and in-service teacher training.

Teachers' organizations play an active role in promoting professional ethics. Education International and its member organizations adopted a declaration on professional ethics in 2001.[92] Its stated objectives are to raise consciousness about the norms and ethics of the profession, to help increase job satisfaction in education, to enhance status and self-esteem and to increase respect for the profession in communities.

Preventing and combating corruption

Implementing policies to improve education is one thing, assuring compliance is another. If fees are abolished but other payment is demanded, if textbooks are supposed to be free but in fact are sold at high costs, the learners' interests are not served.[93]

It is important to distinguish between graft and corruption. Graft is a relatively minor form of rule breaking, often stemming from *force majeur*: teachers who are sometimes absent because their salaries are so low and irregular that they needs additional income are not being thoroughly corrupt. Graft cannot be eliminated by enforcement alone; better policy and, more generally, poverty alleviation are required.

Corruption is not only more severe, it also has a bigger impact on the quality of learning. Several studies conducted in the 1990s emphasize the negative influence of corruption on economic, political and social development.[94] Corruption increases transaction costs, reduces the efficiency and quality of services, distorts the decision-making process and undermines social values. In education, bribes in teacher recruitment and promotion tend to lower the quality of teachers, and illegal payments demanded for school entrance, along with other hidden costs, contribute to low enrolment and high dropout rates.[95] Since such practices affect the poorest most, equity in education is at stake, and so is public confidence in the education system.

While poverty and low salaries are at the roots of graft, the causes of corruption seem less overt. They are likely to include monopoly and discretionary power, poor supervision at all levels, poor public information on government decisions and lack of transparency with regard to foreign aid. The increasingly complex nature of the education sector due to decentralization, privatization and outsourcing has opened new opportunities for corrupt behaviour. Corruption can takes many forms and affect both access and quality, as Table 4.13 shows.

The most successful three strategies in combating corruption in education are setting up and maintaining regulatory systems, strengthening management capacities and increasing ownership of the management process.

Establishing and maintaining *regulatory systems* involves adapting legal frameworks to focus them more on corruption (via rewards and penalties), designing clear norms and criteria for procedures (regarding, for instance, fund allocation or procurement), developing codes of conduct (discussed above) and defining well-

---

92. The Education International Declaration on Professional Ethics was adopted at the third World Congress of Education International in Jomtien, Thailand (25–29 July 2001).

93. See Leguéré (2003).

94. This section draws heavily on documents and discussions from the IIEP Expert Workshop on Ethics and Corruption in Education (Paris, 28–9 November 2001); see Hallak and Poisson (2002).

95. For further discussion on corruption and education, see Bray (2003), Eckstein (2003) and Leguéré (2003).

targeted measures, particularly for fund allocation.

Strengthening *management capacities* entails setting up effective control mechanisms against fraud, ensuring that regulations are enforced by increasing institutional capacities, and promoting ethical behaviour.

Enhancing ownership involves developing decentralized, participatory mechanisms, increasing access to information (particularly via information and communications technology) and empowering communities to exert stronger social control.

Conclusions

The essential conclusions of this chapter are largely straightforward. They reflect the framework for improving quality shown in Figure 4.1:[96]

■ Understand the diverse need of learners, especially multiple disadvantaged learners.

■ Give priority to where teaching and learning actually takes place – the classroom.

■ Support reforms that focus on teaching and learning outcomes: appropriate goals and relevant content; values as well as skills; sufficient and effective instructional time; structured teaching in child-centred classrooms; assessment for learning improvement.

■ Get the enabling environment right, with good learning materials that are used well by teachers; a safe, healthy infrastructure; professional, motivated teachers; and well-organised, well-led schools – the central institutions for improving quality.

■ Build strong professional support systems and knowledge infrastructures.

■ Develop and maintain sound, coherent, long-term education sector policies and a nationally owned, financially realistic framework for quality-related reforms.

■ Address barriers to reform: build partnerships; develop accountability and combat corruption.

Table 4.13: **The main forms of corruption in the education sector**

Areas of planning/management involved	Corrupt practices
Building of schools	Fraud in public tendering Embezzlement School mapping
Equipment, textbooks, food	Fraud in public tendering Embezzlement Circumvention of criteria
Teacher appointment/management	Favouritism Nepotism Bribes
Teacher behaviour	'Ghost teachers' Bribes (for school entrance, assessment, exams, etc.)
Finances	Distortion of rules and procedures Inflation of costs and activities Opacity of financial flows
Allowances (e.g. fellowships, subsidies)	Favouritism Nepotism Bribes Circumvention of criteria
Examinations and diplomas	Information selling Favouritism Nepotism Bribes Academic fraud
Information systems	Data manipulation Data selection/censorship

Source: Hallak and Poisson (2004*b*)

While the list may be straightforward, giving it effect is not. Yet, none of these proposals, suggestions or strategies is a purely abstract idea. All reflect practice in many countries around the world. Their interpretation, sequencing and prioritization may vary, but even the relatively small store of recorded evidence on which this Report has drawn demonstrates that everything is possible. The scope for improving the quality of education is vast and the technical understanding is there. Urgently needed now are the political will and the resources to make it happen.

96. A regional exercise along similar lines is reflected in the Havana Declaration by Ministers of Education from Latin America and the Caribbean on the Follow-up Model of the Regional Project for Latin America and the Caribbean (PRELAC) – Support Monitoring and Assessment. It identified five strategic focuses: education content and practice enabling construction of meanings in regard to ourselves, others and the world in which we live; teachers and strengthening their participation in education change so they may better satisfy student learning needs; culture of schools, converting them into participatory learning communities; management of education systems, making them more flexible and offering effective lifelong opportunities; and social responsibility for education, generating commitment to its development and results (UNESCO-Santiago, 2003).

Chapter 5

Meeting our international commitments

As this Report shows, improving the quality of education while expanding access, so the entire eligible age group can participate in primary education, requires a level of sustained investment that would be beyond the reach of many poor countries even if national budgets for education were to rise. External assistance, whether aimed at developing the education sector in general or addressing specific quality objectives, will remain a key dimension of the international effort to achieve universal primary education (UPE) and all other EFA goals. This chapter examines whether international commitments to provide more aid more effectively, and in a well-coordinated way, are being met, four years after Dakar and two years after the International Conference on Finance for Development in Monterrey.

Reconstructing education systems is a foundation on which to rebuild society.
Afghanistan 2002

EFA Global Monitoring Report 2005

Aid flows to education

Each year, the *EFA Global Monitoring Report* analyses the level and distribution of international aid to education, particularly basic education. Drawing primarily on the international database of the OECD's Development Assistance Committee (DAC), the latest analysis shows a modest upturn in the level of net official development assistance (ODA) disbursements. It also shows substantial differences, however, in the priority that various agencies assign to education generally and to basic education. The chapter also examines the extent to which recent international pledges and initiatives could significantly increase the level of support to basic education.

Total aid – a modest upturn

In 2002, the total level of net disbursements of ODA increased to surpass the level of 1992 (Figure 5.1). From 2001 to 2002, bilateral funds[1] increased slightly more than multilateral aid but were still marginally below their 1992 level, while multilateral aid reached its highest value since that year. Preliminary data indicate that total real ODA will reach its highest level to date in 2003, thanks to several factors, including continuing growth in bilateral grants, the start of reconstruction aid to Iraq and a cyclical fall in the level of contributions to multilateral concessional funds – i.e. those providing loans with a grant element of at least 25% (OECD-DAC, 2004b). The trend has also been attributed to early initial fulfilment of pledges made in Monterrey (United Nations, 2003a).

In 2003, a high-level dialogue on financing for development took place during the fifty-eighth session of the United Nations General Assembly. The United Nations Secretary-General presented an overview of aid pledges made by donor countries at Monterrey (United Nations, 2003b), which showed that, if they were fulfilled, aid levels would rise by US$16 billion, or about 30% in real terms, by 2006.[2] World Bank estimates presented at the IMF/World Bank Development Committee Meeting in 2004 suggest that Monterrey pledges will amount to US$18.5 billion by 2006 (World Bank, 2004e). Although both figures indicate a significant potential increase, they fall well below the additional US$50 billion per year estimated to be required to achieve all the Millennium Development Goals (MDGs) – which include two EFA goals.[3] Furthermore, there is some concern that much of the extra funds will not be directed to financing the incremental costs of meeting the MDGs. In 2002, about 80% of the increase was taken up by debt relief and technical cooperation, not all of which necessarily benefited programmes designed to achieve the MDGs (World Bank, 2004e).

Bilateral aid to education – commitments and priorities

After particularly low levels of bilateral commitments to education at the turn of the century, the next two years saw a marked increase. In 2002, ODA commitments to education exceeded US$4 billion for the first time since 1999 and represented about 9% of total commitments (Figure 5.2). It is expected that further increases will follow, given the pledges for education made since Dakar.[4]

As Table 5.1 shows, over 2001 and 2002, eight countries[5] each committed an annual average of at least US$100 million to education, together accounting for 85% of bilateral education aid. As the *EFA Global Monitoring Report 2003/4* (UNESCO, 2003a) explained, the OECD-DAC reporting system has some problems fully capturing aid to education, particularly for countries directing much of their aid through support to the recipient country's general budget

Figure 5.1: Total official development assistance (net disbursements in US$ billions), 1992–2002

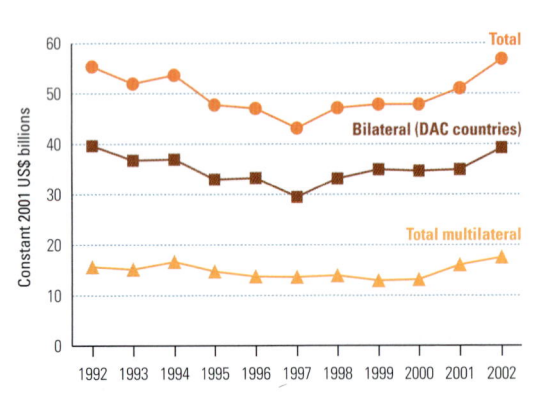

Notes: Net disbursements are defined as total disbursements less repayments of loan principal during the period. DAC deflators, used for producing constant price estimates, adjust for both inflation in the domestic currency and changes in the exchange rate between the domestic currency and the US dollar.
Source: DAC online database (OECD-DAC, 2004a, Table 2a).

---

1. Unless otherwise specified, in this Report the data on bilateral donors refer to the DAC members minus the Commission of the European Communities (EC: European Commission), which is considered a multilateral donor. The other DAC members are Australia, Austria, Belgium, Canada, Denmark, Finland, France, Germany, Greece, Ireland, Italy, Japan, Luxembourg, the Netherlands, New Zealand, Norway, Portugal, Spain, Sweden, Switzerland, the United Kingdom and the United States.

2. This figure includes the United States commitments for the Millennium Challenge Account.

3. The Zedillo Report prepared for the Monterrey Conference estimates that an additional US$50 billion per year is needed (United Nations, 2001b). Devarajan, Miller and Swanson (2002) suggest US$40–60 billion per year.

4. The European Commission, Canada, Japan, the Netherlands, Norway, the United Kingdom, the United States and the World Bank have all made new commitments of ODA to education from 2002 (UNESCO, 2002a, Table 5.8).

5. Canada, France, Germany, Japan, the Netherlands, Spain, the United Kingdom and the United States.

(part of which benefits the education sector) or through projects that target more than one sector. In such cases the figure reported for education is almost certainly an underestimate.[6]

Using the case of the United Kingdom's Department for International Development (DFID), Box 5.1 illustrates the extent to which additional resources to education may miss being captured under current international reporting arrangements. It suggests there is a strong case for developing a standard international approach to reporting (DFID, 2004).

These important caveats should be borne in mind when examining the final column of Table 5.1, which presents an indicator measuring the relative priority donors give to education. It expresses the proportion of aid assigned to

Figure 5.2: Bilateral aid commitments to education, 1990-2002

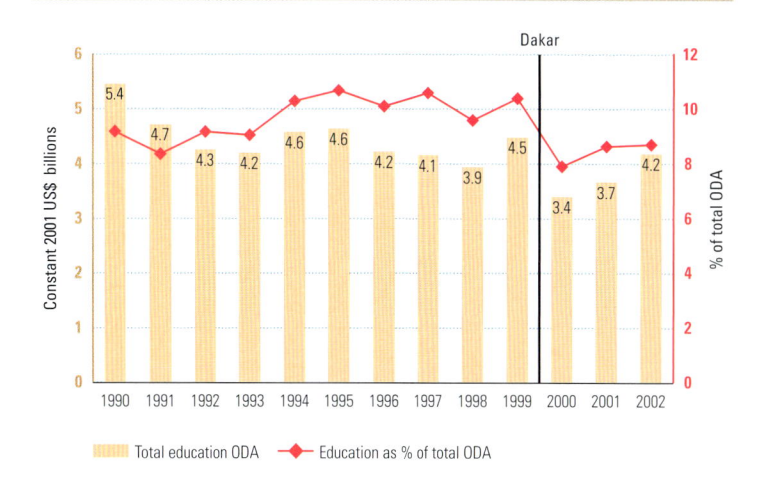

Note: DAC deflators were used to calculate constant prices.
Source: DAC online database (OECD-DAC, 2004a, Table 5).

Table 5.1: Bilateral aid commitments[1] (total and education), two-year averages for 2001-2002

Country	Total (Constant 2001 US$ millions)	Education (Constant 2001 US$ millions)	% of total education aid	Education as % of total aid[2]	Relative priority assigned to education aid[3]
Japan	10 702	883	22.5	8.7	0.9
France	3 830	821	20.9	24.6	2.5
Germany	3 896	611	15.6	17.9	1.8
United States	10 794	300	7.6	3.6	0.4
Netherlands	3 244	250	6.4	8.8	0.9
Canada	1 481	165	4.2	13.0	1.3
United Kingdom	3 051	155	3.9	5.4	0.5
Spain	1 159	138	3.5	13.0	1.3
Norway	1 035	94	2.4	10.2	1.0
Belgium	605	75	1.9	14.0	1.4
Austria	421	61	1.6	15.1	1.5
Italy	879	58	1.5	7.8	0.8
Sweden	1 121	56	1.4	5.9	0.6
Denmark	857	45	1.2	5.8	0.6
Australia	670	45	1.1	8.8	0.9
Ireland	213	42	1.1	20.7	2.1
Portugal	176	32	0.8	19.5	2.0
Switzerland	678	29	0.7	6.4	0.6
Finland	287	28	0.7	11.8	1.2
New Zealand	84	26	0.7	34.8	3.5
Greece	90	8	0.2	9.3	0.9
Total DAC countries	**45 273**	**3 921**	**100**	**10**	**1**

Notes: Figures are rounded. Data are not available for Luxembourg.
1. Most bilateral agencies report commitments to DAC, but a few, including that of the United Kingdom, report disbursements, which complicates comparison among agencies and within the ODA disbursement figures.
2. The education aid shown in the second column of data is expressed as a proportion of the total aid shown in the first column minus multi-sector aid and general programme assistance
3. This is the ratio between the proportion of total aid assigned to education by each agency and the mean for all agencies. The indicator is calculated as follows:

$$\text{Relative priority assigned to education aid} = \frac{EA_i / TA_i}{\sum_{i=1}^{22} EA_i / \sum_{i=1}^{22} TA_i}$$

where: i = a DAC country
EA = Education aid
TA = Total aid

Source: DAC online database (OECD-DAC, 2004a, Table 5).

[6]. Foster (2004) argues that general budget support should be broken down by sector in the same proportion as the allocation of public expenditure by sector by the recipient government. Although this could improve accounting of aid to education at individual donor level, lack of data makes it impossible to conduct this exercise at global level.

> Sub-Saharan Africa, East Asia and the Pacific, and the Arab States account for three-quarters of the total bilateral aid committed to education

Box 5.1 Notional sector classification of budget support: the DFID experience

In recent years, the United Kingdom's Department for International Development has sought to ensure that its spending figures for key development sectors reflects expenditure channelled through budget support aimed at poverty reduction. This effort reflects the changing way aid is delivered and responds to three significant facts:

- The rising use of budget support means an increasing proportion of DFID expenditure is not allocated by sector.

- In existing OECD-DAC reporting mechanisms, all forms of aid channelled through national budgets (including budget support) are accounted for as separate instruments rather than classified as expenditure for a sector such as education or health. Thus, aid to those sectors tends to be under-reported.

- There is strong political and public demand for information on how much the United Kingdom spends on different development sectors.

How DFID's approach evolved

As the share of budget support within the DFID programme grew, so did demand for the department to give Parliament sectoral breakdowns for such allocations. Hence DFID analysed budget support by sector and derived a working average for spending on each sector. There was no fixed methodology for this. One approach was to extrapolate from the budget of the recipient government, another to use notional earmarking figures, where available. Among the results was an estimate that 20% of budget support was spent on education.

In early 2004, DFID approved a standard methodology for this process, referred to as notional sector classification of budget support. It is a developmental approach, designed to provide consistent and comparable figures, based on country-specific data. Budget support expenditure is attributed pro rata to the ODA-eligible parts of the recipient government's budget. The focus on ODA-eligible expenditure explicitly excludes elements such as defence. The new methodology, which DFID began using in April 2004, is designed to promote greater transparency on how each country receiving British aid uses it. At the stage of commitment to a budget support programme, recipient countries will be required to allocate the aid by sector. They will later also be required to report on its use by sector. It is explicitly understood that the sectoral allocations are only indicative, being based on notional allocations derived from budget plans.

What this means for education spending

In the three years from 2000/2001 to 2002/2003, DFID provided, on average, some £250 million per year as budget support (including sectoral budget support) in twenty countries. Applying the 20% average for education, DFID estimates that it has channelled £150 million of investment in education through budget support over this period.

Source: DFID (2004)

education by each donor as a percentage of the DAC mean.[7] A value above 1 means that the donor is giving more importance to education than the average for all agencies, while a value below 1 indicates that the funding agency allocates more of its aid budget to other sectors than the average. The highest value is that for New Zealand, at 3.5, indicating that it gives 3.5 times more priority to education than the average DAC donor. Conversely, the lowest value, 0.4 for the United States, shows that this country gives education a lower than average priority (in relative terms, one-tenth that of New Zealand). Of the the larger donors among the twenty-one DAC countries for which data are available, France, Germany, Canada and Spain give particularly high relative priority to education in their aid programmes.

Sub-Saharan Africa, East Asia and the Pacific, and the Arab States account for three-quarters of the total bilateral aid committed to education, with 30%, 27% and 18%, respectively. Figure 5.3 shows the regions that receive the highest percentage of aid to education by donor as an average for 2001 and 2002. Sub-Saharan Africa receives the highest share of aid for eleven donors. East Asia and the Pacific is the main recipient for only three donors, but since two of them, Japan and Germany, are the first and third biggest donors to education, the region is second in its overall share of aid. The Arab States region,

---

7. The percentage has been calculated after subtracting general programme assistance and multi-sector aid from total aid, since, as noted above, part of these allocations may go to education.

which includes North Africa, is the main education aid target for two major donors: France and the United States. Spain focuses primarily on Latin America, and the United Kingdom allocates almost half its education aid to South and West Asia. The patterns tend to reflect historical associations and current geo-political interests and do not necessarily imply a clear international understanding of where the greatest need lies – which was the basis of the priority accorded to sub-Saharan Africa and South and West Asia in Dakar (UNESCO, 2000a).

Table 5.2 shows the average annual bilateral support to education and to basic education over 2001–02,[8] when bilateral aid to basic education was more than US$900 million per year.[9] With the exception of Spain, the eight biggest bilateral donors to basic education are also the most important contributors to total education aid.

As with Table 5.1, the last column of Table 5.2 shows the relative priority assigned to basic education by each donor, showing in this case

Figure 5.3: Bilateral education aid commitments: percentage of donor's education aid to its most favoured region, two-year averages for 2001-2002

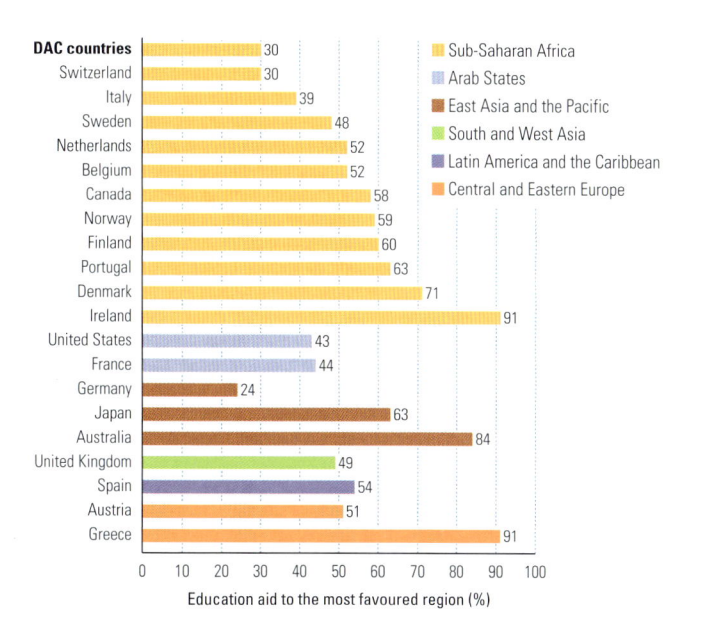

Country	%
DAC countries	30
Switzerland	30
Italy	39
Sweden	48
Netherlands	52
Belgium	52
Canada	58
Norway	59
Finland	60
Portugal	63
Denmark	71
Ireland	91
United States	43
France	44
Germany	24
Japan	63
Australia	84
United Kingdom	49
Spain	54
Austria	51
Greece	91

Regions: Sub-Saharan Africa, Arab States, East Asia and the Pacific, South and West Asia, Latin America and the Caribbean, Central and Eastern Europe

Source: CRS online database (OECD-DAC, 2004a).

Table 5.2: Bilateral aid commitments to education and to basic education, two-year averages for 2001-2002

	Bilateral aid commitments (Constant 2001 US$ millions) Education	Basic education	% of total bilateral aid to basic education	Basic education as % of total education[1]	Relative priority assigned to basic education aid[2]
United States	300	210	22.4	72.2	2.5
Netherlands	250	182	19.4	81.6	2.8
France	821	146	15.6	20.3	0.7
Japan	883	93	9.9	12.6	0.4
United Kingdom	155	66	7.0	85.0	2.9
Canada	165	56	6.0	43.3	1.5
Germany	611	56	5.9	9.7	0.3
Norway	94	35	3.7	43.1	1.5
Australia	45	20	2.1	53.1	1.8
Spain	138	19	2.1	21.5	0.7
Denmark	45	14	1.5	68.4	2.4
Sweden	56	11	1.2	38.3	1.3
Switzerland	29	10	1.0	42.2	1.5
Belgium	75	7	0.8	11.1	0.4
Finland	28	6	0.6	65.0	2.2
Portugal	32	4	0.4	16.8	0.6
New Zealand	26	2	0.2	8.8	0.3
Austria	66	1	0.1	1.5	0.1
Italy	58	0	0.0	1.2	0.1
Greece	8	0	0.0	0.0	0.0
Total DAC countries	**3 925**	**938**	**100.0**	**29.0**	**1.0**

Notes: Figures are rounded. Because of the relatively short period covered, the conclusions to be drawn from these data should be treated with caution. Data are not available for Luxembourg and Ireland.
1. Calculated by dividing aid to basic education by aid to total education minus 'level unspecified' aid, which is not shown in the table.
2. Calculated as in note to Table 5.1 except that basic education aid (BA) and education aid (EA) replace education aid (EA) and total aid (TA), respectively.
Source: DAC online database (OECD-DAC, 2004a, Table 5).

8. DAC education aid is classified into three main levels or subsectors: basic education, which includes primary education, basic life skills for youth and adults, and early childhood education; secondary education and post-secondary education. What cannot be assigned to any of these appears in a category labelled 'level unspecified'. Undifferentiated support provided to the whole education sector is included in this last category (OECD-DAC, 2000).

9. Again, the DAC reporting system cannot fully capture aid to basic education; UNESCO (2003a) shows that part of the 'level unspecified' aid can be attributed to basic education.

Table 5.3: Bilateral aid priorities for education and basic education, 2001-2002

Country	Relative priority assigned to education aid	Relative priority assigned to basic education aid
Group I	**>1**	**>1**
Canada	1.31	1.50
Finland	1.18	2.24
Norway	1.02	1.49
Group II	**<1**	**>1**
Australia	0.88	1.83
Denmark	0.58	2.36
Netherlands	0.88	2.82
Sweden	0.59	1.32
Switzerland	0.64	1.46
United Kingdom	0.54	2.94
United States	0.36	2.49
Group III	**>1**	**<1**
Austria	1.51	0.05
Belgium	1.40	0.38
France	2.46	0.70
Germany	1.80	0.33
New Zealand	3.49	0.30
Portugal	1.96	0.58
Spain	1.30	0.74
Group IV	**<1**	**<1**
Greece	0.93	0.00
Italy	0.78	0.04
Japan	0.88	0.43

Note: Data are not available for Luxembourg and Ireland.
Source: Tables 5.1 and 5.2.

Figure 5.4: Comparison of priorities assigned to overall education aid and basic education aid, 2001-2002

[Scatter plot showing priority assigned to basic education (y-axis, relative to DAC average) versus priority assigned to education (x-axis, relative to DAC average). Fit line: $y = -1.0386\ln(x) + 1.2534$, $R^2 = 0.3494$. Points labeled: United Kingdom, Netherlands, United States, Denmark, Finland, Australia, Switzerland, Norway, Sweden, Canada, Spain, Japan, Portugal, Belgium, France, Germany, Italy, Greece, Austria, New Zealand.]

Source: Table 5.3.

allocate more than 70% of their education aid to basic education and thus, in terms of their overall education aid, give much greater priority to basic education than the average for DAC countries. The three largest contributors to education, however – France, Japan and Germany – give more emphasis to other subsectors (levels) of education, mainly post-secondary (as Table 5.4 will show)

Table 5.3 groups bilateral donors by how they prioritized education and basic education in their aid programmes over 2001–2002. In the first group, Canada, Finland and, to a lesser extent, Norway gave more aid to education and to basic education than the average for all the bilateral agencies. In a second group, seven donors gave education less importance than average, but put relatively high priority on basic education within their overall education allocations. Seven other donors (Group III) did the reverse: they gave high priority to education, but to higher levels rather than to basic education (Table 5.4). The remaining three donors in Group IV fall below the average for both categories; Japan is the only one of the eight major donors in this group.

Figure 5.4 translates the data from Table 5.3 to show a negative correlation between the priority assigned to education and that assigned to basic education: the bilateral donors that are giving relatively more to the education sector as a whole are giving relatively less to basic education. Conversely, the agencies that give relatively higher priority to basic education, on average, give a lower priority to overall support for education.

Table 5.4 shows a more detailed breakdown of education aid. With the exception of Finland, all countries giving relatively high priority to education (Groups I and III in Table 5.3) make post-secondary education the most important level. Of the countries giving lower priority to education, basic education is the most important subsector for Australia, Denmark, the Netherlands, Switzerland, the United Kingdom and the United States.

For the countries giving priority to post-secondary education, a certain proportion of this support is accounted for by what DAC directives call 'imputed student costs' (OECD-DAC, 2000, Box 9.1). This category covers support to

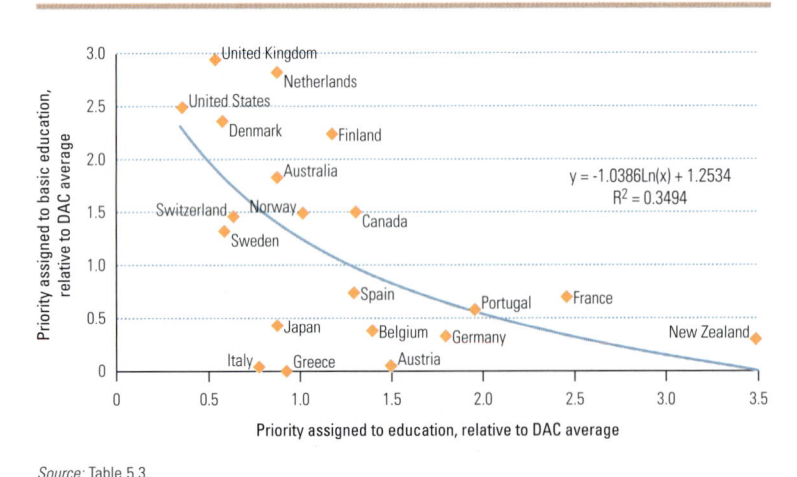

which donors contribute more to basic education than to education as a whole. The Netherlands, the United Kingdom and the United States

Table 5.4: Composition of bilateral education assistance, two-year averages for 2001-2002 (percentage)

Donor groupings*	Donors	Level unspecified as % of total	Basic education	Secondary education (ISCED 2+3)	Post-secondary education
Donors putting high priority onto education aid	Canada	21	43	7	50
	Finland	56	65	17	18
	Norway	14	43	7	50
	Austria	11	1	10	89
	Belgium	14	11	15	74
	France	12	20	8	71
	Germany	6	10	10	80
	New Zealand	5	8	13	79
	Portugal	27	17	31	52
	Spain	34	21	31	48
Donors putting lower priority onto education aid	Australia	17	53	18	29
	Denmark	56	68	2	29
	Netherlands	11	82	0	18
	Sweden	49	39	7	54
	Switzerland	20	42	27	31
	United Kingdom	50	85	11	4
	United States	3	72	0	28
	Greece	39	0	1	99
	Italy	71	2	31	67
	Japan	16	13	15	73
Total DAC countries		17	29	10	61

Percentage distribution of aid by level of education (less 'level unspecified')

Notes: Data are not available for Luxembourg and Ireland.
Figures are rounded. Bold figures indicate the level where the percentage is the highest.
Percentages were calculated using the reported subsector figure rather than the figure for total aid.
*The donors shown as putting high priority on aid for education are those listed in Groups I and III in Table 5.3.
The countries shown as putting lower priority on aid are those listed in Groups II and IV in Table 5.3.
Source: DAC online database (OECD-DAC, 2004a, Table 5).

students from developing countries who are attending university in developed countries. Support for tuition fees and living expenses in donor countries is counted as ODA if the presence of students reflects a conscious policy of development cooperation by the host country. Although DAC recommends reporting this as multi-sector aid, most donors still report imputed student costs and scholarships as aid to post-secondary education.

While it has not been possible to determine the share of imputed costs in aid to post-secondary education, it seems clear that this form of education aid is at least partly driven by policies favouring the internationalization of national universities. For example, as far back as 1983, Japan set a goal of increasing the number of international students in national institutions from about 10,000 to 100,000 by the beginning of the twenty-first century (Tsuruta, 2003). Japan's government has provided generous incentives to students from overseas, partly because of a strong belief that they play an important role in enriching the academic life of all students. The costs of these grants and subsidies to students and their host institutions have been counted as part of aid to education.

Multilateral aid: not much change

Support to education from multilateral agencies (excluding the World Bank) amounted to nearly US$660 million per year for 2001 and 2002. This is slightly more than the World Bank's concessional finance to education through the International Development Association (IDA) but is the equivalent of about 17% of total bilateral aid to education (Table 5.1). Table 5.5 shows that the European Commission (EC) dominates multilateral flows to education, excluding the World Bank, even though EC aid to education fell to 4% of total EC aid in 2001–2002 and the absolute amount involved was slightly less than what the Netherlands gave for education in its bilateral programme (Table 5.1). Between

Japan's government has provided generous incentives to students from overseas

194 / CHAPTER 5

Table 5.5: Average annual multilateral aid commitments (excluding World Bank), two-year averages for 1999-2000 and 2001-2002

Donors	Total (Constant 2001 US$ millions) 1999-2000	Total (Constant 2001 US$ millions) 2001-2002	Education (Constant 2001 US$ millions) 1999-2000	Education (Constant 2001 US$ millions) 2001-2002	Education as % of total 1999-2000	Education as % of total 2001-2002
African Development Fund	499	455	73	70	15	15
Asian Development Fund	1 163	1 093	95	90	8	8
Inter American Development Bank	494	482	29	28	6	6
European Commission	7 191[1]	5 811	390[1]	227	5[1]	4
UNICEF	594	585	49	52	8	9
UNRWA	303	374	173	178	57	48
Other	197	556	12	14	6	2
Total multilateral	10 441	9 355	820	658	8	7

1. 2000 only
Source: DAC on-line database (OECD-DAC, 2004a, Table 5).

Figure 5.5: World Bank education lending per year, 1963-2003

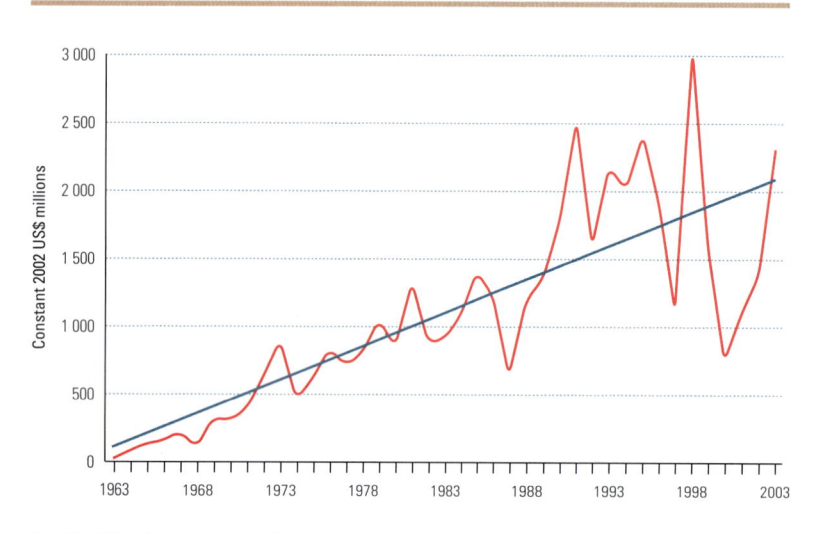

Note: The DAC deflator for the United States has been used to produce constant prices series.
Source: Calculated from http//devdata.worldbank.org/edstats

10. The loans concerned are of two types: IDA loans, which are made on concessional terms, and those of the World Bank's main arm, the International Bank for Reconstruction and Development (IBRD), which are unsubsidized. The former are usually counted as aid.

11. Separate figures for IDA and IBRD lending are not available.

12. This may appear to contradict the trends shown in Figures 5.5 and 5.6, but as Figure 5.5 makes clear, aid fluctuates substantially from year to year, so the apparent declining trend in Figure 5.7 reflects lower lending in certain years.

1999–2000 and 2001–2002, the only multilateral agency listed that increased its overall level of support to education was the United Nations Relief and Works Agency for Palestinian Refugees in the Near East (UNRWA), and even its education aid fell as a proportion of its total aid flows. For the remaining agencies, education as a percentage of total aid remained fairly constant between the two periods shown, although both total aid and aid to education fell – the latter by nearly 20%.

The World Bank remains the biggest single external supporter of education. Figure 5.5 shows total World Bank lending for education since 1963.[10] Starting from an average of less than US$0.2 billion in the 1960s, lending rose steadily until the mid-1980s. In the 1990s, although the average volume of lending grew, flows became more volatile. For example, after the peak in 1998, when total lending to education reached almost US$300 billion, lending for education fell back, for two years, to around its average level for the 1970s.

Education is one of the five corporate priorities in the World Bank's overall assistance strategy (World Bank, 2003a). Figure 5.6 shows that the share of total lending devoted to education sector rose from 3% in the 1960s to around 7% in the 1990s.

In the first two editions of the *EFA Global Monitoring Report* (UNESCO, 2002a and 2003a), the allocation of World Bank education loans to different education subsectors was estimated using individual project information. Now the World Bank's website provides subsector breakdowns, shown in Figure 5.7.[11] Average lending in 2001–2003 was lower than the three-year averages in the entire preceding decade.[12] The figure also shows that the composition of education lending has changed. Although basic education remains the largest subsector, its share dropped slightly over the decade, while general education, which includes projects covering more than one subsector, increased from 4.5% of education lending in 1992–94 to 31.5% in 2001–2003. This rise may reflect the increasing emphasis on support for sector programmes. The extent to which these support basic education will depend on how the recipient government allocates its education budget.

MEETING OUR INTERNATIONAL COMMITMENTS / 195

Figure 5.6: World Bank education lending as proportion of total lending, 1960s to 1990s

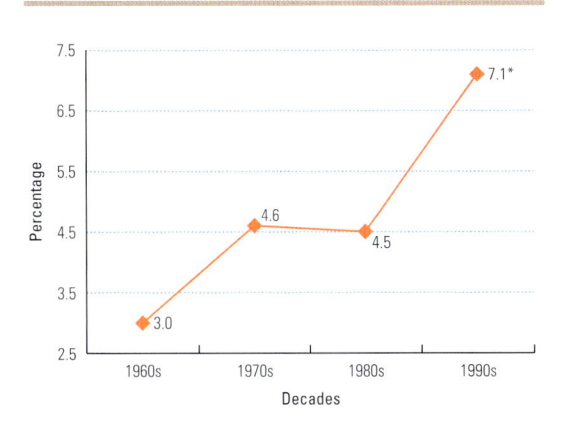

[Line chart showing percentage: 1960s: 3.0; 1970s: 4.6; 1980s: 4.5; 1990s: 7.1*]

*The figure for the 1990s was exceptionally high because of the 1998 financial crisis. If the data for fiscal year 1998 are excluded, the figure falls to 6.2%.
Source: World Bank (2003a)

Prospects for bridging the financing gap

Table 5.6 summarizes total bilateral and multilateral aid to education in 1999–2000 and 2001–2002. Total support to education and basic education declined slightly between the two periods, although aid to basic education was maintained at roughly the same level. This variation is explained by the different tendencies of bilateral and multilateral aid. Aid from multilateral agencies as a group decreased for education overall, and particularly for basic education, primarily because the level of EC aid fell. Bilateral agencies' overall education aid was roughly stable but the proportion allocated to basic education grew. This increase almost matches the level of multilateral decline, so total support to basic education was almost unchanged.

As regards future aid requirements for EFA, it is clear that a significant financing gap remains even if new pledges for increased ODA are fulfilled. The United Kingdom government has proposed an International Finance Facility (IFF) to 'front-load' an additional US$50 billion per year into existing aid programmes, in an effort to meet the MDGs by 2015 (H. M. Treasury, 2003).[13] The idea is to issue bonds in the international capital markets and repay bondholders from long-term donor contributions. If the additional funding were to be raised from bilateral and

13. In July 2004, the United Kingdom announced that its ODA budget would increase to £6.5 billion a year (over US$12 billion) by 2007/2008, to reach 0.47 % of gross national income (H. M. Treasury, 2004).

Figure 5.7: Composition of total World Bank education lending, three-year averages for 1992-2003

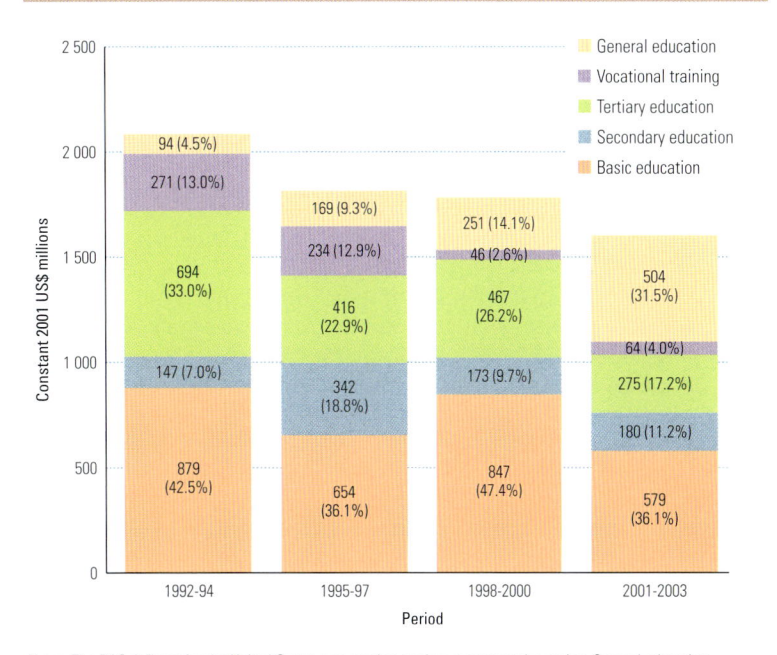

[Stacked bar chart, Constant 2001 US$ millions, categories: General education, Vocational training, Tertiary education, Secondary education, Basic education]

1992-94:
- Vocational training: 94 (4.5%)
- Tertiary education: 271 (13.0%)
- (General/Tertiary): 694 (33.0%)
- Secondary: 147 (7.0%)
- Basic: 879 (42.5%)

1995-97:
- General education: 169 (9.3%)
- Vocational training: 234 (12.9%)
- Tertiary: 416 (22.9%)
- Secondary: 342 (18.8%)
- Basic: 654 (36.1%)

1998-2000:
- General education: 251 (14.1%)
- Vocational training: 46 (2.6%)
- Tertiary: 467 (26.2%)
- Secondary: 173 (9.7%)
- Basic: 847 (47.4%)

2001-2003:
- General education: 504 (31.5%)
- Vocational training: 64 (4.0%)
- Tertiary: 275 (17.2%)
- Secondary: 180 (11.2%)
- Basic: 579 (36.1%)

Notes: The DAC deflator for the United States was used to produce constant price series. General education includes projects covering more than one level. Basic education is defined as pre-primary, primary and non-formal education and adult literacy programmes.
Source: World Bank (2004b)

Table 5.6: Bilateral and multilateral commitments to education, two-year averages for 1999-2000 and 2001-2002
(Constant 2001 US$ billions)

	Education 1999-2000	Education 2001-2002	Basic education 1999-2000	Basic education 2001-2002
Bilateral[1]	3.96	3.97	0.73	0.95
Multilateral	1.61	1.48	0.83	0.59
IDA (World Bank)[2]	0.56	0.59	0.23	0.22
European Commission[3]	0.39	0.23	0.26	0.02
UNESCO	0.23	0.23	0.04	0.06
Inter American Development Bank[4]	0.03	0.03	0.01	0.01
Asian Development Fund[4]	0.09	0.09	0.04	0.03
African Development Fund[4]	0.07	0.07	0.03	0.03
UNICEF	0.05	0.05	0.05	0.05
UNRWA	0.17	0.18	0.15	0.15
Other multilateral[4]	0.01	0.01	0.00	0.01
Total	5.57	5.45	1.53	1.54

1. The share of bilateral education aid allocated to basic education was 18% in 1999–2000 and 24% in 2001-2002. These figures include contributions from non-DAC bilateral agencies: Republic of Korea, Czech Republic and Turkey.
2. The allocation of total World Bank lending (IDA + IBRD) to basic education was 41% in 1999–2000 and 37% in 2001–2002. It is assumed that these percentages can be applied to IDA on its own.
3. Basic education accounted for 66% of EC education aid in 2000 (data for 1999 are not available) and 11% in 2001-2002.
4. The percentages used for IDA commitments to basic education are also used to estimate allocations from the Inter American Development Bank, Asian Development Fund, African Development Fund and other multilateral agencies. IDA and UNESCO commitments are for fiscal years and therefore do not match calendar years exactly. UNESCO data are derived from two-year budgets extracted from UNESCO's Approved Programme and Budget. The data for basic education are the amounts allocated to the Basic Education for All programme and do not include the budget of UNESCO education institutes.
Sources: DAC online database (OECD-DAC, 2004a); World Bank (2004e); UNESCO (2000b and 2002b).

> **Box 5.2 Philanthropic funding of education**
>
> The literature on international aid has paid relatively little attention to the role of philanthropic foundations in development efforts. Neither the scale of their activities nor the magnitude of funding flows is very well known. A recent OECD study, drawing on commissioned analyses covering the United States, Europe and Asia, estimates that such organizations contribute US$3 billion annually to development. This estimate, however, is subject to many caveats.*
>
> While no sector breakdown is available, the OECD reports that, for the American foundations, which account for more than half of the US$3 billion, education is the second largest sector, after health and family planning, with 13.7% of total aid flows from United States foundations in 2000. Of this, 84% goes to graduate professional training and higher education, so the support for basic education must be comparatively low. The scant information available on European foundations' support by sector includes two surveys, one of which notes that thirty European foundations were involved in 'education and research' (Schluter, Then and Walkenhorse, 2001) and the other of which reports that seventy-eight had an interest in education (European Foundation Centre, 2002).
>
> *Some foundations prefer to remain out of the public eye, often from a sense that publicizing such work is undignified or improper; hence, the overall picture is incomplete. In addition, private foundations do not always distinguish between developing and transitional countries or between 'development' and other activities (OECD, 2003a).
>
> Source: OECD (2003a)

multilateral agencies in the same ratios as in the recent past, and if recent allocations to education and basic education were maintained, the IFF would bring an additional US$4.3 billion and US$1.24 billion per year to education and basic education, respectively.[14]

Similarly, if the Monterrey follow-up estimate of an additional US$16 billion of development aid by 2006 is fulfilled and, again, donors' participation and sectoral breakdowns remain constant, an additional US$0.4 billion of aid per year to basic education would result[15]. The possible gains from the IFF and post-Monterrey pledges combined would mean an increase in total international resources for basic education of US$1.6 billion a year – doubling the existing level. Without some shifting of aid-budget priorities, however, even the boldest initiative to increase development funds is unlikely to provide the estimated US$5.6 billion a year in additional resources required just to achieve UPE and gender parity in schooling (UNESCO, 2002a).

Although ODA is almost certain to be the main type of additional aid to education, the level of international philanthropic support to education is not insignificant, though this area is under-researched. As Box 5.2 shows, such funding is not directed primarily towards basic education. More information and analysis of non-government support for EFA is needed.

Conclusion

While modest improvements in overall aid levels and the volume of assistance to basic education are trends that deserve a cautious welcome, they do not come close to matching the level of increased external funding that achievement of the EFA goals requires. The pledges made in the light of the Monterrey Consensus hold out some promise for increased levels of funding for basic education, but there is as yet no assurance that funds will be allocated in ways that will fulfil this expectation.

Using aid effectively for EFA

Aid for development outcomes

Although education aid is insufficient and its distribution less than optimal for the achievement of EFA, ODA donors do provide at least US$5.5 billion each year for education, about 30% of which supports basic education. How these resources are used and whether they are effective in helping individual countries meet the EFA goals is a matter of considerable international interest, in part because the likelihood of additional funds being made available is influenced by the extent to which good use is made of education aid today.

The substantial literature on aid effectiveness is devoted primarily to the impact of specific projects and programmes. However, with the advent of a global coalition committed to achieving the MDGs, a broader international consensus is emerging on aid for which the key performance indicator is sustainable improvements in poor people's lives (UNDP, 2003). This means using aid in support of national and international strategies designed to achieve well-specified development outcomes that increase people's well-being (Managing for Development Results, 2004).

Three core principles of international good practice have emerged to underpin this effort:

---

14. This set of assumptions is employed for illustrative purposes only. It is likely that not all donors would join the facility and that proportionate contributions would vary.

15. The United Nations (2003b) does not provide a breakdown of individual donors' contributions to the additional US$16 billion. It cannot be assumed that the sum will be distributed in line with existing aid disbursements; some donors will increase their development aid more than others. Again, these assumptions are for illustrative purposes only.

the importance of sound, nationally owned policies; close alignment of funding agency support with national governments' priorities and harmonization of donor practice. Figure 5.8 illustrates these, drawing on the work of the OECD-DAC Task Team on Harmonization and Alignment (OECD-DAC, 2004c), which is part of the follow-up to the Rome Declaration on Harmonization (OECD-DAC, 2003).

At the apex of the pyramid are individual governments' priorities and the policies, which, in low-income countries, increasingly find expression in Poverty Reduction Strategy Papers (PRSPs) and related education sector and basic education subsector plans. Over fifty low- and middle-income countries are developing PRSPs, which are gradually, if not uniformly, providing a basis for aid alignment and a focus for the harmonization of donor policies and assistance programmes. At their best, these strategies are driven by pro-poor outcomes, and build on a strong, broad sense of national ownership.[16] A recent World Bank review concluded that progress continues to depend on effective capacity-building to meet skills needs, on strong country leadership and on sustained commitment by development partners (IMF/IDA, 2003). An OECD-DAC working party has noted that 'the evolving PRS approach is bringing about closer links between external support and national processes…but the process is partial and suggests considerable scope for further alignment' (OECD-DAC, 2003: 4).

Growing evidence suggests that sound national policies designed to eliminate poverty are an increasingly important consideration for funding agencies in determining where their aid goes. A study of forty-one agencies indicates that the agencies putting the most explicit emphasis on poverty alleviation are increasingly stressing the content and balance of recipient government policies more than other agencies (Dollar and Levin, 2004).

This move towards donor alignment with country policies and towards working through national systems is exemplified by the recent memorandum of understanding (MOU) between the Government of Zambia, eight bilateral agencies, the World Bank and the United Nations system (Box 5.3). Based on eight central principles, the MOU covers reform, review,

Figure 5.8: Harmonization and alignment

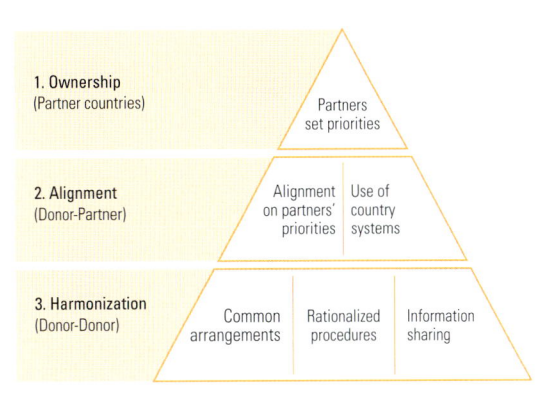

1. Ownership (Partner countries) — Partners set priorities
2. Alignment (Donor-Partner) — Alignment on partners' priorities | Use of country systems
3. Harmonization (Donor-Donor) — Common arrangements | Rationalized procedures | Information sharing

Source: OECD-DAC (2004c)

capacity-building and procedures in the implementation of aid policy (Zambia, 2004). Work along similar lines is taking place in over fifty countries.[17] In addition, the European Commission is considering a common legal framework for aid implementation procedures (European Commission, 2004).

Aid to education is part of this wider international process, and any analysis of education aid should be set within the context of these international developments, especially where aid is given through sector and budget support rather than project or subsector assistance.

Against this backdrop, the effectiveness of education aid is analysed in three ways: by providing an overview of how OECD-DAC countries distribute their education aid to see whether it is dispersed cost-effectively; by examining the findings of three recent international evaluations of aid to basic education; and by assessing the recent experience of education aid use in a small sample of highly aid-dependent countries.

Distribution of aid to education

All aid agencies make choices about where their aid should be used. The nature of these choices can affect the impact of aid on educational outcomes. One way of examining the aid distribution resulting from these choices is to measure how widely or narrowly such aid is dispersed among a portfolio of potential recipients, as an indicator of 'aid proliferation'

> Evidence suggests that sound national policies to eliminate poverty are increasingly important in determining where aid goes

16. See www.worldbank.org/poverty/strategies/overview

17. For details, see www.aidharmonization.org/ah-cla/secondary-pages/cla-country

> **Box 5.3 Coordination and harmonization of government and donor practices in Zambia**
>
> The parties to the MOU agreed on the following broad coordination and harmonization principles:
>
> 1. Delivery of development assistance in accordance with Zambia's needs and priorities as outlined in her PRSP.
> 2. Alignment with GRZ (Government of the Republic of Zambia) systems such as national budget cycles, financial systems and PRSP/MDG monitoring processes, where these provide reasonable assurance that cooperation resources are used for agreed purposes.
> 3. Working with GRZ to address institutional capacity limitations and other constraints that prevent reasonable assurance on use of cooperation resources.
> 4. Review of the multiplicity of different donor missions, reviews, conditionalities and documentation with the aim of reducing transaction costs for GRZ.
> 5. Promotion of coordination and harmonization at all levels.
> 6. Working towards delegated cooperation ('silent partnerships') among donors at country level, where it is possible legally and administratively.
> 7. Improvement of information sharing and understanding of commonalities and differences in our policies, procedures and practices.
> 8. Further formulation of a division of labour, based on the PRSP themes and objectives and formatted along the lines of a Comprehensive Development Framework (CDF).
>
> *Source:* Zambia (2004)

Table 5.7: Recipients of bilateral aid, 2001-2002

Donor countries by amount of aid committed*		Total number of recipient countries (A)	Number of recipient countries accounting for 75% of donors' education aid commitments (B)	(B)/(A) in percentage
Major donors	Netherlands	46	6	13
	United States	56	12	21
	Japan	126	15	12
	France	136	21	15
Medium-sized donors	Germany	126	32	25
	United Kingdom	39	4	10
	Sweden	24	5	21
	Austria	84	10	12
	Italy	94	11	12
	Canada	53	12	23
	Norway	72	13	18
	Spain	97	15	15
Small donors	Belgium	66	20	30
	Greece	8	2	25
	Denmark	31	3	10
	Portugal	38	4	11
	Australia	30	5	17
	Ireland	61	5	8
	Switzerland	30	10	33
	Finland	45	10	22
Total DAC countries		149	38	26
Average DAC countries		63	11	17

Note: Data are not available for Luxembourg and New Zealand.
*Major donors are those with commitments of over US$250 million in 2001–2002; medium-sized donors, below US$250 million and above US$50 million; small donors, below US$50 million.
Source: CRS online database (OECD-DAC, 2004a).

(e.g. Acharya, Fuzzo de Lima and Moore, 2004). A donor that distributes its aid to a large number of countries 'proliferates' more than one that concentrates its efforts on relatively few countries. Aid proliferation has significant implications for transaction costs.

Using a specially prepared data set for 2001–2002 based on the OECD-DAC Creditor Reporting System (CRS) database, it is possible to assess the incidence of aid proliferation in the education sector. The data set shows levels and destinations of aid for twenty bilateral donors and 149 ODA-eligible countries.[18] Table 5.7, showing the recipients of education aid from bilateral donors, indicates that while the twenty DAC countries together gave support to 149 countries in all, the number of recipients per donor varied widely. France, Germany and Japan each made commitments to education in more than 100 countries; at the other end of the spectrum, Greece supported only eight countries. The average was sixty-three. The table also shows that three-quarters of bilateral education commitments went to thirty-eight countries,

---

18. The analysis is based on all aid commitments to education except those not allocable to specific countries (the latter amount to 12% of education aid for all DAC countries and ranges from 0% for Japan to 42% for Belgium). After the inclusion of Japanese Technical Cooperation, which is not reported to CRS, 90% of all DAC education aid is covered, according to a personal communication with OECD-DAC.

or 26% of all the countries receiving such aid. Three-quarters of the commitments of France, Germany and Japan are allocated to less than one-quarter of their recipient countries.[19]

Table 5.8 ranks the twenty DAC countries by the extent to which they disperse their aid budget among recipients. The table uses an index of donor proliferation (IDP),[20] which takes into account the number of countries that receive aid and the share that each receives of total education aid by individual donor. Proliferation is greater when aid is shared among a larger number of recipients and each receives a similar share.[21] The table shows that Germany has a very high level of dispersion in its education aid budget while Sweden, the Netherlands and the United Kingdom, for instance, have a much higher degree of concentration. There are some interesting contrasts. While Japan supports over 120 countries, for example, it is ranked ninth by IDP because most of its aid is concentrated among just a few of those countries.[22]

If the proliferation of education aid commitments is set against a measure of the proliferation of total ODA disbursements, a strong correlation emerges (Figure 5.9).[23] This suggests that aid proliferation in the education sector is partly explained by total aid proliferation: donors with widely dispersed total aid budgets spread out their education aid budgets, too. But proliferation is an interesting characteristic of aid to education in its own right. Compare the ranking of countries in Table 5.8 with the relative priority they accord to basic education in Table 5.3, for example. While seven of the first nine countries in Table 5.8 (Austria, Belgium, Canada, France, Germany, Italy, Japan, Norway and Spain) do not give relatively high priority to basic education, with the exception of Portugal, the bottom nine (Australia, Denmark, Finland, the Netherlands, Sweden, Switzerland, the United Kingdom and the United States) do. Thus, the countries that invest significantly in basic education do so in a relatively small number of countries.

To look at the situation from the point of view of aid recipients, the CRS data can be used to establish the number of bilateral donors with which each recipient is dealing. This is a measure of the 'donor fragmentation' affecting individual countries. Figure 5.10, grouping recipient countries by EFA region, shows that countries dealt on average with seven to twelve bilateral donors in 2001–2002. In most regions there is a significant difference between the

Each recipient country dealt on average with seven to twelve bilateral donors in 2001-2002

Table 5.8: Index of donor proliferation in education aid

Country	IDP value	Ranking
Germany	214	1
France	159	2
Belgium	154	3
Spain	139	4
Canada	118	5
Norway	117	6
Austria	116	7
Italy	111	8
Japan	109	9
Switzerland	105	10
Finland	105	11
United States	103	12
Ireland	88	13
Australia	87	14
Netherlands	87	14
Sweden	79	16
Portugal	78	17
United Kingdom	74	18
Denmark	71	19
Greece	63	20

Notes: Data are not available for Luxembourg and New Zealand. Smaller IDP values mean that aid was concentrated on a smaller group of countries.
Source: Calculated by the EFA Global Monitoring Report Team using data from the CRS online database.

---

19. Because donors report differently regarding the total number of countries supported, these data should be treated with caution. The main aid agencies usually report commitment data at the level of individual activities, but some provide data at the activity component level (e.g. they split a regional project by components per recipient country). Furthermore, activities such as government/NGO joint financing can widen the geographic spread of aid to education if the donor reports individual projects rather than a total corresponding to the subsidy to all NGOs combined. The more accurate a donor's reporting, the greater the apparent dispersion of its aid. Similarly, donors that provide information on the country of origin of students benefiting from scholarships appear to have more aid recipients than those reporting aggregates. These problems can be minimized by excluding activities of a low monetary value; thus, the number of larger aid recipients, accounting for at least 75% of education aid, is a better indicator.

20. The IDP is a measure of how widely each donor disperses a budget of US$$x$, where x can take any value. It is the inverse of the Theil index (an indicator of concentration) multiplied by 100 to eliminate decimal places.

$$IPD = \frac{1}{T} \cdot 100$$

If we define the portion of a donor's total aid going to recipient i as x_i, and the number of recipient countries n, then the Theil index is equal to

$$T = log(n) - H(x) = \sum_{i=1}^{n} x_i \, log(n) \, x_i$$
$$0 \leq T \leq log(n)$$

The minimum value of T ($T = 0$), or maximum of IPD, is reached when an equal amount of aid is given to all n countries, each receiving a proportion $1/n$. T reaches its maximum ($T = log(n)$), or minimum of IPD, when the aid is received by only one recipient.

21. The IDP makes it possible to differentiate between countries such as Germany and Japan. Although they operate in the same number of countries, thirty-two countries account for 75% of Germany's commitments to education, while the equivalent number for Japan is fifteen. Thus, Germany has a higher IDP than Japan.

22. In fact, 42% of the Japanese education aid reported to CRS went to China.

23. The data are not strictly comparable because slightly different time periods and types of aid data are used for the index calculation. This does not, however, invalidate the strong relationship observed.

Figure 5.9: Education Index of Donor Proliferation for 2001-2002 against total Index of Donor Proliferation for 1999-2001

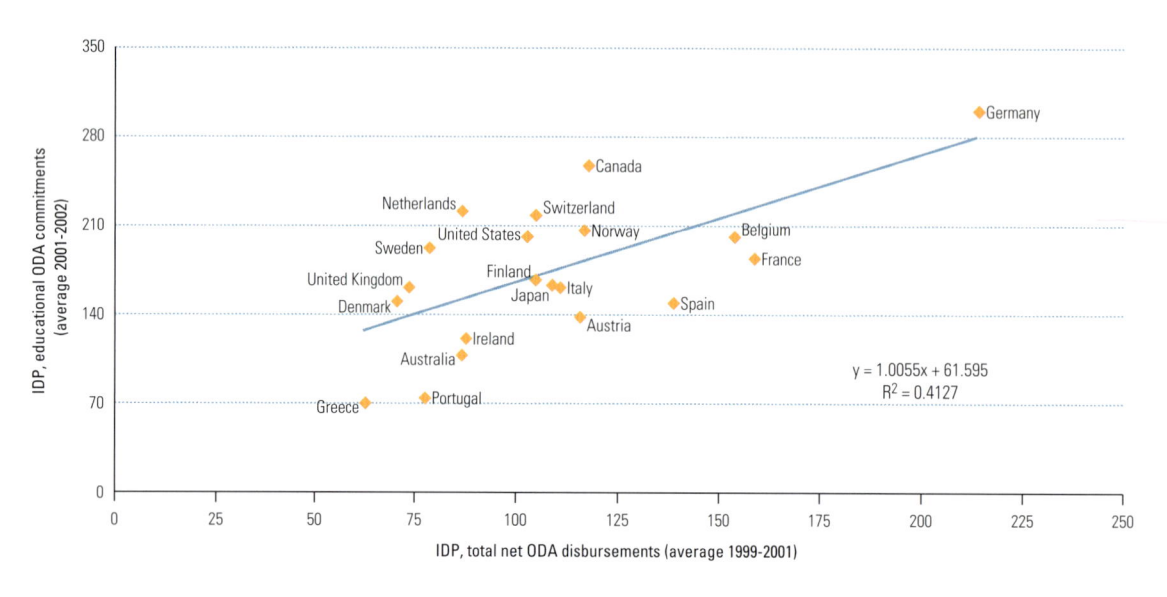

$y = 1.0055x + 61.595$
$R^2 = 0.4127$

Y-axis: IDP, educational ODA commitments (average 2001-2002)
X-axis: IDP, total net ODA disbursements (average 1999-2001)

Source: Table 5.8 and Acharya, Fuzzo de Lima and Moore, 2004.

maximum and minimum values. For instance, in sub-Saharan Africa, two bilateral donors supported education in the Comoros and nineteen in South Africa. This may suggest that the smaller the country, the fewer the donors, which would seem to be borne out by the size of the countries named at the bottom of each regional column. However, in situations of emergency and conflict, this does not hold. For example, a relatively large number of agencies are involved in Serbia and Montenegro and the Palestinian Autonomous Territories.

Figure 5.10: Recipient countries by region and number of bilateral donors making education aid commitments, 2001-2002

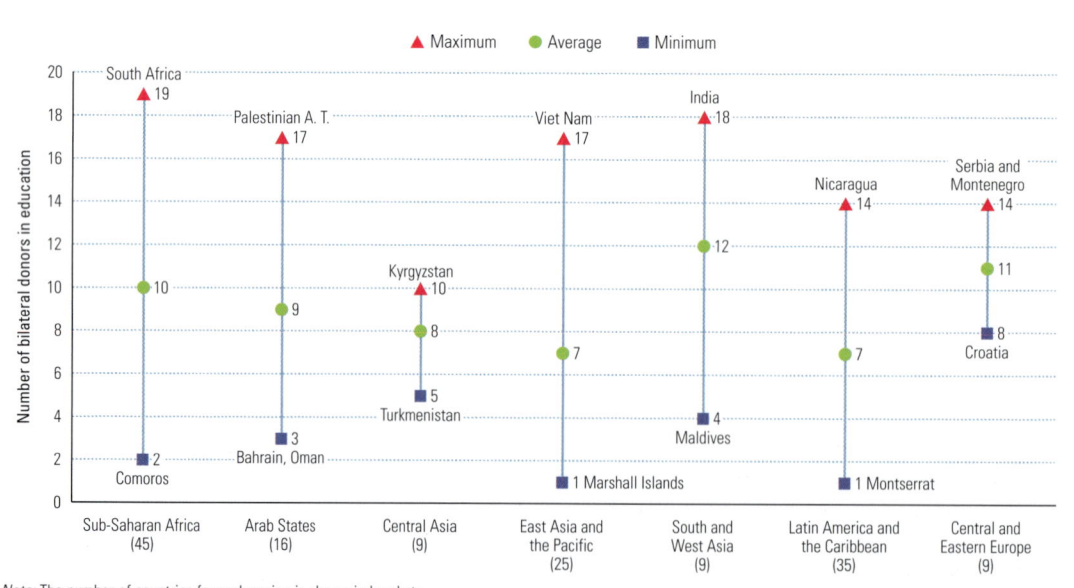

▲ Maximum   ● Average   ■ Minimum

Y-axis: Number of bilateral donors in education

Sub-Saharan Africa (45): South Africa ▲19, Average ●10, Comoros ■2
Arab States (16): Palestinian A. T. ▲17, Average ●9, Bahrain, Oman ■3
Central Asia (9): Kyrgyzstan ▲10, Average ●8, Turkmenistan ■5
East Asia and the Pacific (25): Viet Nam ▲17, Average ●7, Marshall Islands ■1
South and West Asia (9): India ▲18, Average ●12, Maldives ■4
Latin America and the Caribbean (35): Nicaragua ▲14, Average ●7, Montserrat ■1
Central and Eastern Europe (9): Serbia and Montenegro ▲14, Average ●11, Croatia ■8

Note: The number of countries for each region is shown in brackets.
Source: CRS online database (OECD-DAC, 2004a).

In general, one might expect that the efficiency of aid allocation and its use would be maximized if each donor focused its aid programme on a few recipients and if total world education aid was divided more equally among all agencies. This would be consistent with aid recipients having to deal with only a few individual agencies. Some large countries clearly recognize the potential benefits: India, for example, decided recently to curtail its acceptance of aid from some bilateral donors, judging the transaction costs to be greater than the benefits. There are lessons here both for aid agencies and for other aid recipients with highly fragmented programmes.

The distribution of recipients' costs related to donor fragmentation depends on how much donor harmonization exists and how aid is provided (e.g. through separate projects or through budget support, which have different implications for transaction costs). If governments have to work with many diverse donor procedures, especially where project aid predominates, transaction costs are likely to be high. Having to deal with multiple languages and fiscal calendars may compound the costs, and all of this may have a negative effect on the value of aid (see, for example, Knack and Rahman, 2004).

Conclusion
Patterns of proliferation and fragmentation in aid for education give some insights into how wisely individual agencies use their aid budgets, and into the degree of transaction costs likely to be involved. This type of analysis has further potential value in starting to address a more fundamental question: whether aid is allocated to and concentrated in the countries where the challenge of EFA is most pronounced.

Learning from international evaluations

Three recent international evaluations give complementary insights into the use of aid for basic education: a study of EC education aid compares two main modalities of aid (Development Researchers' Network, 2002); the Joint Evaluation of External Support to Basic Education in Developing Countries identifies effective partnerships as key (Netherlands Ministry of Foreign Affairs, 2003a–f) and an evaluation of United Kingdom aid to primary education assesses performance (Al-Samarrai, Bennell and Colclough, 2002). Although different in orientation, all three recognize the importance of partnerships for coherent policies designed to achieve major education goals. All acknowledge the complexity and scale of the task as well.

Projects or programmes?
The analysis of EC aid looks at the effectiveness of support to education in countries of Africa, the Caribbean and the Pacific (the ACP countries) from 1993 to 2000. It focuses on the relevance and effectiveness of both project and programme aid (Box 5.4). It examines EC support to sixteen countries,[24] representing 50% of the funding allocated to education under the seventh and eighth European Development Funds. The study comes out firmly in favour of an evolving approach to aid known as the 'sector-wide approach' or SWAp,[25] calling it 'the optimal way to implement education programme aid'. Such programme aid, the study finds, is more predictable and more easily disbursed than project aid, enabling payment on some recurrent charges (e.g. teachers' salaries), facilitating expenditure at local prices and reducing costs. The report makes clear that programme aid is not effective if governments' policy and management capacity is weak, but where the capacity exists or can be built, programme aid is both an inducement for, and a product of, good policy dialogue.

Effective partnerships
The Joint Evaluation of External Support to Basic Education in Developing Countries was commissioned by thirteen bilateral and multilateral agencies in association with Bolivia, Burkina Faso, Uganda and Zambia. Its central thesis is that sound partnerships underpin the effective use of aid. Although it recognizes considerable strengths in programme aid, it also finds merit in project aid if it is well integrated into sector-wide frameworks (Netherlands Ministry of Foreign Affairs, 2003a–f). Box 5.5 summarizes the study's six main conclusions. The key conclusion is one of caution. It suggests that what donors most lack 'is a willingness and determination to improve basic education through locally developed solutions, which are most relevant to the particular contexts of partner countries and which are built from the "ground-up" rather than through the application of blueprints and templates developed at a global level' (Netherlands Ministry of Foreign Affairs 2003a: xiv-xv).

Programme aid is not effective if governments' policy and management capacity is weak

24. Antigua, Botswana, Burkina Faso, Dominican Republic, Ethiopia, Ghana, Guinea, Mali, Mozambique, Namibia, Papua New Guinea, United Republic of Tanzania, Uganda, Vanuatu, Zambia and Zimbabwe.

25. Though there is no single definition of this approach, generally accepted guidelines include coordinated support to a sector, guided by a single-sector policy and expenditure programme, under government leadership, preferably relying on government procedures for disbursement (Foster et al., 2000; Riddell, 2002; Samoff, 2003).

Box 5.4 European Development Funds: relevance and effectiveness of programme and project aid to education

	Relevance	Effectiveness
Project aid	• Consistent with national education policy and budget frameworks • Meets the very specific needs of a target group • Facilitates pilot activity • Is used for institution-building for organizations that plan to be self-financing	• Works for lower- to middle-income countries within existing reform and budgetary frameworks • Assesses approaches and demonstrates best practice
Programme aid	• Appropriate for sector plans, especially for basic education, as it allows for increased support for teachers (including salaries) and learning materials, and for attention to the needs of the most disadvantaged • Appropriate in countries where efforts are focused on increasing access, requiring stable and predictable sources of funding	• Depends on whether support is through a SWAp or in the framework of macroeconomic budget support • Depends on the choice and effective use of performance indicators • Depends on government 'maturity', capacities within ministries of education and the weight given to institution- and capacity-building

Sources: Orivel (2004); Development Researchers' Network (2002).

Box 5.5 Conclusions of Joint Evaluation of External Support to Basic Education in Developing Countries

1. Greater emphasis is needed on the relevance of external support to local needs and capacities for more tailored local solutions within a global consensus on goals.

2. The shift to programme support is an indication of the commitment of external agencies to strengthen partnership. However, this form of support does not necessarily improve partnerships if implemented as a blueprint rather than a process.

3. The movement to supporting basic education through SWAps and other forms of programme support needs to be accompanied by an understanding of the positive role of project assistance, especially in supporting innovations and providing targeted support to marginalized groups. Projects that can be integrated into programme approaches strengthen the positive aspects of both.

4. A very heavy burden of planning, coordination and monitoring has been made more difficult by uneven progress in agencies' development of common administrative procedures and a reluctance to accept local processes as adequate.

5. Agencies and national partners alike have focused their activities mainly on formal primary schooling, to the detriment of other basic education. Progress has been made in providing access to primary schooling but serious, persistent problems remain in improving the quality of basic education.

6. Agency funding levels have not kept pace with expectations or implied commitments, at least partly because of the complexity of planning and resource allocation processes as well as problems in the absorptive capacity of partner governments.

Source: Netherlands Ministry of Foreign Affairs (2003a)

> **Box 5.6 DFID aid to primary schooling: issues and lessons**
>
> **Increased local ownership by government and civil society and better donor coordination**
> - Tension exists between efforts to maximize local ownership, on the one hand, and increase donor involvement in policy and management, on the other.
> - Each government requires a 'champion' with sufficient authority and leadership to prevent donor domination and a one-sided partnership.
> - Effective donor coordination requires clarity about the role of a lead agency and continuous, intensive consultation.
>
> **Improved sector planning and performance**
> - A predictable resource envelope is crucial for sector-wide planning, including a medium-term budgetary and expenditure framework.
> - Subsector SWAps inhibit overall sector coherence.
> - Involvement by multiple ministries and levels of government makes planning difficult.
> - Strategies should be output and outcome driven, and incorporate clearly focused work programmes.
> - More attention is needed to strengthening the capacity of ministries of education and thus avoiding the formation of de facto parallel structures with overuse of short-term external consultants.
>
> **Lower transaction costs**
> - Overall numbers of expatriate personnel have decreased.
> - Agencies need to invest in developing policy analysis, monitoring and communication skills at sector adviser level.
> - Lack of confidence in government financial management systems has slowed the movement of funding for sector budgets, reflecting the similarly slow pace of public service reform.
> - Fully harmonized implementation procedures are rare.
>
> **Better monitoring and evaluation**
> - Some governments have found joint review processes overly critical.
> - SWAps have increased donor imposition of conditions, with disbursement linked to target attainment, but too many conditions make SWAps impossible to enforce.
> - Most ministry data are lacking in comprehensiveness and/or accuracy.
>
> *Source:* Al-Samarrai, Bennell and Colclough (2002)

The Joint Evaluation suggests that partnerships work best when characterized by great openness, honesty and respect[26] on the part of donors and governments alike, despite differences in power and influence. Partnerships are promoted or impeded by the extent to which attention is given to the continuity of engagement of donors and ministries, and the development of administrative and technical capacity in agencies and governments. Joint agreement on well-defined roles and responsibilities is critical, as is agency adaptability to context and attention to issues of local relevance.

Assessing performance
A study of aid from DFID, the United Kingdom agency, to primary education from 1988 to 2001 in Bangladesh, Ghana, India, Indonesia, Kenya and Malawi concludes that, while it is too early to assess the impact of relatively new approaches, both the benefits and the risks associated with SWAp-type programme aid are potentially greater than in project aid (Al-Samarrai, Bennell and Colclough, 2002).

The study identifies four key issues for better performance. Like the Joint Evaluation, it finds local ownership and better donor coordination to be important factors. A sector-wide approach underpinned by a predictable medium-term expenditure framework is essential. Common approaches by donors to joint funding and to harmonized aid procedures, the third key factor, are important but remain rare. Finally, the study stresses the importance of much better monitoring and evaluation (Box 5.6).

Getting the modalities right

All three studies assess the relative merits of different aid modalities.[27] Broadly, they conclude that, while there is a welcome move in the direction of a more coherent, consistent and coordinated approach to providing support to education, geared to sector or subsector policies, the actual choice of instrument should be sensitive and appropriate to context. This is broadly in line with a recent paper for the World Bank on donor contributions to EFA (Foster, 2004). It argues that

26. A recent analysis of Finnish support for education (Sack, Cross and Moulton, 2003) also identified respect as a key strength.

27. The literature on SWAps and other forms of aid is growing. See, for example, Buchert (2002) on Burkina Faso, Ghana and Mozambique; Samoff (2003) on Burkina Faso; IHSD (2003) on Rwanda, Uganda and Zambia; and Moulton (2003) on World Bank aid to education in Africa. Riddell (2004), among others, notes that the experience of African and Asian countries is different. Most African countries are heavily aid dependent, which has implications for the ability of governments to take clear charge of their own education policies and practices.

> **Box 5.7 How should financial aid for education be provided?**
>
> - **General budget support** is appropriate where the macro policy framework is generally agreed, the central budget process for resource allocation is effective and accountability exists.
>
> - **Sector budget support** may be appropriate if collective decision making on overall budget allocation works imperfectly and/or donor input in sector-level decisions is greater than would be the case with general budget support.
>
> - **Programme support** using government systems is especially important in highly aid-dependent environments, where the costs of dealing with large numbers of donor projects are unmanageable.
>
> - **Project aid** can help pilot new approaches and may be preferred in circumstances where agreement on the policy framework is lacking or severe governance or accountability issues exist.
>
> *Source:* Foster (2004)

the strengths and weaknesses of public expenditure management are a critical consideration in choosing between general or sector budget support, programme assistance or project aid (Box 5.7). Building management capacity in the education sector thus becomes a critical element of aid, especially in countries where the scale of the EFA challenge is considerable but management capacity is weak.

Countries in emergency

While the case for providing aid to support sound policies and good governance is strong, many poor people live in countries that are poorly governed and characterized by conflict and emergency. In its work on Development Cooperation in Difficult Partnerships, the OECD-DAC has highlighted ten key principles for action in such cases, which warrant attention in the education sector as well as more generally (OECD-DAC, 2002: 6):

- Remain engaged.

- Improve analysis of country issues and conflict.

- Adopt specific strategies to address problems of difficult partnership.

- Promote change that will nurture the political environment that leads to more responsive and capable government.

- Maintain services for poor people to the extent possible, working pragmatically with organizations inside and outside of government that have commitment and capability.

- Assess the case for aid against the 'without aid' risks for the international community and poor people.

- Intensify coordination but make it economical.

- Address coherence issues across government.

- Support locally owned peer pressure mechanisms.

- Consider the role of neighbouring countries and key regional leaders.

Cause and effect – aid and quality

The three studies agreed that identifying clear causal relationships between education aid and education quality is difficult. Assessing aid effectiveness in terms of its impact on quality is also problematic. First, national governments and aid agencies interpret quality in different ways, e.g. expressing it in terms of specific targets or as a set of general objectives. Second, and more practically speaking, even where the quality of inputs and processes can be monitored, it is not always possible, with the data available, to monitor and judge educational outcomes.

The study on EC aid to education, for instance,[28] notes that in the five countries its evaluation team visited,[29] the only indicators available were measures of input and efficiency; no indicators for learning outcomes existed (Development Researchers' Network, 2002). Difficult as it is to establish cause and effect with project aid,[30] doing so with pooled funding and budget support is even more complicated.

The Joint Evaluation concludes (Netherlands Ministry of Foreign Affairs, 2003a: 47-8):

> It would perhaps not be an overstatement to say that…achieving quality in basic education has been the most difficult problem for externally supported basic education efforts. …The globally focused Document Review and each of the four Country Studies (Bolivia, Burkina Faso, Uganda and Zambia) iterate

---

28. This study defines 'quality in education' as 'a function of increased opportunities (access) and availability of educational inputs (classrooms, teachers, textbooks, etc.), the quality of these inputs, the quality of the learning outcomes and, finally, …the quality of [the] education system's administration'.

29. Botswana, Burkina Faso, Dominican Republic, Uganda and Zambia.

30. One recent exception is a study linking the provision of textbooks and improved school infrastructure by the World Bank in Ghana to levels of attainment and achievement (World Bank, 2004b). An overview of aid to India (Singh, 2003) suggests that the long-term relationship between India, the World Bank, the European Union, DFID, UNICEF and the Netherlands in piloting and then developing the District Primary Education Programme provided strategic support for policy and service delivery issues, attention to girls and socially and geographically disadvantaged groups, information-based planning, and programme development through rigorous evaluation and review, and that these might not have become such significant elements of national and state policy otherwise.

very strongly that efforts to expand access and improve coverage with the use of national and externally provided resources have met with much more apparent success than efforts to improve quality at each level of the system.[31]

The study suggests four factors that help explain this conclusion:

- weak links between programme design and systematic analysis of what works locally, especially regarding teacher education, curriculum reform, development of materials, pedagogical approaches and the internal management of schools;

- the prevalence of 'pilot study cultures' in which innovations are carried out with project funds, studied at local level but not linked to larger programmes for national funding or extended to the whole system;

- perceptions that formal schooling is insufficiently relevant to prepare primary school leavers to participate in the work force, especially in rural areas.;

- the large size of many primary schools, which seems to be detrimental to quality.

These findings seem to imply that external models of good practice, and their application in aid programmes, are insufficiently attuned to local circumstances, though government policies may also be inappropriate or inefficient.

Thus, the impact of education aid on quality may need to be assessed differently. Evidence of coherent education sector policies that can be financed is an important intermediate indicator of attention to quality. Such policies are likely to have clear objectives for access, equity and quality, with well-defined targets and indicators, even if these are reviewed and changed in the light of experience. The indicators then become important benchmarks for governments in their pursuit of education objectives and for agencies in their assessment of progress. In this regard attention to regular monitoring and review takes on particular significance. Aid that contributes to good policy and governance, technically sound monitoring processes and the strengthening of capacity for outcome-driven programmes is a significant means of improving quality in education.

Plans, partnerships and quality

No shortage of plans

If, as the OECD-DAC model suggests, good national policy is the starting point for the effective use of aid, there is no apparent shortage of national education sector and subsector plans on which to build effective aid-related partnerships. Table 5.9 presents the incidence of plans by EFA region and Table 5.10 by country category. As Table 5.9 shows, 105 countries (59% of the total excluding Western Europe and North America) are recorded as having education

31. While this study does not define education quality, it notes that quality is not only about measurable outcomes in literacy and numeracy but also has multiple dimensions concerning aims and objectives of education in each country.

Table 5.9: PRSPs and education plans by EFA region

		Context			PRSP				
	LDCs	Countries in transition	Countries in armed conflicts in 2002*	E-9 (high population countries)	I-PRSP	PRSP	Education sector plan	EFA action plan	EFA Fast-Track Initiative
Sub-Saharan Africa (45)	31	0	12	1	10	18	42	40	6
Arab States (20)	4	0	3	1	1	2	8	15	2
Central Asia (9)	0	8	0	0	0	6	5	7	0
East Asia and the Pacific (33)	8	0	3	2	2	2	14	25	1
South and West Asia (9)	5	0	6	3	1	3	4	5	0
Latin America and the Caribbean (41)	1	0	1	2	1	4	26	18	3
North America and Western Europe (26)	–	–	–	–	–	–	–	5	0
Central and Eastern Europe (20)	0	19	2	0	2	3	6	5	0
World (203)	**49**	**27**	**27**	**9**	**17**	**38**	**105**	**120**	**12**

*An armed conflict is defined here as a political conflict in which armed combat involves the armed forces of at least one state (or one or more armed factions seeking to gain control of all or part of the state), and in which at least 1,000 people have been killed by the fighting during the course of the conflict. An armed conflict is added to the annual list of current armed conflicts in the year in which the death toll reaches the threshold of 1,000. (Project Ploughshares, 2003)

Source: Compiled by EFA Global Monitoring Report team from sources posted at www.efareport.unesco.org.

Table 5.10: PRSPs and education plans by country classification

Category and regions	Number of countries	Education I-PRSP	Education PRSP	Education sector plan	EFA action plan	EFA Fast-Track Initiative
Least-developed countries	49	11	20	43	39	7
Sub-Saharan Africa	31	8	16	29	27	5
Arab States	4	1	2	3	3	2
East Asia and the Pacific	8	1	1	7	8	0
South and West Asia	5	1	1	3	1	0
Latin America and the Caribbean	1	0	0	1	nd	0
Countries in transition*	27	2	8	11	10	0
Central Asia	8	0	5	5	6	0
Central and Eastern Europe	19	2	3	6	4	0
Countries in armed conflicts in 2002	27	4	9	18	21	1
Sub-Saharan Africa	12	3	5	11	9	1
Arab States	3	0	0	0	2	0
East Asia and the Pacific	3	1	0	3	3	0
South and West Asia	6	0	3	2	5	0
Latin America and the Caribbean	1	0	0	1	1	0
Central and Eastern Europe	2	0	1	1	1	0
E-9 (high-population) countries	9	2	1	7	7	0
Sub-Saharan Africa	1	0	0	1	0	0
Arab States	1	0	0	0	1	0
East Asia and the Pacific	2	1	0	2	2	0
South and West Asia	3	1	1	2	2	0
Latin America and the Caribbean	2	0	0	2	2	0

*In this table, countries in transition include Central and Eastern Europe minus Turkey and Central Asia minus Mongolia.
Source: Compiled by EFA Global Monitoring Report team from sources posted at www.efareport.unesco.org.

---

sector plans, while 120 (59% of all EFA countries) have EFA plans and 55 countries have full or interim PRSPs. In sub-Saharan Africa, where EFA indicators are poorest, virtually every country has an education plan. Furthermore, as the breakdown in Table 5.10 shows, 43 out of 49 least-developed countries (LDCs) have an education plan and, perhaps a little surprisingly, two-thirds of the countries in which armed conflicts were taking place in 2002, or 18 out of 27, had education sector plans, though many may be quite dated.

Tables 5.9 and 5.10 indicate that education plans exist in a majority of developing countries, including those with some of the poorest EFA indicators, though it is unclear to what extent education plans are integrated in PRSPs and whether they provide the basis for financing and programme-implementation decisions. Some plans are clearly broad statements of intent, written in some cases to meet international requirements. This makes it difficult to review the status and implementation of national EFA and other education sector plans (UNESCO, 2004a).[32] Such work is needed, however, and to this end, an international database will be developed to inform future editions of the *EFA Global Monitoring Report*. Meanwhile, using reports from UNESCO offices, it is possible to gauge some developments concerning EFA plans and planning at regional and subregional levels (Box 5.8). The reports suggest that work remains to be done to include all the EFA goals fully in education plans.

While there is no shortage of planning activity, more important in the context of this chapter is the extent to which good planning in aid-dependent countries is providing a basis for better alignment and coordination of aid.

Policy dialogue for coherent sector strategies

Many countries in sub-Saharan Africa are highly aid-dependent. Table 5.11 illustrates this phenomenon for three countries. In some instances, aid may finance more than 50% of

---

32. The EFA High-Level Group indicated at its meeting in 2003 that it would find such a review useful.

Box 5.8 EFA plan developments: some regional experiences

■ **Political commitment:**

Of fourteen EFA plans and draft plans in the **Arab States**, those of Yemen and Jordan committed the government to finance and implement the plans. In **Latin America**, participation by finance and planning ministries was limited except in Costa Rica, the Dominican Republic and Ecuador. In **sub-Saharan Africa**, a review prepared for the Eighth Conference of Ministers of Education of African Member States (MINEDAF VIII) in 2002 noted that EFA plans were not always clearly integrated with wider national sector plans.

■ **Participation:**

Despite commitments made in Dakar regarding consultation with civil society, information sharing was more prevalent than longer-term consultation. In the **Arab States** only Saudi Arabia's plan pointed explicitly to some wider consultation process. For **sub-Saharan Africa**, the MINEDAF review emphasized participation by other partners (other ministry departments, local bodies, private sector, civil society, teachers, parents, religious bodies, etc.) in fewer than half the plans surveyed. In **Latin America**, where a more detailed analysis has been undertaken, participation was concentrated in initial planning and plan validation but not the diagnostic process. Parents, students, the media and many government departments had a minimal role, and teacher participation was uneven. National EFA coordinators and civil society organizations pointed to excessive centralization and scant representation from outside major cities. Eleven of eighteen countries surveyed had EFA Forums, which in some cases (e.g. in Ecuador, Guatemala, Honduras and Nicaragua) served as mechanisms for wider debate on education and human development. The initiative for founding forums came from government, civil society organizations/NGOs (in El Salvador) and international organizations (UNICEF and UNESCO in Ecuador and Chile). In Brazil, existing channels for participation and policy dialogue were deemed sufficient.

■ **EFA goals:**

In most of the **Arab States** surveyed, national ECCE goals were only labels, with no target groups, implementation timelines or indicators specified and no budgeting data or funding sources. The gender goal was limited to primary education and only the plans of Egypt, Sudan and Yemen emphasized girls' education. In **the Pacific**, EFA goals on ECCE and education quality had priority in the fourteen EFA plans of Pacific Island states.* Learning opportunities and life-skills programmes for youth and adults were the third highest priority, reflecting a need for appropriate curricula in these areas. All plans also addressed adult literacy and gender disparities but gave them less priority. In **sub-Saharan Africa**, diagnosis of challenges to EFA in education supply and demand needs to be strengthened in many plans, particularly for literacy and the training of youth and adults.

■ **Monitoring and review:**

In the **Arab States**, with some exceptions, EFA plans did not include time-bound action programmes and, except in Yemen, integration of EFA plans within wider national strategies for economic and social development and poverty reduction was weak. In most cases the EFA plans did not include cost estimates, and only two specified clear monitoring and assessment mechanisms with easily measurable indicators. In **Latin America**, most countries still had to define follow-up and monitoring mechanisms. In the **Pacific Island states**, EFA plans were reviewed and adjusted annually to reflect progress and new priorities. In **sub-Saharan Africa**, most plans included measurable targets and action programmes and, to a lesser extent, cost estimates, but performance indicators and monitoring mechanisms still had to be defined.

*All the Pacific Island states with EFA plans are working together through the Pacific Islands Forum on a Pacific Islands Forum Basic Education Action Plan. The governments of the island states are preparing or strengthening sector-wide strategies consistent with national objectives and regional and international goals. These efforts are supported by the Pacific Regional Initiatives for the Delivery of Basic Education (PRIDE), a programme co-funded by the European Commission (under the ninth EDF Regional Indicative Programme) and New Zealand Aid. The major implementing partner is the University of the South Pacific. Special attention is being paid to resolving common problems and enhancing education agencies' capacity for planning and delivering good-quality basic education (Chandra, 2004; Pacific Islands Forum Secretariat, 2001).

Sources: UNESCO-BREDA (2003), document review from twenty-one countries; UNESCO-Santiago (2004), survey questionnaires from nineteen countries (Latin America only); UNESCO-Beirut (2004a), document review from fourteen countries (not counting North Africa).

---

sector budgets. Furthermore, aid-dependent countries are supported by a relatively large number of donor agencies and other organizations, including NGOs. This is the environment within which dialogue on education sector policy takes place.

In 2000, Mozambique depended on external funds for 28% of its education sector expenditure, and there are risks of this level of dependence increasing over the next decade (Takala, 2004). This means the quality and effectiveness of the aid relationship are vitally important. The relationship is being developed through a SWAp, whose history (Box 5.9) shows that the process has been complex; but strong government leadership is bringing progress on policy and plan development.

Table 5.11: Aid dependence in education in three African countries: budgets and agencies

Country	Aid dependence	Agencies supporting education in the country
Mozambique	28% of education budget externally funded	Canada, Denmark, Finland, France, Germany, Ireland, Italy, Netherlands, Portugal, Spain, Sweden, United Kingdom African Development Bank, European Commission, Islamic Development Bank, United Nations agencies, World Bank
Uganda	54% of primary education recurrent budget externally funded	Austria, Belgium, Canada, Denmark, Finland, France, Germany, Greece, Ireland, Italy, Japan, Netherlands, Norway, Spain, United States European Commission, World Bank, UNICEF
Zambia	43% of education budget externally funded	Belgium, Canada, Denmark, Finland, France, Germany, Ireland, Italy, Japan, Netherlands, Norway, Spain, United Kingdom, United States African Development Bank, Save the Children, UNICEF, World Bank

Sources: Mozambique: Buchert (2002); OECD-DAC (2004a); Takala (2004); European Commission (2001).
Uganda: Netherlands Ministry of Foreign Affairs (2003d); OECD-DAC (2004a).
Zambia: Netherlands Ministry of Foreign Affairs (2003c); OECD-DAC (2004a); Zambia Ministry of Education (2002).

Zambia's recent history in this area has been even more complicated. After ten years of policy reform, the Basic Education Sub-Sector Investment Programme (BESSIP)[33] was agreed with all major funding partners in the late 1990s. Its development has been accompanied by some problems stemming from donor fragmentation and aid proliferation. It was conceived as a programme in which aid funds would be pooled and managed by the Ministry of Education, but funding agencies' financing requirements eventually had to be accommodated in four main ways (Table 5.12). An analysis of how funds were allocated to the nine major BESSIP programme components further highlights the complexity of the situation (Table 5.13). It shows a rough division between pooled funding for such 'softer' elements as training and curriculum development, and project funding for infrastructure development and other 'hardware' components. The high proportion of non-pooled funding for HIV/AIDS

Box 5.9 Evolution of the sector approach in education in Mozambique

Mozambique's high dependence on external funding has had a fundamental influence on the development of its education sector. Until the mid-1990s, as many as fifty agencies funded hundreds of projects, making it hard for the government to set priorities and leading to serious imbalances in resource allocation, both geographically and among subsectors. Operational responsibility for project implementation was typically entrusted to separate units, each with weak links to the core government administrative systems. Meanwhile the Ministry of Education's capacity to contribute to project planning and monitoring was overstretched.

In 1995, the government issued a new National Education Policy, covering the entire sector. It was followed by a SWAp called the Education Sector Strategic Plan (ESSP) – the product of a process led by the ministry and involving consultation with its main external partners, local NGOs and other civil society representatives. The SWAp was strongly espoused by some external funding agencies. ESSP I, prepared for 1999-2003, was in fact not truly sector wide: it covered only primary school (grades 1-7) and non-formal basic education. More recently, however, it has been complemented by strategies for general secondary and vocational education.

Though it has taken more time than expected to harmonize the funding agencies' management procedures, the agencies have established a common planning and monitoring cycle with annual review meetings and a series of joint technical missions has taken place. A major step forward was the establishment of the Education Sector Support Fund – an off-budget arrangement for the pooling of several agencies' contributions. This seen as an intermediate stage on the way to sector, or even general, budget support and eventually as a means of improving equity in the allocation of funds to different parts of Mozambique. Initially the fund is targeting activities to improve quality in basic education, including familiarizing primary teachers with the new curriculum, training adult literacy instructors and producing materials for adult literacy classes. Some non-earmarked funds support flexible procurement of technical assistance, contracted directly by the ministry.

ESSP also provides a policy framework for externally funded projects designed to contribute to its implementation. They are managed according to agency-specific procedures, but are better coordinated than when they were stand-alone projects. The process is not easy, but all parties acknowledge the progress that has been made.

Source: Takala (2004)

---

33. BESSIP defines 'basic education' as grades 1–9. It is one of the six education components of Zambia's PRSP, approved in 2002.

prevention and for nutrition can be explained by support from donors that do not pool funds (UNICEF and the United States). The actual flow of funds also illustrates some of the uncertainties relating to aid flows, including the relatively slow pace of disbursement, which to some extent reflects the degree of donor confidence in the Ministry of Education (Table 5.14).

Tables 5.12–5.14 show part of a complex story in which, gradually and sometimes sporadically, the Ministry of Education has moved towards control over its own national policy – to a point where the World Bank has declared its confidence regarding the continuity of the BESSIP process, even with changes in political leadership in Zambia (World Bank, 2002c). National management mechanisms have emerged: e.g. a Joint Steering Committee overseeing policy development, a Programme Co-ordinating Committee with oversight of overall BESSIP management and a Management Implementation Team for day-to-day matters. All three bodies include donor representation. In addition, the government and the donors have reached agreement on a joint monitoring process. The effectiveness of these mechanisms has been enhanced by a technical assistance programme to build capacity within the ministry (Volan, 2003; Netherlands Ministry of Foreign Affairs, 2003c).

The extent to which the Zambian example demonstrates strong mutuality of purpose and a genuine partnership involving a relatively large number of donors, ministries and local civil society representatives is an open question. Some believe the strength of the partnership depends on the personalities of the key individuals involved (Riddell, 2002). A strong dialogue about the national education policy has certainly been established and considerable progress has been made towards greater alignment of donor funding in support of BESSIP. Greater donor coordination is also gradually evolving. The new MOU referred to in Box 5.3 may spur more effective coordination.

A comprehensive view of quality

One important potential advantage of a sector-wide approach to policy development is the emergence of a broad, comprehensive view of education quality and how it can be improved. In Mozambique, for instance, such a strategic

Table 5.12: Types of funding under BESSIP, 2001

	Control of funds	Features	Donors*
Case 1	Pooled funding: funds controlled by ministry, deposited in a common bank account	Possible to earmark	Denmark, Finland, Ireland, Netherlands, Norway, United Kingdom
Case 2	Funds controlled by ministry, in separate accounts, for all agreed BESSIP components		World Bank
Case 3	Funds controlled by ministry, in separate accounts, for limited number of BESSIP components	Project-like earmarking of funds to specified activities	Ireland, Netherlands African Development Bank, OPEC
Case 4	Separate funds managed by individual donors	Conventional project fund management and flow	Denmark, Finland, Japan, United Kingdom, United States Red Barna, UNICEF

Sources: L. T. Associates (2002a); Netherlands Ministry of Foreign Affairs (2003c).
*Where inconsistencies occur in categorization of donors between the two sources, the first source is used.

Table 5.13: BESSIP budget by component and funding type, 2002

	Budget (US$ thousands)	Pooled (%)	Non-pooled (%)
Overall management	5 829	60.7	39.3
Infrastructure	38 412	12.6	87.4
Teacher development	13 247	52.8	47.2
Education materials	5 738	30.0	70.0
Gender and equity	10 118	53.4	46.6
Health and nutrition	2 930	28.9	71.1
Curriculum	593	77.4	22.6
Capacity-building	3 957	81.5	18.5
HIV/AIDS	4 745	39.6	60.4
Total	85 571	33.8	66.2

Source: L. T. Associates (2002b)

Table 5.14: Zambia Ministry of Education expenditure, 1998–2002
(Constant 2001 Kwacha billions)

		1998	1999	2000	2001	2002
Domestic:	Budget	…	…	264	362	412
	Actual	270	250*	254*	346*	396**
External aid:	Budget	…	…	209	255	305
	Actual	2***	72*	100*	139*	168**

*Includes case 4 funding, **Estimate, ***Government of Zambia accounts.
Source: Ministry of Education Planning Unit data, cited in Netherlands Ministry of Foreign Affairs (2003c).

> **Box 5.10 Policy dialogue on quality in Mozambique**
>
> **A sector-wide strategy for improving quality**
>
> Improving the quality of education is one of three main components of the Education Sector Strategic Plan (the others are expanding access and developing institutional capacity). ESSP I (1999-2003) took a comprehensive view of education quality in a context of accelerated enrolment growth that could have overwhelmed capacity to the point of jeopardizing minimum quality standards. ESSP is a commitment to policies designed to both maintain and enhance quality through:
> - systematic monitoring of quality through national surveys of learning achievement;
> - thorough revision of the primary curriculum;
> - high priority on development of pre-service and in-service teacher training and subsequent pedagogical support;
> - higher salaries and better conditions of service for teachers;
> - better training for school directors;
> - provision of textbooks and other essential materials to all pupils, and kits of basic materials to teachers.
>
> **Building on existing knowledge**
>
> Knowledge about quality is based on annual collection of data for quality-related indicators and newly established national studies of learning achievement. Curriculum reform was launched when the sector-wide approach was adopted.
>
> **Sector-wide analysis**
>
> Taking a sector-wide approach has facilitated comprehensive analysis of complex issues and helped in defining ways to overcome the fragmentation of activities that arose from one project to another. Dialogue on teacher education and the development of the teaching profession has been productive. Trade-offs between sustainable expansion and preserving or improving quality in basic education have also been examined, especially in respect of teacher qualifications and remuneration.
>
> **Building capacity**
>
> Institutional capacity-building aimed at improving quality in basic education, in the context of ESSP, has developed through policy dialogue, implementation and monitoring, rather than through a well-conceived, systematic long-term plan. It has been enhanced by technical assistance with preparation of subsector strategies for teacher education and adult education, and by project support to curriculum development and learning achievement studies at the National Institute for Educational Development.
>
> *Source:* Takala (2004)

view is developing as a direct result of policy dialogue. A clearer overall view of the meaning of quality serves as a foundation for more effective programming and donor assistance (Box 5.10).

Monitoring quality

Uganda, like Mozambique and Zambia, is heavily dependent on external aid. Between 1998 and 2002, 54%–61% of its primary education budget was aid funded. Under its Education Strategic Investment Plan (ESIP) the Ugandan Ministry of Education, in dialogue with partner agencies, has defined a set of indicators, some of which concern the quality of primary education.[34] Table 5.15 itemizes these indicators, which suggest that progress so far in improving quality has been rather limited, though it should be recalled that extraordinary expansion in primary enrolment, from 3.1 million in 1996 to 7.4 million in 2002, is the fundamental context for these trends.

Immediately after the introduction of free primary education in 1997, pupil/teacher ratios rose significantly and untrained teachers were deployed en masse. National upgrading of teachers and better teacher deployment and management, plus slower rates of enrolment growth have helped to lower pupil/teacher ratios to their current levels.

As Table 5.15 indicates, Uganda places considerable weight on teaching quality (with indicators on pupil/teacher ratios and teachers' qualification and training), pupil achievement (mastery of key curriculum content – literacy and numeracy in particular – at grades 3 and 6) and school profile (minimum school quality standards defined by the ministry). In addition to annual monitoring of national progress on key indicators, the government (working with funding agencies) carries out six-monthly monitoring reviews to set targets for assessment.

---

34. Under ESIP, a National Assessment System has been set up to monitor pupil achievement, and the School Inspectorate has been restructured as the Education Standards Agency, with responsibility for overall quality control.

Table 5.15: Initial ESIP indicators relating to quality, 2000/2001–2003/2004

Indicator	Source of data	Status 2000/2001	Status 2001/2002	Status 2002/2003	Status 2003/2004
Percentage of primary school teachers with the required academic background (finished grade 7 or above):	EMIS[1]				
a) Total		98	98	98	97
b) Men		98	98	98	98
c) Women		98	98	98	97
Percentage of primary school teachers who are professionally certified according to national standards, i.e. have at least a grade III teaching certificate:	EMIS[1]				
a) Total		75	75	74	75
b) Men		73	73	73	73
c) Women		78	78	77	77
Pupil/teacher ratio:	EMIS[1]				
a) Primary		55:1	58:1	55:1	52:1
b) Secondary		17:1	20:1	18:1	18:1
Percentage of pupils having reached at least grade 3 who have mastered nationally defined basic competencies in:	NAPE[2]/ UNEB[3]				
a) Literacy		18	…		
b) Numeracy		39	…		
c) Science		…	85	20	
d) Social studies		…	96	39	
Percentage of pupils having reached at least grade 6 who master nationally defined basic competencies in:	NAPE[2]/ UNEB[3]				
a) Literacy		…	…		
b) Numeracy		…	…		
c) Science		13	17		
d) Social studies		42	32		
Percentage of schools meeting minimum quality standards	Inspectorate	66	66	–	–

1. Education Management and Information System.
2. National Assessment of Progress in Education.
3. Uganda National Examination Board.
Source: Uganda Ministry of Education and Sports (2003*a*)

For example, at the tenth Education Sector Review, in November 2003, district-level targets were set on pupil/teacher ratios, pupil/classroom ratios and the ratios of pupils to core textbooks (Uganda Ministry of Education and Sports, 2003*b*).

Ethiopia has a similar approach. Under its Education Sector Development Programme (ESDP) I and II, it has identified five main categories of performance indicator: budget and expenditure, access, quality, efficiency and equity. Among the six quality indicators, three relate to the qualifications of teachers at different levels, two deal with pupil/textbook ratios and one is on assessment of learning at grade 4 (Ethiopia, 2003).

It is not the intention here to reflect on whether Uganda or Ethiopia is demonstrating progress in improving the quality of education. Rather, these examples and that of Mozambique represent the growing number of cases in which some funding agencies use the government's own core indicators as the basis for measuring progress, instead of targets specific to an individual donor activity or programme. Not all agencies are at the point where this approach fits easily with their philosophy or their aid monitoring and reporting procedures and regulations. But the approach is consistent with both the OECD-DAC work on harmonization and alignment, and with the notion of partnership that underpins the Joint Evaluation.

In a growing number of cases, funding agencies use the government's own core indicators as the basis for measuring progress

Uganda and Ethiopia are relatively advanced in having reached agreement on a set of core indicators to which all the main partners in ESIP and ESDP subscribe. A recent study covering Bolivia, Ethiopia, Namibia, Pakistan and Tunisia observed that agreement on core indicators is 'beset by difficulties, primarily because definitions and underlying concepts vary significantly from country to country' (Span Consultants, 2003: 8). The study concluded that acceptance and use of a common set of indicators depends on whether:

- data availability and quality are adequate, both in the education sector and outside of it;

- the incentives for educational institutions to misrepresent data can be overcome;

- data collection and analysis capacity is sufficient at all levels of the system.

Building capacity

> There is increasing agreement on the need for a more strategic approach to building capacity

Just as there is a growing consensus on the need for a system-wide view of quality, so too there is increasing agreement on the need for a more strategic approach to building capacity. The emerging view is that capacity-building should be integrated with system development rather than conceived as isolated, short-term training activities associated with individual projects.

One recent study sees capacity development as an issue that is not limited to those working in educational institutions and programmes (Buchert, 2002). Government officials and aid agency personnel will need to enhance their skills if government resources and aid are to be combined effectively in pursuit of education goals. This is a major human development agenda in its own right.

Individual countries' experience in this respect vary. Burkina Faso's Ten Year Plan for the Development of Basic Education includes provisions on building managerial, administrative and evaluative capacity, but in practice external technical assistance still holds sway. Several key officials from Mozambique underwent training at the UNESCO International Institute for Educational Planning early in the development of ESSP, although capacity-building requirements were apparently identified only as the SWAp evolved. In Ghana in the mid-1990s, understanding of the Free, Compulsory and Universal Basic Education Programme was very uneven across the Ministry of Education. This was partly due to unequal sharing of information and dispersed planning functions within the Ministry.

Looking at a particular subsector, a multi-country study on teacher education (Lewin and Stuart, 2003) concluded that external assistance was often the only source of exposure to new ideas and practices for both lecturers and managers at teacher training institutions. Realizing national goals is very difficult unless the building of key institutional capacity is a part of sector reform and quality improvement nationwide. In the United Republic of Tanzania, the Primary Education Development Plan (2002–2006) recognizes human resource development as central and identifies the teacher as the main instrument for bringing about qualitative improvements in learning. The plan puts priority on professional development of teachers, tutors, inspectors and other leaders in education, within the framework of overall government strategy (United Republic of Tanzania, 2001).

Conclusion

While there is a body of agency literature that records success in meeting programme objectives, it is much more difficult to find substantive evidence of a clear relationship between aid and better learning outcomes at national and international level. SWAps and budget support hold out some promise but have yet to deliver. Projects involve significant weaknesses but have their place, particularly in supporting innovation.

For the present, governments and aid agencies in aid-dependent countries are defining intermediate measures of good practice: sound policy, clearly defined objectives, national targets and indicators, well-managed monitoring and review processes and consistent attention to building strong institutional capacity. The growing body of evidence coming out of regular monitoring reviews should give some idea of whether better coordinated, sector-based aid is proving more effective than previous approaches. That is a topic to which this Report will return in the future.

International coordination

Assessing success

Imagine a retrospective evaluation, conducted in 2015, of how international coordination had affected progress towards EFA. Such a review would require judgements as to whether:

- the international community mobilized substantial new *resources* to help in achieving the six EFA goals, especially for countries lacking the resources to implement national plans for EFA;

- the global store of *knowledge* about policies that strongly help improve equitable access to an education of good quality has been enhanced, shared and used;

- international aid is better *harmonized and aligned* and has been used effectively to support sound, nationally owned education-sector policies;

- EFA has been fully integrated in wider international discourse and action in support of the MDGs and poverty eradication.

These priorities are essentially those set out in the global initiative recommended at the World Education Forum in Dakar (UNESCO, 2000a). The aim was an initiative that would increase aid and make its flow more predictable, quicken debt relief, improve coordination of education aid provision (including through sector-wide approaches) and establish regular EFA monitoring processes. Although a global initiative in the sense intended at Dakar has not come to fruition, proactive and well-coordinated international action designed to address the needs identified by the World Education Forum is as necessary in 2004 as it was at the beginning of the millennium.

The Fast-Track Initiative (FTI) offers one distinctive international response to this challenge. After a relatively protracted debate over its core objectives and functions, it has emerged as a mechanism with objectives that can be assessed in terms of resource flows, knowledge, types of aid and its wider development influence. UNESCO is the other main international actor. It benefits from a strong mandate, given to it by the international community at Dakar, but, as this Report's predecessor explained, it has seen its primary role as facilitating international dialogue and demonstrating the importance of partnerships for EFA through its own diverse programmes (UNESCO, 2003a). These two endeavours are considered in turn.

The Fast-Track Initiative

The FTI is an international partnership designed to accelerate progress towards the achievement by 2015 of universal primary completion (UPC, another way of expressing a core EFA goal, UPE). Launched by the Development Committee of the World Bank and International Monetary Fund at its 2002 spring meeting, the FTI passed two important milestones in 2004. Its partner agencies agreed a framework to guide its development (World Bank-FTI Secretariat, 2004), and the Development Committee concluded, albeit with some caution, that the FTI deserved the strong support of the international community.[35]

As noted in previous EFA Global Monitoring Reports (UNESCO, 2002a and 2003a), the FTI was conceived initially as a direct response to the commitment made in Dakar that 'no countries seriously committed to education for all will be thwarted in their achievement of this goal by a lack of resources' (UNESCO, 2000a). It has since come to be seen as a test case of the Monterrey Consensus as regards the need to establish new development partnerships to meet the MDGs (United Nations, 2000).

As of 2004, the FTI partnership comprises over thirty multilateral and bilateral agencies and regional development banks, though their levels of engagement vary considerably.[36] It also counts the Global Campaign for Education among its supporters and is seeking to extend its partnership with civil society.

Since its latest meetings, in Oslo (November 2003) and Washington (March 2004),[37] the FTI has acquired greater clarity of intent and a broad base of international support. It is now defined as being global in character and open to all interested funding agencies and low-income countries.[38] It promotes six core aims and will follow five guiding principles (Box 5.11), the latter

---

[35]. 'The Fast Track Initiative (FTI) was designed to address the data, policy, capacity and resource gaps that constrain progress in achieving Education for All. Its implementation has highlighted the potential as well as the challenges associated with scaling up the MDG agenda more generally and in particular, the need for credible, effective and predictable financing in support of adequate policies and programs. The experience of FTI so far has demonstrated that it should be anchored in countries' Poverty Reduction Strategies if it is to be effective. We urged all countries, developed and developing, to take the additional steps required to make this initiative succeed and requested the Bank Board to continue to monitor progress' (World Bank/IMF, 2004).

[36]. The partners are the funding agencies of Australia, Austria, Belgium, Canada, Denmark, Finland, France, Germany, Greece, Ireland, Italy, Japan, the Netherlands, New Zealand, Norway, Portugal, the Russian Federation, Spain, Sweden, Switzerland, the United Kingdom and the United States, along with the European Commission, Asian Development Bank, African Development Bank, DAC-OECD, Inter American Development Bank, UNAIDS, UNDP, UNESCO, UNICEF and the World Bank (World Bank, 2004c).

[37]. The FTI involves three types of regular meetings. Annual partnership meetings (Oslo, 2003; Brasilia, 2004) bring together representatives of the FTI countries, funding agencies and NGOs to give strategic policy direction. Steering Committee meetings involve two co-chairs – one from the G8 Presidency and one from a non-G8 country – plus the World Bank, UNESCO and one outgoing co-chair, to oversee coordination. Funding agency meetings have been instrumental in developing the FTI Framework (World Bank-FTI Secretariat, 2004).

[38]. Low-income refers to the World Bank classification for the determination of IDA eligibility (World Bank-FTI Secretariat, 2004).

> **Box 5.11 Fast-Track Initiative: goals and principles**
>
> ■ **Goals**
>
> The FTI aims to accelerate UPC by promoting:
>
> - **more efficient aid for primary education** through actions of development partners to maximize coordination, complementarities and harmonization in aid delivery and reduce transaction costs for FTI recipient countries;
> - **sustained increases in aid for primary education** where countries demonstrate the ability to utilize it effectively;
> - **sound sector policies in education** through systematic review and indicative benchmarking of recipient countries' education policies and performance;
> - **adequate and sustainable domestic financing for education** within the framework of a national poverty reduction strategy, medium-term expenditure framework or other country statement as appropriate;
> - **increased accountability for sector results** through annual reporting on policy progress and key sector outcomes, using a set of appropriate indicators in participating countries, and sharing of results.
>
> Globally, the FTI also aims to promote:
>
> - **mutual learning on what works** to improve primary education outcomes and advance EFA goals.
>
> ■ **Guiding principles**
>
> - **Country ownership:** The FTI is a country-driven process, with the primary locus of activity and decision-making at the country level. It fosters a long-term development partnership at the country level between the government and other partners, in support of the country's effort to accelerate progress towards EFA goals, focusing on UPC. The FTI presents a framework to further coordination, complementarities and harmonization of partner efforts, in a manner that strengthens country governments' ability to manage their own development process more effectively.
> - **Benchmarking:** The FTI encourages the use of indicative benchmarks (the FTI Indicative Framework) locally adapted to enlighten debate, in-country reporting on policies and performance, and mutual learning on what works to improve primary education outcomes which can provide lessons learned across countries for the acceleration of UPC.
> - **Support linked to performance:** The FTI links increased funding to country performance. It is the first global initiative to operationalize the Monterrey Consensus as a partnership between developing countries and the donor community, at the international and country level. The FTI is intended to provide more sustained, predictable and flexible financial support to countries that have demonstrated commitment to the goal of UPC, have adopted policies in full consideration of a locally adapted FTI Indicative Framework, and have demonstrated a need for, and the capacity to use effectively, incremental external resources.
> - **Lower transaction costs:** The FTI encourages donor actions to provide resources to developing countries in a manner which minimizes the transaction costs for recipient countries. The FTI promotes improved coordination, complementarity and harmonization in donor practices and financing to flexibly support country-owned education-sector strategies. The FTI implies moving towards a sector-wide approach, wherever appropriate, in fast-track countries.
> - **Transparency:** The FTI encourages the open sharing of information on the policies and practices of participating countries and donors alike, through indicative benchmarking, systematic cross-country monitoring, strengthened donor collaboration and harmonization, and making best efforts to provide resources in a predictable and sustained manner.
>
> *Source:* World Bank-FTI Secretariat (2004: 2-3)

being closely aligned with the OECD-DAC objectives on harmonization. The aims are ambitious in their coverage, setting UPC within wider education-sector and poverty-reduction frameworks. They are intended to have an impact equivalent to the indicators of success set out at the beginning of this section on international coordination.

The FTI is conceived as an international partnership designed to support the development and implementation of national education-sector policies through well-coordinated technical and financial support at the country level. Figure 5.11, which is from the FTI Framework Document, shows how the FTI process is intended to add value by supporting the development of national education-sector programmes, monitoring aid flows, enhancing donor coordination and, should it prove necessary, mobilizing additional resources internationally.

Figure 5.11: The EFA-FTI process

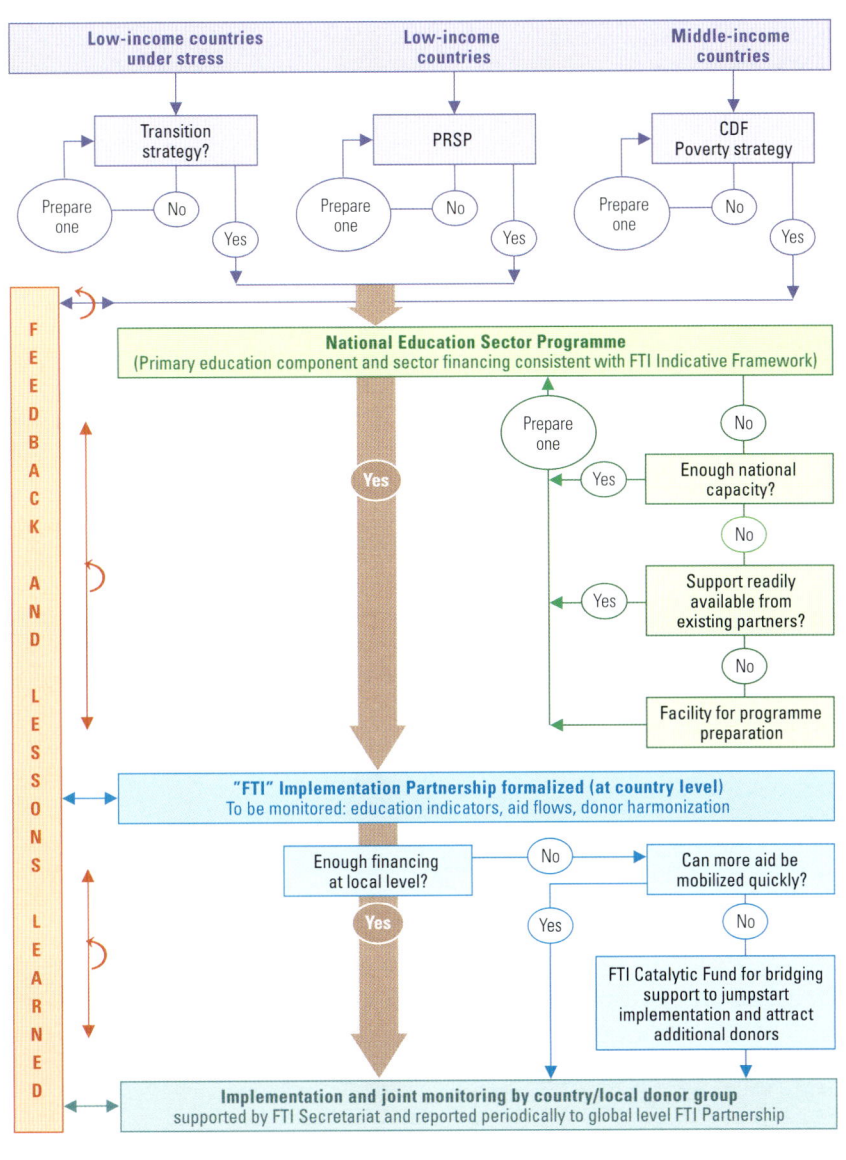

Source: World Bank-FTI Secretariat (2004: 6)

> The FTI needs to be consistent with, and complement, wider international work on donor harmonization

As the Development Committee of the World Bank and IMF has acknowledged, the two-year process that led to agreement of the FTI Framework Document illustrates the challenges involved in giving effect to the principles of the Monterrey Consensus. The FTI demonstrates this in relation to six of its defining characteristics:

- While the FTI has a clear, subsector, *single-goal focus* in UPC (a fact that continues to draw criticism because some see this as too narrow an interpretation of EFA), it also stipulates that policies and strategies designed to attain this goal should be very clearly articulated in national education-sector and poverty-reduction strategies.

- As the FTI supports *donor harmonization* with government policies and programmes,[39] it needs to be consistent with, and complement, wider international work on donor harmonization.

- The FTI is open to all interested agencies and low-income countries but remains a process that

---

39. An FTI working group is to be formed to this end, focusing on SWAps, budget support and financial baseline data, so as to provide a more accurate picture of aid flows in FTI countries.

Table 5.16: Status of countries in relation to FTI, February 2004

Current FTI countries, 2003	Potential FTI countries, 2004	Potential FTI countries, 2005
Burkina Faso Gambia Ghana Guinea Guyana Honduras Mauritania Mozambique Nicaragua Niger Viet Nam Yemen	Albania Armenia Bangladesh Bolivia Cambodia Cameroon Chad D. R. Congo Djibouti Ethiopia Guinea-Bissau India Madagascar Malawi Mali Mongolia Nepal Pakistan Rwanda Senegal Tajikistan U.R. Tanzania Uganda Zambia	Benin Bosnia and Herzegovina Georgia Kenya Lao PDR Lesotho Nigeria Rep. of Moldova Sao Tome and Principe
12	24	9

Note: All the countries in the left hand column of the table have had a PRSP approved and a sector plan endorsed by FTI that takes account of the Indicative Framework and has a mechanism in place that allows FTI to track donor flows of aid to education.
Source: www1.worldbank.org/hdnetwork/efa/PPT/fti%20expansion.ppt.

works on the basis of *eligibility* and *endorsement*. National sector plans and their primary education components are reviewed to determine whether a country is ready to be invited to join the Initiative. Table 5.16 shows that, as of February 2004, twelve countries had been endorsed and thirty-three others could potentially join the Initiative in 2004/5. The FTI's all-encompassing approach will undoubtedly continue to raise expectations on what it will deliver.

■ The FTI is developing frameworks for *country level assessment* and using the Indicative Framework for EFA/Education Sector Plans developed by the World Bank as a key benchmarking tool. This framework (Table 5.17) has been expanded in the past year to take quality and efficiency into account, measuring student flows, hours of instruction and construction cost per classroom. The Indicative Framework has been a significant part of the policy dialogue with the initial FTI countries, though now the emphasis is on applying it flexibly and with attention to context. It will be important to ensure that FTI tools are aids to policy rather than checklists to observe.

■ The FTI provides a new means of identifying and providing *technical support*. One possible development, for instance, is a Facility for Programme Development that would enable countries to undertake preparatory studies, capacity-building and national consultation processes early in the development of education-sector plans. In this regard, the FTI is a new technical facility, but it should avoid duplication of existing technical assistance work in individual countries.

■ The FTI's direct-funding and resource-mobilization role now appears more modest than many developing countries had expected. It has become more a *donor of last resort*, either encouraging agencies working in a country

Table 5.17: Policy benchmarks* for universal primary completion by 2015

Service delivery	Average annual teacher salary Pupil/teacher ratio Non-salary spending Average repetition rate Annual hours of instruction	3.5 x per capita GDP 40:1 33% of recurrent education spending 10% or lower 850–1000 hours
Student flow	Girls' and boys' grade 1 intake rate Girls' and boys' primary completion rate	Trend rate to 100% by 2010 Trend rate to 100% by 2015
System expansion	Construction cost per classroom (furnished and equipped, including sanitation)	US$10,000 or less
System financing	Government revenue Education spending Primary education spending	14%–18% of GDP 20% of government revenue 50% of total education recurrent expenditure

*Benchmarks to be applied flexibly, depending on country circumstances and trend rates towards sustainability by 2015.
Source: World Bank (2004c).

to mobilize additional national and donor resources or drawing the international community's attention to shortfalls.[40] A multi-donor trust fund set up in 2003 finances the FTI Catalytic Fund to help prime the pump of short-term funding and thereby leverage longer-term financing. Expectations as to the resource benefits accruing to FTI countries will need to be met or assuaged.

Recent developments in the FTI point to a real appreciation of the fact that a uniform model of support for UPC and EFA is insufficiently sensitive to context and need. Some donors are growing more amenable to investing modestly in a risk-taking mechanism to provide quick, incremental support to countries whose short-term policy development and programme implementation are blocked by lack of funding. So far, however, there are no signs that the FTI is seen as a channel for major education-aid disbursement.

Remaining questions

Some larger questions remain. While proposals to establish a global fund were rejected in Dakar, the debate on the FTI from its launch in 2002 until Oslo in 2003 focused on the need to assure substantially increased levels of financing for education. Dakar and Monterrey (and the related G8 commitments) raised high expectations in this regard. While some bilateral agencies have responded positively within their existing ODA ceilings, the additional funds raised globally remain far short of the US$5.6 billion per year of additional aid required just to achieve UPE and eliminate gender disparities[41] and do not even cover the immediate needs of the initial FTI countries, as has been noted elsewhere in this chapter.[42] As has been shown, the upturns in overall ODA and in support for basic education are modest and, while initiatives such as the United States's Millennium Challenge Account[43] are welcome additions, it is clear that funding for EFA will continue to fall short. The fact that the World Bank and IMF Development Committee suggested no specific actions finance ministers might take to let the FTI Initiative make a real difference in resource terms underlines this (World Bank/IMF, 2004).[44]

A second question concerns the extent to which the FTI will or can become a framework for all education sector work in developing countries, and the means of approving sector plans. The FTI Framework Document states:

> The FTI encourages a general consensus among in-country donors to endorse a country's sector plan. When the in-country donors are satisfied that key issues have been adequately addressed, the sector plan is considered endorsed for FTI support. The lead donor is requested to ensure the preparation of a report of the conclusions of the review meeting, for the Government and the FTI partnership (through the FTI Secretariat) for broader dissemination and information. (World Bank-FTI Secretariat 2004: 9)

Whether the World Bank and the programming departments of bilateral and other multilateral agencies truly accept this remains unclear. There is a risk of FTI procedures being seen as an additional hoop through which both governments and agencies have to jump, particularly if substantial additional resources do not automatically result. An FTI working group on communications has been set up to ensure that the FTI's purposes and procedures are clearly understood.

Third, questions remain as to whether eligibility criteria will limit the inclusion of countries where

There is a risk of FTI procedures being seen as an additional hoop through which both governments and agencies have to jump

---

40. As of April 2004, the EFA-FTI Catalytic Fund had received US$236 million (from the Netherlands, Norway, Italy and Belgium) for 2004–2007. The fund is intended to provide transitional grant financing for two to three years at most. In 2004, the United Kingdom committed some US$21 million to the Catalytic Fund and a new trust fund to support the FTI Secretariat, which is based at the World Bank. France has also pledged US$100,000 to the Secretariat over two years. All the available money has been used or allocated. In 2003, US$6 million was disbursed to the Niger and US$5 million was committed to Mauritania. For 2004, grant agreements have been signed with Mauritania (US$2 million) and Yemen (US$10 million) and are being finalized with the Niger, the Gambia, Nicaragua and Guyana (a total of US$22 million). Meanwhile, Pakistan, Ghana, Ethiopia and Timor-Leste, among other countries, have requested support from the Catalytic Fund. (World Bank, 2004d; World Bank-FTI Secretariat, 2004; World Bank, 2004c).

41. Existing flows to basic education totalled some US$1.4 billion in 2000. The *EFA Global Monitoring Report 2002* estimated that an additional US$5.6 billion per year was needed to close the gap, making US$7 billion in all (UNESCO, 2002a, Table 5.7).

42. For the first ten countries endorsed for FTI support, the financing gap is estimated at US$204.5 million for 2004 and US$231.5 million for 2005 (World Bank, 2004c).

43. The United States launched the Millennium Challenge Account (MCA) in response to the Monterrey Consensus. The eligible countries exclude Cape Verde and Vanuatu but otherwise there is close correspondence with the FTI-eligible countries. The MCA provides grants to countries that 'rule justly, invest in their people, and encourage economic freedom' (www.mcc.gov). The initial funding for fiscal year 2004 is US$1 billion, and the intent is to increase the amount to US$5 billion by fiscal year 2006. Countries accepted for the FTI may need to develop new proposals for MCA funding.

44. In the recent Copenhagen Consensus meetings, where experts discussed how best to spend US$50 billion on development, no education projects were among the final ranking, and the concluding report stated: 'Experience suggests that it is easy to waste large sums on education initiatives.' This may indicate just how far the arguments for EFA have to extend beyond education circles (Copenhagen Consensus, 2004).

Developing countries continue to ask whether the international community is fulfilling its part of the contract established in Dakar and Monterrey

the EFA challenge is greatest.[45] Catalytic funding to give impetus to new policies may be a good start on addressing this issue. In addition, a stronger focus on integrating primary education plans with wider sector and anti-poverty reforms should help ensure that due attention is paid to systemic reform in the education sector as a whole, not at subsector level alone.

Some developing countries continue to ask nevertheless whether the international community is fulfilling its part of the contract established in Dakar and Monterrey. It remains to be seen whether innovative bridging funding can make a true difference to countries that would otherwise be neglected, whether new ways of assessing policy and measuring progress against benchmark criteria will result in substantive improvements in national practice and whether closer monitoring of aid flows and needs can help spur mobilization of new resources and greater equity in their allocation. But it is clear that the FTI is attempting to respond to the four priorities set out at the beginning of this section and will be judged on its ability to make a difference in all four areas.

UNESCO

The mandate given to UNESCO at the World Education Forum – to continue its role in coordinating EFA partners and in maintaining their collaborative momentum – remains challenging and complex. In a recent strategic review of its post-Dakar role, written for its Executive Board, UNESCO notes that five main areas of activity are at the centre of its current international role (UNESCO, 2004e):

■ broadening and deepening the partnerships and alliances within the EFA movement by bringing in new or under-represented partners (e.g. civil society and the private sector);

■ building consensus;

■ harmonizing the partners' contributions and participation;

■ promoting dialogue on emerging issues;

■ ensuring that the post-Dakar coordination mechanisms are welcoming, useful and effective.

Earlier editions of the *EFA Global Monitoring Report* (UNESCO, 2002a; UNESCO, 2003a) have reflected on various difficulties associated with defining and managing these processes in ways that can make a real difference in progress towards achieving the EFA goals.[46] In its strategic review, UNESCO also recognizes some of the limitations of focusing primarily on dialogue facilitation. It concludes: 'it is increasingly clear that UNESCO's lead co-ordination role needs to be enhanced and needs to be exercised in a more assertive, proactive and creative manner, drawing not only upon UNESCO's Dakar mandate but also its role as the specialized agency for education within the United Nations System' (UNESCO, 2004e: para. 116).

The strategic review can be expected to stimulate debate on UNESCO's opportunities to strengthen its leadership role by developing a stronger, more influential policy voice. This is an important way for UNESCO to enhance its visibility, influence and authority, not only in EFA coordination mechanisms but also in its wider dealings within the United Nations system and vis-à-vis the World Bank, governments, bilateral agencies and civil society.

Strengthening this function will not be without its difficulties. As UNESCO is not a funding agency, it lacks the immediate international leverage and influence of the World Bank and the major bilateral funding agencies, which can more easily command the attention of aid recipients and agencies. UNESCO's influence is likely increasingly to derive from its policy work on strategies for achieving the EFA goals. It brings to this work a dispassionate, evidence-based approach that is not tied to a single issue or a particular political agenda.

In recent years, wherever UNESCO has articulated clear and well-defended policy positions, its standing and influence have been enhanced. Its work on the right to education, on language policy and on education and emergencies, for example, commands respect and influences international practice. The applied research work of the UNESCO Institutes,[47] in areas such as education planning, HIV/AIDS, statistical indicator development, adult education and curriculum analysis, also stands UNESCO in good stead. In addition, innovative work at the regional level on topics such as girls' education,

---

45. This issue was also raised in earlier editions of the *EFA Global Monitoring Report*.

46. One significant recent advance is a move towards greater integration of high-level EFA-related mechanisms. For example, in November 2004 the EFA High-Level Group and the FTI Partners' Group will hold back-to-back meetings in Brasilia, and may eventually establish a single planning mechanism.

47. These include the UNESCO Institute for Statistics in Montreal, the International Institute for Educational Planning in Paris, the International Bureau of Education in Geneva and the UNESCO Institute for Education in Hamburg.

health and education and the educational needs of minorities has influenced government policies and programmes.[48]

Other types of policy work could further enhance UNESCO's ability to command international attention in world forums and strengthen its ability to promote better EFA policy coordination. Among these are the articulation and analysis of national and international strategies for EFA, including work on investment choices, on overall sector planning, on the governance and efficient use of resources for education and on further demonstration of the links between education and broader policies for social and economic development.

In this context, UNESCO's role as guardian of the international EFA agenda is significant. UNESCO rightly emphasizes that programmes driven solely by the need to achieve UPE provide insufficient response to the Dakar goals. But much further work is needed to demonstrate how governments can best develop broad sector strategies to meet all the EFA goals, as well as frameworks for the necessary expenditure. In much of the world, the financing of EFA remains uncharted territory. Related issues include better identification of synergies within the education sector and between basic education and poverty reduction. The rhetoric of partnerships for better education is often not backed up by sound analysis of what makes them work. Changes in the modalities of aid and its coordination receive scrutiny mainly by aid agencies themselves rather than from a more neutral external standpoint. More immediately, UNESCO's leadership role in the United Nations decades for literacy (from 2003) and education for sustainable development (from 2005) gives it a chance to initiate high-profile work in two significant policy arenas. These and other strategic issues offer fertile ground for a new policy agenda.

Some recent examples of influential international policy work illustrate the potential benefits. UNICEF's promotion of 'adjustment with a human face' (Cornia, Jolly and Stewart, 1987) was based on high-quality analysis that ran counter to what was then the conventional wisdom at the World Bank and IMF. UNICEF became influential in the adjustment debate internationally, even though it had relatively few core staff members working exclusively on policy

analysis. Similarly, the United Nations Development Programme, through its Human Development Report, has become an influential voice in the development debate, although it started from what was arguably a less promising basis for effective prognosis than that of UNESCO. More recently, the World Bank's work developing policy benchmarks in its Indicative Framework for achieving universal primary completion has been both influential and controversial in international debate, especially in countries seeking assistance via the FTI.

In each of these cases, expertise from both within and outside the respective agencies was brought together in ways that enabled dedicated work to be done on major issues of international development policy. UNESCO can harness expertise in Paris, at its Institutes and in its regional and cluster offices to direct and carry out such work. It can also draw upon an extraordinary diversity of international networks and research bodies. Thus, it clearly has a very real opportunity to undertake policy work that could not only be highly significant and influential in its own right, but could also strengthen UNESCO's international EFA coordination role substantially, enable the organization to be more proactive in such endeavours as the FTI working groups and enhance its own technical programmes at the regional and country levels. The benefits of cultivating a core capacity for work on macro-level policy issues, and of pursuing an organization-wide approach to international coordination, could produce significant dividends for UNESCO and for the international community more generally.

Other international activities

EFA Flagships
The nine initiatives known as EFA Flagships[49] constituted the main theme of the fourth meeting of the EFA Working Group, held in Paris in 2003 (UNESCO, 2004c). A booklet published after the meeting defined a flagship initiative as a structured set of activities, carried out by voluntary partners under the leadership of one or more of the United Nations specialized agencies, to address specific challenges in achieving the EFA goals (UNESCO, 2004d).

Some flagships have been seeking recently to strengthen their mandates and working

United Nations decades for literacy (from 2003) and education for sustainable development (from 2005) offer fertile ground for a new policy agenda

48. One example is the work of UNESCO-Bangkok on HIV/AIDS and school health.

49. The Initiative on the Impact of HIV/AIDS on Education; Early Childhood Care and Education; the Right to Education of Persons with Disabilities: Towards Inclusion; Education for Rural People; Education in Situations of Emergency and Crisis; Focusing Resources on Effective School Health (FRESH); Teachers and the Quality of Education; the ten-year United Nations Girls Education Initiative (UNGEI) and Literacy in the Framework of the United Nations Literacy Decade.

methods. The International Labour Office, UNESCO and Education International reached a Memorandum of Agreement defining their respective roles and responsibilities on Teachers and the Quality of Education. UNICEF established an international advisory group on improving integration of the United Nations Girls' Education Initiative (UNGEI) activities with national and regional programmes, and is preparing to mark 2005 as gender parity year. The initiative designed to accelerate the education sector response to HIV/AIDS in Africa has been supporting the development of plans and follow-up actions at subregional and national level (e.g. in Gabon in May 2003; Abuja and Ondo, Nigeria, June 2003; Mozambique, February 2004; and Ethiopia, February 2004). An informal consultation of United Nations agencies working on disability and education was convened in March 2004.

As the booklet on flagships notes, it is too early to judge the impact of these nine initiatives, but eventually their added value should be assessed through the range of activities undertaken at country level, their appropriation by governments and their synchronization or integration with national priorities and wider development frameworks.

E-9 Initiative

The E-9 Initiative[50] was revitalized in 2003, ten years after its launch. The nine countries (Bangladesh, Brazil, China, Egypt, India, Indonesia, Mexico, Nigeria and Pakistan) originally came together with support from UNESCO, UNICEF, the United Nations Population Fund and the World Bank to promote political commitment for EFA after Jomtien, to facilitate information exchange and to mobilize aid. Together these countries account for over 71% of the world's adult illiterates and more than half of its out-of-school children. After an evaluation concluded that there was a lack of ownership of the initiative among its member countries and little sign of donor support (Bibeau, Kester-McNees and Reddy, 2003), it was agreed to establish a focal point in each country to coordinate E-9 activities and ensure that clear links exisited with other international EFA mechanisms, such as the High-Level Group and the Working Group on EFA, the FTI and the EFA Flagships (E-9, 2003). It was also agreed to re-energize technical cooperation in specific areas and the sharing of best practices and to encourage involvement by other partners, such as civil society organizations and the private sector. UNESCO was directed to lead the coordination of donor partners.

Other forums

In October 2003, education ministers from 53 Commonwealth countries representing 1.7 billion people agreed the Edinburgh Action Plan,[51] which, among other provisions, encourages countries to share their understanding of what constitutes an 'excellent education system.' In May 2004, at a forum organized by the Southeast Asian Ministers of Education Organization, UNESCO and UNICEF, ten education ministers from South-East Asian countries endorsed the Bangkok Declaration, reaffirming their commitment to a shared vision of quality and equity in education and a determination to promote a comprehensive definition of quality within their systems.[52] At the Arab Regional Conference on Education for All, held in Beirut in January 2004, all participating countries reaffirmed their commitment to the Arab Framework for Action adopted in Cairo in 2000 (UNESCO, 2000a).The participating countries also adopted a platform of action at the state, regional and international levels and identified high-priority projects in individual countries that deserve international support (UNESCO-Beirut, 2004b).

Conclusion

International efforts to improve coordination for EFA remain focused on mechanisms and initiatives. Some progress has been made but it is not yet commensurate with the challenge, especially in translating international dialogue into national action. Galvanizing political will and commitment in all nations, which lies at the heart of the Dakar Framework for Action, remains the most pressing need.

> Galvanizing political will and commitment in all nations, which lies at the heart of the Dakar Framework for Action, remains the most pressing need

---

50. See www.unesco.org/education/e9/initiative

51. See www.thecommonwealth.org/Templates/STPDInternal.asp

52. *Bangkok Post*, 30 May 2004.

Students call for better quality during a demonstration in front of the Ministry of Education in Honduras (2002)

Chapter 6

Towards EFA: the quality imperative

Whether a particular education system is of high or low quality can be judged only in terms of the extent to which its objectives are being met. Evaluations will consequently differ according to whose objectives are deemed decisive. Those of governments, international organizations, non-governmental organizations, teachers, families and pupils are by no means always in accord. For most of these groups, however, the objectives of education include at least two elements. First, the improvement of cognitive skills is a consistent and universal aim of education systems. Second, all societies intend education to promote behavioural traits, attitudes and values that are judged necessary for good citizenship and effective life in the community. The sets of non-cognitive skills required differ by culture and by level of development. Accordingly, some important aspects of education quality are always rooted in the local context.

Education systems that lack a strong, clear respect for human rights cannot be said to be of high quality

Some attributes of a high-quality learning process have achieved independent status as part of the definition of education quality. Most centrally, these can be summarized as the need for education systems to be equitable, inclusive and relevant to local circumstances. Where the access to or the process of education is characterized by gender inequality, or by discrimination against particular groups on ethnic or cultural grounds, the rights of individuals and groups are ignored. Thus, education systems that lack a strong, clear respect for human rights cannot be said to be of high quality. By the same token, any shift towards equity is an improvement in quality.

The status of other aspects of the education process is more contested. Despite the near universal agreement as to what cognitive skills comprise, they are not entirely culturally neutral. Moreover, there remains great debate about how they can best be taught and learned. For example, while most if not all experts judge rote learning to be indicative of poor-quality education, there is debate between those in favour of structured instruction and advocates of more child-centred approaches. In principle, such questions can be settled empirically – by investigating, for example, which methods of class organization and teaching behaviour work best in different contexts. Yet, the evidence is often more ambiguous than we would wish. The question is even more complex in adult learning.

Overall, however, judgements about the quality of education depend upon how it performs intrinsically, as a process, and upon its effectiveness in forming desired cognitive and non-cognitive skills. This final chapter brings together the major arguments and evidence on these questions presented in this Report and asks what implications they have for the prospects of improving the quality of education, particularly in lower-income countries. First, however, the state of progress towards each of the EFA goals is briefly assessed.

Progress towards the EFA goals

The Education for All Development Index (EDI) provides a summary quantitative measure of the extent to which different countries are meeting four of the six EFA goals: universal primary education (UPE), gender parity, literacy and quality.[1] It shows that massive educational deprivation continues to be concentrated in sub-Saharan Africa, some of the Arab States and South and West Asia. Significant efforts are still required to reach the goals in Latin America and the Caribbean, East Asia and the Pacific and Central Asia; meanwhile, most countries of North America and Western Europe and of Central and Eastern Europe have already reached the goals or are close. Progress between 1998 and 2001 was widespread but not universal: about three-quarters of the seventy-four countries with available data for both years registered an increase in their index value. Moreover, for the seventy-four countries as a group, the average gain in the EDI over the period was modest, at just over 2%. On the other hand, some low-income countries that are still far from achieving EFA saw strong gains of 15% or more, with improvements in each of the measured goals in some cases. This demonstrates that rapid progress towards EFA can be made – even in the poorest countries – given commitment and appropriate policies.

Goal 1 – ECCE. Progress since 1998 in the provision of early childhood care and education has been slow and took place mainly in countries with already significant levels of enrolment. Average stay in ECCE programmes ranges from 0.3 years in sub-Saharan Africa to 2.2 years in North America and Western Europe. It is less than a year in most developing countries outside Latin America and the Caribbean.

Goal 2 – UPE. The expansion of schooling is translating into a slow reduction of the number of out-of-school children in the primary-school age group, from 106.7 million in 1998 to 103.5 million in 2001. This is insufficient to achieve UPE by 2015. Indeed, out of the 100-plus countries that had data for both gross enrolment ratio (GER) and net enrolment ratio (NER) and had NERs below 95%, over forty combined GERs below 100% with NERs below 90%, which points to a need to increase the capacity of their school systems. Half a dozen sub-Saharan African countries still have NERs below 50%. There has been some convergence, however, with NERs generally increasing in cases where they had been below 70% in 1990. Meanwhile, the completion of primary schooling remains a major

1. Where not otherwise specified, figures refer to 2001.

cause for concern: delayed enrolment is widespread, survival rates to grade 5 are low (below 75% in thirty of the ninety-one countries with the relevant data) and grade repetition is frequent (in 2001 more than 10% of students were repeating a grade in a third of the eighty-one countries with data).

Goal 3 – Life Skills. Skills development is a crucial link between education and economy. While it is difficult to monitor globally, country experience shows that investments and participation in this area are low if not marginal and that provision is highly diverse.

Goal 4 – Literacy. Nearly 800 million adults – 18% of the world's adult population – were illiterate as of 2002. Some 70% of adult illiterates lived in just nine countries, led by India (33%), China (11%), Bangladesh (7%) and Pakistan (6%). Realization of EFA goal 4 crucially depends on policies implemented in those four countries. Both India and China registered significant progress over the 1990s.

Goal 5 – Gender. Enrolment and performance disparities detrimental to girls and women are still pervasive. Almost two-thirds of the world's adult illiterates (64%) are women. The gender parity index for primary schooling is 0.63 in South and West Asia, 0.69 in the Arab States and 0.77 in sub-Saharan Africa. The situation is slowly improving, although progress over the 1990s was very uneven: by 2001, 57% of out-of-school children of primary school age were girls (more than 60% in the Arab States and South and West Asia), as against 60% in 1998 and seventy-one of the 175 countries with data available still had a GPI in primary GER below 0.97. Girls enrolled in primary schools have higher survival rates than boys but are less present in secondary education. The disparities between the sexes are more extreme in secondary and in higher education. Of eighty-three developing countries with available data, half had achieved parity in primary GER by 2001, less than one-fifth had achieved it at secondary level and only four had in tertiary education.

Goal 6 – Quality. Progress towards better quality in education is assessed (Chapter 3) by examining trends in the resources available to schools, in the availability of teachers and in learning achievements as measured by tests of cognitive skills. As regards the first two,[2] one important conclusion is that, over the long term, quantity and quality in education are complements rather than substitutes: the countries that are farthest from achieving quantitative goals 1 to 5 are also farthest from achieving qualitative goal 6. Nevertheless, low-enrolment countries may experience dynamic trade-offs between expanding coverage and improving quality, or between various elements of quality.

Public expenditure on education represents a higher proportion of GDP in rich countries that have achieved EFA goals (the regional median for North America and Western Europe is 5.2%) than in poorer countries that need to expand already under-resourced school systems of insufficient coverage (the equivalent proportion is 4.1% in India and the regional medians are 3.3% in sub-Saharan Africa and 3.9% in East Asia and the Pacific). Changes between 1998 and 2001 showed no particular trend: government expenditure either dramatically increased or decreased in several developing countries.

Correspondingly, pupil/teacher ratios (PTRs) are low where enrolment is high (North America and Western Europe, Central and Eastern Europe and Central Asia have PTRs of less than 20:1) and high where enrolment is low, especially in sub-Saharan Africa and South and West Asia. PTRs in those regions are typically above 35:1, and in several African countries above 55:1. The regional median for sub-Saharan Africa increased from 40:1 to 44:1 between 1990 and 2001, while that for South and West Asia was stable at around 40:1. Some countries, especially in southern Africa, face the additional challenge of the AIDS pandemic. For example, over 800 primary-school teachers died of AIDS in Zambia in 2000, equivalent to half the total number of new teachers trained that year.

The quality of teachers, which is crucial, remains insufficient in many developing countries. The qualifications required to become a government primary-school teacher vary quite widely – for example, from twelve to seventeen years of education in twenty-six sub-Saharan African countries – and they are often not met. Furthermore, the distribution of teachers is very unequal within countries, since disadvantaged areas typically receive those with less training.

Quantity and quality in education are complements rather than substitutes

2. The third is returned to in a later section.

Formal qualifications, however, matter less than the skills and behaviour of teachers; there is evidence that insufficient mastery of curricula and absenteeism are widespread in many parts of the world.

What is an education of good quality worth?

There is good evidence that the benefits of education to individuals and society are enhanced when its quality is high. For example, better learning outcomes – as represented by pupils' achievement test scores – are closely related to higher earnings in the labour market; thus, differences in quality are likely to indicate differences in individual worker productivity. Furthermore, the wage impact of education quality appears to be stronger for workers in developing countries than for those in more industrialized societies. Empirical research has also demonstrated that good schooling improves national economic potential – the quality of the labour force, again as measured by test scores, appears to be an important determinant of economic growth, and thus of the ability of governments to alleviate poverty.

Benefits do not arise only from the cognitive development that education brings. It is clear that honesty, reliability, determination, leadership ability and willingness to work within the hierarchies of modern life are all characteristics that society rewards. These skills are, in part, formed and nourished by schools. Similarly, evidence shows that bright but undisciplined male school drop-outs who lack persistence and reliability earn less than others with the same levels of ability and cognitive achievement, and will continue to do so beyond school. Schools that encourage the above characteristics more successfully than others will bring greater long-term earnings benefits to the individuals who attend them. Schools also try to encourage creativity, originality and intolerance of injustice – non-cognitive skills that can help people challenge and transform society's hierarchies rather than accept them. These, too, are important results of good schooling, having broader benefits for society, irrespective of their impact on personal earnings.

Good quality in education also affects other aspects of individual behaviour in ways that bring strong social benefits. It is well known, for example, that the acquisition of literacy and numeracy, especially by women, has an impact upon fertility behaviour. More recently it has become clear that the cognitive skills required to make informed choices about HIV/AIDS risk and behaviour are strongly related to levels of education and literacy. For example, HIV/AIDS incidence in Uganda has fallen substantially in recent years for those with some primary or secondary education, whereas infection rates have remained unchanged for those with no schooling. It seems that the higher levels of cognitive achievement fostered by better schools enhance the skills required to process and respond to information about HIV/AIDS from a wide variety of sources.

Higher cognitive achievement is also strongly correlated with the likelihood of staying in school longer. Thus, higher-quality schools and school systems tend to have lower rates of dropout and repetition than others. The potential benefit is not insignificant: for schools that are dysfunctional and have high rates of grade repetition, some improvements in school quality may be largely self-financing because they reduce the average time completers spend in school.

In all these ways, the quality of education influences the speed with which societies become richer and the extent to which individuals can improve their own personal efficacy, productivity and incomes, as well as the ways in which society can become more equitable and less vulnerable to disease and ill health. Accordingly, the quality of education makes a significant difference to the prospects of achieving a wide range of individual and development goals.

Quantity alone is not enough

From a policy perspective, one fundamental reason why focusing simply upon the quantitative UPE goals will not deliver EFA is that in many parts of the world an enormous gap exists between the numbers graduating from schools and those among them who have managed to master a minimum set of cognitive skills. In these circumstances, given the demonstrable link between cognitive achievement and many of the benefits of basic education, schooling does not benefit a large proportion of those who attend.

National and international assessments show that performance levels are very weak in low- and middle-income countries. In seven southern African countries included in the SACMEQ study (1995–98), between 1% and 37% of tested grade-6 students reached the 'desirable' level in reading and between 22% and 65% reached the 'minimum' level. Six of these countries repeated the survey in 2000/2001 and three of them found that achievement levels had fallen significantly. In six countries of French-speaking Africa covered in the PASEC study (1996–2001), 14% to 43% of grade-5 pupils had 'low' achievement in either French or mathematics. In seven low- and middle-income countries included in PIRLS (2001), between 44% and 84% of grade-4 pupils scored in the bottom quartile of the International Reading Literacy Scale, compared with between 2% and 23% in eleven high-income countries. Finally, the PISA study (2000–02), covering thirty-five high- and middle-income countries, showed that 18% of 15-year-olds scored at or below 'level 1' in reading literacy, which indicates very limited reading skills. Regional and socio-economic disparities are pervasive within the countries concerned.

Table 6.1 illustrates the scale of this problem for a group of African countries and one country in Latin America. It shows that, while NERs in many of them are high, only a small proportion of school leavers have achieved minimum mastery levels as defined by their own national governments. Thus, for example, in Malawi, where about 90% of children attended primary school in the mid-1990s, only about 30% stayed in school to grade 5, and as few as 7% achieved the minimum acceptable reading standards in grade 6. The fact that the NER in Malawi at the time was close to 70% seems rather irrelevant to whether the average child was benefiting in a minimally acceptable way from attending primary school. Although Malawi is something of an extreme case, on average for the countries shown, fewer than one-third of children achieved minimum mastery levels in grades 4 to 6, although the average NER for the countries was 65%. A policy aimed exclusively at pushing net enrolment towards 100 in these countries could, at least in the short term, ignore the learning needs of those who attend, and thereby entail the loss, for a substantial majority of children, of

National and international assessments show that performance levels are very weak in low- and middle-income countries

Table 6.1: Quantitative versus qualitative indicators of participation in primary schooling

Study	Country	Cohort	% ever enrolled (ages 6-14)[1]	% that survived to grade 5[2]	% that achieved minimum mastery[3]	NER in primary for the period before the test[4]
SACMEQ (1995) Grade 6 reading test	Malawi	100	91	31 (34)	7 (22)	69
	Mauritius	100	99	98 (99)	52 (53)	99
	Namibia	100	97	74 (76)	19 (26)	84
	U. R. Tanzania	100	87	70 (81)	18 (26)	54
PIRLS (2001) Grade 4 reading test	Colombia	100	98	60 (61)	27 (45)	87
	Morocco	100	99	77 (78)	59 (77)	81
PASEC (mid-1990s) Grade 5 French test	Burkina Faso	100	35	25 (72)	21 (83)	28
	Cameroon	100	88	45 (51)	33 (73)	73
	Côte d'Ivoire	100	65	45 (70)	38 (84)	49
	Guinea	100	48	32 (66)	21 (65)	36
	Madagascar	100	78	31 (40)	20 (64)	63
	Senegal	100	48	42 (87)	25 (59)	51
	Togo	100	82	49 (60)	40 (81)	66

Notes and sources:
1. Data are for the year closest to the test year in each country. World Bank, 2004.
2. The percentage of the cohort that survived to grade 5 is calculated by multiplying survival rates to grade 5 (in brackets) by the percentage of children ever enrolled. Survival rates are taken from the EFA Assessment 2000 CD-ROM for SACMEQ I and PASEC, for the year of the test or the closest to it, and the Statistical annex, Table 7, for PIRLS.
3. The percentage that achieved mastery is calculated by multiplying the percentage of children in the study who achieved the minimum standards (in brackets) by the percentage of children who survived to grade 5. The criteria for considering a student to have achieved minimum standards is different in each study, so the results are not comparable (see Box 3.7). For SACMEQ I countries, data are from Kulpoo (1998), Machingaidze, Pfukani and Shumba (1998), Milner et al. (2001), Nassor and Mohammed (1998), Nkamba and Kanyika (1998), Nzomo, Kariuki and Guantai (2001) and Voigts (1998). For PASEC and PIRLS countries, data are from Bernard (2003) and Mullis et al. (2003), respectively.
4. The averages were calculated for each country using the years available. For SACMEQ I and PASEC countries, data are from the EFA Assessment 2000 CD-ROM; for PIRLS countries, data are from the Statistical annex, Table 5.

> The learning process is very complicated, but at its centre is the relationship between learners and teachers

some of the most important benefits of school attendance.

The main determinants of better quality in education

Identifying the best ways of improving learning outcomes is not easy, and it has been tackled in many different ways. The learning process is very complicated, but at its centre is the relationship between learners and teachers. Learning is smoother where there is close correspondence between the values and objectives of both of these groups. However, the relationship is strongly conditioned by the resources available to schools, by their curriculum objectives and by the teaching practices followed. The evidence reviewed in this Report provides general guidance on these matters, which is confirmed by results from several different research approaches.

No general theory as to what determines the quality of education has been validated by empirical research. Many approaches in the economic tradition have assumed that there is a workable analogy between schools and factories, in the sense that a set of inputs to schooling is transformed by teachers and pupils into a set of outputs in a fairly uniform way. However, attempts to assess the extent to which changing the mix of inputs affects the outputs, so as to identify the most cost-effective policy levers for quality improvement, have often proved inconclusive.

The results for the more developed economies, where data are more generally available, suggest that increasing resources for schools sometimes helps, but that often it apparently does not. In many OECD countries, test scores have not significantly increased for decades, despite large increases in real per-pupil spending. This is partly because those societies have become richer over time, and the expenditure increases partly reflect the consequent increase in real earnings in the education sector. It is likely that the earnings of education workers, relative to those of other professions (the ratio has declined in many cases), are more intrinsically related to changes in productivity in the sector. The law of diminishing returns probably plays a role as well, once certain levels of resourcing (and, perhaps, of average cognitive achievement) have been reached.

In the case of developing countries, the results appear to be more positive: a majority of studies in which significant relationships are found suggest that cognitive achievement, as measured by standardized tests, increases as school expenditure, teacher education and school facilities are enhanced. As one would expect, in low-income environments where resources are scarce, additional inputs appear to have an effect. There are few uncontested results even here, however, and the technical problems involved in interpreting them are considerable.

Other evidence from a growing body of experimental studies does demonstrate much stronger links between school resources and performance, however. Increasingly such studies are being conducted in low-income countries. They show that levels of cognitive achievement are significantly improved by provision of textbooks and other pedagogic materials (Kenya, the Philippines), by reductions in class size (India, Israel, South Africa) and by provision of child-friendly remedial education by locally recruited parateachers (India). These studies are methodologically superior to those in the 'production function' tradition discussed above. They offer grounds for believing that resources are extremely important to the quality of schooling, particularly in resource-poor circumstances.

Schools are definitely not factories producing outputs according to recipe in a technically deterministic way. Crucial to their effectiveness is the education process itself, in which teachers and pupils use the available inputs and interact with each other in creative ways. A strong research tradition, recognizing this fact, has studied the education process, particularly in schools, with a view to identifying, and learning from, success.

Such 'school effectiveness' research shows that successful primary schools are typically characterized by strong leadership, an orderly school and classroom environment and teachers who focus on the basics of the curriculum, hold high expectations of their students' potential and performance and provide them with frequent assessment and feedback. In richer countries, these studies explain a relatively small proportion of the variation in cognitive achievement. For developing countries, however, the results are stronger; they emphasize that structured instruction, face-to-face instructional time, the adequacy of textbooks and other materials, and teacher quality are factors that help account for higher student performance.

As regards teachers themselves, the evidence shows that how they spend their time has a major effect on learning outcomes. Monitoring how well students are progressing requires time and energy in the classroom, beyond the time spent teaching. Ability grouping by whole classes is ineffective, particularly for less able children, but grouping for the specific skill being taught works well for all children, particularly in reading and mathematics. Teachers' subject mastery and verbal skills, their expectations of students and their own passion for learning are significant factors for school quality.

Other evidence from 'instructional effectiveness' research confirms these results. It suggests that structured teaching methods, bringing a strongly ordered approach to learning tasks – with clear learning goals, sequenced introduction to new material, clear explanations, regular checking of understanding, time for pupils to practise new skills, completion of learning tasks and frequent testing and feedback – are helpful ingredients in strategies for quality improvement and reform.

These factors add up to an ambitious programme for reform, particularly in low-income countries where class sizes are large and teachers often have scarcely more formal education than their pupils. Nevertheless, some countries have put all, or most, into effect, with a significant impact on the quality of learning in their schools. Studies of country experience suggest that common to these successes was the central importance assigned to the quality of the teaching profession – its training, support, recruitment standards and pay – relative to other professional groups. These countries' experience also suggests that successful qualitative reforms require a strong leading role by the government. Each case showed a continuity of policy over several decades, remaining stable even when regimes changed. Thus, a robust long-term vision for education, with quality as a persistent theme, appears to be a vital ingredient. The ways of building such commitment are context-specific; they cannot be universalized in any helpful way. Nevertheless, study of best-practice approaches at a more micro level leads to many insights. These are addressed in the next section, which aims to describe key opportunities to improve education quality in ways relevant to the world's poorest nations.

Policies for improved learning

Judging by their broad statements of education policy, most governments recognize the importance of improving the quality of education. Most are also under pressure from students, parents, employers and educators not only to expand educational opportunities, but also to make educational institutions and programmes work better. However, governments of low-income countries, and others working within severe resource constraints, face difficult choices. Where enrolments are low, responding to expansionary pressures with a 'more of the same' model may further constrain resource availability. Moreover, the human, material and financial costs of treating quality improvement in an integrated and comprehensive manner – as advocated in this Report – may prove burdensome. Shortage of funds, the limited capacity of systems and institutions to manage change effectively, the myriad constraints on teacher effectiveness and the absence of a strong political alliance supporting quality in education can constitute major barriers to change. As this Report demonstrates, however, much can be achieved by making better use of existing resources and focusing on targeted interventions that respond to specific weaknesses.

This is not an argument, however, for neglecting the broader vision of education of good quality. Specific policies can be articulated within a medium-term framework that highlights the rights of all learners to a basic education of good quality. Schools are at the heart of the institutional map of education, and a vision of what makes a good school is important, even if achieving the ideal for all takes time.

One approach is to define a minimum package of essentials – an entitlement that every learner and every school has the right to expect. The

Teachers' subject mastery and verbal skills, their expectations of students and their own passion for learning are significant factors for school quality

Better organization and management of existing resources can yield great gains

evidence of this Report suggests that such a package should include a commitment to provide a stated minimum of instructional time for each pupil or student, a safe and healthy place in which to learn, individual access to learning materials, and teachers who have mastered content and pedagogy. Each of these requirements has resource implications, but better organization and management of existing resources can yield great gains. Placing specific values on these benchmarks might involve minimum instructional time of 850-1,000 hours per year; basic safety and health standards for each school, associated with the provision of particular school facilities; agreed time frames for improving standards of textbook provision and revised standards of competency for teachers.

An emphasis on minimum standards, however, can restrict more innovative activities emerging from a given context. Taking this risk into account, the following seven action points suggest priorities for policy that are not necessarily beyond the reach of the most resource-constrained countries that are farthest from EFA.

First, in many countries, present styles and methods of teaching are not serving children well. Pedagogy needs to respond to cultural and classroom contexts. Structured approaches to teaching, as defined above, are not at odds with a child-friendly learning environment. Where such approaches are introduced, reforms to teacher training and school management will usually be required. Pedagogically sound language policy – allowing children to learn in their mother tongue for at least their first few school years – is particularly important.

Second, investment in teachers is critical. It is clear that teachers' subject knowledge is a key factor in their effectiveness. Paying more attention to recruitment practice, by emphasizing talents and motivation as criteria alongside formal educational attainment, also pays dividends. Traditional, institutional pre-service training is less effective than school-based pre- and in-service training. Teachers' pay and conditions of service are a fundamental determinant of their status in society and of their incentives to join and remain in the profession. Teacher absenteeism, a major problem in many countries, usually indicates that these are too low. In some cases the problem can be lessened through better central support for the management and supervision of schools and more timely payment of salaries. In others, closer management of the allocation of teachers among schools and districts can allow increases in average PTRs at little cost to quality. Double-shift arrangements and the use of locally recruited, highly motivated parateachers can provide a boost to quality at relatively low cost in some circumstances.

Third, the quality and availability of learning materials strongly affect what teachers can do. National book policies can usefully provide a framework for the growth and development of local publishers and enable schools to choose which books they use. Gains can be made by managing students' use of books in schools better and helping teachers use books well in support of learning.

Fourth, those who work in and with schools need help to find their own solutions to improving quality. Schools can be given greater freedom provided that accountability frameworks are well defined. Head teachers and principals are critically important to this endeavour. The nature of their leadership can influence the quality of schools strongly. Community leaders and others providing support to schools at local and district levels can also help to give leadership and direction. Decentralization can provide greater scope for schools to attract additional resources, both financial and in-kind, though in low-income contexts especially this can involve a heavy risk of regressive patterns in school quality, where poorer communities have poorer schools. Generally, accountability at the school level needs to be mirrored by greater central accountability. Governments should increasingly publish information on expenditure and resource levels in education, disaggregated to district level and made available locally. Examples are indicators of pupil/teacher ratios, textbook provision and expenditure per student. Such information provides an important means of strengthening the political voice of the poor and improving their potential access to educational resources.

Fifth, relationships among different parts and aspects of the education sector, which the compartmentalized machinery of government may obscure or ignore, can be exploited to help improve quality. ECCE helps with subsequent achievement in school and further lifelong learning. Literacy improves adults' commitment to their children's education, in addition to being desirable in its own right. Gender-sensitive policies in education and more broadly based gender reforms in society directly improve the quality of education and its outcomes. While few governments invest heavily in these areas, a policy environment that enables changes to occur in these areas can strongly support the quality of education at an affordable cost.

Sixth, the existence of special needs in education often needs to be more strongly acknowledged. Uniform models of reform, which ignore the multiple disadvantages many people face, will fail. Useful educational approaches for those who live with HIV/AIDS, emergency, disability and child labour are emerging, and need to be given more support.

Finally, knowledge can make a major difference to the quality of education. Many initiatives require research and/or knowledge that is specific to context and local circumstances. It can often be generated by those who work in the locality or region. Investment in services, networks and structures designed to develop and share educational knowledge can yield significant returns, by enabling schools to make much better use of limited resources.

Although policy reform is not without cost in any of the above areas, much can be achieved in each, given a strong commitment to improve education quality in these ways. It is clear from the evidence in this Report that many countries are not yet able to obtain the human development and economic benefits ascribed to better learning outcomes. In these countries and elsewhere, the scope for improving the quality of learning is enormous. Creating consensus around quality is both a first step and a primary political requirement. It is in that sequence and context that the resource requirements in each society can best be addressed.

International dimensions

Recent estimates of the additional resources likely to be forthcoming in the follow-up to Monterrey, together with those that may arise from the proposed International Finance Facility and through the US Millennium Challenge Account, suggest that total aid to basic education might be expected roughly to double by 2006, to between about US$3 billion and US$3.5 billion. Though the increase is substantial, this remains well short of the roughly US$7 billion per year in external aid to basic education that is likely to be required through to 2015[3] if the EFA goals for universal participation in primary education of a reasonable quality are to be achieved, let alone the other EFA goals. The likely shortage of resources places a particular premium on ensuring that aid is used as effectively as possible and that it is directed towards the countries that most need it.

How, then, can aid better support quality in education? All agencies providing aid for education clearly want to achieve a mix of quantitative and qualitative goals. No one is unconcerned with quality. Nevertheless, the objective of improving education quality is often not well served by aid. This situation has two main dimensions. First, excessive fragmentation of aid programmes, from the point of view of recipients, often involves such high transaction costs that the benefits of the potential transfer of resources can be undermined. Donors often have political reasons for maintaining relationships with large numbers of recipients, many of whom may receive relatively small amounts of aid, but it is unlikely that such justification helps improve the quality of the assistance provided – to education or other sectors. Substantially reducing the average number of countries receiving bilateral aid[4] to education, from the present level of over sixty per donor, would strengthen the quality of aid support. Addressing this issue would require collective attention to which countries are being supported by which donors and to what extent. It would also increase the pressure on agencies to work together to coordinate their aid programming. The potential benefits in terms of efficiency of aid use are clear, however. Some such rationalization of patterns of support needs to be incorporated in the medium-term objectives of the aid community.

The other important dimension of the current situation involves external models of good practice in education, advocated without any

Excessive fragmentation of aid programmes often involves such high transaction costs that the benefits can be undermined

---

3. Existing flows to basic education total some US$1.5 billion per year, and an estimated US$ 5.6 billion of additional resources is needed annually over the period to 2015 to achieve universal participation in primary education, gender parity and enhanced quality, making US$7 billion in all. See Chapter 5 and UNESCO (2002*a*).

4. That is, aid from twenty-one of the member countries of the OECD Development Assistance Committee.

Although external assistance can help, it cannot make up for the absence of a societal project for improving education

particular consistency by different groups of agencies, and often found to be insufficiently attuned to local circumstances. There is evidence, however, that the increasing use of sector-wide approaches is helping increase consistency and reduce underperformance of aid. Such approaches also seem to help strengthen national ownership of aid-supported educational programmes and thus improve the sense of partnership between aid agencies and recipient governments. On the other hand, the shift away from project approaches has increased the amount of policy dialogue required and the number of conditions attached to aid. These circumstances can challenge local ownership of the process, enhance the need for donor coordination and slow the pace of implementation, particularly where government financial management is weak. For all these reasons, the impact of aid on education quality has not yet been markedly positive.

Clear benefits can be gained from the further development of sector approaches. Some agencies traditionally paid special attention to a specific input, such as teacher upgrading or textbook provision. This approach often overlooked the complementary measures needed for education quality to be enhanced. In principle, aid support that is provided in a context of comprehensive sector analysis and reform is likely to be better placed to bring positive consequences for education quality. The introduction of new aid modalities, such as budget support and the possibility of financing part of the cost of teachers' salaries, provides new opportunities to support quality.

It remains the case, however, that although external assistance can help in achieving appropriate resource levels and managing school systems, it cannot make up for the absence of a societal project for improving education. That must come from within each society and cannot be engineered by outsiders. Ultimately, then, the most important lever is the domestic political process. If it favours educational change, the chances that external assistance will facilitate a move towards higher-quality universal education are profoundly better than is the case where such political circumstances are absent. ∎

Mandela Twilimuli gets ready for school.
Nairobi, Kenya

… EFA Global Monitoring Report 2005

Annex

Appendix

The Education for All Development Index 236

Statistical annex

Introduction 248

Tables

Table 1: Background statistics 254
Table 2: Adult and youth literacy 262
Table 3: Early childhood care and education (ECCE) 270
Table 4: Access to primary education 278
Table 5: Participation in primary education 286
Table 6: Internal efficiency: repetition in primary education 294
Table 7: Internal efficiency: dropout and survival in primary education 302
Table 8: Participation in secondary and post-secondary
non-tertiary education 310
Table 9: Participation in tertiary education 318
Table 10: Tertiary education: distribution of students by field
of study and female share in each field, 2001 326
Table 11: Tertiary education: distribution of graduates
by ISCED level and female share in each level 334
Table 12: Tertiary education: distribution of graduates
by field of study and female share in each field, 2001 338
Table 13A: Teaching staff in pre-primary and primary education 346
Table 13B: Teaching staff in secondary and tertiary education 354
Table 14: Private enrolment and education finance 362
Table 15: Trends in basic or proxy indicators
to measure EFA goals 1, 2 and 3 370
Table 16: Trends in basic or proxy indicators
to measure EFA goals 4 and 5 378
Table 17: Trends in basic or proxy indicators to measure EFA goal 6 386

Glossary 394

References 398

Abbreviations 428

Appendix

The Education for All Development Index

As Chapter 3 explains, if an Education for All Development Index is to measure overall progress towards EFA, its constituents should ideally reflect all six Dakar goals. In practice, however, this is difficult, since not all the goals have a clear definition or target. For example, goal 3 – learning and life skills programmes – is not yet conducive to quantitative measurement. For rather different reasons, early childhood care and education (goal 1) cannot easily be incorporated yet, because the national data are insufficiently standardized and are, in any case, available for only a small minority of states. Accordingly, for the time being, the EFA Development Index (EDI) only incorporates indicators for the four goals of universal primary education (UPE), adult literacy, gender parity and the quality of education.

In accordance with the principle of considering each goal to be equally important, one indicator is used as a proxy measure for each of the four EDI components,[1] thus giving the same weight to each index constituent. The EDI value for a particular country is the arithmetical mean of the observed values for each constituent. As the constituents are all expressed as percentages, the EDI value can vary from 0 to 100%, or, when expressed as a ratio, from 0 to 1. The closer a country's EDI value is to the maximum, the greater the extent of its EFA achievement and the nearer the country is to the goal.

The EDI constituents and related indicators are:

- UPE: net enrolment ratio in primary education;

- Adult literacy: literacy rate of the group aged 15 years and over;

- Quality of education: survival rate to grade 5 of primary education;

- Gender parity: the gender-specific EFA index, which is the simple average of the values of the gender parity index (GPI) for gross enrolment ratios in primary education and secondary education, and for adult literacy rates.

Choice of indicators as proxy measures of EDI constituents

In selecting indicators, the issue of data availability must be taken into account. This should not, however, be at the expense of the relevance of the indicator as a measure of the index component. A balance between these considerations is needed. Thus, among a range of indicators that might be used as proxies for various aspects of a given component such as education quality, one of the most relevant and for which the data coverage is acceptable should be chosen.

Universal primary education
The indicator selected to measure UPE achievement is the net enrolment ratio (NER), which reflects the percentage of school-age children who are enrolled in school. Its value varies from 0% to 100%. An NER of 100% means that all eligible children are enrolled in school. If a country maintains that level over time, it implies as well that all the children enrolled are completing their studies.

Adult literacy
The adult literacy rate is used as a proxy to measure progress towards EFA goal 4. However, the existing data on literacy are not entirely satisfactory. In middle- and low-income countries they are generally derived from methods of self-declaration or third-party reporting (e.g. a household head responding on behalf of other household members) used in censuses or household surveys.[2] In other cases they are based on data on years of school attended – for example, the percentage of the

---

1. One of the indicators, that of the EDI's gender component, is itself a composite index, as explained below.

2. Usually during a census or household survey, a question is asked concerning whether those surveyed can read and write, with understanding, a simple short statement on their everyday life. In many cases data derived from this method are of dubious quality, not only because they result from third-party reporting but particularly because they are not based on any test.

population having only three or fewer years of schooling is considered a proxy for illiteracy in OECD countries.[3] Both methods are subject to bias (underestimation of illiteracy in the case of developing countries, overestimation of literacy as regards developed nations), which affects the quality and accuracy of the data on literacy. New methodologies, based on tests and on the definition of literacy as a continuum of skills and a multi-dimensional concept, are being developed, to improve the literacy data. The main ones are the International Adult Literacy Survey (IALS) and the Adult Literacy and Lifeskills Survey (ALL), for OECD countries, and the Literacy Assessment and Monitoring Programme (LAMP) for developing countries. Providing a new data series for all countries will take some years, however, and the literacy estimates now used are the best currently available internationally. As regards relevance, it should be noted that the adult literacy indicator is a statement about the stock of human capital. As such, it is slow to change, and it could be argued that it is not a good 'leading indicator' of year-by-year progress towards improvement in literacy levels.

Quality of education

Student learning outcome measures are widely used as a proxy for the quality of education, particularly among countries at similar levels of development. They are incomplete in that they tell us nothing about values, capacities or other non-cognitive skills that are the other important aims of education (Chapter 2, pp. 43-44). They also tell us nothing about the cognitive value added by schooling (as opposed to home background) or the distribution of ability levels of the children enrolled in schools.[4] Nevertheless, learning outcomes would probably be the most appropriate single proxy for the average quality of education. Due to the lack of comparable data for a large number of countries, however, it is not yet possible to use them in the EDI.

Among the feasible proxies available for a large number of countries, survival rate to grade 5 was selected as the quality constituent for the EDI[5]. Figure A1 shows that there is a clear positive link between such survival rates and educational achievement in three of the international assessments that compare children at primary level across countries – the Latin American Laboratory for the Assessment of Quality in Education (LLECE), the Southern and Eastern African Consortium for Monitoring Educational Quality (SACMEQ II) and the Progress in International Reading Literacy Study (PIRLS).[6] The coefficients of determination vary from

Figure A1: Survival rate to grade 5 and learning outcomes

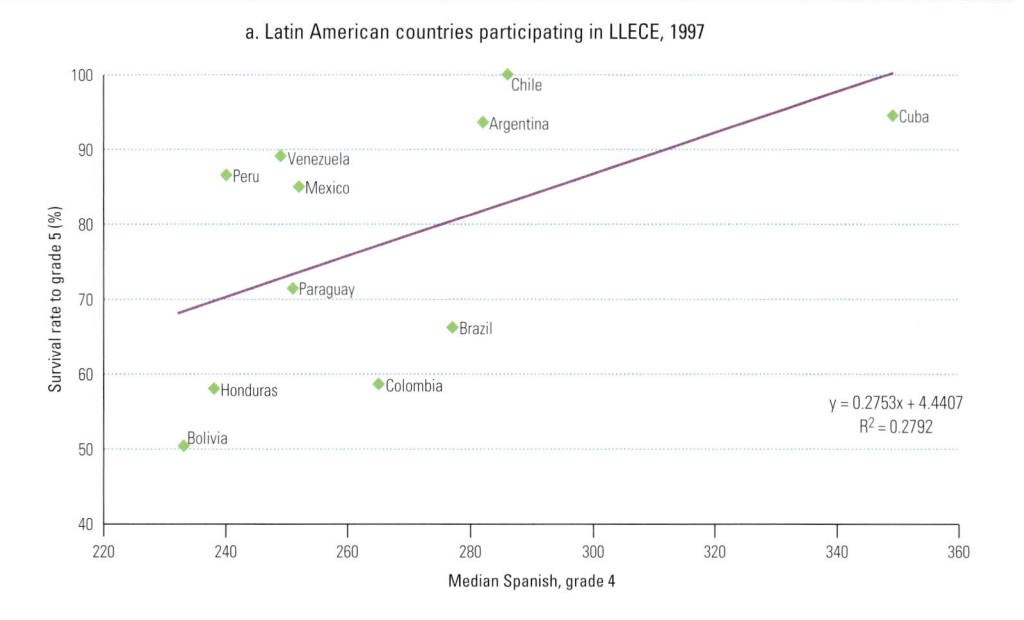

a. Latin American countries participating in LLECE, 1997

$y = 0.2753x + 4.4407$
$R^2 = 0.2792$

Note: Data for Chile and Venezuela are from 1995 and those for Mexico and Peru from 1998.
Sources: Willms and Somers (2001); EFA 2000 assessment CD-ROM.

---

3. This method, based on the percentage of the adult population with no more than three years of schooling as reported in the European Social Survey, seems the closest to the common definition of literacy used to derive literacy rates in developing countries. On the grounds that one or two years of schooling are unlikely to have instilled reading capacity, especially among old people, it permits to measure the percentage of absolute illiterates in developed countries (Carr-Hill, 2004b).

4. Strictly speaking, it would be necessary to compare average levels of cognitive achievement for pupils completing a given school grade, across countries with similar levels and distributions of income and with similar levels of NER, so as to account for home background and ability cohort effects.

5. See the *EFA Global Monitoring Report 2003/4*, Appendix 2, for background.

6. The data allow comparison within each study but not among the studies themselves. Among the factors preventing such comparison are differences in the age or education grouping of the target population, dissimilar assessment methods and the years of the different tests. For detailed discussion on international assessments, see Chapters 2 and 3 and Postlethwaite (2004).

238 / ANNEX

Figure A1 (continued)

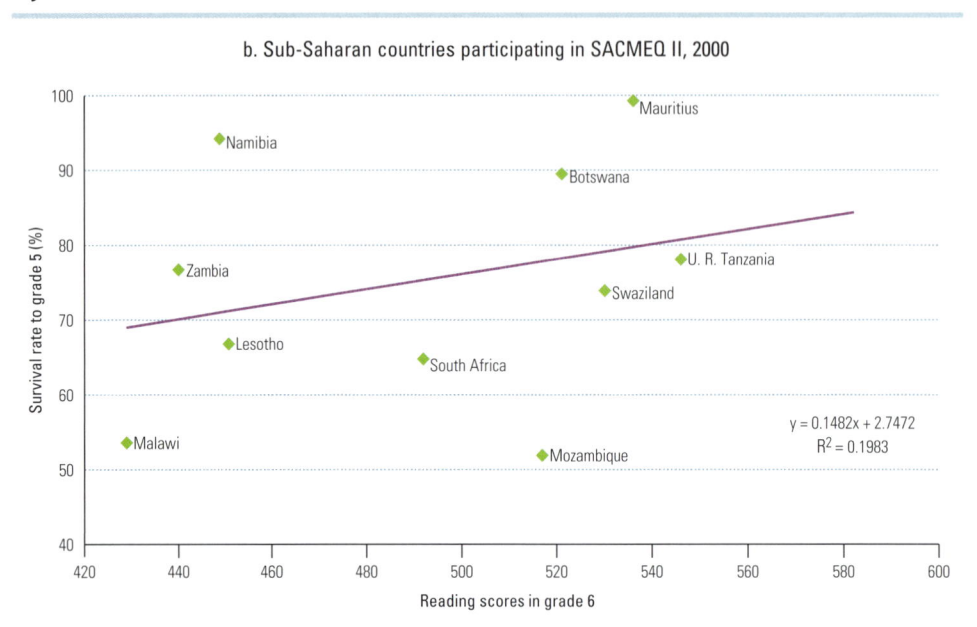

b. Sub-Saharan countries participating in SACMEQ II, 2000

[Scatter plot: Survival rate to grade 5 (%) vs Reading scores in grade 6. Countries: Mauritius, Namibia, Botswana, U. R. Tanzania, Zambia, Swaziland, Lesotho, South Africa, Malawi, Mozambique. Trend line: y = 0.1482x + 2.7472, R^2 = 0.1983]

Sources: Murimba (2003); Statistical annex, Table 7.

Figure A1 (continued)

c. Countries participating in PIRLS, 2001

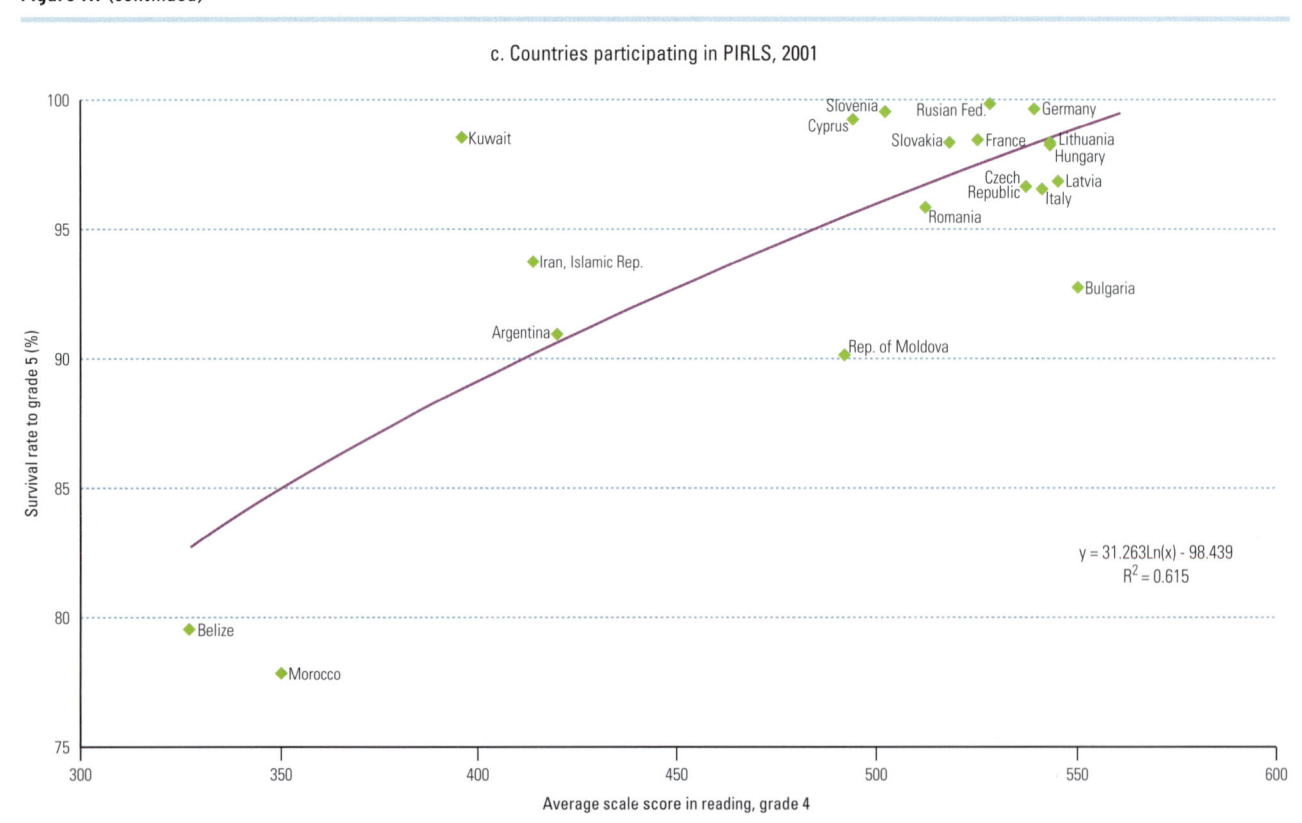

[Scatter plot: Survival rate to grade 5 (%) vs Average scale score in reading, grade 4. Countries: Slovenia, Cyprus, Rusian Fed., Germany, Slovakia, France, Lithuania, Hungary, Czech Republic, Latvia, Italy, Kuwait, Romania, Iran Islamic Rep., Bulgaria, Argentina, Rep. of Moldova, Belize, Morocco. Trend line: y = 31.263Ln(x) − 98.439, R^2 = 0.615]

Sources: Mullis et al. (2003); Statistical annex, Table 7.

around 20% in sub-Saharan Africa to almost 60% in the countries participating in PIRLS, implying that a significant proportion of the variation of learning outcomes among countries can be proxied by the variation in survival rates. Education systems capable of retaining a larger proportion of their pupils to grade 5 are performing better, on average, on international tests.

The survival rate to grade 5 is associated even more strongly with learning outcomes in lower secondary school. Figure A2 shows that the

Figure A2: Survival rate to grade 5 and learning outcomes at lower secondary level

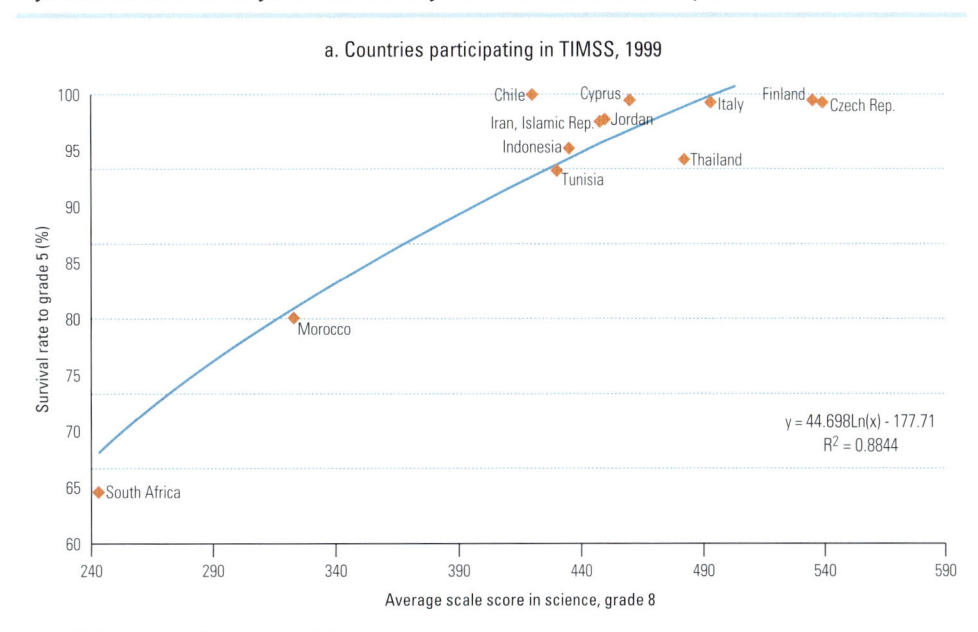

a. Countries participating in TIMSS, 1999

$y = 44.698 \ln(x) - 177.71$
$R^2 = 0.8844$

Sources: Mullis et al. (2000); Statistical annex, Table 7.

Figure A2 (continued)

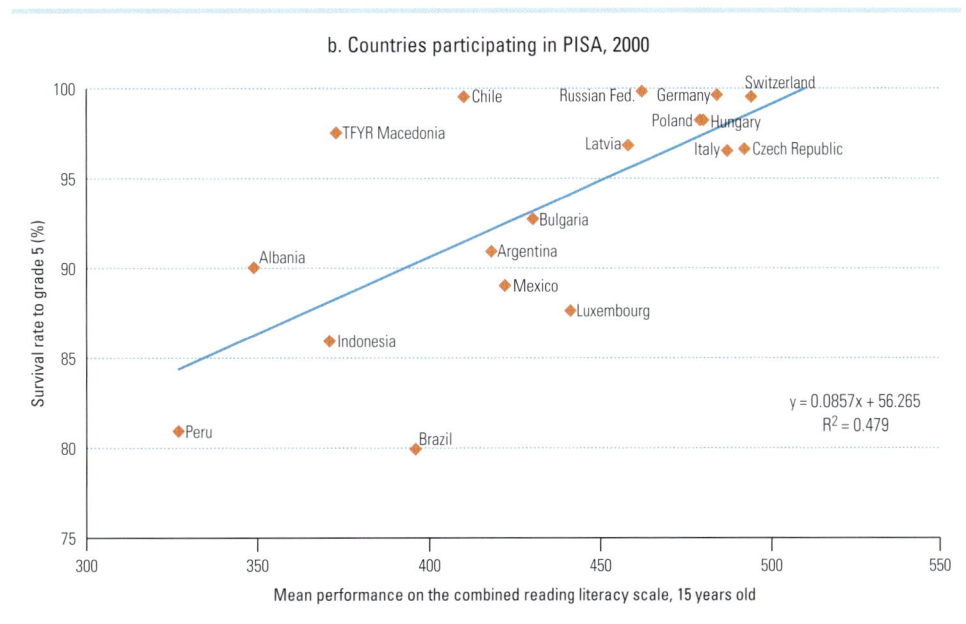

b. Countries participating in PISA, 2000

$y = 0.0857x + 56.265$
$R^2 = 0.479$

Sources: OECD/UNESCO Institute for Statistics (2003); Statistical annex, Table 7.

240 / ANNEX

variation in one variable explains about 50% of the variation in the other one in Programme for International Student Assessment (PISA) results and about 90% in the Third International Mathematics and Science Study (TIMSS).[7]

The relationships between learning outcomes and two other proxies of quality were similarly examined. First, learning outcomes are positively associated with the extent to which the teaching force is trained. In Latin America and sub-Saharan Africa, countries with a higher proportion of trained teachers also show better student scores.[8] In both cases, however, the proportion of variation in student scores explained by teacher training is lower than that explained by survival rates to grade 5.

Second, the data from all the assessments at primary level show that learning outcomes are strongly and negatively associated with pupil/teacher ratios (PTRs). In fact, the proportion of variation in learning outcomes explained by PTRs is higher than that for survival rates to grade 5 in the LLECE and SACMEQ II countries, though lower in the PIRLS countries. PTRs at primary level are also correlated with learning outcomes at lower secondary level, though in both PISA and TIMSS the percentage of variation in student achievement explained by the PTR is lower than that attributed to the survival rate.

Thus, the PTR would seem a good proxy for learning outcomes. As the empirical literature discussed in Chapter 2 shows, however, other evidence is ambiguous. In a multivariate context, PTRs are associated with higher learning outcomes in some studies, but in many others they are not. In addition, the relationship seems to vary by the level of mean test scores. Figure A3 presents PTRs and learning outcomes in PIRLS countries. The relationship between the two variables is exponential. For low levels of test scores, a decrease in pupils per teacher has a positive impact on learning outcomes, but for higher levels of test scores, additional teachers have only limited impact. For example, the test scores of students in Bulgaria and the Czech Republic, where PTRs are around 18:1, are the same level as those of students in Hungary and

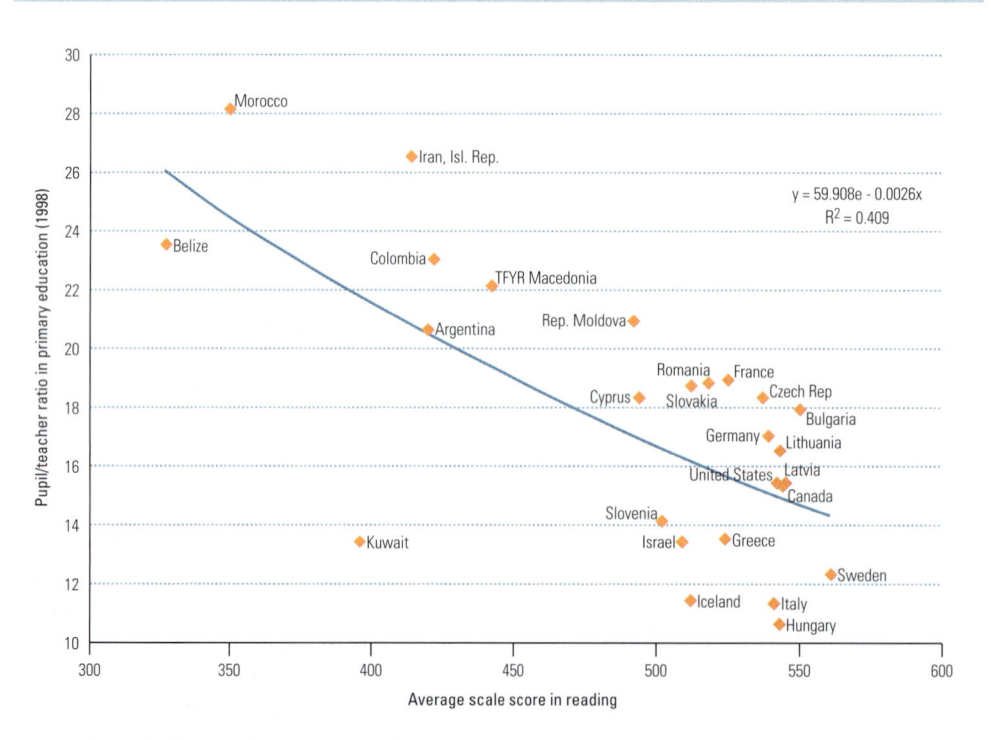

Figure A3: Pupil/teacher ratios and learning outcomes in primary education
(countries participating in PIRLS, 2001)

$y = 59.908e - 0.0026x$
$R^2 = 0.409$

Source: Statistical annex, Table 13A; Mullis et al. (2003).

7. If South Africa and Morocco are excluded from Figure A2a, the results remain unchanged (the coefficients of determination and the slope of the line are basically the same as those shown).

8. The coefficients of determination for simple linear relationships are 0.20 and 0.12, respectively. Data are from LLECE and SACMEQ II studies. No similar analysis is possible for PIRLS, TIMSS and PISA, because data on the percentage of trained teachers are not available for a number of countries that participated in these studies.

Italy, where PTRs are around 11:1. Below 20:1, further decreases in PTRs appear to make no difference to average text scores.

For these reasons, survival rates are retained as a safer proxy for learning outcomes and hence for education quality.[9] The fifth year of primary schooling is often taken as the threshold for acquisition of sustainable literacy. The survival rate to grade 5 also captures aspects of grade repetition, promotion policy and early dropout, and thus incorporates some comparison of the internal efficiency of education systems.

Gender

The fourth EDI component is measured by a composite index, the gender-specific EFA index (GEI). Ideally, the GEI should reflect the whole spirit of the gender-related EFA goal, which calls for 'eliminating gender disparities in primary and secondary education by 2005, and achieving gender equality in education by 2015, with a focus on ensuring girls' full and equal access to and achievement in basic education of good quality'. Two sub-goals are distinguished: gender parity (achieving equal participation of girls and boys in primary and secondary education) and gender equality (ensuring educational equality between boys and girls).

The first sub-goal is measured by the GPIs for the gross enrolment ratios at primary and secondary levels. Measuring and monitoring the broader aspects of equality in education is difficult, as the *EFA Global Monitoring Report 2003/4* demonstrated (UNESCO 2003a). Essentially, outcome measures, disaggregated by sex, are needed for a range of educational levels. No such measures are available on an internationally comparable basis. As a step in that direction, however, the GEI includes gender parity for adult literacy. Thus, the GEI is calculated as a simple average of three GPIs: for gross enrolment ratio in primary education, gross enrolment ratio in secondary education, and for adult literacy rate. That means the GEI does not fully reflect the second aspect of the EFA gender goal. However, this is a priority area and a challenge for future reports.

Calculating the GEI

The GPI, when expressed as the ratio of females to males in enrolment ratios or the literacy rate, can exceed unity when more girls/women are enrolled or literate than boys/men. For the purposes of the index, in cases where the GPI is higher than 1, the F/M formula is inverted to M/F. This solves mathematically the problem of including the GEI in the EDI (where all components have a theoretical limit of 1, or 100%) while keeping the indicator's capacity to show gender disparity. Figure A4 shows how 'transformed GPIs' are arrived at to highlight gender disparities to the disadvantage of males.

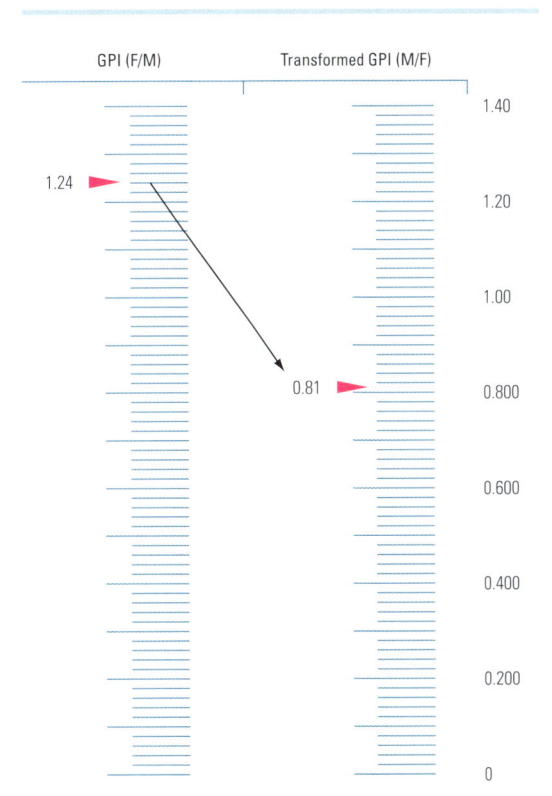

Figure A4: Calculating 'transformed' GPIs

Once all three GPI values have been calculated and converted into 'transformed' GPIs (from 0 to 1) where needed, the composite GEI is obtained by calculating a simple average of the three GPIs, each being equally weighted: those for gross enrolment ratio in primary education, gross enrolment ratio in secondary education, and adult literacy rate.

9. Another reason is that, unlike the pupil-teacher ratios, survival rates, like the other EDI constituents, range from 0 to 100%. Therefore the use of survival rate to grade 5 in the EDI avoids a need to rescale the data.

242 / ANNEX

The following illustration of the calculation uses data for the Dominican Republic in 2001. The GPIs in primary education, secondary education and adult literacy were 1.01, 1.24 and 1.00 respectively.

GEI = 1/3 (transformed GPI in primary)
+ 1/3 (transformed GPI in secondary)
+ 1/3 (transformed GPI in adult literacy)

GEI = 1/3 (0.99) + 1/3 (0.81) + 1/3 (1.00) = 0.93

Figure A5: Calculating the GEI

Transformed GPIs (M/F)

Primary education	Secondary education	Adult literacy	GEI
0.99	0.81	1.00	0.93

Calculating the EDI

Once the GEI has been calculated, determining the EDI is straightforward. It is the arithmetical mean value of its four constituents – NER in primary education, adult literacy rate, GEI and survival rate to grade 5. The EDI value falls between 0 and 1. The closer to 1 a country's EDI is, the nearer it is to achieving EFA overall. A country with an EDI of 0.5 may be considered as being halfway towards its goals. As a simple average, the EDI may mask important variations between its constituents. In other words, since the EDI gives the same weight to each constituent, the results for goals on which a country has made less progress will offset its advances on the others, as Box A1 shows. But since all the EFA goals are equally important, a country that concentrates only on some of them would hardly be considered as having achieved EFA. The objective of a synthetic indicator such as the EDI is to inform the policy debate on the prominence of all EFA goals and to highlight the synergy among them.

Figure A6: Calculating the EDI

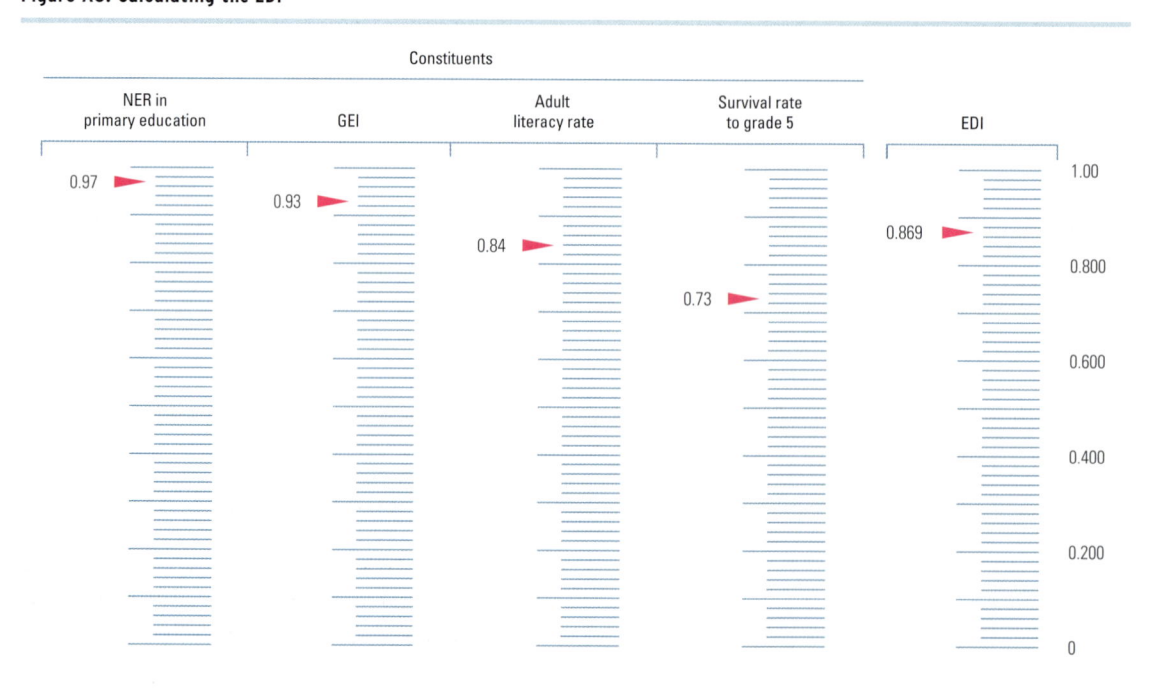

Constituents

NER in primary education	GEI	Adult literacy rate	Survival rate to grade 5	EDI
0.97	0.93	0.84	0.73	0.869

Box 1 Balance between quantity and quality

The following case is an example of a situation where the EDI masks significant variations among its constituents, resulting from unbalanced education policies. The case is simple but extreme, for illustrative purposes.

	Cohort Population	Grade 1	2	3	4	5	6	NIR (%)	NER (%)	Progress to G5 (%)	EDI element
A	100	50	50	50	50	50	50	50%	50%	100%	0.38
B	100	100	80	70	60	50	40	100%	67%	50%	0.29
C	100	100	90	80	75	70	65	100%	80%	70%	0.38

Consider the three examples as different countries (though they could represent the same country at different times). In each, there is a six-grade primary system; the population for every age cohort is 100; all pupils, except in country A, attend in the first year of official schooling; and there is no grade repetition. In country A there is low intake and low participation but high retention, with 100% of the intake progressing to grade 5. The contribution to the proposed EDI is 0.38 (out of a possible 0.50) for the two relevant indicators.

In country B, access to the first grade is widened to the whole population but there is significant dropout. The same number of children progress to grade 5 as in country A, though this now represents only 50% of the intake. The NER is higher than for country A but the decrease in progression to grade 5 is much greater, so the EDI element for these two indicators falls to 0.29. The conceptual underpinning for this is that the increase in access in country B is outweighed by the decrease in education quality suggested by the reduced retention to grade 5.

For a country with 100% intake to achieve A's EDI element of 0.38, it would need to retain 70% of entrants to grade 5, as in country C. Country C may be seen as being closer to achieving EFA than country A, especially as its increased access would be more likely to reach the poor, ethnic minorities and (if disadvantaged in primary education) girls. Yet not all children in C who have access to school are able to complete their education, because of early dropout, which generally affects the poorest. In this sense, although more children may be involved in primary schooling in country C, its education quality may well be lower than that of country A.

Source: EFA Gobal Monitoring Report Team

To illustrate the EDI's calculation, the Dominican Republic is again taken as an example. For NER, adult literacy rate and survival rate to grade 5, the values for this country in 2001 were 0.971, 0.844 and 0.729, respectively.

$$EDI = \frac{1}{4}(NER) + \frac{1}{4}(GEI) + \frac{1}{4}(\text{adult literacy rate}) + \frac{1}{4}(\text{survival rate to grade 5})$$

$$EDI = \frac{1}{4}(0.971) + \frac{1}{4}(0.93) + \frac{1}{4}(0.844) + \frac{1}{4}(0.729) = 0.869$$

Data sources

Almost all the data used to calculate the EDI for 1998 and 2001 (or 2000, where more recent data were not available) were drawn from the UNESCO Institute for Statistics (UIS) database, with two exceptions. First, survival rates to grade 5 were missing from the database for some countries and were obtained from the Education for All 2000 Assessment country reports. Second, adult literacy data for the OECD countries, for which UIS estimates were not available, were based on the results of the European Social Survey that took place in 2002 or 2003 (Carr-Hill, 2004b).

Only countries with a complete set of the indicators required to calculate the EDI are included in this analysis. They currently number 127. This means it will be some time before a comprehensive global overview and monitoring of progress towards the EFA goals is possible.

Table A1: The EFA Development index and its constituents (2001)

Ranking according to level of EDI	Countries	EDI	NER in primary	Adult literacy rate	Gender-specific EFA index (GEI)	Survival rate to grade 5
High EDI						
1	Norway	0.995	0.999	0.999	0.993	0.990
2	Denmark	0.994	1.000	1.000	0.984	0.990
3	Netherlands	0.992	0.994	1.000	0.984	0.990
4	Republic of Korea	0.990	0.999	0.980	0.992	0.990
5	Finland	0.990	1.000	0.998	0.963	0.999
6	Switzerland	0.988	0.988	0.997	0.976	0.993
7	Poland	0.987	0.980	0.997	0.986	0.985
8	Barbados	0.987	0.998	0.997	1.000	0.953
9	Belgium	0.987	1.000	0.997	0.961	0.990
10	Israel	0.981	0.999	0.953	0.984	0.990
11	Estonia	0.981	0.958	0.998	0.980	0.987
12	Luxembourg	0.981	0.962	0.996	0.975	0.990
13	United Kingdom	0.980	1.000	0.998	0.933	0.990
14	Sweden	0.980	0.998	1.000	0.932	0.990
15	Slovenia	0.980	0.931	0.997	0.996	0.995
16	Lithuania	0.979	0.943	0.996	0.992	0.983
17	Ireland	0.978	0.955	0.999	0.969	0.988
18	Italy	0.978	0.992	0.980	0.973	0.965
19	Cyprus	0.976	0.959	0.968	0.981	0.994
20	Maldives	0.973	0.962	0.972	0.975	0.983
21	Greece	0.971	0.968	0.951	0.976	0.990
22	Seychelles	0.971	0.997	0.919	0.978	0.990
23	Argentina	0.970	0.998	0.970	0.981	0.931
24	Malta	0.970	0.966	0.926	0.988	0.999
25	Belarus	0.969	0.942	0.997	0.980	0.956
26	Spain	0.968	0.997	0.918	0.968	0.990
27	Hungary	0.968	0.908	0.992	0.990	0.982
28	Trinidad and Tobago	0.968	0.941	0.985	0.963	0.982
29	Austria	0.967	0.899	1.000	0.980	0.990
30	Cuba	0.965	0.957	0.969	0.983	0.953
31	Tajikistan	0.964	0.975	0.995	0.922	0.965
32	Croatia	0.962	0.885	0.981	0.983	0.999
33	Albania	0.961	0.972	0.987	0.987	0.900
34	Portugal	0.961	0.998	0.908	0.950	0.990
35	Slovakia	0.961	0.870	0.997	0.993	0.983
36	Czech Republic	0.958	0.885	0.996	0.986	0.966
37	Latvia	0.958	0.876	0.997	0.990	0.968
38	Chile	0.958	0.888	0.957	0.986	0.999
39	Kazakhstan	0.956	0.895	0.994	0.989	0.948
40	Georgia	0.954	0.907	0.973	0.975	0.938
41	Fiji	0.954	0.998	0.929	0.967	0.920
Medium EDI						
42	Romania	0.949	0.884	0.973	0.983	0.958
43	Bulgaria	0.949	0.904	0.986	0.980	0.927
44	Costa Rica	0.948	0.906	0.958	0.991	0.937
45	Tonga	0.943	0.999	0.988	0.955	0.829
46	Kyrgyzstan	0.943	0.900	0.976	0.982	0.913
47	Armenia	0.942	0.845	0.994	0.973	0.957
48	Mexico	0.941	0.994	0.905	0.961	0.905
49	Panama	0.941	0.990	0.923	0.964	0.886
50	Venezuela	0.941	0.924	0.931	0.945	0.963
51	Jordan	0.940	0.913	0.909	0.960	0.977
52	Bahrain	0.932	0.910	0.885	0.942	0.991
53	Mauritius	0.931	0.932	0.843	0.957	0.993
54	China	0.930	0.946	0.909	0.885	0.980
55	Samoa	0.930	0.949	0.987	0.958	0.826
56	Azerbaijan	0.930	0.798	0.973	0.973	0.974
57	Uruguay	0.927	0.895	0.977	0.949	0.885
58	Macao, China	0.925	0.857	0.913	0.935	0.994
59	Jamaica	0.923	0.952	0.876	0.959	0.903
60	Thailand	0.921	0.863	0.926	0.955	0.941
61	Ecuador	0.918	0.995	0.910	0.987	0.780
62	Mongolia	0.916	0.866	0.978	0.933	0.885
63	Republic of Moldova	0.914	0.783	0.990	0.983	0.901
64	Viet Nam	0.914	0.940	0.903	0.925	0.890

Note: Data in blue indicate that gender disparities are at the expense of boys or men.
Sources: Statistical annex, Tables 2,5,7,and 8; Education for All 2000 Assessment country reports; European Social Survey 2002-2003; Demographic and Health Survey.

Table A1 (continued)

Ranking according to level of EDI	Countries	EDI	NER in primary	Adult literacy rate	Gender-specific EFA index (GEI)	Survival rate to grade 5
Medium EDI						
65	Indonesia	0.912	0.921	0.879	0.957	0.892
66	Peru	0.912	0.999	0.850	0.937	0.861
67	Kuwait	0.906	0.846	0.829	0.963	0.985
68	Lebanon	0.906	0.898	0.869	0.916	0.940
69	Qatar	0.906	0.945	0.842	0.961	0.875
70	Philippines	0.904	0.930	0.926	0.967	0.793
71	Syrian Arab Republic	0.902	0.975	0.829	0.882	0.924
72	Brazil	0.899	0.965	0.882	0.951	0.799
73	Cape Verde	0.895	0.994	0.757	0.903	0.928
74	Paraguay	0.893	0.915	0.916	0.970	0.772
75	Tunisia	0.887	0.969	0.732	0.894	0.955
76	Bolivia	0.882	0.942	0.867	0.939	0.780
77	Belize	0.877	0.962	0.769	0.963	0.815
78	Namibia	0.877	0.782	0.833	0.952	0.942
79	United Arab Emirates	0.876	0.808	0.773	0.947	0.975
80	Iran, Islamic Republic of	0.872	0.865	0.770	0.918	0.937
81	Dominican Republic	0.869	0.971	0.844	0.933	0.729
82	Algeria	0.868	0.951	0.689	0.873	0.960
83	Botswana	0.863	0.809	0.789	0.959	0.895
84	Zimbabwe	0.847	0.827	0.900	0.927	0.733
85	Oman	0.843	0.745	0.744	0.919	0.962
86	Colombia	0.841	0.867	0.921	0.967	0.609
87	South Africa	0.839	0.895	0.860	0.954	0.648
88	El Salvador	0.830	0.889	0.797	0.962	0.672
89	Swaziland	0.823	0.767	0.809	0.975	0.739
90	Egypt	0.822	0.903	0.556	0.840	0.989
91	Myanmar	0.805	0.819	0.853	0.951	0.599
92	Saudi Arabia	0.801	0.589	0.779	0.895	0.940
Low EDI						
93	Lesotho	0.797	0.844	0.814	0.863	0.668
94	Zambia	0.773	0.660	0.799	0.865	0.767
95	Nicaragua	0.768	0.819	0.767	0.945	0.542
96	Cambodia	0.750	0.862	0.694	0.741	0.704
97	Morocco	0.749	0.884	0.507	0.768	0.837
98	Guatemala	0.748	0.850	0.699	0.886	0.558
99	Togo	0.745	0.918	0.596	0.624	0.843
100	U. R. Tanzania	0.741	0.544	0.771	0.868	0.781
101	Papua New Guinea	0.735	0.775	0.653	0.832	0.680
102	Lao PDR	0.721	0.828	0.664	0.769	0.623
103	Ghana	0.712	0.602	0.738	0.845	0.663
104	Rwanda	0.709	0.840	0.692	0.904	0.400
105	India	0.700	0.823	0.613	0.750	0.614
106	Equatorial Guinea	0.697	0.846	0.848	0.769	0.326
107	Bangladesh	0.692	0.866	0.411	0.838	0.655
108	Malawi	0.688	0.810	0.618	0.788	0.536
109	Comoros	0.677	0.562	0.562	0.811	0.771
110	Nepal	0.651	0.705	0.440	0.683	0.778
111	Gambia	0.648	0.729	0.389	0.774	0.702
112	Djibouti	0.647	0.340	0.665	0.706	0.877
113	Eritrea	0.634	0.425	0.576	0.712	0.821
114	Côte d'Ivoire	0.631	0.626	0.486	0.635	0.777
115	Yemen	0.629	0.671	0.490	0.497	0.860
116	Benin	0.623	0.713	0.398	0.542	0.840
117	Burundi	0.609	0.534	0.504	0.758	0.640
118	Mauritania	0.601	0.667	0.412	0.776	0.547
119	Senegal	0.594	0.579	0.393	0.729	0.675
120	Liberia	0.562	0.699	0.559	0.655	0.334
121	Mozambique	0.558	0.597	0.465	0.651	0.519
122	Ethiopia	0.541	0.462	0.415	0.672	0.613
123	Pakistan	0.537	0.591	0.415	0.645	0.497
124	Chad	0.507	0.583	0.458	0.533	0.453
125	Guinea-Bissau	0.450	0.452	0.410	0.558	0.381
126	Niger	0.448	0.342	0.171	0.567	0.710
127	Burkina Faso	0.429	0.350	0.128	0.599	0.637

Table A2: Countries ranked according to the value of EDI and its constituents (2001)

Countries	EDI	NER in primary	Adult literacy rate	Gender-specific EFA index (GEI)	Survival rate to grade 5	Countries	EDI	NER in primary	Adult literacy rate	Gender-specific EFA index (GEI)	Survival rate to grade 5
Norway	1	5	5	4	12	Indonesia	65	54	68	61	71
Denmark	2	3	1	17	14	Peru	66	9	74	75	78
Netherlands	3	18	3	18	15	Kuwait	67	87	80	50	28
Republic of Korea	4	6	33	6	13	Lebanon	68	66	70	86	55
Finland	5	1	9	49	4	Qatar	69	44	78	54	77
Switzerland	6	23	16	33	8	Philippines	70	52	52	46	88
Poland	7	24	11	15	29	Syrian Arab Republic	71	26	81	93	63
Barbados	8	10	13	1	51	Brazil	72	32	67	66	87
Belgium	9	4	12	55	21	Cape Verde	73	20	93	88	61
Israel	10	7	46	19	16	Paraguay	74	56	57	41	94
Estonia	11	37	8	27	27	Tunisia	75	29	96	90	49
Luxembourg	12	33	20	34	19	Bolivia	76	47	71	74	91
United Kingdom	13	2	7	78	23	Belize	77	35	91	48	86
Sweden	14	11	4	80	24	Namibia	78	101	79	65	53
Slovenia	15	51	17	2	5	United Arab Emirates	79	98	88	70	37
Lithuania	16	45	18	5	31	Iran, Isl. Rep.	80	81	90	85	59
Ireland	17	39	6	42	26	Dominican Republic	81	28	76	79	99
Italy	18	21	32	38	41	Algeria	82	41	100	94	45
Cyprus	19	36	43	25	6	Botswana	83	97	86	58	70
Maldives	20	34	40	37	32	Zimbabwe	84	92	65	81	98
Greece	21	30	47	32	18	Oman	85	104	94	84	44
Seychelles	22	15	55	31	11	Colombia	86	78	54	45	115
Argentina	23	12	41	26	60	South Africa	87	68	72	64	109
Malta	24	31	51	11	1	El Salvador	88	70	85	52	105
Belarus	25	46	15	30	48	Swaziland	89	103	83	35	97
Spain	26	16	56	43	20	Egypt	90	63	110	99	25
Hungary	27	59	24	8	33	Myanmar	91	94	73	67	116
Trinidad and Tobago	28	48	30	51	34	Saudi Arabia	92	116	87	89	56
Austria	29	65	2	29	17	Lesotho	93	89	82	97	106
Cuba	30	38	42	23	50	Zambia	94	111	84	96	96
Tajikistan	31	25	21	83	42	Nicaragua	95	95	92	71	119
Croatia	32	72	31	22	3	Cambodia	96	83	98	111	101
Albania	33	27	27	13	69	Morocco	97	75	111	108	82
Portugal	34	13	62	68	22	Guatemala	98	85	97	91	117
Slovakia	35	77	14	3	30	Togo	99	55	106	121	80
Czech Republic	36	73	19	16	40	U. R. Tanzania	100	120	89	95	89
Latvia	37	76	10	9	39	Papua New Guinea	101	102	103	101	103
Chile	38	71	45	14	2	Lao PDR	102	91	102	106	112
Kazakhstan	39	67	22	10	52	Ghana	103	113	95	98	107
Georgia	40	60	37	36	57	Rwanda	104	90	99	87	124
Fiji	41	14	49	44	64	India	105	93	105	110	113
Romania	42	74	39	21	46	Equatorial Guinea	106	86	75	107	127
Bulgaria	43	62	29	28	62	Bangladesh	107	80	121	100	108
Costa Rica	44	61	44	7	58	Malawi	108	96	104	103	120
Tonga	45	8	26	62	83	Comoros	109	119	108	102	95
Kyrgyzstan	46	64	36	24	65	Nepal	110	107	117	115	92
Armenia	47	88	23	40	47	Gambia	111	105	125	105	102
Mexico	48	19	63	53	66	Djibouti	112	127	101	114	76
Panama	49	22	53	47	73	Eritrea	113	124	107	113	85
Venezuela	50	53	48	72	43	Côte d'Ivoire	114	112	114	120	93
Jordan	51	57	61	56	36	Yemen	115	109	113	127	79
Bahrain	52	58	66	73	10	Benin	116	106	123	125	81
Mauritius	53	50	77	60	9	Burundi	117	121	112	109	110
China	54	43	60	92	35	Mauritania	118	110	120	104	118
Samoa	55	42	28	59	84	Senegal	119	118	124	112	104
Azerbaijan	56	99	38	39	38	Liberia	120	108	109	117	126
Uruguay	57	69	35	69	74	Mozambique	121	114	115	118	121
Macao, China	58	84	58	76	7	Ethiopia	122	122	118	116	114
Jamaica	59	40	69	57	67	Pakistan	123	115	119	119	122
Thailand	60	82	50	63	54	Chad	124	117	116	126	123
Ecuador	61	17	59	12	90	Guinea-Bissau	125	123	122	124	125
Mongolia	62	79	34	77	75	Niger	126	126	126	123	100
Republic of Moldova	63	100	25	20	68	Burkina Faso	127	125	127	122	111
Viet Nam	64	49	64	82	72						

Sources: Statistical annex, Tables 2, 5, 7, and 8; Education for All 2000 Assessment country reports; European Social Survey 2002-2003; Demographic and Health Survey.

Table A3: Change in the EDI and its constituents between 1998 and 2001

Countries	EFA Development Index 1998	EFA Development Index 2001	Variation 1998-2001	Adult literacy rate	NER in primary	Gender-specific EFA index (GEI)	Survival rate to grade 5
High EDI							
Barbados	0.979	0.987	0.8	0.1	0.1	2.0	1.3
Estonia	0.984	0.981	-0.3	-1.2	0.0	0.3	-0.4
Italy	0.982	0.978	-0.5	-0.5	0.0	-1.4	-0.1
Cyprus	0.965	0.976	1.1	0.4	0.2	0.5	3.5
Maldives	0.981	0.973	-0.9	-3.5	0.7	-0.6	0.0
Argentina	0.972	0.970	-0.2	-0.2	0.4	0.6	-1.7
Belarus	0.964	0.969	0.5	1.3	0.1	0.7	0.0
Hungary	0.960	0.968	0.9	1.5	0.0	0.7	1.4
Trinidad and Tobago	0.968	0.968	-0.1	1.3	0.4	-0.4	-1.5
Cuba	0.964	0.965	0.1	-3.2	0.6	1.6	1.7
Tajikistan	0.959	0.964	0.6	0.3	0.5	-1.2	2.7
Chile	0.952	0.958	0.6	1.0	0.3	1.1	0.1
Georgia	0.980	0.954	-2.7	-4.8	0.0	-1.5	-4.4
Medium EDI							
Bulgaria	0.961	0.949	-1.3	-5.4	0.4	0.1	-0.2
Kyrgyzstan	0.939	0.943	0.4	-1.1	0.0	0.3	2.4
Mexico	0.941	0.941	0.0	-0.1	0.1	-1.3	1.7
Venezuela	0.903	0.941	4.2	7.6	1.4	2.0	6.0
Jordan	0.927	0.940	1.4	1.9	2.7	1.2	0.0
Bahrain	0.930	0.932	0.2	-3.1	2.1	0.2	1.7
Mauritius	0.933	0.931	-0.2	0.0	0.8	-1.2	-0.1
Samoa	0.929	0.930	0.2	0.7	0.2	-0.3	0.0
Azerbaijan	0.936	0.930	-0.7	-0.4	0.0	-1.4	-1.0
Ecuador	0.906	0.918	1.3	2.6	0.2	1.0	1.3
Mongolia	0.932	0.916	-1.7	-3.1	0.0	2.0	-5.9
Viet Nam	0.903	0.914	1.2	-2.8	0.0	1.1	7.5
Peru	0.917	0.912	-0.6	0.1	0.0	-0.4	-2.0
Kuwait	0.899	0.906	0.8	-4.1	2.9	-0.6	4.8
Lebanon	0.888	0.906	2.0	2.6	2.3	0.3	3.0
Qatar	0.912	0.906	-0.7	-2.7	0.0	0.0	0.0
Syrian Arab Republic	0.890	0.902	1.4	4.8	0.0	0.0	0.7
Paraguay	0.875	0.893	2.1	-0.2	0.0	0.5	10.3
Tunisia	0.858	0.887	3.4	3.1	6.9	0.9	3.7
Bolivia	0.878	0.882	0.5	-1.9	3.1	2.4	-1.8
Belize	0.863	0.877	1.6	2.0	0.0	0.0	4.8
Namibia	0.841	0.877	4.3	0.4	3.4	0.9	12.9
United Arab Emirates	0.851	0.876	2.9	3.3	3.0	-0.1	5.5
Iran, Islamic Republic of	0.849	0.872	2.7	6.3	4.5	2.1	-1.2
Dominican Republic	0.846	0.869	2.7	10.0	1.8	1.1	-2.9
Algeria	0.847	0.868	2.6	3.3	7.3	0.0	1.1
Botswana	0.841	0.863	2.6	2.8	4.7	1.2	2.2
Oman	0.819	0.843	2.9	-1.8	8.7	2.7	2.7
Colombia	0.858	0.841	-2.0	0.0	1.2	0.0	-11.7
South Africa	0.866	0.839	-3.0	-2.0	1.8	0.9	-14.6
El Salvador	0.792	0.830	4.8	9.8	2.7	-0.8	9.6
Swaziland	0.821	0.823	0.1	-1.3	3.6	0.3	-2.1
Egypt	0.807	0.822	1.8	-0.7	3.6	1.7	3.2
Saudi Arabia	0.784	0.801	2.1	3.7	5.0	2.4	-1.4
Low EDI							
Lesotho	0.742	0.797	7.4	30.9	0.0	5.2	-3.0
Zambia	0.768	0.773	0.7	-3.6	4.7	2.9	-1.9
Nicaragua	0.759	0.768	1.3	5.1	0.0	0.7	-1.5
Cambodia	0.683	0.750	9.9	4.5	4.3	9.4	25.0
Morocco	0.685	0.749	9.3	20.9	8.1	6.5	2.2
Guatemala	0.703	0.748	6.4	11.1	4.1	2.0	9.8
Togo	0.633	0.745	17.7	2.2	9.5	8.5	63.4
United Republic of Tanzania	0.713	0.741	3.8	18.8	6.1	0.8	-3.5
Papua New Guinea	0.719	0.735	2.2	3.6	4.6	1.0	0.0
Lao PDR	0.679	0.721	6.2	3.2	5.3	3.8	14.7
Ghana	0.767	0.712	-7.2	4.0	6.9	3.6	-32.7
Bangladesh	0.697	0.692	-0.7	-4.1	5.7	-0.6	0.2
Comoros	0.585	0.677	15.7	14.3	1.4	0.3	59.2
Gambia	0.609	0.648	6.4	9.5	13.2	6.5	0.0
Djibouti	0.603	0.647	7.3	8.6	6.7	-0.3	14.3
Eritrea	0.639	0.634	-0.8	25.4	6.8	-1.6	-13.8
Côte d'Ivoire	0.586	0.631	7.7	12.8	4.3	0.6	12.5
Yemen	0.546	0.629	15.4	16.9	11.5	16.9	15.6
Burundi	0.632	0.609	-3.7	43.9	10.3	-3.0	-30.4
Mauritania	0.605	0.601	-0.7	6.5	5.1	3.5	-16.1
Senegal	0.587	0.594	1.2	0.0	10.4	12.8	-12.0
Liberia	0.477	0.562	17.7	59.2	10.5	3.8	0.0
Mozambique	0.483	0.558	15.4	26.2	11.4	4.1	24.2
Ethiopia	0.480	0.541	12.7	29.1	12.6	6.0	9.9
Chad	0.495	0.507	2.3	6.6	16.3	8.7	-17.8
Niger	0.393	0.448	13.9	31.0	13.8	3.6	15.8
Burkina Faso	0.430	0.429	-0.3	4.5	0.0	4.7	-6.7

Sources: Statistical annex, Tables 2, 5, 7, and 8; Education for All 2000 Assessment country reports; Demographic and Health Survey.

Statistical annex

Introduction

The most recent data on pupils, students, teachers and expenditure presented in these statistical tables refer to the school year 2001/2002. They are based on survey results reported to the UNESCO Institute for Statistics (UIS) by the end of May 2004. Data received after this date will be used in the next EFA Global Monitoring Report. The school year for 2001/2002 includes countries with a 2001 calendar school year and those whose school year runs into 2002. These statistics refer to all formal schools, both public and private, by level of education. They are supplemented by demographic and economic statistics collected or produced by other international organizations, including the United Nations Population Division and the World Bank.

A total of 203 countries and territories are listed in the statistical tables. Most of them report their data to UIS using standard questionnaires issued by the institute. For some countries, however, education data are collected via surveys carried out under the auspices of the World Education Indicators project (WEI) funded by the World Bank, or are provided by the Organisation for Economic Co-operation and Development (OECD) and the Statistical Office of the European Communities (Eurostat). As an aid to the reader, symbols are used in the tables to distinguish countries in these two categories from the other Member States: o for countries whose education data are collected through the UNESCO/OECD/Eurostat (UOE) questionnaires and w for WEI countries.

Population

The indicators on access and participation in the statistical tables were calculated using the population estimates produced by the United Nations Population Division, in its 2002 revision. Thus, because of possible differences between national population estimates and those of the United Nations, these indicators may differ from those published by individual countries or by other organizations, such as the OECD, or in the framework of projects such as the WEI. As part of the United Nations, UIS uses UN population estimates for calculating enrolment ratios and other indicators. The only exception to this agreed rule within the UN system is for countries with a total population in 2000 below 100,000, for which the UN population by age is not available. In this case, national population, when available, was used to calculate enrolment ratios.

ISCED classification

Education data reported to UIS are in conformity with the 1997 revision of the International Standard Classification of Education (ISCED). In some cases, data have been adjusted to comply with the ISCED97 classification. Data for 1990/1991 may conform to the previous version of the classification, ISCED76, and therefore may not be comparable in some countries to those for years after 1997. ISCED is used to harmonize data and introduce more international comparability among national education systems. Countries may have their own definitions of education levels that do not correspond to ISCED, however, so differences between nationally and internationally reported enrolment ratios may be due to the use of nationally defined education levels rather than the ISCED standard, in addition to the population issue raised above.

Adult participation in basic education

ISCED does not classify education programmes by participants' age. For example, any programme with a content equivalent to primary education, or ISCED 1, may be classed as ISCED 1 even if provided to adults. However, the guidance provided by UIS for respondents to the regular annual education survey asks countries to exclude 'data on programmes designed for people beyond regular school age'. The guidance for UOE and WEI questionnaires states that 'activities classified as "continuing", "adult" or "non-formal" education should be included' if they 'involve studies with subject content similar to regular educational programmes' or if 'the underlying programmes lead to similar potential qualifications' as do the regular programmes.

As a result of these distinctions, data from WEI countries and those for which statistics are collected via the UOE questionnaires, particularly concerning secondary education, may include programmes for older students. Despite the UIS instructions, data from countries in the regular UIS survey may also include pupils who are substantially above the official age for basic education.

Literacy data

UNESCO has long defined literacy as the ability to read and write, with understanding, a short simple statement related to one's daily life. UIS has traditionally estimated literacy by inputting data from censuses and surveys into a statistical model. Such data are largely based on the 'self-declaration' method: respondents are asked to say whether they are literate, as opposed to being asked to demonstrate the skill. Some countries assume that children who complete a certain level of schooling are literate. Literacy information gathered via these varied methodologies has been fed into the statistical model, which projects literacy rates from the most recent data into the future. For many countries the last observed data are more than ten or even twenty years old. As definitions and methodologies used for data collection differ by country, data need to be used with caution.

Literacy data in this report that are derived through these measures refer to 1990 and 2000-2004:

1) 1990 data represent the output of the statistical model used in earlier EFA reports, rebased to the 2002 UN population revision. The UIS estimation methodology can be reviewed at the UIS website (www.uis.unesco.org).

2) 2000-2004 data are derived from the March 2004 UIS Literacy Assessment, which uses directly reported national figures together with UIS estimates. National literacy estimates are published in the statistical tables when available. They were obtained from national censuses or surveys taken between 1995 and 2004; the reference year and literacy definition for each country are presented after this introduction. Figures dated before 2000 will be replaced as soon as UIS gets more recent national estimates. For countries that did not report literacy data for the 2000-2004 reference period, the tables publish UIS estimates for 2002, generated in July 2002 and based on national data collected before 1995. All literacy figures were rebased to the 2002 UN population revision.

As the 'self declaration' method has been widely superseded by a more operational definition of literacy as used in everyday life, UIS is seeking to encourage the replacement of this method by a direct assessment of literacy. To this end, a new method called LAMP (for Literacy Assessment and Monitoring Programme) is being introduced in developing countries. Following the example of the International Adult Assessment Survey (IALS), LAMP is based on actual, functional assessment of literacy skills. It aims to provide literacy data of higher quality and in line with the concept of a continuum of literacy skills rather than the common literate/illiterate dichotomy.

Data gaps

Gaps in the statistical tables may occur for a number of reasons. In some cases data do not exist at country level – where countries are in conflict, for example, or where they do not have the capacity to collect the data concerned. In other countries data may exist but were not reported to UIS.

Both actual and estimated data are presented throughout the statistical tables. When data are not reported to UIS using the standard questionnaires, estimates are often necessary. Wherever possible, UIS encourages countries to make their own estimates, which are presented as national estimates. When UIS obtains the necessary data from other sources, they are presented as UIS estimates unless officially attributed to another source.

Gaps in the tables may also arise where data submitted by a country are found to be inconsistent. UIS makes every attempt to resolve such problems with countries, but reserves the final decision to omit data it regards as problematic.

Net enrolment ratios are now available for over 90% of countries that submitted data (i.e. not including countries in conflict and other non-respondents) or for which estimates have been made. Survival rates remain the indicator with the lowest availability, covering some 50% of countries. To fill the gaps in the annex tables, data for previous school years were included when information for 2001/02 was not available. Such cases are indicated by footnote.

Data processing timetable

The timetable for collection and publication of data used in this report was as follows.

- June 2002: the final school year in the data collection period ended;

- January 2003: questionnaires were sent to countries asking for data submission;

- July 2003: after sending reminders by email, fax and post, UIS began to process data and calculate indicators;

- November 2003: provisional statistical tables were produced and draft indicators sent to member states;

- February 2004: the first draft tables were produced for the EFA Global Monitoring Report;

- June 2004: the final statistical tables were sent to the EFA GMR team.

UIS constantly seeks to speed up its data collection. Questionnaires for data on the 2002/2003 school year were sent to countries in November 2003, two months earlier than in the previous survey cycle. OECD and EU member states tend to be the last to send in their data; for this report UIS received them in provisional form in January 2004.

Data require extensive verification and checking, which can involve protracted discussion with countries about how particular figures were produced. Once problems encountered in processing the raw data have been addressed, indicators are calculated. Further checking is often necessary after this step, requiring a further round of questions to countries.

There is a trade-off between data quality and timeliness. Data can be collected directly from schools at the beginning of the school year, when a large number of pupils are registered, or at the end of the year, after some have dropped out. They can be collected before they are checked and aggregated by national statisticians, or culled from published national reports. In general, UIS collects data after national statisticians compile their reports; hence there may be some lag between data publication at country level and their availability at international level.

Regional averages

Regional figures for gross and net enrolment ratios are overall weighted averages, taking into account the relative size of the school-age population of each country in each region. The averages are derived from both published data and broad estimates for countries for which no reliable data are available. The figures for the countries with higher population-thus have a proportionately greater influence on the regional aggregates. Where not enough reliable data are available to produce an overall weighted mean, a median figure is calculated for countries with available data in the statistical tables.

Capped figures

There are cases where an indicator theoretically should not exceed 100 (the net enrolment ratio, for example), but data inconsistencies may have resulted nonetheless in the indicator exceeding the theoretical limit. In those cases the indicator is 'capped' to 100 but the gender balance is maintained (the highest value, whether for male or female, is set equal to 100 and the other two indicators are then recalculated) so that the gender parity index for the capped figures is the same as that for the uncapped figures.

Footnotes to the tables, along with the glossary following the tables, provide additional help in interpreting the data and information.

Symbols used in the statistical tables

* National estimate

** UIS estimate

... Missing data

– Magnitude nil or negligible

. Category not applicable

./. Data included under another category

o Countries whose education data are collected through UOE questionnaires

w World Education Indicators (WEI) project countries

Composition of regions

World classification

■ Countries in transition:
Countries members of Commonwealth of Independent States, including 4 in Central and Eastern Europe (Belarus, Republic of Moldova, Russian Federation, Ukraine) and the countries of Central Asia (minus Mongolia).

■ Developed countries:
North America and Western Europe (minus Cyprus and Israel); Central and Eastern Europe (minus Belarus, Republic of Moldova, Russian Federation, Ukraine, and Turkey); Australia, Bermuda, Japan and New Zealand.

■ Developing countries:
Arab States; East Asia and the Pacific (minus Australia, Japan and New Zealand); Latin America and the Caribbean (minus Bermuda); South and West Asia; sub-Saharan Africa; and Cyprus, Israel, Mongolia and Turkey.

EFA regions

■ Arab States (20 countries/territories)
Algeria, Bahrain, Djibouti, Egypt, Iraq, Jordan, Kuwait, Lebanon, Libyan Arab Jamahiriya, Mauritania, Morocco, Oman, Palestinian Autonomous Territories, Qatar, Saudi Arabia, Sudan, Syrian Arab Republic, Tunisia, United Arab Emirates, Yemen.

■ Central and Eastern Europe (20 countries)
Albania, Belarus, Bosnia and Herzegovina, Bulgaria, Croatia, Czech Republic, Estonia, Hungary, Latvia, Lithuania, Poland, Republic of Moldova, Romania, Russian Federation, Serbia and Montenegro, Slovakia, Slovenia, The former Yugoslav Republic of Macedonia, Turkey, Ukraine.

■ Central Asia (9 countries)
Armenia, Azerbaijan, Georgia, Kazakhstan, Kyrgyzstan, Mongolia, Tajikistan, Turkmenistan, Uzbekistan.

■ East Asia and the Pacific
(33 countries/territories)
Australia, Brunei Darussalam, Cambodia, China, Cook Islands, Democratic People's Republic of Korea, Fiji, Indonesia, Japan, Kiribati, Lao People's Democratic Republic, Macao (China), Malaysia, Marshall Islands, Micronesia (Federated States of), Myanmar, Nauru, New Zealand, Niue, Palau, Papua New Guinea, Philippines, Republic of Korea, Samoa, Singapore, Solomon Islands, Thailand, Timor-Leste, Tokelau, Tonga, Tuvalu, Vanuatu, Viet Nam.

■ Latin America and the Caribbean
(41 countries/territories)
Anguilla, Antigua and Barbuda, Argentina, Aruba, Bahamas, Barbados, Belize, Bermuda, Bolivia, Brazil, British Virgin Islands, Cayman Islands, Chile, Colombia, Costa Rica, Cuba, Dominica, Dominican Republic, Ecuador, El Salvador, Grenada, Guatemala, Guyana, Haiti, Honduras, Jamaica, Mexico, Montserrat, Netherlands Antilles, Nicaragua, Panama, Paraguay, Peru, Saint Kitts and Nevis, Saint Lucia, Saint Vincent and the Grenadines, Suriname, Trinidad and Tobago, Turks and Caicos Islands, Uruguay, Venezuela.

■ North America and Western Europe
(26 countries)
Andorra, Austria, Belgium, Canada, Cyprus, Denmark, Finland, France, Germany, Greece, Iceland, Ireland, Israel, Italy, Luxembourg, Malta, Monaco, Netherlands, Norway, Portugal, San Marino, Spain, Sweden, Switzerland, United Kingdom, United States.

■ South and West Asia (9 countries)
Afghanistan, Bangladesh, Bhutan, India, Islamic Republic of Iran, Maldives, Nepal, Pakistan, Sri Lanka.

■ Sub-Saharan Africa (45 countries)
Angola, Benin, Botswana, Burkina Faso, Burundi, Cameroon, Cape Verde, Central African Republic, Chad, Comoros, Congo, Côte d'Ivoire, Democratic Republic of the Congo, Equatorial Guinea, Eritrea, Ethiopia, Gabon, Gambia, Ghana, Guinea, Guinea-Bissau, Kenya, Lesotho, Liberia, Madagascar, Malawi, Mali, Mauritius, Mozambique, Namibia, Niger, Nigeria, Rwanda, Sao Tome and Principe, Senegal, Seychelles, Sierra Leone, Somalia, South Africa, Swaziland, Togo, Uganda, United Republic of Tanzania, Zambia, Zimbabwe.

Reference dates for 2000-2004 national literacy data

Year	Country	Data Source	Literacy definition	Mode
2001	Albania	Census		Not specified
2001	Armenia	Population Census (preliminary results)		Not specified
2000	Belize	Census	Literates are persons of 14+ years who have 7 or 8 years at primary level or from secondary level up.	Educational attainment proxies
2001	Bolivia	Census	Illiterates are persons who declare that they cannot read or write a simple statement on their everyday life.	Self-declaration
2002	Brazil	IBGE National Household Sample Survey	A person is considered literate if he/she is able to read and write a simple sentence in a known language. A previously literate person who has become physically or mentally disabled is also considered literate. If the person has previously learned to read and write but has forgotten, he/she is considered illiterate. A person who is only able to write his/her own name is also considered illiterate.	Self-declaration
2001	Brunei Darussalam	National Census		Not specified
1996	Burkina Faso	Recensement Général de la Population et de l'Habitat	Literates are persons who declare that they can read and write in either a national language or a foreign language.	Self-declaration
2000/01	Cameroon	Deuxième Enquête auprès des Ménages - ECAMII	Literacy is the ability of people aged 15+ to read and write in French or in English.	Self-declaration
2000	Central African Republic	MICS	Literacy is defined as the ability to read easily or with difficulty a letter or a newspaper.	Self-declaration
2002	Chile	National Census		Not specified
2000	China	Population Census	In urban areas: literate refers to a person who knows a minimum of 2,000 characters. In rural areas: literate refers to a person who knows a minimum of 1,500 characters.	Self-declaration
2000	Côte d'Ivoire	MICS		Not specified
2001	Croatia	Census	Literate is any person, with or without schooling, who is able to read and write a composition concerning everyday life, for example a letter, irrespective of the language or script he or she reads or writes in.	Self-declaration
2001	Cyprus	Census	Literate is a person who can read and write simple sentences.	Self-declaration
2001	Ecuador	National Population Census	Illiterate persons are those who declare that they cannot read and write.	Self-declaration
1996	Egypt	Population Census	Literates are persons who can read and write.	Self-declaration
2000	Estonia	Census		Not specified
1996	Fiji	National Census		Not specified
2001	Honduras	Population Census	Literate refers to those who can read and write.	Self-declaration
2001	India	National Census	Illiterate persons were identified during National Family Health Survey as those who could not read or write.	Not specified
2002	Iran, Islamic Republic of	Household Employment and Unemployment Survey		Not specified
2000	Latvia	Population and Housing Census	Illiterate is a person who is not able to read and write.	Self-declaration
2001	Lesotho	Demographic survey	Literates are persons who can read and write.	Self-declaration
2001	Lithuania	Census	Illiterate is marked for a person unable to read (with understanding) or write a simple sentence on topics of everyday life.	Self-declaration
2001	Macao, China	Census	A person aged 15+ is defined as literate if he can, with understanding, both read and write a short, simple statement on his everyday life.	Self-declaration
2000	Malaysia	Census	Literate refers to persons aged 10 and over who have been to school.	Educational attainment proxies

INTRODUCTION / 253

Year	Country	Data Source	Literacy definition	Mode
1998	Mali	National Census		Not specified
2000	Mauritius	Housing and Population Census	A person is considered literate if he/she can, with understanding, both read and write a short, simple statement on his/her everyday life, in any language.	Self-declaration
2000	Mexico	Census	The ability to write and read is determined taking as base the population from 6 to 14 years old. Illiterates are persons aged 15+ who cannot read or write.	Self-declaration
2000	Mongolia	Census		Not specified
1996	New Caledonia	Population Census	Literate is a person who knows how to write and read the French language.	Self-declaration
2001	Nicaragua	Survey	Literate is a person who can read and write; illiterate is a person who can only read or who cannot read and write.	Self-declaration
1998	Pakistan	Population Census	A person who can read a newspaper and write a simple letter in any language is treated as literate.	Self-declaration
2000/1	Paraguay	Encuesta Integrada de Hogares	Illiterates are defined as people aged 15+ who have not attained grade 2 of education.	Educational attainment proxies
2002	Peru	National Household Survey - INEI		Not specified
2000	Philippines	Population and Housing Census	1 - Simple literacy is the ability to read and write a simple message. A person is literate when he can both read and write a simple message in any language or dialect. A person who cannot both read and write a simple message like "Census 2000 count me in" is illiterate. Also considered illiterate is a person capable only of reading and writing his own name or reading and writing numbers, as well as a person who can read but not write or vice versa. 2 - A person who knows how to read and write but at the time of the census can no longer read and/or write due to some physical defect or illness is considered illiterate. Example: an aged person who knows how to read and write but can no longer perform these activities due to poor eyesight. 3 - Disabled persons who can read and write through any means such as Braille are considered literate.	Self-declaration
1997	Qatar	Population Census		Self-declaration
2002	Romania	Population and Housing Census	Literates = primary level + secondary level + post-secondary level + people who read and write. Illiterates = people who read but cannot write + people who can neither read nor write.	Educational attainment proxies
2003	Seychelles	Census	A person aged 12 or more who can read and write a simple sentence in any language.	Self-declaration
2000	Singapore	Population Census		Not specified
2001	Slovakia	Population and Housing Census		Not specified
2002	Syrian Arab Republic		Illiterates are individuals who cannot read and write the Arabic language.	Self-declaration
2000	Tajikistan	Population Census	A literate person is an individual who can read and write.	Self declaration
2000	Thailand	Population and Housing Census	Literate persons are defined as persons aged 5 and over who are able to read and write simple statements with understanding, in any language. If a person can read but cannot write, then he/she is classified as illiterate.	Self-declaration
1996	Tonga	National Population Census		Self-declaration
2000	Turkey	General Population Census	Literate is a person who knows how to read and write.	Self-declaration
1995	Turkmenistan	Population Census	Literate is a person aged 7+ who can read and write or only read, no matter the language used; illiterate is a person who cannot read.	Self-declaration
1999	Viet Nam	Population and Housing Census		Not specified

Table 1
Background statistics

Country or territory	Total population (000) 2001	Average annual growth rate (%) 2000-2005	Life expectancy at birth (years) 2000-2005 Total	Life expectancy at birth (years) 2000-2005 Female	Total fertility rate (children per woman) 2000-2005	Infant mortality rate (‰) 2000-2005	HIV prevalence rate (%) in adults (ages 15-49) 2001 Total	HIV[3] prevalence rate (%) in young people (ages 15-24) 2001 Male	HIV[3] prevalence rate (%) in young people (ages 15-24) 2001 Female	Number of children orphaned by AIDS (000) 2001
Arab States										
Algeria	30 746	1.7	69.7	71.3	2.8	43.9	0.1	…	…	…
Bahrain	693	2.2	74.0	75.9	2.7	14.2	0.3	…	…	…
Djibouti	681	1.6	45.7	46.8	5.7	102.4	…	…	…	…
Egypt[w]	69 124	2.0	68.8	71.0	3.3	40.6	<0.1	…	…	…
Iraq	23 860	2.7	60.7	62.3	4.8	83.3	<0.1	…	…	…
Jordan[w]	5 183	2.7	71.0	72.5	3.6	23.9	<0.1	…	…	…
Kuwait[6]	2 353	3.5	76.6	79.0	2.7	10.8	…	…	…	…
Lebanon	3 537	1.6	73.5	75.1	2.2	17.2	…	…	…	…
Libyan Arab Jamahiriya[6]	5 340	1.9	72.8	75.4	3.0	20.7	0.2	…	…	…
Mauritania	2 724	3.0	52.5	54.1	5.8	96.7	…	…	…	…
Morocco	29 585	1.6	68.7	70.5	2.7	42.1	0.1	…	…	…
Oman	2 688	2.9	72.4	74.4	5.0	19.7	0.1	…	…	…
Palestinian Autonomous Territories	3 310	3.6	72.4	74.0	5.6	20.7	…	…	…	…
Qatar[6]	591	1.5	72.2	75.4	3.2	12.3	…	…	…	…
Saudi Arabia	22 829	2.9	72.3	73.7	4.5	20.6	…	…	…	…
Sudan	32 151	2.2	55.6	57.1	4.4	77.0	2.6	1.5	4.2	62
Syrian Arab Republic	16 968	2.4	71.9	73.1	3.3	22.3	…	…	…	…
Tunisia[w]	9 624	1.1	72.8	74.9	2.0	23.3	…	…	…	…
United Arab Emirates[6]	2 879	1.9	74.7	77.4	2.8	13.6	…	…	…	…
Yemen	18 651	3.5	60.0	61.1	7.0	70.6	0.1	…	…	…
Central and Eastern Europe										
Albania[o]	3 122	0.7	73.7	76.7	2.3	25.0	…	…	…	…
Belarus[6]	9 986	-0.5	70.1	75.3	1.2	11.3	0.3	0.8	0.3	…
Bosnia and Herzegovina[o]	4 067	1.1	74.0	76.7	1.3	13.5	<0.1	…	…	…
Bulgaria[o, 6]	8 033	-0.8	70.9	74.6	1.1	15.2	<0.1	…	…	…
Croatia	4 445	-0.2	74.2	78.1	1.7	8.1	<0.1	0	0	…
Czech Republic[o, 6]	10 257	-0.1	75.4	78.7	1.2	5.6	<0.1	0	0	…
Estonia[o, 6]	1 353	-1.1	71.7	76.8	1.2	9.4	1.0	3.2	0.8	…
Hungary[o, 6]	9 968	-0.5	71.9	76.0	1.2	8.8	0.1	0.1	0.03	…
Latvia[o, 6]	2 351	-0.9	71.0	76.2	1.1	14.2	0.4	1.1	0.3	…
Lithuania[o, 6]	3 484	-0.6	72.7	77.6	1.3	8.7	0.1	0.2	0.1	…
Poland[o, 6]	38 651	-0.1	73.9	78.0	1.3	9.1	0.1	0.1	0.1	…
Republic of Moldova	4 276	-0.1	68.9	72.2	1.4	18.1	0.2	…	…	…
Romania[o, 6]	22 437	-0.2	70.5	74.2	1.3	20.0	<0.1	…	…	…
Russian Federation[w, 6]	144 877	-0.6	66.8	73.1	1.1	15.9	0.9	2.2	0.8	…
Serbia and Montenegro	10 545	-0.1	73.2	75.6	1.7	13.0	0.2	…	…	…
Slovakia[6]	5 394	0.1	73.7	77.6	1.3	8.0	<0.1	0	0	…
Slovenia[o]	1 988	-0.1	76.3	79.8	1.1	5.5	<0.1	0	0	…
The former Yugoslav Rep. of Macedonia[o]	2 035	0.5	73.6	75.8	1.9	16.0	<0.1	…	…	…
Turkey[o]	69 303	1.4	70.5	73.2	2.4	39.5	<0.1	…	…	…
Ukraine[6]	49 290	-0.8	69.7	74.7	1.2	13.8	1.0	2.5	1.1	…
Central Asia										
Armenia	3 088	-0.5	72.4	75.6	1.2	17.3	0.2	0.3	0.1	…
Azerbaijan	8 226	0.9	72.2	75.5	2.1	29.3	<0.1	0.1	0.02	…
Georgia	5 224	-0.9	73.6	77.6	1.4	17.6	<0.1	0.1	0.03	…
Kazakhstan	15 533	-0.4	66.3	71.9	2.0	51.7	0.1	…	…	…
Kyrgyzstan	4 995	1.4	68.6	72.3	2.6	37.0	<0.1	0	0	…
Mongolia	2 528	1.3	63.9	65.9	2.4	58.2	<0.1	…	…	…
Tajikistan	6 144	0.9	68.8	71.4	3.1	50.0	<0.1	0	0	…
Turkmenistan	4 720	1.5	67.1	70.4	2.7	48.6	<0.1	0	0	…
Uzbekistan	25 313	1.5	69.7	72.5	2.4	36.7	<0.1	0.01	0	…
East Asia and the Pacific										
Australia[o]	19 352	1.0	79.2	82.0	1.7	5.5	0.1	0.1	0.02	…
Brunei Darussalam[6]	342	2.3	76.3	78.9	2.5	6.1	…	…	…	…
Cambodia	13 478	2.4	57.4	59.5	4.8	73.2	2.7	1.2	3.0	55

1. United Nations Population Division statistics.
2. Joint United Nations Programme on HIV/AIDS (UNAIDS).
3. Data are high estimates.
4. World Bank statistics.
5. *Human Development Report 2003.*
6. Data on net aid per capita refer to net official aid.
(z) Data are for 2000.

Table 1

	GNP[4]			AID AND POVERTY[5]		EXTERNAL DEBT[5]					
Average annual growth rate (%)	GNP per capita			Net aid per capita, current US$	Population living on less than $2 per day (%)	Total debt, current US$ (millions)	Total debt service, current US$ (millions)	Total debt as % of GNP	Public debt service as % of government current revenue	Total debt service as % of exports	Country or territory
	Current US$	PPP US$									
1998-2001	2001	2001		2001	1990-2001	2001	2001	2001	2001	2001	

Arab States

5.3	1 650	5 910	5.9	15.1	22 503	4 375	8.3	21.3	19.5	Algeria
8.1	11 130	15 390	25.8	...	...	...	...	...	...	Bahrain
3.9	890	2 420	80.9	...	...	11	...	...	5.4[z]	Djibouti
6.1	1 530	3 560	18.2	43.9	29 234	1 932	1.9	...	8.8	Egypt[w]
...	...	...	5.1	...	...	...	...	...	...	Iraq
4.2	1 750	3 880	83.3	7.4	7 479	669	7.6	26.0	14.7	Jordan[w]
6.8	18 270	21 530	1.5	...	...	...	...	...	...	Kuwait[6]
1.3	4 010	4 400	68.1	...	12 450	1 457	8.3	...	40.5	Lebanon
...	...	...	1.9	...	...	...	...	...	...	Libyan Arab Jamahiriya[6]
0.7	360	1 940	96.1	68.7	2 164	89	9.1	...	16.5	Mauritania
-1.3	1 190	3 500	17.5	14.3	16 962	2 628	7.9	...	21.9	Morocco
...	...	10 720	0.6	...	6 025	1 667	...	14.7	6.8	Oman
...	...	...	261.3	...	...	...	...	...	...	Palestinian Autonomous Territories
...	...	...	1.7	...	...	...	...	...	...	Qatar[6]
7.7	8 460	13 290	1.2	...	...	...	...	...	...	Saudi Arabia
2.6	340	1 750	5.3	...	15 348	56	0.5	...	3.2	Sudan
8.7	1 040	3 160	9.0	...	21 305	266	1.4	...	2.1	Syrian Arab Republic
0.1	2 070	6 090	39.2	10.0	10 884	1 355	7.1	...	13.4	Tunisia[w]
...	...	...	1.0	...	...	...	...	...	...	United Arab Emirates[6]
11.8	450	730	22.8	45.2	4 954	288	3.4	...	6.3	Yemen

Central and Eastern Europe

11.0	1 340	3 810	86.1	...	1 094	36	0.8	...	3.1	Albania[o]
-7.1	1 290	7 630	3.9	...	869	232	1.9	5.4	2.7	Belarus[6]
3.5	1 240	6 250	157.2	...	2 226	300	6.0	...	18.3	Bosnia and Herzegovina[o]
2.1	1 650	6 740	43.1	...	9 615	1 368	10.3	19.1	15.5	Bulgaria[o, 6]
-2.8	4 550	8 930	25.7	...	10 742	2 960	15.0	16.9	13.7	Croatia
-0.4	5 310	14 320	30.7	...	21 691	4 779	8.7	9.7	4.4	Czech Republic[o, 6]
0.6	3 870	9 650	50.6	...	2 852	383	7.3	2.3	0.9	Estonia[o, 6]
3.7	4 830	11 990	41.9	...	30 289	13 729	27.2	...	8.5	Hungary[o, 6]
7.3	3 230	7 760	45.2	...	5 710	516	6.8	4.9	2.9	Latvia[o, 6]
4.0	3 350	8 350	37.4	...	5 248	1 936	16.4	11.1	5.9	Lithuania[o, 6]
3.6	4 230	9 370	25.0	...	62 393	15 378	8.8	11.4	11.5	Poland[o, 6]
-3.1	400	2 300	27.9	...	1 214	189	12.0	40.6	15.3	Republic of Moldova
3.8	1 720	5 780	28.9	...	11 653	2 607	6.8	16.4	13.7	Romania[o, 6]
3.5	1 750	6 880	7.7	...	152 649	17 322	5.8	12.0	12.0	Russian Federation[w, 6]
...	930	...	122.6	...	11 740	109	1.0	...	2.0	Serbia and Montenegro
-2.7	3 760	11 780	30.4	...	11 121	2 615	13.0	14.0	6.2	Slovakia[6]
-1.5	9 760	17 060	63.0	...	...	...	...	...	...	Slovenia[o]
-1.3	1 690	6 040	121.7	...	1 423	194	5.7	...	10.3	The former Yugoslav Rep. of Macedonia[o]
-10.6	2 530	5 830	2.4	10.3	115 118	22 387	15.3	26.0	24.6	Turkey[o]
-3.5	720	4 270	10.6	...	12 811	2 255	6.1	8.2	6.5	Ukraine[6]

Central Asia

4.4	570	2 730	68.7	...	1 001	55	2.5	...	8.1	Armenia
5.7	650	2 890	27.5	...	1 219	132	2.5	...	4.7	Azerbaijan
-5.5	590	2 580	55.5	...	1 714	77	2.5	15.2	8.1	Georgia
-1.0	1 350	6 150	9.5	...	14 372	3 331	15.7	18.6	4.7	Kazakhstan
-2.3	280	2 630	37.7	...	1 717	177	12.1	...	12.0	Kyrgyzstan
1.9	400	1 710	83.9	50.0	885	45	4.4	11.6	7.9	Mongolia
-6.7	180	1 140	25.9	...	1 086	80	7.8	25.5	6.3	Tajikistan
26.4	950	4 240	15.2	...	...	...	...	...	14.4	Turkmenistan
-9.4	550	2 410	6.1	...	4 627	833	7.5	...	20.6	Uzbekistan

East Asia and the Pacific

-0.2	19 900	24 630	...	...	...	...	...	...	...	Australia[o]
...	...	...	1.0	...	...	...	...	...	...	Brunei Darussalam[6]
4.9	270	1 790	30.3	...	2 704	21	0.6	...	1.1	Cambodia

Table 1 (continued)

Country or territory	Total population (000) 2001	Average annual growth rate (%) 2000-2005	Life expectancy at birth (years) 2000-2005 Total	Life expectancy at birth (years) 2000-2005 Female	Total fertility rate (children per woman) 2000-2005	Infant mortality rate (‰) 2000-2005	HIV prevalence rate (%) in adults (ages 15-49) 2001 Total	HIV[3] prevalence rate (%) in young people (ages 15-24) 2001 Male	HIV[3] prevalence rate (%) in young people (ages 15-24) 2001 Female	Number of children orphaned by AIDS (000) 2001
China[w]	1 285 229	0.7	71.0	73.3	1.8	36.6	0.1	0.2	0.1	76
Cook Islands	18	0.2	...	...	...	...	...	...	...	...
Democratic People's Republic of Korea	22 409	0.5	63.1	66.0	2.0	45.1	...	...	...	...
Fiji	822	1.0	69.8	71.5	2.9	17.8	0.1	...	...	...
Indonesia[w]	214 356	1.3	66.8	68.8	2.4	41.6	0.1	0.1	0.1	18
Japan[o]	127 271	0.1	81.6	85.1	1.3	3.2	<0.1	0.02	0.04	2
Kiribati	85	1.4	...	...	...	...	...	...	...	...
Lao People's Democratic Republic	5 403	2.3	54.5	55.8	4.8	88.0	<0.1	0.1	0.03	...
Macao, China	455	0.9	78.9	81.2	1.1	8.6	...	...	...	...
Malaysia[w]	23 492	1.9	73.1	75.7	2.9	10.1	0.4	0.8	0.1	14
Marshall Islands	52	1.2	...	...	...	...	...	...	...	...
Micronesia (Federated States of)	107	0.8	68.6	69.1	3.8	33.9	...	...	...	...
Myanmar	48 205	1.3	57.3	60.2	2.9	83.5	...	...	...	...
Nauru	12	2.3	...	...	...	...	...	...	...	...
New Zealand[o]	3 815	0.8	78.3	80.7	2.0	5.8	0.1	0.1	0.02	...
Niue	2	-1.2	...	...	...	...	...	...	...	...
Palau	20	2.1	...	...	...	...	...	...	...	...
Papua New Guinea	5 460	2.2	57.6	58.7	4.1	62.1	0.7	0.5	0.5	4
Philippines[w]	77 151	1.8	70.0	72.0	3.2	29.0	<0.1	0.02	0.02	4
Republic of Korea[o, 6]	47 142	0.6	75.5	79.3	1.4	5.0	<0.1	0.03	0.01	1
Samoa	175	1.0	70.0	73.4	4.1	26.1	...	...	...	...
Singapore[6]	4 105	1.7	78.1	80.3	1.4	2.9	0.2	0.2	0.2	...
Solomon Islands	450	2.9	69.2	70.7	4.4	20.7	...	...	...	...
Thailand[w]	61 555	1.0	69.3	73.5	1.9	19.8	1.8	1.3	2.0	290
Timor-Leste	711	4.0	49.5	50.4	3.8	123.7	...	...	...	...
Tokelau	2	-0.1	...	...	...	...	...	...	...	...
Tonga	102	1.0	68.6	69.1	3.7	33.9	...	...	...	...
Tuvalu	10	1.2	...	...	...	...	...	...	...	...
Vanuatu	202	2.4	68.8	70.5	4.1	28.5	...	...	...	...
Viet Nam	79 197	1.3	69.2	71.6	2.3	33.6	0.3	0.4	0.2	22
Latin America and the Caribbean										
Anguilla	11	1.7	...	...	...	...	...	...	...	...
Antigua and Barbuda	72	0.5	...	...	...	...	...	...	...	...
Argentina[w]	37 529	1.2	74.2	77.7	2.4	20.0	0.7	1.0	0.4	25
Aruba	96	2.0	...	...	...	...	...	...	...	...
Bahamas[6]	307	1.1	67.1	70.3	2.3	17.7	3.5	3.6	4.1	3
Barbados	268	0.4	77.2	79.5	1.5	10.9	1.2	...	...	...
Belize	245	2.1	71.4	73.0	3.2	31.1	2.0	1.3	2.4	1
Bermuda	80	0.7	...	...	...	...	...	...	...	...
Bolivia	8 481	1.9	63.9	66.0	3.8	55.6	0.1	0.2	0.1	1
Brazil[w]	174 029	1.2	68.1	72.6	2.2	38.4	0.7	0.8	0.6	130
British Virgin Islands	20	1.8	...	...	...	...	...	...	...	...
Cayman Islands	38	3.0	...	...	...	...	...	...	...	...
Chile[w]	15 419	1.2	76.1	79.0	2.4	11.6	0.3	0.5	0.2	4
Colombia	42 826	1.6	72.2	75.3	2.6	25.6	0.4	1.2	0.3	21
Costa Rica	4 013	1.9	78.1	80.6	2.3	10.5	0.6	0.8	0.4	3
Cuba	11 238	0.3	76.7	78.7	1.6	7.3	<0.1	0.1	0.1	1
Dominica	78	0.3	...	...	...	...	...	...	...	...
Dominican Republic	8 485	1.5	66.7	69.2	2.7	35.7	2.5	2.5	3.3	33
Ecuador	12 616	1.5	70.8	73.5	2.8	41.5	0.3	0.4	0.2	7
El Salvador	6 313	1.6	70.7	73.7	2.9	26.4	0.6	1.0	0.5	13
Grenada	81	-0.3	...	...	...	...	...	...	...	...
Guatemala	11 728	2.6	65.8	68.9	4.4	41.2	1.0	1.2	1.1	32
Guyana	762	0.2	63.2	66.3	2.3	51.2	2.7	4.4	5.4	4
Haiti	8 111	1.3	49.5	50.0	4.0	63.2	6.1	5.5	6.7	200
Honduras	6 619	2.3	68.9	71.4	3.7	32.1	1.6	1.4	1.8	14
Jamaica[w]	2 603	0.9	75.7	77.8	2.4	19.9	1.2	1.0	1.0	5
Mexico[o]	100 456	1.5	73.4	76.4	2.5	28.2	0.3	0.5	0.1	27
Montserrat	3	0.3	...	...	...	...	...	...	...	...

1. United Nations Population Division statistics.
2. Joint United Nations Programme on HIV/AIDS (UNAIDS).
3. Data are high estimates.
4. World Bank statistics.
5. *Human Development Report 2003*.
6. Data on net aid per capita refer to net official aid.
(z) Data are for 2000.

Table 1

	GNP[4]			AID AND POVERTY[5]		EXTERNAL DEBT[5]					
Average annual growth rate (%)	GNP per capita Current US$	GNP per capita PPP US$		Net aid per capita, current US$	Population living on less than $2 per day (%)	Total debt, current US$ (millions)	Total debt service, current US$ (millions)	Total debt as % of GNP	Public debt service as % of government current revenue	Total debt service as % of exports	Country or territory
1998-2001	2001	2001		2001	1990-2001	2001	2001	2001	2001	2001	
7.0	890	3 950		1.1	47.3	170 110	24 297	2.1	…	4.2	China[w]
…	…	…		…	…	…	…	…	…	…	Cook Islands
…	…	…		5.3	…	…	…	…	…	…	Democratic People's Republic of Korea
2.8	2 150	4 920		31.6	…	…	26	…	…	1.5	Fiji
15.7	690	2 830		7.0	55.4	135 704	15 530	11.1	22.4	13.8	Indonesia[w]
1.8	35 610	25 550		…	…	…	…	…	…	…	Japan[o]
-7.5	…	…		…	…	…	…	…	…	…	Kiribati
10.3	300	1 540		45.0	73.2	2 495	44	2.6	…	9.0	Lao People's Democratic Republic
-1.6	14 380	21 630		…	…	…	…	…	…	…	Macao, China
5.3	3 330	7 910		1.1	9.3	43 351	6 229	7.8	…	3.6	Malaysia[w]
2.5	2 190	…		…	…	—	…	…	…	…	Marshall Islands
5.1	2 150	…		…	…	—	…	…	…	…	Micronesia (Federated States of)
…	…	…		2.6	…	5 670	84	…	…	2.8	Myanmar
…	…	…		…	…	…	…	…	…	…	Nauru
-2.3	13 250	18 250		…	…	…	…	…	…	…	New Zealand[o]
…	…	…		…	…	…	…	…	…	…	Niue
5.1	6 780	…		…	…	—	…	…	…	…	Palau
-8.0	580	2 450		37.2	…	2 521	268	9.5	…	7.1	Papua New Guinea
3.4	1 030	4 070		7.5	46.4	52 356	7 776	10.3	49.4	13.3	Philippines[w]
10.6	9 460	15 060		-2.4	<2.0	110 109	26 040	6.2	…	7.1	Republic of Korea[o, 6]
3.8	1 490	6 130		246.6	…	…	7	…	…	7.1[z]	Samoa
-0.3	21 500	22 850		0.2	…	…	…	…	…	…	Singapore[6]
-3.7	590	1 910		130.7	…	…	7	…	…	2.7[z]	Solomon Islands
-0.1	1 940	6 230		4.6	32.5	67 384	20 073	18.0	24.3	7.9	Thailand[w]
…	…	…		…	…	…	…	…	…	…	Timor-Leste
…	…	…		…	…	…	…	…	…	…	Tokelau
-5.0	1 530	…		…	…	…	2	…	…	…	Tonga
…	…	…		…	…	…	…	…	…	…	Tuvalu
-2.2	1 050	3 110		156.5	…	…	2	…	…	1.1	Vanuatu
7.1	410	2 070		18.1	63.7	12 578	1 216	3.7	17.2	6.5	Viet Nam

Latin America and the Caribbean

…	…	…		…	…	…	…	…	…	…	Anguilla
3.3	9 150	9 550		118.9	…	…	…	…	…	…	Antigua and Barbuda
-3.7	6 940	10 980		4.0	…	136 709	24 254	9.3	43.6	48.6	Argentina[w]
…	…	…		…	…	…	…	…	…	…	Aruba
…	…	15 680		27.5	…	…	…	…	…	…	Bahamas[6]
5.1	9 750	15 110		-4.3	…	…	69	…	…	4.3[z]	Barbados
6.6	2 940	5 150		87.1	…	…	98	…	…	24.5	Belize
…	…	…		…	…	…	…	…	…	…	Bermuda
-2.4	950	2 240		85.9	34.3	4 682	544	7.0	17.4	16.1	Bolivia
-14.4	3 070	7 070		2.0	23.7	226 362	54 322	11.3	…	28.6	Brazil[w]
…	…	…		…	…	…	…	…	…	…	British Virgin Islands
…	…	…		…	…	…	…	…	…	…	Cayman Islands
-3.5	4 590	8 840		3.7	8.7	38 360	6 634	10.4	8.0	5.2	Chile[w]
-6.5	1 890	6 790		8.9	26.5	36 699	6 297	7.9	…	28.1	Colombia
5.0	4 060	9 260		0.6	14.3	4 586	695	4.4	16.9	8.2	Costa Rica
…	…	…		4.5	<2.0	…	…	…	…	…	Cuba
-1.3	3 200	4 920		254.5	…	…	16	…	…	11.9	Dominica
10.3	2 230	6 650		12.4	<2.0	5 093	621	3.1	…	6.6	Dominican Republic
-4.4	1 080	2 960		13.6	52.3	13 910	1 550	9.6	…	22.0	Ecuador
4.4	2 040	5 160		37.1	45.0	4 683	384	2.9	…	7.4	El Salvador
4.3	3 610	6 290		142.6	…	…	17	…	…	5.4[z]	Grenada
2.2	1 680	4 380		19.2	37.4	5 037	435	2.2	…	8.5	Guatemala
-1.2	840	4 280		133.6	6.1	…	44	…	…	8.0	Guyana
-0.1	480	1 870		20.4	…	1 250	26	0.7	…	4.5	Haiti
7.3	900	2 760		102.4	44.4	5 051	340	5.4	…	5.7	Honduras
0.4	2 800	3 490		20.7	13.3	4 956	644	8.8	21.6	16.8	Jamaica[w]
14.0	5 530	8 240		0.8	24.3	158 290	48 300	8.1	…	14.1	Mexico[o]
…	…	…		…	…	…	…	…	…	…	Montserrat

Table 1 (continued)

Country or territory	DEMOGRAPHY[1] Total population (000) 2001	Average annual growth rate (%) 2000-2005	Life expectancy at birth (years) 2000-2005 Total	Life expectancy at birth (years) 2000-2005 Female	Total fertility rate (children per woman) 2000-2005	Infant mortality rate (‰) 2000-2005	HIV/AIDS[2] HIV prevalence rate (%) in adults (ages 15-49) 2001 Total	HIV[3] prevalence rate (%) in young people (ages 15-24) 2001 Male	HIV[3] prevalence rate (%) in young people (ages 15-24) 2001 Female	Number of children orphaned by AIDS (000) 2001
Netherlands Antilles	217	0.8	76.3	79.2	2.1	12.6	...	...	...	...
Nicaragua	5 204	2.4	69.5	71.9	3.7	35.7	0.2	0.3	0.1	2
Panama	3 007	1.8	74.7	77.4	2.7	20.6	1.5	2.4	1.6	8
Paraguay[w]	5 604	2.4	70.9	73.1	3.8	37.0	...	0.2	...	...
Peru[w]	26 362	1.5	69.8	72.4	2.9	33.4	0.4	0.5	0.2	17
Saint Kitts and Nevis	42	-0.3	...	...	...	...	...	...	...	...
Saint Lucia	147	0.8	72.5	74.1	2.3	14.8	...	...	...	...
Saint Vincent and the Grenadines	118	0.6	74.1	75.6	2.2	15.7	...	...	...	...
Suriname	429	0.8	71.1	73.7	2.5	25.7	1.2	1.6	2.1	2
Trinidad and Tobago	1 294	0.3	71.3	74.4	1.6	14.1	2.5	3.3	4.4	4
Turks and Caicos Islands	19	3.5	...	...	...	...	...	...	...	...
Uruguay[w]	3 366	0.7	75.3	78.9	2.3	13.1	0.3	0.6	0.2	3
Venezuela	24 752	1.9	73.7	76.7	2.7	18.9	0.5	0.7	...	...
North America and Western Europe										
Andorra	67	2.6	...	...	...	...	...	...	...	...
Austria[o]	8 106	0.05	78.5	81.5	1.3	4.7	0.2	0.3	0.1	...
Belgium[o]	10 273	0.2	78.8	81.9	1.7	4.2	0.2	0.1	0.1	...
Canada[o]	31 025	0.8	79.3	81.9	1.5	5.3	0.3	0.3	0.2	...
Cyprus[o,6]	789	0.8	78.3	80.5	1.9	7.7	0.3	...	...	...
Denmark[o]	5 338	0.2	76.6	79.1	1.8	5.0	0.2	0.2	0.1	...
Finland[o]	5 188	0.2	78.0	81.5	1.7	4.0	<0.1	0.04	0.03	...
France[o]	59 564	0.5	79.0	82.8	1.9	5.0	0.3	0.3	0.2	...
Germany[o]	82 349	0.1	78.3	81.2	1.4	4.5	0.1	0.1	0.1	...
Greece[o]	10 947	0.1	78.3	80.9	1.3	6.4	0.2	0.2	0.1	...
Iceland[o]	285	0.8	79.8	81.9	2.0	3.4	0.2	...	...	...
Ireland[o]	3 865	1.1	77.0	79.6	1.9	5.8	0.1	0.1	0.1	...
Israel[o,6]	6 174	2.0	79.2	81.0	2.7	5.9	0.1	...	...	...
Italy[o]	57 521	-0.1	78.7	81.9	1.2	5.4	0.4	0.3	0.3	...
Luxembourg[o]	441	1.3	78.4	81.4	1.7	5.4	0.2	...	...	...
Malta[o]	391	0.4	78.4	80.7	1.8	7.1	0.1	...	...	...
Monaco	34	0.9	...	...	...	...	...	...	...	...
Netherlands[o]	15 982	0.5	78.3	81.0	1.7	4.5	0.2	0.2	0.1	...
Norway[o]	4 494	0.4	78.9	81.9	1.8	4.5	0.1	0.1	0.1	...
Portugal[o]	10 033	0.1	76.2	79.6	1.5	6.1	0.5	0.5	0.2	...
San Marino	27	1.0	...	...	...	...	...	...	...	...
Spain[o]	40 875	0.2	79.3	82.8	1.2	5.1	0.5	0.6	0.3	...
Sweden[o]	8 860	0.1	80.1	82.6	1.6	3.4	0.1	0.1	0.1	...
Switzerland[o]	7 173	0.0	79.1	82.3	1.4	4.8	0.5	0.6	0.5	...
United Kingdom[o]	58 881	0.3	78.2	80.7	1.6	5.4	0.1	0.1	0.1	...
United States[o]	288 025	1.0	77.1	79.9	2.1	6.7	0.6	0.6	0.3	...
South and West Asia										
Afghanistan	22 083	3.9	43.1	43.3	6.8	161.7	...	...	...	...
Bangladesh	140 880	2.0	61.4	61.8	3.5	64.0	<0.1	0.01	0.01	2
Bhutan	2 125	3.0	63.2	64.5	5.0	53.6	<0.1	...	...	...
India[w]	1 033 395	1.5	63.9	64.6	3.0	64.5	0.8	0.5	1.0	...
Iran, Islamic Republic of	67 245	1.2	70.3	71.9	2.3	33.3	<0.1	...	...	...
Maldives	300	3.0	67.4	67.0	5.3	38.3	0.1	...	...	...
Nepal	24 060	2.2	59.9	59.6	4.3	70.9	0.5	0.4	0.4	13
Pakistan	146 277	2.4	61.0	60.9	5.1	86.5	0.1	0.1	0.1	25
Sri Lanka[w]	18 752	0.8	72.6	75.9	2.0	20.1	<0.1	0.03	0.04	2
Sub-Saharan Africa										
Angola	12 768	3.2	40.1	41.5	7.2	140.3	5.5	2.9	7.3	100
Benin	6 387	2.6	50.6	53.0	5.7	92.7	3.6	1.4	4.5	34
Botswana	1 750	0.9	39.7	40.5	3.7	56.6	38.8	19.3	45.0	69
Burkina Faso	12 259	3.0	45.7	46.2	6.7	93.2	6.5	4.8	11.7	270
Burundi	6 412	3.1	40.9	41.4	6.8	107.4	8.3	6.3	14.1	240
Cameroon	15 429	1.8	46.2	47.4	4.6	88.1	11.8	6.6	15.3	210

1. United Nations Population Division statistics.
2. Joint United Nations Programme on HIV/AIDS (UNAIDS).
3. Data are high estimates.
4. World Bank statistics.
5. *Human Development Report 2003*.
6. Data on net aid per capita refer to net official aid.

(z) Data are for 2000.

STATISTICAL ANNEX / 259

Table 1

	GNP[4]		AID AND POVERTY[5]		EXTERNAL DEBT[5]					
Average annual growth rate (%)	GNP per capita		Net aid per capita, current US$	Population living on less than $2 per day (%)	Total debt, current US$ (millions)	Total debt service, current US$ (millions)	Total debt as % of GNP	Public debt service as % of government current revenue	Total debt service as % of exports	Country or territory
	Current US$	PPP US$								
1998-2001	2001	2001	2001	1990-2001	2001	2001	2001	2001	2001	
...	...	...	...	...	...	...	...	...	...	Netherlands Antilles
...	...	178.4	178.4	94.5	6 391	337	...	...	22.2	Nicaragua
3.0	3 260	5 440	9.3	17.9	8 245	1 178	12.2	...	11.2	Panama
-5.9	1 350	5 180	10.9	49.3	2 817	359	5.0	22.7	8.3	Paraguay[w]
-1.5	1 980	4 470	17.1	41.4	27 512	2 190	4.1	20.5	20.8	Peru[w]
6.5	6 630	10 190	253.0	...	...	21	...	...	13.5	Saint Kitts and Nevis
2.4	3 950	4 960	110.5	...	...	25	...	...	6.9	Saint Lucia
2.9	2 740	4 980	73.0	...	...	14	...	...	6.9	Saint Vincent and the Grenadines
-12.9	1 810	...	54.1	...	...	...	...	...	...	Suriname
13.1	5 960	8 620	-1.3	39.0	2 422	234	2.8	...	3.8	Trinidad and Tobago
...	...	...	...	...	...	...	...	...	...	Turks and Caicos Islands
-5.6	5 710	8 250	4.6	<2.0	9 706	1 489	8.1	26.3	30.3	Uruguay[w]
9.5	4 760	5 590	1.8	32.0	34 660	7 544	6.1	23.1	20.9	Venezuela
										North America and Western Europe
...	...	...	...	...	...	...	...	...	...	Andorra
-3.9	23 940	26 380	...	...	...	...	...	...	...	Austria[o]
-2.8	23 850	26 150	...	...	...	...	...	...	...	Belgium[o]
5.0	21 930	26 530	...	...	...	...	...	...	...	Canada[o]
-0.2	12 320	21 110	63.0	...	...	...	...	...	...	Cyprus[o, 6]
-2.4	30 600	28 490	...	...	...	...	...	...	...	Denmark[o]
-1.9	23 780	24 030	...	...	...	...	...	...	...	Finland[o]
-3.4	22 730	24 080	...	...	...	...	...	...	...	France[o]
-4.8	23 560	25 240	...	...	...	...	...	...	...	Germany[o]
-2.1	11 430	17 520	...	...	...	...	...	...	...	Greece[o]
-2.1	28 910	28 850	...	...	...	...	...	...	...	Iceland[o]
3.9	22 850	27 170	...	...	...	...	...	...	...	Ireland[o]
3.0	16 750	19 630	27.9	...	...	...	...	...	...	Israel[o, 6]
-2.9	19 390	24 530	...	...	...	...	...	...	...	Italy[o]
-4.2	39 840	48 560	...	...	...	...	...	...	...	Luxembourg[o]
1.7	9 210	13 140	4.4	...	...	137	...	...	2.6	Malta[o]
...	...	...	...	...	...	...	...	...	...	Monaco
-0.4	24 330	27 390	...	...	...	...	...	...	...	Netherlands[o]
3.9	35 630	29 340	...	...	...	...	...	...	...	Norway[o]
-1.1	10 900	17 710	...	...	...	...	...	...	...	Portugal[o]
...	...	...	...	...	...	...	...	...	...	San Marino
-0.5	14 300	19 860	...	...	...	...	...	...	...	Spain[o]
-4.3	25 400	23 800	...	...	...	...	...	...	...	Sweden[o]
-1.1	38 330	30 970	...	...	...	...	...	...	...	Switzerland[o]
-0.1	25 120	24 340	...	...	...	...	...	...	...	United Kingdom[o]
4.7	34 280	34 280	...	...	...	...	...	...	...	United States[o]
										South and West Asia
...	...	...	14.7	...	...	...	...	...	...	Afghanistan
1.8	360	1 600	7.3	82.8	15 216	672	1.4	...	9.0	Bangladesh
10.6	640	...	27.9	...	...	6	...	...	3.3	Bhutan
5.0	460	2 820	1.7	79.9	97 320	9 283	2.0	13.1	12.6	India[w]
3.5	1 680	5 940	1.7	7.3	7 483	1 283	1.1	...	4.1	Iran, Islamic Republic of
4.4	2 000	...	83.2	...	...	22	...	...	4.3	Maldives
5.0	250	1 360	16.1	82.5	2 700	89	1.5	13.5	6.2	Nepal
-2.1	420	1 860	13.2	65.6	32 019	2 958	5.1	23.1	21.3	Pakistan
1.4	880	3 260	17.6	45.4	8 529	716	4.4	19.5	9.2	Sri Lanka[w]
										Sub-Saharan Africa
13.8	500	1 690	21.0	...	9 600	1 865	23.7	...	26.0	Angola
0.4	380	970	42.8	...	1 665	50	2.1	...	10.0	Benin
-0.9	3 100	7 410	16.6	50.1	370	52	1.1	...	1.7	Botswana
-0.5	220	1 120	31.7	85.8	1 490	38	1.5	...	11.0	Burkina Faso
-7.9	100	680	20.4	89.2	1 065	23	3.4	...	36.3	Burundi
-0.9	580	1 580	25.8	64.4	8 338	342	4.3	...	9.9	Cameroon

Table 1 (continued)

	DEMOGRAPHY[1]					HIV/AIDS[2]			
	Total population (000)	Average annual growth rate (%)	Life expectancy at birth (years)		Total fertility rate (children per woman)	Infant mortality rate (‰)	HIV prevalence rate (%) in adults (ages 15-49)	HIV[3] prevalence rate (%) in young people (ages 15-24)		Number of children orphaned by AIDS (000)
Country or territory	2001	2000-2005	2000-2005 Total	2000-2005 Female	2000-2005	2000-2005	2001 Total	2001 Male	2001 Female	2001
Cape Verde	445	2.0	70.2	72.8	3.3	29.7	...	...	...	...
Central African Republic	3 770	1.3	39.5	40.6	4.9	100.4	12.9	7.0	16.3	110
Chad	8 103	3.0	44.7	45.7	6.7	115.3	3.6	3.2	5.8	72
Comoros	726	2.8	60.8	62.2	4.9	67.0	...	...	...	...
Congo	3 542	2.6	48.2	49.7	6.3	84.0	7.2	4.4	10.5	78
Côte d'Ivoire	16 098	1.6	41.0	41.2	4.7	101.3	9.7	...	...	...
Democratic Rep. of the Congo	49 785	2.9	41.8	42.8	6.7	119.6	4.9	...	...	...
Equatorial Guinea	468	2.6	49.1	50.5	5.9	100.9	3.4	1.9	3.7	...
Eritrea	3 847	3.7	52.7	54.2	5.4	73.0	2.8	3.6	5.5	24
Ethiopia	67 266	2.5	45.5	46.3	6.1	100.4	6.4	...	...	990
Gabon	1 283	1.8	56.6	57.5	4.0	56.8	...	...	...	...
Gambia	1 351	2.7	54.1	55.5	4.7	80.5	1.6	0.7	1.8	5
Ghana	20 028	2.2	57.9	59.3	4.1	57.8	3.0	1.8	3.9	200
Guinea	8 242	1.6	49.1	49.5	5.8	101.7	...	...	...	...
Guinea-Bissau	1 407	2.9	45.3	46.9	7.1	120.0	2.8	1.4	4.0	4
Kenya	31 065	1.5	44.6	45.6	4.0	69.3	15.0	7.2	18.7	890
Lesotho	1 794	0.1	35.1	37.7	3.8	92.1	31.0	23.5	51.4	73
Liberia	3 099	4.0	41.4	42.2	6.8	147.4	...	...	...	...
Madagascar	16 439	2.8	53.6	54.8	5.7	91.5	0.3	0.1	0.28	6
Malawi	11 627	2.0	37.5	37.7	6.1	115.4	15.0	7.6	17.9	470
Mali	12 256	3.0	48.6	49.1	7.0	118.7	1.7	1.8	2.8	70
Mauritius	1 198	1.0	72.0	75.8	1.9	16.0	0.1	...	...	...
Mozambique	18 204	1.8	38.1	39.6	5.6	122.0	13.0	7.8	18.8	420
Namibia	1 930	1.4	44.3	45.6	4.6	59.8	22.5	13.3	29.2	47
Niger	11 134	3.6	46.2	46.5	8.0	125.7	...	...	...	...
Nigeria	117 823	2.5	51.5	51.8	5.4	78.8	5.8	3.6	7.0	1 000
Rwanda	8 066	2.2	39.3	39.7	5.7	111.5	8.9	5.9	13.4	260
Sao Tome and Principe	153	2.5	69.9	72.8	4.0	31.6	...	...	...	...
Senegal	9 621	2.4	52.9	55.1	5.0	60.7	0.5	0.2	0.7	15
Seychelles	80	0.9	...	...	...	...	...	...	...	...
Sierra Leone	4 573	3.8	34.2	35.5	6.5	177.2	7.0	3.4	10.2	42
Somalia	9 088	4.2	47.9	49.5	7.3	117.7	1.0	...	...	...
South Africa	44 416	0.6	47.7	50.7	2.6	47.9	20.1	12.8	30.8	660
Swaziland	1 058	0.8	34.4	35.4	4.5	78.3	33.4	18.3	47.4	35
Togo	4 686	2.3	49.7	51.1	5.3	81.5	6.0	2.5	7.1	63
Uganda	24 225	3.2	46.2	46.9	7.1	86.1	5.0	2.4	5.6	880
United Republic of Tanzania	35 565	1.9	43.3	44.1	5.1	99.8	7.8	4.3	9.7	810
Zambia	10 570	1.2	32.4	32.1	5.6	104.8	21.5	9.7	25.2	570
Zimbabwe[w]	12 756	0.5	33.1	32.6	3.9	58.4	33.7	14.9	39.6	780

	Sum	Weighted average								
World	6 134 038	1.2	67.0	69.1	2.7	43.7	...	...	...	...
Countries in transition	281 672	-0.3	68.1	73.4	1.4	21.3	...	...	...	...
Developed countries	988 390	0.4	77.8	80.9	1.8	6.2	...	...	...	...
Developing countries	4 863 977	1.5	64.8	66.3	2.9	52.7	...	...	...	...
Arab States	283 518	2.2	66.9	68.6	3.7	46.2	...	...	...	...
Central and Eastern Europe	405 861	-0.1	69.8	74.5	1.4	18.3	...	...	...	...
Central Asia	75 771	0.7	69.1	72.7	2.2	39.4	...	...	...	...
East Asia and the Pacific	2 041 186	0.9	70.7	73.2	2.0	34.3	...	...	...	...
Latin America and the Caribbean	523 091	1.4	70.5	73.9	2.5	31.2	...	...	...	...
North America and Western Europe	716 706	0.6	78.0	80.9	1.8	5.7	...	...	...	...
South and West Asia	1 455 118	1.7	63.4	64.0	3.3	66.2	...	...	...	...
Sub-Saharan Africa	632 788	2.3	46.1	47.0	5.4	91.5	...	...	...	...

1. United Nations Population Division statistics.
2. Joint United Nations Programme on HIV/AIDS (UNAIDS).
3. Data are high estimates.
4. World Bank statistics.
5. *Human Development Report 2003*.
6. Data on net aid per capita refer to net official aid.
(z) Data are for 2000.

Table 1

	GNP[4]		AID AND POVERTY[5]		EXTERNAL DEBT[5]					
Average annual growth rate (%)	GNP per capita Current US$	GNP per capita PPP US$	Net aid per capita, current US$	Population living on less than $2 per day (%)	Total debt, current US$ (millions)	Total debt service, current US$ (millions)	Total debt as % of GNP	Public debt service as % of government current revenue	Total debt service as % of exports	Country or territory
1998-2001	2001	2001	2001	1990-2001	2001	2001	2001	2001	2001	
3.0	1 340	5 540	171.9	...	...	14	...	...	7.0	Cape Verde
-2.1	260	1 300	20.2	84.0	822	13	1.4	...	11.5	Central African Republic
-1.8	200	1 060	22.1	...	1 104	23	1.5	...	10.0	Chad
1.2	380	1 890	38.1	...	...	2	...	...	5.6	Comoros
17.2	640	680	21.1	...	4 496	92	4.8	9.2	3.3	Congo
-6.6	630	1 400	11.6	49.4	11 582	618	6.3	16.6	8.1	Côte d'Ivoire
-6.1	80	630	5.0	...	11 392	18	0.4	...	0.03	Democratic Rep. of the Congo
3.9	700	...	28.3	...	...	5	...	...	0.1	Equatorial Guinea
-1.5	160	1 030	72.8	...	410	7	1.0	...	4.5	Eritrea
-1.5	100	800	16.1	98.4	5 697	182	3.0	...	20.6	Ethiopia
-2.6	3 160	5 190	6.7	...	3 409	456	12.1	...	13.6	Gabon
-2.2	320	2 010	37.7	82.9	489	11	2.8	...	13.8	Gambia
-11.2	290	2 170	32.5	78.5	6 759	316	6.2	...	8.9	Ghana
-5.7	410	1 900	33.0	...	3 254	105	3.6	...	9.2	Guinea
-1.5	160	890	41.7	...	668	23	12.7	...	0.7	Guinea-Bissau
-0.1	350	970	14.6	58.6	5 833	464	4.1	...	11.4	Kenya
-4.9	530	2 980	30.1	65.7	592	69	7.0	...	12.4	Lesotho
11.3	140	...	11.5	...	1 987	1	0.2	...	0.6	Liberia
7.4	260	820	21.5	83.3	4 160	67	1.5	...	3.4	Madagascar
0.4	160	560	34.5	76.1	2 602	39	2.3	...	15.5	Malawi
-0.4	230	770	28.6	90.6	2 890	80	3.2	...	4.5	Mali
3.0	3 830	9 860	18.1	...	1 724	201	4.5	15.8	4.7	Mauritius
-3.2	210	1 050	51.3	78.4	4 466	87	2.6	...	2.7	Mozambique
-2.6	1 960	7 410	56.5	55.8	...	...	...	...	...	Namibia
-1.9	180	880	22.3	85.3	1 555	25	1.3	...	6.6	Niger
9.2	290	790	1.6	90.8	31 119	2 562	6.7	...	11.5	Nigeria
-5.3	220	1 240	36.0	84.6	1 283	19	1.1	...	7.6	Rwanda
5.4	280	...	248.2	...	...	4	...	...	21.3	Sao Tome and Principe
-0.4	490	1 480	43.5	67.8	3 461	214	4.7	20.0	9.3	Senegal
-1.5	6 530	...	169.7	...	...	13	...	...	2.1	Seychelles
3.5	140	460	73.0	74.5	1 188	96	13.1	...	74.3	Sierra Leone
...	...	...	16.4	...	2 532	0.2	...	...	...	Somalia
-5.7	2 820	10 910	9.6	14.5	24 050	4 355	4.0	8.1	6.8	South Africa
-1.8	1 300	4 430	27.6	...	308	28	2.2	...	2.5	Swaziland
-3.9	270	1 620	9.9	...	1 406	32	2.6	...	5.9	Togo
-5.2	260	1 460	32.3	96.4	3 733	50	0.9	4.9	9.7	Uganda
4.0	270	520	34.7	59.7	6 676	152	1.6	...	7.3	United Republic of Tanzania
5.0	320	750	35.3	87.4	5 671	129	3.7	...	13.4	Zambia
18.1	480	2 220	12.5	64.2	3 780	136	1.5	...	3.4	Zimbabwe[w]

	Weighted average		Weighted average		Weighted average					
...	...	...	...	...	...	...	...	...	...	World
...	...	...	...	...	...	...	...	...	...	Countries in transition
...	...	...	...	...	...	...	...	...	...	Developed countries
...	...	...	...	...	...	...	...	...	11.0	Developing countries
...	2 220	5 430	17.9	...	...	...	...	...	8.6	Arab States
...	...	...	...	...	...	...	...	...	...	Central and Eastern Europe
...	...	...	...	...	...	...	...	...	...	Central Asia
...	900	3 790	3.9	...	...	...	...	...	6.4	East Asia and the Pacific
...	3 580	6 900	11.4	...	...	...	...	...	19.7	Latin America and the Caribbean
...	...	...	...	...	...	...	...	...	...	North America and Western Europe
...	...	...	...	...	...	...	...	...	...	South and West Asia
...	460	1 750	20.6	...	...	...	...	...	9.0	Sub-Saharan Africa

Table 2
Adult and youth literacy[1]

	ADULT LITERACY RATE (15 and over) (%)						ADULT ILLITERATES (15 and over)			
	1990			2000-2004[2]			1990		2000-2004[2]	
Country or territory	Total	Male	Female	Total	Male	Female	Total (000)	% F	Total (000)	% F
Arab States										
Algeria	52.9	64.3	41.3	68.9	78.0	59.6	6 799	62	6 486	65
Bahrain	82.1	86.8	74.6	88.5	91.5	84.2	60	55	57	55
Djibouti	53.0	66.8	39.7	…	…	…	141	65	…	…
Egypt[w]	47.1	60.4	33.6	55.6*	67.2*	43.6*	17 432	63	20 468	64*
Iraq	35.7	51.3	19.7	…	…	…	6 208	62	…	…
Jordan[w]	81.5	90.0	72.1	90.9	95.5	85.9	320	72	299	74
Kuwait	76.7	79.3	72.6	82.9	84.7	81.0	317	47	302	42
Lebanon	80.3	88.3	73.1	…	…	…	347	72	…	…
Libyan Arab Jamahiriya	68.1	82.8	51.1	81.7	91.8	70.7	773	71	686	77
Mauritania	34.8	46.3	23.9	41.2	51.5	31.3	743	60	939	60
Morocco	38.7	52.7	24.9	50.7	63.3	38.3	9 089	62	10 108	63
Oman	54.7	67.3	38.3	74.4	82.0	65.4	457	57	424	55
Palestinian Autonomous Territories	…	…	…	…	…	…	…	…	…	…
Qatar	77.0	77.4	76.0	84.2*	84.9*	82.3*	78	28	70	35*
Saudi Arabia	66.2	76.2	50.2	77.9	84.1	69.5	3 287	59	3 218	61
Sudan	45.8	60.0	31.5	59.9	70.8	49.1	7 836	63	7 942	64
Syrian Arab Republic	64.8	81.8	47.5	82.9*	91.0*	74.2*	2 351	75	1 864	74*
Tunisia[w]	59.1	71.6	46.5	73.2	83.1	63.1	2 081	65	1 869	69
United Arab Emirates	71.0	71.2	70.6	77.3	75.6	80.7	421	28	499	25
Yemen	32.7	55.2	12.9	49.0	69.5	28.5	3 820	66	5 033	70
Central and Eastern Europe										
Albania[o]	77.0	86.8	66.7	98.7*	99.2*	98.3*	509	71	29	67*
Belarus	99.5	99.7	99.3	99.7	99.8	99.6	42	76	26	67
Bosnia and Herzegovina[o]	…	…	…	94.6*	98.4*	91.1*	…	…	181	85*
Bulgaria[o]	97.2	98.3	96.2	98.6	99.1	98.1	195	70	97	69
Croatia	96.9	99.0	94.9	98.1*	99.3*	97.1*	121	85	68	83*
Czech Republic[o]	…	…	…	…	…	…	…	…	…	…
Estonia[o]	99.8	99.8	99.8	99.8*	99.8*	99.8*	3	53	2	55*
Hungary[o]	99.1	99.3	98.9	…	…	…	78	63	…	…
Latvia[o]	…	…	…	99.7*	99.8*	99.7*	…	…	5	63*
Lithuania[o]	99.3	99.5	99.1	99.6*	99.6*	99.6*	20	67	10	54*
Poland[o]	99.6	99.6	99.5	…	…	…	119	60	…	…
Republic of Moldova	97.5	99.1	96.1	99.0	99.6	98.6	80	83	32	80
Romania[o]	97.1	98.6	95.6	97.3*	98.4*	96.3*	519	77	501	71*
Russian Federation[w]	99.2	99.6	98.9	99.6	99.7	99.5	857	76	496	69
Serbia and Montenegro	…	…	…	…	…	…	…	…	…	…
Slovakia	…	…	…	99.7*	99.7*	99.7*	…	…	14	49*
Slovenia[o]	99.6	99.6	99.5	99.7	99.7	99.6	7	58	6	56
The former Yugoslav Rep. of Macedonia[o]	…	…	…	…	…	…	…	…	…	…
Turkey[o]	77.9	89.2	66.4	86.5*	94.4*	78.5*	8 066	75	6 592	79*
Ukraine	99.4	99.7	99.2	99.6	99.8	99.5	237	77	147	70
Central Asia										
Armenia	97.5	98.9	96.1	99.4*	99.7*	99.2*	63	80	14	73*
Azerbaijan	…	…	…	…	…	…	…	…	…	…
Georgia	…	…	…	…	…	…	…	…	…	…
Kazakhstan	98.8	99.5	98.2	99.4	99.7	99.2	136	79	64	73
Kyrgyzstan	…	…	…	…	…	…	…	…	…	…
Mongolia	…	…	…	97.8*	98.0*	97.5*	…	…	38	56*
Tajikistan	98.2	99.2	97.2	99.5*	99.7*	99.3*	55	77	20	68*
Turkmenistan	…	…	…	98.8*	99.3*	98.3*	…	…	38	73*
Uzbekistan	98.7	99.5	97.9	99.3	99.6	98.9	164	80	122	74
East Asia and the Pacific										
Australia[o]	…	…	…	…	…	…	…	…	…	…
Brunei Darussalam	85.5	91.0	79.4	93.9*	96.3*	91.4*	24	66	15	68*
Cambodia	62.0	77.7	48.8	69.4	80.8	59.3	2 032	73	2 454	70
China[w]	78.3	87.2	68.9	90.9*	95.1*	86.5*	181 331	70	89 788	73*

1. For countries indicated with (*), national literacy data are used; for all others, the UIS estimates (July 2002 assessment) are used.
2. See Introduction note to the Statistical annex for broader explanation of national literacy definition, sources and years of data.

STATISTICAL ANNEX / 263

Table 2

	YOUTH LITERACY RATE (15-24) (%)						YOUTH ILLITERATES (15-24)				
	1990			2000-2004[2]			1990		2000-2004[2]		
	Total	Male	Female	Total	Male	Female	Total (000)	% F	Total (000)	% F	Country or territory

Arab States

Total	Male	Female	Total	Male	Female	Total (000)	% F	Total (000)	% F	Country or territory
77.3	86.1	68.1	89.9	94.0	85.6	1 158	69	691	70	Algeria
95.6	96.2	95.0	98.6	98.4	98.9	3	54	2	38	Bahrain
73.2	82.2	64.2	...	...	...	28	67	...	...	Djibouti
61.3	70.9	51.0	73.2*	79.0*	66.9*	3 970	62	3 974	60*	Egypt[w]
41.0	56.4	24.9	...	...	...	2 063	62	...	...	Iraq
96.7	97.9	95.3	99.4	99.3	99.5	23	66	7	40	Jordan[w]
87.5	87.9	87.2	93.1	92.2	93.9	46	51	26	40	Kuwait
92.1	95.5	88.6	...	...	...	48	71	...	...	Lebanon
91.0	98.9	82.7	97.0	99.8	94.0	78	94	40	97	Libyan Arab Jamahiriya
45.8	55.5	36.1	49.6	57.4	41.8	214	59	275	58	Mauritania
55.3	68.0	42.0	69.5	77.4	61.3	2 254	64	1 924	62	Morocco
85.6	95.4	75.4	98.5	99.6	97.3	43	82	8	87	Oman
...	...	...	...	...	...	...	...	...	...	Palestinian Autonomous Territories
90.3	88.3	93.0	94.8*	94.1*	95.8*	6	29	4	40*	Qatar
85.4	91.2	78.6	93.5	95.4	91.6	446	68	278	63	Saudi Arabia
65.0	75.6	54.0	79.1	83.9	74.2	1 752	65	1 348	61	Sudan
79.9	92.2	66.9	95.2*	97.1*	93.0*	520	81	199	70*	Syrian Arab Republic
84.1	92.8	75.2	94.3	97.9	90.6	264	77	117	81	Tunisia[w]
84.7	81.7	88.6	91.4	88.2	95.0	48	27	37	26	United Arab Emirates
50.0	73.5	25.0	67.9	84.3	50.9	1 134	73	1 245	75	Yemen

Central and Eastern Europe

Total	Male	Female	Total	Male	Female	Total (000)	% F	Total (000)	% F	Country or territory
94.8	97.4	91.9	99.4*	99.4*	99.5*	34	75	3	42*	Albania[o]
99.8	99.8	99.8	99.8	99.8	99.8	3	50	3	49	Belarus
...	...	...	99.6*	99.6*	99.7*	...	...	2	41*	Bosnia and Herzegovina[o]
99.4	99.5	99.3	99.7	99.8	99.6	7	59	4	67	Bulgaria[o]
99.6	99.7	99.6	99.6*	99.6*	99.7*	2	52	2	48*	Croatia
...	...	...	...	...	...	...	...	...	...	Czech Republic[o]
99.8	99.7	99.8	99.8*	99.7*	99.8*	0.5	42	1	39*	Estonia[o]
99.7	99.8	99.7	...	...	...	4	56	...	...	Hungary[o]
...	...	...	99.7*	99.7*	99.8*	...	...	1	43*	Latvia[o]
99.8	99.8	99.8	99.7*	99.7*	99.7*	1	45	2	42*	Lithuania[o]
99.8	99.8	99.8	...	...	...	11	49	...	...	Poland[o]
99.8	99.8	99.8	99.8	99.8	99.8	1	48	2	49	Republic of Moldova
99.3	99.3	99.2	97.8*	97.7*	97.8*	28	54	79	49*	Romania[o]
99.8	99.8	99.8	99.8	99.8	99.8	42	47	47	49	Russian Federation[w]
...	...	...	...	...	...	...	...	...	...	Serbia and Montenegro
...	...	...	99.6*	99.6*	99.7*	...	...	3	42*	Slovakia
99.8	99.7	99.8	99.8	99.8	99.8	1	45	1	48	Slovenia[o]
...	...	...	...	...	...	...	...	...	...	The former Yugoslav Rep. of Macedonia[o]
92.7	97.1	88.3	95.5*	97.8*	93.2*	838	79	616	75*	Turkey[o]
99.8	99.8	99.9	99.9	99.9	99.9	11	43	8	34	Ukraine

Central Asia

Total	Male	Female	Total	Male	Female	Total (000)	% F	Total (000)	% F	Country or territory
99.5	99.7	99.4	99.8*	99.7*	99.9*	3	63	1	35*	Armenia
...	...	...	...	...	...	...	...	...	...	Azerbaijan
...	...	...	...	...	...	...	...	...	...	Georgia
99.8	99.8	99.8	99.8	99.8	99.8	6	45	6	50	Kazakhstan
...	...	...	...	...	...	...	...	...	...	Kyrgyzstan
...	...	...	97.7*	97.0*	98.4*	...	...	13	34*	Mongolia
99.8	99.8	99.8	99.8*	99.8*	99.8*	2	55	2	49*	Tajikistan
...	...	...	99.8*	99.8*	99.8*	...	...	2	49*	Turkmenistan
99.6	99.7	99.6	99.7	99.7	99.6	14	57	18	58	Uzbekistan

East Asia and the Pacific

Total	Male	Female	Total	Male	Female	Total (000)	% F	Total (000)	% F	Country or territory
...	...	...	...	...	...	...	...	...	...	Australia[o]
97.9	97.6	98.1	99.1*	99.0*	99.3*	1	43	1	42*	Brunei Darussalam
73.5	81.5	65.6	80.3	84.5	75.9	476	65	588	61	Cambodia
95.3	97.5	93.1	98.9*	99.2*	98.5*	11 709	72	2 314	63*	China[w]

Table 2 (continued)

Country or territory	ADULT LITERACY RATE (15 and over) (%) 1990 Total	Male	Female	2000-2004[2] Total	Male	Female	ADULT ILLITERATES (15 and over) 1990 Total (000)	% F	2000-2004[2] Total (000)	% F
Cook Islands	...	...	...	...	...	...	...	...	...	...
Democratic People's Republic of Korea	...	...	...	...	...	...	...	...	...	...
Fiji	88.6	91.6	85.5	92.9*	94.5*	91.4*	51	63	39	60*
Indonesia[w]	79.5	86.7	72.5	87.9	92.5	83.4	23 800	68	18 432	69
Japan[o]	...	...	...	...	...	...	...	...	...	...
Kiribati	...	...	...	...	...	...	...	...	...	...
Lao People's Democratic Republic	56.5	70.3	42.8	66.4	77.4	55.5	1 017	67	1 081	67
Macao, China	90.5	94.6	86.8	91.3*	95.3*	87.8*	26	73	32	75*
Malaysia[w]	80.7	86.9	74.4	88.7*	92.0*	85.4*	2 190	66	1 804	64*
Marshall Islands	...	...	...	...	...	...	...	...	...	...
Micronesia (Federated States of)	...	...	...	...	...	...	...	...	...	...
Myanmar	80.7	87.4	74.2	85.3	89.2	81.4	4 905	68	4 876	64
Nauru	30.4	47.4	14.0	...	...	...	7 546	61	...	...
New Zealand[o]	...	...	...	...	...	...	...	...	...	...
Niue	...	...	...	...	...	...	...	...	...	...
Palau	...	...	...	...	...	...	...	...	...	...
Papua New Guinea	56.6	64.4	48.2	...	...	...	1 046	57	...	...
Philippines[w]	91.7	92.2	91.2	92.6*	92.5*	92.7*	2 986	53	3 687	50*
Republic of Korea[o]	95.9	98.4	93.4	...	...	...	1 307	80	...	...
Samoa	98.0	98.5	97.4	98.7	98.9	98.4	2	61	1	58
Singapore	88.8	94.4	83.2	92.5	96.6	88.6	265	75	244	77
Solomon Islands	...	...	...	...	...	...	...	...	...	...
Thailand[w]	...	...	...	92.6*	94.9*	90.5*	...	...	3 402	66*
Timor-Leste	...	...	...	...	...	...	...	...	...	...
Tokelau	...	...	...	...	...	...	...	...	...	...
Tonga	...	...	...	98.8*	98.8*	98.9*	...	...	1	48*
Tuvalu	...	...	...	...	...	...	...	...	...	...
Vanuatu	...	...	...	...	...	...	...	...	...	...
Viet Nam	...	...	...	90.3*	93.9*	86.9*	...	...	5 273	69*
Latin America and the Caribbean										
Anguilla	...	...	...	...	...	...	...	...	...	...
Antigua and Barbuda	...	...	...	...	...	...	...	...	...	...
Argentina[w]	95.7	95.9	95.6	97.0	97.0	97.0	964	54	831	52
Aruba	...	...	...	...	...	...	...	...	...	...
Bahamas	94.4	93.6	95.2	...	...	...	10	44	...	...
Barbados	99.4	99.4	99.3	99.7	99.7	99.7	1	57	1	51
Belize	...	...	...	76.9*	76.7*	77.1*	...	...	36	49*
Bermuda	...	...	...	...	...	...	...	...	...	...
Bolivia	78.1	86.8	69.8	86.7*	93.1*	80.7*	862	71	700	74*
Brazil[w]	82.0	82.9	81.2	88.2*	88.0*	88.3*	17 336	53	14 958	51*
British Virgin Islands	...	...	...	...	...	...	...	...	...	...
Cayman Islands	...	...	...	...	...	...	...	...	...	...
Chile[w]	94.0	94.4	93.6	95.7*	95.8*	95.6*	550	55	483	52*
Colombia	88.4	88.8	88.1	92.1	92.1	92.2	2 584	53	2 320	51
Costa Rica	93.9	93.9	93.8	95.8	95.7	95.9	121	50	119	48
Cuba	95.1	95.2	95.1	96.9	97.0	96.8	398	51	278	52
Dominica	...	...	...	...	...	...	...	...	...	...
Dominican Republic	79.4	79.8	79.0	84.4	84.3	84.4	894	50	910	49
Ecuador	87.6	90.2	85.1	91.0*	92.3*	89.7*	775	60	770	57*
El Salvador	72.4	76.1	69.1	79.7	82.4	77.1	835	59	848	58
Grenada	...	...	...	...	...	...	...	...	...	...
Guatemala	61.0	68.8	53.2	69.9	77.3	62.5	1 843	60	2 069	62
Guyana	97.2	98.0	96.4	...	...	...	13	66	...	...
Haiti	39.7	42.6	36.9	51.9	53.8	50.0	2 328	54	2 407	54
Honduras	68.1	68.9	67.3	80.0*	79.8*	80.2*	851	51	804	49*
Jamaica[w]	82.2	78.0	86.1	87.6	83.8	91.4	274	40	224	36
Mexico[o]	87.3	90.6	84.3	90.5*	92.6*	88.7*	6 471	64	6 471	62*
Montserrat	...	...	...	...	...	...	...	...	...	...
Netherlands Antilles	95.6	95.6	95.7	96.7	96.7	96.7	6	53	6	52
Nicaragua	62.7	62.7	62.8	76.7*	76.8*	76.6*	764	51	723	51*
Panama	89.0	89.7	88.4	92.3	92.9	91.7	171	53	162	54

1. For countries indicated with (*), national literacy data are used; for all others, the UIS estimates (July 2002 assessment) are used.
2. See Introduction note to the Statistical annex for broader explanation of national literacy definition, sources and years of data.

Table 2

\multicolumn{6}{c	}{YOUTH LITERACY RATE (15-24) (%)}	\multicolumn{4}{c	}{YOUTH ILLITERATES (15-24)}	
\multicolumn{3}{c	}{1990}	\multicolumn{3}{c	}{2000-2004²}	\multicolumn{2}{c	}{1990}	\multicolumn{2}{c	}{2000-2004²}	
Total	Male	Female	Total	Male	Female	Total (000)	% F	Total (000)	% F	Country or territory
…	…	…	…	…	…	…	…	…	…	Cook Islands
…	…	…	…	…	…	…	…	…	…	Democratic People's Republic of Korea
97.8	98.1	97.6	99.3*	99.1*	99.4*	3	54	1	39*	Fiji
95.0	96.6	93.4	98.0	98.5	97.6	1 873	65	835	62	Indonesia ʷ
…	…	…	…	…	…	…	…	…	…	Japan ᵒ
…	…	…	…	…	…	…	…	…	…	Kiribati
70.1	79.47	60.56	79.3	85.8	72.7	235	66	226	65	Lao People's Democratic Republic
97.2	99.2	95.8	99.6*	99.4*	99.8*	2	88	0.3	26*	Macao, China
94.8	95.3	94.2	97.2*	97.2*	97.3*	179	55	122	48*	Malaysia ʷ
…	…	…	…	…	…	…	…	…	…	Marshall Islands
…	…	…	…	…	…	…	…	…	…	Micronesia (Federated States of)
88.2	90.1	86.2	91.4	91.6	91.1	972	58	830	51	Myanmar
46.6	67.0	27.3	…	…	…	1 867	67	…	…	Nauru
…	…	…	…	…	…	…	…	…	…	New Zealand ᵒ
…	…	…	…	…	…	…	…	…	…	Niue
…	…	…	…	…	…	…	…	…	…	Palau
68.6	74.4	62.4	…	…	…	277	60	…	…	Papua New Guinea
97.3	97.1	97.4	95.1*	94.5*	95.7*	342	46	787	43*	Philippines ʷ
99.8	99.8	99.8	…	…	…	18	49	…	…	Republic of Korea ᵒ
99.0	99.1	98.9	99.5	99.4	99.5	0.3	50	0.2	43	Samoa
99.0	98.8	99.2	99.5	99.4	99.6*	6	39	3	38*	Singapore
…	…	…	…	…	…	…	…	…	…	Solomon Islands
…	…	…	98.0*	98.1*	97.8*	…	…	233	53*	Thailand ʷ
…	…	…	…	…	…	…	…	…	…	Timor-Leste
…	…	…	…	…	…	…	…	…	…	Tokelau
…	…	…	99.2*	99.2*	99.1*	…	…	0.2	51*	Tonga
…	…	…	…	…	…	…	…	…	…	Tuvalu
…	…	…	…	…	…	…	…	…	…	Vanuatu
94.1	94.5	93.6	…	…	…	801	54	…	…	Viet Nam

Latin America and the Caribbean

Total	Male	Female	Total	Male	Female	Total (000)	% F	Total (000)	% F	Country or territory
…	…	…	…	…	…	…	…	…	…	Anguilla
…	…	…	…	…	…	…	…	…	…	Antigua and Barbuda
98.2	98.0	98.4	98.6	98.4	98.9	97	44	91	41	Argentina ʷ
…	…	…	…	…	…	…	…	…	…	Aruba
96.5	95.4	97.5	…	…	…	2	34	…	…	Bahamas
99.8	99.8	99.8	99.8	99.8	99.8	0.1	49	0.1	49	Barbados
…	…	…	84.2*	83.9*	84.6*	…	…	8	48*	Belize
…	…	…	…	…	…	…	…	…	…	Bermuda
92.6	96.2	89.0	97.3*	98.5*	96.1*	98	74	44	72*	Bolivia
91.8	90.5	93.1	96.3*	95.1*	97.5*	2 363	42	1 292	34*	Brazil ʷ
…	…	…	…	…	…	…	…	…	…	British Virgin Islands
…	…	…	…	…	…	…	…	…	…	Cayman Islands
98.1	97.9	98.3	99.0*	98.8*	99.2*	48	44	26	40*	Chile ʷ
94.9	94.3	95.5	97.2	96.5	97.9	369	44	229	38	Colombia
97.4	97.1	97.7	98.4	98.1	98.7	15	43	13	39	Costa Rica
99.3	99.3	99.2	99.8	99.8	99.8	17	51	3	49	Cuba
…	…	…	…	…	…	…	…	…	…	Dominica
87.5	86.8	88.2	91.7	91.0	92.5	184	46	144	44	Dominican Republic
95.5	96.0	94.9	96.4*	96.4*	96.5*	95	56	92	48*	Ecuador
83.8	85.1	82.6	88.9	89.6	88.1	172	55	144	53	El Salvador
…	…	…	…	…	…	…	…	…	…	Grenada
73.4	80.5	66.2	80.1	86.2	73.8	457	63	498	65	Guatemala
99.8	99.8	99.8	…	…	…	0.3	51	…	…	Guyana
54.8	55.8	53.8	66.2	65.8	66.5	580	51	638	49	Haiti
79.7	78.5	80.8	88.9*	86.9*	90.9*	201	47	157	40*	Honduras
91.2	87.1	95.2	94.5	91.3	97.8	42	28	29	20	Jamaica ʷ
95.2	95.9	94.4	96.6*	96.8*	96.5*	889	58	687	52*	Mexico ᵒ
…	…	…	…	…	…	…	…	…	…	Montserrat
97.5	97.3	97.7	98.3	98.2	98.5	1	46	1	45	Netherlands Antilles
68.2	67.7	68.7	86.2*	83.6*	88.8*	246	50	157	40*	Nicaragua
95.3	95.7	94.8	97.0	97.4	96.6	24	54	17	56	Panama

Table 2 (continued)

Country or territory	ADULT LITERACY RATE (15 and over) (%) 1990 Total	1990 Male	1990 Female	2000-2004[2] Total	2000-2004[2] Male	2000-2004[2] Female	ADULT ILLITERATES (15 and over) 1990 Total (000)	1990 % F	2000-2004[2] Total (000)	2000-2004[2] % F
Paraguay[w]	90.3	92.4	88.3	91.6*	93.1*	90.2*	237	60	294	59*
Peru[w]	...	...	...	85.0*	91.3*	80.3*	...	...	2 519	69*
Saint Kitts and Nevis	...	...	...	...	...	...	...	...	...	...
Saint Lucia	...	...	...	...	...	...	...	...	...	...
Saint Vincent and the Grenadines	...	...	...	...	...	...	...	...	...	...
Suriname	...	...	...	...	...	...	...	...	...	...
Trinidad and Tobago	96.8	98.1	95.6	98.5	99.0	97.9	26	70	15	69
Turks and Caicos Islands	...	...	...	...	...	...	...	...	...	...
Uruguay[w]	96.5	96.0	97.0	97.7	97.3	98.1	80	46	58	43
Venezuela	88.9	90.1	87.7	93.1	93.5	92.7	1 340	55	1 163	53
North America and Western Europe										
Andorra	...	...	...	...	...	...	...	...	...	...
Austria[o]	...	...	...	...	...	...	...	...	...	...
Belgium[o]	...	...	...	...	...	...	...	...	...	...
Canada[o]	...	...	...	...	...	...	...	...	...	...
Cyprus[o]	94.3	97.7	91.0	96.8*	98.6*	95.1*	29	80	20	79*
Denmark[o]	...	...	...	...	...	...	...	...	...	...
Finland[o]	...	...	...	...	...	...	...	...	...	...
France[o]	...	...	...	...	...	...	...	...	...	...
Germany[o]	...	...	...	...	...	...	...	...	...	...
Greece[o]	94.9	97.6	92.3	...	...	...	419	77	...	...
Iceland[o]	...	...	...	...	...	...	...	...	...	...
Ireland[o]	...	...	...	...	...	...	...	...	...	...
Israel[o]	91.4	94.9	88.0	95.3	97.3	93.4	267	71	214	72
Italy[o]	97.7	98.3	97.1	...	...	...	1 103	65	...	...
Luxembourg[o]	...	...	...	...	...	...	...	...	...	...
Malta[o]	88.4	87.9	88.9	92.6	91.8	93.4	32	49	23	46
Monaco	...	...	...	...	...	...	...	...	...	...
Netherlands[o]	...	...	...	...	...	...	...	...	...	...
Norway[o]	...	...	...	...	...	...	...	...	...	...
Portugal[o]	87.2	90.9	83.8	...	...	...	1 013	66	...	...
San Marino	...	...	...	...	...	...	...	...	...	...
Spain[o]	96.3	97.8	94.8	...	...	...	1 186	71	...	...
Sweden[o]	...	...	...	...	...	...	...	...	...	...
Switzerland[o]	...	...	...	...	...	...	...	...	...	...
United Kingdom[o]	...	...	...	...	...	...	...	...	...	...
United States[o]	...	...	...	...	...	...	...	...	...	...
South and West Asia										
Afghanistan	...	...	...	...	...	...	...	...	...	...
Bangladesh	34.2	44.3	23.7	41.1	50.3	31.4	41 606	56	52 209	57
Bhutan	...	...	...	...	...	...	...	...	...	...
India[w]	49.3	61.9	35.9	61.3*	...	...	272 279	61	270 466	...
Iran, Islamic Republic of	63.2	72.2	54.0	...	83.5*	70.4*	11 506	61	10 543	64*
Maldives	94.8	95.0	94.6	97.2	97.3	97.2	6	50	5	50
Nepal	30.4	47.4	14.0	44.0	61.6	26.4	7 546	61	8 204	65
Pakistan	35.4	49.3	20.1	41.5*	53.4*	28.5*	41 368	60	51 536	60*
Sri Lanka[w]	88.7	92.9	84.7	92.1	94.7	89.6	1 262	65	1 099	64
Sub-Saharan Africa										
Angola	...	...	...	...	...	...	...	...	...	...
Benin	26.4	38.1	15.5	39.8	54.8	25.5	1 773	59	2 152	64
Botswana	68.1	65.7	70.3	78.9	76.1	81.5	234	49	225	45
Burkina Faso	...	...	...	12.8*	18.5*	8.1*	...	...	5 611	56*
Burundi	37.0	48.4	26.6	50.4	57.7	43.6	1 929	61	1 744	60
Cameroon	57.9	68.7	47.5	67.9*	77.0*	59.8*	2 701	64	2 876	64*
Cape Verde	63.8	76.2	54.3	75.7	85.4	68.0	67	71	65	72
Central African Republic	33.2	47.1	20.7	48.6*	64.7*	33.5*	1 119	63	1 122	67*
Chad	27.7	37.0	18.8	45.8	54.5	37.5	2 299	58	2 409	59
Comoros	53.8	61.4	46.4	56.2	63.5	49.1	129	59	188	58
Congo	67.1	77.1	57.9	82.8	88.9	77.1	443	66	331	68

1. For countries indicated with (*), national literacy data are used; for all others, the UIS estimates (July 2002 assessment) are used.
2. See Introduction note to the Statistical annex for broader explanation of national literacy definition, sources and years of data.

STATISTICAL ANNEX / 267

Table 2

\multicolumn{6}{c	}{YOUTH LITERACY RATE (15-24) (%)}	\multicolumn{4}{c	}{YOUTH ILLITERATES (15-24)}	
\multicolumn{3}{c	}{1990}	\multicolumn{3}{c	}{2000-2004²}	\multicolumn{2}{c	}{1990}	\multicolumn{2}{c	}{2000-2004²}	
Total	Male	Female	Total	Male	Female	Total (000)	% F	Total (000)	% F	Country or territory
95.6	95.9	95.2	96.3*	96.2*	96.5*	36	53	42	47*	Paraguay ʷ
94.5	96.9	92.1	96.6*	97.7*	95.6*	243	71	177	65*	Peru ʷ
...	...	...	...	...	...	...	...	...	...	Saint Kitts and Nevis
...	...	...	...	...	...	...	...	...	...	Saint Lucia
...	...	...	...	...	...	...	...	...	...	Saint Vincent and the Grenadines
...	...	...	...	...	...	...	...	...	...	Suriname
99.6	99.7	99.6	99.8	99.8	99.8	1	51	1	50	Trinidad and Tobago
...	...	...	...	...	...	...	...	...	...	Turks and Caicos Islands
98.7	98.3	99.1	99.1	98.8	99.4	6	34	5	32	Uruguay ʷ
96.0	95.4	96.6	98.2	97.6	98.9	153	42	86	30	Venezuela
										North America and Western Europe
...	...	...	...	...	...	...	...	...	...	Andorra
...	...	...	...	...	...	...	...	...	...	Austria ᵒ
...	...	...	...	...	...	...	...	...	...	Belgium ᵒ
...	...	...	...	...	...	...	...	...	...	Canada ᵒ
99.7	99.5	99.8	99.8*	99.7*	99.8*	0.3	29	0.3	40*	Cyprus ᵒ
...	...	...	...	...	...	...	...	...	...	Denmark ᵒ
...	...	...	...	...	...	...	...	...	...	Finland ᵒ
...	...	...	...	...	...	...	...	...	...	France ᵒ
...	...	...	...	...	...	...	...	...	...	Germany ᵒ
99.5	99.4	99.7	...	...	...	7	37	...	...	Greece ᵒ
...	...	...	...	...	...	...	...	...	...	Iceland ᵒ
...	...	...	...	...	...	...	...	...	...	Ireland ᵒ
98.7	99.0	98.4	99.5	99.6	99.4	10	61	5	59	Israel ᵒ
99.8	99.8	99.8	...	...	...	18	49	...	...	Italy ᵒ
...	...	...	...	...	...	...	...	...	...	Luxembourg ᵒ
97.5	96.0	99.1	98.7	97.6	99.8	1	18	1	7	Malta ᵒ
...	...	...	...	...	...	...	...	...	...	Monaco
...	...	...	...	...	...	...	...	...	...	Netherlands ᵒ
...	...	...	...	...	...	...	...	...	...	Norway ᵒ
99.5	99.5	99.6	...	...	...	8	44	...	...	Portugal ᵒ
...	...	...	...	...	...	...	...	...	...	San Marino
99.6	99.6	99.6	...	...	...	27	44	...	...	Spain ᵒ
...	...	...	...	...	...	...	...	...	...	Sweden ᵒ
...	...	...	...	...	...	...	...	...	...	Switzerland ᵒ
...	...	...	...	...	...	...	...	...	...	United Kingdom ᵒ
...	...	...	...	...	...	...	...	...	...	United States ᵒ
										South and West Asia
...	...	...	...	...	...	...	...	...	...	Afghanistan
42.0	50.7	33.2	49.7	57.8	41.1	12 842	56	14 740	57	Bangladesh
...	...	...	...	...	...	...	...	...	...	Bhutan
64.3	73.4	54.2	...	...	...	58 555	61	...	...	India ʷ
86.3	91.7	80.8	...	...	...	1 425	68	...	...	Iran, Islamic Republic of
98.1	98.1	98.1	99.2	99.1	99.2	1	48	1	46	Maldives
46.6	67.0	27.3	62.7	78.1	46.0	1 867	67	1 797	70	Nepal
47.4	62.5	30.6	53.9*	65.5*	42.0*	10 697	63	13 537	61*	Pakistan
95.1	95.9	94.2	97.0	97.2	96.9	157	57	105	51	Sri Lanka ʷ
										Sub-Saharan Africa
...	...	...	...	...	...	...	...	...	...	Angola
40.4	56.6	24.7	55.5	72.7	38.5	497	64	610	70	Benin
83.3	79.3	87.2	89.1	85.5	92.8	48	38	44	33	Botswana
...	...	...	19.4*	25.5*	14.0*	...	...	2 087	54*	Burkina Faso
51.6	58.4	44.8	66.1	67.2	65.1	517	57	490	52	Burundi
81.1	86.4	75.9	...	...	...	414	64	...	...	Cameroon
81.5	87.1	76.2	89.1	92.0	86.3	13	65	11	63	Cape Verde
52.1	65.6	39.4	58.5*	70.3*	46.9*	258	65	321	65*	Central African Republic
48.0	58.4	37.7	69.9	75.8	64.0	569	60	481	60	Chad
56.7	63.8	49.6	59.0	65.6	52.2	45	58	66	58	Comoros
92.5	94.9	90.3	97.8	98.4	97.3	36	66	16	64	Congo

268 / ANNEX

Table 2 (continued)

| | ADULT LITERACY RATE (15 and over) (%) |||||| ADULT ILLITERATES (15 and over) ||||
| | 1990 ||| 2000-2004[2] ||| 1990 || 2000-2004[2] ||
Country or territory	Total	Male	Female	Total	Male	Female	Total (000)	% F	Total (000)	% F
Côte d'Ivoire	38.5	50.5	25.7	...	...	...	4 119	57	...	...
Democratic Rep. of the Congo	47.5	61.4	34.4	...	...	...	10 400	64	...	...
Equatorial Guinea	73.3	85.8	61.1	...	...	...	55	74	...	...
Eritrea	46.4	58.5	34.8	...	...	...	900	62	...	...
Ethiopia	28.6	37.3	19.8	41.5	49.2	33.8	18 993	57	21 955	57
Gabon	...	...	...	...	...	...	...	...	...	...
Gambia	25.6	31.7	19.7	...	...	...	397	55	...	...
Ghana	58.5	70.1	47.2	73.8	81.9	65.9	3 455	65	3 213	66
Guinea	27.2	42.3	12.9	...	...	...	406	61	...	...
Guinea-Bissau	...	...	...	...	...	...	...	...	...	...
Kenya	70.8	80.9	60.8	84.3	90.0	78.5	3 489	68	2 897	69
Lesotho	78.0	65.4	89.5	81.4*	73.7*	90.3*	184	28	184	32*
Liberia	39.2	55.4	22.8	55.9	72.3	39.3	691	64	765	69
Madagascar	58.0	66.4	49.8	...	...	...	2 768	60	...	...
Malawi	51.8	68.8	36.2	61.8	75.5	48.7	2 450	69	2 446	69
Mali	...	...	...	19.0*	26.7*	11.9*	...	...	5 184	56*
Mauritius	79.8	84.8	75.0	84.3*	88.2*	80.5*	150	62	142	63*
Mozambique	33.5	49.3	18.4	46.5	62.3	31.4	4 867	65	5 638	68
Namibia	74.9	77.4	72.4	83.3	83.8	82.8	201	57	186	54
Niger	11.4	18.0	5.1	17.1	25.1	9.3	3 391	54	4 775	55
Nigeria	48.7	59.4	38.4	66.8	74.4	59.4	23 678	61	22 168	61
Rwanda	53.3	62.9	44.0	69.2	75.3	63.4	1 660	61	1 412	64
Sao Tome and Principe	...	...	...	...	...	...	...	...	...	...
Senegal	28.4	38.2	18.6	39.3	49.0	29.7	2 822	58	3 387	59
Seychelles	...	...	...	91.9*	91.4*	92.3*	...	...	–	–*
Sierra Leone	...	...	...	...	...	...	...	...	...	...
Somalia	...	...	...	...	...	...	...	...	...	...
South Africa	81.2	82.2	80.2	86.0	86.7	85.3	4 252	54	4 190	54
Swaziland	71.6	73.7	69.9	80.9	82.0	80.0	129	58	115	57
Togo	44.2	60.5	28.7	59.6	74.3	45.4	1 049	65	1 088	69
Uganda	56.1	69.3	43.5	68.9	78.8	59.2	3 940	66	3 890	67
United Republic of Tanzania	62.9	75.5	51.0	77.1	85.2	69.2	5 128	68	4 556	68
Zambia	68.2	78.6	58.7	79.9	86.3	73.8	1 400	67	1 148	66
Zimbabwe[w]	80.7	86.6	75.0	90.0	93.8	86.3	1 085	66	732	69

	Weighted average						Sum	% F	Sum	% F
World	75.4	81.8	69.1	81.7	87.0	76.5	871 750	63	799 147	64
Countries in transition	99.2	99.6	98.8	99.6	99.7	99.4	1 759	78	998	70
Developed countries	98.0	98.5	97.5	98.9	99.1	98.6	14 864	64	9 151	62
Developing countries	67.0	75.9	57.9	76.4	83.4	69.3	855 127	63	788 999	64
Arab States	50.0	63.7	35.6	62.2	73.1	50.6	63 023	63	69 298	64
Central and Eastern Europe	96.2	98.0	94.6	97.3	98.7	96.1	11 500	75	8 464	77
Central Asia	98.7	99.4	98.0	99.4	99.6	99.1	572	79	333	70
East Asia and the Pacific	81.8	88.9	74.5	91.3	94.9	87.6	232 255	69	134 978	71
Latin America and the Caribbean	85.0	86.7	83.3	89.2	90.1	88.5	41 742	56	39 383	55
North America and Western Europe	97.9	98.4	97.4	98.8	99.1	98.6	11 326	64	6 946	61
South and West Asia	47.5	59.7	34.4	58.3	70.9	45.0	382 353	60	402 744	64
Sub-Saharan Africa	49.9	60.0	40.3	62.0	70.1	54.2	128 980	61	137 000	61

1. For countries indicated with (*), national literacy data are used; for all others, the UIS estimates (July 2002 assessment) are used.
2. See Introduction note to the Statistical annex for broader explanation of national literacy definition, sources and years of data.

Table 2

YOUTH LITERACY RATE (15-24) (%)

1990			2000-2004[2]			YOUTH ILLITERATES (15-24) 1990		2000-2004[2]		Country or territory
Total	Male	Female	Total	Male	Female	Total (000)	% F	Total (000)	% F	
52.6	64.9	40.3	59.9	69.6	51.5*	1 046	62	1 426	61*	Côte d'Ivoire
68.9	80.3	57.6	...	...	...	2 213	68	...	...	Democratic Rep. of the Congo
92.7	96.6	88.8	...	...	...	5	77	...	...	Equatorial Guinea
60.9	72.5	49.3	...	...	...	236	65	...	...	Eritrea
43.0	51.5	34.1	57.4	63.0	51.8	5 326	58	5 752	57	Ethiopia
...	...	...	...	...	...	...	...	...	...	Gabon
42.2	50.5	34.1	...	...	...	95	58	...	...	Gambia
81.8	88.2	75.4	92.2	94.2	90.1	538	67	348	63	Ghana
44.1	62.2	26.5	...	...	...	107	66	...	...	Guinea
...	...	...	...	...	...	...	...	...	...	Guinea-Bissau
89.8	92.9	86.7	95.8	96.4	95.1	473	65	314	58	Kenya
87.2	77.2	97.1	...	...	...	38	12	...	...	Lesotho
57.2	75.4	38.6	70.8	86.3	55.4	176	71	190	76	Liberia
72.2	77.8	66.6	...	...	...	635	60	...	...	Madagascar
63.2	75.7	51.2	72.5	81.9	62.8	643	68	641	68	Malawi
...	...	...	24.2*	32.3*	16.9*	...	...	1 938	55*	Mali
91.1	91.2	91.1	94.5*	93.7*	95.4*	18	49	11	42*	Mauritius
48.8	66.1	31.7	62.8	76.6	49.2	1 365	68	1 363	69	Mozambique
87.4	85.9	89.0	92.3	90.6	94.0	36	44	29	39	Namibia
17.0	24.9	9.3	24.5	34.0	15.1	1 211	54	1 684	55	Niger
73.6	80.8	66.5	88.6	90.7	86.5	4 243	63	2 780	58	Nigeria
72.7	78.0	67.4	84.9	86.3	83.6	363	60	268	59	Rwanda
...	...	...	...	...	...	...	...	...	...	Sao Tome and Principe
40.1	50.0	30.2	52.9	61.3	44.5	829	58	960	59	Senegal
...	...	...	99.1*	98.8*	99.4*	...	...	–	–*	Seychelles
...	...	...	...	...	...	...	...	...	...	Sierra Leone
...	...	...	...	...	...	...	...	...	...	Somalia
88.5	88.6	88.4	91.8	91.8	91.7	882	51	771	50	South Africa
85.1	84.7	85.5	91.2	90.4	92.1	25	52	21	46	Swaziland
63.5	79.4	47.7	77.4	88.3	66.6	242	72	219	74	Togo
70.1	79.8	60.5	80.2	86.3	74.0	1 003	66	1 001	66	Uganda
83.1	89.2	77.2	91.6	93.8	89.4	882	69	642	63	United Republic of Tanzania
81.2	86.4	76.2	89.2	91.5	86.9	311	64	247	61	Zambia
93.9	96.6	91.3	97.6	98.9	96.2	128	72	74	78	Zimbabwe[w]

Weighted average						Sum	% F	Sum	% F	
84.3	88.2	80.1	87.6	90.9	84.0	156 430	62	136 710	63	World
99.2	99.2	99.2	99.4	99.4	99.3	332	49	304	50	Countries in transition
99.7	99.7	99.6	99.7	99.7	99.7	471	51	354	49	Developed countries
80.9	85.8	75.8	85.2	89.3	81.0	155 627	62	136 052	63	Developing countries
66.6	77.3	55.3	78.2	84.4	71.8	14 203	66	12 946	64	Arab States
98.3	99.2	97.4	98.8	99.3	98.3	1 023	75	790	69	Central and Eastern Europe
97.7	97.8	97.7	98.3	98.3	98.3	281	50	257	50	Central Asia
95.4	97.2	93.6	97.8	98.2	97.4	17 383	68	7 446	58	East Asia and the Pacific
92.7	92.7	92.7	95.5	95.2	95.9	6 351	50	4 589	46	Latin America and the Caribbean
99.7	99.7	99.7	99.8	99.8	99.8	310	49	203	49	North America and Western Europe
61.5	71.1	51.0	72.3	81.5	62.5	87 276	61	79 344	65	South and West Asia
67.5	74.8	60.2	76.6	81.0	72.3	29 603	61	31 135	59	Sub-Saharan Africa

270 / ANNEX

Table 3
Early childhood care and education (ECCE)

	Country or territory	Age group 2001	1998 Total	1998 Male	1998 Female	1998 GPI (F/M)	2001 Total	2001 Male	2001 Female	2001 GPI (F/M)
	Arab States									
1	Algeria	4-5	2.5	2.5	2.5	1.01	4.2	4.2	4.2	1.00
2	Bahrain	3-5	32.9	33.7	32.0	0.95	34.9	35.8	34.0	0.95
3	Djibouti	3-5	0.4	0.4	0.5	1.50	0.5	0.5	0.5	1.02
4	Egypt[w]	4-5	10.1	10.4	9.8	0.95	12.8	13.2	12.4	0.94
5	Iraq	4-5	5.2	5.3	5.2	0.98	5.5[y]	5.5[y]	5.4[y]	0.99[y]
6	Jordan[w]	4-5	28.6	29.9	27.2	0.91	31.0	32.2	29.6	0.92
7	Kuwait	4-5	78.3	77.8	78.8	1.01	73.5	73.8	73.2	0.99
8	Lebanon	3-5	66.0	66.9	65.0	0.97	73.9	74.4	73.4	0.99
9	Libyan Arab Jamahiriya	4-5	5.0	5.0**	4.9**	0.98**	7.8	8.0	7.7	0.96
10	Mauritania	3-5	...	...	...	...	...	...	...	...
11	Morocco	4-5	64.3	83.9	44.0	0.52	59.7	75.1	43.6	0.58
12	Oman	4-5	5.6	6.0	5.2	0.87	5.2	5.5	4.8	0.87
13	Palestinian Autonomous Territories	4-5	39.9	40.6	39.1	0.97	31.1	31.9	30.1	0.94
14	Qatar	3-5	25.6	26.0	25.3	0.98	31.7	31.8	31.5	0.99
15	Saudi Arabia	3-5	5.1	5.4	4.9	0.91	4.9	5.1	4.7	0.93
16	Sudan	4-5	21.3	...	...	...	19.6	19.7	19.5	0.99
17	Syrian Arab Republic	3-5	8.4	8.8	7.9	0.90	9.8	10.2	9.3	0.91
18	Tunisia[w]	3-5	13.5	13.9	13.2	0.95	19.8	20.0	19.6	0.98
19	United Arab Emirates	4-5	61.6	62.4	60.8	0.97	70.8	70.6	70.9	1.00
20	Yemen	3-5	0.7	0.7	0.6	0.87	0.40**	0.41**	0.38**	0.92**
	Central and Eastern Europe									
21	Albania[o]	3-5	41.7**	40.0**	43.5**	1.09**	44.4[z]	42.9[z]	46.0[z]	1.07[z]
22	Belarus	3-5	81.2	84.5	77.7	0.92	98.7	99.8	97.5	0.98
23	Bosnia and Herzegovina[o]	3-5	...	...	...	...	...	...	...	...
24	Bulgaria[o]	3-6	64.3	64.7	63.8	0.99	70.4	70.7	70.0	0.99
25	Croatia	3-6	41.1	41.6	40.6	0.98	38.4	39.5	37.2	0.94
26	Czech Republic[o]	3-5	90.5	87.8	93.4	1.06	95.6	95.6	95.6	1.00
27	Estonia[o]	3-6	86.8	87.5	86.0	0.98	105.7	106.2	105.1	0.99
28	Hungary[o]	3-6	79.4	80.1	78.6	0.98	79.5	80.3	78.6	0.98
29	Latvia[o]	3-6	50.9	52.1	49.6	0.95	60.2	62.1	58.3	0.94
30	Lithuania[o]	3-6	50.2	51.0	49.4	0.97	55.3	56.6	53.9	0.95
31	Poland[o]	3-6	49.8	49.7	50.0	1.01	49.0	48.9	49.1	1.00
32	Republic of Moldova	3-6	35.7**	36.3**	35.1**	0.97**	39.4	40.2	38.5	0.96
33	Romania	3-6	61.8	61.1	62.6	1.02	75.7	74.4	77.0	1.03
34	Russian Federation[w]	4-6	...	...	...	...	91.9	94.5**	89.3**	0.94**
35	Serbia and Montenegro[2]	3-6	44.1	44.3	43.8	0.99	43.7[z]	43.5[z]	44.0[z]	1.01[z]
36	Slovakia	3-5	81.7	...	...	...	82.9	84.2	81.5	0.97
37	Slovenia[o]	3-6	72.0	75.3	68.6	0.91	73.2	75.0	71.3	0.95
38	The former Yugoslav Rep. of Macedonia[o]	3-6	27.3	27.2	27.5	1.01	28.2	28.1	28.3	1.01
39	Turkey[o]	3-5	6.0	6.2	5.8	0.94	6.8	7.0	6.6	0.94
40	Ukraine	3-6	47.5	47.9	47.1	0.98	52.0	52.4	51.5	0.98
	Central Asia									
41	Armenia	3-6	...	...	...	...	30.5	29.6	31.4	1.06
42	Azerbaijan	3-5	16.4	17.4	15.4	0.89	23.1	23.2	23.1	1.00
43	Georgia	3-5	30.1	30.2	30.0	0.99	41.0	40.4	41.6	1.03
44	Kazakhstan	3-6	13.9	14.3	13.6	0.95	12.8	12.8	12.7	0.99
45	Kyrgyzstan	3-5	13.9	14.3**	13.5**	0.94**	14.3	14.5	14.1	0.97
46	Mongolia	3-7	24.7	22.4	27.1	1.21	31.6	29.2	34.2	1.17
47	Tajikistan	3-6	8.5	9.6	7.3	0.76	9.6	10.2	9.0	0.88
48	Turkmenistan	3-6	...	...	...	...	...	...	...	...
49	Uzbekistan	3-6	...	...	...	...	21.4**	21.5**	21.4**	0.99**
	East Asia and the Pacific									
50	Australia[o]	4-4	...	...	...	...	104.2	104.2	104.3	1.00
51	Brunei Darussalam	3-5	50.6	50.0	51.3	1.03	43.7	43.9	43.5	0.99
52	Cambodia	3-5	5.2**	5.1**	5.3**	1.03**	7.4	7.2	7.7	1.08

1. GER in ECCE includes pre-primary education and other early childhood care and education programmes.
2. National population data were used to calculate enrolment ratios.

(y) Data are for 1999/2000.
(z) Data are for 2000/2001.

STATISTICAL ANNEX / 271

Table 3

	GROSS ENROLMENT RATIO (GER) IN ECCE[1] (%)									NEW ENTRANTS TO THE FIRST GRADE OF PRIMARY EDUCATION WITH ECCE EXPERIENCE (%)			
	1998				2001				2001			
	Total	Male	Female	GPI (F/M)	Total	Male	Female	GPI (F/M)	Total	Male	Female	
	...	...	...	...	...	...	...	...	2.7 z	2.6 z	2.8 z	1
	...	...	...	...	...	...	...	...	...	...	...	2
	.	.	.	.	.	.	.	.	2.7 z	2.2 z	3.5 z	3
	...	...	...	...	...	...	...	...	...	...	...	4
	...	...	...	...	...	...	...	...	...	...	...	5
	...	...	...	...	...	...	...	...	61.7	64.5	58.8	6
	...	...	...	...	...	...	...	...	92.3	91.9	92.8	7
	...	...	...	...	...	...	...	...	95.4	95.3	95.5	8
	...	...	...	...	...	...	...	...	...	...	...	9
	.	.	.	.	.	.	.	.	...	...	...	10
	65.4	85.0	45.1	0.53	60.9	76.3	44.7	0.59	...	...	...	11
	...	...	...	...	...	...	...	...	...	...	...	12
	...	...	...	...	...	...	...	...	76.4 z	81.0 z	71.6 z	13
	...	...	...	...	...	...	...	...	...	...	...	14
	...	...	...	...	...	...	...	...	...	...	...	15
	.	.	.	.	.	.	.	.	45.6 y	42.1 y	50.1 y	16
	...	...	...	...	...	...	...	...	12.0 z	12.0 z	12.0 z	17
	...	...	...	...	...	...	...	...	...	...	...	18
	...	...	...	...	...	...	...	...	37.1**	37.8**	36.3**	19
	...	...	...	...	...	...	...	...	...	...	...	20
	.	.	.	.	.	.	.	.	...	...	...	21
	...	...	...	...	...	...	...	...	...	...	...	22
	...	...	...	...	...	...	...	...	...	...	...	23
	.	.	.	.	.	.	.	.	.	...	.	24
	...	...	...	...	...	...	...	...	...	...	...	25
	.	.	.	.	.	.	.	.	...	...	...	26
	.	.	.	.	.	.	.	.	...	...	...	27
	...	...	...	...	...	...	...	...	...	...	...	28
	.	.	.	.	.	.	.	.	...	...	...	29
	...	...	...	...	61.7	63.0	60.3	0.96	...	...	...	30
	.	.	.	.	.	.	.	.	...	...	...	31
	...	...	...	...	...	...	...	...	...	...	...	32
	.	.	.	.	.	.	.	.	...	...	...	33
	...	...	...	...	...	...	...	...	70.0 z	70.0 z	70.0 z	34
	...	...	...	...	...	...	...	...	...	...	...	35
	...	...	...	...	...	...	...	...	...	...	...	36
	...	...	...	...	88.0	90.2	85.5	0.95	...	...	...	37
	...	...	...	...	31.0	30.8	31.1	1.01	...	...	...	38
	.	.	.	.	.	.	.	.	...	...	...	39
	...	...	...	...	...	...	...	...	...	...	...	40
	...	...	...	...	...	...	...	...	...	...	...	41
	...	...	...	...	...	...	...	...	7.7	8.0	7.3	42
	...	...	...	...	...	...	...	...	...	...	...	43
	...	...	...	...	...	...	...	...	49.2	49.3	49.2	44
	...	...	...	...	...	...	...	...	7.1	7.3	6.9	45
	...	...	...	...	...	...	...	...	–	...	–	46
	...	...	...	...	...	...	...	...	0.4	0.4	0.4	47
	...	...	...	...	...	...	...	...	...	...	...	48
	...	...	...	...	...	...	...	...	...	...	...	49
	.	.	.	.	.	.	.	.	...	...	...	50
	...	...	...	...	...	...	...	...	94.6 z	94.0 z	95.1 z	51
	...	...	...	...	...	...	...	...	8.6	8.1	9.2	52

Table 3 (continued)

	Country or territory	Age group 2001	GER 1998 Total	Male	Female	GPI (F/M)	GER 2001 Total	Male	Female	GPI (F/M)
53	China[w]	3-6	27.8	28.4	27.1	0.95	27.1	28.1	26.0	0.93
54	Cook Islands[2]	4-4	...	...	...	...	85.9**,[z]	86.4**,[z]	85.4**,[z]	0.99**,[z]
55	Democratic People's Republic of Korea	4-5	...	...	...	...	...	...	...	...
56	Fiji	3-5	15.4**	15.2**	15.5**	1.02**	...	...	...	...
57	Indonesia[w]	5-6	...	...	...	...	20.3	19.5	21.1	1.08
58	Japan[o]	3-5	83.1	82.2**	84.0**	1.02**	84.2	83.2**	85.3**	1.03**
59	Kiribati	3-5	...	...	...	...	...	...	...	...
60	Lao People's Democratic Republic	3-5	7.9	7.5	8.3	1.11	7.6	7.3	7.8	1.07
61	Macao, China	3-5	86.9	89.0	84.7	0.95	86.5	89.5	83.4	0.93
62	Malaysia[w]	5-5	109.5	110.2	108.8	0.99	88.7	85.3	92.3	1.08
63	Marshall Islands	4-5	...	...	...	...	...	...	...	...
64	Micronesia (Federated States of)	3-5	36.6	...	...	...	...	...	...	...
65	Myanmar	3-4	1.9	...	...	...	1.9**,[y]	...	...	...
66	Nauru[2]	5-5	140.9**	143.9**	137.9**	0.96**	...	...	...	...
67	New Zealand[o]	3-4	...	...	...	...	86.8	86.0	87.6	1.02
68	Niue[2]	4-4	128.6	120.8	138.9	1.15	147.8	133.3	163.6	1.23
69	Palau[2]	3-5	62.5	56.2	69.2	1.23	65.5**,[z]	61.9**,[z]	69.5**,[z]	1.12**,[z]
70	Papua New Guinea	6-6	33.5	34.3	32.6	0.95	38.8**	40.4**	37.1**	0.92**
71	Philippines[w]	5-5	30.7	30.0	31.5	1.05	33.0	32.3	33.8	1.05
72	Republic of Korea[o]	5-5	...	...	...	...	79.6	79.4	79.7	1.00
73	Samoa	3-4	55.5	51.9	59.3	1.14	54.5	48.9	60.3	1.23
74	Singapore	3-5	...	...	...	...	...	...	...	...
75	Solomon Islands	5-5	...	...	...	...	...	...	...	...
76	Thailand[w]	3-5	86.6	87.5	85.6	0.98	85.7	86.6	84.8	0.98
77	Timor-Leste	4-5	...	...	...	...	11.2	...	...	...
78	Tokelau	3-4	...	...	...	...	...	...	...	...
79	Tonga	3-4	21.7	20.2	23.3	1.15	29.4**,[z]	26.7**,[z]	32.2**,[z]	1.21**,[z]
80	Tuvalu[2]	3-5	79.5**	71.2**	89.2**	1.25**	...	...	...	...
81	Vanuatu	4-5	73.2**	69.6**	77.1**	1.11**	75.6	74.6	76.8	1.03
82	Viet Nam	3-5	40.2	41.5	38.8	0.94	43.1	43.4	42.7	0.98
	Latin America and the Caribbean									
83	Anguilla[2]	3-4	...	...	...	...	116.1	117.8	114.6	0.97
84	Antigua and Barbuda[3]	3-4	...	...	...	...	...	...	...	...
85	Argentina[w]	3-5	57.0	56.3	57.6	1.02	60.6	60.1	61.0	1.02
86	Aruba[2]	4-5	96.9	96.8	97.0	1.00	99.8	101.7	97.9	0.96
87	Bahamas	3-4	...	...	...	...	30.0	30.3	29.8	0.99
88	Barbados	3-4	82.2	82.9	81.5	0.98	89.1	88.3	90.0	1.02
89	Belize	3-4	27.8	27.4	28.2	1.03	28.0[z]	27.2[z]	28.9[z]	1.06[z]
90	Bermuda[2]	4-4	...	...	...	...	54.6[z]	...	...	...
91	Bolivia	4-5	44.1	43.9	44.3	1.01	46.5	46.3	46.8	1.01
92	Brazil[w]	4-6	53.5	53.3	53.7	1.01	67.3	67.4	67.2	1.00
93	British Virgin Islands[2]	3-4	61.6	57.0	66.3	1.16	85.4	92.0	78.5	0.85
94	Cayman Islands[3]	3-4	...	...	...	...	...	...	...	...
95	Chile[w]	3-5	73.6	74.0	73.3	0.99	77.5[z]	77.5[z]	77.4[z]	1.00[z]
96	Colombia	3-5	34.8	34.4	35.2	1.02	36.6	36.4	36.7	1.01
97	Costa Rica	5-5	...	...	...	...	115.5	114.7	116.3	1.01
98	Cuba	3-5	102.0	100.2	103.9	1.04	110.6	109.5	111.8	1.02
99	Dominica[2]	3-4	76.1	72.1	80.3	1.11	75.7[z]	73.9**,[z]	77.6**,[z]	1.05**,[z]
100	Dominican Republic	3-5	35.2	35.0	35.4	1.01	35.1	36.1	34.0	0.94
101	Ecuador	5-5	63.6	62.5	64.7	1.04	73.0	71.8	74.2	1.03
102	El Salvador	4-6	40.2	39.3	41.1	1.05	45.9	44.7	47.1	1.05
103	Grenada[2]	3-4	...	...	...	...	67.9[z]	67.2[z]	68.6[z]	1.02[z]
104	Guatemala	5-6	37.3*	37.5*	37.1*	0.99*	55.2	54.8	55.6	1.01
105	Guyana	4-5	120.2	120.6	119.9	0.99	117.9[y]	118.3[y]	117.4[y]	0.99[y]
106	Haiti	3-5	...	...	...	...	...	...	...	...
107	Honduras	4-6	...	...	...	...	21.4**	20.9**	22.0**	1.05**
108	Jamaica[w]	3-5	83.6	80.5	86.8	1.08	86.8	84.7	89.0	1.05
109	Mexico[o]	4-5	74.0	73.1	74.9	1.02	75.8	74.9	76.7	1.02
110	Montserrat[2]	3-4	...	...	...	...	82.9	...	...	...
111	Netherlands Antilles	4-5	100.3	99.0	101.6	1.03	86.2	87.1	85.2	0.98

1. GER in ECCE includes pre-primary education and other early childhood care and education programmes.
2. National population data were used to calculate enrolment ratios.
3. Enrolment ratios were not calculated, due to lack of United Nations population data by age.

(y) Data are for 1999/2000.
(z) Data are for 2000/2001.

STATISTICAL ANNEX / **273**

Table 3

	GROSS ENROLMENT RATIO (GER) IN ECCE[1] (%)							NEW ENTRANTS TO THE FIRST GRADE OF PRIMARY EDUCATION WITH ECCE EXPERIENCE (%)			
	1998				2001				2001		
Total	Male	Female	GPI (F/M)	Total	Male	Female	GPI (F/M)	Total	Male	Female	
...	...	...	...	...	...	...	...	...	...	...	53
...	...	...	...	...	...	...	...	...	...	...	54
...	...	...	...	...	...	...	...	...	...	...	55
...	...	...	...	...	...	...	...	...	...	...	56
...	...	...	...	...	...	...	...	...	...	...	57
...	...	...	...	97.9	...	...	...	...	...	...	58
...	...	...	...	...	...	...	...	...	...	...	59
...	...	...	...	...	...	...	...	7.9	7.1	8.7	60
...	...	...	...	...	...	...	...	94.1	94.3	94.0	61
...	...	...	...	...	...	...	...	...	...	...	62
...	...	...	...	...	...	...	...	...	...	...	63
...	...	...	...	...	...	...	...	...	...	...	64
...	...	...	...	...	...	...	...	...	...	...	65
...	...	...	...	...	...	...	...	...	...	...	66
.	.	.	.	.	.	.	.	...	...	...	67
...	...	...	...	...	...	...	...	...	...	...	68
...	...	...	...	...	...	...	...	...	...	...	69
...	...	...	...	...	...	...	...	...	...	...	70
...	...	...	...	...	...	...	...	53.5	52.8	54.2	71
.	.	.	.	.	.	.	.	...	...	...	72
...	...	...	...	...	...	...	...	59.9[z]	55.6[z]	64.6[z]	73
...	...	...	...	...	...	...	...	...	...	...	74
...	...	...	...	...	...	...	...	...	...	...	75
...	...	...	...	...	...	...	...	...	...	...	76
...	...	...	...	...	...	...	...	...	...	...	77
...	...	...	...	...	...	...	...	...	...	...	78
...	...	...	...	...	...	...	...	26.2*,[y]	30.2*,[y]	21.5*,[y]	79
...	...	...	...	...	...	...	...	...	...	...	80
...	...	...	...	...	...	...	...	...	...	...	81
...	...	...	...	...	...	...	...	...	...	...	82
...	...	...	...	...	...	...	...	100.0	100.0	100.0	83
...	...	...	...	...	...	...	...	96.0[y]	94.2[y]	96.6[y]	84
...	...	...	...	...	...	...	...	89.7	89.5	89.9	85
...	...	...	...	...	...	...	...	83.7	85.0	82.4	86
...	...	...	...	...	...	...	...	...	...	...	87
...	...	...	...	...	...	...	...	100.0	100.0	100.0	88
...	...	...	...	...	...	...	...	...	...	...	89
...	...	...	...	...	...	...	...	50.4[z]	45.6[z]	54.8[z]	90
...	...	...	...	...	...	...	...	59.2*	59.2*	59.2*	91
.	.	.	.	.	.	.	.	...	...	...	92
...	...	...	...	...	...	...	...	89.9**	89.3**	90.6**	93
...	...	...	...	...	...	...	...	89.3	90.5	88.1	94
...	...	...	...	...	...	...	...	...	...	...	95
...	...	...	...	...	...	...	...	...	...	...	96
...	...	...	...	118.3	117.7	118.9	1.01	81.4[z]	80.8[z]	82.0[z]	97
...	...	...	...	...	...	...	...	99.4	99.4	99.3	98
...	...	...	...	...	...	...	...	100.0[z]	100.0[z]	100.0[z]	99
.	.	.	.	.	.	.	.	...	...	...	100
...	...	...	...	...	...	...	...	50.4	49.4	51.4	101
...	...	...	...	...	...	...	...	...	...	...	102
...	...	...	...	...	...	...	...	...	...	...	103
...	...	...	...	...	...	...	...	.	...	.	104
...	...	...	...	...	...	...	...	86.9[y]	...	...	105
...	...	...	...	...	...	...	...	...	...	...	106
...	...	...	...	...	...	...	...	...	...	...	107
...	...	...	...	...	...	...	...	94.3**	94.3**	94.3**	108
.	.	.	.	.	.	.	.	...	...	...	109
...	...	...	...	...	...	...	...	...	...	...	110
...	...	...	...	...	...	...	...	100.0[y]	100.0[y]	100.0[y]	111

Table 3 (continued)

	Country or territory	Age group 2001	GROSS ENROLMENT RATIO (GER) IN PRE-PRIMARY EDUCATION (%)							
			1998				2001			
			Total	Male	Female	GPI (F/M)	Total	Male	Female	GPI (F/M)
112	Nicaragua	3-6	24.7	24.4	24.9	1.02	25.9	25.7	26.1	1.02
113	Panama	4-5	37.7**	38.5**	36.9**	0.96**	50.8	50.3	51.4	1.02
114	Paraguay[w]	3-5	25.5	25.1	25.9	1.03	30.3	29.9	30.6	1.02
115	Peru[w]	3-5	56.1	55.5	56.8	1.02	60.3	59.6	60.9	1.02
116	Saint Kitts and Nevis[2]	3-4	...	...	...	...	141.6[z]	135.6[z]	147.9[z]	1.09[z]
117	Saint Lucia	3-4	85.2	85.6**	84.8**	0.99**	65.4	63.9	66.9	1.05
118	Saint Vincent and the Grenadines	3-4	...	...	...	...	...	...	...	...
119	Suriname	4-5	...	...	...	...	96.4	97.3	95.4	0.98
120	Trinidad and Tobago	3-4	59.8**	59.5**	60.2**	1.01**	63.0**	62.5**	63.4**	1.01**
121	Turks and Caicos Islands[2]	4-5	...	...	...	...	134.2	144.1	124.5	0.86
122	Uruguay[w]	3-5	56.0	55.6	56.4	1.01	62.7	62.0	63.5	1.02
123	Venezuela	3-5	44.2	43.6	44.7	1.03	51.6	51.3	51.9	1.01
	North America and Western Europe									
124	Andorra[3]	3-5	...	...	...	...	...	...	...	...
125	Austria[o]	3-5	81.5	81.7	81.3	0.99	83.9	83.9	83.8	1.00
126	Belgium[o]	3-5	109.9	110.7	109.1	0.99	113.8	114.0	113.7	1.00
127	Canada[o]	4-5	66.0	65.8	66.3	1.01	64.7[z]	64.8[z]	64.5[z]	0.99[z]
128	Cyprus[o,2]	3-5	59.8	59.2	60.4	1.02	59.3	59.2	59.3	1.00
129	Denmark[o]	3-6	91.0	90.9	91.0	1.00	90.0	90.2	89.9	1.00
130	Finland[o]	3-6	48.3	48.5	48.1	0.99	55.2	55.5	55.0	0.99
131	France[o]	3-5	110.6	110.7	110.6	1.00	113.6	113.5	113.6	1.00
132	Germany[o]	3-5	93.6	94.4	92.7	0.98	100.7	101.6	99.8	0.98
133	Greece[o]	4-5	68.4	67.8	69.1	1.02	68.2	66.8	69.6	1.04
134	Iceland[o]	3-5	108.3	108.7	108.0	0.99	116.7	115.8	117.6	1.02
135	Ireland[o]	3-3	...	...	...	...	...	...	...	...
136	Israel[o]	3-5	106.0	106.8	105.2	0.98	107.7	107.8	107.7	1.00
137	Italy[o]	3-5	95.4	96.1	94.6	0.98	98.4	99.1	97.6	0.99
138	Luxembourg[o]	3-5	72.9	73.4	72.4	0.99	83.7	83.8	83.6	1.00
139	Malta[o]	3-4	102.7	103.0	102.4	0.99	100.7	102.1	99.2	0.97
140	Monaco[3]	3-5	...	...	...	...	...	...	...	...
141	Netherlands[o]	4-5	97.8	98.3	97.3	0.99	97.6	98.3	96.9	0.99
142	Norway[o]	3-5	75.4	73.4	77.6	1.06	80.8	78.6**	83.2**	1.06**
143	Portugal[o]	3-5	66.3	66.4	66.1	1.00	70.2	...	...	...
144	San Marino[3]	3-5	...	...	...	...	...	...	...	...
145	Spain[o]	3-5	99.4	99.8	99.0	0.99	106.1	106.4	105.9	1.00
146	Sweden[o]	3-6	76.1	75.7	76.5	1.01	75.1	75.5	74.6	0.99
147	Switzerland[o]	5-6	93.9	94.5	93.2	0.99	97.2	97.6	96.8	0.99
148	United Kingdom[o]	3-4	77.5	77.1	77.9	1.01	83.2	83.2	83.2	1.00
149	United States[o]	3-5	57.4	58.3	56.5	0.97	61.3	60.4	62.3	1.03
	South and West Asia									
150	Afghanistan	3-6	...	...	...	...	...	...	...	...
151	Bangladesh	3-5	22.3	21.6	23.2	1.08	19.2	18.6	19.8	1.06
152	Bhutan[4]	4-5	...	...	...	...	...	...	...	...
153	India[w]	3-5	19.5	19.6	19.4	0.99	29.7**	29.7**	29.7**	1.00**
154	Iran, Islamic Republic of	5-5	13.3	13.0	13.6	1.05	23.0	21.9	24.1	1.10
155	Maldives	3-5	45.9	46.0	45.9	1.00	48.1	47.2	49.1	1.04
156	Nepal	3-5	12.1**	13.9**	10.2**	0.73**	12.5	13.5	11.5	0.85
157	Pakistan[5]	3-4	...	...	...	...	54.7*,[z]	62.7*,[z]	46.2*,[z]	0.74*,[z]
158	Sri Lanka[w]	4-4	...	...	...	...	...	...	...	...
	Sub-Saharan Africa									
159	Angola	3-5	...	...	...	...	...	...	...	...
160	Benin	4-5	4.6	4.7	4.5	0.94	6.2**	6.4**	6.0**	0.95**
161	Botswana	3-5	...	...	...	...	...	...	...	...
162	Burkina Faso	4-6	1.7	1.7	1.7	1.01	1.1**	1.0**	1.1**	1.07**
163	Burundi	4-6	0.8	0.8	0.8	1.01	1.3	1.4	1.3	0.95
164	Cameroon	4-5	11.6	11.9	11.3	0.95	14.3	14.3	14.3	1.00
165	Cape Verde	3-5	...	...	...	...	55.5	55.4	55.6	1.00
166	Central African Republic	4-5	...	...	...	...	...	...	...	...

1. GER in ECCE includes pre-primary education and other early childhood care and education programmes.
2. National population data were used to calculate enrolment ratios.
3. Enrolment ratios were not calculated, due to lack of United Nations population data by age.
4. Enrolment ratios were not calculated due to inconsistencies between enrolment and the United Nations population data.
5. Data include enrolment in 'katchi' programmes.

Table 3

	GROSS ENROLMENT RATIO (GER) IN ECCE[1] (%)								NEW ENTRANTS TO THE FIRST GRADE OF PRIMARY EDUCATION WITH ECCE EXPERIENCE (%)			
	1998				2001				2001			
Total	Male	Female	GPI (F/M)	Total	Male	Female	GPI (F/M)	Total	Male	Female	
...	...	...	...	...	...	...	...	38.3	36.8	40.0	112
...	...	...	...	...	...	...	...	69.2**	67.0**	71.6**	113
...	...	...	...	...	...	...	...	66.9	65.9	68.1	114
...	...	...	...	...	...	...	...	...	...	...	115
...	...	...	...	...	...	...	...	98.2 y	98.1 y	98.4 y	116
...	...	...	...	85.7	83.5	88.0	1.05	...	...	...	117
...	...	...	...	...	...	...	...	...	...	...	118
...	...	...	...	...	...	...	...	...	...	...	119
...	...	...	...	...	...	...	...	77.0 z	77.0**,z	77.0**,z	120
...	...	...	...	...	...	...	...	100.0	100.0	100.0	121
...	...	...	...	...	...	...	...	80.9**	80.6**	81.1**	122
52.8	52.4	53.2	1.02	56.7	56.3	57.1	1.01	...	...	...	123
...	...	...	...	...	...	...	...	...	...	...	124
...	...	...	...	88.3	88.4	88.2	1.00	...	...	...	125
.	.	.	.	.	.	.	.	...	...	...	126
.	.	.	.	.	.	.	.	...	...	...	127
...	...	...	...	90.4	90.8	89.8	0.99	...	...	...	128
.	.	.	.	.	.	.	.	...	...	...	129
.	.	.	.	.	.	.	.	...	...	...	130
.	.	.	.	.	.	.	.	...	...	...	131
.	.	.	.	.	.	.	.	...	...	...	132
.	.	.	.	.	.	.	.	...	...	...	133
.	.	.	.	.	.	.	.	...	...	...	134
.	.	.	.	.	.	.	.	...	...	...	135
.	.	.	.	.	.	.	.	...	...	...	136
.	.	.	.	.	.	.	.	...	...	...	137
.	.	.	.	.	.	.	.	...	...	...	138
.	.	.	.	.	.	.	.	...	...	...	139
...	...	...	...	...	...	...	...	...	...	...	140
.	.	.	.	.	.	.	.	...	...	...	141
.	.	.	.	.	.	.	.	...	...	...	142
.	.	.	.	.	.	.	.	...	...	...	143
...	...	...	...	...	...	...	...	...	...	...	144
.	.	.	.	.	.	.	.	...	...	...	145
.	.	.	.	.	.	.	.	...	...	...	146
.	.	.	.	.	.	.	.	...	...	...	147
.	.	.	.	.	.	.	.	...	...	...	148
.	.	.	.	.	.	.	.	...	...	...	149
...	...	...	...	...	...	...	...	...	...	...	150
...	...	...	...	...	...	...	...	22.7	23.3	22.1	151
...	...	...	...	...	...	...	...	...	...	...	152
...	...	...	...	...	...	...	...	...	...	...	153
...	...	...	...	...	...	...	...	...	...	...	154
...	...	...	...	...	...	...	...	91.4 z	91.2 z	91.6 z	155
...	...	...	...	...	...	...	...	12.9	13.5	12.2	156
...	...	...	...	...	...	...	...	...	...	...	157
...	...	...	...	...	...	...	...	...	...	...	158
...	...	...	...	...	...	...	...	...	...	...	159
.	.	.	.	.	.	.	.	...	...	...	160
...	...	...	...	...	...	...	...	...	...	...	161
...	...	...	...	...	...	...	...	4.1 z	3.7 z	4.7 z	162
...	...	...	...	...	...	...	...	2.7	2.4	3.1	163
.	.	.	.	.	.	.	.	...	...	...	164
.	.	.	.	.	.	.	.	.	...	.	165
.	.	.	.	.	.	.	.	...	...	...	166

(y) Data are for 1999/2000.
(z) Data are for 2000/2001.

Table 3 (continued)

	Country or territory	Age group 2001	GROSS ENROLMENT RATIO (GER) IN PRE-PRIMARY EDUCATION (%)							
			1998				2001			
			Total	Male	Female	GPI (F/M)	Total	Male	Female	GPI (F/M)
167	Chad	3-5	...	...	...	...	...	...	...	...
168	Comoros	3-5	2.2	2.1	2.2	1.07	1.7 y	1.6**,y	1.8**,y	1.07**,y
169	Congo	3-5	1.8	1.4	2.2	1.59	4.2	4.0	4.3	1.07
170	Côte d'Ivoire	3-5	2.6	2.6	2.5	0.97	3.2	3.2	3.2	0.99
171	Democratic Rep. of the Congo	3-5	...	...	...	...	0.8**	0.8**	0.8**	0.98**
172	Equatorial Guinea	3-6	30.9	30.2	31.5	1.04	35.1	...	...	...
173	Eritrea	5-6	5.3	5.6	5.0	0.89	5.3	5.5	5.0	0.92
174	Ethiopia	4-6	1.5	1.5	1.5	0.97	1.8	1.9	1.8	0.96
175	Gabon	3-5	...	...	...	...	13.2**	...	...	...
176	Gambia	4-6	19.7	20.7	18.7	0.91	19.7**,y	...	...	...
177	Ghana	3-5	37.0	37.2	36.9	0.99	41.5	41.6	41.3	0.99
178	Guinea	3-6	...	...	...	...	...	...	...	...
179	Guinea-Bissau	4-6	...	...	...	...	3.2 y	3.1 y	3.3 y	1.05 y
180	Kenya	3-5	38.3	37.1	39.6	1.07	44.4	44.8	44.0	0.98
181	Lesotho	3-5	24.9	23.4*	26.5*	1.13*	21.4**	21.3**	21.6**	1.02**
182	Liberia	3-5	43.3	49.8	36.8	0.74	56.1 y	59.4 y	52.8 y	0.89 y
183	Madagascar	3-5	...	...	...	...	3.4**	3.3**	3.4**	1.02**
184	Malawi	3-5	...	...	...	...	...	...	...	...
185	Mali	4-6	2.2	...	...	...	1.6	1.6	1.6	1.00
186	Mauritius	4-5	98.0	97.1	99.0	1.02	87.5	86.4	88.5	1.02
187	Mozambique	3-5	...	...	...	...	...	...	...	...
188	Namibia	3-5	20.1**	19.1**	21.2**	1.11**	23.4	21.4	25.4	1.19
189	Niger	4-6	1.1	1.1	1.1	1.03	1.3	1.3	1.3	0.97
190	Nigeria	3-5	...	...	...	...	8.2**	8.5**	7.9**	0.94**
191	Rwanda	4-6	...	...	...	...	2.5**	2.5**	2.5**	0.99**
192	Sao Tome and Principe	3-6	25.5**	24.8**	26.2**	1.06**	25.8	24.5	27.1	1.11
193	Senegal	4-6	2.9	2.9	2.9	1.00	3.3	3.1	3.5	1.13
194	Seychelles[2]	4-5	112.8	111.3	114.3	1.03	91.5	93.1	89.8	0.96
195	Sierra Leone	3-5	...	...	...	...	4.1 z	...	...	...
196	Somalia	3-5	...	...	...	...	...	...	...	...
197	South Africa	6-6	24.2*	24.3*	24.1*	0.99*	35.1	35.0	35.2	1.00
198	Swaziland	3-5	...	...	...	...	...	...	...	...
199	Togo	3-5	2.7	2.7	2.7	1.00	2.7	2.7	2.8	1.03
200	Uganda	4-5	4.0	4.0	4.0	1.00	4.2**	4.1**	4.2**	1.03**
201	United Republic of Tanzania	5-6	...	...	...	...	...	...	...	...
202	Zambia	3-6	2.3*	2.1*	2.5*	1.19*	...	...	...	...
203	Zimbabwe w	3-5	...	...	...	...	38.7**	38.2**	39.2**	1.03**

I	World[6]	...	44.1	44.3	43.8	0.99	48.6	48.1	49.1	1.02
II	Countries in transition	...	23.3	23.8	22.7	0.95	30.5	29.6	31.4	1.06
III	Developed countries	...	76.1	75.7	76.5	1.01	81.9	81.4	82.4	1.01
IV	Developing countries	...	31.9	32.0	31.8	0.99	35.0	36.0	34.0	0.95
V	Arab States	...	13.5	13.9	13.2	0.95	19.6	19.7	19.5	0.99
VI	Central and Eastern Europe	...	50.6	51.6	49.5	0.96	60.2	62.1	58.3	0.94
VII	Central Asia	...	15.2	15.9	14.5	0.91	22.3	22.4	22.3	1.00
VIII	East Asia and the Pacific	...	50.6	50.0	51.3	1.03	54.5	48.9	60.3	1.23
IX	Latin America and the Caribbean	...	57.0	56.3	57.6	1.02	67.3	67.4	67.2	1.00
X	North America and Western Europe	...	86.3	86.3	86.2	1.00	87.0	87.1	86.9	1.00
XI	South and West Asia	...	19.5	19.6	19.4	0.99	26.4	25.8	26.9	1.04
XII	Sub-Saharan Africa	...	5.0	5.2	4.8	0.92	5.8	6.0	5.5	0.92

1. GER in ECCE includes pre-primary education and other early childhood care and education programmes.
2. National population data were used to calculate enrolment ratios.
3. Enrolment ratios were not calculated, due to lack of United Nations population data by age.
4. Enrolment ratios were not calculated, due to inconsistencies between enrolment and the United Nations population data.
5. Data include enrolment in 'katchi' programmes.

STATISTICAL ANNEX / 277

Table 3

	GROSS ENROLMENT RATIO (GER) IN ECCE[1] (%)								NEW ENTRANTS TO THE FIRST GRADE OF PRIMARY EDUCATION WITH ECCE EXPERIENCE (%)			
	1998				2001				2001			
Total	Male	Female	GPI (F/M)	Total	Male	Female	GPI (F/M)	Total	Male	Female	
...	...	...	...	...	...	...	...	...	...	...	167
...	...	...	...	...	...	...	...	...	...	...	168
.	.	.	.	.	.	.	.	2.8	2.7	2.9	169
.	.	.	.	.	.	.	.	11.4**,z	10.5**,z	12.6**,z	170
...	...	...	...	...	...	...	...	...	...	...	171
.	.	.	.	.	.	.	.	...	...	...	172
.	.	.	.	.	.	.	.	...	...	...	173
...	...	...	...	...	...	...	...	...	...	...	174
...	...	...	...	...	...	...	...	...	...	...	175
...	...	...	...	...	...	...	...	...	...	...	176
...	...	...	...	...	...	...	...	...	...	...	177
.	.	.	.	.	.	.	.	...	...	...	178
.	.	.	.	.	.	.	.	...	...	...	179
...	...	...	...	...	...	...	...	...	...	...	180
.	.	.	.	.	.	.	.	...	...	...	181
...	...	...	...	67.3y	72.3y	62.3y	0.86y	...	...	...	182
...	...	...	...	...	...	...	...	...	...	...	183
...	...	...	...	...	...	...	...	...	...	...	184
...	...	...	...	...	...	...	...	...	...	...	185
.	.	.	.	.	.	.	.	100.0z	100.0z	100.0z	186
...	...	...	...	...	...	...	...	...	...	...	187
...	...	...	...	...	...	...	...	...	...	...	188
.	.	.	.	.	.	.	.	6.5z	5.5z	8.0z	189
...	...	...	...	...	...	...	...	...	...	...	190
...	...	...	...	...	...	...	...	...	...	...	191
...	...	...	...	...	...	...	...	...	...	...	192
...	...	...	...	...	...	...	...	...	...	...	193
.	.	.	.	.	.	.	.	100.0	100.0	100.0	194
...	...	...	...	...	...	...	...	5.3y	4.8y	5.9y	195
...	...	...	...	...	...	...	...	...	...	...	196
...	...	...	...	...	...	...	...	...	...	...	197
.	.	.	.	.	.	.	.	...	...	...	198
.	.	.	.	.	.	.	.	1.9z	1.7z	2.1z	199
...	...	...	...	...	...	...	...	...	...	...	200
...	...	...	...	...	...	...	...	...	...	...	201
...	...	...	...	...	...	...	...	11.3z	10.8z	11.7z	202
...	...	...	...	...	...	...	...	...	...	...	203

...	...	...	...	...	...	...	...	...	...	...	I
...	...	...	...	...	...	...	...	...	...	...	II
...	...	...	...	...	...	...	...	...	...	...	III
...	...	...	...	...	...	...	...	...	...	...	IV
...	...	...	...	...	...	...	...	...	...	...	V
...	...	...	...	...	...	...	...	...	...	...	VI
...	...	...	...	...	...	...	...	...	...	...	VII
...	...	...	...	...	...	...	...	...	...	...	VIII
...	...	...	...	...	...	...	...	...	...	...	IX
...	...	...	...	...	...	...	...	...	...	...	X
...	...	...	...	...	...	...	...	...	...	...	XI
...	...	...	...	...	...	...	...	...	...	...	XII

6. All values shown are medians.
(y) Data are for 1999/2000.
(z) Data are for 2000/2001.

Table 4
Access to primary education

	Country or territory	Compulsory education (age group)	Legal guarantee of free education[1]	New entrants (000) 1998	New entrants (000) 2001	GIR 1998 Total	GIR 1998 Male	GIR 1998 Female	GIR 1998 GPI (F/M)	GIR 2001 Total	GIR 2001 Male	GIR 2001 Female	GIR 2001 GPI (F/M)
	Arab States												
1	Algeria[2]	6-16	Yes	744.9	697.8	101.3	102.2	100.2	0.98	100.9	101.7	100.1	0.98
2	Bahrain	...	Yes	13.1	13.0**	95.9	94.3	97.5	1.03	88.3**	89.9**	86.6**	0.96**
3	Djibouti	6-15	No	5.8	7.8	32.1	36.9**	27.3**	0.74**	39.4	44.7	34.0	0.76
4	Egypt[w, 3]	6-13	Yes	1 449.2**	1 533.8**	88.8**	90.5**	87.1**	0.96**	95.4**	96.5**	94.4**	0.98**
5	Iraq	6-11	Yes	708.9**	709.2[y]	112.1**	119.3**	104.5**	0.88**	111.0[y]	117.9[y]	103.8[y]	0.88[y]
6	Jordan[w, 2]	6-16	No	125.6	139.5	99.0	98.9	99.2	1.00	102.9	102.5	103.2	1.01
7	Kuwait[2]	6-14	Yes	34.9	38.9	99.0	98.9	99.0	1.00	95.3	95.8	94.8	0.99
8	Lebanon[2, 3]	6-12	Yes	71.4	68.9	96.5	100.0	92.8	0.93	96.9	97.9	95.9	0.98
9	Libyan Arab Jamahiriya[2]	6-15	Yes	...	...	...	...	...	...	...	...	...	...
10	Mauritania[3]	6-14	Yes	...	88.4	...	...	...	...	112.2	114.2	110.2	0.96
11	Morocco	6-14	Yes	731.1	718.2	115.8	119.2	112.2	0.94	117.2	119.2	115.2	0.97
12	Oman	...	Yes	51.7	49.6	81.1	81.2	80.9	1.00	74.1	73.8	74.4	1.01
13	Palestinian A. T.	6-15	...	95.2	100.6	104.2	103.5	104.9	1.01	99.7	99.2	100.1	1.01
14	Qatar[3]	6-17	Yes	11.1**	11.4**	113.8**	115.0**	112.4**	0.98**	107.6**	107.0**	108.1**	1.01**
15	Saudi Arabia[3]	6-11	Yes	379.0	405.8	65.2	65.5	64.9	0.99	67.7	67.9	67.4	0.99
16	Sudan[3]	6-13	Yes	...	446.8[y]	...	...	...	...	53.1[y]	58.4[y]	47.7[y]	0.82[y]
17	Syrian Arab Republic[2]	6-12	Yes	465.9	522.7	107.6	110.7	104.4	0.94	122.5	124.4	120.6	0.97
18	Tunisia[w]	6-16	Yes	203.9	182.3	100.6	100.8	100.5	1.00	98.5	97.8	99.3	1.01
19	United Arab Emirates[3]	6-11	Yes	46.9	51.6**	89.7	91.0	88.4	0.97	101.9**	102.2**	101.5**	0.99**
20	Yemen[3]	6-14	Yes	439.6	551.5[z]	77.3	89.8	64.3	0.72	91.7[z]	103.8[z]	79.1[z]	0.76[z]
	Central and Eastern Europe												
21	Albania[o]	6-13	Yes	66.9**	65.1[z]	99.9**	100.6**	99.2**	0.99**	101.8[z]	102.6[z]	100.9[z]	0.98[z]
22	Belarus[3]	6-14	Yes	...	...	...	...	...	...	...	...	...	...
23	Bosnia and Herzegovina[o, 3]	...	Yes	...	...	...	...	...	...	...	...	...	...
24	Bulgaria[o, 2, 3]	7-16	Yes	93.1	79.7	97.9	98.8	96.9	0.98	98.1	97.9	98.3	1.00
25	Croatia	7-14	Yes	49.8	48.2	96.8	97.8	95.6	0.98	97.3	96.9	97.8	1.01
26	Czech Republic[o]	6-15	Yes	123.8**	116.5**,[z]	100.8**	101.8**	99.9**	0.98**	101.7**,[z]	102.3**,[z]	101.0**,[z]	0.99**,[z]
27	Estonia[o]	7-15	Yes	18.4	13.6	99.7	100.5	98.8	0.98	94.5	93.6	95.4	1.02
28	Hungary[o]	7-16	Yes	126.9	112.0	104.0	105.7	102.3	0.97	96.8	97.4	96.2	0.99
29	Latvia[o, 3]	7-15	Yes	32.3	23.6	96.2	96.5**	95.9**	0.99**	89.7	89.5	89.8	1.00
30	Lithuania[o, 2]	7-16	Yes	54.2	41.9	104.0	104.5	103.5	0.99	92.3	92.7	91.9	0.99
31	Poland[o, 4]	7-18	Yes	534.9**	463.3	100.6**	100.0**	101.2**	1.01[a]**	97.4	97.4**	97.5**	1.00**
32	Republic of Moldova[3]	6-16	Yes	63.9**	56.0	87.2**	...	...	...	93.2	94.7	91.6	0.97
33	Romania[o, 3]	7-16	Yes	268.6	245.6	93.7	94.1	93.4	0.99	107.1	107.7	106.4	0.99
34	Russian Federation[w, 3]	6-15	Yes	1 659.0	1 495.1	87.2	87.7**	86.6**	0.99**	101.6	...	...	...
35	Serbia and Montenegro[5]	7-14	...	...	93.7[z]	...	...	...	...	99.7[z]	99.4[z]	100.0[z]	1.01[z]
36	Slovakia[2]	6-16	Yes	75.3	62.7	101.5	102.1	100.8	0.99	94.2	94.4	94.1	1.00
37	Slovenia[o, 2]	7-15	Yes	21.1	21.7	95.3	95.7	94.9	0.99	110.5	110.3	110.8	1.00
38	TFYR Macedonia[o, 2]	7-15	Yes	32.4	29.5	103.3	103.3	103.2	1.00	97.5	97.0	97.9	1.01
39	Turkey[o, 3]	6-14	Yes	...	...	...	...	...	...	...	...	...	...
40	Ukraine[3]	7-15	Yes	622.8	602.5	93.6	94.3**	92.9**	0.98**	118.5	118.9**	118.2**	0.99**
	Central Asia												
41	Armenia[3]	7-17	Yes	...	44.2	...	...	...	...	96.2	97.1	95.3	0.98
42	Azerbaijan[3]	6-16	Yes	171.5	154.4	91.0	90.2	91.8	1.02	89.7	91.4	87.8	0.96
43	Georgia[3]	6-14	Yes	...	59.3	...	...	...	...	92.1	92.6	91.6	0.99
44	Kazakhstan	7-17	Yes	312.7	283.4	96.3	96.0	96.5	1.01	106.5	107.1	105.9	0.99
45	Kyrgyzstan[3]	7-16	Yes	121.2	118.3	104.4	104.3	104.6	1.00	107.1	108.4	105.8	0.98
46	Mongolia	8-15	No	69.9	58.4	110.4	110.4	110.4	1.00	101.2	99.8	102.6	1.03
47	Tajikistan[3]	7-15	Yes	177.5	178.1	105.5	108.5	102.4	0.94	114.5	116.6	112.3	0.96
48	Turkmenistan	7-15	Yes	...	...	...	...	...	...	...	...	...	...
49	Uzbekistan[3]	7-15	Yes	...	633.3**	...	...	...	...	104.2**	104.1**	104.2**	1.00**
	East Asia and the Pacific												
50	Australia[o]	5-15	Yes	...	...	...	...	...	...	...	...	...	...
51	Brunei Darussalam	5-16	No	7.9	7.2	109.8	110.6	108.9	0.99	96.6	96.1	97.2	1.01
52	Cambodia[3]	...	Yes	403.7**	651.6	111.4**	114.6**	108.1**	0.94**	167.4	173.6	161.0	0.93
53	China[w, 3, 6]	6-14	Yes	20 451.3	19 639.4**	92.7	92.1	93.4	1.01	98.5**	98.1**	98.8**	1.01**

1. *Source:* Tomasevsky (2003). Background paper for the *EFA Global Monitoring Report 2003/4.*
2. Information on compulsory education come from the Reports under the United Nations Human Rights Treaties.
3. Primary school fees continue to be charged despite the legal guarantee for free education, according to a World Bank study in 2002. See the *EFA Global Monitoring Report 2003/4,* World Bank (2002e).

STATISTICAL ANNEX / 279

Table 4

	NET INTAKE RATE (NIR) IN PRIMARY EDUCATION (%)								SCHOOL LIFE EXPECTANCY (expected number of years of formal schooling)						
	1998				2001				1998			2001			
	Total	Male	Female	GPI (F/M)	Total	Male	Female	GPI (F/M)	Total	Male	Female	Total	Male	Female	
	77.7	78.7	76.6	0.97	91.9	92.8	90.9	0.98	11.3**	…	…	…	…	…	1
	81.2	79.2	83.3	1.05	74.7**	75.3**	74.1**	0.98**	12.8**	12.3**	13.5**	…	…	…	2
	23.6	27.0	20.1	0.75	28.7**,z	32.5**,z	24.9**,z	0.76**,z	3.5**	4.1**	2.9**	3.9**	4.6**	3.2**	3
	…	…	…	…	85.9**	87.1**	84.7**	0.97**	12.4**	…	…	…	…	…	4
	86.5**	91.1**	81.8**	0.90**	84.0**,y	88.1**,y	79.8**,y	0.91**,y	8.9**	10.1**	7.5**	9.0**,y	10.4**,y	7.6**,y	5
	66.5**	65.9**	67.2**	1.02**	68.0	67.5	68.5	1.01	…	…	…	12.6**	12.5**	12.7**	6
	63.0	64.1	61.8	0.96	69.2	70.4	67.9	0.96	13.5**	12.9**	14.3**	…	…	…	7
	71.1**	72.6**	69.6**	0.96**	83.6	84.3	82.9	0.98	12.6**	12.4**	12.7**	13.1**	12.8**	13.3**	8
	…	…	…	…	…	…	…	…	…	…	…	16.5**	15.9**	17.0**	9
	…	…	…	…	33.8**	34.3**	33.2**	0.97**	6.9**	…	…	6.9**	7.2**	6.5**	10
	52.4	54.4	50.4	0.93	82.9	84.6**	81.1**	0.96**	8.2**	9.1**	7.3**	9.1**,z	9.9**,z	8.4**,z	11
	65.6	65.3	65.9	1.01	59.1	58.8	59.5	1.01	…	…	…	10.4**	10.5**	10.4**	12
	…	…	…	…	76.1**	75.9**	76.3**	1.00**	11.9	11.7	11.9	12.7	12.2	12.9	13
	…	…	…	…	72.9**	73.0**	72.9**	1.00**	13.3**	12.6**	14.3**	12.9**	12.4**	13.5**	14
	39.9	47.2	32.2	0.68	44.7	52.9	36.2	0.68	9.7**	9.8**	9.5**	9.6**	9.7**	9.5**	15
	…	…	…	…	27.7 y	29.2 y	26.1 y	0.89 y	5.1**	…	…	…	…	…	16
	60.7	61.3	60.1	0.98	62.5**	63.4**	61.5**	0.97**	9.0**	…	…	…	…	…	17
	85.5**	86.0**	85.1**	0.99**	83.2	82.8	83.6	1.01	12.7**	12.8**	12.5**	13.4**,z	13.4**,z	13.4**,z	18
	46.7	46.7	46.7	1.00	51.8**	51.2**	52.5**	1.03**	10.8**	…	…	…	…	…	19
	25.7	30.4	20.8	0.68	29.6**,y	34.2**,y	24.8**,y	0.73**,y	7.8**	10.5**	4.9**	8.2**,y	10.6**,y	5.5**,y	20
	77.6**	77.7**	77.5**	1.00**	79.0**,z	79.2**,z	78.9**,z	1.00**,z	…	…	…	11.3**,z	11.0**,z	11.5**,z	21
	…	…	…	…	…	…	…	…	13.0**	12.7**	13.3**	14.0	13.7	14.4	22
	…	…	…	…	…	…	…	…	…	…	…	…	…	…	23
	…	…	…	…	82.1	81.9	82.3	1.00	12.7	12.2	13.1	12.5	12.3	12.6	24
	70.0	71.2	68.7	0.97	71.5	71.8	71.2	0.99	12.7	12.4	12.9	12.9	12.6	13.1	25
	…	…	…	…	50.3**,z	47.1**,z	53.7**,z	1.14**,z	…	…	…	14.7	14.5	14.8	26
	…	…	…	…	78.8**	78.4**	79.3**	1.01**	13.9	13.2	14.6	15.6	14.4	16.5	27
	…	…	…	…	63.3**	65.2**	61.4**	0.94**	14.0**	13.8**	14.3**	15.3	14.6	15.6	28
	…	…	…	…	69.0**	69.0**	69.0**	1.00**	13.7	12.8	14.4	14.9	13.7	15.8	29
	…	…	…	…	72.0**	72.9**	71.1**	0.98**	…	…	…	15.4	14.6	16.0	30
	…	…	…	…	…	…	…	…	…	…	…	15.1**,z	14.6**,z	15.6**,z	31
	…	…	…	…	…	…	…	…	9.9**	9.7**	10.2**	10.0	9.6	10.2	32
	…	…	…	…	76.7**	77.2**	76.2**	0.99**	11.8	11.6	12.0	12.4	12.1	12.7	33
	…	…	…	…	…	…	…	…	…	…	…	13.3	12.7	13.8	34
	…	…	…	…	…	…	…	…	13.2**	13.0**	13.3**	12.8**,z	12.6**,z	12.9**,z	35
	53.5**	50.6**	56.5**	1.12**	49.8**	46.8**	52.9**	1.13**	13.1**	13.0**	13.3**	13.7	13.5	13.9	36
	…	…	…	…	72.6	72.5	72.7	1.00	14.3**	13.6**	14.8**	15.9	15.0	16.5	37
	…	…	…	…	74.1	75.0	73.2	0.98	11.9	11.9	11.9	12.1**	11.9**	12.2**	38
	…	…	…	…	…	…	…	…	…	…	…	10.7**	11.6**	9.8**	39
	…	…	…	…	67.0	67.2**	66.8**	0.99**	…	…	…	13.5**	13.1**	13.7**	40
	…	…	…	…	61.4	60.8	62.0	1.02	…	…	…	10.8**	10.4**	11.2**	41
	57.9**	57.9**	57.9**	1.00**	57.1	58.6	55.4	0.95	10.1**	10.2**	10.0**	10.5	10.6	10.3	42
	…	…	…	…	76.3	75.6	77.1	1.02	10.8**	10.5**	11.0**	11.1**	10.9**	11.3**	43
	61.6**	62.4**	60.7**	0.97**	68.2**	69.7**	66.6**	0.96**	11.5	11.3	11.7	12.9	12.5	13.1	44
	61.2**	61.9**	60.4**	0.98**	66.5**	68.3**	64.6**	0.95**	11.9	11.7	12.1	12.7	12.3	12.8	45
	82.2	82.4	82.0	1.00	61.1	61.0	61.2	1.00	8.8	7.8	9.7	10.3**	9.3**	11.2**	46
	96.8**	100.0**	93.5**	0.94**	97.7**	100.0**	95.4**	0.95**	10.0**	10.8**	9.2**	10.7**	11.7**	9.7**	47
	…	…	…	…	…	…	…	…	…	…	…	…	…	…	48
	…	…	…	…	86.7**	…	…	…	…	…	…	11.4**	…	…	49
	…	…	…	…	…	…	…	…	…	…	…	20.1**	19.8**	20.4**	50
	…	…	…	…	…	…	…	…	13.1**	12.7**	13.4**	13.2**	12.8**	13.6**	51
	65.3**	66.5**	64.0**	0.96**	68.0	69.0	66.9	0.97	…	…	…	9.0**	9.8**	8.2**	52
	66.2	65.7**	66.7**	1.01**	57.8**	…	…	…	10.2**	…	…	10.4**	…	…	53

4. No tuition fees are charged but some direct costs have been reported, according to a World Bank study in 2002. See the *EFA Global Monitoring Report 2003/4*, World Bank (2002e).
5. National population data were used to calculate enrolment ratios.
6. Children can enter primary school at age 6 or 7.
(y) Data are for 1999/2000.
(z) Data are for 2000/2001.

280 / ANNEX

Table 4 (continued)

	Country or territory	Compulsory education (age group)	Legal guarantee of free education[1]	New entrants (000) 1998	New entrants (000) 2001	GIR 1998 Total	GIR 1998 Male	GIR 1998 Female	GIR 1998 GPI (F/M)	GIR 2001 Total	GIR 2001 Male	GIR 2001 Female	GIR 2001 GPI (F/M)
54	Cook Islands[7]	5-15	...	0.7	0.6**,z	...	...	...	...	...	...	...	...
55	DPR Korea	6-15	Yes	...	...	...	...	...	...	...	...	...	...
56	Fiji	6-15	No	21.8**	20.5**	122.5**	123.9**	121.0**	0.98**	111.7**	114.7**	108.5**	0.95**
57	Indonesia[w]	7-15	No	...	5 018.5	...	...	...	...	116.1	119.0	113.1	0.95
58	Japan[o, 4]	6-15	Yes	...	...	...	...	...	...	...	...	...	...
59	Kiribati	...	No	...	...	...	...	...	...	...	...	...	...
60	Lao PDR	6-14	No	180.5	192.6	121.0	127.8	114.0	0.89	125.5	133.3	117.5	0.88
61	Macao, China	5-14	...	6.5	5.8	88.1	87.4	88.8	1.02	95.4	98.5	92.3	0.94
62	Malaysia[w]	...	No	...	531.1	...	...	...	...	92.9	92.7	93.1	1.00
63	Marshall Islands[2, 5]	6-14	No	1.4	1.6	...	...	...	...	120.3**,y	128.2**,y	112.4**,y	0.88**,y
64	Micronesia	6-13	No	...	...	...	...	...	...	...	...	...	...
65	Myanmar	5-9	No	1 225.5	1 259.6	113.9	...	...	...	116.1	115.6	116.7	1.01
66	Nauru[5]	6-16	No	...	...	...	...	...	...	...	...	...	...
67	New Zealand[o, 4]	5-16	Yes	...	59.0 y	...	...	...	...	98.5 y	98.6 y	98.4 y	1.00 y
68	Niue[5]	5-16	...	0.04	0.03	95.3	112.5	73.7	0.65	110.0	123.1	100.0	0.81
69	Palau[2, 5]	6-17	Yes	0.4	...	120.2	119.8	120.7	1.01	...	...	...	...
70	Papua New Guinea	6-14	No	151.8	151.6**	106.6	110.5	102.3	0.93	96.4**	102.0**	90.5**	0.89**
71	Philippines[w, 4]	6-12	Yes	2 550.5**	2 578.3	133.5**	136.8**	129.9**	0.95**	132.1	136.7	127.3	0.93
72	Republic of Korea[o, 2, 4]	6-15	Yes	...	695.9	...	...	...	...	100.9	101.9	99.7	0.98
73	Samoa	...	No	5.2	5.7	107.9	107.3	108.5	1.01	116.3	115.5	117.1	1.01
74	Singapore	6-16	No	...	...	...	...	...	...	...	...	...	...
75	Solomon Islands	...	No	...	...	...	...	...	...	...	...	...	...
76	Thailand[w]	6-14	No	1 037.4**	1 012.8**,z	97.4**	101.0**	93.6**	0.93**	95.6**,z	98.7**,z	92.5**,z	0.94**,z
77	Timor-Leste	7-15	...	...	...	...	...	...	...	...	...	...	...
78	Tokelau	...	...	...	...	...	...	...	...	...	...	...	...
79	Tonga	6-14	No	2.8	2.8	110.4	111.0	109.7	0.99	106.1	104.7	107.6	1.03
80	Tuvalu[5]	7-14	No	0.2**	...	86.0**	84.8**	87.5**	1.03**	...	...	...	...
81	Vanuatu	...	No	5.7**	6.8**	104.9**	101.3**	108.8**	1.07**	121.2**	118.9**	123.8**	1.04**
82	Viet Nam[3]	6-14	Yes	2 035.3	1 741.6	108.4	112.5	104.2	0.93	100.2	103.1	97.1	0.94
	Latin America and the Caribbean												
83	Anguilla[5]	5-17	...	0.22	0.20	...	...	...	...	104.3	88.2	127.3	1.44
84	Antigua and Barbuda[7]	5-16	Yes	...	1.6 y	...	...	...	...	...	...	...	...
85	Argentina[w, 2]	5-15	Yes	792.7	775.0	116.2	115.7	116.8	1.01	112.2	112.0	112.4	1.00
86	Aruba[5]	...	...	1.5	1.6	106.2	109.4	102.9	0.94	110.7	112.2	109.2	0.97
87	Bahamas	5-16	No	...	7.1**	...	...	...	...	112.1**	115.7**	108.4**	0.94**
88	Barbados	5-15	Yes	4.0	3.5	109.3	109.8	108.9	0.99	103.2	103.3	103.1	1.00
89	Belize	5-14	Yes	8.4	7.1 z	129.0	130.3	127.8	0.98	107.4 z	107.2 z	107.7 z	1.01 z
90	Bermuda	5-16	...	...	0.8 z	...	...	...	...	102.9 z	...	...	...
91	Bolivia[3]	...	Yes	272.5**	278.2	122.7**	122.8**	122.6**	1.00**	119.8	119.1	120.6	1.01
92	Brazil[w, 3]	7-14	Yes	4 226.6	4 089.1	125.5	...	...	...	124.7	130.5	118.8	0.91
93	British Virgin Islands[5]	5-16	...	0.4**	0.4**	105.7**	108.6**	102.7**	0.95**	103.5**	102.6**	104.4**	1.02**
94	Cayman Islands[7]	5-16	...	0.62	0.60	...	...	...	...	...	...	...	...
95	Chile[w, 2]	6-14	Yes	287.8	282.2 z	97.7	98.2	97.2	0.99	96.5 z	97.2 z	95.9 z	0.99 z
96	Colombia[2]	5-15	No	1 258.0**	1 222.4	135.1**	137.7**	132.4**	0.96**	127.5	130.3	124.5	0.96
97	Costa Rica	...	Yes	...	83.1	...	...	...	...	101.1	100.7	101.4	1.01
98	Cuba	...	Yes	160.8**	141.9	97.2**	99.1**	95.3**	0.96**	95.4	95.2	95.6	1.00
99	Dominica[5]	5-17	No	1.8	1.6 z	105.1	111.4**	98.6**	0.88**	100.1 z	99.3 z	100.9 z	1.02 z
100	Dominican Republic[3]	5-13	Yes	259.4	262.3	139.6	144.0	135.0	0.94	142.8	148.0	137.3	0.93
101	Ecuador	5-14	Yes	374.4	396.3	132.1	132.4	131.9	1.00	138.5	139.0	138.0	0.99
102	El Salvador	...	Yes	185.9	198.6	128.2	130.6	125.8	0.96	131.3	134.5	127.9	0.95
103	Grenada[5]	5-16	No	...	2.0**,z	...	...	...	...	93.7**,z	103.2**,z	84.2**,z	0.82**,z
104	Guatemala[3]	...	Yes	...	423.6	...	...	...	...	124.9	126.2	123.4	0.98
105	Guyana[3]	6-15	Yes	18.4	19.1 y	121.0	118.0	124.1	1.05	124.4 y	127.5 y	121.3 y	0.95 y
106	Haiti	6-11	No	...	...	...	...	...	...	...	...	...	...
107	Honduras[2]	6-13	Yes	...	256.5**	...	...	...	...	138.7**	138.7**	138.8**	1.00**
108	Jamaica[w]	6-11	No	...	54.2**	...	...	...	...	98.9**	99.0**	98.9**	1.00**
109	Mexico[o, 3]	6-15	Yes	2 508.9	2 475.3	111.3	111.2	111.5	1.00	109.4	109.2	109.6	1.00
110	Montserrat[5]	5-14	...	0.07	0.06	...	...	...	...	139.1	...	...	...
111	Netherlands Antilles	6-15	...	3.8**	3.3**	100.8**	97.5**	104.1**	1.07**	89.1**	85.2**	93.1**	1.09**
112	Nicaragua[3]	7-12	Yes	...	207.0	...	...	...	...	138.2	142.4	133.9	0.94

1. *Source:* Tomasevsky (2003). Background paper for the *EFA Global Monitoring Report 2003/4*.
2. Information on compulsory education come from the Reports under the United Nations Human Rights Treaties.
3. Primary school fees continue to be charged despite the legal guarantee for free education, according to a World Bank study in 2002. See the *EFA Global Monitoring Report 2003/4*, World Bank (2002e).

STATISTICAL ANNEX / 281

Table 4

	NET INTAKE RATE (NIR) IN PRIMARY EDUCATION (%)							SCHOOL LIFE EXPECTANCY (expected number of years of formal schooling)						
	1998				2001				1998			2001		
	Total	Male	Female	GPI (F/M)	Total	Male	Female	GPI (F/M)	Total	Male	Female	Total	Male	Female
54	...	...	...	...	...	...	...	...	...	...	...	...	...	...
55	...	...	...	...	...	...	...	...	...	...	...	...	...	...
56	80.5**	81.2**	79.9**	0.98**	77.3**	79.3**	75.1**	0.95**	...	...	...	...	...	...
57	...	...	...	...	46.4	46.9	45.8	0.98	...	...	...	10.9	11.0	10.7
58	...	...	...	...	...	...	...	...	14.3**	14.5**	14.2**	14.7**	14.8**	14.5**
59	...	...	...	...	...	...	...	...	...	...	...	...	...	...
60	54.7	55.7	53.7	0.96	61.7	62.6	60.9	0.97	8.4**	9.3	7.4**	8.9**	9.8**	7.9**
61	62.5	60.3	64.7	1.07	72.8	73.3	72.3	0.99	12.1**	12.2**	11.9**	14.8**	16.1**	13.7**
62	...	...	...	...	92.9	92.7	93.1	1.00	12.0**	11.7**	12.2**	12.3**,z	12.0**,z	12.6**,z
63	...	...	...	...	...	...	...	...	...	...	...	...	...	...
64	...	...	...	...	...	...	...	...	...	...	...	...	...	...
65	78.0**	...	...	...	93.2	92.8	93.6	1.01	...	...	...	7.4**,z	7.3**,z	7.5**,z
66	...	...	...	...	...	...	...	...	8.1**	...	...	...	...	...
67	...	...	...	...	...	...	...	...	...	...	...	17.7**,y	16.8**,y	18.6**,y
68	84.8	100.0	65.5	0.65	89.4	100.0	81.3	0.81	12.3	...	...	12.8	...	...
69	...	...	...	...	...	...	...	...	...	...	...	...	...	...
70	...	...	...	...	...	...	...	...	5.7**	6.1**	5.3**	...	...	...
71	46.5**	47.7**	45.3**	0.95**	46.7	44.4	49.1	1.11	11.7**	11.4**	11.9**	12.0**	11.9**	12.0**
72	...	...	...	...	95.0	95.8	94.1	0.98	14.9**	15.7**	14.0**	15.7**	16.7**	14.6**
73	79.4	81.5	77.2	0.95	76.3**	74.1**	78.6**	1.06**	11.7**	11.5**	12.0**	11.8**	11.6**	12.0**
74	...	...	...	...	...	...	...	...	...	...	...	...	...	...
75	...	...	...	...	...	...	...	...	...	...	...	...	...	...
76	...	...	...	...	...	...	...	...	...	...	...	12.5**,z	12.7**,z	12.3**,z
77	...	...	...	...	...	...	...	...	...	...	...	11.4**	...	...
78	...	...	...	...	...	...	...	...	...	...	...	...	...	...
79	60.9	60.4	61.6	1.02	87.0	84.9	89.1	1.05	...	...	...	13.4**	13.2**	13.7**
80	86.0**	84.8**	87.5**	1.03**	...	...	...	...	10.9**	...	...	...	...	...
81	...	...	...	...	55.1**	54.1**	56.3**	1.04**	...	...	...	9.4**	...	...
82	80.8	...	...	...	82.9**	...	...	...	10.3**	10.8**	9.8**	10.5**	11.0**	10.1**
83	...	...	...	...	82.8	70.8	100.0	1.41	...	...	...	...	...	...
84	...	...	...	...	...	...	...	...	...	...	...	...	...	...
85	...	...	...	...	93.7	93.6	93.9	1.00	14.9**	14.3**	15.6**	16.3	15.1	17.1
86	87.6	88.6	86.5	0.98	86.3	88.6	84.0	0.95	13.3**	13.2**	13.4**	13.5	13.2	13.7
87	...	...	...	...	80.8**	81.1**	80.6**	0.99**	...	...	...	...	...	...
88	85.4**	85.8**	84.9**	0.99**	85.1	85.4	84.8	0.99	15.0**	14.4**	15.6**	14.2**,z	13.5**,z	15.0**,z
89	78.9**	80.6**	77.2**	0.96**	71.3**,z	72.5**,z	70.0**,z	0.97**,z	...	...	...	...	...	...
90	...	...	...	...	...	...	...	...	...	...	...	15.3**,z	...	...
91	64.2**	63.9**	64.4**	1.01**	67.6	66.8	68.3	1.02	12.9**	13.6**	12.1**	14.3**	...	...
92	...	...	...	...	...	...	...	...	...	...	...	14.9	14.3	15.2
93	73.3**	70.3**	76.4**	1.09**	74.3**	71.2**	77.6**	1.09**	15.8**	...	...	15.0**	14.0**	16.0**
94	...	...	...	...	...	...	...	...	...	...	...	...	...	...
95	37.7**	37.3**	38.1**	1.02**	37.1**,z	36.8**,z	37.3**,z	1.01**,z	12.7**	12.8**	12.6**	13.3**,z	13.4**,z	13.2**,z
96	55.8**	...	...	...	57.3**	58.5**	55.9**	0.96**	11.1**	10.9**	11.4**	10.7**	10.5**	10.9**
97	...	...	...	...	60.9**	59.7**	62.1**	1.04**	...	...	...	11.0**	10.8**	11.1**
98	95.4**	97.0**	93.6**	0.96**	94.0	93.8	94.2	1.00	12.1**	...	...	12.8**	12.8**	12.9**
99	76.2	78.4	73.8	0.94**	68.9**,z	67.5**,z	70.4**,z	1.04**,z	11.8**	...	...	...	...	...
100	61.0	60.9	61.2	1.01	62.8	65.3	60.2	0.92	...	...	...	...	...	...
101	82.8	82.3	83.3	1.01	86.3	85.9	86.6	1.01	...	...	...	...	...	...
102	...	...	...	...	59.2	59.4	59.0	0.99	10.7**	10.7**	10.6**	11.0**	11.0**	10.9**
103	...	...	...	...	54.1**,z	57.0**,z	51.2**,z	0.90**,z	...	...	...	...	...	...
104	...	...	...	...	61.3	62.3	60.3	0.97	...	...	...	...	...	...
105	88.0**	86.4**	89.6**	1.04**	87.2**,y	88.8**,y	85.6**,y	0.96**,y	...	...	...	...	...	...
106	...	...	...	...	...	...	...	...	...	...	...	...	...	...
107	...	...	...	...	48.6**	48.6**	48.6**	1.00**	...	...	...	...	...	...
108	...	...	...	...	80.8**	78.9**	82.8**	1.05**	...	...	...	11.8**	11.3**	12.4**
109	...	...	...	...	83.1**	81.5**	84.8**	1.04**	11.8**	11.8**	11.7**	12.3	12.2	12.4
110	...	...	...	...	65.2	...	...	...	...	...	...	13.6	...	...
111	69.2**	64.6**	74.0**	1.15**	61.5**	54.8**	68.4**	1.25**	12.3**	12.0**	12.6**	11.5	11.0	11.9
112	...	...	...	...	38.2	39.6	36.7	0.93	...	...	...	...	...	...

4. No tuition fees are charged but some direct costs have been reported, according to a World Bank study in 2002. See the *EFA Global Monitoring Report 2003/4*, World Bank (2002e).
5. National population data were used to calculate enrolment ratios.

7. Enrolment ratios were not calculated due to lack of United Nations population data by age.
(y) Data are for 1999/2000.
(z) Data are for 2000/2001.

Table 4 (continued)

	Country or territory	Compulsory education (age group)	Legal guarantee of free education[1]	New entrants (000) 1998	New entrants (000) 2001	GIR 1998 Total	GIR 1998 Male	GIR 1998 Female	GIR 1998 GPI (F/M)	GIR 2001 Total	GIR 2001 Male	GIR 2001 Female	GIR 2001 GPI (F/M)
113	Panama	...	Yes	...	74.6	...	...	...	...	118.8	120.3	117.1	0.97
114	Paraguay[w, 3]	6-14	Yes	173.0	169.1	120.4	121.7	119.1	0.98	113.3	114.4	112.2	0.98
115	Peru[w, 3]	6-16	Yes	726.5	710.0	120.1	119.7	120.5	1.01	115.9	115.9	115.8	1.00
116	Saint Kitts and Nevis[5]	5-17	No	...	0.95[z]	...	...	...	...	115.4[z]	112.6[z]	118.3[z]	1.05[z]
117	Saint Lucia	5-16	No	3.5**	3.2	106.1**	106.0**	106.3**	1.00**	96.2	91.9	101.0	1.10
118	St Vincent/Grenad.	5-15	No	...	2.4**	...	...	...	...	102.4**	105.9**	98.8**	0.93**
119	Suriname[3]	7-12	Yes	...	8.9**	...	...	...	...	103.8**	105.7**	102.0**	0.96**
120	Trinidad and Tobago[2, 3]	5-12	Yes	20.3	17.8**	97.2	96.7**	97.6**	1.01**	96.9**	96.3**	97.6**	1.01**
121	Turks and Caicos Islands[5]	4-16	...	0.27	0.37	...	...	...	...	109.7	100.0	118.8	1.19
122	Uruguay[w]	6-15	Yes	56.8	58.3	102.1	99.3	105.0	1.06	103.7	103.6	103.8	1.00
123	Venezuela	6-15	Yes	547.1**	585.8	99.1**	100.2**	97.8**	0.98**	105.6	106.9	104.2	0.97

North America and Western Europe

	Country or territory	Compulsory	Legal	1998	2001	Total	Male	Female	GPI	Total	Male	Female	GPI
124	Andorra[2, 7]	6-16	...	...	0.69	...	...	...	...	...	...	...	...
125	Austria[o, 2, 4]	6-15	Yes	99.6	100.5**,[z]	105.3	106.4	104.2	0.98	106.4**,[z]	107.6**,[z]	105.2**,[z]	0.98**,[z]
126	Belgium[o, 4]	6-18	Yes	...	...	...	...	...	...	...	...	...	...
127	Canada[o]	6-16	Yes	...	...	...	...	...	...	...	...	...	...
128	Cyprus[o, 2]	6-15	Yes	...	10.1	...	...	...	...	98.2	98.1	98.3	1.00
129	Denmark[o]	7-16	Yes	66.1**	71.5	100.2**	100.2**	100.2**	1.00**	103.0	102.9	103.2	1.00
130	Finland[o]	7-16	Yes	65.4**	64.8	100.4**	100.4**	100.4**	1.00**	99.5	99.6	99.4	1.00
131	France[o]	6-16	Yes	735.5	704.8[y]	100.8	...	...	...	97.8[y]	98.4[y]	97.2[y]	0.99[y]
132	Germany[o]	6-18	Yes	869.2**	787.8	100.3**	100.5**	100.2**	1.00**	97.6	97.9	97.2	0.99
133	Greece[o, 2]	6-15	Yes	...	107.3	...	...	...	...	100.9	104.4	97.2	0.93
134	Iceland[o]	6-16	Yes	4.5	4.3	98.4	99.8	96.8	0.97	93.4	94.5	92.2	0.98
135	Ireland[o]	6-15	Yes	57.3	48.4	104.8	106.0	103.5	0.98	110.5	110.4	110.7	1.00
136	Israel[o, 3]	5-15	Yes	...	...	...	...	...	...	...	...	...	...
137	Italy[o, 2]	6-16	Yes	557.6**	514.4**	100.0**	100.6**	99.3**	0.99**	93.4**	94.0**	92.8**	0.99**
138	Luxembourg[o]	6-15	Yes	...	5.8**	...	...	...	...	99.9**	99.4**	100.4**	1.01**
139	Malta[o, 2]	5-16	Yes	5.4	4.9	102.0	102.2	101.7	0.99	100.7	101.1	100.3	0.99
140	Monaco[2]	6-16	No	...	...	...	...	...	...	...	...	...	...
141	Netherlands[o, 2, 4]	6-17	Yes	198.8	195.0	99.9	100.6	99.2	0.99	97.7	98.4	97.0	0.99
142	Norway[o]	6-16	Yes	61.3**	...	100.3**	101.1**	99.6**	0.99**	...	...	...	...
143	Portugal[o, 2]	6-15	Yes	...	...	...	...	...	...	...	...	...	...
144	San Marino[2, 7]	6-16	No	...	1.2[y]	...	...	...	...	...	...	...	...
145	Spain[o]	6-16	Yes	...	...	...	...	...	...	...	...	...	...
146	Sweden[o]	7-16	Yes	127.2**	114.4	103.9**	104.9**	102.9**	0.98**	98.5	98.3	98.7	1.00
147	Switzerland[o]	7-15	Yes	82.4**	77.1	97.6**	96.0**	99.3**	1.03**	93.5	91.7	95.4	1.04
148	United Kingdom[o]	5-16	Yes	...	...	...	...	...	...	...	...	...	...
149	United States[o]	6-17	No	4 321.9	...	103.4	106.0	100.6	0.95	...	...	...	...

South and West Asia

	Country or territory												
150	Afghanistan	7-12	...	...	...	...	...	...	...	...	...	—	...
151	Bangladesh	6-10	Yes	3 986.1**	3 998.8	111.1**	114.1**	108.0**	0.95**	107.0	105.9	108.3	1.02
152	Bhutan[3, 8]	6-16	Yes	11.8	12.9	...	...	...	...	...	...	...	...
153	India[w]	6-14	Yes	29 639.5	28 621.0	127.7	138.5	116.2	0.84	121.3	132.0	109.9	0.83
154	Iran, Islamic Republic of	6-10	Yes	1 563.0	1 299.0	90.3	90.5	90.0	0.99	86.2	86.1	86.2	1.00
155	Maldives	6-12	No	8.2**	7.7	102.4**	103.0**	101.7**	0.99**	91.5	92.3	90.7	0.98
156	Nepal[3]	6-10	Yes	640.6**	807.0	102.4**	114.9**	89.1**	0.78**	122.3	127.5	116.6	0.91
157	Pakistan	5-9	No	...	3 891.0**,[z]	...	...	...	...	93.9**,[z]	108.1**,[z]	78.8**,[z]	0.73**,[z]
158	Sri Lanka[w, 2]	5-14	Yes	345.5	...	107.7	107.5	107.9	1.00	...	...	...	...

Sub-Saharan Africa

	Country or territory												
159	Angola[2, 3]	6-14	Yes	347.7	319.3	94.4	107.5	81.4	0.76	79.3	...	...	...
160	Benin	6-11	No	...	237.7**	...	...	...	...	121.1**	136.3**	106.0**	0.78**
161	Botswana	6-15	Yes	50.5	52.3	110.3	112.6	108.0	0.96	112.3	114.9	109.6	0.95
162	Burkina Faso	6-16	No	153.6	177.1**	43.5	51.0	35.9	0.70	45.8**	52.9**	38.6**	0.73**
163	Burundi	7-12	No	135.7**	163.6	68.9**	76.6**	61.3**	0.80**	82.3	91.8	72.7	0.79
164	Cameroon	6-11	No	334.7**	482.0*	77.4**	85.3**	69.4**	0.81**	107.1**	114.6*	99.4*	0.87*
165	Cape Verde[2]	6-16	No	13.1**	12.6	106.3**	107.4**	105.2**	0.98**	104.7	106.6	102.9	0.97
166	Central African Republic	...	No	...	71.3*	...	...	...	...	64.4*	76.1*	52.9*	0.70*
167	Chad[2, 3]	6-14	Yes	174.9	208.5**	75.9	88.9	62.8	0.71	82.0**	94.0**	70.0**	0.74**

1. *Source:* Tomasevsky (2003). Background paper for the *EFA Global Monitoring Report 2003/4*.
2. Information on compulsory education come from the Reports under the United Nations Human Rights Treaties.
3. Primary school fees continue to be charged despite the legal guarantee for free education, according to a World Bank study in 2002. See the *EFA Global Monitoring Report 2003/4*, World Bank (2002e).
4. No tuition fees are charged but some direct costs have been reported, according to a World Bank study in 2002. See the *EFA Global Monitoring Report 2003/4*, World Bank (2002e).
5. National population data were used to calculate enrolment ratios.

STATISTICAL ANNEX / 283

Table 4

NET INTAKE RATE (NIR) IN PRIMARY EDUCATION (%)

SCHOOL LIFE EXPECTANCY
(expected number of years of formal schooling)

	1998				2001				1998			2001			
	Total	Male	Female	GPI (F/M)	Total	Male	Female	GPI (F/M)	Total	Male	Female	Total	Male	Female	
	...	...	...	...	84.8**	83.8**	85.8**	1.02**	...	...	...	12.2**,y	11.8**,y	12.7**,y	113
	70.8**	69.8**	71.9**	1.03**	67.2	66.0	68.5	1.04	...	...	...	11.7**	11.6**	11.8**	114
	...	...	...	...	85.2**	85.4**	85.0**	1.00**	...	...	...	14.0**	13.8**	14.0**	115
	...	...	...	...	31.6z	28.6z	34.8z	1.22z	...	...	...	...	...	...	116
	74.8**	74.0**	75.5**	1.02**	66.3**	61.9**	71.2**	1.15**	13.4**	13.2**	13.7**	12.5**	11.8**	13.2**	117
	...	...	...	...	43.4**	39.6**	47.4**	1.20**	...	...	...	...	...	...	118
	...	...	...	...	69.0**	64.3**	73.8**	1.15**	...	...	...	12.5**	11.7**	13.4**	119
	69.2	68.0**	70.5**	1.04**	67.4**	65.2**	69.7**	1.07**	11.9**	11.7**	12.1**	12.1**	11.6**	12.4**	120
	...	...	...	...	68.8	57.3	79.5	1.39	...	...	...	...	...	...	121
	38.1**	36.2**	40.1**	1.11**	34.8**	33.4**	36.4**	1.09**	...	...	...	14.6	13.5	15.5	122
	61.0**	60.8**	61.2**	1.01**	64.8	64.5	65.1	1.01	...	...	...	11.2**	10.8**	11.6**	123
	...	...	...	...	...	...	...	...	...	...	...	...	...	...	124
	...	...	...	...	...	...	...	...	15.2**	15.2**	15.1**	14.8	14.4	14.9	125
	...	...	...	...	...	...	...	...	17.8**	17.4**	18.2**	18.9**	18.0**	19.6**	126
	...	...	...	...	...	...	...	...	16.0**	15.7**	16.3**	16.1**,z	15.7**,z	16.4**,z	127
	...	...	...	...	91.0	90.2	91.8	1.02	12.5	12.3	12.7	13.0	12.7	13.2	128
	...	...	...	...	99.8	99.7	100.0	1.00	16.1**	15.6**	16.6**	16.6	15.7	17.2	129
	...	...	...	...	95.0**	94.0**	96.1**	1.02**	17.5**	16.7**	18.2**	18.1	16.5	18.9	130
	...	...	...	...	...	...	...	...	15.6**	15.3**	15.8**	15.4	15.0	15.7	131
	...	...	...	...	...	...	...	...	16.0**	16.2**	15.8**	15.7**	15.5**	15.6**	132
	...	...	...	...	94.3	97.1	91.2	0.94	...	...	...	14.9**,z	14.6**,z	15.1**,z	133
	...	...	...	...	92.7	93.8	91.6	0.98	...	...	...	17.6	16.2	18.6	134
	...	...	...	...	51.4**	48.4**	54.6**	1.13**	16.2**	15.7**	16.6**	16.7	15.9	17.4	135
	...	...	...	...	...	...	...	...	14.8**	14.4**	15.2**	15.8	14.8	16.2	136
	...	...	...	...	90.3**	90.6**	89.9**	0.99**	14.7**	14.5**	14.9**	15.4	15.0	15.6	137
	...	...	...	...	85.9**	85.5**	86.3**	1.01**	...	...	...	13.5**	13.4**	13.7**	138
	...	...	...	...	71.3**	70.7**	72.0**	1.02**	...	...	...	14.0	13.8	14.1	139
	...	...	...	...	...	...	...	...	...	...	...	...	...	...	140
	99.3	100.0	98.6	0.99	97.7	98.4	97.0	0.99	16.5**	16.7**	16.2**	16.5	16.4	16.4	141
	...	...	...	...	...	...	...	...	17.5**	16.9**	18.0**	17.3	16.0	18.1	142
	...	...	...	...	...	...	...	...	15.8**	15.5**	16.1**	16.1	15.4	16.6	143
	...	...	...	...	...	...	...	...	...	...	...	...	...	...	144
	...	...	...	...	...	...	...	...	...	...	...	16.0	15.4	16.4	145
	...	...	...	...	95.1	95.3	94.8	0.99	19.0**	17.3**	20.8**	19.0	16.8	20.7	146
	...	...	...	...	58.5**	58.5**	58.5**	1.00**	15.5**	16.0**	15.0**	15.7	15.6	15.3	147
	...	...	...	...	...	...	...	...	20.0**	19.3**	20.7**	21.8	19.7	23.3	148
	...	...	...	...	...	...	...	...	...	...	...	15.6	14.5	16.1	149
	...	...	...	...	...	...	...	...	...	...	...	...	...	...	150
	83.3**	84.6**	82.0**	0.97**	80.6	79.0	82.2	1.04	8.5**	8.7**	8.2**	8.4	8.3	8.5	151
	...	...	...	...	...	...	...	...	6.5**	7.0**	5.8**	7.5**	7.8**	6.8**	152
	...	...	...	...	...	...	...	...	...	...	...	9.0**	10.0**	7.9**	153
	43.8**	44.3**	43.2**	0.97**	41.4**,z	41.9**,z	40.8**,z	0.97**,z	11.6**	12.2**	10.9**	11.5**	12.0**	10.9**	154
	...	...	...	...	81.2	81.2	81.2	1.00	11.6	...	...	12.3**	...	...	155
	...	...	...	...	...	...	...	...	...	...	...	9.6**	10.5**	8.5**	156
	...	...	...	...	...	...	...	...	...	...	...	...	...	...	157
	...	...	...	...	...	...	...	...	...	...	...	...	...	...	158
	25.8**	28.7**	22.9**	0.80**	...	...	...	...	5.2**	...	...	4.4**,y	4.7**,y	4.0**,y	159
	...	...	...	...	...	...	...	...	6.7**	8.4**	4.9**	7.1**,y	8.9**,y	5.3**,y	160
	21.5	20.2	22.9	1.14	23.9	22.6	25.4	1.12	11.4**	11.2**	11.5**	11.6**	11.5**	11.7**	161
	18.6	21.9	15.2	0.69	20.3**	23.9**	16.7**	0.70**	...	...	...	3.4**	4.0**	2.8**	162
	25.2**	27.2**	23.3**	0.86**	30.5**	33.3**	27.6**	0.83**	3.7**	4.0**	3.3**	5.2**	5.9**	4.5**	163
	...	...	...	...	...	...	...	...	7.6**	...	...	9.3**	10.0**	8.5**	164
	68.6**	67.8**	69.5**	1.03**	71.4	70.9	71.8	1.01	...	...	...	11.6**	11.7**	11.5**	165
	...	...	...	...	...	...	...	...	...	...	...	...	...	...	166
	23.0	26.8	19.1	0.71	27.6**	31.7**	23.5**	0.74**	...	...	...	5.3**,y	6.9**,y	3.7**,y	167

7. Enrolment ratios were not calculated due to lack of United Nations population data by age.
8. Enrolment ratios were not calculated due to inconsistencies between enrolment and the United Nations population data.

(y) Data are for 1999/2000.
(z) Data are for 2000/2001.

Table 4 (continued)

	Country or territory	Compulsory education (age group)	Legal guarantee of free education[1]	New entrants (000) 1998	New entrants (000) 2001	GIR 1998 Total	GIR 1998 Male	GIR 1998 Female	GIR 1998 GPI (F/M)	GIR 2001 Total	GIR 2001 Male	GIR 2001 Female	GIR 2001 GPI (F/M)
168	Comoros[2]	6-14	No	13.3	16.7	69.5	75.6	63.3	0.84	80.5	87.3	73.4	0.84
169	Congo[3]	6-16	Yes	...	71.8	...	...	...	...	64.2	66.9	61.4	0.92
170	Côte d'Ivoire	6-15	No	309.0	322.7**	69.0	76.4	61.6	0.81	72.1**	82.4**	61.8**	0.75**
171	D. R. Congo[3]	6-15	Yes	766.7	...	52.2	50.5	54.0	1.07	...	...	...	...
172	Equatorial Guinea	7-11	Yes	...	16.2	...	...	...	...	121.9	135.2	108.6	0.80
173	Eritrea	7-13	No	57.3	74.9	54.9	60.3	49.3	0.82	64.7	70.4	58.9	0.84
174	Ethiopia	7-12	No	1 536.9	1 714.6	81.6	96.8	66.3	0.68	84.9	96.2	73.6	0.77
175	Gabon	6-16	No	...	34.0**	...	...	...	...	93.0**	94.4**	91.6**	0.97**
176	Gambia[3]	...	Yes	30.2	31.1[z]	89.5	91.6	87.4	0.95	88.2[z]	88.4[z]	87.9[z]	0.99[z]
177	Ghana[2,3]	6-15	Yes	468.7	466.7	87.9	90.9	84.9	0.93	85.0	86.3	83.6	0.97
178	Guinea	7-16	No	118.6	169.0	53.6	59.6	47.3	0.79	72.0	77.1	66.7	0.87
179	Guinea-Bissau[3]	7-12	Yes	35.8**	36.5[y]	93.1**	110.0**	76.3**	0.69**	91.9[y]	105.6[y]	78.3[y]	0.74[y]
180	Kenya	6-13	No	916.1	892.0[y]	104.6	107.3	101.9	0.95	103.3[y]	105.1[y]	101.5[y]	0.97[y]
181	Lesotho	6-12	No	52.5	69.6	108.9	109.3	108.5	0.99	148.6	157.7	139.3	0.88
182	Liberia[2]	6-16	No	49.7	...	63.0	77.0	48.8	0.63	...	...	...	...
183	Madagascar[3]	6-14	Yes	494.8	585.8	109.4	110.6	108.2	0.98	117.9	119.4	116.4	0.98
184	Malawi	...	Yes	...	616.2[y]	...	...	...	...	182.6[y]	181.9[y]	183.3[y]	1.01[y]
185	Mali[3]	7-15	Yes	172.9**	233.1	48.5**	55.0**	41.9**	0.76**	59.7	65.4	53.9	0.82
186	Mauritius	6-11	Yes	22.2	20.1	104.3	104.0	104.5	1.00	91.0	89.5	92.6	1.03
187	Mozambique	6-12	No	521.4**	648.7	100.5**	109.0**	92.0**	0.84**	119.3	126.2	112.3	0.89
188	Namibia[3]	6-15	Yes	55.3	57.1	101.2	100.3	102.0	1.02	97.3	96.5	98.2	1.02
189	Niger[3]	7-12	Yes	132.7	204.1	42.1	49.6	34.4	0.69	58.0	67.4	48.2	0.72
190	Nigeria	6-11	Yes	...	4 155.7**	...	...	...	...	115.6**	127.8**	103.1**	0.81**
191	Rwanda	7-12	Yes	295.3	314.0	153.7	136.0	171.3	1.26	132.8	132.1	133.5	1.01
192	Sao Tome and Principe	7-13	Yes	4.0	4.6	105.5	107.9	103.1	0.96	109.3	112.1	106.5	0.95
193	Senegal[3]	7-12	Yes	190.1	240.1	71.0	72.5**	69.4**	0.96**	86.3	86.9	85.7	0.99
194	Seychelles[5]	6-15	Yes	1.6	1.5	113.4	111.2	115.7	1.04	104.8	106.4	103.1	0.97
195	Sierra Leone	...	No	...	98.9[y]	...	...	...	...	79.8[y]	81.2[y]	78.5[y]	0.97[y]
196	Somalia	6-13	...	...	...	...	...	...	...	...	...	...	...
197	South Africa	7-15	No	1 264.9	1 040.1	123.6	126.0	121.1	0.96	101.5	109.0	94.0	0.86
198	Swaziland	6-12	No	31.4**	30.6	102.6**	105.2**	100.0**	0.95**	97.9	100.1	95.6	0.96
199	Togo	6-15	No	139.4	154.6	107.7	113.9	101.3	0.89	110.3	116.6	103.9	0.89
200	Uganda	...	No	...	...	...	...	...	...	...	...	...	...
201	United Republic of Tanzania	7-13	Yes	669.0	1 105.2	65.9	66.8	65.0	0.97	103.2	106.6	99.8	0.94
202	Zambia	7-13	No	248.8	275.6[z]	82.2	83.1	81.3	0.98	86.7[z]	86.4[z]	87.0[z]	1.01[z]
203	Zimbabwe[w]	6-12	No	...	445.9	...	...	...	...	119.7	121.4	118.0	0.97

						Median 1998 Total	Male	Female	GPI	Median 2001 Total	Male	Female	GPI
I	World	...	...	...	...	101.0	...	...	...	101.2	100.3	102.0	1.02
II	Countries in transition	...	...	...	...	93.6	94.3	92.9	0.99	102.9	...	...	...
III	Developed countries	...	...	...	...	100.3	101.1	99.6	0.99	98.3	98.3	98.4	1.00
IV	Developing countries	...	...	...	...	103.4	104.4	102.5	0.98	103.2	105.0	101.5	0.97
V	Arab States	...	...	...	...	99.0	98.9	99.2	1.00	98.5	99.2	99.3	1.02
VI	Central and Eastern Europe	...	...	...	...	98.8	99.7	97.9	0.98	97.5	97.0	97.9	1.01
VII	Central Asia	...	...	...	...	104.4	104.3	104.6	1.00	102.7	102.0	103.4	1.01
VIII	East Asia and the Pacific	...	...	...	...	108.4	112.5	104.2	0.93	108.1	113.9	103.8	0.91
IX	Latin America and the Caribbean	...	...	...	...	111.3	111.2	111.5	1.00	109.6	104.6	114.2	1.09
X	North America and Western Europe	...	...	...	...	100.4	100.8	100.0	0.99	98.5	98.3	98.7	1.00
XI	South and West Asia	...	...	...	...	105.1	111.2	98.5	0.89	100.5	107.0	93.6	0.87
XII	Sub-Saharan Africa	...	...	...	...	88.7	91.3	86.2	0.94	93.0	94.4	91.6	0.97

1. *Source:* Tomasevsky (2003). Background paper for the *EFA Global Monitoring Report 2003/4*.
2. Information on compulsory education come from the Reports under the United Nations Human Rights Treaties.
3. Primary school fees continue to be charged despite the legal guarantee for free education, according to a World Bank study in 2002. See the *EFA Global Monitoring Report 2003/4*, World Bank (2002e).
4. No tuition fees are charged but some direct costs have been reported, according to a World Bank study in 2002. See the *EFA Global Monitoring Report 2003/4*, World Bank (2002e).
5. National population data were used to calculate enrolment ratios.

STATISTICAL ANNEX / 285

Table 4

NET INTAKE RATE (NIR) IN PRIMARY EDUCATION (%)

	1998				2001			
Total	Male	Female	GPI (F/M)	Total	Male	Female	GPI (F/M)	
15.5	18.2**	12.7**	0.70**	...	...	...	...
...	...	...	...	...	...	...	...
28.2	31.4	25.0	0.80	27.8**	31.8**	23.6**	0.74**
23.5	22.5	24.5	1.09	...	...	...	...
...	...	...	...	48.3	61.2	35.3	0.58
17.4	18.3	16.5	0.90	26.3	28.3	24.2	0.86
21.4	23.8	19.0	0.80	24.3	25.6	22.9	0.89
...	...	...	...	...	...	...	...
43.0**	43.8**	42.2**	0.96**	42.7**,y	43.0**,y	42.4**,y	0.98**,y
29.8**	30.2**	29.4**	0.97**	...	...	...	...
20.4	21.9	18.9	0.86	27.6	29.0	26.2	0.90
...	...	...	...	27.7**,y	31.3**,y	24.1**,y	0.77**,y
30.5**	30.0**	31.0**	1.03**	30.1**,y	29.4**,y	30.9**,y	1.05**,y
18.1	18.3	17.9	0.97	57.1	56.4	57.8	1.02
...	...	...	...	...	...	...	...
...	...	...	...	37.1	36.1	38.2	1.06
...	...	...	...	...	...	...	...
...	...	...	...	...	...	...	...
...	...	...	...	...	...	...	...
27.0	27.1	27.0	1.00	24.5	24.1	24.8	1.03
17.4**	18.1**	16.8**	0.93**	25.0	25.6	24.4	0.95
56.1	54.6	57.6	1.06	56.8	55.4	58.3	1.05
26.8	32.0	21.3	0.67	38.4	45.1	31.5	0.70
...	...	...	...	...	...	...	...
...	...	...	...	63.4	62.6	64.2	1.03
...	...	...	...	...	...	...	...
39.5	40.3**	38.6**	0.96**	...	...	...	...
68.2	67.6	68.7	1.02	66.8	67.2	66.4	0.99
...	...	...	...	...	...	...	...
...	...	...	...	...	...	...	...
46.8	46.4	47.1	1.02	58.2	59.0	57.3	0.97
43.4**	42.3**	44.5**	1.05**	44.8	43.7	45.9	1.05
43.7	46.4	40.9	0.88	46.5	49.0	43.8	0.89
...	...	...	...	...	...	...	...
11.3	10.5	12.2	1.15	29.4	28.5	30.4	1.07
36.9	36.2	37.5	1.04	38.5**,z	37.3**,z	39.7**,z	1.07**,z
...	...	...	...	44.4	43.9	45.0	1.03

SCHOOL LIFE EXPECTANCY
(expected number of years of formal schooling)

	1998			2001			
Total	Male	Female	Total	Male	Female		
6.5**	7.0**	5.9**	6.9**,y	7.5**,y	6.3**,y	168
...	...	...	7.7**	8.3**	7.0**	169
6.4**	7.7**	5.1**	...	...	...	170
...	...	...	...	...	...	171
...	...	...	9.0**,y	9.5**,y	8.3**,y	172
4.4**	4.9**	3.7**	5.0**	5.7**	4.1**	173
4.0**	4.8**	3.0**	5.2**	6.1**	4.2**	174
12.1**	12.2**	11.7**	...	...	...	175
...	...	...	...	...	...	176
...	...	...	7.5**	8.0**	6.9**	177
...	...	...	...	...	...	178
...	...	...	5.5**,y	6.4**,y	4.2**,y	179
...	...	...	8.5**	8.7**	8.3**	180
9.7**	9.0**	10.3	10.7	10.4	11.0	181
...	...	...	10.3 y	11.4 y	8.7 y	182
6.2**	6.2**	6.0**	...	...	...	183
11.5**	12.0**	10.8**	...	...	...	184
3.9**	...	...	...	...	...	185
11.8**	11.9**	11.8**	12.4**	12.3**	12.4**	186
...	...	...	5.4**,y	6.1**,y	4.5**,y	187
12.1**	11.4**	12.3**	11.7**	11.2**	11.7**	188
...	...	...	2.9**	3.5**	2.3**	189
...	...	...	...	...	...	190
7.9**	...	...	8.2**	8.2**	8.0**	191
...	...	...	9.6**	10.0**	9.2**	192
5.6**	...	...	...	...	...	193
13.4	...	...	13.7**	...	...	194
...	...	...	6.8**,z	7.9**,z	5.7**,z	195
...	...	...	...	...	...	196
13.5**	13.2**	13.7**	12.9**	12.8**	12.9**	197
10.3**	10.4**	10.0**	9.8**	9.9**	9.5**	198
10.8**	13.0**	8.5**	10.4**,y	12.4**,y	8.3**,y	199
11.9**	12.1**	11.0**	11.5**	11.5**	11.1**	200
5.0**	4.8**	4.9**	...	...	...	201
6.9**	7.2**	6.5**	6.9**,z	7.2**,z	6.5**,z	202
...	...	...	9.8**	10.1**	9.4**	203

	Median								Weighted average					
...	...	...	...	67.2	66.0	68.5	1.04	10.0	10.4	9.5	10.3	10.7	9.8	I
...	...	...	...	67.6	68.5	66.7	0.97	12.0	11.9	12.1	12.5	12.2	12.6	II
...	...	...	...	76.7	77.2	76.2	0.99	15.7	15.5	15.9	15.9	15.2	16.4	III
60.8	...	...	...	62.5	63.4	61.5	0.97	9.2	9.8	8.6	9.5	10.1	8.9	IV
64.3	64.7	63.9	0.99	69.2	70.4	67.9	0.96	9.8	10.5	9.0	10.0	10.6	9.4	V
...	...	...	...	72.0	72.9	71.1	0.98	11.8	11.8	11.8	12.7	12.7	12.7	VI
61.6	62.4	60.7	0.97	67.4	69.0	65.6	0.95	11.1	11.2	11.0	11.4	11.5	11.3	VII
...	...	...	...	...	...	...	...	10.5	10.8	10.3	10.9	11.3	10.5	VIII
...	...	...	...	67.6	66.0	69.0	1.05	12.2	12.1	12.2	13.0	12.7	13.2	IX
...	...	...	...	...	...	...	...	16.2	15.9	16.5	16.3	15.4	16.8	X
...	...	...	...	...	...	...	...	8.4	9.4	7.4	8.6	9.5	7.6	XI
26.8	32.0	21.3	0.67	37.1	36.1	31.5	0.87	6.7	7.3	6.0	7.1	7.6	6.4	XII

6. Children can enter primary school at age 6 or 7.
7. Enrolment ratios were not calculated due to lack of United Nations population data by age.
8. Enrolment ratios were not calculated due to inconsistencies between enrolment and the United Nations population data.

(y) Data are for 1999/2000.
(z) Data are for 2000/2001.

Table 5
Participation in primary education

	Country or territory	Age group 2001	School-age population (000) 2001	Enrolment 1998 Total (000)	1998 % F	Enrolment 2001 Total (000)	2001 % F	GER 1998 Total	1998 Male	1998 Female	1998 GPI (F/M)	GER 2001 Total	2001 Male	2001 Female	2001 GPI (F/M)
	Arab States														
1	Algeria	6-11	4 326	4 779	47	4 692	47	106.8	111.4	102.0	0.92	108.4	112.5	104.3	0.93
2	Bahrain	6-11	83	76	49	81	49	100.7	100.4	101.0	1.01	98.0	98.4	97.5	0.99
3	Djibouti	6-11	110	38	41	44	43	38.1	44.6	31.5	0.71	40.3	45.7	34.8	0.76
4	Egypt[w]	6-10	8 103	8 086**	47**	7 855**	47**	98.6**	102.9**	94.2**	0.92**	96.9**	99.9**	93.8**	0.94**
5	Iraq	6-11	3 816	3 604	44	3 639[y]	44[y]	99.5	109.2	89.3	0.82	98.8[y]	108.5[y]	88.7[y]	0.82[y]
6	Jordan[w]	6-11	777	706	49	766	49	96.5	96.4	96.7	1.00	98.6	98.4	98.7	1.00
7	Kuwait	6-9	158	140	49	149	49	101.9	101.5	102.2	1.01	94.3	94.6	94.1	0.99
8	Lebanon	6-11	440	395	49	452	48	106.7	108.9	104.3	0.96	102.7	104.6	100.9	0.96
9	Libyan Arab Jamahiriya	6-11	657	822	49	750	49	115.7	116.6	114.8	0.98	114.1	114.2	114.1	1.00
10	Mauritania	6-11	434	346	48	376	49	86.5	89.1	83.9	0.94	86.5	88.4	84.6	0.96
11	Morocco	6-11	3 764	3 462	44	4 029	46	89.2	98.2	79.9	0.81	107.0	113.2	100.6	0.89
12	Oman	6-11	382	316	48	317	48	85.7	87.2	84.1	0.96	82.9	83.7	82.2	0.98
13	Palestinian A. T.	6-9	386	368	49	402	49	105.7	104.9	106.4	1.01	104.1	103.7	104.6	1.01
14	Qatar	6-11	61	61	48	64	48	108.0	109.9	106.1	0.97	105.9	107.9	103.8	0.96
15	Saudi Arabia	6-11	3 442	2 260	48	2 316	48	68.7	69.9	67.6	0.97	67.3	68.2	66.3	0.97
16	Sudan	6-11	4 922	2 513**	45**	2 889	45	54.5**	58.7**	50.1**	0.85**	58.7	63.3	54.0	0.85
17	Syrian Arab Republic	6-11	2 602	2 738	47	2 905	47	103.6	108.0	98.9	0.92	111.6	115.4	107.8	0.93
18	Tunisia[w]	6-11	1 188	1 443	47	1 326	48	114.9	118.0	111.6	0.95	111.6	113.8	109.3	0.96
19	United Arab Emirates	6-11	310	270	48	286	48	89.1	90.9	87.2	0.96	92.2	94.1	90.3	0.96
20	Yemen	6-11	3 435	2 303	35	2 783	39	73.3	93.2	52.5	0.56	81.0	97.0	64.3	0.66
	Central and Eastern Europe														
21	Albania[o]	6-9	251	287**	48**	274[z]	49[z]	108.2**	108.7**	107.7**	0.99**	106.6[z]	106.6[z]	106.6[z]	1.00[z]
22	Belarus	6-9	464	632	48	512	48	109.0	111.2	106.6	0.96	110.3	111.2	109.4	0.98
23	Bosnia and Herzegovina[o]	6-9	193	...	...	...	...	...	...	...	...	...	...	...	...
24	Bulgaria[o]	7-10	352	412	48	350	48	103.4	104.7	102.0	0.97	99.4	100.5	98.2	0.98
25	Croatia	7-10	202	203	49	193	49	95.7	96.4	94.9	0.98	95.6	96.0	95.0	0.99
26	Czech Republic[o]	6-10	583	655	49	604	49	104.0	104.5	103.5	0.99	103.6	104.3	102.9	0.99
27	Estonia[o]	7-12	107	127	48	109	48	102.2	104.0	100.4	0.97	101.4	103.2	99.5	0.96
28	Hungary[o]	7-10	474	503	48	478	48	103.5	104.4	102.5	0.98	100.8	101.5	100.1	0.99
29	Latvia[o]	7-10	119	141	48	114	48	99.1	100.1	98.0	0.98	95.9	96.8	95.0	0.98
30	Lithuania[o]	7-10	195	220	48	197	49	101.5	102.3	100.6	0.98	101.2	101.8	100.5	0.99
31	Poland[o]	7-12	3 114	...	...	3 105	49	...	...	...	...	99.7	100.1	99.3	0.99
32	Republic of Moldova	7-10	267	262	49	227	49	84.3	84.2	84.4	1.00	85.3	85.7	85.0	0.99
33	Romania[o]	7-10	1 049	1 285	49	1 029	48	104.3	105.2	103.3	0.98	98.0	99.1	96.9	0.98
34	Russian Federation[w, 1]	7-9	4 883	...	...	5 555	...	...	...	...	...	113.8	114.0	113.5	1.00
35	Serbia and Montenegro[2]	7-10	...	418	49	381[z]	49[z]	103.9	104.6	103.1	0.99	98.8[z]	98.9[z]	98.7[z]	1.00[z]
36	Slovakia	6-9	280	317	49	284	49	102.5	103.3	101.8	0.99	101.4	101.7	101.1	0.99
37	Slovenia[o]	7-10	83	92	49	86	49	97.7	98.2	97.2	0.99	103.3	103.8	102.8	0.99
38	TFYR Macedonia[o]	7-10	123	130	48	121	49	101.8	102.7	100.8	0.98	98.7	98.1	99.3	1.01
39	Turkey[o]	6-11	8 692	...	...	8 211**	47**	...	...	...	...	94.5**	98.2**	90.7**	0.92**
40	Ukraine	6-9	2 262	2 200	49	2 047	49	77.8	78.4	77.2	0.99	90.5	90.6	90.4	1.00
	Central Asia														
41	Armenia	7-9	149	...	...	144	49	...	...	...	...	96.3	97.1	95.5	0.98
42	Azerbaijan	6-9	723	691	49	669	48	90.9	90.9	90.9	1.00	92.6	93.4	91.7	0.98
43	Georgia	6-9	276	302	49	254	49	95.3	95.3	95.4	1.00	92.0	92.1	91.8	1.00
44	Kazakhstan	7-10	1 166	1 249	49	1 158	49	93.0	93.0	93.0	1.00	99.3	99.8	98.8	0.99
45	Kyrgyzstan	7-10	454	471	49	455	49	101.3	102.2	100.4	0.98	100.2	101.8	98.6	0.97
46	Mongolia	8-11	244	251	50	241	50	98.2	96.4	99.9	1.04	98.7	97.1	100.4	1.03
47	Tajikistan	7-10	641	690	48	685	48	103.1	106.0	100.1	0.95	106.8	109.4	104.1	0.95
48	Turkmenistan	7-10	478	...	...	...	...	...	...	...	...	...	...	...	...
49	Uzbekistan	7-10	2 495	...	...	2 559**	49**	...	...	...	...	102.6**	102.9**	102.2**	0.99**
	East Asia and the Pacific														
50	Australia[o]	5-11	1 869	...	...	1 914	49	...	...	...	...	102.4	102.4	102.5	1.00
51	Brunei Darussalam	6-11	42	45	47	44	48	114.5	115.7	113.1	0.98	106.3	106.6	105.9	0.99
52	Cambodia	6-11	2 211	2 127	46	2 729	47	96.5	103.5	89.2	0.86	123.4	130.3	116.4	0.89

1. In countries where two or more education structures exist, indicators were calculated on the basis of the most common or widespread structure. In the Russian Federation this is three grades of primary education starting at age 7. However, a four-grade structure also exists, in which about one-third of primary pupils are enrolled. Gross enrolment ratios may be overestimated.

2. National population data were used to calculate enrolment ratios.
(y) Data are for 1999/2000.
(z) Data are for 2000/2001.

STATISTICAL ANNEX / 287

Table 5

\multicolumn{8}{c	}{NET ENROLMENT RATIO (NER) IN PRIMARY EDUCATION (%)}	\multicolumn{6}{c	}{OUT-OF-SCHOOL CHILDREN (000)}	
\multicolumn{4}{c	}{1998}	\multicolumn{4}{c	}{2001}	\multicolumn{3}{c	}{1998}	\multicolumn{3}{c	}{2001}	
Total	Male	Female	GPI (F/M)	Total	Male	Female	GPI (F/M)	Total	Male	Female	Total	Male	Female	
92.1	94.0	90.2	0.96	95.1	96.3	93.7	0.97	352.8	138.0	214.9	213.2	80.9	132.4	1
93.9	93.0	94.9	1.02	91.0**	90.7**	91.3**	1.01**	4.6	2.7	1.9	7.4**	3.9**	3.5**	2
31.3	36.3	26.2	0.72	34.0**	38.3**	29.6**	0.77**	68.9	32.1	36.8	72.7**	34.2**	38.5**	3
90.9**	94.0**	87.6**	0.93**	90.3**	92.2**	88.3**	0.96**	745.6**	249.7**	495.9**	786.2**	321.2**	465.0**	4
91.2	98.2	83.8	0.85	90.5 y	97.6 y	83.2 y	0.85 y	320.1	33.1	286.9	348.5 y	45.5 y	303.0 y	5
89.6	89.2	89.9	1.01	91.3	90.9	91.6	1.01	76.4	40.4	36.0	67.8	36.2	31.6	6
88.2	88.1	88.3	1.00	84.6	85.0	84.3	0.99	16.2	8.4	7.8	24.2	12.2	12.1	7
87.5**	89.0**	85.9**	0.97**	89.8**	90.1**	89.4**	0.99**	46.2**	20.7**	25.5**	45.0**	22.2**	22.8**	8
…	…	…	…	…	…	…	…	…	…	…	…	…	…	9
62.6	64.5	60.7	0.94	66.7**	68.2**	65.2**	0.96**	149.5	71.2	78.4	144.6**	69.3**	75.3**	10
73.1	78.6	67.3	0.86	88.4	91.5	85.1	0.93	1 044.8	422.5	622.3	437.4	162.0	275.4	11
75.9	76.0	75.8	1.00	74.5	74.1	74.9	1.01	88.8	45.2	43.6	97.3	50.6	46.7	12
96.9	96.5	97.4	1.01	95.1	94.8	95.4	1.01	10.7	6.2	4.5	18.8	10.2	8.6	13
97.1	96.6	97.7	1.01	94.5	95.3	93.6	0.98	1.6	1.0	0.6	3.4	1.5	1.9	14
56.8	58.7	54.8	0.93	58.9	61.1	56.5	0.92	1 420.1	695.3	724.8	1 415.1	684.6	730.4	15
…	…	…	…	…	…	…	…	…	…	…	…	…	…	16
93.0**	96.4**	89.5**	0.93**	97.5	100.0	94.9	0.95	185.1**	48.3**	136.7**	64.8	–	64.8	17
94.0	95.1	92.9	0.98	96.9	97.1	96.6	0.99	75.2	31.5	43.6	37.4	17.7	19.7	18
78.2	79.1	77.3	0.98	80.8	81.9	79.7	0.97	66.1	32.3	33.8	59.4	28.6	30.8	19
57.4	71.8	42.4	0.59	67.1**,z	…	…	…	1 336.6	453.2	883.4	1 096.1**,z	…	…	20
99.1**	99.4**	98.7**	0.99**	97.2 z	97.3 z	97.0 z	1.00 z	2.5**	0.8**	1.6**	7.2 z	3.6 z	3.7 z	21
93.0**	95.0**	91.0**	0.96**	94.2**	95.0**	93.4**	0.98**	40.3**	15.0**	25.4**	26.9**	12.0**	14.9**	22
…	…	…	…	…	…	…	…	…	…	…	…	…	…	23
95.6	96.5	94.8	0.98	90.4	91.0	89.7	0.99	17.4	7.2	10.2	33.9	16.2	17.7	24
88.4	89.0	87.6	0.98	88.5	89.2	87.8	0.98	24.7	11.9	12.8	23.3	11.2	12.1	25
90.2	89.9	90.6	1.01	88.5	88.5	88.4	1.00	61.5	32.6	28.9	67.3	34.4	32.9	26
97.0**	97.9**	96.1**	0.98**	95.8	96.4	95.2	0.99	3.7**	1.4**	2.3**	4.5	2.0	2.5	27
89.5	89.8	89.2	0.99	90.8	91.4	90.1	0.99	51.1	25.4	25.8	43.8	20.9	22.9	28
91.0	91.6	90.5	0.99	87.6	87.3	87.9	1.01	12.8	6.2	6.6	14.7	7.7	7.0	29
94.5	95.0	94.0	0.99	94.3	94.7	93.9	0.99	11.8	5.5	6.3	11.2	5.3	5.9	30
…	…	…	…	98.0	97.9	98.1	1.00	…	…	…	61.2	32.9	28.2	31
78.2**	…	…	…	78.3	78.7	77.8	0.99	67.7**	…	…	57.9	29.0	29.0	32
95.7	96.0	95.4	0.99	88.4	88.8	88.0	0.99	52.8	25.0	27.8	121.2	59.9	61.3	33
…	…	…	…	…	…	…	…	…	…	…	…	…	…	34
79.8**	80.3**	79.2**	0.99**	74.9 z	74.8 z	75.0 z	1.00 z	81.4**	40.5**	40.9**	96.9 z	49.9 z	47.0 z	35
…	…	…	…	87.0	86.2	87.8	1.02	…	…	…	36.5	19.8	16.7	36
93.9	94.4	93.5	0.99	93.1	93.4	92.8	0.99	5.7	2.7	3.0	5.8	2.8	2.9	37
94.5	95.6	93.4	0.98	92.3	92.0	92.6	1.01	7.0	2.9	4.1	9.5	5.1	4.4	38
…	…	…	…	87.9**	91.0**	84.8**	0.93**	…	…	…	1 048.5**	396.8**	651.7**	39
71.6	72.1	71.1	0.99	81.5	81.6**	81.4**	1.00**	803.2	402.8	400.3	418.4	213.3**	205.1**	40
…	…	…	…	84.5	84.9	84.2	0.99	…	…	…	23.1	11.5	11.5	41
80.1**	80.0**	80.2**	1.00**	79.8	80.5	79.1	0.98	151.3**	78.1**	73.2**	145.8	72.4	73.4	42
95.3**	95.3**	95.4**	1.00**	90.7	90.9	90.5	1.00	14.8**	7.7**	7.1**	25.6	12.8	12.7	43
83.5**	83.4**	83.5**	1.00**	89.5	90.0	89.0	0.99	222.1**	113.1**	109.0**	122.3	59.1	63.2	44
91.0*	92.0*	90.0*	0.98*	90.0	91.7	88.4	0.96	41.7*	18.9*	22.9*	45.2	19.1	26.1	45
89.4	87.8	91.1	1.04	86.6	85.4	87.9	1.03	27.1	15.8	11.3	32.7	18.2	14.5	46
97.2**	100.0**	94.3**	0.94**	97.5	100.0	95.0	0.95	18.8**	–**	18.8**	15.7	–	15.7	47
…	…	…	…	…	…	…	…	…	…	…	…	…	…	48
…	…	…	…	…	…	…	…	…	…	…	…	…	…	49
…	…	…	…	96.0	95.5	96.4	1.01	…	…	…	75.4	43.1	32.4	50
…	…	…	…	…	…	…	…	…	…	…	…	…	…	51
82.5**	86.5**	78.4**	0.91**	86.2**	89.0**	83.2**	0.93**	387.0**	151.1**	235.9**	305.9**	122.7**	183.1**	52

Table 5 (continued)

	Country or territory	Age group 2001	School-age population (000) 2001	Enrolment 1998 Total (000)	1998 % F	Enrolment 2001 Total (000)	2001 % F	GER 1998 Total	1998 Male	1998 Female	1998 GPI (F/M)	GER 2001 Total	2001 Male	2001 Female	2001 GPI (F/M)
53	China[w,3]	7-11	108 264	135 480	48	125 757	47	119.5	119.0	120.1	1.01	116.2	116.1	116.3	1.00
54	Cook Islands[4]	5-10	...	3	48	3**,z	46**,z	...	...	...	...	...	...	...	...
55	DPR Korea	6-9	1 639	...	...	...	...	...	...	...	...	...	...	...	...
56	Fiji	6-11	106	116**	48**	115**	48**	110.5**	111.0**	110.0**	0.99**	108.8**	109.1**	108.6**	1.00**
57	Indonesia[w]	7-12	26 082	...	...	28926	49	...	...	...	...	110.9	112.1	109.7	0.98
58	Japan[o]	6-11	7 273	7 692	49	7 326	49	101.4	101.4	101.3	1.00	100.7	100.7	100.8	1.00
59	Kiribati[2]	6-11	...	18	49	...	...	130.8	129.6	132.1	1.02	...	...	...	...
60	Lao PDR	6-10	743	828	45	853	46	116.7	126.0	107.0	0.85	114.8	123.1	106.3	0.86
61	Macao, China	6-11	43	47	47	44	47	99.1	101.4	96.6	0.95	104.1	107.4	100.6	0.94
62	Malaysia[w]	6-11	3 178	2 877	49	3 025	49	97.4	97.4	97.4	1.00	95.2	95.1	95.3	1.00
63	Marshall Islands[4]	6-11	...	8	48	9	47	...	...	...	...	...	...	...	...
64	Micronesia	6-11	73	...	...	...	...	...	...	...	...	...	...	...	...
65	Myanmar	5-9	5 345	4 733	49	4 789	50	90.1	90.9	89.3	0.98	89.6	89.5	89.7	1.00
66	Nauru[2]	6-11	...	2**	51**	...	...	81.0**	79.6**	82.4**	1.04**	...	...	...	...
67	New Zealand[o]	5-10	359	...	...	356	48	...	...	...	...	99.0	99.5	98.6	0.99
68	Niue[2]	5-10	...	0.3	43	0.2	46	102.9	109.6	95.3	0.87	117.6	121.0	113.8	0.94
69	Palau[2]	6-10	...	2	47	2**,z	48**,z	113.8	118.0	109.4	0.93	116.1**,z	120.1**,z	112.0**,z	0.93**,z
70	Papua New Guinea	7-12	856	581	45	663**	45**	74.8	77.4	71.8	0.93	77.5**	81.6**	73.0**	0.89**
71	Philippines[w]	6-11	11 446	12 503	49	12826	49	113.1	113.3	113.0	1.00	112.1	112.7	111.4	0.99
72	Republic of Korea[o]	6-11	4 014	...	...	4 100	47	...	...	...	...	102.1	102.3	102.0	1.00
73	Samoa	5-10	28	27	49	29	48	99.4	98.9	99.9	1.01	102.5	103.7	101.3	0.98
74	Singapore	6-11	384	...	...	...	...	...	...	...	...	...	...	...	...
75	Solomon Islands	6-11	75	...	...	...	...	...	...	...	...	...	...	...	...
76	Thailand[w]	6-11	6 375	6 120	48	6 228	49	94.1	96.5	91.8	0.95	97.7	99.6	95.7	0.96
77	Timor-Leste	6-11	128	...	...	184	...	...	...	...	...	143.3	...	...	...
78	Tokelau	5-10	...	...	...	...	...	...	...	...	...	...	...	...	...
79	Tonga	5-10	15	16	46	17	47	110.4	112.2	108.5	0.97	112.4	113.6	111.1	0.98
80	Tuvalu[2]	6-11	...	1**	46**	1	50	103.6**	105.8**	101.1**	0.96**	...	...	...	...
81	Vanuatu	6-11	33	34**	47**	36	48	109.2**	111.2**	107.1**	0.96**	111.6	111.9	111.3	0.99
82	Viet Nam	6-10	9 030	10 250	47	9 337	48	109.4	113.8	104.9	0.92	103.4	107.0	99.7	0.93

Latin America and the Caribbean

	Country or territory	Age group	Pop.	1998 Total	% F	2001 Total	% F	1998 T	M	F	GPI	2001 T	M	F	GPI
83	Anguilla[2]	5-11	...	2	50	1	49	...	...	...	...	98.6	99.3	97.9	0.99
84	Antigua and Barbuda[4]	5-11	...	...	...	13[y]	62[y]	...	...	...	...	...	...	...	...
85	Argentina[w]	6-11	4 098	4 821	49	4 900	49	119.7	119.6	119.8	1.00	119.6	119.8	119.4	1.00
86	Aruba[2]	6-11	...	9	49	10	48	112.2	113.5	110.8	0.98	114.6	117.6	111.4	0.95
87	Bahamas	5-10	37	...	...	34	50	...	...	...	...	92.2	91.6	92.8	1.01
88	Barbados	5-10	22	28	49	23	49	104.3	104.8	103.8	0.99	108.3	108.3	108.2	1.00
89	Belize	5-10	39	44	49	45[z]	49[z]	118.1	119.8	116.3	0.97	117.6[z]	119.4[z]	115.8[z]	0.97[z]
90	Bermuda[2]	5-10	...	...	...	5[z]	50[z]	...	...	...	...	103.2[z]	...	...	...
91	Bolivia	6-11	1 321	1 400	49	1 501	49	112.5	113.7	111.2	0.98	113.6	114.3	112.9	0.99
92	Brazil[w]	7-10	13 287	...	...	19728	48	...	...	...	...	148.5	152.7	144.2	0.94
93	British Virgin Islands[2]	5-11	...	3	49	3	48	111.6	113.5	109.8	0.97	109.1	111.5	106.6	0.96
94	Cayman Islands[4]	5-10	...	3	47	4	49	...	...	...	...	...	...	...	...
95	Chile[w]	6-11	1 755	1 777	48	1 799[z]	49[z]	102.7	104.1	101.2	0.97	102.7[z]	103.9[z]	101.4[z]	0.98[z]
96	Colombia	6-10	4 684	5 062	49	5 131	49	112.0	112.0	112.0	1.00	109.6	110.1	109.0	0.99
97	Costa Rica	6-11	510	...	...	552	49	...	...	...	...	108.4	108.5	108.3	1.00
98	Cuba	6-11	969	1 074	48	972	48	105.3	107.2	103.2	0.96	100.3	102.2	98.3	0.96
99	Dominica[2]	5-11	...	12	48	11	48	98.8	101.2	96.3	0.95	...	...	...	...
100	Dominican Republic	6-11	1 110	1 315**	49**	1 400	49	116.7**	117.7**	115.6**	0.98**	126.1	125.4	126.8	1.01
101	Ecuador	6-11	1 696	1 899	49	1 983	49	113.4	113.5	113.3	1.00	116.9	117.0	116.8	1.00
102	El Salvador	7-12	866	926	49	968	48	111.6	113.3	109.9	0.97	111.8	114.1	109.4	0.96
103	Grenada[4]	5-11	...	...	...	17	48	...	...	...	...	...	...	...	...
104	Guatemala	7-12	1 913	1 685*	46*	1 972	47	94.0*	99.3*	88.4*	0.89*	103.0	107.0	98.9	0.92
105	Guyana	6-11	90	107	49	109[y]	49[y]	116.9	117.9	115.9	0.98	120.2[y]	122.2[y]	118.3[y]	0.97[y]
106	Haiti	6-11	1 254	...	...	...	...	...	...	...	...	...	...	...	...
107	Honduras	7-12	1 054	...	...	1 116**	50**	...	...	...	...	105.8**	104.8**	106.9**	1.02**
108	Jamaica[w]	6-11	328	316**	49**	330	49	95.4**	95.6**	95.3**	1.00**	100.5	100.9	100.1	0.99
109	Mexico[o]	6-11	13 452	14 698	49	14843	49	110.9	111.7	110.1	0.99	110.3	110.7	110.0	0.99
110	Montserrat[2]	5-11	...	0.4	44	0.5	45	...	...	...	...	116.0	...	...	...
111	Netherlands Antilles	6-11	22	25	48	23	49	115.5	118.2	112.7	0.95	104.3	104.2	104.4	1.00

2. National population data were used to calculate enrolment ratios.
3. Children enter primary school at age 6 or 7. Since 7 is the most common entrance age, enrolment ratios were calculated using the 7-11 age group for both enrolments and population.
4. Enrolment ratios were not calculated due to lack of United Nations population data by age.
(y) Data are for 1999/2000.
(z) Data are for 2000/2001.

Table 5

	NET ENROLMENT RATIO (NER) IN PRIMARY EDUCATION (%)							OUT-OF-SCHOOL CHILDREN (000)						
	1998				2001				1998			2001		
	Total	Male	Female	GPI (F/M)	Total	Male	Female	GPI (F/M)	Total	Male	Female	Total	Male	Female
53	...	...	...	...	94.6**	94.3**	95.0**	1.01**	...	...	...	5 819.9**	3 261.8**	2 558.1**
54	...	...	...	...	...	...	...	...	...	...	...	...	...	...
55	...	...	...	...	...	...	...	...	...	...	...	...	...	...
56	99.4**	99.3**	99.5**	1.00**	99.8**	99.6**	100.0**	1.00**	0.6**	0.4**	0.2**	0.2**	0.2**	–**
57					92.1	92.6	91.7	0.99				2 049.1	983.0	1 066.1
58	100.0	100.0	99.9	1.00	100.0	100.0	100.0	1.00	2.8	–	2.8	1.9	1.9	–
59	...	...	...	...	...	...	...	...	...	...	...	...	...	...
60	80.2	83.6	76.6	0.92	82.8	86.1	79.4	0.92	140.6	59.0	81.6	128.0	52.7	75.3
61	84.3	83.9	84.6	1.01	85.7	86.6	84.8	0.98	7.5	3.9	3.5	6.1	2.9	3.2
62	97.4	97.4	97.4	1.00	95.2	95.1	95.3	1.00	76.4	38.9	37.5	153.5	80.2	73.2
63	...	...	...	...	...	...	...	...	...	...	...	...	...	...
64	...	...	...	...	...	...	...	...	...	...	...	...	...	...
65	82.5**	83.1**	81.8**	0.99**	81.9	81.8	82.0	1.00	920.8**	448.4**	472.4**	968.3	491.6	476.7
66	81.0**	79.6**	82.4**	1.04**	...	...	...	...	0.4**	0.2**	0.2**	...	...	...
67	...	...	...	...	98.4	98.8	98.0	0.99	...	...	...	5.7	2.2	3.5
68	93.9	100.0	87.0	0.87	97.2	100.0	94.1	0.94	0.02	–	0.02	0.01	–	0.01
69	96.8**	99.4**	93.9**	0.94**	96.6**,z	100.0**,z	93.1**,z	0.93**,z	0.05**	0.01**	0.05**	0.1**,z	–**,z	0.1**,z
70	74.8*	77.4*	71.8*	0.93*	77.5**	81.6**	73.0**	0.89**	196.0	92.8*	103.2*	192.6**	82.1**	110.5**
71	...	...	...	...	93.0	91.9	94.1	1.02	...	...	...	803.1	470.6	332.5
72	...	...	...	...	99.9	100.0	99.7	1.00	...	...	...	5.2	–	5.2
73	94.2	93.2	95.2	1.02	94.9	95.6	94.2	0.99	1.6	1.0	0.6	1.4	0.6	0.8
74	...	...	...	...	...	...	...	...	...	...	...	...	...	...
75	...	...	...	...	...	...	...	...	...	...	...	...	...	...
76	79.6**	81.6**	77.6**	0.95**	86.3**	87.5**	85.1**	0.97**	1 327.0**	605.5**	721.5**	872.7**	404.3**	468.4**
77	...	...	...	...	...	...	...	...	...	...	...	...	...	...
78	...	...	...	...	...	...	...	...	...	...	...	...	...	...
79	91.7	91.9	91.6	1.00	99.9	100.0	99.8	1.00	1.2	0.6	0.6	0.0	–	0.0
80	97.9**	100.0**	95.5**	0.96**	...	...	...	...	0.0**	–**	0.0**	...	...	...
81	89.8**	91.2**	88.3**	0.97**	93.2	92.4	94.0	1.02	3.2**	1.4**	1.7**	2.2	1.3	0.9
82	96.7				94.0**				361.0			544.4**		
83	...	...	...	...	96.6	96.3	96.9	1.01	...	...	...	0.05	0.03	0.02
84	...	...	...	...	...	...	...	...	...	...	...	...	...	...
85	100.0*	100.0*	100.0*	1.00*	99.8	100.0	99.6	1.00	0.2*	–*	0.2*	7.7	–	7.7
86	97.8	97.4	98.1	1.01	98.4	99.1	97.6	0.98	0.2	0.1	0.1	0.1	0.0	0.1
87	...	...	...	...	86.4**	85.2**	87.6**	1.03**	...	...	...	5.1**	2.8**	2.3**
88	99.7	100.0	99.3	0.99	99.8	99.6	100.0	1.00	0.1	–	0.1	0.04	0.04	–
89	94.3**	94.5**	94.1**	1.00**	96.2**,z	96.1**,z	96.4**,z	1.00**,z	2.1**	1.0**	1.1**	1.5**,z	0.8**,z	0.7**,z
90	...	...	...	...	100.0z	...	...	...	...	...	...	–z	...	...
91	96.0	96.3	95.7	0.99	94.2	94.0	94.4	1.00	50.0	23.4	26.6	76.2	40.2	36.0
92	...	...	...	...	96.5	95.7	97.4	1.02	...	...	...	460.8	288.6	172.2
93	95.6**	94.5**	96.7**	1.02**	93.9	94.7	93.0	0.98	0.1**	0.1**	0.0**	0.2	0.1	0.1
94	...	...	...	...	...	...	...	...	...	...	...	...	...	...
95	87.9	88.4	87.4	0.99	88.8z	89.4z	88.3z	0.99z	209.9	102.5	107.5	195.6z	94.9z	100.7z
96	86.7	...	...	...	86.7	87.1**	86.3**	0.99**	600.2	...	...	621.4	307.0**	314.4**
97	...	...	...	...	90.6	89.9	91.3	1.02	...	...	...	47.9	26.4	21.4
98	98.9	100.0	97.8	0.98	95.7	96.2	95.2	0.99	11.0	–	11.0	41.7	18.9	22.8
99	82.9**	85.9**	79.9**	0.93**	...	...	...	...	2.1**	0.9**	1.2**	...	...	...
100	88.3**	87.5**	89.2**	1.02**	97.1	99.1	95.1	0.96	131.5**	71.9**	59.6**	32.0	5.2	26.8
101	97.0	96.4	97.5	1.01	99.5	99.0	100.0	1.01	50.8	30.3	20.5	8.5	8.5	–
102	81.0	74.7	87.5	1.17	88.9	89.0	88.9	1.00	157.7	106.8	51.0	96.0	48.5	47.5
103	...	...	...	...	...	...	...	...	...	...	...	...	...	...
104	76.5**	79.0**	73.8**	0.93**	85.0	86.9	82.9	0.95	421.8**	192.1**	229.7**	287.8	128.0	159.8
105	95.7**	96.2**	95.2**	0.99**	98.4y	99.7y	97.1y	0.97y	4.0**	1.8**	2.2**	1.5y	0.2y	1.3y
106	...	...	...	...	...	...	...	...	...	...	...	...	...	...
107	...	...	...	...	87.4**	86.7**	88.3**	1.02**	...	...	...	132.3**	71.6**	60.8**
108	90.3**	90.2**	90.4**	1.00**	95.2	95.1	95.3	1.00	32.0**	16.4**	15.6**	15.8	8.2	7.6
109	99.5	99.1	100.0	1.01	99.4	98.8	100.0	1.01	60.8	60.8	–	84.7	84.7	–
110	...	...	...	...	100.0	...	...	...	...	...	...	–	...	...
111	96.1	95.7	96.5	1.01	88.4	86.1	90.7	1.05	0.9	0.5	0.4	2.6	1.6	1.0

Table 5 (continued)

	Country or territory	Age group 2001	School-age population (000) 2001	Enrolment Primary 1998 Total (000)	1998 %F	Enrolment 2001 Total (000)	2001 %F	GER 1998 Total	1998 Male	1998 Female	1998 GPI (F/M)	GER 2001 Total	2001 Male	2001 Female	2001 GPI (F/M)
112	Nicaragua	7-12	829	783	50	868	49	99.9	98.6	101.2	1.03	104.7	104.4	105.1	1.01
113	Panama	6-11	371	391**	48**	408	48	108.1**	109.9**	106.3**	0.97**	110.0	111.7	108.3	0.97
114	Paraguay[w]	6-11	864	909**	49**	967**	48**	109.6**	110.4**	108.7**	0.98**	111.8**	113.8**	109.8**	0.96**
115	Peru[w]	6-11	3 600	4 299	49	4 317	49	122.6	123.4	121.7	0.99	119.9	120.2	119.7	1.00
116	Saint Kitts and Nevis[4]	5-11	...	...	...	6**	49	...	...	...	...	...	...	...	...
117	Saint Lucia	5-11	22	26	49	25	49	114.8	115.9	113.6	0.98	111.3	110.6	112.0	1.01
118	St Vincent/Grenad.	5-11	18	...	...	18	48	...	...	...	...	101.2	103.1	99.2	0.96
119	Suriname	6-11	51	...	...	64	49	...	...	...	...	125.8	126.7	124.8	0.98
120	Trinidad and Tobago	6-11	147	172	49	155**	49**	101.7	102.3	101.1	0.99	105.1**	105.6**	104.5**	0.99**
121	Turks and Caicos Islands[2]	6-11	2	2	49	2	49	...	...	...	...	101.4	103.6	99.1	0.96
122	Uruguay[w]	6-11	332	365	49	360	48	112.8	113.5	112.2	0.99	108.3	109.3	107.1	0.98
123	Venezuela	6-11	3 310	3 261	49	3 507	49	100.3	101.2	99.4	0.98	105.9	107.0	104.9	0.98

North America and Western Europe

124	Andorra[4]	6-11	...	...	...	4	47	...	...	...	...	...	...	...	...
125	Austria[o]	6-9	375	389	49	386	49	102.2	102.6	101.8	0.99	103.0	103.4	102.6	0.99
126	Belgium[o]	6-11	730	763	49	768	49	103.8	104.3	103.2	0.99	105.2	105.6	104.7	0.99
127	Canada[o]	6-11	2 449	2 404	49	2 456[z]	49[z]	97.7	97.7	97.7	1.00	99.6[z]	99.5[z]	99.7[z]	1.00[z]
128	Cyprus[o,2]	6-11	...	64	48	64	48	97.4	97.6	97.2	1.00	97.8	97.7	97.8	1.00
129	Denmark[o]	7-12	397	372	49	415	49	101.9	102.1	101.8	1.00	104.5	104.5	104.6	1.00
130	Finland[o]	7-12	385	383	49	393	49	99.2	99.4	99.0	1.00	102.0	102.3	101.8	0.99
131	France[o]	6-10	3 638	3 944	49	3 808	49	105.6	106.2	104.9	0.99	104.7	105.2	104.1	0.99
132	Germany[o]	6-9	3 358	3 767	49	3 373	49	105.7	106.0	105.3	0.99	100.5	100.7	100.2	0.99
133	Greece[o]	6-11	652	646	48	646	48	95.5	95.7	95.3	1.00	99.1	99.3	98.8	0.99
134	Iceland[o]	6-12	32	30	49	31	49	98.5	99.4	97.6	0.98	99.8	100.0	99.7	1.00
135	Ireland[o]	4-11	425	457	49	446	49	104.1	104.2	103.9	1.00	105.0	104.9	105.2	1.00
136	Israel[o]	6-11	671	722	49	760	49	112.9	113.4	112.3	0.99	113.4	113.5	113.2	1.00
137	Italy[o]	6-10	2 770	2 876	49	2 790	48	102.5	103.1	102.0	0.99	100.7	101.7	99.7	0.98
138	Luxembourg[o]	6-11	34	31	49	34	49	99.6	99.0	100.3	1.01	100.4	100.9	99.9	0.99
139	Malta[o]	5-10	31	35	49	33	48	106.3	106.0	106.7	1.01	105.3	105.8	104.8	0.99
140	Monaco[4]	6-10	...	2	50	2[z]	49[z]	...	...	...	...	...	...	...	...
141	Netherlands[o]	6-11	1 195	1 268	48	1 287	48	108.3	109.5	107.0	0.98	107.7	108.8	106.5	0.98
142	Norway[o]	6-12	424	412	49	429	49	101.1	101.1	101.0	1.00	101.2	101.1	101.3	1.00
143	Portugal[o]	6-11	663	815	48	770	48	123.1	125.7	120.3	0.96	116.1	118.2	114.0	0.96
144	San Marino[4]	6-10	...	...	...	1[y]	48[y]	...	...	...	...	...	...	...	...
145	Spain[o]	6-11	2 321	2 580	48	2 491	48	107.4	108.4	106.4	0.98	107.3	108.2	106.4	0.98
146	Sweden[o]	7-12	712	763	49	786	49	109.7	108.1	111.3	1.03	110.4	109.0	111.9	1.03
147	Switzerland[o]	7-12	500	530	49	536	49	106.3	106.9	105.7	0.99	107.2	107.7	106.7	0.99
148	United Kingdom[o]	5-10	4 522	4 661	49	4 536	49	101.8	101.4	102.3	1.01	100.3	100.4	100.3	1.00
149	United States[o]	6-11	25 314	24 938	50	24 855	49	100.6	99.3	102.0	1.03	98.2	97.8	98.6	1.01

South and West Asia

150	Afghanistan[5]	7-12	3 416	1 046	7**	774	–	32.7	59.0**	4.5**	0.08**	22.6	43.8	–	...
151	Bangladesh	6-10	18 106	17 627**	48**	17 659	49	101.8**	103.4**	100.1**	0.97**	97.5	96.8	98.3	1.02
152	Bhutan[6]	6-12	134	78	45	88	47	...	...	...	...	...	...	...	...
153	India[w]	6-10	116 032	110 986	43	113 883	44	97.9	106.9	88.2	0.83	98.1	106.0	89.7	0.85
154	Iran, Islamic Republic of	6-10	8 154	8 667	47	7 513	48	95.6	98.1	93.0	0.95	92.1	93.8	90.4	0.96
155	Maldives	6-12	57	74	49	71	48	134.1	133.5	134.6	1.01	124.9	125.3	124.5	0.99
156	Nepal	6-10	3 168	3 349**	42**	3 854	45	112.3**	125.7**	97.9**	0.78**	121.6	129.8	112.9	0.87
157	Pakistan	5-9	20 210	...	...	14 562*,z	41*,z	...	...	...	...	73.2*,z	83.7*,z	62.0*,z	0.74*,z
158	Sri Lanka[w]	5-9	1 597	1 802	49	1 763	49	109.2	110.7	107.6	0.97	110.4	110.9	109.8	0.99

Sub-Saharan Africa

159	Angola	6-9	1 512	1 342	46	...	...	97.1	106.1	88.1	0.83	...	...	...	...
160	Benin	6-11	1 107	872	39	1 153	41	82.7	100.4	65.0	0.65	104.1	122.2	86.0	0.70
161	Botswana	6-12	319	321	50	329	50	102.8	102.8	102.9	1.00	103.3	103.2	103.4	1.00
162	Burkina Faso	7-12	2 127	816	40	927**	41**	41.8	49.6	34.0	0.68	43.6**	50.9**	36.2**	0.71**
163	Burundi	7-12	1 151	562**	45**	817	44	50.2**	55.3**	45.1**	0.82**	71.0	79.5	62.4	0.79
164	Cameroon	6-11	2 570	2 134	45	2 742*	46*	87.5	95.9	79.0	0.82	106.7*	114.6*	98.6*	0.86*
165	Cape Verde	6-11	73	92	49	90	49	125.6	128.5	122.7	0.96	122.6	124.9	120.2	0.96
166	Central African Republic	6-11	621	...	...	411*	40*	...	...	...	...	66.1*	79.4*	53.0*	0.67*

2. National population data were used to calculate enrolment ratios.
4. Enrolment ratios were not calculated, due to lack of United Nations population data by age.
5. During the Taliban rule, there were officially no girls enrolled in government schools.
6. Enrolment ratios were not calculated, due to inconsistencies between enrolment and the United Nations population data.
(g) Projected at the national level (593 districts) on the basis of data by age collected for ISCED level 1 in a sample of 193 districts under the District Information System on Education.

STATISTICAL ANNEX / 291

Table 5

NET ENROLMENT RATIO (NER) IN PRIMARY EDUCATION (%)								OUT-OF-SCHOOL CHILDREN (000)						
1998				2001				1998			2001			
Total	Male	Female	GPI (F/M)	Total	Male	Female	GPI (F/M)	Total	Male	Female	Total	Male	Female	
77.9**	76.9**	79.0**	1.03**	81.9	81.6	82.2	1.01	173.1**	92.0**	81.1**	150.2	77.7	72.5	112
96.5**	96.7**	96.2**	0.99**	99.0	99.2	98.8	1.00	12.8**	6.0**	6.8**	3.8	1.5	2.3	113
91.7	91.3	92.1	1.01	91.5**	91.3**	91.8**	1.01**	69.0	36.6	32.4	73.5**	38.4**	35.0**	114
99.8	100.0	99.6	1.00	99.9	99.8	100.0	1.00	7.2	–	7.2	3.8	3.8	–	115
...	...	...	...	...	...	...	...	...	...	...	...	...	...	116
98.0**	100.0**	95.9**	0.96**	99.2**	100.0**	98.3**	0.98**	0.5**	–**	0.5**	0.2**	–**	0.2**	117
...	...	...	...	91.9**	92.3**	91.6**	0.99**	...	...	...	1.4**	0.7**	0.7**	118
...	...	...	...	97.3**	96.7**	98.1**	1.01**	...	...	...	1.4**	0.9**	0.5**	119
92.9	92.9	92.9	1.00	94.1**	94.2**	94.0**	1.00**	12.0	6.1	6.0	8.7**	4.3**	4.3**	120
...	...	...	...	88.0	87.9	88.0	1.00	...	...	...	0.3	0.1	0.1	121
92.4	92.1	92.7	1.01	89.5	89.3	89.8	1.01	24.8	13.1	11.6	34.7	18.2	16.6	122
85.9	85.5	86.4	1.01	92.4	92.0	92.7	1.01	457.3	240.7	216.6	253.0	135.0	118.1	123
...	...	...	...	...	...	...	...	...	...	...	...	...	...	124
89.9	89.2	90.5	1.01	89.9	89.2	90.6	1.02	38.5	21.0	17.5	37.9	20.8	17.2	125
99.4	99.5	99.4	1.00	100.0	100.0	100.0	1.00	4.3	2.0	2.3	0.1	–	0.1	126
96.9	96.9	96.9	1.00	99.6**,z	99.5**,z	99.7**,z	1.00**,z	75.4	38.8	36.7	9.7**,z	6.2**,z	3.5**,z	127
95.5	95.5	95.5	1.00	95.9	95.8	96.1	1.00	3.0	1.5	1.4	2.7	1.4	1.2	128
99.4	99.4	99.4	1.00	100.0	100.0	100.0	1.00	2.2	1.1	1.1	0.04	0.04	–	129
98.7	98.9	98.5	1.00	100.0	99.9	100.0	1.00	5.0	2.2	2.8	0.1	0.1	–	130
100.0	100.0	99.9	1.00	99.6	99.6	99.7	1.00	1.1	–	1.1	13.7	7.9	5.8	131
...	...	...	...	...	...	...	...	...	...	...	...	...	...	132
93.4	93.5	93.3	1.00	96.8	96.9	96.7	1.00	44.5	22.7	21.9	20.9	10.4	10.5	133
98.3	99.2	97.5	0.98	99.7	99.8	99.6	1.00	0.5	0.1	0.4	0.1	0.0	0.1	134
93.8	93.3	94.4	1.01	95.5	94.7	96.3	1.02	27.2	15.2	12.0	19.2	11.6	7.6	135
99.9	100.0	99.8	1.00	99.9	99.7	100.0	1.00	0.7	–	0.7	1.0	1.0	–	136
99.7	100.0	99.3	0.99	99.2	99.4	99.0	1.00	9.5	–	9.5	21.9	8.4	13.5	137
96.0	95.1	97.0	1.02	96.2	96.2	96.2	1.00	1.3	0.8	0.5	1.3	0.7	0.6	138
99.1	98.3	100.0	1.02	96.6	96.6	96.7	1.00	0.3	0.3	–	1.0	0.5	0.5	139
...	...	...	...	...	...	...	...	...	...	...	...	...	...	140
99.5	100.0	98.9	0.99	99.4	100.0	98.8	0.99	6.1	–	6.1	6.8	–	6.8	141
100.0	100.0	99.9	1.00	99.9	99.8	100.0	1.00	0.2	–	0.2	0.4	0.4	–	142
...	...	...	...	99.8	99.6	100.0	1.00	...	...	...	1.3	1.3	–	143
...	...	...	...	...	...	...	...	...	...	...	...	...	...	144
99.6	100.0	99.2	0.99	99.7	100.0	99.4	0.99	9.0	–	9.0	6.7	–	6.7	145
99.8	100.0	99.5	1.00	99.8	100.0	99.6	1.00	1.7	–	1.7	1.5	–	1.5	146
97.9	98.4	97.4	0.99	98.8	99.2	98.5	0.99	10.5	4.2	6.3	5.9	2.2	3.8	147
99.6	99.2	100.0	1.01	100.0	100.0	99.9	1.00	19.6	19.6	–	1.8	–	1.8	148
93.8	93.8	93.8	1.00	92.7	92.2	93.3	1.01	1 526.7	782.2	744.5	1 841.3	1 013.7	827.5	149
...	...	...	...	...	...	...	...	...	...	...	...	...	...	150
90.3**	91.6**	88.8**	0.97**	86.6	85.7	87.5	1.02	1 686.8**	743.1**	943.6**	2 425.1	1 325.0	1 100.1	151
...	...	...	...	...	...	...	...	...	...	...	...	...	...	152
...	...	...	...	82.3 g	88.5 g	75.7 g	0.86 g	...	...	...	20 549.0	6 918.7	13 630.4	153
81.4**	82.6**	80.2**	0.97**	86.5	...	...	...	1 682.2**	806.9**	875.3**	1 097.2	...	...	154
99.7**	99.4**	100.0**	1.01**	96.2	96.0	96.5	1.01	0.2**	0.2**	–**	2.2	1.2	1.0	155
68.5*	76.1*	60.3*	0.79*	70.5**,z	74.6**,z	66.0**,z	0.88**,z	940.2*	370.1*	570.1*	917.7**,z	407.8**,z	509.9**,z	156
...	...	...	...	59.1**,z	67.5**,z	50.0**,z	0.74**,z	...	...	...	8 144.6**,z	3 331.8**,z	4 812.7**,z	157
99.8	99.7	100.0	1.00	99.9	99.7	100.0	1.00	2.5	2.5	–	2.2	2.2	–	158
61.3	65.8	56.8	0.86	...	...	...	...	535.6	235.4	300.2	...	...	...	159
...	...	...	...	71.3**,y	84.4**,y	58.1**,y	0.69**,y	...	...	...	307.6**,y	83.4**,y	224.2**,y	160
78.7	77.0	80.4	1.04	80.9	79.2	82.7	1.04	66.6	36.2	30.4	60.9	33.5	27.4	161
33.5	39.8	27.1	0.68	35.0**	41.0**	28.9**	0.71**	1 298.9	590.2	708.8	1 383.3**	631.6**	751.7**	162
37.1**	40.4**	33.9**	0.84**	53.4**	58.8**	48.0**	0.82**	703.3**	333.3**	370.0**	536.6**	237.1**	299.4**	163
...	...	...	...	...	...	...	...	...	...	...	...	...	...	164
99.7**	100.0**	99.4**	0.99**	99.4	100.0	98.9	0.99	0.2**	–**	0.2**	0.4	–	0.4	165
...	...	...	...	...	...	...	...	...	...	...	...	...	...	166

(y) Data are for 1999/2000.
(z) Data are for 2000/2001.

Table 5 (continued)

	Country or territory	Age group 2001	School-age population (000) 2001	Enrolment 1998 Total (000)	1998 % F	Enrolment 2001 Total (000)	2001 % F	GER 1998 Total	1998 Male	1998 Female	1998 GPI (F/M)	GER 2001 Total	2001 Male	2001 Female	2001 GPI (F/M)
167	Chad	6-11	1 385	840	37	1 016**	39**	67.0	84.8	49.3	0.58	73.4**	89.9**	56.8**	0.63**
168	Comoros	6-11	116	83	45	104	44	75.2	81.2	69.0	0.85	89.6	98.4	80.6	0.82
169	Congo	6-11	614	276	49	525	48	49.6	50.8	48.4	0.95	85.5	88.4	82.6	0.93
170	Côte d'Ivoire	6-11	2 635	1 911	43	2 116	42	73.1	83.7	62.4	0.75	80.3	92.3	68.2	0.74
171	D. R. Congo	6-11	8 518	4 022	47	...	...	49.6	52.2	47.1	0.90	...	...	...	...
172	Equatorial Guinea	7-11	62	75	48**	78	48	131.3	137.5**	125.0**	0.91**	126.2	132.2	120.2	0.91
173	Eritrea	7-11	546	262	45	330	44	53.2	58.0	48.4	0.83	60.5	66.9	54.0	0.81
174	Ethiopia	7-12	11 285	5 168	38	7 213	41	49.9	62.1	37.6	0.60	63.9	74.8	53.0	0.71
175	Gabon	6-11	210	265	50	282	50	134.1	134.1	134.1	1.00	134.4	134.9	133.9	0.99
176	Gambia	7-12	204	150	46	161**	48**	79.9	86.2	73.6	0.85	78.9**	82.3**	75.4**	0.92**
177	Ghana	6-11	3 177	2 377	47	2 586	48	76.8	81.0	72.5	0.90	81.4	85.0	77.7	0.91
178	Guinea	7-12	1 294	727	38	998	42	58.4	71.3	45.1	0.63	77.1	88.1	65.8	0.75
179	Guinea-Bissau	7-12	230	...	...	150 y	40 y	...	...	...	...	69.7 y	83.6 y	55.9 y	0.67 y
180	Kenya	6-12	6 074	5 481	49	5 828	49	90.2	90.9	89.5	0.98	96.0	96.8	95.1	0.98
181	Lesotho	6-12	334	370	52	415	50	109.2	104.9	113.6	1.08	124.3	123.2	125.5	1.02
182	Liberia	6-11	524	396	42	496 y	42 y	89.6	102.9	76.2	0.74	105.4 y	122.1 y	88.6 y	0.73 y
183	Madagascar	6-10	2 311	2 012	49	2 408	49	95.6	97.3	93.9	0.97	104.2	106.2	102.2	0.96
184	Malawi	6-11	1 952	2 525	49**	2 846	49	146.2	150.1**	142.3**	0.95**	145.8	148.8	142.8	0.96
185	Mali	7-12	2 151	959	41	1 227	42	48.8	56.9	40.5	0.71	57.0	65.0	48.9	0.75
186	Mauritius	6-11	126	131	49	134	49	107.6	107.5	107.6	1.00	106.0	106.1	106.0	1.00
187	Mozambique	6-10	2 585	1 968**	42**	2 556	44	81.2**	93.2**	69.1**	0.74**	98.9	110.3	87.3	0.79
188	Namibia	6-12	376	387	50	398	50	113.9	113.5	114.3	1.01	106.0	105.7	106.3	1.01
189	Niger	7-12	1 900	530	39	761	40	30.9	37.0	24.7	0.67	40.0	47.4	32.4	0.68
190	Nigeria	6-11	20 093	16 046**	43**	19 385**	44**	86.1**	97.5**	74.3**	0.76**	96.5**	107.0**	85.6**	0.80**
191	Rwanda	7-12	1 312	1 289	50	1 535	50	118.6	120.2	117.1	0.97	117.0	117.6	116.3	0.99
192	Sao Tome and Principe	7-12	23	24	49	29**	48**	107.1	109.3	104.9	0.96	126.4**	130.4**	122.4**	0.94**
193	Senegal	7-12	1 590	1 034	46**	1 197	47	68.6	73.6**	63.5**	0.86**	75.3	79.0	71.5	0.91
194	Seychelles[2]	6-11	...	10	49	10	49	112.8	113.8	111.8	0.98	115.7	116.3	115.2	0.99
195	Sierra Leone	6-11	729	...	...	554 z	42 z	...	...	...	...	78.9 z	92.9 z	65.2 z	0.70 z
196	Somalia	6-12	1 772	...	...	...	...	...	...	...	...	...	...	...	...
197	South Africa	7-13	7 052	7 998*	49*	7 413	49	114.4*	116.1*	112.8*	0.97*	105.1	107.1	103.1	0.96
198	Swaziland	6-12	211	212	49	212	49	104.3	107.1	101.4	0.95	100.4	103.2	97.6	0.95
199	Togo	6-11	787	954	43	978	45	132.3	150.2	114.3	0.76	124.2	136.5	111.9	0.82
200	Uganda	6-12	5 059	6 591	47	6 901	49	143.3	150.4	136.1	0.90	136.4	139.1	133.7	0.96
201	United Republic of Tanzania	7-13	6 979	4 043	50	4 845	49	61.8	61.9	61.6	0.99	69.4	70.2	68.7	0.98
202	Zambia	7-13	2 063	1 557	48	1 626	48	81.2	84.3	78.1	0.93	78.8	81.4	76.1	0.94
203	Zimbabwe w	6-12	2 561	...	...	2 535	49	...	...	...	...	99.0	100.3	97.6	0.97

			Sum	Sum	% F	Sum	% F				Weighted average				
I	World	...	648 593	656 538	47	651 913	47	100.7	104.6	96.5	0.92	100.6	104.3	96.7	0.93
II	Countries in transition	...	14 259	15 930	49	14 767	49	96.0	96.6	95.3	0.99	103.6	104.2	102.9	0.99
III	Developed countries	...	67 948	70 406	49	65 552	49	102.1	101.8	102.3	1.00	100.6	100.7	100.6	1.00
IV	Developing countries	...	566 386	570 207	46	569 617	46	100.6	105.2	95.8	0.91	100.5	104.7	96.1	0.92
V	Arab States	...	39 396	34 725	46	36 252	46	89.7	95.7	83.5	0.87	92.0	97.0	86.8	0.89
VI	Central and Eastern Europe	...	24 079	25 484	48	23 677	48	94.6	96.5	92.6	0.96	99.9	101.5	98.3	0.97
VII	Central Asia	...	6 627	6 949	49	6 667	49	98.9	99.6	98.3	0.99	100.6	101.5	99.7	0.98
VIII	East Asia and the Pacific	...	189 557	219 912	48	211 108	48	113.0	113.5	112.5	0.99	111.4	112.0	110.8	0.99
IX	Latin America and the Caribbean	...	58 064	78 585	49	69 660	48	121.3	122.7	120.0	0.98	119.9	121.4	118.4	0.98
X	North America and Western Europe	...	51 664	52 858	49	49 643	49	102.5	102.1	103.0	1.01	100.8	100.8	100.8	1.00
XI	South and West Asia	...	170 874	158 096	44	160 398	44	94.7	103.0	85.7	0.83	93.9	101.1	86.2	0.85
XII	Sub-Saharan Africa	...	108 332	80 406	45	91 972	46	79.1	85.9	72.2	0.84	84.9	91.3	78.4	0.86

1. In countries where two or more education structures exist, indicators were calculated on the basis of the most common or widespread structure. In the Russian Federation this is three grades of primary education starting at age 7. However, a four-grade structure also exists, in which about one-third of primary pupils are enrolled. Gross enrolment ratios may be overestimated.

2. National population data were used to calculate enrolment ratios.

3. Children enter primary school at age 6 or 7. Since 7 is the most common entrance age, enrolment ratios were calculated using the 7-11 age group for both enrolments and population.

4. Enrolment ratios were not calculated, due to lack of United Nations population data by age.

Table 5

NET ENROLMENT RATIO (NER) IN PRIMARY EDUCATION (%)

	1998				2001			
	Total	Male	Female	GPI (F/M)	Total	Male	Female	GPI (F/M)
167	54.7	67.6	41.8	0.62	58.3**	69.7**	46.8**	0.67**
168	49.2	53.2	45.1	0.85	…	…	…	…
169	…	…	…	…	…	…	…	…
170	55.5	63.2	47.8	0.76	62.6	72.0	53.1	0.74
171	34.6	35.5	33.7	0.95	…	…	…	…
172	88.0	96.4**	79.7**	0.83**	84.6	91.4	77.8	0.85
173	33.9	36.2	31.6	0.87	42.5	45.8	39.2	0.86
174	35.8	42.4	29.2	0.69	46.2	51.5	40.8	0.79
175	…	…	…	…	78.3**,z	78.9**,z	77.8**,z	0.99**,z
176	66.6	70.9	62.3	0.88	72.9**	76.0**	69.7**	0.92**
177	57.9**	59.8**	55.9**	0.93**	60.2	61.4	59.0	0.96
178	45.3	53.6	36.7	0.69	61.5	69.1	53.7	0.78
179	…	…	…	…	45.2 y	52.9 y	37.5 y	0.71 y
180	65.8**	65.3**	66.3**	1.01**	69.9**	69.4**	70.5**	1.02**
181	64.5	60.3	68.7	1.14	84.4	81.2	87.6	1.08
182	43.9	49.7	38.1	0.77	69.9 y	78.6 y	61.1 y	0.78 y
183	64.5	64.3	64.8	1.01	68.6	68.2	68.9	1.01
184	…	…	…	…	81.0**	81.0**	81.0**	1.00**
185	38.3**	44.5**	32.0**	0.72**	…	…	…	…
186	93.2	93.1	93.2	1.00	93.2	93.2	93.2	1.00
187	47.3**	51.6**	43.0**	0.83**	59.7	63.4	55.9	0.88
188	77.9	75.4	80.4	1.07	78.2	75.8	80.7	1.06
189	26.1	31.3	20.8	0.66	34.2	40.7	27.5	0.68
190	…	…	…	…	…	…	…	…
191	…	…	…	…	84.0	82.8	85.1	1.03
192	85.5	86.5	84.4	0.98	97.1**	100.0**	94.2**	0.94**
193	57.9	61.5**	54.1**	0.88**	57.9	61.2	54.5	0.89
194	99.1	100.0	98.3	0.98	99.7	100	99.3	0.99
195	…	…	…	…	…	…	…	…
196	…	…	…	…	…	…	…	…
197	91.3*	90.8*	91.8*	1.01*	89.5	89.2	89.8	1.01
198	77.7**	77.1**	78.3**	1.02**	76.7	76.3	77.0	1.01
199	89.8	100.0	79.5	0.80	91.8	100.0	83.6	0.84
200	…	…	…	…	…	…	…	…
201	45.8	45.1	46.6	1.03	54.4	54.3	54.5	1.00
202	68.5	69.6	67.4	0.97	66.0**	66.4**	65.6**	0.99**
203	…	…	…	…	82.7	82.4	83.1	1.01

OUT-OF-SCHOOL CHILDREN (000)

	1998			2001		
	Total	Male	Female	Total	Male	Female
167	567.7	202.8	364.9	578.3**	210.0**	368.3**
168	55.9	26.1	29.9	…	…	…
169	…	…	…	…	…	…
170	1 163.3	482.8	680.6	985.2	369.5	615.8
171	5 306.0	2 619.5	2 686.5	…	…	…
172	6.8	1.0**	5.8**	9.6	2.7	6.9
173	325.2	157.8	167.4	313.8	149.0	164.8
174	6 650.8	2 987.1	3 663.7	6 076.1	2 741.1	3 335.0
175	…	…	…	44.8**,z	22.0**,z	22.8**,z
176	62.9	27.4	35.4	55.4**	24.6**	30.8**
177	1 304.1**	625.5**	678.6**	1 264.9	617.1	647.8
178	680.5	292.6	388.0	498.3	203.0	295.2
179	…	…	…	118.0 y	50.6 y	67.4 y
180	2 076.6**	1 056.8**	1 019.8**	1 826.0**	934.4**	891.6**
181	120.2	67.5	52.7	52.1	31.5	20.6
182	247.6	111.5	136.1	141.7 y	50.4 y	91.3 y
183	746.1	375.5	370.6	726.3	367.3	359.0
184	…	…	…	370.9**	185.7**	185.2**
185	1 212.3**	552.6**	659.7**	…	…	…
186	8.3	4.2	4.1	8.6	4.4	4.2
187	1 277.0**	589.5**	687.5**	1 042.1	474.7	567.4
188	75.0	41.8	33.1	81.8	45.6	36.2
189	1 264.4	597.5	666.9	1 249.7	572.5	677.2
190	…	…	…	…	…	…
191	…	…	…	209.9	111.3	98.6
192	3.2	1.5	1.7	0.7**	–**	0.7**
193	635.4	292.6**	342.8**	669.4	310.9	358.5
194	0.1	–	0.1	0.0	–	0.0
195	…	…	…	…	…	…
196	…	…	…	…	…	…
197	607.8*	321.9*	285.9*	738.4	380.6	357.8
198	45.4**	23.3**	22.1**	49.2	25.0	24.3
199	73.6	–	73.6	64.3	–	64.3
200	…	…	…	…	…	…
201	3 544.8	1 803.3	1 741.5	3 183.5	1 599.6	1 583.9
202	604.3	292.3	312.0	701.7**	347.4**	354.3**
203	…	…	…	442.5	226.3	216.2

Weighted average / Sum

Total	Male	Female	GPI	Total	Male	Female	GPI	Total	Male	Female	Total	Male	Female	
84.2	87.3	80.9	0.93	84.0	86.5	81.5	0.94	106 915.6	44 062.3	62 853.3	103 466.3	44 984.8	58 481.5	I
84.6	85.0	84.1	0.99	90.1	90.3	89.8	0.99	2 563.1	1 273.9	1 289.2	1 418.6	705.5	713.1	II
96.4	96.5	96.4	1.00	95.6	95.4	95.9	1.00	2 447.5	1 251.1	1 196.4	2 991.7	1 612.1	1 379.6	III
82.7	86.3	78.9	0.92	82.5	85.3	79.5	0.93	101 905.0	41 537.3	60 367.7	99 056.0	42 667.2	56 388.8	IV
78.1	82.3	73.7	0.90	81.1	85.1	76.9	0.90	8 491.4	3 500.6	4 990.8	7 441.4	2 991.9	4 449.6	V
86.7	88.1	85.3	0.97	88.8	89.9	87.7	0.98	3 580.7	1 639.5	1 941.2	2 688.1	1 245.3	1 442.8	VI
87.5	88.0	87.0	0.99	94.1	95.0	93.2	0.98	878.6	428.5	450.1	390.5	168.7	221.8	VII
96.0	96.1	95.8	1.00	93.7	93.7	93.6	1.00	7 829.6	3 912.3	3 917.2	11 993.2	6 158.5	5 834.7	VIII
94.2	94.8	93.5	0.99	95.7	95.6	95.9	1.00	3 758.7	1 699.4	2 059.3	2 468.4	1 300.2	1 168.1	IX
96.3	96.3	96.4	1.00	95.4	95.1	95.7	1.01	1 884.3	967.0	917.3	2 385.7	1 300.6	1 085.1	X
80.2	87.5	72.3	0.83	79.0	84.7	73.0	0.86	37 410.3	12 179.3	25 231.0	35 807.7	13 518.5	22 289.2	XI
57.6	61.4	53.8	0.88	62.8	66.4	59.2	0.89	43 081.9	19 735.6	23 346.3	40 291.3	18 301.1	21 990.2	XII

5. During the Taliban rule, there were officially no girls enrolled in government schools.
6. Enrolment ratios were not calculated, due to inconsistencies between enrolment and the United Nations population data.
(g) Projected at the national level (593 districts) on the basis of data by age collected for ISCED level 1 in a sample of 193 districts under the District Information System on Education.

(y) Data are for 1999/2000.
(z) Data are for 2000/2001.

Table 6
Internal efficiency: repetition in primary education

	Country or territory	Duration[1] of primary education 2001	Grade 1 Total	Grade 1 Male	Grade 1 Female	Grade 2 Total	Grade 2 Male	Grade 2 Female	Grade 3 Total	Grade 3 Male	Grade 3 Female
	Arab States										
1	Algeria	6	11.4	12.8	9.8	9.6	11.4	7.6	9.9	12.2	7.3
2	Bahrain	6	4.8**	4.4**	5.2**	3.6**	3.8**	3.4**	3.7**	4.8**	2.7**
3	Djibouti	6	7.9	8.2	7.5	8.1	7.5	8.8	8.2	7.8	8.7
4	Egypt[w]	5	–	–	–	3.6**	4.3**	2.8**	4.2**	5.2**	3.1**
5	Iraq	6	10.9**,x	11.9**,x	9.7**,x	10.8**,x	12.4**,x	8.9**,x	10.7**,x	12.5**,x	8.5**,x
6	Jordan[w]	6	...	...	...	...	...	...	...	...	...
7	Kuwait	4	3.6	3.3	3.9	2.5	2.5	2.4	3.6	3.9	3.3
8	Lebanon	6	4.9	5.7	3.9	6.2	7.5	4.8	6.5	7.9	5.0
9	Libyan Arab Jamahiriya	6	...	...	...	...	...	...	...	...	...
10	Mauritania	6	12.8	12.8	12.8	14.2	13.5	14.9	13.9	13.8	13.9
11	Morocco	6	17.1	17.8	16.2	13.5**	13.8**	13.0**	14.8**	17.2**	12.0**
12	Oman	6	5.0	5.2	4.8	5.3	6.0	4.7	4.5	5.2	3.8
13	Palestinian Autonomous Territories	4	1.1	0.9	1.4	0.8	1.1	0.6	1.7	1.9	1.4
14	Qatar	6	...	...	...	...	...	...	...	...	...
15	Saudi Arabia	6	8.0**	9.6**	6.1**	4.8	6.7	2.8	5.6	7.6	3.4
16	Sudan	6	11.2**,x	10.6**,x	12.1**,x	10.2**,x	8.8**,x	12.0**,x	11.6**,x	11.7**,x	11.5**,x
17	Syrian Arab Republic	6	13.8	14.9	12.5	9.2	10.5	7.6	5.8	6.8	4.8
18	Tunisia[w]	6	1.6	1.8	1.4	10.9	12.5	9.1	12.1	14.0	9.9
19	United Arab Emirates	6	3.4	3.1	3.7	2.9	2.8	3.0	2.3	2.3	2.4
20	Yemen	6	5.6**,y	5.8**,y	5.3**,y	6.1**,y	6.1**,y	5.9**,y	8.3**,y	8.6**,y	7.7**,y
	Central and Eastern Europe										
21	Albania[o]	4	5.2[y]	5.6[y]	4.7[y]	4.2[y]	5.0[y]	3.3[y]	3.0[y]	3.4[y]	2.7[y]
22	Belarus	4	...	...	...	...	...	...	...	...	...
23	Bosnia and Herzegovina[o]	4	...	...	...	...	...	...	...	...	...
24	Bulgaria[o]	4	1.4	1.6	1.2	3.4	4.2	2.6	2.5	3.0	1.9
25	Croatia	4	1.0	1.2	0.9	0.3	0.4	0.2	0.2	0.2	0.1
26	Czech Republic[o]	5	1.5**	1.7**	1.3**	1.0**	1.1**	0.8**	0.9**	1.0**	0.7**
27	Estonia[o]	6	1.3	1.7	0.9	1.2	1.5	0.8	1.4	2.0	0.9
28	Hungary[o]	4	4.7	5.4	3.9	2.1	2.4	1.7	1.5	1.9	1.2
29	Latvia[o]	4	3.9	5.3	2.3	1.4	1.9	0.8	1.1	1.5	0.6
30	Lithuania[o]	4	1.4	1.8	1.0	0.4	0.5	0.3	0.3	0.4	0.2
31	Poland[o]	6	0.6	0.6**	0.6**	0.3	0.3**	0.3**	0.3	0.3**	0.3**
32	Republic of Moldova	4	1.2	1.2	1.2	0.7	0.7	0.7	0.7	0.7	0.7
33	Romania[o]	4	5.2	6.0	4.4	2.4	3.0	1.8	2.2	2.6	1.6
34	Russian Federation[w]	3	1.2	...	...	0.7	...	...	0.7	...	...
35	Serbia and Montenegro	4	...	...	...	...	...	...	...	...	...
36	Slovakia	4	4.6	4.9	4.4	2.1	2.3	1.9	1.4	1.7	1.2
37	Slovenia[o]	4	1.1	1.3	0.9	0.7	0.7	0.6	0.6	0.8	0.4
38	The former Yugoslav Rep. of Macedonia[o]	4	0.2	0.2	0.1	0.1	0.1	0.1	0.1	0.1	0.1
39	Turkey[o]	6	...	...	...	...	...	...	...	...	...
40	Ukraine	4	...	...	...	...	...	...	...	...	...
	Central Asia										
41	Armenia	3	.	.	.	0.1	0.1	0.1	0.2	0.2	0.1
42	Azerbaijan	4	0.2	0.2	0.2	0.3	0.3	0.3	0.3	0.3	0.3
43	Georgia	4	0.3	0.4	0.2	0.3	0.5	0.1	0.3	0.5	0.1
44	Kazakhstan	4	0.1	0.1	0.1	0.3	0.3	0.2	0.2	0.2	0.1
45	Kyrgyzstan	4	0.2	0.2	0.1	0.2	0.3	0.1	0.2	0.2	0.1
46	Mongolia	4	1.1	1.1	1.2	0.6	0.7	0.5	0.4	0.4	0.3
47	Tajikistan	4	0.2	0.2	0.2	0.4	0.3	0.5	0.4	0.3	0.5
48	Turkmenistan	4	...	...	...	...	...	...	...	...	...
49	Uzbekistan	4	–	–	–	–	–	–	–	–	–
	East Asia and the Pacific										
50	Australia[o]	7	.	.	.	.	.	.	.	.	.
51	Brunei Darussalam	6	.	.	.	.	.	.	.	.	.
52	Cambodia	6	18.3	19.0	17.6	10.8	11.7	9.7	8.4	9.2	7.4
53	China[w]	5	1.2**	...	...	0.2**	...	...	0.2**	...	...
54	Cook Islands	6	5.1[x]	...	...	0.5[x]	0.9[x]	–	0.3[x]	0.5[x]	–

1. Duration in this table is defined according to ISCED97 and may differ from that reported nationally.

(x) Data are for 1998/1999.
(y) Data are for 1999/2000.
(z) Data on the percentage of Repeaters all grades are for 2000/2001.

STATISTICAL ANNEX / 295

Table 6

\multicolumn{12}{c	}{**REPETITION RATES BY GRADE IN PRIMARY EDUCATION (%), 2000**}	\multicolumn{3}{c	}{**REPEATERS, ALL GRADES (%)**}	
\multicolumn{3}{c	}{Grade 4}	\multicolumn{3}{c	}{Grade 5}	\multicolumn{3}{c	}{Grade 6}	\multicolumn{3}{c	}{Grade 7}	\multicolumn{3}{c	}{2001}	
Total	Male	Female	Total	Male	Female	Total	Male	Female	Total	Male	Female	Total	Male	Female	
11.0	13.6	8.1	11.5	14.3	8.3	16.5	19.4	13.0	.	.	.	11.7	14.2	9.0	1
4.1**	5.0**	3.2**	4.1**	5.1**	3.0**	3.0**	4.0**	1.8**	.	.	.	3.8**	4.4**	3.2**	2
6.6**	6.7**	6.5**	6.6**	6.5**	6.6**	27.4**	27.1**	27.8**	.	.	.	10.9	10.9	10.9	3
6.6**	8.0**	4.9**	10.6**	12.8**	8.0**	.	.	.	.	.	.	5.1**	6.3**	3.8**	4
12.7**,x	14.9**,x	9.9**,x	22.1**,x	25.0**,x	18.1**,x	6.1**,x	7.7**,x	3.9**,x	.	.	.	12.3 y	14.1 y	10.0 y	5
...	...	...	...	...	...	...	...	...	...	...	...	0.5	0.5	0.5	6
1.8	2.3	1.3	.	.	.	.	.	.	.	.	.	2.8	2.9	2.7	7
14.5	16.5	12.3	9.5	10.9	7.9	10.0	11.6	8.4	.	.	.	8.7	10.1	7.2	8
...	...	...	...	...	...	...	...	...	...	...	...	...	...	...	9
11.2	10.8	11.6	14.4	14.1	14.8	25.0	23.2	27.0	.	.	.	14.1	13.8	14.4	10
11.8**	14.2**	8.9**	10.1**	12.3**	7.3**	7.6**	9.5**	5.2**	.	.	.	12.6	14.1	10.8	11
4.4	5.9	2.7	3.7	5.0	2.3	2.4	3.5	1.2	.	.	.	4.3	5.2	3.3	12
2.7	3.0	2.3	.	.	.	.	.	.	.	.	.	1.5	1.7	1.4	13
...	...	...	...	...	...	...	...	...	...	...	...	...	...	...	14
4.9	5.1	4.7	5.4	6.2	4.6	2.0	2.2	1.7	.	.	.	5.2	6.3	3.9	15
13.0**,x	12.6**,x	13.5**,x	12.3**,x	12.4**,x	12.2**,x	11.0**,x	11.4**,x	10.6**,x	.	.	.	11.3 y	10.9 y	11.8 y	16
3.9	4.7	3.0	2.4	2.9	1.9	3.6	4.6	2.5	.	.	.	6.8	7.7	5.7	17
10.0	12.0	7.8	13.3	15.4	10.8	8.6	10.1	7.1	.	.	.	9.8	11.5	8.0	18
3.2	4.3	2.1	3.0	3.8	2.1	3.3	3.2	1.4	.	.	.	2.8	3.2	2.4	19
9.2**,y	9.9**,y	7.7**,y	9.2**,y	10.1**,y	7.1**,y	8.2**,y	9.1**,y	5.9**,y	.	.	.	9.0 z	11.1 z	5.6 z	20
3.3 y	3.8 y	2.8 y	.	.	.	.	.	.	.	.	.	4.1 z	4.6 z	3.5 z	21
...	...	...	...	...	...	...	...	...	...	...	...	0.3	...	...	22
...	...	...	...	...	...	...	...	...	...	...	...	...	...	...	23
2.2	2.5	1.8	.	.	.	.	.	.	.	.	.	2.5	3.0	2.0	24
0.2	0.2	0.1	.	.	.	.	.	.	.	.	.	0.4	0.5	0.3	25
1.0**	1.2**	0.7**	0.9**	1.1**	0.6**	.	.	.	.	.	.	1.1	1.3	0.9	26
1.8	2.5	0.9	2.1	3.3	0.8	3.0	4.6	1.3	.	.	.	2.0	2.9	1.0	27
1.6	2.0	1.2	.	.	.	.	.	.	.	.	.	2.5	3.0	2.0	28
1.0	1.4	0.6	.	.	.	.	.	.	.	.	.	1.9	2.7	1.2	29
0.4	0.5	0.2	.	.	.	.	.	.	.	.	.	0.7	0.9	0.4	30
0.6	0.6**	0.6**	0.8	0.8**	0.8**	0.8	0.8**	0.8**	.	.	.	0.6	0.6**	0.6**	31
0.8	0.8	0.8	.	.	.	.	.	.	.	.	.	0.9	0.9	0.9	32
2.2	2.6	1.7	.	.	.	.	.	.	.	.	.	3.1	3.7	2.5	33
.	.	.	.	.	.	.	.	.	.	.	.	0.9	...	...	34
...	...	...	...	...	...	...	...	...	...	...	...	1.1 z	1.1**,z	1.1**,z	35
1.5	1.6	1.4	.	.	.	.	.	.	.	.	.	2.5	2.7	2.3	36
0.6	0.8	0.4	.	.	.	.	.	.	.	.	.	0.8	0.9	0.6	37
0.1	0.1	0.1	.	.	.	.	.	.	.	.	.	0.1	0.1	0.1	38
...	...	...	...	...	...	...	...	...	...	...	...	...	...	...	39
...	...	...	...	...	...	...	...	...	...	...	...	...	...	...	40
.	.	.	.	.	.	.	.	.	.	.	.	0.1	0.1	0.1	41
0.3	0.3	0.3	.	.	.	.	.	.	.	.	.	0.3	0.3	0.3	42
0.3	0.4	0.2	.	.	.	.	.	.	.	.	.	0.3	0.5	0.2	43
0.1	0.2	0.1	.	.	.	.	.	.	.	.	.	0.2	0.2	0.1	44
0.1	0.2	0.1	.	.	.	.	.	.	.	.	.	0.2	0.2	0.1	45
0.3	0.4	0.3	.	.	.	.	.	.	.	.	.	0.6	0.7	0.6	46
0.5	0.5	0.6	.	.	.	.	.	.	.	.	.	0.4	0.3	0.4	47
...	...	...	...	...	...	...	...	...	...	...	...	...	...	...	48
–	–	–	.	.	.	.	.	.	.	.	.	–	–	–	49
...	...	...	...	...	...	...	...	...	...	...	...	...	...	...	50
.	.	.	.	.	.	.	.	.	.	.	.	.	.	.	51
5.8	6.5	4.9	3.7	4.1	3.2	2.4	2.6	2.2	.	.	.	9.6	10.2	8.9	52
0.1**	...	...	0.1**	...	...	.	.	.	.	.	.	0.3**	...	...	53
2.4 x	2.7 x	2.1 x	1.7 x	2.3 x	1.1 x	3.2 x	4.0 x	2.4 x	.	.	.	2.6 y	...	...	54

Table 6 (continued)

	Country or territory	Duration[1] of primary education 2001	Grade 1 Total	Grade 1 Male	Grade 1 Female	Grade 2 Total	Grade 2 Male	Grade 2 Female	Grade 3 Total	Grade 3 Male	Grade 3 Female
55	Democratic People's Republic of Korea	4	...	...	...	...	...	...	...	...	...
56	Fiji	6	.	.	.	.	.	.	.	.	.
57	Indonesia[w]	6	10.8	11.0	10.6	6.6	6.8	6.4	5.4	5.6	5.2
58	Japan[o]	6	...	...	...	...	...	...	...	...	...
59	Kiribati	6	...	...	...	...	...	...	...	...	...
60	Lao People's Democratic Republic	5	35.7	36.4	34.9	20.6	22.1	18.8	13.1	14.7	11.2
61	Macao, China	6	2.3	2.8	1.8	3.1	4.3	1.8	5.4	7.0	3.6
62	Malaysia[w]	6	–	–	–	–	–	–	–	–	–
63	Marshall Islands	6	.	.	.	.	.	.	.	.	.
64	Micronesia (Federated States of)	6	.	.	.	.	.	.	.	.	.
65	Myanmar	5	1.2	1.2	1.2	0.7	0.7	0.7	0.6	0.6	0.6
66	Nauru	6									
67	New Zealand[o]	6									
68	Niue	6	.	.	.	.	.	.	.	.	.
69	Palau	6									
70	Papua New Guinea	5	–	–	–	–	–	–	–	–	–
71	Philippines[w]	6	5.2	6.1	4.1	2.7	3.5	1.8	1.9	2.5	1.2
72	Republic of Korea[o]	6	.	.	.	.	.	.	.	.	.
73	Samoa	6	2.6	3.0	2.2	0.7	1.1	0.4	0.4	0.4	0.5
74	Singapore	6	–	–	–	–	–	–	–	–	–
75	Solomon Islands	6	...	...	...	...	...	...	...	...	...
76	Thailand[w]	6	9.7**,y	9.5**,y	10.0**,y	3.9**,y	3.8**,y	4.0**,y	3.6**,y	4.9**,y	2.1**,y
77	Timor-Leste	6	...	...	...	...	...	...	...	...	...
78	Tokelau	6									
79	Tonga	6	.	.	.	.	.	.	.	.	.
80	Tuvalu	6									
81	Vanuatu	6	10.6	11.8	9.3	7.4	8.4	6.3	6.9	7.6	6.0
82	Viet Nam	5	5.4	6.3	4.4	2.5	3.0	2.1	1.7	2.1	1.3
	Latin America and the Caribbean										
83	Anguilla	7	2.0**	1.7**	2.5**	0.5	1.0	–	0.5	–	1.0
84	Antigua and Barbuda	7	...	...	...	...	...	...	...	...	...
85	Argentina[w]	6	10.4	11.8	8.9	7.3	8.5	6.0	6.4	7.6	5.2
86	Aruba	6	14.1	17.2	10.6	10.3	11.9	8.7	8.9	10.2	7.5
87	Bahamas	6	–	–	–	–	–	–	–	–	–
88	Barbados	6	–	–	–	–	–	–	–	–	–
89	Belize	6	14.1 y	15.6 y	12.4 y	8.3 y	9.3 y	7.2 y	8.3 y	9.9 y	6.7 y
90	Bermuda	6	–	–	–	.	.	.	.	.	.
91	Bolivia	6	2.8	2.9	2.8	2.4	2.5	2.4	2.6	2.7	2.4
92	Brazil[w]	4	31.1	31.0	31.2	19.1	19.2**	19.0**	16.1	16.6**	15.6**
93	British Virgin Islands	7	3.9**	4.8**	3.0**	1.3**	1.1**	1.5**	2.3**	2.1**	2.4**
94	Cayman Islands	6	...	...	...	...	...	...	...	...	...
95	Chile[w]	6	0.9 y	1.0 y	0.8 y	3.9 y	4.4 y	3.3 y	0.8 y	0.9 y	0.6 y
96	Colombia	5	11.5	12.4	10.4	6.2	6.8	5.5	5.1	5.6	4.5
97	Costa Rica	6	15.1	16.6	13.3	8.9	10.2	7.5	7.3	8.5	6.0
98	Cuba	6	–	–	–	1.9	2.5	1.2	–	–	–
99	Dominica	7	7.0	8.4	5.4	4.7	6.5	2.8	2.9	3.5	2.2
100	Dominican Republic	6	2.6**	3.0**	2.1**	2.9**	3.3**	2.4**	12.1**	14.8**	9.4**
101	Ecuador	6	4.0	4.4	3.7	2.8	3.1	2.4	1.9	2.2	1.6
102	El Salvador	6	14.6**	15.8**	13.2**	5.6**	6.4**	4.8**	4.3**	4.8**	3.7**
103	Grenada	7	4.5**	6.3**	2.5**	3.4**	4.5**	2.2**	2.9**	3.9**	1.9**
104	Guatemala	6	27.0	28.0	25.9	14.5	15.3	13.6	10.8	11.4	10.1
105	Guyana	6	4.0 x	4.6 x	3.3 x	2.6 x	3.0 x	2.1 x	2.6 x	2.9 x	2.4 x
106	Haiti	6	...	...	...	...	...	...	...	...	...
107	Honduras	6	...	...	...	...	...	...	...	...	...
108	Jamaica[w]	6	4.6	5.8	3.3	1.5	2.0	1.0	1.0	1.4	0.7
109	Mexico[o]	6	9.6	10.8	8.2	8.0	9.4	6.6	6.4	7.5	5.2
110	Montserrat	7	14.5	9.1	20.7	29.5	37.1	19.2	18.8	26.5	10.0
111	Netherlands Antilles	6	17.8	23.1	11.8	12.4	15.2	9.6	12.4	14.3	10.2
112	Nicaragua	6	10.9	11.9	9.8	6.3	7.1	5.4	6.8	8.1	5.6
113	Panama	6	10.0	11.3	8.6	8.8	10.0	7.4	6.1	7.2	4.9
114	Paraguay[w]	6	13.5**	15.0**	11.9**	10.7**	12.5**	8.7**	8.0**	9.2**	6.8**

1. Duration in this table is defined according to ISCED97 and may differ from that reported nationally.

(x) Data are for 1998/1999.
(y) Data are for 1999/2000.
(z) Data on the percentage of repeaters all grades are for 2000/2001.

STATISTICAL ANNEX / 297

Table 6

REPETITION RATES BY GRADE IN PRIMARY EDUCATION (%), 2000 | REPEATERS, ALL GRADES (%)

Grade 4 Total	Male	Female	Grade 5 Total	Male	Female	Grade 6 Total	Male	Female	Grade 7 Total	Male	Female	2001 Total	Male	Female	
...	...	...	...	...	...	...	...	...	...	...	...	...	...	...	55
.	.	.	.	.	.	.	.	.	.	.	.	.	.	.	56
4.2	4.4	4.1	2.9	3.1	2.8	0.5	0.5	0.4	.	.	.	5.3	5.5	5.1	57
...	...	...	...	...	...	...	...	...	...	...	...	...	...	...	58
...	...	...	...	...	...	...	...	...	...	...	...	0.8**,y	0.8**,y	0.8**,y	59
8.1	9.6	6.3	5.2	6.5	3.7	.	.	.	.	.	.	20.0	21.2	18.5	60
7.8	9.8	5.5	9.5	12.1	6.7	8.5	9.8	7.1	.	.	.	6.6	8.1	4.8	61
–	–	–	–	–	–	–	–	–	.	.	.	–	–	–	62
.	.	.	.	.	.	.	.	.	.	.	.	.	.	.	63
...	...	...	...	...	...	...	...	...	...	...	...	...	...	...	64
0.5	0.5	0.5	0.3	0.3	0.3	.	.	.	.	.	.	0.7	0.7	0.7	65
...	...	...	...	...	...	...	...	...	...	...	...	...	...	...	66
...	...	...	...	...	...	...	...	...	...	...	...	...	...	...	67
.	.	.	.	.	.	.	.	.	.	.	.	.	.	.	68
.	.	.	–	–	–	.	.	.	.	.	.	.	.	.	69
1.3	1.8	0.8	1.0	1.5	0.6	0.5	0.7	0.3	.	.	.	2.3	2.9	1.6	71
.	.	.	.	.	.	.	.	.	.	.	.	.	.	.	72
0.6	0.9	0.4	0.6	0.9	0.3	0.3	0.4	0.1	.	.	.	0.9	1.1	0.7	73
–	–	–	–	–	–	–	–	–	.	.	.	–	–	–	74
...	...	...	...	...	...	...	...	...	...	...	...	...	...	...	75
...	...	...	...	...	...	1.2**,y	1.2**,y	1.2**,y	.	.	.	3.9**,z	4.0**,z	3.7**,z	76
...	...	...	...	...	...	...	...	...	...	...	...	...	...	...	77
...	...	...	...	...	...	...	...	...	...	...	...	...	...	...	78
.	.	.	.	.	.	28.9**	31.2**	26.2**	.	.	.	6.2	6.9	5.4	79
...	...	...	...	...	...	...	...	...	...	...	...	...	...	...	80
5.5	4.1	7.1	5.9	6.7	5.0	5.8	6.7	4.8	.	.	.	6.7	7.5	5.9	81
1.6	1.9	1.2	0.2	0.3	0.2	.	.	.	.	.	.	2.4	2.8	1.9	82
–	–	–	0.5	0.9	–	–	–	–	0.9	0.9	0.9	0.6**	0.7**	0.6**	83
...	...	...	...	...	...	...	...	...	...	...	...	...	...	...	84
5.5	6.7	4.4	4.7	5.7	3.7	3.9	4.8	3.0	.	.	.	6.2	7.3	5.0	85
7.0	7.8	6.0	6.4	7.7	5.1	2.6	3.3	2.0	.	.	.	7.9	9.3	6.5	86
–	–	–	–	–	–	–	–	–	.	.	.	–	–	–	87
–	–	–	–	–	–	–	–	–	.	.	.	–	–	–	88
9.8 y	11.8 y	7.8 y	8.8 y	10.6 y	6.9 y	9.1 y	10.8 y	7.3 y	.	.	.	9.8 z	11.5 z	8.1 z	89
.	.	.	.	.	.	.	.	.	.	.	.	.	.	.	90
2.3	2.5	2.1	2.5	2.7	2.3	4.4	5.0	3.7	.	.	.	2.7	2.9	2.5	91
14.2	14.8**	13.6**	.	.	.	.	.	.	.	.	.	21.5	21.8**	21.1**	92
1.5**	2.1**	1.0**	1.7**	1.9**	1.5**	2.6**	3.5**	1.7**	6.5**	5.9**	7.2**	2.8	3.0	2.6	93
...	...	...	...	...	...	...	...	...	...	...	...	...	...	...	94
2.5 y	3.1 y	2.0 y	2.3 y	2.9 y	1.6 y	1.6 y	2.0 y	1.1 y	.	.	.	2.0 z	2.4 z	1.6 z	95
4.0	4.6	3.4	3.0	3.4	2.5	.	.	.	.	.	.	6.6	7.3	5.9	96
9.1	10.6	7.6	7.2	8.6	5.8	0.7	0.8	0.6	.	.	.	8.2	9.5	6.9	97
1.7	2.4	0.9	1.0	1.4	0.5	0.3	0.5	0.2	.	.	.	1.2	1.8	0.6	98
1.6	1.8	1.4	3.4	4.9	1.6	3.5	5.4	1.5	7.0	9.0	4.8	4.5	5.9	3.0	99
7.5**	8.9**	6.1**	6.1**	7.5**	4.7**	4.8**	6.0**	3.7**	.	.	.	5.9	7.1	4.6	100
1.5	1.7	1.2	0.9	1.1	0.8	0.4	0.5	0.4	.	.	.	2.1	2.3	1.8	101
3.9**	4.5**	3.3**	3.0**	3.5**	2.4**	2.6**	3.0**	2.2**	.	.	.	6.5	7.3	5.7	102
2.6**	2.9**	2.2**	3.1**	4.6**	1.5**	3.5**	5.1**	1.7**	5.3**	5.7**	4.9**	4.1	5.3	2.9	103
7.7	8.2	7.1	4.8	5.1	4.4	2.0	2.2	1.9	.	.	.	14.2	14.8	13.5	104
1.7 x	1.9 x	1.4 x	1.2 x	1.3 x	1.1 x	2.0 x	1.8 x	2.2 x	.	.	.	2.3 y	2.6 y	2.1 y	105
...	...	...	...	...	...	...	...	...	...	...	...	...	...	...	106
...	...	...	...	...	...	...	...	...	...	...	...	...	...	...	107
7.2	10.0	4.2	0.8	1.0	0.7	5.2	4.9	5.5	.	.	.	3.5	4.3	2.6	108
4.6	5.6	3.6	3.2	4.0	2.4	1.1	1.2	1.0	.	.	.	5.7	6.7	4.6	109
17.0	22.2	10.0	25.3	20.9	31.3	12.1	16.7	7.1	16.2	5.9	25.0	17.3	18.4	16.0	110
12.2	12.9	11.2	11.2	12.4	9.9	6.3	6.3	6.4	.	.	.	12.6	15.6	9.6	111
6.3	7.5	5.1	4.4	5.3	3.4	2.4	2.7	2.1	.	.	.	6.7	7.7	5.7	112
4.0	4.8	3.1	2.7	3.6	1.8	0.9	1.0	0.7	.	.	.	5.6	6.6	4.6	113
6.1**	7.2**	4.9**	3.9**	4.6**	3.1**	1.8**	2.3**	1.3**	.	.	.	8.0**	9.2**	6.7**	114

Table 6 (continued)

	Country or territory	Duration[1] of primary education 2001	Grade 1 Total	Grade 1 Male	Grade 1 Female	Grade 2 Total	Grade 2 Male	Grade 2 Female	Grade 3 Total	Grade 3 Male	Grade 3 Female
115	Peru[w]	6	6.0	6.2	5.8	17.7	18.1	17.4	14.5	14.8	14.2
116	Saint Kitts and Nevis	7	1.9	1.2	2.6	1.9	1.3	2.5	1.8	2.2	1.5
117	Saint Lucia	7	5.4	5.7	5.1	1.4	2.2	0.6	1.2	1.7	0.8
118	Saint Vincent and the Grenadines	7	–	–	–	–	–	–	–	–	–
119	Suriname	6	...	...	...	...	...	...	...	...	...
120	Trinidad and Tobago	7	10.7**	12.1**	9.1**	6.6**	7.6**	5.5**	6.2**	7.4**	4.9**
121	Turks and Caicos Islands	6	3.1	5.1	1.5	5.4	4.9	5.9	3.9	5.9	1.5
122	Uruguay[w]	6	18.6	21.4	15.6	11.3	12.8	9.7	8.5	10.0	7.0
123	Venezuela	6	12.6**	14.3**	10.7**	9.6**	11.5**	7.5**	9.5**	11.8**	7.1**
	North America and Western Europe										
124	Andorra	6	...	...	...	...	...	...	...	...	...
125	Austria[o]	4	1.8**,y	2.1**,y	1.5**,y	1.7**,y	1.9**,y	1.5**,y	1.4**,y	1.7**,y	1.1**,y
126	Belgium[o]	6	...	...	...	...	...	...	...	...	...
127	Canada[o]	6	...	...	...	...	...	...	...	...	...
128	Cyprus[o]	6	...	...	...	...	...	...	...	...	...
129	Denmark[o]	6	.	.	.	.	.	.	.	.	.
130	Finland[o]	6	0.8	1.0	0.6	0.9	1.2	0.7	0.4	0.6	0.3
131	France[o]	5	5.6[x]	5.5**,x	5.6**,x	6.2[x]	6.2**,x	6.2**,x	3.1[x]	3.1**,x	3.1**,x
132	Germany[o]	4	1.7	1.8	1.6	2.2	2.4	2.1	1.7	1.8	1.5
133	Greece[o]	6	...	...	...	...	...	...	...	...	...
134	Iceland[o]	7	–	–	–	–	–	–	–	–	–
135	Ireland[o]	8	1.1	1.2	1.0	2.3	2.6	2.0	1.8	2.0	1.5
136	Israel[o]	6	...	...	...	...	...	...	...	...	...
137	Italy[o]	5	0.4	0.5	0.3	0.3	0.4	0.2	0.2	0.3	0.2
138	Luxembourg[o]	6	6.7**	7.4**	5.8**	5.1**	6.1**	4.1**	6.6**	8.1**	5.1**
139	Malta[o]	6	0.8	1.0	0.5	0.8	0.7	0.8	0.7	0.8	0.5
140	Monaco	5	...	...	...	...	...	...	...	...	...
141	Netherlands[o]	6	.	.	.	.	.	.	.	.	.
142	Norway[o]	7	...	...	...	...	...	...	...	...	...
143	Portugal[o]	6	...	...	...	...	...	...	...	...	...
144	San Marino	5	...	...	...	...	...	...	...	...	...
145	Spain[o]	6	...	...	...	...	...	...	...	...	...
146	Sweden[o]	6	...	...	...	...	...	...	...	...	...
147	Switzerland[o]	6	1.1	1.1	1.1	2.3	2.3	2.3	2.4	2.5	2.3
148	United Kingdom[o]	6	...	...	...	...	...	...	...	...	...
149	United States[o]	6	...	...	...	...	...	...	...	...	...
	South and West Asia										
150	Afghanistan	6	...	...	...	...	...	...	...	...	...
151	Bangladesh	5	6.3	6.5	6.1	5.6	5.8	5.3	8.0	7.6	8.4
152	Bhutan	7	14.8	15.5	14.0	13.7	14.4	12.9	14.0	14.8	13.1
153	India[w]	5	3.5	3.5	3.6	2.7	2.6	2.8	3.9	3.8	4.1
154	Iran, Islamic Republic of	5	7.2	8.0	6.4	4.9	6.1	3.6	3.1	3.9	2.2
155	Maldives	7	–	–	–	...	...	...	...	...	...
156	Nepal	5	39.9	40.1	39.6	17.1	16.7	17.5	12.4	12.5	12.4
157	Pakistan	5	...	...	...	...	...	...	...	...	...
158	Sri Lanka[w]	5	...	...	...	...	...	...	...	...	...
	Sub-Saharan Africa										
159	Angola	4	...	...	...	...	...	...	...	...	...
160	Benin	6	15.5**	15.2**	15.9**	15.6**	15.4**	16.0**	29.4**	29.1**	29.7**
161	Botswana	7	4.1	4.7	3.4	2.2	2.6	1.8	2.1	2.6	1.6
162	Burkina Faso	6	11.7**	11.8**	11.6**	12.8**	13.1**	12.5**	17.1**	...	...
163	Burundi	6	27.1	26.6	27.7	26.8	26.7	26.8	25.0	24.6	25.5
164	Cameroon	6	24.2**	24.8**	23.4**	21.5**	22.7**	20.2**	30.7**	31.3**	30.0**
165	Cape Verde	6	.	.	.	27.8	31.1	24.1	.	.	.
166	Central African Republic	6	...	...	...	...	...	...	...	...	...
167	Chad	6	30.8**	31.0**	30.6**	26.7**	...	...	25.4**	...	...
168	Comoros	6	34.5**	35.3**	33.5**	29.8**	31.8**	27.3**	30.4**	33.2**	27.2**
169	Congo	6	28.0**	28.1**	28.0**	...	...	...	...	...	...
170	Côte d'Ivoire	6	21.1	20.6**	21.7**	19.3	18.8	19.8	21.8	20.8	23.0

1. Duration in this table is defined according to ISCED97 and may differ from that reported nationally.

(x) Data are for 1998/1999.
(y) Data are for 1999/2000.
(z) Data on the percentage of repeaters all grades are for 2000/2001.

STATISTICAL ANNEX / 299

Table 6

REPETITION RATES BY GRADE IN PRIMARY EDUCATION (%), 2000 / REPEATERS, ALL GRADES (%)

	Grade 4			Grade 5			Grade 6			Grade 7			2001			
	Total	Male	Female	Total	Male	Female	Total	Male	Female	Total	Male	Female	Total	Male	Female	
	10.7	10.9	10.4	8.5	8.8	8.2	3.9	4.0	3.7	.	.	.	10.7	10.9	10.4	115
	1.3	1.1	1.5	1.4	0.6	2.4	1.6	1.4	1.8	2.0	2.5	1.5	1.8	1.5	2.1	116
	0.9	1.1	0.6	0.9	1.0	0.8	3.0	3.6	2.4	4.1	4.9	3.3	2.5	3.0	2.0	117
	–	–	–	–	–	–	–	–	–				–	–	–	118
	...	...	...	...	...	...	...	...	...	...	...	...	11.4**,z	...	...	119
	5.3**	6.4**	4.0**	6.9**	8.2**	5.6**	7.0**	8.4**	5.5**	1.8**	1.5**	2.1**	6.3**	7.4**	5.2**	120
	3.6	6.9	0.5	3.1	1.9	4.4	17.2	20.3	13.2	.	.	.	6.8	8.8	4.8	121
	6.3	7.6	5.0	5.2	6.4	4.0	2.3	2.8	1.9	.	.	.	9.0	10.5	7.4	122
	7.1**	8.8**	5.3**	4.7**	6.0**	3.5**	1.8**	2.2**	1.4**	.	.	.	7.7	9.3	5.9	123
	...	...	...	...	...	...	...	...	...	...	...	...	–	–	–	124
	1.2**,y	1.4**,y	1.0**,y	...	...	...	...	...	...	...	...	...	1.5**,z	1.8**,z	1.3**,z	125
	...	...	...	...	...	...	...	...	...	...	...	...	...	...	...	126
	...	...	...	...	...	...	...	...	...	...	...	...	0.3	0.3	0.2	128
	.	.	.	.	.	.	.	.	.	.	.	.	.	.	.	129
	0.3	0.4	0.1	0.2	0.3	0.1	0.2	0.3	0.1	.	.	.	0.5	0.6	0.3	130
	2.5 x	2.5**,x	2.5**,x	3.4 x	3.4**,x	3.4**,x	.	.	.	.	.	.	4.2 y	4.2**,y	4.2**,y	131
	1.1	1.3	1.0	...	...	...	...	...	...	...	...	...	1.7	1.9	1.6	132
	...	...	...	...	...	...	...	...	...	...	...	...	...	...	...	133
	–	–	–	–	–	–	–	–	–	–	–	–	–	–	–	134
	1.1	1.3	0.9	0.8	0.8	0.7	0.8	0.7	0.8	0.6	0.5	0.6	1.2	1.4	1.1	135
	...	...	...	...	...	...	...	...	...	...	...	...	1.7	2.1	1.2	136
	0.2	0.3	0.1	0.3	0.4	0.3	.	.	.	.	.	.	0.3	0.4	0.2	137
	4.0**	4.8**	3.2**	4.1**	5.2**	3.0**	0.4**	0.5**	0.4**	.	.	.	4.5**	5.4**	3.7**	138
	0.8	0.8	0.9	0.7	0.8	0.7	8.6	9.9	7.2	.	.	.	2.3	2.6	2.0	139
	...	...	...	...	...	...	...	...	...	...	...	...	–	–	–	140
	.	.	.	.	.	.	.	.	.	.	.	.	.	.	.	141
	...	...	...	...	...	...	...	...	...	...	...	...	...	...	...	142
	...	...	...	...	...	...	...	...	...	...	...	...	...	...	...	143
	...	...	...	...	...	...	...	...	...	...	...	...	...	...	...	144
	...	...	...	...	...	...	...	...	...	...	...	...	...	...	...	145
	...	...	...	...	...	...	...	...	...	...	...	...	...	...	...	146
	2.1	2.3	1.8	1.8	2.3	1.4	1.1	1.3	0.8	.	.	.	1.7	1.8	1.6	147
	...	...	...	...	...	...	...	...	...	...	...	...	...	...	...	148
	...	...	...	...	...	...	...	...	...	...	...	...	...	...	...	149
	...	...	...	...	...	...	...	...	...	...	...	...	...	...	...	150
	6.6	7.3	5.9	5.1	6.0	4.2	.	.	.	.	.	.	6.4	6.7	6.0	151
	11.5	12.5	10.4	15.0	15.6	14.4	11.9	11.6	12.2	11.8	11.0	12.8	12.9	13.5	12.3	152
	4.2	4.2	4.2	4.5	4.6	4.4	.	.	.	.	.	.	3.7	3.7	3.7	153
	3.5	4.6	2.4	1.9	2.5	1.3	.	.	.	.	.	.	4.3	5.2	3.3	154
	...	...	...	...	...	...	...	...	...	...	...	...	...	...	...	155
	12.8	12.8	12.7	9.0	9.0	8.9	.	.	.	.	.	.	21.6	21.8	21.4	156
	...	...	...	...	...	...	...	...	...	...	...	...	...	...	...	157
	...	...	...	...	...	...	...	...	...	...	...	...	0.8	...	...	158
	...	...	...	...	...	...	...	...	...	...	...	...	29.0**,y	29.0**,y	29.0**,y	159
	22.7**	21.6**	24.4**	30.4**	29.5**	32.0**	26.8**	26.9**	26.5**	.	.	.	20.1**	20.1**	20.1**	160
	10.5	12.8	8.1	1.5	1.8	1.1	1.1	1.4	0.8	0.2	0.2	0.1	3.2	4.0	2.5	161
	15.8**	...	...	18.2**	...	...	38.4**	37.2**	40.2**	.	.	.	17.6**	17.5**	17.7**	162
	24.4	24.0	25.0	33.7	32.3	35.5	42.7	42.0	43.5	.	.	.	26.3	25.6	27.2	163
	23.6**	24.1**	23.0**	27.5**	27.9**	26.9**	27.4**	29.2**	25.5**	.	.	.	25.2*	25.9*	24.4*	164
	24.4	26.9	21.7	.	.	.	16.7	18.3	15.0	.	.	.	13.3	15.1	11.4	165
	...	...	...	...	...	...	...	...	...	...	...	...	...	...	...	166
	23.3**	...	...	18.2**	...	...	26.0**	...	...	.	.	.	25.5**	25.3**	25.9**	167
	27.6**	29.7**	24.9**	26.6**	28.0**	25.0**	29.5**	32.4**	26.1**	.	.	.	28.0	29.3	26.3	168
	...	...	...	...	...	...	...	...	...	...	...	...	24.8**	25.1**	24.4**	169
	21.9	23.5	19.7	23.1	22.2	24.4	38.8	39.6	37.5	.	.	.	23.3**	23.1**	23.7**	170

Table 6 (continued)

	Country or territory	Duration[1] of primary education 2001	Grade 1 Total	Grade 1 Male	Grade 1 Female	Grade 2 Total	Grade 2 Male	Grade 2 Female	Grade 3 Total	Grade 3 Male	Grade 3 Female
171	Democratic Rep. of the Congo	6	...	...	...	...	...	...	...	...	...
172	Equatorial Guinea	5	48.1**	44.6**	51.7**	40.2**	38.1**	42.3**	33.6**	32.8**	34.4**
173	Eritrea	5	25.4	25.2	25.6	15.0	15.2	14.7	17.6	17.3	17.9
174	Ethiopia	6	17.3	16.0	18.9	7.9	7.0	9.0	7.1	6.3	8.4
175	Gabon	6	50.3	51.3	49.1	35.0	35.8	34.1	39.6	41.1	38.1
176	Gambia	6	...	...	...	...	...	...	...	...	...
177	Ghana	6	8.0y	8.1y	7.8y	5.1y	5.2y	4.9y	4.6y	4.7y	4.5y
178	Guinea	6	23.3	22.2	24.6	19.2	16.8	22.5	23.8	21.9	26.4
179	Guinea-Bissau	6	23.9**,x	23.9**,x	23.8**,x	26.9**,x	26.1**,x	28.1**,x	24.4**,x	24.1**,x	24.7**,x
180	Kenya	7	7.2**,y	7.7**,y	6.7**,y	...	...	...	...	...	...
181	Lesotho	7	23.3	24.9	21.4	28.5	31.9	24.8	18.5	21.7	15.2
182	Liberia	6	...	...	...	...	...	...	...	...	...
183	Madagascar	5	37.8	39.0	36.6	29.6	31.1	27.9	31.4	32.4	30.5
184	Malawi	6	19.0	19.3	18.8	17.2	17.4	16.9	15.9	16.2	15.6
185	Mali	6	12.5	12.5	12.5	14.4	14.2	14.7	20.1	19.8	20.5
186	Mauritius	6	–	–	–	–	–	–	–	–	–
187	Mozambique	5	27.1	26.7	27.5	25.8	25.2	26.6	25.8	25.0	27.1
188	Namibia	7	14.9	16.8	12.9	11.9**	14.1**	9.6**	11.6**	14.0**	9.2**
189	Niger	6	1.2	1.1	1.3	5.8	5.7	5.9	7.5	7.1	8.0
190	Nigeria	6	...	...	...	...	...	...	...	...	...
191	Rwanda	6	36.7	37.2	36.2	27.0	27.0	27.1	28.5	28.7	28.3
192	Sao Tome and Principe	6	32.6	34.6	30.2	29.0	30.1	27.7	23.7	23.7	23.6
193	Senegal	6	10.5	10.6	10.5	11.0	10.9	11.1	13.3	13.1	13.4
194	Seychelles	6	.	.	.	.	.	.	.	.	.
195	Sierra Leone	6	...	...	...	...	...	...	...	...	...
196	Somalia	7	...	...	...	...	...	...	...	...	...
197	South Africa	7	8.4y	9.5y	7.1y	7.3y	8.3y	6.1y	8.7y	10.3y	7.0y
198	Swaziland	7	19.3	22.0	16.3	16.8	19.7	13.4	18.5	21.5	15.1
199	Togo	6	29.7	29.9	29.6	23.6	23.1	24.1	25.6	24.7	26.6
200	Uganda	7	...	...	...	...	...	...	...	...	...
201	United Republic of Tanzania	7	3.5	3.4	3.5	2.4	2.4	2.4	2.6	2.5	2.6
202	Zambia	7	4.0**	4.1**	4.0**	4.9**	4.9**	4.8**	5.1**	5.2**	5.0**
203	Zimbabwe[w]	7	.	.	.	.	.	.	.	.	.

I	World[2]	...	6.5	6.9	5.9	5.4	5.5	5.3	5.2	6.1	4.3
II	Countries in transition	...	0.2	0.2	0.2	0.3	0.4	0.2	0.3	0.4	0.2
III	Developed countries	...	1.4	1.7	1.1	1.5	1.9	1.1	1.4	1.8	1.0
IV	Developing countries	...	10.7	12.1	9.1	7.9	8.2	7.8	7.7	7.4	8.2
V	Arab States	...	6.8	7.0	6.4	6.2	7.5	4.8	6.5	7.9	5.0
VI	Central and Eastern Europe	...	1.4	1.6	1.2	1.0	1.1	0.8	0.9	1.0	0.7
VII	Central Asia	...	0.2	0.2	0.2	0.3	0.5	0.1	0.3	0.3	0.3
VIII	East Asia and the Pacific	...	...	...	...	...	...	...	...	...	...
IX	Latin America and the Caribbean	...	10.0	11.3	8.6	6.2	6.9	5.5	6.2	7.4	4.9
X	North America and Western Europe	...	...	...	...	...	...	...	...	...	...
XI	South and West Asia	...	7.2	8.0	6.4	5.6	5.8	5.3	8.0	7.6	8.4
XII	Sub-Saharan Africa	...	22.2	21.4	23.1	19.2	16.8	22.5	20.9	20.3	21.7

1. Duration in this table is defined according to ISCED97 and may differ from that reported nationally.
2. All values shown are medians.

(x) Data are for 1998/1999.
(y) Data are for 1999/2000.
(z) Data on the percentage of repeaters all grades are for 2000/2001.

STATISTICAL ANNEX / 301

Table 6

REPETITION RATES BY GRADE IN PRIMARY EDUCATION (%), 2000 | REPEATERS, ALL GRADES (%)

Grade 4 Total	Grade 4 Male	Grade 4 Female	Grade 5 Total	Grade 5 Male	Grade 5 Female	Grade 6 Total	Grade 6 Male	Grade 6 Female	Grade 7 Total	Grade 7 Male	Grade 7 Female	2001 Total	2001 Male	2001 Female	
...	...	...	...	...	...	...	...	...	...	...	...	...	...	...	171
32.5**	33.0**	32.0**	33.5**	32.0**	35.0**	.	.	.	.	.	.	40.5	38.1	43.1	172
20.1	19.5	20.9	13.6	13.7	13.5	.	.	.	.	.	.	17.5	17.1	18.0	173
9.3	8.0	11.4	8.8	7.1	11.9	5.5	4.6	7.3	.	.	.	8.1	7.3	9.3	174
...	...	...	...	...	...	...	...	...	...	...	...	34.4	35.1	33.7	175
...	...	...	...	...	...	...	...	...	...	...	...	7.7 z	8.0 z	7.4 z	176
4.1 y	4.3 y	4.0 y	3.6 y	3.8 y	3.5 y	3.8 y	4.0 y	3.5 y	.	.	.	6.9	7.0	6.8	177
22.5	20.4	25.5	23.0	21.2	26.0	.	.	.	.	.	.	20.8	19.7	22.4	178
23.9**,x	23.2**,x	25.0**,x	20.6**,x	20.5**,x	20.7**,x	27.9**,x	26.8**,x	29.7**,x	.	.	.	24.0 y	23.6 y	24.5 y	179
...	...	...	...	...	...	...	...	...	...	...	...	...	...	...	180
20.0	23.3	16.8	15.8	18.0	13.8	12.0	13.0	11.1	11.3	11.5	11.1	19.7	22.1	17.3	181
...	...	...	...	...	...	...	...	...	...	...	...	...	...	...	182
25.0	25.2	24.7	22.5	22.5	22.6	.	.	.	.	.	.	30.5	31.5	29.4	183
12.1	12.3	11.9	9.2	8.7	10.0	8.5	8.2	8.9	.	.	.	14.4	14.4	14.4	184
24.4	23.3	26.1	30.1	28.4	32.6	30.8	28.9	34.0	.	.	.	19.3	19.0	19.7	185
–	–	–	–	–	–	21.7**	24.2**	19.0**	.	.	.	4.3**	4.9**	3.7**	186
22.4	21.4	23.8	20.2	19.5	21.2	.	.	.	.	.	.	22.9	22.5	23.4	187
12.4**	14.6**	10.2**	19.0**	20.9**	17.0**	11.3**	12.1**	10.5**	...	...	...	13.0**	14.8**	11.3**	188
10.1	9.8	10.6	12.7	12.0	13.6	34.5	34.3	34.8	.	.	.	8.6	8.5	8.8	189
...	...	...	...	...	...	...	...	...	...	...	...	6.4**	6.7**	6.0**	190
31.3	30.7	31.8	32.4	31.3	33.4	29.6	28.4	31.1	.	.	.	36.1	36.0	36.2	191
18.2	18.7	17.7	18.5**	18.9**	18.2**	35.6**	37.1**	34.1**	.	.	.	25.8**	27.0**	24.5**	192
12.6	12.4	12.8	15.3	14.8	15.8	26.1	25.2	27.2	.	.	.	13.7	13.7	13.6	193
.	.	.	.	.	.	.	.	.	.	.	.	.	.	.	194
...	...	...	...	...	...	...	...	...	...	...	...	...	...	...	195
...	...	...	...	...	...	...	...	...	...	...	...	...	...	...	196
10.5 y	12.3 y	8.5 y	9.7 y	11.9 y	7.5 y	7.1 y	7.9 y	6.2 y	5.6 y	6.4 y	4.9 y	8.8 z	10.2 z	7.4 z	197
17.0	19.2	14.8	16.3	17.4	15.2	15.4	15.4	15.3	9.2	10.4	8.0	16.7	18.9	14.4	198
21.0	20.1	22.2	20.8	19.9	22.2	12.6	11.6	14.2	.	.	.	22.5	21.9	23.2	199
...	...	...	...	...	...	...	...	...	...	...	...	...	...	...	200
8.8	8.6	8.9	0.1	0.1	0.1	0.0	0.0	0.0	0.0	0.0	0.0	2.5	2.5	2.6	201
6.3**	6.4**	6.2**	6.3**	6.5**	6.2**	7.2**	7.4**	6.9**	12.9**	13.8**	11.7**	6.2**	6.5**	5.9**	202
.	.	.	.	.	.	.	.	.	.	.	.	.	.	.	203

5.3	6.4	4.0	...	...	...	...	...	...	...	...	...	5.6	6.6	4.6	I
0.3	0.3	0.2	...	...	...	...	...	...	...	...	...	0.3	...	...	II
1.1	1.3	0.9	...	...	...	...	...	...	...	...	...	1.7	1.8	1.6	III
7.5	8.9	6.1	6.3	6.5	6.2	5.8	6.7	4.8	...	...	...	7.7	9.3	5.9	IV
6.6	6.7	6.5	9.5	10.9	7.9	7.9	9.3	5.5	...	...	...	7.7	8.9	6.4	V
1.0	1.3	0.7	...	...	...	...	...	...	...	...	...	1.1	1.1	1.1	VI
0.3	0.3	0.2	...	...	...	...	...	...	...	...	...	0.3	0.3	0.3	VII
...	...	...	...	...	...	...	...	...	...	...	...	...	...	...	VIII
5.3	6.4	4.0	3.2	4.0	2.4	2.6	3.3	2.0	...	...	...	6.2	7.4	5.2	IX
...	...	...	...	...	...	...	...	...	...	...	...	...	...	...	X
6.6	7.3	5.9	5.1	6.0	4.2	...	...	...	...	...	...	5.3	5.9	4.7	XI
20.6	19.8	21.5	18.5	18.9	18.2	23.8	...	...	...	...	...	19.5	20.5	18.5	XII

Table 7
Internal efficiency: dropout and survival in primary education

DROPOUT RATES BY GRADE IN PRIMARY EDUCATION (%), 2000

	Country or territory	Duration[1] of primary education 2001	Grade 1 Total	Grade 1 Male	Grade 1 Female	Grade 2 Total	Grade 2 Male	Grade 2 Female	Grade 3 Total	Grade 3 Male	Grade 3 Female	Grade 4 Total	Grade 4 Male	Grade 4 Female	Grade 5 Total	Grade 5 Male	Grade 5 Female
	Arab States																
1	Algeria	6	1.1	1.0	1.2	0.6	0.9	0.2	0.8	1.3	0.2	1.2	1.4	1.0	2.3	2.9	1.6
2	Bahrain	6	–	–	–	–	–	–	–	–	–	–	–	–	0.5**	0.7**	0.4**
3	Djibouti	6	2.3	2.7	1.9	3.5	3.9	2.8	1.9	0.8	3.4	4.3**	2.6**	6.4**	–	–	–
4	Egypt[w]	5	0.7**	–	1.9**	0.2**	–	1.5**	0.0**	0.8**	–	0.1**	1.7**	–	.	.	.
5	Iraq	6	10.1**,x	9.4**,x	10.9**,x	7.6**,x	6.9**,x	8.5**,x	5.8**,x	5.9**,x	5.7**,x	11.8**,x	10.3**,x	13.8**,x	19.1**,x	17.8**,x	20.9**,x
6	Jordan[w]	6	...	...	...	...	...	...	...	...	...	...	...	...	...	...	...
7	Kuwait	4	0.9	0.5	1.4	–	–	–	0.6	0.3	1.0	...	...	...			
8	Lebanon	6	1.4	1.5	1.4	0.8	1.1	0.5	0.9	1.2	0.5	2.5	3.2	1.7	3.0	4.0	2.0
9	Libyan Arab Jamahiriya	6	...	...	...	...	...	...	...	...	...	...	...	...	...	...	...
10	Mauritania	6	6.8	7.8	5.9	10.9	11.3	10.4	13.2	13.3	13.1	17.5	17.7	17.4	22.4	22.9	21.7
11	Morocco	6	3.7	2.7	4.7	3.6**	4.7**	2.5**	3.7**	3.2**	4.2**	3.9**	3.8**	4.0**	6.3**	6.3**	6.4**
12	Oman	6	1.2	1.4	1.0	0.5	0.5	0.5	0.5	0.3	0.7	1.4	1.5	1.3	1.1	1.2	0.9
13	Palestinian A. T.	4	1.6	2.2	0.9	0.1	–	0.4	0.5	0.6	0.3	...	...	...			
14	Qatar	6	...	...	...	...	...	...	...	...	...	...	...	...	...	...	...
15	Saudi Arabia	6	2.6**	2.7**	2.6**	0.5	0.3	0.7	1.3	1.7	0.9	1.2	0.9	1.6	1.9	1.7	2.0
16	Sudan	6	2.4**,x	1.7**,x	3.2**,x	5.0**,x	6.1**,x	3.6**,x	3.8**,x	5.9**,x	1.1**,x	3.9**,x	4.9**,x	2.7**,x	7.3**,x	7.7**,x	6.9**,x
17	Syrian Arab Republic	6	1.3	1.0	1.6	1.0	0.9	1.1	1.8	1.8	1.8	3.2	3.1	3.5	4.3	3.6	5.0
18	Tunisia[w]	6	0.8	0.7	0.8	0.7	0.6	0.8	1.1	1.2	1.0	1.6	1.8	1.5	3.1	3.4	2.7
19	United Arab Emirates	6	3.0	3.0	3.1	0.3	0.8	–	–	–	–	0.0	0.2	–	1.6	2.0	1.1
20	Yemen	6	9.2**,y	8.4**,y	10.3**,y	3.4**,y	5.2**,y	0.6**,y	–	–	–	3.4**,y	4.5**,y	1.0**,y	1.6**,y	3.6**,y	–
	Central and Eastern Europe																
21	Albania[o]	4	0.9[y]	2.0[y]	–	3.2[y]	5.5[y]	0.6[y]	5.9[y]	6.0[y]	5.8[y]	.	.	.	.	.	.
22	Belarus	4	–	–	–	–	–	–	–	–	–	.	.	.			
23	Bosnia and Herzegovina[o]	4	...	...	...	...	...	...	...	...	...	.	.	.			
24	Bulgaria[o]	4	3.6	3.9	3.4	2.3	2.2	2.3	1.4	1.3	1.5	.	.	.			
25	Croatia	4	0.2	0.3	0.0	–	–	–	0.0	–	0.2	.	.	.			
26	Czech Republic[o]	5	1.5**	1.7**	1.3**	0.6**	0.8**	0.4**	0.6**	0.6**	0.6**	0.6**	0.8**	0.5**	.	.	.
27	Estonia[o]	6	0.1	0.3	–	0.7	1.1	0.4	0.4	0.3	0.5	0.1	0.0	0.1	0.2	–	0.5
28	Hungary[o]	4	2.5	3.5	1.4	0.7	0.3	1.0	–	–	–	.	.	.			
29	Latvia[o]	4	2.2	2.6	1.9	0.2	–	1.0	0.6	0.5	0.8	.	.	.			
30	Lithuania[o]	4	0.6	0.5	0.8	0.6	0.5	0.6	0.5	1.0	–	.	.	.			
31	Poland[o]	6	0.6	0.7**	0.5**	0.3	0.3**	0.2**	0.3	0.1**	0.5**	0.3	0.3**	0.4**	0.4	0.4**	0.3**
32	Republic of Moldova	4	6.9	7.6	6.1	1.6	2.0	1.2	1.6	0.9	2.3	.	.	.			
33	Romania[o]	4	2.1	2.3	2.0	1.0	1.2	0.7	1.0	1.0	0.9	.	.	.			
34	Russian Federation[w]	3	0.9	–	–	–	–	–	...	...	...						
35	Serbia and Montenegro	4	...	...	...	...	...	...	...	...	...	.	.	.			
36	Slovakia	4	1.3	1.9	0.6	0.3	0.4	0.2	0.0	–	0.2	.	.	.			
37	Slovenia[o]	4	1.1	1.2	1.0	–	–	–	0.3	0.1	0.6	.	.	.			
38	TFYR Macedonia[o]	4	0.9	1.2	0.5	0.7	0.9	0.5	0.9	1.4	0.4	.	.	.			
39	Turkey[o]	6	...	...	...	...	...	...	...	...	...	...	...	...	...	...	...
40	Ukraine	4	...	...	...	...	...	...	...	...	...	.	.	.			
	Central Asia																
41	Armenia	3	2.6	2.2	2.9	1.7	1.9	1.6	.	.	.						
42	Azerbaijan	4	0.7	1.9	–	1.1	1.6	0.6	0.9	0.6	1.2	.	.	.			
43	Georgia	4	2.4	3.0	1.9	2.3	1.8	2.8	1.6	1.3	1.8	.	.	.			
44	Kazakhstan	4	1.3	1.2	1.4	2.0	2.0	2.0	2.1	2.2	1.9	.	.	.			
45	Kyrgyzstan	4	3.8	3.3	4.2	1.8	2.2	1.4	3.4	3.4	3.4	.	.	.			
46	Mongolia	4	6.5	7.0	6.0	2.9	3.3	2.5	2.4	3.1	1.7	.	.	.			
47	Tajikistan	4	–	0.7	–	0.8	1.9	–	0.4	1.4	–	.	.	.			
48	Turkmenistan	4	...	...	...	...	...	...	...	...	...						
49	Uzbekistan	4	...	...	...	...	...	...	...	...	...	.	.	.			
	East Asia and the Pacific																
50	Australia[o]	7	...	...	...	...	...	...	...	...	...	...	...	...	...	...	...
51	Brunei Darussalam	6	...	...	...	...	...	...	...	...	...	...	...	...	...	...	...
52	Cambodia	6	8.9	8.3	9.5	7.2	7.0	7.5	6.1	6.1	6.0	7.6	7.2	8.0	9.3	8.2	10.6
53	China[w]	5	–	–	–	–	–	–	–	0.4**	–	2.1	1.6**	2.7**	.	.	.

1. Duration in this table is defined according to ISCED97 and may differ from that reported nationally.
(x) Data are for 1998/1999.
(y) Data are for 1999/2000.

STATISTICAL ANNEX / 303

Table 7

Grade 6				DROPOUTS, ALL GRADES (%)				SURVIVAL RATE TO GRADE 5 (%)				SURVIVAL RATE TO LAST GRADE (%)				TRANSITION TO SECONDARY EDUCATION (%)					
			2000			2000			2000			2000				
Total	Male	Female	Total	Male	Female	Total	Male	Female	Total	Male	Female	Total	Male	Female	GPI (F/M)	
.	.	.	6.5	8.5	4.4	96.0	94.8	97.3	93.5	91.5	95.6	78.9	75.8	82.5	1.09	1
.	.	.	…	…	…	99.1**	100.0**	98.1**	…	…	…	98.0**	96.1**	100.0**	1.04**	2
.	.	.	…	…	…	87.7**	89.6**	85.2**	…	…	…	48.9**	51.3**	45.3**	0.88**	3
.	.	.	1.1**	1.3**	0.9**	98.9**	98.7**	99.1**	98.9**	98.7**	99.1**	86.4**	80.4**	93.4**	1.16**	4
.	.	.	50.6**,x	48.7**,x	52.8**,x	65.6**,x	67.4**,x	63.3**,x	49.4**,x	51.3**,x	47.2**,x	72.6**,x	78.9**,x	64.2**,x	0.81**,x	5
…	…	…	…	…	…	…	…	…	…	…	…	…	…	…	…	6
.	.	.	1.5	0.8	2.2	.	.	.	98.5	99.2	97.8	97.8	97.9	97.7	1.00	7
.	.	.	9.2	11.8	6.4	94.0	92.3	95.7	90.8	88.2	93.6	86.0	83.2	89.0	1.07	8
…	…	…	…	…	…	…	…	…	…	…	…	…	…	…	…	9
.	.	.	59.6	60.6	58.5	54.7	53.7	55.8	40.4	39.4	41.5	39.6**	40.9**	38.1**	0.93**	10
.	.	.	22.2**	22.1**	22.4**	83.7**	84.0**	83.4**	77.8**	77.9**	77.6**	81.8**	80.9**	82.9**	1.02**	11
.	.	.	4.8	5.2	4.5	96.2	96.1	96.4	95.2	94.8	95.5	97.9	97.3	98.6	1.01	12
.	.	.	2.1	2.5	1.6	.	.	.	97.9	97.5	98.4	96.6**	96.8**	96.3**	0.99**	13
…	…	…	…	…	…	…	…	…	…	…	…	95.5**,y	91.4**,y	100.0**,y	1.09**,y	14
.	.	.	7.8	7.7	7.9	94.0	94.1	94.0	92.2	92.3	92.1	97.0	100.0	93.6	0.94	15
.	.	.	22.9**,x	26.4**,x	18.5**,x	84.1**,x	80.7**,x	88.4**,x	77.1**,x	73.6**,x	81.5**,x	83.4	83.9	82.8	0.99	16
.	.	.	11.7	10.5	12.9	92.4	92.9	91.8	88.3	89.5	87.1	72.3	73.9	70.4	0.95	17
.	.	.	7.9	8.6	7.2	95.5	95.2	95.7	92.1	91.4	92.8	90.8**	90.1**	91.6**	1.02**	18
.	.	.	4.1	4.6	3.6	97.5	97.4	97.5	95.9	95.4	96.4	97.5	95.8	99.5	1.04	19
.	.	.	15.5**,y	21.3**,y	2.6**,y	86.0**,y	81.9**,y	94.2**,y	84.5**,y	78.7**,y	97.4**,y	90.1**,y	87.8**,y	96.0**,y	1.09**,y	20
.	.	.	10.0 y	13.5 y	6.2 y	.	.	.	90.0 y	86.5 y	93.8 y	94.0 y	93.2 y	94.9 y	1.02 y	21
.	.	.	…	…	…	.	.	.	…	…	…	…	…	…	…	22
…	…	…	…	…	…	.	.	.	…	…	…	…	…	…	…	23
.	.	.	7.3	7.4	7.2	.	.	.	92.7	92.6	92.8	96.2	96.1	96.2	1.00	24
.	.	.	0.1	0.0	0.3	.	.	.	99.9	100.0	99.7	99.8	99.9	99.8	1.00	25
.	.	.	3.4**	3.9**	2.8**	96.6**	96.1**	97.2**	96.6**	96.1**	97.2**	95.7**	95.1**	96.4**	1.01**	26
.	.	.	1.5	1.6	1.3	98.7	98.3	99.3	98.5	98.4	98.7	96.5	94.7	98.5	1.04	27
.	.	.	1.8	2.4	1.2	.	.	.	98.2	97.6	98.8	99.0	98.1	100.0	1.02	28
.	.	.	3.2	2.7	3.6	.	.	.	96.8	97.3	96.4	98.9	98.8	99.0	1.00	29
.	.	.	1.7	2.1	1.3	.	.	.	98.3	97.9	98.7	99.8**	100.0**	99.6**	1.00**	30
.	.	.	1.8	1.8**	1.9**	98.5	98.7**	98.4**	98.2	98.2**	98.1**	98.7	100.0**	97.3**	0.97**	31
.	.	.	9.9	10.3	9.4	.	.	.	90.1	89.7	90.6	97.5	97.7	97.3	1.00	32
.	.	.	4.2	4.6	3.7	.	.	.	95.8	95.4	96.3	98.2	98.2	98.2	1.00	33
…	…	…	0.2	…	…	.	.	.	99.8	…	…	92.3	…	…	…	34
…	…	…	…	…	…	.	.	.	…	…	…	…	…	…	…	35
.	.	.	1.7	2.3	1.0	.	.	.	98.3	97.7	99.0	98.2	97.9	98.4	1.01	36
.	.	.	0.5	0.6	0.4	.	.	.	99.5	99.4	99.6	99.6	99.6	99.6	1.00	37
.	.	.	2.5	3.4	1.4	.	.	.	97.5	96.6	98.6	98.4	98.4	98.4	1.00	38
…	…	…	…	…	…	…	…	…	…	…	…	…	…	…	…	39
…	…	…	…	…	…	.	.	.	…	…	…	99.7	100.0**	99.5**	0.99**	40
.	.	.	4.3	4.1	4.4	.	.	.	95.7	95.9	95.6	98.0	98.0	98.1	1.00	41
.	.	.	2.6	4.1	1.0	.	.	.	97.4	95.9	99.0	97.9	98.9	97.0	0.98	42
.	.	.	6.2	6.0	6.3	.	.	.	93.8	94.0	93.7	97.6	98.2	96.8	0.99	43
.	.	.	5.2	5.3	5.2	.	.	.	94.8	94.7	94.8	98.8	98.4	99.2	1.01	44
.	.	.	8.7	8.7	8.7	.	.	.	91.3	91.3	91.3	99.5**,y	98.9**,y	100.0**,y	1.01**,y	45
.	.	.	11.5	13.0	10.0	.	.	.	88.5	87.0	90.0	97.2	96.1	98.2	1.02	46
.	.	.	3.5	6.6	–	.	.	.	96.5	93.4	100.0	98.3	…	…	…	47
…	…	…	…	…	…	.	.	.	…	…	…	…	…	…	…	48
…	…	…	…	…	…	.	.	.	…	…	…	…	…	…	…	49
…	…	…	…	…	…	…	…	…	…	…	…	…	…	…	…	50
…	…	…	…	…	…	…	…	…	…	…	…	95.1	95.3	94.9	1.00	51
.	.	.	36.4	35.0	38.0	70.4	71.1	69.6	63.6	65.0	62.0	82.9	86.5	78.3	0.91	52
.	.	.	2.0	–**	4.2**	98.0	100.0**	95.8**	98.0	100.0**	95.8**	…	…	…	…	53

Table 7 (continued)

	Country or territory	Duration[1] of primary education 2001	Grade 1 Total	Grade 1 Male	Grade 1 Female	Grade 2 Total	Grade 2 Male	Grade 2 Female	Grade 3 Total	Grade 3 Male	Grade 3 Female	Grade 4 Total	Grade 4 Male	Grade 4 Female	Grade 5 Total	Grade 5 Male	Grade 5 Female
54	Cook Islands	6	36.2ˣ	...	...	4.3ˣ	2.7ˣ	6.1ˣ	6.0ˣ	2.3ˣ	10.8ˣ	7.3ˣ	10.1ˣ	4.1ˣ	8.9ˣ	10.0ˣ	7.5ˣ
55	DPR Korea	4	...	...	...	...	...	...	...	...	...	...	...	...	...	...	...
56	Fiji	6	...	...	...	...	...	...	...	...	...	...	...	...	...	...	...
57	Indonesiaʷ	6	2.6	3.8	1.3	1.8	2.0	1.6	3.1	3.8	2.5	2.9	3.6	2.2	3.7	3.7	3.7
58	Japanº	6	–	–	–	–	–	–	–	–	–	–	–	–	–	–	–
59	Kiribati	6	...	...	...	...	...	...	...	...	...	...	...	...	...	...	...
60	Lao PDR	5	12.9	13.1	12.7	7.1	7.3	6.8	6.3	6.1	6.6	6.6	6.1	7.2	.	.	.
61	Macao, China	6	...	...	...	...	...	...	...	...	...	...	...	...	...	...	...
62	Malaysiaʷ	6	1.1	0.7	1.5	0.5	0.5	0.6	1.5	0.9	2.1						
63	Marshall Islands	6	–	–	–	–	–	–									
64	Micronesia	6															
65	Myanmar	5	21.0	21.5	20.5	7.3	7.8	6.8	8.3	7.7	8.8	10.4	10.8	10.0	.	.	.
66	Nauru	6															
67	New Zealandº	6	–	–	–	–	–	–	–	–	–	–	–	–	–	–	–
68	Niue	6	–	–	–												
69	Palau	5															
70	Papua New Guinea	6															
71	Philippinesʷ	6	12.5	13.8	11.0	3.2	4.1	2.2	2.2	3.0	1.3	3.5	4.2	2.7	5.0	6.2	3.9
72	Republic of Koreaº	6	–	–	–	...	...	...	...	...	...	...	...	...	...	...	...
73	Samoa	6	5.1	5.6	4.6	0.6	–	2.5	–	–	–	0.8	–	2.0	–	–	–
74	Singapore	6	...	...	...	...	...	...	...	...	...	...	...	...	...	...	...
75	Solomon Islands	6	...	...	...	...	...	...									
76	Thailandʷ	6	–	0.5**,ʸ	–	0.7**,ʸ	2.3**,ʸ	–	–	–	–	–	–	–			
77	Timor-Leste	6	...	...	...									...			
78	Tokelau	6															
79	Tonga	6	6.3**	5.4**	7.3**	3.0**	3.3**	2.6**	3.6**	2.2**	5.0**	5.5**	4.9**	6.1**	–	–	–
80	Tuvalu	6	...	...	...												
81	Vanuatu	6	4.1	5.4	2.6	–	–	0.1	1.5	2.0	0.9	1.4	3.4	–			
82	Viet Nam	5	3.5	3.0	4.0	2.6	2.7	2.5	2.1	1.7	2.5	3.0	2.6	3.4	.	.	.
	Latin America and the Caribbean																
83	Anguilla	7	–	–	–	3.2	2.9	3.4	3.4	1.0	5.8	6.9	7.8	6.0	2.3	3.7	0.9
84	Antigua and Barbuda	7	...	...	...	...	...	...	...	...	...	...	...	...	...	...	...
85	Argentinaʷ	6	2.5	2.9	2.1	1.0	1.4	0.5	1.1	1.5	0.7	2.0	2.4	1.6	2.2	2.8	1.6
86	Aruba	6	1.0	2.0	–	0.9	0.7	1.1	0.9	2.7	–	–	–	–	–	–	–
87	Bahamas	6	...	...	...	...	...	...	...	...	...	...	...	...	...	...	...
88	Barbados	6	2.6	2.4	2.8	0.1	1.0	–	1.4	1.8	1.0	0.7	0.3	1.1	–	–	–
89	Belize	6	11.9ʸ	12.8ʸ	10.8ʸ	0.2ʸ	–	1.0ʸ	1.5ʸ	2.7ʸ	0.1ʸ	3.4ʸ	1.3ʸ	5.5ʸ	2.2ʸ	3.2ʸ	1.1ʸ
90	Bermuda	6															
91	Bolivia	6	9.7	9.8	9.6	3.9	3.7	4.2	5.7	5.5	6.0	4.0	3.3	4.7	4.5	3.0	6.2
92	Brazilʷ	4	6.1	6.7**	5.3**	4.6	6.6**	2.3**	5.8	6.9**	4.6**	...	...	...			
93	British Virgin Islands	7	...	...	...	...	...	...	...	...	...	...	...	...	...	...	...
94	Cayman Islands	6	...	...	...												
95	Chileʷ	6	–	–	–	1.2ʸ	1.5ʸ	0.9ʸ	–	–	–	–	0.1ʸ	–	0.4ʸ	0.9ʸ	–
96	Colombia	5	18.9	20.1	17.7	7.6	8.1	7.1	8.2	8.4	8.1	7.3	7.6	7.0	.	.	.
97	Costa Rica	6	1.8	1.9	1.8	0.7	0.9	0.4	0.6	0.9	0.4	2.7	2.9	2.4	3.2	3.3	3.1
98	Cuba	6	9.4	11.9	6.6	9.8	12.2	7.1	7.5	9.4	5.3	5.4	6.7	4.1	3.4	4.4	2.4
99	Dominica	7	7.3	6.1	8.6	2.3	2.4	2.2	2.2	1.9	2.6	2.8	2.9	2.7	3.9	3.6	4.3
100	Dominican Republic	6	4.7**	5.6**	3.6**	...	...	...	4.4**	1.2**	7.6**	6.9**	7.9**	5.9**	0.7**	0.8**	0.5**
101	Ecuador	6	12.5	12.5	12.4	3.6	3.7	3.4	3.5	3.9	3.1	3.5	3.6	3.4	2.3	2.3	2.3
102	El Salvador	6	16.1**	16.9**	15.3**	7.9**	9.0**	6.8**	4.7**	5.5**	3.8**	4.7**	4.7**	4.8**	4.3**	4.9**	3.6**
103	Grenada	7	7.1**	8.3**	5.8**	–	–	–	–	–	–	–	–	–	–	–	–
104	Guatemala	6	13.9	13.7	14.2	9.8	9.0	10.6	10.6	9.6	11.7	10.7	9.9	11.6	9.3	9.2	9.5
105	Guyana	6	...	...	...	...	...	...	0.3ˣ	0.5ˣ	0.1ˣ	5.1ˣ	3.5ˣ	6.8ˣ	4.8ˣ	7.3ˣ	2.3ˣ
106	Haiti	6															
107	Honduras	6	...	...	...	...	...	...	...	...	...	...	...	...	...	...	...
108	Jamaicaʷ	6	–	–	–	1.6**	1.8**	1.4**	–	–	0.4**	8.2**	9.8**	6.3**	3.4**	4.7**	2.1**
109	Mexicoº	6	3.9	4.2	3.7	0.4	0.5	0.3	2.8	3.0	2.7	1.9	2.1	1.7	1.6	1.9	1.3
110	Montserrat	7	1.6	9.1	–	–	–	–	–	–	–	12.8	7.4	20.0	–	2.3	–
111	Netherlands Antilles	6	4.9	1.8	8.4	2.8	4.8	0.9	...	...	...	–	–	–			
112	Nicaragua	6	18.8	20.4	17.1	11.6	12.8	10.2	8.1	9.2	7.0	13.2	14.1	12.3	4.3	5.2	3.5
113	Panama	6	4.9	4.9	4.8	2.4	2.4	2.5	1.7	1.8	1.6	1.9	2.2	1.5	2.7	2.9	2.4

1. Duration in this table is defined according to ISCED97 and may differ from that reported nationally.

(x) Data are for 1998/1999.
(y) Data are for 1999/2000.

Table 7

	Grade 6		DROPOUTS, ALL GRADES (%) 2000			SURVIVAL RATE TO GRADE 5 (%) 2000			SURVIVAL RATE TO LAST GRADE (%) 2000			TRANSITION TO SECONDARY EDUCATION (%) 2000				
Total	Male	Female	Total	Male	Female	Total	Male	Female	Total	Male	Female	Total	Male	Female	GPI (F/M)	
.	.	.	53.1 x	50.0 x	56.7 x	51.5 x	55.7 x	46.8 x	46.9 x	50.0 x	43.3 x	87.7 x	94.0 x	81.6 x	0.87 x	54
...	...	...	...	...	...	.	.	.	...	...	...	...	...	...	...	55
...	...	...	...	...	...	...	...	...	...	...	...	98.4**	100.0**	96.6**	0.97**	56
.	.	.	14.1	16.7	11.3	89.2	86.6	92.2	85.9	83.3	88.7	79.5**	78.7**	80.4**	1.02**	57
.	.	.	...	...	...	...	...	...	...	...	...	...	...	...	...	58
...	...	...	...	...	...	...	...	...	...	...	...	...	...	...	...	59
.	.	.	37.7	38.1	37.3	62.3	61.9	62.7	62.3	61.9	62.7	77.0	79.5	73.8	0.93	60
...	...	...	...	...	...	...	...	...	...	...	...	85.6	83.2	88.2	1.06	61
...	...	...	...	...	...	...	...	...	...	...	...	99.7	100.0	99.5	0.99	62
.	.	.	...	...	...	...	...	...	...	...	...	...	...	...	...	63
.	.	.	...	...	...	...	...	...	...	...	...	...	...	...	...	64
.	.	.	40.1	40.7	39.5	59.9	59.3	60.5	59.9	59.3	60.5	69.8	72.1	67.3	0.93	65
.	.	.	...	...	...	...	...	...	...	...	...	...	...	...	...	66
.	.	.	...	...	...	...	...	...	...	...	...	...	...	...	...	67
.	.	.	...	...	...	...	...	...	...	...	...	91.5 x	92.0 x	90.9 x	0.99 x	68
.	.	.	...	...	...	...	...	...	...	...	...	...	...	...	...	69
.	.	.	...	...	...	...	...	...	...	...	...	70.4**	70.8**	69.9**	0.99**	70
.	.	.	24.7	28.9	20.2	79.3	75.8	83.1	75.3	71.1	79.8	97.8	98.2	97.4	0.99	71
.	.	.	...	...	...	...	...	...	...	...	...	99.6 y	99.6 y	99.7 y	1.00 y	72
.	.	.	...	...	...	93.8	96.0	91.5	...	...	...	97.5	95.7	99.4	1.04	73
...	...	...	...	...	...	...	...	...	...	...	...	...	...	...	...	74
...	...	...	...	...	...	...	...	...	...	...	...	...	...	...	...	75
.	.	.	...	...	...	...	...	...	...	...	...	91.7**	91.2**	92.2**	1.01**	76
.	.	.	...	...	...	...	...	...	...	...	...	82.1**	...	...	...	77
...	...	...	...	...	...	...	...	...	...	...	...	...	...	...	...	78
.	.	.	...	...	...**	82.9**	85.0**	80.6**	...	...	...	80.3**	80.6**	79.9**	0.99**	79
...	...	...	...	...	...	...	...	...	...	...	...	...	...	...	...	80
.	.	.	...	...	...	95.1	93.4	97.0	...	...	...	42.7	42.0	43.4	1.03	81
.	.	.	11.0	10.0	12.1	89.0	90.0	87.9	89.0	90.0	87.9	94.6	94.8	94.4	1.00	82
2.9	2.9	2.9	13.6	15.7	10.5	91.1	90.1	93.1	86.4	84.3	89.5	97.3	100.0	94.8	0.95	83
...	...	...	...	...	...	...	...	...	...	...	...	...	...	...	...	84
.	.	.	9.1	11.4	6.7	93.1	91.3	94.9	90.9	88.6	93.3	94.1	92.9	95.4	1.03	85
.	.	.	4.8	9.3	–	96.5	93.3	100.0	95.2	90.7	100.0	99.9	99.7	100.0	1.00	86
...	...	...	...	...	...	...	...	...	...	...	...	...	...	...	...	87
.	.	.	...	...	...	95.3	94.7	95.9	...	...	...	98.0	98.5	97.5	0.99	88
.	.	.	20.5 y	21.4 y	19.5 y	81.5 y	81.5 y	81.5 y	79.5 y	78.6 y	80.5 y	85.8 y	83.6 y	88.3 y	1.06 y	89
...	...	...	...	...	...	...	...	...	...	...	...	93.3	87.0**	100.0**	1.15**	90
.	.	.	25.6	23.5	27.8	78.0	78.9	77.1	74.4	76.5	72.2	88.3	87.5	89.2	1.02	91
...	...	...	20.1	24.2**	15.5**	.	.	.	79.9	75.8**	84.5**	84.0	86.3**	81.6**	0.95**	92
...	...	...	...	...	...	...	...	...	...	...	...	65.9**	59.8**	72.3**	1.21**	93
...	...	...	...	...	...	...	...	...	...	...	...	90.8	89.0	92.9	1.04	94
.	.	.	0.5 y	1.0 y	– y	99.9 y	100.0 y	99.9 y	99.5 y	99.0 y	100.0 y	97.5 y	96.8 y	98.3 y	1.02 y	95
.	.	.	39.1	41.0	37.0	60.9	59.0	63.0	60.9	59.0	63.0	89.6	89.4	89.8	1.01	96
.	.	.	9.5	10.5	8.5	93.7	92.8	94.6	90.5	89.5	91.5	82.4	83.3	81.4	0.98	97
.	.	.	31.2	37.8	23.2	...	...	...	68.8	62.2	76.8	95.7	94.3	97.2	1.03	98
–	–	–	15.4	12.8	18.0	85.4	86.6	84.3	84.6	87.2	82.0	92.9	100.0	85.4	0.85	99
.	.	.	27.6**	37.4**	16.7**	72.9**	63.1**	83.8**	72.4**	62.6**	83.3**	85.3**	83.1**	87.4**	1.05**	100
.	.	.	23.8	24.4	23.2	78.0	77.4	78.6	76.2	75.6	76.8	72.8	75.0	70.4	0.94	101
.	.	.	35.8**	38.6**	32.6**	67.2**	64.7**	70.0**	64.2**	61.4**	67.4**	90.8**	89.8**	91.8**	1.02**	102
–	–	–	...	...	...	...	...	...	...	...	...	97.9**	96.0**	100.0**	1.04**	103
.	.	.	49.7	48.1	51.4	55.8	57.5	54.0	50.3	51.9	48.6	92.5	92.8	92.2	0.99	104
.	.	.	7.3 x	4.8 x	10.0 x	94.8 x	100.0 x	89.6 x	92.7 x	95.2 x	90.0 x	67.6 x	64.7 x	70.7 x	1.09 x	105
...	...	...	...	...	...	...	...	...	...	...	...	...	...	...	...	106
...	...	...	...	...	...	...	...	...	...	...	...	...	...	...	...	107
.	.	.	12.8**	16.1**	9.3**	90.3**	88.0**	92.7**	87.2**	83.9**	90.7**	95.2**	100.0**	90.7**	0.91**	108
.	.	.	11.0	12.1	9.9	90.5	89.7	91.3	89.0	87.9	90.1	91.8	93.0	90.5	0.97	109
15.5	10.0	21.4	...	...	...	...	...	...	...	...	...	90.3	100.0	82.1	0.82	110
...	...	...	...	...	...	...	...	...	...	...	...	52.1	38.9	72.8	1.87	111
.	.	.	48.2	52.2	43.8	54.2	50.5	58.3	51.8	47.8	56.2	97.6	100.0	95.5	0.95	112
.	.	.	13.8	14.5	13.0	88.6	88.1	89.2	86.2	85.5	87.0	63.9**	63.1**	64.8**	1.03**	113

306 / ANNEX

Table 7 (continued)

DROPOUT RATES BY GRADE IN PRIMARY EDUCATION (%), 2000

	Country or territory	Duration¹ of primary education 2001	Grade 1 Total	Grade 1 Male	Grade 1 Female	Grade 2 Total	Grade 2 Male	Grade 2 Female	Grade 3 Total	Grade 3 Male	Grade 3 Female	Grade 4 Total	Grade 4 Male	Grade 4 Female	Grade 5 Total	Grade 5 Male	Grade 5 Female
114	Paraguay[w]	6	9.6**	9.9**	9.2**	3.9**	3.9**	4.0**	3.7**	4.0**	3.3**	5.1**	5.3**	4.9**	5.8**	6.1**	5.4**
115	Peru[w]	6	5.5	5.7	5.3	2.7	3.1	2.3	2.8	2.5	3.2	1.9	1.6	2.3	5.5	5.0	6.0
116	Saint Kitts and Nevis	7	11.3	13.9	8.7	4.2	6.0	2.3	–	–	2.2	10.8	16.5	4.2	11.4	10.4	12.6
117	Saint Lucia	7	–	–	–	1.3	–	3.0	0.6	0.4	0.7	1.2	1.5	0.9	3.3	3.8	2.9
118	St Vincent/Grenad.	7	–	–	…	–	–	–	–	–	–	–	–	–	…	…	…
119	Suriname	6	–	–	–	…	…	…	…	…	…	–	–	–	…	…	…
120	Trinidad and Tobago	7	–	–	–	–	–	–	–	–	–	–	–	–	–	–	–
121	Turks and Caicos Islands	6	3.6	–	6.5	6.6	3.1	9.9	–	–	0.7	15.1	5.3	24.4	–	–	–
122	Uruguay[w]	6	3.0	3.0	2.9	3.5	3.6	3.4	1.1	1.4	0.7	3.0	3.4	2.5	2.0	2.1	2.0
123	Venezuela	6	–	1.2**	–	–	–	–	2.1**	2.4**	1.8**	1.3**	1.5**	1.0**	–	–	–

North America and Western Europe

124	Andorra	6	…	…	…	…	…	…	…	…	…	…	…	…	…	…	…
125	Austria[o]	4	…	…	…	…	…	…	…	…	…						
126	Belgium[o]	6	–	–	–	–	–	–	–	–	–	–	–	–	–	–	–
127	Canada[o]	6	–	–	–	–	–	–	–	–	–	–	–	–	–	–	–
128	Cyprus[o]	6	–	–	–	–	–	–	–	–	–	–	–	–	–	–	–
129	Denmark[o]	6	–	–	–	–	–	–	–	–	–	–	–	–	–	–	–
130	Finland[o]	6	–	0.2	–	–	–	–	–	–	0.0	–	–	–	–	–	–
131	France[o]	5	0.1[x]	0.5**,[x]	–**,[x]	1.1[x]	1.3**,[x]	0.9**,[x]	0.2[x]	–**,[x]	0.6**,[x]	0.6[x]	–**,[x]	1.3**,[x]	.	.	.
132	Germany[o]	4	–	0.3	–	–	–	–	0.8	0.8	0.7	.	.	.	.	.	.
133	Greece[o]	6	–	–	–	–	–	–	–	–	–	–	–	–	–	–	–
134	Iceland[o]	7	–	–	–	–	–	–	–	–	–	–	–	–	–	–	–
135	Ireland[o]	8	1.6	2.2	1.0	–	–	–	–	–	–	–	–	–	–	–	–
136	Israel[o]	6	…	…	…	…	…	…	…	…	…	…	…	…	…	…	…
137	Italy[o]	5	–	0.5	–	1.0	0.9	1.1	1.6	1.6	1.5	1.1	1.0	1.1	.	.	.
138	Luxembourg[o]	6	–	–	–	0.1**	–	1.4**	–	–	–	2.6**	3.2**	2.0**	11.1**	11.8**	10.2**
139	Malta[o]	6	0.3	0.3	0.3	0.1	0.1	0.0	–	–	0.0	–	–	–	–	–	0.6
140	Monaco	5	…	…	…	…	…	…	…	…	…	…	…	…			
141	Netherlands[o]	6	–	–	–	–	–	–	–	–	–	–	–	–	–	–	–
142	Norway[o]	7	–	–	–	–	–	–	–	–	–	–	–	–	–	–	–
143	Portugal[o]	6	…	…	…	…	…	…	…	…	…	…	…	…	…	…	…
144	San Marino	5	…	…	…	…	…	…	…	…	…	…	…	…			
145	Spain[o]	6	–	–	–	–	–	–	–	–	–	–	–	–	–	–	–
146	Sweden[o]	6	…	…	…	…	…	…	…	…	…	…	…	…	…	…	…
147	Switzerland[o]	6	–	–	–	0.6	0.7	0.5	0.2	0.2	0.3	0.4	0.5	0.3	–	–	–
148	United Kingdom[o]	6	…	…	…	…	…	…	…	…	…	…	…	…	…	…	…
149	United States[o]	6	…	…	…	…	…	…	…	…	…	…	…	…	…	…	…

South and West Asia

150	Afghanistan	6	…	…	…	…	…	…	…	…	…	…	…	…	…	…	…
151	Bangladesh	5	8.3	10.0	6.4	8.5	8.6	8.3	9.1	9.6	8.5	11.7	11.9	11.4	…	…	…
152	Bhutan	7	0.7	0.5	0.9	2.3	2.7	1.7	2.8	3.3	2.2	2.3	3.2	1.3	5.1	5.7	4.3
153	India[w]	5	20.3	21.1	19.3	10.1	11.2	8.7	9.6	10.7	8.3	3.5	2.8	4.4	.	.	.
154	Iran, Islamic Republic of	5	2.4	2.4	2.3	1.3	1.3	1.3	0.9	0.9	0.9	1.6	1.5	1.7	.	.	.
155	Maldives	7	…	…	…	…	…	…	…	…	…	…	…	…	…	…	…
156	Nepal	5	10.2	10.2	10.1	1.2	2.8	–	1.1	1.6	0.6	2.5	2.9	2.0	.	.	.
157	Pakistan	5	…	…	…	…	…	…	…	…	…	…	…	…			
158	Sri Lanka[w]	5	…	…	…	…	…	…	…	…	…	…	…	…			

Sub-Saharan Africa

159	Angola	4	…	…	…	…	…	…	…	…	…						
160	Benin	6	…	…	…	…	…	…	…	…	…	…	…	…	…	…	…
161	Botswana	7	7.0	7.9	6.1	1.0	1.1	0.9	0.8	2.1	–	1.5	2.0	0.9	1.6	2.4	0.8
162	Burkina Faso	6	10.1**	9.5**	10.9**	5.7**	…	…	10.3**	…	…	10.2**	…	…	11.2**	…	…
163	Burundi	6	10.5	9.0	12.3	4.6	2.7	7.0	9.0	8.5	9.6	6.2	6.0	6.5	7.1	8.5	5.4
164	Cameroon	6	…	…	…	…	…	…	…	…	…	…	…	…	…	…	…
165	Cape Verde	6	–	–	–	2.2	2.9	1.5	–	–	0.5	3.9	6.2	1.4	2.9	1.5	4.2
166	Central African Republic	6	–	–	–	…	…	…	…	…	…	…	…	…	…	…	…
167	Chad	6	13.2**	…	…	7.1**	…	…	13.7**	…	…	17.6**	…	…	23.2**	…	…
168	Comoros	6	…	…	…	…	…	…	…	…	…	…	…	…	…	…	…
169	Congo	6	…	…	…	…	…	…	…	…	…	…	…	…	…	…	…

1. Duration in this table is defined according to ISCED97 and may differ from that reported nationally.

(x) Data are for 1998/1999.
(y) Data are for 1999/2000.

STATISTICAL ANNEX / 307

Table 7

	Grade 6			DROPOUTS, ALL GRADES (%) 2000			SURVIVAL RATE TO GRADE 5 (%) 2000			SURVIVAL RATE TO LAST GRADE (%) 2000			TRANSITION TO SECONDARY EDUCATION (%) 2000				
	Total	Male	Female	Total	Male	Female	Total	Male	Female	Total	Male	Female	Total	Male	Female	GPI (F/M)	
	.	.	.	27.4**	28.8**	26.0**	77.2**	76.1**	78.4**	72.6**	71.2**	74.0**	91.2**	91.5**	90.8**	0.99**	114
	.	.	.	19.1	18.7	19.6	86.1	86.1	86.1	80.9	81.3	80.4	93.8	95.4	92.0	0.96	115
	–	–	3.2	27.5	24.3	29.8	78.4	74.5	83.3	72.5	75.7	70.2	96.1	92.2	100.0	1.08	116
	–	–	–	0.9	1.8	–	97.2	96.4	98.0	99.1	98.2	100.0	65.3	56.0	75.1	1.34	117
	–	–	–	…	…	…	…	…	…	…	…	…	58.6**	45.9**	70.9	1.54**	118
	…	…	…	…	…	…	…	…	…	…	…	…	12.1**	14.5**	9.9**	0.68**	119
	–	–	–	…	…	…	…	…	…	…	…	…	97.4**	94.8**	100.0**	1.06**	120
	.	.	.	…	…	…	…	…	…	…	…	…	67.9	65.4	71.1	1.09	121
	.	.	.	13.4	14.6	12.1	88.5	87.4	89.7	86.6	85.4	87.9	79.6	…	…	…	122
	.	.	.	…	…	…	96.3**	95.0**	97.5**	…	…	…	98.4**	96.9**	100.0**	1.03**	123
	…	…	…	…	…	…	…	…	…	…	…	…	…	…	…	…	124
	…	…	…	…	…	…	.	.	.	…	…	…	95.3**,y	90.8**,y	100.0**,y	1.10**,y	125
	.	.	.	…	…	…	…	…	…	…	…	…	…	…	…	…	126
	.	.	.	…	…	…	…	…	…	…	…	…	…	…	…	…	127
	.	.	.	…	…	…	…	…	…	…	…	…	99.3	100.0	98.5	0.99	128
	.	.	.	…	…	…	…	…	…	…	…	…	100.0	100.0	99.9	1.00	129
	.	.	.	…	…	…	99.9	99.9	100.0	…	…	…	99.9	99.8	100.0	1.00	130
	.	.	.	…	…	…	…	…	…	…	…	…	98.9 y	…	…	…	131
	.	.	.	0.4	0.7	–	.	.	.	99.6	99.3	100.0	99.7	100.0	99.4	0.99	132
	.	.	.	…	…	…	…	…	…	…	…	…	…	…	…	…	133
	–	–	–	…	…	…	…	…	…	…	…	…	99.8	100.0	99.5	1.00	134
	–	–	–	…	…	…	98.8	97.7	100.0	…	…	…	98.1	96.3	100.0	1.04	135
	…	…	…	…	…	…	…	…	…	…	…	…	72.6	72.3	72.9	1.01	136
	.	.	.	3.5	4.0	3.0	96.5	96.0	97.0	96.5	96.0	97.0	99.9	100.0	99.7	1.00	137
	.	.	.	12.4**	13.2**	11.7**	99.0**	99.2**	98.7**	87.6**	86.8**	88.3**	…	…	…	…	138
	.	.	.	1.0	–	2.1	99.9	99.8	100.0	99.0	100.0	97.9	91.5	91.4	91.6	1.00	139
	…	…	…	…	…	…	…	…	…	…	…	…	…	…	…	…	140
	.	.	.	…	…	…	…	…	…	…	…	…	98.9 y	97.9 y	100.0 y	1.02 y	141
	–	–	–	…	…	…	…	…	…	…	…	…	…	…	…	…	142
	…	…	…	…	…	…	…	…	…	…	…	…	…	…	…	…	143
	…	…	…	…	…	…	…	…	…	…	…	…	…	…	…	…	144
	.	.	.	…	…	…	…	…	…	…	…	…	…	…	…	…	145
	…	…	…	…	…	…	…	…	…	…	…	…	…	…	…	…	146
	.	.	.	…	…	…	99.3	100.0	98.6	…	…	…	99.7	99.3	100.0	1.01	147
	.	.	.	…	…	…	…	…	…	…	…	…	…	…	…	…	148
	.	.	.	…	…	…	…	…	…	…	…	…	…	…	…	…	149
	…	…	…	…	…	…	…	…	…	…	…	…	…	…	…	…	150
	…	…	…	34.5	36.6	32.2	65.5	63.4	67.8	65.5	63.4	67.8	84.1	79.2	89.1	1.13	151
	4.4	5.3	3.3	18.7	22.0	14.9	91.0	89.2	93.2	81.3	78.0	85.1	82.5	82.4	82.6	1.00	152
	.	.	.	38.6	40.3	36.5	61.4	59.7	63.5	61.4	59.7	63.5	88.9	90.4	86.9	0.96	153
	.	.	.	6.3	6.3	6.3	93.7	93.7	93.7	93.7	93.7	93.7	90.8	90.5	91.0	1.01	154
	…	…	…	…	…	…	…	…	…	…	…	…	…	…	…	…	155
	.	.	.	22.2	24.6	19.2	77.8	75.4	80.8	77.8	75.4	80.8	81.7	82.8	80.2	0.97	156
	…	…	…	…	…	…	…	…	…	…	…	…	…	…	…	…	157
	…	…	…	…	…	…	…	…	…	…	…	…	…	…	…	…	158
	…	…	…	…	…	…	…	…	…	…	…	…	…	…	…	…	159
	…	…	…	…	…	…	…	…	…	…	…	…	64.6	64.4	65.1	1.01	160
	3.5	3.8	3.3	15.1	18.6	11.5	89.5	86.7	92.3	84.9	81.4	88.5	96.1	95.1	97.0	1.02	161
	.	.	.	45.1**	…	…	63.7**	…	…	54.9**	…	…	33.3**	34.2**	32.0**	0.93**	162
	.	.	.	44.1	41.4	47.4	64.0	68.3	58.8	55.9	58.6	52.6	32.3**	36.9**	26.7**	0.72**	163
	…	…	…	…	…	…	…	…	…	…	…	…	26.7**,y	27.8**,y	25.4**,y	0.91**,y	164
	.	.	.	9.9	12.2	7.7	92.8	89.2	96.4	90.1	87.8	92.3	69.4	69.1	69.7	1.01	165
	…	…	…	…	…	…	…	…	…	…	…	…	…	…	…	…	166
	.	.	.	67.7**	…	…	45.3**	…	…	32.3**	…	…	47.2 x	48.4 x	43.8 x	0.90 x	167
	.	.	.	…	…	…	…	…	…	…	…	…	56.6**	57.6**	55.5**	0.96**	168
	…	…	…	…	…	…	…	…	…	…	…	…	81.2**,y	100.0**,y	61.8**,y	0.62**,y	169

Table 7 (continued)

DROPOUT RATES BY GRADE IN PRIMARY EDUCATION (%), 2000

	Country or territory	Duration[1] of primary education 2001	Grade 1 Total	Grade 1 Male	Grade 1 Female	Grade 2 Total	Grade 2 Male	Grade 2 Female	Grade 3 Total	Grade 3 Male	Grade 3 Female	Grade 4 Total	Grade 4 Male	Grade 4 Female	Grade 5 Total	Grade 5 Male	Grade 5 Female
170	Côte d'Ivoire	6	...	...	...	...	...	...	...	...	...	...	...	...	...	...	...
171	D. R. Congo	6	...	...	...	...	...	...	...	...	...	...	...	...	...	...	...
172	Equatorial Guinea	5	23.3**	26.8**	19.6**	3.1**	0.5**	5.5**	10.2**	7.9**	12.5**	12.8**	12.9**	12.6**	.	.	.
173	Eritrea	5	8.1	7.3	9.2	0.8	–	2.7	–	–	–	5.5	3.4	8.0			
174	Ethiopia	6	16.6	16.8	16.3	8.9	8.0	10.2	7.4	7.2	7.8	7.0	6.4	7.9	8.5	8.8	8.0
175	Gabon	6															
176	Gambia	6	...	...	...	...	...	...	...	...	...	...	...	...	...	...	...
177	Ghana	6	11.1 y	10.9 y	11.2 y	6.8 y	6.3 y	7.4 y	8.2 y	7.9 y	8.6 y	10.7 y	10.4 y	11.1 y	10.2 y	9.6 y	11.0 y
178	Guinea	6															
179	Guinea-Bissau	6	28.5**,x	26.0**,x	31.8**,x	9.8**,x	10.3**,x	9.2**,x	10.9**,x	8.9**,x	13.7**,x	13.1**,x	13.0**,x	13.2**,x	21.7**,x	20.2**,x	24.2**,x
180	Kenya	7	...	...	...	...	...	...	...	...	...	...	...	...	...	...	...
181	Lesotho	7	14.7	17.1	11.9	1.3	1.6	0.9	5.4	7.0	3.7	7.5	9.0	6.0	8.1	9.9	6.6
182	Liberia	6															
183	Madagascar	5	16.3	16.1	16.4	12.2	12.6	11.8	17.6	17.5	17.7	17.8	17.8	17.7	.	.	.
184	Malawi	6	20.5	19.9	21.2	6.1	5.2	6.9	15.1	14.0	16.2	4.8	–	13.1	21.5	26.7	14.9
185	Mali	6	0.9	0.7	1.1	3.1	1.7	4.9	4.0	3.3	4.9	5.3	4.2	6.8	7.0	6.6	7.7
186	Mauritius	6	0.2	–	0.6	–	–	–	0.3	1.0	–	0.5	0.3	0.8	0.9**	1.2**	0.6**
187	Mozambique	5	12.7	10.6	15.1	8.4	7.5	9.6	11.9	11.7	12.3	11.4	10.2	13.1	.	.	.
188	Namibia	7	4.5**	4.7**	4.3**	0.8**	1.3**	0.3**	1.2**	1.1**	1.3**	–	–	–	5.5**	8.4**	2.4**
189	Niger	6	7.1	5.8	9.0	8.8	8.2	9.7	7.6	7.3	7.9	7.3	7.2	7.4	7.4	7.6	7.1
190	Nigeria	6															
191	Rwanda	6	15.7	15.6	15.8	11.2	11.8	10.5	11.9	12.5	11.3	15.4	15.4	15.4	17.9	17.3	18.4
192	Sao Tome and Principe	6	5.3	2.4	8.6	4.4	8.1	–	4.7	5.1	4.2	19.0**	20.6**	17.3**	4.5**	8.9**	0.1**
193	Senegal	6	12.4	11.3	13.6	7.9	7.1	8.7	7.3	7.0	7.6	5.4	4.6	6.4	10.5	9.3	11.9
194	Seychelles	6	–	–	–	–	–	–	–	–	–	–	–	–	–	–	–
195	Sierra Leone	6	...	...	...	...	...	...	...	...	...	...	...	...	...	...	...
196	Somalia	7															
197	South Africa	7	19.7 y	18.3 y	21.0 y	6.9 y	6.7 y	7.2 y	4.1 y	3.6 y	4.6 y	6.0 y	7.1 y	4.9 y	4.9 y	4.2 y	5.6 y
198	Swaziland	7	5.8	5.9	5.7	3.9	5.2	2.5	7.6	9.0	6.0	6.5	7.9	5.0	7.8	8.4	7.3
199	Togo	6	5.0	4.4	5.6	0.2	–	0.8	3.7	3.0	4.6	2.7	1.3	4.3	1.5	–	3.9
200	Uganda	7															
201	United Republic of Tanzania	7	6.4	6.3	6.6	4.4	4.4	4.4	3.1	4.5	1.7	8.6	9.4	7.8	4.7	5.6	3.9
202	Zambia	7	9.0**	8.2**	9.9**	3.4**	2.7**	4.2**	3.8**	3.6**	4.0**	8.0**	7.6**	8.4**	6.6**	6.6**	6.7**
203	Zimbabwe w	7	...	...	...	...	...	...	...	...	...	...	...	...	–	–	–

I	World[2]	...	4.0	4.8	3.1	2.3	2.4	2.2	2.1	2.4	1.9	...	...	...	...	...	...
II	Countries in transition	...	1.9	2.1	1.6	1.7	1.9	1.6	1.6	1.1	2.0	...	...	...	...	...	...
III	Developed countries	...	...	...	...	...	...	...	...	...	...	...	...	...	...	...	...
IV	Developing countries	...	6.4	6.3	6.6	3.2	3.5	2.8	3.4	1.0	5.8	4.8	2.3	8.9	...	...	...
V	Arab States	...	1.9	2.5	1.4	0.8	1.1	0.5	1.2	1.5	1.0	2.9	3.1	2.6	3.0	4.0	2.0
VI	Central and Eastern Europe	...	1.1	1.2	1.0	0.7	0.6	0.8	0.6	0.6	0.6	...	...	...	...	...	...
VII	Central Asia	...	2.5	2.6	2.4	1.8	2.2	1.4	1.8	1.8	1.9	...	...	...	...	...	...
VIII	East Asia and the Pacific	...	...	...	...	...	...	...	...	...	...	...	...	...	...	...	...
IX	Latin America and the Caribbean	...	5.8	6.2	5.3	3.0	3.8	2.2	2.2	1.9	2.6	4.3	4.0	4.7	3.3	3.8	2.9
X	North America and Western Europe	...	...	...	...	...	...	...	...	...	...	...	...	...	...	...	...
XI	South and West Asia	...	8.3	10.0	6.4	2.3	2.7	1.7	2.8	3.3	2.2	2.5	2.9	2.0	...	...	...
XII	Sub-Saharan Africa	...	10.5	9.0	12.3	4.6	2.7	7.0	7.5	7.2	7.9	7.3	7.2	7.4	...	...	...

1. Duration in this table is defined according to ISCED97 and may differ from that reported nationally.
2. All values shown are medians.

(x) Data are for 1998/1999.
(y) Data are for 1999/2000.

STATISTICAL ANNEX / 309

Table 7

	Grade 6			DROPOUTS, ALL GRADES (%)			SURVIVAL RATE TO GRADE 5 (%)			SURVIVAL RATE TO LAST GRADE (%)			TRANSITION TO SECONDARY EDUCATION (%)				
				2000			2000			2000			2000				
	Total	Male	Female	Total	Male	Female	Total	Male	Female	Total	Male	Female	Total	Male	Female	GPI (F/M)	
	…	…	…	…	…	…	…	…	…	…	…	…	39.7	41.9	36.3	0.87	170
	…	…	…	…	…	…	…	…	…	…	…	…	…	…	…	…	171
	.	.	.	67.4**	66.2**	68.7**	32.6**	33.8**	31.3**	32.6**	33.8**	31.3**	…	…	…	…	172
	.	.	.	17.9	10.6	26.3	82.1	89.4	73.7	82.1	89.4	73.7	82.7	88.1	76.2	0.87	173
	.	.	.	44.4	43.1	46.3	61.3	62.8	59.0	55.6	56.9	53.7	96.9	95.3	100.0	1.05	174
	…	…	…	…	…	…	…	…	…	…	…	…	…	…	…	…	175
	…	…	…	…	…	…	…	…	…	…	…	…	88.9 y	87.9 y	90.2 y	1.03 y	176
	.	.	.	40.7 y	39.4 y	42.2 y	66.3 y	67.3 y	65.2 y	59.3 y	60.6 y	57.8 y	90.3	89.5	91.2	1.02	177
	…	…	…	…	…	…	…	…	…	…	…	…	53.0**	54.6**	49.8**	0.91**	178
	.	.	.	72.5**,x	69.5**,x	76.6**,x	38.1**,x	41.2**,x	33.8**,x	27.5**,x	30.5**,x	23.4**,x	62.9**,x	65.5**,x	58.4**,x	0.89**,x	179
	…	…	…	…	…	…	…	…	…	…	…	…	73.1	75.4	70.9	0.94	180
8.3	9.3	7.4	45.6	53.5	37.4	66.8	59.9	74.2	54.4	46.5	62.6	66.1	67.5	65.1	0.96		181
	…	…	…	…	…	…	…	…	…	…	…	…	…	…	…	…	182
	.	.	.	66.4	67.2	65.6	33.6	32.8	34.4	33.6	32.8	34.4	55.0	55.4	54.5	0.98	183
	.	.	.	59.1	57.0	61.1	53.6	60.8	46.6	40.9	43.0	38.9	76.1**	77.6**	74.5**	0.96**	184
	.	.	.	24.8	20.6	30.6	84.1	87.9	79.1	75.2	79.4	69.4	56.3**	57.7**	53.8**	0.93**	185
	.	.	.	1.7**	2.0**	1.3**	99.3	99.2	99.3	98.3**	98.0**	98.7**	63.2	58.8	68.0	1.15	186
	.	.	.	48.1	44.0	53.2	51.9	56.0	46.8	51.9	56.0	46.8	58.8	58.5	59.3	1.01	187
1.5**	1.4**	1.6**	13.7**	17.3**	10.3**	94.2**	94.3**	94.1**	86.3**	82.7**	89.7**	81.6 y	80.6 y	82.4 y	1.02 y		188
	.	.	.	35.0	33.4	37.2	71.0	72.8	68.4	65.0	66.6	62.8	38.5	39.0	37.6	0.96	189
	…	…	…	…	…	…	…	…	…	…	…	…	…	…	…	…	190
	.	.	.	71.4	71.4	71.4	40.0	39.2	40.7	28.6	28.6	28.6	…	…	…	…	191
	.	.	.	42.3**	48.5**	35.8**	61.5**	58.3**	64.7**	57.7**	51.5**	64.2**	64.5**	66.4**	62.6**	0.94**	192
	.	.	.	40.9	37.6	44.4	67.5	70.1	64.8	59.1	62.4	55.6	39.2	40.5	37.3	0.92	193
	.	.	.	…	…	…	…	…	…	…	…	…	98.8	98.3	99.4	1.01	194
	…	…	…	…	…	…	…	…	…	…	…	…	…	…	…	…	195
	…	…	…	…	…	…	…	…	…	…	…	…	…	…	…	…	196
5.8 y	5.3 y	6.3 y	42.6 y	41.5 y	43.7 y	64.8 y	65.2 y	64.2 y	57.4 y	58.5 y	56.3 y	91.9 y	90.7 y	93.0 y	1.03 y		197
10.8	11.5	10.0	41.8	46.9	36.3	73.9	68.8	79.2	58.2	53.1	63.7	76.2	79.7	72.8	0.91		198
	.	.	.	17.9	12.2	24.9	84.3	88.1	79.7	82.1	87.8	75.1	71.3	73.4	68.1	0.93	199
	…	…	…	…	…	…	…	…	…	…	…	…	40.6	38.3	43.6	1.14	200
6.8	7.1	6.6	30.7	33.0	28.3	78.1	76.4	79.9	69.3	67.0	71.7	19.9	20.5	19.3	0.94		201
7.9**	5.6**	10.5**	34.8**	31.3**	38.3**	76.7**	78.7**	74.8**	65.2**	68.7**	61.7**	49.8**	49.7**	49.9**	1.01**		202
—	—	—	…	…	…	…	…	…	…	…	…	…	…	…	…	203

	…	…	…	13.6	15.7	10.5	…	…	…	86.2	85.5	87.0	90.8	89.8	91.8	1.02	I
	…	…	…	4.8	4.7	4.8	…	…	…	95.3	95.3	95.2	98.0	98.0	98.1	1.00	II
	…	…	…	…	…	…	…	…	…	…	…	…	98.9	98.8	99.0	1.00	III
	…	…	…	22.2	22.1	22.4	83.3	84.5	82.0	77.5	75.8	79.6	84.0	86.3	81.6	0.95	IV
	…	…	…	7.9	8.2	7.6	94.0	92.3	95.7	92.1	91.4	92.8	88.3	84.1	94.7	1.13	V
	…	…	…	1.8	1.8	1.9	…	…	…	98.2	97.6	98.8	98.3	98.2	98.4	1.00	VI
	…	…	…	5.2	5.3	5.2	…	…	…	94.8	94.7	94.8	98.0	98.0	98.1	1.00	VII
	…	…	…	…	…	…	…	…	…	…	…	…	87.7	91.6	89.6	0.98	VIII
	…	…	…	19.1	18.7	19.6	88.5	87.4	89.7	80.9	81.3	80.4	90.8	89.8	91.8	1.02	IX
	…	…	…	…	…	…	…	…	…	…	…	…	99.3	100.0	98.5	0.99	X
	…	…	…	22.2	24.6	19.2	77.8	75.4	80.8	77.8	75.4	80.8	84.1	79.2	89.1	1.13	XI
	…	…	…	42.1	47.7	36.1	66.6	63.6	69.7	58.0	52.3	64.0	63.9	62.6	65.3	1.04	XII

Table 8
Participation in secondary[1] and post-secondary non-tertiary[2] education

	Country or territory	Age group 2001	School-age population (000) 2001	Total enrolment 1998 Total (000)	1998 % F	Total enrolment 2001 Total (000)	2001 % F	Enrolment in technical and vocational education 2001 Total (000)	2001 % F	GER 1998 Total	GER 1998 Male	GER 1998 Female	GPI (F/M)
	Arab States												
1	Algeria	12-17	4 408	2 809	50	3 157	51	86	33	65.8	64.9	66.8	1.03
2	Bahrain	12-17	68	59	51	64	51	13	41	93.9	90.2	97.8	1.08
3	Djibouti	12-18	105	16	42	21	38	1	38	16.2	18.9	13.5	0.72
4	Egypt[w]	11-16	9 813	7 671**	47**	8 645**	47**	2 533**	45**	80.8**	84.3**	77.2**	0.92**
5	Iraq	12-17	3 380	1 105	38	1 224[y]	37[y]	76[y]	17[y]	35.7	43.6	27.5	0.63
6	Jordan[w]	12-17	701	579	49	605	50	42	36	86.9	85.8	88.0	1.03
7	Kuwait	10-17	286	235**	49**	244**	50**	4**	34**	97.8**	96.8**	98.8	1.02**
8	Lebanon	12-17	434	372	52	336	52	41	40	77.5	74.1	80.9	1.09
9	Libyan Arab Jamahiriya	12-17	787	...	...	825	51	183	53	...	...	...	...
10	Mauritania	12-17	364	63**	42**	79	43	2	34	18.7**	21.7**	15.8**	0.73**
11	Morocco	12-17	3 924	1 470	43	1 608**,[z]	44**,[z]	105**,[z]	45**,[z]	37.7	42.0	33.3	0.79
12	Oman	12-17	340	229	49	267	49	...	...	71.7	71.9	71.5	0.99
13	Palestinian A. T.	10-17	642	444	50	545	50	4	28	78.8	77.5	80.3	1.04
14	Qatar	12-17	54	44	51	49	50	1	...	92.3	89.6	95.1	1.06
15	Saudi Arabia	12-17	2 882	1 774	46	1 996	46	40	14	67.9	72.7	62.9	0.87
16	Sudan	12-16	3 572	965**	...	1 141	...	31	33	28.5**	...	...	...
17	Syrian Arab Republic	12-17	2 652	1 030	47	1 182	47	118	46	40.6	42.5	38.7	0.91
18	Tunisia[w]	12-18	1 478	1 059	49	1 169	50	64	38	72.9	72.3	73.6	1.02
19	United Arab Emirates	12-17	285	202	50	226	50	2	...	82.1	79.0	85.5	1.08
20	Yemen	12-17	2 800	1 042	26	1 249**,[z]	28**,[z]	...	...	41.9	60.3	22.5	0.37
	Central and Eastern Europe												
21	Albania[o]	10-17	484	363**	49**	377[z]	49[z]	16**,[z]	30**,[z]	75.8**	74.6**	77.1**	1.03**
22	Belarus	11-17	1 168	1 003	50	982	50	5	33	85.2	83.6	87.0	1.04
23	Bosnia and Herzegovina[o]	10-17	498	...	...	...	...	...	...	...	...	...	...
24	Bulgaria[o]	11-17	735	700	48	693	48	188	39	89.4	90.3	88.5	0.98
25	Croatia	11-18	455	427	50	402	49	155	47	89.8	88.5	91.2	1.03
26	Czech Republic[o]	11-18	1 042	928	50	999	50	392	47	82.5	80.9	84.3	1.04
27	Estonia[o]	13-18	108	116	50	123	49	18	33	92.7	91.0	94.6	1.04
28	Hungary[o]	11-18	978	1 007	49	1 013	49	65	40	95.3	94.5	96.0	1.02
29	Latvia[o]	11-18	294	255	50	278	49	40	39	88.4	86.8	90.1	1.04
30	Lithuania[o]	11-18	441	...	...	443	49	38	36	...	...	...	...
31	Poland[o]	13-18	3 838	...	...	3 950	48	...	...	...	...	...	...
32	Republic of Moldova	11-17	572	418	49	414	50	23	37	72.7	72.4	73.0	1.01
33	Romania[o]	11-18	2 679	2 218	49	2 255	49	617	44	78.9	78.3	79.4	1.01
34	Russian Federation[w]	10-16	16 060	...	...	14 769	49	1 399	34	...	...	...	...
35	Serbia and Montenegro[3]	11-18	...	814	49	761[z]	49[z]	267[z]	47[z]	92.3	92.0	92.6	1.01
36	Slovakia	10-18	745	674	50	666	49	210	47	85.2	84.3	86.2	1.02
37	Slovenia[o]	11-18	205	220	50	221	49	87	46	98.7	97.4	100.1	1.03
38	TFYR Macedonia[o]	11-18	261	219	48	219	48	58	43	82.3	83.4	81.1	0.97
39	Turkey[o]	12-16	7 237	...	...	5 500**	43**	1 240	39**	...	...	...	...
40	Ukraine	10-16	5 150	...	...	4 983	49	334	33	...	...	...	...
	Central Asia												
41	Armenia	10-16	436	...	...	378	51	5	35	...	...	...	...
42	Azerbaijan	10-16	1 305	929	49	1 040	48	22	32	76.9	77.2	76.7	0.99
43	Georgia	10-16	581	449	50	456	51	20	76	74.2	73.0	75.3	1.03
44	Kazakhstan	11-17	2 276	1 966	49	2 020	49	87	38	87.4	87.8	87.1	0.99
45	Kyrgyzstan	11-17	796	633	50	689	50	26	36	85.4	84.3	86.4	1.02
46	Mongolia	12-17	371	207	56	282	54	13	51	58.9	51.9	66.0	1.27
47	Tajikistan	11-17	1 096	773	46	899	45	25	28	76.1	81.9	70.2	0.86
48	Turkmenistan	11-17	789	...	...	...	...	...	...	...	...	...	...
49	Uzbekistan	11-17	4 296	...	...	4 237**	49**	374**	44**	...	...	...	...
	East Asia and the Pacific												
50	Australia[o]	12-17	1 625	...	...	2 500	48	1 111	46	...	...	...	...
51	Brunei Darussalam	12-18	42	33	51	37	50	2	36	81.6	77.7	85.6	1.10

1. Refers to lower and upper secondary education (ISCED levels 2 and 3).
2. Corresponds to ISCED level 4. Like secondary education, it includes general as well as technical and vocational programmes.
3. National population data were used to calculate enrolment ratios.
(y) Data are for 1999/2000.
(z) Data are for 2000/2001.

STATISTICAL ANNEX / 311

Table 8

	GROSS ENROLMENT RATIO (GER) IN SECONDARY EDUCATION (%) 2001				NET ENROLMENT RATIO (NER) IN SECONDARY EDUCATION (%) 1998				2001				INTERNAL EFFICIENCY Repeaters in general secondary education (%) 2001			POST-SECONDARY NON-TERTIARY EDUCATION Total enrolment 2001		
	Total	Male	Female	GPI (F/M)	Total	Male	Female	GPI (F/M)	Total	Male	Female	GPI (F/M)	Total	Male	Female	Total (000)	% F	
	71.6	69.0	74.4	1.08	57.8**	57.5**	58.1**	1.01**	62.0**	60.4**	63.7**	1.06**	...	...	...	...	...	1
	95.0	91.1	99.2	1.09	80.6	76.5	84.9	1.11	81.4**	76.9**	86.2**	1.12**	6.5	7.8	5.4	6.6	31	2
	19.6	24.2	14.9	0.62	...	...	...	...	17.1**	21.0**	13.2**	0.63**	6.0**	6.1**	5.8**	–	–	3
	88.1**	91.3**	84.8**	0.93**	...	...	...	...	80.8**	83.1**	78.5**	0.95**	8.3**	9.7**	6.8**	128.8**,z	47**,z	4
	38.3y	47.2y	29.0y	0.62y	31.4	37.7	24.8	0.66	33.0y	39.7y	26.0y	0.66y	27.5y	30.5y	22.7y	11.3y	44y	5
	86.3	85.3	87.4	1.02	78.5**	76.0**	81.0**	1.07**	80.3	79.3	81.4	1.03	1.1	1.2	0.9	.	.	6
	85.2**	82.8**	87.8	1.06**	88.0**	87.3**	88.8**	1.02**	77.2**	75.2**	79.3**	1.05**	11.0	12.9	9.1	16.8y	55y	7
	77.4	73.9	81.0	1.10	...	...	...	...	...	...	...	...	11.5	12.0	11.0	1.0	41	8
	104.8	101.6	108.0	1.06	...	...	...	...	...	...	...	...	...	...	...	...	...	9
	21.7	24.6	18.7	0.76	...	...	...	...	14.5**	15.9**	13.1**	0.83**	14.0**	13.7**	14.5**	0.9	47	10
	40.9**,z	45.2**,z	36.5**,z	0.81**,z	...	...	...	...	31.2**,y	34.0**,y	28.3**,y	0.83**,y	17.7z	19.5z	15.4z	64.1y	45y	11
	78.5	79.5	77.5	0.98	61.6	60.8	62.5	1.03	68.1	68.0	68.3	1.00	7.7	10.8	4.5	16.2**,y	36**,y	12
	84.9	82.4	87.6	1.06	75.6	74.2	77.2	1.04	80.7**	78.3**	83.2**	1.06**	2.1	2.4	1.9	6.9**,y	55**,y	13
	90.2	88.0	92.6	1.05	78.0	74.9	81.2	1.08	78.0**	75.6**	80.4**	1.06**	...	...	...	.	.	14
	69.2	73.0	65.3	0.89	...	...	...	...	52.9**	54.7**	51.0**	0.93**	7.4**	9.0**	5.4**	36.3	41**	15
	32.0	...	...	...	...	...	...	...	...	...	...	...	...	...	...	.	.	16
	44.6	46.8	42.3	0.90	36.4	37.9	34.8	0.92	38.7	40.5	36.9	0.91	9.9	11.5	8.1	37.7	60	17
	79.1	77.6	80.7	1.04	...	...	...	...	67.8**	66.7**	69.1**	1.04**	16.7	18.8	14.6	3.6	38	18
	79.4	77.1	81.8	1.06	74.4	71.7	77.2	1.08	71.9**	70.0**	73.8	1.05**	4.9	6.2	3.5	.	.	19
	46.3**,z	64.7**,z	26.9**,z	0.42**,z	32.6*	45.8*	18.6*	0.41*	34.5**,y	46.9**,y	21.4**,y	0.46**,y	...	...	...	19.1z	16z	20
	78.4z	77.2z	79.6z	1.03z	71.5**	70.5**	72.7**	1.03**	73.9z	72.9z	75.0z	1.03z	6.1z	6.8z	5.5z	.	.	21
	84.1	82.5	85.8	1.04	...	...	...	...	77.5**	76.0**	79.1**	1.04**	0.3	0.3**	0.3**	133.4	38	22
	...	...	...	...	...	...	...	...	...	...	...	...	...	...	...	...	...	23
	94.3	95.5	93.0	0.97	83.2	83.8	82.5	0.98	86.7	87.6	85.7	0.98	1.7	2.3	1.1	3.6	51	24
	88.4	87.5	89.2	1.02	85.4	84.4	86.3	1.02	86.4	85.3	87.5	1.03	0.6	0.9	0.3	...	...	25
	95.8	94.5	97.1	1.03	...	...	...	...	89.5	88.9	90.1	1.01	1.1	1.4	0.7	48.3	45	26
	95.9	95.0	96.9	1.02	...	...	...	...	86.8	85.5	88.2	1.03	3.0	4.2	2.0	11.4	62	27
	103.6	103.2	104.1	1.01	84.7**	84.2**	85.2**	1.01**	92.1	92.0	92.2	1.00	2.2	2.9	1.6	99.7	52	28
	94.5	94.2	94.9	1.01	85.0	83.8	86.2	1.03	87.6**	87.0**	88.2**	1.01**	0.6	0.9	0.4	7.5	66	29
	100.5	101.2	99.9	0.99	...	...	...	...	92.9	92.6	93.1	1.01	0.7	1.0	0.3	7.6	63	30
	102.9	104.5	101.2	0.97	...	...	...	...	91.3	90.0	92.7	1.03	...	...	...	191.6	60	31
	72.4	71.4	73.5	1.03	69.3**	...	...	...	68.5	67.4	69.6	1.03	0.9	1.0	0.9	.	.	32
	84.2	83.6	84.8	1.01	74.4**	73.6**	75.3**	1.02**	80.0	79.0	81.0	1.03	2.2	3.1	1.3	72.7	63	33
	92.0	91.6	92.3	1.01	...	...	...	...	...	...	...	...	0.8	...	...	246.1	41	34
	88.7z	88.2z	89.2z	1.01z	86.4**	86.3**	86.5**	1.00**	82.9**,z	82.6**,z	83.3**,z	1.01**,z	2.1**,z	2.1**,z	2.0**,z	6.5z	5z	35
	89.5	89.0	89.9	1.01	...	...	...	...	86.6	86.1	87.2	1.01	1.5	1.9	1.1	5.8	66	36
	107.6	107.4	107.8	1.00	89.5	87.9	91.1	1.04	92.7	92.1	93.3	1.01	1.7	3.0	0.4	1.0	70	37
	84.0	85.0	82.9	0.97	79.1**	80.1**	78.0**	0.97**	81.2**	82.2**	80.1**	0.97**	0.6	0.8	0.4	0.2	8	38
	76.0**	86.2**	65.5**	0.76**	...	...	...	...	...	...	...	...	...	...	...	.	.	39
	96.8	97.0	96.5	1.00	...	...	...	...	90.5**	90.5**	90.6**	1.00**	0.1	0.1**	0.1**	178.7	54	40
	86.5	83.9	89.2	1.06	...	...	...	...	84.6	82.9	86.4	1.04	0.3	0.4	0.1	29.4	67	41
	79.7	80.8	78.5	0.97	74.8**	74.7**	74.8**	1.00**	75.7**	76.3**	75.2**	0.99**	0.6	0.6	0.6	.	.	42
	78.6	75.7	81.7	1.08	71.2**	70.0**	72.4**	1.03**	...	...	...	...	0.3	0.4	0.2	10.4	28	43
	88.8	89.7	87.8	0.98	81.7**	81.8**	81.7**	1.00**	84.1	85.3	82.9	0.97	0.2	0.3	0.1	196.2	58	44
	86.5	86.4	86.7	1.00	...	...	...	...	...	...	...	...	0.2	0.3	0.1	26.5	66	45
	76.1	69.3	82.9	1.20	55.5	49.1	62.1	1.26	71.5	65.3	77.8	1.19	0.1	0.1	0.1	2.0	46	46
	82.0	89.9	73.9	0.82	72.8**	77.8**	67.7**	0.87**	79.0**	85.8**	72.2**	0.84**	0.8	...	...	23.8	49	47
	...	...	...	...	...	...	...	...	...	...	...	...	...	...	...	.	.	48
	98.6**	100.1**	97.1**	0.97**	...	...	...	...	...	...	...	...	–	–	–	.	.	49
	153.8	154.8	152.8	0.99	...	...	...	...	88.5**	87.2**	89.8**	1.03**	...	...	...	171.2	50	50
	87.7	85.0	90.5	1.06	...	...	...	...	...	...	...	...	...	...	...	0.1	24	51

Table 8 (continued)

	Country or territory	Age group 2001	School-age population (000) 2001	Enrolment in secondary education Total enrolment 1998 Total (000)	1998 % F	2001 Total (000)	2001 % F	Enrolment in technical and vocational education 2001 Total (000)	2001 % F	GER 1998 Total	1998 Male	1998 Female	GPI (F/M)
52	Cambodia	12-17	2 230	318**	34**	476	37	9	34	16.0**	20.8**	11.0**	0.53**
53	China w	12-17	135 029	81 488	...	90 723	...	...	...	65.0	...	...	...
54	Cook Islands 4	11-18	...	2	51	...	...	...	...	...	...	...	...
55	DPR Korea	10-15	2 323	...	...	...	...	...	...	...	...	...	...
56	Fiji	12-18	120	...	...	96**	50**	3**	38**	...	...	...	...
57	Indonesia w	13-18	26 146	...	...	15 141	49	...	...	...	...	...	...
58	Japan o	12-17	8 184	8 959	49	8 394	49	1 092	45	101.8	101.1	102.4	1.01
59	Kiribati	12-16	...	...	...	...	...	...	...	...	...	...	...
60	Lao PDR	11-16	790	240	40	320	41	5	34	33.4	39.4	27.3	0.69
61	Macao, China	12-17	48	32	51	42	50	3	48	75.5	71.8	79.4	1.10
62	Malaysia w	12-18	3 227	2 154	51	2 247	51	134	43	69.4	65.9	73.1	1.11
63	Marshall Islands 3	12-17	...	6	51	6	50	...	...	...	...	...	...
64	Micronesia (Federated States of)	12-17	65	19	...	...	...	...	...	109.2	...	...	...
65	Myanmar	10-15	6 037	2 059	50	2 373	48	...	...	34.9	35.0	34.8	0.99
66	Nauru 3	12-17	...	1**	51**	...	...	...	...	53.9**	52.3**	55.6**	1.06**
67	New Zealand o	11-17	403	...	...	456	...	...	...	...	...	...	...
68	Niue 3	11-16	...	0.3	47	0.2	50	...	...	101.4	111.9	91.7	0.82
69	Palau 3	11-17	...	2	49	2**,z	48**,z	...	...	101.2	98.2	104.5	1.07
70	Papua New Guinea	13-18	705	133	40	160**	41**	15**	26**	20.4	23.2	17.3	0.75
71	Philippines w	12-15	7 106	5 117	51	5 817	51	...	...	75.8	72.5	79.3	1.09
72	Republic of Korea o	12-17	4 135	...	...	3 768	48	657	49	...	...	...	...
73	Samoa	11-17	30	22	50	22	50	...	...	74.9	71.2	78.9	1.11
74	Singapore	12-15	221	...	...	...	...	...	...	...	...	...	...
75	Solomon Islands	12-18	73	...	...	...	...	...	...	...	...	...	...
76	Thailand w	12-17	6 664	...	...	5 577 z	48 z	635 z	48 z	...	...	...	...
77	Timor-Leste	12-17	135	...	...	47	...	...	...	...	...	...	...
78	Tokelau	...	...	...	...	...	...	...	...	...	...	...	...
79	Tonga	11-16	14	14	51	14	49	1**	40**	93.3	87.8	99.3	1.13
80	Tuvalu 3	12-17	...	1**	45**	1	46	...	...	78.3**	83.1**	73.1**	0.88**
81	Vanuatu	12-18	34	10**	43**	10	49	1	45	33.1**	36.1**	29.9**	0.83**
82	Viet Nam	11-17	12 608	7 401	47	8 783	47	195	51	61.9	65.1	58.6	0.90
Latin America and the Caribbean													
83	Anguilla 3	12-16	...	1	53	1	51	0.1**	62**	...	...	...	...
84	Antigua and Barbuda 4	12-16	...	...	...	5 y	72 y	1 y	37 y	...	...	...	...
85	Argentina w	12-17	3 970	3 556	51	3 954	51	1 210	50	89.0	85.7	92.5	1.08
86	Aruba 3	12-16	...	6	51	7	52	1	37	100.6	98.6	102.7	1.04
87	Bahamas	11-16	35	...	...	32	50	...	...	...	...	...	...
88	Barbados	11-15	20	22**	51**	21	49	0.1	28	104.0**	101.3**	106.7**	1.05**
89	Belize	11-16	35	22	51	24 z	51 z	1 z	61 z	64.8	62.3	67.4	1.08
90	Bermuda 3	11-17	...	...	...	5	52	...	...	...	...	...	...
91	Bolivia	12-17	1 124	756	47	949	48	65	59	72.3	75.4	69.1	0.92
92	Brazil w	11-17	24 591	...	...	26 441	52	...	...	...	...	...	...
93	British Virgin Islands 3	12-16	...	2	47	2	51	0.3	42	98.8	103.3	94.1	0.91
94	Cayman Islands 4	11-16	...	2	48	2	50	...	...	...	...	...	...
95	Chile w	12-17	1 656	1 246	50	1 391 z	50 z	378 z	47 z	79.6	78.0	81.3	1.04
96	Colombia	11-16	5 178	3 549	52	3 378	52	...	...	70.6	66.9	74.5	1.11
97	Costa Rica	12-16	430	...	...	287	49	59	43	...	...	...	...
98	Cuba	12-17	1 005	740	50	896	49	257	38	79.4	77.1	81.8	1.06
99	Dominica 3	12-16	...	7	53	8	52	...	...	85.5	78.5	92.8	1.18
100	Dominican Republic	12-17	1 122	610**	55**	756	54	37	55	56.1**	49.5**	63.0**	1.27**
101	Ecuador	12-17	1 633	904	50	966	49	203	53	56.4	55.7	57.2	1.03
102	El Salvador	13-18	780	402	49	436	50	86	52	50.2	50.4	50.0	0.99
103	Grenada 3	12-16	...	...	...	6	49	...	...	...	...	...	...
104	Guatemala	13-17	1 654	400*	47*	548	47	156	51	30.7*	31.9*	29.5*	0.92*
105	Guyana	12-16	75	66	50	69 y	50 y	7**,y	37**,y	81.1	80.5	81.8	1.02
106	Haiti	12-18	1 482	...	...	...	...	...	...	...	...	...	...
107	Honduras	13-18	919	...	...	...	...	...	...	...	...	...	...
108	Jamaica w	12-16	273	231**	50**	228	50	0.4	44	84.1**	83.2**	85.1**	1.02**
109	Mexico o	12-17	12 806	8 722	50	9 693	51	1 449	57	69.1	68.3	69.9	1.02

3. National population data were used to calculate enrolment ratios.
4. Enrolment ratios were not calculated, due to lack of United Nations population data by age.
(y) Data are for 1999/2000.
(z) Data are for 2000/2001.

STATISTICAL ANNEX / 313

Table 8

GROSS ENROLMENT RATIO (GER) IN SECONDARY EDUCATION (%)				NET ENROLMENT RATIO (NER) IN SECONDARY EDUCATION (%)								INTERNAL EFFICIENCY — Repeaters in general secondary education (%)			POST-SECONDARY NON-TERTIARY EDUCATION — Total enrolment		
2001				1998				2001				2001			2001		
Total	Male	Female	GPI (F/M)	Total	Male	Female	GPI (F/M)	Total	Male	Female	GPI (F/M)	Total	Male	Female	Total (000)	% F	
21.3	26.7	15.9	0.60	14.3**	18.6**	10.0**	0.54**	20.8**	26.0**	15.5**	0.60**	3.2	3.9	2.1	9.5	24	52
67.2	...	...	...	...	...	...	...	...	...	...	...	...	...	...	691.8	36	53
...	...	...	...	...	...	...	...	...	...	...	...	4.3**,z	...	...	0.04**,z	69**,z	54
...	...	...	...	...	...	...	...	...	...	...	...	...	...	...	...	...	55
80.4**	77.6**	83.2**	1.07**	...	...	...	...	76.0**	73.4**	78.7**	1.07**	.	.	.	.	.	56
57.9	58.3	57.5	0.99	...	...	...	...	47.4**,y	48.5**,y	46.2**,y	0.95**,y	0.3	0.5	0.2	.	.	57
102.6	102.2	102.9	1.01	...	...	...	...	100.0**	...	...	...	...	...	...	14.5	63	58
...	...	...	...	...	...	...	...	...	...	...	...	...	...	...	...	...	59
40.6	46.8	34.1	0.73	26.7	29.9	23.5	0.79	31.4	34.6	28.1	0.81	2.3	3.1	1.1	16.8	43	60
87.1	84.5	89.8	1.06	61.9	58.4	65.6	1.12	71.6	68.0	75.4	1.11	12.2	14.3	10.1	.	.	61
69.6	66.3	73.1	1.10	68.9	65.4	72.6	1.11	69.4	66.0	72.9	1.10	...	...	...	156.9	45	62
...	...	...	...	...	...	...	...	...	...	...	...	3.1**	3.1**	3.2**	0.05	27	63
...	...	...	...	...	...	...	...	...	...	...	...	.	.	.	.	.	64
39.3	40.5	38.1	0.94	31.2**	31.4**	31.0**	0.99**	35.3	36.5	34.2	0.94	2.2	2.2	2.3	.	.	65
...	...	...	...	...	...	...	...	...	...	...	...	...	...	...	...	...	66
113.2	...	...	...	...	...	...	...	91.6**,z	90.7**,z	92.5**,z	1.02**,z	...	...	...	32.1	49	67
93.8	94.6	93.0	0.98	...	...	...	...	93.8	94.6	93.0	0.98	.	.	.	.	.	68
88.8**,z	88.6**,z	88.9**,z	1.00**,z	...	...	...	...	...	...	...	...	...	...	...	...	...	69
22.7**	25.2**	19.9**	0.79**	20.4*	23.2*	17.3*	0.75*	22.7**	25.2**	19.9**	0.79**	–	–	–	.	.	70
81.9	78.0	85.9	1.10	50.8	48.6	53.1	1.09	56.5	51.3	61.8	1.20	2.6	4.0	1.2	438.5	.	71
91.1	91.0	91.2	1.00	...	...	...	...	88.6	88.5	88.8	1.00	.	.	.	.	.	72
74.5	70.8	78.6	1.11	65.8	62.9	69.1	1.10	61.0	57.6	64.7	1.12	2.2	2.4	2.0	0.2	59	73
...	...	...	...	...	...	...	...	...	...	...	...	–	–	–	.	.	74
...	...	...	...	...	...	...	...	...	...	...	...	...	...	...	.	.	75
82.8 z	84.8 z	80.7 z	0.95 z	...	...	...	...	...	...	...	...	...	...	...	18.5	72	76
34.6	...	...	...	...	...	...	...	20.3**,z	...	...	...	...	...	...	.	.	77
...	...	...	...	...	...	...	...	...	...	...	...	...	...	...	.	.	78
99.6	94.0	106.1	1.13	68.5	64.2	73.2	1.14	71.8**,z	67.5**,z	76.6**,z	1.13**,z	5.7	5.8	5.6	1.2	40	79
...	...	...	...	...	...	...	...	...	...	...	...	6.3**	5.8**	6.8**	...	...	80
28.6	28.2	29.0	1.03	...	...	...	...	27.5	27.3	27.7	1.01	.	.	.	2.1	37	81
69.7	72.4	66.8	0.92	49.4**	...	...	...	65.3**	...	...	...	1.3**	...	...	.	.	82
101.9	103.0	100.7	0.98	...	...	...	...	98.8**	100.0**	97.6**	0.98**	–	–	–	0.0	63	83
...	...	...	...	...	...	...	...	...	...	...	...	–	–	–	1.3 y	63 y	84
99.6	96.6	102.7	1.06	73.6	71.0	76.3	1.07	80.8	78.5	83.0	1.06	...	...	...	.	.	85
101.5	98.1	104.8	1.07	79.3	76.4	82.1	1.07	77.5	74.5	80.5	1.08	12.4	13.5	11.5	0.1 y	41 y	86
91.5	90.2	92.8	1.03	...	...	...	...	79.0**	78.6**	79.3**	1.01**	.	.	.	...	...	87
103.3	103.2	103.4	1.00	88.2**	86.4**	90.0**	1.04**	86.8	87.1	86.4	0.99	–	–	–	3.6	43	88
70.7**	68.0**	73.5 z	1.08**	56.4**	54.2**	58.7**	1.08**	60.4 z	58.3 z	62.6 z	1.07 z	7.1 z	7.9 z	6.4 z	0.8 y	29 y	89
86.1 z	...	...	...	...	...	...	...	...	...	...	...	...	...	...	...	...	90
84.4	86.0	82.8	0.96	61.7**	63.9**	59.4**	0.93**	67.3**,z	68.1**,z	66.5**,z	0.98**,z	3.6*	4.3*	2.8*	...	...	91
107.5	102.4	112.8	1.10	...	...	...	...	71.6	68.9	74.5	1.08	18.0	18.0**	18.0**	...	...	92
95.2	94.3	96.2	1.02	79.8**	81.1**	78.4**	0.97**	78.0**	74.6**	81.5**	1.09**	8.2**	10.2**	6.5**	0.7 z	63 z	93
...	...	...	...	...	...	...	...	...	...	...	...	...	...	...	0.0*	54*	94
85.5 z	84.5 z	86.5 z	1.02 z	70.3	68.8	71.9	1.05	74.5 z	73.5 z	75.6 z	1.03 z	2.7 z	3.2 z	2.2 z	.	.	95
65.2	62.1	68.5	1.10	...	...	...	...	53.5	50.9**	56.2**	1.10**	4.5	5.3	3.7	7.4	74	96
66.8	66.0	67.7	1.03	...	...	...	...	50.7	48.2	53.4	1.11	8.3	9.6	7.0	8.3 y	51 y	97
89.1	89.6	88.6	0.99	75.2	71.4	79.3	1.11	83.4	83.2	83.6	1.01	1.6	2.2	1.0	19.3	83	98
95.4 z	89.5 z	101.5 z	1.13 z	65.5	55.7	75.7	1.36	84.3 z	81.8 z	86.8 z	1.06 z	12.1	15.6	8.8	0.8	61	99
67.4	60.3	74.8	1.24	39.5**	34.6**	44.7**	1.29**	40.8	34.9	47.0	1.34	3.1	4.0	2.4	.	.	100
59.2	58.9	59.4	1.01	46.1	45.4	46.8	1.03	50.0	49.5	50.5	1.02	4.2	5.0	3.3	21.7 z	55 z	101
55.9	55.7	56.0	1.01	39.6**	39.9**	39.4**	0.99**	46.0	45.4	46.5	1.02	2.4**	3.1**	1.7**	.	.	102
62.6 z	84.0 z	40.6 z	0.48 z	...	...	...	...	45.5**,z	...	...	...	9.3	12.0	6.8	1.2	39	103
39.3	40.7	37.8	0.93	21.3**	21.7**	20.8**	0.96**	29.3**	29.9**	28.7**	0.96**	3.4**	3.8**	2.9**	.	.	104
87.1 y	85.6 y	88.7 y	1.04 y	74.2**	72.2**	76.3**	1.06**	75.2**,y	71.6**,y	78.9**,y	1.10**,y	9.9 y	11.3 y	8.7 y	2.3 y	77 y	105
...	...	...	...	...	...	...	...	...	...	...	...	...	...	...	...	...	106
...	...	...	...	...	...	...	...	...	...	...	...	...	...	...	.	.	107
83.6	82.2	85.0	1.03	73.9**	73.3**	74.5**	1.02**	74.9	73.5	76.4	1.04	1.4	2.0	0.8	41.7	59	108
75.7	73.3	78.2	1.07	54.9**	55.1**	54.8**	1.00**	60.2**	59.2**	61.1**	1.03**	2.1	2.7	1.5	.	.	109

314 / ANNEX

Table 8 (continued)

	Country or territory	Age group 2001	School-age population (000) 2001	Enrolment in secondary education Total enrolment 1998 Total (000)	1998 % F	2001 Total (000)	2001 % F	Enrolment in technical and vocational education 2001 Total (000)	2001 % F	GER 1998 Total	1998 Male	1998 Female	GPI (F/M)
110	Montserrat[3]	12-16	...	0.3	47	0.3	48	...	...	...	...	...	...
111	Netherlands Antilles	12-17	21	15	54	15	52	6	43	74.9	69.0	80.9	1.17
112	Nicaragua	13-17	625	287**	54**	354	54	19	57	48.4**	44.3**	52.5**	1.18**
113	Panama	12-17	353	229**	51**	244	51	101	51	67.5**	65.0**	70.1**	1.08**
114	Paraguay[w]	12-17	784	368	51	498	50	40	47	50.8	49.6	52.1	1.05
115	Peru[w]	12-16	2 795	2 212	48	2 486**	48**	...	...	81.7	84.0	79.4	0.95
116	Saint Kitts and Nevis[4]	12-16	...	...	...	4**	51**	...	...	...	...	...	...
117	Saint Lucia	12-16	15	12	57	13	57	...	...	76.4	66.6	86.1	1.29
118	St Vincent/Grenad.	12-16	14	...	...	10	54	2	36	...	...	...	...
119	Suriname	12-17	...	...	...	42	57	19	53	...	...	...	...
120	Trinidad and Tobago	12-16	136	117**	52**	109**	52**	3**	52**	81.7**	78.5**	85.0**	1.08**
121	Turks and Caicos Islands[3]	12-16	...	1	51	1	50	...	...	...	...	...	...
122	Uruguay[w]	12-17	311	...	...	316	52	61	43	...	...	...	...
123	Venezuela	12-16	2 640	1 439	54	1 811	53	54	51	56.9	51.2	62.8	1.23
	North America and Western Europe												
124	Andorra[4]	12-17	...	...	...	3	53	0.2	45	...	...	...	...
125	Austria[o]	10-17	762	748	48	756	48	266	43	98.8	100.9	96.6	0.96
126	Belgium[o]	12-17	732	1 033	51	1 149	52	663	52	142.4	137.3	147.7	1.08
127	Canada[o]	12-17	2 490	2 565	49	2 621[z]	49[z]	102[z]	36[z]	105.3	105.6	105.0	0.99
128	Cyprus[o,3]	12-17	...	63	50	64	49	4	17	93.2	91.8	94.7	1.03
129	Denmark[o]	13-18	337	422	50	435	50	118	45	125.6	122.1	129.2	1.06
130	Finland[o]	13-18	390	480	51	493	52	172	50	120.9	115.8	126.2	1.09
131	France[o]	11-17	5 427	5 955	49	5 852	49	1 444	44	109.6	109.5	109.6	1.00
132	Germany[o]	10-18	8 485	8 185	48	8 465	48	1 753	43	98.2	99.0	97.3	0.98
133	Greece[o]	12-17	755	771	49	743[z]	49[z]	135[z]	44[z]	93.9	93.3	94.5	1.01
134	Iceland[o]	13-19	30	32	50	33	50	8	40	109.4	106.2	112.7	1.06
135	Ireland[o]	12-16	308	346	50	323	51	...	...	105.4	102.2	108.7	1.06
136	Israel[o]	12-17	642	569	49	606	49	126	40	90.8	91.0	90.6	1.00
137	Italy[o]	11-18	4 602	4 450	49	4 516	48	720	45	91.7	92.2	91.1	0.99
138	Luxembourg[o]	12-18	35	...	...	34	50	11	48	...	...	...	...
139	Malta[o]	11-17	40	...	...	36	48	3	27	...	...	...	...
140	Monaco[4]	11-17	...	3	51	3[z]	48[z]	0.5[z]	44[z]	...	...	...	...
141	Netherlands[o]	12-17	1 144	1 365	48	1 398	48	477	46	124.4	127.1	121.6	0.96
142	Norway[o]	13-18	329	378	49	373	49	119	45	120.3	118.9	121.7	1.02
143	Portugal[o]	12-17	695	848	51	797	50	115	44	109.5	105.3	114.0	1.08
144	San Marino[4]	11-18	...	...	...	1[y]	48[y]	...	...	...	...	...	...
145	Spain[o]	12-17	2 686	...	...	3 107	50	444	50	...	...	...	...
146	Sweden[o]	13-18	641	964	55	935	54	276	55	160.1	141.0	180.2	1.28
147	Switzerland[o]	13-19	562	544	47	550	47	175	40	99.9	103.8	95.8	0.92
148	United Kingdom[o]	11-17	5 376	8 092	52	9 630	54	5 255	58	157.6	149.0	166.5	1.12
149	United States[o]	12-17	24 952	...	...	23 196	49	...	...	...	...	...	...
	South and West Asia												
150	Afghanistan	13-18	2 907	...	...	362	—	...	...	...	...	...	...
151	Bangladesh	11-17	22 805	9 134	47	10 691	51	124	25	42.4	43.3	41.5	0.96
152	Bhutan[5]	13-16	58	17	44	26	45	0.4	38	...	...	...	...
153	India[w]	11-17	151 602	67 090	39	76 216	41	619	17	46.6	54.4	38.1	0.70
154	Iran, Islamic Republic of	11-17	12 894	9 727	47	9 916	48	736	37	77.4	80.2	74.4	0.93
155	Maldives	13-17	37	12	51	25	51	2	40	36.5	35.7	37.3	1.05
156	Nepal	11-17	3 853	1 265	40	1 690	41	21	20	35.5	41.2	29.3	0.71
157	Pakistan	10-16	24 855	...	...	5 790 *,[z]	38 *,[z]	83 *,[z]	17 *,[z]	...	...	...	...
158	Sri Lanka[w]	10-17	2 760	2 135**	51**	2 229	...	...	...	74.4**	72.0**	76.8**	1.07**
	Sub-Saharan Africa												
159	Angola	10-16	2 168	292	...	414	44	77	39	14.7	...	...	...
160	Benin	12-18	1 106	213	31	287**	32**	24**	33**	21.1	29.1	13.2	0.45
161	Botswana	13-17	216	148	52	157	51	5	30	71.2	67.7	74.6	1.10
162	Burkina Faso	13-19	2 004	173	38	205**	39**	18**	51**	9.4	11.8	7.1	0.60
163	Burundi	13-19	1 143	73**	46**	122**	42**	9**	33**	7.1**	7.7**	6.5**	0.84**

3. National population data were used to calculate enrolment ratios.
4. Enrolment ratios were not calculated, due to lack of United Nations population data by age.
5. Enrolment ratios were not calculated due to inconsistencies between enrolment and the United Nations population data.

STATISTICAL ANNEX / 315

Table 8

	GROSS ENROLMENT RATIO (GER) IN SECONDARY EDUCATION (%) 2001				NET ENROLMENT RATIO (NER) IN SECONDARY EDUCATION (%) 1998				2001				INTERNAL EFFICIENCY Repeaters in general secondary education (%) 2001			POST-SECONDARY NON-TERTIARY EDUCATION Total enrolment 2001		
	Total	Male	Female	GPI (F/M)	Total	Male	Female	GPI (F/M)	Total	Male	Female	GPI (F/M)	Total	Male	Female	Total (000)	% F	
	102.0	...	...	...	...	...	...	...	94.6	...	...	...	0.3	.	0.7	0.0	56	110
	72.6	68.6	76.7	1.12	70.8	65.2	76.3	1.17	64.6	62.6	66.6	1.06	–	–	–	0.4	86	111
	56.6	51.9	61.3	1.18	...	...	...	...	37.0	34.0	40.1	1.18	6.2	7.3	5.1	.	.	112
	69.2	66.9	71.6	1.07	60.1**	58.2**	62.2**	1.07**	62.4**	59.6**	65.4**	1.10**	5.1	6.4	3.8	2.6	60	113
	63.5	62.8	64.2	1.02	42.1**	40.8**	43.5**	1.07**	50.1**	48.9**	51.4**	1.05**	1.2	1.6	0.8	.	.	114
	89.0**	92.0**	85.8**	0.93**	62.2	62.9	61.6	0.98	65.8**,z	66.9**,z	64.7**,z	0.97**,z	5.3	6.1	4.3	263.6	66	115
	...	...	...	...	...	...	...	...	...	...	...	...	4.0	4.4	3.6	1.3	69	116
	86.0	74.7	97.1	1.30	65.4	60.3	70.4	1.17	70.5**	61.4**	79.4**	1.29**	0.2	0.1	0.2	1.1	56	117
	68.1	61.8	74.4	1.20	...	...	...	...	51.8	46.9	56.9	1.21	–	–	–	1.2	58	118
	73.6	61.8	86.0	1.39	...	...	...	...	63.4**	52.4**	74.8**	1.43**	–	–	–	.	.	119
	80.2**	76.5**	83.9**	1.10**	72.5**	70.0**	74.9**	1.07**	69.2**	66.2**	72.3**	1.09**	3.5**	3.4**	3.6**	8.3	63	120
	85.3	84.2	86.5	1.03	...	...	...	...	76.2	74.1	78.4	1.06	1.6	1.7	1.4	0.6	65	121
	101.4	95.0	108.2	1.14	...	...	...	...	71.7**	68.0**	75.6**	1.11**	12.4	15.3	9.9	2.3	35	122
	68.6	63.5	73.8	1.16	48.0	43.0	53.2	1.24	57.5**	53.0**	62.2**	1.17**	9.4	11.2	7.9	.	.	123
	...	...	...	...	...	...	...	...	...	...	...	...	–	–	–	.	.	124
	99.1	101.4	96.8	0.95	...	...	...	...	88.5	88.9	88.1	0.99	...	...	...	56.3	59	125
	157.1	148.3	166.3	1.12	...	...	...	...	95.4**	94.5**	96.3**	1.02**	...	...	...	48.5	53	126
	106.2 z	106.5 z	105.8 z	0.99 z	94.0**	94.3**	93.7**	0.99**	97.6**	97.4**	97.9**	...	...	...	...	313.8 z	43 z	127
	96.9	95.9	98.0	1.02	87.8	86.2	89.6	1.04	91.7	90.3	93.1	1.03	1.8	2.6	1.0	.	.	128
	128.8	125.8	131.9	1.05	89.0**	87.6**	90.4**	1.03**	92.9	91.5	94.4	1.03	.	.	.	1.0	19	129
	126.5	119.8	133.5	1.11	94.9**	94.5**	95.2**	1.01**	94.4	93.7	95.1	1.02	0.4	0.5	0.3	8.9	45	130
	107.8	107.5	108.2	1.01	93.3**	92.5**	94.3**	1.02**	93.3**	92.4**	94.2**	1.02**	...	...	...	24.0	64	131
	99.8	100.4	99.1	0.99	...	...	...	...	...	...	...	...	3.4	3.9	2.8	444.8	47	132
	95.7 z	94.8 z	96.6 z	1.02 z	84.9**	83.5**	86.4**	1.03**	84.9 z	83.6 z	86.4 z	1.03 z	...	...	...	42.9	53	133
	111.3	107.9	114.9	1.07	84.7**	82.3**	87.2**	1.06**	84.6	82.9	86.5	1.04	–	–	–	0.3	26	134
	104.8	100.2	109.7	1.10	82.1	80.1	84.1	1.05	82.4	79.4	85.5	1.08	2.6	2.5	2.7	46.9	54	135
	94.4	95.0	93.8	0.99	86.8**	86.3**	87.3**	1.01**	88.9	88.5	89.4	1.01	2.1	3.2	0.9	14.3	51	136
	98.1	100.1	96.1	0.96	84.8**	84.4**	85.2**	1.01**	90.5	90.4	90.7	1.00	3.1**	4.0**	2.2**	38.9	60	137
	96.1	92.9	99.5	1.07	...	...	...	...	79.9	77.0	82.9	1.08	...	...	...	1.0	20	138
	91.3	91.8	90.8	0.99	...	...	...	...	82.0	81.4	82.6	1.01	0.8	0.5	1.0	0.7	23	139
	...	...	...	...	...	...	...	...	...	...	...	...	–	–	–	.	.	140
	122.2	123.9	120.4	0.97	92.2**	91.8**	92.7**	1.01**	90.4**	90.2**	90.5**	1.00**	4.6	5.0	4.3	6.3	13	141
	113.4	112.2	114.6	1.02	96.1**	95.7**	96.5**	1.01**	95.0	94.5	95.6	1.01	...	...	...	5.7	23	142
	114.7	112.0	117.6	1.05	85.3**	81.8**	89.0**	1.09**	84.5	81.8	87.4	1.07	...	...	...	.	.	143
	...	...	...	...	...	...	...	...	...	...	...	...	...	...	...	1.1 y	49 y	144
	115.7	112.1	119.4	1.06	...	...	...	...	94.0	92.2	95.9	1.04	...	...	...	30.9	50	145
	145.7	132.0	160.2	1.21	97.8**	95.7**	100.0**	1.05**	98.6	98.2	99.0	1.01	...	...	...	11.6	48	146
	98.0	101.0	94.8	0.94	88.2**	91.3**	85.0**	0.93**	87.2	89.5	84.7	0.95	2.2	2.4	2.0	28.5	69	147
	179.1	159.9	199.4	1.25	94.8*	94.7*	94.9*	1.00*	95.6	94.4	96.7	1.02	...	...	...	–	–	148
	93.0	93.5	92.4	0.99	...	...	...	...	85.3	85.3	85.4	1.00	...	...	...	1 672.5 z	57 z	149
	12.5	24.0	–	...	...	...	...	...	...	...	...	...	...	...	...	.	.	150
	46.9	44.7	49.2	1.10	39.4	40.3	38.5	0.95	43.8	41.9	45.9	1.10	5.1	5.2	4.9	19.8	40	151
	...	...	...	...	...	...	...	...	...	...	...	...	10.7	9.2	12.6	3.4	35	152
	50.3	57.5	42.5	0.74	...	...	...	...	...	...	...	...	4.8	5.2	4.3	523.4	26	153
	76.9	78.8	74.9	0.95	...	...	...	...	...	...	...	...	...	...	...	804.9	15 *	154
	66.0	63.9	68.2	1.07	...	...	...	...	31.4 y	29.5 y	33.3 y	1.13 y	...	...	...	0.2	...	155
	43.9	49.8	37.4	0.75	...	...	...	...	...	...	...	...	8.9	8.4	9.6	.	.	156
	23.9*,z	28.6*,z	18.9*,z	0.66*,z	...	...	...	...	...	...	...	...	...	...	...	923.6*,z	45*,z	157
	80.8	...	...	...	...	...	...	...	...	...	...	...	...	...	...	.	.	158
	19.1	21.4	16.8	0.78	...	...	...	...	...	...	...	...	...	...	...	.	.	159
	26.0**	35.5**	16.5**	0.46**	15.7**	21.5**	9.9**	0.46**	20.1**,z	27.2**,z	12.9**,z	0.48**,z	21.2	21.1	21.4	...	...	160
	72.7	70.5	75.0	1.06	52.7**	48.2**	57.4**	1.19**	54.6**,z	50.7**,z	58.5**,z	1.15**,z	...	...	...	14.1	49	161
	10.2**	12.4**	8.0**	0.65**	8.3	10.5	6.1	0.58	8.0**,z	9.7**,z	6.3**,z	0.65**,z	...	...	...	.	.	162
	10.7**	12.4**	9.0**	0.73**	...	...	...	...	8.3**	9.5**	7.1**	0.75**	...	...	...	.	.	163

(y) Data are for 1999/2000.
(z) Data are for 2000/2001.

Table 8 (continued)

	Country or territory	Age group 2001	School-age population (000) 2001	Enrolment in secondary education — Total enrolment 1998 Total (000)	1998 % F	2001 Total (000)	2001 % F	Enrolment in technical and vocational education 2001 Total (000)	2001 % F	GER 1998 Total	1998 Male	1998 Female	GPI (F/M)
164	Cameroon	12-18	2 562	626**	45**	836**	45**	161**	38**	26.5**	29.1**	24.0**	0.82**
165	Cape Verde	12-17	70	40**	...	46	51	1	40	61.7**	...	...	...
166	Central African Republic	12-18	603	...	...	...	...	...	...	...	...	...	...
167	Chad	12-18	1 273	123	21	137**,z	22**,z	3**,z	32**,z	10.7	17.1	4.4	0.26
168	Comoros	12-18	122	29	44	34	45	0.2	40	24.8	27.4	22.2	0.81
169	Congo	12-18	571	...	...	183**	42**	18**	52**	...	...	...	...
170	Côte d'Ivoire	12-18	2 847	592**	35**	620**,y	35**,y	...	...	22.5**	29.2**	15.7**	0.54**
171	Democratic Rep. of the Congo	12-17	7 140	...	...	...	...	...	...	...	...	...	...
172	Equatorial Guinea	12-18	71	...	...	21**	36**	1	20	...	...	...	...
173	Eritrea	12-17	553	115	41	153	39	2	21	23.3	27.6	19.1	0.69
174	Ethiopia	13-18	9 104	1 060	40	1 734	38	9**	23**	12.9	15.4	10.4	0.67
175	Gabon	12-18	207	87	46	105**	...	8	34	45.7	49.2	42.3	0.86
176	Gambia	13-18	171	47	40	59**	41**	0.4**	69**	30.8	37.1	24.5	0.66
177	Ghana	12-17	2 943	1 024	44	1 107**	45**	15**	13**	36.7	41.2	32.2	0.78
178	Guinea	13-19	1 283	172**	26**	...	...	...	...	13.9**	20.2**	7.3**	0.36**
179	Guinea-Bissau	13-17	154	...	...	26 y	35 y	1 y	27 y	...	...	...	...
180	Kenya	13-17	4 162	1 156**	47**	1 331	47	25	42	29.9**	31.5**	28.3**	0.90**
181	Lesotho	13-17	236	72	58	80	56	1	50	31.7	26.5	36.9	1.39
182	Liberia	12-17	445	114	39	137 y	40 y	45 y	40 y	30.5	37.0	23.9	0.65
183	Madagascar	11-17	2 643	347**	49**	...	...	...	...	14.3**	14.6**	14.0**	0.96**
184	Malawi	12-17	1 526	519	41**	518	44	...	...	36.1	42.9**	29.5**	0.69**
185	Mali	13-18	1 748	218	34	...	...	...	...	13.6	17.7	9.4	0.53
186	Mauritius	12-18	137	102	50	109	48	11**	22**	70.3	69.9	70.6	1.01
187	Mozambique	11-17	3 035	270**	40**	402	39	21	28	9.8**	11.7**	8.0**	0.68**
188	Namibia	13-17	213	110	54	131	53	...	...	57.3	53.2	61.4	1.15
189	Niger	13-19	1 727	105	38	112	39	3	34	6.7	8.1	5.2	0.63
190	Nigeria	12-17	16 854	...	...	...	...	...	...	...	...	...	...
191	Rwanda	13-18	1 156	91	50	167**	50**	21**	48**	9.6	10.2	9.0	0.88
192	Sao Tome and Principe	13-17	19	...	...	7**	45**	0.04	25	...	...	...	...
193	Senegal	13-19	1 559	239**	39**	291**	40**	6**	45**	16.7**	20.2**	13.0**	0.64**
194	Seychelles[3]	12-16	...	8	49	8	51	...	...	114.0	114.1	113.9	1.00
195	Sierra Leone	12-17	611	...	...	156 z	42**,z	21 z	44**,z	...	...	...	...
196	Somalia	...	...	...	...	...	...	...	...	...	...	...	...
197	South Africa	14-18	4 894	4 244*	53*	4 229**	52**	200**	42**	89.8*	84.5*	95.1*	1.13*
198	Swaziland	13-17	136	61	50	61	50	0.3**	23**	48.4	48.4	48.5	1.00
199	Togo	12-18	761	232	29	261**,y	31**,y	17**,y	25**,y	33.6	47.9	19.2	0.40
200	Uganda	13-18	3 388	304	39	571**	43**	31**	30**	9.8	12.0	7.7	0.64
201	United Republic of Tanzania	14-19	4 943	250**	45**	271**,y	45**,y	24**,y	31**,y	5.5**	6.1**	5.0**	0.82**
202	Zambia	14-18	1 232	226	43**	297	44	7	6	19.8	22.4**	17.1**	0.77**
203	Zimbabwe w	13-18	2 021	...	...	866	47	...	...	...	...	...	...

			Sum	Sum	% F	Sum	% F	Sum	% F	Weighted average			
I	World	...	752 008	424 925	46	477 586	47	57 348	44	60.2	63.1	57.2	0.91
II	Countries in transition	...	34 524	...	...	31 272	49	2 319	36	...	...	...	...
III	Developed countries	...	84 628	87 210	49	85 816	49	17 676	49	103.5	103.2	103.9	1.01
IV	Developing countries	...	632 856	311 079	45	358 392	46	37 311	43	52.5	56.1	48.7	0.87
V	Arab States	...	38 975	21 997	46	24 823	46	3 360	44	59.3	62.9	55.6	0.88
VI	Central and Eastern Europe	...	43 829	37 881	49	38 288	48	6 224	39	...	...	...	...
VII	Central Asia	...	11 946	5 754	49	10 406	49	571	43	85.5	86.1	84.8	0.98
VIII	East Asia and the Pacific	...	217 947	137 952	...	149 732	47	25 640	43	66.5	...	...	...
IX	Latin America and the Caribbean	...	66 291	41 871	51	57 159	51	5 716	52	71.9	68.8	75.0	1.09
X	North America and Western Europe	...	61 486	63 630	49	63 508	50	12 311	51	105.4	105.1	105.7	1.01
XI	South and West Asia	...	221 771	95 750	41	107 017	42	1 621	27	45.6	52.0	38.6	0.74
XII	Sub-Saharan Africa	...	89 764	20 358	44	24 073	44	1 855	37	24.6	27.3	22.0	0.80

1. Refers to lower and upper secondary education (ISCED levels 2 and 3).
2. Corresponds to ISCED level 4. Like secondary education, it includes general as well as technical and vocational programmes.
3. National population data were used to calculate enrolment ratios.
4. Enrolment ratios were not calculated, due to lack of United Nations population data by age.

STATISTICAL ANNEX / 317

Table 8

	GROSS ENROLMENT RATIO (GER) IN SECONDARY EDUCATION (%)				NET ENROLMENT RATIO (NER) IN SECONDARY EDUCATION (%)									INTERNAL EFFICIENCY Repeaters in general secondary education (%)			POST-SECONDARY NON-TERTIARY EDUCATION Total enrolment		
	2001				1998				2001					2001			2001		
	Total	Male	Female	GPI (F/M)	Total	Male	Female	GPI (F/M)	Total	Male	Female	GPI (F/M)		Total	Male	Female	Total (000)	% F	
	32.6**	35.9**	29.4**	0.82**	...	...	...	...	...	...	...	...		...	...	...	...	...	164
	65.9	64.4	67.4	1.05	...	...	...	...	53.4	52.4	54.3	1.04		21.6	22.6	20.7	0.6	55	165
	...	...	...	...	...	...	...	...	...	...	...	...		...	...	...	...	...	166
	11.2**,z	17.4**,z	4.9**,z	0.28**,z	7.5	11.6	3.4	0.29	7.5**,z	11.5**,z	3.6**,z	0.31**,z		16.1**,z	16.1**,z	16.1**,z	.	.	167
	27.7	30.0	25.3	0.84	...	...	...	...	...	...	...	...		19.2	19.2	19.1	0.4	45	168
	32.0**	37.4**	26.6**	0.71**	...	...	...	...	...	...	...	...		30.8	28.0	34.8	...	...	169
	22.8**,y	29.6**,y	16.0**,y	0.54**,y	...	...	...	...	...	...	...	...		17.2 y	17.8**,y	16.0**,y	...	...	170
	...	...	...	...	...	...	...	...	...	...	...	...		...	...	...	...	...	171
	29.7**	37.8**	21.6**	0.57**	23.4**	...	...	...	26.2**,y	33.2**,y	19.2**,y	0.58**,y		...	...	...	.	.	172
	27.6	33.4	21.8	0.65	18.9**	21.0**	16.8**	0.80**	21.3**	24.4**	18.1**	0.74**		20.3	18.5	23.1	1.3	16	173
	19.0	23.5	14.6	0.62	11.4**	13.3**	9.4**	0.71**	15.0**	18.7**	11.4**	0.61**		...	...	...	9.5	39	174
	50.9**	...	...	...	...	...	...	...	...	...	...	...		21.7	...	...	0.3	52	175
	34.3**	40.1**	28.4**	0.71**	25.2	29.8	20.7	0.70	27.9**	32.0**	23.9**	0.75**		...	...	...	0.1**,z	98**,z	176
	37.6**	41.2**	34.0**	0.82**	31.1**	34.1**	28.0**	0.82**	32.0**	34.3**	29.7**	0.87**		...	...	...	18.8	31	177
	...	...	...	...	12.0**	17.2**	6.5**	0.38**	...	...	...	...		...	...	...	...	...	178
	17.8 y	23.0 y	12.5 y	0.54 y	...	...	...	...	...	...	...	...		18.7 y	17.8 y	20.4 y	.	.	179
	32.0	33.6	30.3	0.90	...	...	...	...	24.0**	24.4**	23.6**	0.97**		...	...	...	...	...	180
	33.7	29.8	37.6	1.26	14.0**	9.7**	18.3**	1.89**	21.9	17.1	26.6	1.56		...	...	...	1.6	56	181
	34.1 y	40.3 y	27.8 y	0.69 y	...	...	...	...	17.9**,y	22.8**,y	13.0**,y	0.57**,y		...	...	...	15.6 y	43 y	182
	...	...	...	...	11.5**	11.3**	11.6**	1.03**	...	...	...	...		...	...	...	13.2**	34**	183
	34.0	38.6	29.4	0.76	26.9**	30.3**	23.5**	0.78**	29.3	32.4	26.2	0.81		...	...	...	13.6 z	35 z	184
	...	...	...	...	...	...	...	...	...	...	...	...		...	...	...	.	.	185
	79.5	81.0	78.0	0.96	62.4**	62.1**	62.7**	1.01**	62.1	59.9	64.5	1.08		12.8	14.0	11.7	3.3**	23**	186
	13.3	16.0	10.5	0.66	7.9**	9.3**	6.6**	0.72**	10.8	12.7	8.7	0.69		22.2	20.9	24.0	.	.	187
	61.4	57.4	65.4	1.14	30.3	24.6	36.1	1.47	38.2	32.4	44.1	1.36		10.9**	9.7**	12.0**	1.6	27	188
	6.5	7.8	5.1	0.65	5.8**	7.0**	4.6**	0.65**	5.5	6.5	4.3	0.66		22.9	22.5	23.6	0.2	41	189
	...	...	...	...	...	...	...	...	...	...	...	...		...	...	...	...	...	190
	14.4**	15.4**	13.5**	0.88**	...	...	...	...	...	...	...	...		13.2**	11.5**	15.0**	.	.	191
	39.2**	42.4**	35.9**	0.84**	...	...	...	...	...	...	...	...		23.5**	20.7**	26.8**	...	...	192
	18.7**	22.3**	15.0**	0.67**	...	...	...	...	...	...	...	...		14.0	13.5	14.8	...	...	193
	110.0	107.5	112.6	1.05	99.4	98.8	100.0	1.01	97.6	95.2	100.0	1.05		...	...	...	1.7	53	194
	26.4 z	31.0**,z	21.8**,z	0.70**,z	...	...	...	...	...	...	...	...		7.8 z	7.0 z	8.9 z	40.1 z	57 z	195
	...	...	...	...	...	...	...	...	...	...	...	...		...	...	...	...	...	196
	86.4**	82.6**	90.2**	1.09**	59.4*	55.4*	63.4*	1.15*	62.0**,z	58.8**,z	65.1**,z	1.11**,z		...	...	...	356.0	40	197
	45.2	45.1	45.3	1.00	37.1	35.3	38.8	1.10	32.2	29.2	35.2	1.21		12.5	12.6	12.5	...	...	198
	36.5**,y	50.6**,y	22.3**,y	0.44**,y	23.1	32.1	14.1	0.44	26.6**,y	35.9**,y	17.3**,y	0.48**,y		20.9**	21.3 y	20.0 y	...	...	199
	16.8**	19.1**	14.6**	0.77**	...	...	...	...	14.0 z	15.1 z	13.0 z	0.86 z		...	...	...	.	.	200
	5.8**,y	6.4**,y	5.2**,y	0.81**,y	...	...	...	...	...	...	...	...		0.2 y	0.2 y	0.1 y	–	–	201
	24.1	26.8	21.4	0.80	15.9**	17.3**	14.6**	0.84**	20.0**	21.7**	18.4**	0.85**		12.3**	11.4**	13.4**	.	.	202
	42.9	45.4	40.3	0.89	...	...	...	...	40.2	42.2	38.3	0.91		.	.	.	1.5	...	203

	Weighted average				Weighted average									Median					
	63.7	66.2	60.9	0.92	51.3	...	...	...	54.9**	58.1**	51.5	0.89		4.4	...	...	...	...	I
	90.6	90.8	90.3	0.99	...	...	...	...	85.0	84.8	85.2	1.00		0.3	0.4	0.2	...	...	II
	105.9	104.7	107.2	1.02	87.9	87.7	88.1	1.00	90.0	89.5	90.4	1.01		...	...	...	...	...	III
	56.6	59.8	53.1	0.89	...	...	...	...	48.5**	52.4**	44.4	0.85		7.4	9.0	5.4	...	...	IV
	63.7	67.1	60.1	0.90	50.8	53.5	48.1	0.90	55.3	57.7	52.9	0.92		8.3	9.7	6.8	...	...	V
	90.1	91.7	88.4	0.96	...	...	...	...	82.7	83.4	82.0	0.98		1.1	1.4	0.7	...	...	VI
	87.1	88.2	86.0	0.98	81.6	82.3	80.9	0.98	83.6	84.8	82.4	0.97		0.3	0.4	0.1	...	...	VII
	68.7	70.9	66.3	0.93	...	...	...	...	...	...	...	...		...	...	...	...	...	VIII
	86.2	83.2	89.3	1.07	52.9	50.7	55.1	1.09	63.8	61.9	65.7	1.06		4.2	5.0	3.3	...	...	IX
	107.6	105.9	109.3	1.03	89.4	89.5	89.3	1.00	89.2	88.8	89.6	1.01		...	...	...	...	...	X
	48.3	53.8	42.3	0.79	...	...	...	...	...	...	...	...		...	...	...	...	...	XI
	26.8	30.0	23.7	0.79	18.0	19.7	16.3	0.83	21.3	23.1	19.4	0.84		...	...	...	...	...	XII

5. Enrolment ratios were not calculated due to inconsistencies between enrolment and the United Nations population data.

(y) Data are for 1999/2000.
(z) Data are for 2000/2001.

Table 9
Participation in tertiary education

		\multicolumn{9}{c}{ENROLMENT IN TERTIARY EDUCATION}
		\multicolumn{6}{c}{Total students enrolled (000)}	\multicolumn{4}{c}{Gross enrolment ratio (GER) (%)}
		\multicolumn{3}{c}{1998}	\multicolumn{3}{c}{2001}	\multicolumn{4}{c}{1998}
	Country or territory	Total	Male	Female	Total	Male	Female	Total	Male	Female	GPI (F/M)
	Arab States										
1	Algeria	456**	...	...	...	...	...	15.1**	...	...	...
2	Bahrain	11	4**	7**	...	...	...	20.7	15.0**	27.8**	1.85**
3	Djibouti	0.2	0.1	0.1	0.7	0.4	0.3	0.3	0.3	0.3	1.00
4	Egyptw	2 447**	...	...	...	...	...	38.3**	...	...	...
5	Iraq	272	179	93	318**	210**	108**	12.9	16.7	9.1	0.54
6	Jordanw	...	...	...	163	83	80	...	...	...	...
7	Kuwait	32**	10**	22**	...	...	...	20.9**	12.2**	31.6**	2.59**
8	Lebanon	113	56	57	143	67	76	35.5	35.1	35.9	1.02
9	Libyan Arab Jamahiriya	308	158**	150**	359	175	185	56.1	56.8**	55.4**	0.98**
10	Mauritania	13	...	...	8	6	2	5.5	...	...	...
11	Morocco	273	159	114	315**	177**	138**	9.4	10.8	8.0	0.74
12	Oman	...	...	...	20**	8**	12**	...	...	...	...
13	Palestinian Autonomous Territories	66	36	30	89	46	43	24.8	26.2	23.3	0.89
14	Qatar	9**	3**	6**	8	2	6	25.2**	11.7**	45.7**	3.91**
15	Saudi Arabia	350	150	199	445**	183**	261**	20.2	16.8	23.8	1.42
16	Sudan	201	106	95	...	...	...	6.8	7.1	6.5	0.92
17	Syrian Arab Republic	94**,mk	...	...	...	...	...	5.7**,mk	...	...	...
18	Tunisiaw	157**	81**	76**	226**	...	...	17.3**	17.5**	17.0**	0.97**
19	United Arab Emirates	21**	...	...	...	...	...	10.2**	...	...	...
20	Yemen	164	130	34	173**,y	137**,y	36**,y	11.2	17.1	4.8	0.28
	Central and Eastern Europe										
21	Albaniao	...	...	...	41z	16z	25z	...	...	...	...
22	Belarus	353	155	198	464	200	263	48.4	41.6	55.4	1.33
23	Bosnia and Herzegovinao	...	...	...	...	...	...	...	...	...	...
24	Bulgariao	270	109	161	228	105	123	43.5	34.5	52.9	1.53
25	Croatia	96	45	51	113	54	59	31.9	29.6	34.2	1.16
26	Czech Republico	231	116	115	284	139	146	26.1	25.7	26.5	1.03
27	Estoniao	49	21	28	61	23	37	51.0	42.3	60.0	1.42
28	Hungaryo	279	128	151	354	159	196	33.4	29.9	37.1	1.24
29	Latviao	82	32	51	111	43	68	50.5	38.5	62.6	1.63
30	Lithuaniao	107	43	64	149	59	90	45.5	36.1	55.0	1.52
31	Polando	1 399	601	798	1 906	803	1 104	45.7	38.5	53.1	1.38
32	Republic of Moldova	105	47	59	108	47	61	30.0	26.5	33.4	1.26
33	Romaniao	408	200	208	582	266	316	21.3	20.4	22.1	1.08
34	Russian Federationw	...	...	...	8 030	3 477	4 553	...	...	...	...
35	Serbia and Montenegro2	197	92	106	209z	97z	112z	34.0	31.1	37.0	1.19
36	Slovakia	123	59	64	152	73	79	26.5	25.2	27.9	1.11
37	Sloveniao	79	35	44	99	42	57	52.8	45.3	60.7	1.34
38	The former Yugoslav Rep. of Macedoniao	35	16	19	45	20	25	22.0	19.3	24.7	1.28
39	Turkeyo	...	...	...	1 678	984	694	...	...	...	...
40	Ukraine	1 583	751*	833*	2 135	995*	1 139*	43.2	40.4*	46.1*	1.14*
	Central Asia										
41	Armenia	...	...	...	75	35	41	...	...	...	...
42	Azerbaijan	146**	79**	67**	171	82	88	21.9**	24.1**	19.7**	0.82**
43	Georgia	130	63	68	149	75	74	32.2	30.4	34.1	1.12
44	Kazakhstan	324	151	173	515	228	287	23.7	22.0	25.5	1.16
45	Kyrgyzstan	131	65	67	209	98	111	30.4	29.8	30.9	1.04
46	Mongolia	65	23	42	90	33	57	26.1	18.1	34.1	1.88
47	Tajikistan	76	57	19	85	64	21	14.1	20.8	7.3	0.35
48	Turkmenistan	...	...	...	...	...	...	...	...	...	...
49	Uzbekistan	...	...	...	227**	...	...	...	...	...	...
	East Asia and the Pacific										
50	Australiao	...	...	...	869	398	471	...	...	...	...
51	Brunei Darussalam	3	1	2	4.5	1.6	2.8	9.4	6.5	12.4	1.91

1. Data are included in ISCED level 5A.
2. National population data were used to calculate enrolment ratios.
(hf) Data refer to ISCED level 5A only.
(eo) Full-time only.
(mk) Data refer to Bâat University only.
(kb) Not including Islamic Azad University.
(l) Data refer to ISCED level 5B only.
(j) Data refer to ISCED levels 5A and 6 only.
(v) Data do not include ISCED level 6.
(q) Data cover only 80% of students.
(y) Data are for 1999/2000.

STATISTICAL ANNEX / 319

Table 9

	ENROLMENT IN TERTIARY EDUCATION				DISTRIBUTION OF STUDENTS BY ISCED LEVEL						FOREIGN STUDENTS (000)						
	Gross enrolment ratio (GER) (%)				Total students (%)			Percentage of female in each level									
	2001				2001			2001			1998			2001			
	Total	Male	Female	GPI (F/M)	Level 5A	Level 5B	Level 6	Level 5A	Level 5B	Level 6	Total	Male	Female	Total	Male	Female	
	...	...	...	...	...	...	...	...	...	...	...	...	...	...	...	...	1
	...	...	...	...	...	...	...	...	...	...	...	...	...	0.02 y	0.02 y	0.0 y	2
	1.2	1.3	1.1	0.85	52.9	47.1	.	40.8	48.7	.	–	...	–	–	...	–	3
	...	...	...	...	...	...	...	...	...	...	...	...	...	...	...	...	4
	14.1**	18.2**	9.8**	0.54**	...	...	...	...	...	...	...	...	...	8.3 y	7.0 y	1.2 y	5
	31.0	30.7	31.3	1.02	87.8	11.8	0.4	49.1	48.1	25.2	...	...	...	4.4 j	...	...	6
	...	...	...	...	...	...	...	...	...	...	...	...	...	...	...	...	7
	44.7	41.8	47.6	1.14	86.3	12.7	1.0	54.9	40.9	33.2	15.6	...	...	15.2	10.1	5.1	8
	58.1	55.5	60.7	1.09	72.1	25.7	2.2	52.5	49.6	38.0	...	...	...	...	...	...	9
	3.2	5.0	1.4	0.28	95.0	5.0	.	21.4	18.1	.	...	...	...	0.3	...	...	10
	10.3**	11.4**	9.2**	0.81**	84.5**	10.8**	4.6**	44.9**	39.8**	31.6**	4.2	3.5	0.7	4.5 z	3.7 z	0.8 z	11
	7.5**	5.7**	9.6**	1.68**	98.5**	.	1.5**	58.5**	.	22.2**	...	...	...	0.05 y	0.01 y	0.04 y	12
	30.6	30.9	30.2	0.98	94.0	6.0	.	47.5	54.9	.	2.8	2.0	0.8	0.4 z	0.2 z	0.1 z	13
	23.3	12.7	34.1	2.69	100.0	.	.	72.5	.	.	...	...	...	1.6	0.6	1.0	14
	22.0**	17.7**	26.5**	1.50**	84.9**	13.1**	2.1**	61.8**	42.4**	37.4**	6.1	4.5	1.5	7.6 y	5.6 y	2.0 y	15
	...	...	...	...	...	...	...	...	...	...	...	...	...	...	...	...	16
	...	...	...	...	...	...	...	...	...	...	...	...	...	...	...	...	17
	23.2**	...	...	...	77.5**	15.5**	7.1**	...	...	...	2.7 j	...	...	2.5	...	...	18
	...	...	...	...	...	...	...	...	...	...	...	...	...	...	...	...	19
	11.1**,y	17.1**,y	4.8**,y	0.28**,y	85.1**,y	14.9**,y	0.0**,y	22.1**,y	13.3**,y	5.9**,y	...	...	...	...	...	...	20
	15.1 z	11.3 z	19.1 z	1.69 z	97.0 z	3.0 z	./.1	60.8 z	79.9 z	./.1	...	...	...	0.6 z	0.5 z	0.1 z	21
	62.1	52.6	72.0	1.37	65.3	33.5	1.2	57.0	56.8	47.2	2.7	...	...	2.6	...	...	22
	...	...	...	...	...	...	...	...	...	...	...	...	...	...	...	...	23
	37.7	33.9	41.7	1.23	91.0	7.3	1.8	53.7	58.7	49.5	8.4	4.9	3.5	8.0	4.9	3.1	24
	36.4	34.0	39.0	1.15	67.8	32.2	./.1	54.3	48.6	./.1	0.5 j	...	...	0.7	0.4	0.3	25
	33.7	32.2	35.2	1.09	83.4	9.8	6.8	50.4	69.0	36.1	...	...	...	9.8	5.1	4.6	26
	63.9	48.3	80.1	1.66	84.6	13.0	2.5	59.0	78.5	56.3	0.8	0.3	0.5	0.5	...	...	27
	44.1	38.6	49.8	1.29	95.3	2.7	2.0	55.5	57.3	42.3	8.9 j	4.1	4.8	11.8 j	6.4	5.4	28
	68.5	52.0	85.5	1.64	84.0	14.8	1.2	63.6	49.7	59.5	1.8 j	...	...	3.3	1.6	1.7	29
	64.5	50.2	79.1	1.58	70.4	28.1	1.4	59.4	63.2	57.1	0.5	0.4	0.1	0.7	0.5	0.2	30
	58.5	48.3	69.1	1.43	97.5	1.0	1.5	57.9	79.9	45.4	5.7 j	3.0	2.7	7.4 j	3.4	4.0	31
	28.7	24.6	32.9	1.34	82.5	15.9	1.6	56.4	57.6	58.0	...	...	...	2.9	2.0	0.9	32
	30.4	27.2	33.8	1.24	90.5	9.5	./.1	53.6	61.8	./.1	13.3	8.0	5.3	10.6	6.1	4.5	33
	69.9	59.9	80.0	1.34	67.6	30.8	1.7	58.0	54.6	44.7	41.2	...	...	70.7 v	...	...	34
	36.0 z	32.8 z	39.4 z	1.20 z	75.3 z	24.4 z	0.3 z	55.4 z	48.6 z	35.7 z	1.3	0.8	0.5	0.8 z	0.5 z	0.3 z	35
	32.1	30.2	34.1	1.13	90.6	4.0	5.4	51.6	80.3	38.7	...	...	0.5	1.6	1.0	0.7	36
	66.0	54.6	78.1	1.43	51.4	48.6	./.1	60.9	54.0	./.1	0.7	0.4	0.3	1.0	0.5	0.5	37
	27.1	23.7	30.6	1.29	93.0	7.0	./.1	56.1	43.2	./.1	0.3	0.2	0.1	0.1	0.1	0.1	38
	24.8	28.5	20.9	0.73	74.7	24.0	1.3	41.0	42.8	36.0	18.3 v	13.1	5.2	16.3	11.7	4.6	39
	58.0	53.5*	62.5*	1.17*	72.5	26.3	1.2	53.4*	53.5*	49.1*	18.3	...	–	17.2	...	...	40
	26.7	24.5	28.8	1.18	98.3	.	1.8	54.0	.	34.0	...	...	...	–	...	–	41
	24.0	23.8	24.3	1.02	70.6	28.8	0.6	44.3	70.5	31.4	1.7	1.1	0.6	2.2	2.0	0.2	42
	36.5	36.1	36.8	1.02	98.9	.	1.2	49.7	.	59.0	0.3	...	...	0.4	...	...	43
	38.4	33.9	42.8	1.26	100.0	.	1.0	55.2	.	63.0	7.5	...	...	6.0 z	...	...	44
	45.2	42.3	48.2	1.14	99.1	.	0.9	52.9	.	64.1	1.1	...	...	11.9	6.4	5.6	45
	34.7	25.3	44.1	1.74	94.9	4.0	1.1	62.8	73.3	63.7	0.3	0.1	0.1	0.2 z	0.1 z	0.1 z	46
	14.8	22.2	7.3	0.33	99.0	.	1.0	24.3	.	40.9	5.0	...	...	3.9	...	...	47
	...	...	...	...	...	...	...	...	...	...	...	...	...	...	...	...	48
	9.4**	...	...	...	95.0**	3.6**	1.4**	...	...	...	...	...	...	...	...	...	49
	64.6	57.8	71.8	1.24	75.0	21.7	3.3	55.6	50.2	47.9	...	...	...	121.0	64.3	56.7	50
	13.4	9.7	17.2	1.77	57.6	42.3	0.1	63.2	63.3	33.3	0.1	0.05	0.05	0.2	0.1	0.1	51

(z) Data are for 2000/2001.
± Partial data.

Table 9 (continued)

		colspan="6"	ENROLMENT IN TERTIARY EDUCATION				colspan="4"	
		colspan="6"	Total students enrolled (000)				colspan="4"	Gross enrolment ratio (GER) (%)
		colspan="3"	1998	colspan="3"	2001	colspan="4"	1998
	Country or territory	Total	Male	Female	Total	Male	Female	Total	Male	Female	GPI (F/M)
---	---	---	---	---	---	---	---	---	---	---	---
52	Cambodia	...	...	...	32	23	9	...	...	...	...
53	China[w]	7 364	...	...	12 144	...	...	7.2	...	...	...
54	Cook Islands	...	...	...	...	...	...	...	...	...	...
55	Democratic People's Republic of Korea	...	...	...	...	...	...	...	...	...	...
56	Fiji	...	...	...	...	...	...	...	...	...	...
57	Indonesia[w]	...	...	...	3 176	1 717	1 458	...	...	...	...
58	Japan[o]	3 941	2 180	1 760	3 967	2 177	1 790	43.7	47.3	40.0	0.85
59	Kiribati	...	...	...	...	...	...	...	...	...	...
60	Lao People's Democratic Republic	12	8	4	29	18	11	2.6	3.4	1.7	0.50
61	Macao, China	7	4	3	20	13	8	27.6	31.4	24.1	0.77
62	Malaysia[w]	443	216	226	557	...	...	22.9	22.0	23.8	1.08
63	Marshall Islands[3]	...	...	...	0.9	0.4	0.5	...	...	...	...
64	Micronesia (Federated States of)	2	...	...	...	...	...	15.3	...	...	...
65	Myanmar	...	...	...	555**	...	...	...	...	...	...
66	Nauru	.	.	.	.	.	.	.	.	.	.
67	New Zealand[o]	...	...	...	178	73	104	...	...	...	...
68	Niue	.	.	.	.	.	.	.	.	.	.
69	Palau[3]	...	...	...	0.5**	0.2**	0.3**	...	...	...	...
70	Papua New Guinea	10	6	4	...	...	...	2.1	2.8	1.5	0.54
71	Philippines[w]	2 209	995	1 213	2 467	1 096	1 371	29.4	26.0	32.8	1.26
72	Republic of Korea[o]	...	...	...	3 130	2 002	1 128	...	...	...	...
73	Samoa	1	1	1	1**	1**	1**	8.1	8.3	7.8	0.94
74	Singapore	...	...	...	...	...	...	...	...	...	...
75	Solomon Islands	.	.	.	.	.	.	.	.	.	.
76	Thailand[w]	1 814	846	969	2 155	1 033	1 122	30.7	28.6	32.8	1.15
77	Timor-Leste	...	...	...	6*	3*	3*	...	...	...	...
78	Tokelau	.	.	.	.	.	.	.	.	.	.
79	Tonga	...	...	...	0.4**	0.2**	0.2**	...	...	...	...
80	Tuvalu	.	.	.	.	.	.	.	.	.	.
81	Vanuatu	...	...	...	1	...	...	...	...	...	...
82	Viet Nam	810	462	348	785	449	336	10.9	12.4	9.4	0.76
	Latin America and the Caribbean										
83	Anguilla	.	.	.	.	.	.	.	.	.	.
84	Antigua and Barbuda	.	.	.	.	.	.	.	.	.	.
85	Argentina[w]	1 527	...	...	1 919	782	1 136	46.9	...	...	...
86	Aruba[2]	1	1	1	2	1	1	26.3	24.5	28.0	1.14
87	Bahamas	...	...	...	...	...	...	...	...	...	...
88	Barbados	7	2	5	8[z]	2[z]	5[z]	32.0	19.6	44.6	2.28
89	Belize	...	...	...	...	...	...	...	...	...	...
90	Bermuda[2]	...	...	...	2[z]	1[z]	1[z]	...	...	...	...
91	Bolivia	228	148**	80**	302	...	...	30.9	40.0**	21.8**	0.55**
92	Brazil[w]	2 204	992	1 211	3 126	1 372	1 753	13.6	12.3	15.0	1.22
93	British Virgin Islands[2]	.	.	.	0.8	0.2	0.5	.	.	.	.
94	Cayman Islands[3]	0.4**	0.1**	0.3**	0.4[z]	0.1[z]	0.3[z]	...	...	...	...
95	Chile[w]	407	219	187	452[z]	239[z]	213[z]	33.8	36.0	31.5	0.88
96	Colombia	823**	400**	423**	977	471	506	21.2**	20.4**	21.9**	1.07**
97	Costa Rica	58**	27**	30**	79	37	42	16.8**	15.5**	18.2**	1.17**
98	Cuba	156*	...	...	191	87	104	18.9*	...	...	...
99	Dominica	.	.	.	.	.	.	.	.	.	.
100	Dominican Republic	...	...	...	...	...	...	...	...	...	...
101	Ecuador	...	...	...	...	...	...	...	...	...	...
102	El Salvador	118**	53**	65**	110	50	60	18.3**	16.5**	20.2**	1.22**
103	Grenada	...	...	...	...	...	...	...	...	...	...
104	Guatemala	...	...	...	...	...	...	...	...	...	...
105	Guyana	...	...	...	...	...	...	...	...	...	...
106	Haiti	...	...	...	...	...	...	...	...	...	...
107	Honduras	78	35**	43**	90**	40**	51**	13.1	11.5**	14.6**	1.27**
108	Jamaica[w]	...	...	...	45	14	31	...	...	...	...
109	Mexico[o]	1 838	950	888	2 147	1 088	1 059	18.3	19.2	17.4	0.91

2. National population data were used to calculate enrolment ratios.
3. Enrolment ratios were not calculated, due to lack of United Nations population data by age.

(hf) Data refer to ISCED level 5A only.
(eo) Full-time only.
(mk) Data refer to Bâat University only.

(kb) Not including Islamic Azad University.
(l) Data refer to ISCED level 5B only.
(j) Data refer to ISCED levels 5A and 6 only.

STATISTICAL ANNEX / 321

Table 9

ENROLMENT IN TERTIARY EDUCATION				DISTRIBUTION OF STUDENTS BY ISCED LEVEL						FOREIGN STUDENTS (000)						
Gross enrolment ratio (GER) (%)				Total students (%)			Percentage of female in each level			1998			2001			
2001				2001			2001										
Total	Male	Female	GPI (F/M)	Level 5A	Level 5B	Level 6	Level 5A	Level 5B	Level 6	Total	Male	Female	Total	Male	Female	
3.0	4.3	1.7	0.40	100.0	.	.	28.8	.	.	0.02	0.02	0.0	0.04	0.02	0.02	52
12.7	...	...	...	54.6	44.7	0.7	...	...	26.0	...	...	...	...	...	...	53
...	...	...	...	...	...	...	...	...	...	...	...	...	...	...	...	54
...	...	...	...	...	...	...	...	...	...	...	...	...	...	...	...	55
...	...	...	...	...	...	...	...	...	...	...	...	...	...	...	...	56
15.2	16.3	14.1	0.87	74.6	23.6	1.8	43.2	55.5	34.4	0.3	...	...	0.4	...	...	57
49.2	52.7	45.5	0.86	73.6	24.7	1.7	38.8	65.2	27.1	56.6	32.0	24.5	74.9	39.8	35.1	58
...	...	...	...	...	...	...	...	...	...	...	...	...	...	...	...	59
5.5	6.9	4.1	0.59	26.7	73.3	.	36.0	37.4	.	0.1	0.1	0.0	0.1	0.1	0.0	60
66.4	89.5	46.1	0.52	87.3	12.3	0.3	32.6	67.4	30.4	...	...	...	13.1	9.9	3.2	61
26.6	...	...	...	51.9	47.3	0.8	...	...	...	3.1 j	...	...	3.0 j	...	...	62
...	...	...	...	13.6	86.4	.	56.9	56.4	.	...	...	...	0.03	0.01	0.02	63
...	...	...	...	...	...	...	...	...	...	...	...	...	...	...	...	64
11.5**	...	...	...	99.3**	0.5**	0.2**	...	32.9**	...	...	...	...	...	...	...	65
.	.	.	.	.	.	.	.	.	.	.	.	.	.	.	.	66
71.7	57.3	87.1	1.52	72.7	25.4	1.9	58.4	60.1	47.7	6.9	3.4	3.5	11.1	5.5	5.6	67
.	.	.	.	.	.	.	.	.	.	.	.	.	.	.	.	68
...	...	...	...	100.0**	.	.	63.4**	.	.	...	...	...	0.01 z	...	...	69
...	...	...	...	...	...	...	...	...	...	0.3	0.2	0.1	...	...	...	70
31.1	27.1	35.1	1.30	90.7	8.8	0.5	55.6	54.6	62.5	3.5	...	...	2.6	...	...	71
82.0	101.9	61.0	0.60	57.9	41.0	1.1	36.3	35.9	26.1	2.9	1.7	1.2	3.9	2.2	1.7	72
6.5**	6.8**	6.2**	0.91**	19.6**	80.3**	.	39.8**	45.5**	.	0.1	0.1	0.0	0.1 z	...	...	73
...	...	...	...	...	...	...	...	...	...	...	...	...	...	...	...	74
.	.	.	.	.	.	.	.	.	.	.	.	.	.	.	.	75
36.7	35.0	38.3	1.09	79.1	20.7	0.2	54.0	44.5	53.5	1.9 j	...	...	4.1 j,q	...	...	76
12.0*	9.7*	15.3*	1.58*	...	...	...	...	...	...	...	...	...	...	...	...	77
.	.	.	.	.	.	.	.	.	.	.	.	.	.	.	.	78
3.6**	3.0**	4.2**	1.40**	...	...	...	...	...	...	...	...	...	...	...	...	79
.	.	.	.	.	.	.	.	.	.	.	.	.	.	.	.	80
4.0	...	...	...	98.8	.	1.2	...	...	...	...	...	...	...	...	.	81
10.0	11.4	8.6	0.75	69.6	27.7	2.7	51.7	21.1	36.7	0.5	0.4	0.1	0.9	0.7	0.2	82
.	.	.	.	.	.	.	.	.	.	.	.	.	.	.	.	83
.	.	.	.	.	.	.	.	.	.	.	.	.	.	.	.	84
56.3	45.4	67.4	1.48	74.6	25.1	0.3	55.6	70.0	56.1	2.8 l	...	...	3.3 l	...	...	85
28.8	23.2	34.2	1.47	26.6	73.4	.	76.2	54.7	.	...	...	...	...	...	...	86
...	...	...	...	...	...	...	...	...	...	...	...	...	...	...	...	87
36.0 z	20.4 z	52.0 z	2.55 z	52.2 z	47.6 z	...	66.1 z	77.3 z	...	...	...	...	0.6 z	...	...	88
...	...	...	...	...	...	...	...	...	...	...	...	...	...	...	...	89
61.8 z	...	...	...	.	100.0 z	.	...	55.1 z	.	...	...	...	...	...	...	90
39.1	...	...	...	91.3**	7.1**	1.6**	...	...	...	1.1	...	...	...	...	...	91
18.2	15.9	20.6	1.30	...	...	...	...	...	...	...	...	...	...	...	...	92
51.4	31.0	72.7	2.35	67.7	32.3	.	75.0	56.3	.	.	.	.	...	...	...	93
...	...	...	...	79.5 z	20.5 z	.	71.6 z	86.3 z	.	...	...	...	0.1 z	...	...	94
37.5 z	39.1 z	35.9 z	0.92 z	80.5 z	17.8 z	1.7 z	47.5 z	46.4 z	39.6 z	...	...	...	3.5 z	...	...	95
24.2	23.0	25.3	1.10	75.7	18.3	6.0	53.2	46.9	49.5	...	...	...	.	...	...	96
20.5	18.9	22.2	1.17	82.4	17.4	0.2	52.8	52.2	55.9	...	...	...	1.8	...	—	97
27.4	24.4	30.4	1.25	99.2	.	0.8	54.4	.	57.3	3.7 hf	...	...	10.7	...	.	98
.	.	.	.	.	.	.	.	.	.	.	.	.	.	.	.	99
...	...	...	...	...	...	...	...	...	...	...	...	...	...	...	...	100
...	...	...	...	...	...	...	...	...	...	...	...	...	...	...	...	101
16.7	15.2	18.1	1.19	75.4**	15.4**	9.2**	52.6**	61.9**	54.4**	0.6	...	...	0.5	0.2	0.3	102
...	...	...	...	...	...	...	...	...	...	...	...	...	...	...	...	103
...	...	...	...	...	...	...	...	...	...	...	...	...	...	...	...	104
...	...	...	...	...	...	...	...	...	...	...	...	...	...	...	...	105
...	...	...	...	...	...	...	...	...	...	...	...	...	...	...	...	106
14.3**	12.3**	16.2**	1.32**	93.2**	5.1**	1.7**	56.3**	58.7**	40.9**	...	...	...	...	...	...	107
17.2	10.7	23.9	2.23	37.0	56.9	6.2	71.5	66.9	69.9**	0.6	...	...	0.8 y	...	...	108
21.5	22.0	21.0	0.95	96.7	2.9	0.5	49.6	42.9	39.8	2.3	...	...	1.9	...	...	109

(v) Data do not include ISCED level 6.
(q) Data cover only 80% of students.
(y) Data are for 1999/2000.
(z) Data are for 2000/2001.
± Partial data.

Table 9 (continued)

ENROLMENT IN TERTIARY EDUCATION

	Country or territory	Total students enrolled (000) 1998 Total	Male	Female	2001 Total	Male	Female	Gross enrolment ratio (GER) (%) 1998 Total	Male	Female	GPI (F/M)
110	Montserrat	.	.	.	.	.	.	.	.	.	.
111	Netherlands Antilles	2	1	1	2	1	1	14.4	13.3	15.4	1.16
112	Nicaragua	...	...	...	...	...	...	...	...	...	...
113	Panama	...	...	...	89**,y	34**,y	55**,y	...	...	...	...
114	Paraguay[w]	...	...	...	97	41	55	...	...	...	...
115	Peru[w]	...	...	...	824**	422**	402**	...	...	...	...
116	Saint Kitts and Nevis	.	.	.	.	.	.	.	.	.	.
117	Saint Lucia	4	2**	2**	0.2	0.1	0.2	...	...	...	...
118	Saint Vincent and the Grenadines	.	.	.	.	.	.	.	.	.	.
119	Suriname	...	...	...	5	2	3	...	...	...	...
120	Trinidad and Tobago	8	3	4	10	4	6	6.0	5.0	7.0	1.40
121	Turks and Caicos Islands[3]	0.03	–	0.03	0.01z	0.00z	0.01z	...	...	...	...
122	Uruguay[w]	94	34	60	99	36	63	34.8	24.6	45.3	1.84
123	Venezuela	...	...	...	650**	280**	370**	...	...	...	...

North America and Western Europe

124	Andorra	...	...	...	...	...	...	...	...	...	...
125	Austria[o]	253	126	127	224	106	118	52.8	51.6	54.1	1.05
126	Belgium[o]	352	168	183	367	172	195	55.9	52.6	59.2	1.13
127	Canada[o]	1 193	529	664	1 212z	533z	679z	58.9	51.0	67.1	1.32
128	Cyprus[3]	11	5	6	14	6	8	21.9	19.7	24.0	1.22
129	Denmark[o]	190	83	107	196	84	113	54.6	46.8	62.7	1.34
130	Finland[o]	263	121	142	284	130	154	83.3	75.1	91.9	1.22
131	France[o]	2 012	917	1 095	2 029	917	1 112	51.4	46.1	57.0	1.24
132	Germany[o]	2 185**	1 163**	1 022**	2 255**	1 161**	1 094**	48.4**	50.4**	46.3**	0.92**
133	Greece[o]	...	...	...	528	257	271	...	...	...	...
134	Iceland[o]	...	...	...	12	4	7	...	...	...	...
135	Ireland[o]	151	70	81	176	79	97	44.5	40.5	48.7	1.20
136	Israel[o]	247	105	142	300	130	169	49.1	40.5	58.2	1.44
137	Italy[o]	1 797	806	991	1 854	811	1 043	45.3	39.9	50.9	1.28
138	Luxembourg[o]	3	1	1	3	1**	2**	10.3	9.9	10.8	1.09
139	Malta[o]	6	3	3	7	3	4	19.8	18.6	21.1	1.13
140	Monaco[o]	.	.	.	.	.	.	.	.	.	.
141	Netherlands[o]	470	238	232	517	255	262	48.9	48.6	49.1	1.01
142	Norway[o]	187	80	108	197	80	118	64.8	54.2	75.8	1.40
143	Portugal[o]	357	157	199	397	170	226	43.9	38.3	49.6	1.30
144	San Marino[3]	...	...	...	0.9y	0.4y	0.5y	...	...	...	...
145	Spain[o]	1 787	839	948	1 833	859	974	52.9	48.6	57.5	1.18
146	Sweden[o]	335	142	193	383	155	228	62.3	51.8	73.3	1.42
147	Switzerland[o]	156	91	65	170	96	74	38.6	43.9	33.0	0.75
148	United Kingdom[o]	2 081	974	1 107	2 241	1 003	1 238	59.2	55.2	63.2	1.14
149	United States[o]	...	...	...	15 928	6 961	8 967	...	...	...	...

South and West Asia

150	Afghanistan	...	...	...	...	...	...	...	...	...	...
151	Bangladesh	709	480	229	855	582	274	5.6	7.3	3.7	0.51
152	Bhutan[4]	1.3**	0.9**	0.4**	2**	1**	1**	...	...	...	...
153	India[w]	...	...	...	10 577	6 441	4 135	...	...	...	...
154	Iran, Islamic Republic of	1 308	740	568	1 567	798	768	20.2	22.4	17.9	0.80
155	Maldives	.	.	.	.	.	.	.	.	.	.
156	Nepal	...	...	...	120	95	25	...	...	...	...
157	Pakistan	...	...	...	...	...	...	...	...	...	...
158	Sri Lanka[w]	...	...	...	...	...	...	...	...	...	...

Sub-Saharan Africa

159	Angola	8	5	3	8y	5y	3y	0.8	0.9	0.6	0.67
160	Benin	16	13	3	19y	15y	4y	3.3	5.3	1.4	0.26
161	Botswana	6	3	2	8	5	4	3.1	3.5	2.8	0.80
162	Burkina Faso	...	...	...	16	12	4	...	...	...	...
163	Burundi	5	4	1	11	7	3	1.0	1.5	0.6	0.40

3. Enrolment ratios were not calculated, due to lack of United Nations population data by age.
4. Enrolment ratios were not calculated, due to inconsistencies between enrolment and the United Nations population data.

(hf) Data refer to ISCED level 5A only.
(eo) Full-time only.
(mk) Data refer to Bâat University only.

(kb) Not including Islamic Azad University.
(l) Data refer to ISCED level 5B only.
(j) Data refer to ISCED levels 5A and 6 only.

Table 9

	ENROLMENT IN TERTIARY EDUCATION				DISTRIBUTION OF STUDENTS BY ISCED LEVEL						FOREIGN STUDENTS (000)						
	Gross enrolment ratio (GER) (%)				Total students (%)			Percentage of female in each level									
	2001				2001			2001			1998			2001			
	Total	Male	Female	GPI (F/M)	Level 5A	Level 5B	Level 6	Level 5A	Level 5B	Level 6	Total	Male	Female	Total	Male	Female	
	.	.	.	.	.	.	.	.	.	.	.	.	.	.	.	.	110
	14.0	11.3	16.7	1.48	15.1	64.2	20.7	44.2	59.1	72.9	...	...	...	...	...	...	111
	...	...	...	...	...	...	...	...	...	...	...	...	...	...	...	...	112
	33.6**,y	25.2**,y	42.1**,y	1.67**,y	...	...	...	...	...	...	...	...	...	...	...	...	113
	18.6	15.7	21.5	1.37	64.0	35.8	0.3**	51.0	68.4	.	...	...	...	...	...	...	114
	31.8**	32.2**	31.4**	0.98**	52.9**	45.9**	1.2**	43.0	55.7	.	...	...	...	—	...	...	115
	.	.	.	.	.	.	.	.	.	.	.	.	.	.	.	.	116
	1.4	0.7	2.2	3.14	.	100.0	.	.	76.9	.	.	.	.	.	.	.	117
	.	.	.	.	.	.	.	.	.	.	.	.	.	.	.	.	118
	12.2	9.2	15.4	1.67	62.7**	37.3**	.	49.1**	83.6**	.	...	...	...	.	...	.	119
	7.3	5.7	8.8	1.54	82.2**	16.3	1.4**	59.0**	67.1	47.9**	1.0	0.5	0.5	1.2	0.4*	0.8*	120
	...	...	...	...	.	100.0z	.	.	75.0z	.	...	...	...	—	...	—	121
	37.1	26.5	48.1	1.82	76.3	21.1	2.6**	60.0	77.2	...	...	...	...	2.1z	...	...	122
	27.1**	22.9**	31.4**	1.37**	61.7**	32.5**	5.8**	52.7	65.8**	52.7**	...	...	...	0.3	0.1	0.2	123
	...	...	...	...	...	...	...	...	...	...	...	...	...	...	...	...	124
	48.3	44.2	52.6	1.19	81.2	11.9	6.9	51.6	66.0	43.1	29.8	15.2	14.6	28.5	13.7	14.7	125
	59.8	55.1	64.7	1.17	46.6	51.7	1.7	49.9	56.5	38.3	36.1	18.9	17.2	40.4	20.4	20.0	126
	59.1z	50.7z	67.8z	1.34z	...	...	...	...	...	...	35.5j	20.0	15.6	40.0j,y	...	...	127
	25.6	22.8	28.4	1.25	22.1	77.3	0.6	77.7	48.4	45.6	1.9	1.1	0.7	3.1	1.9	1.1	128
	62.6	52.2	73.4	1.41	87.4	10.3	2.4	59.8	40.7	43.0	12.3	4.8	7.5	14.5	6.5	7.9	129
	85.7	77.1	94.6	1.23	91.7	0.9	7.4	54.5	49.8	49.2	4.8	2.8	2.0	6.8	3.7	3.0	130
	53.6	47.4	60.0	1.27	70.5	24.8	4.7	55.7	53.9	46.8	131.0±	...	...	165.4±	...	...	131
	49.9**	50.4**	49.4**	0.98**	81.4**	14.4**	...	46.7	62.3	...	178.2	96.2	82.0	219.0	112.1	106.9	132
	68.3	64.7	72.1	1.11	65.1	32.3	2.6	52.7	49.5	42.4	...	...	...	8.6	...	...	133
	54.6	39.5	70.1	1.77	92.9	6.8	0.3	64.1	50.8	55.3	0.2	0.1	0.1	0.5	0.2	0.3	134
	49.9	43.7	56.4	1.29	59.1	38.9	2.0	56.5	53.4	46.3	7.2eo	...	...	9.2	4.4	4.8	135
	57.6	48.7	67.1	1.38	76.5	21.1	2.5	57.3	54.1	52.4	...	...	...	...	...	...	136
	53.1	45.6	61.0	1.34	97.4	1.2	1.4	56.2	64.9	51.7	23.5	11.7	11.8	28.4	12.5	16.0	137
	11.5	10.8**	12.2**	1.13**	60.2	39.8	.	46.1**	63.0**	.	0.7j	...	...	...	...	...	138
	24.4	20.4	28.7	1.41	81.6	18.3	0.1	55.9	61.7	37.5	0.3j	0.1	0.2	0.4	0.2	0.1	139
	.	.	.	.	.	.	.	.	.	.	.	.	.	.	.	.	140
	57.0	55.0	59.1	1.07	97.4	1.4	1.2	50.7	55.9	40.5	13.6	7.4	6.3	18.9	9.2	9.7	141
	74.1	58.5	90.4	1.55	92.9	4.7	2.4	60.6	50.1	41.0	9.0	4.2	4.8	9.5	5.2	4.3	142
	53.1	44.9	61.5	1.37	95.0	1.8	3.2	57.2	55.3	53.5	...	...	...	11.2y	5.6y	5.6y	143
	...	...	...	...	13.9y	86.1y	.	58.8y	57.7y	.	...	...	...	...	...	...	144
	58.9	53.9	64.2	1.19	84.1	12.3	3.6	53.7	50.1	51.0	33.0	16.2	16.7	44.9	19.7	25.2	145
	76.2	60.2	92.9	1.54	90.9	3.6	5.5	60.8	47.7	45.6	24.4	13.5	11.0	28.7	15.6	13.1	146
	44.4	49.2	39.3	0.80	71.5	20.4	8.1	44.6	40.9	37.2	25.3	14.2	11.1	29.3	16.6	12.7	147
	63.6	57.0	70.2	1.23	64.5	31.7	3.8	53.7	59.8	42.8	232.5*	124.2	108.3	227.3	117.1	110.1	148
	81.4	69.5	93.7	1.35	76.1z	21.7z	2.2z	56.4z	55.4z	42.6z	451.9*	262.6	189.4	583.0	327.4	255.6	149
	...	...	...	...	...	...	...	...	...	...	...	...	...	...	...	...	150
	6.3	8.3	4.1	0.49	99.8	...	0.2	32.0	...	24.4	...	...	...	0.4	...	...	151
	...	...	...	...	23.5**	76.5**	.	31.9**	34.3**	.	...	...	...	...	...	...	152
	11.4	13.4	9.3	0.70	98.7	0.8	0.6	39.2	34.3	36.3	...	...	...	8.1	...	...	153
	20.3	20.2	20.4	1.01	76.9	22.1	0.9	51.1	43.0	23.3	...	...	...	1.3kb	1.0	0.3	154
	.	.	.	.	.	.	.	.	.	.	.	.	.	.	.	.	155
	5.4	8.2	2.3	0.28	85.6	.	14.4	20.7	.	20.2	...	...	...	...	...	...	156
	.	.	.	.	.	.	.	.	.	.	.	.	.	.	.	.	157
	...	...	...	...	...	...	...	...	...	...	...	...	...	...	...	...	158
	0.7y	0.9y	0.5y	0.56y	100.0y	.	.	39.0y	.	.	0.05	0.02	0.03	...	...	0.6y	159
	3.6y	5.9y	1.4y	0.24y	82.1y	17.7y	0.2y	18.9y	24.4y	22.6y	...	...	...	...	...	...	160
	4.4	4.8	3.9	0.81	88.5	11.4	0.1	46.8	29.9	55.6	...	...	...	...	...	...	161
	1.4	2.1	0.7	0.33	...	...	...	...	...	...	...	...	...	...	...	...	162
	1.9	2.7	1.2	0.44	66.2**	33.6**	0.2**	32.1**	27.3**	9.1**	0.1	...	...	...	...	...	163

(v) Data do not include ISCED level 6.
(q) Data cover only 80% of students.
(y) Data are for 1999/2000.
(z) Data are for 2000/2001.
± Partial data.

Table 9 (continued)

			ENROLMENT IN TERTIARY EDUCATION							
			Total students enrolled (000)					Gross enrolment ratio (GER) (%)			
			1998				2001				1998			
	Country or territory	Total	Male	Female	Total	Male	Female	Total	Male	Female	GPI (F/M)
---	---	---	---	---	---	---	---	---	---	---	---
164	Cameroon	67	...	...	78	48**	30**	5.1	...	...	...
165	Cape Verde	...	...	...	2	1	1	...	...	...	...
166	Central African Republic	6	5	1	6 y	5 y	1 y	1.9	3.3	0.6	0.18
167	Chad	...	...	...	6 y	5 y	1 y	...	...	...	...
168	Comoros	0.6	0.4	0.3	0.7 y	0.4**,y	0.3**,y	1.0	1.2	0.9	0.75
169	Congo	...	...	...	12	10	2	...	...	...	...
170	Côte d'Ivoire	97	71	25	...	...	...	7.1	10.4	3.7	0.36
171	Democratic Rep. of the Congo	60**	...	...	...	...	...	1.4**	...	...	...
172	Equatorial Guinea	...	...	...	1.0 y	0.7 y	0.3 y	...	...	...	...
173	Eritrea	4	3	1	6	5	1	1.2	2.2	0.3	0.14
174	Ethiopia	52	43	10	102	75	27	1.0	1.6	0.4	0.25
175	Gabon	7	5	3	...	...	...	6.8	8.9	4.8	0.54
176	Gambia	...	...	...	...	...	...	...	...	...	...
177	Ghana	...	...	...	68	49	19	...	...	...	...
178	Guinea	...	...	...	...	...	...	...	...	...	...
179	Guinea-Bissau	...	...	...	0.5 y	0.4 y	0.1 y	...	...	...	...
180	Kenya	...	...	...	99**	64**	34**	...	...	...	...
181	Lesotho	4	1	3	5	2	3	2.2	1.7	2.7	1.59
182	Liberia	...	...	...	44 y	25 y	19 y	...	...	...	...
183	Madagascar	31	17	14	33	18	15	2.3	2.5	2.1	0.84
184	Malawi	3	2	1	...	...	...	0.3	0.5	0.2	0.40
185	Mali	19	...	...	27	...	...	1.8	...	...	...
186	Mauritius	8	4	3	13	6	7	7.1	7.6	6.6	0.87
187	Mozambique	...	...	...	9**,y	5**,y	4**,y	...	...	...	...
188	Namibia	11	5	6	13	7	6	6.6	6.2	7.1	1.15
189	Niger	...	...	...	14**	10**	3**	...	...	...	...
190	Nigeria	...	...	...	...	...	...	...	...	...	...
191	Rwanda	6	...	...	14**	9**	5**	0.9	...	...	...
192	Sao Tome and Principe	.	.	.	0.2**	0.1**	0.1**	.	.	.	.
193	Senegal	29	...	...	...	...	...	3.7	...	...	...
194	Seychelles	.	.	.	.	.	.	.	.	.	.
195	Sierra Leone	...	...	...	9**	6**	3**	...	...	...	...
196	Somalia	...	...	...	...	...	...	...	...	...	...
197	South Africa	634	293	341	659	306	352	15.3	14.2	16.3	1.15
198	Swaziland	5	3	2	5	2	3	4.9	5.3	4.5	0.85
199	Togo	15	12	3	15 y	13 y	3 y	3.8	6.4	1.3	0.20
200	Uganda	41	27**	14**	72**	47**	25**	2.0	2.7**	1.4**	0.52**
201	United Republic of Tanzania	19	15	4	22 z	19 z	3 z	0.6	1.0	0.3	0.30
202	Zambia	23	16	7	25**,z	17**,z	8**,z	2.3	3.2	1.5	0.47
203	Zimbabwe w	...	...	...	60**	38**	22**	...	...	...	...

		Sum			Sum			Median			
I	World	...	...	...	...	...	...	20.7	...	...	...
II	Countries in transition	...	...	...	...	...	...	30.2	28.2	32.2	1.14
III	Developed countries	...	...	...	...	...	...	45.6	37.3	54.1	1.45
IV	Developing countries	...	...	...	...	...	...	10.2	...	...	...
V	Arab States	...	...	...	...	...	...	16.2	...	...	...
VI	Central and Eastern Europe	...	...	...	...	...	...	38.6	35.8	41.6	1.16
VII	Central Asia	...	...	...	...	...	...	24.9	20.1	29.8	1.49
VIII	East Asia and the Pacific	...	...	...	...	...	...	...	...	...	...
IX	Latin America and the Caribbean	...	...	...	...	...	...	...	...	...	...
X	North America and Western Europe	...	...	...	...	...	...	50.3	43.3	57.6	1.33
XI	South and West Asia	...	...	...	...	...	...	...	...	...	...
XII	Sub-Saharan Africa	...	...	...	...	...	...	2.3	...	...	...

1. Data are included in ISCED level 5A.
2. National population data were used to calculate enrolment ratios.
3. Enrolment ratios were not calculated, due to lack of United Nations population data by age.
4. Enrolment ratios were not calculated, due to inconsistencies between enrolment and the United Nations population data.
5. Data are included in ISCED level 5B.

STATISTICAL ANNEX / 325

Table 9

	ENROLMENT IN TERTIARY EDUCATION				DISTRIBUTION OF STUDENTS BY ISCED LEVEL						FOREIGN STUDENTS (000)						
	Gross enrolment ratio (GER) (%)				Total students (%)			Percentage of female in each level			1998			2001			
	2001				2001			2001									
	Total	Male	Female	GPI (F/M)	Level 5A	Level 5B	Level 6	Level 5A	Level 5B	Level 6	Total	Male	Female	Total	Male	Female	
	5.4	6.6**	4.2**	0.64**	...	...	...	...	...	...	...	...	...	...	...	...	164
	3.6	3.9	3.3	0.85	...	...	...	...	...	...	...	...	...	...	...	...	165
	1.9 y	3.3 y	0.6 y	0.18 y	91.4**,y	8.6**,y	...	16.9**,y	9.2**,y	...	...	...	...	...	...	...	166
	0.9 y	1.5 y	0.3 y	0.20 y	88.6 y	7.1 y	4.3 y	13.7 y	28.2 y	20.2 y	...	...	...	...	...	...	167
	1.1 y	1.3**,y	0.9**,y	0.69**,y	64.3 y	35.7 y	.	33.8**,y	56.5**,y	.	.	.	.	.	.	–	168
	3.8	6.5	1.2	0.18	84.4	15.0	0.6	16.3	12.5	32.0	...	...	...	.	.	.	169
	...	...	...	...	...	...	...	...	...	...	...	...	...	...	...	...	170
	...	...	...	...	...	...	...	...	...	...	...	...	...	...	...	...	171
	2.7 y	3.8 y	1.6 y	0.42 y	88.1 y	11.9 y	.	33.3 y	8.4 y	...	...	...	...	.	...	.	172
	1.5	2.6	0.4	0.15	100.0	./.¹	./.¹	13.4	./.¹	./.¹	0.1	0.1	0.0	0.05 y	0.03 y	0.02 y	173
	1.7	2.5	0.9	0.36	100.0	./.¹	./.¹	26.4	./.¹	./.¹	...	...	...	...	...	...	174
	...	...	...	...	...	...	...	...	...	...	0.4	...	...	...	...	...	175
	...	...	...	...	...	...	...	...	...	...	...	...	...	0.1 y	0.1 y	0.0 y	176
	3.4	4.8	1.9	0.40	57.7**	37.2**	5.2**	29.4**	25.9**	22.7**	...	...	...	.	...	...	177
	...	...	...	...	...	...	...	...	...	...	...	...	...	...	...	...	178
	0.4 y	0.7 y	0.1 y	0.14 y	./.⁵	100.0 y	./.⁵	./.⁵	15.6 y	./.⁵	...	...	...	–	...	–	179
	2.9**	3.8**	2.0**	0.53**	47.0**	49.6**	3.4**	39.2**	31.0**	25.4**	...	...	...	...	...	...	180
	2.5	2.2	2.8	1.27	59.5	40.5	.	51.6	67.6	.	1.0	0.5	0.5	0.13 z	0.07 z	0.06 z	181
	16.9 y	19.2 y	14.6 y	0.76 y	60.8 y	36.6 y	2.6 y	43.3 y	42.1 y	40.8 y	...	...	...	...	...	...	182
	2.2	2.4	2.0	0.83	77.3	20.3	2.4	45.5	45.0	45.2	1.1	...	...	1.2	0.9	0.3	183
	...	...	...	...	...	...	...	...	...	...	–	...	...	–	...	...	184
	2.5	...	...	...	99.0	–	1.0	...	–	...	1.2	...	...	...	...	...	185
	11.3	9.9	12.7	1.28	44.0	55.0	1.1	47.9	62.5	38.6	...	...	...	...	...	...	186
	0.6**,y	0.7**,y	0.5**,y	0.71**,y	...	...	...	...	...	...	...	...	...	...	...	...	187
	7.5	8.2	6.8	0.83	55.3	44.7	0.0	54.1	35.2	16.7	...	...	...	...	...	...	188
	1.5**	2.2**	0.7**	0.32**	84.3**	14.9**	0.7**	23.9**	30.0**	25.2**	...	...	...	0.1 y	0.1 y	0.0 y	189
	...	...	...	...	...	...	...	...	...	...	...	...	...	...	...	...	190
	1.7**	2.6**	1.0**	0.38**	...	...	...	...	...	...	–	...	...	0.1 z	0.1 z	0.0 z	191
	1.0**	1.3**	0.7**	0.54**	100.0**	.	.	36.1**	.	.	.	.	.	.	.	.	192
	...	...	...	...	...	...	...	...	...	...	1.3	...	...	...	...	...	193
	.	.	.	.	...	...	...	...	...	...	.	.	.	.	.	.	194
	2.2**	3.1**	1.2**	0.39**	43.9**	56.1**	.	16.0**	38.8**	.	...	...	...	–	...	–	195
	...	...	...	...	...	...	...	...	...	...	...	...	...	...	...	...	196
	15.0	14.0	15.9	1.14	84.8	14.3	1.0	51.4	66.7	38.0	15.5	8.4*	7.1*	...	...	...	197
	4.7	4.3	5.0	1.16	...	...	...	...	...	...	0.1	...	...	0.1 y	0.0 y	0.1 y	198
	3.7 y	6.2 y	1.3 y	0.21 y	98.3 y	1.7 y	./.¹	17.2 y	2.3 y	./.¹	0.5	0.4	0.2	...	...	0.2 y	199
	3.2**	4.3**	2.2**	0.51**	57.2**	42.7**	0.1**	37.5**	30.5**	...	...	...	...	...	...	...	200
	0.7 z	1.2 z	0.2 z	0.17 z	...	...	...	...	...	...	...	...	...	0.5 z	...	...	201
	2.4**,z	3.3**,z	1.5**,z	0.45**,z	58.4**,z	40.8**,z	0.8**,z	37.7**,z	23.3**,z	14.4**,z	...	...	...	...	...	...	202
	4.4**	5.6**	3.2**	0.57**	29.7**	67.1**	3.2**	28.8**	40.6	...	...	...	...	...	...	...	203

	Median				Median			Median			Sum			Sum			
	23.2	...	...	...	80.5	17.8	1.7	51.7	21.1	36.7	...	...	...	...	...	...	I
	36.5	36.1	36.8	1.02	95.0	3.6	1.4	53.7	...	41.6	...	...	...	...	...	...	II
	54.6	39.5	70.1	1.80	81.6	18.3	0.1	55.6	50.2	47.9	...	...	...	...	...	...	III
	11.3	9.9	12.7	1.28	77.3	20.3	2.4	46.2	37.5	50.4	...	...	...	...	...	...	IV
	22.0	17.7	26.5	1.50	85.7	13.8	0.5	49.1	48.1	25.2	...	...	...	...	...	...	V
	37.7	33.9	41.7	1.23	83.4	9.8	6.8	56.1	43.2	...	...	...	...	...	...	...	VI
	30.7	24.9	36.5	1.46	98.6	...	1.5	52.9	...	64.1	...	...	...	...	...	...	VII
	13.4	...	...	...	73.6	24.7	1.7	...	...	...	...	...	...	...	...	...	VIII
	25.7	23.0	28.4	1.24	71.2	28.7	0.2	52.8	52.2	55.9	...	...	...	...	...	...	IX
	57.0	55.0	59.1	1.07	81.2	11.9	6.9	55.9	61.7	44.4	...	...	...	...	...	...	X
	...	...	...	...	85.6	...	14.4	32.0	...	24.4	...	...	...	...	...	...	XI
	2.5	...	...	...	82.1	17.7	0.2	33.6	32.5	...	...	...	...	...	...	...	XII

(hf) Data refer to ISCED level 5A only.
(eo) Full-time only.
(mk) Data refer to Bâat University only.
(kb) Not including Islamic Azad University.
(l) Data refer to ISCED level 5B only.
(j) Data refer to ISCED levels 5A and 6 only.
(v) Data do not include ISCED level 6.
(q) Data cover only 80% of students.
(y) Data are for 1999/2000.
(z) Data are for 2000/2001.
± Partial data.

326 / ANNEX

Table 10. Tertiary education: distribution of students by field of study and female share in each field, 2001

Country or territory	Total enrolment (000)	% F	Education	Humanities and arts	Social sciences, business and law	Science	Engineering, manufacturing and construction	Agriculture	Health and welfare	Services	Not known or unspecified
Arab States											
Algeria	...	...	...	...	...	...	...	...	...	...	...
Bahrain	...	...	...	...	...	...	...	...	...	...	...
Djibouti	0.7	44.5	...	...	...	...	...	...	...	...	100.0
Egypt[w]	...	...	...	...	...	...	...	...	...	...	...
Iraq	318**	34.0**	22.9[y]	20.3[y]	9.3[y]	0.5[y]	10.0[y]	2.9[y]	6.0[y]	.	28.1[y]
Jordan[w]	163	48.9	...	...	...	...	...	...	...	...	100.0
Kuwait	...	...	...	...	...	...	...	...	...	...	...
Lebanon	143	52.9	2.5	20.0	39.8	15.8	11.5	0.4	7.0	2.5	0.4
Libyan Arab Jamahiriya	359	51.4	11.7[y]	18.6[y]	18.3[y]	10.2[y]	20.6[y]	2.6[y]	17.0[y]	...	1.0[y]
Mauritania	8.2	21.3	...	...	...	...	...	...	...	...	100.0
Morocco	315**	43.7**	5.0[z]	25.3[z]	44.8[z]	15.3[z]	5.3[z]	0.7[z]	3.4[z]	0.2[z]	–
Oman	20**	57.9**	...	...	...	...	...	...	...	...	100.0**
Palestinian A. T.	89	47.9	14.8	16.3	32.6	13.3	6.7	0.5	11.1	0.1	4.6
Qatar	7.8	72.5	20.3	15.0	38.5	10.8	3.5	0.0	–	–	11.8
Saudi Arabia	445**	58.8**	49.7[y]	15.0[y]	7.6[y]	6.6[y]	8.1[y]	1.1[y]	3.4[y]	.	8.6[y]
Sudan	...	...	...	...	...	...	...	...	...	...	...
Syrian Arab Republic	...	...	...	...	...	...	...	...	...	...	...
Tunisia[w]	226**	...	...	...	...	...	...	...	...	...	100.0**
United Arab Emirates	...	...	...	...	...	...	...	...	...	...	...
Yemen	173**,[y]	20.8**,[y]	...	...	...	...	...	...	...	...	100.0**,[y]
Central and Eastern Europe											
Albania[o]	41[z]	61.4[z]	35.9[z]	8.6[z]	34.8[z]	2.0[z]	6.6[z]	2.7[z]	8.1[z]	1.3[z]	–
Belarus	464	56.8	...	...	...	...	...	...	...	...	100.0
Bosnia and Herzegovina[o]	...	...	...	...	...	...	...	...	...	...	...
Bulgaria[o]	228	54.0	9.0	9.1	39.7	4.9	22.7	2.4	6.1	6.0	0.1
Croatia	113	52.5	4.6	10.0	32.4	7.0	18.6	3.8	8.5	15.1	–
Czech Republic[o]	284	51.2	11.8	8.3	24.4	8.6	20.7	3.5	12.0	3.6	7.1
Estonia[o]	61	61.5	10.5	11.5	38.2	9.2	11.7	5.8	6.8	6.2	–
Hungary[o]	354	55.3	14.5	8.9	39.2	5.0	13.0	3.4	7.4	8.6	–
Latvia[o]	111	61.5	16.2	7.1	51.0	7.2	10.2	1.8	3.6	3.0	–
Lithuania[o]	149	60.5	15.1	7.7	35.7	5.5	20.2	2.9	8.5	4.3	–
Poland[o]	1 906	57.9	12.3	8.6	43.3	5.6	13.6	2.1	2.5	4.6	7.3
Republic of Moldova	108	56.6	...	...	...	...	...	...	...	...	100.0
Romania[o]	582	54.4	4.2	10.9	43.7	5.0	20.1	4.0	5.8	3.0	3.3
Russian Federation[w]	8 030	56.7	...	...	...	...	...	...	...	...	100.0
Serbia and Montenegro	209[z]	53.7[z]	4.4[z]	9.6[z]	32.6[z]	5.2[z]	24.4[z]	4.8[z]	12.2[z]	6.7[z]	0.3[z]
Slovakia	152	52.1	15.8	5.8	27.2	8.6	19.1	4.5	12.3	6.6	–
Slovenia[o]	99	57.5	13.5	6.2	43.0	4.6	16.7	2.7	6.4	6.9	–
TFYR Macedonia[o]	45	55.2	11.7	11.3	25.9	8.3	20.5	6.2	9.4	6.8	–
Turkey[o]	1 678	41.4	12.8	5.7	18.4	7.3	13.1	3.4	5.7	2.4	31.1
Ukraine	2 135	53.4*	8.1	6.1	39.7	4.3	22.8**	5.5**	6.0**	5.2**	2.2**
Central Asia											
Armenia	75	53.7	16.0**	6.8**	9.9**	0.9**	6.9**	2.9**	8.1**	1.8**	46.6**
Azerbaijan	171	51.8	...	...	...	...	...	...	...	...	100.0
Georgia	149	49.8	7.2	19.0	32.6	5.0	21.0	3.5	8.8	2.9	0.02
Kazakhstan	515	55.8	...	...	...	...	...	...	...	...	100.0
Kyrgyzstan	209	53.0	24.4	7.3	33.9	6.2	16.5	1.4	2.6	7.8	–
Mongolia	90	63.2	13.2	10.0	26.5	6.2	17.8	3.7	6.3	4.6	11.7
Tajikistan	85	24.5	14.2	38.9	20.5	10.8	7.5	3.3	4.1	0.8	–
Turkmenistan	...	...	...	...	...	...	...	...	...	...	...
Uzbekistan	227**	...	...	...	...	...	...	...	...	...	100.0**
East Asia and the Pacific											
Australia[o]	869	54.2	8.3	13.6	34.3	14.2	11.5	1.8	13.0	2.3	1.2
Brunei Darussalam	4.5	63.2	54.5	8.4	12.8	5.5	5.1	.	11.2	.	2.6
Cambodia	32	28.8	0.8	10.8	57.3	14.0	2.5	3.4	2.9	5.2	3.1
China[w]	12 144	...	...	...	...	...	...	...	...	...	100.0**

(y) Data are for 1999/2000.   (z) Data are for 2000/2001.

Table 10

PERCENTAGE OF FEMALES IN EACH FIELD

Education	Humanities and arts	Social sciences, business and law	Science	Engineering, manufacturing and construction	Agriculture	Health and welfare	Services	Not known or unspecified	Country or territory
									Arab States
...	...	...	...	...	...	...	...	...	Algeria
...	...	...	...	...	...	...	...	...	Bahrain
...	...	...	...	...	...	...	...	44.5	Djibouti
...	...	...	...	...	...	...	...	...	Egypt [w]
50.7 [y]	24.7 [y]	33.7 [y]	51.5 [y]	22.2 [y]	25.2 [y]	34.5 [y]	.	32.1 [y]	Iraq
...	...	...	...	...	...	...	...	48.9	Jordan [w]
...	...	...	...	...	...	...	...	...	Kuwait
95.4	71.2	54.3	41.1	20.4	49.7	64.2	34.9	66.6	Lebanon
...	...	...	...	...	...	...	...	...	Libyan Arab Jamahiriya
...	...	...	...	...	...	...	...	21.3	Mauritania
49.4 [z]	50.5 [z]	43.3 [z]	32.2 [z]	34.4 [z]	22.3 [z]	61.3 [z]	55.0 [z]	–	Morocco
...	...	...	...	...	...	...	...	57.9**	Oman
70.3	64.7	34.7	46.9	30.2	18.6	45.3	62.6	47.9	Palestinian Autonomous Territories
90.7	93.9	63.2	68.9	–	–	–	–	69.4	Qatar
81.7 [y]	42.3 [y]	32.4 [y]	40.5 [y]	0.6 [y]	28.4 [y]	39.6 [y]	.	25.0 [y]	Saudi Arabia
...	...	...	...	...	...	...	...	...	Sudan
...	...	...	...	...	...	...	...	...	Syrian Arab Republic
...	...	...	...	...	...	...	...	...	Tunisia [w]
...	...	...	...	...	...	...	...	...	United Arab Emirates
...	...	...	...	...	...	...	...	20.8**,[y]	Yemen
									Central and Eastern Europe
77.5 [z]	70.4 [z]	49.2 [z]	63.5 [z]	24.0 [z]	33.4 [z]	72.4 [z]	56.4 [z]	–	Albania [o]
...	...	...	...	...	...	...	...	56.8	Belarus
...	...	...	...	...	...	...	...	...	Bosnia and Herzegovina [o]
70.7	65.1	59.3	55.2	34.6	43.1	62.9	44.4	58.9	Bulgaria [o]
91.2	71.9	65.0	43.8	25.7	43.9	72.5	28.7	–	Croatia
73.7	60.3	56.9	35.9	21.0	51.2	73.4	38.4	59.6	Czech Republic [o]
86.9	75.0	62.5	39.4	29.0	75.7	82.1	45.0	–	Estonia [o]
71.9	62.8	61.1	31.9	21.5	44.8	75.4	44.5	–	Hungary [o]
80.6	78.4	64.9	35.8	22.8	43.7	81.0	43.4	–	Latvia [o]
80.5	73.8	67.7	40.3	29.3	51.8	81.5	42.3	–	Lithuania [o]
73.1	69.3	63.0	44.4	22.2	54.9	70.7	46.7	68.7	Poland [o]
...	...	...	...	...	...	...	...	56.6	Republic of Moldova
76.2	67.9	61.7	59.3	27.8	40.3	64.1	52.5	41.0	Romania [o]
...	...	...	...	...	...	...	...	56.7	Russian Federation [w]
84.6 [z]	75.2 [z]	60.4 [z]	59.0 [z]	28.8 [z]	41.5 [z]	72.7 [z]	32.3 [z]	35.7 [z]	Serbia and Montenegro
73.9	53.3	58.1	34.8	28.6	34.7	74.0	35.4	–	Slovakia
81.0	72.8	63.0	31.0	24.5	53.8	79.3	42.7	–	Slovenia [o]
77.9	67.9	60.8	58.9	28.2	38.0	72.5	42.8	–	The former Yugoslav Rep. of Macedonia [o]
48.5	52.3	44.1	39.0	21.7	35.6	56.4	33.5	42.2	Turkey [o]
53.4	...	...	...	...	...	...	...	...	Ukraine
									Central Asia
78.5**	65.7**	44.1**	48.4**	26.1**	38.1**	49.4**	34.5**	52.1**	Armenia
...	...	...	...	...	...	...	...	51.8	Azerbaijan
65.9	79.5	39.5	66.8	28.2	29.2	74.8	8.0	21.7	Georgia
...	...	...	...	...	...	...	...	55.8	Kazakhstan
79.1	67.0	44.2	56.4	43.2	13.2	57.3	19.9	–	Kyrgyzstan
77.1	70.4	64.1	49.9	49.3	63.8	84.2	29.7	69.4	Mongolia
...	...	...	...	...	...	...	...	...	Tajikistan
...	...	...	...	...	...	...	...	...	Turkmenistan
...	...	...	...	...	...	...	...	...	Uzbekistan
									East Asia and the Pacific
75.3	65.6	55.1	38.3	18.6	44.4	75.5	60.1	52.9	Australia [o]
66.9	55.1	60.0	47.8	40.8	.	72.9	.	61.0	Brunei Darussalam
30.7	32.3	32.3	16.5	4.1	14.0	30.1	40.8	22.2	Cambodia
...	...	...	...	...	...	...	...	...	China [w]

Table 10 (continued)

	Total enrolment		PERCENTAGE DISTRIBUTION BY FIELD OF STUDY								
Country or territory	(000)	% F	Education	Humanities and arts	Social sciences, business and law	Science	Engineering, manufacturing and construction	Agriculture	Health and welfare	Services	Not known or unspecified
Cook Islands	...	...	...	...	...	...	...	...	...	...	...
DPR Korea	...	...	...	...	...	...	...	...	...	...	...
Fiji	...	...	...	...	...	...	...	...	...	...	...
Indonesia[w]	3 176	45.9	...	...	...	...	...	...	...	...	100.0
Japan[o]	3 967	45.1	6.7	16.7	29.8	3.0	17.5	2.2	10.9	6.8	6.3
Kiribati	...	...	...	...	...	...	...	...	...	...	...
Lao PDR	29	37.0	21.4	11.7	21.2	4.8	8.6	4.9	2.0	2.2	23.1
Macao, China	20	36.9	4.5	3.9	81.0	3.4	1.5	–	4.3	1.3	–
Malaysia[w]	557	...	...	...	...	...	...	...	...	...	100.0
Marshall Islands	0.9	56.5	...	...	...	...	...	...	...	...	100.0
Micronesia	...	...	...	...	...	...	...	...	...	...	...
Myanmar	555**	...	0.7[z]	32.2[z]	22.9[z]	36.6[z]	5.4[z]	0.8[z]	1.4[z]	0.0[z]	–
Nauru	.	.	.	.	.	.	.	.	.	.	.
New Zealand[o]	178	58.6	10.8	18.7	29.0	13.8	6.5	1.7	11.2	4.2	4.1
Niue	...	...	...	...	...	...	...	...	...	.	...
Palau	0.5**	63.4**	...	...	...	...	...	...	...	...	100.0**
Papua New Guinea	...	...	...	...	...	...	...	...	...	...	...
Philippines[w]	2 467	55.6	...	...	...	...	...	...	...	...	100.0
Republic of Korea[o]	3 130	36.0	5.4	17.6	20.3	9.8	34.5	1.9	6.5	4.1	.
Samoa	1.2**	44.4**	23.1[z]	7.5[z]	34.0[z]	9.4[z]	4.8[z]	10.7[z]	2.6[z]	2.9[z]	5.0[z]
Singapore	...	...	...	...	...	...	...	...	...	...	...
Solomon Islands	.	.	.	.	.	.	.	.	.	.	.
Thailand[w]	2 155	52.1	...	...	...	...	...	...	...	...	100.0
Timor-Leste	6.3*	52.9*	...	...	...	...	...	...	...	...	100.0*
Tokelau	.	.	.	.	.	.	.	.	.	.	.
Tonga	0.4**	57.9**	...	...	...	...	...	...	...	...	100.0**
Tuvalu	.	.	.	.	.	.	.	.	.	.	.
Vanuatu	0.7	...	...	...	...	...	...	...	...	...	100.0
Viet Nam	785	42.8	23.0	3.8	38.6	–	19.7	5.9	3.5	–	5.5
Latin America and the Caribbean											
Anguilla	.	.	.	.	.	.	.	.	.	.	.
Antigua and Barbuda	.	.	.	.	.	.	.	.	.	.	.
Argentina[w]	1 919	59.2	3.0	7.0	35.0	8.0	7.5	2.9	10.2	0.7	25.7
Aruba	2	60.4	12.8	.	48.4	.	24.1	.	14.8	.	–
Bahamas	...	...	...	...	...	...	...	...	...	...	...
Barbados	8[z]	71.4[z]	...	...	...	...	...	...	...	...	100.0[z]
Belize	...	...	...	...	...	...	...	...	...	...	...
Bermuda	2[z]	55.1[z]	.	12.0[z]	17.0[z]	8.4[z]	.	.	.	.	62.6[z]
Bolivia	302	...	...	...	...	...	...	...	...	...	100.0
Brazil[w]	3 126	56.1	...	...	...	...	...	...	...	...	100.0
British Virgin Islands	0.8	69.0	...	...	...	...	...	...	...	...	100.0
Cayman Islands	0.4[z]	74.6[z]	...	...	...	...	...	...	...	...	100.0[z]
Chile[w]	452[z]	47.2[z]	...	...	...	...	...	...	...	...	100.0[z]
Colombia	977	51.8	11.3	3.1	43.1	2.6	29.0	1.9	9.0	.	–
Costa Rica	79	52.7	18.6	7.0	30.2	11.5	12.6	4.6	5.9	1.7	7.9
Cuba	191	54.4	...	...	...	...	...	...	...	...	100.0
Dominica	.	.	.	.	.	.	.	.	.	.	.
Dominican Republic	...	...	...	...	...	...	...	...	...	...	...
Ecuador	...	...	...	...	...	...	...	...	...	...	...
El Salvador	110	54.2	...	...	...	...	...	...	...	...	100.0
Grenada	...	...	...	...	...	...	...	...	...	...	...
Guatemala	...	...	...	...	...	...	...	...	...	...	...
Guyana	...	...	...	...	...	...	...	...	...	...	...
Haiti	...	...	...	...	...	...	...	...	...	...	...
Honduras	90**	56.1**	...	...	...	...	...	...	...	...	100.0**
Jamaica[w]	45	68.8	...	...	...	...	...	...	...	...	100.0
Mexico[o]	2 147	49.3	12.0	3.7	41.5	12.5	18.9	2.1	7.9	2.0	0.01
Montserrat	.	.	.	.	.	.	.	.	.	.	.
Netherlands Antilles	2	59.7	5.2[z]	–	40.8[z]	–	32.2[z]	–	21.9[z]	–	–
Nicaragua	...	...	...	...	...	...	...	...	...	...	...

(y) Data are for 1999/2000.   (z) Data are for 2000/2001.

STATISTICAL ANNEX / 329

Table 10

PERCENTAGE OF FEMALES IN EACH FIELD

Education	Humanities and arts	Social sciences, business and law	Science	Engineering, manufacturing and construction	Agriculture	Health and welfare	Services	Not known or unspecified	Country or territory
...	...	...	...	...	...	...	...	...	Cook Islands
...	...	...	...	...	...	...	...	...	Democratic People's Republic of Korea
...	...	...	...	...	...	...	...	...	Fiji
...	...	...	...	...	...	...	...	45.9	Indonesia[w]
70.6	67.6	32.6	24.7	11.6	40.0	65.1	80.2	50.0	Japan[o]
...	...	...	...	...	...	...	...	...	Kiribati
42.4	39.7	42.4	39.4	10.2	21.0	53.2	21.6	38.9	Lao People's Democratic Republic
...	...	...	...	...	...	...	...	...	Macao, China
...	...	...	...	...	...	...	...	54.3	Malaysia[w]
...	...	...	...	...	...	...	...	56.5	Marshall Islands
...	...	...	...	...	...	...	...	...	Micronesia (Federated States of)
...	...	...	...	...	...	...	...	...	Myanmar
.	.	.	.	.	.	.	.	.	Nauru
80.3	64.0	57.2	40.9	26.6	41.5	80.5	51.3	52.3	New Zealand[o]
.	.	.	.	.	.	.	.	.	Niue
...	...	...	...	...	...	...	...	63.4**	Palau
...	...	...	...	...	...	...	...	...	Papua New Guinea
...	...	...	...	...	...	...	...	55.6	Philippines[w]
67.7	56.6	35.4	33.7	17.5	27.9	61.2	34.6	.	Republic of Korea[o]
66.7[z]	57.3[z]	37.3[z]	41.4[z]	3.5[z]	28.6[z]	80.6[z]	11.8[z]	44.1[z]	Samoa
...	...	...	...	...	...	...	...	...	Singapore
.	.	.	.	.	.	.	.	.	Solomon Islands
...	...	...	...	...	...	...	...	52.1	Thailand[w]
...	...	...	...	...	...	...	...	52.9*	Timor-Leste
.	.	.	.	.	.	.	.	.	Tokelau
...	...	...	...	...	...	...	...	57.9**	Tonga
.	.	.	.	.	.	.	.	.	Tuvalu
...	...	...	...	...	...	...	...	...	Vanuatu
55.6	68.8	48.6	–	14.4	34.0	40.1	–	43.4	Viet Nam

Latin America and the Caribbean

...	...	...	...	...	...	...	...	...	Anguilla
.	.	.	.	.	.	.	.	.	Antigua and Barbuda
77.8	63.8	57.4	46.4	29.5	43.9	66.8	56.7	69.7	Argentina[w]
86.7	.	68.6	.	11.2	.	91.1	.	–	Aruba
...	...	...	...	...	...	...	...	...	Bahamas
...	...	...	...	...	...	...	...	71.4[z]	Barbados
...	...	...	...	...	...	...	...	...	Belize
.	66.5[z]	72.4[z]	3.7[z]	.	.	.	.	55.0[z]	Bermuda
...	...	...	...	...	...	...	...	...	Bolivia
...	...	...	...	...	...	...	...	56.1	Brazil[w]
...	...	...	...	...	...	...	...	69.0	British Virgin Islands
...	...	...	...	...	...	...	...	74.6[z]	Cayman Islands
...	...	...	...	...	...	...	...	47.2[z]	Chile[w]
63.8	47.5	58.0	51.5	33.4	36.4	71.2	.	–	Colombia
70.9	57.6	53.3	39.7	29.7	37.6	66.2	43.5	59.5	Costa Rica
...	...	...	...	...	...	...	...	54.4	Cuba
.	.	.	.	.	.	.	.	.	Dominica
...	...	...	...	...	...	...	...	...	Dominican Republic
...	...	...	...	...	...	...	...	...	Ecuador
...	...	...	...	...	...	...	...	54.2	El Salvador
...	...	...	...	...	...	...	...	...	Grenada
...	...	...	...	...	...	...	...	...	Guatemala
...	...	...	...	...	...	...	...	...	Guyana
...	...	...	...	...	...	...	...	...	Haiti
...	...	...	...	...	...	...	...	56.1**	Honduras
...	...	...	...	...	...	...	...	68.8	Jamaica[w]
67.1	55.3	56.1	41.2	23.3	27.8	61.7	52.2	24.9	Mexico[o]
...	...	...	...	...	...	...	...	...	Montserrat
95.2[z]	–	72.2[z]	–	14.7[z]	–	85.3[z]	–	–	Netherlands Antilles
...	...	...	...	...	...	...	...	...	Nicaragua

Table 10 (continued)

	Total enrolment		PERCENTAGE DISTRIBUTION BY FIELD OF STUDY								
Country or territory	(000)	% F	Education	Humanities and arts	Social sciences, business and law	Science	Engineering, manufacturing and construction	Agriculture	Health and welfare	Services	Not known or unspecified
Panama	89**,y	61.9**,y	...	...	...	...	...	...	...	...	100.0**,y
Paraguay[w]	97	57.2	...	...	...	...	...	...	...	...	100.0
Peru[w]	824**	48.8**	...	...	...	...	...	...	...	...	100.0**
Saint Kitts and Nevis	.	.	.	.	.	.	.	.	.	.	.
Saint Lucia	0.2	76.9	...	...	...	...	...	...	...	...	100.0
St Vincent/Grenad.	.	.	.	.	.	.	.	.	.	.	.
Suriname	5	62.0	38.0	3.0	35.1	8.4	10.1	1.1	.	1.3	3.0
Trinidad and Tobago	10	60.2	11.4	12.3	25.3	14.4	20.7	3.5	10.6	1.8	0.01
Turks and Caicos Islands	0.01[z]	75.0[z]	...	...	...	...	...	...	...	...	100.0[z]
Uruguay[w]	99	63.7	...	...	...	...	...	...	...	...	100.0
Venezuela	650**	56.9**	...	...	...	...	...	...	...	...	100.0**

North America and Western Europe

Andorra	.	.	.	.	.	.	.	.	.	.	.
Austria[o]	224	52.7	11.1[y]	11.8[y]	40.0[y]	11.6[y]	14.0[y]	1.9[y]	8.3[y]	1.2[y]	0.2[y]
Belgium[o]	367	53.1	13.0	10.9	32.3	10.7	11.3	2.1	18.1	1.5	0.1
Canada[o]	1 212[z]	56.0[z]	7.0[y]	10.5[y]	26.4[y]	9.7[y]	10.1[y]	1.6[y]	9.0[y]	4.2[y]	21.5[y]
Cyprus[o]	14	54.8	12.9	8.5	41.9	12.8	3.7	0.1	4.5	15.6	–
Denmark[o]	196	57.4	10.1	16.5	24.3	10.0	9.9	1.9	24.7	2.1	0.5
Finland[o]	284	54.1	5.5	15.0	22.6	11.4	25.8	2.4	13.2	4.1	–
France[o]	2 029	54.8	...	...	...	...	...	...	...	...	100.0
Germany[o]	2 255**	48.5**	7.1**	15.8**	26.2**	13.7**	14.7**	1.4**	14.6**	2.3**	4.3**
Greece[o]	528	51.4	7.1	13.3	32.1	16.0	13.8	5.6	7.0	5.1	–
Iceland[o]	12	63.2	18.0	14.0	34.8	12.1	6.0	0.5	12.4	2.2	–
Ireland[o]	176	55.1	4.2	15.2	19.6	15.7	11.3	1.2	8.4	3.0	21.4
Israel[o]	300	56.5	16.9	11.7	33.5	10.5	20.1	0.5	5.9	.	1.0
Italy[o]	1 854	56.2	5.6	15.7	39.1	7.5	16.4	2.2	11.7	1.8	0.1
Luxembourg[o]	3	52.8**	21.7	12.6	40.6	10.5	7.6	–	7.0	–	–
Malta[o]	7	56.9	20.6	10.0	36.4	5.0	7.2	0.4	20.0	0.4	–
Monaco	.	.	.	.	.	.	.	.	.	.	.
Netherlands[o]	517	50.7	13.9	8.0	41.0	5.9	10.6	1.7	16.0	2.3	0.5
Norway[o]	197	59.6	16.0	10.3	28.5	11.5	6.4	1.1	17.5	2.7	6.1
Portugal[o]	397	57.0	14.4[y]	8.0[y]	35.6[y]	9.4[y]	17.9[y]	3.1[y]	7.6[y]	4.1[y]	–
San Marino	0.9[y]	57.9[y]	...	...	...	...	...	...	...	...	100.0[y]
Spain[o]	1 833	53.1	8.4	10.7	34.4	13.2	17.1	2.7	9.0	4.3	0.3
Sweden[o]	383	59.5	14.3	13.0	25.7	10.6	18.1	0.8	15.5	1.6	0.2
Switzerland[o]	170	43.3	9.7	12.8	37.6	11.6	14.3	1.4	9.2	3.0	0.5
United Kingdom[o]	2 241	55.2	8.8	19.2	23.6	16.4	10.1	1.1	19.9	1.0	–
United States[o]	15 928	56.3	...	...	...	...	...	...	...	...	100.0

South and West Asia

Afghanistan	...	...	...	...	...	...	...	...	...	...	...
Bangladesh	855	32.0	2.2	31.9	39.3	9.6	1.5	0.8	13.3	0.1	1.2
Bhutan	2**	33.8**	...	...	...	...	...	...	...	...	100.0**
India[w]	10 577	8.1	1.1	–	51.9	15.1	5.0	–	1.4	–	25.5
Iran, Islamic Republic of	1 567	49.1	2.3[z]	14.5[z]	27.2[z]	14.7[z]	19.3[z]	6.3[z]	13.4[z]	2.1[z]	0.3[z]
Maldives	.	.	.	.	.	.	.	.	.	.	.
Nepal	120	20.6	...	...	...	...	...	...	...	...	100.0
Pakistan	...	...	...	...	...	...	...	...	...	...	...
Sri Lanka[w]	...	...	...	...	...	...	...	...	...	...	...

Sub-Saharan Africa

Angola	8[y]	39.0[y]	34.6[y]	.	37.0[y]	9.7[y]	8.6[y]	–	7.4[y]	.	2.7[y]
Benin	19[y]	19.8[y]	...	...	...	...	...	...	...	...	100.0[y]
Botswana	8	44.8	25.6	22.5	29.2	14.4	4.2	1.3	2.4	0.4	–
Burkina Faso	16	25.4	...	...	...	...	...	...	...	...	100.0
Burundi	11	30.4	25.2	14.1	28.2	4.9	4.7	3.7	6.4	.	12.8
Cameroon	78	38.8**	...	...	...	...	...	...	...	...	100.0
Cape Verde	2	46.8	...	...	...	...	...	...	...	...	100.0
Central African Republic	6[y]	16.2[y]	9.1[y]	32.7[y]	18.9[y]	13.3[y]	1.7[y]	0.5[y]	23.8[y]	–	–
Chad	6[y]	15.0[y]	...	...	...	...	...	...	...	...	100.0[y]

(y) Data are for 1999/2000.   (z) Data are for 2000/2001.

STATISTICAL ANNEX / 331

Table 10

PERCENTAGE OF FEMALES IN EACH FIELD

Education	Humanities and arts	Social sciences, business and law	Science	Engineering, manufacturing and construction	Agriculture	Health and welfare	Services	Not known or unspecified	Country or territory
...	...	...	...	...	...	...	...	61.9**,y	Panama
...	...	...	...	...	...	...	...	...	Paraguay[w]
...	...	...	...	...	...	...	...	48.8**	Peru[w]
.	.	.	.	.	.	.	.	.	Saint Kitts and Nevis
...	...	...	...	...	...	...	...	76.9	Saint Lucia
.	.	.	.	.	.	.	.	.	Saint Vincent and the Grenadines
59.8	80.8	68.5	66.7	33.1	66.7	.	78.8	69.4	Suriname
74.2	78.3	70.0	56.9	26.5	58.4	56.9	71.7	100.0	Trinidad and Tobago
...	...	...	...	...	...	...	...	75.0[z]	Turks and Caicos Islands
...	...	...	...	...	...	...	...	63.7	Uruguay[w]
...	...	...	...	...	...	...	...	56.9**	Venezuela

North America and Western Europe

.	.	.	.	.	.	.	.	.	Andorra
67.4[y]	69.5[y]	50.0[y]	32.9[y]	18.6[y]	54.3[y]	58.4[y]	37.1[y]	54.7[y]	Austria[o]
71.2	59.5	53.1	28.9	20.5	48.3	72.0	49.4	56.0	Belgium[o]
74.6[y]	62.1[y]	58.4[y]	38.2[y]	20.3[y]	49.6[y]	77.1[y]	56.7[y]	60.0[y]	Canada[o]
90.7	80.3	54.2	36.8	7.5	–	70.0	35.0	–	Cyprus[o]
69.9	64.0	47.6	33.2	30.9	48.6	81.7	26.1	49.0	Denmark[o]
80.5	71.6	63.2	41.8	18.8	48.9	83.6	69.1	–	Finland[o]
...	...	...	...	...	...	...	...	54.8	France[o]
69.3	64.3	46.3	33.0	18.9	45.7	72.5	54.5	...	Germany[o]
70.5	72.9	53.7	37.3	27.1	43.2	72.1	41.9	–	Greece[o]
84.4	66.2	59.6	38.9	26.3	36.8	79.5	77.4	–	Iceland[o]
84.0	66.2	61.0	44.0	17.9	39.8	77.3	55.9	56.1	Ireland[o]
83.5	67.4	57.7	37.9	29.1	55.9	77.0	.	60.2	Israel[o]
88.4	74.7	56.8	49.1	26.4	43.6	64.2	46.8	57.7	Italy[o]
...	...	...	...	...	–	...	–	–	Luxembourg[o]
74.8	59.1	53.2	30.7	27.6	28.6	62.2	34.6	–	Malta[o]
.	.	.	.	.	.	.	.	.	Monaco
74.6	57.3	46.4	23.0	11.9	46.7	75.4	51.1	29.1	Netherlands[o]
77.8	61.6	56.2	32.7	23.6	52.4	81.4	42.8	59.8	Norway[o]
79.9[y]	67.3[y]	59.7[y]	40.8[y]	29.5[y]	54.9[y]	73.8[y]	49.3[y]	–	Portugal[o]
...	...	...	...	...	...	...	...	57.9[y]	San Marino
77.1	61.6	58.3	36.9	26.6	44.0	75.6	59.3	39.1	Spain[o]
77.9	64.0	61.5	43.7	29.2	54.4	81.5	59.1	77.8	Sweden[o]
70.0	57.9	42.9	25.3	13.1	42.6	62.8	51.8	42.1	Switzerland[o]
69.7	63.8	51.5	39.2	15.9	54.9	77.9	62.0	–	United Kingdom[o]
...	...	...	...	...	...	...	...	56.3	United States[o]

South and West Asia

...	...	...	...	...	...	...	...	...	Afghanistan
36.1	40.5	31.4	30.8	10.6	17.5	18.5	26.3	16.1	Bangladesh
...	...	...	...	...	...	...	...	33.8**	Bhutan
43.5	–	42.3	39.1	24.9	–	40.6	–	35.2	India[w]
56.9[z]	66.2[z]	51.3[z]	52.6[z]	16.3[z]	43.3[z]	60.4[z]	24.8[z]	72.7[z]	Iran, Islamic Republic of
.	.	.	.	.	.	.	.	.	Maldives
...	...	...	...	...	...	...	...	20.6	Nepal
...	...	...	...	...	...	...	...	...	Pakistan
...	...	...	...	...	...	...	...	...	Sri Lanka[w]

Sub-Saharan Africa

42.7[y]	.	37.3[y]	37.6[y]	20.5[y]	–	57.5[y]	.	27.3[y]	Angola
...	...	...	...	...	...	...	...	19.8[y]	Benin
51.5	55.9	44.2	24.5	16.4	14.3	68.5	34.3	–	Botswana
...	...	...	...	...	...	...	...	25.4	Burkina Faso
32.9	19.3	39.7	17.6	8.6	15.1	22.8	.	38.8	Burundi
...	...	...	...	...	...	...	...	38.8	Cameroon
...	...	...	...	...	...	...	...	46.8	Cape Verde
6.6[y]	15.4[y]	14.5[y]	13.2[y]	2.8[y]	11.8[y]	19.0[y]	–	–	Central African Republic
...	...	...	...	...	...	...	...	15.0[y]	Chad

Table 10 (continued)

Country or territory	Total enrolment (000)	% F	Education	Humanities and arts	Social sciences, business and law	Science	Engineering, manufacturing and construction	Agriculture	Health and welfare	Services	Not known or unspecified
Comoros	0.7 y	41.9 **,y	...	...	...	...	...	...	...	...	100.0 y
Congo	12	15.8	7.7	27.3	33.8	10.2	1.0	3.1	3.8	0.2	13.0
Côte d'Ivoire	...	...	...	...	...	...	...	...	...	...	...
Democratic Rep. of the Congo	...	...	...	...	...	...	...	...	...	...	...
Equatorial Guinea	1 y	30.3 y	...	...	...	...	...	...	...	...	100.0 y
Eritrea	6	13.4	18.5	1.4	26.5	17.0	–	6.4	3.6	.	26.5
Ethiopia	102	26.4	32.1	1.5	35.2	3.2	9.2	5.9	4.9	0.0	8.0
Gabon	...	...	...	...	...	...	...	...	...	...	...
Gambia	...	...	...	...	...	...	...	...	...	...	...
Ghana	68	27.8	8.7	27.4	28.9	11.7	13.8	4.4	4.0	1.3	–
Guinea	...	...	...	...	...	...	...	...	...	...	...
Guinea-Bissau	0.5 y	15.6 y	...	...	...	...	...	...	...	...	100.0 y
Kenya	99 **	34.7 **	22.9 z	7.6 z	21.4 z	10.4 z	18.6 z	7.3 z	9.4 z	1.3 z	1.2 z
Lesotho	5	58.0	50.6	7.2	28.9	8.0	–	5.0	0.3	–	–
Liberia	44 y	42.8 y	5.0 y	18.4 y	32.3 y	7.3 y	3.9 y	2.5 y	21.6 y	6.8 y	2.3 y
Madagascar	33	45.4	3.2	10.1	54.1	12.8	7.0	2.3	9.3	0.1	1.0
Malawi	...	...	...	...	...	...	...	...	...	...	...
Mali	27	...	...	...	...	...	...	...	...	...	100.0
Mauritius	13	55.8	31.8	5.1	24.1	8.2	15.8	2.1	12.1	0.5	0.4
Mozambique	9 **,y	44.2 **,y	...	...	...	...	...	...	...	...	100.0 **,y
Namibia	13	45.6	32.5	3.2	39.5	6.1	4.2	2.3	5.4	3.4	3.3
Niger	14 **	24.8 **	21.4 z	15.5 z	29.6 z	4.9 z	1.8 z	19.7 z	5.1 z	1.9 z	– z
Nigeria	...	...	...	...	...	...	...	...	...	...	...
Rwanda	14 **	33.7 **	...	...	...	...	...	...	...	...	100.0 **
Sao Tome and Principe	0.2 **	36.1 **	49.2 z	21.0 z	29.8 z	.	.	.	.	.	.
Senegal	...	...	...	...	...	...	...	...	...	...	...
Seychelles	.	.	.	.	.	.	.	.	.	.	.
Sierra Leone	9 **	28.8 **	43.3 z	18.1 z	11.0 z	6.8 z	0.9 z	15.3 z	4.0 z	0.7 z	–
Somalia	...	...	...	...	...	...	...	...	...	...	...
South Africa	659	53.5	21.2	6.6	47.0	10.6	6.7	1.4	5.3	1.0 z	–
Swaziland	5	54.6	14.3 **,z	16.7 **,z	32.4 **,z	5.3 **,z	5.6 **,z	4.5 **,z	4.3 **,z	...	...
Togo	15 y	16.9 y	7.6 y	43.6 y	33.0 y	5.9 y	1.7 y	1.1 y	7.1 y	– y	– y
Uganda	72 **	34.5 **	43.7 z	4.5 z	32.7 z	2.4 z	5.4 z	2.9 z	3.3 z	3.3 z	1.8 z
United Republic of Tanzania	22 z	13.3 z	...	...	...	...	...	...	...	...	100.0 z
Zambia	25 **,z	31.6 **,z	...	...	...	...	...	...	...	...	100.0 **,z
Zimbabwe w	60 **	36.7 **	...	...	...	...	...	...	...	...	100.0 **
World[1]	...	...	...	...	...	...	...	...	...	...	...
Countries in transition	...	...	...	...	...	...	...	...	...	...	...
Developed countries	...	...	11.0	15.3	34.5	12.7	10.3	1.8	9.8	2.7	2.1
Developing countries	...	...	...	...	...	...	...	...	...	...	...
Arab States	...	...	...	...	...	...	...	...	...	...	...
Central and Eastern Europe	...	...	12.1	8.5	33.9	7.1	17.2	2.8	7.3	4.1	7.2
Central Asia	...	...	14.2	38.9	20.5	10.8	7.5	3.3	4.1	0.8	–
East Asia and the Pacific	...	...	...	...	...	...	...	...	...	...	...
Latin America and the Caribbean	...	...	...	...	...	...	...	...	...	...	...
North America and Western Europe	...	...	11.1	11.8	40.0	11.6	14.0	1.9	8.3	1.2	0.2
South and West Asia	...	...	...	...	...	...	...	...	...	...	...
Sub-Saharan Africa	...	...	...	...	...	...	...	...	...	...	...

1. All values shown are medians. (y) Data are for 1999/2000. (z) Data are for 2000/2001.

Table 10

PERCENTAGE OF FEMALES IN EACH FIELD

Education	Humanities and arts	Social sciences, business and law	Science	Engineering, manufacturing and construction	Agriculture	Health and welfare	Services	Not known or unspecified	Country or territory
...	...	...	...	...	...	...	...	41.9 y	Comoros
9.2	12.5	15.8	16.0	10.3	31.1	26.5	44.4	19.4	Congo
...	...	...	...	...	...	...	...	...	Côte d'Ivoire
...	...	...	...	...	...	...	...	...	Democratic Rep. of the Congo
...	...	...	...	...	...	...	...	30.3 y	Equatorial Guinea
8.8	32.1	19.2	7.0	–	10.2	11.5	.	14.7	Eritrea
19.4	39.0	40.3	24.7	8.2	16.5	25.1	26.1	20.0	Ethiopia
...	...	...	...	...	...	...	...	...	Gabon
...	...	...	...	...	...	...	...	...	Gambia
30.9	35.1	29.0	24.7	8.3	19.7	33.3	70.6	–	Ghana
...	...	...	...	...	...	...	...	...	Guinea
...	...	...	...	...	...	...	...	15.6 y	Guinea-Bissau
...	...	...	...	...	...	...	...	...	Kenya
68.3	55.4	50.3	30.7	–	46.0	94.1	–	–	Lesotho
44.6 y	41.2 y	38.4 y	50.6 y	24.8 y	14.3 y	35.0 y	7.4 y	...	Liberia
44.8	59.3	48.7	31.3	19.6	36.6	52.3	51.1	39.8	Madagascar
...	...	...	...	...	...	...	...	...	Malawi
...	...	...	...	...	...	...	...	...	Mali
64.3	65.5	53.6	49.3	22.5	49.0	86.5	10.5	–	Mauritius
...	...	...	...	...	...	...	...	44.2**,y	Mozambique
54.7	59.6	55.6	40.5	16.4	34.7	81.0	62.3	50.3	Namibia
15.9 z	28.0 z	16.6 z	14.2 z	15.4 z	15.2 z	28.8 z	– z	– z	Niger
...	...	...	...	...	...	...	...	...	Nigeria
...	...	...	...	...	...	...	...	33.7**	Rwanda
25.8 z	60.5 z	35.2 z	.	.	.	.	.	.	Sao Tome and Principe
...	...	...	...	...	...	...	...	...	Senegal
.	.	.	.	.	.	.	.	.	Seychelles
32.7 z	31.0 z	21.4 z	27.4 z	25.0 z	19.6 z	28.5 z	34.5 z	–	Sierra Leone
...	...	...	...	...	...	...	...	...	Somalia
71.1 z	65.4 z	53.2 z	43.5 z	16.6 z	37.4 z	71.9 z	75.0 z	–	South Africa
43.2 z	62.3 z	47.5 z	40.9 z	15.3 z	32.6 z	72.4 z	...	...	Swaziland
17.1 y	19.8 y	14.9 y	7.3 y	6.3 y	7.2 y	21.1 y	– y	– y	Togo
32.8 z	37.6 z	37.7 z	24.2 z	17.7 z	16.7 z	41.7 z	56.4 z	48.5 z	Uganda
...	...	...	...	...	...	...	...	13.3 z	United Republic of Tanzania
...	...	...	...	...	...	...	...	31.6**,z	Zambia
...	...	...	...	...	...	...	...	36.7**	Zimbabwe w

Education	Humanities and arts	Social sciences, business and law	Science	Engineering, manufacturing and construction	Agriculture	Health and welfare	Services	Not known or unspecified	Country or territory
...	...	...	...	...	...	...	...	...	World[1]
...	...	...	...	...	...	...	...	...	Countries in transition
73.9	66.8	53.6	36.9	22.6	47.9	69.5	44.2	53.5	Developed countries
...	...	...	...	...	...	...	...	...	Developing countries
...	...	...	...	...	...	...	...	...	Arab States
73.4	64.8	60.0	40.2	21.6	53.1	72.1	42.6	64.2	Central and Eastern Europe
...	...	...	...	...	...	...	...	...	Central Asia
...	...	...	...	...	...	...	...	...	East Asia and the Pacific
...	...	...	...	...	...	...	...	...	Latin America and the Caribbean
67.4	69.5	50.0	32.9	18.6	54.3	58.4	37.1	54.7	North America and Western Europe
...	...	...	...	...	...	...	...	...	South and West Asia
...	...	...	...	...	...	...	...	...	Sub-Saharan Africa

334 / ANNEX

Table 11. Tertiary education: distribution of graduates by ISCED level and female share in each level

	Country or territory	Number of graduates 2001 Total (000)	% F	DISTRIBUTION OF GRADUATES BY ISCED LEVEL Total graduates (%) 2001 Level 5A	Level 5B	Level 6	Percentage female in each level 2001 Level 5A	Level 5B	Level 6	
	Arab States									
1	Algeria	...	...	...	...	...	...	...	...	1
2	Bahrain	...	...	...	...	...	...	...	...	2
3	Djibouti	0.5 z	41.7 z	47.4 z	52.6 z	. z	27.7 z	54.4 z	. z	3
4	Egypt w	...	...	...	...	...	...	...	...	4
5	Iraq	55 y	36.4 y	...	...	...	...	...	...	5
6	Jordan w	28	54.1	86.9	13.1	–	51.0	74.3	–	6
7	Kuwait	...	...	...	...	...	...	...	...	7
8	Lebanon	17	54.7	87.6	9.7	2.8	55.8	48.8	39.3	8
9	Libyan Arab Jamahiriya	...	...	...	...	...	...	...	...	9
10	Mauritania	...	...	...	...	.	...	...	.	10
11	Morocco	44 z	43.7 z	64.6 z	30.6 z	4.8 z	43.9 z	45.0 z	32.0 z	11
12	Oman	3	62.5	...	.	...	...	.	...	12
13	Palestinian Autonomous Territories	12 z	50.4 z	82.7 z	17.3 z	.	48.4 z	60.2 z	.	13
14	Qatar	1	...	100.0	.	.	78.6	.	.	14
15	Saudi Arabia	56 y	58.3 y	77.4 y	20.2 y	2.4 y	57.4 y	64.8 y	33.1 y	15
16	Sudan	...	...	...	...	...	...	...	...	16
17	Syrian Arab Republic	...	...	...	...	...	...	...	...	17
18	Tunisia w	26 **	48.5 **	...	...	...	50.2	42.2	...	18
19	United Arab Emirates	...	...	...	...	...	...	...	...	19
20	Yemen	...	...	...	...	...	...	...	...	20
	Central and Eastern Europe									
21	Albania o	5 z	31.4 z	94.2 z	5.8 z	. z	32.4 z	14.6 z	. z	21
22	Belarus	91	...	48.8	49.9	1.3	...	59.3	...	22
23	Bosnia and Herzegovina o	...	...	...	...	...	...	...	...	23
24	Bulgaria o	51	57.7	89.9	9.4	0.8	57.1	63.9	53.0	24
25	Croatia	15	55.4	61.4	36.8	1.7	58.1	51.3	49.0	25
26	Czech Republic o	44	56.5	79.5	17.5	3.0	53.9	72.4	34.3	26
27	Estonia o	8	68.2	75.7	21.8	2.4	64.8	80.9	59.6	27
28	Hungary o	62	60.5	95.3	3.1	1.6	60.7	59.7	44.8	28
29	Latvia o	19	69.4	85.3	14.5	0.3	71.8	55.5	71.2	29
30	Lithuania o	30	64.4	67.6	31.1	1.3	62.8	68.3	56.3	30
31	Poland o	460	64.9	98.0	1.0	1.0	64.9	83.0	44.5	31
32	Republic of Moldova	20	56.2	65.0	33.6	1.4	56.5	55.9	52.9	32
33	Romania o	93	57.4	85.1	14.9	–	55.6	67.6	–	33
34	Russian Federation w	1 354	...	53.1	45.0	2.0	...	...	...	34
35	Serbia and Montenegro	19 z	58.2 z	72.2 z	25.6 z	2.2 z	...	...	...	35
36	Slovakia	28	55.3	88.4	9.0	2.6	53.1	81.3	40.6	36
37	Slovenia o	14	59.4	47.2	50.5	2.2	62.2	57.3	45.3	37
38	The former Yugoslav Rep. of Macedonia o	4	61.7	90.0	8.6	1.4	62.5	54.0	54.9	38
39	Turkey o	287	42.4	64.6	34.5	0.9	41.2	44.8	33.7	39
40	Ukraine	466	...	67.1	31.7	1.2	...	...	...	40
	Central Asia									
41	Armenia	12	56.5	97.0	.	3.0	57.4	.	27.8	41
42	Azerbaijan	36	51.0	67.2	32.1	0.7	38.9	76.7	35.5	42
43	Georgia	22	52.7	98.0	.	2.0	53.0	.	40.2	43
44	Kazakhstan	...	...	...	...	...	...	...	...	44
45	Kyrgyzstan	18 z	53.0 z	93.7 z	4.1 z	2.2 z	52.7 z	54.8 z	61.9 z	45
46	Mongolia	18	66.6	92.7	7.1	0.3	66.4	70.2	43.8	46
47	Tajikistan	12	...	98.3	.	1.7	...	.	...	47
48	Turkmenistan	...	...	...	...	...	...	...	...	48
49	Uzbekistan	...	...	...	...	...	...	...	...	49
	East Asia and the Pacific									
50	Australia o	152 z	56.1 z	95.4 z	2.2 z	2.4 z	56.9 z	39.9 z	40.0 z	50
51	Brunei Darussalam	1	67.4	45.8	54.2	–	69.0	66.1	–	51
52	Cambodia	3	25.1	100.0	.	.	25.1	.	.	52
53	China w	1 948	...	...	...	...	...	...	...	53

1. Data are included in ISCED level 5A.
(y) Data are for 1999/2000.
(z) Data are for 2000/2001.

Table 11 (continued)

DISTRIBUTION OF GRADUATES BY ISCED LEVEL

	Country or territory	Number of graduates 2001 Total (000)	% F	Total graduates (%) 2001 Level 5A	Level 5B	Level 6	Percentage female in each level 2001 Level 5A	Level 5B	Level 6	
54	Cook Islands	.	.	.	.	.	.	.	.	54
55	Democratic People's Republic of Korea	...	...	...	...	...	...	...	...	55
56	Fiji									56
57	Indonesia[w]	506	45.2	68.9	29.3	1.7	42.8	51.2	38.3	57
58	Japan[o]	1 048	48.8	59.5	39.2	1.3	38.0	66.1	23.1	58
59	Kiribati	...	...	...	...	...	...	...	...	59
60	Lao People's Democratic Republic	5	37.2	43.1	56.9	.	34.2	39.5	.	60
61	Macao, China	5	38.8	85.8	14.2	0.0	33.6	70.5	–	61
62	Malaysia[w]	125 [y]	51.3 [y]	...	...	...	...	...	...	62
63	Marshall Islands	...	...	...	...	...	...	...	...	63
64	Micronesia (Federated States of)	...	...	...	...	...	...	...	...	64
65	Myanmar	...	...	...	...	...	...	...	...	65
66	Nauru	.	.	.	.	.	.	.	.	66
67	New Zealand[o]	43 [z]	61.9 [z]	...	...	...	...	...	...	67
68	Niue	.	.	.	.	.	.	.	.	68
69	Palau	0.1 [z]	60.1 [z]	100.0 [z]	.	.	60.1 [z]	.	.	69
70	Papua New Guinea	...	...	...	...	...	...	...	...	70
71	Philippines[w]	364	61.0	87.0	12.5	0.4	61.8	55.7	63.0	71
72	Republic of Korea[o]	563	48.6	...	...	...	...	...	...	72
73	Samoa	0.4 [z]	43.1 [z]	13.3 [z]	86.7 [z]	.	38.9 [z]	43.8 [z]	.	73
74	Singapore	...	...	...	...	...	...	...	...	74
75	Solomon Islands	.	.	.	.	.	.	.	.	75
76	Thailand[w]	394	55.6	52.7	47.1	0.1	58.6	52.3	53.0	76
77	Timor-Leste	...	...	...	...	...	...	...	...	77
78	Tokelau	.	.	.	.	.	.	.	.	78
79	Tonga	...	...	...	...	...	...	...	...	79
80	Tuvalu	.	.	.	.	.	.	.	.	80
81	Vanuatu	...	...	...	...	...	...	...	...	81
82	Viet Nam	125	45.1	74.9	22.5	2.7	53.2	19.7	33.2	82
	Latin America and the Caribbean									
83	Anguilla	.	.	.	.	.	.	.	.	83
84	Antigua and Barbuda	.	.	.	.	.	.	.	.	84
85	Argentina[w]	140	63.2	45.4	54.4	0.1	56.3	69.1	46.8	85
86	Aruba	0.3	55.6	...	...	.	...	...	.	86
87	Bahamas	...	...	...	...	...	...	...	...	87
88	Barbados	0.9 [z]	66.0**,[z]	...	...	...	...	...	...	88
89	Belize	...	...	...	...	...	...	...	...	89
90	Bermuda	0.1 [z]	76.8 [z]	.	100.0 [z]	. [z]	.	76.8 [z]	. [z]	90
91	Bolivia	23	...	...	...	...	...	...	...	91
92	Brazil[w]	422	61.6	93.8	./.[1]	6.2	62.4	./.[1]	50.0	92
93	British Virgin Islands	...	...	...	...	...	...	...	...	93
94	Cayman Islands	...	...	...	...	...	...	...	...	94
95	Chile[w]	53 [z]	46.2 [z]	...	...	...	...	...	...	95
96	Colombia	...	...	...	...	...	...	...	...	96
97	Costa Rica	23	61.1	96.9	2.9	0.1	61.3	54.0	59.4	97
98	Cuba	17	62.6	...	.	...	...	.	...	98
99	Dominica	.	.	.	.	.	.	.	.	99
100	Dominican Republic	...	...	...	...	...	...	...	...	100
101	Ecuador	...	...	...	...	...	...	...	...	101
102	El Salvador	...	...	...	...	...	...	...	...	102
103	Grenada	...	...	...	...	...	...	...	...	103
104	Guatemala	...	...	...	...	...	...	...	...	104
105	Guyana	...	...	...	...	...	...	...	...	105
106	Haiti	...	...	...	...	...	...	...	...	106
107	Honduras	3 [z]	73.7 [z]	...	...	...	73.7 [z]	...	...	107
108	Jamaica[w]	6 [z]	70.9 [z]	...	...	...	...	...	...	108
109	Mexico[o]	339	52.2	94.8	4.6	0.5	52.7	42.7	38.9	109
110	Montserrat	.	.	.	.	.	.	.	.	110
111	Netherlands Antilles	0.6**,[z]	19.2**,[z]	...	...	...	...	...	...	111
112	Nicaragua	...	...	...	...	...	...	...	...	112

1. Data are included in ISCED level 5A.   (y) Data are for 1999/2000.
(z) Data are for 2000/2001.

Table 11 (continued)

	Country or territory	Number of graduates 2001 Total (000)	2001 % F	Total graduates (%) 2001 Level 5A	Level 5B	Level 6	Percentage female in each level 2001 Level 5A	Level 5B	Level 6	
113	Panama	...	...	...	...	...	...	...	...	113
114	Paraguay[w]	15	66.3	46.1	53.7	0.2**	60.4	71.4	...	114
115	Peru[w]	...	...	...	...	...	...	...	...	115
116	Saint Kitts and Nevis	.	.	.	.	.	.	.	.	116
117	Saint Lucia	...	...	...	...	...	...	...	...	117
118	Saint Vincent and the Grenadines	.	.	.	.	.	.	.	.	118
119	Suriname	...	...	...	...	...	...	...	...	119
120	Trinidad and Tobago	2	66.8	65.0	33.9	1.1	61.7	76.8	55.6	120
121	Turks and Caicos Islands	...	...	...	...	...	...	...	...	121
122	Uruguay[w]	7**	69.3**	49.8	39.3	10.9**	59.7	85.3	55.6**	122
123	Venezuela	61[y]	62.8[y]	54.9[y]	45.1[y]	–[y]	62.9[y]	62.7[y]	–[y]	123
	North America and Western Europe									
124	Andorra	.	.	.	.	.	.	.	.	124
125	Austria[o]	27[z]	51.5[z]	61.8[z]	31.3[z]	6.9[z]	49.2[z]	59.2[z]	37.1[z]	125
126	Belgium[o]	73	56.7	46.9	51.1	1.9	51.8	62.0	35.8	126
127	Canada[o]	225[y]	57.4[y]	66.8[y]	31.4[y]	1.8[y]	58.1[y]	57.1[y]	39.0[y]	127
128	Cyprus[o]	3	62.2	20.5	79.4	0.1	77.2	58.4	–	128
129	Denmark[o]	39	56.5	82.2	15.9	1.9	61.2	34.0	41.1	129
130	Finland[o]	37	61.1	88.0	7.2	4.9	62.7	51.3	45.9	130
131	France[o]	532	55.5	70.0	28.1	2.0	56.7	53.4	42.7	131
132	Germany[o]	294	52.2	59.9	32.0	8.1	48.6	62.9	36.4	132
133	Greece[o]	44	55.2	66.0	31.4	2.6	56.8	53.2	38.4	133
134	Iceland[o]	2[y]	64.4[y]	86.6[y]	13.3[y]	0.1[y]	66.9[y]	48.3[y]	50.0[y]	134
135	Ireland[o]	45	57.1	66.7	32.1	1.2	59.7	52.3	40.2	135
136	Israel[o]	72**	57.3**	57.5	41.3**	1.2	60.6	53.0**	47.4	136
137	Italy[o]	218	57.3	95.5	2.7	1.8	57.4	55.9	51.9	137
138	Luxembourg[o]	0.7[y]	...	34.1[y]	65.9[y]	.	...	...	.	138
139	Malta[o]	2	52.0	83.9	15.5	0.6	52.7	50.2	–	139
140	Monaco	.	.	.	.	.	.	.	.	140
141	Netherlands[o]	86	55.4	94.3	2.8	3.0	55.8	58.9	38.5	141
142	Norway[o]	30	60.3	87.8	9.7	2.5	61.9	51.6	36.8	142
143	Portugal[o]	58[y]	65.0[y]	87.9[y]	9.4[y]	2.7[y]	64.9[y]	70.5[y]	49.2[y]	143
144	San Marino	...	...	...	...	...	...	...	...	144
145	Spain[o]	278[z]	57.2[z]	76.1[z]	21.6[z]	2.3[z]	59.0[z]	52.6[z]	42.9[z]	145
146	Sweden[o]	46	60.0	83.5	8.8	7.7	62.4	54.1	40.6	146
147	Switzerland[o]	58	43.2	41.0	54.1	4.9	41.1	45.6	33.9	147
148	United Kingdom[o]	524	56.5	75.8	22.0	2.2	55.7	60.7	41.5	148
149	United States[o]	2 238	57.3	82.9	15.2	2.0	57.3	58.6	46.3	149
	South and West Asia									
150	Afghanistan	...	...	...	...	...	...	...	...	150
151	Bangladesh	187	31.4	90.2	9.4	0.4	33.3	13.9	23.1	151
152	Bhutan	...	...	...	...	...	...	...	...	152
153	India[w]	...	...	...	...	...	...	...	...	153
154	Iran, Islamic Republic of	...	...	...	...	...	...	...	...	154
155	Maldives	.	.	.	.	.	.	.	.	155
156	Nepal	...	...	...	.	.	...	.	.	156
157	Pakistan	...	...	...	...	...	...	...	...	157
158	Sri Lanka[w]	...	...	...	...	...	...	...	...	158
	Sub-Saharan Africa									
159	Angola	0.3[y]	45.9[y]	100.0[y]	.	.	45.9[y]	.	.	159
160	Benin	...	...	...	...	...	...	...	...	160
161	Botswana	...	...	...	...	...	...	...	...	161
162	Burkina Faso	...	...	...	...	...	...	...	...	162
163	Burundi	0.8[z]	37.9[z]	71.3[z]	28.7[z]	–[z]	31.5[z]	53.9[z]	–[z]	163

1. Data are included in ISCED level 5A.
(y) Data are for 1999/2000.
(z) Data are for 2000/2001.

Table 11 (continued)

	Country or territory	Number of graduates 2001 Total (000)	2001 % F	Total graduates (%) 2001 Level 5A	Level 5B	Level 6	Percentage female in each level 2001 Level 5A	Level 5B	Level 6	
164	Cameroon	...	...	...	...	...	...	...	...	164
165	Cape Verde	...	...	...	...	...	...	...	...	165
166	Central African Republic	...	...	...	...	...	...	...	...	166
167	Chad	0.7 y	12.7 y	71.5 y	27.4 y	1.1 y	10.4 y	19.4 y	–	167
168	Comoros	...	...	...	...	...	...	...	...	168
169	Congo	0.1 y	25.7 y	...	...	...	...	...	...	169
170	Côte d'Ivoire	...	...	...	...	...	...	...	...	170
171	Democratic Rep. of the Congo	...	...	...	...	...	...	...	...	171
172	Equatorial Guinea	...	...	...	...	...	...	...	...	172
173	Eritrea	1	15.5	100.0	.	.	15.5	.	.	173
174	Ethiopia	18	23.8	100.0	.	.	23.8	.	–	174
175	Gabon	...	...	...	...	...	...	...	...	175
176	Gambia	1 y	22.4 y	.	100.0 y	.	.	22.4 y	.	176
177	Ghana	14 z	27.0 z	49.2 z	45.2 z	5.6 z	26.5 z	30.0 z	8.0 z	177
178	Guinea	...	...	...	...	...	...	...	...	178
179	Guinea-Bissau	...	...	...	...	...	...	...	...	179
180	Kenya	28 y	36.4 y	38.1 y	57.9 y	4.0 y	34.9 y	37.6 y	32.2 y	180
181	Lesotho	0.9	50.1**	58.3	41.7	.	...	...	...	181
182	Liberia	7 y	46.2 y	32.1 y	60.4 y	7.5 y	42.2 y	49.1 y	40.3 y	182
183	Madagascar	7	47.3	89.4	7.4	3.2	48.0	40.9	42.7	183
184	Malawi	...	...	...	...	...	...	...	...	184
185	Mali	...	...	...	...	...	...	...	...	185
186	Mauritius	2	48.1	51.1	48.5	0.4	54.3	41.7	25.0	186
187	Mozambique	...	...	...	...	...	...	...	...	187
188	Namibia	3	45.8	87.1	12.9	–	...	...	–	188
189	Niger	0.8 z	27.3 z	80.8 z	7.8 z	11.5 z	27.3 z	35.9 z	21.3 z	189
190	Nigeria	...	...	...	...	...	...	...	...	190
191	Rwanda	...	...	...	...	...	...	...	...	191
192	Sao Tome and Principe	...	...	...	...	...	...	...	...	192
193	Senegal	...	...	...	...	...	...	...	...	193
194	Seychelles	.	.	.	.	.	.	.	.	194
195	Sierra Leone	6 y	43.8 y	21.9 y	78.1 y	. y	47.7 y	40.8 y	. y	195
196	Somalia	...	...	...	...	...	...	...	...	196
197	South Africa	98	57.0	81.8	17.3	0.9	53.9	73.0	34.0	197
198	Swaziland	1 y	51.5 y	98.7 y	1.3 y	– y	51.6 y	38.5 y	– y	198
199	Togo	6 y	15.0 y	97.2 y	2.8 y	.	15.4 y	2.4 y	.	199
200	Uganda	25 z	21.5 z	63.0 z	36.9 z	0.1 z	16.1 z	30.7 z	25.0 z	200
201	United Republic of Tanzania	...	...	...	...	...	...	...	...	201
202	Zambia	...	...	...	...	...	...	...	...	202
203	Zimbabwe w	6 z	...	...	...	...	...	...	...	203

I	World[2]	...	...	...	...	...	...	...	...	I
II	Countries in transition	...	...	67.2	32.1	0.7	...	...	...	II
III	Developed countries	...	...	80.9	16.7	2.5	57.4	57.3	49.1	III
IV	Developing countries	...	...	...	...	...	...	...	...	IV
V	Arab States	...	...	...	...	...	...	...	...	V
VI	Central and Eastern Europe	...	...	75.7	21.8	2.4	58.1	51.3	49.0	VI
VII	Central Asia	...	...	95.4	2.1	2.6	53.0	...	40.2	VII
VIII	East Asia and the Pacific	...	...	...	...	...	...	...	...	VIII
IX	Latin America and the Caribbean	...	...	...	...	...	...	...	...	IX
X	North America and Western Europe	...	...	75.8	22.0	2.2	57.8	56.5	45.5	X
XI	South and West Asia	...	...	...	...	...	...	...	...	XI
XII	Sub-Saharan Africa	...	...	...	...	...	...	...	...	XII

1. Data are included in ISCED level 5A.
2. All values shown are medians.
(y) Data are for 1999/2000.
(z) Data are for 2000/2001.

338 / ANNEX

Table 12. Tertiary education: distribution of graduates by field of study and female share in each field, 2001

	Number of graduates		PERCENTAGE DISTRIBUTION BY FIELD OF STUDY								
Country or territory	Total (000)	% F	Education	Humanities and arts	Social sciences, business and law	Science	Engineering, manufacturing and construction	Agriculture	Health and welfare	Services	Not known or unspecified
Arab States											
Algeria	...	...	...	...	...	...	...	...	...	...	...
Bahrain	...	...	...	...	...	...	...	...	...	...	...
Djibouti	0.5z	41.7z	–z	6.9z	50.4z	25.4z	2.6z	–z	–z	–z	14.7z
Egyptw	...	...	...	...	...	...	...	...	...	...	...
Iraq	55y	36.4y	22.5y	12.2y	10.4y	5.2y	10.3y	3.8y	5.6y	.	29.9y
Jordanw	28	54.1	...	...	...	...	...	...	...	...	100.0
Kuwait	...	...	...	...	...	...	...	...	...	...	...
Lebanon	17	54.7	3.3	16.8	43.2	9.6	13.1	0.8	10.1	3.1	–
Libyan Arab Jamahiriya	...	...	...	...	...	...	...	...	...	...	...
Mauritania	...	...	...	...	...	...	...	...	...	...	...
Morocco	44z	43.7z	...	...	...	...	...	...	...	...	100.0z
Oman	3	62.5	...	...	...	...	...	...	...	.	100.0
Palestinian A. T.	12z	50.4z	10.2z	21.7z	34.5z	13.8z	7.0z	0.9z	9.8z	0.3z	1.9z
Qatar	1.2	...	37.3	11.2	31.4	11.9	5.1	–	3.2	–	–
Saudi Arabia	56y	58.3y	...	...	...	...	...	...	...	...	100.0y
Sudan	...	...	...	...	...	...	...	...	...	...	...
Syrian Arab Republic	...	...	...	...	...	...	...	...	...	...	...
Tunisiaw	26**	48.5**	...	...	...	...	...	...	...	...	100.0**
United Arab Emirates	...	...	...	...	...	...	...	...	...	...	...
Yemen	...	...	...	...	...	...	...	...	...	...	...
Central and Eastern Europe											
Albaniao	5z	31.4z	35.5z	13.8z	29.3z	1.7z	3.9z	1.7z	12.8z	1.3z	–z
Belarus	91	...	14.6	17.9	24.7	2.4	22.9	8.5	7.8	...	...
Bosnia and Herzegovinao	...	...	...	...	...	...	...	...	...	...	...
Bulgariao	51	57.7	9.7	7.5	42.0	5.5	21.1	2.0	7.0	5.3	–
Croatia	15	55.4	9.0	11.0	27.1	7.4	15.4	4.2	8.1	17.9	–
Czech Republico	44	56.5	15.1	8.1	29.5	11.3	11.9	3.5	14.4	3.7	2.4
Estoniao	8	68.2	12.2	11.5	40.2	6.1	10.1	1.5	11.7	6.7	–
Hungaryo	62	60.5	19.4	8.4	39.0	3.1	9.3	3.6	8.4	8.9	–
Latviao	19	69.4	20.3	6.4	50.6	6.2	7.7	1.0	3.3	4.5	–
Lithuaniao	30	64.4	17.5	7.7	33.6	4.5	18.7	2.8	10.3	4.9	–
Polando	460	64.9	12.4	6.4	39.6	3.6	7.2	1.6	1.9	3.6	23.6
Republic of Moldova	20	56.2	...	...	...	...	...	...	...	...	100.0
Romaniao	93	57.4	6.9	11.1	43.9	5.4	16.5	3.0	6.1	3.8	3.3
Russian Federationo	1 354	...	...	...	...	...	...	...	...	...	100.0
Serbia and Montenegro	19z	58.2z	...	...	...	...	...	...	...	...	100.0
Slovakia	28	55.3	16.1	5.9	27.8	8.6	16.6	3.7	14.7	6.5	–
Sloveniao	14	59.4	11.9	6.9	41.6	3.9	16.1	3.1	9.9	6.7	–
TFYR Macedoniao	4	61.7	16.9	11.1	24.6	9.2	17.2	4.3	12.1	4.6	–
Turkeyo	287	42.4	15.1	7.0	23.1	7.7	15.3	4.1	6.3	3.0	18.5
Ukraine	466	...	7.6	5.6	38.7	3.7	24.2	6.1	7.1	4.4	2.7
Central Asia											
Armenia	12	56.5	13.7	3.7	32.3	–	7.2	2.2	8.0	2.3	30.6
Azerbaijan	36	51.0	...	...	...	...	...	...	...	...	100.0
Georgia	22	52.7	7.9	22.9	32.1	6.4	15.6	3.2	9.8	2.1	0.01
Kazakhstan	...	...	...	...	...	...	...	...	...	...	...
Kyrgyzstan	18z	53.0z	13.7z	7.8z	46.2z	7.6z	11.8z	2.5z	4.7z	3.5z	2.1z
Mongolia	18	66.6	16.0	11.1	33.4	5.5	13.6	3.5	5.6	2.9	8.4
Tajikistan	12	...	14.4	34.1	22.6	8.0	9.8	4.1	6.4	0.5	–
Turkmenistan	...	...	...	...	...	...	...	...	...	...	...
Uzbekistan	...	...	...	...	...	...	...	...	...	...	...
East Asia and the Pacific											
Australiao	152z	56.1z	11.1z	13.8z	35.7z	11.8z	7.9z	1.6z	14.8z	3.2z	–z
Brunei Darussalam	1	67.4	49.8	8.2	9.2	4.7	7.4	.	17.6	.	3.1
Cambodia	3	25.1	8.0	9.9	56.2	12.4	2.4	4.4	5.5	1.3	–
Chinaw	1 948	...	...	...	...	...	...	...	...	...	100.0

(y) Data are for 1999/2000.   (z) Data are for 2000/2001.

Table 12

PERCENTAGE OF FEMALES IN EACH FIELD

Education	Humanities and arts	Social sciences, business and law	Science	Engineering, manufacturing and construction	Agriculture	Health and welfare	Services	Not known or unspecified	Country or territory
									Arab States
...	...	...	...	...	...	...	...	...	Algeria
...	...	...	...	...	...	...	...	...	Bahrain
–z	52.9z	51.2z	23.0z	–z	–z	–z	–z	43.8z	Djibouti
...	...	...	...	...	...	...	...	...	Egypt w
58.9y	39.2y	36.6y	70.5y	20.8y	20.5y	31.4y	.	20.7y	Iraq
...	...	...	...	...	...	...	...	54.1	Jordan w
...	...	...	...	...	...	...	...	...	Kuwait
85.6	68.6	55.8	47.5	20.7	40.7	71.4	46.8	–	Lebanon
...	...	...	...	...	...	...	...	...	Libyan Arab Jamahiriya
...	...	...	...	...	...	...	...	...	Mauritania
...	...	...	...	...	...	...	...	43.7z	Morocco
...	...	...	...	...	...	...	.	62.5	Oman
69.5z	61.2z	39.4z	55.5z	20.7z	23.8z	58.5z	19.4z	73.5z	Palestinian Autonomous Territories
86.9	88.3	70.9	65.1	–	...	100.0	...	–	Qatar
...	...	...	...	...	...	...	...	58.3y	Saudi Arabia
...	...	...	...	...	...	...	...	...	Sudan
...	...	...	...	...	...	...	...	...	Syrian Arab Republic
...	...	...	...	...	...	...	...	48.5**	Tunisia w
...	...	...	...	...	...	...	...	...	United Arab Emirates
...	...	...	...	...	...	...	...	...	Yemen
									Central and Eastern Europe
21.4z	22.3z	41.8z	29.1z	79.8z	80.5z	23.6z	38.7z	–z	Albania o
...	...	...	...	...	...	...	...	...	Belarus
...	...	...	...	...	...	...	...	...	Bosnia and Herzegovina o
76.6	68.2	63.1	59.0	34.6	44.8	69.2	46.1	–	Bulgaria o
93.9	76.6	66.4	51.5	28.6	44.0	72.3	26.3	–	Croatia
77.2	61.1	59.7	26.8	30.4	48.1	79.4	51.0	24.9	Czech Republic o
92.9	77.8	67.6	42.6	38.3	45.8	91.8	42.9	–	Estonia o
77.5	69.3	62.4	34.7	25.5	48.3	75.7	42.4	–	Hungary o
87.4	83.2	70.7	51.5	29.3	46.0	85.8	40.4	–	Latvia o
83.8	75.2	67.8	47.5	34.3	59.7	80.8	53.9	–	Lithuania o
76.2	76.3	67.7	57.1	24.2	55.2	68.6	54.4	66.8	Poland o
...	...	...	...	...	...	...	...	56.2	Republic of Moldova
77.6	71.1	62.5	64.5	27.4	39.2	64.3	54.6	45.0	Romania o
...	...	...	...	...	...	...	...	...	Russian Federation o
...	...	...	...	...	...	...	...	58.2	Serbia and Montenegro
74.4	50.5	59.6	38.1	31.2	38.8	78.1	36.6	–	Slovakia
86.1	72.8	64.9	37.1	21.6	43.7	84.0	37.5	–	Slovenia o
77.9	65.2	67.4	71.0	29.7	44.7	75.8	42.9	–	The former Yugoslav Rep. of Macedonia o
46.3	50.2	46.7	42.9	24.1	41.9	57.4	36.0	41.7	Turkey o
...	...	...	...	...	...	...	...	...	Ukraine
									Central Asia
72.6	65.1	44.8	–	31.0	46.5	48.6	10.1	72.9	Armenia
...	...	...	...	...	...	...	...	51.0	Azerbaijan
65.5	76.4	40.2	67.5	26.9	27.1	74.6	20.4	–	Georgia
...	...	...	...	...	...	...	...	...	Kazakhstan
86.5z	71.3z	45.8z	60.4z	35.7z	20.0z	62.4z	23.5z	63.3z	Kyrgyzstan
79.8	69.7	68.0	53.1	50.9	64.8	88.5	20.6	68.0	Mongolia
...	...	...	...	...	...	...	...	...	Tajikistan
...	...	...	...	...	...	...	...	...	Turkmenistan
...	...	...	...	...	...	...	...	...	Uzbekistan
									East Asia and the Pacific
74.7z	67.1z	51.8z	40.6z	21.3z	41.6z	75.9z	51.3z	–z	Australia o
71.1	60.2	62.6	51.0	37.5	.	75.3	.	93.9	Brunei Darussalam
31.0	45.1	23.9	21.4	1.4	4.4	24.1	38.5	–	Cambodia
...	...	...	...	...	...	...	...	...	China w

Table 12 (continued)

	Number of graduates		PERCENTAGE DISTRIBUTION BY FIELD OF STUDY								
Country or territory	Total (000)	% F	Education	Humanities and arts	Social sciences, business and law	Science	Engineering, manufacturing and construction	Agriculture	Health and welfare	Services	Not known or unspecified
Cook Islands	.	.	.	.	.	.	.	.	.	.	.
DPR Korea	…	…	…	…	…	…	…	…	…	…	…
Fiji	…	…	…	…	…	…	…	…	…	…	…
Indonesia[w]	506	45.2	…	…	…	…	…	…	…	…	100.0
Japan[o]	1 048	48.8	6.8	16.4	25.4	2.8	19.4	2.3	11.9	11.0	4.1
Kiribati	…	…	…	…	…	…	…	…	…	…	…
Lao PDR	5	37.2	24.8	28.7	16.4	8.0	9.2	6.6	3.0	3.4	–
Macao, China	5	38.8	4.9	2.4	80.7	2.8	1.0	–	6.5	1.7	–
Malaysia[w]	125[y]	51.3[y]	…	…	…	…	…	…	…	…	100.0[y]
Marshall Islands	…	…	…	…	…	…	…	…	…	…	…
Micronesia	…	…	…	…	…	…	…	…	…	…	…
Myanmar	…	…	…	…	…	…	…	…	…	…	…
Nauru	.	.	.	.	.	.	.	.	.	.	.
New Zealand[o]	43[z]	61.9[z]	16.8[z]	19.1[z]	26.7[z]	10.5[z]	5.0[z]	1.6[z]	11.5[z]	6.4[z]	–
Niue	.	.	.	.	.	.	.	.	.	.	.
Palau	0.1[z]	60.1[z]	2.8[z]	–	37.1[z]	–	16.1[z]	4.2[z]	9.1[z]	9.8[z]	21.0[z]
Papua New Guinea	…	…	…	…	…	…	…	…	…	…	…
Philippines[w]	364	61.0	…	…	…	…	…	…	…	…	100.0
Republic of Korea[o]	563	48.6	7.1	17.6	20.4	9.0	32.0	2.1	8.0	3.8	–
Samoa	0.4[z]	43.1[z]	18.7[z]	8.1[z]	30.5[z]	12.8[z]	5.7[z]	9.9[z]	1.2[z]	5.9[z]	7.1[z]
Singapore	…	…	…	…	…	…	…	…	…	…	…
Solomon Islands	.	.	.	.	.	.	.	.	.	.	.
Thailand[w]	394	55.6	…	…	…	…	…	…	…	…	100.0
Timor-Leste	…	…	…	…	…	…	…	…	…	…	…
Tokelau	.	.	.	.	.	.	.	.	.	.	.
Tonga	…	…	…	…	…	…	…	…	…	…	…
Tuvalu	.	.	.	.	.	.	.	.	.	.	.
Vanuatu	…	…	…	…	…	…	…	…	…	…	…
Viet Nam	125	45.1	22.0	3.9	44.6	–	14.7	5.3	3.9	–	5.7

Latin America and the Caribbean

Anguilla	.	.	.	.	.	.	.	.	.	.	.
Antigua and Barbuda	…	…	…	…	…	…	…	…	…	…	…
Argentina[w]	140	63.2	3.0	2.8	20.9	3.8	4.5	1.8	8.2	0.6	54.5
Aruba	0.3	55.6	12.8	.	47.1	.	24.1	.	16.0	.	–
Bahamas	…	…	…	…	…	…	…	…	…	…	…
Barbados	0.9[z]	66.0**,[z]	…	…	…	…	…	…	…	…	100.0[z]
Belize	…	…	…	…	…	…	…	…	…	…	…
Bermuda	0.1[z]	76.8[z]	.	20.2[z]	43.4[z]	5.1[z]	10.1[z]	.	12.1[z]	8.1[z]	1.0[z]
Bolivia	23	…	…	…	…	…	…	…	…	…	100.0
Brazil[w]	422	61.6	…	…	…	…	…	…	…	…	100.0
British Virgin Islands	…	…	…	…	…	…	…	…	…	…	…
Cayman Islands	…	…	…	…	…	…	…	…	…	…	…
Chile[w]	53[z]	46.2[z]	…	…	…	…	…	…	…	…	100.0[z]
Colombia	…	…	…	…	…	…	…	…	…	…	…
Costa Rica	23	61.1	32.5	2.2	39.3	4.3	8.9	1.3	11.1	0.4	0.0
Cuba	17[z]	66.0[z]	…	…	…	…	…	…	…	…	100.0[z]
Dominica	.	.	.	.	.	.	.	.	.	.	.
Dominican Republic	…	…	…	…	…	…	…	…	…	…	…
Ecuador	…	…	…	…	…	…	…	…	…	…	…
El Salvador	…	…	…	…	…	…	…	…	…	…	…
Grenada	…	…	…	…	…	…	…	…	…	…	…
Guatemala	…	…	…	…	…	…	…	…	…	…	…
Guyana	…	…	…	…	…	…	…	…	…	…	…
Haiti	…	…	…	…	…	…	…	…	…	…	…
Honduras	3[z]	73.7[z]	…	…	…	…	…	…	…	…	100.0[z]
Jamaica[w]	6[z]	70.9[z]	…	…	…	…	…	…	…	…	100.0[z]
Mexico[o]	339	52.2	16.3	2.9	42.7	10.1	15.0	2.1	8.9	2.0	0.1
Montserrat	.	.	.	.	.	.	.	.	.	.	.
Netherlands Antilles	0.6**,[z]	19.2**,[z]	…	…	…	…	…	…	…	…	100.0**,[z]
Nicaragua	…	…	…	…	…	…	…	…	…	…	…

(y) Data are for 1999/2000.   (z) Data are for 2000/2001.

Table 12

PERCENTAGE OF FEMALES IN EACH FIELD

Education	Humanities and arts	Social sciences, business and law	Science	Engineering, manufacturing and construction	Agriculture	Health and welfare	Services	Not known or unspecified	Country or territory
.	.	.	.	.	.	.	.	.	Cook Islands
...	...	...	...	...	...	...	...	...	Democratic People's Republic of Korea
...	...	...	...	...	...	...	...	...	Fiji
...	...	...	...	...	...	...	...	45.2	Indonesia[w]
76.0	71.1	34.5	25.2	12.5	40.4	69.8	78.7	55.3	Japan[o]
...	...	...	...	...	...	...	...	...	Kiribati
45.7	41.3	38.2	43.8	11.2	17.4	43.9	24.0	–	Lao People's Democratic Republic
...	...	...	...	...	...	...	...	...	Macao, China
...	...	...	...	...	...	...	...	51.3[y]	Malaysia[w]
...	...	...	...	...	...	...	...	...	Marshall Islands
...	...	...	...	...	...	...	...	...	Micronesia (Federated States of)
...	...	...	...	...	...	...	...	...	Myanmar
.	.	.	.	.	.	.	.	.	Nauru
80.9[z]	63.9[z]	55.0[z]	43.3[z]	32.5[z]	39.0[z]	79.8[z]	65.6[z]	–	New Zealand[o]
.	.	.	.	.	.	.	.	.	Niue
100.0[z]	–	79.2[z]	–	4.3[z]	16.7[z]	84.6[z]	50.0[z]	66.7[z]	Palau
...	...	...	...	...	...	...	...	...	Papua New Guinea
...	...	...	...	...	...	...	...	61.0	Philippines[w]
75.7	68.5	47.4	45.3	28.1	36.6	70.9	53.2	–	Republic of Korea[o]
78.9[z]	66.7[z]	31.5[z]	34.6[z]	–	30.0[z]	100.0[z]	–	65.5[z]	Samoa
...	...	...	...	...	...	...	...	...	Singapore
.	.	.	.	.	.	.	.	.	Solomon Islands
...	...	...	...	...	...	...	...	55.6	Thailand[w]
...	...	...	...	...	...	...	...	...	Timor-Leste
.	.	.	.	.	.	.	.	.	Tokelau
...	...	...	...	...	...	...	...	...	Tonga
.	.	.	.	.	.	.	.	.	Tuvalu
...	...	...	...	...	...	...	...	...	Vanuatu
62.8	61.2	48.7	–	13.5	25.9	36.6	–	43.2	Viet Nam

Latin America and the Caribbean

Education	Humanities and arts	Social sciences, business and law	Science	Engineering, manufacturing and construction	Agriculture	Health and welfare	Services	Not known or unspecified	Country or territory
.	.	.	.	.	.	.	.	.	Anguilla
...	...	...	...	...	...	...	...	...	Antigua and Barbuda
78.1	70.2	56.0	51.5	30.6	40.5	63.9	54.9	69.1	Argentina[w]
18.2	.	70.2	.	22.6	.	92.7	.	–	Aruba
...	...	...	...	...	...	...	...	...	Bahamas
...	...	...	...	...	...	...	...	66.0**,[z]	Barbados
...	...	...	...	...	...	...	...	...	Belize
.	75.0[z]	95.3[z]	60.0[z]	10.0[z]	.	100.0[z]	50.0[z]	–	Bermuda
...	...	...	...	...	...	...	...	...	Bolivia
...	...	...	...	...	...	...	...	61.6	Brazil[w]
...	...	...	...	...	...	...	...	...	British Virgin Islands
...	...	...	...	...	...	...	...	...	Cayman Islands
...	...	...	...	...	...	...	...	46.2[z]	Chile[w]
...	...	...	...	...	...	...	...	...	Colombia
80.7	55.5	54.8	39.6	27.9	33.7	66.1	49.0	33.3	Costa Rica
...	...	...	...	...	...	...	...	66.0[z]	Cuba
.	.	.	.	.	.	.	.	.	Dominica
...	...	...	...	...	...	...	...	...	Dominican Republic
...	...	...	...	...	...	...	...	...	Ecuador
...	...	...	...	...	...	...	...	...	El Salvador
...	...	...	...	...	...	...	...	...	Grenada
...	...	...	...	...	...	...	...	...	Guatemala
...	...	...	...	...	...	...	...	...	Guyana
...	...	...	...	...	...	...	...	...	Haiti
...	...	...	...	...	...	...	...	73.7[z]	Honduras
...	...	...	...	...	...	...	...	70.9[z]	Jamaica[w]
65.4	58.3	57.1	45.7	24.3	28.6	62.6	49.6	45.1	Mexico[o]
.	.	.	.	.	.	.	.	.	Montserrat
...	...	...	...	...	...	...	...	19.2**,[z]	Netherlands Antilles
...	...	...	...	...	...	...	...	...	Nicaragua

Table 12 (continued)

	Number of graduates		\multicolumn{9}{c	}{PERCENTAGE DISTRIBUTION BY FIELD OF STUDY}
Country or territory	Total (000)	% F	Education	Humanities and arts	Social sciences, business and law	Science	Engineering, manufacturing and construction	Agriculture	Health and welfare	Services	Not known or unspecified
Panama	...	...	...	...	...	...	...	...	...	...	...
Paraguay[w]	15	66.3	...	...	...	...	...	...	...	...	100.0
Peru[w]	...	...	...	...	...	...	...	...	...	...	...
Saint Kitts and Nevis	.	.	.	.	.	.	.	.	.	.	.
Saint Lucia	...	...	...	...	...	...	...	...	...	...	...
St Vincent/Grenad.	.	.	.	.	.	.	.	.	.	.	.
Suriname	...	...	...	...	...	...	...	...	...	...	...
Trinidad and Tobago	2	66.8	31.6	9.5	22.3	8.7	11.3	3.3	7.4	5.8	–
Turks and Caicos Islands	...	...	...	...	...	...	...	...	...	...	...
Uruguay[w]	7**	69.3**	...	...	...	...	...	...	...	...	100.0
Venezuela	61[y]	62.8[y]	18.3[y]	0.6[y]	42.9[y]	7.0[y]	19.5[y]	1.2[y]	7.3[y]	3.2[y]	–
North America and Western Europe											
Andorra	.	.	.	.	.	.	.	.	.	.	.
Austria[o]	27[z]	51.5[z]	20.8[z]	8.3[z]	26.4[z]	6.8[z]	20.6[z]	3.2[z]	10.4[z]	3.3[z]	0.3[z]
Belgium[o]	73	56.7	15.4	10.0	31.1	8.3	10.5	1.7	20.7	2.3	0.0
Canada[o]	225[y]	57.4[y]	11.1[y]	12.2[y]	34.4[y]	10.4[y]	10.9[y]	2.0[y]	11.3[y]	5.9[y]	–
Cyprus[o]	3	62.2	15.2	7.4	36.5	7.5	5.6	0.6	4.9	22.2	–
Denmark[o]	39	56.5	10.3	12.7	23.7	9.1	13.0	2.4	25.8	2.9	–
Finland[o]	37	61.1	6.6	11.3	23.0	7.3	22.2	2.3	21.7	5.5	–
France[o]	532	55.5	6.8	12.7	39.1	13.3	16.5	0.3	7.2	4.0	0.2
Germany[o]	294	52.2	8.3	10.3	21.5	9.2	16.9	2.4	26.9	4.1	0.4
Greece[o]	44	55.2	...	...	...	...	...	...	...	...	100.0
Iceland[o]	2[y]	64.4[y]	22.3[y]	13.2[y]	30.9[y]	13.5[y]	6.2[y]	0.6[y]	13.3[y]	–	–
Ireland[o]	45	57.1	7.1	12.1	31.9	18.4	10.6	1.1	10.7	4.0	4.1
Israel[o]	72**	57.3**	...	...	...	...	...	...	...	...	100.0
Italy[o]	218	57.3	8.8	13.8	35.6	7.5	14.7	1.9	12.8	4.5	0.3
Luxembourg[o]	0.7[y]	...	16.6[y]	13.2[y]	49.3[y]	10.7[y]	3.8[y]	–	6.3[y]	–	–
Malta[o]	2	52.0	26.3	7.8	42.9	4.0	4.4	1.2	13.1	0.3	–
Monaco	.	.	.	.	.	.	.	.	.	.	.
Netherlands[o]	86	55.4	17.1	6.7	34.1	5.4	10.4	2.3	21.2	2.7	0.0
Norway[o]	30	60.3	18.7	7.3	25.8	8.1	7.3	1.0	24.5	3.0	4.3
Portugal[o]	58[y]	65.0[y]	18.1[y]	8.0[y]	36.9[y]	5.4[y]	12.2[y]	2.3[y]	13.3[y]	3.7[y]	–[y]
San Marino	...	...	...	...	...	...	...	...	...	...	...
Spain[o]	278[z]	57.2[z]	12.1[z]	9.4[z]	32.0[z]	10.5[z]	16.2[z]	2.3[z]	11.9[z]	5.4[z]	0.1[z]
Sweden[o]	46	60.0	16.7	5.9	20.7	10.0	21.9	1.2	21.5	2.0	–
Switzerland[o]	58	43.2	12.7	7.7	36.7	10.6	12.7	1.6	12.1	5.7	0.2
United Kingdom[o]	524	56.5	10.9	15.1	26.6	16.8	10.1	1.3	18.1	1.2	–
United States[o]	2 238	57.3	11.6	12.2	40.1	9.4	8.0	2.2	11.8	4.7	0.0
South and West Asia											
Afghanistan	...	...	...	...	...	...	...	...	...	...	...
Bangladesh	187	31.4	5.9	27.5	36.4	11.4	0.4	0.8	11.0	–	6.5
Bhutan	...	...	...	...	...	...	...	...	...	...	...
India[w]	...	...	...	...	...	...	...	...	...	...	...
Iran, Islamic Republic of	...	...	...	...	...	...	...	...	...	...	...
Maldives	.	.	.	.	.	.	.	.	.	.	.
Nepal	...	...	...	...	...	...	...	...	...	...	...
Pakistan	...	...	...	...	...	...	...	...	...	...	...
Sri Lanka[w]	...	...	...	...	...	...	...	...	...	...	...
Sub-Saharan Africa											
Angola	0.3[y]	45.9[y]	22.2[y]	.	44.1[y]	5.7[y]	5.7[y]	–	21.5[y]	.	0.7[y]
Benin	...	...	...	...	...	...	...	...	...	...	...
Botswana	...	...	...	...	...	...	...	...	...	...	...
Burkina Faso	...	...	...	...	...	...	...	...	...	...	...
Burundi	0.8[z]	37.9[z]	32.8[z]	11.4[z]	45.8[z]	–	4.5[z]	–	5.5[z]	–	–
Cameroon	...	...	...	...	...	...	...	...	...	...	...
Cape Verde	...	...	...	...	...	...	...	...	...	...	...
Central African Republic	...	...	...	...	...	...	...	...	...	...	...
Chad	0.7[y]	12.7[y]	16.4[y]	40.6[y]	29.4[y]	13.7[y]	.	.	.	.	–

(y) Data are for 1999/2000. (z) Data are for 2000/2001.

Table 12

PERCENTAGE OF FEMALES IN EACH FIELD

Education	Humanities and arts	Social sciences, business and law	Science	Engineering, manufacturing and construction	Agriculture	Health and welfare	Services	Not known or unspecified	Country or territory
...	...	...	...	...	...	...	...	...	Panama
...	...	...	...	...	...	...	...	66.3	Paraguay w
...	...	...	...	...	...	...	...	...	Peru w
.	.	.	.	.	.	.	.	.	Saint Kitts and Nevis
...	...	...	...	...	...	...	...	...	Saint Lucia
.	.	.	.	.	.	.	.	.	Saint Vincent and the Grenadines
...	...	...	...	...	...	...	...	...	Suriname
76.8	80.6	72.9	62.0	27.1	69.6	46.9	73.9	–	Trinidad and Tobago
...	...	...	...	...	...	...	...	...	Turks and Caicos Islands
...	...	...	...	...	...	...	...	69.3	Uruguay w
85.0 y	48.4 y	65.5 y	53.1 y	39.1 y	37.8 y	78.8 y	40.7 y	–	Venezuela

North America and Western Europe

Education	Humanities and arts	Social sciences, business and law	Science	Engineering, manufacturing and construction	Agriculture	Health and welfare	Services	Not known or unspecified	Country or territory
.	.	.	.	.	.	.	.	.	Andorra
78.7 z	59.3 z	52.7 z	39.0 z	15.1 z	39.1 z	68.4 z	64.9 z	41.7 z	Austria o
73.5	62.5	55.7	31.3	19.4	39.6	74.0	52.7	13.3	Belgium o
75.3 y	61.7 y	59.9 y	42.0 y	19.8 y	50.5 y	79.1 y	55.4 y	–	Canada o
93.0	79.1	68.0	50.2	15.6	–	75.5	40.6	–	Cyprus o
70.6	68.6	48.4	31.8	26.2	39.1	82.3	19.8	–	Denmark o
84.7	75.3	67.1	46.7	20.2	50.6	85.8	68.5	–	Finland o
70.9	74.1	63.1	40.7	20.8	50.8	76.0	53.2	36.9	France o
77.7	66.6	45.6	33.8	17.1	33.5	74.3	51.1	52.3	Germany o
...	...	...	...	...	...	...	...	55.2	Greece o
90.2 y	67.1 y	55.5 y	44.0 y	24.5 y	–	81.8 y	...	–	Iceland o
79.2	67.3	60.2	46.5	16.2	36.5	84.5	42.1	65.6	Ireland o
...	...	...	...	...	...	...	...	57.3 **	Israel o
78.2	79.6	55.5	53.6	27.5	43.8	63.9	52.2	60.1	Italy o
...	...	...	...	...	–	...	–	–	Luxembourg o
67.8	53.4	47.1	29.7	22.0	34.8	53.9	60.0	.	Malta o
.	.	.	.	.	.	.	.	.	Monaco
78.1	59.5	49.4	27.8	12.7	45.9	74.8	53.3	18.9	Netherlands o
76.6	61.5	51.3	32.2	21.4	45.0	82.7	36.1	51.8	Norway o
83.7 y	67.1 y	65.0 y	45.7 y	34.6 y	57.6 y	77.7 y	58.1 y	– y	Portugal o
...	...	...	...	...	...	...	...	...	San Marino
79.4 z	62.8 z	62.5 z	40.8 z	25.1 z	41.9 z	77.1 z	57.8 z	38.1 z	Spain o
80.0	61.2	60.3	48.0	28.5	56.4	81.6	61.2	–	Sweden o
73.0	56.3	39.2	20.8	10.8	25.9	68.8	48.0	56.6	Switzerland o
72.2	62.6	54.4	41.6	18.3	55.5	79.5	65.7	–	United Kingdom o
76.7	61.6	55.5	42.9	19.3	48.9	79.6	55.2	54.2	United States o

South and West Asia

Education	Humanities and arts	Social sciences, business and law	Science	Engineering, manufacturing and construction	Agriculture	Health and welfare	Services	Not known or unspecified	Country or territory
...	...	...	...	...	...	...	...	...	Afghanistan
35.4	39.8	32.5	29.3	9.9	17.6	17.1	–	17.2	Bangladesh
...	...	...	...	...	...	...	...	...	Bhutan
...	...	...	...	...	...	...	...	...	India w
...	...	...	...	...	...	...	...	...	Iran, Islamic Republic of
.	.	.	.	.	.	.	.	.	Maldives
...	...	...	...	...	...	...	...	...	Nepal
...	...	...	...	...	...	...	...	...	Pakistan
...	...	...	...	...	...	...	...	...	Sri Lanka w

Sub-Saharan Africa

Education	Humanities and arts	Social sciences, business and law	Science	Engineering, manufacturing and construction	Agriculture	Health and welfare	Services	Not known or unspecified	Country or territory
45.2 y	.	42.3 y	50.0 y	25.0 y	–	58.3 y	.	50.0 y	Angola
...	...	...	...	...	...	...	...	...	Benin
...	...	...	...	...	...	...	...	...	Botswana
...	...	...	...	...	...	...	...	...	Burkina Faso
38.4 z	27.6 z	45.3 z	–	–	–	26.2 z	–	–	Burundi
...	...	...	...	...	...	...	...	...	Cameroon
...	...	...	...	...	...	...	...	...	Cape Verde
...	...	...	...	...	...	...	...	...	Central African Republic
9.4 y	11.7 y	20.0 y	4.1 y	.	.	.	.	–	Chad

344 / ANNEX

Table 12 (continued)

	Number of graduates		PERCENTAGE DISTRIBUTION BY FIELD OF STUDY								
Country or territory	Total (000)	% F	Education	Humanities and arts	Social sciences, business and law	Science	Engineering, manufacturing and construction	Agriculture	Health and welfare	Services	Not known or unspecified
Comoros	...	...	...	...	...	...	...	...	...	...	...
Congo	0.1 y	25.7 y	...	...	...	...	...	...	...	...	100.0 y
Côte d'Ivoire	...	...	...	...	...	...	...	...	...	...	...
Democratic Rep. of the Congo	...	...	...	...	...	...	...	...	...	...	...
Equatorial Guinea	...	...	...	...	...	...	...	...	...	...	...
Eritrea	1	15.5	17.0	1.3	50.7	11.3	6.0	7.3	6.4	.	–
Ethiopia	18	23.8	34.6	1.1	37.8	3.7	6.9	8.6	7.1	0.1	0.1
Gabon	...	...	...	...	...	...	...	...	...	...	...
Gambia	1 y	22.4 y	...	...	...	...	...	...	...	...	100.0 y
Ghana	14 z	27.0 z	...	...	...	...	...	...	...	...	100.0
Guinea	...	...	...	...	...	...	...	...	...	...	...
Guinea-Bissau	...	...	...	...	...	...	...	...	...	...	...
Kenya	28 y	36.4 y	21.0 y	6.6 y	26.0 y	12.2 y	17.9 y	6.3 y	9.0 y	1.0 y	–
Lesotho	0.9	50.1 **	48.4	9.9	25.2	4.5	–	8.3	–	–	3.8
Liberia	7 y	46.2 y	5.3 y	6.1 y	24.3 y	18.3 y	9.1 y	1.8 y	26.8 y	8.3 y	–
Madagascar	7	47.3	1.1	13.8	54.9	17.8	4.4	1.0	6.6	0.3	–
Malawi	...	...	...	...	...	...	...	...	...	...	...
Mali	...	...	...	...	...	...	...	...	...	...	...
Mauritius	2	48.1	30.7	2.9	34.9	8.1	15.1	8.3	.	.	–
Mozambique	...	...	...	...	...	...	...	...	...	...	...
Namibia	3	45.8	70.5	1.2	20.0	1.2	0.3	1.2	4.7	0.8	0.1
Niger	0.8 z	27.3 z	9.5 z	10.1 z	26.8 z	19.0 z	.	13.6 z	15.1 z	5.8 z	–
Nigeria	...	...	...	...	...	...	...	...	...	...	...
Rwanda	...	...	...	...	...	...	...	...	...	...	...
Sao Tome and Principe	...	...	...	...	...	...	...	...	...	...	...
Senegal	...	...	...	...	...	...	...	...	...	...	...
Seychelles	.	.	.	.	.	.	.	.	.	.	.
Sierra Leone	6 y	43.8 y	67.9 y	15.7 y	5.7 y	2.0 y	0.6 y	4.9 y	2.7 y	0.5 y	–
Somalia	...	...	...	...	...	...	...	...	...	...	...
South Africa	98	57.0	...	...	...	...	...	...	...	...	...
Swaziland	1 y	51.5 y	25.9 y	12.1 y	35.4 y	4.6 y	0.3 y	8.2 y	9.2 y	1.3 y	2.9 y
Togo	6 y	15.0 y	2.1 y	46.8 y	31.6 y	5.7 y	2.8 y	1.8 y	9.2 y	– y	– y
Uganda	25 z	21.5 z	...	...	...	...	...	...	...	...	100.0 z
United Republic of Tanzania	...	...	...	...	...	...	...	...	...	...	...
Zambia	...	...	...	...	...	...	...	...	...	...	...
Zimbabwe w	6 z	...	...	...	...	...	...	...	...	...	...
World [1]	...	...	...	...	...	...	...	...	...	...	...
Countries in transition	...	...	13.7	5.8	39.3	...	9.5	2.4	6.4	2.9	16.3
Developed countries	...	...	12.6	7.1	38.2	7.1	10.0	1.6	7.0	4.7	11.9
Developing countries	...	...	...	...	...	...	...	...	...	...	...
Arab States	...	...	...	...	...	...	...	...	...	...	...
Central and Eastern Europe	...	...	14.9	13.0	27.1	6.9	17.4	6.0	11.1	...	...
Central Asia	...	...	13.7	7.8	46.2	7.6	11.8	2.5	4.7	3.5	2.1
East Asia and the Pacific	...	...	...	...	...	...	...	...	...	...	...
Latin America and the Caribbean	...	...	...	...	...	...	...	...	...	...	...
North America and Western Europe	...	...	12.7	7.7	36.7	10.6	12.7	1.6	12.1	5.7	0.2
South and West Asia	...	...	...	...	...	...	...	...	...	...	...
Sub-Saharan Africa	...	...	...	...	...	...	...	...	...	...	...

1. All values shown are medians.   (y) Data are for 1999/2000.   (z) Data are for 2000/2001.

Table 12

PERCENTAGE OF FEMALES IN EACH FIELD

Education	Humanities and arts	Social sciences, business and law	Science	Engineering, manufacturing and construction	Agriculture	Health and welfare	Services	Not known or unspecified	Country or territory
...	...	...	...	...	...	...	...	...	Comoros
...	...	...	...	...	...	...	...	25.7 y	Congo
...	...	...	...	...	...	...	...	...	Côte d'Ivoire
...	...	...	...	...	...	...	...	...	Democratic Rep. of the Congo
...	...	...	...	...	...	...	...	...	Equatorial Guinea
12.5	21.4	20.7	4.1	1.5	10.1	20.3	.	–	Eritrea
17.7	24.5	35.9	22.9	4.9	8.5	26.5	22.7	15.8	Ethiopia
...	...	...	...	...	...	...	...	...	Gabon
...	...	...	...	...	...	...	...	22.4 y	Gambia
...	...	...	...	...	...	...	...	27.0	Ghana
...	...	...	...	...	...	...	...	...	Guinea
...	...	...	...	...	...	...	...	...	Guinea-Bissau
42.7 y	32.0 y	50.6 y	29.6 y	13.0 y	27.2 y	44.3 y	48.3 y	–	Kenya
...	...	...	...	...	...	–	–	...	Lesotho
37.0 y	53.1 y	44.8 y	80.5 y	31.8 y	22.3 y	38.9 y	20.4	–	Liberia
34.2	64.2	48.2	37.0	20.0	50.7	51.3	60.9	–	Madagascar
...	...	...	...	...	...	...	...	...	Malawi
...	...	...	...	...	...	...	...	...	Mali
51.5	71.9	50.8	53.7	19.1	62.4	.	.	–	Mauritius
...	...	...	...	...	...	...	...	...	Mozambique
50.6	63.2	24.2	43.6	...	30.8	76.8	...	–	Namibia
20.5 z	25.3 z	44.1 z	7.7 z	.	31.3 z	34.7 z	–	–	Niger
...	...	...	...	...	...	...	...	...	Nigeria
...	...	...	...	...	...	...	...	...	Rwanda
...	...	...	...	...	...	...	...	...	Sao Tome and Principe
...	...	...	...	...	...	...	...	...	Senegal
.	.	.	.	.	.	.	.	.	Seychelles
41.5 y	43.9 y	49.9 y	73.0 y	25.0 y	52.1 y	56.3 y	48.5 y	–	Sierra Leone
...	...	...	...	...	...	...	...	...	Somalia
...	...	...	...	...	...	...	...	...	South Africa
50.6 y	55.4 y	44.1 y	54.3 y	33.3 y	28.0 y	83.7 y	38.5 y	100.0 y	Swaziland
26.4 y	16.3 y	14.1 y	6.0 y	2.4 y	7.7 y	20.2 y	– y	– y	Togo
...	...	...	...	...	...	...	...	21.5 z	Uganda
...	...	...	...	...	...	...	...	...	United Republic of Tanzania
...	...	...	...	...	...	...	...	...	Zambia
...	...	...	...	...	...	...	...	...	Zimbabwe w

Education	Humanities and arts	Social sciences, business and law	Science	Engineering, manufacturing and construction	Agriculture	Health and welfare	Services	Not known or unspecified	
...	...	...	...	...	...	...	...	...	World [1]
79.6	68.2	45.3	...	33.4	33.3	55.5	16.8	68.1	Countries in transition
74.6	66.3	53.5	39.0	17.5	40.6	68.7	51.2	61.7	Developed countries
...	...	...	...	...	...	...	...	...	Developing countries
...	...	...	...	...	...	...	...	...	Arab States
...	...	...	...	...	...	...	...	...	Central and Eastern Europe
86.5	71.3	45.8	60.4	35.7	20.0	62.4	23.5	63.3	Central Asia
...	...	...	...	...	...	...	...	...	East Asia and the Pacific
...	...	...	...	...	...	...	...	...	Latin America and the Caribbean
73.0	7.7	39.2	20.8	10.8	25.9	68.8	48.0	56.6	North America and Western Europe
...	...	...	...	...	...	...	...	...	South and West Asia
...	...	...	...	...	...	...	...	...	Sub-Saharan Africa

Table 13A
Teaching staff in pre-primary and primary education

	PRE-PRIMARY EDUCATION											
	Total teachers				Trained teachers (%)						Pupil/teacher ratio	
	1998		2001		1998			2001			1998	2001
Country or territory	Total (000)	% F	Total (000)	% F	Total	Male	Female	Total	Male	Female		
Arab States												
Algeria	1.3	93	2.0**	88**	...	...	...	...	...	...	28	28**
Bahrain	0.7	100	0.7**	100**	18.3	–	18.4	...	...	...	21	21**
Djibouti	0.01	100	0.01	100	...	...	...	...	...	...	29	29
Egypt^w	13.7**	99**	17.7	99	...	...	...	...	...	...	24**	23
Iraq	4.6	100	4.9^y	100^y	...	...	...	100.0^y	–^y	100.0^y	15	15^y
Jordan^w	3.3	100	4.1	99	...	...	...	...	...	...	22	21
Kuwait	3.8	100	4.4	100	100.0	100.0	100.0	...	...	...	15	14
Lebanon	10.7	96	8.3	100	...	...	...	12.1	22.9	12.0	13	18
Libyan Arab Jamahiriya	1.2	100	1.8	99	...	...	...	...	...	...	8	10
Mauritania	...	...	0.3^z	99^z	...	...	...	...	...	...	...	...
Morocco	40.1	40	37.7	44	...	...	...	...	...	...	20	20
Oman	0.4	100	0.4**	100**	92.5	–	92.5	92.5**	–**	92.5**	20	19**
Palestinian A. T.	2.7	100	3.3**	98**	...	...	...	...	...	...	29	20**
Qatar	0.4**	96**	0.6	98	...	...	...	...	...	...	21**	17
Saudi Arabia	8.7	100	8.2	100	...	...	...	72.3	–	72.3	11	11
Sudan	12.3**	85**	14.5	...	...	...	...	...	...	...	30**	25
Syrian Arab Republic	4.6	96	4.9	99	87.1	84.5	87.2	...	...	...	24	26
Tunisia^w	3.9	95	5.4	95	...	...	...	...	...	...	20	19
United Arab Emirates	3.5	100	3.9	100	59.3	71.4**	59.2**	61.3	80.0	61.2	19	18
Yemen	0.8	93	0.8**,y	93**,y	...	...	...	...	...	...	17	17**,y
Central and Eastern Europe												
Albania°	3.9**	100**	3.9^z	100^z	...	...	...	...	...	...	21**	21^z
Belarus	53.6	...	53.4	99	...	...	...	58.3	19.0	58.8	5	5
Bosnia and Herzegovina°	...	...	...	...	...	...	...	...	...	...	...	...
Bulgaria°	19.3	100**	17.5	100	...	...	...	...	...	...	11	11
Croatia	6.4	100	6.9	100	76.3	85.7	76.3	77.7	90.9	77.6	13	11
Czech Republic°	17.0	100**	16.2^y	100^y	...	...	...	...	...	...	18	18^y
Estonia°	6.9	100	6.4**	...	...	...	...	...	...	...	8	8**
Hungary°	32.0	100	32.7	99	...	...	...	...	...	...	12	11
Latvia°	1.3	100	1.3	98	...	...	...	...	...	...	46	41
Lithuania°	12.7	99	11.1	100	...	...	...	...	...	...	7	8
Poland°	...	...	73.7^z	97^z	...	...	...	...	...	...	...	12^z
Republic of Moldova	10.6**	...	9.0	...	91.7**	...	...	91.7	...	...	9**	9
Romania°	36.6	100**	34.6	100	...	...	...	...	...	...	17	18
Russian Federation°	618.3	99**	605.3	99**	...	...	...	...	...	...	...	6
Serbia and Montenegro	11.8	68**	11.9^z	...	95.5	95.5**	95.5**	95.1^z	...	...	14	14^z
Slovakia	16.3	100	15.5	100	...	...	...	...	...	...	10	10
Slovenia°	3.2	99**	3.0	100	...	...	...	...	...	...	18	18
TFYR Macedonia°	3.2	99	2.9	99	...	...	...	...	...	...	10	12
Turkey°	17.1	68	18.1	...	...	...	...	...	...	...	15	16
Ukraine	142.6	100	121.2	99	...	...	...	...	...	...	8	8
Central Asia												
Armenia	...	...	6.9	100	...	...	...	...	...	...	...	7
Azerbaijan	11.9	100	11.0	100	77.5	–	77.5	83.0	–	83.0	7	10
Georgia	4.9	100	7.1	100	...	...	...	...	...	...	13	10
Kazakhstan	18.5	...	23.9	98	...	...	...	...	...	...	9	5
Kyrgyzstan	3.8	100	2.3	100	42.2	–	42.2	35.2	–	35.2	12	19
Mongolia	3.0	100	3.2	99	98.9	75.0	99.0	...	...	...	25	26
Tajikistan	5.2	42**	4.6	46**	...	...	...	100.0	...	...	11	13
Turkmenistan	...	...	...	...	...	...	...	...	...	...	...	...
Uzbekistan	...	...	67.0**	95**	...	...	...	100.0**	100.0**	100.0**	...	7**
East Asia and the Pacific												
Australia°	...	...	...	...	...	...	...	...	...	...	...	...
Brunei Darussalam	0.5*	82*	0.5*	78*	...	...	...	...	...	...	21*	20*
Cambodia	2.2**	99**	3.2	99	...	...	...	93.8	...	...	27**	28
China^w	872.4	94	856.5^z	94^z	...	...	...	...	...	...	27	26^z

(y) Data are for 1999/2000. (z) Data are for 2000/2001.

Table 13A

PRIMARY EDUCATION

Total teachers 1998 Total (000)	1998 % F	2001 Total (000)	2001 % F	Trained teachers (%) 1998 Total	1998 Male	1998 Female	2001 Total	2001 Male	2001 Female	Pupil/teacher ratio 1998	2001	Country or territory
												Arab States
169.5	46	170.0	48	93.7	92.0	95.7	97.1	96.1	98.2	28	28	Algeria
...	...	5.0**	76**	...	...	...	...	...	...	...	16**	Bahrain
1.0	28	1.3**	30**	...	...	...	...	...	...	40	34**	Djibouti
346.0**	52**	349.2**	53**	...	...	...	...	...	...	23**	23**	Egypt w
141.5	72	170.1 y	73 y	...	...	...	100.0 y	100.0 y	100.0 y	26	21 y	Iraq
...	...	38.3**	63**	...	...	...	...	...	...	...	20**	Jordan w
10.4	73	10.9	79	100.0	100.0	100.0	...	...	...	13	14	Kuwait
28.4	83	26.8	87	...	...	...	14.9	15.6	14.7	14	17	Lebanon
...	...	94.1**,y	...	...	...	...	...	...	...	...	8**,y	Libyan Arab Jamahiriya
7.4	26	9.6	26	...	...	...	...	...	...	47	39	Mauritania
123.0	39	142.3	42	...	...	...	...	...	...	28	28	Morocco
12.4	52	13.6**	59**	99.6	99.8	99.4	99.8**	99.8**	99.8**	25	23**	Oman
...	...	12.9**,z	54**,z	...	...	...	...	...	...	...	31**,z	Palestinian A. T.
4.6	75	5.2	82	...	...	...	...	...	...	13	12	Qatar
184.8	54	187.6	49	...	...	...	...	...	...	12	12	Saudi Arabia
...	...	...	...	...	...	...	...	...	...	...	...	Sudan
110.5**	68**	120.9**	68**	...	...	...	95.6**	98.0**	94.5**	25**	24**	Syrian Arab Republic
60.5	50	60.6	50	...	...	...	...	...	...	24	22	Tunisia w
16.9	73	18.7	76	...	...	...	...	...	...	16	15	United Arab Emirates
77.2**	21**	...	...	...	...	...	...	...	...	30**	...	Yemen
												Central and Eastern Europe
12.7**	75**	12.6 z	74 z	...	...	...	...	...	...	23**	22 z	Albania o
32.3	99	30.7	99	...	...	...	97.9	97.6	97.9	20	17	Belarus
...	...	...	...	...	...	...	...	...	...	...	...	Bosnia and Herzegovina o
23.0	91**	20.8	92	...	...	...	...	...	...	18	17	Bulgaria o
10.6	89	10.8	89	...	...	...	100.0	100.0	100.0	19	18	Croatia
35.8	85**	34.8**	84**	...	...	...	...	...	...	18	17**	Czech Republic o
8.1	...	7.7**	...	...	...	...	...	...	...	16	14**	Estonia o
47.3	86	46.5	86	...	...	...	...	...	...	11	10	Hungary o
9.2	97	7.9	97	...	...	...	...	...	...	15	14	Latvia o
13.3	98	12.5	...	...	...	...	...	...	...	17	16	Lithuania o
...	...	209.6	84**	...	...	...	...	...	...	...	15	Poland o
12.6**	97**	11.7	96	...	...	...	...	...	...	21**	20	Republic of Moldova
68.6**	85**	59.0	87	...	...	...	...	...	...	19**	17	Romania o
348.0	98	325.6	99	...	...	...	...	...	...	...	17	Russian Federation o
...	...	19.2 z	82 z	...	...	...	100.0 z	100.0 z	100.0 z	...	20 z	Serbia and Montenegro
16.9	93	14.9	93	...	...	...	...	...	...	19	19	Slovakia
6.5	97	6.9	96	...	...	...	...	...	...	14	13	Slovenia o
5.9	67	5.7	69	...	...	...	...	...	...	22	21	TFYR Macedonia o
...	...	...	...	...	...	...	...	...	...	...	...	Turkey o
107.4	99	105.2	99	...	...	...	99.7	...	...	21	20	Ukraine
												Central Asia
...	...	7.6	99	...	...	...	...	...	...	...	19	Armenia
36.8	83	41.3	84	100.0	100.0	100.0	100.0	100.0	100.0	19	16	Azerbaijan
17.4	92	18.4	85	...	...	...	76.9	...	...	17	14	Georgia
69.6**	97**	61.3	97	...	...	...	...	...	...	18**	19	Kazakhstan
19.2	95	18.9	97	47.7	48.8	47.7	49.3	49.2	49.3	25	24	Kyrgyzstan
7.8	93	7.6	94	...	...	...	...	...	...	32	32	Mongolia
31.4	56	31.4	60	...	...	...	81.6	...	...	22	22	Tajikistan
...	...	...	...	...	...	...	...	...	...	...	...	Turkmenistan
...	...	...	...	...	...	...	...	...	...	...	...	Uzbekistan
												East Asia and the Pacific
...	...	...	...	...	...	...	...	...	...	...	...	Australia o
3.2*	66*	3.2*	70*	...	...	...	...	...	...	14*	14*	Brunei Darussalam
44.5**	37**	48.5	39	...	...	...	96.0	...	...	48**	56	Cambodia
7 139.0	50**	6 430.8	53	...	...	...	96.8	...	...	19	20**	China w

Table 13A (continued)

	\multicolumn{11}{c	}{PRE-PRIMARY EDUCATION}
	\multicolumn{4}{c	}{Total teachers}	\multicolumn{6}{c	}{Trained teachers (%)}	\multicolumn{2}{c	}{Pupil/teacher ratio}
	\multicolumn{2}{c	}{1998}	\multicolumn{2}{c	}{2001}	\multicolumn{3}{c	}{1998}	\multicolumn{3}{c	}{2001}	1998	2001
Country or territory	Total (000)	% F	Total (000)	% F	Total	Male	Female	Total	Male	Female		
---	---	---	---	---	---	---	---	---	---	---	---	---
Cook Islands	0.03	...	0.03**,z	100**,z	...	...	...	...	...	...	15	14**,z
DPR Korea	...	...	...	...	...	...	...	...	...	...	...	...
Fiji	...	...	...	...	...	...	...	...	...	...	...	...
Indonesia[w]	...	...	130.7	98	...	...	...	...	...	...	...	13
Japan[o]	96.0	...	99.8	...	...	...	...	...	...	...	31	30
Kiribati	...	...	...	...	...	...	...	...	...	...	...	...
Lao People's Democratic Republic	2.1	100	2.3	100	85.6	100.0	85.6	83.0	50.0	83.2	18	16
Macao, China	0.5	100	0.5	100	92.8	–	92.8	97.9	–	98.1	31	29
Malaysia[w]	23.1	100	22.3	100	...	...	...	...	...	...	26	23
Marshall Islands	0.1	...	0.1	61	...	...	...	100.0	100.0	100.0	11	12
Micronesia (Federated States of)	...	...	...	...	...	...	...	...	...	...	...	...
Myanmar	1.9	...	1.9**,y	...	...	...	...	...	...	...	22	22**,y
Nauru	...	...	...	...	...	...	...	...	...	...	...	...
New Zealand[o]	...	...	7.5 z	99 z	...	...	...	...	...	...	...	14 z
Niue	0.0	100	0.01	100	...	...	...	100.0	–	100.0	14	6
Palau	...	...	0.1**,z	98**,z	...	...	...	...	...	...	...	10**,z
Papua New Guinea	1.4	41	2.1**	42**	100.0	100.0	100.0	100.0**	100.0**	100.0**	34	29**
Philippines[w]	18.0	92	21.6	97	100.0**	...	...	...	...	...	33	30
Republic of Korea[o]	...	...	24.7	100	...	...	...	...	...	...	...	22
Samoa	...	...	0.1	94	...	...	...	...	...	...	...	42
Singapore	...	...	...	...	...	...	...	...	...	...	...	...
Solomon Islands	...	...	...	...	...	...	...	...	...	...	...	...
Thailand[w]	111.3	79	111.2 y	79 y	...	...	...	...	...	...	25	25 y
Timor-Leste	...	...	...	...	...	...	...	...	...	...	...	...
Tokelau	...	...	...	...	...	...	...	...	...	...	...	...
Tonga	0.1	100	0.1**,z	100**,z	50.4	...	50.4	...	...	...	10	18**,z
Tuvalu	...	...	0.04	100	...	...	...	32.5	–	32.5	...	18
Vanuatu	...	...	0.8	99	...	...	...	42.0	–	42.7	...	11
Viet Nam	94.0	100	103.1	100	43.6	...	43.6	...	...	...	23	21
Latin America and the Caribbean												
Anguilla	0.03	100	0.04	100	38.5	...	38.5	38.9	–	38.9	18	13
Antigua and Barbuda	...	...	0.3 y	100 y	...	...	...	45.1 y	– y	45.1 y	...	6 y
Argentina[w]	55.0	96	60.1**	...	...	...	...	...	...	...	21	21**
Aruba	0.1	100	0.1	99	100.0	–	100.0	100.0	100.0	100.0	26	24
Bahamas	...	...	0.3	100	...	...	...	59.8	–	59.8	...	11
Barbados	0.3**	95**	0.4**	99**	84.3**	82.4**	84.4**	84.5**	25.0**	85.1**	18**	16**
Belize	0.2	99	0.2 z	98 z	...	...	...	68.1	25.0	68.9 z	19	18 z
Bermuda	...	...	0.1	100	...	...	...	100.0	–	100.0	...	7
Bolivia	...	...	5.1	94	...	...	...	80.4	68.2	81.2	...	44
Brazil[w]	265.7	98	352.7	98	...	...	...	...	...	...	20	19
British Virgin Islands	0.1	99	0.05	100	...	...	...	...	...	...	7	14
Cayman Islands	0.1	96	0.1	98	...	...	...	96.6	100.0	96.6	10	10
Chile[w]	...	...	18.6 z	99 z	...	...	...	90.5**,z	...	...	...	24 z
Colombia	58.3	...	51.9	95	...	...	...	...	...	...	17	20
Costa Rica	...	...	5.1	93	...	...	...	84.7	...	...	...	19
Cuba	25.7	98	25.4	100	97.9	...	100.0	100.0	–	100.0	19	18
Dominica	0.1	100	0.1	100	75.0	...	75.0	...	...	...	18	16
Dominican Republic	8.2	95	7.2	96	53.6	59.5	53.3	38.6	85.7	36.5	24	27
Ecuador	10.2	90	11.6	88	...	...	...	69.3	58.4	70.7	18	18
El Salvador	...	...	8.0**	...	...	...	...	...	...	...	...	27**
Grenada	...	...	0.2	100	...	...	...	31.6	–	31.6	...	15
Guatemala	9.2*	...	16.9	...	...	...	...	100.0	...	...	27*	23
Guyana	2.1	99	2.2 y	99 y	38.4	40.9	38.3	37.6	13.6 y	37.8 y	18	17 y
Haiti	...	...	...	...	...	...	...	...	...	...	...	...
Honduras	...	...	6.3**	...	...	...	...	...	...	...	...	20**
Jamaica[w]	...	...	6.0	...	...	...	...	...	...	...	...	24
Mexico[o]	150.1	94	159.0	95**	...	...	...	...	...	...	22	22
Montserrat	0.01	100	0.01	100	...	...	...	100.0	...	100.0	12	11
Netherlands Antilles	0.3	99	0.3	100	100.0	100.0	100.0	100.0	100.0	100.0	21	20
Nicaragua	4.7	97	6.5	97	35.2	23.9	35.6	29.4	9.6	29.9	31	25

(y) Data are for 1999/2000.   (z) Data are for 2000/2001.

STATISTICAL ANNEX / 349

Table 13A

PRIMARY EDUCATION

Total teachers 1998 Total (000)	1998 % F	Total teachers 2001 Total (000)	2001 % F	Trained teachers (%) 1998 Total	1998 Male	1998 Female	Trained teachers (%) 2001 Total	2001 Male	2001 Female	Pupil/teacher ratio 1998	Pupil/teacher ratio 2001	Country or territory
0.1	...	0.1**,z	86**,z	...	...	...	...	...	...	19	18**,z	Cook Islands
...	...	...	...	...	...	...	...	...	...	...	...	DPR Korea
5.1**	57**	4.1**	57**	97.5**	96.9**	97.9**	...	...	...	23**	28**	Fiji
...	...	1 383.9	52	...	...	...	...	...	...	...	21	Indonesia[w]
366.6	...	365.5	...	...	...	...	...	...	...	21	20	Japan[o]
0.7	64	...	...	...	...	...	...	...	...	24	...	Kiribati
27.1	43	28.5	44	75.7	68.6	85.2	76.1	68.9	85.3	31	30	Lao People's Democratic Republic
1.5	87	1.6	89	81.0	61.9	83.9	89.7	74.7	91.5	31	28	Macao, China
132.4	63	154.2	67	96.6**	...	...	...	...	...	22	20	Malaysia[w]
0.6	...	0.5	34	...	...	...	...	...	...	15	17	Marshall Islands
...	...	...	...	...	...	...	...	...	...	...	...	Micronesia (Federated States of)
154.7	73	146.7	77	77.9**	80.0**	77.2**	...	...	...	31	33	Myanmar
0.1**	82**	...	...	...	...	...	...	...	...	23**	...	Nauru
...	...	20.4	84	...	...	...	...	...	...	...	18	New Zealand[o]
0.01	100	0.01	100	...	...	...	100.0	—	100.0	24	18	Niue
0.1	82	0.1**,y	82**,y	...	...	...	...	...	...	15	18**,y	Palau
16.1	38	18.5**	39**	100.0	100.0	100.0	100.0**	100.0**	100.0**	36	36**	Papua New Guinea
360.4	87	362.4	87	100.0**	...	...	...	...	...	35	35	Philippines[w]
...	...	128.0	72	...	...	...	...	...	...	...	32	Republic of Korea[o]
1.1**	73**	1.2	73	...	...	...	...	...	...	25**	25	Samoa
...	...	...	...	...	...	...	...	...	...	...	...	Singapore
...	...	...	...	...	...	...	...	...	...	...	...	Solomon Islands
297.6	63	326.3	58	...	...	...	...	...	...	21	19	Thailand[w]
...	...	3.6	30	...	...	...	...	...	...	...	51	Timor-Leste
...	...	...	...	...	...	...	...	...	...	...	...	Tokelau
0.8	70	0.8	68	87.2	74.8	92.6	100.0	100.0	100.0	22	21	Tonga
...	...	0.1	84	...	...	...	...	...	...	...	26	Tuvalu
1.6**	44**	1.2	58	...	...	...	100.0	100.0	100.0	22**	29	Vanuatu
336.8	78	354.6	78	77.6	75.1	78.4	87.0	87.0	87.0	30	26	Viet Nam

Latin America and the Caribbean

0.1	87	0.1	92	76.1	77.8	75.8	73.8	71.4**	74.0**	22	17	Anguilla
...	...	0.7[y]	79[y]	...	...	...	46.9[y]	58.8[y]	43.7[y]	...	19[y]	Antigua and Barbuda
234.1	89	244.5**	...	...	...	...	...	...	...	21	20**	Argentina[w]
0.5	78	0.5	80	100.0	100.0	100.0	100.0	100.0	100.0	19	19	Aruba
...	...	2.0	93	...	...	...	94.8	89.7	95.2	...	17	Bahamas
1.4**	75**	1.4**	75**	84.4**	71.6**	88.6**	76.7**	68.2**	79.4**	20**	16**	Barbados
1.9**	64**	2.0[z]	65[z]	...	...	...	40.9[z]	38.1[z]	42.4[z]	24**	23[z]	Belize
...	...	0.5	88	...	...	...	100.0	100.0**	100.0**	...	9	Bermuda
...	...	59.5**	60**	...	...	...	...	...	...	...	25**	Bolivia
941.4	94	858.8	92	...	...	...	...	...	...	...	23	Brazil[w]
0.2	86	0.2	88**	71.9	54.5	74.8	...	...	...	18	17	British Virgin Islands
0.2	89	0.2	81	...	...	...	99.2	97.8	99.5	16	15	Cayman Islands
53.5	78	55.8[z]	78[z]	...	...	...	92.5**,[z]	...	...	33	32[z]	Chile[w]
220.5	...	197.2	77	...	...	...	...	...	...	23	26	Colombia
...	...	22.7	79	...	...	...	89.5	...	...	...	24	Costa Rica
91.2	79	71.8	79	100.0	100.0	100.0	100.0	100.0	100.0	12	14	Cuba
0.6	77	0.6	79	64.0	48.9	68.4	60.1	45.5	63.9	20	19	Dominica
33.7**	75**	36.2**	83**	...	...	...	58.5**	...	...	39**	39**	Dominican Republic
70.6	68	81.0	69	...	...	...	68.6	69.0	68.4	27	25	Ecuador
...	...	37.8**	...	...	...	...	...	...	...	...	26**	El Salvador
...	...	0.8**	79**	...	...	...	69.7**	64.3**	71.2**	...	22**	Grenada
46.5*	...	65.7	...	...	...	...	100.0	...	...	36*	30	Guatemala
4.0	86	4.2[y]	85[y]	51.7	52.0	51.7	51.4[y]	51.5[y]	51.4[y]	27	26[y]	Guyana
...	...	...	...	...	...	...	...	...	...	...	...	Haiti
...	...	32.8**	...	...	...	...	...	...	...	...	34**	Honduras
...	...	9.8	...	...	...	...	...	...	...	...	34	Jamaica[w]
539.9	67**	552.4	66**	...	...	...	...	...	...	27	27	Mexico[o]
0.02	84	0.02	96	...	...	...	91.3	100.0	90.9	21	20	Montserrat
1.3	86	1.1	86	100.0	100.0	100.0	100.0	100.0	100.0	20	20	Netherlands Antilles
21.1	83	23.6	82	73.6	62.3	75.9	72.9	53.5	77.0	37	37	Nicaragua

Table 13A (continued)

	\multicolumn{12}{c}{PRE-PRIMARY EDUCATION}
	\multicolumn{4}{c}{Total teachers}	\multicolumn{6}{c}{Trained teachers (%)}	\multicolumn{2}{c}{Pupil/teacher ratio}
	\multicolumn{2}{c}{1998}	\multicolumn{2}{c}{2001}	\multicolumn{3}{c}{1998}	\multicolumn{3}{c}{2001}	1998	2001
Country or territory	Total (000)	% F	Total (000)	% F	Total	Male	Female	Total	Male	Female		
Panama	2.1**	97**	3.5	98	…	…	…	37.4	13.6	38.0	22**	19
Paraguay^w	4.6**	92**	…	…	…	…	…	…	…	…	25**	…
Peru^w	35.2	96	…	…	…	…	…	…	…	…	30	…
Saint Kitts and Nevis	…	…	0.3	100	…	…	…	54.5**	–**	54.5**	…	9
Saint Lucia	0.5	96**	0.4	100**	…	…	…	…	…	…	12	12
Saint Vincent and the Grenadines	…	…	…	…	…	…	…	…	…	…	…	…
Suriname	…	…	0.7	99**	…	…	…	…	…	100.0**	…	25
Trinidad and Tobago	1.7**	100**	1.8**	99**	20.4**	–**	20.4**	20.1**	…	20.2**	14**	12**
Turks and Caicos Islands	0.1**	95**	0.1	94	…	…	…	97.1**	50.0**	100.0**	15**	13
Uruguay^w	3.1	98**	3.8	…	…	…	…	…	…	…	31	28
Venezuela	…	…	…	…	…	…	…	…	…	…	…	…
North America and Western Europe
Andorra	…	…	0.2	91	…	…	…	…	…	…	…	15
Austria^o	14.1	99	14.0**,y	99**,y	…	…	…	…	…	…	16	16**,y
Belgium^o	…	…	27.4**	93**	…	…	…	…	…	…	…	15**
Canada^o	…	…	28.6^z	68^z	…	…	…	…	…	…	…	18^z
Cyprus^o	1.0	…	0.8	98	…	…	…	…	…	…	19	20
Denmark^o	45.2	92	45.4^z	…	…	…	…	…	…	…	6	6^z
Finland^o	10.4	96	11.2	97	…	…	…	…	…	…	12	13
France^o	128.4	78	135.2	79	…	…	…	…	…	…	19	18
Germany^o	116.3	97	123.9	…	…	…	…	…	…	…	20	19
Greece^o	9.0	…	10.3	…	…	…	…	…	…	…	16	14
Iceland^o	2.8	98	2.9^y	99^y	…	…	…	…	…	…	5	5^y
Ireland^o	0.2	92	0.2**	94**	…	…	…	…	…	…	18	18**
Israel^o	…	…	…	…	…	…	…	…	…	…	…	…
Italy^o	119.2	100	125.5	98	…	…	…	…	…	…	13	13
Luxembourg^o	…	…	0.9	98	…	…	…	…	…	…	…	15
Malta^o	0.9	99	1.1	99	…	…	…	…	…	…	12	8
Monaco	0.1**	100**	0.04^z	100^z	…	…	…	…	…	…	18**	24^z
Netherlands^o	…	…	…	…	…	…	…	…	…	…	…	…
Norway^o	27.3	…	27.3**,y	95**,y	…	…	…	…	…	…	5	5**,y
Portugal^o	…	…	14.3	98**	…	…	…	…	…	…	…	17
San Marino	…	…	0.1^y	99^y	…	…	…	…	…	…	…	8^y
Spain^o	67.5	93	80.2	92	…	…	…	…	…	…	17	15
Sweden^o	…	…	33.1	…	…	…	…	…	…	…	…	10
Switzerland^o	9.7	99	9.6**	99**	…	…	…	…	…	…	16	16**
United Kingdom^o	…	…	48.7**	97**	…	…	…	…	…	…	…	24**
United States^o	326.6	95	348.3**	89**	…	…	…	…	…	…	22	22**
South and West Asia
Afghanistan	–	…	–	…	…	…	…	…	…	…	…	…
Bangladesh	64.7	32	58.2	32	…	…	…	…	…	…	38	38
Bhutan	0.02	81	0.03	48	87.5	…	…	72.4	73.3	71.4	22	18*
India^w	…	…	535.3**	90**	…	…	…	…	…	…	…	40**
Iran, Islamic Republic of	9.5	98	13.8	92	…	…	…	…	…	…	23	24
Maldives	0.4	90	0.6	91	46.8	25.0	49.2	56.6	56.0	56.7	32	22
Nepal	9.9**	31**	12.7	41	…	…	…	…	…	…	24**	20
Pakistan	…	…	…	…	…	…	…	…	…	…	…	…
Sri Lanka^w	…	…	…	…	…	…	…	…	…	…	…	…
Sub-Saharan Africa
Angola	…	…	…	…	…	…	…	…	…	…	…	…
Benin	0.6	61	0.8**	72**	100.0	100.0	100.0	…	…	…	28	30**
Botswana	…	…	…	…	…	…	…	…	…	…	…	…
Burkina Faso	…	…	0.5**	66**	…	…	…	…	…	…	…	29**
Burundi	0.2**	99**	0.3*	93*	…	…	…	…	…	…	28**	32*
Cameroon	4.4	97	5.5*	96**	…	…	…	…	…	…	23	24*
Cape Verde	…	…	0.8	100	…	…	…	7.5	–	7.5	…	25
Central African Republic	…	…	…	…	…	…	…	…	…	…	…	…
Chad	…	…	…	…	…	…	…	…	…	…	…	…

(y) Data are for 1999/2000. (z) Data are for 2000/2001.

STATISTICAL ANNEX / 351

Table 13A

PRIMARY EDUCATION

Total teachers 1998 Total (000)	1998 % F	2001 Total (000)	2001 % F	Trained teachers (%) 1998 Total	1998 Male	1998 Female	2001 Total	2001 Male	2001 Female	Pupil/teacher ratio 1998	2001	Country or territory
15.1**	75**	16.8	75	...	...	...	75.7	80.4	74.1	26**	24	Panama
48.9**	76**	...	...	...	...	...	...	...	...	19**	...	Paraguay[W]
170.2	60	147.4	64	...	...	...	...	...	...	25	29	Peru[W]
...	...	0.4	87	...	...	...	54.4	54.9**	54.3**	...	17**	Saint Kitts and Nevis
1.2	84**	1.1	84	...	...	...	77.8	70.6	79.1	22	24	Saint Lucia
...	...	1.0**	71**	...	...	...	...	...	...	...	17**	Saint Vincent and the Grenadines
...	...	3.3	85	...	...	...	100.0	100.0	100.0	...	20	Suriname
8.1	76	8.0**	78**	71.5	73.9	70.7	78.1**	78.1**	78.1**	21	19**	Trinidad and Tobago
0.1**	93**	0.1	87	...	...	...	100.0	100.0	100.0	21**	18	Turks and Caicos Islands
17.7	92**	17.3	...	...	...	...	...	...	...	21	21	Uruguay[W]
...	...	...	...	...	...	...	...	...	...	...	...	Venezuela

North America and Western Europe

...	...	0.3	75	...	...	...	...	...	...	...	12	Andorra
28.9	89	29.2**,y	89**,y	...	...	...	...	...	...	14	14**,y	Austria[o]
...	...	64.3**	79**	...	...	...	...	...	...	...	12**	Belgium[o]
156.9	68	141.0[z]	68[z]	...	...	...	...	...	...	15	17[z]	Canada[o]
3.5	67	3.3	82	...	...	...	...	...	...	18	19	Cyprus[o]
37.1	63	39.9[z]	64[z]	...	...	...	...	...	...	10	10[z]	Denmark[o]
22.2	71	25.3	74	...	...	...	...	...	...	17	16	Finland[o]
208.6	78	204.3	79	...	...	...	...	...	...	19	19	France[o]
221.3	82	236.0	...	...	...	...	...	...	...	17	14	Germany[o]
47.7	...	51.6	...	...	...	...	...	...	...	14	13	Greece[o]
2.7**	76**	2.9**,y	78**,y	...	...	...	...	...	...	11**	11**,y	Iceland[o]
21.1	74	22.0**	81**	...	...	...	...	...	...	22	20**	Ireland[o]
53.9	...	61.3[z]	83[z]	...	...	...	...	...	...	13	12	Israel[o]
253.7	95	263.4	95	...	...	...	...	...	...	11	11	Italy[o]
...	...	2.9	68	...	...	...	...	...	...	...	12	Luxembourg[o]
1.8	87	1.7	87	...	...	...	...	...	...	20	19	Malta[o]
0.1**	87**	0.1[z]	87[z]	...	...	...	...	...	...	16**	22[z]	Monaco
...	...	131.0[z]	78[z]	...	...	...	...	...	...	...	10[z]	Netherlands[o]
...	...	...	...	...	...	...	...	...	...	...	...	Norway[o]
...	...	69.6	81**	...	...	...	...	...	...	...	11	Portugal[o]
...	...	0.2[y]	91[y]	...	...	...	...	...	...	...	5[y]	San Marino
171.5	68	177.8	71	...	...	...	...	...	...	15	14	Spain[o]
61.9	80	68.5	...	...	...	...	...	...	...	12	12	Sweden[o]
39.5	72	39.4**	73**	...	...	...	...	...	...	13	14**	Switzerland[o]
244.5	76	264.1	82	...	...	...	...	...	...	19	17	United Kingdom[o]
1 617.8	87	1 638.0[z]	87[z]	...	...	...	...	...	...	15	15[z]	United States[o]

South and West Asia

32.6	...	11.7[z]	...	...	...	...	...	...	...	32	43[z]	Afghanistan
309.6	31	320.7	36	62.9	62.4	63.8	65.6	64.4	67.6	57**	55	Bangladesh
2.1	41	2.2	35	99.7	99.8	99.6	91.6	92.0	90.7	38	40	Bhutan
3 135.3*	33*	2 832.9**	36**	...	...	...	...	...	...	40*	40**	India[W]
327.0	53	308.1	54	...	...	...	96.5**,z	96.5**,z	96.5**,z	27	24	Iran, Islamic Republic of
2.8	58	3.2	61	68.9	70.8	67.5	66.9	66.5	67.2	26	23	Maldives
82.0**	22**	96.7	25	52.0**	55.2**	40.6**	...	...	...	41**	40	Nepal
...	...	329.8*,z	37*,z	...	...	...	...	...	...	...	44*,z	Pakistan
...	...	...	...	...	...	...	...	...	...	...	...	Sri Lanka[W]

Sub-Saharan Africa

32.1*	25*	33.5**,z	41**,z	...	...	...	...	...	...	42*	35**,z	Angola
16.3	23	21.8	19	...	...	...	...	...	...	53	53	Benin
11.7	82	12.4	80	91.8	87.0	92.9	89.5	84.3	90.8	28	27	Botswana
16.7	25	19.6**	23**	...	...	...	...	...	...	49	47**	Burkina Faso
12.2**	54**	16.7	54	...	...	...	...	...	...	46**	49	Burundi
41.1	36	45.1**	35**	...	...	...	...	...	...	52	61*	Cameroon
3.2**	62**	3.1	65	...	...	...	67.2	67.5	67.0	29**	29	Cape Verde
...	...	6.2**,z	18**,z	...	...	...	...	...	...	...	74**,z	Central African Republic
12.4	9	14.3**	10**	...	...	...	...	...	...	68	71**	Chad

Table 13A (continued)

	\multicolumn{12}{c}{PRE-PRIMARY EDUCATION}
	\multicolumn{4}{c}{Total teachers}	\multicolumn{6}{c}{Trained teachers (%)}	\multicolumn{2}{c}{Pupil/teacher ratio}
	\multicolumn{2}{c}{1998}	\multicolumn{2}{c}{2001}	\multicolumn{3}{c}{1998}	\multicolumn{3}{c}{2001}	1998	2001
Country or territory	Total (000)	% F	Total (000)	% F	Total	Male	Female	Total	Male	Female		
Comoros	0.1**	94**	0.04 y	...	...	...	...	...	...	...	26**	26 y
Congo	0.6	100	1.0	100	...	...	...	...	...	...	10	15
Côte d'Ivoire	1.6	96	2.1	87	...	...	...	...	...	...	23	21
Democratic Rep. of the Congo	...	...	1.7**	88**	...	...	...	...	...	...	...	25**
Equatorial Guinea	0.4	36	0.4 z	82 z	...	...	...	...	...	...	43	55 z
Eritrea	0.3	97	0.4	98	64.8	22.2	66.0	66.9	33.3	67.4	36	36
Ethiopia	2.5	93	3.7	91	63.0	37.1	65.1	63.2	53.7	64.2	36	32
Gabon	...	...	0.5**	98**	...	...	...	...	...	...	...	30**
Gambia	...	...	...	...	...	...	...	...	...	...	...	...
Ghana	24.2**	92**	27.9	89	26.6**	15.6**	27.6**	22.2	21.3	22.3	25**	25
Guinea	...	...	...	...	...	...	...	...	...	...	...	...
Guinea-Bissau	...	...	0.2 y	73 y	...	...	...	22.7 y	26.9 y	21.1 y	...	21 y
Kenya	37.8	99	47.1	...	...	...	...	47.4	...	...	27	25
Lesotho	2.0	100	1.6 z	99 z	...	...	...	...	...	...	18	19 z
Liberia	...	...	4.3 y	70 y	...	...	...	...	...	...	...	36 y
Madagascar	...	...	2.9**,z	98**,z	...	...	...	...	...	...	...	18**,z
Malawi	...	...	...	...	...	...	...	...	...	...	...	...
Mali	1.1	80	1.0	73	...	...	...	...	...	...	24	21
Mauritius	2.6	100	2.4	100	100.0	–	100.0	89.8	–	89.8	17	16
Mozambique	...	...	...	...	...	...	...	...	...	...	...	...
Namibia	1.3**	88**	1.6**	89**	...	...	...	...	...	...	27**	27**
Niger	0.5	98	0.6	98	...	...	...	96.7	100.0	96.6	22	26
Nigeria	...	...	...	...	...	...	...	...	...	...	...	...
Rwanda	...	...	0.6**	86**	...	...	...	...	...	...	...	35**
Sao Tome and Principe	...	...	0.2	94	...	...	...	54.9	75.0	53.5	...	25
Senegal	1.3	78	1.4	73	...	...	...	100.0	100.0	100.0	19	21
Seychelles	0.2	100	0.2	100	88.1	–	88.1	80.5	100.0	80.4	17	14
Sierra Leone	...	...	0.9 z	83 z	...	...	...	76.3 z	94.7 z	72.6 z	...	19 z
Somalia	...	...	...	...	...	...	...	...	...	...	...	...
South Africa	7.0**	79**	...	...	65.8**	67.7**	65.3**	...	...	...	36**	...
Swaziland	...	...	...	...	...	...	...	...	...	...	...	...
Togo	0.6	97	0.7	91	...	...	...	61.3	77.3	59.7	20	17
Uganda	2.6**	70**	3.0**	71**	...	...	...	...	...	...	25**	25**
United Republic of Tanzania	...	...	...	...	...	...	...	...	...	...	...	...
Zambia	0.7	57	...	...	100.0	100.0	100.0	...	...	...	43*	...
Zimbabwe w	...	...	...	...	...	...	...	...	...	...	...	...
World [1]	...	98	...	98	...	...	...	...	...	...	19	18
Countries in transition	...	100	...	99	...	...	...	87.4	...	...	9	8
Developed countries	...	99	...	99	...	...	...	...	...	...	16	14
Developing countries	...	97	...	98	...	...	...	...	...	...	22	21
Arab States	...	100	...	99	...	...	...	...	...	...	20	19
Central and Eastern Europe	...	100	...	100	...	...	...	...	...	...	12	11
Central Asia	...	100	...	100	...	...	...	...	...	...	12	10
East Asia and the Pacific	...	...	...	99	...	...	...	...	...	...	...	21
Latin America and the Caribbean	...	98	...	99	...	...	...	74.9	63.3	76.0	19	18
North America and Western Europe	...	97	...	97	...	...	...	...	...	...	16	15
South and West Asia	...	81	...	69	...	...	...	...	...	...	24	23
Sub-Saharan Africa	...	...	...	90	...	...	...	...	...	...	...	25

1. All values shown are medians. (y) Data are for 1999/2000. (z) Data are for 2000/2001.

Table 13A

PRIMARY EDUCATION

Total teachers 1998 Total (000)	1998 % F	2001 Total (000)	2001 % F	Trained teachers (%) 1998 Total	1998 Male	1998 Female	2001 Total	2001 Male	2001 Female	Pupil/teacher ratio 1998	2001	Country or territory
2.4	26	2.7	...	...	...	...	...	...	...	35	39	Comoros
4.5	42	9.3	38	...	...	...	...	...	...	61	56	Congo
44.7	20	48.2	22	...	...	...	...	...	...	43	44	Côte d'Ivoire
154.6	22	...	...	...	...	...	...	...	...	26	...	Democratic Rep. of the Congo
...	...	1.8**,z	24**,z	...	...	...	...	...	...	...	43**,z	Equatorial Guinea
5.6	35	7.5	38	72.8	74.8	69.1	72.6	82.2	57.2	47	44	Eritrea
112.4	28	126.9	31	...	...	...	69.3	62.3	85.1	46	57	Ethiopia
6.0	42	5.7**	41**	...	...	...	...	...	...	44	49**	Gabon
4.6	30	4.2**	30**	72.5	72.5**	72.4**	...	...	...	33	38**	Gambia
80.3	32	80.6	32	71.8	64.0	88.5	64.9	56.7	82.5	30	32	Ghana
15.5	25	21.1	24	...	...	...	...	...	...	47	47	Guinea
...	...	3.4y	20y	...	...	...	35.1y	33.3y	42.4y	...	44y	Guinea-Bissau
192.3	42	184.1	42	96.6	96.1	97.3	98.0	97.3	98.9	29	32	Kenya
8.3**	80**	8.8	80	76.7**	73.8**	77.4**	74.8	60.9	78.3	44**	47	Lesotho
10.0	19	13.0y	28y	...	...	...	...	...	...	39	38y	Liberia
42.7	58	50.7	58	...	...	...	...	...	...	47	48	Madagascar
39.9**	40**	47.8z	38z	46.1**	47.9**	43.4**	51.2z	52.2z	49.4z	63**	63**,y	Malawi
15.4*	23*	21.8	25	...	...	...	...	...	...	62*	56	Mali
5.1	53	5.4	57	100.0	100.0	100.0	100.0	100.0	100.0	26	25	Mauritius
31.5	25	38.8	27	32.7	32.6	32.9	59.9	57.8	65.6	63**	66	Mozambique
12.0	67	12.6	60	29.1	28.7	29.2	37.0**	31.1**	40.8**	32	32	Namibia
12.9	31	18.4	34	...	...	...	72.7	83.7	51.3	41	41	Niger
516.7**	39**	487.3**	49**	...	...	...	...	...	...	31**	40**	Nigeria
23.7	55	26.0	50	...	...	...	81.2	80.8	81.6	54	59	Rwanda
0.7	...	0.9**	62**	...	...	...	...	...	...	36	33**	Sao Tome and Principe
21.3	...	24.5	23	...	...	...	90.5	96.1	71.7	49	49	Senegal
0.7	88	0.7	86	83.7	77.6	84.5	77.7	101.0	73.9	15	14	Seychelles
...	...	14.9z	38z	...	...	...	78.9z	82.6z	72.9z	...	37z	Sierra Leone
...	...	...	...	...	...	...	...	...	...	...	...	Somalia
216.0**	78**	199.8	78	63.1**	65.9**	62.4**	67.6	60.6	69.6	37**	37	South Africa
6.4	75	6.6	75	91.1	89.1	91.8	...	...	...	33	32	Swaziland
23.1	14	27.8	12	...	...	...	80.5	82.6	65.4	41	35	Togo
109.7	33	127.0	...	...	...	...	...	...	...	60	54	Uganda
106.3	44	105.0	45	44.1	44.2	44.0	...	...	...	38	46	United Republic of Tanzania
34.8	48	36.2**	51**	88.8	86.2	91.7	100.0z	100.0z	100.0z	45	45**	Zambia
...	...	66.5	48	...	...	...	95.3**	...	...	...	38	Zimbabwe w

...	72	...	73	...	...	...	...	...	...	24	22	World[1]
...	97	...	97	...	...	...	89.8	...	...	20	19	Countries in transition
...	85	...	83	...	...	...	...	...	...	16	15	Developed countries
...	61	...	61	...	...	...	...	...	...	28	28	Developing countries
...	52	...	59	...	...	...	...	...	...	25	22	Arab States
...	93	...	91	...	...	...	...	...	...	19	17	Central and Eastern Europe
...	92	...	94	...	...	...	...	...	...	20	19	Central Asia
...	66	...	69	...	...	...	...	...	...	23	25	East Asia and the Pacific
...	79	...	79	...	...	...	78.0	74.4	78.6	22	21	Latin America and the Caribbean
...	76	...	80	...	...	...	...	...	...	15	14	North America and Western Europe
...	37	...	36	...	...	...	...	...	...	38	40	South and West Asia
...	36	...	38	...	...	...	...	...	...	43	44	Sub-Saharan Africa

354 / ANNEX

Table 13B
Teaching staff in secondary and tertiary education

	SECONDARY EDUCATION[1]				Trained teachers (%)		
	Total teachers				1998		
	1998		2001				
Country or territory	Total (000)	% F	Total (000)	% F	Total	Male	Female
Arab States							
Algeria	154.6	47	161.6	49	96.9	95.6	98.4
Bahrain	...	...	5.2**	54**	...	...	...
Djibouti	0.7	22	0.7**	23**	...	...	...
Egypt[w]	454.0**	41**	497.0**	41**	...	...	...
Iraq	56.1**	69**	62.0[y]	69[y]	...	...	...
Jordan[w]	...	...	33.8**	59**	...	...	...
Kuwait	22.3**	56**	23.7**	56**	100.0**	100.0**	100.0**
Lebanon	42.1**	51**	46.8**	53**	...	...	...
Libyan Arab Jamahiriya	...	...	...	...	...	...	...
Mauritania	...	...	2.7[z]	10[z]	...	...	...
Morocco	87.9**	33**	90.8**,[y]	32**,[y]	...	...	...
Oman	12.9	50	15.2**	50**	100.0	100.0	100.0
Palestinian Autonomous Territories	...	...	16.7**,[z]	50**,[z]	...	...	...
Qatar	4.4**	57**	4.9	55	...	...	...
Saudi Arabia	138.8	55	159.1	48	...	...	...
Sudan	...	...	...	...	...	...	...
Syrian Arab Republic	70.2**	47**	62.8**,[z]	51**,[z]	...	...	...
Tunisia[w]	56.5**	40**	58.3**	46**	...	...	...
United Arab Emirates	16.3	55	17.8	55	51.7	46.2	56.2
Yemen	73.8**	19**	...	...	...	...	...
Central and Eastern Europe							
Albania[o]	22.2**	54**	22.3[z]	54[z]	...	...	...
Belarus	...	...	105.9**	78**	...	...	...
Bosnia and Herzegovina[o]	...	...	...	...	...	...	...
Bulgaria[o]	56.0	73**	57.4	76	...	...	...
Croatia	34.5	64	37.7	66	...	...	...
Czech Republic[o]	72.3	62**	70.8[y]	68[y]	...	...	...
Estonia[o]	11.1	...	12.3**	...	...	...	...
Hungary[o]	100.2	72	93.3	73	...	...	...
Latvia[o]	24.8	80	24.5	81	...	...	...
Lithuania[o]	36.3**	79**	42.6**	...	...	...	...
Poland[o]	...	...	238.9	68**	...	...	...
Republic of Moldova	31.8**	72**	31.3	75	...	...	...
Romania[o]	177.3**	64**	176.2	66	...	...	...
Russian Federation[w]	...	...	874.0**,[z]	76**,[z]	...	...	...
Serbia and Montenegro	54.3**	63**	56.4[z]	61[z]	100.0**	100.0**	100.0**
Slovakia	53.7**	72**	52.6	73	...	...	...
Slovenia[o]	16.8	69	16.9	70	...	...	...
The former Yugoslav Rep. of Macedonia[o]	13.4	49	13.6	51	...	...	...
Turkey[o]	...	...	...	...	...	...	...
Ukraine	...	...	369.8**	...	...	...	...
Central Asia							
Armenia	...	...	46.9**	81**	...	...	...
Azerbaijan	118.5**	63**	121.9**	64**	...	...	...
Georgia	59.7**	77**	49.4**	80**	...	...	...
Kazakhstan	...	...	170.3**	85**	...	...	...
Kyrgyzstan	48.0**	68**	51.4	70	...	...	...
Mongolia	11.0	67	12.9	70	...	...	...
Tajikistan	40.8**	42**	50.3	45	...	...	...
Turkmenistan	...	...	...	...	...	...	...
Uzbekistan	...	...	...	...	...	...	...
East Asia and the Pacific							
Australia[o]	...	...	...	...	...	...	...
Brunei Darussalam	3.1*	48*	3.4*	52*	...	...	...
Cambodia	18.1**	27**	22.0	29	...	...	...
China[w]	4 763.0	41**	4 792.8	43	...	...	...

1. Refers to lower and upper secondary education (ISCED levels 2 and 3).
(y) Data are for 1999/2000.
(z) Data are for 2000/2001.

STATISTICAL ANNEX / 355

Table 13B

Trained teachers (%) 2001 Total	Male	Female	Pupil/teacher ratio 1998	2001	Total teachers 1998 Total (000)	% F	2001 Total (000)	% F	Country or territory
									Arab States
98.0	97.1	99.0	18	20	16.3**	23**	...	...	Algeria
...	...	...	...	12**	...	...	...	...	Bahrain
...	...	...	23	28**	0.02	30	0.1**	15**	Djibouti
...	...	...	17**	17**	...	...	...	...	Egypt[w]
100.0[y]	100.0[y]	100.0[y]	20**	20[y]	11.8	31	14.7**	...	Iraq
...	...	...	...	18**	...	...	6.6	19	Jordan[w]
...	...	...	11**	10**	2.2**	...	...	...	Kuwait
...	...	...	9**	7**	8.9	28	11.0	30	Lebanon
...	...	...	...	...	11.7	13**	15.0	13**	Libyan Arab Jamahiriya
...	...	...	...	28[z]	...	...	0.2	...	Mauritania
...	...	...	17**	17**,[y]	16.2	23	18.0**	22**	Morocco
100.0**	100.0**	100.0**	18	18**	...	...	0.6	11	Oman
...	...	...	...	30**,[z]	3.2	13	4.0	14	Palestinian Autonomous Territories
...	...	...	10**	10	0.7**	32**	0.6	33	Qatar
...	...	...	13	13	19.7	36	21.9**	34**	Saudi Arabia
...	...	...	...	...	4.4	23	...	...	Sudan
...	...	...	15**	18**,[z]	4.3**	...	...	...	Syrian Arab Republic
...	...	...	19**	20**	5.9	...	11.4	35	Tunisia[w]
51.6	49.2	53.7	12	13	1.6**	...	...	...	United Arab Emirates
...	...	...	14**	...	4.9	1	5.2**,[y]	1**,[y]	Yemen
									Central and Eastern Europe
...	...	...	16**	17[z]	...	...	3.0[z]	...	Albania[o]
97.9**	97.9**	97.9**	...	9**	30.3	51**	42.5	54	Belarus
...	...	...	...	...	...	...	...	...	Bosnia and Herzegovina[o]
...	...	...	13	12	24.4	41**	22.3	45	Bulgaria[o]
70.5	63.3	74.2	12	11	6.7	35	7.6	35	Croatia
...	...	...	13	14[y]	19.2	...	21.0[z]	40[z]	Czech Republic[o]
...	...	...	11	10**	6.2	49	6.9**	48**	Estonia[o]
...	...	...	10	11	21.3	...	23.9	40	Hungary[o]
...	...	...	10	11	5.6	52	5.3	54	Latvia[o]
...	...	...	...	10**	15.2	50	14.0	53**	Lithuania[o]
...	...	...	...	...	...	...	83.5	...	Poland[o]
...	...	...	13**	13	...	...	7.3	52	Republic of Moldova
...	...	...	13**	13	26.0	37	28.7	40	Romania[o]
...	...	...	...	...	525.2**	56**	575.4	56	Russian Federation[w]
100.0[z]	100.0[z]	100.0[z]	15**	14[z]	12.8	36	11.6[z]	38[z]	Serbia and Montenegro
...	...	...	13**	13	11.3**	38**	13.2	42	Slovakia
...	...	...	13	13	2.5	21	3.1	29**	Slovenia[o]
...	...	...	16	16	2.7	42	2.7	44	The former Yugoslav Rep. of Macedonia[o]
...	...	...	...	...	60.1	...	71.3	37	Turkey[o]
...	...	...	...	14**	132.9	...	168.6	...	Ukraine
									Central Asia
...	...	...	...	8**	...	...	11.8	46	Armenia
100.0**	100.0**	100.0**	8**	9**	17.9**	44**	19.5	48	Azerbaijan
...	...	...	8**	9**	13.5**	49**	14.9	48	Georgia
...	...	...	...	12**	27.1	58	34.5	58	Kazakhstan
68.5	64.9	70.0	13**	13	7.7	32	10.5	34	Kyrgyzstan
...	...	...	19	22	5.7	47**	5.3	52	Mongolia
...	...	...	19**	18	5.9	29	6.1	31	Tajikistan
...	...	...	...	...	...	...	...	...	Turkmenistan
...	...	...	...	...	...	...	23.7**	38**	Uzbekistan
									East Asia and the Pacific
...	...	...	...	...	...	...	...	...	Australia[o]
...	...	...	11*	11*	0.5	28	0.5	33	Brunei Darussalam
99.0	98.9**	99.4**	18**	22	1.1	19	2.1	18	Cambodia
...	...	...	17	19**	523.3	...	679.9	45	China[w]

Table 13B (continued)

	SECONDARY EDUCATION[1]						
	Total teachers				Trained teachers (%)		
	1998		2001		1998		
Country or territory	Total (000)	% F	Total (000)	% F	Total	Male	Female
Cook Islands	...	...	...	...	...	...	...
Democratic People's Republic of Korea	...	...	...	...	...	...	...
Fiji	...	...	5.8**	49**	...	...	...
Indonesia[w]	...	...	1 114.8	40	...	...	...
Japan[o]	629.8	...	619.5	...	...	...	...
Kiribati	...	...	...	...	...	...	...
Lao People's Democratic Republic	11.8	40	13.3	42	97.6	97.1	98.2
Macao, China	1.4	56	1.8	57	58.8	49.8	66.0
Malaysia[w]	111.2**	60**	125.6**	63**	...	...	...
Marshall Islands	0.3	...	0.4	39	...	...	...
Micronesia (Federated States of)	...	...	...	...	...	...	...
Myanmar	68.4	77	76.2	78	69.5**	72.6**	68.5**
Nauru	...	...	...	...	...	...	...
New Zealand[o]	...	...	36.5	59	...	...	...
Niue	0.02	60	0.02**	50**	...	...	...
Palau	0.2	52	0.1**,y	59**,y	...	...	...
Papua New Guinea	6.0	35	7.7**	35**	100.0	100.0	100.0
Philippines[w]	150.2	76	151.8	76	100.0**	...	...
Republic of Korea[o]	...	...	189.3	46	...	...	...
Samoa	1.1**	56**	1.1	60	...	...	...
Singapore	...	...	...	...	...	...	...
Solomon Islands	...	...	...	...	...	...	...
Thailand[w]	241.7	60	237.9	54	...	...	...
Timor-Leste	...	...	1.6	...	...	...	...
Tokelau	...	...	...	...	...	...	...
Tonga	1.4	32	1.0**,z	50**,z	59.3	45.3	89.8
Tuvalu	...	...	0.04	83	...	...	...
Vanuatu	0.4**	47**	0.4z	49z	...	...	...
Viet Nam	258.3	65	334.2	65	...	...	...
Latin America and the Caribbean							
Anguilla	0.1**	65**	0.1**	63**	60.0**	65.2**	57.1**
Antigua and Barbuda	...	...	0.4y	71y	...	...	...
Argentina[w]	257.8	69	321.2**	...	...	...	...
Aruba	0.4**	49**	0.4**	49**	100.0**	100.0**	100.0**
Bahamas	...	...	2.1	67	...	...	...
Barbados	1.2**	58**	1.3**	49**	63.8**	63.2**	64.3**
Belize	0.9**	62**	1.1z	65z	...	...	...
Bermuda	...	...	0.7	67	...	...	...
Bolivia	...	...	37.5**	53**	...	...	...
Brazil[w]	...	...	1 367.5	78	...	...	...
British Virgin Islands	0.1**	62**	0.2**	63**	...	...	...
Cayman Islands	0.2**	52**	0.2**	55**	...	...	...
Chile[w]	...	...	47.4z	63z	...	...	...
Colombia	...	...	177.2**	51**	...	...	...
Costa Rica	...	...	14.3	53	...	...	...
Cuba	64.9	61	77.0	58	94.4	94.5	94.4
Dominica	0.3**	68**	0.4	67	29.9**	26.9**	31.3**
Dominican Republic	22.1**	58**	23.9**	74**	...	...	...
Ecuador	53.9**	50**	71.2	49	...	...	...
El Salvador	...	...	7.3z	...	...	...	...
Grenada	...	...	0.3	90**	...	...	...
Guatemala	27.2*	...	40.0	...	...	...	...
Guyana	3.6**	63**	3.8**,y	60**,y	58.2**	59.2**	57.6**
Haiti	...	...	...	...	...	...	...
Honduras	...	...	...	...	...	...	...
Jamaica[w]	...	...	11.8**	67**	...	...	...
Mexico[o]	...	...	571.4	45**	...	...	...
Montserrat	0.03**	69**	0.03**	55**	...	...	...
Netherlands Antilles	1.0	53	1.2**	55**	100.0	100.0	100.0
Nicaragua	7.7*	58*	10.6*	62*	44.2*	35.8*	50.4*

1. Refers to lower and upper secondary education (ISCED levels 2 and 3).
(y) Data are for 1999/2000.
(z) Data are for 2000/2001.

Table 13B

\multicolumn{5}{c	}{SECONDARY EDUCATION[1]}	\multicolumn{4}{c	}{TERTIARY EDUCATION}	
\multicolumn{3}{c	}{Trained teachers (%)}	\multicolumn{2}{c	}{Pupil/teacher ratio}	\multicolumn{4}{c	}{Total teachers}	
\multicolumn{3}{c	}{2001}	1998	2001	\multicolumn{2}{c	}{1998}	\multicolumn{2}{c	}{2001}	
Total	Male	Female			Total (000)	% F	Total (000)	% F	Country or territory
…	…	…	…	…	.	.	.	.	Cook Islands
…	…	…	…	…	…	…	…	…	Democratic People's Republic of Korea
…	…	…	…	17**	…	…	…	…	Fiji
…	…	…	…	14	…	…	251.5	40	Indonesia[W]
…	…	…	14	14	465.1	…	482.0	…	Japan[o]
…	…	…	…	…	…	…	…	…	Kiribati
96.5	96.0	97.2	20	24	1.1	31	1.5	37	Lao People's Democratic Republic
60.1	47.0	70.0	23	24	0.7	…	1.2	36	Macao, China
…	…	…	19**	18**	…	…	30.3	45	Malaysia[W]
…	…	…	22	17	…	…	0.05	52	Marshall Islands
…	…	…	…	…	0.1	…	…	…	Micronesia (Federated States of)
66.4	68.4	65.9	30	31	…	…	10.5[z]	70**,[z]	Myanmar
…	…	…	…	…	.	.	.	.	Nauru
…	…	…	…	13	…	…	11.7	45	New Zealand[o]
…	…	…	14	12**	.	.	.	.	Niue
…	…	…	13	14**,[y]	…	…	0.05**	46**	Palau
100.0**	100.0**	100.0**	22	21**	1.1	20	…	…	Papua New Guinea
…	…	…	34	38	93.7	…	99.0	55	Philippines[W]
…	…	…	…	20	…	…	150.9	27	Republic of Korea[o]
…	…	…	20**	21	0.2	37	0.1**	43**	Samoa
…	…	…	…	…	…	…	…	…	Singapore
…	…	…	…	…	.	.	.	.	Solomon Islands
…	…	…	…	…	50.2	53	64.1	47	Thailand[W]
…	…	…	…	28	…	…	0.1*	9*	Timor-Leste
…	…	…	…	…	.	.	.	.	Tokelau
…	…	…	10	15**,[z]	0.1**	21**	0.1**,[z]	22**,[z]	Tonga
…	…	…	…	25	.	.	.	.	Tuvalu
85.4[z]	100.0[z]	70.4[z]	27**	27[z]	0.01	40	0.0	…	Vanuatu
91.8**	90.6**	92.4**	29	26	28.0	37	35.9	39	Viet Nam
									Latin America and the Caribbean
90.2**	86.7**	92.3**	16**	13**	.	.	.	.	Anguilla
52.5[y]	65.5**,[y]	47.1**,[y]	…	13[y]	.	.	.	.	Antigua and Barbuda
…	…	…	14	12**	116.1	53	112.7[z]	54[z]	Argentina[W]
100.0**	100.0**	100.0**	16**	15**	0.2	43	0.2	47	Aruba
100.0*	100.0*	100.0*	…	15	…	…	…	…	Bahamas
91.0**	90.8**	91.1**	18**	16**	0.6**	42**	0.6**,[z]	51**,[z]	Barbados
40.9[z]	38.0[z]	42.5[z]	24**	23[z]	…	…	…	…	Belize
100.0	100.0	100.0	…	7	…	…	0.1**	55**	Bermuda
77.1**,[z]	74.1**,[z]	80.0**,[z]	…	25**	11.5	…	13.7	…	Bolivia
…	…	…	…	19	165.1	42	203.4	42	Brazil[W]
39.2**	41.0**	38.1**	10**	10**	.	.	0.1	54	British Virgin Islands
100.0**	100.0**	100.0**	9**	10**	0.02	42	0.02[z]	32[z]	Cayman Islands
87.1**,[z]	…	…	…	29[z]	…	…	…	…	Chile[W]
…	…	…	…	19**	…	…	88.7	34	Colombia
84.6	…	…	…	20	…	…	3.9	…	Costa Rica
84.1	83.6	84.5	11	12	23.5	47	24.2	46	Cuba
35.0	35.1	34.9	22**	17	.	.	.	.	Dominica
…	…	…	28**	32**	…	…	…	…	Dominican Republic
67.4	60.9	74.0	17**	14	…	…	15.3[z]	…	Ecuador
…	…	…	…	…	7.3	32	6.8**	32**	El Salvador
31.4**	39.4**	30.5**	…	20	…	…	…	…	Grenada
100.0	…	…	15*	14	…	…	…	…	Guatemala
75.1**,[y]	59.5**,[y]	85.3**,[y]	19**	18**,[y]	…	…	…	…	Guyana
…	…	…	…	…	…	…	…	…	Haiti
…	…	…	…	…	5.5	…	5.5**	36**	Honduras
…	…	…	…	19**	1.5	…	2.0	60	Jamaica[W]
…	…	…	…	17	192.4	…	219.8	…	Mexico[o]
57.6**	33.3**	77.8**	11**	9**	.	.	.	.	Montserrat
100.0**	100.0**	100.0**	15	13**	0.2**	42**	0.3**	34**	Netherlands Antilles
44.6*	37.5*	49.1*	37**	33*	…	…	…	…	Nicaragua

Table 13B (continued)

	SECONDARY EDUCATION[1]						
	Total teachers				Trained teachers (%)		
	1998		2001		1998		
Country or territory	Total (000)	% F	Total (000)	% F	Total	Male	Female
Panama	14.3**	55**	15.2	56	...	...	...
Paraguay[w]	...	...	38.7	62	...	...	...
Peru[w]	128.4**	41**	114.4**,z	44**,z	...	...	...
Saint Kitts and Nevis	...	...	0.4**	61**	...	...	...
Saint Lucia	0.7**	64**	0.7**	64**	...	...	...
Saint Vincent and the Grenadines	...	...	0.4**	60**	...	...	...
Suriname	...	...	2.8	68**	...	...	...
Trinidad and Tobago	5.4**	59**	6.0**	59**	55.7**	59.2**	53.2**
Turks and Caicos Islands	0.1**	61**	0.1**	61**	...	...	...
Uruguay[w]	15.9	...	22.5	...	...	...	...
Venezuela	...	...	...	...	...	...	...
North America and Western Europe							
Andorra	...	...	0.4	54	...	...	...
Austria[o]	72.6	58	75.7**,y	...	...	...	...
Belgium[o]	...	...	...	...	...	...	...
Canada[o]	143.2**	68**	147.9[z]	68[z]	...	...	...
Cyprus[o]	4.9**	51**	5.3	59	...	...	...
Denmark[o]	44.2	45	43.9[z]	48[z]	...	...	...
Finland[o]	39.3	64	...	...	...	...	...
France[o]	495.2	57	510.5	57	...	...	...
Germany[o]	532.6	51	590.0	...	...	...	...
Greece[o]	74.7	...	84.3	...	...	...	...
Iceland[o]	2.5**	58**	2.6**,y	58**,y	...	...	...
Ireland[o]	...	...	...	...	...	...	...
Israel[o]	54.9	...	72.4[z]	72[z]	...	...	...
Italy[o]	422.1	65	440.7	65	...	...	...
Luxembourg[o]	...	...	3.2**	42**	...	...	...
Malta[o]	3.6	48	3.7	54	...	...	...
Monaco	0.4**	60**	0.3[z]	58[z]	...	...	...
Netherlands[o]	...	...	103.8**	42**	...	...	...
Norway[o]	...	...	...	...	...	...	...
Portugal[o]	...	...	89.6	69**	...	...	...
San Marino	...	...	...	...	...	...	...
Spain[o]	...	...	407.0**,z	52**,z	...	...	...
Sweden[o]	63.1	...	70.2	...	...	...	...
Switzerland[o]	50.3	39	48.0**	40**	...	...	...
United Kingdom[o]	469.5	56	471.4[z]	59[z]	...	...	...
United States[o]	1 503.9	56	1 522.6[z]	56[z]	...	...	...
South and West Asia							
Afghanistan	...	...	...	...	...	...	...
Bangladesh	251.5	13	285.1	15	...	...	...
Bhutan	0.5	33	0.8**	36**	100.0	100.0	100.0
India[w]	...	...	2 357.8	34	...	...	...
Iran, Islamic Republic of	322.0	45	343.3	46	...	...	...
Maldives	0.7	24	1.9	41	75.6	74.5	78.9
Nepal	39.9	10	58.2	14	...	...	...
Pakistan	...	...	...	...	...	...	...
Sri Lanka[w]	...	...	...	...	...	...	...
Sub-Saharan Africa							
Angola	16.0	33	17.7*	29*	...	...	...
Benin	9.0**	12**	11.9**,z	11**,z	...	...	...
Botswana	8.5**	46**	7.7**	47**	80.4**	82.8**	77.6**
Burkina Faso	6.2**	...	...	...	...	...	...
Burundi	4.2**	...	5.5**,z	22**,z	...	...	...
Cameroon	26.4**	28**	...	...	...	...	...
Cape Verde	1.7**	...	2.0	36	...	...	...
Central African Republic	...	...	...	...	...	...	...
Chad	3.6	5	4.3**,z	5**,z	...	...	...

1. Refers to lower and upper secondary education (ISCED levels 2 and 3).
(y) Data are for 1999/2000.
(z) Data are for 2000/2001.

Table 13B

SECONDARY EDUCATION[1]						TERTIARY EDUCATION					
Trained teachers (%)			Pupil/teacher ratio		Total teachers					
2001			1998	2001	1998		2001		
Total	Male	Female			Total (000)	% F	Total (000)	% F	Country or territory
93.5	91.3	95.2	16**	16	...	...	5.0**,y	...	Panama
...	...	...	...	13	...	...	1.8 y	71 y	Paraguay w
76.1**,z	...	...	17**	21**,z	54.5	...	...	...	Peru w
36.6**	39.5**	34.8**	...	11**	.	.	.	.	Saint Kitts and Nevis
58.2**	53.9**	60.6**	18**	18**	0.2	39**	0.2	77	Saint Lucia
...	...	...	...	23**	.	.	.	.	Saint Vincent and the Grenadines
100.0	100.0**	100.0**	...	15	...	...	0.6**	48**	Suriname
48.2**	48.6**	47.9**	22**	18**	0.5	31	0.6	32	Trinidad and Tobago
97.9**	98.2**	97.7**	9**	9**	0.0	33	0.0**,z	33**,z	Turks and Caicos Islands
...	...	...	...	14	12.7	...	11.7	...	Uruguay w
...	...	...	...	...	...	...	53.6 y	38 y	Venezuela

North America and Western Europe

...	...	...	...	8	.	.	.	.	Andorra
...	...	...	10	10**,y	25.7	...	26.5**,y	...	Austria o
...	...	...	...	...	...	...	23.3	39	Belgium o
...	...	...	18**	18 z	125.5	...	133.5 z	41 z	Canada o
...	...	...	13**	12	1.1	34	1.1	38	Cyprus o
...	...	...	10	...	...	...	...	...	Denmark o
...	...	...	12	...	...	...	17.6**	46**	Finland o
...	...	...	12	12	102.3	...	129.0	34	France o
...	...	...	15	14	271.7	...	277.0	32	Germany o
...	...	...	10	...	17.2	...	21.1	...	Greece o
...	...	...	13**	12**,y	1.4	...	1.7**,z	43**,z	Iceland o
...	...	...	...	...	10.3	33	12.0**	42**	Ireland o
...	...	...	10	8	...	...	...	...	Israel o
...	...	...	11	10	73.0	...	80.3	31	Italy o
...	...	...	...	11**	...	...	0.1 y	...	Luxembourg o
...	...	...	...	10	0.7	25	0.6	23	Malta o
...	...	...	8**	11 z	.	.	.	.	Monaco
...	...	...	...	14**	...	...	44.2	33	Netherlands o
...	...	...	...	...	14.1	...	16.3**	36**	Norway o
...	...	...	...	9	...	...	...	...	Portugal o
...	...	...	...	...	...	...	...	...	San Marino
...	...	...	...	8**,z	107.7	...	133.5	37	Spain o
...	...	...	15	13	28.9	...	33.7	40	Sweden o
...	...	...	11	12**	26.1	...	28.0	28	Switzerland o
...	...	...	17	18 z	92.2	...	98.3	35	United Kingdom o
...	...	...	...	15 z	991.8	...	1 113.2	41**	United States o

South and West Asia

...	...	...	...	...	...	...	1.5 z	...	Afghanistan
...	...	...	36	38	44.9	14	63.6	12	Bangladesh
88.5**	88.5**	88.7**	39	32**	...	...	0.2**,z	27**,z	Bhutan
...	...	...	...	32	...	...	428.6	37	India w
...	...	...	30	29	65.4	17	79.2	18	Iran, Islamic Republic of
62.8	68.9	54.1	17	13	.	.	.	.	Maldives
28.2	29.4	20.7	32	29	3.0**	...	4.6**,z	...	Nepal
...	...	...	...	...	...	...	...	...	Pakistan
...	...	...	...	...	...	...	...	...	Sri Lanka w

Sub-Saharan Africa

...	...	...	18	23*	0.8	...	0.8**,z	20**,z	Angola
...	...	...	24**	22**,z	...	...	0.6 y	9 y	Benin
...	...	...	17**	20**	0.5**	28**	...	...	Botswana
...	...	...	28**	...	...	...	...	...	Burkina Faso
...	...	...	17**	21**,z	0.4	...	0.6	10**	Burundi
...	...	...	24**	...	2.6	...	3.0	...	Cameroon
...	...	...	24**	24	...	...	...	...	Cape Verde
...	...	...	...	...	0.3	5	0.3 y	9 y	Central African Republic
...	...	...	34	32**,z	...	...	0.4 y	5 y	Chad

Table 13B (continued)

	SECONDARY EDUCATION[1]						
	Total teachers				Trained teachers (%)		
	1998		2001		1998		
Country or territory	Total (000)	% F	Total (000)	% F	Total	Male	Female
Comoros	...	...	2.6**	13**	...	...	...
Congo	...	...	7.7**,z	10**,z	...	...	...
Côte d'Ivoire	20.1**	...	23.2**,z	...	...	...	...
Democratic Rep. of the Congo	...	...	...	...	...	...	...
Equatorial Guinea	0.9**	5**	0.9**,y	4**,y	...	...	...
Eritrea	2.3	12	3.1	11	56.5	55.2	65.7
Ethiopia	...	...	15.0z	...	...	...	...
Gabon	3.1**	16**	...	...	...	...	...
Gambia	1.9	15	2.2z	17z	81.5**	81.4**	81.7**
Ghana	52.2	22	59.6**	21**	74.2	69.9	89.4
Guinea	5.8**	11**	5.3z	...	...	...	...
Guinea-Bissau	...	...	1.2**,y	5**,y	...	...	...
Kenya	44.3**	35**	48.0**,z	35**,z	92.5**	90.9**	95.6**
Lesotho	3.1**	51**	3.5**	54**	84.5**	84.7**	84.3**
Liberia	6.6	16	6.8y	20y	...	...	...
Madagascar	20.4**	44**	...	...	...	...	...
Malawi	9.3**	39**	12.8**,z	20**,z	...	...	...
Mali	7.7*	14*	6.0z	...	...	...	...
Mauritius	...	...	5.4**,z	48**,z	...	...	...
Mozambique	...	...	14.8	19	...	...	...
Namibia	5.1**	48**	5.5	58	...	...	...
Niger	4.3	18	4.2	19	...	...	...
Nigeria	...	...	...	...	...	...	...
Rwanda	...	...	...	...	...	...	...
Sao Tome and Principe	...	...	...	...	...	...	...
Senegal	9.4**	14**	10.7**	14**	...	...	...
Seychelles	0.6**	53**	0.5**	57**	87.6**	85.4**	89.5**
Sierra Leone	...	...	5.8z	27z	...	...	...
Somalia	...	...	...	...	...	...	...
South Africa	143.8**	50**	141.4**	50**	89.1**	85.6**	92.5**
Swaziland	3.4**	46**	...	...	99.2**	99.4**	98.9**
Togo	6.6	13	8.4**,y	11**,y	...	...	...
Uganda	25.0**	21**	31.0z	...	...	...	...
United Republic of Tanzania	...	...	...	...	...	...	...
Zambia	10.0	26	10.1**,y	27**,y	...	...	...
Zimbabwe[w]	...	...	34.2z	48z	...	...	...

World[2]	...	52	...	54	...	...	...
Countries in transition	...	...	...	76	...	...	...
Developed countries	...	62	...	59	...	...	...
Developing countries	...	48	...	50	...	...	...
Arab States	...	48	...	50	...	...	...
Central and Eastern Europe	...	69	...	70	...	...	...
Central Asia	...	67	...	70	...	...	...
East Asia and the Pacific	...	...	...	51	...	...	...
Latin America and the Caribbean	...	...	...	61	...	...	...
North America and Western Europe	...	57	...	57	...	...	...
South and West Asia	...	24	...	35	...	...	...
Sub-Saharan Africa	...	21	...	20	...	...	...

1. Refers to lower and upper secondary education (ISCED levels 2 and 3).
2. All values shown are medians.

(y) Data are for 1999/2000.
(z) Data are for 2000/2001.

Table 13B

\multicolumn{3}{c	}{SECONDARY EDUCATION[1]}	\multicolumn{2}{c	}{}	\multicolumn{4}{c	}{TERTIARY EDUCATION}	
\multicolumn{3}{c	}{Trained teachers (%)}	\multicolumn{2}{c	}{Pupil/teacher ratio}	\multicolumn{4}{c	}{Total teachers}	
\multicolumn{3}{c	}{2001}	1998	2001	\multicolumn{2}{c	}{1998}	\multicolumn{2}{c	}{2001}	
Total	Male	Female			Total (000)	% F	Total (000)	% F	Country or territory
...	...	...	...	13**	0.1	10	0.1 y	...	Comoros
...	...	...	...	26**,z	...	...	0.7 z	5 z	Congo
...	...	...	29**	29**,z	...	...	...	...	Côte d'Ivoire
...	...	...	...	...	3.8	6	...	...	Democratic Rep. of the Congo
...	...	...	...	23**,y	...	...	0.2 y	16 y	Equatorial Guinea
...	...	...	51	49	0.2	13	0.3 z	12 z	Eritrea
...	...	...	...	...	2.2	6	3.3	8	Ethiopia
...	...	...	28**	...	0.6	17	...	...	Gabon
89.0 z	87.9 z	94.5 z	24	26 z	0.1	15	...	...	Gambia
...	...	...	20	19**	2.3**	14**	3.5 z	12 z	Ghana
...	...	...	30**	...	...	...	...	...	Guinea
...	...	...	...	21**,y	...	...	0.03 y	19 y	Guinea-Bissau
...	...	...	26**	26**,z	...	...	...	...	Kenya
...	...	...	23**	23**	0.4	45**	0.4**	...	Lesotho
...	...	...	17	20 y	0.7	16	0.8**,z	16**,z	Liberia
...	...	...	17**	...	1.5	31	1.9	26	Madagascar
26.9**,z	26.1**,z	30.4**,z	56**	60**,y	0.5	25	...	...	Malawi
...	...	...	28*	...	1.0	...	...	...	Mali
...	...	...	...	19**,z	0.6**	26**	...	...	Mauritius
57.2	55.4	64.8	...	27	...	...	1.0**,y	23**,y	Mozambique
60.6	67.2	55.7	22**	24	0.6	...	0.9	31	Namibia
67.1	68.1	62.8	24	27	...	...	0.8 z	15**,z	Niger
...	...	...	...	...	...	...	...	...	Nigeria
...	...	...	...	...	0.4	10	1.3 z	15 z	Rwanda
...	...	...	...	...	.	.	0.0**,z	33**,z	Sao Tome and Principe
...	...	...	25**	27**	...	...	...	...	Senegal
...	...	...	15**	15**	.	.	.	.	Seychelles
...	...	...	...	27 z	...	...	1.2**	15**	Sierra Leone
...	...	...	...	...	...	...	...	...	Somalia
...	...	...	30**	30**	...	...	38.6	48	South Africa
...	...	...	18**	...	0.2	32	0.3	35**	Swaziland
...	...	...	35	31**,y	0.4	10	...	...	Togo
...	...	...	12**	...	2.2	18	4.9**	18**	Uganda
...	...	...	...	...	2.1	14	2.2 z	14 z	United Republic of Tanzania
...	...	...	23	23**,y	...	...	...	...	Zambia
...	...	...	...	25 z	...	...	...	...	Zimbabwe w
...	...	...	17	17	...	...	...	35	World[2]
...	...	...	...	12	...	49	...	48	Countries in transition
...	...	...	13	12	...	...	...	40	Developed countries
...	...	...	19	20	...	...	...	33	Developing countries
...	...	...	16	18	...	23	...	19	Arab States
...	...	...	13	13	...	41	...	43	Central and Eastern Europe
...	...	...	13	12	...	45	...	47	Central Asia
...	...	...	20	20	...	...	...	41	East Asia and the Pacific
80.6	78.8	82.2	16	16	...	...	...	...	Latin America and the Caribbean
...	...	...	12	12	...	...	...	37	North America and Western Europe
...	...	...	32	31	...	...	...	...	South and West Asia
...	...	...	24	24	...	...	...	15	Sub-Saharan Africa

Table 14
Private enrolment and education finance

| | | \multicolumn{6}{c|}{PRIVATE ENROLMENT AS % OF TOTAL ENROLMENT} | \multicolumn{8}{c|}{EDUCATION FINANCE} |
	Country or territory	\multicolumn{2}{c	}{Pre-primary education}	\multicolumn{2}{c	}{Primary education}	\multicolumn{2}{c	}{Secondary education}	\multicolumn{2}{c	}{Total public expenditure on education as % of GNP}	\multicolumn{2}{c	}{Total public expenditure on education as % of total government expenditure}	\multicolumn{2}{c	}{Public current expenditure on education as % of total public expenditure on education}	\multicolumn{2}{c	}{Public current expenditure on primary education per pupil (unit cost) in constant 2001 US$}
		1998	2001	1998	2001	1998	2001	1998	2001	1998	2001	1998	2001	1998	2001
	Arab States														
1	Algeria	.	.	.	.	...	...	...	...	...	...	...	...	...	...
2	Bahrain	100.0	99.3	18.8	21.1	13.2	14.9	...	3.1 z	...	11.4 z	...	97.1 z	...	...
3	Djibouti	100.0	100.0	8.5	11.0	13.8	15.3	3.4**	...	...	...	...	...	...	...
4	Egypt w	...	48.5 z	...	8.1**,z	...	5.2**,y	...	...	...	...	...	...	...	...
5	Iraq	.	.	...	...	...	...	...	...	...	...	...	...	...	...
6	Jordan w	99.6	96.9	29.3	29.4	16.5	16.2	6.2**	4.6	...	20.6 y	...	88.7**	211	243**
7	Kuwait	24.4	30.5	32.2	30.4	26.9**	27.6**	...	...	...	...	...	...	...	...
8	Lebanon	77.9	75.1	65.6	63.5	55.1	51.0	2.0	2.8	10.4	11.1 z	...	96.5	...	...
9	Libyan Arab Jamahiriya	.	15.4	.	2.5	...	2.8	...	...	...	...	...	...	...	...
10	Mauritania	...	...	1.9	3.3	...	8.8	4.0**	3.6**,y	16.6**	...	...	...	...	...
11	Morocco	100.0	100.0	4.2	4.9	4.8	5.0**,z	...	5.2	...	...	...	92.9	...	193
12	Oman	100.0	100.0	4.5	4.1	0.9	0.9	4.3	4.4**	...	...	93.1	89.3**,y	...	787
13	Palestinian A. T.	99.9	99.9	8.7	8.3	4.7	4.3	...	...	...	...	...	...	...	...
14	Qatar	100.0	97.8	37.3	41.2	26.2	30.4	...	...	...	...	...	93.9*	...	...
15	Saudi Arabia	50.4	48.8	6.0	6.7	5.2	6.3	8.2	...	...	...	...	...	...	...
16	Sudan	90.4**	90.4	2.4**	4.7	8.6**	12.6	...	...	...	...	...	...	...	...
17	Syrian Arab Republic	66.6	63.1	4.2	4.4	4.9	4.5	3.8**	4.2	12.2**	11.1 z	...	...	...	641 z
18	Tunisia w	88.4	86.5	0.7	0.8	8.2	4.0	7.9	7.2**,z	...	17.4**,z	...	85.5**,z	...	275**,z
19	United Arab Emirates	67.8	70.9	44.5	50.7	30.7	35.9	1.8	...	...	...	...	97.3	...	...
20	Yemen	...	32.4**	1.3	1.3**	1.2	1.3**,z	...	10.6**	...	32.8 z	...	...	...	...
	Central and Eastern Europe														
21	Albania o	.	2.2 z	.	2.2 z	...	...	...	...	...	...	...	...	...	...
22	Belarus	–	–	0.1	0.1	0.1	0.1	...	6.0 y	...	...	...	...	...	...
23	Bosnia and Herzegovina o	...	...	...	...	...	...	...	...	...	...	...	...	...	...
24	Bulgaria o	0.1	0.2	0.3	0.3	0.6	0.8	3.3	3.6	...	...	...	98.9**	209	283**
25	Croatia	5.4	8.0	0.1	0.2	0.7	0.9	4.3**	4.3**,y	10.4**	...	...	...	...	...
26	Czech Republic o	1.7	1.5	0.8	1.0	5.8	6.7	4.3	4.5	...	9.6	85.4	90.6	519	620
27	Estonia o	0.7	1.5	1.3	1.9	1.0	1.6	6.9	6.2	...	...	...	88.0**	554	753**
28	Hungary o	3.1	3.9	4.7	5.2	6.4	9.7	4.8	5.3	...	14.1 z	91.3**	90.4**	760**	1 003**
29	Latvia o	1.0	1.4	1.0	0.8	0.8	1.1	6.8	5.9	...	...	...	...	...	646**,z
30	Lithuania o	...	0.3	...	0.4	...	0.3	...	6.1	...	...	...	97.2**	...	...
31	Poland o	3.3	5.3	...	1.2	...	5.0 z	5.5	5.5	...	12.2 z	...	93.1**	...	1 205**,z
32	Republic of Moldova	8.1**	–	–	1.0	...	1.4	...	3.8 z	...	15.0 z	...	94.9 z	...	...
33	Romania o	...	0.9	...	0.2	...	0.6	3.6**	3.4	...	...	...	92.2**	...	...
34	Russian Federation w	...	2.3**	...	0.4	...	0.3	3.7**	3.2	...	11.5	...	...	...	...
35	Serbia and Montenegro	...	.	...	.	...	– z	...	5.1**,y	...	...	...	...	...	...
36	Slovakia	0.4	0.6	3.9	4.0	5.3	5.8	...	4.2	...	7.5	...	93.9**	...	425**
37	Slovenia o	1.0	1.0	0.1	0.1	0.8	2.3	...	...	...	...	...	...	...	...
38	TFYR Macedonia o	.	.	.	.	...	0.5	...	4.2**,y	...	...	...	...	...	...
39	Turkey o	...	6.3	...	1.7**	...	2.0**	2.9	3.7	...	...	...	94.4**	...	245**
40	Ukraine	0.0	0.4	0.3	0.4	...	0.3	4.5	4.4 z	15.7	15.0 z	97.1	89.3 z	...	...
	Central Asia														
41	Armenia	...	1.2	...	0.5	...	0.4	...	3.1	...	...	...	98.6	...	...
42	Azerbaijan	.	–	.	–	...	...	...	3.7	...	23.1	...	98.8	...	...
43	Georgia	0.1	0.1 z	0.5	1.8	0.7	1.4	2.2	2.5	11.3	13.1	...	...	...	...
44	Kazakhstan	10.1	11.9	0.5	0.6	...	0.9	...	...	...	...	...	...	...	...
45	Kyrgyzstan	1.0	0.9	0.2	0.3	0.2	0.3	...	3.2	...	18.6	...	98.7	...	...
46	Mongolia	3.7	3.0 z	0.5	2.3	0.1	1.6	...	6.6**,z	...	...	...	...	...	...
47	Tajikistan	.	.	.	.	.	.	2.2**	2.5	...	...	...	...	...	...
48	Turkmenistan	...	...	...	...	...	...	...	...	...	...	...	...	...	...
49	Uzbekistan	...	.	...	.	...	.	...	...	...	...	...	...	...	...
	East Asia and the Pacific														
50	Australia o	...	62.6	...	27.6	...	24.1	...	4.7	...	13.6	...	96.6**	...	2 934**
51	Brunei Darussalam	66.4	60.6	35.5	33.8	11.6	11.4	3.0	...	9.3**	9.1**,z	94.8	98.3 z	...	...

(y) Data are for 1999/2000.   (z) Data are for 2000/2001.

STATISTICAL ANNEX / 363

Table 14

EDUCATION FINANCE

	Public current expenditure on primary education per pupil (unit cost) in PPP US$		Public current expenditure on primary education as % of GNP		Public current expenditure on primary education per pupil as % of GNP per capita		Public current expenditure on primary education as % of public current expenditure on education		Primary education textbooks and other teaching material as % of public current expenditure on primary education		Primary teachers' salaries as % of public current expenditure on primary education		Teachers' salaries as % of public current expenditure on education		Salaries of all personnel of primary education as % of public current expenditure on primary education		Salaries of all personnel in education as % of public current expenditure on education		
	1998	2001	1998	2001	1998	2001	1998	2001	1998	2001	1998	2001	1998	2001	1998	2001	1998	2001	
	...	...	...	...	...	...	...	...	...	...	...	...	...	...	...	...	...	...	1
	...	...	...	...	...	...	...	...	...	4.0**	...	96.0**	...	...	...	96.0**	...	...	2
	...	...	...	...	...	...	...	...	...	...	...	...	...	...	...	...	...	...	3
	...	...	...	...	...	...	...	...	...	...	...	...	...	...	...	...	...	...	4
	...	...	...	...	...	...	...	...	...	...	...	...	...	...	...	...	...	...	5
	446	536**	1.9	2.1**	13.0	14.2	...	51.5**	...	...	...	89.3	...	89.3	...	95.6	...	...	6
	...	...	...	...	...	...	...	...	...	...	...	...	...	...	...	...	...	...	7
	...	...	...	0.9**,y	...	7.6 y	...	49.6**,y	...	...	...	...	...	...	...	...	...	98.3	8
	...	...	...	...	...	...	...	12.1**,y	...	...	...	...	...	...	...	...	...	...	9
	...	...	...	...	...	4.7 y	...	...	...	...	...	...	...	...	...	...	...	...	10
	...	593	...	2.3	...	17.2	...	48.6	...	...	...	...	...	...	...	...	...	92.6	11
	1 270	...	1.5	1.3	12.0	10.9	38.8	35.9**,y	...	1.4	...	83.8	...	...	...	98.6	...	...	12
	...	...	...	...	...	...	...	...	...	...	...	...	...	...	...	...	...	...	13
	...	...	...	...	...	...	...	...	...	...	...	...	...	...	...	...	...	...	14
	...	...	...	...	...	...	...	...	...	...	...	...	...	...	...	...	...	...	15
	...	...	...	...	...	...	...	...	...	...	...	...	...	...	...	...	...	...	16
	...	1 600 z	...	2.0 z	...	11.7 z	...	56.9 z	...	1.9 z	...	...	...	...	...	91.8 z	...	90.0 z	17
	...	955**,z	...	2.3**,z	...	16.3 z	...	38.3**,z	...	...	...	...	...	...	...	97.8 z	...	...	18
	...	...	...	...	...	...	...	...	...	...	...	...	...	...	...	91.3	...	89.9	19
	...	...	...	...	...	...	...	...	...	...	...	...	...	...	...	...	...	...	20
	...	...	...	...	...	...	...	...	...	...	...	...	...	...	...	...	...	...	21
	...	...	...	...	...	...	...	...	...	...	...	...	...	...	...	...	...	...	22
	...	...	...	...	...	...	...	...	...	...	...	...	...	...	...	...	...	...	23
	802	1 153**	0.7	0.7**	14.6	17.1	...	20.8**	...	...	...	53.3	...	45.2	...	76.2	...	69.4	24
	...	...	...	...	...	...	...	...	...	...	...	...	...	...	...	...	...	...	25
	1 281	1 644	0.7	0.7	10.3	11.4	17.9	16.3	...	...	...	49.9	...	43.2	...	69.9	...	61.9	26
	1 260	1 891**	1.4	1.6**	15.9	19.5	...	28.6**	...	...	...	...	...	...	...	71.6	...	66.4	27
	1 748**	2 427**	0.9**	1.0**	17.5	19.9	20.1**	19.9**	...	...	...	...	...	...	...	76.3	...	71.0	28
	...	1 544**,z	...	1.1**,z	...	21.6 z	...	20.8**,z	...	...	...	...	...	...	...	82.1	...	85.3	29
	...	...	...	...	...	...	...	...	...	...	...	...	...	...	...	...	...	...	30
	...	2 544**,z	...	2.2**,z	...	26.5 z	...	46.7**,z	...	...	...	...	...	...	...	76.5	...	75.6	31
	...	...	...	...	...	...	...	...	...	11.9 z	...	...	...	...	...	56.9 z	...	62.0 z	32
	...	...	...	...	...	...	...	...	...	...	...	...	...	...	...	84.7	...	72.2	33
	...	...	...	...	...	...	...	...	...	...	...	...	...	...	...	...	...	...	34
	...	...	...	...	...	...	...	...	...	...	...	...	...	...	...	78.4 z	...	71.8 z	35
	...	1 342**	...	0.6**	...	11.4	...	15.3**	...	...	...	59.3	...	53.7	...	74.9	...	72.6	36
	...	...	...	...	...	...	...	...	...	...	...	...	...	...	...	...	...	...	37
	...	...	...	...	...	...	...	...	...	...	...	...	...	...	...	...	...	...	38
	...	646**	...	1.4**	...	11.8	...	40.0**	...	...	...	94.7	...	69.3	...	93.0 z	...	89.6	39
	...	...	...	...	...	...	...	...	...	...	...	...	...	...	...	...	...	...	40
	...	...	...	...	...	...	...	...	...	...	...	...	...	...	...	...	...	...	41
	...	...	...	...	...	...	...	...	...	...	...	...	...	...	...	...	...	64.4	42
	...	...	...	...	...	...	...	...	...	...	...	...	...	...	...	...	...	...	43
	...	...	...	...	...	...	...	...	...	...	...	...	...	...	...	...	...	...	44
	...	...	...	...	...	...	...	...	...	...	...	56.4	...	35.0	...	72.3	...	51.5	45
	...	...	...	...	...	...	0.2	...	56.1	...	39.8	...	56.1	...	39.8	...	...	...	46
	...	...	...	...	...	...	...	...	...	...	...	...	...	...	...	...	...	...	47
	...	...	...	...	...	...	...	...	...	...	...	...	...	...	...	...	...	...	48
	...	...	...	...	...	...	...	...	...	...	...	...	...	...	...	...	...	...	49
	...	3 913**	...	1.6**	...	15.8	...	34.2**	...	...	...	56.6	...	...	...	70.6	...	69.4 z	50
	...	...	...	...	...	...	...	...	...	...	...	...	...	...	...	...	...	...	51

Table 14 (continued)

		\multicolumn{6}{c}{PRIVATE ENROLMENT AS % OF TOTAL ENROLMENT}	\multicolumn{8}{c}{EDUCATION FINANCE}
		\multicolumn{2}{c}{Pre-primary education}	\multicolumn{2}{c}{Primary education}	\multicolumn{2}{c}{Secondary education}	\multicolumn{2}{c}{Total public expenditure on education as % of GNP}	\multicolumn{2}{c}{Total public expenditure on education as % of total government expenditure}	\multicolumn{2}{c}{Public current expenditure on education as % of total public expenditure on education}	\multicolumn{2}{c}{Public current expenditure on primary education per pupil (unit cost) in constant 2001 US$}
	Country or territory	1998	2001	1998	2001	1998	2001	1998	2001	1998	2001	1998	2001	1998	2001
52	Cambodia	22.5**	27.4	1.6	0.9	0.6**	0.4	1.4	2.1	10.2	15.3	63.8	95.3	6	18
53	China^w	...	...	...	...	...	...	2.2	...	13.0	...	93.2**	...	48**	...
54	Cook Islands	25.9	24.6^y	15.1	15.0^y	11.4	12.6^y	0.4	0.4^y	13.1**	...	98.6	98.4^y	...	...
55	DPR Korea	...	...	...	...	...	...	...	...	...	...	...	...	...	...
56	Fiji	...	...	...	...	...	...	5.6**	5.6**	16.2**	19.4**	...	...	...	...
57	Indonesia^w	...	98.8	...	16.0	...	42.7	...	1.4	...	9.8	...	87.8**	...	23**
58	Japan^o	65.3	65.1	0.9	0.9	...	18.6	3.4	3.6	...	10.5	...	88.8**	...	6 415**
59	Kiribati	...	...	...	...	...	...	...	...	...	...	...	...	...	...
60	Lao PDR	18.4	19.5	1.9	2.0	0.7	0.8	2.5	3.4	...	10.6	...	...	...	...
61	Macao, China	93.8	92.0	94.7**	94.2**	93.6**	92.8**	3.5	3.0	10.8	16.0	...	...	...	1 133**,z
62	Malaysia^w	53.0	41.1	0.9	3.8	...	6.6	...	8.5	...	20.0	...	63.5	351**	424
63	Marshall Islands	...	18.3	...	24.1	...	34.4	14.3	8.9	...	...	...	97.2	...	...
64	Micronesia	...	...	...	...	...	...	5.1**	6.7**	...	...	...	...	...	...
65	Myanmar	89.9	89.9**,y	.	.	...	...	0.6	1.3^z	8.0	18.1*,z	63.8	66.5^z	...	...
66	Nauru	...	...	...	...	...	...	...	...	7.0**	6.9**	...	95.3**,z	...	...
67	New Zealand^o	...	47.1	...	2.0	...	11.3	...	6.9	...	...	...	99.8**	...	2 569**
68	Niue	.	.	...	...	...	...	...	...	...	10.1	...	97.3	...	...
69	Palau	23.9	19.5^y	18.1	18.4^y	27.2	29.1^y	8.6**	9.9**	...	20.0**,y	...	...	...	...
70	Papua New Guinea	...	0.8**	...	1.4**	...	2.0**	2.1**	2.4**,z	17.5**	17.5**,z	...	...	...	...
71	Philippines^w	...	46.0	...	7.1	...	21.5	4.0	3.1	...	14.0	90.4	92.3**	117	99
72	Republic of Korea^o	...	77.5	...	1.4	...	38.4	4.1	3.6	...	13.1	...	...	...	1 410**,z
73	Samoa	100.0	100.0	15.4	16.6	...	31.7	4.5	4.5**	13.3	14.6**	98.9	...	...	141^z
74	Singapore	...	...	...	...	...	...	...	3.5^z	...	23.6**,z	...	72.9^z	...	...
75	Solomon Islands	...	...	...	...	...	...	3.3	3.5**,z	15.4**	15.4**,y	...	...	...	...
76	Thailand^w	18.9	20.2	12.9	13.6	...	6.4	4.9	5.1	...	28.3	77.8	93.1**	190	291**
77	Timor-Leste	...	...	...	...	...	...	...	...	...	...	...	...	...	...
78	Tokelau	...	...	...	...	...	...	...	...	...	...	...	...	...	...
79	Tonga	...	100.0^y	...	9.2	...	72.8^y	5.3**	5.0	15.0**	13.1	...	77.5	...	170
80	Tuvalu	...	...	...	...	...	...	...	...	...	16.8**,y	...	...	...	...
81	Vanuatu	...	100.0	...	3.8	...	13.5	8.9	10.7	17.4	26.7	...	59.3	...	165
82	Viet Nam	48.6	59.9	0.3	0.3	10.6	10.9	...	...	...	...	...	...	...	...
	Latin America and the Caribbean														
83	Anguilla	100.0	100.0	5.0	7.5	...	...	...	...	14.4	...	...	...	...	...
84	Antigua and Barbuda	...	100.0^y	...	38.2^y	...	20.1^y	...	3.5^y	...	...	...	100.0^y	...	...
85	Argentina^w	28.8	28.2	20.1	20.0	25.3	25.0	4.1	4.7**,z	...	13.7**,z	98.6	97.8**,z	854	916**,z
86	Aruba	83.3	80.8	82.9	80.7	90.8	91.5	...	...	17.5	17.2	73.9	89.4^y	...	...
87	Bahamas	...	79.5	...	24.6	...	27.9	...	...	...	...	...	...	...	...
88	Barbados	18.2	18.4	8.8	11.3	7.5**	5.9	5.3	6.7	15.4	16.7	91.6	90.1	1 114	1 737**
89	Belize	100.0	100.0^z	87.2**	87.1^z	54.1	74.1^z	6.2**	6.8^z	17.1**	20.9^z	...	80.9^z	...	416^z
90	Bermuda	...	.	...	35.2	...	41.2	...	...	17.0	...	73.5	...	...	...
91	Bolivia	6.7	24.2	6.8	20.7	13.6	29.0	5.6	6.2	25.0	18.4	86.5	89.8	107**	112
92	Brazil^w	...	28.7	...	8.1	...	11.3	...	4.2	...	10.4^z	...	94.0**	...	290**
93	British Virgin Islands	100.0	100.0	13.3	16.3	...	2.8	...	...	...	9.0	...	79.8	...	...
94	Cayman Islands	87.8	91.7	36.4	38.3	25.1	25.3	...	...	...	...	...	...	...	...
95	Chile^w	45.3	45.7^z	43.6	45.5^z	45.9	49.7^z	3.8	4.0^z	16.1	17.5^z	...	88.8**,z	514	539**,z
96	Colombia	45.1	40.5	19.6	18.8	33.4	28.1	4.0	4.6	18.1*	18.0*	...	...	...	...
97	Costa Rica	...	14.7	...	6.8	...	12.2	...	5.0	...	21.1	...	97.6	...	580
98	Cuba	.	.	.	.	.	.	6.8	8.7^z	12.2	16.8	...	92.6^z	...	...
99	Dominica	100.0	100.0	24.3	27.2	26.7	33.9	7.6	5.6**,y	...	...	65.4*	...	644*	...
100	Dominican Republic	44.9	38.3	11.6**	14.4	32.2**	23.0	2.6**	2.5	15.7**	13.2	...	95.3	...	154**
101	Ecuador	39.4	46.2	21.2	27.4	24.3	32.3	2.8	1.1**	14.2	8.0**	...	...	...	...
102	El Salvador	22.3	20.6	11.0	10.8	24.9	21.4	2.4	2.5**	16.4	19.4**	96.8	...	39**	198**,z
103	Grenada	...	52.2	...	9.2	...	9.6	...	4.5**,y	...	...	...	...	...	...
104	Guatemala	...	19.3	...	12.8	...	56.0	1.4	1.7^z	...	11.4^z	...	88.5^y	...	136
105	Guyana	1.2	0.1^y	1.0	0.9^y	0.8	...	5.1**	4.5**,y	8.6**	8.6**,y	...	...	...	...
106	Haiti	...	...	...	...	...	...	...	1.1**,z	...	10.9**,z	...	...	...	...
107	Honduras	...	...	...	...	...	...	4.2**	...	...	...	...	...	...	...
108	Jamaica^w	87.7	88.8	...	4.8	...	2.9	6.6	6.8	...	12.3	...	91.1	...	423
109	Mexico^o	9.0	10.2	7.0	7.9	15.1	16.0	4.3	5.3	...	24.3	94.4**	97.0**	539**	834**

(y) Data are for 1999/2000.   (z) Data are for 2000/2001.

Table 14

EDUCATION FINANCE

Public current expenditure on primary education per pupil (unit cost) in PPP US$		Public current expenditure on primary education as % of GNP		Public current expenditure on primary education per pupil as % of GNP per capita		Public current expenditure on primary education as % of public current expenditure on education		Primary education textbooks and other teaching material as % of public current expenditure on primary education		Primary teachers' salaries as % of public current expenditure on primary education		Teachers' salaries as % of public current expenditure on education		Salaries of all personnel of primary education as % of public current expenditure on primary education		Salaries of all personnel in education as % of public current expenditure on education		
1998	2001	1998	2001	1998	2001	1998	2001	1998	2001	1998	2001	1998	2001	1998	2001	1998	2001	
37	117	0.5	1.5	2.7	7.2	52.1	73.1	...	...	...	...	...	...	...	...	...	...	52
200 **	...	0.7 **	...	6.6	...	34.3 **	...	...	...	...	...	...	...	...	...	...	...	53
...	...	0.2	0.2 y	...	...	53.0	51.1 y	...	...	...	...	...	...	...	...	...	...	54
...	...	...	...	...	...	...	...	...	...	...	...	...	...	...	...	...	...	55
...	...	...	...	...	...	...	...	...	...	...	...	...	...	...	...	...	...	56
...	95 **	...	0.5 **	...	3.6	...	39.4 **	...	...	...	78.3	...	...	...	80.8	...	89.5	57
...	4 946 **	...	1.1 **	...	19.4	...	35.3 **	...	...	...	...	...	...	...	88.1	...	78.6	58
...	...	...	...	...	...	...	...	...	...	...	...	...	...	...	...	...	...	59
...	...	...	...	...	...	...	...	...	...	...	...	...	...	...	...	...	...	60
...	1 792 **,z	...	0.9 **,z	...	8.7 z	...	...	...	...	...	...	...	...	...	89.5 z	...	...	61
747 **	1 002	1.4 **	1.6	10.7	12.2	37.5 **	29.0	...	...	...	67.2	...	54.5	...	79.0	...	66.5	62
...	...	...	3.9	...	...	...	45.0	...	1.7	...	68.6	...	59.6	...	78.9	...	76.9	63
...	...	...	...	...	...	...	...	...	...	...	...	...	...	...	...	...	...	64
...	...	0.2	0.5 z	2.3	4.8 z	59.6	57.6 z	...	...	...	...	...	...	...	...	...	...	65
...	...	...	...	...	...	...	45.6 **,z	...	...	...	...	...	...	...	...	...	...	66
...	3 757 **	...	1.9 **	...	20.4	...	27.7 **	...	...	...	...	...	...	...	...	...	...	67
...	...	...	...	...	...	31.9	29.1	...	...	...	...	...	...	...	...	...	...	68
...	...	...	...	...	...	...	...	...	...	...	...	...	...	...	...	...	...	69
...	...	...	...	...	...	...	...	...	...	...	...	...	...	...	...	...	...	70
468	417	2.2	1.7	12.6	10.1	59.8	59.5 **	...	...	...	87.5	...	84.8	...	87.5	...	84.8	71
...	2 289 **,z	...	1.3 **,z	...	15.6 z	...	43.5 **,z	...	...	...	77.6	...	68.3	...	86.1	...	80.8	72
...	625 z	...	1.8 z	...	11.3 z	...	42.9 z	...	...	...	...	...	...	...	...	...	...	73
...	...	...	...	...	...	...	...	...	...	...	...	...	...	...	...	...	...	74
...	...	...	...	...	...	...	...	...	...	...	...	...	...	...	...	...	...	75
616	995 **	1.2	1.6 **	11.8	15.8	32.0	33.6 **	...	...	...	...	...	...	...	...	...	...	76
...	...	...	...	...	...	...	...	...	...	...	...	...	...	...	...	...	...	77
...	...	...	...	...	...	...	...	...	...	...	...	...	...	...	...	...	...	78
...	...	...	2.3	...	13.7	...	59.1	...	...	...	...	...	...	...	...	...	...	79
...	...	...	...	...	...	...	...	...	...	...	...	...	...	...	...	...	...	80
...	497	...	2.8	...	15.4	...	43.9	...	1.2	...	98.8	...	94.5	...	98.8	...	97.9	81
...	...	...	...	...	...	...	...	...	...	...	...	...	...	...	...	...	...	82
...	...	...	...	...	...	...	...	...	...	...	...	...	...	...	...	...	...	83
...	...	...	...	...	...	...	...	...	6.8 y	...	66.4 y	...	56.1 y	...	84.9 y	...	74.2 y	84
1 261	1 418 **,z	1.4	1.6 **,z	10.8	12.2 z	35.2	35.1 **,z	...	...	...	49.2 **,z	...	51.1 **,z	...	56.8 z	...	60.3 **,z	85
...	...	...	...	...	...	31.2	30.0 y	...	...	...	...	...	...	...	96.4	...	92.2	86
...	...	...	...	...	...	...	...	...	...	...	...	...	...	...	...	...	...	87
1 576	2 629 **	1.3	1.5 **	12.0	17.3	26.5	25.1 **	0.1 **	1.4 **,z	93.9 **	...	98.1	...	93.9 **	73.5 **	98.1	77.0	88
...	705 z	...	2.6 z	...	14.0 z	...	48.2 z	...	0.8 z	...	97.5 *,z	...	75.5 *,z	...	97.5 *,z	...	75.5 *,z	89
...	...	...	...	...	...	43.0	...	...	...	...	...	...	...	...	...	...	...	90
245 **	276	2.0 **	2.2	11.3	12.2	40.8 **	39.0	...	...	...	86.8	...	85.7	...	...	...	98.4	91
...	731 **	...	1.2 **	...	10.4	...	29.6 **	...	...	...	77.4	...	...	...	77.4	...	79.7	92
...	...	...	...	...	...	...	29.5	...	...	...	...	...	...	...	96.1	...	...	93
...	...	...	...	...	...	...	...	...	...	...	...	...	...	...	...	...	...	94
1 016	1 145 **,z	1.5	1.6 **,z	12.5	13.2 z	...	43.5 **,z	...	...	...	...	...	...	...	...	...	...	95
...	...	...	...	...	...	...	...	...	...	...	91.0 *	...	91.0	...	...	...	...	96
...	1 319	2.9	2.1	...	14.9	...	42.5	...	...	...	...	...	96.4	...	...	...	...	97
...	...	...	2.9 *,z	...	32.0 z	...	32.2	...	1.2	...	...	...	...	...	67.1	...	57.7	98
865 *	...	3.0 *	...	19.1	...	61.0 *	...	...	...	...	...	...	...	...	...	...	...	99
...	435 **	...	1.1 **	...	6.5	...	45.5 **	...	1.7	...	...	...	...	...	79.7	...	70.6	100
...	...	...	...	...	...	...	...	...	...	...	...	...	...	...	...	...	82.4 z	101
90 **	467 **,z	0.3 **	1.4 **,z	1.9	9.0 z	12.7 **	54.2 **,z	...	...	...	...	...	...	...	93.7 z	...	89.6 z	102
...	...	...	...	...	...	...	...	...	...	...	...	...	...	...	...	...	...	103
...	342	...	1.3	...	7.7	...	...	...	1.8	...	89.1	...	89.6	...	89.1	...	89.6	104
...	...	...	...	...	...	...	...	...	...	...	...	...	...	...	...	...	...	105
...	...	...	...	...	...	...	...	...	...	...	...	...	...	...	...	...	...	106
...	...	...	...	...	...	...	...	...	...	...	...	...	...	...	...	...	...	107
...	523	...	1.9	...	15.1	...	31.0	...	...	...	73.3	...	63.1	...	81.5	...	79.5	108
694 **	1 131 **	1.5 **	2.0 **	9.5	13.7	35.6 **	39.8 **	...	...	...	86.4	...	78.2	...	95.6	...	91.3	109

STATISTICAL ANNEX / 365

Table 14 (continued)

	Country or territory	\multicolumn{6}{c	}{PRIVATE ENROLMENT AS % OF TOTAL ENROLMENT}	\multicolumn{8}{c	}{EDUCATION FINANCE}
		\multicolumn{2}{c	}{Pre-primary education}	\multicolumn{2}{c	}{Primary education}	\multicolumn{2}{c	}{Secondary education}	\multicolumn{2}{c	}{Total public expenditure on education as % of GNP}	\multicolumn{2}{c	}{Total public expenditure on education as % of total government expenditure}	\multicolumn{2}{c	}{Public current expenditure on education as % of total public expenditure on education}	\multicolumn{2}{c	}{Public current expenditure on primary education per pupil (unit cost) in constant 2001 US$}
		1998	2001	1998	2001	1998	2001	1998	2001	1998	2001	1998	2001	1998	2001
110	Montserrat	.	14.0 y	38.0	38.6	...	...	...	...	6.8**	3.3	58.9	47.3 y	...	...
111	Netherlands Antilles	75.1	75.4	73.9	73.1	78.9	78.8	...	...	14.1**	12.8	...	93.4	...	...
112	Nicaragua	...	16.8	...	16.0	...	...	5.7	...	8.2	13.0**	...	...	...	...
113	Panama	...	19.3	...	10.0	...	14.9	5.3**	4.5	...	7.3	96.1**	96.5	532**	420
114	Paraguay w	31.6	28.5	15.3**	14.9**	29.3	26.3	4.5	4.8**	...	9.7**	...	95.4**	...	154**
115	Peru w	...	15.5	...	13.5	...	17.2**	3.3	3.5 y	...	21.1 y	86.2	87.9 y	134	129 y
116	Saint Kitts and Nevis	...	64.4	...	13.4**	...	3.5**	6.0	8.5	13.8	19.0	...	53.2	...	624**
117	Saint Lucia	100.0	100.0	2.3**	2.8	...	3.6 y	8.3	7.7**,z	20.7	20.7**,z	81.4	78.5 y	...	650 y
118	St Vincent/Grenad.	...	.	...	5.0	...	31.6**	9.3**	10.0 z	12.2**	13.4**,z	...	70.7 z	...	600 z
119	Suriname	...	45.8	...	47.8	...	21.4	...	...	...	...	...	...	...	...
120	Trinidad and Tobago	100.0**	100.0**	5.0	5.7**	7.6**	17.5**	3.4	4.3	...	13.4	90.2	90.6	515	897**
121	Turks and Caicos Islands	47.5	58.9	18.0	17.9	8.6	10.9	...	...	13.6	16.0	91.1 z	64.1 z	...	...
122	Uruguay w	22.6	18.1	14.7	12.7	...	11.9	2.3	2.4	...	10.0	...	90.3**	...	377**
123	Venezuela	19.9	18.4	15.0	14.4	30.0	25.8	...	...	...	...	...	...	...	...
	North America and Western Europe														
124	Andorra	...	...	...	...	...	...	...	...	...	...	...	...	...	...
125	Austria o	24.8	25.9	4.3	4.3	8.5	8.7	6.4	5.9	...	11.2	93.0**	96.7**	5 145**	5 363**
126	Belgium o	55.6	53.7	55.1	54.3	...	57.4	...	5.7 y	...	11.6 y	...	...	...	4 027**
127	Canada o	5.4	7.8 z	4.5	6.5 z	5.9	6.4 z	5.7	5.3	...	12.7	98.6**	98.1**	...	...
128	Cyprus o	54.3	43.3	4.0	5.2	10.0	11.1	...	5.9	...	...	...	90.6**	...	2 367**
129	Denmark o	...	2.7 y	10.8	11.0	11.8	11.1	8.4	8.5	...	15.4	95.2**	93.2**	7 174**	6 508**
130	Finland o	9.9	7.1	1.1	1.2	5.9	8.0	...	6.4	...	12.7	...	93.1**	...	3 780**
131	France o	12.6	12.6	14.6	14.6	25.0	25.1	5.8	5.7	...	11.4 z	87.6	91.6**	3 108	3 624**
132	Germany o	54.3	59.0	2.1	2.6	6.5	7.0	4.7	4.6	...	9.5	91.9**	92.7**	3 488**	3 480**
133	Greece o	3.2	3.5	6.9	7.1	5.0	5.8 z	3.3	3.9	...	7.0 y	80.2**	81.5**	1 457**	1 698**
134	Iceland o	4.9	7.8	1.5	1.3	3.8	4.7	7.3	6.7	...	...	87.5**	88.3**	...	4 868**
135	Ireland o	45.5	49.6	0.9	1.1	0.4	0.8	5.0	5.1 z	...	13.5 z	93.3**	89.1**,z	2 363**	2 942**,z
136	Israel o	7.0	4.6	...	–	...	...	7.8	7.6 z	...	...	91.5**	93.9**,z	3 334**	3 539**,z
137	Italy o	30.0	27.5	7.0	6.7	5.9	5.2	4.8	5.0	...	10.3	95.3**	94.4**	4 020**	4 410**
138	Luxembourg o	5.4	5.8	7.0	6.7	...	17.9	...	4.5	...	9.8	...	83.7**	...	7 921**
139	Malta o	37.3	38.3	35.5	37.1	25.2	27.9	4.9	4.9	...	...	90.3	...	892	...
140	Monaco	26.0	25.5 z	31.0	29.9 z	23.4	24.7 z	...	...	...	...	...	93.5 z	...	...
141	Netherlands o	68.8	69.3**	68.4	68.4**	84.7	83.2	4.9	5.0	...	10.7	95.7**	96.7**	3 240**	3 808**
142	Norway o	40.4	39.5	1.5	1.7	6.7	6.8	7.7	7.2	...	16.2 z	89.6	91.8**	9 450**	8 901**,z
143	Portugal o	52.3	51.2**	9.4	10.5	11.8	14.2	...	6.1	...	12.7	...	94.6**	...	2 498**
144	San Marino	...	...	...	...	...	...	...	...	...	...	...	...	...	...
145	Spain o	32.3	34.4	33.5	33.6	...	29.4	4.6	4.5	...	11.3	91.1**	92.0**	2 279**	2 611**
146	Sweden o	9.9	13.4	3.0	4.6	1.8	3.9	8.1	7.8	...	12.8	...	100.0**	...	5 579**
147	Switzerland o	5.7	7.4	3.3	3.6	7.9	7.2	5.1	5.1	...	15.1 z	90.2**	85.6**	6 912**	7 304**
148	United Kingdom o	6.1	6.2	4.6	4.9	52.3	52.4 z	4.6	4.5	...	11.4	...	92.3**	...	3 304**
149	United States o	34.2	44.6	11.6	10.3	9.7	8.8	5.0	5.6	...	17.1	...	...	...	7 386**
	South and West Asia														
150	Afghanistan	...	...	...	...	...	...	...	...	...	...	...	...	...	...
151	Bangladesh	...	...	36.3**	38.7	95.2	95.9	2.3	2.2	15.7	15.8	63.7	63.7	13**	15
152	Bhutan	100.0	100.0*	1.5	1.4	...	0.3**	...	5.9 z	...	12.9 z	...	67.6 z	...	...
153	India w	...	3.7**	...	15.5	...	42.0**	3.2	4.1 z	12.6	12.7 z	...	99.5**,z	...	62**,z
154	Iran, Islamic Republic of	...	8.2	...	3.8	...	5.2	4.6	5.0	18.7	21.7	90.9	91.8	...	620
155	Maldives	27.3	40.1	...	2.0	...	12.9	4.2**	...	11.2**	...	76.4**	...	...	...
156	Nepal	...	83.9 z	...	7.0	...	15.9 z	2.8**	3.3	12.5**	13.9	73.6**	74.9	15**	19
157	Pakistan	...	...	...	...	...	...	1.9**	1.8**,z	8.5**	7.8**,z	...	...	...	...
158	Sri Lanka w	...	...	...	1.9	...	...	3.1	1.3	...	...	...	75.4	...	...
	Sub-Saharan Africa														
159	Angola	...	...	5.2	5.2**,y	...	...	3.1	3.4**	...	...	88.7	93.7**	...	...
160	Benin	20.4	31.4 z	7.2	7.3	18.3	15.8**	2.5	3.3**	...	...	...	93.8**,y	...	34
161	Botswana	...	...	4.3	4.7	5.7	4.2	...	2.3 z	...	25.6 z	...	...	...	144 z
162	Burkina Faso	33.5	34.0**,y	10.8	12.0**	33.1	34.4**	...	...	...	...	...	...	...	...
163	Burundi	49.0	51.3	0.8**	1.3	...	13.3**,z	4.0**	3.7**	...	20.7**	...	94.9**	...	12**

(y) Data are for 1999/2000. (z) Data are for 2000/2001.

STATISTICAL ANNEX / 367

Table 14

EDUCATION FINANCE

Public current expenditure on primary education per pupil (unit cost) in PPP US$ 1998	2001	Public current expenditure on primary education as % of GNP 1998	2001	Public current expenditure on primary education per pupil as % of GNP per capita 1998	2001	Public current expenditure on primary education as % of public current expenditure on education 1998	2001	Primary education textbooks and other teaching material as % of public current expenditure on primary education 1998	2001	Primary teachers' salaries as % of public current expenditure on primary education 1998	2001	Teachers' salaries as % of public current expenditure on education 1998	2001	Salaries of all personnel of primary education as % of public current expenditure on primary education 1998	2001	Salaries of all personnel in education as % of public current expenditure on education 1998	2001	
...	...	...	...	...	...	...	...	...	4.0 z	...	92.4 z	...	58.1 z	...	92.5	...	65.7 z	110
...	...	...	...	...	...	...	...	...	...	...	...	...	...	...	...	...	...	111
...	...	...	...	...	...	...	...	...	...	...	...	...	...	...	...	...	...	112
821**	688	1.9**	1.5	14.1	11.0	38.3**	34.6	...	...	...	82.1	...	65.3	...	82.1	...	65.3	113
...	626**	...	2.2**	...	12.6	...	47.9**	...	...	...	...	...	...	...	...	...	...	114
282	308 y	1.1	1.2 y	6.7	7.2 y	40.4	40.4 y	...	...	...	...	...	...	...	...	...	...	115
...	926**	...	1.3	...	...	...	28.7	0.7	1.9	80.0	80.2 z	78.9	66.9	90.2	...	88.6	82.0	116
...	738 y	...	2.4 y	...	13.9 y	...	38.7 y	...	2.0 y	...	87.6 y	...	88.4 y	...	94.9 y	...	94.5 y	117
...	1 038 z	...	3.4 z	...	21.3 z	...	48.9 z	...	1.6 z	...	94.0 z	...	84.2 z	...	94.7 z	...	88.2 z	118
...	...	...	...	...	...	...	...	...	...	...	...	...	...	...	...	...	...	119
655	1 209**	1.3	1.6	9.5	13.5	41.3	41.9	...	...	...	77.5 y	...	78.7 y	...	93.1	...	84.3 y	120
...	...	...	...	...	...	...	29.7 y	...	3.5**,z	75.0**	59.4**,z	55.1	63.9 z	83.3**	79.5**	57.9	76.0	121
...	571**	...	0.7**	...	6.5	...	32.6**	...	...	...	...	...	...	...	47.6	...	56.2	122
...	...	...	...	...	...	...	...	...	...	...	...	...	...	...	...	...	...	123
...	...	...	...	...	...	...	...	...	...	...	...	...	...	...	...	...	...	124
5 542**	6 183**	1.1**	1.1**	23.8	23.4	19.3**	19.4**	...	...	...	68.0	...	59.1	...	74.9	...	72.6	125
...	4 603**	...	1.3**	...	17.6	...	...	...	...	...	73.7	...	70.4	...	86.2	...	82.4	126
...	...	...	...	...	...	...	...	...	...	...	...	...	51.4	...	...	...	73.7	127
...	4 179**	...	1.7**	...	18.4	...	31.3**	...	...	...	79.2	...	79.7	...	89.1	...	88.7	128
6 438**	6 261**	1.8**	1.7**	25.2	21.9	22.2**	21.4**	...	...	...	51.3	...	51.4	...	78.8	...	78.6	129
...	3 964**	...	1.3**	...	16.5	...	21.1**	...	...	...	57.6	...	49.1	...	67.9	...	65.0	130
3 163	3 929**	1.0	1.0**	15.2	16.4	19.9	20.2**	...	...	...	...	...	...	...	82.0	...	80.8	131
3 716**	3 934**	0.8**	0.6**	16.5	15.6	17.5**	14.9**	...	...	...	...	...	...	...	83.8	...	82.4	132
2 110**	2 677**	0.9**	0.9**	14.6	15.8	32.8**	29.4**	...	...	...	93.8	...	76.2	...	93.8	...	78.1	133
...	5 344**	...	2.1**	...	18.7	...	35.1**	...	...	...	...	...	...	...	68.7	...	73.4	134
2 513**	3 193**,z	1.5**	1.4**,z	12.5	12.4 z	32.8**	31.8**,z	...	...	...	...	...	...	...	77.5 z	...	65.8 z	135
3 699**	4 094**,z	2.4**	2.4**,z	19.6	19.7 z	34.1**	35.3	...	...	...	...	...	...	...	76.1	...	75.3	136
4 983**	5 791**	1.1**	1.1**	22.8	23.4	25.1**	24.0**	...	...	...	65.6	...	60.1	...	80.9	...	77.3	137
...	10 133**	...	1.6**	...	20.9	...	42.5**	...	...	...	70.2	...	70.0	...	87.9	...	86.4	138
1 226	...	1.0	...	10.5	...	21.7	...	...	...	...	57.7	...	60.0	...	89.2	...	85.9	139
...	...	...	...	...	...	...	16.2 z	...	1.3 z	...	...	...	...	...	98.7 z	...	97.6 z	140
3 577**	4 369**	1.2**	1.3**	14.8	15.9	25.2**	26.4**	...	...	...	...	...	...	...	71.8	...	72.4	141
7 130**	6 916**,z	2.5**	2.3**,z	26.6	23.8 z	35.7**	36.7**,z	...	...	...	...	...	...	...	83.1	...	78.4	142
...	4 138**	...	1.8**	...	23.4	...	31.3**	...	...	...	...	...	...	...	96.8	...	91.1	143
...	...	...	...	...	...	...	...	...	...	...	...	...	...	...	...	...	...	144
3 031**	3 718**	1.1**	1.1**	17.8	18.6	27.4**	27.4**	...	...	...	78.0	...	73.9	...	87.4	...	85.3	145
...	5 719**	...	2.1**	...	23.9	...	27.3**	...	...	...	51.4	...	...	...	69.3	...	63.9	146
5 484**	6 006**	1.5**	1.4**	19.8	19.2	31.6**	33.1**	...	...	...	71.1	...	67.1	...	84.0	...	83.0	147
...	3 296**	...	1.0**	...	13.6	...	25.0**	...	...	...	52.1	...	...	...	75.2	...	75.5	148
...	7 186**	...	1.8**	...	21.1	...	...	...	...	...	55.7	...	48.5	...	81.0	...	77.0	149
...	...	...	...	...	...	...	...	...	...	...	...	...	...	...	...	...	...	150
56**	66	0.6	0.5	4.3	4.3	38.9	38.2	...	...	...	...	...	...	...	...	...	...	151
...	...	...	...	...	...	...	...	...	...	...	...	...	...	...	...	...	...	152
...	382**,z	...	1.5**,z	...	13.8 z	...	37.6**,z	...	...	...	87.5 z	...	...	...	92.6 z	...	93.9 z	153
...	2 106	...	1.2	...	11.1	...	26.9	...	...	...	...	...	...	...	98.9 y	...	...	154
...	...	...	...	...	...	...	...	...	...	...	...	...	...	...	...	...	...	155
79**	106	1.1**	1.3	7.4	8.1	52.7**	53.0	...	...	...	...	...	...	...	...	...	...	156
...	...	...	...	...	...	...	...	...	...	...	...	...	...	...	...	...	...	157
...	...	...	...	...	...	...	...	...	...	...	...	...	...	...	26.6	...	71.4	158
...	...	...	...	...	...	...	...	...	...	...	...	...	...	...	...	...	...	159
...	91	...	1.7	...	9.2	...	...	...	...	...	...	...	...	...	...	...	...	160
...	379 z	...	1.0 z	...	5.6 z	...	...	...	...	...	...	...	...	...	...	...	...	161
...	...	...	...	...	...	...	...	...	...	...	...	...	...	...	...	...	...	162
...	80**	...	1.4**	...	11.0	...	40.2**	...	...	...	...	...	...	...	99.6	...	81.1	163

Table 14 (continued)

	Country or territory	\multicolumn{6}{c}{PRIVATE ENROLMENT AS % OF TOTAL ENROLMENT}	\multicolumn{8}{c}{EDUCATION FINANCE}
		\multicolumn{2}{c}{Pre-primary education}	\multicolumn{2}{c}{Primary education}	\multicolumn{2}{c}{Secondary education}	\multicolumn{2}{c}{Total public expenditure on education as % of GNP}	\multicolumn{2}{c}{Total public expenditure on education as % of total government expenditure}	\multicolumn{2}{c}{Public current expenditure on education as % of total public expenditure on education}	\multicolumn{2}{c}{Public current expenditure on primary education per pupil (unit cost) in constant 2001 US$}
		1998	2001	1998	2001	1998	2001	1998	2001	1998	2001	1998	2001	1998	2001
164	Cameroon	57.0	61.3	27.7	24.9*	31.6**	33.4**	2.7**	3.4z	10.9**	12.5z	...	...	40	...
165	Cape Verde	–	–	–	...	...	...	4.4**	...	...	...	...	...	...	...
166	Central African Republic	...	...	...	...	...	...	1.9**	...	...	...	...	...	...	...
167	Chad	...	...	25.0	27.8y	14.0	14.9y	1.8**	2.0**,y	...	...	...	...	...	...
168	Comoros	100.0	100.0y	12.4	10.1	46.2	34.1	3.8	...	...	...	...	...	...	...
169	Congo	84.7	75.1	10.0	19.0	...	12.6**	6.7	4.6	21.2	12.6	96.1	85.9	...	...
170	Côte d'Ivoire	46.3	45.7	11.6	10.9	...	...	4.0	4.9z	...	21.5z	88.3	94.0z	83	90y
171	Democratic Rep. of the Congo	...	93.2z	19.4	...	...	...	...	...	...	...	...	...	...	...
172	Equatorial Guinea	36.9	36.9**,y	32.8	32.8**,y	...	...	...	2.2	...	1.6	...	65.9	...	23**
173	Eritrea	96.7	93.3	11.1	8.3	6.5	5.7	4.8	2.7	...	...	69.5	...	...	...
174	Ethiopia	100.0	100.0	4.5	6.0	3.6	1.2	4.3**	4.8z	...	13.8z	...	63.8z	...	...
175	Gabon	...	71.9**	17.2	29.0	29.3	29.8**	3.8	4.6**,z	...	...	87.3	87.3**,y	187	...
176	Gambia	...	...	...	2.0z	...	20.8z	...	2.8**,z	...	14.2**,z	...	86.8**,z	...	45y
177	Ghana	26.2	34.8	13.3	18.3	7.1	10.5z	...	4.2**,y	...	...	...	...	...	...
178	Guinea	...	...	14.7	20.6	...	...	1.8**	1.9**,z	25.8**	25.6**,z	...	...	...	...
179	Guinea-Bissau	...	62.2y	...	19.4y	...	12.8y	...	2.3y	...	4.8y	...	...	...	...
180	Kenya	...	10.4y	...	5.6	...	4.2	6.7	6.3**,z	...	22.3**,z	95.5	...	...	...
181	Lesotho	100.0	100.0**	3.1	0.0	11.1	...	10.2	8.0z	25.5	18.4z	74.1	92.0**,z	81	76z
182	Liberia	38.6	18.0y	38.4	...	37.2	...	...	...	...	...	...	...	...	...
183	Madagascar	...	93.6**	21.9	21.7	...	...	1.9	2.5	10.2	...	79.6	68.4	...	13
184	Malawi	...	...	...	...	...	...	4.7	4.2**,y	24.6	...	81.8	...	...	...
185	Mali	...	...	...	...	...	...	3.0	2.9**,y	...	...	89.6	89.6**,y	31	29**,y
186	Mauritius	82.7	82.6	23.6	24.0	73.9	67.8	4.2	3.3	17.7	13.3z	91.1	...	343	348y
187	Mozambique	...	...	1.7**	1.8	10.1**	6.7	2.7	2.5**,y	12.3	12.3**,y	67.2	...	...	...
188	Namibia	100.0**	100.0	4.0	4.2	4.5	4.1	7.9	7.7y	...	21.0y	93.9	92.8y	332	319y
189	Niger	33.1	31.3	4.0	3.8	16.4	15.9	...	2.4	...	...	...	...	...	...
190	Nigeria	...	...	...	...	...	...	...	...	...	...	...	...	...	...
191	Rwanda	...	100.0**	–	–	49.0	44.1**	2.6**	2.8**,z	...	...	...	...	...	...
192	Sao Tome and Principe	–	–	–	–	...	...	...	...	...	...	...	...	...	...
193	Senegal	68.5	69.9	12.1	11.0	28.4**	24.6**	3.5*	3.2**,z	...	...	...	...	...	43**
194	Seychelles	3.9	4.3	3.7	3.9	2.8	3.3	6.3	7.8**,y	10.7	...	84.4	...	734	...
195	Sierra Leone	...	58.7z	...	...	...	1.9z	1.0	...	...	...	98.5	...	...	...
196	Somalia	...	...	...	...	...	...	...	...	...	...	...	...	...	...
197	South Africa	17.5*	10.8	0.9*	2.0	1.2*	2.4**	6.2	5.8y	22.2	18.1y	98.1	94.3y	352*	332y
198	Swaziland	...	...	...	...	...	...	6.0	5.4	...	...	100.0	100.0y	108	...
199	Togo	53.1	61.2	35.6	40.9	17.7	...	4.5	4.9z	24.4	23.2z	96.8	91.2z	24	22**,z
200	Uganda	...	100.0z	...	4.9y	57.6**	...	...	2.5**,y	...	...	...	...	...	...
201	United Republic of Tanzania	...	...	0.2	0.2y	...	...	2.2**	...	...	...	...	...	...	...
202	Zambia	100.0*	...	2.0**	...	2.6**	...	2.5	2.0y	17.6	...	99.4	...	...	...
203	Zimbabwew	...	...	...	87.3	...	71.3	...	11.1**,y	...	...	...	...	...	115**

		1998	2001	1998	2001	1998	2001	1998	2001	1998	2001	1998	2001	1998	2001
I	World[1]	39.9	40.1	7.1	7.2	...	11.7	4.3	4.5	...	13.6	...	...	...	...
II	Countries in transition	...	1.1	...	0.5	...	0.4	...	3.2	...	15.0	...	...	...	...
III	Developed countries	9.9	7.8	4.3	4.2	5.9	7.1	5.0	5.1	...	11.6	...	92.9	...	3 480
IV	Developing countries	54.3	55.5	11.6	10.9	...	14.9	4.0	4.2	...	14.8	...	...	...	...
V	Arab States	95.0	86.5	7.3	7.4	8.6	7.6	...	...	...	...	...	...	...	...
VI	Central and Eastern Europe	1.0	1.5	0.6	0.8	...	1.1	4.3	4.4	...	...	...	93.1	...	...
VII	Central Asia	...	1.2	...	0.6	...	0.9	...	3.2	...	...	...	...	...	...
VIII	East Asia and the Pacific	...	59.9	...	8.2	...	16.1	3.8	3.6	...	15.3	...	...	...	...
IX	Latin America and the Caribbean	45.2	43.1	15.2	14.7	...	22.2	4.5	4.6	...	13.4	...	90.2	...	...
X	North America and Western Europe	26.0	25.7	6.9	6.7	8.2	8.8	5.1	5.6	...	11.6	91.5	92.7	3 334	3 808
XI	South and West Asia	...	40.1	...	3.8	...	14.4	3.1	3.3	12.6	13.4	75.4	74.9	...	...
XII	Sub-Saharan Africa	...	61.8	11.0	9.2	16.4	13.3	3.8	3.4	...	...	...	...	...	...

1. All values shown are medians.   (y) Data are for 1999/2000.   (z) Data are for 2000/2001.

Table 14

EDUCATION FINANCE

Public current expenditure on primary education per pupil (unit cost) in PPP US$		Public current expenditure on primary education as % of GNP		Public current expenditure on primary education per pupil as % of GNP per capita		Public current expenditure on primary education as % of public current expenditure on education		Primary education textbooks and other teaching material as % of public current expenditure on primary education		Primary teachers' salaries as % of public current expenditure on primary education		Teachers' salaries as % of public current expenditure on education		Salaries of all personnel of primary education as % of public current expenditure on primary education		Salaries of all personnel in education as % of public current expenditure on education		
1998	2001	1998	2001	1998	2001	1998	2001	1998	2001	1998	2001	1998	2001	1998	2001	1998	2001	
112	...	1.2	...	8.0	...	...	...	...	...	...	...	...	...	...	...	...	...	164
...	...	...	...	...	...	...	...	...	...	...	...	...	...	...	...	...	...	165
...	...	...	...	...	...	...	...	...	...	...	...	...	...	...	...	...	...	166
...	...	...	...	...	...	...	...	...	...	...	...	...	...	...	...	...	...	167
...	...	...	...	...	...	...	...	...	...	...	...	...	...	...	...	...	...	168
...	...	...	...	...	...	...	...	...	...	...	...	...	...	...	...	...	...	169
183	212 y	1.6	1.8 y	12.7	14.5 y	45.3	43.4 y	...	...	...	83.2 y	...	61.0 y	...	...	...	...	170
...	...	...	...	...	...	...	...	...	...	...	...	...	...	...	...	...	...	171
...	...	...	0.4**	...	2.4	...	27.1**	...	...	...	...	...	...	...	...	...	...	172
...	...	1.6	1.2	21.6	14.3	49.1	45.8	...	...	...	...	...	...	...	96.8	...	75.5	173
...	...	...	...	...	...	...	...	...	...	...	...	...	...	...	...	...	...	174
300	...	1.3	...	5.8	...	38.6	...	...	...	...	...	...	...	...	...	...	...	175
...	312 y	...	2.1 y	...	17.2 y	...	80.3 y	...	...	...	...	...	...	...	...	...	...	176
...	...	...	...	...	...	...	...	...	...	...	...	...	...	...	98.2	...	96.8	177
...	...	...	...	...	...	...	...	...	...	...	...	...	...	...	...	...	...	178
...	...	...	...	...	...	...	...	...	...	...	...	...	...	...	...	...	...	179
...	...	...	...	...	...	...	...	...	...	...	...	...	...	...	...	...	...	180
460	494 z	3.2	3.5 z	15.3	15.0 z	42.8	46.7**,z	...	...	...	92.3 y	...	...	...	75.6 z	...	62.6 z	181
...	...	...	...	...	...	...	...	...	...	...	...	...	...	...	...	...	...	182
...	39	...	0.7	...	4.8	...	41.4	...	...	...	...	...	...	...	...	...	...	183
...	...	...	...	...	...	...	...	...	...	...	...	...	...	...	...	...	...	184
99	96**,y	1.3	1.3**,y	15.6	14.2 y	48.9	48.9**,y	...	...	...	...	...	...	...	...	...	...	185
854	926 y	1.2	1.2 y	11.0	10.7 y	31.9	34.1 y	...	...	...	...	...	...	...	...	...	...	186
...	...	...	...	...	...	...	...	...	...	...	...	...	...	...	...	...	...	187
1 300	1 324 y	4.4	4.2 y	20.6	20.4 y	59.4	59.4 y	...	8.6 y	...	91.4 y	...	79.2 y	...	91.4 y	...	79.2 y	188
...	...	...	...	...	...	...	...	...	...	...	...	...	...	...	...	...	...	189
...	...	...	...	...	...	...	...	...	...	...	...	...	...	...	...	...	...	190
...	...	...	...	...	...	...	...	...	...	...	...	...	...	...	...	...	...	191
...	...	...	...	...	...	...	...	...	...	...	...	...	...	...	...	...	...	192
...	137**	...	1.1**	...	9.2	...	38.4**	...	...	...	...	...	...	...	...	...	...	193
...	...	1.1	...	8.9	...	20.8	...	...	...	...	...	...	...	...	...	...	...	194
...	...	0.4	...	...	...	38.7	...	...	...	...	...	...	...	...	...	...	...	195
...	...	...	...	...	...	...	...	...	...	...	...	...	...	...	...	...	...	196
1 411 *	1 415 y	2.8	2.6 y	14.8	14.4 y	45.2	47.9 y	...	1.9 z	...	90.2 z	...	68.5 z	...	95.9 z	...	75.3 z	197
383	...	2.0	...	9.4	...	33.2	...	...	...	...	...	...	...	...	...	...	...	198
139	153**,z	1.9	2.0**,z	8.6	9.5 z	43.9	44.2**,z	...	...	...	84.3**,y	...	70.7 y	...	...	...	...	199
...	...	...	...	...	...	...	...	...	...	...	...	...	...	...	...	...	...	200
...	...	...	...	...	...	...	...	...	...	...	...	...	...	...	...	...	...	201
...	...	...	...	...	...	...	...	...	...	...	...	...	...	...	95.3 z	...	96.5 z	202
...	372**	...	3.3**	...	16.7	...	...	...	...	...	...	...	...	...	97.6	...	96.9	203

...	...	...	...	...	...	...	...	...	...	...	...	...	...	...	...	...	...	I
...	...	...	...	...	...	...	...	...	...	...	...	...	...	...	...	...	...	II
...	3 934	...	1.3	...	19.2	...	26.9	...	...	...	...	...	...	...	79.9	...	75.6	III
...	...	...	...	...	...	...	...	...	...	...	...	...	...	...	...	...	...	IV
...	...	...	...	...	...	...	...	...	...	...	...	...	...	...	...	...	...	V
...	...	...	...	...	...	...	...	...	...	...	...	...	...	...	76.3	...	71.8	VI
...	...	...	...	...	...	...	...	...	...	...	...	...	...	...	...	...	...	VII
...	...	...	...	...	...	...	43.5	...	...	...	...	...	...	...	...	...	...	VIII
...	...	...	1.6	...	...	...	38.7	...	...	...	...	...	...	...	...	...	79.6	IX
3 699	4 369	1.1	1.4	17.8	18.7	25.2	27.4	...	...	...	66.8	...	60.1	...	82.0	...	78.3	X
...	...	...	...	...	...	...	...	...	...	...	...	...	...	...	...	...	...	XI
...	...	...	...	...	...	...	...	...	...	...	...	...	...	...	...	...	...	XII

370 / ANNEX

Table 15. Trends in basic or proxy indicators to measure EFA goals 1, 2 and 3

	GOAL 1					
	Early childhood care and education (ECCE)					
	GER IN PRE-PRIMARY EDUCATION					
	1990		1998		2001	
Country or territory	Total GER (%)	GPI (F/M)	Total GER (%)	GPI (F/M)	Total GER (%)	GPI (F/M)
Arab States						
Algeria	...	...	2.5	1.01	4.2	1.00
Bahrain	27.1	1.02	32.9	0.95	34.9	0.95
Djibouti	0.7	1.46	0.4	1.50	0.5	1.02
Egypt[w]	6.1	0.99	10.1	0.95	12.8	0.94
Iraq	7.8	0.95	5.2	0.98	5.5[y]	0.99[y]
Jordan[w]	20.8	0.88	28.6	0.91	31.0	0.92
Kuwait	32.9	1.01	78.3	1.01	73.5	0.99
Lebanon	...	...	66.0	0.97	73.9	0.99
Libyan Arab Jamahiriya	...	...	5.0	0.98**	7.8	0.96
Mauritania	...	...	...	...	...	...
Morocco	60.7	0.46	64.3	0.52	59.7	0.58
Oman	3.1	0.89	5.6	0.87	5.2	0.87
Palestinian Autonomous Territories	13.8	...	39.9	0.97	31.1	0.94
Qatar	28.3	0.93	25.6	0.98	31.7	0.99
Saudi Arabia	6.8	0.87	5.1	0.91	4.9	0.93
Sudan	19.7	0.57	21.3	...	19.6	0.99
Syrian Arab Republic	6.2	0.88	8.4	0.90	9.8	0.91
Tunisia[w]	7.7	...	13.5	0.95	19.8	0.98
United Arab Emirates	53.0	0.97	61.6	0.97	70.8	1.00
Yemen	0.7	0.94	0.7	0.87	0.40**	0.92**
Central and Eastern Europe						
Albania[o]	58.6	...	41.7**	1.09**	44.4[z]	1.07[z]
Belarus	84.1	...	81.2	0.92	98.7	0.98
Bosnia and Herzegovina[o]	...	...	...	...	...	...
Bulgaria[o]	91.6	1.01	64.3	0.99	70.4	0.99
Croatia	28.2	0.99	41.1	0.98	38.4	0.94
Czech Republic[o]	95.0	0.97	90.5	1.06	95.6	1.00
Estonia[o]	74.9	0.99	86.8	0.98	105.7	0.99
Hungary[o]	113.4	0.97	79.4	0.98	79.5	0.98
Latvia[o]	44.7	1.01	50.9	0.95	60.2	0.94
Lithuania[o]	57.5	1.01	50.2	0.97	55.3	0.95
Poland[o]	46.7	...	49.8	1.01	49.0	1.00
Republic of Moldova	72.7	0.95	35.7**	0.97**	39.4	0.96
Romania[o]	76.0	1.04	61.8	1.02	75.7	1.03
Russian Federation[w]	74.0	...	...	...	91.9	0.94**
Serbia and Montenegro[1]	...	...	44.1	0.99	43.7[z]	1.01[z]
Slovakia	86.1	...	81.7	...	82.9	0.97
Slovenia[o]	73.6	0.95	72.0	0.91	73.2	0.95
The former Yugoslav Rep. of Macedonia[o]	...	...	27.3	1.01	28.2	1.01
Turkey[o]	4.2	0.92	6.0	0.94	6.8	0.94
Ukraine	85.0	0.92	47.5	0.98	52.0	0.98
Central Asia						
Armenia	36.6	...	...	...	30.5	1.06
Azerbaijan	18.8	0.84	16.4	0.89	23.1	1.00
Georgia	58.9	...	30.1	0.99	41.0	1.03
Kazakhstan	72.4	...	13.9	0.95	12.8	0.99
Kyrgyzstan	33.5	1.02	13.9	0.94**	14.3	0.97
Mongolia	39.1	1.24	24.7	1.21	31.6	1.17
Tajikistan	15.8	...	8.5	0.76	9.6	0.88
Turkmenistan	...	...	...	...	...	...
Uzbekistan	73.1	...	...	...	21.4**	0.99**
East Asia and the Pacific						
Australia[o]	71.3	1.00	...	...	104.2	1.00
Brunei Darussalam	47.2	0.95	50.6	1.03	43.7	0.99

1. National population data were used to calculate enrolment ratios.
(y) Data are for 1999/2000.
(z) Data are for 2000/2001.

STATISTICAL ANNEX / 371

Table 15

GOAL 2 — Universal primary education — NER IN PRIMARY EDUCATION						GOAL 3 — Learning needs of all youth and adults — YOUTH LITERACY RATE (15-24)					
1990		1998		2001		1990		2000-2004		
Total NER (%)	GPI (F/M)	Total NER (%)	GPI (F/M)	Total NER (%)	GPI (F/M)	Total (%)	GPI (F/M)	Total (%)	GPI (F/M)	Country or territory
										Arab States
93.2	0.88	92.1	0.96	95.1	0.97	77.3	0.79	89.9	0.91	Algeria
99.0	1.00	93.9	1.02	91.0**	1.01**	95.6	0.99	98.6	1.00	Bahrain
31.3	0.71**	31.3	0.72	34.0**	0.77**	73.2	0.78	...	...	Djibouti
83.7**	0.84**	90.9**	0.93**	90.3**	0.96**	61.3	0.72	73.2*	0.85*	Egypt [w]
94.2**	0.88**	91.2	0.85	90.5 [y]	0.85 [y]	41.0	0.44	...	...	Iraq
94.1	1.01	89.6	1.01	91.3	1.01	96.7	0.97	99.4	1.00	Jordan [w]
49.0**	0.93**	88.2	1.00	84.6	0.99	87.5	0.99	93.1	1.02	Kuwait
77.8**	0.96**	87.5**	0.97**	89.8**	0.99**	92.1	0.93	...	...	Lebanon
96.1**	0.96**	...	...	...	...	91.0	0.84	97.0	0.94	Libyan Arab Jamahiriya
35.3**	0.74**	62.6	0.94	66.7**	0.96**	45.8	0.65	49.6	0.73	Mauritania
56.8	0.70	73.1	0.86	88.4	0.93	55.3	0.62	69.5	0.79	Morocco
69.3	0.95	75.9	1.00	74.5	1.01	85.6	0.79	98.5	0.98	Oman
...	...	96.9	1.01	95.1	1.01	...	...	...	...	Palestinian Autonomous Territories
89.4	0.98	97.1	1.01	94.5	0.98	90.3	1.05	94.8*	1.02*	Qatar
58.7	0.81	56.8	0.93	58.9	0.92	85.4	0.86	93.5	0.96	Saudi Arabia
43.3**	0.75**	...	...	...	...	65.0	0.71	79.1	0.88	Sudan
92.3	0.91	93.0**	0.93**	97.5	0.95	79.9	0.73	95.2*	0.96*	Syrian Arab Republic
93.9	0.92	94.0	0.98	96.9	0.99	84.1	0.81	94.3	0.93	Tunisia [w]
99.1	0.98	78.2	0.98	80.8	0.97	84.7	1.08	91.4	1.08	United Arab Emirates
51.7**	0.38**	57.4	0.59	67.1**,[z]	...	50.0	0.34	67.9	0.60	Yemen
										Central and Eastern Europe
95.1**	1.01**	99.1**	0.99**	97.2 [z]	1.00 [z]	94.8	0.94	99.4*	1.00*	Albania [o]
86.2**	0.95**	93.0**	0.96**	94.2**	0.98**	99.8	1.00	99.8	1.00	Belarus
...	...	...	...	...	...	...	...	99.6*	1.00*	Bosnia and Herzegovina [o]
86.1	0.99	95.6	0.98	90.4	0.99	99.4	1.00	99.7	1.00	Bulgaria [o]
74.2	1.00	88.4	0.98	88.5	0.98	99.6	1.00	99.6*	1.00*	Croatia
86.7**	1.00**	90.2	1.01	88.5	1.00	...	...	...	...	Czech Republic [o]
99.5**	0.99**	97.0**	0.98**	95.8	0.99	99.8	1.00	99.8*	1.00*	Estonia [o]
91.3	1.01	89.5	0.99	90.8	0.99	99.7	1.00	...	...	Hungary [o]
92.1**	0.99**	91.0	0.99	87.6	1.01	...	...	99.7*	1.00*	Latvia [o]
...	...	94.5	0.99	94.3	0.99	99.8	1.00	99.7*	1.00*	Lithuania [o]
96.7	1.00	...	...	98.0	1.00	99.8	1.00	...	...	Poland [o]
88.8**	0.99**	78.2**	...	78.3	0.99	99.8	1.00	99.8	1.00	Republic of Moldova
81.2**	1.00**	95.7	0.99	88.4	0.99	99.3	1.00	97.8*	1.00*	Romania [o]
98.6**	1.00**	...	...	...	...	99.8	1.00	99.8	1.00	Russian Federation [w]
69.4	1.02	79.8**	0.99**	74.9 [z]	1.00 [z]	...	...	...	...	Serbia and Montenegro [1]
...	...	...	...	87.0	1.02	...	...	99.6*	1.00*	Slovakia
99.7**	1.01**	93.9	0.99	93.1	0.99	99.8	1.00	99.8	1.00	Slovenia [o]
94.4	0.99	94.5	0.98	92.3	1.01	...	...	...	...	The former Yugoslav Rep. of Macedonia [o]
89.5	0.92**	...	...	87.9**	0.93**	92.7	0.91	95.5*	0.95*	Turkey [o]
80.2**	1.00**	71.6	0.99	81.5	1.00**	99.8	1.00	99.9	1.00	Ukraine
										Central Asia
...	...	...	...	84.5	0.99	99.5	1.00	99.8*	1.00*	Armenia
100.0**	1.00**	80.1**	1.00**	79.8	0.98	...	...	...	...	Azerbaijan
97.1**	1.00**	95.3**	1.00**	90.7	1.00	...	...	...	...	Georgia
87.6**	0.99**	83.5**	1.00**	89.5	0.99	99.8	1.00	99.8	1.00	Kazakhstan
92.3**	1.00**	91.0*	0.98*	90.0	0.96	...	...	...	...	Kyrgyzstan
90.1**	1.02**	89.4	1.04	86.6	1.03	...	...	97.7*	1.01*	Mongolia
76.7**	0.98**	97.2**	0.94**	97.5	0.95	99.8	1.00	99.8*	1.00*	Tajikistan
...	...	...	...	...	...	...	...	99.8*	1.00*	Turkmenistan
78.2**	0.99**	...	...	...	...	99.6	1.00	99.7	1.00	Uzbekistan
										East Asia and the Pacific
99.2	1.00	...	...	96.0	1.01	...	...	...	...	Australia [o]
89.7**	0.95**	...	...	...	...	97.9	1.01	99.1*	1.00*	Brunei Darussalam

Table 15 (continued)

Country or territory	GOAL 1 — Early childhood care and education (ECCE) — GER IN PRE-PRIMARY EDUCATION					
	1990 Total GER (%)	1990 GPI (F/M)	1998 Total GER (%)	1998 GPI (F/M)	2001 Total GER (%)	2001 GPI (F/M)
Cambodia	3.9	0.90	5.2**	1.03**	7.4	1.08
China[w]	22.7	0.99	27.8	0.95	27.1	0.93
Cook Islands[1]	...	...	...	...	85.9**,z	0.99**,z
Democratic People's Republic of Korea	...	...	...	...	...	...
Fiji	13.4	1.06	15.4**	1.02**	...	...
Indonesia[w]	18.1	...	...	...	20.3	1.08
Japan[o]	48.1	1.02	83.1	1.02**	84.2	1.03**
Kiribati	...	...	...	...	...	...
Lao People's Democratic Republic	7.3	0.87	7.9	1.11	7.6	1.07
Macao, China	88.8	0.98	86.9	0.95	86.5	0.93
Malaysia[w]	35.0	1.02	109.5	0.99	88.7	1.08
Marshall Islands	...	...	...	...	...	...
Micronesia (Federated States of)	...	...	36.6	...	...	...
Myanmar	...	...	1.9	...	1.9**,y	...
Nauru[1]	...	...	140.9**	0.96**	...	...
New Zealand[o]	74.5	1.00	...	...	86.8	1.02
Niue[1]	...	...	128.6	1.15	147.8	1.23
Palau[1]	...	...	62.5	1.23	65.5**,z	1.12**,z
Papua New Guinea	0.4	1.00	33.5	0.95	38.8**	0.92**
Philippines[w]	11.7	...	30.7	1.05	33.0	1.05
Republic of Korea[o]	55.4	0.98	...	...	79.6	1.00
Samoa	...	...	55.5	1.14	54.5	1.23
Singapore	...	...	...	...	...	...
Solomon Islands	32.1	0.93	...	...	...	...
Thailand[w]	43.4	0.99	86.6	0.98	85.7	0.98
Timor-Leste	...	...	...	...	11.2	...
Tokelau	...	...	...	...	...	...
Tonga	...	...	21.7	1.15	29.4**,z	1.21**,z
Tuvalu[1]	...	...	79.5**	1.25**	...	...
Vanuatu	...	...	73.2**	1.11**	75.6	1.03
Viet Nam	28.5	...	40.2	0.94	43.1	0.98
Latin America and the Caribbean						
Anguilla[1]	...	...	...	...	116.1	0.97
Antigua and Barbuda[2]	...	...	...	...	...	...
Argentina[w]	...	...	57.0	1.02	60.6	1.02
Aruba[1]	...	...	96.9	1.00	99.8	0.96
Bahamas	...	...	...	...	30.0	0.99
Barbados	...	...	82.2	0.98	89.1	1.02
Belize	23.2	1.13	27.8	1.03	28.0 z	1.06 z
Bermuda[1]	...	...	...	...	54.6 z	...
Bolivia	31.5	1.00	44.1	1.01	46.5	1.01
Brazil[w]	46.5	...	53.5	1.01	67.3	1.00
British Virgin Islands[1]	...	...	61.6	1.16	85.4	0.85
Cayman Islands[2]	...	...	...	...	...	...
Chile[w]	82.4	1.01	73.6	0.99	77.5 z	1.00 z
Colombia	13.0	...	34.8	1.02	36.6	1.01
Costa Rica	60.1	1.01	...	...	115.5	1.01
Cuba	101.0	0.82	102.0	1.04	110.6	1.02
Dominica[1]	...	...	76.1	1.11	75.7 z	1.05**,z
Dominican Republic	...	...	35.2	1.01	35.1	0.94
Ecuador	41.9	...	63.6	1.04	73.0	1.03
El Salvador	...	...	40.2	1.05	45.9	1.05
Grenada[1]	...	...	...	...	67.9 z	1.02 z
Guatemala	...	...	37.3*	0.99*	55.2	1.01
Guyana	73.6	1.03	120.2	0.99	117.9 y	0.99 y
Haiti	34.2	0.95	...	...	...	...
Honduras	...	...	...	...	21.4**	1.05**
Jamaica[w]	78.1	1.03	83.6	1.08	86.8	1.05
Mexico[o]	64.5	1.03	74.0	1.02	75.8	1.02

1. National population data were used to calculate enrolment ratios.
2. Enrolment ratios were not calculated, due to lack of United Nations population data by age.
(y) Data are for 1999/2000.
(z) Data are for 2000/2001.

Table 15

GOAL 2
Universal primary education
NER IN PRIMARY EDUCATION

GOAL 3
Learning needs of all youth and adults
YOUTH LITERACY RATE (15-24)

1990 Total NER (%)	1990 GPI (F/M)	1998 Total NER (%)	1998 GPI (F/M)	2001 Total NER (%)	2001 GPI (F/M)	1990 Total (%)	1990 GPI (F/M)	2000-2004 Total (%)	2000-2004 GPI (F/M)	Country or territory
66.6**	0.83**	82.5**	0.91**	86.2**	0.93**	73.5	0.81	80.3	0.90	Cambodia
97.4	0.96	…	…	94.6**	1.01**	95.3	0.95	98.9*	0.99*	China w
…	…	…	…	…	…	…	…	…	…	Cook Islands 1
…	…	…	…	…	…	…	…	…	…	Democratic People's Republic of Korea
99.6**	1.01**	99.4**	1.00**	99.8**	1.00**	97.8	1.00	99.3*	1.00*	Fiji
96.7	0.96	…	…	92.1	0.99	95.0	0.97	98.0	0.99	Indonesia w
99.7	1.00	100.0	1.00	100.0	1.00	…	…	…	…	Japan o
…	…	…	…	…	…	…	…	…	…	Kiribati
62.6**	0.85**	80.2	0.92	82.8	0.92	70.1	0.76	79.3	0.85	Lao People's Democratic Republic
81.1**	0.98**	84.3	1.01	85.7	0.98	97.2	0.97	99.6*	1.00*	Macao, China
93.7**	1.00**	97.4	1.00	95.2	1.00	94.8	0.99	97.2*	1.00*	Malaysia w
…	…	…	…	…	…	…	…	…	…	Marshall Islands
…	…	…	…	…	…	…	…	…	…	Micronesia (Federated States of)
97.8**	0.96**	82.5**	0.99**	81.9	1.00	88.2	0.96	91.4	1.00	Myanmar
…	…	81.0**	1.04**	…	…	46.6	0.41	…	…	Nauru 1
99.6	0.99	…	…	98.4	0.99	…	…	…	…	New Zealand o
…	…	93.9	0.87	97.2	0.94	…	…	…	…	Niue 1
…	…	96.8**	0.94**	96.6**,z	0.93**,z	…	…	…	…	Palau 1
66.0**	0.86**	74.8*	0.93*	77.5**	0.89**	68.6	0.84	…	…	Papua New Guinea
96.5**	0.99**	…	…	93.0	1.02	97.3	1.00	95.1*	1.01*	Philippines w
99.7	1.01	…	…	99.9	1.00	99.8	1.00	…	…	Republic of Korea o
95.6**	1.09**	94.2	1.02	94.9	0.99	99.0	1.00	99.5	1.00	Samoa
96.4**	0.99**	…	…	…	…	99.0	1.00	99.5*	1.00*	Singapore
83.2**	0.86**	…	…	…	…	…	…	…	…	Solomon Islands s
75.9**	0.97**	79.6**	0.95**	86.3**	0.97**	…	…	98.0*	1.00*	Thailand w
…	…	…	…	…	…	…	…	…	…	Timor-Leste
…	…	…	…	…	…	…	…	…	…	Tokelau
91.8	0.96	91.7	1.00	99.9	1.00	…	…	99.2*	1.00*	Tonga
…	…	97.9**	0.96**	…	…	…	…	…	…	Tuvalu 1
70.6**	1.01**	89.8**	0.97**	93.2	1.02	…	…	…	…	Vanuatu
90.5**	0.92**	96.7	…	94.0**	…	94.1	0.99	…	…	Viet Nam

Latin America and the Caribbean

…	…	…	…	96.6	1.01	…	…	…	…	Anguilla 1
…	…	…	…	…	…	…	…	…	…	Antigua and Barbuda 2
93.8**	1.00**	100.0*	1.00*	99.8	1.00	98.2	1.00	98.6	1.00	Argentina w
…	…	97.8	1.01	98.4	0.98	…	…	…	…	Aruba 1
89.6**	1.03**	…	…	86.4**	1.03**	96.5	1.02	…	…	Bahamas
80.1**	0.99**	99.7	0.99	99.8	1.00	99.8	1.00	99.8	1.00	Barbados
94.0**	0.99**	94.3**	1.00**	96.2**,z	1.00**,z	…	…	84.2*	1.01*	Belize
…	…	…	…	100.0 z	…	…	…	…	…	Bermuda 1
90.8	0.92	96.0	0.99	94.2	1.00	92.6	0.93	97.3*	0.98*	Bolivia
85.6	0.94**	…	…	96.5	1.02	91.8	1.03	96.3*	1.02*	Brazil w
…	…	95.6**	1.02**	93.9	0.98	…	…	…	…	British Virgin Islands 1
…	…	…	…	…	…	…	…	…	…	Cayman Islands 2
87.7	0.98**	87.9	0.99	88.8 z	0.99 z	98.1	1.00	99.0*	1.00*	Chile w
68.1**	1.15**	86.7	…	86.7	0.99**	94.9	1.01	97.2	1.01	Colombia
87.3	1.01	…	…	90.6	1.02	97.4	1.01	98.4	1.01	Costa Rica
91.7	1.00	98.9	0.98	95.7	0.99	99.3	1.00	99.8	1.00	Cuba
…	…	82.9**	0.93**	…	…	…	…	…	…	Dominica 1
58.2**	2.20**	88.3**	1.02**	97.1	0.96	87.5	1.02	91.7	1.02	Dominican Republic
97.8**	1.01**	97.0	1.01	99.5	1.01	95.5	0.99	96.4*	1.00*	Ecuador
72.8**	1.02**	81.0	1.17	88.9	1.00	83.8	0.97	88.9	0.98	El Salvador
…	…	…	…	…	…	…	…	…	…	Grenada 1
64.0**	0.91**	76.5**	0.93**	85.0	0.95	73.4	0.82	80.1	0.86	Guatemala
88.9	1.00	95.7**	0.99**	98.4 y	0.97 y	99.8	1.00	…	…	Guyana
22.1	1.05	…	…	…	…	54.8	0.96	66.2	1.01	Haiti
89.9**	1.02**	…	…	87.4**	1.02**	79.7	1.03	88.9*	1.05*	Honduras
95.7	1.00	90.3**	1.00**	95.2	1.00	91.2	1.09	94.5	1.07	Jamaica w
98.8	0.98**	99.5	1.01	99.4	1.01	95.2	0.98	96.6*	1.00*	Mexico o

Table 15 (continued)

	GOAL 1						
	Early childhood care and education (ECCE)					
	GER IN PRE-PRIMARY EDUCATION					
	1990		1998		2001	
Country or territory	Total GER (%)	GPI (F/M)	Total GER (%)	GPI (F/M)	Total GER (%)	GPI (F/M)
Montserrat[1]	...	...	...	...	82.9	...
Netherlands Antilles	...	...	100.3	1.03	86.2	0.98
Nicaragua	12.1	1.09	24.7	1.02	25.9	1.02
Panama	53.4	1.00	37.7**	0.96**	50.8	1.02
Paraguay[w]	27.1	1.03	25.5	1.03	30.3	1.02
Peru[w]	29.6	...	56.1	1.02	60.3	1.02
Saint Kitts and Nevis[1]	...	...	...	...	141.6[z]	1.09[z]
Saint Lucia	54.4	...	85.2	0.99**	65.4	1.05
Saint Vincent and the Grenadines	44.6	1.11	...	...	...	...
Suriname	79.2	0.99	...	...	96.4	0.98
Trinidad and Tobago	8.8	1.02	59.8**	1.01**	63.0**	1.01**
Turks and Caicos Islands[1]	...	...	...	...	134.2	0.86
Uruguay[w]	42.6	1.03	56.0	1.01	62.7	1.02
Venezuela	40.8	1.02	44.2	1.03	51.6	1.01
North America and Western Europe						
Andorra[2]	...	...	...	...	...	...
Austria[o]	68.9	0.99	81.5	0.99	83.9	1.00
Belgium[o]	104.0	1.00	109.9	0.99	113.8	1.00
Canada[o]	60.8	1.00	66.0	1.01	64.7[z]	0.99[z]
Cyprus[o,1]	48.0	0.99	59.8	1.02	59.3	1.00
Denmark[o]	99.0	1.00	91.0	1.00	90.0	1.00
Finland[o]	33.6	...	48.3	0.99	55.2	0.99
France[o]	83.3	1.00	110.6	1.00	113.6	1.00
Germany[o]	...	...	93.6	0.98	100.7	0.98
Greece[o]	56.7	1.00	68.4	1.02	68.2	1.04
Iceland[o]	...	...	108.3	0.99	116.7	1.02
Ireland[o]	101.2	0.98	...	...	...	...
Israel[o]	85.4	...	106.0	0.98	107.7	1.00
Italy[o]	93.9	1.01	95.4	0.98	98.4	0.99
Luxembourg[o]	92.4	...	72.9	0.99	83.7	1.00
Malta[o]	102.6	0.93	102.7	0.99	100.7	0.97
Monaco[2]	...	...	...	...	...	...
Netherlands[o]	99.2	1.01	97.8	0.99	97.6	0.99
Norway[o]	88.4	...	75.4	1.06	80.8	1.06**
Portugal[o]	52.7	0.99	66.3	1.00	70.2	...
San Marino[2]	...	...	...	...	...	...
Spain[o]	59.4	1.03	99.4	0.99	106.1	1.00
Sweden[o]	64.7	...	76.1	1.01	75.1	0.99
Switzerland[o]	59.7	1.00	93.9	0.99	97.2	0.99
United Kingdom[o]	53.2	0.99	77.5	1.01	83.2	1.00
United States[o]	62.7	0.97	57.4	0.97	61.3	1.03
South and West Asia						
Afghanistan	...	...	...	...	...	...
Bangladesh	...	...	22.3	1.08	19.2	1.06
Bhutan[3]	...	...	...	...	...	...
India[w]	3.4	0.89	19.5	0.99	29.7**	1.00**
Iran, Islamic Republic of	11.9	0.95	13.3	1.05	23.0	1.10
Maldives	...	...	45.9	1.00	48.1	1.04
Nepal	...	...	12.1**	0.73**	12.5	0.85
Pakistan[4]	...	...	...	...	54.7*,[z]	0.74*,[z]
Sri Lanka[w]	...	...	...	...	...	...
Sub-Saharan Africa						
Angola	54.4	0.51	...	...	...	...
Benin	2.6	0.83	4.6	0.94	6.2**	0.95**
Botswana	...	...	...	...	...	...
Burkina Faso	0.7	1.01	1.7	1.01	1.1**	1.07**
Burundi	...	...	0.8	1.01	1.3	0.95

1. National population data were used to calculate enrolment ratios.
2. Enrolment ratios were not calculated, due to lack of United Nations population data by age.
3. Enrolment ratios were not calculated, due to inconsistencies between enrolment and the United Nations population data.

STATISTICAL ANNEX / 375

Table 15

GOAL 2 — Universal primary education — NER IN PRIMARY EDUCATION							GOAL 3 — Learning needs of all youth and adults — YOUTH LITERACY RATE (15-24)					
1990		1998		2001		1990		2000-2004		
Total NER (%)	GPI (F/M)	Total NER (%)	GPI (F/M)	Total NER (%)	GPI (F/M)	Total (%)	GPI (F/M)	Total (%)	GPI (F/M)	Country or territory
...	...	...	...	100.0	...	...	...	...	...	Montserrat [1]
...	...	96.1	1.01	88.4	1.05	97.5	1.00	98.3	1.00	Netherlands Antilles
72.2	1.04	77.9**	1.03**	81.9	1.01	68.2	1.01	86.2*	1.06*	Nicaragua
91.5	1.00	96.5**	0.99**	99.0	1.00	95.3	0.99	97.0	0.99	Panama
92.8	0.99	91.7	1.01	91.5**	1.01**	95.6	0.99	96.3*	1.00*	Paraguay [w]
87.8**	0.99**	99.8	1.00	99.9	1.00	94.5	0.95	96.6*	0.98*	Peru [w]
...	...	...	...	...	...	...	...	...	...	Saint Kitts and Nevis [1]
95.1**	0.97**	98.0**	0.96**	99.2**	0.98**	...	...	...	...	Saint Lucia
...	...	...	...	91.9**	0.99**	...	...	...	...	Saint Vincent and the Grenadines
78.4**	1.03**	...	...	97.3**	1.01**	...	...	...	...	Suriname
90.9	0.99	92.9	1.00	94.1**	1.00**	99.6	1.00	99.8	1.00	Trinidad and Tobago
...	...	...	...	88.0	1.00	...	...	...	...	Turks and Caicos Islands [1]
91.9**	1.01**	92.4	1.01	89.5	1.01	98.7	1.01	99.1	1.01	Uruguay [w]
88.1	1.03	85.9	1.01	92.4	1.01	96.0	1.01	98.2	1.01	Venezuela
										North America and Western Europe
...	...	...	...	...	...	...	...	...	...	Andorra [2]
87.7**	1.02**	89.9	1.01	89.9	1.02	...	...	...	...	Austria [o]
96.2	1.02	99.4	1.00	100.0	1.00	...	...	...	...	Belgium [o]
97.7	1.00	96.9	1.00	99.6**,z	1.00**,z	...	...	...	...	Canada [o]
86.9	1.00	95.5	1.00	95.9	1.00	99.7	1.00	99.8*	1.00*	Cyprus [o,1]
98.3	1.00	99.4	1.00	100.0	1.00	...	...	...	...	Denmark [o]
98.3**	1.00**	98.7	1.00	100.0	1.00	...	...	...	...	Finland [o]
100.0	1.00	100.0	1.00	99.6	1.00	...	...	...	...	France [o]
84.3**	1.03**	...	...	...	...	...	...	...	...	Germany [o]
94.6	0.99	93.4	1.00	96.8	1.00	99.5	1.00	...	...	Greece [o]
99.6**	0.99**	98.3	0.98	99.7	1.00	...	...	...	...	Iceland [o]
90.4	1.02	93.8	1.01	95.5	1.02	...	...	...	...	Ireland [o]
91.9**	1.03**	99.9	1.00	99.9	1.00	98.7	0.99	99.5	1.00	Israel [o]
99.8**	1.00**	99.7	0.99	99.2	1.00	99.8	1.00	...	...	Italy [o]
81.4**	1.10**	96.0	1.02	96.2	1.00	...	...	...	...	Luxembourg [o]
97.0	0.99	99.1	1.02	96.6	1.00	97.5	1.03	98.7	1.02	Malta [o]
...	...	...	...	...	...	...	...	...	...	Monaco [2]
95.3	1.04	99.5	0.99	99.4	0.99	...	...	...	...	Netherlands [o]
100.0	1.00	100.0	1.00	99.9	1.00	...	...	...	...	Norway [o]
99.8	1.00	...	...	99.8	1.00	99.5	1.00	...	...	Portugal [o]
...	...	...	...	...	...	...	...	...	...	San Marino [2]
99.8	1.00	99.6	0.99	99.7	0.99	99.6	1.00	...	...	Spain [o]
99.8	1.00	99.8	1.00	99.8	1.00	...	...	...	...	Sweden [o]
83.7	1.02	97.9	0.99	98.8	0.99	...	...	...	...	Switzerland [o]
98.3	0.97	99.6	1.01	100.0	1.00	...	...	...	...	United Kingdom [o]
96.8	1.00	93.8	1.00	92.7	1.01	...	...	...	...	United States [o]
										South and West Asia
26.5**	0.55**	...	...	...	...	...	...	...	...	Afghanistan
71.2	0.87	90.3**	0.97**	86.6	1.02	42.0	0.65	49.7	0.71	Bangladesh
...	...	...	...	...	...	...	...	...	...	Bhutan [3]
...	...	...	...	82.3	0.86	64.3	0.74	...	...	India [w]
92.3**	0.92**	81.4**	0.97**	86.5	...	86.3	0.88	...	...	Iran, Islamic Republic of
86.7**	1.00**	99.7**	1.01**	96.2	1.01	98.1	1.00	99.2	1.00	Maldives
81.2**	0.61**	68.5*	0.79*	70.5**,z	0.88**,z	46.6	0.41	62.7	0.59	Nepal
34.7**	...	...	...	59.1**,z	0.74**,z	47.4	0.49	53.9*	0.64*	Pakistan [4]
89.9**	0.96**	99.8	1.00	99.9	1.00	95.1	0.98	97.0	1.00	Sri Lanka [w]
										Sub-Saharan Africa
58.0**	0.95**	61.3	0.86	...	...	...	...	...	...	Angola
44.8**	0.52**	...	...	71.3**,y	0.69**,y	40.4	0.44	55.5	0.53	Benin
84.9	1.09	78.7	1.04	80.9	1.04	83.3	1.10	89.1	1.09	Botswana
26.2	0.63	33.5	0.68	35.0**	0.71**	...	...	19.4*	0.55*	Burkina Faso
53.2**	0.85**	37.1**	0.84**	53.4**	0.82**	51.6	0.77	66.1	0.97	Burundi

4. ECCE data include enrolment in 'katchi' programmes.
(y) Data are for 1999/2000.
(z) Data are for 2000/2001.

Table 15 (continued)

	GOAL 1 Early childhood care and education (ECCE) GER IN PRE-PRIMARY EDUCATION					
	1990		1998		2001	
Country or territory	Total GER (%)	GPI (F/M)	Total GER (%)	GPI (F/M)	Total GER (%)	GPI (F/M)
Cameroon	12.4	1.01	11.6	0.95	14.3	1.00
Cape Verde	...	...	...	...	55.5	1.00
Central African Republic	5.7	...	...	...	...	...
Chad	...	...	...	...	...	...
Comoros	...	...	2.2	1.07	1.7 y	1.07**,y
Congo	2.3	1.00	1.8	1.59	4.2	1.07
Côte d'Ivoire	0.9	0.94	2.6	0.97	3.2	0.99
Democratic Rep. of the Congo	...	...	...	...	0.8**	0.98**
Equatorial Guinea	...	...	30.9	1.04	35.1	...
Eritrea	...	...	5.3	0.89	5.3	0.92
Ethiopia	1.6	1.01	1.5	0.97	1.8	0.96
Gabon	...	...	...	...	13.2**	...
Gambia	...	...	19.7	0.91	19.7**,y	...
Ghana	...	...	37.0	0.99	41.5	0.99
Guinea	...	...	...	...	...	...
Guinea-Bissau	...	...	...	...	3.2 y	1.05 y
Kenya	32.9	1.13	38.3	1.07	44.4	0.98
Lesotho	...	...	24.9	1.13*	21.4**	1.02**
Liberia	...	...	43.3	0.74	56.1 y	0.89 y
Madagascar	...	...	...	...	3.4**	1.02**
Malawi	...	...	...	...	...	...
Mali	...	...	2.2	...	1.6	1.00
Mauritius	56.0	0.99	98.0	1.02	87.5	1.02
Mozambique	...	...	...	...	...	...
Namibia	14.2	1.13	20.1**	1.11**	23.4	1.19
Niger	1.5	0.94	1.1	1.03	1.3	0.97
Nigeria	...	...	...	...	8.2**	0.94**
Rwanda	...	...	...	...	2.5**	0.99**
Sao Tome and Principe	...	...	25.5**	1.06**	25.8	1.11
Senegal	2.4	1.04	2.9	1.00	3.3	1.13
Seychelles[1]	...	...	112.8	1.03	91.5	0.96
Sierra Leone	...	...	...	...	4.1 z	0.78 z
Somalia	...	...	...	...	...	...
South Africa	16.5	1.03	24.2*	0.99*	35.1	1.00
Swaziland	14.0	1.83	...	...	...	...
Togo	3.2	0.98	2.7	1.00	2.7	1.03
Uganda	...	...	4.0	1.00	4.2**	1.03**
United Republic of Tanzania	...	...	...	...	...	...
Zambia	...	...	2.3*	1.19*	...	...
Zimbabwe w	...	...	...	...	38.7**	1.03**

	Median					
World	...	...	43.7	0.86	48.6	1.02
Countries in transition	72.4	...	23.3	0.95	30.5	1.06
Developed countries	72.5	0.98	76.1	1.01	81.9	1.01
Developing countries	...	...	31.9	0.99	35.0	0.95
Arab States	10.8	...	13.5	0.95	19.6	0.99
Central and Eastern Europe	74.0	...	50.6	0.96	60.2	0.94
Central Asia	37.9	...	15.2	0.91	22.3	1.00
East Asia and the Pacific	32.1	0.93	50.6	1.03	54.5	1.23
Latin America and the Caribbean	43.6	1.07	57.0	1.02	67.3	1.00
North America and Western Europe	68.9	0.99	86.3	1.00	87.0	1.00
South and West Asia	...	...	19.5	0.99	26.4	1.04
Sub-Saharan Africa	...	...	5.0	0.92	5.8	0.92

1. National population data were used to calculate enrolment ratios.
2. Enrolment ratios were not calculated, due to lack of United Nations population data by age.
3. Enrolment ratios were not calculated, due to inconsistencies between enrolment and the United Nations population data.

Table 15

GOAL 2
Universal primary education
NER IN PRIMARY EDUCATION

GOAL 3
Learning needs of all youth and adults
YOUTH LITERACY RATE (15-24)

1990 Total NER (%)	1990 GPI (F/M)	1998 Total NER (%)	1998 GPI (F/M)	2001 Total NER (%)	2001 GPI (F/M)	1990 Total (%)	1990 GPI (F/M)	2000-2004 Total (%)	2000-2004 GPI (F/M)	Country or territory
73.6**	0.87**	...	...	...	...	81.1	0.88	...	...	Cameroon
93.8**	0.95**	99.7**	0.99**	99.4	0.99	81.5	0.87	89.1	0.94	Cape Verde
53.5	0.66	...	...	...	...	52.1	0.60	58.5*	0.67*	Central African Republic
36.5**	0.45**	54.7	0.62	58.3**	0.67**	48.0	0.65	69.9	0.84	Chad
56.7**	0.73**	49.2	0.85	...	...	56.7	0.78	59.0	0.79	Comoros
79.3**	0.93**	...	...	...	...	92.5	0.95	97.8	0.99	Congo
45.6	0.71**	55.5	0.76	62.6	0.74	52.6	0.62	59.9*	0.74*	Côte d'Ivoire
54.5	0.78	34.6	0.95	...	...	68.9	0.72	...	...	Democratic Rep. of the Congo
90.5**	0.97**	88.0	0.83**	84.6	0.85	92.7	0.92	...	...	Equatorial Guinea
16.1**	0.99**	33.9	0.87	42.5	0.86	60.9	0.68	...	...	Eritrea
23.3**	0.75**	35.8	0.69	46.2	0.79	43.0	0.66	57.4	0.82	Ethiopia
86.0**	1.00**	...	...	78.3**,z	0.99**,z	...	...	...	...	Gabon
48.0**	0.71**	66.6	0.88	72.9**	0.92**	42.2	0.68	...	...	Gambia
52.4**	0.87**	57.9**	0.93**	60.2	0.96	81.8	0.86	92.2	0.96	Ghana
25.5**	0.51**	45.3	0.69	61.5	0.78	44.1	0.43	...	...	Guinea
38.0**	0.56**	...	...	45.2 y	0.71 y	...	...	...	...	Guinea-Bissau
74.3**	1.00**	65.8**	1.01**	69.9**	1.02**	89.8	0.93	95.8	0.99	Kenya
73.0	1.24	64.5	1.14	84.4	1.08	87.2	1.26	...	...	Lesotho
...	...	43.9	0.77	69.9 y	0.78 y	57.2	0.51	70.8	0.64	Liberia
64.8**	1.00**	64.5	1.01	68.6	1.01	72.2	0.86	...	...	Madagascar
49.8	0.92	...	...	81.0**	1.00**	63.2	0.68	72.5	0.77	Malawi
20.4	0.61	38.3**	0.72**	...	...	...	...	24.2*	0.52*	Mali
94.9	1.01	93.2	1.00	93.2	1.00	91.1	1.00	94.5*	1.02*	Mauritius
44.7	0.76**	47.3**	0.83**	59.7	0.88	48.8	0.48	62.8	0.64	Mozambique
83.2**	1.09**	77.9	1.07	78.2	1.06	87.4	1.04	92.3	1.04	Namibia
24.0	0.58	26.1	0.66	34.2	0.68	17.0	0.37	24.5	0.44	Niger
59.9**	0.78**	...	...	...	...	73.6	0.82	88.6	0.95	Nigeria
67.4	0.99	...	...	84.0	1.03	72.7	0.86	84.9	0.97	Rwanda
...	...	85.5	0.98	97.1**	0.94**	...	...	...	...	Sao Tome and Principe
47.1**	0.74**	57.9	0.88**	57.9	0.89	40.1	0.60	52.9	0.72	Senegal
...	...	99.1	0.98	99.7	0.99	...	...	99.1	1.01	Seychelles [1]
41.0**	0.73**	...	...	...	...	...	...	...	...	Sierra Leone
8.2**	0.55**	...	...	...	...	...	...	...	...	Somalia
87.9**	1.03**	91.3*	1.01*	89.5	1.01	88.5	1.00	91.8	1.00	South Africa
77.2	1.04	77.7**	1.02**	76.7	1.01	85.1	1.01	91.2	1.02	Swaziland
75.2	0.71	89.8	0.80	91.8	0.84	63.5	0.60	77.4	0.75	Togo
52.7**	0.82**	...	...	...	...	70.1	0.76	80.2	0.86	Uganda
49.6	1.02	45.8	1.03	54.4	1.00	83.1	0.87	91.6	0.95	United Republic of Tanzania
79.1**	0.96**	68.5	0.97	66.0**	0.99**	81.2	0.88	89.2	0.95	Zambia
85.7**	1.00**	...	...	82.7	1.01	93.9	0.95	97.6	0.97	Zimbabwe w

Weighted average

1990 NER	GPI	1998 NER	GPI	2001 NER	GPI	1990	GPI	2000-2004	GPI	
81.7	0.88	84.2	0.93	84.0	0.94	84.3	0.91	87.6	0.92	World
89.0	0.99	84.6	0.99	90.1	0.99	99.2	1.00	99.4	1.00	Countries in transition
96.2	1.00	96.5	1.00	95.6	1.00	99.7	1.00	99.7	1.00	Developed countries
79.5	0.86	82.7	0.92	82.5	0.93	80.9	0.88	85.2	0.91	Developing countries
74.8	0.81	78.1	0.90	81.1	0.90	66.6	0.71	78.2	0.85	Arab States
90.1	0.98	86.7	0.97	88.8	0.98	98.3	0.98	98.8	0.99	Central and Eastern Europe
84.8	0.99	87.5	0.99	94.1	0.98	97.7	1.00	98.3	1.00	Central Asia
95.9	0.96	96.8	1.00	93.7	1.00	95.4	0.96	97.8	0.99	East Asia and the Pacific
86.4	0.99	94.4	0.99	95.7	1.00	92.7	1.00	95.5	1.01	Latin America and the Caribbean
97.0	1.00	96.3	1.00	95.4	1.01	99.7	1.00	99.8	1.00	North America and Western Europe
72.7	0.67	79.4	0.83	79.0	0.86	61.5	0.72	72.3	0.77	South and West Asia
54.5	0.86	57.6	0.88	62.8	0.89	67.5	0.80	76.6	0.89	Sub-Saharan Africa

4. ECCE data include enrolment in 'katchi' programmes.
(y) Data are for 1999/2000.
(z) Data are for 2000/2001.

Table 16. Trends in basic or proxy indicators to measure EFA goals 4 and 5

	GOAL 4				GOAL 5					
	Improving levels of adult literacy				Gender parity in primary education					
	ADULT LITERACY RATE (15 and over)				GROSS ENROLMENT RATIO					
	1990		2000-2004		1990		1998		2001	
Country or territory	Total (%)	GPI (F/M)	Total (%)	GPI (F/M)	Total GER (%)	GPI (F/M)	Total GER (%)	GPI (F/M)	Total GER (%)	GPI (F/M)
Arab States										
Algeria	52.9	0.64	68.9	0.76	100.5	0.85	106.8	0.92	108.4	0.93
Bahrain	82.1	0.86	88.5	0.92	110.0	1.00	100.7	1.01	98.0	0.99
Djibouti	53.0	0.59	...	...	37.7	0.71	38.1	0.71	40.3	0.76
Egypt[w]	47.1	0.56	55.6*	0.65*	91.5	0.83	98.6**	0.92**	96.9**	0.94**
Iraq	35.7	0.38	...	...	115.6	0.84	99.5	0.82	98.8[y]	0.82[y]
Jordan[w]	81.5	0.80	90.9	0.90	100.6	1.01	96.5	1.00	98.6	1.00
Kuwait	76.7	0.91	82.9	0.96	60.2	0.95	101.9	1.01	94.3	0.99
Lebanon	80.3	0.83	...	...	113.2**	0.96**	106.7	0.96	102.7	0.96
Libyan Arab Jamahiriya	68.1	0.62	81.7	0.77	104.7	0.94	115.7	0.98	114.1	1.00
Mauritania	34.8	0.52	41.2	0.61	50.3	0.73	86.5	0.94	86.5	0.96
Morocco	38.7	0.47	50.7	0.61	65.2	0.69	89.2	0.81	107.0	0.89
Oman	54.7	0.57	74.4	0.80	84.9	0.92	85.7	0.96	82.9	0.98
Palestinian Autonomous Territories	...	...	...	...	...	...	105.7	1.01	104.1	1.01
Qatar	77.0	0.98	84.2*	0.97*	100.5	0.93	108.0	0.97	105.9	0.96
Saudi Arabia	66.2	0.66	77.9	0.83	72.7	0.86	68.7	0.97	67.3	0.97
Sudan	45.8	0.53	59.9	0.69	52.3	0.77	54.5**	0.85**	58.7	0.85
Syrian Arab Republic	64.8	0.58	82.9*	0.82*	102.2	0.90	103.6	0.92	111.6	0.93
Tunisia[w]	59.1	0.65	73.2	0.76	113.7	0.89	114.9	0.95	111.6	0.96
United Arab Emirates	71.0	0.99	77.3	1.07	110.8	0.97	89.1	0.96	92.2	0.96
Yemen	32.7	0.23	49.0	0.41	65.4**	0.35**	73.3	0.56	81.0	0.66
Central and Eastern Europe										
Albania[o]	77.0	0.77	98.7*	0.99*	100.2	1.00	108.2**	0.99**	106.6[z]	1.00[z]
Belarus	99.5	1.00	99.7	1.00	96.0	0.96**	109.0	0.96	110.3	0.98
Bosnia and Herzegovina[o]	...	...	94.6*	0.93*	...	...	...	...	...	...
Bulgaria[o]	97.2	0.98	98.6	0.99	97.6	0.97	103.4	0.97	99.4	0.98
Croatia	96.9	0.96	98.1*	0.98*	79.7	0.99	95.7	0.98	95.6	0.99
Czech Republic[o]	...	...	...	...	96.4	1.00	104.0	0.99	103.6	0.99
Estonia[o]	99.8	1.00	99.8*	1.00*	110.8	0.97	102.2	0.97	101.4	0.96
Hungary[o]	99.1	1.00	...	...	94.5	1.00	103.5	0.98	100.8	0.99
Latvia[o]	...	...	99.7*	1.00*	96.5	0.99	99.1	0.98	95.9	0.98
Lithuania[o]	99.3	1.00	99.6*	1.00*	94.0	0.95	101.5	0.98	101.2	0.99
Poland[o]	99.6	1.00	...	...	98.4	0.99	...	...	99.7	0.99
Republic of Moldova	97.5	0.97	99.0	0.99	93.1	1.00	84.3	1.00	85.3	0.99
Romania[o]	97.1	0.97	97.3*	0.98*	91.3	1.00	104.3	0.98	98.0	0.98
Russian Federation[w]	99.2	0.99	99.6	1.00	109.2	1.00	...	...	113.8	1.00
Serbia and Montenegro[1]	...	...	...	...	72.0	1.02	103.9	0.99	98.8[z]	1.00[z]
Slovakia	...	...	99.7*	1.00*	...	...	102.5	0.99	101.4	0.99
Slovenia[o]	99.6	1.00	99.7	1.00	108.3	...	97.7	0.99	103.3	0.99
The former Yugoslav Rep. of Macedonia[o]	...	...	...	...	99.3	0.98	101.8	0.98	98.7	1.01
Turkey[o]	77.9	0.74	86.5*	0.83*	99.1	0.92	...	...	94.5**	0.92**
Ukraine	99.4	0.99	99.6	1.00	88.8	1.00	77.8	0.99	90.5	1.00
Central Asia										
Armenia	97.5	0.97	99.4*	0.99*	...	...	...	...	96.3	0.98
Azerbaijan	...	...	...	...	110.6**	0.99**	90.9	1.00	92.6	0.98
Georgia	...	...	...	...	97.3	1.00	95.3	1.00	92.0	1.00
Kazakhstan	98.8	0.99	99.4	1.00	88.2	0.99**	93.0	1.00	99.3	0.99
Kyrgyzstan	...	...	...	...	92.8	1.00	101.3	0.98	100.2	0.97
Mongolia	...	...	97.8*	0.99*	97.2	1.02	98.2	1.04	98.7	1.03
Tajikistan	98.2	0.98	99.5*	1.00*	91.0	0.98	103.1	0.95	106.8	0.95
Turkmenistan	...	...	98.8*	0.99*	...	...	...	...	...	...
Uzbekistan	98.7	0.98	99.3	0.99	81.4	0.98	...	...	102.6**	0.99**
East Asia and the Pacific										
Australia[o]	...	...	...	...	107.7	0.99	...	...	102.4	1.00
Brunei Darussalam	85.5	0.87	93.9*	0.95*	115.3	0.94	114.5	0.98	106.3	0.99

1. National population data were used to calculate enrolment ratios.
(y) Data are for 1999/2000.
(z) Data are for 2000/2001.

Table 16

GOAL 5
Gender parity in secondary education
GROSS ENROLMENT RATIO

1990 Total GER (%)	1990 GPI (F/M)	1998 Total GER (%)	1998 GPI (F/M)	2001 Total GER (%)	2001 GPI (F/M)	Country or territory
						Arab States
60.9	0.81	65.8	1.03	71.6	1.08	Algeria
99.7	1.03	93.9	1.08	95.0	1.09	Bahrain
11.6	0.66	16.2	0.72	19.6	0.62	Djibouti
70.8	0.79	80.8**	0.92**	88.1**	0.93**	Egypt [w]
49.0	0.64	35.7	0.63	38.3 [y]	0.62 [y]	Iraq
63.3	1.04	86.9	1.03	86.3	1.02	Jordan [w]
42.9	0.98	97.8**	1.02**	85.2**	1.06**	Kuwait
...	...	77.5	1.09	77.4	1.10	Lebanon
85.9	...	...	...	104.8	1.06	Libyan Arab Jamahiriya
13.4	0.46	18.7**	0.73**	21.7	0.76	Mauritania
35.5	0.73	37.7	0.79	40.9**,[z]	0.81**,[z]	Morocco
44.9	0.81	71.7	0.99	78.5	0.98	Oman
...	...	78.8	1.04	84.9	1.06	Palestinian Autonomous Territories
83.6	1.06	92.3	1.06	90.2	1.05	Qatar
43.7	0.79	67.9	0.87	69.2	0.89	Saudi Arabia
21.5	0.79	28.5**	...	32.0	...	Sudan
48.8	0.73	40.6	0.91	44.6	0.90	Syrian Arab Republic
44.4	0.79	72.9	1.02	79.1	1.04	Tunisia [w]
65.4	1.21	82.1	1.08	79.4	1.06	United Arab Emirates
...	...	41.9	0.37	46.3**,[z]	0.42**,[z]	Yemen
						Central and Eastern Europe
78.3	0.86	75.8**	1.03**	78.4 [z]	1.03 [z]	Albania [o]
95.3	...	85.2	1.04	84.1	1.04	Belarus
...	...	...	...	...	...	Bosnia and Herzegovina [o]
75.2	1.04	89.4	0.98	94.3	0.97	Bulgaria [o]
69.2	1.09	89.8	1.03	88.4	1.02	Croatia
91.2	0.97	82.5	1.04	95.8	1.03	Czech Republic [o]
98.5	1.11	92.7	1.04	95.9	1.02	Estonia [o]
78.6	1.01	95.3	1.02	103.6	1.01	Hungary [o]
91.0	1.00	88.4	1.04	94.5	1.01	Latvia [o]
91.7	...	...	...	100.5	0.99	Lithuania [o]
81.5	1.05	...	...	102.9	0.97	Poland [o]
80.0	1.09	72.7	1.01	72.4	1.03	Republic of Moldova
92.0	0.99	78.9	1.01	84.2	1.01	Romania [o]
93.3	1.06	...	...	92.0	1.01	Russian Federation [w]
63.4	1.03	92.3	1.01	88.7 [z]	1.01 [z]	Serbia and Montenegro [1]
...	...	85.2	1.02	89.5	1.01	Slovakia
91.1	...	98.7	1.03	107.6	1.00	Slovenia [o]
55.7	0.99	82.3	0.97	84.0	0.97	The former Yugoslav Rep. of Macedonia [o]
48.2	0.63	...	...	76.0**	0.76**	Turkey [o]
92.8	...	...	...	96.8	1.00	Ukraine
						Central Asia
...	...	...	...	86.5	1.06	Armenia
87.5	1.01	76.9	0.99	79.7	0.97	Azerbaijan
94.9	0.97	74.2	1.03	78.6	1.08	Georgia
97.5	1.04	87.4	0.99	88.8	0.98	Kazakhstan
100.1	1.02	85.4	1.02	86.5	1.00	Kyrgyzstan
82.4	1.14	58.9	1.27	76.1	1.20	Mongolia
102.1	...	76.1	0.86	82.0	0.82	Tajikistan
...	...	...	...	...	...	Turkmenistan
99.4	0.91	...	...	98.6**	0.97**	Uzbekistan
						East Asia and the Pacific
81.7	1.04	...	...	153.8	0.99	Australia [o]
68.7	1.07	81.6	1.10	87.7	1.06	Brunei Darussalam

Table 16 (continued)

Country or territory	GOAL 4 — ADULT LITERACY RATE (15 and over) 1990 Total (%)	GPI (F/M)	2000-2004 Total (%)	GPI (F/M)	GOAL 5 — GROSS ENROLMENT RATIO 1990 Total GER (%)	GPI (F/M)	1998 Total GER (%)	GPI (F/M)	2001 Total GER (%)	GPI (F/M)
Cambodia	62.0	0.63	69.4	0.73	83.4	0.81**	96.5	0.86	123.4	0.89
China[w]	78.3	0.79	90.9*	0.91*	125.2	0.93	119.5	1.01	116.2	1.00
Cook Islands[2]	…	…	…	…	…	…	…	…	…	…
Democratic People's Republic of Korea	…	…	…	…	…	…	…	…	…	…
Fiji	88.6	0.93	92.9*	0.97*	131.4	1.00**	110.5**	0.99**	108.8**	1.00**
Indonesia[w]	79.5	0.84	87.9	0.90	114.3	0.98	…	…	110.9	0.98
Japan[o]	…	…	…	…	99.7	1.00	101.4	1.00	100.7	1.00
Kiribati	…	…	…	…	…	…	130.8	1.02	…	…
Lao People's Democratic Republic	56.5	0.61	66.4	0.72	103.4	0.79	116.7	0.85	114.8	0.86
Macao, China	90.5	0.92	91.3*	0.92*	98.6	0.96	99.1	0.95	104.1	0.94
Malaysia[w]	80.7	0.86	88.7*	0.93*	93.7	1.00	97.4	1.00	95.2	1.00
Marshall Islands[2]	…	…	…	…	…	…	…	…	…	…
Micronesia (Federated States of)	…	…	…	…	…	…	…	…	…	…
Myanmar	80.7	0.85	85.3	0.91	108.6	0.95	90.1	0.98	89.6	1.00
Nauru[1]	30.4	0.30	…	…	…	…	81.0**	1.04**	…	…
New Zealand[o]	…	…	…	…	105.6	0.98	…	…	99.0	0.99
Niue[1]	…	…	…	…	…	…	102.9	0.87	117.6	0.94
Palau[1]	…	…	…	…	…	…	113.8	0.93	116.1**,[z]	0.93**,[z]
Papua New Guinea	56.6	0.75	…	…	66.2	0.86	74.8	0.93	77.5**	0.89**
Philippines[w]	91.7	0.99	92.6*	1.00*	109.5	0.99	113.1	1.00	112.1	0.99
Republic of Korea[o]	95.9	0.95	…	…	104.9	1.01	…	…	102.1	1.00
Samoa	98.0	0.99	98.7	0.99	121.7	1.09	99.4	1.01	102.5	0.98
Singapore	88.8	0.88	92.5	0.92	103.7	0.97	…	…	…	…
Solomon Islands	…	…	…	…	85.8	0.86	…	…	…	…
Thailand[w]	…	…	92.6*	0.95*	98.1	0.96	94.1	0.95	97.7	0.96
Timor-Leste	…	…	…	…	…	…	…	…	143.3	…
Tokelau	…	…	…	…	…	…	…	…	…	…
Tonga	…	…	98.8*	1.00*	105.8	0.96	110.4	0.97	112.4	0.98
Tuvalu[1]	…	…	…	…	…	…	103.6**	0.96**	…	…
Vanuatu	…	…	…	…	96.0	0.98	109.2**	0.96**	111.6	0.99
Viet Nam	…	…	90.3*	0.93*	106.9	0.93**	109.4	0.92	103.4	0.93
Latin America and the Caribbean										
Anguilla[1]	…	…	…	…	…	…	…	…	98.6	0.99
Antigua and Barbuda[2]	…	…	…	…	…	…	…	…	…	…
Argentina[w]	95.7	1.00	97.0	1.00	106.3	1.04**	119.7	1.00	119.6	1.00
Aruba[1]	…	…	…	…	…	…	112.2	0.98	114.6	0.95
Bahamas	94.4	1.02	…	…	95.6	1.03**	…	…	92.2	1.01
Barbados	99.4	1.00	99.7	1.00	93.0	1.00	104.3	0.99	108.3	1.00
Belize	…	…	76.9*	1.01*	111.5	0.98	118.1	0.97	117.6[z]	0.97[z]
Bermuda[1]	…	…	…	…	…	…	…	…	103.2[z]	…
Bolivia	78.1	0.80	86.7*	0.87*	94.8	0.91	112.5	0.98	113.6	0.99
Brazil[w]	82.0	0.98	88.2*	1.00*	105.3	0.94**	…	…	148.5	0.94
British Virgin Islands[1]	…	…	…	…	…	…	111.6	0.97	109.1	0.96
Cayman Islands[2]	…	…	…	…	…	…	…	…	…	…
Chile[w]	94.0	0.99	95.7*	1.00*	99.9	0.98	102.7	0.97	102.7[z]	0.98[z]
Colombia	88.4	0.99	92.1	1.00	102.2	1.15	112.0	1.00	109.6	0.99
Costa Rica	93.9	1.00	95.8	1.00	101.9	0.99	…	…	108.4	1.00
Cuba	95.1	1.00	96.9	1.00	97.7	0.97	105.3	0.96	100.3	0.96
Dominica[1]	…	…	…	…	…	…	98.8	0.95	…	…
Dominican Republic	79.4	0.99	84.4	1.00	94.8**	1.02**	116.7**	0.98**	126.1	1.01
Ecuador	87.6	0.94	91.0*	0.97*	116.5	0.99**	113.4	1.00	116.9	1.00
El Salvador	72.4	0.91	79.7	0.94	81.1	1.01	111.6	0.97	111.8	0.96
Grenada[2]	…	…	…	…	…	…	…	…	…	…
Guatemala	61.0	0.77	69.9	0.81	77.6	0.88**	94.0*	0.89*	103.0	0.92
Guyana	97.2	0.98	…	…	93.6	0.98	116.9	0.98	120.2[y]	0.97[y]
Haiti	39.7	0.87	51.9	0.93	47.8	0.94	…	…	…	…
Honduras	68.1	0.98	80.0*	1.01*	109.0**	1.05**	…	…	105.8**	1.02**
Jamaica[w]	82.2	1.10	87.6	1.09	101.3	0.99	95.4**	1.00**	100.5	0.99
Mexico[o]	87.3	0.93	90.5*	0.96*	113.9	0.98	110.9	0.99	110.3	0.99

1. National population data were used to calculate enrolment ratios.
2. Enrolment ratios were not calculated, due to lack of United Nations population data by age.
(y) Data are for 1999/2000.
(z) Data are for 2000/2001.

Table 16

GOAL 5
Gender parity in secondary education
GROSS ENROLMENT RATIO

1990 Total GER (%)	1990 GPI (F/M)	1998 Total GER (%)	1998 GPI (F/M)	2001 Total GER (%)	2001 GPI (F/M)	Country or territory
28.9	0.43	16.0**	0.53**	21.3	0.60	Cambodia
48.7	0.75	65.0	...	67.2	...	China W
...	...	...	...	...	...	Cook Islands [2]
...	...	...	...	...	...	Democratic People's Republic of Korea
58.2**	...	...	...	80.4**	1.07**	Fiji
45.5	0.83	...	...	57.9	0.99	Indonesia W
97.1	1.02	101.8	1.01	102.6	1.01	Japan O
...	...	...	...	...	...	Kiribati
24.4*	0.62*	33.4	0.69	40.6	0.73	Lao People's Democratic Republic
65.1*	1.11*	75.5	1.10	87.1	1.06	Macao, China
56.3	1.07	69.4	1.11	69.6	1.10	Malaysia W
...	...	...	...	...	...	Marshall Islands [2]
...	...	109.2	...	...	...	Micronesia (Federated States of)
22.4	0.98	34.9	0.99	39.3	0.94	Myanmar
...	...	53.9**	1.06**	...	...	Nauru [1]
89.1	1.02	...	...	113.2	...	New Zealand O
...	...	101.4	0.82	93.8	0.98	Niue [1]
...	...	101.2	1.07	88.8**,z	1.00**,z	Palau [1]
11.5	0.59	20.4	0.75	22.7**	0.79**	Papua New Guinea
70.7	1.04	75.8	1.09	81.9	1.10	Philippines W
89.8	0.97	...	...	91.1	1.00	Republic of Korea O
36.1	1.22	74.9	1.11	74.5	1.11	Samoa
68.1	0.93	...	...	...	...	Singapore
14.0	0.63	...	...	...	...	Solomon Islands
30.8	0.94	...	...	82.8 z	0.95 z	Thailand W
...	...	...	...	34.6	...	Timor-Leste
...	...	...	...	...	...	Tokelau
97.1	1.01	93.3	1.13	99.6	1.13	Tonga
...	...	78.3**	0.88**	...	...	Tuvalu [1]
16.7	0.79	33.1**	0.83**	28.6	1.03	Vanuatu
32.2	...	61.9	0.90	69.7	0.92	Viet Nam

Latin America and the Caribbean

1990 Total GER (%)	1990 GPI (F/M)	1998 Total GER (%)	1998 GPI (F/M)	2001 Total GER (%)	2001 GPI (F/M)	Country or territory
...	...	...	...	101.9	0.98	Anguilla [1]
...	...	...	...	...	...	Antigua and Barbuda [2]
71.1	...	89.0	1.08	99.6	1.06	Argentina W
...	...	100.6	1.04	101.5	1.07	Aruba [1]
...	...	...	...	91.5	1.03	Bahamas
...	...	104.0**	1.05**	103.3	1.00	Barbados
43.9	1.15	64.8	1.08	70.7 z	1.08 z	Belize
...	...	...	...	86.1 z	...	Bermuda [1]
36.7	0.85	72.3	0.92	84.4	0.96	Bolivia
38.4	...	...	...	107.5	1.10	Brazil W
...	...	98.8	0.91	95.2	1.02	British Virgin Islands [1]
...	...	...	...	...	...	Cayman Islands [2]
73.5	1.08	79.6	1.04	85.5 z	1.02 z	Chile W
49.8*	1.13*	70.6	1.11	65.2	1.10	Colombia
43.0	1.05	...	...	66.8	1.03	Costa Rica
88.9	1.14	79.4	1.06	89.1	0.99	Cuba
...	...	85.5	1.18	95.4 z	1.13 z	Dominica [1]
...	...	56.1**	1.27**	67.4	1.24	Dominican Republic
55.3*	...	56.4	1.03	59.2	1.01	Ecuador
26.4*	1.06*	50.2	0.99	55.9	1.01	El Salvador
...	...	...	...	62.6 z	0.48 z	Grenada [2]
...	...	30.7*	0.92*	39.3	0.93	Guatemala
78.7	1.06	81.1	1.02	87.1 y	1.04 y	Guyana
20.6*	0.96*	...	...	...	...	Haiti
...	...	...	...	...	...	Honduras
65.3	1.06	84.1**	1.02**	83.6	1.03	Jamaica W
53.3	1.01	69.1	1.02	75.7	1.07	Mexico O

Table 16 (continued)

	GOAL 4				GOAL 5					
	\multicolumn{4}{c}{Improving levels of adult literacy}	\multicolumn{6}{c}{Gender parity in primary education}
	\multicolumn{4}{c}{ADULT LITERACY RATE (15 and over)}	\multicolumn{6}{c}{GROSS ENROLMENT RATIO}
	1990		2000-2004		1990		1998		2001	
Country or territory	Total (%)	GPI (F/M)	Total (%)	GPI (F/M)	Total GER (%)	GPI (F/M)	Total GER (%)	GPI (F/M)	Total GER (%)	GPI (F/M)
Montserrat[1]	...	...	...	...	...	...	...	...	116.0	...
Netherlands Antilles	95.6	1.00	96.7	1.00	...	...	115.5	0.95	104.3	1.00
Nicaragua	62.7	1.00	76.7*	1.00*	93.5	1.06	99.9	1.03	104.7	1.01
Panama	89.0	0.98	92.3	0.99	106.4	0.96	108.1**	0.97**	110.0	0.97
Paraguay[w]	90.3	0.96	91.6*	0.97*	105.4	0.97	109.6**	0.98**	111.8**	0.96**
Peru[w]	...	...	85.0*	0.88*	118.9	0.97**	122.6	0.99	119.9	1.00
Saint Kitts and Nevis[2]	...	...	...	...	...	...	...	...	...	...
Saint Lucia	...	...	...	...	138.5	0.94	114.8	0.98	111.3	1.01
Saint Vincent and the Grenadines	...	...	...	...	111.6	0.99	...	...	101.2	0.96
Suriname	...	...	...	...	100.2	1.00	...	...	125.8	0.98
Trinidad and Tobago	96.8	0.98	98.5	0.99	96.7	0.99	101.7	0.99	105.1**	0.99**
Turks and Caicos Islands[1]	...	...	...	...	...	...	...	...	101.4	0.96
Uruguay[w]	96.5	1.01	97.7	1.01	108.6	0.99	112.8	0.99	108.3	0.98
Venezuela	88.9	0.97	93.1	0.99	95.7	1.03	100.3	0.98	105.9	0.98
North America and Western Europe										
Andorra[2]	...	...	...	...	...	...	...	...	...	...
Austria[o]	...	...	...	...	100.7	1.00	102.2	0.99	103.0	0.99
Belgium[o]	...	...	...	...	99.9	1.01	103.8	0.99	105.2	0.99
Canada[o]	...	...	...	...	103.8	0.98	97.7	1.00	99.6[z]	1.00[z]
Cyprus[o,1]	94.3	0.93	96.8*	0.96*	90.0	1.00	97.4	1.00	97.8	1.00
Denmark[o]	...	...	...	...	98.3	1.00	101.9	1.00	104.5	1.00
Finland[o]	...	...	...	...	98.8	0.99	99.2	1.00	102.0	0.99
France[o]	...	...	...	...	108.4	0.99	105.6	0.99	104.7	0.99
Germany[o]	...	...	...	...	101.0	1.01**	105.7	0.99	100.5	0.99
Greece[o]	94.9	0.95	...	...	98.4	0.99	95.5	1.00	99.1	0.99
Iceland[o]	...	...	...	...	101.3	0.99**	98.5	0.98	99.8	1.00
Ireland[o]	...	...	...	...	102.5	1.00	104.1	1.00	105.0	1.00
Israel[o]	91.4	0.93	95.3	0.96	97.9	1.03	112.9	0.99	113.4	1.00
Italy[o]	97.7	0.99	...	...	103.7	1.00	102.5	0.99	100.7	0.98
Luxembourg[o]	...	...	...	...	90.2	1.09	99.6	1.01	100.4	0.99
Malta[o]	88.4	1.01	92.6	1.02	107.9	0.96	106.3	1.01	105.3	0.99
Monaco[2]	...	...	...	...	...	...	...	...	...	...
Netherlands[o]	...	...	...	...	102.4	1.03	108.3	0.98	107.7	0.98
Norway[o]	...	...	...	...	100.4	1.00	101.1	1.00	101.2	1.00
Portugal[o]	87.2	0.92	...	...	123.0	0.95	123.1	0.96	116.1	0.96
San Marino[2]	...	...	...	...	...	...	...	...	...	...
Spain[o]	96.3	0.97	...	...	108.6	0.99	107.4	0.98	107.3	0.98
Sweden[o]	...	...	...	...	99.8	1.00	109.7	1.03	110.4	1.03
Switzerland[o]	...	...	...	...	90.3	1.01	106.3	0.99	107.2	0.99
United Kingdom[o]	...	...	...	...	107.4	0.97	101.8	1.01	100.3	1.00
United States[o]	...	...	...	...	103.1	0.98	100.6	1.03	98.2	1.01
South and West Asia										
Afghanistan	...	...	...	...	28.8	0.55	32.7	0.08**	22.6	...
Bangladesh	34.2	0.53	41.1	0.62	79.6	0.86	101.8**	0.97**	97.5	1.02
Bhutan[3]	...	...	...	...	...	...	...	...	...	...
India[w]	49.3	0.58	61.3*	...	98.6	0.76	97.9	0.83	98.1	0.85
Iran, Islamic Republic of	63.2	0.75	...	0.84*	109.3	0.90	95.6	0.95	92.1	0.96
Maldives	94.8	1.00	97.2	1.00	134.1**	0.97**	134.1	1.01	124.9	0.99
Nepal	30.4	0.30	44.0	0.43	113.8	0.61	112.3**	0.78**	121.6	0.87
Pakistan	35.4	0.41	41.5*	0.53*	...	...	...	...	73.2*,[z]	0.74*,[z]
Sri Lanka[w]	88.7	0.91	92.1	0.95	113.2	0.96	109.2	0.97	110.4	0.99
Sub-Saharan Africa										
Angola	...	...	...	...	92.0	0.92*	97.1	0.83	...	...
Benin	26.4	0.41	39.8	0.47	58.6	0.50	82.7	0.65	104.1	0.70
Botswana	68.1	1.07	78.9	1.07	103.0	1.08	102.8	1.00	103.3	1.00
Burkina Faso	...	...	12.8*	0.44*	32.5	0.63	41.8	0.68	43.6**	0.71**
Burundi	37.0	0.55	50.4	0.76	71.5	0.84	50.2**	0.82**	71.0	0.79

1. National population data were used to calculate enrolment ratios.
2. Enrolment ratios were not calculated, due to lack of United Nations population data by age.
3. Enrolment ratios were not calculated, due to inconsistencies between enrolment and the United Nations population data.

(y) Data are for 1999/2000.
(z) Data are for 2000/2001.

Table 16

GOAL 5
Gender parity in secondary education
GROSS ENROLMENT RATIO

1990 Total GER (%)	1990 GPI (F/M)	1998 Total GER (%)	1998 GPI (F/M)	2001 Total GER (%)	2001 GPI (F/M)	Country or territory
...	...	...	...	102.0	...	Montserrat[1]
92.9	1.19	74.9	1.17	72.6	1.12	Netherlands Antilles
40.4	1.37	48.4**	1.18**	56.6	1.18	Nicaragua
61.4	1.07	67.5**	1.08**	69.2	1.07	Panama
30.9	1.04	50.8	1.05	63.5	1.02	Paraguay[W]
67.4	...	81.7	0.95	89.0**	0.93**,[z]	Peru[W]
...	...	...	...	...	...	Saint Kitts and Nevis[2]
52.9	1.45	76.4	1.29	86.0	1.30	Saint Lucia
58.4	1.24	...	...	68.1	1.20	Saint Vincent and the Grenadines
52.1	1.15	...	...	73.6	1.39	Suriname
80.4	1.05	81.7**	1.08**	80.2**	1.10**	Trinidad and Tobago
...	...	...	...	85.3	1.03	Turks and Caicos Islands[1]
81.3	...	...	...	101.4	1.14	Uruguay[W]
34.7	1.38	56.9	1.23	68.6	1.16	Venezuela

North America and Western Europe

1990 Total GER (%)	1990 GPI (F/M)	1998 Total GER (%)	1998 GPI (F/M)	2001 Total GER (%)	2001 GPI (F/M)	Country or territory
...	...	...	...	...	...	Andorra[2]
101.8	0.93	98.8	0.96	99.1	0.95	Austria[o]
101.8	1.01	142.4	1.08	157.1	1.12	Belgium[o]
100.8	1.00	105.3	0.99	106.2[z]	0.99[z]	Canada[o]
72.1	1.02	93.2	1.03	96.9	1.02	Cyprus[o,1]
109.2	1.01	125.6	1.06	128.8	1.05	Denmark[o]
116.4	1.19	120.9	1.09	126.5	1.11	Finland[o]
98.5	1.05	109.6	1.00	107.8	1.01	France[o]
98.2	0.97	98.2	0.98	99.8	0.99	Germany[o]
93.8	0.98	93.9	1.01	95.7[z]	1.02[z]	Greece[o]
99.6	0.96	109.4	1.06	111.3	1.07	Iceland[o]
100.2	1.09	105.4	1.06	104.8	1.10	Ireland[o]
88.1	1.08	90.8	1.00	94.4	0.99	Israel[o]
83.2	1.00	91.7	0.99	98.1	0.96	Italy[o]
76.5	...	...	...	96.1	1.07	Luxembourg[o]
82.8	0.94	...	...	91.3	0.99	Malta[o]
...	...	...	...	...	...	Monaco[2]
119.5	0.92	124.4	0.96	122.2	0.97	Netherlands[o]
103.0	1.03	120.3	1.02	113.4	1.02	Norway[o]
67.2	1.16	109.5	1.08	114.7	1.05	Portugal[o]
...	...	...	...	...	...	San Marino[2]
104.1	1.07	...	...	115.7	1.06	Spain[o]
90.2	1.05	160.1	1.28	145.7	1.21	Sweden[o]
99.1	0.95	99.9	0.92	98.0	0.34	Switzerland[o]
88.0	1.00	157.6	1.12	179.1	1.25	United Kingdom[o]
92.1	1.01	...	...	93.0	0.99	United States[o]

South and West Asia

1990 Total GER (%)	1990 GPI (F/M)	1998 Total GER (%)	1998 GPI (F/M)	2001 Total GER (%)	2001 GPI (F/M)	Country or territory
10.2	...	...	...	12.5	...	Afghanistan
20.2	0.52	42.4	0.96	46.9	1.10	Bangladesh
...	...	...	...	...	...	Bhutan[3]
44.5	0.60	46.6	0.70	50.3	0.74	India[W]
57.5	0.75	77.4	0.93	76.9	0.95	Iran, Islamic Republic of
...	...	36.5	1.05	66.0	1.07	Maldives
33.1	0.44	35.5	0.71	43.9	0.75	Nepal
25.1	0.48	...	...	23.9*,[z]	0.66*,[z]	Pakistan
76.8	1.09	74.4**	1.07**	80.8	...	Sri Lanka[W]

Sub-Saharan Africa

1990 Total GER (%)	1990 GPI (F/M)	1998 Total GER (%)	1998 GPI (F/M)	2001 Total GER (%)	2001 GPI (F/M)	Country or territory
12.1	...	14.7	...	19.1	0.78	Angola
11.7	0.41	21.1	0.45	26.0**	0.46**	Benin
37.6	1.12	71.2	1.10	72.7	1.06	Botswana
6.7	0.52	9.4	0.60	10.2**	0.65**	Burkina Faso
5.5	0.58	7.1**	0.84**	10.7**	0.73**	Burundi

384 / ANNEX

Table 16 (continued)

	GOAL 4				GOAL 5					
	\multicolumn{4}{c|}{Improving levels of adult literacy ADULT LITERACY RATE (15 and over)}	\multicolumn{6}{c}{Gender parity in primary education GROSS ENROLMENT RATIO}				
	1990		2000-2004		1990		1998		2001	
Country or territory	Total (%)	GPI (F/M)	Total (%)	GPI (F/M)	Total GER (%)	GPI (F/M)	Total GER (%)	GPI (F/M)	Total GER (%)	GPI (F/M)
Cameroon	57.9	0.69	67.9*	0.78*	99.5	0.86	87.5	0.82	106.7*	0.86*
Cape Verde	63.8	0.71	75.7	0.80	113.8	0.94**	125.6	0.96	122.6	0.96
Central African Republic	33.2	0.44	48.6*	0.52*	65.5	0.63	…	…	66.1*	0.67*
Chad	27.7	0.51	45.8	0.69	54.7	0.45	67.0	0.58	73.4**	0.63**
Comoros	53.8	0.76	56.2	0.77	75.0	0.73	75.2	0.85	89.6	0.82
Congo	67.1	0.75	82.8	0.87	116.8	0.90	49.6	0.95	85.5	0.93
Côte d'Ivoire	38.5	0.51	…	…	65.1	0.71	73.1	0.75	80.3	0.74
Democratic Rep. of the Congo	47.5	0.56	…	…	70.6	0.75	49.6	0.90	…	…
Equatorial Guinea	73.3	0.71	…	…	162.6**	0.95**	131.3	0.91**	126.2	0.91
Eritrea	46.4	0.59	…	…	21.3	0.94	53.2	0.83	60.5	0.81
Ethiopia	28.6	0.53	41.5	0.69	31.8	0.66	49.9	0.60	63.9	0.71
Gabon	…	…	…	…	141.8**	0.98**	134.1	1.00	134.4	0.99
Gambia	25.6	0.62	…	…	61.1	0.68	79.9	0.85	78.9**	0.92**
Ghana	58.5	0.67	73.8	0.80	72.1	0.83	76.8	0.90	81.4	0.91
Guinea	27.2	0.30	…	…	34.0	0.47	58.4	0.63	77.1	0.75
Guinea-Bissau	…	…	…	…	49.9**	0.55**	…	…	69.7 y	0.67 y
Kenya	70.8	0.75	84.3	0.87	94.5	0.95	90.2	0.98	96.0	0.98
Lesotho	78.0	1.37	81.4*	1.23*	112.1	1.21	109.2	1.08	124.3	1.02
Liberia	39.2	0.41	55.9	0.54	…	…	89.6	0.74	105.4 y	0.73 y
Madagascar	58.0	0.75	…	…	93.6	0.98	95.6	0.97	104.2	0.96
Malawi	51.8	0.53	61.8	0.64	68.0	0.83	146.2	0.95**	145.8	0.96
Mali	…	…	19.0*	0.44*	25.3	0.60	48.8	0.71	57.0	0.75
Mauritius	79.8	0.88	84.3*	0.91*	109.2	1.00	107.6	1.00	106.0	1.00
Mozambique	33.5	0.37	46.5	0.50	63.9	0.76	81.2**	0.74**	98.9	0.79
Namibia	74.9	0.94	83.3	0.99	123.9	1.09	113.9	1.01	106.0	1.01
Niger	11.4	0.28	17.1	0.37	27.8	0.58	30.9	0.67	40.0	0.68
Nigeria	48.7	0.65	66.8	0.80	91.9	0.78	86.1**	0.76**	96.5**	0.80**
Rwanda	53.3	0.70	69.2	0.84	71.3	0.98	118.6	0.97	117.0	0.99
Sao Tome and Principe	…	…	…	…	…	…	107.1	0.96	126.4**	0.94**
Senegal	28.4	0.49	39.3	0.61	57.5	0.73	68.6	0.86**	75.3	0.91
Seychelles[1]	…	…	91.9*	1.01*	…	…	112.8	0.98	115.7	0.99
Sierra Leone	…	…	…	…	50.3	0.69	…	…	78.9 z	0.70 z
Somalia	…	…	…	…	…	…	…	…	…	…
South Africa	81.2	0.98	86.0	0.98	106.6	0.99	114.4*	0.97*	105.1	0.96
Swaziland	71.6	0.95	80.9	0.98	97.7	0.98	104.3	0.95	100.4	0.95
Togo	44.2	0.47	59.6	0.61	110.0	0.66	132.3	0.76	124.2	0.82
Uganda	56.1	0.63	68.9	0.75	68.7	0.80	143.3	0.90	136.4	0.96
United Republic of Tanzania	62.9	0.68	77.1	0.81	67.2	0.98	61.8	0.99	69.4	0.98
Zambia	68.2	0.75	79.9	0.85	93.7	0.91**	81.2	0.93	78.8	0.94
Zimbabwe w	80.7	0.87	90.0	0.92	103.6	0.99	…	…	99.0	0.97

	\multicolumn{4}{c|}{Weighted average}	\multicolumn{6}{c}{Weighted average}				
World	75.4	0.84	81.7	0.88	99.1	0.89	100.7	0.92	100.6	0.93
Countries in transition	99.2	0.99	99.6	1.00	97.0	0.99	96.0	0.99	103.6	0.99
Developed countries	98.0	0.99	98.9	1.00	101.9	0.99	102.1	1.00	100.6	1.00
Developing countries	67.0	0.76	76.4	0.83	98.8	0.87	100.6	0.91	100.5	0.92
Arab States	50.0	0.56	62.2	0.69	85.7	0.80	89.7	0.87	92.0	0.89
Central and Eastern Europe	96.2	0.97	97.3	0.97	98.0	0.98	94.6	0.96	99.9	0.97
Central Asia	98.7	0.99	99.4	1.00	89.4	0.99	98.9	0.99	100.6	0.98
East Asia and the Pacific	81.8	0.84	91.3	0.92	116.9	0.94	113.0	0.99	111.4	0.99
Latin America and the Caribbean	85.0	0.96	89.2	0.98	104.3	0.98	121.3	0.98	119.9	0.98
North America and Western Europe	97.9	0.99	98.8	1.00	104.0	0.99	102.5	1.01	100.8	1.00
South and West Asia	47.5	0.58	58.3	0.63	92.2	0.76	94.7	0.83	93.9	0.85
Sub-Saharan Africa	49.9	0.67	62.0	0.77	73.5	0.83	79.1	0.84	84.9	0.86

1. National population data were used to calculate enrolment ratios.
2. Enrolment ratios were not calculated, due to lack of United Nations population data by age.
3. Enrolment ratios were not calculated, due to inconsistencies between enrolment and the United Nations population data.

(y) Data are for 1999/2000.
(z) Data are for 2000/2001.

Table 16

GOAL 5

Gender parity in secondary education

GROSS ENROLMENT RATIO

1990 Total GER (%)	1990 GPI (F/M)	1998 Total GER (%)	1998 GPI (F/M)	2001 Total GER (%)	2001 GPI (F/M)	Country or territory
27.5	0.71	26.5**	0.82**	32.6**	0.82**	Cameroon
20.9*	...	61.7**	...	65.9	1.05	Cape Verde
11.5	0.40	...	...	...	...	Central African Republic
7.0	0.20	10.7	0.26	11.2**,z	0.28**,z	Chad
17.6*	0.65*	24.8	0.81	27.7	0.84	Comoros
46.2	0.72	...	...	32.0**	0.71**	Congo
21.3	0.48	22.5**	0.54**	22.8**,y	0.54**,y	Côte d'Ivoire
...	...	...	...	...	...	Democratic Rep. of the Congo
...	...	...	...	29.7**	0.57**	Equatorial Guinea
...	...	23.3	0.69	27.6	0.65	Eritrea
13.5	0.75	12.9	0.67	19.0	0.62	Ethiopia
...	...	45.7	0.86	50.9**	...	Gabon
18.4	0.49	30.8	0.66	34.3**	0.71**	Gambia
34.7	0.63	36.7	0.78	37.6**	0.82**	Ghana
9.5	0.33	13.9**	0.36**	...	...	Guinea
...	...	...	...	17.8 y	0.54 y	Guinea-Bissau
23.8	0.74	29.9**	0.90**	32.0	0.90	Kenya
25.4	1.47	31.7	1.39	33.7	1.26	Lesotho
...	...	30.5	0.65	34.1 y	0.69 y	Liberia
17.6	0.97	14.3**	0.96**	...	...	Madagascar
8.0	0.46	36.1	0.69**	34.0	0.76	Malawi
6.6	0.51	13.6	0.53	...	...	Mali
52.9	1.01	70.3	1.01	79.5	0.96	Mauritius
6.9	0.57	9.8**	0.68**	13.3	0.66	Mozambique
38.9	1.26	57.3	1.15	61.4	1.14	Namibia
6.5	0.43	6.7	0.63	6.5	0.65	Niger
24.8	0.77	...	...	...	...	Nigeria
8.2	0.76	9.6	0.88	14.4**	0.88**	Rwanda
...	...	...	...	39.2**	0.84**	Sao Tome and Principe
16.3	0.53	16.7**	0.64**	18.7**	0.67**	Senegal
...	...	114.0	1.00	110.0	1.05	Seychelles [1]
16.6	0.57	...	...	26.4 z	0.70**,z	Sierra Leone
...	...	...	...	...	...	Somalia
66.3	1.16	89.8*	1.13*	86.4**	1.09**	South Africa
41.3	0.93	48.4	1.00	45.2	1.00	Swaziland
22.7	0.34	33.6	0.40	36.5**,y	0.44**,y	Togo
12.5	0.56	9.8	0.64	16.8**	0.77**	Uganda
4.7	0.70	5.5**	0.82**	5.8**,y	0.81**,y	United Republic of Tanzania
19.6	...	19.8	0.77**	24.1	0.80	Zambia
46.9	0.87	...	...	42.9	0.89	Zimbabwe w

Median		Weighted average				
56.3	1.07	60.2	0.91	63.7	0.92	World
95.1	...	...	...	90.6	0.99	Countries in transition
91.7	...	103.5	1.01	105.9	1.02	Developed countries
39.7	...	52.5	0.87	56.6	0.89	Developing countries
48.8	0.73	59.3	0.88	63.7	0.90	Arab States
86.3	1.03			90.1	0.96	Central and Eastern Europe
97.5	1.04	85.5	0.98	87.1	0.98	Central Asia
52.5	0.91	66.5	...	68.7	0.93	East Asia and the Pacific
53.3	1.01	71.9	1.09	86.2	1.07	Latin America and the Caribbean
98.5	1.05	105.4	1.01	107.6	1.03	North America and Western Europe
33.1	0.44	45.6	0.74	48.3	0.79	South and West Asia
17.6	0.81	24.6	0.80	26.8	0.79	Sub-Saharan Africa

386 / ANNEX

Table 17
Trends in basic or proxy indicators to measure EFA goal 6

GOAL 6. Educational quality in primary education

	Country or territory	School Life Expectancy 1990 Total	1990 Male	1990 Female	1998 Total	1998 Male	1998 Female	2001 Total	2001 Male	2001 Female	Survival 1990 Total (%)	1990 GPI (F/M)	1998 Total (%)	1998 GPI (F/M)	2000 Total (%)	2000 GPI (F/M)
	Arab States															
1	Algeria	10.3	...	...	11.3**	...	...	...	...	...	94.5	0.99	95.0	1.02	96.0	1.03
2	Bahrain	13.5	13.2	13.7	12.8**	12.3**	13.5**	...	...	...	89.2	1.01	97.4**	1.01**	99.1**	0.98**
3	Djibouti	...	...	...	3.5**	4.1**	2.9**	3.9**	4.6**	3.2**	87.3	...	76.7	1.19	87.7**	0.95**
4	Egypt[w]	9.7	10.8	8.5	12.4**	...	...	...	...	...	...	...	...	...	98.9**	1.00**
5	Iraq	...	...	...	8.9**	10.1**	7.5**	9.0**,y	10.4**,y	7.6**,y	...	...	65.6**	0.94**	65.6**,x	0.94**,x
6	Jordan[w]	12.5	12.4	12.7	...	...	...	12.6**	12.5**	12.7**	99.1	1.02	97.7	0.99	.	...
7	Kuwait	...	...	...	13.5**	12.9**	14.3**	...	...	...	...	...	...	...	.	...
8	Lebanon	...	...	...	12.6**	12.4**	12.7**	13.1**	12.8**	13.3**	...	...	91.3	1.07	94.0	1.04
9	Libyan Arab Jamahiriya	13.0	...	...	...	...	...	16.5**	15.9**	17.0**	...	...	...	...	...	...
10	Mauritania	4.1	5.0	3.2	6.9**	7.2**	6.5**	6.9**	7.2**	6.5**	75.3	0.99	65.2**	0.92**	54.7	1.04
11	Morocco	6.6	7.8	5.4	8.2**	9.1**	7.3**	9.1**,z	9.9**,z	8.4**,z	75.1	1.02	81.9	1.00	83.7**	0.99**
12	Oman	8.2	8.8	7.7	...	...	...	10.4**	10.5**	10.4**	96.9	0.99	93.7	1.00	96.2	1.00
13	Palestinian A. T.	...	...	...	11.9	11.7	11.9	12.7	12.2	12.9	...	...	...	...	.	...
14	Qatar	12.3	11.8	13.2	13.3**	12.6**	14.3**	12.9**	12.4**	13.5**	64.1	1.02	...	...	...	...
15	Saudi Arabia	7.8	8.4	7.2	9.7**	9.8**	9.5**	9.6**	9.7**	9.5**	82.9	1.03	95.3	1.00	94.0	1.00
16	Sudan	4.4	5.0	3.9	5.1**	...	...	...	...	...	93.8	1.09	84.1**	1.10**	84.1**,x	1.10**,x
17	Syrian Arab Republic	10.0	10.9	8.9	9.0**	...	...	...	...	...	96.0	0.98	91.8	0.99	92.4	0.99
18	Tunisia[w]	10.4	11.3	9.5	12.7**	12.8**	12.5**	13.4**,z	13.4**,z	13.4**,z	86.6	0.83	92.1	1.02	95.5	1.01
19	United Arab Emirates	11.0	10.6	11.7	10.8**	...	...	...	...	...	80.0	0.99	92.4	0.99	97.5	0.99
20	Yemen	...	...	...	7.8**	10.5**	4.9**	8.2**,y	10.6**,y	5.5**,y	...	...	...	...	86.0**,y	1.15**,y
	Central and Eastern Europe															
21	Albania[o]	11.5	11.7	11.3	...	...	...	11.3**,z	11.0**,z	11.5**,z	...	...	...	...	.	...
22	Belarus	13.1	...	...	13.0**	12.7**	13.3**	14.0	13.7	14.4	...	...	...	...	.	...
23	Bosnia and Herzegovina[o]	...	...	...	...	...	...	...	...	...	...	...	...	...	.	...
24	Bulgaria[o]	12.3	12.3	12.3	12.7	12.2	13.1	12.5	12.3	12.6	90.6	0.99	...	...	...	...
25	Croatia	10.2	...	...	12.7	12.4	12.9	12.9	12.6	13.1	...	...	...	...	...	...
26	Czech Republic[o]	11.9	12.1	11.7	...	...	...	14.7	14.5	14.8	...	...	98.3	1.01	96.6**	1.01**
27	Estonia[o]	12.8	12.6	13.0	13.9	13.2	14.6	15.6	14.4	16.5	...	...	99.1	1.01	98.7	1.01
28	Hungary[o]	11.4	11.4	11.4	14.0**	13.8**	14.3**	15.3	14.6	15.6	97.6	...	...	...	...	...
29	Latvia[o]	12.4	12.2	12.5	13.7	12.8	14.4	14.9	13.7	15.8	...	...	...	...	.	...
30	Lithuania[o]	...	...	...	...	...	...	15.4	14.6	16.0	...	...	...	...	.	...
31	Poland[o]	12.2	12.0	12.4	...	...	...	15.1**,z	14.6**,z	15.6**,z	97.8	...	...	...	98.5	1.00
32	Republic of Moldova	11.9	...	...	9.9**	9.7**	10.2**	10.0	9.6	10.2	...	...	...	...	...	...
33	Romania[o]	11.5	11.5	11.4	11.8	11.6	12.0	12.4	12.1	12.7	...	...	...	...	...	...
34	Russian Federation[w]	12.5	12.0	13.0	...	...	...	13.3	12.7	13.8	...	...	...	...	...	...
35	Serbia and Montenegro	...	...	...	13.2**	13.0**	13.3**	12.8**,z	12.6**,z	12.9**,z	...	...	...	...	...	...
36	Slovakia	...	...	...	13.1**	13.0**	13.3**	13.7	13.5	13.9	...	...	...	...	...	...
37	Slovenia[o]	...	...	...	14.3**	13.6**	14.8**	15.9	15.0	16.5	...	...	...	...	...	...
38	TFYR Macedonia[o]	11.0	11.0	11.0	11.9	11.9	11.9	12.1**	11.9**	12.2**	...	...	...	...	...	...
39	Turkey[o]	8.5	9.5	7.4	...	...	...	10.7**	11.6**	9.8**	97.6	0.99	...	...	.	...
40	Ukraine	12.3	...	...	...	...	...	13.5**	13.1**	13.7**	97.7	...	...	...	.	...
	Central Asia															
41	Armenia	...	...	...	...	...	...	10.8**	10.4**	11.2**	...	...	...	...	...	...
42	Azerbaijan	10.5	10.8	10.3	10.1**	10.2**	10.0**	10.5	10.6	10.3	...	...	...	...	...	...
43	Georgia	12.4	12.3	12.4	10.8**	10.5**	11.0**	11.1**	10.9**	11.3**	...	...	...	...	...	...
44	Kazakhstan	12.4	...	...	11.5	11.3	11.7	12.9	12.5	13.1	...	...	...	...	...	...
45	Kyrgyzstan	10.4	...	...	11.9	11.7	12.1	12.7	12.3	12.8	...	...	...	...	...	...
46	Mongolia	9.4	8.8	10.0	8.8	7.8	9.7	10.3**	9.3**	11.2**	...	...	...	...	...	...
47	Tajikistan	11.7	...	...	10.0**	10.8**	9.2**	10.7**	11.7**	9.7**	...	...	...	...	...	...
48	Turkmenistan	...	...	...	...	...	...	...	...	...	...	...	...	...	...	...
49	Uzbekistan	11.6	...	...	...	...	...	11.4**	...	...	...	...	...	...	...	...
	East Asia and the Pacific															
50	Australia[o]	13.2	13.0	13.4	...	...	...	20.1**	19.8**	20.4**	...	...	...	...	...	...
51	Brunei Darussalam	...	...	...	13.1**	12.7**	13.4**	13.2**	12.8**	13.6**	...	...	...	...	...	...

(x) Data are for 1998/1999.   (y) Data are for 1999/2000.   (z) Data are for 2000/2001.

STATISTICAL ANNEX / 387

Table 17

GOAL 6. Educational quality in primary education

PUPIL/TEACHER RATIO			% FEMALE TEACHERS			TRAINED TEACHERS as % of total		PUBLIC CURRENT EXPENDITURE ON PRIMARY EDUCATION AS % GNP			PUBLIC CURRENT EXPENDITURE ON PRIMARY EDUCATION PER PUPIL (unit cost) in constant 2001 US$			PUBLIC CURRENT EXPENDITURE ON PRIMARY EDUCATION PER PUPIL (unit cost) in US$ at PPP			
1990	1998	2001	1990	1998	2001	1998	2001	1990	1998	2001	1990	1998	2001	1990	1998	2001	
28	28	28	39	46	48	93.7	97.1	...	...	...	...	...	...	...	...	...	1
19	...	16**	54	...	76**	...	...	...	...	...	...	...	...	...	...	...	2
43	40	34**	37	28	30**	...	...	2.0	...	...	403	...	...	...	...	...	3
24	23**	23**	52	52**	53**	...	...	...	...	...	...	...	...	...	...	...	4
25	26	21 y	70	72	73 y	...	100.0 y	...	...	...	...	...	...	...	...	...	5
25	...	20**	62	...	63**	...	...	...	1.9	2.1**	...	211	243**	...	446	536**	6
18	13	14	61	73	79	100.0	...	1.5	...	...	...	...	...	...	...	...	7
...	14	17	...	83	87	...	14.9	...	...	0.9**,y	...	...	...	...	...	...	8
14	...	8**,y	...	...	...	...	...	...	...	...	...	...	...	...	...	...	9
45	47	39	18	26	26	...	...	1.3	...	...	...	...	...	...	...	...	10
27	28	28	37	39	42	...	...	...	...	2.3	...	...	193	...	...	593	11
28	25	23**	47	52	59**	99.6	99.8**	1.7	1.5	1.3	...	...	787	910	1 270	...	12
...	...	31**,z	...	...	54**,z	...	...	...	...	...	...	...	...	...	...	...	13
11	13	12	72	75	82	...	...	...	...	...	...	...	...	...	...	...	14
16	12	12	48	54	49	...	...	...	...	...	...	...	...	...	...	...	15
34	...	...	51	...	...	...	...	...	...	...	...	...	...	...	...	...	16
25	25**	24**	64	68**	68**	...	95.6**	...	...	2.0 z	...	...	641 z	...	...	1 600 z	17
28	24	22	45	50	50	...	...	...	...	2.3**,z	...	...	275**,z	...	...	955**,z	18
18	16	15	64	73	76	...	...	...	...	...	...	...	...	...	...	...	19
...	30**	...	...	21**	...	...	...	...	...	...	...	...	...	...	...	...	20
19	23**	22 z	55	75**	74 z	...	...	...	...	...	...	...	...	...	...	...	21
...	20	17	...	99	99	...	97.9	1.6	...	...	...	...	...	...	...	...	22
...	...	...	...	...	...	...	...	...	...	...	...	...	...	...	...	...	23
15	18	17	77	91**	92	...	...	2.6	0.7	0.7**	...	209	283**	...	802	1 153**	24
19	19	18	75	89	89	...	100.0	...	...	...	...	...	...	...	...	...	25
23	18	17**	...	85**	84**	...	...	...	0.7	0.7	...	519	620	...	1 281	1 644	26
...	16	14**	...	...	...	...	...	...	1.4	1.6**	...	554	753**	...	1 260	1 891**	27
13	11	10	84	86	86	...	...	2.3	0.9**	1.0**	905	760**	1 003**	1 840	1 748**	2 427**	28
15	15	14	...	97	97	...	...	...	...	1.1**,z	...	...	646**,z	...	...	1 544**,z	29
18	17	16	94	98	...	...	...	...	...	...	...	...	...	...	...	...	30
16	...	15	...	...	84**	...	...	1.8	...	2.2**,z	...	...	1 205**,z	...	...	2 544**,z	31
23	21**	20	97	97**	96	...	...	...	...	...	...	...	...	...	...	...	32
22	19**	17	84	85**	87	...	...	1.2	...	...	...	...	...	...	...	...	33
22	...	17	99	98	99	...	...	...	...	...	...	...	...	...	...	...	34
...	...	20 z	...	...	82 z	...	100.0 z	...	...	...	...	...	...	...	...	...	35
...	19	19	...	93	93	...	...	...	...	0.6**	...	...	425**	...	...	1 342**	36
...	14	13	...	97	96	...	...	...	...	...	...	...	...	...	...	...	37
21	22	21	...	67	69	...	...	...	...	...	...	...	...	...	...	...	38
30	...	...	43	...	...	...	...	1.1	...	1.4**	183	...	245**	392	...	646**	39
22	21	20	98	99	99	...	99.7	...	...	...	...	...	...	...	...	...	40
...	...	19	...	...	99	...	...	...	...	...	...	...	...	...	...	...	41
...	19	16	...	83	84	100.0	100.0	...	...	...	...	...	...	...	...	...	42
17	17	14	92	92	85	...	76.9	...	...	...	...	...	...	...	...	...	43
21	18**	19	96	97**	97	...	...	...	...	...	...	...	...	...	...	...	44
...	25	24	81	95	97	47.7	49.3	...	...	...	...	...	...	...	...	...	45
28	32	32	90	93	94	...	...	...	...	...	...	...	...	...	...	...	46
21	22	22	49	56	60	...	81.6	...	...	...	...	...	...	...	...	...	47
...	...	...	...	...	...	...	...	...	...	...	...	...	...	...	...	...	48
24	...	...	79	...	...	...	...	...	...	...	...	...	...	...	...	...	49
...	...	...	...	...	...	...	...	...	...	1.6**	...	...	2 934**	...	...	3 913**	50
...	14*	14*	...	66*	70*	...	...	0.5	...	...	...	...	...	...	...	...	51

Table 17 (continued)

GOAL 6. Educational quality in primary education

| | Country or territory | SCHOOL LIFE EXPECTANCY (expected number of years of formal schooling) ||||||||| SURVIVAL RATE TO GRADE 5 ||||||
| | | 1990 ||| 1998 ||| 2001 ||| 1990 || 1998 || 2000 ||
		Total	Male	Female	Total	Male	Female	Total	Male	Female	Total (%)	GPI (F/M)	Total (%)	GPI (F/M)	Total (%)	GPI (F/M)
52	Cambodia	7.0	...	...	...	...	...	9.0**	9.8**	8.2**	...	...	56.3**	0.93**	70.4	0.98
53	China[w]	9.3	10.0	8.6	10.2**	...	...	10.4**	...	...	86.0	...	99.4	...	98.0	0.96
54	Cook Islands	...	...	...	...	...	...	...	...	...	...	...	51.5	0.84	51.5[x]	0.84[x]
55	DPR Korea	...	...	...	...	...	...	...	...	...	...	...	...	...	...	...
56	Fiji	...	...	...	...	...	...	...	...	...	...	...	92.0**	1.04**	...	...
57	Indonesia[w]	10.1	...	...	...	...	...	10.9	11.0	10.7	83.6	...	...	...	89.2	1.06
58	Japan[o]	13.4	13.7	13.1	14.3**	14.5**	14.2**	14.7**	14.8**	14.5**	100.0	1.00	...	...	...	...
59	Kiribati	...	...	...	...	...	...	...	...	...	93.4	1.14	...	...	...	...
60	Lao PDR	...	...	...	8.4**	9.3	7.4**	8.9**	9.8**	7.9**	...	...	54.3	0.98	62.3	1.01
61	Macao, China	11.5	12.0	11.1	12.1**	12.2**	11.9**	14.8**	16.1**	13.7**	...	...	...	...	...	...
62	Malaysia[w]	9.9	9.8	10.0	12.0**	11.7**	12.2**	12.3**,[z]	12.0**,[z]	12.6**,[z]	98.2	1.00	...	...	...	...
63	Marshall Islands	...	...	...	...	...	...	...	...	...	...	...	...	...	...	...
64	Micronesia	...	...	...	...	...	...	...	...	...	...	...	...	...	...	...
65	Myanmar	6.9	...	...	...	...	...	7.4**,[z]	7.3**,[z]	7.5**,[z]	...	...	...	...	59.9	1.02
66	Nauru	...	...	...	8.1**	...	...	...	...	...	...	...	...	...	...	...
67	New Zealand[o]	14.6	14.5	14.7	...	...	...	17.7**,[y]	16.8**,[y]	18.6**,[y]	92.2	1.02	...	...	...	...
68	Niue	...	...	...	12.3	...	...	12.8	...	...	...	...	75.8	1.03	...	...
69	Palau	...	...	...	...	...	...	...	...	...	...	...	84.2	0.82	...	...
70	Papua New Guinea	...	...	...	5.7**	6.1**	5.3**	...	...	...	59.1	0.98	68.0	1.01	...	...
71	Philippines[w]	10.8	10.6	11.1	11.7**	11.4**	11.9**	12.0**	11.9**	12.0**	...	...	...	...	79.3	1.10
72	Republic of Korea[o]	13.7	14.4	12.9	14.9**	15.7**	14.0**	15.7**	16.7**	14.6**	99.5	1.00	...	...	...	...
73	Samoa	...	...	...	11.7**	11.5**	12.0**	11.8**	11.6**	12.0**	...	...	82.6	0.87	93.8	0.95
74	Singapore	11.9	12.3	11.5	...	...	...	...	...	...	...	...	...	...	...	...
75	Solomon Islands	...	...	...	...	...	...	...	...	...	84.9	...	...	...	...	...
76	Thailand[w]	...	...	...	...	...	...	12.5**,[z]	12.7**,[z]	12.3**,[z]	...	...	94.1**	1.04**	...	...
77	Timor-Leste	...	...	...	...	...	...	11.4**	...	...	...	...	...	...	...	...
78	Tokelau	...	...	...	...	...	...	...	...	...	...	...	...	...	...	...
79	Tonga	...	...	...	...	...	...	13.4**	13.2**	13.7**	89.6	0.89	89.2	0.84	82.9**	0.95**
80	Tuvalu	...	...	...	10.9**	...	...	...	...	...	...	...	...	...	...	...
81	Vanuatu	...	...	...	...	...	...	9.4**	...	...	...	...	91.5**	0.84**	95.1	1.04
82	Viet Nam	7.5	...	...	10.3**	10.8**	9.8**	10.5**	11.0**	10.1**	...	...	82.8	1.08	89.0	0.98
	Latin America and the Caribbean															
83	Anguilla	...	...	...	...	...	...	...	...	...	...	...	...	...	91.1	1.03
84	Antigua and Barbuda	...	...	...	...	...	...	...	...	...	...	...	...	...	...	...
85	Argentina[w]	...	...	...	14.9**	14.3**	15.6**	16.3	15.1	17.1	...	...	94.7	1.03	93.1	1.04
86	Aruba	...	...	...	13.3**	13.2**	13.4**	13.5	13.2	13.7	...	...	96.8	0.99	96.5	1.07
87	Bahamas	...	...	...	...	...	...	...	...	...	...	...	...	...	...	...
88	Barbados	...	...	...	15.0**	14.4**	15.6**	14.2**,[z]	13.5**,[z]	15.0**,[z]	...	...	94.1	0.95	95.3	1.01
89	Belize	...	...	...	...	...	...	...	...	...	67.4	0.96	77.8	1.04	81.5[y]	1.00[y]
90	Bermuda	...	...	...	...	...	...	15.3**,[z]	...	...	...	...	...	...	...	...
91	Bolivia	10.1	...	...	12.9**	13.6**	12.1**	14.3**	...	...	...	...	79.4	0.97	78.0	0.98
92	Brazil[w]	10.3	...	...	...	...	...	14.9	14.3	15.2	...	...	...	...	.	...
93	British Virgin Islands	...	...	...	15.8**	...	...	15.0**	14.0**	16.0**	...	...	...	...	...	...
94	Cayman Islands	...	...	...	...	...	...	...	...	...	...	...	...	...	...	...
95	Chile[w]	...	...	...	12.7**	12.8**	12.6**	13.3**,[z]	13.4**,[z]	13.2**,[z]	...	...	99.8	1.00	99.9[y]	1.00[y]
96	Colombia	8.8	8.3	9.4	11.1**	10.9**	11.4**	10.7**	10.5**	10.9**	62.1	0.63	69.0	1.09	60.9	1.07
97	Costa Rica	9.7	...	...	...	...	...	11.0**	10.8**	11.1**	82.4	1.04	...	...	93.7	1.02
98	Cuba	12.4	11.9	12.9	12.1**	...	...	12.8**	12.8**	12.9**	91.6	...	93.7	1.00	...	...
99	Dominica	...	...	...	11.8**	...	...	...	...	...	...	...	91.1	1.17**	85.4	0.97
100	Dominican Republic	...	...	...	...	...	...	...	...	...	...	...	75.1**	1.11**	72.9**	1.33**
101	Ecuador	11.4	...	...	...	...	...	...	...	...	...	...	77.0	1.01	78.0	1.02
102	El Salvador	9.0	9.1	8.9	10.7**	10.7**	10.6**	11.0**	11.0**	10.9**	...	...	61.3**	1.03**	67.2**	1.08**
103	Grenada	...	...	...	...	...	...	...	...	...	...	...	...	...	...	...
104	Guatemala	...	...	...	...	...	...	...	...	...	...	...	...	...	55.8	0.94
105	Guyana	...	...	...	...	...	...	...	...	...	93.1	0.99	94.8	0.90	94.8[x]	0.90[x]
106	Haiti	...	...	...	...	...	...	...	...	...	...	...	...	...	...	...
107	Honduras	...	...	...	...	...	...	...	...	...	...	...	...	...	...	...
108	Jamaica[w]	11.0	11.0	11.1	...	...	...	11.8**	11.3**	12.4**	...	...	...	...	90.3**	1.05**
109	Mexico[o]	10.8	11.0	10.6	11.8**	11.8**	11.7**	12.3	12.2	12.4	79.5	...	89.0	1.02	90.5	1.02

(x) Data are for 1998/1999. (y) Data are for 1999/2000. (z) Data are for 2000/2001.

Table 17

GOAL 6. Educational quality in primary education

PUPIL/TEACHER RATIO			% FEMALE TEACHERS			TRAINED TEACHERS as % of total		PUBLIC CURRENT EXPENDITURE ON PRIMARY EDUCATION AS % GNP			PUBLIC CURRENT EXPENDITURE ON PRIMARY EDUCATION PER PUPIL (unit cost) in constant 2001 US$			PUBLIC CURRENT EXPENDITURE ON PRIMARY EDUCATION PER PUPIL (unit cost) in US$ at PPP			
1990	1998	2001	1990	1998	2001	1998	2001	1990	1998	2001	1990	1998	2001	1990	1998	2001	
33	48**	56	31	37**	39	...	96.0	...	0.5	1.5	...	6	18	...	37	117	52
22	19	20**	43	50**	53	...	96.8	...	0.7**	...	...	48**	...	...	200**	...	53
...	19	18**,z	...	...	86**,z	...	...	...	0.2	0.2y	...	...	...	...	...	...	54
...	...	...	...	...	...	...	...	...	...	...	...	...	...	...	...	...	55
34	23**	28**	...	57**	57**	97.5**	...	...	...	...	...	...	...	...	...	...	56
23	...	21	51	...	52	...	...	...	...	0.5**	...	...	23**	...	...	95**	57
21	21	20	58	...	...	...	...	...	...	1.1**	...	...	6 415**	...	...	4 946**	58
29	24	...	57	64	...	...	...	...	...	...	...	...	...	...	...	...	59
27	31	30	38	43	44	75.7	76.1	...	...	...	...	...	...	...	...	...	60
...	31	28	...	87	89	81.0	89.7	...	...	0.9**,z	...	...	1 133**,z	...	...	1 792**,z	61
20	22	20	57	63	67	96.6**	...	...	1.4**	1.6	...	351**	424	...	747**	1 002	62
...	15	17	...	...	34	...	...	...	...	3.9	...	...	...	...	...	...	63
...	...	...	...	...	...	...	...	...	...	...	...	...	...	...	...	...	64
48	31	33	62	73	77	77.9**	...	...	0.2	0.5z	...	...	...	...	...	...	65
...	23**	...	...	82**	...	...	...	...	...	...	...	...	...	...	...	...	66
18	...	18	79	...	84	...	...	1.7	...	1.9**	1 823	...	2 569**	2 181	...	3 757**	67
...	24	18	...	100	100	...	100.0	...	...	...	...	...	...	...	...	...	68
...	15	18**,y	...	82	82**,y	...	...	...	...	...	...	...	...	...	...	...	69
32	36	36**	32	38	39**	100.0	100.0**	...	...	...	...	...	...	...	...	...	70
33	35	35	...	87	87	100.0**	...	...	2.2	1.7	...	117	99	...	468	417	71
36	...	32	50	...	72	...	...	1.4	...	1.3**,z	631	...	1 410**,z	880	...	2 289**,z	72
24	25**	25	64	73**	73	...	...	...	...	1.8z	...	...	141z	...	...	625z	73
26	...	...	...	...	...	...	...	...	...	...	...	...	...	...	...	...	74
19	...	...	...	...	...	...	...	...	...	...	...	...	...	...	...	...	75
22	21	19	...	63	58	...	...	1.7	1.2	1.6**	174	190	291**	484	616	995**	76
...	...	51	...	...	30	...	...	...	...	...	...	...	...	...	...	...	77
...	...	...	...	...	...	...	...	...	...	...	...	...	...	...	...	...	78
24	22	21	69	70	68	87.2	100.0	...	...	2.3	...	...	170	...	...	...	79
21	...	26	72	...	84	...	...	...	...	...	...	...	...	...	...	...	80
27	22**	29	40	44**	58	...	100.0	...	...	2.8	...	...	165	...	...	497	81
35	30	26	...	78	78	77.6	87.0	...	...	...	...	...	...	...	...	...	82
...	22	17	...	87	92	76.1	73.8	...	...	...	...	...	...	...	...	...	83
...	...	19y	...	...	79y	...	46.9y	...	...	...	...	...	...	...	...	...	84
...	21	20**	...	89	...	...	...	...	1.4	1.6**,z	...	854	916**,z	...	1 261	1 418**,z	85
...	19	19	...	78	80	100.0	100.0	...	...	...	...	...	...	...	...	...	86
...	...	17	...	...	93	...	94.8	...	...	...	...	...	...	...	...	...	87
18	20**	16**	72	75**	75**	84.4**	76.7**	...	1.3	1.5**	...	1 114	1 737**	...	1 576	2 629**	88
26	24**	23z	70	64**	65z	...	40.9z	2.7	...	2.6z	...	...	416z	...	...	705z	89
...	...	9	...	...	88	...	100.0	1.1	...	...	...	...	...	...	...	...	90
25	...	25**	57	...	60**	...	...	...	2.0**	2.2	...	107**	112	...	245**	276	91
23	...	23	...	94	92	...	...	...	...	1.2**	...	...	290**	...	...	731**	92
19	18	17	...	86	88**	71.9	...	...	...	...	...	...	...	...	...	...	93
...	16	15	...	89	81	...	99.2	...	...	...	...	...	...	...	...	...	94
29	33	32z	75	78	78z	...	92.5**,z	1.4	1.5	1.6**,z	...	514	539**,z	...	1 016	1 145**,z	95
30	23	26	...	...	77	...	...	...	...	...	...	...	...	...	...	...	96
32	...	24	...	...	79	...	89.5	...	2.9	2.1	...	...	580	...	...	1 319	97
13	12	14	79	79	79	100.0	100.0	1.5	...	2.9*,z	...	...	...	...	...	...	98
29	20	19	81	77	79	64.0	60.1	...	3.0*	...	...	644*	...	...	865*	...	99
...	39**	39**	...	75**	83**	...	58.5**	...	...	1.1**	...	...	154**	...	...	435**	100
30	27	25	...	68	69	...	68.6	...	...	...	...	...	...	...	...	...	101
...	...	26**	...	...	...	...	...	...	0.3**	1.4**,z	...	39**	198**,z	...	90**	467**,z	102
...	...	22**	...	...	79**	...	69.7**	...	...	...	...	...	...	...	...	...	103
...	36*	30	...	...	...	...	100.0	0.4	...	1.3	...	...	136	...	...	342	104
30	27	26y	76	86	85y	51.7	51.4y	...	...	...	...	...	...	...	...	...	105
23	...	...	45	...	...	...	...	0.8	...	...	58	...	...	198	...	...	106
...	...	34**	74	...	...	...	...	...	...	...	...	...	...	...	...	...	107
34	...	34	...	...	...	...	...	1.6	...	1.9	307	...	423	325	...	523	108
31	27	27	...	67**	66**	...	...	0.6	1.5**	2.0**	...	539**	834**	...	694**	1 131**	109

Table 17 (continued)

GOAL 6. Educational quality in primary education

	Country or territory	SCHOOL LIFE EXPECTANCY (expected number of years of formal schooling)									SURVIVAL RATE TO GRADE 5					
		1990			1998			2001			1990		1998		2000	
		Total	Male	Female	Total	Male	Female	Total	Male	Female	Total (%)	GPI (F/M)	Total (%)	GPI (F/M)	Total (%)	GPI (F/M)
110	Montserrat	...	...	...	13.6	...	...	...	...	...	60.3	0.93	...	...	...	...
111	Netherlands Antilles	...	...	...	12.3**	12.0**	12.6**	11.5	11.0	11.9	...	...	82.6**	1.04**	...	...
112	Nicaragua	8.3	7.7	8.8	...	...	...	...	...	...	45.6	...	...	...	54.2	1.15
113	Panama	11.2	...	...	...	...	...	12.2**,y	11.8**,y	12.7**,y	...	...	...	...	88.6	1.01
114	Paraguay[w]	8.6	8.7	8.5	...	...	...	11.7**	11.6**	11.8**	70.5	1.04	70.0**	1.03**	77.2**	1.03**
115	Peru[w]	12.2	...	...	...	...	...	14.0**	13.8**	14.0**	...	...	87.9	0.99	86.1	1.00
116	Saint Kitts and Nevis	...	...	...	...	...	...	...	...	...	...	...	...	...	78.4	1.12
117	Saint Lucia	12.9	12.6	13.1	13.4**	13.2**	13.7**	12.5**	11.8**	13.2**	...	...	90.1**	1.20**	97.2	1.02
118	St Vincent/Grenad.	...	...	...	...	...	...	...	...	...	...	...	...	...	...	...
119	Suriname	...	...	...	...	...	...	12.5**	11.7**	13.4**	...	...	...	...	...	...
120	Trinidad and Tobago	11.1	11.1	11.2	11.9**	11.7**	12.1**	12.1**	11.6**	12.4**	97.9	1.04	99.7	1.01	...	...
121	Turks and Caicos Islands	...	...	...	...	...	...	...	...	...	...	...	...	...	...	...
122	Uruguay[w]	12.9	...	...	...	...	...	14.6	13.5	15.5	94.5	1.03	88.3	1.06	88.5	1.03
123	Venezuela	10.8	...	...	...	...	...	11.2**	10.8**	11.6**	86.1	1.09	90.8	1.08	96.3**	1.03**
	North America and Western Europe															
124	Andorra	...	...	...	...	...	...	...	...	...	...	...	...	...	...	...
125	Austria[o]	13.8	14.2	13.4	15.2**	15.2**	15.1**	14.8	14.4	14.9	...	...	...	...	.	.
126	Belgium[o]	14.0	14.0	14.1	17.8**	17.4**	18.2**	18.9**	18.0**	19.6**	...	...	...	...	...	...
127	Canada[o]	16.9	16.4	17.3	16.0**	15.7**	16.3**	16.1**,z	15.7**,z	16.4**,z	...	...	...	...	...	...
128	Cyprus[o]	10.3	10.3	10.4	12.5	12.3	12.7	13.0	12.7	13.2	99.9	...	96.1	1.03	...	...
129	Denmark[o]	14.3	14.1	14.5	16.1**	15.6**	16.6**	16.6	15.7	17.2	94.2	1.00	100.0	1.00	...	...
130	Finland[o]	15.2	14.5	16.0	17.5**	16.7**	18.2**	18.1	16.5	18.9	99.8	1.00	99.8	1.00	99.9	1.00
131	France[o]	14.3	14.0	14.6	15.6**	15.3**	15.8**	15.4	15.0	15.7	96.4	...	98.0	0.99**	...	...
132	Germany[o]	14.5	...	...	16.0**	16.2**	15.8**	15.7**	15.5**	15.6**	...	...	...	...	.	.
133	Greece[o]	13.4	13.5	13.3	...	...	...	14.9**,z	14.6**,z	15.1**,z	99.7	1.00	...	...	...	...
134	Iceland[o]	15.3	15.3	15.3	...	...	...	17.6	16.2	18.6	...	...	...	...	...	...
135	Ireland[o]	12.7	12.6	12.8	16.2**	15.7**	16.6**	16.7	15.9	17.4	99.5	1.01	95.1	1.03	98.8	1.02
136	Israel[o]	13.2	12.9	13.4	14.8**	14.4**	15.2**	15.8	14.8	16.2	...	...	...	...	...	...
137	Italy[o]	13.4	13.5	13.4	14.7**	14.5**	14.9**	15.4	15.0	15.6	99.6	1.01	96.6	1.02	96.5	1.01
138	Luxembourg[o]	...	...	...	...	...	...	13.5**	13.4**	13.7**	...	...	...	...	99.0**	0.99**
139	Malta[o]	12.9	13.2	12.5	...	...	...	14.0	13.8	14.1	99.3	1.01	99.4	0.99	99.9	1.00
140	Monaco	...	...	...	...	...	...	...	...	...	82.9	0.81	...	...	...	...
141	Netherlands[o]	15.2	15.6	14.9	16.5**	16.7**	16.2**	16.5	16.4	16.4	...	...	99.9	1.00	...	...
142	Norway[o]	14.4	14.1	14.7	17.5**	16.9**	18.0**	17.3	16.0	18.1	99.6	1.01	...	...	...	...
143	Portugal[o]	12.5	12.2	12.7	15.8**	15.5**	16.1**	16.1	15.4	16.6	...	...	...	...	...	...
144	San Marino	...	...	...	...	...	...	...	...	...	88.1	1.27	...	...	...	...
145	Spain[o]	14.6	14.3	14.8	...	...	...	16.0	15.4	16.4	...	...	...	...	...	...
146	Sweden[o]	13.1	12.8	13.4	19.0**	17.3**	20.8**	19.0	16.8	20.7	99.8	1.00	...	...	...	...
147	Switzerland[o]	13.8	14.2	13.3	15.5**	16.0**	15.0**	15.7	15.6	15.3	79.7	0.98	...	...	99.3	0.99
148	United Kingdom[o]	14.2	14.4	14.0	20.0**	19.3**	20.7**	21.8	19.7	23.3	...	...	...	...	...	...
149	United States[o]	15.3	14.9	15.7	...	...	...	15.6	14.5	16.1	...	...	...	...	...	...
	South and West Asia															
150	Afghanistan	2.5	...	...	...	...	...	...	...	...	...	...	...	...	...	...
151	Bangladesh	5.6	6.4	4.7	8.5**	8.7**	8.2**	8.4	8.3	8.5	...	...	65.4**	1.19**	65.5	1.07
152	Bhutan	...	...	...	6.5**	7.0**	5.8**	7.5**	7.8**	6.8**	...	...	87.5	1.03	91.0	1.04
153	India[w]	8.1	9.6	6.6	...	...	...	9.0**	10.0**	7.9**	...	...	62.0	0.95	61.4	1.06
154	Iran, Islamic Republic of	9.7	10.7	8.6	11.6**	12.2**	10.9**	11.5**	12.0**	10.9**	89.9	0.98	...	...	93.7	1.00
155	Maldives	...	...	...	11.6	...	...	12.3**	...	...	...	...	...	...	...	...
156	Nepal	7.7	9.8	5.5	...	...	...	9.6**	10.5**	8.5**	...	...	...	...	77.8	1.07
157	Pakistan	4.7	6.1	3.2	...	...	...	...	...	...	...	...	...	...	...	...
158	Sri Lanka[w]	12.0	11.9	12.1	...	...	...	...	...	...	94.4	1.01	...	...	...	...
	Sub-Saharan Africa															
159	Angola	4.8	...	...	5.2**	...	...	4.4**,y	4.7**,y	4.0**,y	...	...	...	...	...	...
160	Benin	4.2	5.7	2.6	6.7**	8.4**	4.9**	7.1**,y	8.9**,y	5.3**,y	55.1	1.02	...	...	...	...
161	Botswana	9.4	9.1	9.8	11.4**	11.2**	11.5**	11.6**	11.5**	11.7**	96.6	1.07	87.6	1.08	89.5	1.06
162	Burkina Faso	2.5	3.1	1.9	...	...	...	3.4**	4.0**	2.8**	69.7	0.96	68.3	1.05	63.7**	...
163	Burundi	4.9	5.4	4.4	3.7**	4.0**	3.3**	5.2**	5.9**	4.5**	61.8	0.89	...	...	64.0	0.86

(x) Data are for 1998/1999. (y) Data are for 1999/2000. (z) Data are for 2000/2001.

STATISTICAL ANNEX / 391

Table 17

GOAL 6. Educational quality in primary education

	PUPIL/TEACHER RATIO			% FEMALE TEACHERS			TRAINED TEACHERS as % of total		PUBLIC CURRENT EXPENDITURE ON PRIMARY EDUCATION AS % GNP			PUBLIC CURRENT EXPENDITURE ON PRIMARY EDUCATION PER PUPIL (unit cost) in constant 2001 US$			PUBLIC CURRENT EXPENDITURE ON PRIMARY EDUCATION PER PUPIL (unit cost) in US$ at PPP			
	1990	1998	2001	1990	1998	2001	1998	2001	1990	1998	2001	1990	1998	2001	1990	1998	2001	
	...	21	20	...	84	96	...	91.3	...	...	...	...	...	...	...	...	...	110
	...	20	20	...	86	86	100.0	100.0	...	...	...	...	...	...	...	...	...	111
	33	37	37	87	83	82	73.6	72.9	...	...	...	...	...	...	...	...	...	112
	23	26**	24	...	75**	75	...	75.7	1.8	1.9**	1.5	313	532**	420	422	821**	688	113
	25	19**	...	...	76**	...	...	...	0.5	...	2.2**	...	...	154**	...	...	626**	114
	29	25	29	...	60	64	...	...	...	1.1	1.2y	...	134	129y	...	282	308y	115
	22	...	17**	74	...	87	...	54.4	...	...	1.3	...	...	624**	...	...	926**	116
	29	22	24	83	84**	84	...	77.8	2.6	...	2.4y	...	...	650y	...	...	738y	117
	20	...	17**	67	...	71**	...	...	...	...	3.4z	...	...	600z	...	...	1 038z	118
	22	...	20	84	...	85	...	100.0	5.0	...	...	2 577	...	...	...	...	...	119
	26	21	19**	70	76	78**	71.5	78.1**	1.6	1.3	1.6	446	515	897**	514	655	1 209**	120
	...	21**	18	...	93**	87	...	100.0	...	...	...	...	...	...	...	...	...	121
	22	21	21	...	92**	...	...	...	1.1	...	0.7**	...	...	377**	...	...	571**	122
	23	...	...	75	...	...	...	...	0.5	...	...	...	...	...	...	...	...	123
	...	...	12	...	...	75	...	...	...	...	...	...	...	...	...	...	...	124
	11	14	14**,y	82	89	89**,y	...	...	0.9	1.1**	1.1**	3 469	5 145**	5 363**	3 273	5 542**	6 183**	125
	...	...	12**	...	...	79**	...	...	1.1	...	1.3**	2 886	...	4 027**	2 799	...	4 603**	126
	15	15	17z	69	68	68z	...	...	...	...	...	...	...	...	...	...	...	127
	21	18	19	60	67	82	...	...	1.1	...	1.7**	1 045	...	2 367**	1 495	...	4 179**	128
	...	10	10z	...	63	64z	...	...	...	1.8**	1.7**	...	7 174**	6 508**	...	6 438**	6 261**	129
	...	17	16	...	71	74	...	...	1.6	...	1.3**	3 878	...	3 780**	3 398	...	3 964**	130
	...	19	19	...	78	79	...	...	0.9	1.0	1.0**	2 237	3 108	3 624**	2 020	3 163	3 929**	131
	...	17	14	...	82	...	...	...	...	0.8**	0.6**	...	3 488**	3 480**	...	3 716**	3 934**	132
	19	14	13	52	...	...	...	...	0.7	0.9**	0.9**	713	1 457**	1 698**	909	2 110**	2 677**	133
	...	11**	11**,y	...	76**	78**,y	...	...	2.5	...	2.1**	4 590	...	4 868**	4 147	...	5 344**	134
	27	22	20**	77	74	81**	...	...	1.5	1.5**	1.4**,z	1 536	2 363**	2 942**,z	1 393	2 513**	3 193**,z	135
	15	13	12	82	...	83z	...	...	1.9	2.4**	2.4**,z	1 651	3 334**	3 539**,z	1 611	3 699**	4 094**,z	136
	12	11	11	91	95	95	...	...	0.8	1.1**	1.1**	2 435	4 020**	4 410**	2 669	4 983**	5 791**	137
	13	...	12	51	...	68	...	...	...	...	1.6**	...	...	7 921**	...	...	10 133**	138
	21	20	19	79	87	87	...	...	0.9	1.0	...	624	892	...	687	1 226	...	139
	...	16**	22z	...	87**	87z	...	...	...	...	...	...	...	...	...	...	...	140
	17	...	10z	53	...	78z	...	...	0.9	1.2**	1.3**	2 303	3 240**	3 808**	2 215	3 577**	4 369**	141
	...	...	...	...	...	...	...	...	2.5	2.5**	2.3**,z	9 154	9 450**	8 901**,z	6 214	7 130**	6 916**,z	142
	14	...	11	82	...	81**	...	...	1.6	...	1.8**	1 269	...	2 498**	1 718	...	4 138**	143
	6	...	5y	89	...	91y	...	...	...	...	...	...	...	...	...	...	...	144
	22	15	14	73	68	71	...	...	0.9	1.1**	1.1**	1 339	2 279**	2 611**	1 562	3 031**	3 718**	145
	10	12	12	77	80	...	...	...	3.4	...	2.1**	9 457	...	5 579**	8 026	...	5 719**	146
	...	13	14**	...	72	73**	...	...	2.0	1.5**	1.4**	11 646	6 912**	7 304**	8 363	5 484**	6 006**	147
	20	19	17	78	76	82	...	...	1.2	...	1.0**	2 902	...	3 304**	2 445	...	3 296**	148
	...	15	15z	...	87	87z	...	...	...	...	1.8**	...	...	7 386**	...	...	7 186**	149
	41	32	43z	59	...	...	...	...	...	...	...	...	...	...	...	...	...	150
	63	57**	55	19	31	36	62.9	65.6	...	0.6	0.5	...	13**	15	...	56**	66	151
	...	38	40	...	41	35	99.7	91.6	...	...	...	...	...	...	...	...	...	152
	47	40*	40**	28	33*	36**	...	...	...	...	1.5**,z	...	...	62**,z	...	...	382**,z	153
	31	27	24	53	53	54	...	96.5**,z	...	...	1.2	...	...	620	...	...	2 106	154
	...	26	23	...	58	61	68.9	66.9	...	...	...	...	...	...	...	...	...	155
	39	41**	40	...	22**	25	52.0**	...	...	1.1**	1.3	...	15**	19	...	79**	106	156
	...	...	44*,z	27	...	37*,z	...	...	...	...	...	...	...	...	...	...	...	157
	29	...	...	...	...	...	...	...	...	...	...	...	...	...	...	...	...	158
	32	42*	35**,z	...	25*	41**,z	...	...	4.2	...	...	...	...	...	...	...	...	159
	36	53	53	25	23	19	...	...	...	...	1.7	...	...	34	...	...	91	160
	32	28	27	80	82	80	91.8	89.5	...	...	1.0z	...	...	144z	...	...	379z	161
	57	49	47**	27	25	23**	...	...	...	...	...	...	...	...	...	...	...	162
	67	46**	49	46	54**	54	...	...	1.6	...	1.4**	19	...	12**	110	...	80**	163

Table 17 (continued)

GOAL 6. Educational quality in primary education

| | Country or territory | SCHOOL LIFE EXPECTANCY (expected number of years of formal schooling) ||||||||| SURVIVAL RATE TO GRADE 5 ||||||
| | | 1990 ||| 1998 ||| 2001 ||| 1990 || 1998 || 2000 ||
		Total	Male	Female	Total	Male	Female	Total	Male	Female	Total (%)	GPI (F/M)	Total (%)	GPI (F/M)	Total (%)	GPI (F/M)
164	Cameroon	8.3	...	...	7.6**	...	...	9.3**	10.0**	8.5**	...	...	80.7**	1.29**	...	...
165	Cape Verde	...	...	...	...	...	...	11.6**	11.7**	11.5**	...	...	96.7**	1.07**	92.8	1.08
166	Central African Republic	4.9	6.2	3.6	...	...	...	...	...	...	24.0	0.90	...	...	...	...
167	Chad	...	...	...	...	...	...	5.3**,y	6.9**,y	3.7**,y	53.1	0.75	55.1	0.86	45.3**	...
168	Comoros	...	...	...	6.5**	7.0**	5.9**	6.9**,y	7.5**,y	6.3**,y	...	...	...	...	...	...
169	Congo	11.0	12.1	9.9	...	...	...	7.7**	8.3**	7.0**	62.7	1.15	...	...	...	...
170	Côte d'Ivoire	...	...	...	6.4**	7.7**	5.1**	...	...	...	73.0	0.94	69.1	0.89	...	...
171	D. R. Congo	...	...	...	...	...	...	...	...	...	54.7	0.86	...	...	...	...
172	Equatorial Guinea	...	...	...	...	...	...	9.0**,y	9.5**,y	8.3**,y	...	...	...	...	32.6**	0.93**
173	Eritrea	...	...	...	4.4**	4.9**	3.7**	5.0**	5.7**	4.1**	...	...	95.3	0.95	82.1	0.82
174	Ethiopia	2.8	3.4	2.3	4.0**	4.8**	3.0**	5.2**	6.1**	4.2**	...	...	55.8	1.03	61.3	0.94
175	Gabon	...	...	...	12.1**	12.2**	11.7**	...	...	...	...	...	...	...	...	...
176	Gambia	...	...	...	...	...	...	...	...	...	...	...	70.2**	0.82**	...	...
177	Ghana[1]	6.5	7.5	5.6	...	...	...	7.5**	8.0**	6.9**	80.5	0.98	98.5	0.97	66.3y	0.97y
178	Guinea	2.8	4.0	1.7	...	...	...	...	...	...	58.8	0.76	86.9	0.86	...	...
179	Guinea-Bissau	...	...	...	...	...	...	5.5**,y	6.4**,y	4.2**,y	...	...	38.1**	0.82**	38.1**,x	0.82**,x
180	Kenya	8.4	8.8	7.9	...	...	...	8.5**	8.7**	8.3**	...	...	...	...	...	...
181	Lesotho	9.8	8.8	10.8	9.7**	9.0**	10.3	10.7	10.4	11.0	70.7	1.42	68.9	1.23	66.8	1.24
182	Liberia	...	...	...	...	...	...	10.3y	11.4y	8.7y	...	...	...	...	...	...
183	Madagascar	6.3	6.4	6.2	6.2**	6.2**	6.0**	...	...	...	21.7	0.95	51.1	1.02	33.6	1.05
184	Malawi	6.3	7.1	5.5	11.5**	12.0**	10.8**	...	...	...	64.5	0.80	44.1	0.78**	53.6	0.77
185	Mali	2.0	2.5	1.4	3.9**	...	...	...	...	...	72.5	0.95	78.3**	0.97**	84.1	0.90
186	Mauritius	10.3	10.4	10.3	11.8**	11.9**	11.8**	12.4**	12.3**	12.4**	98.4	1.00	99.4	1.01	99.3	1.00
187	Mozambique	...	...	...	...	...	...	5.4**,y	6.1**,y	4.5**,y	32.9	0.76	41.8	0.83	51.9	0.84
188	Namibia	...	...	...	12.1**	11.4**	12.3**	11.7**	11.2**	11.7**	...	...	83.4	1.09	94.2**	1.00**
189	Niger	2.2	...	...	...	...	...	2.9**	3.5**	2.3**	62.4	1.06	...	...	71.0	0.94
190	Nigeria	...	...	...	...	...	...	...	...	...	...	...	...	...	...	...
191	Rwanda	...	...	...	7.9**	...	...	8.2**	8.2**	8.0**	60.0	0.97	45.4	0.89	40.0	1.04
192	Sao Tome and Principe	...	...	...	9.6**	10.0**	...	9.2**	...	...	...	...	61.5**	1.11**	...	...
193	Senegal	4.8	...	...	5.6**	...	...	...	...	...	84.5	...	...	...	67.5	0.92
194	Seychelles	...	...	...	13.4	...	...	13.7**	...	...	...	...	...	...	...	...
195	Sierra Leone	4.8	...	...	...	...	...	6.8**,z	7.9**,z	5.7**,z	...	...	...	...	...	...
196	Somalia	...	...	...	...	...	...	...	...	...	...	...	...	...	...	...
197	South Africa	11.5	11.4	11.6	13.5**	13.2**	13.7**	12.9**	12.8**	12.9**	75.3	1.09	75.9*	1.02*	64.8y	0.98y
198	Swaziland	9.4	9.6	9.1	10.3**	10.4**	10.0**	9.8**	9.9**	9.5**	76.2	1.05	75.5**	1.15**	73.9	1.15
199	Togo	8.8	11.3	6.3	10.8**	13.0**	8.5**	10.4**,y	12.4**,y	8.3**,y	50.7	0.81	...	...	84.3	0.90
200	Uganda	5.2	5.9	4.5	11.9**	12.1**	11.0**	11.5**	11.5**	11.1**	...	...	...	...	...	...
201	United Republic of Tanzania	5.3	...	...	5.0**	4.8**	4.9**	...	...	...	78.9	1.05	80.9	1.06	78.1	1.05
202	Zambia	7.8	...	...	6.9**	7.2**	6.5**	6.9**,z	7.2**,z	6.5**,z	...	...	78.2	0.87	76.7**	0.95**
203	Zimbabwe[w]	9.8	...	...	...	...	...	9.8**	10.1**	9.4**	92.4	0.85	...	...	...	...

		Weighted average									Median					
I	World	9.3	9.9	8.43	10.0	10.4	9.5	10.3	10.7	9.8	...	...	...	...	...	...
II	Countries in transition	12.2	11.9	12.80	12.0	11.9	12.1	12.5	12.2	12.6	...	...	...	...	...	...
III	Developed countries	14.2	14.1	14.3	15.7	15.5	15.9	15.9	15.2	16.4	...	...	...	...	...	...
IV	Developing countries	8.4	9.2	7.36	9.2	9.8	8.6	9.5	10.1	8.9	...	...	84.1	1.01	83.3	0.97
V	Arab States	8.6	9.1	7.3	9.8	10.5	9.0	10.0	10.6	9.4	87.3	...	92.0	1.01	94.0	1.04
VI	Central and Eastern Europe	11.4	...	...	11.8	11.8	11.8	12.7	12.7	12.7	...	...	...	...	...	...
VII	Central Asia	11.6	...	...	11.1	11.2	11.0	11.4	11.5	11.3	...	...	...	...	...	...
VIII	East Asia and the Pacific	9.6	10.4	9.2	10.5	10.8	10.3	10.9	11.3	10.5	...	...	...	...	...	...
IX	Latin America and the Caribbean	10.4	...	...	12.2	12.1	12.2	13.0	12.7	13.2	...	...	88.7	1.04	88.5	1.03
X	North America and Western Europe	14.7	14.6	15.0	16.2	15.9	16.5	16.3	15.4	16.8	99.5	1.01	...	...	...	...
XI	South and West Asia	7.6	9.0	6.2	8.4	9.4	7.4	8.6	9.5	7.6	...	...	...	...	77.8	1.07
XII	Sub-Saharan Africa	6.0	6.6	5.5	6.7	7.3	6.0	7.1	7.6	6.4	64.5	0.80	75.7	1.08	66.6	1.10

1. The survival rate in Ghana in 1998 is inflated because substantially more children were reported in several grades in 1999 than 1998, suggesting relatively that large numbers of children who had previously dropped out re-entered school that year.

STATISTICAL ANNEX / 393

Table 17

GOAL 6. Educational quality in primary education

PUPIL/TEACHER RATIO			% FEMALE TEACHERS			TRAINED TEACHERS as % of total		PUBLIC CURRENT EXPENDITURE ON PRIMARY EDUCATION AS % GNP			PUBLIC CURRENT EXPENDITURE ON PRIMARY EDUCATION PER PUPIL (unit cost) in constant 2001 US$			PUBLIC CURRENT EXPENDITURE ON PRIMARY EDUCATION PER PUPIL (unit cost) in US$ at PPP			
1990	1998	2001	1990	1998	2001	1998	2001	1990	1998	2001	1990	1998	2001	1990	1998	2001	
51	52	61*	30	36	35**	...	...	...	1.2	...	...	40	...	...	112	...	164
...	29**	29	...	62**	65	...	67.2	...	...	...	...	...	...	...	...	...	165
77	...	74**,z	25	...	18**,z	...	...	1.1	...	...	29	...	...	124	...	...	166
66	68	71**	6	9	10**	...	...	...	...	...	...	...	...	...	...	...	167
37	35	39	...	26	...	...	...	...	...	...	...	...	...	...	...	...	168
65	61	56	32	42	38	...	...	...	...	...	...	...	...	...	...	...	169
37	43	44	18	20	22	...	...	...	1.6	1.8y	...	83	90y	...	183	212y	170
40	26	...	24	22	...	...	...	...	...	...	...	...	...	...	...	...	171
...	...	43**,z	...	...	24**,z	...	...	...	...	0.4**	...	...	23**	...	...	...	172
...	47	44	45	35	38	72.8	72.6	...	1.6	1.2	...	...	...	...	...	...	173
36	46	57	24	28	31	...	69.3	1.5	...	...	31	...	...	217	...	...	174
...	44	49**	...	42	41**	...	...	...	1.3	...	...	187	...	...	300	...	175
31	33	38**	31	30	30**	72.5	...	1.3	...	2.1y	37	...	45y	230	...	312y	176
29	30	32	36	32	32	71.8	64.9	0.8	...	...	14	...	...	95	...	...	177
40	47	47	23	25	24	...	...	...	...	...	...	...	...	...	...	...	178
...	...	44y	...	...	20y	...	35.1y	...	...	...	...	...	...	...	...	...	179
31	29	32	38	42	42	96.6	98.0	3.2	...	...	...	...	...	...	...	...	180
55	44**	47	80	80**	80	76.7**	74.8	...	3.2	3.5z	...	81	76z	...	460	494z	181
...	39	38y	...	19	28y	...	...	...	...	...	...	...	...	...	...	...	182
40	47	48	...	58	58	...	...	...	...	0.7	...	...	13	...	...	39	183
61	63**	63**,y	31	40**	38z	46.1**	51.2z	1.1	...	...	...	...	...	...	...	...	184
47	62*	56	25	23*	25	...	...	...	1.3	1.3**,y	...	31	29**,y	...	99	96**,y	185
21	26	25	44	53	57	100.0	100.0	1.2	1.2	1.2y	254	343	348y	557	854	926y	186
55	63**	66	23	25	27	32.7	59.9	1.0	...	...	14	...	...	66	...	...	187
...	32	32	...	67	60	29.1	37.0**	...	4.4	4.2y	...	332	319y	...	1 300	1 324y	188
42	41	41	33	31	34	...	72.7	...	...	...	...	...	...	...	...	...	189
41	31**	40**	43	39**	49**	...	...	...	...	...	...	...	...	...	...	...	190
57	54	59	46	55	50	...	81.2	...	...	...	...	...	...	...	...	...	191
...	36	33**	...	...	62**	...	...	...	...	...	...	...	...	...	...	...	192
53	49	49	27	...	23	...	90.5	1.7	...	1.1**	...	...	43**	...	...	137**	193
...	15	14	...	88	86	83.7	77.7	2.3	1.1	...	784	734	...	...	...	...	194
35	...	37z	...	...	38z	...	78.9z	...	0.4	...	...	...	...	...	...	...	195
...	...	...	...	...	...	...	...	...	...	...	...	...	...	...	...	...	196
...	37**	37	...	78**	78	63.1**	67.6	4.1	2.8	2.6y	534	352*	332y	1 914	1 411*	1 415y	197
33	33	32	79	75	75	91.1	...	1.4	2.0	...	...	108	...	...	383	...	198
58	41	35	19	14	12	...	80.5	1.6	1.9	2.0**,z	26	24	22**,z	133	139	153**,z	199
29	60	54	30	33	...	...	...	...	...	...	...	...	...	...	...	...	200
35	38	46	41	44	45	44.1	...	...	...	...	...	...	...	...	...	...	201
44	45	45**	...	48	51**	88.8	100.0z	...	...	...	...	...	...	...	...	...	202
36	...	38	39	...	48	...	95.3**	4.3	...	3.3**	166	...	115**	445	...	372**	203

Median			Median			Median		Median			Median			Median			
27	24	22	57	72	73	...	...	...	...	...	...	...	...	...	...	...	I
22	20	19	94	97	97	...	89.8	...	...	...	...	...	...	...	...	...	II
18	16	15	77	85	83	...	...	1.4	...	1.3	...	...	3 480	...	...	3 934	III
30	28	28	47	61	61	...	...	...	...	...	...	...	...	...	...	...	IV
25	25	22	51	52	59	...	...	...	...	...	...	...	...	...	...	...	V
20	19	17	84	93	91	...	...	...	...	...	...	...	...	...	...	...	VI
21	20	19	85	92	94	...	...	...	...	...	...	...	...	...	...	...	VII
26	23	25	...	66	69	...	...	...	...	...	...	...	...	...	...	...	VIII
25	22	21	...	79	79	...	78.0	...	...	1.6	...	...	...	...	...	...	IX
15	15	14	77	76	80	...	...	1.2	1.1	1.4	2 369	3 334	3 808	2 330	3 699	4 369	X
40	38	40	28	37	36	...	...	...	...	...	...	...	...	...	...	...	XI
40	43	44	31	36	38	...	...	...	...	...	...	...	...	...	...	...	XII

(x) Data are for 1998/1999. (y) Data are for 1999/2000. (z) Data are for 2000/2001.

Glossary

Achievement. Examination results or test performance. The term is sometimes used interchangeably with educational quality when describing the evolution of the education system or comparing the situation of a school or group of schools.

Adult literacy rate (estimated). Number of literate persons aged 15 and above, expressed as a percentage of the total population in that age group. A person is considered literate if he/she can read and write with understanding a simple statement related to his/her everyday life.

Basic education. The whole range of educational activities, taking place in various settings, that aim to meet basic learning needs as defined in the World Declaration on Education for All (Jomtien, Thailand, 1990). According to the ISCED, basic education comprises primary education (first stage of basic education) and lower secondary education (second stage). It also covers a wide variety of non-formal and informal public and private activities intended to meet the basic learning needs of people of all ages.

Compulsory education. Educational programmes that children and young people are legally obliged to attend, usually defined in terms of a number of grades or an age range, or both.

Constant prices. A way of expressing values in real terms, enabling comparisons across a period of years. To measure real national income, economists use consumer prices as deflators to value total production in each year at constant prices; that is, at the set of prices that applied in a chosen base year.

Dropout rate by grade. Percentage of pupils or students who drop out from a given grade in a given school year. It is the difference between 100% and the sum of the promotion and repetition rates.

Early childhood care and education (ECCE). Programmes that, in addition to providing children with care, offer a structured and purposeful set of learning activities either in a formal institution (pre-primary or ISCED 0) or as part of a non-formal child development programme. ECCE programmes are normally designed for children from age 3 and include organized learning activities that constitute, on average, the equivalent of at least two hours per day and 100 days per year.

Education for All Development Index (EDI). Composite index aimed at measuring overall progress towards EFA. For the time being, the EDI incorporates only the four most quantifiable EFA goals – universal primary education as measured by the net enrolment ratio, adult literacy as measured by the adult literacy rate, gender parity as measured by the gender-specific EFA index, and quality of education as measured by the survival rate to grade five. Its value is the arithmetical mean of the observed values of these four indicators.

Enrolment. Number of pupils or students enrolled at a given level of education, regardless of age. See also gross enrolment ratio and net enrolment ratio.

Entrance age (official). Age at which pupils or students would enter a given programme or level of education assuming they had started at the official entrance age for the lowest level, studied full-time throughout and progressed through the system without repeating or skipping a grade. The theoretical entrance age to a given programme or level may be very different from the actual or even the most common entrance age.

Fields of study in tertiary or higher education.
Education: teacher training and education science.
Humanities and arts: humanities, religion and theology, fine and applied arts.
Social sciences, business and law: social and behavioural sciences, journalism and information, business and administration, law.
Science: life and physical sciences, mathematics, statistics and computer sciences.
Engineering, manufacturing and construction: engineering and engineering trades, manufacturing and processing, architecture and building.
Agriculture: agriculture, forestry and fishery, veterinary.
Health and welfare: medical sciences and health-related sciences, social services.
Services: personal services, transport services, environmental protection, security services

Foreign students. Students enrolled in an education programme in a country of which they are not permanent residents.

Gender parity index (GPI). Ratio of female to male values (or male to female, in certain cases) of a given indicator. A GPI of 1 indicates parity between sexes; a GPI between 0 and 1 means a disparity in favour of boys/men; a GPI greater than 1 indicates a disparity in favour of girls/women.

Gender-specific EFA index (GEI). Composite index measuring relative achievement in gender parity in total participation in primary and secondary education as well as gender parity in adult literacy. The GEI is calculated as an arithmetical mean of the gender parity indices of the primary and secondary gross enrolment ratios and of the adult literacy rate.

Grade. Stage of instruction usually covered in one school year.

Graduate. A person who has successfully completed the final year of a level or sub-level of education. In some countries completion occurs as a result of passing an examination or a series of examinations. In other countries it occurs after a requisite number of course hours have been accumulated. Sometimes both types of completion occur within a country.

Gross enrolment ratio (GER). Total enrolment in a specific level of education, regardless of age, expressed as a percentage of the population in the official age group corresponding to this level of education. The GER can exceed 100% due to late entry or/and repetition.

Gross intake rate (GIR). Total number of new entrants in the first grade of primary education, regardless of age, expressed as a percentage of the population at the official primary-school entrance age.

Gross domestic product (GDP). Sum of gross value added by all resident producers in the economy, including distributive trades and transport, plus any product taxes and minus any subsidies not included in the value of the products.

Gross national product (GNP). Gross domestic product plus net receipts of income from abroad. As these receipts may be positive or negative, GNP may be greater or smaller than GDP.

Gross national product per capita. GNP divided by the total population

HIV prevalence rate in a given age group. Estimated number of people of a given age group living with HIV/AIDS at the end of a given year, expressed as a percentage of the total population of the corresponding age group.

Illiterate. A person who cannot read and write with understanding a simple statement related to his/her everyday life.

Infant mortality rate. Number of deaths of children under age 1 per 1,000 live births in a given year.

International Standard Classification of Education (ISCED). Classification system designed to serve as an instrument suitable for assembling, compiling and presenting comparable indicators and statistics of education both within individual countries and internationally. The system, introduced in 1976, was revised in 1997 (ISCED97).

Life expectancy at birth. Theoretical number of years a newborn infant would live if prevailing patterns of age-specific mortality rates in the year of birth were to stay the same throughout the child's life.

Net attendance rate (NAR). Number of pupils in the official age group for a given level of education who attend school in that level, expressed as a percentage of the population in that age group.

Net enrolment ratio (NER). Enrolment of the official age group for a given level of education, expressed as a percentage of the population in that age group.

Net intake rate (NIR). New entrants to the first grade of primary education who are of the official primary-school entrance age, expressed as a percentage of the population of that age.

New entrants. Pupils entering a given level of education for the first time; the difference between enrolment and repeaters in the first grade of the level.

Number of children orphaned by AIDS. Estimated number of children up to age 14 who have lost one or both parents to AIDS.

Out-of-school children. Children in the official school-age range who are not enrolled.

Percentage of new entrants to the first grade of primary education with ECCE experience. Number of new entrants to the first grade of primary school who have attended the equivalent of at least 200 hours of organized ECCE programmes, expressed as a percentage of the total number of new entrants to the first grade.

Percentage of repeaters. Number of pupils enrolled in the same grade or level as the previous year, expressed as a percentage of the total enrolment in that grade or level.

Post-secondary non-tertiary education (ISCED level 4). Programmes that lie between the upper secondary and tertiary levels from an international point of view, even though they might clearly be considered upper-secondary or tertiary programmes in a national context. They are often not significantly more advanced than programmes at ISCED 3 (upper secondary) but they serve to broaden the knowledge of students who have completed a programme at that level. The students are usually older than those at ISCED level 3. ISCED 4 programmes typically last between six months and two years.

Pre-primary education (ISCED level 0). Programmes at the initial stage of organized instruction, primarily designed to introduce very young children, aged at least 3 years, to a school-type environment and provide a bridge between home and school. Variously referred to as infant education, nursery education, pre-school education, kindergarten or early childhood education, such programmes are the more formal component of ECCE. Upon completion of these programmes, children continue their education at ISCED 1 (primary education).

Primary education (ISCED level 1). Programmes normally designed on a unit or project basis to give pupils a sound basic education in reading, writing and mathematics and an elementary understanding of subjects such as history, geography, natural sciences, social sciences, art and music. Religious instruction may also be featured. These subjects serve to develop pupils' ability to obtain and use information they need about their home, community, country, etc. Sometimes called elementary education.

Private enrolment. Number of children enrolled in an institution that is not operated by a public authority but controlled and managed, whether for profit or not, by a private body such as a non-governmental organization, religious body, special interest group, foundation or business enterprise.

Public current expenditure on education as percentage of total public expenditure on education. Recurrent public expenditure on education expressed as a percentage of total public expenditure on education (current and capital). It covers public expenditure for both public and private institutions. Current expenditure includes expenditure for goods and services that are consumed within a given year and have to be renewed the following year, such as staff salaries and benefits; contracted or purchased services; other resources, including books and teaching materials; welfare services and items such as furniture and equipment, minor repairs, fuel, telecommunications, travel, insurance and rent. Capital expenditure includes expenditure for construction, renovation and major repairs of buildings and the purchase of heavy equipment or vehicles.

Public current expenditure on primary education as percentage of GNP. Current expenditure on primary education by local, regional and national governments, including municipalities, expressed as percentage of GNP.

Public current expenditure on primary education as percentage of total public current expenditure on education. The share of public current expenditure on education that is devoted to primary education.

Public current expenditure on primary education per pupil (unit cost). The average public spending on a pupil in primary education.

Public current expenditure on primary education per pupil as percentage of per capita GNP. An indicator measuring the average public spending on a pupil in primary education in relation to a country's per capita GNP. In other words, the unit cost of primary education as a share of per capita GNP.

Public expenditure on education. Total public finance devoted to education by local, regional and national governments, including municipalities. Household contributions are excluded. Includes both current and capital expenditure.

Public expenditure on education as percentage of GNP. Total current and capital expenditure on education at every level of administration, i.e. by central, regional and local authorities, expressed as a percentage of GNP.

Public expenditure on education as percentage of total government expenditure. Total current and capital expenditure on education at every level of administration, i.e. central, regional and local authorities, expressed as a percentage of total government expenditure (on health, education, social services, etc.).

Pupil. A child enrolled in pre-primary or primary education. Youth and adults enrolled at more advanced levels are referred to as students.

Pupil/teacher ratio (PTR). Average number of pupils per teacher at a specific level of education, based on headcounts for both pupils and teachers.

Purchasing power parity (PPP). An exchange rate that accounts for price differences among countries, allowing international comparisons of real output and incomes. A given sum of money, when converted into US dollars at the PPP rate (PPP$), will buy the same basket of goods and services in all countries.

Repetition rate by grade. Number of repeaters in a given grade in a given school year, expressed as a percentage of enrolment in that grade the previous school year.

School life expectancy (SLE). Number of years a child of school entrance age is expected to spend at school or university, including years spent on repetition. It is the sum of the age-specific enrolment ratios for primary, secondary, post-secondary non-tertiary and tertiary education (the gross enrolment ratio is used as a proxy to compensate for the lack of data by age for tertiary and partial data for the other ISCED levels).

School-age population. Population of the age group officially corresponding to a given level of education, whether enrolled in school or not.

Secondary education. Programmes at ISCED levels 2 and 3. Lower secondary education (ISCED 2) is generally designed to continue the basic programmes of the primary level but the teaching is typically more subject-focused, requiring more specialized teachers for each subject area. The end of this level often coincides with the end of compulsory education. In upper secondary education (ISCED 3), the final stage of secondary education in most countries, instruction is often organized even more along subject lines and teachers typically need a higher or more subject-specific qualification than at ISCED level 2.

Survival rate by grade. Percentage of a cohort of pupils who enrolled in the first grade of an education cycle in a given school year and are expected to reach a specified grade, regardless of repetition.

Teachers or teaching staff. Number of persons employed full time or part time in an official capacity to guide and direct the learning experience of pupils and students, irrespective of their qualifications or the delivery mechanism, i.e. face-to-face and/or at a distance. Excludes educational personnel who have no active teaching duties (e.g. headmasters, headmistresses or principals who do not teach) and persons who work occasionally or in a voluntary capacity.

Teachers' salaries as percentage of public current expenditure on education. The share of teachers' salaries and other remuneration in total public current expenditure on education

Technical and vocational education. Programmes designed mainly to prepare students for direct entry into a particular occupation or trade (or class of occupations or trades). Successful completion of such programmes normally leads to a labour-market-relevant vocational qualification recognized by the competent authorities (ministry of education, employers' associations, etc.) in the country in which it is obtained.

Tertiary or higher education. Programmes with an educational content more advanced than what is offered at ISCED levels 3 and 4. The first stage of tertiary education, ISCED level 5, covers level 5A, composed of largely theoretically based programmes intended to provide sufficient qualifications for gaining entry to advanced research programmes and professions with high skill requirements; and level 5B, where programmes are generally more practical, technical and/or occupationally specific. The second stage of tertiary education, ISCED level 6, comprises programmes devoted to advanced study and original research, and leading to the award of an advanced research qualification.

Total debt service. Sum of principal repayments and interest paid in foreign currency, goods or services on long-term debt, or interest paid on short-term debt, as well as repayments (repurchases and charges) to the International Monetary Fund.

Total fertility rate. Average number of children that would be born to a woman if she were to live to the end of her childbearing years (15 to 49) and bear children at each age in accordance with prevailing age-specific fertility rates.

Trained teacher. Teacher who has received the minimum organized teacher training (pre-service or in-service) normally required for teaching at the relevant level in a given country.

Transition rate to secondary education. New entrants to the first grade of secondary education in a given year, expressed as a percentage of the number of pupils enrolled in the final grade of primary education in the previous year.

Youth literacy rate (estimated). Number of literate persons aged 15 to 24, expressed as a percentage of the total population in that age group. A person is considered literate if he/she can read and write with understanding a simple statement related to his/her everyday life.

References*

Acharya, A.; Fuzzo de Lima, A.; Moore, M. 2004. *Aid proliferation: how responsible are the donors?* Working Paper No. 214, Brighton, Institute of Development Studies.

Adams, D. 1993. *Defining Educational Quality*. Arlington, VA, Institute for International Research. (IEQ Publication No. 1. Biennial Report.)

ADEA. 2003. *The Challenge of Learning: Improving the Quality of Basic Education in Sub-Saharan Africa*. Discussion paper for the ADEA Biennial Meeting, Grand Baie, Mauritius, 3-6 December. Paris, Association for the Development of Education in Africa.

AfDB. 1998. *African Development Report 1998: Human Capital Development in Africa*. African Development Bank.

Akerlof, G. A.; Kranton, R. E. 2002. Identity and Schooling: Some Lessons for the Economics of Education. *Journal of Economic Literature*, Vol. 40, December: 1167-201.

Akyeampong, K. 2004. Aid for Self-Help Effort? A Sustainable Alternative Route to Basic Education in Northern Ghana. *Journal of International Co-operation in Education* (Hiroshima), Vol. 7, No. 1, April: 41-52.

Akyeampong, K.; Ampiah, J.; Fletcher, J.; Kutor, N.; Sokpe, B. 2000. *Learning to Teach in Ghana: An Evaluation of Curriculum Delivery*. Brighton, Centre for International Education, University of Sussex. (MUSTER Discussion Paper No. 17.)

Akyeampong, K.; Furlong, D.; Lewin, K. M. 2000. *The Costs and Financing of Teacher Education in Ghana*. Brighton, Centre for International Education, University of Sussex. (MUSTER Discussion Paper No. 18.)

Alderman, H.; Behrman, J. R.; Ross, D. R. Sabot, R. 1996. The returns to endogenous human capital in Pakistan's rural wage labor market. *Oxford Bulletin of Economics and Statistics,* Vol. 58: 29-55.

Al-Samarrai, S. 2002. *Achieving Education for All: How Much Does Money Matter?* Brighton, Institute of Development Studies. (Working Paper No. 175, December).

Al-Samarrai, S.; Bennell, P.; Colclough, C. 2002. *From Projects to SWAPs: an evaluation of British aid to primary schooling 1988-2001*. London, Department for International Development.

Altonji, J. G.; Pierret, C. R. 2001. Employer learning and statistical discrimination. *Quarterly Journal of Economics*, Vol. 116, No. 1, February: 313-350.

Amadio, M.; Truong, N.; Ressler, D.; Gross, S. 2004. *Quality Education for All? World trends in educational aims and goals between the 1980s and the 2000s*. Background paper for *EFA Global Monitoring Report 2005* through the UNESCO International Bureau of Education, Geneva.

Anderson, C. S. 1982. The search for school climate: A review of the research. *Review of Educational Research*, Vol. 52, No. 3: 368-420.

Anderson, L. W. 2004. *Increasing Teacher Effectiveness*. 2nd ed. Paris, UNESCO International Institute for Educational Planning.

Anderson, S. (ed.). 2002. *School improvement through teacher development: Case studies of the Aga Khan Foundation projects in East Africa*. Lisse, the Netherlands, Swets & Zeitlinger.

Anderson Pillsbury, A. 2004. *Education in Emergencies*. Background paper for *EFA Global Monitoring Report 2005*.

Angrist, J. D.; Lavy, V. 1997. The effect of a change in language of instruction on the returns to schooling in Morocco. *Journal of Labor Economics*, Vol. 15: 48-76.

— 1999. Using Maimonides' Rule to Estimate the Effect of Class Size on Scholastic Achievement. *Quarterly Journal of Economics*, Vol. 114, No. 2, May: 533-75.

*All background papers for *EFA Global Monitoring Report 2005* are available at www.efareport.unesco.org

— 2001. Does Teacher Training Affect Pupil Learning? Evidence from Matched Comparisons in Jerusalem Public Schools. *Journal of Labor Economics*, Vol. 19, No. 2, April: 343-69.

Apple, M. W. 1978, Ideology, reproduction, and educational reform. *Comparative Education Review*, Vol. 22, No. 3.

Arab Republic of Egypt Ministry of Education. 2002. *Mubarak and Education, Qualitative Development in the National Project of Education: Application of Principles of Total Quality*. Cairo, Rose El Youssef Printing House.

Arnove, R. F.; Graff, H. J. (eds.). 1987. *National Literacy Campaigns: Historical and Comparative Perspectives.* New York, Plenum Press.

Asian Network of Research and Training Institutions in Educational Planning. Forthcoming. *Improving school management in Asia through capacity building of head teachers.* Paris, UNESCO International Institute for Educational Planning.

Askerud, P. 1997. *A guide to Sustainable Book Provision*. Paris, UNESCO.

Aspland, R.; Brown, G. 1993. Keeping Teaching Professional. In: D. Bridges and T. Kerry (eds.), *Developing Teachers Professionally: reflections for initial and in-service trainers.* London, Routledge.

Atchoarena; D.; Nozawa; M. 2004. *Skills Development to Meet the Learning Needs of the Excluded*. Background paper for *EFA Global Monitoring Report 2005*.

Avalos, B. 1980. Teacher Effectiveness: Research in the Third World – Highlights of a Review. *Comparative Education*, Vol. 16, No. 1: 45-54.

Babu, S.; R. Mendro. 2003. *Teacher Accountability: HLM-Based Teacher Effectiveness Indices in the Investigation of Teacher Effects on Student Achievement in a State Assessment Program.* Paper delivered to the American Educational Research Association Annual Meeting, Chicago, April 21-25.

Badcock-Walters, P.; Desmond, C.; Wilson, D.; Heard, W. 2003. *Educator mortality in service in KwaZulu Natal: A consolidated study of HIV/AIDS impact and trends.* Mobile Task Team on the Impact of HIV/AIDS on Education, Health Economics and HIV/AIDS Research Division, University of Natal.

Badcock-Walters, P; Kelly, M.; Görgens, M. 2004. *Does Knowledge Equal Change? HIV/AIDS Education and Behaviour Change*. Background paper for *EFA Global Monitoring Report 2005*.

Banerjee, A.; Cole, S.; Duflo, E.; Linden, L. 2003. *Remedying Education: Evidence from Two Randomized Experiments in India*. Cambridge, MA, Massachusetts Institute of Technology (Poverty Action Lab Paper No. 4, September).

Banerjee, A.; Kremer, M.; with Lanjouw, J.; Lanjouw, P. 2002. Teacher-Student Ratios and School Performance in Udaipur, India: A Prospective Evaluation. Cambridge, MA, Harvard University. (Mimeograph)

Bangert, R. L.; Kulik, J. A.; Kulik, C. C. 1983. Individualized systems of instruction in secondary schools. *Review of Educational Research*, Vol. 53: 143-58.

Barber, M. 2000. The very big picture. *Improving Schools,* Vol. 3, No. 2: 5-13.

Barro, R. J.; Lee, J. 2001. International data on educational attainment: Updates and implications. *Oxford Economic Papers,* Vol. 53, No.3, July: 541-63.

Barro, R. J.; Sala-i-Martin, X. 2003. Economic growth. 2nd ed. Cambridge, MIT Press.

Barth, R. 1990. *Improving Schools from Within*. San Francisco, Jossey-Bass.

Basu, A. 2002. Why Does Education Lead to Lower Fertility? A critical review of some of the possibilities. *World Development*, Vol. 30, 10 October: 1779-90.

Baudelot, C.; Leclercq, F.; Châtard, A.; Gobille, B.; Satchkova, E. 2004. *Les Effets de l'éducation*. Report for the Programme incitatif de recherche en éducation et formation, Laboratoire de Sciences Sociales, Paris, Ecole Normale Supérieure, January.

Baumert, J., Blum, W.; Neubrand, M. 2000. Surveying the Instructional Conditions and Domain-Specific Individual Prerequisites for the Development of Mathematical Competences. (Draft Paper)

Behrman, J. R., Kletzer, L. G.; McPherson, M. S.; Schapiro, M. O. 1998. The microeconomics of college choice, careers, and wages: Measuring the impact of higher education. *Annals of the American Academy of Political and Social Science,* Vol. 559, September: 12-23.

Behrman, J. R.; Ross, D.; Sabot, R. Forthcoming. Improving the Quality Versus Increasing the Quantity of Schooling: Evidence for Rural Pakistan.

Benavot, A. 2004a. *Studies on instructional time.* Background paper for *EFA Global Monitoring Report 2005* through the UNESCO International Bureau of Education, Geneva.

— 2004b. *Factors affecting actual instructional time in African primary schools: a literature review, Part 3.* Paper prepared for the World Bank-IBE Study on Instructional Time. Geneva, UNESCO International Bureau of Education.

Bennell, P. 2004. *Primary School Teachers Taking the Strain in Sierra Leone.* Background paper for *EFA Global Monitoring Report 2005.*

Bennell P.; Hyde, K.; Swainson, N. 2002. *The impact of the HIV/AIDS epidemic on the education sector in sub-Saharan Africa: A synthesis of the findings and recommendations of three country studies.* Brighton, Centre for International Education, University of Sussex.

Bennett, J. 2003. *Review of School Feeding Projects.* London, Department for International Development.

Benson, C. 2004.*The Importance of Mother Tongue-based Schooling for Educational Quality.* Background paper for *EFA Global Monitoring Report 2005.*

Bernard, A. 2004. *Review of Child-Friendly School Initiatives in the EAPRO Region.* Draft Report 3. Bangkok, EAPRO/UNESCO.

Bernard, J.-M. 1999. *Les enseignants du primaire dans cinq pays du Programme d'analyse des systèmes éducatifs de la CONFEMEN : Caractéristiques, conditions de travail et représentations.* Report of the Groupe de travail sur la profession enseignante. Paris, Association for the Development of Education in Africa.

Bernard, J.-M. 2003. *Eléments d'appréciation de la qualité de l'enseignement primaire en Afrique francophone.* Background paper for the ADEA report *The Challenge of Learning: Improving the Quality of Basic Education in Sub-Saharan Africa.* Paris, Association for the Development of Education in Africa.

Bertram, T.; Pascal, C. 2002. *Early Years Education: An International Perspective.* Birmingham, Centre for Research in Early Childhood.

Bibeau, J. R.; Kester-McNees, P.; Reddy, V. 2003. *Report on the Evaluation of UNESCO's E-9 Initiative.* Report commissioned by UNESCO.

Bishop, J. 1989. Is the test score decline responsible for the productivity growth decline? *American Economic Review* Vol. 79, No. 1: 178-97.

— 1991. Achievement, test scores, and relative wages. In: M. H. Kosters (ed.), *Workers and their wages*: 146-86. Washington, DC, AEI Press.

Black, P.; Wiliam, D. 1998. Assessment and Classroom Learning. *Assessment in Education*, Vol. 5, No. 1: 7-74.

— 2002. Inside the Black Box: raising standards through classroom assessment. (www.kcl.ac.uk/depsta/education/publications/blackbox.html)

Blackburn, M. L.; Neumark, D. 1993. Omitted-ability bias and the increase in the return to schooling. *Journal of Labor Economics* Vol. 11, No. 3, July: 521-44.

— 1995. Are OLS estimates of the return to schooling biased downward? Another look. *Review of Economics and Statistics* Vol. 77, No. 2, May: 217-30.

Blackman, D. E. 1995. *B. F. Skinner.* In: R. Fuller (ed.), *Seven Pioneers of Psychology.* London, Routledge.

Bloom, B. 1964. *Stability and Change in Human Characteristics.* New York, Wiley and Sons.

— 1968. *Learning for Mastery.* Washington, DC, ERIC Document Reproduction Service.

— 1956. *Taxonomy of educational objectives: the classification of educational goals. Handbook 1, Cognitive domain.* New York, David McKay.

Bobbitt, F. 1918. *The Curriculum*. Boston, Houghton Mifflin.

Boekaerts, M.; Simons, P. R. J. 1993. *Leren en Instructie. Psychologie van de Leerling en het Leerproces*. Assen, the Netherlands, Dekker & Van de Vegt.

Boissiere, M. X.; Knight, J. B.; Sabot, R. H. 1985. Earnings, schooling, ability, and cognitive skills. *American Economic Review* Vol. 75, No. 5: 1016-30.

Booth, T.; Ainscow, M. 2000. *Index for Inclusion*. Bristol, Centre for Studies on Inclusive Education.

Borovikova, E. 2004. *Review of the textbook research findings in Russia*. (Draft Mimeograph)

Bourdieu, P. 1977. *Outline of a Theory of Practice*. Cambridge, Cambridge University Press.

Bourdieu, P.; Passeron, J.-C. 1964, *Les Héritiers: les étudiants et la culture*. Paris, Minuit.

Bowles, S.; Gintis, H. 1976. *Schooling in Capitalist America: Educational Reform and the Contradictions of Economic Life*. New York, Basic Books.

Bowles, S.; Gintis, H.; Osborne, M. 2001. Incentive-Enhancing Preferences: personality, behaviour and earnings. *American Economic Association Papers and Proceedings,* Vol. 19, No. 2, May: 155-8.

Bray, M. 2000. *Double-Shift Schooling: Design and Operation for Cost-Effectiveness*. Paris/London, UNESCO-IIEP/Commonwealth Secretariat.

— 2003. *Adverse effect of private supplementary tutoring: dimensions, implications and government responses.* Paris, UNESCO International Institute for Educational Planning. (Ethics and Corruption in Education series.)

Brookover, W. B.; Beady, C.; Flood, P.; Schweitzer, J.; Wisenbaker, J. 1979. *School social systems and student achievement – schools can make a difference*. New York, Praeger Publishers.

Brophy, J. E. 2001. Generic Aspects of Effective Teaching. In: M. C. Wang and H. J. Walberg, *Tomorrow's Teachers*. Richmond, CA, McCutchan.

Brophy, J. E.; Good, T. L. 1986. Teacher Behavior and Student Achievement. In: M. C. Wittrock (ed.), *Handbook of Research on Teaching*: 328-75. New York, Macmillan.

Bruns, B.; Mingat, A.; Rakotomalala, R. 2003. *A Chance for Every Child. Achieving Universal Primary Education by 2015*. Washington, DC, World Bank.

Buchert, L. 2002. Towards new partnerships in sector-side approaches: comparative experiences from Burkina Faso, Ghana and Mozambique. *International Journal of Educational Development*, Vol. 22: 69-84.

Burtless, G. 1995. The Case for Randomized Field Trials in Economic and Policy Research. *Journal of Economic Perspectives*, Vol. 9, No. 2, Spring: 63-84.

Caldwell, B. J. 1998. *Self-managing schools and improved learning outcomes*. Canberra, Department of Employment, Education, Training and Youth Affairs.

Cambodia. 1999. *Education in Cambodia*. Phnom Penh, Kingdom of Cambodia, Ministry of Education, Youth and Sport, Department of Planning.

Card, D. 1999. The Causal Effect of Education on Earnings. In: O. C. Ashenfeller and D. Card (eds.), *Handbook of Labor Economics*, Vol. 3A, Chapter 30. Amsterdam, North-Holland (Elsevier).

Carnegie Corporation of New York. 1994. *Starting Points: Meeting the Needs of our Youngest Children*. New York, The Carnegie Corporation of New York.

Carneiro, P.; Heckman, J. J. 2003. *Human Capital Policy*. Cambridge, MA, National Bureau of Economic Research. (NBER Working Paper 9495, February.)

Carnoy, M. 2004. *Education for all and the quality of education: a reanalysis*. Background paper for *EFA Global Monitoring Report 2005*.

Carnoy, M.; Gove, A; Marshall, J. H. Forthcoming. *Why Do Students Achieve More in Some Countries Than in Others? A Comparative Study of Brazil, Chile, and Cuba*.

Carr-Hill, R. A. 2004a. *HIV/AIDS, poverty and educational statistics in Africa: Evidence and indicators*. Montreal, UNESCO Institute for Statistics. (Processed)

Carr-Hill, R. A. 2004b. *Additional material on literacy rates*. Background paper for *EFA Global Monitoring Report 2005*.

Carr-Hill, R. A.; Kweka, A. N.; Rusimbi, M.; Chengelele, R. 1991. *The Functioning and Effects of the Tanzanian Literacy Programme*. Paris, UNESCO International Institute for Educational Planning. (IIEP Research Report No. 93.)

Carroll, J. B. 1963. A model of school learning. *Teachers College Record*, Vol. 64: 722-33.

— 1989. The Carroll Model, a 25-year retrospective and prospective view. *Educational Researcher*, Vol. 18: 6-31.

Carron, G.; Mwiria, K.; Righa, G. 1989. *The Functioning and Effects of the Kenya Literacy Programme*. Paris, UNESCO International Institute for Educational Planning. (IIEP Research Report No. 76.)

Casassus, J.; Cusato, S.; Froemel, J. E.; Palafox, J. C. 2002. *First International Comparative Study of Language, Mathematics and Associated Factors for Students in the Third and Fourth Grade of Primary School. Second Report*. Santiago, OREALC/UNESCO.

Case, A.; Deaton, A. 1999. School Inputs and Educational Outcomes in South Africa. *Quarterly Journal of Economics*, Vol. 114, No. 3, August: 1047-84.

Case, A.; Yogo, M. 1999. *Does School Quality Matter? Returns to Education and the Characteristics of Schools in South Africa*. Cambridge, MA, National Bureau of Economic Research. (NBER Working Paper 7399, October.)

Cawthera, A. 2003. *Nijera Shikhi & Adult Literacy*. (www.eldis.org/fulltext/nijerashikhi.pdf)

Centre of Excellence for Early Childhood Development. 2004. Encyclopedia on Early Childhood Development. Montreal, Quebec. (www.excellence-earlychildhood.ca)

CERI. 1999. *Education Policy Analysis*. Paris, Centre for Educational Research and Innovation, OECD.

— 2002. *Educational Research and Development in England: Examiners' Report*. Paris, Centre for Educational Research and Innovation, OECD.

Chabbott, C. 2004. *UNICEF's Child-Friendly Schools' Framework. A Desk Review*. Report to UNICEF.

Chandra, R. 2004. Speech for the launch of the PRIDE Project. Suva, Fiji, University of the South Pacific, 14 May.

Chazée, L. 1999. *The Peoples of Laos: Rural and Ethnic Diversities*. Bangkok, White Lotus.

Chelu, F.; Mbulwe, F. 1994. The Self-Help Action Plan for Primary Education (SHAPE) in Zambia. In: A. Little, W. Hoppers and R. Gardner (eds.), *Beyond Jomtien: Implementing Primary Education for All*: 99-23. London, Macmillan.

Chisholm, L. 2004. *The quality of primary education in South Africa*. Background paper for *EFA Global Monitoring Report 2005*.

Chiswick, B.; Patrinos, H.; Tamyo, S. 1996. *The Economics of Language: Application to Education*. Washington, DC, World Bank.

Cogneau, D. 2003. *Colonisation, School and Development in Africa: An empirical Analysis*. Paris, Développement et Insertion Internationale (DIAL Working Paper 2003/01.)

Cohen, D. K. 1988. Teaching practice ... Plus ça change ... In: P. Jackson (ed.), *Contributing to Educational Change: Perspectives on Research and Practice*. Berkeley, CA, McCutchan.

Cohen, M. 1982. Effective schools: Accumulating research findings. *American Education*, January-February: 13-16.

Colclough, C. 1991. Wage flexibility in Sub-Saharan Africa. In: G. Standing and V. Tokman (eds.), *Towards Social Adjustment*: 211-32. Geneva, International Labour Organisation.

— 1997. Economic Stagnation and Earnings Decline in Zambia 1975-91. In: C. Colclough (ed.), *Public Sector Pay and Adjustment: lessons from five countries*: 68-12. London, Routledge.

Colclough, C. with Lewin, K. M. 1993. *Educating All the Children: Strategies for Primary Schooling in the South*. Oxford: Clarendon Press.

Coleman, J. S.; Campbell, E. Q.; Hobson, C. J.; McPartland, J.; Mood, A. M.; Weinfield, F. D.; York, R. L. 1966. *Equality of Educational Opportunity*. Washington, DC, United States Government Printing Office.

Collins, A.; Brown, J. S.; Newman, S. E. 1989. Cognitive apprenticeship: teaching the crafts of reading, writing and mathematics. In: L. B. Resnick (ed.), *Knowing, learning and instruction*: 453-95. Hillsdale, NJ, Lawrence Erlbaum Associates.

Collins, A.; Stevens, A. 1982. Goals and strategies of inquiry teachers. In: R. Glaser (ed.), *Advances in Instructional Psychology*, Vol. 2: 65-119 Hillsdale, NJ, Lawrence Erlbaum Associates.

CONFEMEN. 2004. Les résultats des études PASEC. In: *Confemen infos*, Vol. 1, No. 1.

Copenhagen Consensus. 2004. *Copenhagen Consensus: The Results*. 24-28 May. (www.copenhagenconsensus.com/Files/Filer/CC/Press/UK/copenhagen_consensus_result_FINAL.pdf)

Cornia, G. A.; Jolly, R.; Stewart, F. 1987. *Adjustment with a Human Face*. Oxford, Oxford University Press.

Corrales, J. 1999. *The Politics of Education Reform: Bolstering the Supply and Demand: Overcoming Institutional Blocks*. Washington, DC, World Bank. (Education Reform and Management Series, Vol. II, No. 1.)

Cotton, K. 1995. *Effective schooling practices: A research synthesis*. Portland, OR, Northwest Regional Educational Laboratory. (School Improvement Research Series, update.)

Cox, C. 2004. *Innovation and reform to improve the quality of primary education: Chile*. Background paper for *EFA Global Monitoring Report 2005*.

Crahay, M. 2000. *L'école peut-elle être juste et efficace? De l'égalité des chances à l'égalité des acquis*. Brussels, De Boeck Université.

Craig, H. J.; Kraft, R. J.; du Plessis, J. 1998. *Teacher development: Making an impact*. Washington, DC, World Bank.

Creemers, B. P. M. 1994. *The Effective Classroom*. London, Cassell.

Croft, A. 2002. Teachers, student teachers and pupils; a study of teaching and learning in lower primary classes in Southern Malawi. Unpublished D. Phil. Thesis. University of Sussex.

Crouch, L.; Fasih, T. 2004. *Patterns of Educational Development: Implications for Further Efficiency Analysis*. Washington, DC, World Bank. (Mimeograph)

Crouch, L.; Lewin, K. M. 2003. Turbulence or Orderly Change? Teacher supply and demand in South Africa - current status, future needs, and the impact of HIV/AIDS. In: K. M. Lewin, M. Samuel and Y. Sayed (eds.), *Changing Patterns of Teacher Education in South Africa: Policy, Practice and Prospects*: 45-71. Sandown, Heinemann Press.

Cunningham, D J. 1991. In defence of extremism. *Educational Technology*, Vol.. 31, No. 9: 26-27.

Currie, C.; Roberts, C.; Morgan, A.; Smith, R.; Settertobulte, W.; Samdal, O.; Barnekow Rasmussen, V. 2004. *Young people's health in context. Health Behaviour in School-Aged Children (HBSC) study: international report from the 2001/2002 survey*. Geneva, WHO. (Health Policy for Children and Adolescents, No. 4.)

Currie, J. 2001. Early Childhood Education Programs. *Journal of Economic Perspectives*, Vol. 15, No. 2, Spring: 213-38.

Dalin, P. 1994. *How Schools Improve*. London/New York, Cassell.

Darling-Hammond, L. 2000. Teacher Quality and Student Achievement: A Review of State Policy Evidence. *Education Policy Analysis Archives*, Vol. 8, No. 1. (http://olam.ed.asu.edu/epaa/v8n1)

De Grauwe, A. 2001. *School supervision in four African countries. Vol. I, Challenges and Reforms.* Paris, UNESCO International Institute for Educational Planning.

— 2004. *School-based Management (SBM): Does it Improve Quality?* Background paper for *EFA Global Monitoring Report 2005*.

De Grauwe, A.; Carron, G. Undated. *Resource Centres as a close-to-school Support Service.* (Mimeograph)

De Ketele, J. M. 2004. *La scolarisation primaire universelle et une éducation de qualité pour tous: Un défi considérable pour toutes les régions du monde.* Background paper for *EFA Global Monitoring Report 2005*.

De Walque, D. 2004. *How Does the Impact of an HIV/AIDS Information Campaign Vary with Educational Attainment: Evidence from Rural Uganda?* Washington, DC, World Bank, Development Research Group.

DEA. 1996. *The Case for Development Education.* London, Development Education Association.

Delors, J.; Al Mufti, I.; Amagi, I.; Carneiro, R.; Chung, F.; Geremek, B.; Gorham, W.; Kornhauser, A.; Manley, M.; Padrón Quero, M.; Savané, M.-A.; Singh, K.; Stavenhagen, R.; Myong Won Suhr; Zhou Nanzhao. 1996. *Learning: The Treasure Within: Report to UNESCO of the International Commission on Education for the Twenty-first Century.* Paris, UNESCO. (www.unesco.org/delors/)

Dembélé, M.; Miaro-II, B. 2003. *Pedagogical Renewal and Teacher Development in Sub-Saharan Africa: A Thematic Synthesis.* Background paper for the ADEA Biennial Meeting, Grand Baie, Mauritius, 3-6 December.

Dempster, N. 2000. Guilty or Not: The Impact and Effects of Site-Based Management on Schools. *Journal of Educational Administration,* Vol. 38, No. 1: 47-63.

Devarajan, S.; Miller, M. J.; Swanson, E. V. 2002. *Goals for Development: History, Prospects and Costs.* Washington, DC, World Bank. (World Bank Policy Research Working Paper 2819.)

Development Researchers' Network. 2002. *Evaluation of EC Support to the Education Sector in ACP Countries: Synthesis Report.* Brussels, Development Researchers' Network.

Dewey, J. 1916. *Democracy and Education.* New York, Macmillan.

DFID, 2004. *National Sector Classification of Budget Support.* Notes prepared by the UK Department for International Development for *EFA Global Monitoring Report 2005*.

DFID/Ministry of Education. 2002. Review of the Primary Reading Programme: Report and Recommendations, Lusaka, Zambia Ministry of Education.

Disability Awareness in Action. 2004. It's Our World, Too! The international disability & human rights network. (www.daa.org.uk/itisourworldtoo.htm)

Döbert, H.; Klieme, E.; Sroka, W. (eds.). 2004. *Conditions of School Performance in Seven Countries: A Quest for Understanding the International Variation of PISA Results.* Münster, Waxmann.

Dolata, S.; Ikeda, M.; Murimba, S. 2004. Different pathways to EFA for different school systems. *IIEP Newsletter*, Vol. XXII, No. 1, January-March 2004.

Doll, R. C. 1996. *Curriculum Improvement: Decision Making and Process.* Needham Heights, MA, Allyn & Bacon.

Dollar, D.; Levin, K. 2004. *The Increasing Selectivity of Foreign Aid, 1984-2002.* Washington, DC, World Bank. (World Bank Policy Research Working Paper 3299, May.) (http://econ.worldbank.org/files/35475_wps3299.pdf)

Dougherty, K. 1981. After the fall: Research on school effects since the Coleman report. *Harvard Educational Review,* Vol. 51: 301-8.

Doyle, W. 1985. Effective secondary classroom practices. In: M. J. Kyle (ed.), *Reaching for excellence. An effective schools sourcebook.* Washington, DC, United States Government Printing Office.

Drake, L.; Maier, C.; Jukes, M.; Patrikios, A.; Bundy, D.; Gardner, A.; Dolan, C. 2002. School-Age Children: their nutrition and health. *Standing Committee on Nutrition (SCN) News*, No. 25, December.

Drèze, J.; Sen., A., 2002, *India: Development and Participation,* New Delhi, Oxford University Press.

Duffy, T. M.; Jonassen, D. H. 1992. *Constructivism and the Technology of Instruction: A Conversation.* Hillsdale, NJ, Lawrence Erlbaum Associates.

Duflo, E. 2003. Scaling Up and Evaluation. In: *Annual Bank Conference in Development Economics Proceedings.* Washington, DC, World Bank.

Duflo, E.; Kremer, M. 2003. *Use of Randomization in the Evaluation of Development Effectiveness.* Paper prepared for the World Bank Operations Evaluation Department Conference on Evaluation and Development Effectiveness, Washington, DC, 15-16 July.

Dugan, D. J. 1976. Scholastic achievement: its determinants and effects in the education industry. In: J. T. Froomkin, Dean T. Jamison and Roy Radner (eds.), *Education as an industry*: 53-83. Cambridge, MA, A: Ballinger.

Durkheim, E., 1956. *Education and Sociology.* Translated by S. D. Fox. Glencoe, IL, Free Press. As excerpted by A. Giddens, 1972, *Émile Durkheim: Selected Writings*, quoted in M. Haralambos, 1990, *Sociology, Themes and Perspectives.* London, Unwin.

E-9. 2003. *Declaration of the E-9 Countries.* Fifth Ministerial Review Meeting, Cairo, 19-21 December.

Eckstein, M. A. 2003. *Combating academic fraud: towards a culture of integrity*. Paris, UNESCO International Institute for Educational Planning. (Ethics and Corruption in Education series.)

Edmonds, R. R. 1979. Effective schools for the urban poor. *Educational Leadership,* Vol. 37, No. 1: 15-27.

Education Watch. 2001. *A Question of Quality: State of Primary Education in Bangladesh.* Dhaka, University Press Limited.

European Foundation Centre. 2002. *Independent Funding: A directory of foundation and corporate members of the European Foundation Centre.* Brussels, European Foundation Centre.

Egulu, L. 2004. *Trade Union Participation in the PRSP Process.* Washington, DC, World Bank. (Social Protection Discussion Paper No. 0417.)
(http://wbln0018.worldbank.org/HDNet/hddocs.nsf/0/7a0f881805ec10bc85256ee600757c0d/$FILE/0417.pdf)

Eilor, J.; Okurut, H. E.; Opolot, M. J.; Mulyalya, C.; Nansamba, J. F.; Nakayenga, J.; Zalwango, C.; Omongin, O.; Nantume, O.; Apolot, F. 2003. *Impact of Primary Education Reform Program (PERP) on the Quality of Basic Education in Uganda.* Paper presented at the ADEA Biennial Meeting, Grand Baie, Mauritius, 3-6 December.

El Salvador. 2003. *Fundamentación y Resultados Logros de aprendizaje en educación básica 2001 y PAES 2002.* San Salvador, Sistema nacional de Evaluación de los Aprendizajes.

Elias, J. L.; Merriam, S. 1980. *Philosophical Foundations of Adult Education.* Malabar, FL, Krieger.

ELRC. 2003. Collective Agreement Number 4 of 2003, 10 April. Post and Salary Structure for Education. South Africa, Education Labour Relations Council. (www.elrc.co.za/Negotiations.asp?ID=1)

ERNWACA. 2003. *Emerging Trends in Research on the Quality of Education; A Synthesis of Educational Research Reviews from 1992-2002 in eleven Countries of West and Central Africa.* Background paper for the ADEA Biennial Meeting, Grand Baie, Mauritius, 3-6 December.

Ethiopia Ministry of Education. 1999. *Education Sector Development Programme: Action Plan.* Addis Ababa.

Ethiopia. 2003. *Education Sector Development Programme II. 2002/03-2004/05. Joint Review Mission Report.* Government of Ethiopia.

European Commission. 2001. Mozambique-European Community Country Strategy Paper and National Indicative Programme for the period 2001-2007. (http://europa.eu.int/comm/development/body/csp_rsp/print/mz_csp_en.pdf)

— 2004. Commission Acts to Boost Efficiency of EU Development Aid through Better Co-ordination and Harmonisation. Press release, 11 March. (http://europa-eu-un.org/articles/de/article_3285_de.htm)

Farrell, J. P. 2002. The Aga Khan Foundation experience compared with emerging alternatives to schooling. In: S. E. Anderson (ed.), *School improvement through teacher development: Case studies of the Aga Khan Foundation projects in East Africa*: 247-70. Lisse, the Netherlands, Swets & Zeitlinger.

Faure, E.; Herrera, F.; Kaddoura, A.; Lopes, H.; Petrovsky, A.; Rahnema, M; Ward, F. C. 1972. *Learning to be: the world of education today and tomorrow*. Paris/London, UNESCO/Harrap.

Fenwick, T. 2001. *Experiential Learning: A Theoretical Critique from Five Perspectives*. Columbus, OH, ERIC Clearinghouse on Adult, Career, and Vocational Education. (Information Series No. 385.)

Fiedrich, M.; Jellema, A. 2003. *Literacy, Gender and Social Agency: Adventures in Empowerment*. London, Department for International Development. (DFID Educational Paper 53.)

Finland Ministry for Foreign Affairs. 2002. *Welfare Development: The Finnish Experience*. Helsinki, Department for International Development Cooperation.

Finland Ministry of Education. 2003. *Ministry of Education Strategy 2015*. Helsinki, Publications of the Ministry of Education, Finland (No. 2003:35) (www.minedu.fi/julkaisut/hallinto/2003/opm35/opm35.pdf)

Finland National Board of Education. 1996. *An independent evaluation of comprehensive curriculum reform in Finland*. Helsinki, Yliopistopaino [Helsinki University Press].

Finnie, R.; Meng, R. 2002. Minorities, cognitive skills, and incomes of Canadians. *Canadian Public Policy*, Vol. 28: 257-73.

Fiske, E; Ladd, H. 2004. Balancing public and private resources for basic education: school fees in post-apartheid South Africa. In: L. Chisholm (ed.), *Changing Class: Education and Social Change in Post-Apartheid South Africa*: 57-87. Cape Town/London, Human Sciences Research Council/Zed Press.

Foster, M. 2004. *Accounting for Donor Contributions to Education for All: How Should Finance be Provided? How Should it be Monitored?* Final report to the World Bank. (Mimeograph)

Foster, M.; Norton, A.; Brown, A.; Naschold, F. 2000. *The Status of Sector-Wide Approaches*. A framework paper for the meeting of the Like-minded Donor Working Group on Sector Wide Approaches, Dublin. 3rd draft. London, Overseas Development Institute.

Foucault, M. 1977. *Discipline and Punish: The Birth of the Prison*. Translated by A. Sheridan. Harmondsworth, Penguin.

Freire, P. 1985, *The Politics of Education: Culture, Power and Liberation*. Translated by D. Macedo. London, Macmillan.

Fullan, M. 1993. *Change Forces: Probing the Depths of Educational Reform*. London, Falmer Press.

— 2000. The return of large-scale reform. *Journal of Educational Change*, Vol. 2, No. 1: 5-28.

Fullan, M.; Watson, N. 2000. School-Based Management: Re-conceptualizing to Improve Learning Outcome. *School Effectiveness and School Improvement*, Vol. 11, No. 4: 453-73.

Fuller, B.; Clarke, P. 1994. Raising School Effects While Ignoring Culture? Local conditions and the influence of classrooms, tools, rules and pedagogy. *Review of Educational Research*, Vol. 64, No. 1 :119-57.

Gage, N. 1965. Desirable behaviors of teachers. *Urban Education*, Vol. 1: 85-95.

— 1986. *Comment tirer un meilleur parti des recherches sur les processus d'enseignement?* In: M. Crahay and D. Lafontaine (eds.), *L'art et la science de l'enseignement*: 304-25. Brussels, Labor.

Gajardo, M.; Gómez, F. 2003. *Social Dialogue in Education in Latin America: A Regional Survey*. Background document for the Working Group on Social Dialogue in Education, Joint ILO/UNESCO Committee of Experts on the Application of the Recommendations concerning Teaching Personnel, Paris, 15-19 September. (ILO Sectoral Activities Working Paper, forthcoming.)

Gasperini, L. 2000. *The Cuban Education System: Lessons and Dilemmas*. Washington, DC, World Bank. (World Bank Country Studies. Education Reform and Management Publication Series, Vol. 1, No. 5.)

Gauthier, C.; Dembélé, M. 2004. *Qualité de l'enseignement et qualité de l'éducation. Revue des résultats de recherche*. Background paper for *EFA Global Monitoring Report 2005*.

Gaziel, H. 1998. School-based management as a factor in school effectiveness. *International Review of Education*, Vol. 44, No. 4: 319-33.

George, J.; Quamina-Aiyejina, L. 2003. *An Analysis of Primary Teacher Education in Trinidad and Tobago*. Multi-Site Teacher Education Research Project (MUSTER) Country Report Four. London, Department for International Development. (DFID Educational Paper 49e.)

Gerdes, P. 2001. Ethnomathematics as a New Research Field, Illustrated by Studies of Mathematical Ideas in African History. In: J. J Saldaña et al. (eds.), *Science and Cultural Diversity: Filling a Gap in the History of Science, Cuadernos de Quipu* No. 5: 10-34. Mexico City, Sociedad Latinoamericana de Historia de las Ciencias y la Tecnología.

Ghana Education Service. 1999. *Whole School Development: Training Programme for Head Teachers and other Stakeholders*. Teacher Education Division, Ghana Education Service.

— 2004. *WSD (Whole School Development) Status Report*. Accra, Ministry of Education.

Gibbons, M.; Limoges, C.; Nowotny, H.; Schwartzman, S.; Trow, M. 1994. *The New Production of Knowledge: the Dynamics of Science and Research in Contemporary Societies*. London, Sage.

Giroux, H. 1993. *Living Dangerously*. New York, Peter Lang.

Glewwe, P. 1996. The relevance of standard estimates of rates of return to schooling for educational policy: A critical assessment. *Journal of Development Economics*, Vol. 51: 267-90.

— 2002. Schools and Skills in Developing Countries: Education Policies and Socioeconomic Outcomes. *Journal of Economic Literature*, Vol. 40, No. 2, June: 436-82.

Glewwe, P.; Kremer, M.; Moulin, S. 2000. Textbooks and Test Scores: evidence from the Prospective Evaluation in Kenya. Working Paper. Cambridge, MA, Harvard University, November. (http://post.economics.harvard.edu/faculty/kremer/webpapers/Textbooks_Test_Scores.pdf)

Glewwe, P.; Nauman, I; Kremer, M. 2003. *Teacher Incentives*. Cambridge, MA, National Bureau of Economic Research (NBER Working Paper 9671, May.)

Good, T. L.; Biddle, B. J.; Brophy, J. E. 1983. *Teaching effectiveness: Research findings and policy implications*. Columbia, University of Missouri Center for Research in Social Behavior. (Technical Report No. 319.)

Good, T. L.; Brophy, J. E. 1986. School effects. In: M. C. Wittrock (ed.), *Handbook of Research on Teaching*: 328-75. New York, Macmillan.

Greaney, V.; Khandker, S. R.; Alam, M. 1999. *Bangladesh: Assessing Basic Learning Skills*. Washington, DC, World Bank.

Green, D. A.; Riddell, W. Craig. 2003. Literacy and earnings: An investigation of the interaction of cognitive and unobserved skills in earnings generation. *Labour Economics*, Vol. 10: 165-84.

Grimes, B. F. (ed.). 2000. *Ethnologue: Languages of the World*. 14th ed. Dallas, SIL International. (www.ethnologue.com/web.asp)

Grogger, J. T.; Eide, E. 1993. Changes in college skills and the rise in the college wage premium. *Journal of Human Resources*, Vol. 30, No. 2, Spring: 280-310.

Guadalupe, C.; Louzano, P. 2003. *Measuring universal primary completion in Latin America*. Santiago, OREALC/UNESCO.

Gundlach, E.; Woessmann, L.; Gmelin, J. 2001. The Decline of Schooling Productivity in OECD Countries. *Economic Journal*, Vol. 111, No. 471, May: 135-47.

Gupta, S.; Verhoeven, M.; Tiongson, E. 1999. *Does Higher Government Spending Buy Better Results in Education and Health Care?* Washington, International Monetary Fund. (Working Paper No. 99/21, February).

Gusso, D. 2004. *Brazil Report*. Background paper for *EFA Global Monitoring Report 2005*.

Hallak, J.; Poisson, M. 2002. *Ethics and corruption in education: Results from the Expert Workshop held at IIEP, Paris, 28-29 November 2001*. Paris, UNESCO International Institute for Educational Planning. (Observatory Programme, Policy Forum No. 15.)

— 2004a. *Teachers' codes of conduct: How can they help improve quality?* Background paper for *EFA Global Monitoring Report 2005* through the UNESCO International Institute for Educational Planning, Paris.

— 2004b. *Corruption in Education: What impact on quality, equity and ethics?* Background paper for *EFA Global Monitoring Report 2005* through the UNESCO International Institute for Educational Planning, Paris.

Hanushek, E. A. 1995. Interpreting Recent Research on Schooling in Developing Countries. *World Bank Research Observer*, Vol. 10, No. 2, August: 227-46.

— 1997. Assessing the Effects of School Resources on Student Performance: An Update. *Education Evaluation and Policy Analysis*, Vol. 19, No. 2, Summer: 141-64.

— 2002a. Evidence, Politics, and the Class Size Debate. In: L. Mishel and R. Rothstein (eds.), *The Class Size Debate*: 37-65. Washington, DC, Economic Policy Institute.

— 2002b. Publicly Provided Education. In: A. J. Auerbach and M. Feldstein (eds.), *Handbook of Public Economics*, Vol. 4, Chapter 30: 2045-141. Oxford, Elsevier Science Ltd.

— 2003a. The Failure of Input-based Schooling Policies, *Economic Journal*, Vol. 113, No. 485, February: 64-98.

— 2003b. The Importance of School Quality. In: P. E. Peterson (ed.), *Our Schools and Our Future: Are We Still at Risk?:* 141-73. Stanford, Calif., Hoover Institution Press.

— 2004. *Economic Analysis of School Quality.* Background paper for *EFA Global Monitoring Report 2005.*

Hanushek, E. A.; Kain, J. F.; Rivkin, S. G. 1999. *Do Higher Salaries Buy Better Teachers?* Cambridge, MA, National Bureau of Economic Research. (NBER Working Paper 7082, April).

— 2004. Why Public Schools Lose Teachers. *Journal of Human Resources*, Vol. 39, No. 2: 326-54.

Hanushek, E. A.; Kimko, D. D. 2000. Schooling, Labor-Force Quality, and the Growth of Nations. *American Economic Review*, Vol. 90, No. 5, December: 1184-208.

Hanushek, E. A.; Luque, J. A. 2003. Efficiency and Equity in Schools around the World, *Economics of Education Review*, Vol. 22, No. 5, October: 481-502.

Hanushek, E. A.; Pace, R. R. 1995. Who chooses to teach (and why)? *Economics of Education Review,* Vol. 14, No. 2, June: 101-17.

Hanushek, E. A.; Rivkin, S. G. 2003. Does Public School Competition Affect Teacher Quality? In: C. M. Hoxby (ed.), *The Economics of School Choice.* Chicago, University of Chicago Press.

Hanushek, E. A.; Rivkin, S. G.; Taylor, L. L. 1996. Aggregation and the estimated effects of school resources. *Review of Economics and Statistics,* Vol. 78, No. 4, November: 611-27.

Hargreaves, A.; Lieberman, A.; Fullan, M.; Hopkins, D. (eds.). 1998. *International Handbook of Educational Change 4.* Dordrecht, Kluwer Academic Press.

Hargreaves, D. 1999. Revitalising Educational Research: Lessons from the Past and Proposals for the Future. *The Cambridge Journal of Education,* Vol. 29, No. 2: 242-60.

— The production, mediation and use of professional knowledge among teachers and doctors: a comparative analysis. In: CERI, *Knowledge Management in the Learning Society*: 219-38. Paris, Centre for Educational Research and Innovation, OECD.

Hargreaves, D.; Hopkins, D. 1994. *Development Planning for School Improvement.* London, Cassell.

Harlen, W.; James, M. 1997. Assessment and Learning: differences and relationships between formative and summative assessment. *Assessment in Education*, Vol. 4, No. 3: 365-79.

Hattie, J. 1992. *Self-concept.* Hillsdale, NJ, Lawrence Erlbaum Associates.

Heckman, J. J.; Rubinstein, Y. 2001. The Importance of Noncognitive Skills: Lessons from the GED Testing Program. *American Economic Review*, Vol. 19, No. 2, May: 145-9.

Heckman, J. J.; Vytlacil, E. 2001. Identifying the role of cognitive ability in explaining the level of and change in the return to schooling. *Review of Economics and Statistics*, Vol. 83, No. 1, February: 1–12.

Hedges, J. 2002. The importance of posting and interaction with the education bureaucracy in becoming a teacher in Ghana. *International Journal of Educational Development*, Vol. 22, Nos. 3/4: 353–66.

Helvetas. 2002. *10 key stages towards effective participatory curriculum development: learning from practice and experience in the Social Forestry Support Programme, Vietnam, and other Helvetas-supported projects*. Zurich, Helvetas. (Experience and Learning in International Cooperation, No. 2.)

Heston, A.; Summers, R.; Aten, B. 2002. *Penn World Table Version 6.1*. Philadelphia, Center for International Comparison, University of Pennsylvania.

High/Scope Educational Research Foundation. 2004. *The IEA Preprimary Project Age 7 Follow-up*. Ypsilanti, MI, High/Scope.

H. M. Treasury. 2003. *International Finance Facility*. London, H. M. Treasury.

— 2004. Stability, security and opportunity for all: investing for Britain's long-term future. *2004 Spending Review: new public spending plans 2005–2008*, July.

Hoeven-Van Doornum, A. A.; Jungbluth, P. 1987. De bijdrage van schoolkenmerken aan schooleffectiviteit [The relevance of school characteristics for school effectiveness]. In: J. Scheerens and W. G. R. Stoel (eds.), *Effectiviteit van onderwijsorganisaties* [Effectiveness of educational organizations]. Lisse, the Netherlands, Swets & Zeitlinger.

Honduras Ministry of Education. 2003. *Informe Nacional de Rendimiento Académico 2002 Tercero y Sextos grados*. Tegucigalpa, Unidad Externa de Medición de la Calidad de la Educación. Universidad Pedagógica Nacional Francisco Morazán.

Hopkin, A. G. 1997. Staff Perspectives on Teaching and Learning Styles in Teacher Education in Botswana. *Journal of the International Society for Teacher Education*, Vol. 1, No. 1: 1–11.

Hopkins, D. 2001. *School Improvement for Real*. London/New York, Routledge/Falmer.

Hopkins, D.; Ainscow, M.; West, M. 1994. *School Improvement in an Era of Change*. London, Cassell.

Hoppers, W. 1998. Teachers' Resource Centers in Southern Africa; an Investigation into Local Autonomy and Educational Change. *International Journal of Educational Development*, Vol. 18, No. 3: 229–46.

— 2001. About How to Reach the Truth in Development Cooperation: ODA/DFID's Education Papers. *International Journal of Educational Development*, Vol. 21, No. 5: 463–70.

— 2004. *Knowledge Infrastructures for Quality Improvement*. Background paper for *EFA Global Monitoring Report 2005*.

Horsley, M. 2004. *An Expert Teacher's Use of Textbooks in the Classroom*. University of Sydney. (http://alex.edfac.usyd.edu.au/Year1/cases/Case%2014/Expert_teacher's_use_of_te.html.)

Hoxby, C. 2000. The Effects of Class Size on Student Achievement: New Evidence from Population Variation. *Quarterly Journal of Economics*, Vol. 115, No. 4, November: 1239–85.

Hunt, J. 1961. *Intelligence and Experience*. New York, Ronald Press.

IHSD. 2003. *Sector Wide Approaches in Education*. London, Institute for Health Sector Development.

Illich, I. 1971. *Deschooling Society*. New York, Harper & Row.

ILO. 2000. *Lifelong learning in the twenty-first century: The changing role of educational personnel*. Geneva, International Labour Office.

— 2002. *A Future without Child Labour: Global Report under the Follow-up to the ILO Declaration on Fundamental Principles and Rights at Work 2002*. Geneva, International Labour Office.

— 2004. *IPEC action against child labour 2002–2003: progress and future priorities*. Geneva, International Labour Office, International Programme on the Elimination of Child Labour.

IMF/IDA. 2003. *Poverty Reduction Strategy Papers: Progress in Implementation*. Washington, DC, International Monetary Fund and International Development Association.

Indonesia Ministry of Education and Culture. 1998. *Impact Evaluation of Non-Formal Education Program in Batch I and II Intensive Kecamatan*. Final Report. Jakarta, Directorate General of Out-of-School Education, Youth and Sports, Directorate of Community Education.

INEP. 2002. *Geografia da Educação Brasileira: Statistical Handbook*. Brasilia, Instituto Nacional de Estudos e Pesquisas Educacionais Anísio Teixeira.

IRFOL. 2004. *Distance Learning and Improving the Quality of Education*. Background paper for *EFA Global Monitoring Report 2005* through the International Research Foundation for Open Learning, Cambridge.

Jaramillo, A.; Mingat, A. 2003. *Early Childhood Care and Education in Sub-Saharan Africa: What would it take to meet the Millennium Development Goals?* Washington, DC, World Bank.

Jarousse, J.-P.; Mingat, A.; Richard, M. 1992. La scolarisation maternelle à 2 ans: effets pédagogiques et sociaux. *Education et formations*, n° 31, avril-juin: 3-9.

Jarvis, P. 1983. *Adult and Continuing Education: Theory and Practice*. London, Croom Helm.

Jencks, C.; Bartlett, S.; Corcoran, M.; Crouse, J.; Eaglesfield, D.; Jackson, G.; McClelland, K.; Mueser, P.; Olneck, M.; Schwartz, J.; Ward, S.; Williams, J. 1979. *Who gets ahead? The Determinants of Success in America*. New York, Basic Books.

Jepsen, C.; Rivkin, S. 2002. *What is the Tradeoff between Smaller Classes and Teacher Quality?* Cambridge, MA, National Bureau of Economic Research. (NBER Working Paper 9205, September).

Jessee, C.; Mchazime, H.; Dowd, A. J.; Winicki, F; Harris, A.; Schubert, J. 2003. *Exploring factors that influence teaching and learning: Summary findings from the IEQ/Malawi longitudinal study 1999-2002*. Washington, DC, USAID, Improving Educational Quality Project. (www.ieq.org/pdf/Exploration_into_Findings.pdf) (USAID document No. PN-ACU-230, September.)

Jimenez, E.; Sawada, Y. 1998. *Do community-managed schools work? An evaluation of El Salvador's EDUCO program*. Washington, DC, World Bank, Development Economics Research Group. (Working Paper No. 8, Series on Impact Evaluation of Education Reforms.)

Jolliffe, D. 1998. Skills, schooling, and household income in Ghana. *World Bank Economic Review*, Vol. 12: 81-104.

Jonassen, D. H. 1992. Evaluating constructivist learning. In: T. M. Duffy and D. H. Jonassen (eds.), *Constructivism and the Technology of Instruction: A Conversation*: 138-48. Hillsdale, NJ, Lawrence Erlbaum Associates.

Juel, C. 1991. Beginning Reading. In: R. Barr, M.L. Kamil, P.B. Mosenthal and P.D. Pearson (eds.), *Handbook of Reading Research*, Vol. 2, Chapter 27. New York, Longman.

Kagitçbasi, Ç. 1996. *Family and Human Development Across Cultures: A View from the Other Side*. Mahwah, N.J., Lawrence Erlbaum Associates.

Kanyika, J. 2004. *National Assessment: Preliminary Results*. Paper presented to the National Assessment Steering Committee, Zambia, February.

Kapoor, J. M.; Roy, P. 1970. *Retention of literacy*. New Delhi, Council for Social Development, India International Centre.

Karlekar, M. (ed.). 2000. *Reading the World: Understanding the Literacy Campaigns in India*. Mumbai, Asian South Pacific Bureau of Adult Education.

Kasprzyk, D. 1999. *Measuring teacher qualifications*. Washington, DC, US Department of Education, National Center for Education Statistics. (NCES Working Paper Series, No. 1999-2004.)

Kassam, Y. 1995. Julius Nyerere. In: Z. Morsy (ed.), *Thinkers on Education*. Paris, UNESCO.

Keating, D.; Hertzman, C. (eds.). 1999. *Developmental Health and the Wealth of Nations*. New York, Guilford Press.

Keddie, N. 1971. Classroom Knowledge. In: M. Young, *Knowledge and Control*: 133-60. London, Collins-Macmillan.

KEDI. 1979. *The Long-Term Prospect for Educational Development 1978–91*. Seoul, Korean Educational Development Institute.

Keeves, J. P. 1995. *The World of School Learning: Selected Key Findings from 35 Years of IEA Research*. The Hague, International Association for the Evaluation of Educational Achievement.

Keeves, J. P.; Schleicher, A. 1992. Changes in Science Achievement 1970–84. In: Keeves, J. P. (ed.), *The IEA Study of Science: Changes in Science Education and Achievement: 1970 to 1984*: Chapter 9. Oxford, Pergamon Press.

Kellaghan, T.; Greaney, V. 2001. *Using Assessment to Improve the Quality of Education*. Paris, UNESCO International Institute for Educational Planning.

Kelly, M. J. 2000. *Planning for education in the context of HIV/AIDS*. Paris, UNESCO International Institute For Educational Planning.

Kigotho, W. 2004. Teachers battling heavy odds. *School & Career*, 6 May 2004.

King, E.; Ozler, B. 1998. *What's Decentralization Got to do with Learning? The Case of Nicaragua's School Autonomy Reform*. Washington, DC, World Bank, Development Economics Research Group. (Working Paper No. 9, series on Impact Evaluation of Education Reforms.)

Kingdon, G. 1996. *Student Achievement and Teacher Pay: A Case-Study of India*. London, London School of Economics, Suntory and Toyota International Centres for Economics and Related Disciplines. (STICERD Discussion Paper No. 74, August).

Kingdon, G.; Teal, F. 2003. *Does Performance-Related Pay for Teachers Improve Student Performance? Some Evidence from India*. Working Paper. Department of Economics, University of Oxford, November.

Kingsada, T. 2003. Languages and Ethnic Classification in the Lao PDR. *Waalasaan phasaa lae xiwit, Language and Life Journal*, Vol. 1, 2003: 24-39.

Kirk, J; Winthrop, R. 2004. *IRC Healing Classrooms Initiative: An initial study in Ethiopia*. New York, International Rescue Committee.

Kloprogge, J.; van Oijen, P.; Riemersma, F.; van Tilborg, L.; Walraven, G.;Wind, D. 1995. *Educational Research and Development in the Netherlands; The State of the Art from the Perspective of the Education Support Structure*. The Hague, SVO.

Knack, S.; Rahman, A. 2004. *Donor Fragmentation and Bureaucratic Quality in Aid Recipients*. Washington, DC, World Bank. (World Bank Policy Research Working Paper 3186.)

Knamiller, G. (ed.). 1999. *The Effectiveness of Teacher Resource Center Strategy*. London, Department for International Development. (Education Research, Serial No. 34.)

Knight, J. B.; Sabot, R. H. 1990. *Education, productivity, and inequality*. New York, Oxford University Press.

Knowles, M. S. 1980. *The Modern Practice of Adult Education*. Englewood Cliffs, NJ, Prentice Hall.

Kolb, D. 1984. *Experiential Learning: Experience as a Source of Learning and Development*. Englewood Cliffs, NJ, Prentice Hall.

Kosonen, K. 2004. *Education in Local Languages: Policy and Practice in South-East Asia*. A paper prepared for the SEAMEO-UNESCO Education Congress, Bangkok, 27–29 May.

Kotta, M. N. 1986. *Tutors' and student-teachers' reactions to discovery methods in diploma colleges of education: a case study of Morogoro and Dar es Salaam Colleges*. Dar es Salaam, University of Dar es Salaam, Department of Education.

Kotze, K.; Higgins, C. 1999. Breakthrough to Icibemba Pilot: An Evaluation. (Mimeograph)

Kremer, M. ; Moulin, S. ; Namunyu, R. 2003. *Decentralization: A Cautionary Tale*. Working Paper. Cambridge, MA, Harvard University, March.

Kremer, M.; Moulin, S.; Namunyu, R.; Myatt, D. 1997. *The Quantity-Quality Tradeoff in Education: Evidence from a Prospective Evaluation in Kenya.* Working Paper. Cambridge, MA, Harvard University.

Krueger, A. B. 1999. Experimental Estimates of Education Production Functions. *Quarterly Journal of Economics*, Vol. 114, No. 2, May: 497-534.

— 2003. Economic Considerations and Class Size. *Economic Journal*, Vol. 13, No. 485, February: 34-63.

Krueger, A. B.; Whitmore, D. M. 2002. Would Smaller Classes Help Close the Black-White Achievement Gap? In: J. Chubb and T. Loveless (eds.), *Bridging the Achievement Gap*. Washington, DC, Brookings Institution Press.

Kulik, C. L. C.; Kulik, J. A. 1982. Effects of ability grouping on secondary school students: a meta-analysis of research findings. *American Educational Research Journal*, Vol. 19: 415-28.

Kulpoo, D. 1998. *The Quality of Education: Some Policy Suggestions Based on a Survey of Schools, Mauritius.* SACMEQ Policy Research Report No. 1. Ministry of Education and Human Resource Development, Mauritius, and UNESCO International Institute for Educational Planning.

Kunje, D. 2002. The Malawi Integrated In-service Teacher Education Programme: an experiment with mixed-mode training. *International Journal of Educational Development*, Vol. 22, Nos.3/4: 305-20.

Kunje, D.; Chirembo, S. 2000. *The Malawi Integrated In-Service Teacher Education Programme and its School-Based Components.* Brighton, Centre for International Education, University of Sussex. (MUSTER Discussion Paper No. 12.)

Kunje, D.; Lewin, K. M. 2000. *The Costs and Financing of Teacher Education in Malawi.* Brighton, Centre for International Education, University of Sussex. (MUSTER Discussion Paper No. 2.)

Kunje, D.; Lewin, K. M.; Stuart, J. S. 2003. *Primary Teacher Education in Malawi: Insights into Practice and Policy.* Multi-Site Teacher Education Research Project (MUSTER) Country Report Three. London, Department for International Development. (DFID Educational Paper 49d.)

Kyle, M. J. (ed.). 1985. *Reaching for Excellence: An Effective Schools Sourcebook.* Washington, DC, United States Government Printing Office.

Lambert, S. 2004. *Pay and Conditions: An Assessment of Recent Trends in Africa.* Background paper for *EFA Global Monitoring Report 2005.*

Lancy, D. (ed.). 1978. The Indigenous Mathematics Project. *Papua New Guinea Journal of Education*, Vol. 14, Special Issue: 1-217.

Latif, S. 2004. *Improvements in the Quality of Primary Education in Bangladesh 1990-2002.* Background paper for *EFA Global Monitoring Report 2005.*

Lavy, V. 2003. *Paying for Performance: The Effects of Teachers' Financial Incentives on Students' Scholastic Outcomes.* Cambridge, MA, Harvard University, Bureau for Research and Economic Analysis of Development. (BREAD Working Paper No. 022, February.)

Lawler, E. E. 1986. *High involvement management.* San Francisco, Jossey-Bass.

Laws, K.; Horsley, M. 2004. *Educational Equity? Textbooks in New South Wales Secondary Schools.* University of Sydney. (http://alex.edfac.usyd.edu.au/Year1/cases/Case%2014/Textbooks_in_Secondary_Sch.html)

Lazear, E. P. 2003. Teacher incentives. *Swedish Economic Policy Review*, Vol. 10: 179-214.

Lee, J.; Barro, R. J. 2001. Schooling Quality in a Cross-Section of Countries. *Economica*, Vol. 38, No. 272, November: 465-88.

Leguéré, J.-P. 2003. *Approvisionnement en livres scolaires: vers plus de transparence. Afrique francophone.* Paris, UNESCO International Institute for Educational Planning. (Ethics and Corruption in Education series.)

Leithwood, K.; Jantzi, D.; Steinbach, R. 1999. *Changing Leadership for Changing Times.* Buckingham, PA, Open University Press.

Leithwood, K.; Menzies, T. 1998. A Review of Research Concerning the Implementation of Site-Based Management. *School Effectiveness and School Improvement*, Vol. 9, No. 33.

Levine, D. K.; Lezotte, L. W. 1990. *Unusually Effective Schools: A Review and Analysis of Research and Practice.* Madison, WI, National Center for Effective Schools Research and Development.

Levinger, B. 1994. *Nutrition, Health and Education for All.* Newton, MA/New York, Education Development Center, Inc./UNDP.

Lewin, K. M. 1999. *Counting the Cost of Teacher Education: Cost and Quality Issues.* Brighton, Centre for International Education, University of Sussex. (MUSTER Discussion Paper No. 1.)

— 2002. The costs of supply and demand for teacher education: dilemmas for development. *International Journal of Educational Development,* Vol. 22, Nos. 3/4: 221-42.

— 2004. *The Pre-Service Training of Teachers: Does it Meet its Objectives and How can it be Improved?* Background paper for *EFA Global Monitoring Report 2005*.

Lewin, K. M.; Ntoi, V.; Nenty, H. J.; Mapuru, P. 2000. *Costs and Financing of Teacher Education in Lesotho.* Brighton, Centre for International Education, University of Sussex. (MUSTER Discussion Paper No. 10.)

Lewin, K. M.; Samuel, M.; Sayed, Y. (eds.). 2003. *Changing Patterns of Teacher Education in South Africa: Policy, Practice and Prospects*. Sandown, Heinemann Press.

Lewin, K. M; Stuart, J. S. 2003. *Researching Teacher Education: New Perspectives on Practice, Performance and Policy*. Multi-Site Teacher Education Research Project (MUSTER) Synthesis Report. London, Department for International Development. (DFID Educational Paper 49a.)

Liang, X. 1999. *Teacher Pay in 12 Latin American Countries: How does teacher pay compare to other professions, what determines teacher pay, and who are the teachers?* Washington, DC, World Bank. (Latin America and the Caribbean Region Human Development Paper No. 49.)

Linehan, S. 2004. *Language of Instruction and the Quality of Basic Education in Zambia.* Background paper for *EFA Global Monitoring Report 2005*.

Litteral, R. 2004. *Vernacular Education in Papua New Guinea.* Background paper for *EFA Global Monitoring Report 2005*.

Little, A. W. (ed.). 2000. *Primary Education Reforms in Sri Lanka.* Battaramulla, Sri Lanka Ministry of Education and Higher Education.

Little, A. W. 2004. *Learning and Teaching in Multigrade Settings.* Background paper for *EFA Global Monitoring Report 2005*.

Lopez-Acevedo, G. 2004. *Professional Development and Incentives for Teacher Performance in Schools in Mexico.* Washington, DC, World Bank. (World Bank Policy Research Working Paper 3236, March.)

Low-Beer, D.; Stoneburner, R. 2000. *Social Communications and AIDS population behaviour changes in Uganda compared to other countries.* Johannesburg, Centre for AIDS Development, Research and Evaluation.

— 2001. *In Search of the Magic Bullet: Evaluating And Replicating Prevention Programs.* From Curtailing the HIV Epidemic: The Role of Prevention – Leadership Forum sponsored by the Kaiser Family Foundation, Ford Foundation, Gates Foundation. New York, 22 June.

L. T. Associates, Inc. 2002a. *Review and Analysis of Zambia's Education Sector.* Vol. 1. Lusaka, USAID.

— 2002b. *Review and Analysis of Zambia's Education Sector.* Vol. 2. Lusaka, USAID.

Lubart, T. 2004. *Individual student differences and creativity for quality education.* Background paper for *EFA Global Monitoring Report 2005*.

Lynch, J. 2000. *Inclusion in Education: The Participation of Disabled Learners.* Education for All 2000 Assessment Thematic Study. Paris, UNESCO.

Machingaidze, T.; Pfukani, P.; Shumba, S. 1998. *The Quality of Education: Some Policy Suggestions Based on a Survey of Schools, Zimbabwe.* SACMEQ Policy Research Report No. 3. Ministry of Basic Education and Culture, Zimbabwe, and UNESCO International Institute for Educational Planning.

Magrab, P. R. 2004. *Brief Commentary on Quality Education and Children with Disabilities.* Background paper for *EFA Global Monitoring Report 2005.*

Malderez, A. 2002. I.S.A. Mentor Development. In: D. Hayes (ed.), *Making a Difference: The Experience of Primary English Language Project, Sri Lanka,* Colombo, British Council.

Managing for Development Results. 2004. *Action Plan on Managing for Development Results.* Second Roundtable on Managing for Development Results, Marrakech, 5 February.

Manski, C. F.; Wise, D. A. 1983. *College Choice in America.* Cambridge, MA, Harvard University Press.

Martínez, J. P.; Myers, R. 2003. *En búsqueda de la calidad educativa en centros preescolares.* Unpublished report to the Dirección General de Investigación Educativa. Mexico City.

McBer, H. 2000. *Research into Teacher Effectiveness: A Model of Teacher Effectiveness.* Norwich, Crown Copyright Unit.

McDonnell, I.; Lecomte, H.-B.; Wegimont, L. (eds.). 2003. *Public Opinion and the Fight against Poverty.* Development Centre Studies. Paris, OECD.

McIntosh, S.; Vignoles, A. 2001. Measuring and assessing the impact of basic skills on labor market outcomes. *Oxford Economic Papers,* Vol. 53: 453-81.

McKay, H.; Sinisterra, L.; McKay, A.; Gomez, H.; Lloreda, P. 1978. Improving cognitive ability in chronically deprived children. *Science,* Vol. 200, No. 4339: 270-78.

McLaren, P. 1994. *Life in Schools: An Introduction to Critical Pedagogy in the Foundations of Education.* 2nd ed. New York, Longman.

McLaughlin, M. W. 1987. Learning from experience: Lessons from policy implementation. *Educational Evaluation and Policy Analysis*, Vol. 9, No. 2: 171-78.

McMahon, W. 1999. *Education and Development: Measuring the Social Benefits*, Oxford, Oxford University Press.

Medley, D.; Mitzel, H. 1963. Measuring classroom behavior by systematic observation. In: N. Gage (ed.), *Handbook of Research on Teaching*. Chicago, Rand McNally.

Mehrotra, S.; Buckland, P. 1998. *Managing Teacher Costs for Access and Quality.* New York, UNICEF.

Merrill, M. D. 1991. Constructivism and instruction design. *Educational Technology*, Vol. 31: 45-53.

Michaelowa, K. 2002. *Teacher job satisfaction, student achievement, and the cost of primary education in francophone sub-Saharan Africa.* HWWA Discussion Paper No. 188. Hamburg, Hamburg Institute of International Economics.

— 2004. *Quality and equity of learning outcomes in francophone Africa.* Montreal, UNESCO Institute for Statistics. (Processed)

Michéa, J.-C. 1999. L'enseignement de l'ignorance et ses conditions moderne. Castlenau Le Nez, France, Ed. Climat.

Miguel, E.; Kremer, M. 2004. Worms: Identifying Impact on Education and Health in the Presence of Treatment Externalities. *Econometrica,* Vol. 72, No. 1: 159-217.

Miles, M. B., Saxl, E. R.; Lieberman, A. 1988. What Skills do Educational Change Agents Need? An Empirical View. *Curriculum Enquiry*. Vol. 18, No. 2: 157-93.

Milner, G.; Chimombo, J.; Banda, T.; Mchikoma, C. 2001. *The Quality of Education: Some Policy Suggestions Based on a Survey of Schools, Malawi.* SACMEQ Policy Research Report No. 7. Ministry of Basic Education and Culture, Malawi, and UNESCO International Institute for Educational Planning.

Mingat, A. 2002. *Teacher salary issues in African countries.* World Bank Africa Region, Human Development Analysis and Policy Development Support Team. Washington, DC, World Bank.

Moll, P. G. 1998. Primary schooling, cognitive skills, and wage in South Africa. *Economica,* Vol. 65: 263-84.

Montagnes, I. 2001. *Textbooks and Learning Materials 1990-99.* Education For All 2000 Assessment Thematic Study. London/Paris, Department for International Development/UNESCO.

Mortimore, P.; Sammons, P.; Stoll, L.; Lewis, D.; Ecob, R. 1988. *The junior school project; technical appendices.* London, Inner London Education Authority, Research and Statistics Branch.

Moses, K. 2000. Do you know where your teachers and schools are? *Techknowlogia,* November/December. (http://ict.aed.org/infocentre/pdfs/doyu.pdf)

Moulton, J. 2003. *Improving the Quality of Primary Education in Africa: What has the World Bank Learned?* Draft background paper for ADEA Biennial Meeting, Grand Baie, Mauritius, 3-6 December.

Mulligan, C. B. 1999. Galton versus the human capital approach to inheritance. *Journal of Political Economy,* Vol. 107, No. 6, pt. 2, December: 184-224.

Mullis, I. V. S; Martin, M. O.; Gonzalez, E. J.; Gregory, K. D.; Garden, R. A.; O'Connor, K. M.; Chrostowski, S. J.; Smith, T. A. 2000. *Findings from IEA's Repeat of the Third International Mathematics and Science Study at the Eighth Grade.* Chestnut Hill, MA, International Study Center, Boston College.

Mullis, I. V. S.; Martin, M. O.; Gonzalez, E. J.; Kennedy, A. M. 2003. *PIRLS 2001 International Report: IEA's Study of Reading Literacy Achievement in Primary Schools in 35 Countries.* Chestnut Hill, MA, International Study Center, Boston College.

Murimba, S. 2003. Learning outcomes in primary education; examples from the south. Conference paper presented in Oslo, 11-13 June.

Murnane, R. J. 1981. Interpreting the evidence on school effectiveness. *Teachers College Record,* Vol. 83: 19-35.

Murnane, R. J.; Willet, J. B.; Braatz, M. J.; Duhaldeborde, Y. 2001. Do different dimensions of male high school students' skills predict labor market success a decade later? Evidence from the NLSY. *Economics of Education Review,* Vol. 20, No. 4, August: 311-20.

Murnane, R. J.; Willet, J. B.; Duhaldeborde, Y.; Tyler, J. H. 2000. How important are the cognitive skills of teenagers in predicting subsequent earnings? *Journal of Policy Analysis and Management,* Vol. 19, No. 4, Fall: 547-68.

Murnane, R. J.; Willet, J. B.; Levy, F. 1995. The growing importance of cognitive skills in wage determination. *Review of Economics and Statistics,* Vol. 77, No. 2, May: 251-66.

Mustard, F. 2002. Early Child Development and the Brain – the Base for Health, Learning and Behavior throughout Life. In: M. Young (ed.), *From Early Child Development to Human Development*: 23-61. Washington, DC, World Bank.

Myers, B. 2004. *In Search of Quality in Programmes of Early Childhood Care and Education.* Background paper for *EFA Global Monitoring Report 2005.*

Nassor, S.; Mohammed, A. K. 1998. *The Quality of Education: Some Policy Suggestions Based on a Survey of Schools, Zanzibar.* SACMEQ Policy Research Report No. 4. Ministry of Basic Education, Zanzibar, United Republic of Tanzania, and UNESCO International Institute for Educational Planning.

National Institute of Education of Sri Lanka. 2002. *Performance of Grade 3 students I literacy and numeracy (after 3 years of implementation of Education Reforms).* Maharagama, National Institute of Education.

National Research Council. 2001. *Eager to Learn: Educating Our Preschoolers.* Washington, DC, National Academy Press.

National Statistical Centre. 1997. *Lao Census 1995: Country Report.* Vientiane, National Planning Committee.

Neal, D. A.; Johnson, W. R. 1996. The role of pre-market factors in black-white differences. *Journal of Political Economy,* Vol. 104, No. 5, October: 869-95.

Netherlands Ministry of Foreign Affairs. 2003a. *Joint Evaluation of External Support to Basic Education in Developing Countries. Local Solutions to Global Challenges: towards effective partnership in basic education. Final Report.* The Hague, Netherlands Ministry of Foreign Affairs.

— 2003b. *Joint Evaluation of External Support to Basic Education in Developing Countries. Local Solutions to Global Challenges: towards effective partnership in basic education. Document Review.* The Hague, Netherlands Ministry of Foreign Affairs.

— 2003c. *Joint Evaluation of External Support to Basic Education in Developing Countries. Local Solutions to Global Challenges: towards effective partnership in basic education. Country Study Report- Zambia.* The Hague, Netherlands Ministry of Foreign Affairs.

— 2003d. *Joint Evaluation of External Support to Basic Education in Developing Countries. Local Solutions to Global Challenges: towards effective partnership in basic education. Country Study Report - Uganda.* The Hague, Netherlands Ministry of Foreign Affairs.

— 2003e. *Joint Evaluation of External Support to Basic Education in Developing Countries. Local Solutions to Global Challenges: towards effective partnership in basic education. Country Study Report - Burkina Faso.* The Hague, Netherlands Ministry of Foreign Affairs.

— 2003f. *Joint Evaluation of External Support to Basic Education in Developing Countries. Local Solutions to Global Challenges: towards effective partnership in basic education. Country Study Report - Bolivia.* The Hague, Netherlands Ministry of Foreign Affairs.

Neufeld, E.; Farrar, E.; Miles, M. B. 1983. *A Review of Effective Schools Research: The Message for Secondary Schools.* Report to the National Commission on Excellence in Education.

Newman, J.; Rawlings, L.; Gertler, P. 1994. Using Randomized Control Designs in Evaluating Social Sector Programs in Developing Countries. *World Bank Research Observer*, Vol. 9, No. 2, July: 181–201.

Niane, B. 2004. *Innovation and reform to improve basic education quality in Senegal to achieve EFA goals.* Background paper for *EFA Global Monitoring Report 2005*.

Nicaragua Ministry of Education. 2003. *Evaluación del Rendimiento Académico de los Estudiantes de Tercero y Sexto Grado de Primaria: Informe de Resultados 2002.* Ministerio de Educación, Cultura y Deportes.

Nirantar. 1997. Innovating for change: Women's Education for Empowerment. An Analysis of the Mahila Samakhya Program in Banda District (India). In: W. Mauch and U. Papen (eds.), *Making a difference: Innovations in Adult Education*: 33–47. UNESCO Institute for Education, Hamburg, and the German Foundation for International Development, Frankfurt am Main, Peter Lang, GmbH.

Nkamba, M.; Kanyika, J. 1998. *The Quality of Education: Some Policy Suggestions Based on a Survey of Schools, Zambia.* SACMEQ Policy Research Report No. 5. Ministry of Education, Zambia, and UNESCO International Institute for Educational Planning.

Nordström, K. 2004. *Quality Education for Persons with Disabilities.* Background paper for *EFA Global Monitoring Report 2005*.

Nyerere, J. 1968. *Freedom and Socialism. A Selection from Writings & Speeches, 1965-1967.* Dar es Salaam, Oxford University Press.

Nzomo, J.; Kariuki, M.; Guantai, L. 2001. *The Quality of Education: Some Policy Suggestions Based on a Survey of Schools, Kenya.* SACMEQ Policy Research: Report No. 6. Ministry of Education, Science and Technology, Kenya, and UNESCO International Institute for Educational Planning.

Odden, A.; Busch, C. 1998. *Financing schools for high performance: strategies for improving the use of educational resources.* San Francisco, Jossey-Bass Publishers.

OECD. 1996. *Instructional Time in the Classroom.* Center for Education Research and Innovation, Education at a Glance, OECD Indication. Paris, Organisation for Economic Co-operation and Development.

— 1998. *Education at a glance. OECD Indicators 1998.* Centre for Educational Research and Innovation, Paris, OECD.

— 2001. *Education Policy Analysis.* Paris, Organisation for Economic Co-operation and Development.

— 2003a. Philanthropic Foundations and Development Co-operation. Off-print of the *DAC Journal*, Vol. 4, No. 3. (www.oecd.org/dataoecd/23/4/22272860.pdf)

— 2003b. *Attracting, developing and retaining effective teachers. Country background report for The Netherlands*, paragraphs 85–9. Paris, OECD.

— 2003c. *Education at a Glance: OECD Indicators – 2003*. Paris, OECD.

— 2004a. *Innovation in the Knowledge Economy: Implications for Education and Learning*. Paris, OECD.

— 2004b. *Knowledge Management; New Challenges for Educational Research. A Review of National Educational Research and Development Systems in the Untied Kingdom and New Zealand*. Paris, OECD.

— 2004c. *Raising the quality of educational performance at school*. Policy Brief. Paris, OECD.

— 2004d. *Reviews of National Policies for Education: Chile*. Paris, OECD.

— 2004e. *The Quality of the Teaching Workforce*. Policy Brief. Paris, OECD.

OECD-DAC. 2000. *DAC Statistical Reporting Directives*. Paris, OECD-DAC. (www.oecd.org/dataoecd/44/45/1894833.pdf)

— 2002. *Development Cooperation in Difficult Partnerships*. Note by the Secretariat for the Development Assistance Committee. 16 May. DCD/DAC (2002) 11/REV1. Paris, OECD-DAC.

— 2003. *Progress in Alignment and Harmonisation at a Country Level*. Note by the SPA – Budget Support Working Group. Paris. OECD-DAC. (DAC Working Party on Aid Effectiveness and Donor Practices, Room Document No. 4).

— 2004a. International Development Statistics. Paris, OECD-DAC. (www.oecd.org/dataoecd/50/17/5037721.htm)

— 2004b. *ODA Statistics for 2003 and ODA Outlook*. DCD/DAC(2004/22). Paris, OECD.

— 2004c. *OECD-DAC Survey on Progress in Harmonisation and Alignment: Explanatory Note on the Questionnaire*. Paris, OECD-DAC. (www.oecd.org/dataoecd/29/41/31661156.doc)

OECD/UNESCO Institute for Statistics. 2003. *Literacy Skills for the World of Tomorrow: Further Results From PISA 2000*. Paris/Montreal, OECD/UNESCO-UIS.

Ohanian, S. 1999. *One size fits few: The folly of educational standards*. Portsmouth, N. H. Heinemann.

Okech, A.; Carr-Hill, R.; Katahoire, A. R.; Kakooza, T.; Ndidde, A. N.; Oxenham, J. 2001. *Adult Literacy Programs in Uganda*. Washington, DC, World Bank. (Africa Region Human Development Series.)

Okyere, B.; Mensah, A.; Kugbey, H.; Harris, A. 1997. *What happens to the Textbooks?* Silver Spring, MD, American Institutes for Research, for USAID Improving Educational Quality Project. (www.air.org/pubs/international/textbooks.pdf)

Oliver, R. 1999. *Fertility and women's Schooling in Ghana*. In: P. Glewwe (ed), *The Economics of School Quality Investments in Developing Countries*: 327–44. St. Martin's, Macmillan.

Olweus, D. 2001. Bullying at school: tackling the problem. *OECD Observer*, 30 March 2001.

O'Neill, J. 1990. The role of human capital in earnings differences between black and white men. *Journal of Economic Perspectives*, Vol. 4, No. 4, Fall: 25–46.

Orazem, P. F.; Gunnarsson, V. 2003. *Child labour, school attendance and academic performance: a review*. Working Paper. International Programme on the Elimination of Child Labour. Geneva, International Labour Office.

Orivel, F. 2004. *Evaluation of EC support to the Education sector in ACP countries (May 2002)*. Paper presented at the International Colloquium From Evaluation to Policy and Practice: Aid and Education. The Hague, 22–3 March.

Oxenham, J. 2004. *The Quality of Programs and Policies regarding Literacy and Skills Development*. Background paper for *EFA Global Monitoring Report 2005*.

— Forthcoming. *Review of World Bank and World Experiences in Supporting Non-Formal Education with Literacy for Adults (NFEA)*. Washington, DC, World Bank, Human Development Network, Education Department.

Oxenham, J.; Diallo, A. H.; Katahoire, A. R.; Petkova-Mwangi, A.; Sall, O. 2002. *Skills and Literacy Training for Better Livelihoods: A Review of Approaches and Experiences.* Washington, DC, World Bank. (Africa Region Human Development Series.)

Pacific Islands Forum Secretariat. 2001. *Forum Basic Education Action Plan – 2001.* Auckland, New Zealand, 15 May.

Panchaud, C.; Pii, J.; Poncet, M.; UNESCO-Bangkok. 2004. *Quality analysis of a set of curricula and related material on education for HIV and AIDS prevention in school settings.* Background paper for *EFA Global Monitoring Report 2005*.

Parker, B. 2003. Roles and Responsibilities, Institutional Landscapes and Curriculum Mindscapes: a partial view of teacher education policy in South Africa, 1990-2000. In: K. M. Lewin, M. Samuel, Y. Sayed (eds.), *Changing Patterns of Teacher Education in South Africa: Policy, Practice and Prospects*: 16–44. Sandown, Heinemann Press.

Parsons, T. 1959. The school class as a social system: some of its functions in American society. *Harvard Educational Review*, Vol. 29, Fall: 297–318.

Patrinos, H; Velez, E. 1996. *Costs and Benefits of Bilingual Education in Guatemala: A Partial Analysi.* Washington, DC, World Bank. (Human Capital Working Paper No. 74.)

Peiris, K. 2004. *And that made All the Difference: Developments in improving the quality of education in Sri Lanka.* Background paper for *EFA Global Monitoring Report 2005*.

Peisner-Feinberg, E. S. 2004. Child care and its impact on children 2-5 years of age. In: R. E. Tremblay, R. G. Barr and R. Peters (eds.), *Encyclopedia on Early Childhood Development.* Montreal, Quebec, Centre of Excellence for Early Childhood Development. (Available at www.excellence-earlychildhood.ca)

Pettifor, A. E.; Rees, H. V.; Steffenson, A.; Hlongwa-Madikizela, L.; MacPhail, C.; Vermaak K.; Kleinschmidt, I. 2004. *HIV and sexual behaviour among young South Africans: A national survey of 15-24-year-olds.* Johannesburg, Reproductive Health Research Unit, University of the Witwatersrand.

Piaget, J. 1971. *Structuralism.* Translated and edited by C. Maschler. London, Routledge and Kegan Paul.

— 1972. *The principles of genetic epistemology.* Translated by W. Mays. London, Routledge and Kegan Paul.

Piaget, J.; Inhelder, B. 1969. *The Psychology of the Child.* Translated by H. Weaver. New York, Basic Books.

Pigozzi, M. J. 2004. *Quality Education and HIV/AIDS.* Draft, June. Paris, UNESCO.

Pollitt, E. 1990. *Malnutrition and Infection in the Classroom.* Paris, UNESCO.

Postlethwaite T. N. 2004. *What do International Assessment Studies tell us about the Quality of School Systems?* Background paper for *EFA Global Monitoring Report 2005*.

Presidential Commission on Education & Human Resource Policy. 2002. *The Policy Report on National Human Resources Development in the 21st[t] Century.* Seoul, Presidential Commission on Education & Human Resource Policy.

Pritchett, L. 2003. Basic Education Services. In: World Bank, *World Development Report 2004: Making Services Work for Poor People*, Chapter 7. Washington, DC, World Bank.

— 2004. *Towards a New Consensus for Addressing the Global Challenge of the Lack of Education.* Copenhagen, Copenhagen Consensus Challenge Paper.

PROBE Team. 1999. *Public Report on Basic Education in India.* Delhi, Oxford University Press.

Project Ploughshares. 2003. Countries hosting armed conflicts in 2002. *Armed Conflicts Report 2003.* (www.ploughshares.ca/content/ACR/acr.html)

Purkey, S. C.; Smith, M. S. 1983. Effective schools: a review. *The Elementary School Journal*, Vol. 83, No. 4: 427–52.

Putnam, R. D.; Feldstein, L. M. 2003. *Better Together, Restoring the American Community.* New York, Simon & Schuster.

Rabinow, P. (ed.). 1984. *The Foucault Reader.* London, Penguin.

Radebe, T. 1998. Classroom libraries: South Africa. In: D. Rosenberg (ed.), *Getting Books to School Pupils in Africa*: 37-79. London, Department for International Development.

Raine, A.; Mellingen, K.; Liu, J.; Venables, P. 2003. Effects on Environmental Enrichment at Ages 3-5 Years on Schizotypal Personality and Antisocial Behavior at Ages 17 and 23 Years. *The American Journal of Psychiatry*, Vol. 160: 1627-635.

Ralph, J. H.; Fennessey, J. 1983. Science or reform: some questions about the effective schools model. *Phi Delta Kappan*, Vol. 64, No. 10:. 689-95.

Ramey, C. T.; Ramey, S. L. 1998. Early Intervention and Early Experience. *American Journal of Psycology*, Vol. 53: 109-20.

Ratteree, B. 2004. *Teachers, Their Unions and the Education for All Campaign*. Background paper for *EFA Global Monitoring Report 2005* through the International Labour Office, Geneva.

Ravela, P. 2002. *¿Cómo Presentan sus Resultados los Sistemas Nacionales de Evaluación Educativa en América Latina?* El Programa de Promoción de la Reforma Educativa en América Latina y el Caribe. (www.preal.cl)

Reezigt, G. J. 1993. *Effecten van differentiatie op de basisschool* [Effects of Grouping in Primary Education]. Groningen, Research instituut voor het onderwijs in het noorden, University of Groningen.

Republic of Korea. 2003. *Education in Korea 2003-2004*. Seoul, Ministry of Education and Human Resources.

Resnick, L. B. 1987. *Education and Learning to Think*. Washington, DC, National Academic Press.

Reynolds, D.; Hopkins, D.; Stoll, L. 1993. Linking school effectiveness knowledge and school improvement practice: towards a synergy. *School Effectiveness and School Improvement*, Vol. 4, No. 1.: 37-58.

Richler, D. 2004. *Quality Education for Persons with Disabilities*. Background paper for *EFA Global Monitoring Report 2005*.

Riddell, A. 2002. *Sector-wide Approaches in Education: issues for donor agencies arising from case studies of Zambia and Mozambique*. Paris, UNESCO International Institute for Educational Planning.

— 2004. *UNESCO and Sector Wide Approaches in Education*. (Draft, mimeograph)

Ritzen, J. 1999. *Looking for Eagles; A Short Guide to Bird Watching in an Educational Context*. Washington, World Bank.

Rivkin, S. G. 1995. Black/white differences in schooling and employment. *Journal of Human Resources*, Vol. 30, No. 4, Fall: 826-52.

Rivkin, S. G.; Hanushek, E. A.; Kain, J. F. 2002. *Teachers, Schools and Academic Achievement*. University of Texas-Dallas, Texas Schools Project

Rosenberg, D. (ed.) 1998. *Getting Books to School Pupils in Africa*. London, Department for International Development.

Rosenshine, B. V. 1983. Teaching functions in instructional programs. *Elementary School Journal*, Vol. 3: 335-51.

Rosenshine, B. V.; Furst, N. 1973. The use of direct observation to study teaching. In: R. M. Travers (ed.), *Handbook of Research on Teaching*. 2nd edition. Chicago, Rand McNally.

Rosenshine, B. V.; Stevens, R. 1986. Teaching functions. In: M. C. Wittrock (ed.), *Handbook of Research on Teaching*: 376-391. New York, Macmillan.

Rosenzweig, M. 1995. Why are there returns to schooling? *American Economic Review*, Vol. 76, No. 3:. 470-82.

Rosso, J. M. D.; Marek, T. 1996. *Class Action: improving school performance in the developing world through better health and nutrition*. Washington, DC, World Bank.

Rousseau, J.-J. 1911. *Emile*. Translated by B. Foxley. London, Dent.

Russell, B. 1961. *History of Western Philosophy*. London, Allen and Unwin.

Rutter, M. 1983. School effects on pupil progress: research findings and policy implications. *Child Development*, Vol. 54, No. 1: 1-29.

Rutter, M.; Giller, H.; Hagell, A. 1998. *Antisocial Behaviour by Young People*. Cambridge, Cambridge University Press.

Sack, R.; Cross, M.; Moulton, J. 2003. Evaluation of Finnish education sector development cooperation. Helsinki, Ministry of Foreign Affairs of Finland, Department for Development Policy. (http://global.finland.fi/evaluations/education.pdf)

Sallis, E. J. 1996. *Total quality management in education*. 2nd ed. London, Kogan Page.

Salzano, C. 2002. *Making Book Coordination Work*. Paris, Association for the Development of Education in Africa Working Group on Books and Learning Materials, and UNESCO. (Perspectives on African Book Development, 13.)

Sammons, P.; Hillman, J.; Mortimore, P. 1995. *Key characteristics of effective schools: A review of school effectiveness research*. London, Office for Standards in Education.

Samoff, J. 1993. The Reconstruction of Schooling in Africa. *Comparative Education Review*, Vol. 37, No. 2: 181-222.

— 2003. Sector-based Development Co-operation: evolving strategies, persisting problems – a place for dialogue. In: J. Olsson and L. Wohlgemuth (eds.), *Dialogue in Pursuit of Development*: 286-301. Stockholm, Almqvist & Wiksell International. (Expert Group on Development Issues, Study 2003:2.)

Sampa, F. K. 2003. *Country Case Study. Primary Reading Programme (PRP): Improving Access and Quality Education in Basic Schools*. A study prepared for the Association for the Development of Education in Africa. Paris.

Save the Children. 2004. School Health and Nutrition Newsletter, April 2004. (www.savethechildren.org/publications/SHN_newsletter_April_2004.pdf)

Sayed, Y. 2001. *Continuing Professional Development and Education Policy: Characteristics, Conditions and Change*. Keynote paper for the Ministry of Education, South Africa for the National Teacher Education Policy Conference, 20-21 October.

— 2002. Changing forms of teacher education in South Africa: a case study of policy change. *International Journal of Educational Development*, Vol. 22, Nos.3/4: 381-95.

Sayed, Y.; Heystek, J.; Smit, B. 2002. *Further Diploma in Education (Educational Management) by Distance Education at the University of Pretoria, South Africa*. Brighton, Centre for International Education, University of Sussex. (MUSTER Discussion Paper No. 33.)

Sayed, Y; Akyeampong, K.; Ampiah, J. G. 2000. Partnership and Participation in Whole School Development in Ghana. *Education through Partnership*, Vol. 4, No. 2: 40-5.

Scheerens, J. 1992. *Effective Schooling, Research, Theory and Practice*. London, Cassell.

— 2004. *Review of School and Instructional Effectiveness Research*. Background paper for *EFA Global Monitoring Report 2005*.

Schleicher, A.; Siniscalco, M.; Postlethwaite, T. N. 1995. *The Conditions of Primary Schools: A Pilot Study in the Least Developed Countries*. Report to UNESCO and UNICEF.

Schliesinger, J. 2000. *Ethnic Groups of Thailand: Non-Tai-Speaking Peoples*. Bangkok, White Lotus.

— 2003. *Ethnic Groups of Laos. Vols. 1-4*. Bangkok, White Lotus.

Schluter, A; Then, V; Walkenhorse, P. 2001. *Foundations in Europe: Society, Management and Law*. London Directory of Social Change/CAF.

Schultz, T. P. 1996. Accounting for Public Expenditures on Education: An International Panel Study. In: T. P. Schultz (ed.), *Research in Population Economics*, 8, Greenwich, Conn., JAI Press: 8.

Silanda, A. 2000. Why are there so few books in the schools? *ADEA Newsletter*, Vol. 12, No. 3, July-September.

Sinclair, M. 2001. Education in Emergencies. In: *Learning for a Future: Refugee Education in Developing Countries*, Geneva, UNHCR.

— 2002. *Planning Education in and after Emergencies*. Paris, UNESCO International Institute for Educational Planning. (Fundamentals of Educational Planning No. 73.)

Singh, N. K. 2003. *Aid Management: India Country Report*. Paper to the 5th UN Global Forum on Innovation and Quality in the Government of the 21st Century, Mexico City, 3-7 November.

Siniscalco, M. T. 2004. *Teachers' Salaries*. Background paper for *EFA Global Monitoring Report 2005*.

Skinner, B. F. 1968. *The Technology of Teaching*. Englewood Cliffs, N.J./London, Prentice-Hall.

Slavin, R. E. 1987. *Cooperative learning: student teams*, 2nd edition. Washington, DC, National Education Association Professional Library.

— 1996. *Success for all*. Lisse, the Netherlands, Swets & Zeitlinger.

— 1998. Sands, Bricks, and Seeds: School Change Strategies and Readiness for Reform. In: A. Hargreaves, A. Liebermann, M. Fullan and D. Hopkins (eds.), *International Handbook of Educational Change*, Dordrecht/Boston/London, Kluwer.

Smalley, W. A. 1994. *Linguistic Diversity and National Unity: Language Ecology in Thailand*. Chicago, University of Chicago Press.

Smith, G.; Kippax, S., Aggleton, P. 2000. *HIV and Sexual Health Education in primary and secondary schools: findings from selected Asia-Pacific Countries*. Sydney, National Centre in HIV Social Research.

Somerset, A., 1996. Examinations and educational quality. In: A. Little and A. Wolf (eds.), *Assessment in Transition: learning, monitoring and selection in international perspective*: 263-84. Oxford/Tarrytown/Tokyo, Elsevier Science Ltd.

South Africa Department of Education. 2004. *Draft Policy Framework. Education Management and Leadership Development*. Directorate: Education Management and Governance Development. June.

Sow, M. A.; Brunswic, E.; Valérien, J. 2001. Case Study E: Guinea. In: T. Read, C. Denning and V. Bontoux (eds.), *Upgrading book distribution in Africa*: 127-36. ADEA Working Group on Books and Learning Materials, c/o the Department for International Development, London.

Span Consultants. 2003. *Common Indicators in Education for Development Co-operation*. Final Report Prepared for the European Commission. Utrecht, Span Consultants.

Spiro, R. J.; Feltowich, P. J.; Jacobson, M. J.; Caulson, R. L. 1992. Cognitive flexibility, constructivism and hypertext: random access instruction for advanced knowledge acquisition in ill-structured domains. In: T. M. Duffy and D. H. Jonassen (eds.), *Constructivism and the Technology of Instruction: A Conversation*. Hillsdale, N. J., Lawrence Erlbaum Associates.

Spring , J. 1972. *Education and the Rise of the Corporate State*. Boston, Beacon Press.

Stallings, J. 1985. Effective elementary classroom practices. In: M. J. Kyle (ed.), *Reaching for excellence. An effective schools sourcebook*. Washington, DC, United States Government Printing Office.

Stallings, J.; Mohlman, G. 1981. *School policy, leadership style, teacher change and student behavior in eight schools*. Final Report to the National Institute of Education, Washington, DC.

Steele, M. 2003. Teacher Education Policy: A Provincial Portrait from KZN. Dead Men Walking. In: K. M. Lewin, M. Samuel, Y. Sayed. (eds.), *Changing Patterns of Teacher Education in South Africa: Policy, Practice and Prospects*: 107-17. Sandown, Heinemann Press.

Storeng, M. 2001. *Giving learners a chance: learner-centredness in the reform of Namibian teaching*. Unpublished Ph.D. Thesis. Stockholm, Institute of International Education.

Sweeney, J. 1982. Research synthesis on effective school leadership. *Educational Leadership*, Vol. 39: 346-52.

Tabulawa, R. 1997. *Teachers' perspectives on classroom practice in Botswana: implications for pedagogical change*. Paper presented at the 3rd Biennial National Conference of Teachers' Education. Gaborone, 25-29 August.

Takala, T. 2004. *Contribution of the Sector-wide Approach to Improvement of Quality of Basic Education in Mozambique*. Background paper for *EFA Global Monitoring Report 2005*.

Tan, J.-P. ; Lane, J. ; Lassibille, G. 1999. Outcomes in Philippine Elementary Schools: An Evaluation of Four Experiments. *World Bank Economic Review*, Vol. 13, No. 3, August: 493–508.

Taylor, P. 2004. *How can participatory processes of curriculum development impact on the quality of teaching and learning in developing countries?* Background paper for *EFA Global Monitoring Report 2005* through the Institute of Development Studies, Brighton.

Taylor, P.; Fransman, J. 2004. *Learning and Teaching Participation: Exploring the Role of Higher Learning Institutions as Agents of Development and Social Change*. Brighton, Institute of Development Studies. (Working Paper 219.)

Teddlie, C.; Reynolds, D. 2000. *The International Handbook of School Effectiveness Research*. London/New York, Falmer Press.

Theunynck, S. 2003. *School Construction in Developing Countries: What do we know?* Washington, DC, World Bank.

Thomas, D. 1999. *Fertility, Education and Resources in South Africa*. In: C. Bledsoe, et al., *Critical Perspectives on Schooling and Fertility in the Developing World*. Washington, DC, National Academy Press.

Tobias, S. 1991. An eclectic examination of some issues in the constructivist-ISP controversy. *Educational Technology*, Vol. 31, No. 9: 41-3.

Todd, P. E.; Wolpin, K. I. 2003. On the Specification and Estimation of the Production Function for Cognitive Achievement. *Economic Journal*, Vol. 113, No. 485, February: 3-33.

Torres, R. M. 2003. *Lifelong Learning: A New Momentum and a New Opportunity for Adult Basic Learning and Education (ABLE) in the South*. Stockholm, Swedish International Development Agency.

Touré, Saliou. 1984. Preface. In: Salimata (ed.), *Mathématiques dans l'environnement socio-culturel Africain*. Doumbia, Abidjan, Institut de Recherches Mathématiques d'Abidjan.

Tsuruta, Y. 2003. *On-going Changes to Higher Education in Japan and Some Key Issues.* Paper presented at the seminar Responding to Change and Reforms at the Higher Education Institution. Daiwa Anglo-Japanese Foundation. 26 November.

Tutu, D. 2000. *No Future without Forgiveness*. Cape Town, Image Books.

Tyler, R. W. 1949. *Basic Principles of Curriculum and Instruction*. Chicago, London, University of Chicago Press.

Uganda Bureau of Statistics and ORC Macro. 2002. *DHS EdData Survey 2001: Education Data for Decision-Making*. Calverton, MD, ORC Macro.

Uganda Ministry of Education and Sports. 2003*a*. *Education Sector Six Monthly Report (ESSMR), May – November 2003*. (www.education.go.ug/ESSMR%2016%20VERSION.htm)

Uganda Ministry of Education and Sports. 2003*b*. Final Aide-Mémoire for the 10th Education Sector Review, November.

UIE. 2004. *Quality Adult Learning. Background paper for EFA Global Monitoring Report 2005* through the UNESCO Institute for Education, Hamburg.

UNAIDS/UNICEF. 2003. *Children Orphaned by AIDS in sub-Sahara Africa*. (UNAIDS/UNICEF Fact Sheet).

UNDP. 2003. *Development Effectiveness Report 2003: Partnership for Results*. New York, UNDP.

UNESCO. 1997. *International Standard Classification of Education*. Paris, UNESCO.

— 2000*a*. *The Dakar Framework for Action: Education for All – Meeting our Collective Commitments*. World Education Forum, Dakar, Senegal. 26-28 April. Paris, UNESCO.

— 2000*b*. *Approved Programme and Budget for 2000-2001, 30C/5*. Paris, UNESCO.

— 2002a. *EFA Global Monitoring Report 2002: Education for All – Is the World on Track?* Paris, UNESCO. (www.unesco.org/education/efa/monitoring/monitoring_2002.shtml)

— 2002b. *Approved Programme and Budget for 2002-2003, 31C/5.* Paris, UNESCO.

— 2003a. *EFA Global Monitoring Report 2003/4: Gender and Education for All –The Leap to Equality.* Paris, UNESCO. (http://portal.unesco.org/education/en/ev.php-URL_ID=23023&URL_DO=DO_TOPIC&URL_SECTION=201.html)

— 2003b. *Education in a Multilingual World.* UNESCO Education Position Paper. Paris, UNESCO.

— 2003c. *Educational Reform in Egypt 1996-2003: Achievements and Challenges in the New Century.* Prepared by S. Spaulding, M. Ahmed and G. Gholam for the Ministry of Education, Egypt, September.

— 2004a. *Report 2003: Third High-Level Group Meeting on Education for All.* Paris, UNESCO. (www.unesco.org/education/efa/global_co/policy_group/hlg_2003_report.pdf)

— 2004b. *Decisions Adopted by the Executive Board at its 169th Session.* Paris, 14-28 April. (http://unesdoc.unesco.org/images/0013/001346/134685e.pdf)

— 2004c. *Report of the Fourth Meeting of the Working Group on Education for All.* Paris, UNESCO. (http://unesdoc.unesco.org/images/0013/001318/131853e.pdf)

— 2004d. *EFA Flagship Initiatives: Multi-partner collaborative mechanisms in support of EFA goals.* Paris, UNESCO.

— 2004e. *Report by the Director-General on the Strategic Review of UNESCO's Post-Dakar Role in Education for All (EFA).* 170 EX/8. Paris, 20 August. Paper for the 170th Executive Board Meeting. (http://unesdoc.unesco.org/images/0013/001360/136095e.pdf)

UNESCO-IIEP. 2004. *Promoting Skills Development.* Paris, UNESCO International Institute for Educational Planning.

UNESCO Institute for Statistics. 2001. *Report on the meeting and proposals for the future development of EFA Indicators.* Montreal/Paris, UNESCO Institute for Statistics.

— 2004a. *Global Education Digest 2004.* Montreal/Paris, UNESCO Institute for Statistics.

— 2004b. *The primary completion rate: feasibility as an international indicator.* Montreal/Paris, UNESCO Institute for Statistics. (Processed)

UNESCO Institute for Statistics/OECD. 2003. *Financing Education: Investments and Returns.* Montreal/Paris, UNESCO Institute for Statistics/OECD.

UNESCO/UNDP. 1976. *Experimental World Literacy Programme: Critical Evaluation.* Paris, UNESCO.

UNESCO-Beirut. 2004a. *Comparative Analysis of Education for All National Plans in the Arab States.* Arab Regional Conference on Education for All, EFA National Plans: What Actions Next? Beirut, 20-23 January.

— 2004b. *Future Orientations Adopted by the Drafting Committee.* Arab Regional Conference on Education for All, EFA National Plans: What Actions Next? Beirut, 20-23 January.

UNESCO-BREDA. 2003. *Synthesis of the Progress Made in Africa in the Planning and Achievement of Education for All.* Reference document for the Eighth Conference of Ministers of Education of African Member States (MINEDAF VIII). Dar-es-Salaam, 2-6 December 2002.

UNESCO-Santiago. 2003. *Follow-up Model of the Regional Project for Latin America and the Caribbean (PRELAC) – Support, Monitoring and Assessment – Havana Declaration.* Santiago, OREALC/UNESCO.

— 2004. *Education for All in Latin America: A Goal within our Reach.* Regional EFA Monitoring Report 2003. Santiago, OREALC/UNESCO.

UNICEF. 1999a. Child Domestic Work. *Innocenti Digest*, 5. Florence, UNICEF.

— 1999b. *Education For All?* Florence, Innocenti Research Centre.

— 1999c. *The State of the World's Children 1999.* UNICEF.

— 2000. *Defining Quality in Education.* New York, UNICEF.

United Nations. 2000. United Nations Millennium Declaration. Resolution adopted by the General Assembly. (United Nations A/RES/55/2) (www.un.org/millennium/declaration/ares552e.htm)

— 2001a. Appendix, para. 9. (CRC/GC/2001/1) Committee on the Rights of the Childs, General Comment 1: The Aims of Education.

— 2001b. Report of the High-Level Panel on Financing for Development. (www.un.org/reports/financing/full_report.pdf)

— 2003a. Post-Monterrey development aid report card. (Financing for Development Briefing Note 2.) (www.un.org/esa/ffd/1003brief-Oda.pdf)

— 2003b. *Implementation of and Follow-up to Commitments and Agreements Made at the International Conference on Financing for Development.* Report of the Secretary-General to the Fifty-Eight Session of the General Assembly, A/58/216. United Nations.

United Republic of Tanzania. 2001. *Education Sector Development Programme. Primary Education Development Plan (2002-2006).* Dar-Es-Salaam, Government of the United Republic of Tanzania, Basic Education Development Committee.

Usher, R.; Edwards, R. 1994. *Postmodernism and Education.* New York, Routledge.

Välijärvi, J.; Linnakylä, P.; Kupari, P.; Reinikainen, P.; Arffman, I. 2002. *The Finnish Success in PISA – and Some Reasons Behind It.* Jyvaskyla, Institute for Educational Research, University of Jyvaskyla.

Van Graan, M.; Pokuti, H.; Leczel, D.; Liman, M.; Swarts, P. 2003. *Practising Critical Reflection in Teacher Education: Case Study of three Namibian Teacher Development Programmes.* Background paper for the ADEA Biennial Meeting, Grand Baie, Mauritius, 3-6 December.

Van Laarhoven, P.; de Vries, A. M. 1987. Effecten van de interklassikale groeperingsvorm in het voortgezet onderwijs: resultaten van een literatuurstudie [Effects of heterogeneous grouping in secondary schools]. In: J. Scheerens and W. G. R. Stoel (eds.), *Effectiviteit van onderwijsorganisaties* [Effectiveness of educational organizations]. Lisse, the Netherlands, Swets & Zeitlinger.

Vawda, A.; Patrinos, H. 1998. Cost of Producing Educational Materials in Local Languages. In: W. Kuper (ed.), *Mother-Tongue Languages in Africa: A Reader.* 2nd ed. Eschborn, GTZ.

Vedder, P. H. 1985. *Cooperative learning. A study on processes and effects of cooperation between primary school children.* The Hague, SVO.

Vegas, E.; De Laat, J. 2003. *Do differences in teacher contracts affect student performance? Evidence from Togo.* Background paper for *EFA Global Monitoring Report 2005.*

Vermeersch, C. 2002. *School Meals, Educational Achievement and School Competition: Evidence from a Randomized Experiment.* Working Paper. Cambridge, MA, Harvard University, November.

Vijverberg, Wim P. M. 1999. The impact of schooling and cognitive skills on income from non-farm self-employment. In: P. Gelwwe (ed.), *The economics of school quality investments in developing countries: An empirical study of Ghana.* New York: St. Martin's Press and the University of Oxford.

Vince-Whitman, C.; Aldinger, C.; Levinger, B.; Birdthistle, I. 2001. *School Health and Nutrition.* Education for All 2000 Assessment Thematic Study. Paris, UNESCO.

Voigts, F. 1998. *The Quality of Education: Some Policy Suggestions Based on a Survey of Schools, Namibia.* SACMEQ Policy Research Report No. 2. Ministry of Basic Education and Culture, Namibia, and UNESCO International Institute for Educational Planning.

Volan, S. 2003. *Educational Reform and Change in the South: a matter of restructuring as well as reculturing – experiences from Zambia.* Unpublished D.Phil Thesis. University of Southampton.

VSO. 2002. *What makes teachers tick? A policy research report on teachers' motivation in developing countries.* London, Voluntary Service Overseas.

Vygotsky, L. S. 1962. *Thought and Language.* Cambridge, MA, MIT Press.

— 1978. *Mind in Society: The Development of Higher Psychological Process.* Cambridge, MA, Harvard University Press.

Wade, R. 1990. *Governing the Market: Economic Theory and the Role of Government in East Asian Industrialization.* Princeton, NJ, Princeton University Press.

Walberg, H. 1991. Improving school science in advanced and developing countries. *Review of Educational Research,* Vol. 61, No. 1: 25-69.

Walter, S. L. Forthcoming. *Literacy, Education and Language.* (Draft) Dallas, SIL International.

Wang, M. C.; Haertel, G. D.; Walberg, H. J. 1993. Toward a knowledge base for school learning. *Review of Educational Research,* Vol. 63, No. 3: 249-94.

— 1994. Qu'est-ce qui aide l'élève à apprendre? *Vie pédagogique,* No. 90, septembre-octobre: 45-9.

Weeda, W. C. 1986. Effectiviteitsonderzoek van scholen. In: J. C. van der Wolf and J. J. Hox (eds.), *Kwaliteit van het onderwijs in het geding* [About education quality]. Publicaties van het Amsterdams Pedogogische Centrum, No. 2, Lisse, the Netherlands, Swets & Zeitlinger.

Weikart, D. P.; Montie, J.; Xiang, Z. 2004. *Preschool Experience and Age 7 Child Outcomes: Findings from 10 Countries.* Ypsilanti, MI, High/Scope. (www.highscope.org/Research/iea.htm)

Weikart, D.P.; Olmsted, P.; Montie, J. (eds.). 2003. *IEA Preprimary Project, Phase 2: A World of Experience. Observations in 15 Countries.* Ypsilanti, MI, High/Scope.

Werner, E. E.; Smith, R. 1982. *Vulnerable but Invincible: A Longitudinal Study of Resilient Children and Youth.* New York, McGraw-Hill.

Weva, K. 2003a. *Adaptation of School Curriculum to Local Context.* Background paper for the ADEA Biennial Meeting, Grand Baie, Mauritius, 3-6 December.

— 2003b. *Le rôle et la formation des directeurs d'écoles en Afrique.* Background paper commissioned by the Association for the Development of Education in Africa in the framework of the Challenge of Learning study. Paris, UNESCO International Institute for Educational Planning.

— White, H. 2004. *Using household survey data to measure educational performance: The case of Ghana.* OED Impact Evaluation. Washington, DC, World Bank. (Mimeograph)

WHO. 1997. *Promoting Health through Schools: a summary and recommendations of WHO's Expert Committee on Comprehensive School Health Education and Promotion.* Geneva, World Health Organization. (WHO Technical Report Series, 870.)

— 1998. *Violence Prevention: An Important Element of a Health-Promoting School.* Geneva, World Health Organization. (WHO Information Series on School Health, Document Three.)

Williams, E. 1998. *Investigating Bilingual Literacy : Evidence from Malawi and Zambia.* London, Department for International Development. (DFID Educational Paper 24).

Williams, R. C.; Harold, B.; Robertson, J.; Southworth, G. 1997. Sweeping decentralization of educational decision-making authority: lessons from England and New Zealand. *Phi Delta Kappan,* Vol. 78, No. 8: 626-31.

Willms, J. D. 2003. *Ten Hypotheses about Socioeconomic Gradients and Community Differences in Children's Developmental Outcomes.* Ottawa, Human Resources Development Canada, Applied Research Branch.

Willms, J. D.; Somers, M. A. 2001. *Schooling outcomes in Latin America.* Report prepared for UNESCO.

Wilson, D. 2004. *A Human Rights Contribution to Defining Quality Education.* Background paper for *EFA Global Monitoring Report 2005.*

Wisenthal, M. 1983. *Historical Statistics of Canada: Section W: Education*. Ottawa, Statistics Canada. (www.statcan.ca/english/freepub/11-516-XIE/sectionw/sectionw.htm)

Woessmann, L. 2000. *Schooling Resources, Education Institutions, and Student Performance: The International Evidence*. Kiel Institute of World Economics. (Working Paper No. 983.)

Women's Commission for Refugee Children and Women. 2004. *Global Survey on Education in Emergencies*. New York, Women's Commission for Refugee Children and Women.

Working Group for International Cooperation in Skills Development. 2002. *World Bank Study on: Vocational Skills Development in Sub-Saharan Africa*. Edinburgh, Working Group for International Cooperation in Skills Development. (Debates in Skills Development Paper 7.)

World Bank. 1993. *The East Asian Miracle: Economic Growth and Public Policy*. New York, Oxford University Press.

— 2002a. *Arab Republic of Egypt Education Sector Review: Progress and Priorities for the Future*. EGT Human Development Group, Middle East and North Africa Region. Washington, DC, World Bank. (Report No. 24905, October.)

— 2002b. *Education and HIV/AIDS: A Window of Hope*. Washington, DC, World Bank.

— 2002c. *Zambia Country Assistance Evaluation*. Washington, DC, World Bank, Operations Evaluation Department.

— 2003a. *Opening Doors: Education and the World Bank*, Washington, DC, World Bank, Human Development Network. (www1.worldbank.org/education/pdf/OpenDoors.pdf)

— 2003b. *World Development Indicators*. CD-ROM. Washington, DC, World Bank.

— 2004a. *Books, Buildings, and Learning Outcomes: An Impact Evaluation of World Bank Support to Basic Education in Ghana*. Washington, DC, World Bank Operation Evaluation Department. (www-wds.worldbank.org/servlet/WDSContentServer/WDSP/IB/2004/05/20/000160016_20040520093425/Rendered/PDF/287790GH.pdf)

— 2004b. EdStats, the World Bank database of education statistics. (www.worldbank.org/education/edstats)

— 2004c. *Education for All (EFA) – Fast Track Initiative: Progress Report*. Washington, DC, World Bank. (http://siteresources.worldbank.org/DEVCOMMINT/Documentation/20190709/DC2004-0002(E)-EFA.pdf)

— 2004d. *FTI News*, May. (www1.worldbank.org/education/efafti/documents/news_052804.pdf)

— 2004e. *Global Monitoring Report 2004. Policies and Actions for Achieving the MDGs and Related Outcomes*. Washington, DC, World Bank.

— 2004f. *Improving Primary Education in Ghana: An Impact Evaluation*. Washington, DC, World Bank.

— 2004g. Research Project on Educational Attainment and Enrollment Around the World, database. (www.worldbank.org/research/projects/edattain/edattain.htm)

— 2004h. School Health at a Glance. Core Intervention 2: provision of safe water and sanitation. (http://wbln0018.worldbank.org/HDNet/hddocs.nsf/c840b59b6982d2498525670c004def60/489122cbc270b63185256a4e00697986)

— 2004i. School Health at a Glance. Core Intervention 4: Access to Health and Nutrition Services. (http://wbln0018.worldbank.org/HDNet/HDdocs.nsf/c840b59b6982d2498525670c004def60/652e989def046eb185256a4e006af0f9?OpenDocument)

— 2004j. *World Development Report 2004: Making Services Work for Poor People*. Washington, DC, World Bank.

World Bank/Asian Development Bank. 2003. *Public Expenditure Review 2003*. Washington, DC, World Bank.

World Bank/IMF. 2004. Communiqué of the Development Committee, Spring 2004. (www.imf.org/external/np/cm/2004/042504.htm)

World Bank-FTI Secretariat. 2004. *Education for All Fast-Track Initiative: Framework Document.*
(www1.worldbank.org/education/efafti/documents/FrameworkDocMarch30_04.pdf)

World Education. 2000. *Farmer Field Schools in Nepal: a proven model to promote sustainable agriculture.*
Boston, World Education.

Wormnæs. S. 2004. *Quality of Education for Persons with Disabilities.* Background paper for *EFA Global Monitoring Report 2005.*

Wright, S. P.; Horn, S. P.; Sanders, W. L. 1997. Teacher and Classroom Context. *Personnel Evaluation in Education,* Vol. 11: 57-7.

Young, M. E. (ed.). 2002. *From Early Child Development to Human Development.* Washington, DC, World Bank.

Young, M. F. D. 1971. *Knowledge and Control.* London, Collins-Macmillan.

Zambia Central Statistical Office and ORC Macro. 2003. *DHS EdData Survey 2002: Education Data for Decision-Making.* Calverton, MD, ORC Macro.

Zambia Ministry of Education. 2002. *MOE Annual Report 2002.* Lusaka, Ministry of Education.

Zambia. 2004. *Memorandum of Understanding: Co-ordination and Harmonisation of GRZ/Donor Practices for Aid Effectiveness in Zambia.* Lusaka, Government of the Republic of Zambia.

Zaslavsky, C. 1973. *Africa counts: Number and pattern in African culture.* Boston, Prindle, Weber & Schmidt.

Zeitlin, M.; Ghassemi, H.; Mansour, M. 1990. *Positive Deviance in Child Nutrition with Emphasis on Psychological and Behavioural Aspects and Implications for Development.* Tokyo, United Nations University.

Abbreviations

ACP	Africa, Caribbean and the Pacific
ADEA	Association for the Development of Education in Africa
AfDB	African Development Bank
AIDS	Acquired immune deficiency syndrome
AusAID	Australian Agency for International Development
BESSIP	Basic Education Sub-Sector Investment Programme (Zambia)
BRAC	Bangladesh Rural Advancement Committee
CDF	Comprehensive Development Framework
CERI	Centre for Educational Research and Innovation
CRS	Creditor Reporting System
DAC	Development Assistance Committee (OECD)
DFID	Department for International Development (United Kingdom)
DHS	Demographic and Health Survey
E-9	Nine high-population countries
EC	European Commission
ECCE	Early childhood care and education
EDI	EFA Development Index
EDUCO	Educación con Participación de la Comunidad (El Salvador) [Community Managed Schools Programme]
EFA	Education for All
ERNESA	Educational Research Network in East and Southern Africa
ERNWACA	Educational Research Network for West And Central Africa
ESDP	Education Sector Development Programme
ESIP	Education Strategic Investment Plan
ESSP	Education Sector Strategic Plan
FRESH	Focusing Resources on Effective School Health
FTI	Fast-Track Initiative (EFA)
GCE	Global Campaign for Education
GDP	Gross domestic product
GER	Gross enrolment ratio
GIR	Gross intake rate
GNP	Gross national product
GPI	Gender Parity Index
HIPC	Highly indebted poor countries
HIV/AIDS	Human immunodeficiency virus/acquired immune deficiency syndrome
IALS	International Adult Literacy Survey
IBE	International Bureau of Education (UNESCO)
IBRD	International Bank for Reconstruction and Development
ICT	Information and communications technology
IDA	International Development Association

IDP	Index of donor proliferation
IEA	International Association for the Evaluation of Educational Achievement
IFF	International Finance Facility
IIEP	UNESCO International Institute for Educational Planning
ILO	International Labour Office
IMF	International Monetary Fund
INEE	Inter-Agency Network for Education in Emergencies
INEP	Instituto Nacional de Estudos e Pesquisas Educacionais (Brazil) [National Institute for Educational Studies and Research]
I-PRSP	Interim Poverty Reduction Strategy Paper
IRC	International Rescue Committee
IRFOL	International Research Foundation for Open Learning
ISCED	International Standard Classification of Education
LAMP	Literacy Assessment Monitoring Project
LDCs	Least-developed countries
LLECE	Laboratorio Latinamericano de Evaluacion de la Calidad de la Educación [Latin American Laboratory for the Assessment of Quality in Education]
MCA	Millennium Challenge Account
MDG	Millennium Development Goal
MECE	Programa de Mejoramiento de la Calidad de la Educación (Chile) [Primary Education Improvement Project]
MICS	Multiple Indicator Cluster Surveys
MINEDAF	Conference of Ministers of Education of African Member States
MLA	Monitoring Learning Achievement
MOU	Memorandum of understanding
MUSTER	Multi-site Teacher Education Research Project
NER	Net enrolment ratio
NGO	Non-governmental organization
NRC	National Reading Committee (Zambia)
ODA	Official development assistance
OECD	Organisation for Economic Co-operation and Development
OED	Operations Evaluation Department
OPEC	Organization of Petroleum Exporting Countries
ORC	Opinion Research Corporation
OREALC	UNESCO Regional Office for Latin America and the Caribbean
PASEC	Programme d'analyse des systèmes éducatifs des pays de la CONFEMEN [Programme for the Analysis of the Educational Systems of CONFEMEN Countries]
PCD	Participatory curriculum development
PIRLS	Progress in International Reading Literacy Study
PISA	Programme for International Student Achievement
PNG	Papua New Guinea
PPP	Purchasing power parity
PRELAC	Proyecto Regional de Educación para America Latina y el Caribe [Regional Education Project for Latin America and the Caribbean]
PRISM	Primary School Management Programme (Kenya)

PRP Primary Reading Programme (Zambia)
PRS Poverty Reduction Strategy
PRSP Poverty Reduction Strategy Paper
PTR Pupil/teacher ratio
R&D Research and development
REFLECT Regenerated Freirean Literacy through Empowering Community Techniques
SACMEQ Southern and Eastern African Consortium for Monitoring Educational Quality
SADC Southern African Development Community
SES Socio-economic status
SLE School life expectancy
STAR Tennessee Student-Teacher Achievement Ratio
SWAp Sector-wide approach
TIMSS Trends in International Mathematics and Science Study
UIS UNESCO Institute for Statistics
UN United Nations
UNAIDS Joint United Nations Programme on HIV/AIDS
UNDP United Nations Development Programme
UNESCO United Nations Educational, Scientific and Cultural Organization
UNGEI United Nations Girls' Education Initiative
UNICEF United Nations Children's Fund
UNRWA United Nations Relief and Works Agency for Palestine Refugees in the Near East
UPC Universal primary completion
UPE Universal primary education
VSO Voluntary Service Overseas
WFD World Federation of the Deaf
WHO World Health Organization